T0189894

Lecture Notes in Computer Science 13794

More information about this series at https://link.springer.com/bookseries/558

Shweta Agrawal · Dongdai Lin (Eds.)

Advances in Cryptology – ASIACRYPT 2022

28th International Conference on the Theory
and Application of Cryptology and Information Security
Taipei, Taiwan, December 5–9, 2022
Proceedings, Part IV

Editors
Shweta Agrawal
Indian Institute of Technology Madras
Chennai, India

Dongdai Lin
Chinese Academy of Sciences
Beijing, China

ISSN 0302-9743   ISSN 1611-3349 (electronic)
Lecture Notes in Computer Science
ISBN 978-3-031-22971-8   ISBN 978-3-031-22972-5 (eBook)
https://doi.org/10.1007/978-3-031-22972-5

This Springer imprint is published by the registered company Springer Nature Switzerland AG
The registered company address is: Gewerbestrasse 11, 6330 Cham, Switzerland

Preface

The 28th Annual International Conference on Theory and Application of Cryptology and Information Security (ASIACRYPT 2022) was held in Taiwan during December 5–9, 2022.

The conference covered all technical aspects of cryptology, and was sponsored by the International Association for Cryptologic Research (IACR).

We received a total of 364 submissions from all over the world, and the Program Committee (PC) selected 98 papers for publication in the proceedings of the conference. The two program chairs were supported by a PC consisting of 79 leading experts in aspects of cryptology. Each submission was reviewed by at least three PC members (or their sub-reviewers). The strong conflict of interest rules imposed by IACR ensure that papers are not handled by PC members with a close working relationship with the authors. The two program chairs were not allowed to submit a paper, and PC members were limited to two submissions each. There were approximately 331 external reviewers, whose input was critical to the selection of papers.

The review process was conducted using double-blind peer review. The conference operated a two-round review system with a rebuttal phase. After the reviews and first-round discussions the PC selected 224 submissions to proceed to the second round and the authors were then invited to participate in an interactive rebuttal phase with the reviewers to clarify questions and concerns. The second round involved extensive discussions by the PC members.

Alongside the presentations of the accepted papers, the program of ASIACRYPT 2022 featured two invited talks by Jian Guo and Damien Stehlé. The conference also featured a rump session which contained short presentations on the latest research results of the field.

The four volumes of the conference proceedings contain the revised versions of the 98 papers that were selected. The final revised versions of papers were not reviewed again and the authors are responsible for their contents.

Using a voting-based process that took into account conflicts of interest, the PC selected the three top papers of the conference: "Full Quantum Equivalence of Group Action DLog and CDH, and More" by Hart Montgomery and Mark Zhandry, "Cryptographic Primitives with Hinting Property" by Navid Alamati and Sikhar Patranabis, and "SwiftEC: Shallue–van de Woestijne Indifferentiable Function to Elliptic Curves" by Jorge Chavez-Saab, Francisco Rodriguez-Henriquez, and Mehdi Tibouchi. The authors of all three papers were invited to submit extended versions of their manuscripts to the Journal of Cryptology.

Many people have contributed to the success of ASIACRYPT 2022. We would like to thank the authors for submitting their research results to the conference. We are very grateful to the PC members and external reviewers for contributing their knowledge and expertise, and for the tremendous amount of work that was done with reading papers and contributing to the discussions. We are greatly indebted to Kai-Min Chung and Bo-Yin Yang, the General Chairs, for their efforts and overall organization. We thank

Bart Preneel, Ron Steinfeld, Mehdi Tibouchi, Jian Guo, and Huaxiong Wang for their valuable suggestions and help. We are extremely grateful to Shuaishuai Li for checking all the LaTeX files and for assembling the files for submission to Springer. We also thank the team at Springer for handling the publication of these conference proceedings.

December 2022   Shweta Agrawal
                                                                Dongdai Lin

Organization

General Chairs

Kai-Min Chung   Academia Sinica, Taiwan
Bo-Yin Yang   Academia Sinica, Taiwan

Program Committee Chairs

Shweta Agrawal   Indian Institute of Technology, Madras, India
Dongdai Lin   Institute of Information Engineering, Chinese
       Academy of Sciences, China

Program Committee

Divesh Aggarwal	National University of Singapore, Singapore
Adi Akavia	University of Haifa, Israel
Martin Albrecht	Royal Holloway, University of London, UK
Ghada Almashaqbeh	University of Connecticut, USA
Benny Applebaum	Tel Aviv University, Israel
Lejla Batina	Radboud University, Netherlands
Carsten Baum	Aarhus University, Denmark
Sonia Belaïd	CryptoExperts, France
Mihir Bellare	University of California, San Diego, USA
Andrej Bogdanov	Chinese University of Hong Kong, China
Christina Boura	Université de Versailles, France
Ran Canetti	Boston University, USA
Jie Chen	East China Normal University, China
Yilei Chen	Tsinghua University, China
Jung Hee Cheon	Seoul National University, South Korea
Ilaria Chillotti	Zama, France
Michele Ciampi	The University of Edinburgh, UK
Craig Costello	Microsoft Research, USA
Itai Dinur	Ben-Gurion University, Israel
Nico Döttling	Helmholtz Center for Information Security (CISPA), Germany
Maria Eichlseder	Graz University of Technology, Austria
Saba Eskandarian	University of North Carolina at Chapel Hill, USA
Marc Fischlin	TU Darmstadt, Germany

Pierre-Alain Fouque	Rennes University and Institut Universitaire de France, France
Steven D. Galbraith	University of Auckland, New Zealand
Chaya Ganesh	Indian Institute of Science, India
Juan Garay	Texas A&M University, USA
Sanjam Garg	University of California, Berkeley and NTT Research, USA
Daniel Genkin	Georgia Institute of Technology, USA
Jian Guo	Nanyang Technological University, Singapore
Siyao Guo	New York University Shanghai, China
Mohammad Hajiabadi	University of Waterloo, Canada
Mike Hamburg	Rambus Inc, USA
David Heath	Georgia Institute of Technology, USA
Viet Tung Hoang	Florida State University, USA
Xinyi Huang	Fujian Normal University, China
Takanori Isobe	University of Hyogo, Japan
Tetsu Iwata	Nagoya University, Japan
Khoongming Khoo	DSO National Laboratories, Singapore
Elena Kirshanova	Immanuel Kant Baltic Federal University, Russia
Ilan Komargodski	Hebrew University of Jerusalem and NTT Research, Israel
Gregor Leander	Ruhr-Universität Bochum, Germany
Qipeng Liu	Simons Institute for the Theory of Computing, USA
Tianren Liu	Peking University, China
Shengli Liu	Shanghai Jiao Tong University, China
Zhe Liu	Nanjing University of Aeronautics and Astronautics, China
Hemanta Maji	Purdue University, USA
Giulio Malavolta	Max Planck Institute for Security and Privacy, Germany
Bart Mennink	Radboud University Nijmegen, Netherlands
Tal Moran	Reichman University, Israel
Pratyay Mukherjee	Swirlds/Hedera, USA
Omkant Pandey	State University of New York at Stony Brook, USA
Anat Paskin-Cherniavsky	Ariel University, Israel
Alain Passelègue	Inria and ENS Lyon, France
Svetla Petkova-Nikova	KU Leuven, Belgium and University of Bergen, Norway
Duong Hieu Phan	Télécom Paris, France
Cécile Pierrot	Inria, France
Silas Richelson	UC Riverside, USA

Yu Sasaki	NTT Corporation, Japan
Tobias Schneider	NXP Semiconductors, Austria
Dominique Schröder	Friedrich-Alexander-Universität Erlangen-Nürnberg, Germany
abhi shelat	Northeastern University, USA
Mark Simkin	Ethereum Foundation, USA
Ling Song	Jinan University, Guangzhou, China
Fang Song	Portland State University, USA
Pratik Soni	Carnegie Mellon University, USA
Akshayaram Srinivasan	Tata Institute of Fundamental Research, India
Damien Stehlé	ENS de Lyon, France
Ron Steinfeld	Monash University, Australia
Qiang Tang	University of Sydney, Australia
Yiannis Tselekounis	Carnegie Mellon University, USA
Meiqin Wang	Shandong University, China
Xiaoyun Wang	Tsinghua University, China
David Wu	University of Texas at Austin, USA
Wenling Wu	Institute of Software, Chinese Academy of Sciences, China
Shota Yamada	AIST, Japan
Takashi Yamakawa	NTT Corporation, Japan
Jiang Zhang	State Key Laboratory of Cryptology, China

Additional Reviewers

Behzad Abdolmaleki	Charlotte Bonte	Nai-Hui Chia
Calvin Abou Haidar	Carl Bootland	Arka Rai Choudhuri
Damiano Abram	Katharina Boudgoust	Jiali Choy
Bar Alon	Lennart Braun	Qiaohan Chu
Pedro Alves	Marek Broll	Hien Chu
Ravi Anand	Chris Brzuska	Eldon Chung
Anurag Anshu	BinBin Cai	Sandro Coretti-Drayton
Victor Arribas	Matteo Campanelli	Arjan Cornelissen
Thomas Attema	Federico Canale	Maria Corte-Real Santos
Christian Badertscher	Avik Chakraborti	Anamaria Costache
Anubhab Baksi	Suvradip Chakraborty	Alain Couvreur
Zhenzhen Bao	John Chan	Nan Cui
James Bartusek	Rohit Chatterjee	Benjamin R. Curtis
Christof Beierle	Long Chen	Jan-Pieter D'Anvers
Ritam Bhaumik	Yu Long Chen	Joan Daemen
Alexander Bienstock	Hongyin Chen	Wangchen Dai
Olivier Blazy	Shan Chen	Hannah Davis
Alex Block	Shiyao Chen	Luca De Feo
Maxime Bombar	Rongmao Chen	Gabrielle De Micheli

Thomas Debris-Alazard
Amit Deo
Patrick Derbez
Julien Devevey
Siemen Dhooghe
Benjamin Dowling
Leo Ducas
Yen Ling Ee
Jonathan Eriksen
Daniel Escudero
Muhammed F. Esgin
Thomas Espitau
Andre Esser
Hulya Evkan
Jaiden Fairoze
Joël Felderhoff
Hanwen Feng
Joe Fitzsimons
Antonio Flórez-Gutiérrez
Pouyan Forghani
Cody Freitag
Georg Fuchsbauer
Pierre Galissant
Tommaso Gagliardoni
Daniel Gardham
Pierrick Gaudry
Romain Gay
Chunpeng Ge
Rosario Gennaro
Paul Gerhart
Satrajit Ghosh
Ashrujit Ghoshal
Niv Gilboa
Aarushi Goel
Aron Gohr
Jesse Goodman
Mike Graf
Milos Grujic
Aurore Guillevic
Aldo Gunsing
Chun Guo
Hosein Hadipour
Mathias Hall-Andersen
Shuai Han
Helena Handschuh

Lucjan Hanzlik
Yonglin Hao
Keisuke Hara
Patrick Harasser
Jingnan He
Rachelle Heim-Boissier
Minki Hhan
Shoichi Hirose
Seungwan Hong
Akinori Hosoyamada
James Hsin-Yu Chiang
Zhicong Huang
Senyang Huang
Chloé Hébant
Ilia Iliashenko
Laurent Imbert
Joseph Jaeger
Palak Jain
Ashwin Jha
Mingming Jiang
Zhengzhong Jin
Antoine Joux
Eliran Kachlon
Bhavana Kanukurthi
Alexander Karenin
Shuichi Katsumata
Mojtaba Khalili
Hamidreza Khorasgani
Dongwoo Kim
Duhyeong Kim
Young-Sik Kim
Fuyuki Kitagawa
Kamil Kluczniak
Yashvanth Kondi
Rajendra Kumar
Noboru Kunihiro
Fukang Liu
Russell W. F. Lai
Jason LeGrow
Jooyoung Lee
Hyung Tae Lee
Byeonghak Lee
Charlotte Lefevre
Zeyong Li
Yiming Li

Hanjun Li
Shun Li
Xingjian Li
Xiao Liang
Benoît Libert
Damien Ligier
Chao Lin
Chengjun Lin
Yunhao Ling
Eik List
Jiahui Liu
Feng-Hao Liu
Guozhen Liu
Xiangyu Liu
Meicheng Liu
Alex Lombardi
Patrick Longa
Wen-jie Lu
Yuan Lu
Donghang Lu
You Lyu
Reinhard Lüftenegger
Bernardo Magri
Monosij Maitra
Mary Maller
Lenka Mareková
Mark Marson
Takahiro Matsuda
Alireza Mehrdad
Simon-Philipp Merz
Pierre Meyer
Michael Meyer
Peihan Miao
Tarik Moataz
Hart Montgomery
Tomoyuki Morimae
Fabrice Mouhartem
Tamer Mour
Marta Mularczyk
Michael Naehrig
Marcel Nageler
Yusuke Naito
Mridul Nandi
Patrick Neumann
Ruth Ng

Ky Nguyen
Khoa Nguyen
Ngoc Khanh Nguyen
Jianting Ning
Oded Nir
Ryo Nishimaki
Olga Nissenbaum
Semyon Novoselov
Julian Nowakowski
Tabitha Ogilvie
Eran Omri
Hiroshi Onuki
Jean-Baptiste Orfila
Mahak Pancholi
Omer Paneth
Lorenz Panny
Roberto Parisella
Jeongeun Park
Rutvik Patel
Sikhar Patranabis
Alice Pellet-Mary
Hilder Vitor Lima Pereira
Ludovic Perret
Thomas Peyrin
Phuong Pham
Guru Vamsi Policharla
Sihang Pu
Luowen Qian
Chen Qian
Kexin Qiao
Willy Quach
Rahul Rachuri
Srinivasan Raghuraman
Adrian Ranea
Shahram Rasoolzadeh
Christian Rechberger
Krijn Reijnders
Maxime Remaud
Ling Ren
Mahshid Riahinia
Peter Rindal
Mike Rosulek
Adeline Roux-Langlois
Paul Rösler

Yusuke Sakai
Kosei Sakamoto
Amin Sakzad
Simona Samardjiska
Olga Sanina
Roozbeh Sarenche
Santanu Sarker
Tobias Schmalz
Markus Schofnegger
Jacob Schuldt
Sruthi Sekar
Nicolas Sendrier
Akash Shah
Yaobin Shen
Yixin Shen
Yu Shen
Danping Shi
Rentaro Shiba
Kazumasa Shinagawa
Omri Shmueli
Ferdinand Sibleyras
Janno Siim
Siang Meng Sim
Luisa Siniscalchi
Yongsoo Song
Douglas Stebila
Lukas Stennes
Igors Stepanovs
Christoph Striecks
Ling Sun
Siwei Sun
Bing Sun
Shi-Feng Sun
Akira Takahashi
Abdul Rahman Taleb
Chik How Tan
Adrian Thillard
Sri Aravinda Krishnan
    Thyagarajan
Yan Bo Ti
Elmar Tischhauser
Yosuke Todo
Junichi Tomida
Ni Trieu

Monika Trimoska
Yi Tu
Aleksei Udovenko
Rei Ueno
Mayank Varia
Daniele Venturi
Riad Wahby
Roman Walch
Mingyuan Wang
Haoyang Wang
Luping Wang
Xiao Wang
Yuejun Wang
Yuyu Wang
Weiqiang Wen
Chenkai Weng
Benjamin Wesolowski
Yusai Wu
Yu Xia
Zhiye Xie
Shengmin Xu
Guangwu Xu
Sophia Yakoubov
Hailun Yan
Rupeng Yang
Kang Yang
Qianqian Yang
Shao-Jun Yang
Li Yao
Hui Hui Yap
Kan Yasuda
Weijing You
Thomas Zacharias
Yupeng Zhang
Kai Zhang
Lei Zhang
Yunlei Zhao
Yu Zhou
Chenzhi Zhu
Paul Zimmermann
Lukas Zobernig
matthieu rambaud
Hendrik Waldner
Yafei Zheng

Sponsoring Institutions

- Platinum Sponsor: ZAMA
- Gold Sponsor: BTQ, Hackers in Taiwan, Technology Innovation Institute
- Silver Sponsor: Meta (Facebook), Casper Networks, PQShield, NTT Research, WiSECURE
- Bronze Sponsor: Mitsubishi Electric, Algorand Foundation, LatticeX Foundation, Intel, QSancus, IOG (Input/Output Global), IBM

Contents – Part IV

Cryptanalysis

Quantum Cryptography

Signatures

Recovering the Tight Security Proof of SPHINCS+

Andreas Hülsing[(✉)] and Mikhail Kudinov

Eindhoven University of Technology, Eindhoven, The Netherlands
wotstw@huelsing.net

Abstract. In 2020, Kudinov, Kiktenko, and Fedorov pointed out a flaw in the tight security proof of the SPHINCS+ construction. This work gives a new tight security proof for SPHINCS+. The flaw can be traced back to the security proof for the Winternitz one-time signature scheme (WOTS) used within SPHINCS+. In this work, we give a stand-alone description of the WOTS variant used in SPHINCS+ that we call WOTS-TW. We provide a security proof for WOTS-TW and multi-instance WOTS-TW against non-adaptive chosen message attacks where the adversary only learns the public key after it made its signature query. Afterwards, we show that this is sufficient to give a tight security proof for SPHINCS+. We recover almost the same bound for the security of SPHINCS+, with only a factor w loss compared to the previously claimed bound, where w is the Winternitz parameter that is commonly set to 16. On a more technical level, we introduce new lower bounds on the quantum query complexity for generic attacks against properties of cryptographic hash functions and analyse the constructions of tweakable hash functions used in SPHINCS+ with regard to further security properties.

Keywords: Post-quantum cryptography · hash-based signatures · W-OTS · SPHINCS+ · WOTS-TW · hash functions · undetectability · PRF

1 Introduction

Recently, hash-based signatures have received a lot of attention as they are widely considered the most conservative choice for post-quantum signature schemes. At the time of writing, the stateless hash-based signature scheme SPHINCS+ is a third round alternate candidate in the NIST PQC competition. However, NIST has repeatedly stated the following.

"NIST sees SPHINCS+ as an extremely conservative choice for standard-ization. If NIST's confidence in better performing signature algorithms is

This work was funded by an NWO VIDI grant (Project No. VI.Vidi.193.066). Part of this work was done while M.K. was still affiliated with the Russian Quantum Center, QApp. Date: November 19, 2022.

S. Agrawal and D. Lin (Eds.): ASIACRYPT 2022, LNCS 13794, pp. 3–33, 2022.
https://doi.org/10.1007/978-3-031-22972-5_1

shaken by new analysis, SPHINCS+ could provide an immediately available algorithm for standardization at the end of the third round."
(Dustin Moody on the pqc-forum mailing list after new attacks on Rainbow and GeMSS were published, January 21, 2021)

One more supporting argument for the security of SPHINCS$^+$ would be a tight security reduction that allows one to derive attack complexities for a given set of parameters. However, the tight proof for SPHINCS$^+$ that was given in [BHK+19] turned out to be flawed [KKF20]. The flaw, pointed out by Kudinov, Kiktenko, and Fedorov is related to the proof of security of the used WOTS scheme. Although the flaw could not be translated into an attack, this resulted in an unsatisfactory situation. While there still exists a non-tight reduction for the security of SPHINCS$^+$, this reduction can not support the claimed security of the used SPHINCS$^+$ parameters.

In this work, we give a new tight security proof for SPHINCS$^+$.

Security flaw. To provide context, we first give a brief description of the flaw in the previous security proof. A WOTS signature consists of intermediate values of a collection of hash chains. The security of all WOTS variants relies on the hardness of inverting such a hash chain or finding a longer alternative chain with the same end note. The challenging point in a tight security proof is to deal with the case where the adversary really inverts the hash chain on the signature value, i.e., comes up with a longer hash chain that agrees on the signature value and all following nodes. The straightforward proof approach is to embed a preimage challenge in the chain. However, when targeting standard (EU-CMA) security, this requires the reduction to guess the position used in the signature as it may not be able to answer signature queries otherwise. This guessing causes a significant tightness loss. An alternative approach was taken in [BHK+19], based on [BH19], where the reduction tries to use the adversary to solve a second preimage challenge. This has the advantage that the reduction knows the full chain, hence can answer arbitrary signature queries and so no guessing is necessary. The flaw occurred exactly there: The argument given for why an adversary is likely to provide a second preimage does not apply to preimages that are images of the hash function themselves. This is the issue pointed out by [KKF20]. In this work, we solve the problem using a different approach: We show that for the security of SPHINCS+ it is sufficient if WOTS achieves security under non-adaptive chosen message attacks. Intuitively this is the case as WOTS is used to sign values that are fully under the control of the honest user and entirely independent of the adversaries input. This allows us to go back to the straightforward proof approach and show how to implement it.

Security of hash-based signatures. Analyzing the security of modern hash-based signature schemes is a multi-stage process. First, the security of the signature scheme is related to the complexity of breaking properties of the used (hash) function families. To support the security of specific parameter sets with proofs, we need an expected complexity for attacks that break the assumed properties.

In general, a cryptographic hash function is considered secure if there are no attacks that perform significantly better than generic attacks. Hence, the complexity of generic attacks against these properties is analyzed. In [BHK+19], the abstraction of *tweakable hash functions* (THFs) was introduced to unify the description of schemes that only differ in the inputs that internal hash functions take but follow the same general construction. These THFs are constructed from keyed hash functions (KHFs). When using this abstraction, security of the signature scheme is related to the complexity of breaking the properties of THFs (and possibly further functions, like PRFs, or further KHFs). Security of a THF is then related to the security of the used KHF. Finally, the latter is assessed with regard to generic attacks. In all of these steps, quantum adversaries have to be considered to ensure post-quantum security.

Our contributions. With this work, we contribute to all three levels in the security analysis of SPHINCS$^+$. First, we give a new tight proof for the security of SPHINCS$^+$, assuming the used THFs provide a form of target-collision resistance (TCR), decisional second-preimage resistance (DSPR), preimage resistance (PRE), and undetectability (UD)[1]. As with all previous proofs for SPHINCS$^+$, we require that the KHF used for message compression provides interleaved target-subset resilience (ITSR) and that a secure PRF is available. Note that our new proof closes the gap again without modifying SPHINCS$^+$.

The difference to the previous security proof for SPHINCS$^+$ is in the proof of the used WOTS variant. To make the proof more easily accessible, we first extract this WOTS variant and formally define it, naming it WOTS-TW. WOTS-TW is different from other WOTS variants in that it uses THFs to construct the function chains. We then prove the security of WOTS-TW under non-adaptive chosen message attacks (EU-naCMA) where the adversary receives the public key after it made its signature query. This weaker model allows for a tight security proof for WOTS-TW while also being sufficient for security proofs of schemes like SPHINCS$^+$. A tight proof is possible because a reduction can now generate the WOTS-TW public key based on the signature query instead of guessing the query. This eliminates the loss factor introduced by guessing. At the same time, the notion is sufficient because for SPHINCS$^+$, WOTS-TW is used to sign the roots of hash trees which are generated by the reduction. In short, our new proof combines the work of Dods, Smart, and Stam [DSS05] that uses undetectability to plant preimage challenges, with the second-preimage resistance version of Hülsing [Hül13], and the approach of multi-target mitigation by Hülsing, Rijneveld, and Song [HRS16] and lifts it to the setting of tweakable hash functions. We start with a proof in the single-instance setting for better exposition and move to a proof in a multi-instance setting as used in SPHINCS$^+$ afterwards.

As a second contribution, we analyze the security of THFs with respect to undetectability and preimage resistance. The remaining properties were used in the previous SPHINCS$^+$ proof and were hence already analyzed. We obtain results for the two THF-constructions (*simple* and *robust*) used in SPHINCS$^+$

---

[1] To be precise, we are considering multi-target versions of these notions which we omit in the introduction for the sake of clarity.

that were considered in [BHK+19]. The *simple* construction simply concatenates all inputs and feeds them into the underlying hash function. This construction was previously analyzed in the quantum-accessible random oracle model (QROM). We give tight bounds for PRE and UD in the QROM (the former is based on a conjecture from [BHK+19]). For the robust construction, we show that PRE and UD can be based on PRE and UD of the used KHF, respectively. Due to space constraints we left this part only in the full version of the paper [HK22].

As a third contribution, we complete the picture for the hardness of breaking the properties of (hash) function families via generic attacks (see Table 1 for an overview). We obtain a new result for UD, and improve the result for TCR. Our analysis generally follows the framework of [HRS16], which reduces the problem of distinguishing two distributions over boolean functions to the respective security property. In [HRS16], a distribution over variable weight functions, introduced by Zhandry [Zha12], is used where every input is mapped to 1 with a fixed probability. In this work, we also use distributions over fixed-weight functions where the number of 1's per function is fixed. During this process, we find a useful self-reducibility result for the distinguishing problem with this kind of functions. Moreover, we establish a new bound for PRE, overcoming a previous limitation of the analysis in [HRS16] which only applied to sufficiently compressing functions. Our new approach is a reduction from SPR and DSPR as previously implicitly done in [BH19]. This gives a tight unconditional bound for the single target case. For the multi-target case, we obtain a non-tight unconditional bound and a tight bound based on a previous conjecture made in [BHK+19] regarding the complexity of breaking DSPR in the multi-target case.

Lessons learned. As a result of our work we can conclude that the security analysis is a lot nicer if WOTS is used to only sign signer-generated values. The possibly more important lessons learned concern the general security analysis of hash-based signatures. While the non-tight analysis is relatively well understood, it does not justify the used parameter sets. The tight security analysis which justifies used parameter sets however is largely non-trivial. Proofs are extremely complex which makes them error-prone and hard to verify as demonstrated by recent history. In consequence, an important next step is to actually verify the given proof, for example, using tools from formal verification.

Acknowledgments. We want to thank Sydney Antonov for pointing out wrong bounds in Table 1 of a previous version.

Organization. We introduce necessary definitions and notations in Sect. 2. Section 3 is devoted to the description of the WOTS-TW scheme. The description of the EU-naCMA security model is given in Sect. 4. In Sect. 5 we provide a security reduction for WOTS-TW in the single instance setting and in Sect. 6 we lift the result to the multi-instance setting with possibly dependent messages. The security proof for SPHINCS+ that uses WOTS-TW as a building block is then given in Sect. 7. The summary of the state of the art for generic security bounds and analysis of quantum generic security of UD and TCR properties is given in Sect. 8. The constructions of tweakable hash function from keyed hash function can be found in the full version of the paper [HK22].

2   Preliminaries

In this section we introduce the definitions of building blocks, and security notions for hash functions that we use. We begin with the notion of a tweakable hash function, introduced in the construction of SPHINCS$^+$ [BHK+19], and its security. Beyond the presented notions, we make use of the standard definition for PRFs which for reference can be found in the full paper [HK22]. For signatures we consider the common existential unforgeability notion but under non-adaptive message attacks. In this setting the adversary has to select a set of q messages that it will get signed before it receives the public key. For one-time signatures we have $q = 1$. A detailed formal definition can be found in Sect. 4.

2.1   Tweakable Hash Functions

In this section we recall the definition of tweakable hash functions and related security notions from [BHK+19]. These properties will later be used to prove the security of our WOTS-TW scheme.

Function definition. A *tweakable* hash function takes public parameters P and context information in form of a *tweak* T in addition to the message input. The public parameters might be thought of as a function key or index. The tweak might be interpreted as a nonce.

Definition 1 (Tweakable hash function). *Let $n, m \in \mathbb{N}$, $\mathcal{P}$ the public parameters space and $\mathcal{T}$ the tweak space. A tweakable hash function is an efficient function*

$$\mathbf{Th} : \mathcal{P} \times \mathcal{T} \times \{0,1\}^m \to \{0,1\}^n, \ \mathrm{MD} \leftarrow \mathbf{Th}(P, T, M)$$

mapping an m-bit message M to an n-bit hash value MD using a function key called public parameter $P \in \mathcal{P}$ and a tweak $T \in \mathcal{T}$.

We will sometimes denote $\mathbf{Th}(P, T, M)$ as $\mathbf{Th}_{P,T}(M)$. In SPHINCS$^+$, a public value $Seed$ is used as public parameter which is part of the SPHINCS$^+$ public key (the name comes from a specific construction of a tweakable hash function that uses the public parameters as seed for a PRG). For the tweak, SPHINCS$^+$ uses a so-called hash function address (**ADRS**) that identifies the position of the hash function call within the virtual structure defined by a SPHINCS$^+$ key pair. We use the same approach for WOTS-TW, i.e., the public parameter is a seed value that becomes part of the public key if WOTS-TW is used stand-alone. If it is encompassed in a larger structure like SPHINCS$^+$, the public parameter will typically be that used in the encompassing structure and is therefore only part of that structure's public key. In this case, the hash addresses have to be unique within the entire structure. Therefore, the address usually contains a prefix determined by the calling structure.

Security notions. To provide a security proof for WOTS-TW we require that the used tweakable hash functions have certain security properties. Specifically, we require the following properties or some variations of them which will be discussed below:

- *post-quantum single-function, multi-target collision resistance for distinct tweaks* (PQ-SM-DT-TCR);
- *post-quantum single-function, multi-target preimage resistance for distinct tweaks* (PQ-SM-DT-PRE);
- *post-quantum single-function, multi-target undetectability for distinct tweaks* (PQ-SM-DT-UD).

These properties were already considered in previous work. We slightly adapt them. Moreover, in the context of multi-instance constructions like SPHINCS$^+$, we need another generic extension to collections of tweakable hash functions, discussed at the end of the subsection.

We generally consider post-quantum security in this work. Therefore, we will omit the PQ prefix from now on and consider it understood that we always consider quantum adversaries. Since we are working in the post-quantum setting, we assume that adversaries have access to a quantum computer but honest parties do not. Hence, any oracles that implement secretly-keyed functions only allow for classical queries. Moreover, in all of the properties an adversary can influence the challenges by specifying the tweaks used in challenges. We generally restrict this control in so far as we do not allow more than one challenge for the same tweak (indicated by the DT label). As we have this restriction for all of our properties we omit the DT label in all of the security notions.

Below we will define success probabilities and advantages of the adversaries against different properties of hash functions. Here we define the insecurity of a property Prop for parameter p (which usually denotes the number of targets) of (tweakable) hash function F against time-ξ adversaries as the maximum success probability for finding games or maximum advantage for distinguishing games of any such adversary: $\text{InSec}^{\text{Prop}}(F; \xi, p) = \max_{\mathcal{A}}\{\text{Succ}/\text{Adv}_{F,p}^{\text{Prop}}(\mathcal{A})\}$.

Now we will discuss above properties and their variations. We provide additional intuition for those notions in the full paper [HK22].

Definition 2 (SM-TCR). *In the following let **Th** be a tweakable hash function as defined above. We define the success probability of any adversary $\mathcal{A} = (\mathcal{A}_1, \mathcal{A}_2)$ against the SM-TCR security of **Th**. The definition is parameterized by the number of targets p for which it must hold that $p \leq |\mathcal{T}|$. In the definition, $\mathcal{A}_1$ is allowed to make p classical queries to an oracle $\textbf{Th}(P, \cdot, \cdot)$. We denote the set of $\mathcal{A}_1$'s queries by $Q = \{(T_i, M_i)\}_{i=1}^p$ and define the predicate $\textbf{DIST}(\{T_i\}_{i=1}^p) = (\forall i, k \in [1, p], i \neq k) : T_i \neq T_k$, i.e., $\textbf{DIST}(\{T_i\}_{i=1}^p)$ outputs 1 iff all tweaks are distinct.*

$$\text{Succ}_{\mathbf{Th},p}^{\text{SM-TCR}}(\mathcal{A}) = \Pr[P \leftarrow_{\$} \mathcal{P}; S \leftarrow \mathcal{A}_1^{\mathbf{Th}(P,\cdot,\cdot)}(\ );$$
$$(j,M) \leftarrow \mathcal{A}_2(Q,S,P) : \mathbf{Th}(P,T_j,M_j) = \mathbf{Th}(P,T_j,M)$$
$$\wedge\, M \neq M_j \wedge \mathbf{DIST}(\{T_i\}_{i=1}^p)]$$

Definition 3 (SM-PRE). *In the following let* **Th** *be a tweakable hash function as defined above. We define the success probability of any adversary* $\mathcal{A} = (\mathcal{A}_1, \mathcal{A}_2)$ *against the* SM-PRE *security of* **Th***. The definition is parameterized by the number of targets* p *for which it must hold that* $p \leq |\mathcal{T}|$. *In the definition,* $\mathcal{A}_1$ *is allowed to make* p *classical queries to an oracle* $\mathbf{Th}(P,\cdot,x_i)$, *where* x_i *is chosen uniformly at random for the query* i *(the value of* x_i *stays hidden from* $\mathcal{A}$*). We denote the set of* $\mathcal{A}_1$*'s queries by* $Q = \{T_i\}_{i=1}^p$ *and define the predicate* $\mathbf{DIST}(\{T_i\}_{i=1}^p)$ *as we did in the definition above.*

$$\text{Succ}_{\mathbf{Th},p}^{\text{SM-PRE}}(\mathcal{A}) = \Pr[P \leftarrow_{\$} \mathcal{P}; S \leftarrow \mathcal{A}_1^{\mathbf{Th}(P,\cdot,x_i)}(\ );$$
$$(j,M) \leftarrow \mathcal{A}_2(Q,S,P) : \mathbf{Th}(P,T_j,M) = \mathbf{Th}(P,T_j,x_j) \wedge \mathbf{DIST}(\{T_i\}_{i=1}^p)]$$

Definition 4 (SM-UD). *In the following let* **Th** *be a tweakable hash function as defined above. We define the advantage of any adversary* $\mathcal{A} = (\mathcal{A}_1, \mathcal{A}_2)$ *against the* SM-UD *security of* **Th***. The definition is parameterized by the number of targets* p *for which it must hold that* $p \leq |\mathcal{T}|$. *First the challenger flips a fair coin* b *and chooses a public parameter* $P \leftarrow_{\$} \mathcal{P}$. *Next consider an oracle* $\mathcal{O}_P(\mathcal{T}, \{0,1\})$, *which works the following way:* $\mathcal{O}_P(T,0)$ *returns* $\mathbf{Th}(P,T,x_i)$, *where* x_i *is chosen uniformly at random for the query* i; $\mathcal{O}_P(T,1)$ *returns* y_i, *where* y_i *is chosen uniformly at random for the query* i. *In the definition,* $\mathcal{A}_1$ *is allowed to make* p *classical queries to an oracle* $\mathcal{O}_P(\cdot, b)$. *The goal of* $\mathcal{A}$ *is to distinguish whether the oracle is* $\mathcal{O}_P(\mathcal{T},0)$ *or* $\mathcal{O}_P(\mathcal{T},1)$. *We denote the set of* $\mathcal{A}_1$*'s queries by* $Q = \{T_i\}_{i=1}^p$ *and define the predicate* $\mathbf{DIST}(\{T_i\}_{i=1}^p)$ *as we did above.*

$$\text{Adv}_{\mathbf{Th},p}^{\text{SM-UD}}(\mathcal{A}) =$$
$$|\Pr[P \leftarrow_{\$} \mathcal{P}; S \leftarrow \mathcal{A}_1^{\mathcal{O}_P(\cdot,0)}(\ ); 1 \leftarrow \mathcal{A}_2(Q,S,P) \wedge \mathbf{DIST}(\{T_i\}_{i=1}^p)]$$
$$- \Pr[P \leftarrow_{\$} \mathcal{P}; S \leftarrow \mathcal{A}_1^{\mathcal{O}_P(\cdot,1)}(\ ); 1 \leftarrow \mathcal{A}_2(Q,S,P) \wedge \mathbf{DIST}(\{T_i\}_{i=1}^p)]|$$

At this point, we have finished describing the properties that will be needed to construct a reduction proof for WOTS-TW. But for the further analysis of those properties and analysis of SPHINCS$^+$ one would need several more properties.

Decisional Second Preimage Resistance (DSPR) and its variants were introduced and motivated in [BH19]. Here we present a multi-target version of DSPR which is denoted as SM-DSPR. To do so, we need a second-preimage exists predicate for THFs.

Definition 5 (SP$_{P,T}$). *A second preimage exists predicate of tweakable hash function* **Th** : $\mathcal{P} \times \mathcal{T} \times \{0,1\}^m \rightarrow \{0,1\}^n$ *with a fixed* $P \in \mathcal{P}$, $T \in \mathcal{T}$ *is the function* SP$_{P,T}$: $\{0,1\}^m \rightarrow \{0,1\}$ *defined as follows:*

$$\mathsf{SP}_{P,T}(x) \stackrel{def}{=} \begin{cases} 1 & \text{if } |\mathbf{Th}_{P,T}^{-1}(\mathbf{Th}_{P,T}(x))| \geq 2 \\ 0 & \text{otherwise} \end{cases} \quad,$$

where $\mathbf{Th}_{P,T}^{-1}$ *refers to the inverse of the tweakable hash function with fixed public parameter and a tweak.*

Now we present the definition of SM-DSPR from [BHK+19] for a tweakable hash function. The intuition behind this notion is that the adversary should be unable to find a preimage such that doesn't have a second preimage.

Definition 6 (SM-DSPR). *Let* **Th** *be a tweakable hash function. Let* $\mathcal{A} = (\mathcal{A}_1, \mathcal{A}_2)$ *be a two stage adversary. The number of targets is denoted with* p, *where the following inequality must hold:* $p \leq |\mathcal{T}|$. $\mathcal{A}_1$ *is allowed to make* p *classical queries to an oracle* **Th**$(P, \cdot, \cdot)$. *We denote the query set* $Q = \{(T_i, M_i)\}_{i=1}^p$ *and predicate* DIST$(\{T_i\}_1^p)$ *as in previous definitions.*

$$\mathrm{Adv}_{\mathbf{Th},p}^{\mathrm{SM\text{-}DSPR}}(\mathcal{A}) = \max\{0, \mathsf{succ} - \mathsf{triv}\},$$

where

$$\mathsf{succ} = \Pr[P \leftarrow_{\$} \mathcal{P}; S \leftarrow \mathcal{A}_1^{\mathbf{Th}(P,\cdot,\cdot)}(); (j,b) \leftarrow \mathcal{A}_2(Q,S,P) :$$
$$\mathsf{SP}_{P,T_j}(M_j) = b \wedge \mathsf{DIST}(\{T_i\}_1^p)].$$

$$\mathsf{triv} = \Pr[P \leftarrow_{\$} \mathcal{P}; S \leftarrow \mathcal{A}_1^{\mathbf{Th}(P,\cdot,\cdot)}(); (j,b) \leftarrow \mathcal{A}_2(Q,S,P) :$$
$$\mathsf{SP}_{P,T_j}(M_j) = 1 \wedge \mathsf{DIST}(\{T_i\}_1^p)].$$

Security for a collection of tweakable hash functions. In more complex constructions like SPHINCS$^+$, we make use of a collection of tweakable hash functions which we call **Th**$_\lambda$. In this case **Th**$_\lambda$ consists of a set of tweakable hash functions **Th**$_{m_i}$ for different m_i, the length of messages they process. This notion of a collection of tweakable hash functions is necessary as we use the same public parameters for all functions in the collection. Especially, it is necessary to make the security notions above usable in the context of SPHINCS$^+$. The problem is that when used in constructions like SPHINCS$^+$ or XMSS, queries to the challenge oracle may depend on the outputs of other functions in the collection, or even the same function but with different tweaks. This is incompatible with above definitions as the public parameters are only given to the adversary after all challenge queries are made.

We solve this issue by extending all the above *stand-alone* security properties to the case of collections. The definitions for functions that are part of a collection only differ from the above in a single spot. We give the first part of the adversary $\mathcal{A}_1$, that makes the challenge queries, access to another oracle $\mathbf{Th}_\lambda(P, \cdot, \cdot)$, initialized with P. The oracle takes an input M and a tweak T and, depending on the length $m = |M|$ of M returns $\mathbf{Th}_m(P, T, M)$. The only limitation is that $\mathcal{A}$ is not allowed to use the same tweak in queries to both oracles, the challenge oracle and the collection oracle. In general, $\mathcal{A}$ is allowed to query the challenge oracle as well as $\mathbf{Th}_\lambda$ with a message of length x, as long as the used tweak is never used in a query to the challenge oracle.

Definition 7 (SM-TCR, SM-PRE, SM-UD, SM-DSPR for members of a collection). *Let $\mathbf{Th}_m$ be a THF as defined above with message length m. Moreover, let $\mathbf{Th}_m$ be an element of a collection $\mathbf{Th}_\lambda$ of THFs as described above. Consider an adversary $\mathcal{A} = (\mathcal{A}_1, \mathcal{A}_2)$ against the SM-TCR (, SM-PRE, SM-UD, SM-DSPR) security of $\mathbf{Th}_m$ as part of collection $\mathbf{Th}_\lambda$ (which we denote as $\mathbf{Th}_m \in \mathbf{Th}_\lambda$). Let $\mathbf{Th}_\lambda(P, \cdot, \cdot)$ denote an oracle for $\mathbf{Th}_\lambda$ as described above and denote by $\{T_i^\lambda\}_1^{p_\lambda}$ the tweaks used in the queries made by $\mathcal{A}$. We define the success probability of $\mathcal{A}$ against SM-TCR (, SM-PRE, SM-UD, SM-DSPR) security of $\mathbf{Th}_m$ as part of collection $\mathbf{Th}_\lambda$ as the success probability of $\mathcal{A}$ against stand-alone SM-TCR (, SM-PRE, SM-UD, SM-DSPR) security of $\mathbf{Th}_m$ defined above, when $\mathcal{A}_1$ is additionally given classical oracle access to $\mathbf{Th}_\lambda(P, \cdot, \cdot)$ with the condition that $\{T_i\}_1^p \cap \{T_i^\lambda\}_1^{p_\lambda} = \emptyset$.*

In the case of SM-TCR, we will abuse notation when it comes to the security of SPHINCS$^+$ and consider the joined security of several members of a collection of tweakable hash functions.

3   WOTS-TW

SPHINCS$^+$ [BHK+19] developed its own variant of the Winternitz OTS. However, the authors never explicitly defined that variant. Since the flaw in the SPHINCS$^+$ security proof was in the proof for their WOTS scheme, we give a separate description of the scheme in this section. As the distinguishing feature of this variant is the use of tweakable hash functions, we call it WOTS-TW.

3.1   Parameters

WOTS-TW uses several parameters. The main security parameter is $n \in \mathbb{N}$. The length of messages that are signed is denoted as m. In the case of SPHINCS$^+$, $m = n$. The Winternitz parameter $w \in \mathbb{N}$ determines a base of the representation that is used in the scheme and determines the parameter l:

$$l_1 = \left\lceil \frac{m}{\log(w)} \right\rceil, \quad l_2 = \left\lfloor \frac{\log(l_1(w - 1))}{\log(w)} \right\rfloor + 1, \quad l = l_1 + l_2.$$

The tweak space $\mathcal{T}$ must be at least of size lw. The size of the tweak space should be bigger if we use several instances of WOTS-TW in a bigger construction such as SPHINCS$^+$ so we can use a different tweak for each hash function call. We also need a pseudorandom function $\mathbf{PRF} : \{0,1\}^n \times \mathcal{T} \to \{0,1\}^n$, and a tweakable hash function $\mathbf{Th} : \{0,1\}^n \times \mathcal{T} \times \{0,1\}^n \to \{0,1\}^n$.

3.2   Addressing Scheme

For the tweakable hash functions to guarantee security, they have to be called with different tweaks. This is achieved using what was called an addressing scheme in SPHINCS⁺. Such an addressing scheme assigns a unique address to every tweakable hash function call in the scheme and the address space is part of the tweak space such that addresses can be used as tweaks. We do not specify a concrete addressing scheme in this work (see the SPHINCS⁺ specification [ABB+20] for an example). Abstractly, we achieve unique addresses the following way. A Winternitz key pair defines a structure of l hash chains, each of which makes $w - 1$ calls to the tweakable hash function. For a unique addressing scheme, one may use any injective function that takes as input $i \in [0, l - 1]$, $j \in [0, w - 2]$, and possibly a prefix, and maps into the address space. The prefix is necessary to ensure uniqueness if many instances of WOTS-TW are used in a single construction. We will use **ADRS** to denote that prefix. The tweak associated with the j-th function call in the i-th chain is then defined as the output of this function on input i, j (and a possible prefix) and denoted as $T_{i,j}$. The prefix can also be used to distinguish other parts of a signature scheme such as binary trees or few time signatures. Note that the addresses (**ADRS**, tweaks) can be publicly computed and known to everybody.

3.3   WOTS-TW Scheme

The main difference between WOTS variants is in the way they do hashing. Previously, the distinction was made in the definition of the so-called chaining function that describes how the hash chains are computed. For WOTS-TW this distinction is further shifted into the construction of the tweakable hash function **Th**. The chaining function then looks as follows:

Chaining function $c^{j,k}(x, i, \text{Seed})$: The chaining function takes as inputs a message $x \in \{0, 1\}^n$, iteration counter $k \in \mathbb{N}$, start index $j \in \mathbb{N}$, chain index i, and public parameters Seed. The chaining function then works the following way. In case $k \leq 0$, c returns x, i.e., $c^{j,0}(x, i, \text{Seed}) = x$. For $k > 0$ we define c recursively as

$$c^{j,k}(x, i, \text{Seed}) = \mathbf{Th}(\text{Seed}, T_{i,j+k-1}, c^{j,k-1}(x, i, \text{Seed})).$$

If we consider several instances of WOTS-TW then we will use $c_{\mathbf{ADRS}}^{j,k}(x, i, \text{Seed})$ to denote that tweaks that are used to construct the chain have **ADRS** as a prefix. With this chaining function, we describe the algorithms of WOTS-TW.

Key Generation Algorithm $(\mathsf{SK}, \mathsf{PK}) \leftarrow \mathbf{WOTS\text{-}TW.kg}(\mathcal{C}; \mathcal{S})$: The key generation algorithm optionally takes as input context information $\mathcal{C} = (\text{Seed}, \mathbf{ADRS})$, consisting of a public seed Seed $\in \{0, 1\}^n$ and a global address **ADRS**, as well as randomness $\mathcal{S} \in \{0, 1\}^n$ which we call the secret seed. These inputs are meant for the use in more complex protocols. If they are not provided, key generation randomly samples the seeds and sets **ADRS** to 0. The key generation algorithm then computes the internal secret key $\mathsf{sk} = (\mathsf{sk}_1, \ldots, \mathsf{sk}_l)$ as

$\mathsf{sk}_i \leftarrow \mathbf{PRF}(\mathcal{S}, T_{i,0}))$, i.e., the $l \cdot n$ bit secret key elements are derived form the secret seed using addresses. The element of the public key pk is computed as

$$\mathsf{pk} = (\mathsf{pk}_1, \ldots, \mathsf{pk}_l) = (c^{0,w-1}(\mathsf{sk}_1, 1, \text{Seed}), \ldots, c^{0,w-1}(\mathsf{sk}_l, l, \text{Seed})).$$

The key generation algorithm returns $\mathsf{SK} = (\mathcal{S}, \mathcal{C})$ and $\mathsf{PK} = (\mathsf{pk}, \mathcal{C})$ Note that we can compute sk and pk from SK.

Signature Algorithm $\sigma \leftarrow$ WOTS-TW.sign(M, SK): On input of an m-bit message M, and the secret key $\mathsf{SK} = (\mathcal{S}, \mathcal{C})$, the signature algorithm first computes a base w representation of $M : M = (M_1, \ldots, M_{l_1})$, $M_i \in \{0, \ldots, w - 1\}$. That is, M is treated as the binary representation of a natural number x and then the w-ary representation of x is computed. Next it computes the checksum $C = \sum_{i=1}^{l_1}(w - 1 - M_i)$ and its base w representation $C = (C_1, \ldots, C_{l_2})$. We set $B = (b_1, \ldots, b_l) = M\|C$, the concatenation of the base w representations of M and C. Then the internal secret key is regenerated using $\mathsf{sk}_i \leftarrow \mathbf{PRF}(\mathcal{S}, T_{i,0})$ the same way as during key generation. The signature is computed as

$$\sigma = (\sigma_1, \ldots, \sigma_l) = (c^{0,b_1}(\mathsf{sk}_1, 1, \text{Seed}), \ldots, c^{0,b_l}(\mathsf{sk}_l, l, \text{Seed})).$$

Verification Algorithm ($\{0, 1\} \leftarrow$ WOTS-TW.vf(M, σ, PK)): On input of m-bit message M, a signature σ, and public key $\mathsf{PK} = (\mathsf{pk}, \mathcal{C})$, the verification algorithm computes the $b_i, 1 \le i \le l$ as described above and checks if

$$\mathsf{pk} \overset{?}{=} \mathsf{pk}' = (\mathsf{pk}'_1, \ldots, \mathsf{pk}'_l) = (c^{b_1,w-1-b_1}(\sigma_1, 1, \text{Seed}), \ldots, c^{b_l,w-1-b_l}(\sigma_l, l, \text{Seed})).$$

In case of equality the algorithm outputs true and false otherwise.

The intuition behind the security of WOTS-TW is the following. Assume that you've observed a message and a signature (M, σ). To obtain (M', σ'), where $M' \ne M$ you will have at least one block in some chain that occurs earlier than in σ. This is due to checksum computation.

4   EU-naCMA Model

A standard definition of a Digital signature scheme and a notion of EU-CMA is given in the full paper [HK22]. Here we define existential unforgeability under *non-adaptive* chosen message attack (EU-naCMA). It is defined using the following experiment where S makes the shared state of $\mathcal{A}_1$ and $\mathcal{A}_2$ explicit.

Experiment $\mathsf{Exp}_{\mathsf{Dss}(1^n)}^{\mathsf{EU-naCMA}}(\mathcal{A} = (\mathcal{A}_1, \mathcal{A}_2))$:

    $(\mathsf{sk}, \mathsf{pk}) \leftarrow \mathsf{Kg}(1^n)$.
    $(\{M_1, \ldots, M_q\}, S) \leftarrow \mathcal{A}_1()$.
    Compute $\{(M_i, \sigma_i)\}_{i=1}^q$ using $\mathsf{Sign}(\mathsf{sk}, \cdot)$.
    $(M^\star, \sigma^\star) \leftarrow \mathcal{A}_2(S, \{(M_i, \sigma_i)\}_{i=1}^q, \mathsf{pk})$
    Return 1 iff $\mathsf{Vf}(\mathsf{pk}, \sigma^\star, M^\star) = 1$ and $M^\star \notin \{M_i\}_{i=1}^q$.

Definition 8 (EU-naCMA). *Let* Dss *be a digital signature scheme. We define the success probability of an adversary* $\mathcal{A}$ *against the* EU-naCMA *security of* Dss *as the probability that the above experiment outputs 1:*

$$\text{Succ}_{\text{Dss}(1^n),q}^{\text{EU-naCMA}}(\mathcal{A}) = \Pr\left[\text{Exp}_{\text{Dss}(1^n)}^{\text{EU-naCMA}}(\mathcal{A}) = 1\right],$$

where q *denotes the number of messages that* $\mathcal{A}_1$ *asks the game to sign.*

If we limit the number of queries $q = 1$ to the signing oracle we will call the model one-time EU-naCMA.

5   Security of WOTS-TW

Now we will reduce the security of WOTS-TW in a EU-naCMA model (see Definition 8) to the security properties of the tweakable hash function **Th** and the pseudorandom function family PRF. To do so we will give a standard game-hopping proof. Intuitively the proof goes through the following steps.

– First, we replace the inner secret key elements that are usually generated using PRF by uniformly random values. The two cases must be computationally indistinguishable if PRF is indeed pseudorandom.
– Next we replace the blocks in the chains that become part of the signature by the hash of random values. We need this so that we can later place preimage challenges at these positions of the chain. Here it is important to note that preimage challenges are exactly such hashes of random domain elements and not random co-domain elements. To argue that these two cases are indistinguishable, we need a hybrid argument since for most chains we replace the outcome of several iterations of hashing with a random value.
– Lastly we show that breaking the EU-naCMA property of our scheme in this final case will either allow us to extract a target-collision or a preimage for a given challenge.

Theorem 1. *Let* $n, w \in \mathbb{N}$ *and* $w = poly(n)$. *Let* $\textbf{Th} : \mathcal{P} \times \mathcal{T} \times \{0,1\}^n \to \{0,1\}^n$ *be a* SM-TCR, SM-PRE, *and* SM-UD *function. Let* $\textbf{PRF} : \mathcal{S} \times \mathcal{T} \to \{0,1\}^n$ *be a pseudorandom function. Then the insecurity of the WOTS-TW scheme against one-time EU-naCMA attack is bounded by*

$$\text{InSec}^{\text{EU-naCMA}}(\text{WOTS-TW}; t, 1) \leq$$
$$\text{InSec}^{\text{PRF}}(\textbf{PRF}; \widetilde{t}, l) + \text{InSec}^{\text{SM-TCR}}(\textbf{Th}; \widetilde{t}, lw) +$$
$$\text{InSec}^{\text{SM-PRE}}(\textbf{Th}; \widetilde{t}, l) + w \cdot \text{InSec}^{\text{SM-UD}}(\textbf{Th}; \widetilde{t}, l)$$

with $\widetilde{t} = t + lw$, *where time is given in number of* **Th** *evaluations.*

Proof. First consider the following two games: GAME.1 is the original EU-naCMA game and GAME.2 is the same as GAME.1 but all outputs of

PRF are replaced by random values. We claim that the difference in the success probability of $\mathcal{A}$ playing these games must be bound by $\mathrm{InSec}^{\mathrm{PRF}}(\mathbf{PRF}; \widetilde{t}, l)$.

Next we consider GAME.3 which is the same as GAME.2 but to answer the message signing request we build the signature from nodes that are computed applying **Th** only once instead of b_i times (except if $b_i = 0$, then we return a random value as in the previous game). The public key is constructed from that signature by finishing the chain according to the usual algorithm. We will detail the process in the proof below. We claim that the difference in the success probability of $\mathcal{A}$ playing these games must be bounded by $w \cdot \mathrm{InSec}^{\mathrm{SM\text{-}UD}}(\mathbf{Th}; \widetilde{t}, l)$.

Afterwards, we consider GAME.4, which differs from GAME.3 in that we are considering the game lost if an adversary outputs a valid forgery (M', σ') where there exists an i such that $b_i' < b_i$ and $c^{(b_i', b_i - b_i')}(\sigma_i', i, \mathrm{Seed}) \neq \sigma_i$. We claim that the difference in the success probability of $\mathcal{A}$ playing these games must be bound by $\mathrm{InSec}^{\mathrm{SM\text{-}TCR}}(\mathbf{Th}; \widetilde{t}, lw)$.

If we now consider how $\mathcal{A}$ can win in GAME.4 there is just one viable case left. By the properties of the checksum, there has to be at least one i with $b_i' < b_i$. For any such i the values that get computed from the forgery during verification fully agree with those values that are computed during the verification of the signature by the last game hop. This means that we can use an $\mathcal{A}$ that wins in GAME.4 to find a preimage. We claim that the success probability of the adversary $\mathcal{A}$ in GAME.4 must be bounded by $\mathrm{InSec}^{\mathrm{SM\text{-}PRE}}(\mathbf{Th}; \widetilde{t}, l)$.

In summary, we get the following claims:

Claim 1. $|\mathrm{Succ}^{\mathrm{GAME}.1}(\mathcal{A}) - \mathrm{Succ}^{\mathrm{GAME}.2}(\mathcal{A})| \leq \mathrm{InSec}^{\mathrm{PRF}}(\mathbf{PRF}; \widetilde{t}, l)$.

Claim 2. $|\mathrm{Succ}^{\mathrm{GAME}.2}(\mathcal{A}) - \mathrm{Succ}^{\mathrm{GAME}.3}(\mathcal{A})| \leq w \cdot \mathrm{InSec}^{\mathrm{SM\text{-}UD}}(\mathbf{Th}; \widetilde{t}, l)$.

Claim 3. $|\mathrm{Succ}^{\mathrm{GAME}.3}(\mathcal{A}) - \mathrm{Succ}^{\mathrm{GAME}.4}(\mathcal{A})| \leq \mathrm{InSec}^{\mathrm{SM\text{-}TCR}}(\mathbf{Th}; \widetilde{t}, lw)$.

Claim 4. $\mathrm{Succ}^{\mathrm{GAME}.4}(\mathcal{A}) \leq \mathrm{InSec}^{\mathrm{SM\text{-}PRE}}(\mathbf{Th}; \widetilde{t}, l)$.

The remainder of the proof consists of proving these claims. We then combine the bounds from the claims to obtain the bound of the theorem.

Proof of Claim 1.

Claim 1. $|\mathrm{Succ}^{\mathrm{GAME}.1}(\mathcal{A}) - \mathrm{Succ}^{\mathrm{GAME}.2}(\mathcal{A})| \leq \mathrm{InSec}^{\mathrm{PRF}}(\mathbf{PRF}; \widetilde{t}, l)$.

Proof. We replace **PRF** in GAME.1 by the oracle provided by the PRF game and output 1 whenever $\mathcal{A}$ succeeds. If the oracle is the real **PRF** function keyed with a random secret key, the view of $\mathcal{A}$ is identical to that in GAME.1. If the oracle is the truly random function the argument is a bit more involved. In this case, it is important to note that $\mathcal{A}$ never gets direct access to the oracle but only receives outputs of the oracle. The inputs on which the oracle is queried to obtain these outputs are all unique. Hence, the outputs are uniformly random values. Therefore, the view of $\mathcal{A}$ in this case is exactly that of GAME.2. Consequently, the difference of the probabilities that the reduction outputs 1 in either of the two cases (which is the PRF distinguishing advantage) is exactly the difference of the success probabilities of $\mathcal{A}$ in the two games.

Proof of Claim 2. We first give a more detailed description of GAME.3. In the EU-naCMA game the adversary $\mathcal{A}$ asks to sign a message M without knowing the public key. This message M gets encoded as $B = b_1, \ldots, b_l$. In GAME.3, to answer the query we will perform the following operations. First we generate l values uniformly at random: $u_i \leftarrow_\$ \{0,1\}^n$, $i \in \{1, \ldots, l\}$. Next we answer the signing query with a signature $\sigma = (\sigma_1, \ldots, \sigma_l)$, where $\sigma_i = \mathbf{Th}(\text{Seed}, T_{i,b_i-1}, u_i)$ if $b_i > 0$ and $\sigma_i = u_i$ if $b_i = 0$. Then the public key is constructed as

$$\mathsf{pk} = (\mathsf{pk}_1, \ldots, \mathsf{pk}_l) = (c^{b_1, w-1-b_1}(\sigma_1, 1, \text{Seed}), \ldots, c^{b_l, w-1-b_l}(\sigma_l, l, \text{Seed})), \quad (1)$$

and public key and signature are returned to the adversary. The reason we consider this game is that to bound the final success probability in GAME.4 we will have a reduction replace the u_i with SM-PRE challenges. The resulting signatures have exactly the same distribution as the ones we get here. To show that this cannot change the adversary's success probability significantly, we now prove the following claim.

Claim 2. $|\text{Succ}^{\text{GAME.2}}(\mathcal{A}) - \text{Succ}^{\text{GAME.3}}(\mathcal{A})| \leq w \cdot \text{InSec}^{\text{SM-UD}}(\mathbf{Th}; \widetilde{t}, l)$.

Proof. Consider the following scenario. Let the adversary's query be M. During the signing algorithm M is encoded as $B = \{b_1, \ldots, b_l\}$. Consider two distributions $D_0 = \{\xi_1, \ldots, \xi_l\}$, where $\xi_i \leftarrow_\$ \{0,1\}^n$, $i \in [1, l]$ and $D_{Kg} = \{y_1, \ldots, y_l\}$, where $y_i = c^{0, b_i-1}(\xi_i, i, \text{Seed})$, $\xi_i \leftarrow_\$ \{0,1\}^n$, $i \in [1, l]$. Samples from the first distribution are just random values, and the samples from D_{Kg} are distributed the same way as the $(b_i - 1)$-th values of valid WOTS-TW chains. Assume we play a game where we get access to an oracle $\mathcal{O}_\phi$ that on input B returns $\phi = \{\phi_1, \ldots, \phi_l\}$, either initialized with a sample from D_0 or with a sample from D_{Kg}. Each case occurs with probability $1/2$. Then we can construct an algorithm $\mathcal{M}_{2-3}^{\mathcal{A}}$ as in Algorithm 1 that can distinguish these two cases using a forger $\mathcal{A}$.

Let us consider the behavior of $\mathcal{M}_{2-3}^{\mathcal{A}}$ when $\mathcal{O}_\phi$ samples from D_{Kg}. In this case all the elements in the chains are distributed the same as in GAME.2. The probability that $\mathcal{M}_{2-3}^{\mathcal{A}}$ outputs 1 is the same as the success probability of the adversary in GAME.2. If ϕ instead is from D_0, then the distribution of the elements in the chains is the same as in GAME.3. Hence, the probability that $\mathcal{M}_{UD}^{\mathcal{A}}$ outputs 1 is the same as the success probability of the adversary in GAME.3. By definition, the advantage of $\mathcal{M}_{2-3}^{\mathcal{A}}$ in distinguishing D_0 from D_{Kg} is hence given by

$$\text{Adv}_{D_0, D_{Kg}}(\mathcal{M}_{2-3}^{\mathcal{A}}) = |\text{Succ}^{\text{GAME.2}}(\mathcal{A}) - \text{Succ}^{\text{GAME.3}}(\mathcal{A})| \quad (2)$$

The remaining step is to derive an upper bound for $\text{Adv}_{D_0, D_{Kg}}(\mathcal{M}_{UD}^{\mathcal{A}})$ using the insecurity of the SM-UD property and a hybrid argument.

Let $b_{\max} = \max\{b_1, \ldots, b_l\}$ be the maximum of the values in the message encoding of M. Let H_k be the distribution obtained by computing the values in ϕ as $\phi_i = c^{k, b_i-1-k}(\xi_i, i, \text{Seed})$, $\xi_i \leftarrow_\$ \{0,1\}^n$. Then $H_0 = D_{Kg}$ and $H_{b_{\max}-1} = D_0$ (Note that the chaining function returns the identity when asked to do a negative

---

Algorithm 1: $\mathcal{M}_{2-3}^{\mathcal{A}}$

Input : Access to a distribution oracle $\mathcal{O}_\phi$ and forger $\mathcal{A}$
Output: 0 or 1.

1 Start $\mathcal{A}$ to obtain query with a message M.
2 Encode M as $B = b_1, \dots, b_l$ as in signature algorithm.
3 Call $\mathcal{O}_\phi(B)$ to obtain sample ϕ
4 Construct the signature σ doing one chain step on each sample where $b > 0$ and compute the public key from the signature:
5 **for** $1 \leq i \leq l$ **do**
6   **if** $b_i > 0$ **then**
7      $\sigma_i = c^{b_i - 1, 1}(\phi_i, i, Seed)$
8    $\mathsf{pk}_i = c^{b_i, w - 1 - b_i}(\sigma_i, i, Seed)$
9 Send $\mathsf{PK} = (\mathsf{pk}, Seed)$ and σ to $\mathcal{A}$.
10 **if** $\mathcal{A}$ *returns a valid forgery* (M', σ') **then**
11   **return** *1*
12 **else**
13   **return** *0*

---

amount of steps). As $\mathcal{M}_{2-3}^{\mathcal{A}}$ distinguishes the extreme cases, by a hybrid argument there are two consecutive hybrids H_j and H_{j+1} that can be distinguished with probability $\geq \mathrm{Adv}_{\mathcal{D}_0, \mathcal{D}_{K_g}}(\mathcal{M}_{2-3}^{\mathcal{A}})/(b_{\max} - 1)$.

To bound the success probability of an adversary in distinguishing two such consecutive hybrids, we build a second reduction $\mathcal{M}_{\mathrm{UD}}^{\mathcal{B}}$ that uses $\mathcal{B} = \mathcal{M}_{2-3}^{\mathcal{A}}$ to break SM-UD. For this purpose, $\mathcal{M}_{\mathrm{UD}}^{\mathcal{B}}$ simulates $\mathcal{O}_\phi$. To answer a query for $B = b_1, \dots, b_l$, $\mathcal{M}_{\mathrm{UD}}^{\mathcal{B}}$ plays in the SM-UD game, interacting with the SM-UD oracle $\mathcal{O}_{\mathrm{UD}}(\cdot, b)$ to construct hybrid H_{j+b}, depending on the secret bit b of the oracle. To do so $\mathcal{M}_{\mathrm{UD}}^{\mathcal{B}}$ makes queries to $\mathcal{O}_{\mathrm{UD}}$ with tweaks $\{T_{1,j}, \dots, T_{l,j}\}$. Then, depending on b, the responses ψ of $\mathcal{O}_{\mathrm{UD}}$ are either l random values or $\psi = (c^{j,1}(\xi_1, 1, Seed), \dots, c^{j,1}(\xi_l, l, Seed)$, $\xi_i \leftarrow_\$ \{0,1\}^n$, $i \in [1, l])$. After that $\mathcal{M}_{\mathrm{UD}}^{\mathcal{B}}$ requests Seed from the SM-UD challenger. Next, $\mathcal{M}_{\mathrm{UD}}^{\mathcal{B}}$ applies the hash chain to the oracle responses ψ to compute samples

$$\phi_i = \begin{cases} c^{j+1, b_i - 1 - (j+1)}(\psi_i, i, Seed), & \text{if } j < b_i - 1 \\ \xi_i \leftarrow_\$ \{0,1\}^n, & \text{otherwise,} \end{cases}$$

and returns it to $\mathcal{M}_{2-3}^{\mathcal{A}}$. $\mathcal{M}_{\mathrm{UD}}^{\mathcal{B}}$ returns whatever $\mathcal{M}_{2-3}^{\mathcal{A}}$ returns. If ψ consisted of random values the distribution was H_{j+1}, otherwise H_j. Consequently, the advantage of distinguishing any two hybrids must be bound by $\mathrm{InSec}^{\mathrm{SM\text{-}UD}}(\mathbf{Th}; \xi, l)$. Putting things together, we see that $b_{\max} \leq w$ for any message M. Hence, we get

$$|\mathrm{Succ}^{\mathrm{GAME.2}}(\mathcal{A}) - \mathrm{Succ}^{\mathrm{GAME.3}}(\mathcal{A})| = \mathrm{Adv}_{\mathcal{D}_0, \mathcal{D}_{K_g}}(\mathcal{M}_{2-3}^{\mathcal{A}})$$
$$\leq w \cdot \mathrm{Adv}_{\mathbf{Th}, l}^{\mathrm{SM\text{-}UD}}(\mathcal{M}_{\mathrm{UD}}^{\mathcal{B}}) \leq w \cdot \mathrm{InSec}^{\mathrm{SM\text{-}UD}}(\mathbf{Th}; \xi, l)$$

which concludes the proof of the claim.

Proof of Claim 3. Recall that GAME.4 differs from GAME.3 in that we are considering the game lost if an adversary outputs a valid forgery (M', σ') where there exists i such that $b_i' < b_i$ and $c^{(b_i', b_i - b_i')}(\sigma_i', i, \text{Seed}) \neq \sigma_i$. So the difference in success probability is exactly the probability that $\mathcal{A}$ outputs a valid forgery and there exists an i such that $b_i' < b_i$ and $c^{(b_i', b_i - b_i')}(\sigma_i', i, \text{Seed}) \neq \sigma_i$. We will now prove Claim 3 which claims the following bound on this probability:

Claim 3. $|\text{Succ}^{\text{GAME.3}}(\mathcal{A}) - \text{Succ}^{\text{GAME.4}}(\mathcal{A})| \leq \text{InSec}^{\text{SM-TCR}}(\mathbf{Th}; \tilde{t}, lw)$.

Proof. To prove the claim we construct an algorithm $\mathcal{M}_{\text{TCR}}^{\mathcal{A}}$ that reduces SM-TCR of $\mathbf{Th}$ to the task of forging a signature that fulfills the above condition. The algorithm is based on the following idea. $\mathcal{M}_{\text{TCR}}^{\mathcal{A}}$ simulates GAME.4. In GAME.4 the adversary sends a query to sign a message M. To answer this query and compute the public key, $\mathcal{M}_{\text{TCR}}^{\mathcal{A}}$ interacts with the SM-TCR oracle. This way, $\mathcal{M}_{\text{TCR}}^{\mathcal{A}}$ obtains target-collision challenges corresponding to the nodes in the signature and all intermediate values of the chain computations made to compute the public key. Then $\mathcal{M}_{\text{TCR}}^{\mathcal{A}}$ requests the public parameters P from the SM-TCR challenger. We set the public seed Seed of WOTS-TW equal to P and return the constructed signature and public key to $\mathcal{A}$. When $\mathcal{A}$ returns a forgery (M', σ'), there exists i such that $b_i' < b_i$ and $c^{(b_i', b_i - b_i')}(\sigma_i', i, \text{Seed}) \neq \sigma_i$ per assumption. By a pigeonhole argument there must be a collision on the way to the public key element. $\mathcal{M}_{\text{TCR}}^{\mathcal{A}}$ extracts this collision and returns it. Algorithm 2 gives a detailed description of $\mathcal{M}_{\text{TCR}}^{\mathcal{A}}$ in pseudocode. For the visual representation of the idea described in the mentioned algorithm see Fig. 1 in the full paper [HK22]. The algorithm is broken into two logically separated parts: Challenge placement and obtaining the result.

Here we detail which SM-TCR challenges we create per chain in line 11 of Algorithm 2. Assume we have σ_i at position b_i. Then the first query will be (T_{i,b_i}, σ_i). Let's denote the answer for that query as c_1. The next query will be (T_{i,b_i+1}, c_1). We denote the answer for that query as c_2. In general we will make queries of the form (T_{i,b_i+k}, c_k). And we denote the answers for those queries as c_{k+1}. We make queries until we get c_{w-1-b_i}. We set pk_i to be c_{w-1-b_i}.

As we are set to bound the probability of those cases where the adversary outputs a valid forgery and there exists i such that $b_i' < b_i$ and $c^{(b_i', b_i - b_i')}(\sigma_i', i, \text{Seed}) \neq \sigma_i$, $\mathcal{M}_{\text{TCR}}^{\mathcal{A}}$ never runs into the fail cases in lines 22 and 24. Moreover, the distribution of inputs to $\mathcal{A}$ when run by $\mathcal{M}_{\text{TCR}}^{\mathcal{A}}$ is identical to that in GAME.4. Therefore, $\mathcal{M}_{\text{TCR}}^{\mathcal{A}}$ returns a target-collision with probability $|\text{Succ}^{\text{GAME.3}}(\mathcal{A}) - \text{Succ}^{\text{GAME.4}}(\mathcal{A})|$ which concludes the proof of the claim.

Proof of Claim 4. It remains to prove the last claim. Consider a forgery σ' and the positions b_i' of the σ' elements. There must exist a j such that $b_j' < b_j$ by the properties of the checksum. Remember that in GAME.4, the case where $c^{(b_j', b_j - b_j')}(\sigma_j', j, \text{Seed}) \neq \sigma_j$ is excluded for all such j. Hence, it must hold for these j that $c^{(b_j', b_j - b_j')}(\sigma_j', j, \text{Seed}) = \sigma_j$. Therefore, we can use $\mathcal{A}$ to compute a preimage of σ_j. We use this to prove Claim 4.

Claim 4. $\text{Succ}^{\text{GAME.4}}(\mathcal{A}) \leq \text{InSec}^{\text{SM-PRE}}(\mathbf{Th}; \tilde{t}, l)$.

Algorithm 2: $\mathcal{M}^{\mathcal{A}}_{\text{TCR}}$

Input : Security parameter n, oracle access to SM-TCR challenger C and EU-naCMA forger $\mathcal{A}$.

Output: A pair (j, M) or fail.

1 **begin** Challenge placement
2   Start $\mathcal{A}$ to obtain query with a message M.
3   Encode M as $B = b_1, \ldots, b_l$ as in signature algorithm.
4   **for** $i \in \{1, \ldots, l\}$ **do**
5   **if** $b_i = 0$ **then**
6   Set $\sigma_i \leftarrow_\$ \{0,1\}^n$.
7   **else**
8   Sample $\xi_i \leftarrow_\$ \{0,1\}^n$,
9   Query C for SM-TCR challenge with inputs ξ_i, T_{1,b_i-1}.
10   Store answer as σ_i. // i.e., $\sigma_i = \mathbf{Th}(P, T_{i,b_i-1}, \xi_i)$
11   Compute public key element $\mathsf{pk}_i = c^{b_i, w-1-b_i}(\sigma_i, i, \cdot)$ as in the verification algorithm but using the SM-TCR challenge oracle provided by C in place of $\mathbf{Th}$. // That is why no Seed is needed
12   Get public parameters P from the challenger and set Seed $= P$.
13   Set signature $\sigma = (\sigma_1, \ldots, \sigma_l)$ and $\mathsf{pk} = (\mathsf{pk}_1, \ldots, \mathsf{pk}_l)$.

14 **begin** Obtaining the result
15   Return σ and $\mathsf{PK} = (\mathsf{pk}, \text{Seed})$ to the adversary $\mathcal{A}$.
16   **if** *The adversary returns a valid forgery (M', σ')* **then**
17   Encode M' as $B' = (b'_1, \ldots, b'_l)$ according to sign.
18   **if** $\exists\ i$ *such that $b'_i < b_i$ and $c^{(b'_i, b_i - b'_i)}(\sigma'_i, i, \text{Seed}) \neq \sigma_i$* **then**
19   Let j be the smallest integer such that the chains collide:
          $c^{b_i, j}(y_i, i, \text{Seed}) = c^{b'_i, j}(\sigma'_i, i, \text{Seed}))$.
20   **return** SM-TCR *solution* $(i, c^{b'_i, (j-1)}(\sigma'_i, i, \text{Seed}))$
21   **else**
22   **return** *fail*
23   **else**
24   **return** *fail*

Proof. As for the previous claim, we construct an algorithm $\mathcal{M}^{\mathcal{A}}_{\text{PRE}}$ that uses a forger in GAME.4 to solve a SM-PRE challenge. In the beginning, $\mathcal{M}^{\mathcal{A}}_{\text{PRE}}$ receives a query to sign a message M from the adversary $\mathcal{A}$ and encodes it into b_i's. To answer the query $\mathcal{M}^{\mathcal{A}}_{\text{PRE}}$ interacts with the SM-PRE challenger to receive preimage challenges y_i for tweaks that make the challenges fit into positions b_i. That way, $\mathcal{M}^{\mathcal{A}}_{\text{PRE}}$ can use the challenges as signature values $\sigma_i = y_i$. Then $\mathcal{M}^{\mathcal{A}}_{\text{PRE}}$ asks the SM-PRE challenger to return public parameters P. Given P, $\mathcal{M}^{\mathcal{A}}_{\text{PRE}}$ can construct the public key using the recomputation method used in the signature verification algorithm. $\mathcal{M}^{\mathcal{A}}$ sets the public seed Seed of WOTS-TW to be P and returns the constructed signature and public key to $\mathcal{A}$. When $\mathcal{A}$ returns a valid forgery, this forgery must contain a signature value σ_j with index

---

Algorithm 3: $\mathcal{M}_{PRE}^{\mathcal{A}}$

Input : Security parameter n, access to SM-PRE challenger C and forger $\mathcal{A}$.
Output: A pair (j, M) or fail.

1 **begin** Challenge placement
2 | Run $\mathcal{A}$ to receive initial query for a signature on message M.
3 | Encode M as $B = b_1, \ldots, b_l$ following the steps in the signature algorithm.
4 | **for** $1 \leq i \leq l$ **do**
5 | | **if** $b_i > 0$ **then**
6 | | | Query C for preimage challenge y_i with tweak T_{1,b_i-1}.
   | | | // $y_i = \mathbf{Th}(P, T_{i,b_i-1}, \xi_i)$
7 | | **else**
8 | | | $y_i \leftarrow_\$ \{0,1\}^n$.
9 | | Set $\sigma_i = y_i$.
10 | Get the seed P from C and set Seed $= P$.
11 | Compute public key $\mathsf{pk} = (\mathsf{pk}_1, \ldots \mathsf{pk}_l)$, as $\mathsf{pk}_i = c^{w-1-b_i}(y_i, i, \text{Seed})$.
12 **begin** Obtaining the result
13 | Return σ and $\mathsf{PK} = (\mathsf{pk}, P)$ to $\mathcal{A}$.
14 | **if** $\mathcal{A}$ *returns a valid forgery* (M', σ') **then**
15 | | Compute $B' = (b'_1, \ldots, b'_l)$ encoding M'
16 | | **if** $\exists 1 \leq j \leq l$ *such that* $b'_j < b_j$ *and* $c^{(b'_j, b_j - b'_j)}(\sigma'_j, j, \text{Seed}) = \sigma_j$ **then**
17 | | | **return** SM-PRE *solution* $(j, c^{b'_j,(b_j-b'_j-1)}(\sigma'_j, j, \text{Seed}))$
18 | | **else**
19 | | | **return** *fail*
20 | **else**
21 | | **return** *fail*

---

j such that $b'_j < b_j$ and $c^{b'_j,(b_j-b'_j)}(\sigma'_j, j, \text{Seed}) = \sigma_j$ per definition of the game. $\mathcal{M}_{PRE}^{\mathcal{A}}$ returns preimage $(j, c^{b'_j,(b_j-b'_j-1)}(\sigma'_j, j, \text{Seed}))$. A pseudocode version of $\mathcal{M}_{PRE}^{\mathcal{A}}$ is given as Algorithm 3. For a visual representation of the ideas described in the Algorithm 3 we refer to Fig. 2 in the full paper [HK22]. The algorithm is broken into two logically separated parts: Challenge placement and obtaining the result.

Due to the properties of GAME.4, $\mathcal{M}_{PRE}^{\mathcal{A}}$ succeeds whenever $\mathcal{A}$ succeeds, as the failure case in line 19 never occurs when $\mathcal{A}$ succeeds. Moreover, the distribution of the inputs to $\mathcal{A}$ when run by $\mathcal{M}_{PRE}^{\mathcal{A}}$ is identical to that in GAME.4 (this was ensured in the game hop to GAME.3). Therefore, $\mathcal{M}_{PRE}^{\mathcal{A}}$ returns preimages with probability $\text{Succ}^{GAME.4}(\mathcal{A})$ which proves the claim.

6   Extension to Multiple Instances with Same Public Seed

One-time signatures are often used in more complex constructions. For example, WOTS-TW was developed as part of SPHINCS$^+$. The distinguishing feature of this setting is that many WOTS-TW instances are used within one instance of the complex construction. In this section we will show that we can base the security of multiple WOTS-TW instances on the same multi-target security properties used for a single instance. While, the number of targets increases, we argue in Sect. 8 that the complexity of generic attacks is not influenced by the number of targets for these notions. Hence, there is no decrease in security to be expected when using multiple instances. We will show that this even works when the same public seed is used for all instances, as long as different prefixes are used for the tweaks.

In SPHINCS-like constructions WOTS-TW is used to sign the roots of trees which are not controlled by an adversary against the construction but by the signer. More generally, this is the case in many such constructions. Hence, we use an extension of the EU-naCMA model from last section to d instances. We define EU-naCMA security for d instances of WOTS-TW with respect to a collection of THFs. Our definition is non-generic but tailored to WOTS-TW and the way it is used within SPHINCS$^+$ and other constructions. The reason is that in these settings the THF used in WOTS-TW is a member of the collection of THFs used in the construction and uses the same public parameters. We could have introduced a generic model for this but this would have required the introduction of further abstractions that would unnecessarily complicate the presentation.

The security of multiple WOTS-TW instances is analyzed using the following experiment. In which a two-stage adversary $\mathcal{A} = (\mathcal{A}_1, \mathcal{A}_2)$ is allowed to make signing queries to a signing oracle WOTS-TW.sign$(\cdot, (Seed, \cdot, \mathcal{S}))$ and THF oracle $\mathbf{Th}_\lambda$. The signing oracle takes as inputs a message M and address **ADRS**. As we described in Sect. 3.2 **ADRS** defines a prefix that distinguishes different instances of WOTS-TW and other structures in bigger constructions. First it runs $(\mathsf{SK}, \mathsf{PK}) \leftarrow$ WOTS-TW.kg$(\mathcal{C} = (Seed, \mathbf{ADRS}); \mathcal{S})$. Then it computes $\sigma \leftarrow$ WOTS-TW.sign$(M; \mathsf{SK})$. By PK' we denote PK without $Seed$, i.e. $\mathsf{PK}' = (\mathsf{pk}, \mathbf{ADRS})$. The signing oracle returns $(\sigma, M, \mathsf{PK}')$ to the adversary. We restrict $\mathcal{A}_1$ from querying $\mathbf{Th}_\lambda$ with tweaks for **ADRS**s that are used in signature queries. We define a function $\mathsf{adrs}(\cdot)$ that takes a tweak as an input and returns **ADRS** of that tweak. The set of queries to signing oracle is denoted as $Q = \{(M_i, \mathbf{ADRS}_i)\}_{i=1}^{d}$ and the set of tweaks that are used to query $\mathbf{Th}_\lambda$ is $T = \{T_i\}_{i=1}^{p}$. We analyze one-time signatures, so the number of allowed signing queries for each **ADRS** is restricted to 1.

Experiment $\mathsf{Exp}_{\mathsf{WOTS\text{-}TW}}^{\mathsf{d\text{-}EU\text{-}naCMA}}(\mathcal{A})$

- $Seed \leftarrow_\$ \{0,1\}^n$
- $\mathcal{S} \leftarrow_\$ \{0,1\}^n$
- $state \leftarrow \mathcal{A}_1^{\text{WOTS-TW.sign}(\cdot,(Seed,\cdot,\mathcal{S})),\mathbf{Th}_\lambda(Seed,\cdot,\cdot)}(\ )$
- $(M^\star, \sigma^\star, j) \leftarrow \mathcal{A}_2(state, Seed)$
- Return 1 iff $j \in [1, d] \wedge [\mathsf{Vf}(\mathsf{PK}_j, \sigma^\star, M^\star) = 1] \wedge [M^\star \neq M_j] \wedge [\mathbf{DIST}(\{\mathbf{ADRS}_i\}_{i=1}^{d})] \wedge [\forall \mathbf{ADRS}_i \in Q, \mathbf{ADRS}_i \notin T' = \{\mathsf{adrs}(T_i)\}_{i=1}^{p}]$.

We define the success probability of an adversary $\mathcal{A}$ in the described experiment with d instances as $\mathsf{Succ}_{\mathsf{WOTS\text{-}TW},d}^{\mathsf{d\text{-}EU\text{-}naCMA}}(\mathcal{A}) \overset{\text{def}}{=} \Pr\left[\mathsf{Exp}_{\mathsf{WOTS\text{-}TW}}^{\mathsf{d\text{-}EU\text{-}naCMA}}(\mathcal{A}) = 1\right]$. Note that due to **ADRS** restrictions for the signing oracle the adversary can not obtain more than one signature for the same pk. The following theorem can be proven by generalization of the proof of Theorem 1. The main idea behind the proof is the following. First we use different tweaks in different instances of WOTS-TW as we use different **ADRSs** for each instance. Next point is that we obtain d times more challenges and we separate them in d sets. Each set will be used for one instance of WOTS-TW. Then the proof follows the same path as in Theorem 1.

Theorem 2. *Let $n, w \in \mathbb{N}$ and $w = poly(n)$. Let $\mathbf{F} := \mathbf{Th}_1 : \mathcal{P} \times \mathcal{T} \times \{0,1\}^n \to \{0,1\}^n$ be a SM-TCR, SM-PRE, SM-UD THF as a member of a collection. Let $\mathbf{PRF} : \mathcal{S} \times \mathcal{T} \to \{0,1\}^n$ be a KHF. Then the following inequality holds:*

$$\mathsf{InSec}^{\mathsf{d\text{-}EU\text{-}naCMA}}(\mathsf{WOTS\text{-}TW}; t, d)$$
$$< \mathsf{InSec}^{\mathsf{PRF}}(\mathbf{PRF}; \tilde{t}, d \cdot l) + \mathsf{InSec}^{\mathsf{SM\text{-}TCR}}(\mathbf{F} \in \mathbf{Th}; \tilde{t}, d \cdot lw)$$
$$+ \mathsf{InSec}^{\mathsf{SM\text{-}PRE}}(\mathbf{F} \in \mathbf{Th}; \tilde{t}, d \cdot l) + w \cdot \mathsf{InSec}^{\mathsf{SM\text{-}UD}}(\mathbf{F} \in \mathbf{Th}; \tilde{t}, d \cdot l) \quad (3)$$

with $\tilde{t} = t + d \cdot lw$, where time is given in number of $\mathbf{Th}$ and $\mathbf{PRF}$ evaluations.

Proof sketch. Let us give a brief description how the proof for the multi-instance case is obtained. We have the same game hopping as in Theorem 1.

GAME.1 is the original d-EU-naCMA game and GAME.2 is the same as GAME.1 but the pseudorandom outputs from **PRF** are replaced by truly random values. We claim that

$$\left| \mathsf{Succ}^{\mathsf{GAME.1}}(\mathcal{A}) - \mathsf{Succ}^{\mathsf{GAME.2}}(\mathcal{A}) \right| \leq \mathsf{InSec}^{\mathsf{PRF}}(\mathbf{PRF}; \tilde{t}, d \cdot l).$$

The reasoning here is the same as in Claim 1 in Theorem 1. Note that all inputs on which the oracle in the PRF game is queried are unique due to the unique **ADRSs** for each instance. Hence, the outputs are uniformly random values as desired.

GAME.3 is different from GAME.2 in that for each signing query we answer with a hash of a random value rather than building it with a chaining function. In Claim 2 of Theorem 1 we reduced it to the SM-UD property by using a hybrid argument. Here we need to apply the same reasoning. To obtain the needed hybrids in case of d instances we will do the following. We use an additional index to denote the B-values associated with the i-th message M_i. So M_i is transferred into $b_{i,1}, \ldots, b_{i,l}$. We now consider the d-fold distributions $D_{d\text{-}Kg} = \{y_{1,1}, \ldots, y_{1,l}, \ldots, y_{d,1}, \ldots, y_{d,l}\}$, where $y_{i,j} = c_{\mathbf{ADRS}_i}^{0, b_j - 1}(\xi_{i,j}, j, \mathsf{Seed})$ and $D_{d\text{-}0} = \{\xi_{1,1}, \ldots, \xi_{1,l}, \ldots, \xi_{d,1}, \ldots, \xi_{d,l}\}$, where $\xi_{i,j} \leftarrow_\$ \{0,1\}^n$, $i \in [1,d]$, $j \in [1,l]$. The distinguishing advantage of an adversary against those two distributions is exactly the difference of these two games. To limit this distinguishing advantage we need to build hybrids. We do this in the same manner as in the proof of Theorem 1. Let $b_{\max} = \max\{b_{1,1}, \ldots, b_{1,l} \ldots, b_{d,1}, \ldots, b_{d,l}\}$ be the maximum of the values in the message encoding of all M_i. Let H_k be the distribution obtained by computing the values as $c_{\mathbf{ADRS}_i}^{k, b_{i,j} - 1 - k}(\xi_{i,j}, j, \mathsf{Seed})$, $\xi_{i,j} \leftarrow_\$ \{0,1\}^n$.

One can notice that $H_0 = D_{Kg}$ and $H_{b_{\max}-1} = D_0$. There must be two consecutive hybrids H_γ and $H_{\gamma+1}$ that we can distinguish with probability close to the distinguishing advantage. By playing SM-UD and interacting with the oracle $\mathcal{O}(\cdot, b)$ we can construct hybrid $H_{\gamma+b}$. This is done in just the same way as in Claim 2 of Theorem 1. Hence, we obtain the following bound:

$$|\mathrm{Succ}^{\mathrm{GAME.2}}(\mathcal{A}) - \mathrm{Succ}^{\mathrm{GAME.3}}(\mathcal{A})| \leq w \cdot \mathrm{InSec}^{\mathrm{SM\text{-}UD}}(\mathbf{F} \in \mathbf{Th}; \widetilde{t}, d \cdot l).$$

Notice that in case of one instance we obtained Seed from the SM-UD challenger that we used to construct the hybrids and obtain the WOTS-TW public key. Here instead of using Seed we need to interact with the $\mathbf{Th}_\lambda(\mathrm{Seed}\cdot, \cdot)$ oracle. Only after all of the signing queries are made we will obtain the Seed.

GAME.4 is different from GAME.3 in that we are considering the game lost if an adversary outputs a valid forgery $(M^\star, \sigma^\star, j)$ where there exist such i that $b_{i,j}^\star < b_{i,j}$ and $c_{\mathbf{ADRS}_i}^{(b_{i,j}^\star, b_{i,j}-b_{i,j}^\star)}(\sigma_j^\star, j, \mathrm{Seed}) \neq \sigma_j$. To show the bound we can build a reduction that works as follows. To answer the signature queries and compute the public key, the reduction interacts with the SM-TCR oracle. The difference in case of d instances from one instance is that we will need d times more interactions with the SM-TCR oracle. Per assumption, there must exist at least one chain such that the chain that we built and the chain obtained from the forged signature are different but lead to the same public key. Hence, by a pigeonhole argument there must be a collision on the way to the public key element. This collision is a solution for the SM-TCR challenge. So we proved that

$$|\mathrm{Succ}^{\mathrm{GAME.3}}(\mathcal{A}) - \mathrm{Succ}^{\mathrm{GAME.4}}(\mathcal{A})| \leq \mathrm{InSec}^{\mathrm{SM\text{-}TCR}}(\mathbf{H} \in \mathbf{Th}; \widetilde{t}, d \cdot lw).$$

To give a bound on the success probability for GAME.4 we use the SM-PRE property. To answer signing queries we will interact with the SM-PRE oracle and place challenges obtained from that oracle in place of signatures. To construct public keys of WOTS-TW instances we will behave in the same way as in the undetectability case. By interacting with $\mathbf{Th}_\lambda(\mathrm{Seed}, \cdot, \cdot)$ we can build the chains of WOTS-TW structures. Again there must exist a j such that $b_{i,j}^\star < b_{i,j}$ by the properties of the checksum. And since we excluded the case where $c_{\mathbf{ADRS}_i}^{(b_{i,j}^\star, b_{i,j}-b_{i,j}^\star)}(\sigma_j^\star, j, \mathrm{Seed}) \neq \sigma_j$ we can obtain a preimage by computing $c_{\mathbf{ADRS}_i}^{(b_{i,j}^\star-1, b_{i,j}-b_{i,j}^\star)}(\sigma_j^\star, j, \mathrm{Seed})$. So we obtain

$$|\mathrm{Succ}^{\mathrm{GAME.4}}(\mathcal{A})| \leq \mathrm{InSec}^{\mathrm{SM\text{-}PRE}}(\mathbf{F} \in \mathbf{Th}; \widetilde{t}, d \cdot l).$$

This concludes the sketch of the proof.

7 SPHINCS⁺

In this section we will recap the SPHINCS⁺ structure and afterwards give fixes to the original SPHINCS⁺ proof. To obtain a fixed proof we will utilize the results from Theorem 2. In SPHINCS$^+$ a special function to compute message digest is introduced. An expected property of that function is interleaved target subset-resilience. The formal definition of this property is given in the full paper [HK22]. The part of the proof where we use this property is the same as in the SPHINCS$^+$ paper [BHK+19]. Hence, we will not discuss it in details.

7.1   Brief Description

First we give a brief description of the SPHINCS$^+$ signature scheme. An example of the SPHINCS$^+$ structure is shown in Fig. 3 in the full paper [HK22]. A detailed description can be found in [BHK+19]. The public key consists of two n-bit values: a random public seed **PK**.seed and the root of the top tree in the hypertree structure. **PK**.seed is used as a first argument for all of the tweakable hash functions calls. The private key contains two more n-bit values **SK**.seed and **SK**.prf. We discuss the main parts of SPHINCS$^+$. First we describe the addressing scheme. As SPHINCS$^+$ uses THFs, different tweaks are required for all calls to THFs. The tweaks are instantiated by the addresses. The address is a 32 byte value. Address coding can be done in any convenient way. Each address has a prefix that denotes to which part of the SPHINCS$^+$ structure it belongs. We denoted this prefix as **ADRS** in previous sections.

Then we need to discuss binary trees. In the SPHINCS$^+$ algorithm, binary trees of height γ always have 2^γ leaves. Each leaf L_i, $i \in [0, 2^\gamma - 1]$ is a bit string of length n. Each node of the tree $N_{i,j}$, $0 < j \leq \gamma, 0 \leq i < 2^{\gamma-j}$ is also a bit string of length n. The values of the internal nodes of the tree are calculated from the children of that node using a THF. A leaf of a binary tree is the output of a THF that takes the elements of a WOTS-TW public key as input.

Binary trees and WOTS-TW signature schemes are used to construct a hypertree structure. WOTS-TW instances are used to sign the roots of binary trees on lower levels. WOTS-TW instances on the lowest level are used to sign the public key of a FORS (Forest of Random Subsets) few-time signature scheme instance. FORS is defined with the following parameters: $k \in \mathbb{N}$, $t = 2^a$. This algorithm can sign message digests of length ka-bits.

FORS key pair. The private key of FORS consists of kt pseudorandomly generated n-bit values grouped into k sets of t elements each. To get the public key, k binary hash trees are constructed. The leaves in these trees are k sets (one for each tree) which consist of t values, each. Thus, we get k trees of height a. As roots of k binary trees are calculated they are compressed using a THF. The resulting value will be the FORS public key.

FORS Signature. A message of ka bits is divided into k lines of a bits. Each of these lines is interpreted as a leaf index corresponding to one of the k trees. The signature consists of these leaves and their authentication paths. An authentication path for a leaf is the set of siblings of the nodes on the path from this leaf to the root. The verifier reconstructs the tree roots, compresses them, and verifies them against the public key. If there is a match, it is said that the signature was verified. Otherwise, it is declared invalid.

The last thing to discuss is the way the message digest is calculated. First, a pseudorandom value $\mathbf{R}$ is prepared as $\mathbf{R} = \mathbf{PRF}_{msg}(\mathbf{SK}_{\mathsf{prf}}, \mathsf{OptRand}, M)$ using a dedicated secret key element $\mathbf{SK}.\mathsf{prf}$ and the message. This function can be made non-deterministic initializing the value $\mathsf{OptRand}$ with randomness. The $\mathbf{R}$ value is part of the signature. Using $\mathbf{R}$, we calculate the index of the FORS key pair with which the message will be signed and the message digest itself: $(\mathsf{MD}\|\mathsf{idx}) = \mathbf{H}_{\mathbf{msg}}(\mathbf{R}, \mathbf{PK}.\mathsf{seed}, \mathbf{PK}.\mathsf{root}, M)$.

The signature consists of the randomness $\mathbf{R}$, the FORS signature (under idx from $\mathbf{H}_{\mathbf{msg}}$) of the message digest, the WOTS-TW signature of the corresponding FORS public key, and a set of authentication paths and WOTS-TW signatures of tree roots. To test this chain, the verifier iteratively reconstructs the public keys and tree roots until it gets the root of the top tree. If this matches the root given in the SPHINCS+ public key, the signature is accepted.

7.2 SPHINCS+ Proof

In this part we fix the proof of security of the SPHINCS+ framework. The security had several issues which are described in [KKF20, ABB+20]. The SPHINCS+ construction uses the following functions:

$\mathbf{F} := \mathbf{Th}_1 : \mathcal{P} \times \mathcal{T} \times \{0,1\}^n \to \{0,1\}^n$; $\mathbf{Th}_k : \mathcal{P} \times \mathcal{T} \times \{0,1\}^{kn} \to \{0,1\}^n$;
$\mathbf{PRF} : \{0,1\}^n \times \{0,1\}^{256} \to \{0,1\}^n$; $\mathbf{Th}_l : \mathcal{P} \times \mathcal{T} \times \{0,1\}^{ln} \to \{0,1\}^n$;
$\mathbf{H}_{\mathbf{msg}} : \{0,1\}^n \times \{0,1\}^n \times \{0,1\}^n \times \{0,1\}^* \to \{0,1\}^m$.
$\mathbf{PRF}_{\mathbf{msg}} : \{0,1\}^n \times \{0,1\}^n \times \{0,1\}^* \to \{0,1\}^n$;
$\mathbf{H} := \mathbf{Th}_2 : \mathcal{P} \times \mathcal{T} \times \{0,1\}^{2n} \to \{0,1\}^n$;

In this section, we prove the following Theorem about the standard EU-CMA-security (for a definition see the full paper [HK22]) of SPHINCS+. Note that $\mathbf{F}$, $\mathbf{H}$, $\mathbf{Th}_l$, and $\mathbf{Th}_k$ are members of a collection $\mathbf{Th}$ of tweakable hash functions with different message lengths.

Theorem 3. *For parameters n, w, h, d, m, t, k as described in [BHK+19] and l be the number of chains in WOTS-TW instances the following bound can be obtained:*

$$\mathsf{InSec}^{\mathrm{EU-CMA}}(\text{SPHINCS}^+; \xi, q_s)$$
$$\leq \mathsf{InSec}^{\mathrm{PRF}}(\mathbf{PRF}, \xi, q_1) + \mathsf{InSec}^{\mathrm{PRF}}(\mathbf{PRF_{msg}}, \xi, q_s)$$
$$+ \mathsf{InSec}^{\mathrm{ITSR}}(\mathbf{H_{msg}}, \xi, q_s) + w \cdot \mathsf{InSec}^{\mathrm{SM-UD}}(\mathbf{F} \in \mathbf{Th}; \xi, q_2)$$
$$+ \mathsf{InSec}^{\mathrm{SM-TCR}}(\mathbf{F} \in \mathbf{Th}; \xi, q_3 + q_7) + \mathsf{InSec}^{\mathrm{SM-PRE}}(\mathbf{F} \in \mathbf{Th}; \xi, q_2)$$
$$+ \mathsf{InSec}^{\mathrm{SM-TCR}}(\mathbf{H} \in \mathbf{Th}; \xi, q_4) + \mathsf{InSec}^{\mathrm{SM-TCR}}(\mathbf{Th}_k \in \mathbf{Th}; \xi, q_5)$$
$$+ \mathsf{InSec}^{\mathrm{SM-TCR}}(\mathbf{Th}_l \in \mathbf{Th}; \xi, q_6)$$
$$+ 3 \cdot \mathsf{InSec}^{\mathrm{SM-TCR}}(\mathbf{F} \in \mathbf{Th}; \xi, q_8) + \mathsf{InSec}^{\mathrm{SM-DSPR}}(\mathbf{F} \in \mathbf{Th}; \xi, q_8),$$

where $q_1 < 2^{h+1}(kt + l)$, $q_2 < 2^{h+1} \cdot l$, $q_3 < 2^{h+1} \cdot l \cdot w$, $q_4 < 2^{h+1}k \cdot 2t$, $q_5 < 2^h$, $q_6 < 2^{h+1}$, $q_7 < 2^{h+1}kt$, $q_8 < 2^h \cdot kt$ and q_s denotes the number of signing queries made by $\mathcal{A}$.

Proof. We want to bound the success probability of an adversary $\mathcal{A}$ against the EU-CMA security of SPHINCS$^+$. Towards this end we use the following series of games. We start with GAME.0 which is the EU-CMA experiment for SPHINCS$^+$. Now consider a GAME.1 which is GAME.0 but the experiment makes use of a SPHINCS$^+$ version where all the outputs of PRF, i.e., the WOTS-TW and FORS secret-key elements, get replaced by truly random values.

Next, consider a game GAME.2, which is the same as GAME.1 but in the signing oracle $\mathbf{PRF_{msg}}$(SK.prf, $\cdot$) is replaced by a truly random function.

Afterwards, we consider GAME.3, which differs from GAME.2 in that we are considering the game lost if an adversary outputs a valid forgery (M, SIG) where the FORS signature part of SIG contains only secret values which were contained in previous signatures with that FORS key pair obtained by $\mathcal{A}$ via the signing oracle.

Now consider what are the possibilities of the adversary to win the game. The FORS signature in a forgery must include the preimage of a FORS leaf node that was not previously revealed to it. There are two separate cases for that leaf:

1. The FORS leaf is different to the leaf that we would generate for that place.
2. The FORS leaf is the same to the leaf that we would generate for that place;

Let's consider GAME.4 which differs from GAME.3 in that we are considering that the game is lost in the first "leaf case" scenario.

Now let's analyze those games.

GAME.0 - GAME.3. The hops between GAME.0 and GAME.3 are fully presented in the SHINCS+ paper [BHK+19]. The bound for these games are

$$|\mathrm{Succ}_{\mathcal{A}}^{\mathrm{GAME.0}} - \mathrm{Succ}_{\mathcal{A}}^{\mathrm{GAME.1}}| \leq \mathrm{InSec}^{\mathrm{PRF}}(\mathbf{PRF}, \xi, q_1), \tag{4}$$

$$|\mathrm{Succ}_{\mathcal{A}}^{\mathrm{GAME.1}} - \mathrm{Succ}_{\mathcal{A}}^{\mathrm{GAME.2}}| \leq \mathrm{InSec}^{\mathrm{PRF}}(\mathbf{PRF_{msg}}, \xi, q_s), \tag{5}$$

$$|\mathrm{Succ}_{\mathcal{A}}^{GAME.2} - \mathrm{Succ}_{\mathcal{A}}^{GAME.3}| \leq \mathrm{InSec}^{\mathrm{ITSR}}(\mathbf{H_{msg}}, \xi, q_s), \tag{6}$$

where $q_1 < 2^{h+1}(kt + l)$ and q_s is the number of signing queries made by $\mathcal{A}$.

GAME.3 - GAME.4. Let's break the hop between GAME.3 and GAME.4 into several steps. Since the FORS leaf is different to the leaf that we would generate for that place there are two possible outcomes. First is that the forged signature contains a second preimage for some input of a THF. This can occur in the FORS or WOTS-TW instances, the compression of FORS or WOTS-TW public keys, and in the binary trees. And second case is that a WOTS-TW forgery occurs.

Consider GAME.3.1 in which the game is lost if there is a second preimage contained in the forged signature for an input of $\mathbf{H}$ in a binary tree. The difference for this case can be bounded by building a SM-TCR adversary for $\mathbf{H}$ as a member of a collection. We construct the SPHINCS$^+$ structure using SM-TCR challenger for every input to $\mathbf{H}$ and the oracle $\mathbf{Th}_\lambda$ for the rest. Here we also consider binary trees of FORS as part of the challenge. Hence we obtain

$$|\mathrm{Succ}_\mathcal{A}^{GAME.3} - \mathrm{Succ}_\mathcal{A}^{GAME.3.1}| \leq \mathrm{InSec}^{\text{SM-TCR}}(\mathbf{H} \in \mathbf{Th}; \xi, q_4), \qquad (7)$$

where $q_4 < 2^{h+1} \cdot k \cdot 2t$.

Now we introduce GAME.3.2 which is different from GAME.3.1 in that we are considering the game lost if a second preimage for $\mathbf{Th}_k$ is contained in the FORS tree nodes computed while verifying the forged signature. As in the previous case this can be bounded by

$$|\mathrm{Succ}_\mathcal{A}^{GAME.3.1} - \mathrm{Succ}_\mathcal{A}^{GAME.3.2}| \leq \mathrm{InSec}^{\text{SM-TCR}}(\mathbf{Th}_k \in \mathbf{Th}; \xi, q_5), \qquad (8)$$

where $q_5 < 2^h$.

Next the GAME.3.3 is considered lost if a second preimage for $\mathbf{Th}_l$ is contained in the WOTS-TW public keys computed from the forged signature. Following the same ideas as above we obtain

$$|\mathrm{Succ}_\mathcal{A}^{GAME.3.2} - \mathrm{Succ}_\mathcal{A}^{GAME.3.3}| \leq \mathrm{InSec}^{\text{SM-TCR}}(\mathbf{Th}_l \in \mathbf{Th}; \xi, q_6), \qquad (9)$$

where $q_6 < 2^{h+1}$.

The GAME.3.4 is lost if there is a second preimage in the forged signature for some input for $\mathbf{F}$ outside the WOTS-TW instances, i.e., in as a FORS signature value. The bound for this case is

$$|\mathrm{Succ}_\mathcal{A}^{GAME.3.3} - \mathrm{Succ}_\mathcal{A}^{GAME.3.4}| \leq \mathrm{InSec}^{\text{SM-TCR}}(\mathbf{F} \in \mathbf{Th}; \xi, q_7), \qquad (10)$$

where $q_7 < 2^h \cdot k \cdot t$.

So the only case left to hop to GAME.4 is a WOTS-TW forgery for one out of $d < 2^{h+1}$ instances. Using the bound in Theorem 2 we obtain

$$|\mathrm{Succ}_\mathcal{A}^{GAME.3.4} - \mathrm{Succ}_\mathcal{A}^{GAME.4}| \leq \mathrm{InSec}^{\text{SM-TCR}}(\mathbf{F} \in \mathbf{Th}; \xi, q_3)$$
$$+ \mathrm{InSec}^{\text{SM-PRE}}(\mathbf{F} \in \mathbf{Th}; \xi, q_2 + w \cdot \mathrm{InSec}^{\text{SM-UD}}(\mathbf{F} \in \mathbf{Th}; \xi, q_2), \quad (11)$$

where $q_2 < 2^{h+1} \cdot l$, $q_3 < 2^{h+1} \cdot lw$.

GAME.4. The analysis of GAME.4 can be found in the SPHINCS$^+$ (see paper [BHK+19] Claim 23). Here we note that we cannot use the SM-PRE bound as the reduction is an instance of a T-openPRE game as introduced in [BH19], i.e., the reduction needs to know some preimages. The only difference is that we have already excluded the WOTS-TW preimage case. Hence we obtain the following bound:

$$\mathrm{Succ}_\mathcal{A}^{GAME.4} \leq 3 \cdot \mathrm{InSec}^{\text{SM-TCR}}(\mathbf{F}; \xi, q_8) + \mathrm{InSec}^{\text{SM-DSPR}}(\mathbf{F}; \xi, q_8), \qquad (12)$$

where $q_8 < 2^h \cdot kt$.

Combining the inequalities we obtain the bound from the theorem.

8   Analyzing Quantum Generic Security

In this section we collect bounds on the complexity of generic attacks against the properties discussed so far for THFs and KHFs. The definitions of the properties for KHFs can be found in the full paper [HK22]. A hash function **Th** is commonly considered a good function if there are no attacks known for any security property that perform better against **Th** than a generic attack against a random function. First we discuss the current situation which is summarized in Table 1. Attacks that match the security bound for nonnegligible probability for the UD and PRF properties are shown in the full paper [HK22]. Then we give a new proof for the SM-UD property. To do so we follow the approach of [HRS16] where different instances of average-case distinguishing problems over boolean functions are reduced to breaking the different hash function security properties. The advantage of this approach is that we know lower bounds for these decision problems, even for quantum algorithms. This allows us to derive lower bounds on the complexity of quantum attacks against our security properties. A new proof for the SM-TCR property which improves a previous result from [BHK+19] can be found in the full version of the paper [HK22].

Table 1. Success probability of generic attacks – In the "Success probability" column we give the bound for a quantum adversary $\mathcal{A}$ that makes q quantum queries to the function and p classical queries to the challenge oracle. The security parameter n is the output length of **Th**. We use $X = \sum_{\gamma} \left(1 - \left(1 - \frac{1}{t}\right)^{\gamma}\right)^k \binom{p}{\gamma} \left(1 - \frac{1}{2^h}\right)^{p-\gamma} \frac{1}{2^{h\gamma}}$.

Property	Success probability	Status
SM-TCR	$\Theta((q+1)^2/2^n)$	proven (this work, [BHK+19, HRS16])
SM-DSPR	$\Theta((q+1)^2/2^n)$	conjectured ([BHK+19])
SM-PRE	$\Theta((q+1)^2/2^n)$	based on conjecture ([BH19, BHK+19])
PRF	$\Theta(12q/\sqrt{2^n})$	proven ([XY19])
SM-UD	$\Theta(12q/\sqrt{2^n})$	proven (this work)
ITSR	$\Theta((q+1)^2 \cdot X)$	conjectured ([BHK+19])

8.1   Estimated Security

The success probability of generic attacks against SM-TCR and a reduction to an average-case search problem was given in [BHK+19], but it had several limitations on the adversary. In the full version of this paper (see [HK22]) a proof without extra limitations on the adversary is given. A generic attack using Grover search against plain TCR is given in [HRS16], which is applicable against SM-TCR – as it runs a second preimage search when all information is available – and has a success probability matching the proven bound.

With regard to SM-DSPR, two bounds are proven in [BH19]. On the one hand, the bound $O((q+1)^2/2^n)$ is proven for single-target DSPR of a KHF, which is tight. This proof perfectly transfers to the SM-DSPR notion of a THF by specifying the tweak we analyze $\mathbf{Th}(P, T, \cdot)$ which can be viewed as a KHF with a fixed key. For a T-target version a factor-T lose bound is obtained via a standard plug'n'pray argument, placing the challenge instance at a random position, hoping that that will be the one that gets distinguished by the adversary. In [BHK+19], the authors conjecture that the actual multi-target bound should be the same as the single-target bound. A supporting argument for this conjecture is that the best attack against multi-target DSPR for now is still a second-preimage search which has the same complexity in both cases.

For PRE of a KHF h, a bound of $\mathrm{Succ}_{h,p}^{\mathrm{PRE}}(\mathcal{A}) = \Theta((q+1)^2/2^n)$ is given in [HRS16] that also holds in a multi-function, multi-target setting. The bound is proven for h that are random and compressing by at least a factor 2 in the message length. It is conjectured that it also applies for length preserving hash functions, i.e., functions that map n-bit messages to n-bit outputs, possibly taking additional inputs like function keys or tweaks. A bound for SM-PRE can be proven using SM-TCR and SM-DSPR ($\mathrm{Succ}_{\mathbf{Th},p}^{\mathrm{SM\text{-}PRE}}(\mathcal{A}) \leq 3 \cdot \mathrm{Succ}_{\mathbf{Th},p}^{\mathrm{SM\text{-}TCR}}(\mathcal{A}) + \mathrm{Adv}_{\mathbf{Th},p}^{\mathrm{SM\text{-}DSPR}}(\mathcal{A})$) as shown in [BHK+19, BH19]. With this we derive the same bound of $\mathrm{Succ}_{\mathbf{Th},p}^{\mathrm{SM\text{-}PRE}}(\mathcal{A}) = \Theta((q+1)^2/2^n)$. For the case of multiple targets, the tight bound needs above conjecture for SM-DSPR. A factor-T-loose, unconditional bound follows from the loose bound for SM-DSPR.

The success probability of generic attacks against PRF is analyzed in [XY19]. The analysis is done by reducing to a distinguishing problem between a boolean function of weight 0 and a random boolean function of weight 1.

The notion of undetectability was introduced in [DSS05]. In that work, the authors give a bound for single-target undetectability considering classical adversaries as $\mathcal{O}(q/2^n)$. Below, we give a bound for multi-target undetectability of random $\mathbf{Th}$ considering quantum adversaries.

For all notions we conjecture that the bounds are exactly the same for the case of collections. The reason is that for a random tweakable function, every tweak is related to an independent random function. Hence, giving access to those does not give any information about the targets to the adversary. This is also reflected in the reductions that we know so far. In these, the function for a tweak that is not used for a challenge is simulated by an independent random function and we can give access to this function in parallel to the challenge oracle as we do not touch it in the reduction.

In the full paper [HK22] we also discuss properties of KHFs which are similar to ones discussed above. Specifically DM-SPR, DM-UD, DM-PRE, DM-DSPR. We show that it is possible to obtain exactly the same table of success probabilities by replacing SM-TCR with DM-SPR, SM-DSPR with DM-DSPR, SM-PRE with DM-PRE, and SM-UD with DM-UD. In the following subsection we give a proof for the SM-UD property.

8.2   Decision Problem

Here we define distinguishing problems over boolean functions for which an optimal query complexity bound is known. In our reductions to show lower bounds, we assume we have access to some random functions G and g. Hence, we need to simulate G and g efficiently so that any algorithm with q queries cannot notice a difference. According to [Zha12] this can be simulated using 2q-wise independent hash functions or QPRFs.

Definition 9 ([HRS16]).
Let $\mathcal{F} := \{f : \{0,1\}^m \to \{0,1\}\}$ be the collection of all boolean functions on $\{0,1\}^m$. Let $\lambda \in [0,1]$ and $\varepsilon > 0$. Define a family of distributions D_λ on $\mathcal{F}$ such that $f \leftarrow_\$ D_\lambda$ satisfies

$$f : x \to \begin{cases} 1 & \text{with prob. } \lambda \\ 0 & \text{with prob. } 1 - \lambda \end{cases}$$

for any $x \in \{0,1\}^m$.

We follow the same approach as in [HRS16] and define $\mathsf{Avg} - \mathsf{Search}_\lambda$ to be the problem that given oracle access to $f \leftarrow D_\lambda$, finds an x such that $f(x) = 1$. For any quantum algorithm $\mathcal{A}$ that makes q queries, we define

$$\mathrm{Succ}_\lambda^q(\mathcal{A}) := \Pr_{f \leftarrow D_\lambda} \left[f(x) = 1 : x \leftarrow \mathcal{A}^f(\cdot) \right]$$

Theorem 4 ([HRS16]). $\mathrm{Succ}_\lambda^q(\mathcal{A}) \leq 8\lambda(q+1)^2$ *holds for any quantum algorithm $\mathcal{A}$ with q queries.*

Assume we have a family $\mathcal{F}$ of all n-bit boolean functions. We will call the weight of a boolean function f the result of the following function: $wt(f) = |\{x : f(x) = 1\}|$. Let's denote $S_i = \{f \in \mathcal{F}|wt(f) = i\}$. We define the distinguishing advantage for two sets S_i and S_j as

Definition 10 (Dist-i,j). *Let S_i be as defined above. We define the distinguishing advantage between*

$$\mathrm{Adv}_{S_0,S_1}^q(\mathcal{A}) \stackrel{def}{=} \left| \Pr_{f \leftarrow_\$ S_i} \left[\mathcal{A}^f(\cdot) = 1 \right] - \Pr_{f \leftarrow_\$ S_j} \left[\mathcal{A}^f(\cdot) = 1 \right] \right|.$$

We derive the following lemma from Theorem 9.3.2 [KLM06].

Lemma 1 ([KLM06]). *Let S_i be as defined above. The advantage of any q query quantum algorithm in distinguishing S_0 from S_1 is $\mathrm{Adv}_{S_0,S_1}^q(\mathcal{A}) \leq 6q/\sqrt{2^n}$.*

$\mathsf{Avg} - \mathsf{Search}_\lambda$ is used to prove SM-TCR (the proof can be found in the full paper [HK22]) and SM-UD will be bounded by $\mathrm{Adv}_{S_0,S_1}^q(\mathcal{A})$.

8.3   SM-UD

In this section we analyze the SM-UD property. In our reduction we need sets S_0^l and S_1^l. S_i^l will contain all functions $f : [1,l] \times \{0,1\}^n \to \{0,1\}^n$. Where $f(j, \cdot)$, $j \in [1,l]$ is a random function from S_i. We will now show that distinguishing $f \leftarrow_\$ S_1^l$ from $f \leftarrow_\$ S_0^l$ is as hard as distinguishing $f \leftarrow_\$ S_1$ from $f \leftarrow_\$ S_0$.

Algorithm 4: Dist-1,0 to SM-UD
Input : f, SM-UD adversary $\mathcal{A}$
Output: $b' \in \{0,1\}^n$
1 Choose a random public parameter $P \leftarrow_\$ \mathcal{P}$
2 Construct a random tweakable hash function
$H : \mathcal{P} \times \mathcal{T} \times \{0,1\}^n \to \{0,1\}^n$ using random function
$F : \mathcal{P} \times \mathcal{T} \times \{0,1\}^n \to \{0,1\}^n$ and $e_y : \mathcal{T} \to \{0,1\}^n$ the following way:
3 $$H(p,t,x) : \begin{cases} \text{if } (p = P, f(t,x) = 1) : \text{ Return } e_y(t) \\ \text{Return } F(p,t,x) \end{cases}$$
4 Give oracle access to H to the adversary
5 For each query T_i respond with $e_y(T_i)$, $i \in [1,p]$
6 Give the public parameter P to adversary $\mathcal{A}_2$
7 **return** Output of $\mathcal{A}_2$

Lemma 2. *Consider sets S_0, S_1, S_0^l, S_1^l as defined above. Then $\mathrm{Adv}_{S_0,S_1}^q(\mathcal{A}) = \mathrm{Adv}_{S_0^l,S_1^l}^q(\mathcal{A})$.*

Proof. Assume we can distinguish $f \leftarrow_\$ S_1$ from $f \leftarrow_\$ S_0$ with some algorithm $\mathcal{A}$. Then to distinguish $f \leftarrow_\$ S_1^l$ from $f \leftarrow_\$ S_0^l$ we run $\mathcal{A}$ on $f(1,\cdot)$. Hence, $\mathrm{Adv}_{S_0,S_1}^q(\mathcal{A}) \le \mathrm{Adv}_{S_0^l,S_1^l}^q(\mathcal{A})$.

To show equality we now give the reduction in the opposite direction. Assume we can distinguish $f \leftarrow_\$ S_1^l$ from $f \leftarrow_\$ S_0^l$. Our task is to distinguish $f' \leftarrow_\$ S_1$ from $f' \leftarrow_\$ S_0$. To build f from f' we can sample $z_i \leftarrow_\$ \{0,1\}^n$ using a random function $e : [1,l] \mapsto \{0,1\}^n$, $i \in [1,l]$, and set $f(i,x) \stackrel{\text{def}}{=} f'(x \oplus e(i))$. One can see that if f' was a constant zero function then f is a collection of constant zero functions, so $f \in S_0^l$. If $f' \in S_1$ then $f(i,\cdot)$ outputs 1 for one random value since z_i were chosen uniformly at random, so $f \in S_1^l$. Hence, $\mathrm{Adv}_{S_0,S_1}^q(\mathcal{A}) \ge \mathrm{Adv}_{S_0^l,S_1^l}^q(\mathcal{A})$.

Lemma 3. *Let $n \in \mathbb{N}$, $H : \mathcal{P} \times \mathcal{T} \times \{0,1\}^n \to \{0,1\}^n$ - a random hash function. Any quantum adversary $\mathcal{A}$ that solves SM-UD for p targets making q queries to H can be used to construct a quantum adversary $\mathcal{B}$ that makes $2q$ queries to its oracle and distinguishes S_0 from S_1 with an advantage $\mathrm{Adv}_{H,p}^{\text{SM-UD}}(\mathcal{A}) \le 12q/\sqrt{2^n}$.*

Proof. We give a reduction that distinguishes $S_0^{|\mathcal{T}|}$ from $S_1^{|\mathcal{T}|}$. The lemma follows then by applying Lemmas 1 and 2. Assume we obtain a function f either from $S_0^{|\mathcal{T}|}$ or from $S_1^{|\mathcal{T}|}$. We build the reduction shown in Algorithm 4 for which we refer as quantum adversary $\mathcal{B}$.

As in the single-target case we can see that for any f we construct a truly random tweakable hash function. If $f \in S_0^{|\mathcal{T}|}$ we answer the adversary with random values. If $f \in S_1^{|\mathcal{T}|}$ we answer the queries with outputs of the hash function on randomly chosen inputs.

$$\mathrm{Adv}^{2q}_{S_0^{|\mathcal{T}|}, S_1^{|\mathcal{T}|}}(\mathcal{B}) = | \Pr_{f \leftarrow_\$ S_0^{|\mathcal{T}|}}[\mathcal{B}^f() = 1] - \Pr_{f \leftarrow_\$ S_1^{|\mathcal{T}|}}[\mathcal{B}^f() = 1]| = \mathrm{Adv}^{\mathrm{SM\text{-}UD}}_{H,p}(\mathcal{A}).$$

Combining this with Lemmas 1 and 2 we obtain the final bound:

$$\mathrm{Adv}^{\mathrm{SM\text{-}UD}}_{\mathbf{Th},p}(\mathcal{A}) \leq \mathrm{Adv}^{2q}_{S_0^{|\mathcal{T}|}, S_1^{|\mathcal{T}|}}(\mathcal{B}) = \mathrm{Adv}^{2q}_{S_0, S_1}(\mathcal{B}) \leq 12q/\sqrt{2^n},$$

where q denotes the number of queries to **Th**.

References

[ABB+20] Aumasson, J.-P., et al.: SPHINCS$^+$. Submission to NIST's post-quantum crypto standardization project, v. 3 (2020). http://sphincs.org/data/sphincs+-round3-specification.pdf

[BH19] Bernstein, D.J., Hülsing, A.: Decisional second-preimage resistance: when does SPR imply PRE? In: Galbraith, S.D., Moriai, S. (eds.) ASIACRYPT 2019, Part III. LNCS, vol. 11923, pp. 33–62. Springer, Cham (2019). https://doi.org/10.1007/978-3-030-34618-8_2

[BHK+19] Bernstein, D.J., Hülsing, A., Kölbl, S., Niederhagen, R., Rijneveld, J., Schwabe, P.: The SPHINCS$^+$ signature framework. In: Cavallaro, L., Kinder, J., Wang, X., Katz, J. (eds.) ACM CCS 2019, pp. 2129–2146. ACM Press (2019)

[DSS05] Dods, C., Smart, N.P., Stam, M.: Hash based digital signature schemes. In: Smart, N.P. (ed.) Cryptography and Coding 2005. LNCS, vol. 3796, pp. 96–115. Springer, Heidelberg (2005). https://doi.org/10.1007/11586821_8

[HK22] Hülsing, A., Kudinov, M.: Recovering the tight security proof of SPHINCS$^+$. Cryptology ePrint Archive, Paper 2022/346 (2022). http://eprint.iacr.org/2022/346

[HRS16] Hülsing, A., Rijneveld, J., Song, F.: Mitigating multi-target attacks in hash-based signatures. In: Cheng, C.-M., Chung, K.-M., Persiano, G., Yang, B.-Y. (eds.) PKC 2016, Part I. LNCS, vol. 9614, pp. 387–416. Springer, Heidelberg (2016). https://doi.org/10.1007/978-3-662-49384-7_15

[Hül13] Hülsing, A.: W-OTS+ – shorter signatures for hash-based signature schemes. In: Youssef, A., Nitaj, A., Hassanien, A.E. (eds.) AFRICACRYPT 2013. LNCS, vol. 7918, pp. 173–188. Springer, Heidelberg (2013). https://doi.org/10.1007/978-3-642-38553-7_10

[KKF20] Kudinov, M., Kiktenko, E., Fedorov, A.: [PQC-forum] Round 3 Official Comment: SPHINCS+ (2020). http://csrc.nist.gov/CSRC/media/Projects/post-quantum-cryptography/documents/round-3/official-comments/Sphincs-Plus-round3-official-comment.pdf. Accessed 1 Feb 2022

[KLM06] Kaye, P., Laflamme, R., Mosca, M.: An Introduction to Quantum Computing. Oxford University Press, Oxford (2006)

[XY19] Xagawa, K., Yamakawa, T.: (Tightly) QCCA-secure key-encapsulation mechanism in the quantum random oracle model. In: Ding, J., Steinwandt, R. (eds.) PQCrypto 2019. LNCS, vol. 11505, pp. 249–268. Springer, Cham (2019). https://doi.org/10.1007/978-3-030-25510-7_14

[Zha12] Zhandry, M.: Secure identity-based encryption in the quantum random oracle model. In: Safavi-Naini, R., Canetti, R. (eds.) CRYPTO 2012. LNCS, vol. 7417, pp. 758–775. Springer, Heidelberg (2012). https://doi.org/10.1007/978-3-642-32009-5_44

On Rejection Sampling in Lyubashevsky's Signature Scheme

Julien Devevey[1]([envelope]), Omar Fawzi[1,2], Alain Passelègue[1,2], and Damien Stehlé[1,3]

[1] ENS de Lyon, Lyon, France
julien.devevey@ens-lyon.fr
[2] Inria Lyon, Lyon, France
[3] Institut Universitaire de France, Paris, France

Abstract. Lyubashevsky's signatures are based on the Fiat-Shamir with aborts paradigm, whose central ingredient is the use of rejection sampling to transform secret-dependent signature samples into samples from (or close to) a secret-independent target distribution. Several choices for the underlying distributions and for the rejection sampling strategy can be considered. In this work, we study Lyubashevsky's signatures through the lens of rejection sampling, and aim to minimize signature size given signing runtime requirements. Several of our results concern rejection sampling itself and could have other applications.

We prove lower bounds for compactness of signatures given signing runtime requirements, and for expected runtime of perfect rejection sampling strategies. We also propose a Rényi-divergence-based analysis of Lyubashevsky's signatures which allows for larger deviations from the target distribution, and show hyperball uniforms to be a good choice of distributions: they asymptotically reach our compactness lower bounds and offer interesting features for practical deployment. Finally, we propose a different rejection sampling strategy which circumvents the expected runtime lower bound and provides a worst-case runtime guarantee.

1 Introduction

Lyubashevsky's signature scheme [Lyu09, Lyu12] may be viewed as a lattice variant of Schnorr's group-based signature scheme [Sch91], with a core conceptual difference being the use of rejection sampling and the associated introduction of aborts and repeats in the Fiat-Shamir heuristic [FS86]. The use of rejection sampling in Lyubashesvky's scheme is the focus of the present work. It is hard to overstate the importance of Lyubashevsky's signature scheme in lattice-based cryptography. Thanks to its elementary and flexible design, numerous variants and optimizations have been proposed (see [AFLT16, GLP15, DDLL13, BG14], or [Lyu16], for instance). Notably, it led to the TESLA [ABB+17, AAB+19] and Dilithium [DKL+18, BDK+20] candidates to the NIST standardization project on post-quantum cryptography. It also led to lattice-based zero-knowledge proofs (see [LNP22] and the references therein).

© International Association for Cryptologic Research 2022
S. Agrawal and D. Lin (Eds.): ASIACRYPT 2022, LNCS 13794, pp. 34–64, 2022.
https://doi.org/10.1007/978-3-031-22972-5_2

Lyubashevsky's scheme involves a publicly shared matrix $\mathbf{A} \in \mathbb{Z}_q^{n \times m}$ (note that other algebraic setups are possible, but this is not relevant to the present discussion). The signing key is a matrix $\mathbf{S} \in \mathbb{Z}^{m \times k}$. It is small in the sense that all its entries have absolute values significantly smaller than q. The verification key associated to $\mathbf{S}$ is $\mathbf{T} = \mathbf{AS}$. Given a message $\mu \in \{0,1\}^*$, the signer samples a small masking vector $\mathbf{y} \in \mathbb{Z}^m$ and computes a random-looking commitment com $= \mathbf{Ay}$. By using a hash function H taking small values in $\mathbb{Z}^k$, it computes a challenge $\mathbf{c} = H(\text{com}, \mu)$. Finally, if some (possibly probabilistic) test passes, it outputs a signature $\sigma = (\mathbf{z}, \mathbf{c})$ with $\mathbf{z} = \mathbf{y} + \mathbf{Sc}$, and else it restarts from scratch. Given a signature $\sigma = (\mathbf{z}, \mathbf{c})$ for a message μ, the verifier accepts if and only if $\mathbf{z}$ is small and $H(\mathbf{Az} - \mathbf{Tc}, \mu) = \mathbf{c}$. We refer the reader to Fig. 2 for a formal description. As suggested by the choice of terminology, Lyubashevsky's signature can be viewed as an identification protocol made non-interactive by relying on the Fiat-Shamir heuristic, i.e., by replacing a truly random $\mathbf{c}$ by the output of a hash function. The security proof relies on the Random Oracle Model (ROM) as it models H as a function such that each image is distributed as $\mathbf{c}$ is supposed to be.

Compared to Schnorr's signature scheme, the signing key and mask do not belong to a finite set, preventing the use of a uniform mask $\mathbf{y}$ to hide the sensitive term $\mathbf{Sc}$.[1] One possibility (see, e.g., [DPSZ12]) is to sample $\mathbf{y}$ exponentially larger than $\mathbf{Sc}$ as a function of the security parameter, so that the distributions of $\mathbf{y}$ and $\mathbf{y} + \mathbf{Sc}$ have exponentially small statistical distance. As q must be larger than $\mathbf{y}$ and the smallness of $\mathbf{S}$ relative to q impacts security, this flooding approach leads to large parameters. Instead, Lyubashevsky [Lyu09, Lyu12] put forward the notion of Fiat-Shamir with aborts. This is the reason for the test concerning $\mathbf{z}$ in the signing algorithm: it is so that the output signature $(\mathbf{z}, \mathbf{c})$ follows a distribution that is independent of the sensitive term $\mathbf{Sc}$.

A classic application of rejection sampling (see, e.g., [Dev86, Chapter 2]) is to use a source distribution Q that is convenient to sample from, to create samples from a target distribution P. In Lyubashevsky's scheme, the purpose differs: we start from a pre-source distribution Q for $\mathbf{y}$; it is shifted by $\mathbf{Sc}$, leading to a distribution $Q_{+\mathbf{Sc}}$ for $\mathbf{y} + \mathbf{Sc}$; the latter is the source distribution; it is rejected to a target distribution P for $\mathbf{z}$ that does not depend on the signing key $\mathbf{S}$. The purpose of rejection sampling here is to hide the sensitive data $\mathbf{Sc}$. Diverse choices of pairs of distributions have been put forward in the literature: uniform in hypercubes [Lyu09], Gaussian with the same standard deviation while allowing for some small statistical inaccuracy in the target distribution [Lyu12], a bimodal Gaussian source distribution with a Gaussian target distribution in association with an accomodating arithmetic modification of the scheme [DDLL13] (the modification consists in replacing q with $2q$ and changing key generation to ensure that $\mathbf{T} = -\mathbf{T} = q\mathbf{I} \mod 2q$). The pre-source distribution Q is shifted by $(-1)^b \mathbf{Sc}$ for a uniform bit b, leading to a source distribution $Q_{\pm \mathbf{Sc}}$. We refer

---

[1] If we view $\mathbf{y}$ and $\mathbf{S}$ over $\mathbb{Z}_q$ rather than $\mathbb{Z}$, then they do belong to a finite set; but for security, the masking should preserve smallness relative to q, which the uniform distribution modulo q does not achieve.

to this as the bimodal setting. By opposition, we now refer to the former two cases where the source distribution is $Q_{+\mathbf{Sc}}$ as the unimodal setting. The first choice (uniform distributions in hypercubes) leads to a simple design, whereas the latter two allow for more compact signatures. One may also want to add constraints on the number of loop iterations, notably to guarantee a signing runtime upper bound. In the extreme case of removing rejection altogether, it was recently shown in [ASY22] that a limited flooding suffices, compared to the exponential flooding discussed earlier. This leads us to the question we address in this work:

Given signing runtime requirements, which rejection sampling strategy leads to the most compact signatures?

In a signature $\sigma = (\mathbf{z}, \mathbf{c})$, the second component contributes to a small fraction of the bitsize: the main requirement on $\mathbf{c}$ is that it has sufficiently high min-entropy to make it hard to guess. On the other hand, the contribution of $\mathbf{z}$ towards signature length is mostly driven by $\|\mathbf{z}\|$, as this directly impacts security: for a given security level, the smaller $\|\mathbf{z}\|$, the more compact the signatures. For this reason, we simplify the overall objective to minimizing $\mathbb{E}_{\mathbf{x}\hookleftarrow P}(\|\mathbf{x}\|)$ under signing runtime requirements.

Contributions. Our main contributions concern the optimality of rejection sampling design choices towards optimizing signature sizes and signing runtime. We provide lower bounds, and study ways to reach and circumvent them.

Before describing the main results, we need to quantify the runtime of rejection sampling strategies. We note that for classic rejection sampling with target P and source Q, the expected number of samples needed is $R_\infty(P\|Q)$ where $R_\infty(D_1\|D_2) = \sup_x D_1(x)/D_2(x)$ refers to the Rényi divergence of infinite order. Indeed, for classic rejection sampling, one samples x from Q and accepts with probability $P(x)/(M \cdot Q(x))$, for $M = R_\infty(P\|Q)$. This justifies using $R_\infty(P\|Q)$ to quantify the runtime for rejecting Q to P.

We start with our lower bounds.

- Considering Lyubashevsky's scheme with perfect rejection sampling to the target distribution P (as in [Lyu09]), the relevant quantity measuring the signing runtime is then given by $M = \max_{\mathbf{S},\mathbf{c}} R_\infty(P\|Q_{+\mathbf{Sc}})$. We show (under a mild assumption discussed below) that for all P and Q such that M is finite, the expected norm $\mathbb{E}_{\mathbf{x}\hookleftarrow P}(\|\mathbf{x}\|)$ is $\Omega((m/\log M) \cdot \max_{\mathbf{S},\mathbf{c}} \|\mathbf{Sc}\|)$. Interestingly, this bound is a factor $\sqrt{m}$ lower than what is obtained for the typical choice of P and Q set as uniform distributions in hypercubes.
- In the case of perfect rejection with the accommodating arithmetic modification from [DDLL13], then the relevant quantity for measuring the signing runtime is $M = \max_{\mathbf{S},\mathbf{c}} R_\infty(P\|Q_{\pm\mathbf{Sc}})$, where $Q_{\pm\mathbf{Sc}}$ denotes the balanced mixture of $Q_{+\mathbf{Sc}}$ and $Q_{-\mathbf{Sc}}$. In this case, we show (under the same mild assumption) that for all P and Q such that M is finite, the expected norm $\mathbb{E}_{\mathbf{x}\hookleftarrow P}(\|\mathbf{x}\|)$ is $\Omega(\sqrt{m/\log M} \cdot \max_{\mathbf{S},\mathbf{c}} \|\mathbf{Sc}\|)$. This lower bound is actually reached (up to a constant factor) for P and Q Gaussian as in [DDLL13].

- We show that for any algorithm (terminating with probability 1) that selects one out of many samples from Q to get a sample from P, the expected number of required samples from Q is $\geq R_\infty(P\|Q)$. This lower bound is reached by classic rejection sampling. In the case of Lyubashesvky's signatures with exact rejection sampling, this general result implies that classic rejection sampling is the appropriate strategy when it comes to minimize the expected runtime.

The lower bounds above seem to give little margin of improvement in the design choices of Lyubashevsky's signatures, except for the unimodal case, for which uniform distributions in hypercubes do not reach the lower bound. Our second set of results considers ways to reach or circumvent these lower bounds.

- Concerning the unimodal case, one way to circumvent the results above is to consider imperfect rejection sampling, by allowing for an approximation to P whose accuracy is parameterized by some $\varepsilon > 0$ (as introduced in [Lyu12]). Then the relevant quantity to bound the runtime becomes $\max_{\mathbf{s},\mathbf{c}} R_\infty^\varepsilon(P\|Q_{+\mathbf{Sc}})$, where R_∞^ε is a smoothed variant of R_∞ that we define. In this case, we improve the signature security analysis from [Lyu12] by using the Rényi divergence instead of the statistical distance to quantify the closeness to P of the output distribution. This allows choosing ε larger than previously, leading to a (limited) signature compactness improvement.
- Gaussian distributions provide better signature compactness in the bimodal and imperfect unimodal regimes, than uniforms in hypercubes in the perfect unimodal regime. However, uniforms in hypercubes are sometimes preferred (see, e.g., Dilithium), because they lead to a simpler implementation, which in turn makes protection against timing attacks easier. We consider uniforms in hyperballs as a new alternative for the choice of source and target distributions. We show that this choice reaches the two lower bounds for $\mathbb{E}_{\mathbf{x} \hookleftarrow P}(\|\mathbf{x}\|)$ for perfect rejection sampling and is as good as Gaussians for imperfect rejection sampling (up to a constant factor). Interestingly, the rejection test for uniforms in hyperballs is very simple, similarly to uniforms in hypercubes. We not only study the choice of uniforms in hyperballs in the asymptotic regime, but also compare it to Dilithium.
- Finally, imperfect rejection from Q to P allows us to describe and analyze variants of rejection sampling where the maximum number of loop iterations is bounded. This provides trade-offs between maximum signing runtime and signature sizes. When instantiated to rejection-free sampling, we recover the scheme and analysis from [ASY22], whereas it quickly converges to Lyubashevsky's signature scheme when the signing runtime bound grows.

The results concerning signature compactness for unbounded (perfect and imperfect) rejection sampling are summarized in Table 1.

Technical Overview. In Sect. 2, we provide the background necessary to this work, including rejection sampling and Lyubashevsky's signature scheme.

After identifying the notion of expected number of iterations during rejection sampling with the notion of smooth-Rényi divergence that we define, we start addressing our main question of understanding to which extent the expected norm of a signature can be small for target expected signing runtime constraints.

Table 1. This table expresses the compactness of the signature modeled as $\mathbb{E}_{\mathbf{x} \hookleftarrow P}(\|\mathbf{x}\|)$ given the signing runtime constraint for various choices of distributions P and Q. The column indicates the signing runtime constraint which is modeled in the unimodal case by $\max_{\mathbf{v} \in \mathcal{B}_m(t)} R_\infty^\varepsilon(P\|Q_{+\mathbf{v}}) \leq M$ where ε quantifies the accuracy of rejection sampling and in the bimodal case by $\max_{\mathbf{v} \in \mathcal{B}_m(t)} R_\infty(P\|Q_{\pm\mathbf{v}}) \leq M$. In the first row, P and Q are chosen to be uniform in m-dimensional hypercubes of appropriate side-lengths, in the second row, they are chosen to be m-dimensional Gaussians of appropriate variance. In the third row, they are chosen to be uniform in the m-dimensional hyperballs of appropriate radii. The last row gives a lower bound on the compactness for any choice of P and Q. Multiplicative constants are omitted in this table, and we make the assumption that $\log M \leq m$.

	Unimodal ($\varepsilon = 0$)	Unimodal ($\varepsilon \geq 2^{-o(m)}$ and $\varepsilon = o(1/m)$)	Bimodal ($\varepsilon = 0$)
Hypercube	$\frac{tm^{3/2}}{\log M}$	$\frac{tm^{3/2}}{\log M}$	$\frac{tm^{3/2}}{\log M}$
Gaussian	∞	$\frac{t\sqrt{m}\sqrt{\log \frac{1}{\varepsilon} + \log M}}{\log M}$	$\frac{t\sqrt{m}}{\sqrt{\log M}}$
Hyperball	$\frac{tm}{\log M}$ (Lemma 6)	$\frac{t\sqrt{m}\sqrt{\log \frac{1}{\varepsilon} + \log M}}{\log M}$ (Lemma 6)	$\frac{t\sqrt{m}}{\sqrt{\log M}}$ (Lemma 7)
Lower bound	$\frac{tm}{\log M}$ (Corollary 1)	?	$\frac{t\sqrt{m}}{\sqrt{\log M}}$ (Corollary 2)

Lower Bounds. In Sect. 3, we prove lower bounds in the case of exact rejection sampling in both unimodal and bimodal settings. These lower bounds are obtained following a similar path. In what follows, we focus on the unimodal setting. To ease the analysis, we place ourselves in a slightly simplified setup where shifts belong to a hyperball $\mathcal{B}_m(t)$ of radius t instead of being defined as **Sc**. Given that **S** is unknown, this simplification seems reasonable and allows avoiding significant complications in the proof. In this setting, we prove that for a given constraint $\max_{\mathbf{v} \in \mathcal{B}_m(t)} R_\infty(P\|Q_{+\mathbf{v}}) \leq M$, we have $\mathbb{E}_{\mathbf{x} \hookleftarrow P}(\|\mathbf{x}\|) \geq (t/M^{1/(m-1)} - 1) - \sqrt{m}/2$.

Our lower bounds are obtained in three steps: (1) considering the same setting with continuous distributions, we first prove that we can restrict ourselves to the case of isotropic distributions over $\mathbb{R}^m$, where isotropic means that their densities only depend on the norm. Specifically, we prove that for any two densities f, g, there exist isotropic distributions f^*, g^* satisfying $\max_{\mathbf{v} \in \mathcal{B}_m(t)} R_\infty(f^*\|g^*_{+\mathbf{v}}) \leq M$ as well as $\mathbb{E}_{\mathbf{x} \hookleftarrow f^*}(\|\mathbf{x}\|) = \mathbb{E}_{\mathbf{x} \hookleftarrow f}(\|\mathbf{x}\|)$. The latter distributions are essentially obtained from f, g by averaging their respective densities on hyperspheres. (2) Starting with f and g isotropic, we show that $\mathbb{E}_{\mathbf{x} \hookleftarrow f}(\|\mathbf{x}\|) = \mu_m/\mu_{m-1}$ where $\mu_k = \int_0^\infty r^k f(r)\, dr$. The main technicality consists in proving an intermediate lower bound $\mu_{m-1}/\mu_{m-2} \geq (t/M^{1/(m-1)} - 1)$ which results from the constraint $\max_{\mathbf{v} \in \mathcal{B}_m(t)} R_\infty(f\|g_{+\mathbf{v}}) \leq M$. Our lower bound is then obtained by applying the Cauchy-Schwarz inequality $|\mathbb{E}(XY)|^2 \leq \mathbb{E}(X^2)\mathbb{E}(Y^2)$ to random variables $X = \|\mathbf{x}\|^{m/2}$ and $Y = \|\mathbf{x}\|^{(m-2)/2}$, where $\mathbf{x} \hookleftarrow f$. Indeed, it immediately leads to inequality $\mu_m \cdot \mu_{m-2} \geq (\mu_{m-1})^2$, which results in $\mu_m/\mu_{m-1} \geq \mu_{m-1}/\mu_{m-2} \geq (t/M^{1/(m-1)} - 1)$. (3) A similar lower bound in the discrete setting is obtained by considering the continuous density $p(\mathbf{x}) = P(\lceil \mathbf{x} \rceil)$

with P being a discrete probability. These lower bounds provide us with a target to reach, and we can compare them with the signature size obtained when instantiating the above scheme with various distributions.

On Alternative Rejection Sampling Strategies. In Sect. 3.3, we investigate the question of the relevance of rejection sampling strategies differing from the classic one. We consider the following setting. As above, the goal is to sample from a distribution P given access to a sampler from a distribution Q, and we consider a sequence of samples $(X_i)_{i \geq 1}$ from distribution Q. Any strategy is allowed as long as we output one of the X_i's. A strategy is given by a sequence of algorithms $(A_i)_{i \geq 1}$ that take samples $(X_j)_{j \leq i}$ as input and return either an index $j \in [i]$, which corresponds to halting with output X_j, or a special symbol r which corresponds to rejecting and moving to A_{i+1}. We restrict ourselves to the case of procedures that terminate with probability 1. Considering i^* the random variable denoting the number of samples observed in a strategy, our objective is then to measure how small $\mathbb{E}(i^*)$ can be. We prove that for any P, Q, we have $\mathbb{E}(i^*) \geq R_\infty(P \| Q)$. This result is obtained by proving that for any x, we have $P(x) \leq \mathbb{E}(i^*) \cdot Q(x)$, leading to the former inequality by definition of R_∞.

Rényi-Based Analysis for Imperfect Rejection Sampling. All lower bounds are for perfect rejection sampling, in the sense that one obtains a sample from (exactly) P. In [Lyu12], Lyubashevsky showed that one can consider imperfect rejection sampling, and shows that it is particularly beneficial in the case of Gaussians. We propose an analysis that replaces the use of the statistical distance as done in [Lyu12] by that of the smooth Rényi divergence, and allows loosening the constraints on imperfectness. We first recall that in [Lyu12], the statistical distance is used to bound the statistical distance between a (single) execution of the imperfect rejection sampling algorithm and the target distribution. Using imperfect rejection sampling in a signature scheme and given bound ε for the above statistical distance, one can then bound the distinguishing advantage of an adversary between the real security game and the ideal game (where signatures are simulated by sampling them from the target distribution) by $q_{\text{sig}} \cdot \varepsilon$. Here q_{sig} is a bound on the number of signature queries an adversary can make. In Sect. 4, we prove that for P, Q such that $R_\infty^\varepsilon(P \| Q)$ is finite, the Rényi divergence of infinite order between a (single) execution of the imperfect rejection sampling algorithm and the target distribution is bounded by $1/(1 - \varepsilon)$. Combining this result with the multiplicativity of the Rényi divergence, we can then bound the Rényi divergence of infinite order between the adversary's view in the real game and its view in the ideal game by $1/(1 - \varepsilon)^{q_{\text{sig}}}$ for the resulting signature. The probability preservation property of the Rényi divergence then allows completing the analysis. Our analysis leads to potential improvements as the former statistical bound $q_{\text{sig}} \cdot \varepsilon$ imposes that $\varepsilon = 2^{-\Omega(\lambda)}$, while our bound can be used setting $\varepsilon = 1/q_{\text{sig}}$. Since q_{sig} is a (possibly large) polynomial of the security parameter λ, this puts less constraint on the condition P and Q must satisfy, which results in compactness improvement.

Hyperball Uniforms. We show that (continuous) uniform distributions over hyperballs reach the signature compactness lower bound (up to constant factors) in both unimodal and bimodal settings, as shown in Sect. 5.1. We also show that they are as good as Gaussians for imperfect rejection sampling (up to a constant factor). These results reduce to Rényi divergence computations, which involve geometric properties of hyperballs. We emphasize that while Gaussian distributions also achieve similar signature size (up to a constant factor) in both unimodal and bimodal settings (but only in the case of imperfect rejection sampling with polynomial loss for the unimodal case), using uniform distributions over hyperballs makes the rejection test as simple as computing $\|\mathbf{z}\|$ since it consists only in checking that $\mathbf{z}$ is in the hyperball of the target distribution P. In order to use this distribution in a signature, we propose a generalization of Lyubashevsky's signature that allows for continuous source and target distributions, by adding a rounding step after accepting a sample. Its security relies on the same mechanisms as the discrete case. This strategy could also benefit to Gaussian distributions, by allowing to replace discrete Gaussian sampling with possibly simpler continuous Gaussian sampling. To assess the practicality of this new choice of distributions, we propose parameters for a variant of Dilithium with uniform distributions in hyperballs. If considering the sum of bitsizes of a verification key and a signature, the gains range from $\sim 15\%$ to $\sim 25\%$, depending on the security level.

Bounded Rejection Sampling. We conclude this work by proposing an original strategy to use rejection sampling while guaranteeing a (moderate) worst-case runtime. This could be beneficial in the context of real-time systems. A simple strategy could consist in fixing a (very large) bound i on the number of iterations such that it fails to produce a sample with negligible probability. While this guarantees a worst-case runtime, the change is mainly cosmetic since it has to be large enough for the sampling to succeed. In Sect. 6, we propose an alternative solution that leaves the choice of i open without ever failing: for a fixed bound i, it performs (up to) $i - 1$ iterations of the classic rejection sampling and outputs a sample if it ever succeeds, otherwise, the last (i-th) iteration uses one-shot flooding techniques (as done in [ASY22]) to guarantee an output. The analysis makes heavy use of the smooth Rényi divergence and its properties. Different choices for the bound i offer various trade-offs, ranging from one-shot signatures ($i = 1$) as in [ASY22] to Lyubashevsky's expected polynomial-time signatures (i going to ∞).

Open problems. Our results suggest that instantiating the Fiat-Shamir with aborts using uniform distributions in hyperballs is a relevant choice, both in the unimodal and bimodal settings, as it provides more compact signatures than uniform distributions in hypercubes but also much simpler rejection test than Gaussians. We believe it is an interesting open question to investigate a constant-time implementation with this choice. Regarding further improvements of signatures, our results show that there is not much room for improvement if the goal is to minimize signature size or $\mathbb{E}(i^*)$. However, other quantities could be considered, such as the shape of the tail of the distribution of i^*.

2   Preliminaries

See full version for notations and some standard background.

We introduce a relaxed version of the Rényi divergence, termed the smooth Rényi divergence, where one is able to remove a few problematic points from the support, including those that may lie in $\mathrm{Supp}(p) \setminus \mathrm{Supp}(q)$. Doing so, we can compare a wider set of probability distributions. For instance, while the Rényi divergence of infinite order between $D_{\mathbb{Z}^m, \sigma}$ and $D_{\mathbb{Z}^m, \sigma, \mathbf{v}}$ is infinite when $\mathbf{v} \neq \mathbf{0}$, their smooth divergence is finite, as we show in the full version and is implicit in [Lyu12]. We could give this definition for any order $a \in [1, +\infty]$. However, only the case $a = +\infty$ is relevant for this work.

This definition is useful to link previous works on rejection sampling and the Rényi divergence. A similar quantity has been previously defined in the quantum information literature [Ren05, Dat09], though the specific notion of smoothing we consider here is slightly different.

Definition 1 (Smooth Rényi Divergence). *Let $\varepsilon \geq 0$. Let p, q be two probability densities such that $\int_{\mathrm{Supp}(q)} p(x) \, \mathrm{d}\mu(x) \geq 1 - \varepsilon$. Their ε-smooth Rényi divergence of infinite order is*

$$R_{\infty}^{\varepsilon}(p\|q) := \inf_{\substack{S \subseteq \mathrm{Supp}(q) \\ \int_S p(x) \, \mathrm{d}\mu(x) \geq 1-\varepsilon}} \mathrm{ess\,sup}_{x \in S} \frac{p(x)}{q(x)}.$$

This definition is equivalent to

$$R_{\infty}^{\varepsilon}(p\|q) := \inf\{M > 0 \mid \Pr_{x \leftarrow p}(p(x) \leq Mq(x)) \geq 1 - \varepsilon\}.$$

By convention, if $\int_{\mathrm{Supp}(q)} p(x) \, \mathrm{d}\mu(x) < 1 - \varepsilon$, we define $R_{\infty}^{\varepsilon}(p\|q) = +\infty$.

In the full version, we prove that the two definitions are indeed equivalent and give useful properties of the smooth Rényi divergence.

2.1   Rejection Sampling

Given two close enough densities p_t and p_s, either both continuous or both discrete, rejection sampling is a way to generate samples from p_t given access to samples from p_s, as explained for instance in [Dev86]. It was used mainly to generate samples from complex distributions that were "close" to easier-to-sample distributions. However, in cryptography and particularly in the line of works started with [Lyu09], it found a peculiar use that diverged from its primary use. Given a family of densities $(p_s^{(v)})$, rejection sampling can be used to hide the parameter v given a density p_t that is close to every density in this family. It was later observed in [Lyu12] that an "imperfect" rejection procedure is sufficient for this use and leads to smaller parameters, notably standard deviation of p_s.

In the case of Lyubashevsky's signature scheme [Lyu09, Lyu12], a signature is a pair of vectors $(\mathbf{y} + \mathbf{Sc}, \mathbf{c})$ where $\mathbf{y} \hookleftarrow P_{\mathbf{y}}$ and $\mathbf{c}$ would ideally be sampled from $P_{\mathbf{c}}$. Here $P_{\mathbf{c}} : \mathcal{C} \to \mathbb{R}$ and $P_{\mathbf{y}} : \mathbb{Z}^m \to \mathbb{R}$ are two discrete probability distributions, where $\mathcal{C} \subset \mathbb{Z}^k, m, k \geq 1$, and $\mathbf{S} \in \mathbb{Z}^{m \times k}$ is fixed (it is the signing key). The joint distribution of this pair corresponds to the source distribution $P_s^{(\mathbf{Sc})}$ above, which depends on the sensitive data $\mathbf{Sc}$. Rejection sampling is used to ensure that the output of the signing algorithm is of the form $(\mathbf{z}, \mathbf{c})$ where $\mathbf{z} \hookleftarrow P_{\mathbf{z}}$ and $\mathbf{c} \hookleftarrow P_{\mathbf{c}}$ are statistically independent and $P_{\mathbf{z}}$ is well-chosen. Their joint distribution corresponds to the target distribution P_t above. The case of BLISS [DDLL13] is identical, except that signatures are of the form $(\mathbf{y} + (-1)^b \mathbf{Sc}, \mathbf{c})$, where $b \hookleftarrow U(\{0, 1\})$.

We consider the algorithms from Fig. 1, which take some $M \geq 1$ as a parameter. Algorithm $\mathcal{A}^{\mathsf{ideal}}$ corresponds to what we would like to have, whereas $\mathcal{A}^{\mathsf{real}}$ is the algorithm corresponding to the real distribution. We are typically interested in calling these algorithms until they output something, which is what $\mathcal{B}_\infty^{\mathsf{real}}$ and $\mathcal{B}_\infty^{\mathsf{ideal}}$ do. It remains to understand when the outputs of these algorithms are statistically close. The lemma below is proved in the full version.

Algorithm $\mathcal{A}^{\mathsf{real}}$:	Algorithm $\mathcal{A}^{\mathsf{ideal}}$:
1: $x \hookleftarrow p_s$	1: $x \hookleftarrow p_t$
2: with probability $\min\left(\frac{p_t(x)}{M \cdot p_s(x)}, 1\right)$, return x	2: with probability $\frac{1}{M}$, return x
	3: return $\perp$
3: return $\perp$	
Algorithm $\mathcal{B}_\infty^{\mathsf{real}}$:	Algorithm $\mathcal{B}_\infty^{\mathsf{ideal}}$:
1: $z \leftarrow \perp$	1: $z \leftarrow \perp$
2: **while** $z = \perp$ **do**	2: **while** $z = \perp$ **do**
3: $z \leftarrow \mathcal{A}^{\mathsf{real}}$	3: $z \leftarrow \mathcal{A}^{\mathsf{ideal}}$
4: **end while**	4: **end while**
5: return z	5: return z

Fig. 1. Rejection sampling algorithms.

Lemma 1 Adapted from [Lyu12, Lemma 4.7]). *Assume that $M \geq 1$ and $\varepsilon \in [0, 1/2]$ are such that*

$$\Pr_{z \hookleftarrow p_t} (p_t(z) \leq M \cdot p_s(z)) \geq 1 - \varepsilon,$$

which can be rewritten in terms of smooth Rényi divergence as $R_\infty^\varepsilon(p_t \| p_s) \leq M$. Then the probability $\mathcal{A}^{\mathsf{real}}(\perp)$ that $\mathcal{A}^{\mathsf{real}}$ aborts is such that

$$\frac{M-1}{M} \leq \mathcal{A}^{\mathsf{real}}(\perp) \leq \frac{M-1+\varepsilon}{M}.$$

Moreover, we have

$$\Delta(\mathcal{A}^{\mathsf{real}}, \mathcal{A}^{\mathsf{ideal}}) \leq \varepsilon/M \quad \text{and} \quad \Delta(\mathcal{B}_\infty^{\mathsf{real}}, \mathcal{B}_\infty^{\mathsf{ideal}}) \leq \varepsilon.$$

2.2 Lyubashevsky's Signature Scheme

All the following parameters are functions of a security parameter λ. We let $k, m,$ $n \geq 1$ and $q \geq 2$ specify matrix spaces over $\mathbb{Z}_q$, with $m > n$. The distribution $P_{\mathbf{S}}$ over $\mathbb{Z}^{m \times k}$ is for signing keys and has support $\mathcal{S} = \text{Supp}(P_{\mathbf{S}})$. Let $\mathcal{M}$ be the message space. Let $\mathcal{C} \subset \mathbb{Z}^k$ finite and $H : \mathbb{Z}_q^n \times \mathcal{M} \rightarrow \mathcal{C}$ a hash function, which is modeled as a random oracle in the signature scheme analysis. The parameter $\gamma > 0$ is used in the verification algorithm to quantify the smallness of vectors corresponding to valid signatures. To obtain a 2^λ security against known attacks, one typically sets $m, n, k = \Omega(\lambda)$ and $\gamma, q = \text{poly}(\lambda)$.

Let $\varepsilon \geq 0$ and $M \geq 1$ be parameters related to rejection sampling, for a source distribution Q and a target distribution P over $\mathbb{Z}^m$. Most works directly instantiate these distributions. For example, uniform distributions in well-chosen hypercubes are used in [Lyu09] and $P = Q$ Gaussian are used in [Lyu12]. We assume that the support of Q is contained in $(-q/2, q/2]^m$.

We consider the scheme presented in Fig. 2, borrowed from [Lyu12] with the aforementioned rejection sampling generalization. For simplicity, we assume that the verification key $\mathbf{A} \in \mathbb{Z}_q^{n \times m}$ is in Hermite normal form, i.e., we have $\mathbf{A} = (\mathbf{I}_n | \mathbf{B})$ for some matrix $\mathbf{B}$ and with $\mathbf{I}_n \in \mathbb{Z}_q^{n \times n}$ denoting the identity matrix. Up to mild conditions on k, n, m, q, this is without loss of generality.

$\mathsf{KeyGen}(1^\lambda) :$
1: $\mathbf{B} \hookleftarrow \mathbb{Z}_q^{n \times (m-n)}$ and $\mathbf{S} \hookleftarrow P_{\mathbf{S}}$
2: $\mathbf{A} \leftarrow (\mathbf{I}_n | \mathbf{B})$
3: $\mathbf{T} \leftarrow \mathbf{A} \mathbf{S}$
4: return $\mathsf{vk} = (\mathbf{A}, \mathbf{T})$ and $\mathsf{sk} = (\mathbf{A}, \mathbf{S})$

$\mathsf{Sign}(\mu, \mathbf{A}, \mathbf{S}) :$
1: $\mathbf{y} \hookleftarrow Q$
2: $\mathbf{c} \leftarrow H(\mathbf{A}\mathbf{y}, \mu)$
3: $\mathbf{z} \leftarrow \mathbf{y} + \mathbf{S}\mathbf{c}$
4: $u \hookleftarrow U([0, 1])$
5: if $u \leq \min\left(\frac{P(\mathbf{z})}{M \cdot Q(\mathbf{y})}, 1\right)$ then
6:     return $(\mathbf{z}, \mathbf{c})$
7: else
8:     go to Step 1
9: end if

$\mathsf{Verify}(\mu, \mathbf{z}, \mathbf{c}, \mathbf{A}, \mathbf{T} = \mathbf{A}\mathbf{S}) :$
1: if $\|\mathbf{z}\| \leq \gamma$ and $\mathbf{c} = H(\mathbf{A}\mathbf{z} - \mathbf{T}\mathbf{c}, \mu)$ then
2:     return 1
3: else
4:     return 0
5: end if

Fig. 2. Lyubashevsky's signature scheme.

Runtime and correctness follow from the two lemmas below.

Lemma 2 (Sign Runtime). *Let* $\varepsilon \geq 0$, $M \geq 1$ *and* $B = \lceil \lambda / \log \frac{M}{M-1+\varepsilon} \rceil$. *Assume that P and Q satisfy* $\max_{(\mathbf{S}, \mathbf{c}) \in \mathcal{S} \times \mathcal{C}} R_\infty^\varepsilon(P \| Q_{+\mathbf{S}\mathbf{c}}) \leq M$.

Let $(\mathbf{y}_0^\top|\mathbf{y}_1^\top)^\top \hookleftarrow Q$, where $\mathbf{y}_0$ takes values in $\mathbb{Z}^n$. In the ROM, the number of loop iterations i^* of a Sign execution satisfies

$$\forall i: \Pr(i^* \geq i) \leq \left(1 - \frac{1-\varepsilon}{M}\right)^i + B^2 \cdot 2^{-H_\infty(\mathbf{y}_0|\mathbf{y}_1)_Q} + 2^{-\lambda}.$$

Note that when $M \leq \mathsf{poly}(\lambda)$, $\varepsilon \leq 1 - 1/\mathsf{poly}(\lambda)$ and $2^{-H_\infty(\mathbf{y}_0|\mathbf{y}_1)_Q} \leq \mathsf{negl}(\lambda)$, we have that $B^2 \cdot 2^{-H_\infty(\mathbf{y}_0|\mathbf{y}_1)_Q} + 2^{-\lambda} \leq \mathsf{negl}(\lambda)$.

Lemma 3 (Correctness). *Let $\varepsilon \geq 0$ and $M \geq 1$. Let P and Q satisfying $\max_{(\mathbf{S},\mathbf{c})\in\mathcal{S}\times\mathcal{C}} R_\infty^\varepsilon(P\|Q_{+\mathbf{Sc}}) \leq M$. Let $(\mathbf{y}_0^\top|\mathbf{y}_1^\top)^\top \hookleftarrow Q$, where $\mathbf{y}_0$ takes value in $\mathbb{Z}^n$. Further assume that $2^{-H_\infty(\mathbf{y}_0|\mathbf{y}_1)_Q} \leq \mathsf{negl}(\lambda)$, $\varepsilon \leq \mathsf{negl}(\lambda)$ and the probability that Sign terminates is $\geq 1 - \mathsf{negl}(\lambda)$. Then, in the ROM, the scheme is correct if $\gamma \geq \gamma_P$ with γ_P such that $\Pr_{\mathbf{z}\hookleftarrow P}(\|\mathbf{z}\| \geq \gamma_P) \leq \mathsf{negl}(\lambda)$.*

We only highlight components of typical security proofs that are relevant to our work, and refer to prior works for more details [Lyu09,Lyu12,AFLT16]. The security proofs of Lyubashevsky's signature scheme all proceed by sequences of games and argue that the adversary's advantages in successive games differ by small amounts and that no efficient adversary can solve the last game with a significant advantage.

An early step in the sequence of games is to replace the calls to H at Step 2 of the Sign algorithm by truly uniform and independent samples $\mathbf{c} \leftarrow U(\mathcal{C})$. To ensure that the adversary cannot notice the difference in the ROM, this requires that a given input $(\mathbf{Ay}, \mu)$ to H cannot occur twice. This is obtained by having the conditional min-entropy $H_\infty(\mathbf{y}_0|\mathbf{y}_1)_Q$ satisfy:

$$H_\infty(\mathbf{y}_0|\mathbf{y}_1)_Q = \Omega(\lambda).$$

An important other game hop consists in making Steps 1 to 6 of the Sign algorithm signing-key independent. Concretely, this means arguing that the distributions of the pair $(\mathbf{z}, \mathbf{c})$ in the experiments from Fig. 3 are statistically close, by using Lemma 1. (Note that this also requires programming H consistently with all appearing $\mathbf{c}$'s.)

To complete the security proof, Lyubashevsky [Lyu12] reduces the SIS problem to the sEU-CMA security of a signing-key independent simulation of the Sign algorithm, by relying on the forking lemma. At this stage of the security proof, rejection sampling does not play a role anymore. We only note that the SIS instance has parameters q, m, n and $\beta = 2(\gamma + \gamma')$, with γ as in the Verify algorithm and $\gamma' = \max_{(\mathbf{S},\mathbf{c})\in\mathcal{S}\times\mathcal{C}}\|\mathbf{Sc}\|$. Note that γ is always significantly larger than γ'. We stress that there is a tension in setting γ: it should be sufficiently high to provide correctness (see Lemma 3 above) and as small as possible to provide higher security and hence allow more compact instantiations.

3 Lower Bounds in the Case of Perfect Rejection Sampling

We start by studying *the case of perfect rejection sampling*, which corresponds to the setting of [Lyu09,DDLL13]. That is, we set $\varepsilon = 0$ in the formalism of Sect. 2.2.

1: $\mathbf{y} \hookleftarrow Q$
2: $\mathbf{c} \leftarrow U(\mathcal{C})$
3: $\mathbf{z} \leftarrow \mathbf{y} + \mathbf{Sc}$
4: $u \hookleftarrow U([0,1])$
5: **if** $u \leq \min\left(\frac{P(\mathbf{z})}{M \cdot Q(\mathbf{y})}, 1\right)$ **then**
6:     return $(\mathbf{z}, \mathbf{c})$
7: **else**
8:     return $(\bot, \bot)$
9: **end if**

1: $\mathbf{c} \leftarrow U(\mathcal{C})$
2: $\mathbf{z} \leftarrow P$
3: $u \hookleftarrow U([0,1])$
4: **if** $u \leq \frac{1}{M}$ **then**
5:     return $(\mathbf{z}, \mathbf{c})$
6: **else**
7:     return $(\bot, \bot)$
8: **end if**

Fig. 3. Simulating signatures.

We prove two lower bounds: (1) regarding signature size in both unimodal and bimodal settings (Sects. 3.1 and 3.2), and (2) regarding the expected number of iterations of the rejection step (Sect. 3.3).

First, we analyze to which extent the expected norm of a distribution P can be decreased, under the constraint that we can reject to it using shifted samples from Q, where the Euclidean norm of the shift is bounded from above. This gives lower bounds on the norm of the signature vector $\mathbf{z}$ in Lyubashevsky's signature scheme, as recalled in Sect. 2.2. We start by studying the easier case of continuous distributions, and then provide a way to discretize the results.

Second, we prove than the classical rejection sampling strategy described above is optimal if one aims to minimize the expected number of iterations of the rejection step in the case of perfect rejection sampling from P to Q. Specifically, the expected number of iterations of any strategy is at least $R_\infty(P\|Q)$, which is reached by classical rejection sampling.

3.1 Optimal Compactness in the Unimodal Setting

The main result of this subsection is the following.

Theorem 1. *Let* $m \geq 1, t > 0$, $V = \mathcal{B}_m(t)$ *and* $M > 1$. *Let* $f, g : \mathbb{R}^m \to [0,1]$ *be two probability densities over* $\mathbb{R}^m$ *such that* $\sup_{\mathbf{v} \in V} R_\infty(f\|g_{+\mathbf{v}}) \leq M$. *Then we have:*

$$\mathbb{E}_{\mathbf{x} \hookleftarrow f}(\|\mathbf{x}\|) \geq \frac{t}{M^{1/(m-1)} - 1}.$$

Note that we place ourselves in a setup where shifts belong to a hyperball. In the context of Lyubashesvky's signature scheme, the shift is $\mathbf{Sc}$, where $\mathbf{S}$ is the signing key and $\mathbf{c}$ is the challenge (which is part of the signature). Given that $\mathbf{S}$ is unknown, replacing the set of $\mathbf{Sc}$'s by a hyperball seems to be a reasonable approach. Refining this approximation would lead to significant difficulties in the proof, with unlikely gains.

We now discuss the parameters M and m. As exhibited in Lemma 2, the variable M is related to the rejection probability. The smaller M, the faster we expect signing to be. To obtain a signing algorithm that terminates in polynomial time with overwhelming probability, we are interested in $M \leq \text{poly}(\lambda)$. Recall that we have $m = \Omega(\lambda)$. In this parameter regime, we have $t/(M^{1/(m-1)} - 1) \approx t(m-1)/\log M$.

The role of distribution g in Theorem 1 may seem puzzling, as it does not appear in the result. It acts as a control of the discrepancy of f: distribution f must be sufficiently wide to hide (in the Rényi divergence sense) a version of V that is blurred by g. This forces $\mathbb{E}_{\mathbf{x} \hookleftarrow f}(\|\mathbf{x}\|)$ to be rather large. The proof proceeds in two steps. The first one consists in showing that there is no point favoring any direction and that we can restrict the study to isotropic distributions, i.e., distributions whose density is a function of the norm of the vector. The proof, which may be found in the full version, proceeds by averaging on shells. Theorem 1 is then obtained by integrating the local constraint $\sup_{\mathbf{v} \in V} R_\infty(f\|g_{+\mathbf{v}}) \leq M$ over the whole support, with appropriate scaling.

Lemma 4. *Let $m \geq 1, t > 0$ and $V = \mathcal{B}_m(t)$. Let $f, g : \mathbb{R}^m \to [0,1]$ be two probability densities over $\mathbb{R}^m$ and define $M = \sup_{\mathbf{v} \in V} R_\infty(f\|g_{+\mathbf{v}})$. Then there exist two probability densities f^*, g^* that satisfy*

- $\sup_{\mathbf{v} \in V} R_\infty(f^*\|g^*_{+\mathbf{v}}) \leq M$,
- $\|\mathbf{x}\| = \|\mathbf{y}\| \implies g^*(\mathbf{x}) = g^*(\mathbf{y})$ *and* $f^*(\mathbf{x}) = f^*(\mathbf{y})$,
- $\mathbb{E}_{\mathbf{z} \hookleftarrow f}(\|\mathbf{z}\|) = \mathbb{E}_{\mathbf{z} \hookleftarrow f^*}(\|\mathbf{z}\|)$.

Proof (Theorem 1). Thanks to Lemma 4, we can, without loss of generality, assume that both f and g are isotropic. For $k \geq 0$, we define $\mu_k = \int_0^\infty r^k f(r)\, dr$, which is the k-th order moment of f. In particular, we have $\mu_{m-1} = 1/S_m$ and $\mu_m = \mathbb{E}_{\mathbf{x} \hookleftarrow f}(\|\mathbf{x}\|)/S_m$. Indeed, using a hyperspherical variable change, we see that, for any $\beta \in \{0,1\}$:

$$
\begin{aligned}
\mathbb{E}_{\mathbf{x} \hookleftarrow f}(\|\mathbf{x}\|^\beta) &= \int_{\mathbb{R}^m} \|\mathbf{x}\|^\beta f(\mathbf{x})\, d\mathbf{x} \\
&= \int_0^\infty \rho^{m-1+\beta} f(\rho) \int_{[0,\pi]^{m-2} \times [0,2\pi]} D(\vec{\theta})\, d\vec{\theta}\, d\rho \\
&= S_m \cdot \mu_{m-1+\beta}.
\end{aligned}
$$

The above implies that $\mathbb{E}_{\mathbf{x} \hookleftarrow f}(\|\mathbf{x}\|) = \mu_m/\mu_{m-1}$.

For any $x \geq 0$ and $u \in [-t, t]$, it holds that $f(x) \leq M \cdot g(|x-u|)$. In particular, for $x \geq t$, we have $f(x - t) \leq M \cdot g(x)$. Let us multiply both sides by x^{m-1} and integrate over $[t, +\infty)$. With a change of variable on the left-hand side, this gives

$$
\begin{aligned}
\int_0^\infty (x+t)^{m-1} f(x)\, dx &\leq M \cdot \int_t^\infty x^{m-1} g(x)\, dx \\
&\leq M \cdot \int_0^\infty x^{m-1} g(x)\, dx \\
&= M \cdot \int_0^\infty x^{m-1} f(x)\, dx,
\end{aligned}
$$

by recognizing that the right-hand side is $M \cdot \mu_{m-1}$ (which is the same for f and g). Grouping everything on the same side, we have

$$0 \leq \int_0^\infty \left(Mx^{m-1} - (x+t)^{m-1} \right) f(x) \, \mathrm{d}x. \tag{1}$$

Let $C = t/(M^{1/(m-1)} - 1)$. For $m > 2$, we rewrite the integrand as

$$Mx^{m-1} - (x+t)^{m-1} = \left(M^{\frac{1}{m-1}}x - (x+t) \right) \cdot \sum_{k=0}^{m-2} \left(xM^{\frac{1}{m-1}} \right)^k (x+t)^{m-2-k}$$

$$= \left(M^{\frac{1}{m-1}} - 1 \right) (x - C) \cdot \sum_{k=0}^{m-2} \left(xM^{\frac{1}{m-1}} \right)^k (x+t)^{m-2-k}.$$

For $m = 2$, the above holds by replacing the sum by 1. Now, note that the inequality $xM^{1/(m-1)} \geq x + t$ holds if and only if $x \geq C$. Hence the following upper bound holds for any $x \geq 0$, if $m > 2$:

$$(x - C) \cdot \sum_{k=0}^{m-2} (xM^{\frac{1}{m-1}})^k (x+t)^{m-2-k} \leq (x - C)(m-1)M^{\frac{m-2}{m-1}} x^{m-2}.$$

When $m > 2$, we can divide by $(M^{1/(m-1)} - 1)M^{(m-2)/(m-1)}(m - 1) > 0$ in Equation (1), and obtain:

$$C \cdot \int_0^\infty x^{m-2} f(x) \, \mathrm{d}x \leq \int_0^\infty x^{m-1} f(x) \, \mathrm{d}x.$$

Note that it also holds for $m = 2$. This can be rewritten as $\mu_{m-1}/\mu_{m-2} \geq C$.

Now, observe that $\mu_m \cdot \mu_{m-2} \geq (\mu_{m-1})^2$. Indeed, the Cauchy-Schwarz inequality states that for any real random variables X, Y, it holds that $|\mathbb{E}(XY)|^2 \leq \mathbb{E}(X^2)\mathbb{E}(Y^2)$. We instantiate it with the (non-independent) random variables $X = \|\mathbf{x}\|^{m/2}$ and $Y = \|\mathbf{x}\|^{(m-2)/2}$, where $\mathbf{x} \hookleftarrow f$. Then $XY = \|\mathbf{x}\|^{\frac{m}{2} + \frac{m-2}{2}} = \|\mathbf{x}\|^{m-1}$. To conclude, note $\mu_m \cdot \mu_{m-2} \geq (\mu_{m-1})^2$ implies that $\mu_m/\mu_{m-1} \geq \mu_{m-1}/\mu_{m-2} \geq C$. This completes the proof. $\qquad\square$

For the discrete case, we observe that given a discrete distribution P, letting $f : \mathbf{x} \mapsto P(\lceil \mathbf{x} \rfloor)$ be a probability density over $\mathbb{R}^m$, we have, by the triangle inequality

$$\mathbb{E}_{\mathbf{x} \hookleftarrow f}(\|\mathbf{x}\|) \leq \mathbb{E}_{\mathbf{x} \hookleftarrow P}(\|\mathbf{x}\|) + \frac{\sqrt{m}}{2}.$$

Theorem 1 can then be adapted to the discrete case, up to subtracting $\frac{\sqrt{m}}{2}$ from the lower bound. In all setups considered in this work, this term is significantly smaller than $t/(M^{1/(m-1)} - 1)$.

Corollary 1. *Let $m \geq 1$, $t > 0$, $V = \mathcal{B}_m(t) \cap \mathbb{Z}^m$ and $M > 1$. Let P and Q be two discrete probability distributions over $\mathbb{Z}^m$ such that $\sup_{\mathbf{v} \in V} R_\infty(P \| Q_{+\mathbf{v}}) \leq M$. Then we have:*

$$\mathbb{E}_{\mathbf{x} \hookleftarrow P}(\|\mathbf{x}\|) \geq \frac{t}{M^{1/(m-1)} - 1} - \frac{\sqrt{m}}{2}.$$

3.2   Optimal Compactness in the Bimodal Setting

We obtain the following result in the bimodal setting. The proof, which is similar to the one of Theorem 1, it provided in the full version.

Theorem 2. *Let $m \geq 3, t > 0$, $V = \mathcal{B}_m(t)$ and $M > 1$. Let $f, g : \mathbb{R}^m \to [0, 1]$ be two probability densities over $\mathbb{R}^m$ such that $\sup_{\mathbf{v} \in V} R_\infty(f \| g_{\pm \mathbf{v}}) \leq M$, where $g_{\pm \mathbf{v}}$ is the density $\mathbf{x} \mapsto \frac{1}{2}(g(\mathbf{x} - \mathbf{v}) + g(\mathbf{x} + \mathbf{v}))$. Then the following holds:*

$$\mathbb{E}_{\mathbf{x} \hookleftarrow f}(\|\mathbf{x}\|) \geq \frac{t}{\sqrt{M^{\frac{2}{m-2}} - 1}}.$$

For $M \leq \mathsf{poly}(\lambda)$ and $m = \Omega(\lambda)$ as in the discussion following Theorem 1, we have $t/(M^{2/(m-2)} - 1)^{1/2} \approx t\sqrt{(m-2)/(2 \log M)}$. Similarly to the unimodal case, the lower bound can be adapted to integer distributions with limited loss (for all setups considered in this work).

Corollary 2. *Let $m \geq 3, t > 0, V = \mathcal{B}_m(t) \cap \mathbb{Z}^m$ and $M > 1$. Let P and Q be two discrete probability distributions over $\mathbb{Z}^m$ such that $\sup_{\mathbf{v} \in V} R_\infty(P \| Q_{\pm \mathbf{v}}) \leq M$, where $Q_{\pm \mathbf{v}}$ is as in Theorem 2. Then the following holds:*

$$\mathbb{E}_{\mathbf{x} \hookleftarrow P}(\|\mathbf{x}\|) \geq \frac{t}{\sqrt{M^{\frac{2}{m-2}} - 1}} - \frac{\sqrt{m}}{2}.$$

3.3   Optimality of the Expected Number of Iterations

We now analyze to which extent the expected number of iterations of the rejection step could be reduced in the case of exact rejection sampling from P to Q, and prove the classical strategy to be optimal. This question arises from the variety of rejection sampling techniques that have been studied in other fields.

There exist multiple variants of rejection sampling. For instance, a procedure described in [HJMR07], and recalled in the full version, takes a greedy approach to rejection sampling and differs from the one we presented up until now. We are in the setting where we have access to a sampler from distribution Q. These samples are denoted by $(X_i)_{i \geq 1}$ with $X_i \in \mathcal{X}$ for some set $\mathcal{X}$ and we are required to output a sample from the distribution P over $\mathcal{X}$. Any design of procedure is allowed, as long as the output is one of the observed samples X_i. Let i^* be the random variable denoting the number of samples observed by an algorithm and we wish to determine how small $\mathbb{E}(i^*)$ can be. We note that the work of [HJMR07], establishes that there exists a rejection sampling algorithm achieving $\mathbb{E}(\log i^*) = \log R_1(P \| Q)$ up to lower order terms in $R_1(P \| Q)$, and that this is optimal. Here, we show that the minimum value for $\mathbb{E}(i^*)$ is $R_\infty(P \| Q)$.

We model a rejection sampling algorithm by a family of randomized functions $A_i : \mathcal{X}^i \to \{1, \dots, i\} \cup \{\mathrm{r}\}$. At step i, it sees the new sample X_i and based on $X_1, \dots, X_i$ it computes $A_i(X_1, \dots, X_i)$. If it is equal to r, the algorithm asks for one more sample and otherwise if $A_i(X_1, \dots, X_i) \in \{1, \dots, i\}$, the algorithm terminates and outputs the sample $X_{A_i(X_1, \dots, X_i)}$. Note that the running time of the algorithm is defined by $i^* = \inf\{i \geq 1 : A_i(X_1, \ldots, X_i) \neq r\}$. We only consider algorithms for which $i^* < \infty$ almost surely. We define the random variable $J = A_{i^*}(X_1, \ldots, X_{i^*}) \in \mathbb{N}_+$, note that $J \leq i^*$ and the output of the algorithm is X_J (i.e., the output sample may not be the last one that was generated).

Theorem 3. *Let P, Q be two discrete probability distributions. Any rejection sampling algorithm $(A_i)_{i \geq 1}$ sampling from P satisfies $\mathbb{E}(i^*) \geq R_\infty(P\|Q)$.*

Proof. We have by assumption for any $x \in \mathcal{X}$,

$$P(x) = \Pr[X_J = x] = \sum_{j=1}^{\infty} \Pr[J = j, X_j = x] \leq \sum_{j=1}^{\infty} \Pr[i^* \geq j, X_j = x],$$

where we used the fact that the event $[J = j]$ is contained in $[i^* \geq j]$. Now, observe that the event $[i^* < j]$ only depends on $X_1, \ldots, X_{j-1}$ and as such it is independent of the event $[X_j = x]$. This implies that $[i^* \geq j]$ is independent of $[X_j = x]$. As a result, we have

$$P(x) \leq \sum_{j=1}^{\infty} \Pr[i^* \geq j] \Pr[X_j = x] = \mathbb{E}(i^*) Q(x),$$

which proves the desired result.

In the context of Lyubashevsky's signature schemes with source distribution Q', target distribution P', challenge set $\mathcal{C}$ and signing key $\mathbf{S}$, we would have $P = P' \otimes U(\mathcal{C})$ and Q would be the distribution of the pair $(\mathbf{z}, \mathbf{c})$ obtained by sampling $\mathbf{y}$ from Q', $\mathbf{c}$ from $U(\mathcal{C})$ and defining $\mathbf{z} = \mathbf{y} + \mathbf{Sc}$.

The above proof can be adapted in the setting where P and Q are continuous distributions by considering a sequence of balls converging to $\{x\}$ instead of x.

4   Improved Analysis via the Rényi Divergence

For the rest of the paper, we flip our focus and prove positive results (upper bounds). In this section, we propose an improved analysis of Lyubashevsky's signatures that relies on the Rényi divergence rather than the statistical distance, allowing larger sampling errors in the case of imperfect rejection sampling. Then, in Sect. 5 propose a new choice of distributions that (asymptotically) reaches our lower bounds. Finally, in Sect. 6, we propose a way to circumvent the lower bound for the expected number of iterations by providing an alternate strategy which allows to fix a-priori a maximal number of loop iterations.

Our lower bounds apply to perfect rejection sampling, but rejecting to an inaccurate approximation to the target distribution also allows to instantiate Lyubashevsky's signature, as done in [Lyu12] and already mentioned in Sect. 2.2 (when $\varepsilon > 0$ in Lemma 1). In particular, imperfect rejection sampling is used when instantiating the signature scheme with Gaussian distributions.

In this section, we study the case of imperfect rejection sampling and describe a way to improve the analysis of the digital signature from Sect. 2.2, by replacing the statistical distance (in Lemma 1) with the Rényi divergence to quantify the closeness between ideal and real rejection sampling algorithms. As already observed in prior works (see in particular the discussion in [BLR+18]), the Rényi divergence is well-suited for improving the analyses of digital signatures, as the security game is of a search type. While the analysis based on the statistical distance imposes $\varepsilon = 2^{\Omega(\lambda)}$, as it requires the statistical distance to be negligible, our analysis allows larger sampling errors as it only imposes $\varepsilon \approx 1/q_{\mathsf{sig}}$ where q_{sig} is the number of signing queries (which is $\mathsf{poly}(\lambda) \ll 2^{\Omega(\lambda)}$).

4.1   Rényi Divergence Bounds for Imperfect Rejection Sampling

Let p_t and p_s be two probability densities, both continuous or both discrete. We consider algorithms $\mathcal{A}^{\mathsf{real}}$, $\mathcal{A}^{\mathsf{ideal}}$, $\mathcal{B}^{\mathsf{real}}$ and $\mathcal{B}^{\mathsf{ideal}}$ from Fig. 1.

Lemma 5. *Assume that $M > 1$ and $\varepsilon < 1$ are such that $R_\infty^\varepsilon(p_t \| p_s) \leq M$. Then for any $a \in (1, +\infty)$ we have:*

$$R_a(\mathcal{A}^{\mathsf{real}} \| \mathcal{A}^{\mathsf{ideal}}) \leq \left(\frac{1}{M} + \frac{M - 1 + \varepsilon}{M} \cdot \left(1 + \frac{\varepsilon}{M - 1} \right)^{a-1} \right)^{\frac{1}{a-1}},$$

$$R_a(\mathcal{B}_\infty^{\mathsf{real}} \| \mathcal{B}_\infty^{\mathsf{ideal}}) \leq \frac{1}{(1 - \varepsilon)^{a/(a-1)}}.$$

Moreover, for $a = \infty$, we have:

$$R_\infty(\mathcal{A}^{\mathsf{real}} \| \mathcal{A}^{\mathsf{ideal}}) \leq 1 + \frac{\varepsilon}{M - 1} \quad \text{and} \quad R_\infty(\mathcal{B}_\infty^{\mathsf{real}} \| \mathcal{B}_\infty^{\mathsf{ideal}}) \leq \frac{1}{1 - \varepsilon}.$$

Note that for $\varepsilon = 0$, we recover the distributional equalities $\mathcal{A}^{\mathsf{real}} = \mathcal{A}^{\mathsf{ideal}}$ and $\mathcal{B}_\infty^{\mathsf{real}} = \mathcal{B}_\infty^{\mathsf{ideal}}$ of Lemma 1. We are interested in the case $\varepsilon > 0$.

Proof. Let $\mathcal{A}^{\mathsf{real}}(\bot)$ and $\mathcal{A}^{\mathsf{ideal}}(\bot)$ denote the probabilities that $\mathcal{A}^{\mathsf{real}}$ or $\mathcal{A}^{\mathsf{ideal}}$ output nothing. We have, using results from Lemma 1:

$$R_a(\mathcal{A}^{\mathsf{real}} \| \mathcal{A}^{\mathsf{ideal}})^{a-1} = \left[\int_{\mathsf{Supp}(p_s)} \frac{\left(p_s(x) \min\left(\frac{p_t(x)}{M \cdot p_s(x)}, 1 \right) \right)^a}{(p_t(x)/M)^{a-1}} \, \mathrm{d}x \right] + \frac{(\mathcal{A}^{\mathsf{real}}(\bot))^a}{(\mathcal{A}^{\mathsf{ideal}}(\bot))^{a-1}}$$

$$\leq \int_{\mathsf{Supp}(p_s)} \frac{\left(p_s(x) \frac{p_t(x)}{M \cdot p_s(x)} \right)^a}{(p_t(x)/M)^{a-1}} \, \mathrm{d}x + \frac{(1 - (1 - \varepsilon)/M)^a}{(1 - 1/M)^{a-1}}$$

$$= \int_{\mathsf{Supp}(p_s)} \frac{p_t(x)}{M} \, \mathrm{d}x + \frac{M - 1 + \varepsilon}{M} \cdot \left(\frac{M - 1 + \varepsilon}{M - 1} \right)^{a-1}$$

$$\leq \frac{1}{M} + \frac{M - 1 + \varepsilon}{M} \cdot \left(1 + \frac{\varepsilon}{M - 1} \right)^{a-1}.$$

We move on to bounding the second divergence. For any $x \in \text{Supp}(p_s)$:

$$\mathcal{B}_\infty^{\text{real}}(x) = \frac{\mathcal{A}^{\text{real}}(x)}{1 - \mathcal{A}^{\text{real}}(\bot)}.$$

This also holds for $\mathcal{B}_\infty^{\text{ideal}}$ with $\mathcal{A}^{\text{ideal}}$ instead of $\mathcal{A}^{\text{real}}$. We obtain:

$$R_a(\mathcal{B}_\infty^{\text{real}} \| \mathcal{B}_\infty^{\text{ideal}})^{a-1} = \int_{\text{Supp}(p_s)} \frac{1}{M^{a-1}} \cdot \frac{\left(p_s(x) \min\left(\frac{p_t(x)}{M \cdot p_s(x)}, 1\right)\right)^a}{(\mathcal{A}^{\text{real}}(\bot))^a (p_t(x)/M)^{a-1}}$$

$$\leq \frac{M}{(1-\varepsilon)^a} \int_{\text{Supp}(p_s)} \frac{\left(p_s(x) \min\left(\frac{p_t(x)}{M \cdot p_s(x)}, 1\right)\right)^a}{(p_t(x)/M)^{a-1}}.$$

This sum was already computed just above and is at most $1/M$.

The continuity of $a \mapsto R_a(P_t \| P_s)$ at $a = +\infty$ gives the last bounds.   □

4.2 Improved Analysis of Lyubashevsky's Scheme

We now go back to the scheme described in Sect. 2.2 with imperfect rejection sampling, and show that the analysis above allows setting $\varepsilon \approx 1/q_{\text{sig}}$ instead of $\varepsilon = 2^{-\Omega(\lambda)}$. Here q_{sig} refers to the number of signing queries that an adversary can make. As a signing query requires an interaction with the signer, it is typically considered to be a large polynomial in λ, which is much smaller than $2^{\Omega(\lambda)}$. As a result, this refined analysis puts less stress on the condition that P_s and P_t must satisfy and hence to reach smaller values for $\mathbb{E}_{\mathbf{z} \hookleftarrow P_t}(\|\mathbf{x}\|)$: this is beneficial to security and then allows for smaller parameter sets.

To achieve this improvement, we replace the statistical distance with the Rényi divergence in the scheme analysis, when simulating signature queries (see Fig. 3). By Lemma 5 and the Rényi divergence data processing inequality, replacing $\mathcal{A}^{\text{real}}$ by $\mathcal{A}^{\text{ideal}}$ once in the security proof (i.e., in one loop iteration of one signature query) leads to a multiplicative loss of a factor $\leq 1 + \varepsilon/(M-1)$ in the adversary's advantage. Now, note that the probability that at least one among the q_{sig} sign queries requires more than $B = (\lambda + \log q_{\text{sig}})/\log(M/(M-1+\varepsilon))$ loop iterations is exponentially small. Assuming this is not the case, we can bound the number of times $\mathcal{A}^{\text{real}}$ is replaced by $\mathcal{A}^{\text{ideal}}$ in the security proof by $B \cdot q_{\text{sig}}$. By the Rényi divergence multiplicativity property, this induces a multiplicative loss of a factor $\leq (1 + \varepsilon/(M-1))^{B \cdot q_{\text{sig}}}$ in the adversary's advantage.

5 Reaching the Lower Bounds with Hyperballs

In this section, we show that continuous uniform distributions in hyperballs reach the lower bounds in both the unimodal and bimodal perfect rejection sampling settings. We also consider the imperfect unimodal setting and find parameters that are asymptotically at least as good as the ones obtained for the Gaussian distribution (using our analysis described in Sect. 4). As continuous hyperball uniform distributions are easier both to study and implement than their discrete counterpart, we consider the case of continuous distributions. Further, we show that a slight modification of Lyubashevsky's signature allows for the target and source distributions to be continuous.

We also compare this choice of distributions with the uniform distributions in hypercubes and with Gaussians, both asymptotically and with concrete parameters.

5.1   Uniform Distributions in Hyperballs

The first step is to compute the divergence in the three settings: unimodal, either perfect or imperfect rejection sampling and bimodal perfect rejection sampling. The first case can actually be seen as a particular case of the second one, and we summarize both in the following lemma. We use the notation $I_x(a, b) = B(x; a, b)/B(a, b)$ for $x \in [0, 1]$ and $a, b > 0$, where $B(a, b)$ is the Beta function and $B(x; a, b)$ is the regularized incomplete Beta function.

Lemma 6 (Smooth Divergence). *Let $m \geq 1$ and $\mathbf{v} \in \mathbb{R}^m$. Let $\varepsilon \in [0, 1/2)$ and $\eta \geq 1$ be such that $2\varepsilon = I_{1-1/\eta^2}(\frac{m+1}{2}, \frac{1}{2})$. Let $r, r' > 0$ such that $r'^2 \geq r^2 + \|\mathbf{v}\|^2 + 2r\|\mathbf{v}\|/\eta$. Then it holds that:*

$$R_\infty^\varepsilon \Big(U(\mathcal{B}_m(r)) \| U(\mathcal{B}_m(r', \mathbf{v})) \Big) = \left(\frac{r'}{r}\right)^m.$$

Let $M > 1$. The above is $\leq M$ if $r \geq \|\mathbf{v}\| \cdot \dfrac{\frac{1}{\eta} + \sqrt{\frac{1}{\eta^2} + M^{2/m} - 1}}{M^{2/m} - 1}$ and $r' = M^{1/m}r$.

Note that when $\varepsilon = 0$, we have $\eta = 1$. In that case, we can set $r = \|\mathbf{v}\|/(M^{1/m} - 1)$, which almost matches the lower bound from Theorem 1. For $\varepsilon = 2^{-c \cdot m}$ with a constant $c > 0$, we have that $1/\eta^2$ tends to $1 - 2^{-c}$ when m goes to infinity; for ε satisfying $\varepsilon \geq 2^{-o(m)}$ and $\varepsilon = o(1/m)$ with m going to infinity, we have that $1/\eta^2 \sim -\log(\varepsilon)/m$ (see full version).

Proof. Assume that there exists some cut $\mathcal{C}$ with $\mathrm{vol}(\mathcal{C})/V_m(r) \leq \varepsilon$ such that the divergence is defined, i.e., with $\mathcal{B}_m(r) \setminus \mathcal{C} \subseteq \mathcal{B}_m(r', \mathbf{v})$. Then the divergence is $(r'/r)^m$, as the ratio of densities is constant and equal to $(r'/r)^m$ over $\mathcal{B}_m(r) \setminus \mathcal{C}$. To prove the first claim, it hence suffices to show that such a cut $\mathcal{C}$ exists.

We introduce the cut $\mathcal{C}_\eta := \{\mathbf{x} \in \mathcal{B}_m(r) | \langle \mathbf{x}, \mathbf{v} \rangle \geq -\|\mathbf{v}\| r/\eta\}$. This is the intersection of a ball with an affine half-space, i.e., an m-dimensional hyperspherical cap. Its volume is $\frac{V_m(r)}{2} \cdot I_{1-1/\eta^2}(\frac{m+1}{2}, \frac{1}{2})$ (see full version). The definition of η ensures that $\mathrm{vol}(\mathcal{C}_\eta)/V_m(r) = \varepsilon$. We now check that $\mathcal{B}_m(r) \setminus \mathcal{C}_\eta \subseteq \mathcal{B}_m(r', \mathbf{v})$. Let $\mathbf{x} \in \mathcal{B}_m(r) \setminus \mathcal{C}_\eta$. We have

$$\|\mathbf{x} - \mathbf{v}\| \leq \sqrt{r^2 + \|\mathbf{v}\|^2 + 2r\|\mathbf{v}\|/\eta}.$$

By assumption, the latter is no larger than r', implying that $\mathbf{x} \in \mathcal{B}_m(r', \mathbf{v})$. This completes the proof of the first claim.

If we combine the condition on r and r' and the equality $r' = M^{1/m}r$, we get

$$r^2 + \|\mathbf{v}\|^2 + 2\frac{r\|\mathbf{v}\|}{\eta} \leq M^{2/m}r^2,$$

which is a degree-2 inequality on r. Solving it completes the proof. $\square$

Lemma 7 (Divergence in the Bimodal Setting). *Let $m \geq 1$ and $\mathbf{v} \in \mathbb{R}^m$. Let $r, r' > 0$ such that $r'^2 \geq r^2 + \|\mathbf{v}\|^2$. Let $U(\mathcal{B}_m(r'), \pm\mathbf{v})$ denote the continuous probability distribution which samples $b \hookleftarrow U(\{0, 1\})$ and returns $\mathbf{z} \hookleftarrow U(\mathcal{B}_m(r', (-1)^b\mathbf{v}))$. Then it holds that:*

$$R_\infty\left(U(\mathcal{B}_m(r))\|U(\mathcal{B}_m(r'), \pm\mathbf{v})\right) = \left(1 + \chi_{<r+\|\mathbf{v}\|}(r')\right) \cdot \left(\frac{r'}{r}\right)^m,$$

where $\chi_{<r+\|\mathbf{v}\|}$ denotes the indicator function of reals smaller than $r + \|\mathbf{v}\|$. Let $M > 1$. The above is $\leq M$ if $r \geq \|\mathbf{v}\|/\sqrt{(M/2)^{2/m} - 1}$ and $r' = (M/2)^{1/m}r$.

Note that the choice of r almost matches the lower bound from Theorem 2.

Proof. The support of $U(\mathcal{B}_m(r'), \pm\mathbf{v})$ is exactly $\mathcal{B}_m(r', \mathbf{v}) \cup \mathcal{B}_m(r', -\mathbf{v})$ and its density is $\mathbf{z} \mapsto (\chi_{\mathcal{B}_m(r', \mathbf{v})}(\mathbf{z}) + \chi_{\mathcal{B}_m(r', -\mathbf{v})}(\mathbf{z}))/(2V_m(r'))$. The divergence is finite when $\mathcal{B}_m(r) \subseteq \mathcal{B}_m(r', \mathbf{v}) \cup \mathcal{B}_m(r', -\mathbf{v})$. This is the case if any $\mathbf{x}$ with $\|\mathbf{x}\| \leq r$ satisfies $\|\mathbf{x} - \mathbf{v}\| \leq r'$ or $\|\mathbf{x} + \mathbf{v}\| \leq r'$. Let us assume, w.l.o.g., that $\|\mathbf{x} - \mathbf{v}\| \leq \|\mathbf{x} + \mathbf{v}\|$. Then we write

$$\|\mathbf{x} - \mathbf{v}\| = \sqrt{\|\mathbf{x}\|^2 + \|\mathbf{v}\|^2 - 2\langle\mathbf{x}, \mathbf{v}\rangle} \leq \sqrt{\|\mathbf{x}\|^2 + \|\mathbf{v}\|^2}.$$

Thanks to the assumption on r and r', we conclude that the divergence is finite.

Now, the ratio of the densities only takes three values. If $\mathbf{x} \notin \mathcal{B}_m(r)$ then the ratio is 0. If $\mathbf{x} \in \mathcal{B}_m(r) \cap \mathcal{B}_m(r', \mathbf{v}) \cap \mathcal{B}_m(r', -\mathbf{v})$ then the ratio is $(r'/r)^m$. Finally, if $\mathbf{x}$ belongs to $\mathcal{B}_m(r) \cap \mathcal{B}_m(r', \mathbf{v})$ but not to $\mathcal{B}_m(r', -\mathbf{v})$, then the ratio is $2(r'/r)^m$. This last case only occurs if $\mathcal{B}_m(r) \not\subseteq \mathcal{B}_m(r', -\mathbf{v})$. This is the case only if $r' < r + \|\mathbf{v}\|$. This completes the proof of the first claim.

For the second claim, note that the assumption on r and r' is satisfied, and that the divergence bound is indeed $\leq M$. $\square$

Finally, in order to use the uniform distribution in a hyperball, we verify that there is sufficient min-entropy in the first n coordinates given the remaining $m-n$ coordinates. The proof of the following lemma can be found in the full version.

Lemma 8. *Let $m \geq 6, n \geq 1$ and $r \geq 2\sqrt{m}$. Let $\mathbf{x} = (\mathbf{x}_0^\top|\mathbf{x}_1^\top)^\top$ be a random variable over $\mathbb{R}^m$ whose distribution is $U(\mathcal{B}_m(r))$, where $\mathbf{x}_0$ has dimension n. It holds that*

$$H_\infty\left(\lceil\mathbf{x}_0\rceil | \lceil\mathbf{x}_1\rceil\right)_{U(\mathcal{B}_m(r))} \geq \left(\log_2\frac{1}{0.85}\right) \cdot n .$$

5.2 Lyubashevsky's Signature with Continuous Distributions

We consider continuous distributions over hyperballs, which are not directly compatible with Lyubashevsky's signature scheme, as recalled in Sect. 2. Switching to uniform distributions over the integer points inside hyperballs leads to several difficulties: sampling from such a distribution seems delicate, in particular if the radius of the ball is moderate. Similarly, adapting Lemmas 6 and 7 seems difficult. Rather, we argue that it is possible to extend Lyubashevsky's signature scheme to the case of continuous distributions, and that this comes with very limited complications (in the case of Gaussians, it could be simpler to use continuous Gaussians with this modified scheme, than using discrete Gaussians with the original scheme).

In order to adapt Lyubashevsky's signature scheme to continuous distributions, a rounding step is added after acceptance of a sample, as well as during hashing. Concretely, the changes compared to the construction described in Fig. 2 are as follows: (i) $\mathbf{y}$ is now sampled from a continuous distribution with density g, (ii) $\mathbf{c}$ is now computed as $H(\mathbf{A}\lceil\mathbf{y}\rfloor, \mu)$, (iii) with $\mathbf{z}$ still being defined as $\mathbf{y} + \mathbf{Sc}$, if the test passes, and the returned signature is now $(\lceil\mathbf{z}\rfloor, \mathbf{c})$. This adaptation is discussed in more details in the full version. We note that this leads to the requirement that the min-entropy of $\lceil\mathbf{x}_0\rfloor\|\lceil\mathbf{x}_1\rfloor$ is large, where $\mathbf{x} = (\mathbf{x}_0^\top|\mathbf{x}_1^\top)^\top$ is a random variable over $\mathbb{R}^m$ whose distribution is g and $\mathbf{x}_0$ has dimension n. In the case of the uniform distribution in a hyperball, this is provided by Lemma 8.

We further remark that this applies to the analysis relying on the statistical distance as well as our improved analysis which relies on the Rényi divergence. Also, we note that the modified scheme involves computations over real numbers. These can be securely replaced by finite precision computations, using standard techniques such as described in [Pre17].

5.3 Comparison with Other Distributions

Let $t = \max_{\mathbf{S},\mathbf{c}}\|\mathbf{Sc}\|$. In Table 2, we summarize the expected norm of signatures (up to a constant factor) for diverse distributions P and Q, and for a target expected number of iterations M. We consider three specific pairs of distributions, two of them being previously considered distributions (Gaussians and uniforms in hypercubes), and the last one being uniform distributions in hyperballs, introduced above. We also consider three different scenarios:

- unimodal distributions and perfect rejection sampling, corresponding to the column $\varepsilon = 0$;
- unimodal distributions and imperfect rejection sampling – we use approximations specific to the choice of $\varepsilon \geq 2^{-o(m)}$ and $\varepsilon = o(1/m)$;
- bimodal source distribution and perfect rejection sampling, corresponding to column "Bimodal".

Note that the second scenario relies on our improved analysis relying on the Rényi divergence for the imperfect case (see Sect. 4). This parameter range for ε is not appropriate when using the analysis relying on the statistical distance.

In the last column, we also emphasize if the test that decides to keep or reject a sample is simple or not. For hyperballs, it simply consists in comparing the norm of the sample with the radius of the target hyperball.

The entries in the table are approximations for $m \to \infty$, $t = \omega(1)$ and $M = 2^{o(m)}$, and for a given choice of P, we optimize the parametrization of Q (e.g., the radius in case of a hyperball) to minimize the signature norm.

Table 2. Expected norm of signatures depending on the choice of distributions and (im)perfectness of rejection sampling.

Choices for P and Q	$\varepsilon = 0$	$\varepsilon \geq 2^{-o(m)}$ and $\varepsilon = o(1/m)$	Bimodal	Rejection Test
Hypercubes	$\frac{tm^{3/2}}{\log M}$	$\frac{tm^{3/2}}{\log M}$	$\frac{tm^{3/2}}{\log M}$	Simple
Gaussians	∞	$\frac{t\sqrt{m}\sqrt{\log \frac{1}{\varepsilon} + \log M}}{\log M}$	$\frac{t\sqrt{m}}{\sqrt{\log M}}$	Complex
Hyperballs	$\frac{tm}{\log M}$	$\frac{t\sqrt{m}\sqrt{\log \frac{1}{\varepsilon} + \log M}}{\log M}$	$\frac{t\sqrt{m}}{\sqrt{\log M}}$	Simple

The values of the table are obtained by computing the parameters for the underlying distributions (radii r, r' of the hypercubes or hyperballs and standard deviation σ of Gaussians) for our constraints M and t. This is done by computing their (smooth) Rényi Divergence, as done in Lemmas 6 and 7 for hyperballs. Proofs for hypercubes and Gaussians can be found in the full version. Given these parameters, the expected norm immediately follows ($r\sqrt{m}$ for a hypercube of radius r, σr for a Gaussian of standard deviation σ, and r for a hyperball of radius r). To conclude this section, we emphasize the following points:

- Gaussians and Hyperballs are asymptotically equivalent and reach the lower bounds in the bimodal setting; Hyperballs further reach our lower bound in the exact unimodal setting as well;
- Hyperballs benefits from a significantly simpler rejection test compared to Gaussians;
- The bimodal setting (in both Gaussian and Hyperballs cases) leads to the most compact signatures.

5.4 Concrete Parameters

To study the concrete impact of the choice of distributions on signature size, we consider Dilithium. The left side of Table 3 shows the parameters for three security levels of the round-3 documentation of the CRYSTALS-Dilithium submission to the NIST post-quantum project [BDK+20]. The right side of Table 3 gives updated parameters for Dilithium-G, a modification of Dilithium using Gaussian distributions whose description is available in the first version of the eprint version of [DKL+18]. For this updated version, we set the value of M to 4.

In these schemes, the verification key is a module-LWE sample $\mathbf{Bs}_1 + \mathbf{s}_2$ where $\mathbf{s}_1$ and $\mathbf{s}_2$ have ℓ_∞-norms $\leq \eta$. For each coordinate, the lowest d bits are

Table 3. Parameters for Dilithium and updated Dilithium-G.

	Hypercube-Uniform			Previous Gaussian		
	Medium	Recommended	Very High	Medium	Recommended	Very High
Ring dimension ℓ	256	256	256	256	256	256
q	8380417	8380417	8380417	254977	254977	254977
$(n, m-n)$	$(4,4)$	$(6,5)$	$(8,7)$	$(4,3)$	$(5,4)$	$(7,6)$
η	2	4	2	2	3	2
S	N/A	N/A	N/A	91	134	111
τ	39	49	60	39	49	60
$t = S \cdot \sqrt{\tau}$	N/A	N/A	N/A	568	938	860
B	N/A	N/A	N/A	864K	535K	664K
γ_2	$\frac{q-1}{88}$	$\frac{q-1}{32}$	$\frac{q-1}{32}$	$\frac{q-1}{48}$	$\frac{q-1}{24}$	$\frac{q-1}{32}$
d	13	13	13	11	11	11
M	4.25	5.1	3.85	4	4	4
BKZ block-size b to break SIS	423 (417)	638 (603)	909 (868)	450 (390)	677 (588)	1018 (891)
Best known classical bit-cost	123 (121)	186 (176)	265 (253)	131 (114)	198 (171)	297 (260)
Best known quantum bit-cost	112 (110)	169 (159)	241 (230)	119 (103)	179 (155)	270 (236)
BKZ block-size b to break LWE	422	622	860	403	623	1018
Best known classical bit-cost	123	181	251	117	182	297
Best known quantum bit-cost	111	164	228	1076	165	170
Expected signature size	2420	3293	4595	1737	2372	3478
Expected public key size	1312	1952	2592	672	1312	1600

dropped. A parameter τ is used to control the ℓ_1-norm of any hashed value $\mathbf{c}$, so that $\mathbf{c}$ has sufficient min-entropy. In Dilithium-G, the bound t is $S\sqrt{\tau}$, where S is the median over the key generation randomness of the largest singular value of $(\mathsf{rot}(\mathbf{s}_1)^\top, \mathsf{rot}(\mathbf{s}_2)^\top)^\top$. A rejection step is added in KeyGen to check that the key satisfies this bound. The value of the SIS bound corresponding to unforgeability is computed using [BDK+20, Equation (6)]. The strong unforgeability bound is obtained by multiplying this bound by 2. The security is estimated using block-size optimized BKZ to break the module-SIS or module-LWE instances.[2]

For Dilithium, i.e., the hypercube version, we take $t_\infty = \tau\eta$ as a bound on the ℓ_∞-norm of the secret key, which drives the radius of the hypercube and subsequently the unforgeability SIS bound (in ℓ_∞-norm).

It was argued in [DKL+18] that it seems difficult for BKZ to solve SIS with ℓ_∞-norm bound close to q, i.e., ℓ_2-norm above q. To analyze the runtime of BKZ in the case of an ℓ_2-norm bound $B \geq q$, one can remove the trivial vectors of the input basis (i.e., the vectors with coordinates in $q\mathbb{Z}$) by some randomizing step. This approach was however not considered for Dilithium-G and q was chosen such that $B < q$, leading to bigger parameters overall. Our updated parameters allow for $B \geq q$, for a fairer comparison to Dilithium. We note that for $B > q\sqrt{n}/2$, linear algebra modulo q allows to solve SIS efficiently – our choice of B is always significantly lower than this threshold.

Finally, the computation of the verification key and signature sizes (in bytes) is performed as in [BDK+20] and [DKL+18], respectively. We note that the updated Dilithium-G has signature sizes $\sim 25\%$ smaller than those of Dilithium.

---

[2] We use the scripts from https://github.com/pq-crystals/security-estimates.

To compute signature sizes for Gaussian and Hypercube versions, we rely on a strategy explained in [ETWY22, Section 5].

Table 4. Parameters for hyperball-uniform and improved Dilithium-G.

	Hyperball-Uniform			Improved Gaussian		
	Medium	Recommended	Very High	Medium	Recommended	Very High
Ring dimension ℓ	256	256	256	256	256	256
q	254977	254977	254977	254977	254977	254977
(m, n)	$(4, 3)$	$(6, 4)$	$(8, 6)$	$(4, 3)$	$(5, 4)$	$(7, 6)$
η	2	3	2	2	3	2
S	91	140	115	91	134	111
τ	39	49	60	39	49	60
$t = S \cdot \sqrt{\tau}$	568	980	890	568	938	860
B	741K	1894K	2330K	836K	413K	760K
γ_2	$\frac{q-1}{16}$	$\frac{q-1}{8}$	$\frac{q-1}{8}$	$\frac{q-1}{64}$	$\frac{q-1}{48}$	$\frac{q-1}{48}$
d	10	13	13	12	11	10
M	4	4	4	4	4	4
BKZ block-size b to break SIS	464 (402)	677 (595)	958 (848)	453 (393)	715 (620)	991 (868)
Best known classical bit-cost	135 (117)	198 (174)	280 (248)	132 (114)	209 (181)	289 (253)
Best known quantum bit-cost	123 (106)	179 (157)	254 (224)	120 (104)	189 (164)	262 (230)
BKZ block-size b to break LWE	403	623	953	403	623	1018
Best known classical bit-cost	117	182	278	117	182	297
Best known quantum bit-cost	106	165	252	106	165	170
Expected signature size	1900	2710	3989	1672	2284	3347
Expected public key size	1056	1184	1824	672	1152	1376

We apply to Dilithium-G two modifications introduced in this work. In Table 4 (right side), we show the improvements we obtain when the standard deviation σ is computed using our refined bound (available in the full version) on the smooth Rényi divergence between two Gaussians and instantiated with $\varepsilon = 2^{-64}$ instead of $\varepsilon = 2^{-128}$, as allowed by the use of Rényi divergence (as discussed in Sect. 4). Keeping $M = 4$, the standard deviation σ drops from $11t$ to $6.85t$ and leads to an additional saving of $\sim 5\%$ on the signature size. When compared to Dilithium, we obtain up to $\sim 30\%$ of signature size savings.

Finally, we explore the use of the continuous uniform distributions in hyperballs. We take the algorithms from Dilithium-G, which are adapted to radial distributions and replace the Gaussians with the continuous uniform distributions in hyperballs, adding coefficient-wise rounding to integers when computing commitments. We also emphasize that the rejection step is deterministic. To set parameters, the bound B is computed using the radius of the hyperball instead of the probabilistic upper bound on the norm of a Gaussian vector. In Table 4 (left side), we provide the instantiations that we obtained. We note that the signature sizes are larger than those obtained with Gaussians. The growth of the signature size comes from two factors: first, the bound B is larger than the Gaussian case, likely because of constant factors hidden in the Rényi divergence computations of this section. Second, in order to encode a signature, we use a coordinate-wise

Huffman coding of the rounded vector, which is less efficient than in the Gaussian case, as the Gaussian distribution minimizes entropy across distributions with a fixed standard deviation. When compared to Dilithium, the signature size still drops by $\sim 10\%$ to $\sim 20\%$, which underlines the trade-off offered by the uniform distributions in hyperballs, between the efficiency of Gaussians and the ease of implementation provided by the uniform distributions in hypercubes.

All figures of Tables 3 and 4 can be reproduced using scripts available at https://github.com/jdevevey/security-estimates.

6   Circumventing the Second Lower Bound via Bounded Rejection Sampling

We conclude this work by investigating an alternative way to perform rejection sampling which circumvents our lower bound on the expected number of loop iterations from Sect. 3.3. Notably, this approach makes the resulting signature scheme run within a given amount of time, which may be required in some practical applications (e.g., in real-time systems).

A first solution could be to set a bound on the maximal number of iterations, based on the run-time analysis from Lemma 2. However, this leads to a very large bound, of the order of $\omega(\log \lambda + \log q_{\mathsf{sig}})/\log(M/(M-1+\varepsilon))$, to ensure that with probability $1 - \lambda^{-\omega(1)}$, no signature among q_{sig} requires more iterations.

In the following, we propose a rejection sampling strategy that lets us fix an arbitrary bound $i \geq 1$ on the number of iterations while still guaranteeing an output is produced at the end of the process. This strategy consists in first running $i - 1$ iterations of the rejection sampling procedure. If something was output, then we are done, but if all iterations failed, we have to sample something that is related to the target distribution, in one-shot. For this last step, we use some sort of flooding. Note that, setting $i = 1$, one obtains one-shot signatures based on flooding, as in [ASY22]. Hence, this strategy can be seen as a generalization of both rejection sampling and flooding techniques.

6.1   Bounded Rejection Sampling Lemma

Let $i \geq 1$ be an arbitrary bound for the number of loop iterations. Instead of simply having one distribution P_s to sample from, we now use two distributions P_f and P_s, where P_s is used for the rejection sampling part (the first $i-1$ iterations) and P_f is used in case of $i-1$ successive failures. If the divergences $R_\infty(P_f\|P_s)$ and $R_\infty(P_s\|P_t)$ are small, this strategy works. Moreover, the resulting distribution has a divergence with P_s and is a weighted mean of the classical rejection sampling-resulting distribution and the flooding distribution. This is what we prove in the following lemma.

Lemma 9 (Bounded Rejection Sampling). *Let p_f, p_t, p_s be probability densities, either all continuous or all discrete, and $\varepsilon_0, \varepsilon_1 \geq 0, M_0, M_1 \geq 1$ with*

$$R_\infty^{\varepsilon_0}(p_f\|p_t) \leq M_0 \quad and \quad R_\infty^{\varepsilon_1}(p_t\|p_s) \leq M_1.$$

Then

$$R_\infty^{\frac{M}{M_0}\varepsilon_0}(\mathcal{B}_i^{\text{real}} \| \mathcal{B}_i^{\text{ideal}}) \leq M,$$

where

$$M = \left(1 - \left(1 - \frac{1}{M_1}\right)^{i-1}\right)\frac{1}{1-\varepsilon_1} + \left(1 - \frac{1+\varepsilon_1}{M_1}\right)^{i-1} \cdot M_0,$$

and $\mathcal{B}_i^{\text{real}}$ and $\mathcal{B}_i^{\text{ideal}}$ are defined in Fig. 4.

Note that in the case where $i = 1$, distribution p_s is useless, as $\mathcal{B}_1^{\text{real}}$ samples $z \hookleftarrow p_f$ and returns it: this is flooding. Our lemma captures this situation, as $M = M_0$ in that case. It is then not only a generalization of rejection sampling but also of flooding techniques.

Algorithms $\mathcal{B}_i^{\text{ideal}}$ and $\mathcal{B}_i^{\text{ideal}'}$ produce the same distribution for variable z, and hence Lemma 9 also holds when replacing $\mathcal{B}_i^{\text{ideal}}$ by $\mathcal{B}_i^{\text{ideal}'}$. Algorithm $\mathcal{B}_i^{\text{ideal}'}$ is more convenient when analyzing the adapted Lyubashevsky signature scheme.

Algorithm $\mathcal{B}_i^{\text{real}}$:	Algorithm $\mathcal{B}_i^{\text{ideal}}$:	Algorithm $\mathcal{B}_i^{\text{ideal}'}$:
1: $\ell \leftarrow 1$	1: return $z \hookleftarrow p_t$	1: $\ell \leftarrow 1$
2: **while** $\ell \leq i - 1$ **do**		2: **while** $\ell \leq i - 1$ **do**
3: $\quad z \hookleftarrow p_s$		3: $\quad z \hookleftarrow p_t$
4: $\quad$ with probability $\min(\frac{p_t(z)}{M_1 \cdot p_s(z)}, 1)$,		4: $\quad$ with probability $\frac{1}{M_1}$,
$\quad$ return z		$\quad$ return z
5: $\quad \ell \leftarrow \ell + 1$		5: $\quad \ell \leftarrow \ell + 1$
6: **end while**		6: **end while**
7: return $z \hookleftarrow p_f$		7: return $z \hookleftarrow p_t$

Fig. 4. Bounded rejection sampling algorithms.

Proof. With p_t and p_s, for $\mathsf{t} \in \{\text{real, ideal}\}$, we can view $\mathcal{B}_i^{\mathsf{t}}$ as calling $i - 1$ times $\mathcal{A}^{\mathsf{t}}$ from Fig. 1, returning the value of the first call that does not abort, and if all calls failed, returning some independent sample $z \hookleftarrow p_f$ (or p_t). Using probability bounds from Lemma 1 and letting $\mathcal{A}^{\text{real}}(\bot)$ denote the probability that $\mathcal{A}^{\text{real}}$ aborts, we know that

$$
\begin{aligned}
\mathcal{B}_i^{\text{real}}(x) &= \left[\sum_{0 \leq j \leq i-2} (\mathcal{A}^{\text{real}}(\bot))^j \cdot \min\left(\frac{p_t(x)}{M_1}, p_s(x)\right)\right] + (\mathcal{A}^{\text{real}}(\bot))^{i-1} \cdot p_f(x) \\
&= \frac{1 - (\mathcal{A}^{\text{real}}(\bot))^{i-1}}{1 - \mathcal{A}^{\text{real}}(\bot)} \cdot \min\left(\frac{p_t(x)}{M_1}, p_s(x)\right) + (\mathcal{A}^{\text{real}}(\bot))^{i-1} \cdot p_f(x) \\
&\leq \frac{1 - \left(1 - \frac{1}{M_1}\right)^{i-1}}{\frac{1-\varepsilon_1}{M_1}} \cdot \frac{p_t(x)}{M_1} + \left(\frac{M_1 - 1 + \varepsilon_1}{M_1}\right)^{i-1} \cdot p_f(x).
\end{aligned}
$$

Let us define

$$M = \left(1 - \left(1 - \frac{1}{M_1}\right)^{i-1}\right) \cdot \frac{1}{1-\varepsilon_1} + \left(\frac{M_1 - 1 + \varepsilon_1}{M_1}\right)^{i-1} \cdot M_0.$$

For this to be an upper bound on $R_\infty^{\frac{M}{M_0}\varepsilon_0}(\mathcal{B}_i^{\text{real}}\|\mathcal{B}_i^{\text{ideal}})$, it suffices that

$$\Pr_{x \hookleftarrow \mathcal{B}_i^{\text{real}}}[\mathcal{B}_i^{\text{real}}(x) > M \cdot p_t(x)] \leq \frac{M}{M_0}\varepsilon_0.$$

For any output x such that $\mathcal{B}_i^{\text{real}}(x) > Mp_t(x)$, it holds $p_f(x) > M_0p_t(x)$ according to the above upper bound on $\mathcal{B}_i^{\text{real}}(x)$. This yields, by definition of M_0:

$$\Pr_{x \hookleftarrow p_f}[\mathcal{B}_i^{\text{real}}(x) > M \cdot p_t(x)] \leq \varepsilon_0.$$

The probability is however not taken over the desired distribution for x. Note that if we combine $p_f(x) > M_0 \cdot p_t(x)$ with the above bound on the distribution of the output of $\mathcal{B}_i^{\text{real}}$, we get

$$\mathcal{B}_i^{\text{real}}(x) < \frac{M}{M_0} \cdot p_f(x).$$

Then $\Pr_{x \hookleftarrow \mathcal{B}_i^{\text{real}}}[\mathcal{B}_i^{\text{real}}(x) > Mp_t(x)] < \frac{M}{M_0}\varepsilon_0$. $\qquad\square$

6.2 Lyubashevsky's Signature with Bounded Rejection

In this section, we present a way to modify Lyubashevsky's signature scheme by relying on bounded rejection sampling, as decribed above. This can be seen as a hybrid version between one-shot signatures which use flooding, as in [ASY22], and Lyubashevsky's unbounded signature.

Let $k, n, m, q \geq 1$ specify matrix spaces with $m > n$. Let $\mathcal{M}$ be the message space. Let H be a hash function modeled as a random oracle with domain $\mathbb{Z}_q^n \times \mathcal{M}$ and range some finite set $\mathcal{C} \subseteq \mathbb{Z}^k$. Let $\gamma > 0$. Let $\varepsilon_0, \varepsilon_1 \geq 0, M_0, M_1 \geq 1, i \geq 1$ be parameters related to bounded rejection sampling. Let $\mathcal{S} \subseteq \mathbb{Z}^{m \times k}$. Let P_0, P_1 and P_2 be three probability distributions over $\mathbb{Z}^m$ satisfying

$$\max_{(\mathbf{S},\mathbf{c})\in\mathcal{S}\times\mathcal{C}} R_\infty^{\varepsilon_0}((P_0)_{+\mathbf{Sc}}\|P_1) \leq M_0 \quad \text{and} \quad \max_{(\mathbf{S},\mathbf{c})\in\mathcal{S}\times\mathcal{C}} R_\infty^{\varepsilon_1}(P_1\|(P_2)_{+\mathbf{Sc}}) \leq M_1.$$

Let $(\mathbf{x}_0^\top|\mathbf{x}_1^\top)^\top \hookleftarrow P_0$ and $(\mathbf{y}_0^\top|\mathbf{y}_1^\top)^\top \hookleftarrow P_2$, where $\mathbf{y}_0$ and $\mathbf{x}_0$ take values in $\mathbb{Z}^n$. We present the modified scheme in Fig. 5. The key generation algorithm is unchanged from Fig. 2.

Before moving to the scheme analysis, let us define

$$M = \left(1 - \left(1 - \frac{1}{M_1}\right)^{i-1}\right)\frac{1}{1-\varepsilon_1} + \left(1 - \frac{1+\varepsilon_1}{M_1}\right)^{i-1} \cdot M_0.$$

The runtime of Sign is deterministically bounded, by at most i loop iterations. The correctness statement from Lemma 3 can be adapted as follows.

Lemma 10 (Correctness). *Let $\varepsilon_0, \varepsilon_1 \geq 0$ and $M_0, M_1 \geq 1$. Let P_0, P_1, P_2 satisfy $\max_{(\mathbf{S},\mathbf{c})\in\mathcal{S}\times\mathcal{C}} R_\infty^{\varepsilon_b}(P_b\|P_{b+1,+\mathbf{Sc}}) \leq M_b$ for $b \in \{0,1\}$. Let $(\mathbf{x}_0^\top|\mathbf{x}_1^\top)^\top \hookleftarrow P_0$ and $(\mathbf{y}_0^\top|\mathbf{y}_1^\top)^\top \hookleftarrow P_2$, where $\mathbf{x}_0$ and $\mathbf{y}_0$ take values in $\mathbb{Z}^n$. Assume that $\varepsilon_0 \leq \mathsf{negl}(\lambda)$, $M \leq \mathsf{poly}(\lambda)$ and $2^{-H_\infty(\mathbf{x}_0|\mathbf{x}_1)_{P_0}}, 2^{-H_\infty(\mathbf{y}_0|\mathbf{y}_1)_{P_2}} \leq \mathsf{negl}(\lambda)$. Then, in the ROM, the scheme is correct if $\gamma \geq \gamma_{P_1}$ with γ_{P_1} such that $\Pr_{\mathbf{z}\hookleftarrow P_1}(\|\mathbf{z}\| \geq \gamma_{P_1}) \leq \mathsf{negl}(\lambda)$.*

$\mathsf{Sign}'(\mu, \mathbf{A}, \mathbf{S})$:

1: $\ell \leftarrow 1$
2: **if** $\ell \leq i - 1$ **then**
3:     $\mathbf{y} \hookleftarrow P_2$
4: **else**
5:     $\mathbf{y} \hookleftarrow P_0$
6: **end if**
7: $\mathbf{c} \leftarrow H(\mathbf{Ay}, \mu)$
8: $\mathbf{z} \leftarrow \mathbf{y} + \mathbf{Sc}$
9: $u \hookleftarrow U([0,1])$
10: **if** $u \leq \frac{P_1(\mathbf{z})}{M_1 P_2(\mathbf{y})}$ or $\ell = i$ **then**
11:     return $(\mathbf{z}, \mathbf{c})$
12: **else**
13:     $\ell \leftarrow \ell + 1$
14:     go to Step 2
15: **end if**

$\mathsf{Verify}(\mu, \mathbf{z}, \mathbf{c}, \mathbf{A}, \mathbf{T} = \mathbf{AS})$:

1: **if** $\|\mathbf{z}\| \leq \gamma$ and $\mathbf{c} = H(\mathbf{Az} - \mathbf{Tc}, \mu)$
   then
2:     return 1
3: **else**
4:     return 0
5: **end if**

Fig. 5. Lyubashevsky's signature scheme with bounded rejection.

The main modification towards analyzing the security of the scheme from Fig. 5, compared to the one from Fig. 2, resides in the observation that the distributions of the pair $(\mathbf{z}, \mathbf{c})$ obtained by the two processes from Fig. 6 have $\frac{M}{M_0}\varepsilon_0$-smooth Rényi divergence of infinite order bounded by M. This is obtained by applying Lemma 9. Note that the hash function H needs to be consistently programmed for every $\mathbf{c}$ that is produced, which is why we use the formalism of Algorithm $\mathcal{B}_i^{\mathsf{ideal}'}$ rather than Algorithm $\mathcal{B}_i^{\mathsf{ideal}}$.

By the multiplicativity of the smooth Rényi divergence (see full version), we obtain that the $(q_{\mathsf{sig}} \cdot M\varepsilon_0/M_0)$-smooth Rényi divergence between the adversary's views in games where the changes from Fig. 6 have been applied to all signature queries, is bounded by $M^{q_{\mathsf{sig}}}$. The probability preservation property can then be used meaningfully if $q_{\mathsf{sig}} \cdot M\varepsilon_0/M_0 = 2^{-\Omega(\lambda)}$ and $M^{q_{\mathsf{sig}}} \leq \mathsf{poly}(\lambda)$.

Once the signature queries are simulated without the signing key, the security proof can be completed as in prior works (see [Lyu09, Lyu12, AFLT16]).

Asymptotic Trade-Off. We now discuss the choices of the distributions P_0, P_1 and P_2. We require that $M^{q_{\mathsf{sig}}} = \mathsf{poly}(\lambda)$ and $q_{\mathsf{sig}} \cdot M\varepsilon_0/M_0 = 2^{-\Omega(\lambda)}$, with $\varepsilon_0, \varepsilon_1$, M_0, M_1 and M as in Lemma 9. We are aiming at not too large divergence bounds M_0, M_1, M as signatures typically become less efficient when they increase. For this reason, we set $\varepsilon_0 = 2^{-\Omega(\lambda)}$. As the condition $M^{q_{\mathsf{sig}}} = \mathsf{poly}(\lambda)$ forces M to be close to 1, the condition $q_{\mathsf{sig}} \cdot M\varepsilon_0/M_0 = 2^{-\Omega(\lambda)}$ is already satisfied. We now focus on ε_1, M_0 and M_1.

When i tends to infinity, we have $M \approx 1/(1 - \varepsilon_1)$, so that we can set $\varepsilon_1 \approx 1/q_{\mathsf{sig}}$ as in Sect. 4. For $i = 1$, we have $M = M_0$, and we fall in the regime of [ASY22, Section 4]. Let us now consider the small i case, which is probably the most interesting one for applications requiring a bounded signature time.

1: $\ell \leftarrow 1$
2: **if** $\ell \leq i - 1$ **then**
3:     $\mathbf{y} \hookleftarrow P_2$
4: **else**
5:     $\mathbf{y} \hookleftarrow P_0$
6: **end if**
7: $\mathbf{c} \leftarrow U(\mathcal{C})$
8: $\mathbf{z} \leftarrow \mathbf{y} + \mathbf{Sc}$
9: $u \hookleftarrow U([0,1])$
10: **if** $u \leq \frac{P_1(\mathbf{z})}{M_1 P_2(\mathbf{y})}$ or $\ell = i$ **then**
11:     return $(\mathbf{z}, \mathbf{c})$
12: **else**
13:     $\ell \leftarrow \ell + 1$
14:     go to Step 2
15: **end if**

1: $\ell \leftarrow 1$
2: $\mathbf{y} \hookleftarrow P_1$
3: $\mathbf{c} \leftarrow U(\mathcal{C})$
4: $\mathbf{z} \leftarrow \mathbf{y} + \mathbf{Sc}$
5: $u \hookleftarrow U([0,1])$
6: **if** $u \leq \frac{1}{M_1}$ or $\ell = i$ **then**
7:     return $(\mathbf{z}, \mathbf{c})$
8: **else**
9:     $\ell \leftarrow \ell + 1$
10:     go to Step 2
11: **end if**

Fig. 6. Simulating signatures.

As $M \geq 1/(1 - \varepsilon_1)$ and we must ensure that $M^{q_{\mathsf{sig}}} = \mathsf{poly}(\lambda)$, we set ε_1 at most of the order of $1/q_{\mathsf{sig}}$. This implies that $M \approx 1 + M_0 \cdot (1 - 1/M_1)^{i-1}$, and hence we set $(M_0 - 1) \cdot (1 - 1/M_1)^{i-1} = O(1/q_{\mathsf{sig}})$. For Gaussian and hyperball-uniform instantiations, this leads to a standard deviation (resp. radius) growing polynomially in $q_{\mathsf{sig}}/(1 - 1/M_1)^{i-1}$.

We argue now that the trade-off above (for small i) seems essentially optimal. For $i = 1$, it was showed in [ASY22, Appendix C.2] that the folklore statistical attack against the Gaussian and rejection-free version of Lyubashevsky's signature scheme runs in subexponential time when $M_0 = q_{\mathsf{sig}}^{o(1)}$. Now, for larger i and sufficiently distinct target and flooding distributions, an adversary could consider the signatures for which all loop iterations failed (i.e., the output sample corresponds to the flooding distribution), and run the statistical attack described in [ASY22] for those samples. As the probability of rejecting all samples is essentially $(1 - 1/M_1)^{i-1}$, this attack matches with the trade-off above.

Acknowledgments. The authors thank Wonhee Cho for helpful discussions. The authors were supported by the AMIRAL ANR grant (ANR-21-ASTR-0016), the European Union Horizon 2020 Research and Innovation Program Grant 780701, the PEPR quantique France 2030 programme (ANR-22-PETQ-0008) and the PEPR Cyber France 2030 programme (ANR-22-PECY-0003).

References

AAB+19. Akleylek, S., et al.: qTESLA round-3 candidate to the NIST post-quantum cryptography standardisation project (2019). https://qtesla.org/

ABB+17. Alkim, E., et al.: Revisiting TESLA in the quantum random oracle model. In: Lange, T., Takagi, T. (eds.) PQCrypto 2017. LNCS, vol. 10346, pp. 143–162. Springer, Cham (2017). https://doi.org/10.1007/978-3-319-59879-6_9

AFLT16. Abdalla, M., Fouque, P.-A., Lyubashevsky, V., Tibouchi, M.: Tightly-secure signatures from lossy identification schemes. In: Pointcheval, D., Johansson, T. (eds.) EUROCRYPT 2012. LNCS, vol. 7237, pp. 572–590. Springer, Heidelberg (2012). https://doi.org/10.1007/978-3-642-29011-4_34

ASY22. Agrawal, S., Stehlé, D., Yadav, A.: Round-optimal lattice-based threshold signatures, revisited. In: ICALP (2022)

BDK+20. Bai, S., et al.: CRYSTALS-DILITHIUM round-3 candidate to the NIST post-quantum cryptography standardisation project (2020). https://pq-crystals.org/dilithium/

BG14. Bai, S., Galbraith, S.D.: An improved compression technique for signatures based on learning with errors. In: CT-RSA (2014)

BLR+18. Bai, S., Lepoint, T., Roux-Langlois, A., Sakzad, A., Stehlé, D., Steinfeld, R.: Improved security proofs in lattice-based cryptography: Using the Rényi divergence rather than the statistical distance. J. Cryptol. **31**, 610–640 (2018)

Dat09. Datta, N.: Min-and max-relative entropies and a new entanglement monotone. T. Inform. Theory. **55**, 2816–2826 (2009)

DDLL13. Ducas, L., Durmus, A., Lepoint, T., Lyubashevsky, V.: Lattice signatures and bimodal gaussians. In: Canetti, R., Garay, J.A. (eds.) CRYPTO 2013. LNCS, vol. 8042, pp. 40–56. Springer, Heidelberg (2013). https://doi.org/10.1007/978-3-642-40041-4_3

Dev86. Devroye, L.: Non-Uniform random variate generation (1986)

DKL+18. Ducas, L., et al.: CRYSTALS-DILITHIUM: a lattice-based digital signature scheme. In: TCHES (2018)

DPSZ12. Damgård, I., Pastro, V., Smart, N., Zakarias, S.: Multiparty computation from somewhat homomorphic encryption. In: Safavi-Naini, R., Canetti, R. (eds.) CRYPTO 2012. LNCS, vol. 7417, pp. 643–662. Springer, Heidelberg (2012). https://doi.org/10.1007/978-3-642-32009-5_38

ETWY22. Espitau, T., Tibouchi, M., Wallet, A., Yu, Y.: Shorter hash-and-sign lattice-based signatures. In: Dodis, Y., Shrimpton, T. (eds.) Advances in Cryptology – CRYPTO 2022. CRYPTO 2022. LNCS, vol. 13508, pp. 245–275. Springer, Cham (2022). https://doi.org/10.1007/978-3-031-15979-4_9

FS86. Fiat, A., Shamir, A.: How to prove yourself: practical solutions to identification and signature problems. In: Odlyzko, A.M. (ed.) CRYPTO 1986. LNCS, vol. 263, pp. 186–194. Springer, Heidelberg (1987). https://doi.org/10.1007/3-540-47721-7_12

GLP15. Güneysu, T., Lyubashevsky, V., Pöppelmann, T.: Lattice-based signatures: optimization and implementation on reconfigurable hardware. T. Comput. **64**, 1954–1967 (2015)

HJMR07. Harsha, P., Jain, R., McAllester, D., Radhakrishnan, J.: The communication complexity of correlation. In: CCC 2007 (2007)

LNP22. V. Lyubashevsky, N. K. Nguyen, and M. Plançon. Lattice-based zero-knowledge proofs and applications: shorter, simpler, and more general. In: Dodis, Y., Shrimpton, T. (eds.) Advances in Cryptology – CRYPTO 2022. CRYPTO 2022. LNCS, vol. 13508, pp. 71–101. Springer, Cham (2022). https://doi.org/10.1007/978-3-031-15979-4_3

Lyu09. Lyubashevsky, V.: Fiat-Shamir with aborts: applications to lattice and factoring-based signatures. In: Matsui, M. (ed.) ASIACRYPT 2009. LNCS, vol. 5912, pp. 598–616. Springer, Heidelberg (2009). https://doi.org/10.1007/978-3-642-10366-7_35

Lyu12. Lyubashevsky, V.: Lattice signatures without trapdoors. In: Pointcheval, D., Johansson, T. (eds.) EUROCRYPT 2012. LNCS, vol. 7237, pp. 738–755. Springer, Heidelberg (2012). https://doi.org/10.1007/978-3-642-29011-4_43

Lyu16. Lyubashevsky, V.: Digital signatures based on the hardness of ideal lattice problems in all rings. In: Cheon, J.H., Takagi, T. (eds.) ASIACRYPT 2016. LNCS, vol. 10032, pp. 196–214. Springer, Heidelberg (2016). https://doi.org/10.1007/978-3-662-53890-6_7

Pre17. Prest, T.: Sharper bounds in lattice-based cryptography using the Rényi divergence. In: Takagi, T., Peyrin, T. (eds.) ASIACRYPT 2017. LNCS, vol. 10624, pp. 347–374. Springer, Cham (2017). https://doi.org/10.1007/978-3-319-70694-8_13

Ren05. Renner, R.: Security of quantum key distribution. Ph.D. thesis, ETH Zurich (2005)

Sch91. Schnorr, C.-P.: Efficient signature generation by smart cards. J. Cryptol. 4, 161–174 (1991). https://doi.org/10.1007/BF00196725

HAWK: Module LIP Makes Lattice Signatures Fast, Compact and Simple

Léo Ducas[1,2] 🆔, Eamonn W. Postlethwaite[1](✉) 🆔, Ludo N. Pulles[1] 🆔, and Wessel van Woerden[1] 🆔

[1] CWI, Cryptology Group, Amsterdam, The Netherlands
ewp@cwi.nl
[2] Mathematical Institute, Leiden University, Leiden, The Netherlands

Abstract. We propose the signature scheme HAWK, a concrete instantiation of proposals to use the Lattice Isomorphism Problem (LIP) as a foundation for cryptography that focuses on simplicity. This simplicity stems from LIP, which allows the use of lattices such as $\mathbb{Z}^n$, leading to signature algorithms with no floats, no rejection sampling, and compact precomputed distributions. Such design features are desirable for constrained devices, and when computing signatures inside FHE or MPC. The most significant change from recent LIP proposals is the use of module lattices, reusing algorithms and ideas from NTRUSIGN and FALCON. Its simplicity makes HAWK competitive. We provide cryptanalysis with experimental evidence for the design of HAWK and implement two parameter sets, HAWK-512 and HAWK-1024. Signing using HAWK-512 and HAWK-1024 is four times faster than FALCON on x86 architectures, produces signatures that are about 15% more compact, and is slightly more secure against forgeries by lattice reduction attacks. When floating-points are unavailable, HAWK signs 15 times faster than FALCON.

We provide a worst case to average case reduction for module LIP. For certain parametrisations of HAWK this applies to secret key recovery and we reduce signature forgery in the random oracle model to a new problem called the one more short vector problem.

Keywords: Post-Quantum Cryptography · Signatures · Module Lattice Isomorphism Problem · Concrete Design · Quadratic Forms

1 Introduction

Background. Currently the most efficient lattice based signature scheme, and more generally, one of the most efficient post-quantum signature schemes, is FALCON [32]. Like its predecessor NTRUSIGN it has a hash-then-sign design, but fixes the issue of signature transcript leakage [27] via Discrete Gaussian Sampling (DGS) [19].

Since its introduction much progress has been made into making DGS more efficient [11,12,18], in particular by exploiting ideal or module structures [14,28] such as those of NTRU lattices. Nonetheless, DGS remains particularly difficult

© International Association for Cryptologic Research 2022
S. Agrawal and D. Lin (Eds.): ASIACRYPT 2022, LNCS 13794, pp. 65–94, 2022.
https://doi.org/10.1007/978-3-031-22972-5_3

to implement securely and efficiently, especially on constrained devices, and even more so when side-channel attacks are a concern. In particular, DGS involves high precision floating-point linear algebra and the evaluation of transcendental functions. A decade of research has not provided an entirely satisfactory solution to such issues.

Recently an idea emerged: use a simple lattice, maybe as simple as $\mathbb{Z}^n$ [7,15]. More precisely, use a hidden rotation of it. The idea is to base security on the problem of finding isometries between lattices, i.e. the Lattice Isomorphism Problem (LIP). While this is not only motivation for LIP based cryptography, it was noted in [15] that this avoids the difficult DGS step above: sampling from the $\mathbb{Z}^n$ lattice is much easier.

This work. The work [15], introducing the LIP based cryptography framework, mostly focused on theoretical and asymptotic results. In our work we give a concrete instantiation of their approach, based on simple module lattices, to see if it is practical and competitive. An attractive choice would be to consider the most structured option, namely modules of rank one (ideal lattices) over number fields, however this restricted version of LIP is known to be solvable in classical polynomial time [20,24].

Instead we work with rank two modules, for which the LIP problem has already received some cryptanalytic attention [33]. It was quickly noted that NTRUSIGN signatures [22] were leaking the Gram matrix of the secret key; recovering the secret key from this Gram matrix is precisely LIP. While the NTRUSIGN scheme was ultimately broken, it was only by exploiting a stronger form of leakage, not by solving LIP. In conclusion this module LIP problem is plausibly hard and is clear and simple to state, and therefore appears as a legitimate basis for cryptography.

We consider the ring $R = \mathbb{Z}[X]/(X^n + 1)$ for n a power of two, that is the ring of integers for some power of two cyclotomic field. This ring is naturally viewed as an orthogonal lattice. We must then generate a basis of R^2 following some distribution, which we achieve by mimicking NTRUSIGN key generation and setting the modulus $q = 1$. This allows us to make use of efficient techniques from the literature [22,29,32]. Following the ideas presented in [15] we are able to show that sampling our keys in this manner gives a worst case to average case reduction for module LIP. However, this reduction is limited to a large choice of the parameter that determines the sampling of the public key. In HAWK we make more aggressive choices based on heuristic and experimental cryptanalysis.

The original design of [15] hashed a message to $\{0, \frac{1}{q}, \ldots, \frac{q-1}{q}\}^{2n}$ for some $q = \mathsf{poly}(n)$. Another optimisation we propose is to hash the message to a smaller target space $\{0, \frac{1}{2}\}^{2n}$ to further simplify Gaussian sampling. For this variant we provide a reduction in the programmable random oracle model to a new problem: one more (approximate) SVP. This reduction also requires a specific choice of parameters, and again HAWK makes more aggressive choices. This problem is similar to the recently introduced one more inhomogenous short integer solution problem [1] used to design blind signature schemes from lattices.

We also propose efficient encodings for the public key and signatures of our scheme. Decoding the keys is cheap and recovering redundant parts is done

Table 1. Performance of FALCON and HAWK for $n = 512, 1024$ on an Intel® Core™ i5-4590 @3.30GHz processor with TurboBoost disabled. HAWK was compiled with -O2 and FALCON with -O3. The Sign timings correspond to batch usage; "Gain" is more favourable for HAWK in unbatched usage, see Sect. 5.4.

	[32] FALCON 512	This work HAWK 512	Gain $\left(\frac{\text{FALCON}}{\text{HAWK}}\right)$	[32] FALCON 1024	This work HAWK 1024	Gain $\left(\frac{\text{FALCON}}{\text{HAWK}}\right)$
AVX2 KGen	7.95 ms	4.25 ms	×1.87	23.60 ms	17.88 ms	×1.32
Reference KGen	19.32 ms	13.14 ms	×1.47	54.65 ms	41.39 ms	×1.32
AVX2 Sign	193 μs	50 μs	× 3.9	382 μs	99 μs	× 3.9
Reference Sign	2449 μs	168 μs	×14.6	5273 μs	343 μs	×15.4
AVX2 Vf	50 μs	19 μs	×2.63	99 μs	46 μs	×2.15
Reference Vf	53 μs	178 μs	×0.30	105 μs	392 μs	×0.27
Secret key (bytes)	1281	1153	×1.11	2305	2561	×0.90
Public key (bytes)	897	1006 ± 6	×0.89	1793	2329 ± 11	×0.77
Signature (bytes)	652 ± 3	542 ± 4	×1.21	1261 ± 4	1195 ± 6	×1.05

efficiently with a few number theoretic or fast Fourier transforms. Moreover, we significantly compress the signature by dropping half of it, which is effectively computationally free. Decompressing a signature uses Babai's round-off algorithm [4]. This decompression uses public data during verification, so it is not a target for side-channel or statistical attacks and does not require masking. Its use of rounding also allows us to avoid the need for high precision floats.

Performance and comparison. Following FALCON, we propose a reference implementation and an AVX2 optimised implementation. The reference implementation makes no use of floating-points (though it emulates them during key generation), whereas the AVX2 version uses floating-points.

On AVX2 CPUs, HAWK-512 outperforms FALCON-512 by a factor of about 2 for key generation and verification and a factor of 4 for signing. The situation is similar for HAWK-1024. Without floats, HAWK signs 15 times faster than FALCON, because HAWK uses number theoretic transforms in signing while FALCON emulates floating-points. The verification contains a fast decompression that uses fixed-point arithmetic but uses two number theoretic transforms making it slightly slower than FALCON. Because the numbers are smaller in HAWK's secret key, key generation is faster with HAWK.

Regarding compactness, HAWK-512 signatures are about 110 bytes shorter, but public keys about 110 bytes larger, than FALCON-512; this puts HAWK-512 on par for certificate chain applications, and should be advantageous for other applications. Additionally, secret keys are 128 bytes smaller. In HAWK-1024 we save a little on signatures, but our keys are larger.

We also note that HAWK resists forgery attacks a little better than FALCON. This is a direct result of being able to use the secret key to efficiently sample slightly smaller signatures in $\mathbb{Z}^{2n}$ than is possible in an NTRU lattice.

The recent variant of FALCON named MITAKA [17] also aims to make the signing procedure simpler and free from floating-point arithmetic. They achieve this with some loss in the signing quality compared to FALCON which makes signature forgeries somewhat easier, but their floating-point implementation signs twice as fast. In contrast, by using $\mathbb{Z}^{2n}$ we obtain an even simpler sampler while simultaneously improving the signing quality, efficiency and signature size.

Simplicity as a circuit. We claim that our signature scheme is simpler as a circuit than FALCON and therefore expect the performance gap to be larger on constrained architectures. In fact, we hope that HAWK or a variant of HAWK may be simple enough to be implemented within a Fully Homomorphic Encryption scheme for applications such as blind or threshold signatures [2]. It might also be easier to mask against side-channel attacks, similarly to how the lack of floating-points in the sampler simplifies the masking of MITAKA$_\mathbb{Z}$ [17, Sec. 7.3].

Implementation and source c. Our constant-time C implementation and auxiliary scripts are open source.[1] Included is a SageMath implementation of HAWK.

Roadmap. Section 2 introduces some preliminaries. Section 3 introduces the signature scheme HAWK. Section 4 details our concrete cryptanalytic model for HAWK. Section 5 details the parameters for HAWK, its estimated security, and explains implementation and performance details. Section 6 provides a worst case to average case reduction for smLIP, the search module LIP problem that underlies our key generation design. Throughout references to appendices can be found in the full version of this report [16], where we provide more information on formal reductions and our implementation.

2   Preliminaries

We use bold lowercase letters $\mathbf{v}$ to denote column vectors. Bold uppercase letters $\mathbf{B}$ represent matrices, and $\mathbf{B}^\mathsf{T}$ is the transpose. For a real matrix $\mathbf{B}$ let $\tilde{\mathbf{B}}$ denote the related Gram–Schmidt matrix. Let $[n] = \{1, \ldots, n\}$ for $n \in \mathbb{Z}_{\geq 1}$. Let log without subscript denote the natural logarithm.

Lattices and quadratic forms. A full rank, n dimensional lattice Λ is a discrete subgroup of $\mathbb{R}^n$ and is given by a basis $\mathbf{B} \in \mathbb{R}^{n \times n}$ of $\mathbb{R}$-linearly independent column vectors. A lattice defined by $\mathbf{B}$ is $\Lambda(\mathbf{B}) = \{\mathbf{B} \cdot \mathbf{x} : \mathbf{x} \in \mathbb{Z}^n\}$. Denote by $\lambda_i(\Lambda)$ the ith minima of Λ. This is the smallest radius of a centred and closed ball such that its intersection with Λ contains i linearly independent vectors. Two bases $\mathbf{B}, \mathbf{B}'$ generate the same lattice if there exists a unimodular

---

[1] https://github.com/ludopulles/hawk-aux.

matrix $\mathbf{U} \in \mathrm{GL}_n(\mathbb{Z})$ such that $\mathbf{B} \cdot \mathbf{U} = \mathbf{B}'$. Two lattices Λ, Λ' are *isomorphic* if there exists an orthonormal transformation $\mathbf{O} \in O_n(\mathbb{R})$ such that $\mathbf{O} \cdot \Lambda = \Lambda'$. Recovering this transformation is the Lattice Isomorphism Problem (LIP).

Definition 1 (Lattice Isomorphism Problem). *Given two isomorphic lattices Λ, Λ', find $\mathbf{O} \in O_n(\mathbb{R})$ such that $\mathbf{O} \cdot \Lambda = \{\mathbf{O} \cdot \mathbf{v} \colon \mathbf{v} \in \Lambda\} = \Lambda'$.*

If Λ, Λ' are generated by $\mathbf{B}, \mathbf{B}'$ respectively, then they are isomorphic if there exists an orthonormal transformation $\mathbf{O} \in O_n(\mathbb{R})$ and a unimodular matrix $\mathbf{U} \in \mathrm{GL}_n(\mathbb{Z})$ such that $\mathbf{O} \cdot \mathbf{B} \cdot \mathbf{U} = \mathbf{B}'$. We can remove the real valued orthonormal transformation by moving to quadratic forms. A quadratic form is a positive definite real symmetric matrix $\mathbf{Q} \in \mathcal{S}_n^{>0}(\mathbb{R})$. For any lattice basis $\mathbf{B}$ the Gram matrix $\mathbf{B}^\mathsf{T}\mathbf{B}$, consisting of all pairwise inner products, is a quadratic form. Conversely, given a quadratic form $\mathbf{Q}$, Cholesky decomposition finds a basis $\mathbf{B}_\mathbf{Q}$ such that $\mathbf{B}_\mathbf{Q}^\mathsf{T} \cdot \mathbf{B}_\mathbf{Q} = \mathbf{Q}$ and $\mathbf{B}_\mathbf{Q}$ is an upper triangular matrix. Two quadratic forms $\mathbf{Q}, \mathbf{Q}' \in \mathcal{S}_n^{>0}(\mathbb{R})$ are *equivalent* if there exists a unimodular $\mathbf{U} \in \mathrm{GL}_n(\mathbb{Z})$ such that $\mathbf{U}^\mathsf{T} \cdot \mathbf{Q} \cdot \mathbf{U} = \mathbf{Q}'$. We have that two lattices are isomorphic if and only if their Gram matrices are equivalent; this allows us to restate LIP.

Definition 2 (LIP, restated). *Given two equivalent forms $\mathbf{Q}, \mathbf{Q}'$, find $\mathbf{U} \in \mathrm{GL}_n(\mathbb{Z})$ such that $\mathbf{U}^\mathsf{T} \cdot \mathbf{Q} \cdot \mathbf{U} = \mathbf{Q}'$.*

The inner product with respect to $\mathbf{Q} \in \mathcal{S}_n^{>0}(\mathbb{R})$ is defined as $\langle \cdot, \cdot \rangle_\mathbf{Q} : \mathbb{R}^n \times \mathbb{R}^n \to \mathbb{R}$, $(\mathbf{x}, \mathbf{y}) \mapsto \mathbf{x}^\mathsf{T} \cdot \mathbf{Q} \cdot \mathbf{y}$. The norm with respect to $\mathbf{Q} \in \mathcal{S}_n^{>0}(\mathbb{R})$ is defined as $\|\mathbf{x}\|_\mathbf{Q} = \sqrt{\langle \mathbf{x}, \mathbf{x} \rangle_\mathbf{Q}}$. Note that for a basis $\mathbf{B}$ and vectors $\mathbf{x}, \mathbf{y} \in \mathbb{R}^n$ we have

$$\langle \mathbf{Bx}, \mathbf{By} \rangle = \mathbf{x}^\mathsf{T}\mathbf{B}^\mathsf{T}\mathbf{By} = \langle \mathbf{x}, \mathbf{y} \rangle_{\mathbf{B}^\mathsf{T}\mathbf{B}},$$

and thus the geometry of $\Lambda(\mathbf{B})$ is fully described by $\mathbf{Q} = \mathbf{B}^\mathsf{T}\mathbf{B}$. Moving from lattices to quadratic forms can be viewed as forgetting about the specific embedding of the lattice in $\mathbb{R}^n$, while maintaining all geometric information. Throughout the paper we will talk about lattices and quadratic forms interchangeably.

Discrete gaussian sampling and smoothing. Given a parameter $\sigma \in \mathbb{R}_{>0}$, we define the Gaussian mass $\rho_\sigma : \mathbb{R}^n \to \mathbb{R}$, $\mathbf{x} \mapsto \exp\left(-\|\mathbf{x}\|^2 / 2\sigma^2\right)$. For any $\mathbf{c} \in \mathbb{R}^n$ we denote the discrete Gaussian distribution on $\Lambda + \mathbf{c}$ with parameter σ by $D_{\Lambda + \mathbf{c}, \sigma}$ which assigns the probability $\rho_\sigma(\mathbf{x}) / \sum_{\mathbf{y} \in \Lambda + \mathbf{c}} \rho_\sigma(\mathbf{y})$ to a point $\mathbf{x} \in \Lambda + \mathbf{c}$, and zero otherwise. We also define a Gaussian mass with respect to $\mathbf{Q} \in \mathcal{S}_n^{>0}(\mathbb{R})$ as $\rho_{\mathbf{Q},\sigma} : \mathbb{R}^n \to \mathbb{R}, \mathbf{x} \mapsto \exp\left(-\|\mathbf{x}\|_\mathbf{Q}^2 / 2\sigma^2\right)$. For any $\mathbf{c} \in \mathbb{R}^n$ we denote the discrete Gaussian distribution on $\mathbb{Z}^n + \mathbf{c}$ with respect to $\mathbf{Q}$ and parameter σ by $D_{\mathbf{Q}, \mathbb{Z}^n + \mathbf{c}, \sigma}$, which assigns a probability $\rho_{\mathbf{Q},\sigma}(\mathbf{x}) / \sum_{\mathbf{y} \in \mathbb{Z}^n + \mathbf{c}} \rho_{\mathbf{Q},\sigma}(\mathbf{y})$ to a point $\mathbf{x} \in \mathbb{Z}^n + \mathbf{c}$, and zero otherwise. If $\mathbf{c} \in \mathbb{Z}^n$ we write $D_{\mathbf{Q},\sigma}$. If $\mathbf{Q} = \mathbf{B}^\mathsf{T} \cdot \mathbf{B}$, note that $D_{\mathbf{Q}, \mathbb{Z}^n + \mathbf{c}, \sigma}(\mathbf{x}) = \mathbf{B}^{-1} \cdot D_{\Lambda(\mathbf{B}) + \mathbf{B} \cdot \mathbf{c}, \sigma}(\mathbf{B} \cdot \mathbf{x})$, as $\rho_{\mathbf{Q},\sigma}(\mathbf{x}) = \rho_\sigma(\mathbf{B} \cdot \mathbf{x})$. When σ is large enough compared to the maximum length of a Gram–Schmidt basis vector, we can efficiently sample a discrete Gaussian.

Lemma 1 [8, Lem. 2.3], adapted). *There is a PPT algorithm that on input a quadratic form* $\mathbf{Q} \in \mathcal{S}_n^{>0}(\mathbb{R})$, $\mathbf{c} \in \mathbb{R}^n$ *and parameter* $\sigma \geq \left\| \tilde{\mathbf{B}}_{\mathbf{Q}} \right\| \cdot (1/\pi) \cdot$ $\sqrt{\log(2n+4)/2}$ *outputs a sample according to* $D_{\mathbf{Q},\mathbb{Z}^n+\mathbf{c},\sigma}$.

A discrete Gaussian has a similar tail bound to a continuous Gaussian.

Lemma 2 ([6, Lem. 1.5(ii)]). *For any lattice* $\Lambda \subset \mathbb{R}^n$, *point* $\mathbf{c} \in \mathbb{R}^n$ *and* $\tau \geq 1$, *we have*

$$\Pr_{\mathbf{x} \sim D_{\Lambda+\mathbf{c},\sigma}} \left[\|\mathbf{x}\| > \tau\sigma\sqrt{n} \right] \leq 2 \frac{\rho_\sigma(\Lambda)}{\rho_\sigma(\Lambda+\mathbf{c})} \cdot \tau^n e^{-\frac{n}{2}(\tau^2-1)}.$$

Definition 3. *Let* $\hat{\Lambda}$ *denote the dual of* Λ. *For* $\varepsilon > 0$ *we define the* smoothing parameter $\eta_\varepsilon(\Lambda)$ *as the smallest* $\sigma \in \mathbb{R}_{>0}$ *such that* $\rho_{1/(2\pi\sigma)}\left(\hat{\Lambda} \setminus \{\mathbf{0}\}\right) \leq \varepsilon$.

Note that η_ε is usually defined with respect to a width $s = \sqrt{2\pi}\sigma$. Here its value is a factor $\sqrt{2\pi}$ smaller than usual. If $\sigma \geq \eta_\varepsilon(\Lambda)$ then $D_{\Lambda+\mathbf{c},\sigma}$ exhibits several useful properties. For example, σ is close to the standard deviation of $D_{\Lambda+\mathbf{c},\sigma}$, with the closeness parametrised by ε, see [26, Lem. 4.3], and cosets have similar weights. We may say σ is 'above smoothing' to refer to $\sigma \geq \eta_\varepsilon(\Lambda)$ for some implicit appropriate ε.

Lemma 3 ([26, Proof of Lem. 4.4]). *For any lattice* $\Lambda \subset \mathbb{R}^n$, *point* $\mathbf{c} \in \mathbb{R}^n$, *and* $\varepsilon \in (0,1)$, $\sigma \geq \eta_\varepsilon(\Lambda)$, *we have*

$$(1-\varepsilon) \cdot \frac{\left(\sqrt{2\pi} \cdot \sigma\right)^n}{\det(\Lambda)} \leq \rho_\sigma(\Lambda+\mathbf{c}) = \rho_{\mathbf{Q},\sigma}(\mathbb{Z}^n+\mathbf{c}') \leq (1+\varepsilon) \cdot \frac{\left(\sqrt{2\pi} \cdot \sigma\right)^n}{\det(\Lambda)},$$

where $\mathbf{Q} = \mathbf{B}^{\mathsf{T}}\mathbf{B}$ *and* $\mathbf{c}' = \mathbf{B}^{-1}\mathbf{c}$ *for any basis* $\mathbf{B}$ *of* Λ.

Module lattices and Hermitian forms. A number field $\mathbb{K}$ is an algebraic extension of $\mathbb{Q}$ of finite degree $n = [\mathbb{K} : \mathbb{Q}]$. We write $\mathcal{O}_{\mathbb{K}}$ for the ring of integers of a general number field. In this work, we consider the cyclotomic field $\mathbb{K} = \mathbb{Q}(\zeta_{2n}) = \mathbb{Q}\left(e^{-2\pi i/2n}\right) \cong \mathbb{Q}[X]/(X^n+1)$ where $n \geq 2$ is a power of two. This is a CM field and has conductor $m = 2n$. Many of the facts below are not true for general number fields. The ring of integers $R \cong \mathbb{Z}[X]/(X^n+1)$ of $\mathbb{K}$, or any ideal of it, is a rank n lattice. Indeed, consider its image under the embedding $\sigma : \mathbb{K} \to \mathbb{C}^n$, $x \mapsto (\sigma_1(x), \ldots, \sigma_n(x))$. Here $\sigma_1, \sigma_2, \ldots, \sigma_n$ are the n embeddings of $\mathbb{K}$ into $\mathbb{C}$, ordered such that $\sigma_{i+n/2} = \overline{\sigma_i}$ for $i \in [n/2]$ (for $m \geq 3$ cyclotomic fields have no real embeddings). The subset $\left\{ (x_1, \ldots, x_n) \in \mathbb{C}^n : \forall i \in [n/2], x_{i+n/2} = \overline{x}_i \right\} \subset \mathbb{C}^n$ is isomorphic as an inner product space to $\mathbb{R}^n$ [25, Sec. 2.1]. We implicitly use this isomorphism and write $\sigma : \mathbb{K} \to \mathbb{R}^n$. We also have the coefficient embedding $\mathrm{vec} : \mathbb{K} \to \mathbb{Q}^n$, $a_0 + a_1 X + \cdots + a_{n-1}X^{n-1} \mapsto (a_0, a_1, \ldots, a_{n-1})^{\mathsf{T}}$, which is an additive group isomorphism.

    The algebraic norm and trace are given by $\mathrm{N}(x) = \prod_{i=1}^n \sigma_i(x)$ and $\mathrm{Tr}(x) = \sum_{i=1}^n \sigma_i(x)$ for $x \in \mathbb{K}$. Since the σ_i are ring homomorphisms the algebraic norm is multiplicative and the trace is additive. If $x \in R$ then $N(x), \text{Tr}(x) \in \mathbb{Z}$. The embeddings enable us to view $\mathbb{K}$ as an inner product space over $\mathbb{Q}$ by defining $\langle \cdot, \cdot \rangle : \mathbb{K} \times \mathbb{K} \to \mathbb{Q}$ as

$$\langle f, g \rangle = \frac{1}{n} \cdot \sum_{i=1}^{n} \overline{\sigma_i(f)} \cdot \sigma_i(g).$$

We renormalise by $\frac{1}{n}$ as there is an isometry, up to a scaling factor of n, from the complex embedding to the coefficient embedding, i.e. we have $\langle f, g \rangle = \langle \text{vec}(f), \text{vec}(g) \rangle$ with the right hand inner product over $\mathbb{R}^n$. This gives a (geometric) norm on $\mathbb{K}$ as $\| \cdot \| : \mathbb{K} \to \mathbb{Q}$, $f \mapsto \sqrt{\langle f, f \rangle}$, which agrees with the Euclidean norm of $\text{vec}(f)$. As $\mathbb{K}$ is a CM field, it has an automorphism $\cdot^* : \mathbb{K} \to \mathbb{K}$ that acts as complex conjugation on its embeddings, which we call the adjoint operator. It is the unique automorphism satisfying $\sigma_i(x^*) = \overline{\sigma_i(x)}$ for all $x \in \mathbb{K}$ and $i \in [n]$. Therefore, we have $\langle f, g \rangle = \text{Tr}(f^* g) / n$.

For any $\ell \in \mathbb{Z}_{\geq 1}$, we define $\mathbb{K}^\ell = \overbrace{\mathbb{K} \oplus \cdots \oplus \mathbb{K}}^{\ell \text{ times}}$ (and similarly R^ℓ, which is an R-module). Extend $\text{vec} : \mathbb{K}^\ell \to \mathbb{Q}^{n\ell}$ in the natural way. We extend the inner product and norm to vectors $\mathbf{f}, \mathbf{g} \in \mathbb{K}^\ell$ by

$$\langle \mathbf{f}, \mathbf{g} \rangle = \sum_{i=1}^{\ell} \langle f_i, g_i \rangle \qquad \text{and} \qquad \|\mathbf{f}\| = \sqrt{\langle \mathbf{f}, \mathbf{f} \rangle}.$$

We write $\text{rot}(f) = \big(\text{vec}(f), \text{vec}(Xf), \ldots, \text{vec}(X^{n-1}f)\big) \in \mathbb{Q}^{n \times n}$ for $f \in \mathbb{K}$, which is a basis for the lattice $\sigma(f)$ given by the (possibly fractional) ideal (f), and extend this to matrices $\mathbf{B} \in \mathbb{K}^{k \times \ell}$ in the natural way,

$$\text{rot}(\mathbf{B}) = \begin{pmatrix} \text{rot}(\mathbf{B}_{11}) & \cdots & \text{rot}(\mathbf{B}_{1\ell}) \\ \vdots & \ddots & \vdots \\ \text{rot}(\mathbf{B}_{k1}) & \cdots & \text{rot}(\mathbf{B}_{k\ell}) \end{pmatrix}.$$

We now define a module lattice. Since R is the ring of integers of a number field, it is a Dedekind domain and the notion of rank is well defined for R-modules.

Definition 4. *Let $M \subset \mathbb{K}^k$ be an R-module of rank $\ell \leq k$ and define the map $\boldsymbol{\sigma} = (\sigma, \ldots, \sigma) : \mathbb{K}^k \to \mathbb{R}^{nk}$, $(x_1, \ldots, x_k) \mapsto (\sigma(x_1), \ldots, \sigma(x_k))$. The image $\boldsymbol{\sigma}(M)$ is a rank $n\ell$ lattice in $\mathbb{R}^{nk}$ which we call a module lattice.*

We may refer to 'the module lattice M' to mean $\boldsymbol{\sigma}(M)$. If $\mathbf{B} \in \mathbb{K}^{k \times \ell}$ is a basis for an R-module M then $\text{rot}(\mathbf{B}) \in \mathbb{Q}^{nk \times n\ell}$ is a basis for the module lattice $\boldsymbol{\sigma}(M)$. For $\mathbf{B} \in \mathbb{K}^{k \times \ell}$ we write $\mathbf{B}^*$ to denote the adjoint transpose, and given a vector $\mathbf{f} \in \mathbb{K}^\ell$ we write $\mathbf{f}^*$ for the adjoint transpose row vector.

Definition 5. *For $\ell \geq 1$, the set of Hermitian forms $\mathcal{H}_\ell^{>0}(\mathbb{K})$ consists of all $\mathbf{Q} \in \mathbb{K}^{\ell \times \ell}$ such that $\mathbf{Q}^* = \mathbf{Q}$ and $\text{Tr}(\mathbf{v}^* \mathbf{Q} \mathbf{v}) > 0$ for all $\mathbf{v} \in \mathbb{K}^\ell \setminus \{\mathbf{0}\}$.*

Equivalently, $\mathbf{Q}$ is a Hermitian form whenever $\mathsf{rot}(\mathbf{Q})$ is a quadratic form. For $\mathbf{B} \in \mathbb{K}^{\ell \times \ell}$ the Gram matrix $\mathbf{B}^*\mathbf{B}$ is a Hermitian form. Similar to the general case, we define an inner product with respect to a Hermitian form $\mathbf{Q}$ as

$$\langle \mathbf{f}, \mathbf{g} \rangle_{\mathbf{Q}} = \frac{1}{n} \cdot \mathrm{Tr}(\mathbf{f}^*\mathbf{Q}\mathbf{g}) \qquad \text{and} \qquad \|\mathbf{f}\|_{\mathbf{Q}} = \sqrt{\langle \mathbf{f}, \mathbf{f} \rangle_{\mathbf{Q}}}.$$

Once again, observe that for any $\mathbf{B}$ we have $\langle \mathbf{Bf}, \mathbf{Bg} \rangle = \langle \mathbf{f}, \mathbf{g} \rangle_{\mathbf{B}^*\mathbf{B}}$ and $\|\mathbf{Bf}\| = \|\mathbf{f}\|_{\mathbf{B}^*\mathbf{B}}$. We use the above to define a discrete Gaussian over Hermitian forms. For some $\mathbf{Q} \in \mathcal{H}_\ell^{>0}(\mathbb{K})$ and $\mathbf{x} \in \mathbb{K}^\ell$ set $D_{\mathbf{Q},\sigma}(\mathbf{x}) = D_{\mathsf{rot}(\mathbf{Q}),\sigma}(\mathsf{vec}(\mathbf{x}))$. Due to our choice of $\mathbb{K}$ and the definition of our norm, this is equivalent to the natural definition that follows from $\rho_{\mathbf{Q},\sigma} \colon \mathbb{K}^\ell \to \mathbb{R}$, $\mathbf{x} \mapsto \exp(-\|\mathbf{x}\|_{\mathbf{Q}}^2 /2\sigma^2)$. Note that the normalised trace satisfies $\langle 1, z \rangle = \mathrm{Tr}(z)/n$, which evaluates a polynomial $z = z_0 + z_1 X + \cdots + z_{n-1}X^{n-1}$ to its constant coefficient z_0.

Signature scheme. A signature scheme is a triple of PPT algorithms $\Pi = (\mathsf{KGen}, \mathsf{Sign}, \mathsf{Vf})$ such that Vf is deterministic. On input 1^n, KGen outputs a public and secret key $(\mathsf{pk}, \mathsf{sk})$. We assume n can be determined from either key. On input sk and a message m from a message space that may depend on pk, Sign outputs a signature sig. On input pk, a message m and a signature sig, Vf outputs a bit $b \in \{0,1\}$. We say sig is a valid signature on m if and only if $b = 1$.

In our practical cryptanalysis of Sect. 4 we discuss two types of forgery an adversary may produce, strong and weak. A strong forgery is a signature on a message for which an adversary does not know a signature, whereas a weak forgery is a signature on a message for which an adversary may know signatures. We call a signature scheme Π for which an adversary cannot produce a weak forgery strongly unforgeable, and a signature scheme for which an adversary cannot produce a strong forgery weakly unforgeable. In Appendix B of the full version [16] we consider signature security in a formal game based model.

3   Scheme

In this section we present HAWK.[2] We first give a version of HAWK that performs no compression on its signatures for simplicity, we call this uncompressed HAWK. We then introduce (compressed) HAWK and discuss how the security of HAWK directly reduces to that of the uncompressed HAWK.

3.1   Uncompressed HAWK

The uncompressed version of our signature scheme is based on the scheme presented in [15, Sec. 6], but is adapted to number rings for efficiency. The scheme uses the number ring $R = \mathbb{Z}[X]/(X^n + 1)$ with $n \geq 2$ a power of two, the ring of integers of the number field $\mathbb{Q}(\zeta_{2n})$. We use the simplest rank 2 module lattice, $R^2 \cong \mathbb{Z}^{2n}$. We implicitly move between R^2 and $\mathbb{Z}^{2n}$ via the coefficient

---

[2] See https://github.com/ludopulles/hawk-aux/blob/main/code/hawk.sage.

embedding. The secret key is some basis $\mathbf{B} \in \mathrm{SL}_2(R)$ where $\mathbf{B}$ (resp. $\mathsf{rot}(\mathbf{B})$) generates R^2 (resp. $\mathbb{Z}^{2n}$). In the context of [15, Sec. 6] this matrix represents a basis transformation applied to the trivial basis $\mathbf{I}_2(\mathbb{K})$ of R^2. The public key is the Hermitian form $\mathbf{Q} = \mathbf{B}^* \cdot \mathbf{B}$ associated to the basis $\mathbf{B}$. A signature for a message m is generated by first hashing m and a salt r to a point $\mathbf{h} = (h_0, h_1)^\mathsf{T} \in \{0,1\}^{2n}$. Applying the transformation $\mathbf{B}$ to $\frac{1}{2}\mathbf{h}$ gives us a target $\frac{1}{2}\mathbf{B} \cdot \mathbf{h}$. We then sample a short element $\mathbf{x}$ in the target's coset $R^2 + \frac{1}{2}\mathbf{B} \cdot \mathbf{h}$ via discrete Gaussian samples on $\mathbb{Z}$ and $\mathbb{Z} + 1/2$. By applying the inverse transformation $\mathbf{B}^{-1}$ we compute the signature $\mathbf{s} = \frac{1}{2}\mathbf{h} \pm \mathbf{B}^{-1}\mathbf{x} \in R^2$. This is close to $\frac{1}{2}\mathbf{h}$ with respect to $\|\cdot\|_\mathbf{Q}$, and the sign is chosen to prevent weak forgeries, see Algorithm 2 and below. See Fig. 1 for a visualisation when $n = 1$. Verification checks if the distance $\left\|\frac{1}{2}\mathbf{h} - \mathbf{s}\right\|_\mathbf{Q}$ between $\mathbf{s}$ and $\frac{1}{2}\mathbf{h}$ is not too large, which only requires the public key $\mathbf{Q} = \mathbf{B}^*\mathbf{B}$ and not the secret key $\mathbf{B}$. We have the following parameters:

1. σ_pk: controls the length of $(f, g)^\mathsf{T}$, the first basis vector of $\mathbf{B}$,
2. σ_sec: controls the lower bound on the acceptable length of $(f, g)^\mathsf{T}$,
3. σ_sign: controls the length of of a short coset vector,
4. σ_ver: controls the acceptable distance between signatures and halved hashes,
5. $\mathsf{saltlen}$: controls the probability of hash collisions.

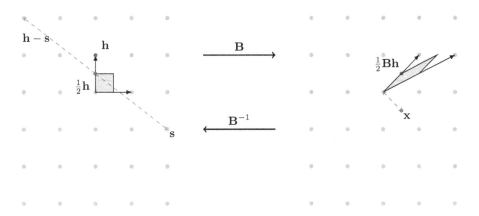

Fig. 1. Illustration of signing. First $\mathbf{h}$ is sampled (left), then $\mathbf{B}$ is applied, a short lattice point $\mathbf{x}$ is sampled from a discrete Gaussian on $\mathbb{Z}^{2n} + \frac{1}{2}\mathbf{B} \cdot \mathbf{h}$ (right). Finally $\mathbf{B}^{-1}$ applied to $\mathbf{x}$ is subtracted from $\frac{1}{2}\mathbf{h}$ to obtain a lattice point $\mathbf{s}$ close to $\mathbf{h}/2$ in $\|\cdot\|_\mathbf{Q}$. We then add $\mathbf{h} - 2\mathbf{s}$ to ensure we satisfy $\mathsf{sym\text{-}break}(h_1 - 2s_1)$.

Algorithm 1. Key generation for HAWK: KGen(1^n)

1: Sample $f, g \in R$ with coefficients from $D_{\mathbb{Z}, \sigma_{pk}}$
2: $q_{00} = f^* f + g^* g$
3: **if** $2 \mid N(f)$ **or** $2 \mid N(g)$ **or** $\|(f, g)\|^2 \leq \sigma_{sec}^2 \cdot 2n$ **then**
4:     **restart**
5: $(F, G)^\mathsf{T} \leftarrow \mathsf{TowerSolve}_{n,1}(f, g)$ [29, Alg. 4], **if** $\perp$, restart
6: $(F, G)^\mathsf{T} \leftarrow (F, G)^\mathsf{T} - \mathsf{ffNP}_R\left(\frac{f^* F + g^* G}{q_{00}}, \mathsf{ffLDL}_R^*(q_{00})\right) \cdot (f, g)^\mathsf{T}$ [14]
7: $\mathbf{B} = \begin{pmatrix} f & F \\ g & G \end{pmatrix}$.
8: $\mathbf{Q} = \begin{pmatrix} q_{00} & q_{01} \\ q_{10} & q_{11} \end{pmatrix} = \mathbf{B}^* \cdot \mathbf{B}$.
9: **return** $(\mathsf{pk}, \mathsf{sk}) = (\mathbf{Q}, \mathbf{B})$

Algorithm 2. Signing for HAWK: $\mathsf{Sign}_\mathbf{B}(m)$

1: $\mathsf{r} \leftarrow U(\{0, 1\}^{\mathsf{saltlen}})$
2: $\mathbf{h} \leftarrow H(m\|\mathsf{r})$
3: $\mathbf{t} \leftarrow \mathbf{B} \cdot \mathbf{h} \pmod 2$
4: $\mathbf{x} \leftarrow D_{\mathbb{Z}^{2n} + \frac{1}{2}\mathbf{t}, \sigma_{sign}}$
5: **if** $\|\mathbf{x}\|^2 > \sigma_{ver}^2 \cdot 2n$ **then**
6:     **restart**   (optional, see Sect. 5.3, § Failure checks.)
7: $\mathbf{s} = (s_0, s_1)^\mathsf{T} = \frac{1}{2}\mathbf{h} - \mathbf{B}^{-1}\mathbf{x}$ (parse $\mathbf{x} \in R^2$ via vec^{-1}.)
8: **if** $\mathsf{sym\text{-}break}(h_1 - 2s_1)$ is **False then**
9:     $\mathbf{s} \leftarrow \mathbf{h} - \mathbf{s}$
10: **return** $\mathsf{sig} = (\mathsf{r}, \mathbf{s})$

Algorithm 3. Verification for HAWK: $\mathsf{Vf}_\mathbf{Q}(m, \mathsf{sig})$

1: $(\mathsf{r}, \mathbf{s}) \leftarrow \mathsf{sig}$
2: $\mathbf{h} \leftarrow H(m\|\mathsf{r})$
3: **if** $\mathbf{s} \in R^2$ **and** $\mathsf{sym\text{-}break}(h_1 - 2s_1)$ is **True and** $\left\|\frac{\mathbf{h}}{2} - \mathbf{s}\right\|_\mathbf{Q}^2 \leq \sigma_{ver}^2 \cdot 2n$ **then**
4:     **return** 1
5: **else**
6:     **return** 0

For uncompressed HAWK we present KGen in Algorithm 1, Sign in Algorithm 2 and Vf in Algorithm 3. The security parameter n is a power of two and we assume the internal parameters can be computed from it. We use previous work [29, Alg. 4] to generate the unimodular transformation $\mathbf{B}$ efficiently, by sampling the first basis vector $(f, g)^\mathsf{T}$, and then completing it (if possible) with a second basis vector $(F, G)^\mathsf{T}$ such that $\det \mathbf{B} = 1$. We combine this with the fast Babai reduction of [14] to obtain a shorter second basis vector $(F, G)^\mathsf{T}$. In KGen checks are performed prior to completing the basis $\mathbf{B}$. In TowerSolvel [29] it is necessary for $N(f)$ or $N(g)$ to be an odd integer. We require both to be odd to use an optimised constant-time greatest common divisor algorithm, identical to the FALCON reference implementation. Also, we require the squared norm of $(f, g)^\mathsf{T}$ to be longer than $\sigma_\mathsf{sec}^2 \cdot 2n$ for our concrete cryptanalysis, see Sect. 4. Note that the signer has $\mathbf{B}^{-1} = \begin{pmatrix} G & -F \\ -g & f \end{pmatrix}$ since $fG - gF = \det \mathbf{B} = 1$.

In Sign and Vf we check the condition $\mathtt{sym\text{-}break}(h_1 - 2s_1)$, which is required for strong unforgeability. Without it $\mathsf{sig}' = (\mathsf{r}, \mathbf{h} - \mathbf{s})$, which can be constructed from public values, is another valid signature on m if $\mathsf{sig} = (\mathsf{r}, \mathbf{s})$ is. Given $e \in R$, we define $\mathtt{sym\text{-}break}(e)$ to be $\mathtt{True}$ if and only if $e \neq 0$ and the first non zero coefficient of $\mathsf{vec}(e)$ is positive. Checking this condition on $h_1 - 2s_1$ in Vf prevents a weak forgery attack.

Signature correctness. Assume Sign is called with message m and outputs $\mathsf{sig} = (\mathsf{r}, \mathbf{s})$. First, note $\mathbf{B}^{-1}\mathbf{x} \in R^2 + \frac{1}{2}\mathbf{h}$ and $\frac{1}{2}\mathbf{h} \pm \frac{1}{2}\mathbf{h} \in R^2$, so $\mathbf{s} = \frac{1}{2}\mathbf{h} \pm \mathbf{B}^{-1}\mathbf{x} \in R^2$. Second, suppose $\mathtt{sym\text{-}break}(h_1 - 2s_1)$ is not satisfied during verification. By lines 8 and 9 of Algorithm 2, this means $\mathtt{sym\text{-}break}(h_1 - 2s_1)$ and $\mathtt{sym\text{-}break}(2s_1 - h_1)$ are both $\mathtt{False}$, therefore $h_1 = 2s_1$. Since $\mathbf{h} \in \{0, 1\}^{2n}$, this implies $h_1 = 0$, i.e. we have found a preimage of $(h_0, 0)^\mathsf{T}$ for H. By choosing a preimage resistant H or modelling it as a random oracle, this happens with $\mathsf{negl}(n)$ probability. We allow this failure probability to simplify (compressed) HAWK.

The signing algorithm terminates only if the condition on line 5 is $\mathtt{False}$. Therefore $\|\mathbf{x}\|^2 \leq \sigma_\mathsf{ver}^2 \cdot 2n$. Thus during verification $\left\| \frac{\mathbf{h}}{2} - \mathbf{s} \right\|_\mathbf{Q}^2 = \left\| \mathbf{B}\left(\frac{\mathbf{h}}{2} - \mathbf{s} \right) \right\|^2 = \|{\pm}\mathbf{x}\|^2 \leq \sigma_\mathsf{ver}^2 \cdot 2n$, with $-\mathbf{x}$ given by line 9 of Sign.

Storing pk *and* sk. We now consider how to efficiently store pk and sk, that is,

$$\mathbf{Q} = \begin{pmatrix} q_{00} & q_{01} \\ q_{10} & q_{11} \end{pmatrix} = \mathbf{B}^* \cdot \mathbf{B} \quad \text{and} \quad \mathbf{B} = \begin{pmatrix} f & F \\ g & G \end{pmatrix}$$

respectively. For $\mathbf{B}$ it is sufficient to only store f and g, but this requires the computationally expensive recovery of F and G in Sign. We note that computing F, G is the most expensive part of KGen. Instead, one stores f, g and F since G can be recovered efficiently from $fG - gF = 1$. The coefficients of f, g and F are small so we use a simple encoding with constant-time decoding for them.

For $\mathbf{Q}$ by construction we have $q_{10} = q_{01}^*$ so one may simply drop q_{10}. Moreover, since $\det(\mathbf{B}) = 1$ we have $q_{00}q_{11} - q_{01}q_{10} = \det \mathbf{Q} = \det(\mathbf{B}^*)\det(\mathbf{B}) = 1$, therefore q_{11} can be dropped and reconstructed as $q_{11} = \frac{1 + q_{01}^* \cdot q_{01}}{q_{00}}$. In addition, q_{00} is self-adjoint and therefore only the first half of its coefficients need to be encoded. More details are given in Sect. 5.2.

3.2 (Compressed) HAWK

HAWK is obtained by dropping s_0 from a signature $\mathbf{s} = (s_0, s_1)^\mathsf{T}$ in Sign and then reconstructing it in Vf using public values $\mathbf{Q}$ and $\mathbf{h}$. There is a probability that s_0 is not correctly recovered, but it is kept small by rejecting 'bad' key pairs in KGen. In Vf, s_0 is recovered by finding a value that makes $\frac{1}{2}\mathbf{h} - (s_0, s_1)^\mathsf{T}$

short with respect to $\|\cdot\|_{\mathbf{Q}}$. Two ways to reconstruct s_0 are Babai's round-off algorithm and Babai's Nearest Plane Algorithm [4]. Given that we work with respect to the norm induced by $\mathbf{Q}$, we must adapt one of these algorithms to quadratic forms. Because of its simplicity and good performance, we use round-off for HAWK. Specifically, we use the following to reconstruct s_0.

$$ s_0' = \left\lceil \frac{h_0}{2} + \frac{q_{01}}{q_{00}} \left(\frac{h_1}{2} - s_1 \right) \right\rfloor, \tag{1} $$

where the rounding is coefficientwise and $\lceil x \rfloor = z$ for $x \in \left(z - \frac{1}{2}, z + \frac{1}{2} \right]$ and $z \in \mathbb{Z}$. Hence Vf is adapted to read a signature $\mathsf{sig} = (\mathsf{r}, s_1)$ and reconstruct s_0' using (1), before setting $\mathbf{s} = (s_0', s_1)^{\mathsf{T}}$. Observe that $s_0' = s_0$ if and only if

$$ \left\lceil \frac{q_{00} \left(\frac{h_0}{2} - s_0 \right) + q_{01} \left(\frac{h_1}{2} - s_1 \right)}{q_{00}} \right\rfloor = 0. $$

The fraction inside the rounding function can be rewritten using $(q_{00}, q_{01}) = (f^*, g^*) \cdot \mathbf{B}$ and $\mathbf{B} \cdot \left(\frac{\mathbf{h}}{2} - \mathbf{s} \right) = (x_0, x_1)^{\mathsf{T}}$ as $\frac{f^* x_0 + g^* x_1}{f^* f + g^* g}$. Thus, we certainly recover the correct s_0 from $\mathbf{Q}$, $\mathbf{h}$ and s_1 if

$$ \frac{f^* x_0 + g^* x_1}{f^* f + g^* g} \in \left(-\frac{1}{2}, \frac{1}{2} \right)^n. \tag{2} $$

Intuitively, when (f, g) is sampled such that the Euclidean norm of $(f^*/q_{00}, g^*/q_{00})$ is sufficiently small, this recovery works almost always. Note

$$ \left\| \left(\frac{f^*}{q_{00}}, \frac{g^*}{q_{00}} \right) \right\|^2 = \frac{1}{n} \mathrm{Tr} \left(\frac{f^* f + g^* g}{q_{00}^2} \right) = \frac{1}{n} \mathrm{Tr}(q_{00}^{-1}) = \langle 1, q_{00}^{-1} \rangle. \tag{3} $$

Hence we choose a bound ν_{dec} such that decompression works almost always for keys satisfying $\langle 1, q_{00}^{-1} \rangle < \nu_{\mathsf{dec}}$. We provide a computation and value for ν_{dec} in Sect. 5.1. In summary, Algorithms 1, 2 and 3 are changed as follows for HAWK.

1. In KGen, restart if $\langle 1, q_{00}^{-1} \rangle \geq \nu_{\mathsf{dec}}$.
2. In Sign, restart if $\mathbf{x} = (x_0, x_1)^{\mathsf{T}}$ does not satisfy (2).
3. In Sign, return a signature as (r, s_1) instead of $(\mathsf{r}, \mathbf{s}) = (\mathsf{r}, (s_0, s_1)^{\mathsf{T}})$.
4. In Vf, given a signature (r, s_1) reconstruct s_0' with (1) and set $\mathbf{s} = (s_0', s_1)^{\mathsf{T}}$.

Given the above, a reconstructed signature is correct. In practice we choose ν_{dec} such that (2) is also satisfied except with small probability and forego item 2. in the list, see Sect. 5.3.

Security relation to the uncompressed variant. Note that an adversary that can create a forgery (strong or weak) against HAWK can also create a forgery (strong or weak) against uncompressed HAWK. Indeed, if $\mathsf{sig} = (\mathsf{r}, s_1)$ is a forgery against HAWK then this implies $\mathsf{sig} = (\mathsf{r}, (s_0', s_1)^{\mathsf{T}})$ is a forgery against uncompressed HAWK. Only public quantities are required to recover s_0'. Therefore, throughout we consider the security of uncompressed HAWK. In Appendix B of the full version [16] we further reduce the forgery security of uncompressed HAWK to an assumption called the one more short vector problem, or omSVP.

4   Cryptanalysis

In this section we provide a concrete cryptanalysis of HAWK. Whereas the formal security arguments we make in Sect. 6 and Appendix B of the full version [16] increase our confidence in the design of HAWK, our results here aid us in choosing parameter sets that are efficient. Throughout we consider uncompressed HAWK. We consider recovering the secret key from public information and forging a new signature given at most $q_s = 2^{64}$ signatures. We report the various parameters, probabilities and blocksizes output by our cryptanalysis in Table 2.

We express the constraints on various quantities in our scheme in terms of Gaussian parameters $\sigma_\bullet$, even if they are not quantities sampled from a distribution. This allows us to present necessary relationships between these quantities as in Fig. 2. In particular for $\mathbf{x} \leftarrow D_{\mathbb{Z}^d,\sigma}$, with σ above smoothing, $\mathbb{E}[\|\mathbf{x}\|] \approx \sigma\sqrt{d}$ [26, Sec. 4]. For example, the verification of signatures is determined by a distance, say ℓ. Instead of referring to ℓ, we use the shorthand $\sigma_{\mathsf{ver}} = \ell/\sqrt{d}$.

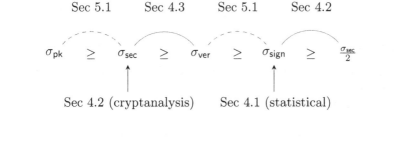

Fig. 2. A summary of the necessary relationships between the various $\sigma_\bullet$.

We stress that the relations of Fig. 2 are necessary, under our experimental analysis, conditions for security – any selection must also satisfy the concrete cryptanalysis below. As a short introduction, σ_{sign} is our fundamental parameter, and we select it first. It ensures that our scheme does not suffer from learning attacks [13,27] if an adversary is given access to signature transcripts. We then choose σ_{pk} which controls key generation in Algorithm 1. It must be large enough that recovering the secret key is hard, and also that the cost of computing a sufficiently good basis to aid with signature forgeries is hard. To this end we heuristically estimate and verify experimentally σ_{sec}, a parameter that represents the shortest a public basis can be before one recovers the secret key. Finally, σ_{pk}

and σ_{ver} are chosen to ensure various rejection steps, in key generation and signing respectively, do not occur too frequently, see Sect. 5.1. The condition $\sigma_{\mathsf{ver}}^2 < \sigma_{\mathsf{sec}}^2 + \sigma_{\mathsf{sign}}^2$ encodes the requirement for a good basis to not help with signature forgeries.

4.1 Choosing σ_{sign}

We choose σ_{sign} large enough to avoid signatures leaking information about a secret key. Following [32, Sec. 2.6], for security parameter λ in the face of an adversary allowed q_s signatures, it is enough to set

$$\sigma_{\mathsf{sign}} \geq \frac{1}{\pi} \cdot \sqrt{\frac{\log(4n(1 + 1/\varepsilon))}{2}} \geq \eta_\varepsilon(\mathbb{Z}^{2n}),$$

for $\varepsilon = 1/\sqrt{q_s \cdot \lambda}$ to lose a small constant number of bits of security. We note that since we sample from $\mathbb{Z}^{2n}$ we may use the orthogonal basis $\mathbf{I}_{2n}(\mathbb{Z})$, and thus the above inequality is also sufficient for efficient sampling via Lemma 1. We ensure that, following the analysis of FALCON [32, Sec. 3.9.3], our probability distribution tables have a Rényi divergence at order 513 from their ideal distributions of less than $1 + 2^{-79}$.[3]

4.2 Key Recovery

In HAWK, the problem of recovering the secret key $\mathbf{B} \in \mathrm{SL}_2(\mathcal{O}_\mathbb{K})$ from the public key $\mathbf{Q} = \mathbf{B}^* \cdot \mathbf{B}$ is a (module) Lattice Isomorphism Problem. For the lattice $R^2 \cong \mathbb{Z}^{2n}$ it is equivalent to finding a $\mathbf{U} \in \mathrm{SL}_2(\mathcal{O}_\mathbb{K})$ such that $\mathbf{U}^* \cdot \mathbf{Q} \cdot \mathbf{U} = \mathbf{I}_2(\mathbb{K})$, i.e. reducing (any lattice basis corresponding to) $\mathbf{Q}$ to an orthonormal basis. As mentioned in [15], all known algorithms to solve LIP for modules of rank at least two require finding at least one shortest vector. Therefore we assume that the best key recovery attack requires one to find a single shortest vector.

Unusual-SVP. The shortest vectors in R^2 have length 1, which is a factor of order $\Theta(\sqrt{n})$ shorter than predicted by the Gaussian heuristic. Recovering such 'unusually' short vectors is easier than generic shortest vectors, and can be achieved by running the BKZ lattice reduction algorithm with blocksize β much lower than the full dimension $2n$. Given that for current cryptanalysis there are no significant speed-ups for solving the structured variant of this unusual-SVP, we treat the problem by considering the unstructured version (i.e. as the form $\mathrm{rot}(\mathbf{Q})$ or some rotation of $\mathbb{Z}^{2n}$). The problem of finding an unusually short vector has received much cryptanalytic attention. This has lead to accurate estimates for the required BKZ blocksize, see [3] for a survey. As an estimate, given that our lattice has unit volume and we search for a vector of unit length, we require a blocksize β such that

$$\sqrt{\beta/d} \approx \delta_\beta^{2\beta - d - 1}, \tag{4}$$

---

[3] See   https://github.com/ludopulles/hawk-aux/blob/main/code/generate_C_tables. sage.

where $\delta_\beta \approx (\beta/2\pi e)^{1/2(\beta-1)}$. Asymptotically this is satisfied for some $\beta \in d/2 + o(d)$. Concrete estimates also simulate the Gram–Schmidt profile, use probabilistic models for the lengths of projected vectors and account for the presence of multiple shortest vectors [5,9,10,30].

In Fig. 4 we plot the estimate given by (4) where the $o(d)$ term is concretised to some constant, the estimate given by the leaky-LWE-estimator [10], which applies the concrete improvements mentioned above, and experimental data. These experiments apply the BKZ2.0 algorithm with lattice point enumeration as implemented in [34] to the public form $\mathbf{Q}$, reporting the BKZ block size required to find a shortest vector. For dimensions which are not powers of two, the experimental data uses a form sampled by [15, Alg. 1], the unstructured generation procedure upon which our key generation is based. For some small power of two dimensions we generate bases via Algorithm 1. We see that below approximately dimension 80 instances can be solved with LLL reduction, and that afterwards the required blocksize approximately increments by one when the dimension increases by two, as (4) would suggest. We also see that above approximately blocksize 70 the model of [10] appears especially accurate. We therefore use this model to determine β_{key} in Table 2. We use a simple progressive strategy where the blocksize increments by one after each tour, which we expect to require a blocksize perhaps two or three larger than a more optimal progressive strategy.

Decreasing σ_{pk}. For the experiments of Fig. 4 we took a large σ_{pk} as an attempt to find a ground truth. We would like to minimise σ_{pk} to minimise the size of our keys and the complexity of computing with them, but without significantly reducing security. To this end we perform a similar experiment where we fix a set of dimensions and reduce forms of these dimensions using various $\sigma_{\mathsf{pk}} < 20$. The results of these experiments are presented in Fig. 3.

For σ_{pk} below a certain threshold instances can be solved by LLL, then as σ_{pk} increases past this threshold the instances become harder, before reaching an empirical "maximum hardness" (at least with respect to these experiments) where further increases in σ_{pk} appear to give no extra security.

When running BKZ one encounters shorter vectors as β grows. In a random lattice of unit volume one expects to encounter vectors of length $\delta_\beta^{d-1} \in \Theta(d)$ when $\beta = d/2 + o(d)$, but for $\mathbb{Z}^d$ this is also the moment that a vector of length 1 is found. In fact, the model of [10] predicts that we suddenly jump from finding vectors of length $\ell_0 = \Theta(d)$ to finding a shortest vector of length 1. This threshold behaviour was observed and discussed in [7, Sec. 6.2]. In our notation the authors observe the threshold effect once vectors of length approximately $\sqrt{d}/2$ are discovered. Our model and experiments suggest the threshold length is $\Theta(d)$ but with a constant smaller than 1. We verified this behaviour for $\mathbb{Z}^d$ experimentally. In Fig. 5 we plot $\sigma_{\mathsf{sec}} = \ell_0/\sqrt{d}$ where ℓ_0 is the length of the shortest basis vector after the penultimate tour concludes.

We see that for large enough dimensions the behaviour matches the unusual-SVP predictions, and we obtain $\sigma_{\mathsf{sec}} = \Theta(\sqrt{d})$. For Table 2 we take σ_{sec} as the output from the prediction of [10]. We assume the value σ_{sec} represents a lower

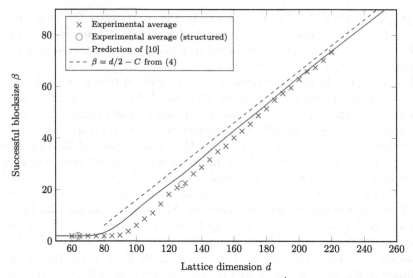

We ran progressive BKZ (one tour per blocksize) over $\mathbb{Z}^d$ using an input form generated with $\sigma_{\mathsf{pk}} = 20$ and report the average successful β that recovered a length one vector over 40 instances. We used the BKZ simulator and probabilistic model of [10], accounting for the d target solutions. See `BKZ_simulator.sage` and `exp_varying_n.sage` at `https://github.com/ludopulles/hawk-aux`.

Fig. 3. Blocksize required to recover a shortest vector via lattice reduction as a function of the standard deviation $\widetilde{\sigma_{\mathsf{pk}}}$.

bound for σ_{pk} such that our public forms exhibit maximum hardness. In practice we take $\sigma_{\mathsf{pk}} > \sigma_{\mathsf{sec}}$ and reject keys where the length of $(f, g)^\mathsf{T}$ is shorter than ℓ_0. If we allow shorter $(f, g)^\mathsf{T}$ then the public key may give information to an adversary that she would not have unless she had already recovered the secret key.

We note that the prediction of [10] in Fig. 5 is inaccurate for $d \leq 180$, similarly (but more noticeably) to Fig. 4. One can improve the accuracy of estimates for these dimensions by using the geometric series assumption, and performing several tours so that basis profiles match it, for small blocksizes (say up to $\beta = 20$). Since our estimates converge in the range of feasible experiments, we choose simplicity instead.

Note that even if the statistical arguments of Sect. 4.1 allow it, we cannot take $\sigma_{\mathsf{sign}} < \sigma_{\mathsf{sec}}/2$. Indeed, $2 \cdot (\frac{1}{2}\mathbf{h} - \mathbf{s}) \in \mathbb{Z}^{2n}$ and if $\sigma_{\mathsf{sign}} < \sigma_{\mathsf{sec}}/2$ then $\left\| 2 \cdot (\frac{1}{2}\mathbf{h} - \mathbf{s}) \right\|_\mathbf{Q} = 2 \|\mathbf{x}\| \approx 2\sigma_{\mathsf{sign}}\sqrt{d} < \sigma_{\mathsf{sec}}\sqrt{d}$. Therefore, doubling a public quantity given by a signature may describe a shorter lattice vector than those seen just before secret key recovery.

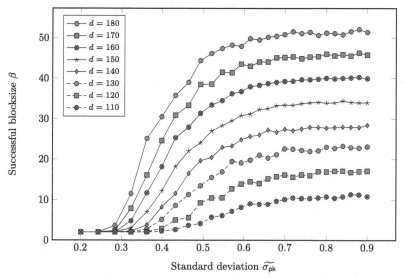

We ran progressive BKZ (one tour per blocksize) over $\mathbb{Z}^d$ using an input form generated with various σ_{pk} and report the average successful β that recovered a length one vector over 80 instances. Note that the range of σ_{pk} includes values below smoothing, for which the actual standard deviation $\widetilde{\sigma_{\mathsf{pk}}}$ can be significantly lower than the Gaussian parameter σ_{pk}. See https://github.com/ludopulles/hawk-aux/blob/main/code/exp_varying_sigma.sage.

Fig. 4. Blocksize required to recover a shortest vector via lattice reduction as a function of dimension d.

4.3 Signature Forgery

Strong Forgery. We consider the general problem of forging a signature for some unsigned message. Specifically, given a target $\frac{1}{2}\mathbf{h}$ for some $\mathbf{h} \in \{0,1\}^{2n}$, return an $\mathbf{s} \in \mathbb{Z}^{2n}$ such that $\left\|\frac{1}{2}\mathbf{h} - \mathbf{s}\right\|_{\mathbf{Q}} \leq \sigma_{\mathsf{ver}}\sqrt{d}$. We use the heuristic that solving such an approximate CVP instance is at least as hard as solving an approximate SVP instance with the same approximation factor over the same lattice. we determine the expected blocksize β using the BKZ simulator [10] such that our first basis vector has norm less than $\sigma_{\mathsf{ver}}\sqrt{d}$, and report it as β_{forge} in Table 2. Note that since we use the BKZ simulator of [10] to estimate both β_{key} and β_{forge}, if $\sigma_{\mathsf{ver}} = \sigma_{\mathsf{sec}}$ then $\beta_{\mathrm{key}} = \beta_{\mathrm{forge}}$. Our approach mandates that $\sigma_{\mathsf{ver}} \leq \sigma_{\mathsf{sec}}$. We make this design decision because in our model it means an adversary should not be able to produce a strong forgery unless the secret key is recovered. Indeed, when $\sigma_{\mathsf{ver}} \leq \sigma_{\mathsf{sec}}$ our assumption on approximate CVP says forging a signature is as hard as finding a vector as short as those found just before key recovery.

Weak Forgery. We consider a weak forgery attack consisting of adding a short lattice vector to an existing signature for some message, and hoping that it remains a valid signature for the same message. This vector might come from

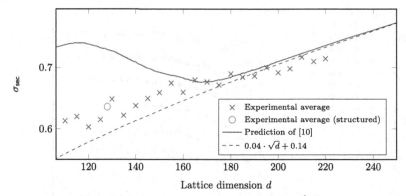

We ran progressive BKZ (one tour per blocksize) over $\mathbb{Z}^d$ using an input form generated with $\sigma_{pk} = 20$ and report the average σ_{sec} determined by the shortest basis vector in the penultimate BKZ tour over 40 instances. See `exp_varying_n.sage` and `predict_varying_n.sage` at `https://github.com/ludopulles/hawk-aux`.

Fig. 5. Shortest basis vector length before the recovery of a length one vector, given in terms of σ_{sec}.

the public key, or from lattice reduction effort on it. Its length is assumed to be at least $\ell_0 = \sigma_{sec} \cdot \sqrt{d}$, see Sect. 4.2. We give arbitrarily many such length ℓ_0 vectors to the adversary for free. We estimate the probability the attack succeeds, i.e. that $\|\mathbf{x} + \mathbf{v}\|^2 \leq d \cdot \sigma_{ver}^2$ for $\mathbf{x} \leftarrow D_{\mathbb{Z}^{2n}, \sigma_{sign}}$ and $\mathbf{v}$ of length ℓ_0.[4] If $\mathbf{x}$ were sampled from a spherical continuous Gaussian, then considering any such $\mathbf{v}$ would give the same distribution of squared lengths. We examine the distribution of $\|\mathbf{x} + \mathbf{v}\|^2$ for two "extremal" choices of $\mathbf{v}$; the first has all its weight in one coordinate, $\mathbf{v} = (\lfloor \ell_0 \rfloor, 0, \ldots, 0)$, and the second is as balanced as possible, e.g. $\mathbf{v} = (1, \ldots, 1, 2, \ldots, 2)$ for $\|\mathbf{v}\| = \lfloor \ell_0 \rfloor$. Note that the distribution of $\|\mathbf{x} + \mathbf{v}\|^2$ is invariant under signed permutations of $\mathbf{v}$. We report our estimate for the success probability of this attack as Pr[weak forgery] in Table 2.

This attack implies the requirement $\sigma_{ver}^2 < \sigma_{sec}^2 + \sigma_{sign}^2$. Even if a vector from a reduced public key is orthogonal to a given signature, then if $\sigma_{ver}^2 \geq \sigma_{sec}^2 + \sigma_{sign}^2$ adding it will likely be sufficient for a weak forgery.

Comparison with FALCON. FALCON uses a different cryptanalytic model to determine the blocksizes reported in Table 2. Our model makes use of recent improvements [10] and enjoys the experimental evidence above. The unusually short vectors in $\mathbb{Z}^d$ are a factor about 1.17 shorter than the NTRU lattice of FALCON, after appropriate renormalisation, and thus key recovery for HAWK will be slightly easier than FALCON in either model. On the other hand, our verification bound σ_{ver} is a factor about 1.15 (HAWK-512) to 1.06 (HAWK-1024) shorter than FALCON after renormalisation, and thus obtaining strong forgeries

---

[4] See `fail_and_forge_probability` at `https://github.com/ludopulles/hawk-aux/blob/main/code/find_params.sage`.

is slightly harder than in FALCON in either model. In both HAWK-512 and FAL-CON-512 key recovery is harder than signature forgery, and thus hardening the latter, as we do, gives a slightly more secure scheme overall. For HAWK-1024 and FALCON-1024 key recovery is easier than signature forgery, and in the FAL-CON model we obtain a slightly less secure scheme overall. See Appendix D of the full version [16] for more detail on FALCON's security methodology, and a comparison to HAWK under it. We also argue there that part of the key recovery methodology of FALCON is overconservative.

5   Parameters and Performance

In Table 2 we list parameters and the output of our concrete cryptanalysis for HAWK.[5] Section 5.1 explains how these parameters were chosen. We explain the encoding used for public keys and signatures, and the simple encoding used for secret keys, in Sect. 5.2. In Sect. 5.3 we explain the design choices made in our constant-time implementation of HAWK, written in C. Finally, Sect. 5.4 contains the details behind Table 1. More details can be found in Appendix C of the full version [16].

5.1   Parameter Selection

In HAWK we set $\mathsf{saltlen} = \lambda + \log_2 q_s$, where $q_s = 2^{64}$ is the limit on the signature transcript size. The probability of a hash collision is then less than $q_s \cdot 2^{-\lambda}$ [32, Section 2.2.2]. Allowing $\mathsf{saltlen}$ to depend on λ implies one must know λ before computing $\mathsf{H}(m\|r)$, which is commonly the case. For simplicity FALCON choose a fixed salt length of 320 bits. This is not optimal for $\lambda = 128$. Here HAWK-512 saves 16 bytes on signatures, though this saving is also available to FALCON-512.

The value of σ_{pk} for HAWK-512 listed in Table 2 is such that the probability of $\|(f,g)\|^2 > \sigma_{\mathsf{sec}}^2 \cdot 2n$ is greater than 99.5% for f, g both with odd algebraic norm and sampled as in KGen. For HAWK-1024, the probability that $\|(f,g)\|^2 > \sigma_{\mathsf{sec}}^2 \cdot 2n$ holds for similar f, g is greater than 80%.

There are two failures that may occur during signing in HAWK. Firstly, $\|\mathbf{x}\|^2$ may be too large. Secondly, (2) may be violated, i.e. decompressing $\mathsf{sig} = (r, s_1)$ may return $s_0' \neq s_0$, the original first component of the signature. We choose parameters σ_{ver} and ν_{dec} to make such failures unlikely.

For HAWK-512, $\mathbf{x}$ is too large with a probability of around 2^{-22}, determined by convolving the necessary distributions together.[6] To obtain a strict upper bound on this probability one can use a looser tail bound analysis via Lemma 2 and Lemma 3, with $\varepsilon = 1/\sqrt{q_s \lambda}$ and $\tau = \sigma_{\mathsf{ver}}/\sigma_{\mathsf{sign}}$, which gives 2^{-17}. Similarly for HAWK-1024, $\mathbf{x}$ is too large with a probability of around 2^{-128} and the tail bound gives a probability of at most 2^{-121}.

---

[5] See https://github.com/ludopulles/hawk-aux/blob/main/code/find_params.sage.

[6] See `fail_and_forge_probabilities` at https://github.com/ludopulles/hawk-aux/blob/main/code/find_params.sage.

Given a fixed secret key $\mathsf{sk} = \mathbf{B}$, we provide a heuristic upper bound on the probability of decompression (1) giving $s_0' \neq s_0$, which is upper bounded by the probability that (2) does not hold. This also upper bounds the probability a compressed signature is correct although $s_0 \neq s_0'$. Heuristically, we assume that x_0, x_1 are independently sampled from a normal distribution on $\mathbb{R}^n$ with mean 0 and standard deviation σ_{sign}. Following Sect. 3.2 the decompression succeeds if $\frac{f^* x_0 + g^* x_1}{q_{00}} \in (-\frac{1}{2}, \frac{1}{2})^n$. Since $\mathbf{B}$ is fixed, each coefficient is normally distributed with mean 0 and variance $\|(f^*/q_{00}, g^*/q_{00})\|^2 \cdot \sigma_{\mathsf{sign}}^2 = \langle 1, q_{00}^{-1} \rangle \cdot \sigma_{\mathsf{sign}}^2$, using (3). Hence the probability that one of the n coefficients is not in the interval $(-\frac{1}{2}, \frac{1}{2})$ is $\mathrm{erfc}\left(\frac{1}{2} / \left(\sqrt{2 \cdot \langle 1, 1/q_{00} \rangle} \cdot \sigma_{\mathsf{sign}}\right)\right)$, where erfc is the complementary error function. By a union bound, the probability that decompression fails is heuristically bounded from above by $n \cdot \mathrm{erfc}\left(1/(\sqrt{8 \cdot \langle 1, 1/q_{00} \rangle} \cdot \sigma_{\mathsf{sign}})\right)$. By rejecting keys for which $\langle 1, q_{00}^{-1} \rangle \geq \nu_{\mathsf{dec}}$, decompression fails for any $\mathbf{B}$ heuristically with probability at most $n \cdot \mathrm{erfc}\left(1/\left(\sqrt{8\nu_{\mathsf{dec}}} \cdot \sigma_{\mathsf{sign}}\right)\right)$.

Taking $\nu_{\mathsf{dec}} = 1/1000$ in HAWK-512 this upper bound is 2^{-105}. This condition on (f, g) in KGen fails in about 9% of cases. We empirically determined this by sampling f and g with odd algebraic norm 100,000 times. Combining this with the small probability that $\|(f, g)\|$ is too small, one can efficiently sample (f, g) until all requirements, before TowerSolvel is invoked, are met.

In HAWK-1024 we take $\nu_{\mathsf{dec}} = 1/3000$ and decompression fails on a signature with probability less than 2^{-315} for a key satisfying $\langle 1, q_{00}^{-1} \rangle < \nu_{\mathsf{dec}}$. This condition fails in about 0.9% of the cases during sampling of (f, g) inside KGen.

Parametrisations for formal reductions. The parameters above are determined by concrete cryptanalysis and do not follow our formal reductions. In Sect. 6 we give a worst case to average case reduction for smLIP, and in Appendix A of the full version [16] show how it applies to the KGen of HAWK. For this reduction to be efficient σ_{pk} must grow exponentially in n. We discuss this in final paragraph of Sect. 6. In Appendix B of the full version [16] we reduce the strong signature forgery security of HAWK's design to omSVP. To ensure the parametrisation of the omSVP problem we reduce to is not easy we require $\sigma_{\mathsf{ver}} < \sqrt{2}\sigma_{\mathsf{sign}}$ and $2\sigma_{\mathsf{sign}} < \sigma_{\mathsf{pk}}$. The existence of plausibly hard parametrisations of omSVP encourages us that there is no inherent flaw in our design. We take σ_{pk} smaller than this requirement and discuss this further in Appendix B of the full version [16].

5.2   Encoding

In HAWK both the secret key and $\mathbf{x}$ in Sign are sampled from a discrete Gaussian. As a consequence, the coefficients of the public key and the signature roughly follow a normal distribution. Therefore, it is beneficial to use the Golomb–Rice coding [21]. This encoding is used for the signatures in FALCON [32].

Table 2. Parameter sets and their estimated security are given. The dimension, bit security and transcript size are used to determine σ_{sign}. Other standard deviations are determined in Sect. 4. We then estimate the probability that a signature fails for being too long. The estimated required blocksizes β for BKZ reduction to achieve key recovery and signature forgery are then given. Finally, we give the estimated probability of finding a weak forgery via the attack in Sect. 4.3.

	HAWK-256	HAWK-512	HAWK-1024
Targeted security	Challenge	NIST-1	NIST-5
Dimension $d = 2n$	512	1024	2048
Bit security λ	64	128	256
Transcript size limit q_s	2^{32}	2^{64}	2^{64}
Signature Std. dev. σ_{sign}	1.010	1.278	1.299
Verif. Std. dev. σ_{ver}	1.040	1.425	1.572
Key Recov. Std. dev. σ_{sec}	1.042	1.425	1.974
Key Gen. Std. dev. σ_{pk}	1.1	1.5	2
Salt Length (bits)	112	192	320
$\log_2(\Pr[\text{sign fail}])$	-2	-22	-128
Key Recov. (BKZ) β_{key}	211	452	940
Strong Forgery (BKZ) β_{forge}	211	452	1009
$\log_2(\Pr[\text{weak forgery}])$	-83	-143	-683

For the coding, we use an altered absolute value $|\cdot|' : \mathbb{Z} \to [0, \infty)$, $x \mapsto x$ for $x \geq 0$ and $x \mapsto -x - 1$ for $x < 0$. The map that sends x to its sign and $|x|'$ gives a bijection $\mathbb{Z} \to \{0, 1\} \times \mathbb{Z}_{\geq 0}$. Given a quantity that is sampled from a discrete Gaussian distribution with (an above smoothing) parameter σ, take an integer k close to $\log_2(\sigma)$. To encode a value $x \in \mathbb{Z}$, first output the sign of x and the lowest k bits of $|x|'$ in binary. Then output $\lfloor |x|'/2^k \rfloor$ in unary, i.e. $\lfloor |x|'/2^k \rfloor$ zeros followed by a one. Note that FALCON uses $|\cdot|$ where we use $|\cdot|'$, but their decoding fails when negative zero is encountered to ensure unique encodings [32, Section 3.11.2]. An advantage of this altered absolute value is that it sometimes saves one bit and is easy to implement: $|\mathtt{x}|'$ is the XOR of x and $-(\mathtt{x} >> 15)$ when x has 16 bits.

We use the Golomb–Rice coding on pk and s_1. In particular, for pk the coefficients of q_{01} and coefficients 1 up to and including $n/2 - 1$ of q_{00} are encoded, with $k = 9$ and $k = 5$ respectively for HAWK-512 and $k = 10$ and $k = 6$ for HAWK-1024. The constant coefficient of q_{00} is output with 16 bits as its size is much larger than the other coefficients. The second half of q_{00} can be deduced from its self-adjointness. For s_1 we use $k = 8$ and $k = 9$ in our implementation for HAWK-512 and HAWK-1024 respectively.

For the secret key, we note the sampler in our implementation of HAWK-512 generates coefficients for f and g with an absolute value at most $13 < 2^4$, we encode these with 5 bits, one of which is the sign. For the remaining polynomial

F of the secret key, we encode with one byte per coefficient (recall G can be reconstructed). We use this simple encoding and decoding for our secret key as it is constant-time. HAWK-1024 requires 6 bits for coefficients of f and g since the sampler generates values of absolute value at most $18 < 2^5$.

5.3   Implementation Details

We implemented HAWK-512 and HAWK-1024 in the C programming language, together with an AVX2 optimised implementation. Due to the many algorithmic similarities between HAWK and FALCON, we were able to reuse a significant portion of the public implementation of FALCON. The code for key generation and signing is isochronous; all is constant-time except the encoding of the public quantities pk and sig. Verification is trivially isochronous as it only uses public information.

Babai reduction. In KGen we perform another reduction step to make $(F, G)^\mathsf{T}$ smaller than the output of TowerSolvel. TowerSolvel returns an element $(F, G)^\mathsf{T}$ whose projection onto the module lattice $M = (f, g)^\mathsf{T} \cdot R$, i.e. the rank n real lattice with basis $\mathbf{C} = \mathrm{rot}((f, g)^\mathsf{T})$, lies in the fundamental parallelepiped defined by $\mathbf{C}$. If this projection is uniformly distributed here, the expectation of its squared norm is $\frac{n}{12} \cdot 2n\sigma_{\mathsf{pk}}^2$. However, line 6 in Algorithm 1 implies the projection of $(F, G)^\mathsf{T}$ onto M lies in the fundamental domain generated by the Gram–Schmidt orthogonalisation of the rotations of $(f, g)^\mathsf{T}$ in bit reversed order. By [31, Lemma 6.9], the ith vector has an expected norm of $\sqrt{\frac{2n+1-i}{2n}} \cdot \|(f, g)\|$ for $i \in [n]$. Therefore, the expected squared norm of a point sampled uniformly from this fundamental domain will be

$$\frac{1}{12} \cdot \frac{(3n+1)n/2}{2n} \cdot 2n\sigma_{\mathsf{pk}}^2 = \frac{3n+1}{48} \cdot 2n\sigma_{\mathsf{pk}}^2 \le \frac{n}{12} \cdot 2n\sigma_{\mathsf{pk}}^2.$$

We observe that the squared norm of (F, G) is reduced by a factor of $4/3$ by line 6 of Algorithm 1. This shrinks the HAWK-512 public key size from 1027 bytes on average to 1006.

Sampling and pseudorandomness. We use the SHAKE256 extendable output function to seed a pseudorandom number generator (PRNG) based on CHACHA20 during sampling in KGen and Sign. As the Gaussian parameters used in the scheme are fixed, DGS can be performed efficiently with precomputed probability tables and this PRNG. KGen uses a sampler that requires 64 bits of randomness. For sampling in Sign we implement DGS for $\mathbb{Z} + \frac{1}{2}t$ with $t \in \{0, 1\}$ that is constant-time over input t and that uses 80 bits of randomness, sufficient for Sect. 4.1. This sampler uses a reverse cumulative distribution table scaled by a factor of 2^{78} similar to [32, Section 3.9.3]. Almost half of the time of Sign is spent on sampling.

Fast polynomial arithmetic. We want all computations to be performed in time $O(n \log n)$. Addition of two polynomials in $R = \mathbb{Z}[X]/(X^n + 1)$ is in $O(n)$, but naïve multiplication in R requires $O(n^2)$ integer multiplications. There are two ways to achieve $O(n \log n)$ via the specific structure of the used number ring. First, one can use the fast Fourier transform (FFT) to perform a multiplication in $O(n \log n)$. Alternatively, one can perform multiplications with the number theoretic transform NTT, which works with a (sufficiently large) prime modulus $p \equiv 1 \pmod{2n}$ and an element $\omega \in \mathbb{F}_p^\times$ of order $2n$. Then, as $\mathbb{F}_p^\times$ is a cyclic group of order $p - 1$ the NTT computes $f(\omega^i) \in R$ for all $i \in (\mathbb{Z}/2n\mathbb{Z})^\times$ in time $O(n \log n)$. When polynomials are transformed with the FFT or NTT, multiplication is coefficientwise. We only use NTT in the reference implementation. Multiplications in R could also be implemented with Karatsuba or Toom–Cook style multiplication. For certain applications such as masking this may have comparable performance for the given parameters. We leave the trade-off between masking techniques and alternative multiplication methods as future work.

For the NTT, multiplying two polynomials $a(X), b(X)$ requires p to be twice larger than the absolute value of any coefficient of $a(X)$, $b(X)$ or $a(X) \cdot b(X)$. This allows one to recover the correct result in $\mathbb{Z}$ via the inverse transformation. In HAWK-512 and HAWK-1024, $p = 12289$ is sufficient for signing. In the reference implementation we use $p = 2^{16} + 1$ since this Fermat prime allows a faster multiplication procedure than using Montgomery reduction with $p = 12289$. Signing using $p = 2^{16} + 1$ is 17% faster than using $p = 12289$. If one wants to reduce memory usage from 15 kB to 8 kB for HAWK-512, one can safely use the prime $p = 18433$ such that values fit in the 16 bits instead of 32.

By demanding coefficients of $\mathbf{s}$ and $\mathbf{Q}$ are within 6 standard deviations of their means, we can bound the integer $\|\mathbf{h} - 2\mathbf{s}\|_\mathbf{Q}$ by a product of two 31 bit primes. Hence, in the reference implementation of Vf, we can compute the norm of a signature by computing it with the NTT modulo these two primes.

The FFT in our implementation uses double precision floating-point numbers (`double`). When a processor has a floating-point unit and AVX2 support, this FFT is much faster than the NTT, but also requires more RAM.

Divisions and signature decompression. During decoding we require a polynomial division in $\mathbb{K}$ to recover $G = (1 + gF)/f$ and $q_{11} = (1 + q_{10}q_{01})/q_{00}$. Since these exact divisions have output in R, they can be computed with either the FFT or NTT, by performing a division coefficientwise in the transformed domain. In KGen, it should be checked that all NTT coefficients of f and q_{00} are nonzero.

The signature decompression requires a division with rounding to the closest integral point in R, which can be done efficiently with the FFT. One can do this with fixed-point arithmetic: it is highly unlikely that the numerical error yields an incorrect rounding. Especially, when we require that the quantity in (2) has to be in $(-0.49, 0.49)^n$, an absolute error of 0.01 is tolerated.

Failure checks. By default we catch invalid signatures before they are issued. The first failure check is line 5 of Algorithm 2. A decompression may also output an incorrect $s_0' \neq s_0$. To catch this we could check with FFT if (2) holds, and restart

Table 3. Performance of dynamic signing for FALCON and HAWK on same PC with same compilation flags as in Table 1.

	FALCON-512	HAWK-512	$\left(\frac{\text{FALCON}}{\text{HAWK}}\right)$	FALCON-1024	HAWK-1024	$\left(\frac{\text{FALCON}}{\text{HAWK}}\right)$
AVX2 Sign	320 µs	58 µs	×5.5	656 µs	114 µs	×5.8
Ref. Sign	5427 µs	168 µs	×32	11868 µs	343 µs	×35

if not. We remove this decompression check, because it is extremely unlikely that it restarts over the lifetime of a key (see Sect. 5.1).

Omitting the first check might be necessary when implementing HAWK as a circuit inside an FHE scheme, where `while` loops are impractical. This comes at the cost of a rare but non negligible probability (see Sect. 5.1) of an invalid signature, which might be mitigated by reparametrising the scheme.

In contrast to FALCON, we sample a new salt whenever Sign restarts as we do not see how reusing the same target can be made compatible with the security argument of [19]. Reusing the salt may lead to a statistical leak for FALCON, though it may be hard to exploit as failures in signing are rare. Nevertheless, we choose to be cautious when it comes to statistical leaks.

5.4   Performance

We report on the performance of our implementation of HAWK-512 and compare it to that of FALCON-512 in Table 1. HAWK was compiled with the `gcc` compiler (version 12.1.0) and compilation flag `-O2` (and `-mavx2` for AVX2), as `-O3` actually made the performance worse. The code for FALCON was taken from the 'Extra' folder in the Round 3 submission package https://falcon-sign.info/falcon-round3.zip, and was compiled with the same `gcc` but had compilation flags `-O3 -march=native`.

Memory usage. The reference implementation of HAWK-512 uses 24kB, 15kB and 18kB of RAM for KGen, Sign and Vf respectively, versus 16kB, 40kB and 4kB for FALCON-512 respectively. HAWK requires more RAM for KGen compared to FALCON to execute line 6 of Algorithm 1. RAM usage of FALCON's KeyGen is more than reported on https://falcon-sign.info as we took the RAM usage of the API functions, which takes sizes of decoded keys into account. The AVX2 optimised implementation of HAWK requires 27kB and 24kB for Sign and Vf respectively, prioritising speed over memory usage. For HAWK-1024 and FALCON-1024 memory usage roughly doubles.

Batched vs. dynamic signing. For consistency with the FALCON report [32], Table 1 reports signing speeds for batched usage, that is, after some precomputation expanding the secret key (called `expand_seckey`). If one needs to start from the secret key without expanding it, the performance of FALCON is significantly affected while the precomputation is much lighter for HAWK. The timings for dynamic signing are given in Table 3.

6 Module LIP Self Reduction

In this section we give a worst to average case reduction for the search module LIP problem, which underlies secret key recovery in HAWK. The average case distribution we give does not match Algorithm 1 exactly, as it does not include some conditions which may cause a restart. We also replace TowerSolvel, which 'completes' f and g into a basis with determinant one via F and G, with HermiteSolve. HermiteSolve fails if and only if it is impossible to complete a particular f, g. We show that the distribution of public keys output by Algorithm 1 after the above changes enjoys a worst to average case reduction. In Appendix A of the full version [16] we discuss the unaltered public key distribution of HAWK and show that the reduction is still applicable to HAWK.

Throughout we are concerned with asymptotic security, in contrast to the main body of the paper where we find efficient parameters that are supported by concrete cryptanalysis. In particular, the choice of σ_{pk} required to make the reduction efficient is larger than is chosen in our parametrisations for HAWK.

6.1 Module Lattice Isomorphism Problem

Here we introduce a generalisation of the Lattice Isomorphism Problem (LIP) to module lattices. Given the Hermitian inner product, the correct generalisation of orthonormal transformations for the module version is to that of unitary matrices. To avoid confusion with $\mathbf{U}$, which is often used for $\mathbf{U} \in \mathrm{GL}_\ell(\mathcal{O}_{\mathbb{K}})$ in lattice based cryptography, we will use $\mathbf{O} \in \mathrm{U}_\ell(\mathbb{K}_{\mathbb{R}}) = \{\mathbf{O} \in \mathbb{K}_{\mathbb{R}}^{\ell \times \ell} : \mathbf{O}^* \cdot \mathbf{O} = \mathbf{I}_\ell(\mathbb{K})\}$ for unitary matrices.

Definition 6 (Module Lattice Isomorphism Problem). *Given two $\mathcal{O}_{\mathbb{K}}$-modules $M, M' \subset \mathbb{K}^\ell$ find $\mathbf{O} \in \mathrm{U}_\ell(\mathbb{K}_{\mathbb{R}})$ such that $\mathbf{O} \cdot M = \{\mathbf{O} \cdot m : m \in M\} = M'$.*

Moving to Hermitian forms, the natural translation becomes equivalence under the action of $\mathrm{GL}_\ell(\mathcal{O}_{\mathbb{K}})$. However, for simplicity we restrict ourselves to equivalence under the action of $\mathrm{SL}_\ell(\mathcal{O}_{\mathbb{K}})$, and we denote the equivalence class by $[\mathbf{Q}]_{\mathrm{sl}} = \{\mathbf{U}^* \cdot \mathbf{Q} \cdot \mathbf{U} : \mathbf{U} \in \mathrm{SL}_2(\mathcal{O}_{\mathbb{K}})\}$. Throughout we implicitly restrict to $\mathbb{K}$ that are CM fields, e.g. all cyclotomic fields. Using (generalisations of) the Gentry–Szydlo algorithm [20,23,24], solving LIP under both actions is equivalent for such fields. We can now define the worst case module LIP variant. Note that our worst case and average case problems are *within* a particular class.

Definition 7 (Worst case smLIP). *Given $\mathbb{K}$ and $\mathbf{Q} \in \mathcal{H}_\ell^{>0}(\mathbb{K})$ an instance of $\mathsf{wc\text{-}smLIP}_{\mathbb{K},\ell}^{\mathbf{Q}}$, the worst case search module Lattice Isomorphism Problem, is given by $\mathbf{Q}$ and any $\mathbf{Q}' \in [\mathbf{Q}]_{\mathrm{sl}}$. A solution is $\mathbf{U} \in \mathrm{SL}_\ell(\mathcal{O}_{\mathbb{K}})$ such that $\mathbf{Q}' = \mathbf{U}^* \mathbf{Q} \mathbf{U}$.*

We now define an average case version of smLIP relevant to HAWK. It is less general than the worst case version in that we implicitly fix $\ell = 2$ and consider only power of two cyclotomics with conductor $m = 2^\kappa = 2n$ for $\mathbb{K}$. We define our average case distribution for any class $[\mathbf{Q}]_{\mathrm{sl}}$, but note that the average case distribution over $[\mathbf{I}_2(\mathbb{K})]_{sl}$ relates to our key generation in Algorithm 1. Finally, we define our average case distribution $\mathsf{AC}_\sigma([\mathbf{Q}]_{sl}, \mathbb{K})$ algorithmically, see Algorithm 6. This algorithm takes as input a particular form $\mathbf{Q}$ and a parameter σ that controls an internal discrete Gaussian sampling procedure, and outputs a sample from $[\mathbf{Q}]_{sl}$. One can think of $\sigma = \sigma_{pk}$ in the case of HAWK.

A subroutine of Algorithm 6 must 'complete' a vector $(f, g)^\mathsf{T} \in \mathcal{O}_\mathbb{K}^2$, if possible, into a basis $\mathbf{Y} \in \mathcal{O}_\mathbb{K}^{2 \times 2}$ with second column $(F, G)^\mathsf{T}$ and determinant one. To perform this operation we define a subroutine called HermiteSolve. This is an algorithm that outputs $\bot$ if and only if the particular vector cannot be completed, and otherwise outputs such a completion.

We also define a procedure Reduce with respect to the form $\mathbf{Q}$. This is a simpler, but less efficient, version of ffNP used in Algorithm 1. It serves two purposes; from a theoretical perspective it ensures that the distribution is well defined, i.e. that the distribution of the output form is independent of the input form being used to sample, and from a practical perspective it ensures the second column of the completed basis is relatively short.

Algorithm 4. HermiteSolve $(\mathbb{K}, f, g)$: completing f, g if possible.

Require: Conductor $m = 2^\kappa$ cyclotomic $\mathbb{K}$, $f, g \in \mathcal{O}_\mathbb{K}$
Ensure: Completion $F, G \in \mathcal{O}_\mathbb{K}$ such that $\det(\mathbf{Y}) = 1$ if it exists, else $\bot$
1: Let $\mathbf{X} = (\mathrm{rot}(f)\ \mathrm{rot}(g))$
2: Find $\mathbf{U} \in \mathrm{GL}_{2n}(\mathbb{Z})$ such that $\mathbf{X} \cdot \mathbf{U}$ is in Hermite Normal Form
3: **if** $\mathbf{X} \cdot \mathbf{U} \neq (\mathbf{I}_n(\mathbb{Z})\ \mathbf{0})$ **then return** $\bot$
4: Let $(\mathrm{vec}(G)\ -\mathrm{vec}(F))^\mathsf{T}$ be the first column of $\mathbf{U}$ **return** F, G

Algorithm 4 uses the Hermite Normal Form over the integers. If there exist F, G such that $fG - gF = 1$ in $\mathcal{O}_\mathbb{K}$, i.e. such that $\det(\mathbf{Y}) = 1$, then the ideal $(f, g) = \mathcal{O}_\mathbb{K}$, and this is equivalent to the Hermite Normal Form of $(\mathrm{rot}(f)\ \mathrm{rot}(g))$ being $(\mathbf{I}_n(\mathbb{Z})\ \mathbf{0}) \in \mathbb{Z}^{n \times 2n}$. One can then check that setting F, G as in Algorithm 4 satisfies $fG - gF = 1$. Given F, G we use Algorithm 5 to find a short, and canonical with respect to $\mathbf{Q}$, pair $F_\mathbf{Q}, G_\mathbf{Q}$ that also satisfy $fG_\mathbf{Q} - gF_\mathbf{Q} = 1$. Note that in Algorithm 5 we require a rounding function that partitions $\mathbb{R}$, i.e. $\lceil \cdot \rfloor : \mathbb{R} \to \mathbb{Z}$ that rounds $a + 1/2$ to $a + 1$ so the preimage of integer a is $[a - 1/2, a + 1/2)$. This rounding is applied coefficientwise.

Algorithm 5. Reduce $(\mathbf{Q}, f, g, F, G)$: reduction of F, G by $\mathbf{Q}$ and (f, g).

Require: Conductor $m = 2^\kappa$ cyclotomic $\mathbb{K}$, $f, g, F, G \in \mathcal{O}_\mathbb{K}$, $\mathbf{Q} \in \mathcal{H}_2^{>0}(\mathbb{K})$
Ensure: Canonical $F_\mathbf{Q}, G_\mathbf{Q}$ reduced with respect to $\mathbf{Q}$ and (f, g)
1: Let $\mathbf{x} = (f, g)^\mathsf{T}$, $\mathbf{y} = (F, G)^\mathsf{T}$, and $\nu = \left\lceil \frac{\mathbf{x}^* \cdot \mathbf{Q} \cdot \mathbf{y}}{\mathbf{x}^* \cdot \mathbf{Q} \cdot \mathbf{x}} \right\rfloor \in \mathcal{O}_\mathbb{K}$
2: Let $F_\mathbf{Q} = F - \nu f$, $G_\mathbf{Q} = G - \nu g$ **return** $F_\mathbf{Q}, G_\mathbf{Q}$

Algorithm 6. $\mathsf{ac}_\sigma(\mathbf{Q}, \mathbb{K})$: sampling from $\mathsf{AC}_\sigma([\mathbf{Q}]_{\mathrm{sl}}, \mathbb{K})$.

Require: Conductor $m = 2^\kappa$ cyclotomic $\mathbb{K}$, $\mathbf{Q} \in \mathcal{H}_2^{>0}(\mathbb{K})$
Ensure: $\mathbf{R} \in [\mathbf{Q}]_{\mathrm{sl}}$ and $\mathbf{Y} \in \mathrm{SL}_2(\mathcal{O}_\mathbb{K})$ such that $\mathbf{R} = \mathbf{Y}^* \cdot \mathbf{Q} \cdot \mathbf{Y}$
1: Parse $\mathbf{y}_1 \leftarrow D_{\mathbf{Q},\sigma}$ as $\mathbf{y}_1 = (f, g)^\mathsf{T} \in \mathcal{O}_\mathbb{K}^2$
2: **if** HermiteSolve($\mathbb{K}, f, g$) returns $\perp$ **then**
3:     **restart**
4: **else** $F, G \leftarrow$ HermiteSolve($\mathbb{K}, f, g$)
5: Let $\mathbf{y}_2 = (F_\mathbf{Q} \; G_\mathbf{Q})^\mathsf{T}$ for $F_\mathbf{Q}, G_\mathbf{Q} \leftarrow$ Reduce($\mathbf{Q}, f, g, F, G$)
6: Let $\mathbf{Y} = (\mathbf{y}_1 \; \mathbf{y}_2)$ and $\mathbf{R} = \mathbf{Y}^* \cdot \mathbf{Q} \cdot \mathbf{Y}$ **return** $(\mathbf{R}, \mathbf{Y})$

The following lemma ensures that a sample $\mathbf{R} \in [\mathbf{Q}]_{\mathrm{sl}}$ output by Algorithm 6 only depends on the class $[\mathbf{Q}]_{\mathrm{sl}}$, and not on the input representative $\mathbf{Q}$. As a result the distribution $\mathsf{AC}_\sigma([\mathbf{Q}]_{\mathrm{sl}}, \mathbb{K})$ is well defined. We can then define our average case module LIP.

Lemma 4. *For any power of two cyclotomic* $\mathbb{K}$, $\mathbf{Q} \in \mathcal{H}_2^{>0}(\mathbb{K})$, $\mathbf{Q}' \in [\mathbf{Q}]_{\mathrm{sl}}$ *and* $\sigma > 0$ *the distributions of* $(\mathbf{R}, \cdot) \leftarrow \mathsf{ac}_\sigma(\mathbf{Q}, \mathbb{K})$ *and* $(\mathbf{R}', \cdot) \leftarrow \mathsf{ac}_\sigma(\mathbf{Q}', \mathbb{K})$ *are equal.*

Proof. For $\mathbf{Q}' \in [\mathbf{Q}]_{\mathrm{sl}}$ there exists a $\mathbf{U} \in \mathrm{SL}_2(\mathcal{O}_\mathbb{K})$ such that $\mathbf{Q}' = \mathbf{U}^* \cdot \mathbf{Q} \cdot \mathbf{U}$. It is sufficient to show that for any $\mathbf{Y}$ created during $\mathsf{ac}_\sigma(\mathbf{Q}, \mathbb{K})$, $\mathbf{Y}' = \mathbf{U}^{-1} \cdot \mathbf{Y}$ is created within $\mathsf{ac}_\sigma(\mathbf{Q}', \mathbb{K})$ with the same probability. Having shown this, since $\mathbf{Y}^* \cdot \mathbf{Q} \cdot \mathbf{Y} = (\mathbf{Y}')^* \cdot \mathbf{Q}' \cdot \mathbf{Y}'$, the two distributions are equal. Firstly, letting $\mathbf{y}_1' = \mathbf{U}^{-1} \cdot \mathbf{y}_1$ we see that $\rho_{\mathbf{Q}',\sigma}(\mathbf{y}_1') = \rho_{\mathbf{Q},\sigma}(\mathbf{y}_1)$. Given that the normalisation constant for a given σ will be equal over all forms in $[\mathbf{Q}]$, the probability of sampling $\mathbf{y}_1' \leftarrow D_{\mathbf{Q}',\sigma}$ is equal to the probability of sampling $\mathbf{y}_1 \leftarrow D_{\mathbf{Q},\sigma}$.

We must now show that, after completing $\mathbf{y}_1'$ to $\mathbf{y}_2'$ via Algorithm 4 and then reducing it with respect to $\mathbf{y}_1'$ and $\mathbf{Q}'$ using Algorithm 5, we have $\mathbf{y}_2' = \mathbf{U}^{-1} \cdot \mathbf{y}_2$. This is precisely the statement that $\mathbf{Y}' = \mathbf{U}^{-1} \cdot \mathbf{Y}$. Note that Algorithm 4 finds a solution if one exists. Since $\mathbf{U}^{-1} \cdot \mathbf{y}_2$ is such a solution, Algorithm 4 succeeds.

We parse $\mathbf{y}_1' = (f' \; g')^\mathsf{T}$ and $\mathbf{y}_2' = (F' \; G')^\mathsf{T}$ so that $f'G' - g'F' = 1$. For fixed (f', g'), any $\tilde{F}, \tilde{G}$ such that $f'\tilde{G} - g'\tilde{F} = 1$ are of the form $\tilde{F} = F' + \lambda \cdot f'$, $\tilde{G} = G' + \lambda \cdot g'$ for some $\lambda \in \mathcal{O}_\mathbb{K}$. For example, one has

$$f' \cdot (G' - \tilde{G}) = g' \cdot (F' - \tilde{F}) \Rightarrow G' - \tilde{G} = g' \cdot \left(G' \cdot (F' - \tilde{F}) - F' \cdot (G' - \tilde{G}) \right)$$

$$\Rightarrow \lambda = -\left(G' \cdot (F' - \tilde{F}) - F' \cdot (G' - \tilde{G}) \right),$$

with the same λ for the $F' - \tilde{F}$ case. If we let $\tilde{\mathbf{y}} = \mathbf{U}^{-1} \cdot \mathbf{y}_2$ it is therefore enough to show that $\tilde{\mathbf{y}}$ is the unique reduced completion of $\mathbf{y}_1'$ into $\mathbf{Y}' \in \mathrm{SL}_2(\mathcal{O}_\mathbb{K})$, i.e. $\mathbf{y}_2'$. We have

$$\left\lceil \frac{\mathbf{y}_1'^* \cdot \mathbf{Q}' \cdot \tilde{\mathbf{y}}}{\mathbf{y}_1'^* \cdot \mathbf{Q}' \cdot \mathbf{y}_1'} \right\rfloor = \left\lceil \frac{(\mathbf{U}^{-1} \cdot \mathbf{y}_1)^* \cdot \mathbf{Q}' \cdot (\mathbf{U}^{-1} \cdot \mathbf{y}_2)}{(\mathbf{U}^{-1} \cdot \mathbf{y}_1)^* \cdot \mathbf{Q}' \cdot (\mathbf{U}^{-1} \cdot \mathbf{y}_1)} \right\rfloor = \left\lceil \frac{\mathbf{y}_1^* \cdot \mathbf{Q} \cdot \mathbf{y}_2}{\mathbf{y}_1^* \cdot \mathbf{Q} \cdot \mathbf{y}_1} \right\rfloor = 0,$$

since $\mathbf{y}_2$ is reduced with respect to $\mathbf{y}_1$ and $\mathbf{Q}$ by the construction of $\mathbf{Y}$ in $\mathsf{ac}_s(\mathbf{Q}, \mathbb{K})$. Therefore $\tilde{\mathbf{y}}$ is reduced with respect to $\mathbf{y}_1'$ and $\mathbf{Q}'$.

Definition 8 (Average case smLIP). *Given some power of two cyclotomic $\mathbb{K}$ and $\mathbf{Q} \in \mathcal{H}_2^{>0}(\mathbb{K})$ an instance of $\mathsf{ac-smLIP}^{\mathbf{Q}}_{\mathbb{K},\sigma}$, the average case search module Lattice Isomorphism Problem, is given by $\mathbf{Q}$ and an element $\mathbf{Q}' \in [\mathbf{Q}]_{\mathrm{sl}}$ sampled from $\mathsf{AC}_\sigma([\mathbf{Q}]_{\mathrm{sl}}, \mathbb{K})$. A solution is $\mathbf{U} \in \mathrm{SL}_2(\mathcal{O}_{\mathbb{K}})$ such that $\mathbf{Q}' = \mathbf{U}^* \cdot \mathbf{Q} \cdot \mathbf{U}$.*

We expect the problem to become harder as the parameter σ increases. In fact, following [15], if σ is large enough we have equivalence with the corresponding worst case problem, assuming that HermiteSolve does not fail too often.

Lemma 5 (Worst case to average case). *Given a machine that can solve $\mathsf{ac-smLIP}^{\mathbf{Q}}_{\mathbb{K},\sigma}$ in time T with probability $\varepsilon > 0$, for $\sigma \geq 2^{\Theta(n)} \cdot \lambda_{2n}([\mathrm{rot}(\mathbf{Q})])$, one may solve $\mathsf{wc-smLIP}^{\mathbf{Q}}_{\mathbb{K},\ell}$ in expected time $T + \mathbb{E}_{samples} \cdot \mathrm{poly}(n, \log \sigma)$ with probability ε. Here $\mathbb{E}_{samples}(n, \sigma) \geq 1$ is the expected number of times $(f\ g)^{\mathsf{T}}$ is (re)sampled in Algorithm 6.*

Proof. As input we receive $\mathbf{Q} \in \mathcal{H}_2^{>0}(\mathbb{K})$ and some $\mathbf{Q}' \in [\mathbf{Q}]_{\mathrm{sl}}$. By first LLL reducing $\mathbf{Q}$ (by considering $\mathrm{rot}(\mathbf{Q}) \in \mathbb{Q}^{2n \times 2n}$) we can sample efficiently from $D_{\mathbf{Q},\sigma}$ via Lemma 1, and thus we can sample $(\mathbf{Q}'', \mathbf{U}'') \leftarrow \mathsf{ac}_\sigma(\mathbf{Q}, \mathbb{K})$ in time $\mathbb{E}_{samples} \cdot \mathrm{poly}(n, \sigma)$ by Algorithm 6. The sample $\mathbf{Q}''$ is distributed as $\mathsf{AC}_\sigma([\mathbf{Q}]_{\mathrm{sl}}, \mathbb{K})$, and we have $\mathbf{Q}'' = \mathbf{U}''^* \mathbf{Q} \mathbf{U}''$. We now have an average case instance between $\mathbf{Q}'$ and $\mathbf{Q}''$, which the machine can solve in time T with probability ε. On success we obtain some $\mathbf{U}'$ such that $\mathbf{Q}'' = \mathbf{U}'^* \mathbf{Q}' \mathbf{U}'$, and $\mathbf{U} = \mathbf{U}''(\mathbf{U}')^{-1}$ gives a solution to the worst case instance, i.e. $\mathbf{Q}' = \mathbf{U}^* \mathbf{Q} \mathbf{U}$.

Following the same argument as [15, Lem 3.10] we may reduce σ in the reduction at the expense of an additive loss from the cost of stronger lattice reduction. In Appendix A of the full version [16] we give a heuristic explanation and matching experimental evidence for why HermiteSolve fails with probability around $\frac{1}{4}$, which gives $\mathbb{E}_{samples} \approx \frac{4}{3}$, and thus the reduction above is in fact efficient.

Acknowledgments. The authors thank Nick Genise, Shane Gibbons, Thomas Prest, Noah Stephens-Davidowitz and the anonymous reviewers for helpful discussions and useful feedback. W. van Woerden was supported by the ERC-ADG-ALGSTRONGCRYPTO project (no. 740972). The research of L. Ducas and E.W. Postlethwaite was supported by the European Union's H2020 Programme under PROMETHEUS project (grant 780701). L. Ducas and L.N. Pulles were supported by the ERC-StG-ARTICULATE project (no. 947821).

References

1. Agrawal, S., Kirshanova, E., Stehle, D., Yadav, A.: Practical, round-optimal lattice-based blind signatures. Cryptology ePrint Archive, Paper 2021/1565 (2021). https://eprint.iacr.org/2021/1565
2. Agrawal, S., Stehle, D., Yadav, A.: Round-optimal lattice-based threshold signatures, revisited. Cryptology ePrint Archive, Paper 2022/634 (2022). https://eprint.iacr.org/2022/634
3. Albrecht, M.R., Ducas, L.: Lattice Attacks on NTRU and LWE: A History of Refinements, pp. 15–40. London Mathematical Society Lecture Note Series, Cambridge University Press (2021). https://doi.org/10.1017/9781108854207.004

4. Babai, L.: On Lovász' lattice reduction and the nearest lattice point problem. Combinatorica **6**(1), 1–13 (1986)
5. Bai, S., Stehlé, D., Wen, W.: Measuring, simulating and exploiting the head concavity phenomenon in BKZ. In: Peyrin, T., Galbraith, S. (eds.) ASIACRYPT 2018. LNCS, vol. 11272, pp. 369–404. Springer, Cham (2018). https://doi.org/10.1007/978-3-030-03326-2_13
6. Banaszczyk, W.: New bounds in some transference theorems in the geometry of numbers. Math. Ann. **296**(1), 625–635 (1993)
7. Bennett, H., Ganju, A., Peetathawatchai, P., Stephens-Davidowitz, N.: Just how hard are rotations of $\mathbb{Z}^n$? algorithms and cryptography with the simplest lattice. Cryptology ePrint Archive, Report 2021/1548 (2021). https://eprint.iacr.org/2021/1548
8. Brakerski, Z., Langlois, A., Peikert, C., Regev, O., Stehlé, D.: Classical hardness of learning with errors. In: Boneh, D., Roughgarden, T., Feigenbaum, J., (eds.) 45th ACM STOC, pp. 575–584. ACM Press (2013). https://doi.org/10.1145/2488608.2488680
9. Chen, Y., Nguyen, P.Q.: BKZ 2.0: better lattice security estimates. In: Lee, D.H., Wang, X. (eds.) ASIACRYPT 2011. LNCS, vol. 7073, pp. 1–20. Springer, Heidelberg (2011). https://doi.org/10.1007/978-3-642-25385-0_1
10. Dachman-Soled, D., Ducas, L., Gong, H., Rossi, M.: LWE with side information: attacks and concrete security estimation. In: Micciancio, D., Ristenpart, T. (eds.) CRYPTO 2020. LNCS, vol. 12171, pp. 329–358. Springer, Cham (2020). https://doi.org/10.1007/978-3-030-56880-1_12
11. Ducas, L., Durmus, A., Lepoint, T., Lyubashevsky, V.: Lattice signatures and bimodal Gaussians. In: Canetti, R., Garay, J.A. (eds.) CRYPTO 2013. LNCS, vol. 8042, pp. 40–56. Springer, Heidelberg (2013). https://doi.org/10.1007/978-3-642-40041-4_3
12. Ducas, L., Nguyen, P.Q.: Faster Gaussian lattice sampling using lazy floating-point arithmetic. In: Wang, X., Sako, K. (eds.) ASIACRYPT 2012. LNCS, vol. 7658, pp. 415–432. Springer, Heidelberg (2012). https://doi.org/10.1007/978-3-642-34961-4_26
13. Ducas, L., Nguyen, P.Q.: Learning a zonotope and more: cryptanalysis of NTRUSign countermeasures. In: Wang, X., Sako, K. (eds.) ASIACRYPT 2012. LNCS, vol. 7658, pp. 433–450. Springer, Heidelberg (2012). https://doi.org/10.1007/978-3-642-34961-4_27
14. Ducas, L., Prest, T.: Fast Fourier orthogonalization. In: Proceedings of the ACM on International Symposium on Symbolic and Algebraic Computation, ISSAC 2016, Association for Computing Machinery, New York, NY, USA, pp. 191–198 (2016). https://doi.org/10.1145/2930889.2930923
15. Ducas, L., van Woerden, W.P.J.: On the lattice isomorphism problem, quadratic forms, remarkable lattices, and cryptography. In: Dunkelman, O., Dziembowski, S. (eds.) EUROCRYPT 2022, Part III. LNCS, vol. 13277, pp. 643–673. Springer, Heidelberg (2022). https://doi.org/10.1007/978-3-031-07082-2_23
16. Ducas, L., Postlethwaite, E.W., Pulles, L.N., van Woerden, W.: Hawk: Module LIP makes lattice signatures fast, compact and simple. Cryptology ePrint Archive, Paper 2022/1155 (2022). https://eprint.iacr.org/2022/1155
17. Espitau, T., et al.: Mitaka: a simpler, parallelizable, maskable variant of falcon. In: Dunkelman, O., Dziembowski, S. (eds.) EUROCRYPT 2022, Part III. LNCS, vol. 13277, pp. 222–253. Springer, Heidelberg (2022). https://doi.org/10.1007/978-3-031-07082-2_9

18. Genise, N., Micciancio, D.: Faster Gaussian sampling for trapdoor lattices with arbitrary modulus. In: Nielsen, J.B., Rijmen, V. (eds.) EUROCRYPT 2018. LNCS, vol. 10820, pp. 174–203. Springer, Cham (2018). https://doi.org/10.1007/978-3-319-78381-9_7

19. Gentry, C., Peikert, C., Vaikuntanathan, V.: Trapdoors for hard lattices and new cryptographic constructions. In: Ladner, R.E., Dwork, C., (eds.) 40th ACM STOC, pp. 197–206. ACM Press (2008). https://doi.org/10.1145/1374376.1374407

20. Gentry, C., Szydlo, M.: Cryptanalysis of the revised NTRU signature scheme. In: Knudsen, L.R. (ed.) EUROCRYPT 2002. LNCS, vol. 2332, pp. 299–320. Springer, Heidelberg (2002). https://doi.org/10.1007/3-540-46035-7_20

21. Golomb, S.: Run-length encodings (corresp.). IEEE Trans. Inf. Theory **12**(3), 399–401 (1966). https://doi.org/10.1109/TIT.1966.1053907

22. Hoffstein, J., Howgrave-Graham, N., Pipher, J., Silverman, J.H., Whyte, W.: NTRUSign: digital signatures using the NTRU lattice. In: Joye, M. (ed.) CT-RSA 2003. LNCS, vol. 2612, pp. 122–140. Springer, Heidelberg (2003). https://doi.org/10.1007/3-540-36563-X_9

23. Kirchner, P.: Algorithms on ideal over complex multiplication order. Cryptology ePrint Archive, Report 2016/220 (2016). https://eprint.iacr.org/2016/220

24. Lenstra, H.W., Silverberg, A.: Lattices with symmetry. J. Cryptol. **30**(3), 760–804 (2016). https://doi.org/10.1007/s00145-016-9235-7

25. Lyubashevsky, V., Peikert, C., Regev, O.: On ideal lattices and learning with errors over rings. In: Gilbert, H. (ed.) EUROCRYPT 2010. LNCS, vol. 6110, pp. 1–23. Springer, Heidelberg (2010). https://doi.org/10.1007/978-3-642-13190-5_1

26. Micciancio, D., Regev, O.: Worst-case to average-case reductions based on Gaussian measures. SIAM J. Comput. **37**(1), 267–302 (2007). https://doi.org/10.1137/S0097539705447360

27. Nguyen, P.Q., Regev, O.: Learning a parallelepiped: cryptanalysis of GGH and NTRU signatures. J. Cryptol. **22**(2), 139–160 (2008). https://doi.org/10.1007/s00145-008-9031-0

28. Peikert, C.: An efficient and parallel Gaussian sampler for lattices. In: Rabin, T. (ed.) CRYPTO 2010. LNCS, vol. 6223, pp. 80–97. Springer, Heidelberg (2010). https://doi.org/10.1007/978-3-642-14623-7_5

29. Pornin, T., Prest, T.: More efficient algorithms for the NTRU key generation using the field norm. In: Lin, D., Sako, K. (eds.) PKC 2019. LNCS, vol. 11443, pp. 504–533. Springer, Cham (2019). https://doi.org/10.1007/978-3-030-17259-6_17

30. Postlethwaite, E.W., Virdia, F.: On the success probability of solving unique SVP via BKZ. In: Garay, J.A. (ed.) PKC 2021. LNCS, vol. 12710, pp. 68–98. Springer, Cham (2021). https://doi.org/10.1007/978-3-030-75245-3_4

31. Prest, T.: Gaussian sampling in lattice-based cryptography. Ph.D. thesis, Ecole normale supérieure-ENS PARIS (2015)

32. Prest, T., et al.: FALCON. Technical report, National Institute of Standards and Technology (2020). https://csrc.nist.gov/projects/post-quantum-cryptography/round-3-submissions

33. Szydlo, M.: Hypercubic lattice reduction and analysis of GGH and NTRU signatures. In: Biham, E. (ed.) EUROCRYPT 2003. LNCS, vol. 2656, pp. 433–448. Springer, Heidelberg (2003). https://doi.org/10.1007/3-540-39200-9_27

34. T.F. development team: fpylll, a Python wraper for the fplll lattice reduction library, Version: 0.5.6 (2021). https://github.com/fplll/fpylll

BLOOM: Bimodal Lattice
One-out-of-Many Proofs and Applications

Vadim Lyubashevsky[1] and Ngoc Khanh Nguyen[2(✉)] [iD]

[1] IBM Research Europe, Ruschlikon, Switzerland
vad@zurich.ibm.com
[2] EPFL, Lausanne, Switzerland
nknguyen007@gmail.com

Abstract. We give a construction of an efficient one-out-of-many proof system, in which a prover shows that he knows the pre-image for one element in a set, based on the hardness of lattice problems. The construction employs the recent zero-knowledge framework of Lyubashevsky et al. (Crypto 2022) together with an improved, over prior lattice-based one-out-of-many proofs, recursive procedure, and a novel rejection sampling proof that allows to use the efficient bimodal rejection sampling throughout the protocol.

Using these new primitives and techniques, we give instantiations of the most compact lattice-based ring and group signatures schemes. The improvement in signature sizes over prior works ranges between 25% and 2X. Perhaps of even more significance, the size of the user public keys, which need to be stored somewhere publicly accessible in order for ring signatures to be meaningful, is reduced by factors ranging from 7X to 15X. In what could be of independent interest, we also provide noticeably improved proofs for integer relations which, together with one-out-of-many proofs are key components of confidential payment systems.

Keywords: Lattices · Zero-knowledge · One-out-of-many proofs · Ring signatures

1 Introduction

Zero-knowledge proofs are the cornerstone of privacy-enabling cryptography and the ones based on lattice assumptions appear to currently be the most practical potentially quantum-resistant variants. The fundamental hard problem upon which lattice cryptography is based on is finding a vector $\vec{s}$ with a small norm satisfying $A\vec{s} = \vec{t} \bmod p$. Rapid recent progress in the area resulted in the proof size for proving pre-image knowledge in this basic equation to be reduced from being on the order of megabytes [LNSW13] to as short as a dozen kilobytes [YAZ+19, ESLL19, BLS19, ALS20, ENS20, LNS21a, LNP22].

A very useful extension of proving knowledge of a pre-image is proving knowledge of a pre-image for one element in a set. That is, given a set $\{\vec{t}_1, \ldots, \vec{t}_m\}$, one

© International Association for Cryptologic Research 2022
S. Agrawal and D. Lin (Eds.): ASIACRYPT 2022, LNCS 13794, pp. 95–125, 2022.
https://doi.org/10.1007/978-3-031-22972-5_4

would like to prove knowledge of a short vector $\vec{s}$ such that $A\vec{s} = t_i \bmod p$ without leaking any information about the $\vec{s}$ or the i. This type of a proof is related to concepts such as set membership proofs and one-out-of-many proofs [GK15].[1] These proofs have applications to ring signatures, group signatures, confidential transactions, anonymous credentials, and various other privacy-enhancing cryptographic primitives.

In this work, we improve upon existing lattice-based one-out-of-many proofs and, based on this new building block, construct the most efficient quantum-safe ring and group signatures. Our improvement uses the high-level idea from the recursive algorithm of [LNS21b], but using a different and simpler recursive step which is made possible in part by being able to prove the base case using the recent framework for zero-knowledge proofs [LNP22]. We also give a general improvement to the rejection sampling step present in most lattice-based zero-knowledge proofs. Specifically, we show that when using the zero-knowledge framework from [LNP22], which gives the most efficient linear-size proofs for quadratic relations, one can use the more efficient bimodal rejection sampling procedure [DDLL13] everywhere. In some cases, this requires an extra short commitment, but in the case of the one-out-of-many proof given in the current work, using the more efficient rejection sampling step comes completely for free and noticeably reduces the proof size. We additionally show how to apply this bimodal rejection technique, together with the framework from [LNP22], to create more efficient proofs for integer relations such as addition and multiplication. Like one-out-of-many proofs, proving integer relations is a component of confidential transaction systems, and we believe that our improved tools can be used to make such systems (e.g. [LNS21b, ESZ21]) more efficient.

1.1   Results and Techniques

One-out-of-Many Proofs. The general equation for a lattice-based one-out-of-m proof can be written as

$$T\vec{v} = A\vec{s} \bmod p \tag{1}$$

where $\vec{v}$ is an m-dimensional unit vector (i.e. a vector consisting of one 1 and the rest zeroes) and $\vec{s}$ is a pre-image to the column in T chosen by the unit vector. For our end application, we would like to prove that $\vec{s}$ has a small norm, but we will give a proof system for slightly more general statements, as the generality is useful in the recursive nature of the protocol. Given a commitment to a vector $\vec{v}$ and $\vec{s}$, we would like to be able to prove that $\vec{v}$ and $\vec{s}$ satisfy (1), $\vec{v}$ is a unit vector, and $\vec{s}$ additionally satisfies some arbitrary quadratic relations $f_i(\vec{s}) = 0$.[2] In applications to group and ring signatures, the dimension of $\vec{s}$ is quite small,

---

[1] The original formal definition of a one-out-of-many proof from [GK15] is more restricted in that $A\vec{s}$ is a commitment to 0 rather than just an evaluation of a one-way function on $\vec{s}$. But we do not need to restrict to this definition in this work.

[2] Being able to prove quadratic relations, of course also allows one to prove that the ℓ_2-norm of $\vec{s}$ is smaller than some bound.

and so it is enough to only strive for proofs that are linear in the input size. Note that to keep the size of the proof linear, we still need it to be logarithmic in m since a unit vector of dimension m only has entropy $\log m$.

The proof of knowledge of (1) follows the commit-and-prove paradigm. That is, we commit to the secrets $\vec{v}$ and $\vec{s}$ and then prove that the committed messages satisfy the requisite relations. Keeping the proof linear in $\log m$ is the main technical challenge in building a one-out-of-many proof since one can't simply commit and open the naive m-dimensional representation of $\vec{v}$. Instead, one can write the unit vector $\vec{v}$ as a tensor product of a logarithmic number of smaller dimensional unit vectors, commit to these unit vectors, and then proceed to recursively prove the relation.

We begin with the base case – proving the knowledge of a unit vector $\vec{v} \in \{0,1\}^d$ (we can think of d being a constant with respect to m) and a vector $\vec{s}$ satisfying $T\vec{v} = A\vec{s}$ where $f_i(\vec{s}) = 0$ for arbitrary quadratic functions f_i. The most efficient known proof for this statement directly follows from the recent framework of [LNP22] where one commits to the vector $\vec{v}$ and $\vec{s}$ using the "ABDLOP" commitment scheme defined in that work (it is a combination of the Ajtai [Ajt96] and BDLOP [BDL+18] commitments – see (11) and Sect. 2.6) and then proves that the committed values satisfy

$$T\vec{v} = A\vec{s} \bmod p, \tag{2}$$

and $f_i(\vec{s}) = 0$, and $\|\vec{v}\| = 1$.[3]

Now suppose, by the inductive hypothesis, that having a commitment to $\vec{s}'$ and (some representation of) $\vec{v}' \in \{0,1\}^m$, we are able to prove that they satisfy the linear relation

$$T'\vec{v}' = A'\vec{s}' \bmod p \tag{3}$$

as well as the quadratic relations $f_i(\vec{s}') = 0$ and that $\vec{v}'$ is a unit vector. We will now show how to prove the relation in (3) for an arbitrary unit vector in $\{0,1\}^{\mathfrak{d} \cdot m}$. First, observe that any unit vector in $\{0,1\}^{\mathfrak{d} \cdot m}$ can be written as $\vec{v} \otimes \vec{v}' \in \{0,1\}^{\mathfrak{d} \cdot m}$, where $\vec{v}$ and $\vec{v}'$ are unit vectors in $\{0,1\}^{\mathfrak{d}}$ and $\{0,1\}^m$, respectively. So by writing an arbitrary $\mathfrak{d} \cdot m$-dimensional unit vector as $\vec{v} \otimes \vec{v}'$, we would like to prove (when having a commitment to $\vec{v}, \vec{v}', \vec{s}$) that

$$T(\vec{v} \otimes \vec{v}') = A\vec{s} \bmod p, \tag{4}$$

that $f_i(\vec{s}) = 0$, and that $\vec{v}, \vec{v}'$ are unit vectors. To prove (4), we will prove that

$$\langle \vec{\varphi}_i, T(\vec{v} \otimes \vec{v}') - A\vec{s} \rangle = \vec{0} \bmod p \tag{5}$$

where $\vec{\varphi}_i$ for $i = 1, \ldots, \mathfrak{l}$ are randomly-chosen challenge vectors in $\mathbb{Z}_p^n$. Proving one such equation for a randomly-chosen $\vec{\varphi}_i$ would result in the proof having soundness error p^{-1}, and so we would like to prove $\mathfrak{l}$ such equations in order to achieve the desired soundness error of $p^{-\mathfrak{l}}$.

---

[3] This only proves that $\vec{v}$ is either a unit vector or a negative unit vector. But this is fine because proving knowledge of $\vec{v}, \vec{s}$ satisfying $\pm T\vec{v} = A\vec{s}$ is equivalent to (1).

To prove (5) for one of $\mathfrak{l}$ different $\vec{\varphi}_i$, we decompose the matrix T as $T = [T_1 \ \ldots \ T_{\mathfrak{d}}]$ where $T_i \in \mathbb{Z}_p^{n \times m}$, and observe that by algebraic manipulation, we can rewrite

$$\langle \vec{\varphi}_i, T(\vec{v} \otimes \vec{v}') - A\vec{s} \rangle = \langle \vec{v}, \vec{w}_i \rangle - \vec{\varphi}_i^T A\vec{s} \bmod p, \tag{6}$$

where

$$\vec{w}_i = \begin{bmatrix} \vec{\varphi}_i^T T_1 \\ \cdots \\ \vec{\varphi}_i^T T_{\mathfrak{d}} \end{bmatrix} \cdot \vec{v}' \in \mathbb{Z}_p^{\mathfrak{d}}. \tag{7}$$

Each of the $\mathfrak{l}$ different $\vec{\varphi}_i$ leads to an equation of the above form and the prover thus commits to $\vec{w}_1, \ldots, \vec{w}_{\mathfrak{l}}$ and then using the inductive hypothesis from (3), he can show that

$$\begin{bmatrix} \vec{w}_1 \\ \cdots \\ \vec{w}_{\mathfrak{l}} \end{bmatrix} = T' \cdot \vec{v}' \bmod p \tag{8}$$

where the matrix T' is defined as

$$T' = \begin{bmatrix} \vec{\varphi}_1^T T_1 \\ \cdots \\ \vec{\varphi}_1^T T_{\mathfrak{d}} \\ \cdots \\ \vec{\varphi}_{\mathfrak{l}}^T T_1 \\ \cdots \\ \vec{\varphi}_{\mathfrak{l}}^T T_{\mathfrak{d}} \end{bmatrix} \in \mathbb{Z}_p^{\mathfrak{l} \cdot \mathfrak{d} \times m}. \tag{9}$$

The inductive hypothesis also allows him to prove that $f_i(\vec{s}) = 0$ and additionally that (the quadratic functions) $\langle \vec{v}, \vec{w}_i \rangle - \vec{\varphi}_i^T A\vec{s} = 0$. To see that the inductive hypothesis is applicable to proving these statements, we define the vector $\vec{s}'$ in (3) as

$$\vec{s}' = \begin{bmatrix} \vec{w} \\ \vec{s} \\ \vec{v} \end{bmatrix}, \text{ where } \vec{w} = \begin{bmatrix} \vec{w}_1 \\ \cdots \\ \vec{w}_{\mathfrak{l}} \end{bmatrix} \tag{10}$$

and the matrix A' as $[\ I \mid 0 \mid 0\ ]$, and thus $T'\vec{v}' = A'\vec{s}' = \vec{w}$. Since we assumed to have commitments to $\vec{v}'$ and we created commitments to all parts of $\vec{s}'$, we can prove (8) and the aforementioned quadratic relations involving $\vec{s}, \vec{w}$, and $\vec{v}$. The main point is that by additionally committing to $\vec{w}$ and $\vec{v}$, we are able to use the inductive hypothesis to prove relations where the unit vector is $\mathfrak{d}$ times longer.

The commitment scheme used in [LNP22] allows to naturally commit to polynomials in the ring $\mathcal{R}_p = \mathbb{Z}_p[X]/(X^d + 1)$ where, for optimal efficiency, $d = 64$ or 128. For efficiency of the protocol, we would then like to pack the $\mathfrak{l}$ commitments to $\vec{w}_i \in \mathbb{Z}_p^{\mathfrak{d}}$ into just one vector $\mathbb{Z}_p^d$, which can then be represented by one polynomial in $\mathcal{R}_p$. We can do this in the trivial way as long as $\mathfrak{d} \cdot \mathfrak{l} \leqslant d$. Then to compute inner products $\langle \vec{v}, \vec{w}_i \rangle$, we simply put the vector $\vec{v} \in \{0,1\}^{\mathfrak{d}}$ into a vector $\mathbb{Z}_p^d$ that contains $\vec{v}$ at the top and has the rest of its coefficients set to 0. Then $\langle \vec{v}, \vec{w}_i \rangle$ is the inner product of an appropriate shift of the vector containing the $\vec{v}$ and the vector containing the $\vec{w}_i$. A downward shift of a committed vector in $\mathbb{Z}_p^d$ whose bottom coefficients are all 0 is simply a multiplication of the commitment by the polynomial X in $\mathcal{R}_p$, which can be performed by the verifier.

Thus proving $T \cdot (\vec{v} \otimes \vec{v}') = A\vec{s}$, where $\vec{v} \otimes \vec{v}'$ is a $\mathfrak{d} \cdot m$ dimensional unit vector, requires the commitments needed for proving (3), an additional commitment to $\vec{v}$, and one more commitment to the $\vec{w}_i$. Since the base case requires one commitment to $\vec{v}$ (and a commitment to $\vec{s}$), the total number of commitments to elements in $\mathcal{R}_p$ for proving (1) when $\vec{v}$ is an $m = \mathfrak{d}^k \cdot d$-dimensional unit vector is $2k + 1$ (and a commitments to $\vec{s}$), which is logarithmic in m and linear in the dimension of $\vec{s}$. In particular, we write the unit vector $\vec{v}$ in (1) as $\vec{v}_1 \otimes \ldots \otimes \vec{v}_k \otimes \vec{v}_{k+1}$ where $\vec{v}_1, \ldots, \vec{v}_k \in \{0,1\}^{\mathfrak{d}}$ and $\vec{v}_{k+1} \in \{0,1\}^d$. Then proving (1), that $\vec{v}_i$ are unit vectors, and $f_i(\vec{s}) = 0$ requires creating an ABDLOP commitment to the vectors $\vec{v}_i, \vec{s}$, and then also creating a commitment to the above-described vector $\vec{w}_i$ at each step of the proof.

Bimodal Gaussian Rejection Sampling Everywhere. The framework of [LNP22] uses the newly-defined ABDLOP commitment scheme to commit to a low-norm polynomial vector $\mathbf{s}_1$ and an arbitrary-norm polynomial vector $\mathbf{m}$. To do this, one generates a low-norm randomness $\mathbf{s}_2$ and outputs the commitment

$$\begin{bmatrix} \mathbf{t}_A \\ \mathbf{t}_B \end{bmatrix} := \begin{bmatrix} \mathbf{A}_1 \\ \mathbf{0} \end{bmatrix} \mathbf{s}_1 + \begin{bmatrix} \mathbf{A}_2 \\ \mathbf{B} \end{bmatrix} \mathbf{s}_2 + \begin{bmatrix} \mathbf{0} \\ \mathbf{m} \end{bmatrix} \bmod q.^4 \qquad (11)$$

Proving knowledge of $\mathbf{s}_1$ and $\mathbf{m}$ is done using the "Fiat-Shamir with Aborts" technique [Lyu09, Lyu12] where, upon generating low-norm masking vectors $\mathbf{y}_1$ and $\mathbf{y}_2$, computing $\mathbf{w} = \mathbf{A}_1 \mathbf{y}_1 + \mathbf{A}_2 \mathbf{y}_2$, and receiving a challenge polynomial c, the prover creates the responses $\mathbf{z}_1 = \mathbf{y}_1 + c\mathbf{s}_1$ and $\mathbf{z}_2 = \mathbf{y}_2 + c\mathbf{s}_2$ which satisfy

$$\mathbf{A}_1 \mathbf{z}_1 + \mathbf{A}_2 \mathbf{z}_2 = c\mathbf{t}_A + \mathbf{w} \bmod q. \qquad (12)$$

He now needs to perform rejection sampling on the $\mathbf{z}_i$ in order to not leak information about the $\mathbf{s}_i$. The generic setup from [Lyu12] that results in the smallest-norm $\mathbf{z}_i$ being sent involves $\mathbf{y}_i$ being sampled from a discrete Gaussian distribution while standard deviation is approximately a factor of 12 larger than $\|c\mathbf{s}_i\|$. With the appropriate rejection sampling step, this results in the polynomial vectors $\mathbf{z}_i$ also being distributed as discrete Gaussians with standard deviation $12 \cdot \|c\mathbf{s}_i\|$.

It was shown in [DDLL13] that if one first chooses a secret bit $b \in \{-1, 1\}$ and creates $\mathbf{z}_i = \mathbf{y}_i + bc\mathbf{s}_i$ (which is a bimodal distribution with two peaks at $\pm c\mathbf{s}_i$), then one can choose the $\mathbf{y}_i$ from a discrete Gaussian distribution with standard deviation $\|c\mathbf{s}_i\|/\sqrt{2}$ and via appropriate rejection sampling, the standard deviation of $\mathbf{z}_i$ ends up being $\|c\mathbf{s}_i\|/\sqrt{2}$ as well, which is around 17X smaller than that

---

4 We use modulus q here instead of p in the previous section to signify that the commitment scheme modulus need not be (and is usually not, though they could be related) the same as the modulus that one wants to prove relations over.

in the previous paragraph. The outputs z_i having a smaller standard deviation means that the proof size will be noticeably smaller, the modulus q can be set smaller as well, which in turn results in a smaller commitment size. The main technical difficulty with using the bimodal distribution is that the bit b needs to remain secret and the z_i need to satisfy the verification Eq. (12) irrespective of the b, which implies that we need to have $\mathbf{A}_1 b \mathbf{s}_1 + \mathbf{A}_2 b \mathbf{s}_2 = c t_A \bmod q$. This set-up exists in the special case of the BLISS signature scheme [DDLL13] where the modulus is set to be even, and one can also force it by modifying the equation being proved as in [TWZ20], but these techniques would extol a high extra cost on the output size of the zero-knowledge proofs.

In our work, we show how one can use the bimodal rejection sampling technique for masking the secret vectors $\mathbf{s}_1$ and $\mathbf{s}_2$ in (11) either completely for free, or at a small increase in the commitment size. We note that using a rejection sampling procedure that had similar properties as bimodal rejection sampling was already employed in [LNS21a] on the *randomness vector* $\mathbf{s}_2$. The rejection step there allowed for a smaller standard deviation at the cost of leaking one bit of $\mathbf{s}_2$. This leakage is not a problem because the commitment scheme from (11) (and the related commitment in [LNS21a]) is used inside a commit-and-prove approach to constructing zero-knowledge proofs. In particular, when trying to prove some relation (e.g. (1)), the prover commits to the secret values ($\vec{s}$ and $\vec{v}$ in the case of (1)) using the commitment in (11) and proves relations about $\mathbf{s}_1$ and $\mathbf{m}$, which in turn implies the initial relation he set out to prove. The important part is that the commitment scheme is only used once – if the prover is to perform another proof, he will create another commitment with different randomness $\mathbf{s}_2$. Thus leaking a small part of the randomness $\mathbf{s}_2$ is not a problem as long as the Module-LWE problem upon which the hiding of the commitment scheme is based on remains hard.

Our work improves on [LNS21a] in two ways. First, we show that directly using the bimodal rejection sampling on $\mathbf{z}_2$ (despite $\mathbf{z}_2$ not being distributed according to a bimodal distribution) only leaks a few more (i.e. $\log q$) bits of $\mathbf{s}_2$ but ends up saving a factor of 2 in the rejection sampling probability. Leaking $\log q$ bits still keeps the entropy of $\mathbf{s}_2$ very high. This problem has been investigated both theoretically and in practice [AP12, ASA16, DDGR20, BJRW21], and it does not seem that the LWE problem is weakened if a few bits of the randomness are leaked. The more interesting improvement is in also being able to use the bimodal rejection sampling on $\mathbf{z}_1$. Here one cannot leak anything because $\mathbf{s}_1$ is where the actual secret message is stored.[5] The new idea is to create a commitment to $b \mathbf{s}_1$, for a random $b \in \{-1, 1\}$ instead of to $\mathbf{s}_1$. We can show that creating such a commitment and then outputting $\mathbf{z}_1 = \mathbf{y}_1 + c b \mathbf{s}_1$ after applying

---

[5] One might be tempted to put the secret message into the $\mathbf{m}$ part of the commitment, which does not leak even if there is leakage in $\mathbf{s}_2$, but this results in a much less efficient commitment scheme because the dimension of the commitment grows linearly with the dimension of $\mathbf{m}$, whereas $\mathbf{s}_1$ has no effect on the size of the commitment. See Sect. 2.6.

the bimodal rejection sampling does not leak anything about $\mathbf{s}_1$ or b as long as the commitment is only used once.

There is, however, an obvious problem with committing to $b\mathbf{s}_1$ – the relation that one may want to prove about the message committed to in $\mathbf{s}_1$ may not hold true when the messages are negated. There are two cases here – the simple case is that what we would like to prove still holds true for the negated messages. In our one-out-of-many proof, we commit to unit vectors $\vec{v}_1, \ldots, \vec{v}_{k+1}$ and a low-norm vector $\vec{s}$ such that $\vec{v}_1 \otimes \ldots \otimes \vec{v}_{k+1} = \vec{v}$ such that (1) is satisfied. Note that if we're tensoring an even number of $\vec{v}_i$, then $\bigotimes_i \vec{v}_i = \bigotimes_i -\vec{v}_i$, and also $\|\vec{v}_i\| = 1 = \| -\vec{v}_i\|$ and $\|\vec{s}\| = \beta = \| -\vec{s}\|$.[6] Therefore proving (1) as well as $\|\vec{v}_i\| = 1$ and $\|\vec{s}\| = \beta$ can be done regardless of whether we committed to the positive or negative of these values.

In the case that we would like to prove some relations on some secret vector $\vec{s}$ which are not sign-independent, we commit to a bit $b \in \{-1, 1\}$ in the $\mathbf{m}$ part of the ABDLOP commitment and to $\vec{s}' = b\vec{s}$, and then prove knowledge of a vector $\vec{s}'$ and a bit $b \in \{-1, 1\}$ satisfying $f_i(b\vec{s}') = 0$. Very importantly, note that $f_i(b\vec{s}')$ is still a quadratic equation because all the quadratic terms in f_i remain the same (since multiplication by $b \in \{-1, 1\}$ does not change them), and it is only the linear terms that get multiplied by b, thus becoming quadratic. We then prove that if the bit b is chosen randomly in $\{-1, 1\}$, then one can use the bimodal rejection sampling on $\mathbf{z}_1 = \mathbf{y}_1 + cb\mathbf{s}_1$ without leaking anything about the secret $\mathbf{s}_1$.

Applications to Ring and Group Signatures. Being able to prove (1) immediately gives us a construction of a ring signature scheme. In particular, every user has a secret/public key pair $\vec{s}_i, \vec{t}_i$, where $\|\vec{s}_i\|$ is small and $A\vec{s}_i = \vec{t}_i \bmod p$. Given a matrix T whose columns are the public keys of a group of users, the signature of user i of a message μ is a zero-knowledge proof of knowledge (with μ being used as an input into the random oracle of the Fiat-Shamir transform) of a unit vector $\vec{v}$ and a short vector $\vec{s}$ satisfying (1). The full details are given in the full version of the paper. In Fig. 1, we compare an instantiation of our ring signature with other known potentially quantum-safe ones. Once the group size within which one wishes to hide is larger than a few hundred members, the size of our signature is the smallest, even including the isogeny-based construction of [BKP20]. Additionally, the size of the public key of our ring signatures can be as small as 128 bytes per user, which is a significant reduction over all prior lattice-based ring signatures.[7] Having small public keys is important because the

---

[6] If we want to prove that $\|\vec{s}\| \leqslant \beta$, then we could create another commitment to a vector $\vec{s}' \in \mathcal{R}_q$ such that $\|\vec{s}\|^2 + \|\vec{s}'\|^2 = \beta^2$ – the existence of such an $\vec{s}'$ is guaranteed by the four squares theorem.

[7] It is of course possible to reduce the public key size of any scheme by hashing it as $\mathsf{pk}' = H(\mathsf{pk})$ for some cryptographic hash function H with the resulting pk' being as small as 32 bytes. This technique is fine for regular signatures, where one can reveal pk as part of the signature; but ring signatures will require a zero-knowledge proof that $\mathsf{pk}' = H(\mathsf{pk})$, which will make the signatures orders of magnitude larger and slower.

	sig. sizes for N: 2^6 2^{12} 2^{21}		asymptotic sig. size	hardness assumption	(user) public key size
Raptor [LAZ19]	81	5161	–	$O(N)$	NTRU	0.9
DualRing-LB [YEL+21]	6	106	–	$O(N)$	MSIS, MLWE	[2.8, 3.4]
Falafl [BKP20]	32	35	39	$O(\log N)$	MSIS, MLWE	1.9
MatRiCT [EZS+19]	31	59	148	$O(\log^{1.7} N)$	MSIS, MLWE	[3.4, 22.7]
MatRiCT+ [ESZ21]	11	18	40(?)	$O(\log^{1.7} N)$	MSIS, MLWE	3
SMILE [LNS21b]	18	19	22	$O(\log N)$	MSIS, E-MLWE	2
Calamari [BKP20]	8	14	23	$O(\log N)$	CSIDH-512	0.06
This Work	**13**	**14**	**16**	$O(\log N)$	**MSIS, E-MLWE**	**0.13**

Fig. 1. Comparison of the different post-quantum ring signature schemes with approximately 128 bits of security. Sizes from previous constructions are either taken from the corresponding prior work or from the recent survey by Buser et al. [BDE+22]. All the values are given in KB. Here, N is the size of the ring. The signatures sizes for [ESZ21,LNS21b] only approximately correspond to the ring sizes (e.g. 18KB signature size is for the ring of 2^{10} users and not 2^{12}). For DualRing-LB and MatRiCT (and MatRiCT+) the public key size grows in the number of users. For MatRiCT+, the public key size for the ring of size 1024 is provided. Further, we extrapolate the signature size for MatRiCT+ with 2^{21} users from the smaller examples and from MatRiCT. In our construction, we rely on the Extended-MLWE problem introduced in Definition 5. Note that this is a different version of the E-MLWE problem compared to the one in [LNS21a] which is used in SMILE [LNS21b] (see Sect. 3.1 for more details).

public keys of *all* users need to be stored somewhere accessible by everyone who wishes to use the ring signature.

The reason for the significant reduction in the public key size over the previous lattice schemes is that we were able to adapt the new framework from [LNP22] as the base case of our recursive one-out-of-many proof. In prior ring signatures (e.g. [EZS+19,ESZ21,LNS21b]) the signer had knowledge of $\vec{v}$ and $\vec{s}$ satisfying (1), but for efficiency would only prove knowledge of an $\vec{s}'$ and an additional low-norm polynomial c with $\|\vec{s}'\| \gg \|\vec{s}\|$ satisfying $T\vec{v} = cA\vec{s}' \bmod p$ (where the right-hand side operations are over a polynomial ring $\mathcal{R}_p$.) Being able to prove knowledge of a vector that has the exact norm of $\vec{s}$ and not have an additional multiplication by c allows us to use a much smaller modulus p, which in turn also allows to reduce the number of rows in A. The public key size can, in fact, be essentially as small as the outputs in the hash function SWIFFT [LMPR08].[8]

One can construct group signatures in a somewhat similar manner as ring signatures. A technique employed in [EZS+19,ESZ21] has the public key of each

---

[8] If we make p too small, then the signature size will increase because a smaller p requires more "garbage terms" in the zero-knowledge proof to increase soundness. In our parameter settings, we chose a particular compromise between the public key size and signature size, but one could make the public key size even smaller at the expense of a few extra kilobytes in the signature size.

member stored in the matrix T, as in the ring signature, and the secret key of user i are the $\vec{v}$ and $\vec{s}$ from (1). The keys are generated by choosing a small-norm random $\vec{s}_i$ and then putting $A\vec{s}_i = \vec{t}_i$ into the public matrix T. To sign, the group member does the same thing as in the ring signature (with an additional encryption and proof required by the group signature). Our group signature works in the same fashion except that the secret key/public key pairs are generated by first generating $\vec{t}_i = H(i)$, for some cryptographic hash function H, and then using a trapdoor for the matrix A to generate a short $\vec{s}_i$ such that $A\vec{s}_i = \vec{t}_i$. The main advantage of generating the keys in this manner is that the public key size no longer needs to be linear in the number of group members, and can just consist of the matrix A (since everyone can now generate T themselves). The disadvantage is that using a trap-door sampler to generate $\vec{s}_i$ results in $\|\vec{s}_i\|$ being larger. But because our one-out-of many proof system can prove exact norms, the proof size does not increase by too much. Using GPV-type trapdoor sampling [GPV08, DP16] along with an optimized NTRU trapdoor [HHGP+03, DLP14] and the parameters used in the Falcon signature scheme [FHK+20], we give an instantiation (in the full version of the paper) of a lattice-based group signature scheme with the smallest public key and signature sizes (see Fig. 2). The only exception when one would want to use a different scheme is in the case that the group sizes are very large – in that case [LNPS21, LNP22] has an advantage over all others in the table due to the fact that the running time for signature generation and verification are independent of the group size, rather than linear.

Other Applications. In addition to ring and group signatures, lattice-based one-out-of-many proofs have recently found applications in the constructions of confidential transaction protocols [EZS+19, LNS21b, ESZ21]. These constructions also used other primitives, notably proofs of addition that were used to make sure that the amounts in the transactions match up. As a side contribution, in the full version of the paper, we also show how to use the new framework of [LNP22] in conjunction with the bimodal rejection sampling technique to construct more efficient proofs of integer addition and multiplication, which improve upon the constructions from [LNS20, ESZ21] that are used in the aforementioned instantiations. We believe that the improved one-out-of-many proof and proof of addition from this paper should noticeably shorten the confidential transaction proof sizes. We leave the integration of these tools as well as the full implementation of the confidential transaction system to future work.

	signature sizes for N:			asymptotic sig. size	anonymity	master public key size
	2^6	2^{10}	2^{21}			
[LNPS21, LNP22]	90	90	90	$O(1)$	CPA	48
[BDK$^+$21][Lattice]	89	91	96	$O(\log N)$	CCA	$2.9 \cdot (N+1)$
MatRiCT [EZS$^+$19]	34	60	148	$O(\log^{1.7} N)$	CPA	$[3.8, 24] \cdot N$
MatRiCT+ [ESZ21]	12	19	45(?)	$O(\log^{1.7} N)$	CPA	$3 \cdot N$
[BDK$^+$21][Isogeny]	6.6	9.0	15.5	$O(\log N)$	CCA	$0.06 \cdot (N+1)$
This Work	**17**	**18**	**20**	$O(\log N)$	CPA	**3.2**

Fig. 2. Comparison of different post-quantum group signature with approximately 128 bits of security. All the values are given in KB. Here, N denotes the size of the group. We note that the schemes from [LNPS21, LNP22] not only do offer constant size signatures but also enjoy signing and verification complexity independent of the group size N which is not the case for all the other works (including ours). Further, the constructions in [BDK+21, EZS+19, ESZ21] are dynamic which results in the linear public key size in the number of users N. For MatRiCT+, the public key size for the group of size 1024 is provided. Since the signature size for MatRiCT+ was not explicitly provided for group size 2^{21}, we set the value to be three times smaller than for MatRiCT which seems to be the case for smaller examples. Finally, we remark that our scheme can achieve CCA anonymity by following the Naor-Yung paradigm [NY90], i.e. encrypting the same message under two different public keys and adding a NIZK proof that both ciphertext encrypt the same message. We estimate that with this modification our group signature sizes will be around 30KB.

2   Preliminaries

2.1   Notation

Denote $\mathbb{Z}_p$ to be the ring of integers modulo p. Let $q = q_1 \cdot \ldots \cdot q_n$ be a product of n odd primes where $q_1 < q_2 < \ldots < q_n$. Usually, we pick $n = 1$ or $n = 2$. In this paper we pick each $q_i = 5 \pmod 8$. We write $\vec{v} \in \mathbb{Z}_q^m$ to denote vectors over a ring $\mathbb{Z}_q$. Matrices over $\mathbb{Z}_q$ will be written as regular capital letters. By default, all vectors are column vectors. For simplicity, we denote $\vec{u}^2 = \vec{u} \circ \vec{u}$. We write $x \leftarrow S$ when $x \in S$ is sampled uniformly at random from the finite set S and similarly $x \leftarrow D$ when x is sampled according to the distribution D. Further, denote $[n] := \{1, \ldots, n\}$.

2.2   Cyclotomic Rings

For a power of two d and a positive integer p, denote $\mathcal{R}$ and $\mathcal{R}_p$ respectively to be the rings $\mathbb{Z}[X]/(X^d + 1)$ and $\mathbb{Z}_p[X]/(X^d + 1)$. Lower-case letters denote elements in $\mathcal{R}$ or $\mathcal{R}_p$ and bold lower-case (resp. upper-case) letters represent column vectors (resp. matrices) with coefficients in $\mathcal{R}$ or $\mathcal{R}_p$. For a polynomial $f \in \mathcal{R}_p$, denote $\vec{f} \in \mathbb{Z}_q^d$ to be the coefficient vector of f. By default, we write its i-th coefficient as its corresponding regular font letter subscript i, e.g. $f_{d/2} \in \mathbb{Z}_p$

is the coefficient corresponding to $X^{d/2}$ of $f \in \mathcal{R}_p$. For the constant coefficient, however, we will denote $\tilde{f} := f_0 \in \mathbb{Z}_p$.

The ring $\mathcal{R}$ has a group of automorphisms $\mathsf{Aut}(\mathcal{R})$ that is isomorphic to $\mathbb{Z}_{2d}^\times$. Let $\sigma_i \in \mathsf{Aut}(\mathcal{R}_q)$ be defined by $\sigma_i(X) = X^i$. For readability, we denote for an arbitrary vector $\mathbf{m} \in \mathcal{R}^k$:

$$\sigma_i(\mathbf{m}) := (\sigma_i(m_1), \ldots, \sigma_i(m_k))$$

and similarly $\sigma_i(\mathbf{R})$ for any matrix $\mathbf{R}$. When we write $\langle \mathbf{u}, \mathbf{v} \rangle \in \mathbb{Z}$ for $\mathbf{u}, \mathbf{v} \in \mathcal{R}^k$, we mean the inner product of their corresponding coefficient vectors.

We recall the result by Lyubashevsky et al. [LNP22] which says that for specific primes p, if $c \in \mathcal{R}_p$ satisfies $\sigma_{-1}(c) = c$ and c is non-zero then c is invertible over $\mathcal{R}_p$.

Lemma 1 ([LNP22]). *Let $p \equiv 5 \pmod 8$ be a prime. Then all non-zero $c \in \mathcal{R}_p$ satisfying $\sigma_{-1}(c) = c$ are invertible.*

In this paper, we will only be interested in the $\sigma := \sigma_{-1}$ automorphism. The main reason is the following observation.

Lemma 2 ([LNP22]). *Let $\mathbf{u}, \mathbf{v} \in \mathcal{R}_q^k$. Then, the constant coefficient of $\sigma(\mathbf{u})^T \mathbf{v}$ is equal to $\langle \mathbf{u}, \mathbf{v} \rangle$.*

Thus, one reduces inner product arguments $\langle \mathbf{u}, \mathbf{v} \rangle = a$ to proving that $\sigma(\mathbf{u})^T \mathbf{v} - a \in \mathcal{R}_q$ has a vanishing constant coefficient.

We introduce the following notation:

$$\langle x \rangle_\sigma := (x, \sigma(x)) \in \mathcal{R}_q^2 \text{ for } x \in \mathcal{R}_q.$$

Similarly, for a vector $\mathbf{x} = (x_1, \ldots, x_n)$, define $\langle \mathbf{x} \rangle_\sigma = (\langle x_1 \rangle_\sigma, \ldots, \langle x_n \rangle_\sigma) \in \mathcal{R}_q^{2n}$. We will use the following simple properties.

Lemma 3. *For any $\mathbf{x}, \mathbf{y} \in \mathcal{R}_q^n$ and any $c \in \mathcal{R}_q$ such that $\sigma(c) = c$:*

$$\langle \mathbf{x} \parallel \mathbf{y} \rangle_\sigma = \langle \mathbf{x} \rangle_\sigma \parallel \langle \mathbf{y} \rangle_\sigma \quad and \quad \langle \mathbf{x} + c\mathbf{y} \rangle_\sigma = \langle \mathbf{x} \rangle_\sigma + c\langle \mathbf{y} \rangle_\sigma.$$

Next, we recall the definition of the discrete Gaussian distribution over $\mathcal{R}$.

Definition 1. *The* discrete Gaussian distribution *on $\mathcal{R}^\ell$ centered around $\mathbf{v} \in \mathcal{R}^\ell$ with standard deviation $\mathfrak{s} > 0$ is given by*

$$D_{\mathbf{v}, \mathfrak{s}}^\ell(\mathbf{z}) = \frac{e^{-\|\mathbf{z} - \mathbf{v}\|^2 / 2\mathfrak{s}^2}}{\sum_{\mathbf{z}' \in \mathcal{R}^\ell} e^{-\|\mathbf{z}'\|^2 / 2\mathfrak{s}^2}}.$$

When it is centered around $\mathbf{0} \in \mathcal{R}^\ell$ we write $D_\mathfrak{s}^\ell = D_{\mathbf{0}, \mathfrak{s}}^\ell$.

We will use the standard tail bound result from [Ban93, Lemma 1.5(i)].

Lemma 4. *Let $\mathbf{z} \leftarrow D_\mathfrak{s}^m$. Then $\Pr\left[\|\mathbf{z}\| > t \cdot \mathfrak{s}\sqrt{md}\right] < \left(te^{\frac{1-t^2}{2}}\right)^{md}.$*

2.3   Module-SIS and Module-LWE Problems

Security of the [BDL+18] commitment scheme used in our protocols relies on
the well-known computational lattice problems, namely Module-LWE (MLWE)
and Module-SIS (MSIS) [LS15]. Both problems are defined over $\mathcal{R}_q$.

Definition 2 (MSIS$_{\kappa,m,B}$). *Given* $\mathbf{A} \leftarrow \mathcal{R}_q^{\kappa \times m}$, *the* Module-SIS *problem with
parameters* $\kappa, m > 0$ *and* $0 < B < q$ *asks to find* $\mathbf{z} \in \mathcal{R}_q^m$ *such that* $\mathbf{Az} = \mathbf{0}$ *over*
$\mathcal{R}_q$ *and* $0 < \|\mathbf{z}\| \leqslant B$. *An algorithm* $\mathcal{A}$ *is said to have advantage* ϵ *in solving*
MSIS$_{\kappa,m,B}$ *if*

$$\Pr\left[0 < \|\mathbf{z}\|_\infty \leqslant B \wedge \mathbf{Az} = \mathbf{0} \mid \mathbf{A} \leftarrow \mathcal{R}_q^{\kappa \times m}; \mathbf{z} \leftarrow \mathcal{A}(\mathbf{A})\right] \geqslant \epsilon.$$

Definition 3 (MLWE$_{m,\lambda,\chi}$). *The* Module-LWE *problem with parameters*
$m, \lambda > 0$ *and an error distribution* χ *over* $\mathcal{R}$ *asks the adversary* $\mathcal{A}$ *to distin-
guish between the following two cases: 1)* $(\mathbf{A}, \mathbf{As} + \mathbf{e})$ *for* $\mathbf{A} \leftarrow \mathcal{R}_q^{m \times \lambda}$, *a secret
vector* $\mathbf{s} \leftarrow \chi^\lambda$ *and error vector* $\mathbf{e} \leftarrow \chi^m$, *and 2)* $(\mathbf{A}, \mathbf{b}) \leftarrow \mathcal{R}_q^{m \times \lambda} \times \mathcal{R}_q^m$. *Then,*
$\mathcal{A}$ *is said to have advantage* ϵ *in solving* MLWE$_{m,\lambda,\chi}$ *if*

$$\left|\Pr\left[b = 1 \mid \mathbf{A} \leftarrow \mathcal{R}_q^{m \times \lambda}; \mathbf{s} \leftarrow \chi^\lambda; \mathbf{e} \leftarrow \chi^m; b \leftarrow \mathcal{A}(\mathbf{A}, \mathbf{As} + \mathbf{e})\right]\right. \tag{13}$$
$$\left. - \Pr\left[b = 1 \mid \mathbf{A} \leftarrow \mathcal{R}_q^{m \times \lambda}; \mathbf{b} \leftarrow \mathcal{R}_q^m; b \leftarrow \mathcal{A}(\mathbf{A}, \mathbf{b})\right]\right| \geqslant \epsilon.$$

2.4   Rejection Sampling

In lattice-based zero-knowledge proofs, the prover will want to output a vector $\mathbf{z}$
whose distribution should be independent of a secret message/randomness vector
$\mathbf{r}$, so that $\mathbf{z}$ cannot be used to gain any information on the prover's secret. During
the protocol, the prover computes $\mathbf{z} = \mathbf{y} + c\mathbf{r}$ where $\mathbf{r}$ is either a secret vector
or randomness used to commit to the prover's secret, $c \leftarrow \mathcal{C}$ is a challenge
polynomial, and $\mathbf{y}$ is a "masking" vector. In order to remove the dependency
of $\mathbf{z}$ on $\mathbf{r}$, one applies *rejection sampling*. We summarise the two most common
techniques for rejection sampling described in [Lyu12, DDLL13].

Lemma 5 (Rejection Sampling [Lyu12, DDLL13]). *Let* $V \subseteq \mathcal{R}^\ell$ *be a set of
polynomials with norm at most* T *and* $\rho: V \to [0,1]$ *be a probability distribution.
Fix the standard deviation* $\mathfrak{s} = \gamma T$. *Then, the following statements hold.*

1. *Let* $M = \exp(14/\gamma + 1/(2\gamma^2))$. *Now, sample* $\mathbf{v} \leftarrow \rho$ *and* $\mathbf{y} \leftarrow D_\mathfrak{s}^\ell$, *set* $\mathbf{z} = \mathbf{y} + \mathbf{v}$,
   and run $b \leftarrow \mathrm{Rej}_1(\mathbf{z}, \mathbf{v}, \mathfrak{s})$ *as defined in Fig. 3. Then, the probability that* $b = 0$
   is at least $(1 - 2^{-128})/M$ *and the distribution of* $(\mathbf{v}, \mathbf{z})$, *conditioned on* $b = 0$,
   is within statistical distance of 2^{-128} *of the product distribution* $\rho \times D_\mathfrak{s}^\ell$.
2. *Let* $M = \exp(1/(2\gamma^2))$. *Now, sample* $\mathbf{v} \leftarrow \rho, \beta \leftarrow \{0,1\}$ *and* $\mathbf{y} \leftarrow D_\mathfrak{s}^\ell$, *set*
   $\mathbf{z} = \mathbf{y} + (-1)^\beta \mathbf{v}$, *and run* $b \leftarrow \mathrm{Rej}_2(\mathbf{z}, \mathbf{v}, \mathfrak{s})$ *as defined in Fig. 3. Then, the
   probability that* $b = 0$ *is equal to* $1/M$ *and the distribution of* $(\mathbf{v}, \mathbf{z})$, *condi-
   tioned on* $b = 0$, *is identical to the product distribution* $\rho \times D_\mathfrak{s}^\ell$.

$\mathrm{Rej}_1(\vec{z}, \vec{v}, s)$	$\mathrm{Rej}_2(\vec{z}, \vec{v}, s)$
01 $u \leftarrow [0, 1)$	01 $u \leftarrow [0, 1)$
02 If $u > \frac{1}{M} \cdot \exp\left(\frac{-2\langle \vec{z}, \vec{v} \rangle + \|\vec{v}\|^2}{2s^2}\right)$	02 If $u > \dfrac{1}{M \exp\left(-\frac{\|\vec{v}\|^2}{2s^2}\right) \cosh\left(\frac{\langle \vec{z}, \vec{v} \rangle}{\sigma^2}\right)}$
03 return 1 (i.e. *reject*)	03 return 1 (i.e. *reject*)
04 Else	04 Else
05 return 0 (i.e. *accept*)	05 return 0 (i.e. *accept*)

Fig. 3. Two rejection sampling algorithms: the one used generally in previous works [Lyu12] (left) and the bimodal Gaussian one [DDLL13] (right).

2.5 Challenge Space

We recall the specific challenge space used in [LNP22]. Namely, we fix $\eta > 0$ and a power-of-two k and set the challenge space $\mathcal{C}$ as:

$$\mathcal{C} := \left\{ c \in S_\kappa : \sigma_{-1}(c) = c \wedge \sqrt[2k]{\|c^{2k}\|_1} \leq \eta \right\}. \tag{14}$$

Roughly speaking, the first condition, i.e. $\sigma_{-1}(c) = c$, is needed to prove quadratic equations in the committed messages which might additionally involve automorphisms, e.g. $m_1 m_2 = \sigma_{-1}(m_3)$ where m_1, m_2, m_3 are the secret messages. On the other hand, the second condition allows us to use [LNP22, Lemma 2.15] and deduce that if $\|\mathbf{r}\| \leq \alpha$ and $c \in \mathcal{C}$ then $\|c\mathbf{r}\| \leq \eta\alpha$.

Further, we denote $\bar{\mathcal{C}} := \{c - c' : c, c' \in \mathcal{C} \text{ and } c \neq c'\}$ to be the set of differences of any two distinct elements in $\mathcal{C}$. We will choose the constant η such that (experimentally) the probability for $c \leftarrow S_\kappa$ to satisfy $\sqrt[2k]{\|c^{2k}\|_1} \leq \eta$ is at least 99%.

For security of our protocols, we need the invertibility property of the challenge space $\mathcal{C}$, i.e. the difference of any two distinct elements of $\mathcal{C}$ is invertible over $\mathcal{R}_q$. To this end, we apply Lemma 1 and thus we only need the condition $\kappa < q_1/2$. Secondly, to achieve negligible soundness error, we will need $|\mathcal{C}|$ to be exponentially large. In Fig. 4 we propose example parameters to instantiate the challenge space $\mathcal{C}$.

d	κ	η	$|\mathcal{C}|$
64	8	140	2^{129}
128	2	59	2^{147}

Fig. 4. Example parameters to instantiate the challenge space $\mathcal{C} := \{c \in S_\kappa : \sigma_{-1}(c) = c \wedge \sqrt[2k]{\|c^{2k}\|_1} \leq \eta\}$ for a modulus q such that its smallest prime divisor q_1 is greater than 16. In our examples we picked $k = 32$.

2.6 ABDLOP Commitment

We recall the ABDLOP commitment scheme defined in [LNP22], which is a generalisation of the Ajtai [Ajt96] and BDLOP [BDL+18] constructions. Concretely, to commit to a message vector $s_1 \in \mathcal{R}_q^{m_1}$ with small coefficients as well as a "full-fledged" polynomial vector $m \in \mathcal{R}_q^\ell$, we sample a randomness vector $s_2 \leftarrow \chi^{m_2}$, where χ is a probability distribution over $\mathcal{R}_q$, and compute:

$$\begin{bmatrix} t_A \\ t_B \end{bmatrix} := \begin{bmatrix} A_1 \\ 0 \end{bmatrix} s_1 + \begin{bmatrix} A_2 \\ B \end{bmatrix} s_2 + \begin{bmatrix} 0 \\ m \end{bmatrix}$$

where $A_1 \leftarrow \mathcal{R}_q^{n \times m_1}, A_2 \leftarrow \mathcal{R}_q^{n \times m_2}, B \leftarrow \mathcal{R}_q^{\ell \times m_2}$. We observe that when $\ell = 0$ (resp. $m_1 = 0$) then this construction ends up being the Ajtai (resp. BDLOP) commitment scheme. In particular, the commitment size does not depend on the length m_1 of s_1 (but it does on ℓ). Hence, our strategy is to commit to long vectors with small coefficients in the "Ajtai" part s_1 and commit to a few *garbage* polynomials used for the proofs in the "BDLOP" part m.

An opening of the commitment is a triple $(s_1, m, s_2)^9$. As usual in lattice-based cryptography, we also consider relaxed openings of a commitment which are defined as follows.

Definition 4. *A relaxed opening of the* ABDLOP *commitment* (t_A, t_B) *is a tuple* (s_1, m, s_2, c) *which satisfies:*

$$A_1 s_1 + A_2 s_2 = t_A$$
$$A_2 s_2 + m = t_B$$
$$c \in \bar{\mathcal{C}} \text{ as defined in Sect. 2.5}$$
$$\|c s_1\| \leqslant B_1 \quad \text{and} \quad \|c s_2\| \leqslant B_2.$$

As shown in [LNP22, Lemma 3.1], the ABDLOP commitment is binding with respect to relaxed openings under the Module-SIS assumption.

Lemma 6 ([LNP22]). *The* ABDLOP *commitment is computationally binding with respect to relaxed openings under the* $\mathsf{MSIS}_{n,m_1+m_2,B}$ *assumption where* $B := 4\eta\sqrt{B_1^2 + B_2^2}$.

The hiding property of the ABDLOP commitment scheme follows from the fact that under the Module-LWE assumption that $\begin{bmatrix} A_2 \\ B \end{bmatrix} s_2$ looks pseudorandom.

2.7 Framework for Proving Lattice Statements

The recently proposed framework by Lyubashevsky et al. [LNP22] can be used to prove various relations in the committed messages. Concretely, one can prove knowledge of the secret messages $(s_1, m) \in \mathcal{R}_q^{m_1+\ell}$ which satisfy all the following conditions:

1. *Quadratic relations over* $\mathcal{R}_q$ *with automorphisms.* For $i \in [N]$ and public triples $(R_{i,2}, r_{i,1}, r_{i,0}) \in \mathcal{R}_q^{2(m_1+\ell) \times 2(m_1+\ell)} \times \mathcal{R}_q^{2(m_1+\ell)} \times \mathcal{R}_q$, we have:

$$\langle s_1 \| m \rangle_\sigma^T R_{i,2} \langle s_1 \| m \rangle_\sigma + r_{i,1}^T \langle s_1 \| m \rangle_\sigma + r_{i,0} = 0. \tag{15}$$

---

[9] Message m does not need to be included in the opening since it can be deterministically computed from t_B and s_2.

2. *Quadratic relations over $\mathbb{Z}_q$ with automorphisms.* For $i \in [M]$ and public triples $(\mathbf{R}'_{i,2}, \mathbf{r}'_{i,1}, r'_{i,0}) \in \mathcal{R}_q^{2(m_1+\ell) \times 2(m_1+\ell)} \times \mathcal{R}_q^{2(m_1+\ell)} \times \mathcal{R}_q$:

const. coeff. of $\langle \mathbf{s}_1 \parallel \mathbf{m} \rangle_\sigma^T \mathbf{R}'_{i,2} \langle \mathbf{s}_1 \parallel \mathbf{m} \rangle_\sigma + \mathbf{r}'^T_{i,1} \langle \mathbf{s}_1 \parallel \mathbf{m} \rangle_\sigma + r'_{i,0}$ equals 0. (16)

3. *Shortness in the infinity norm.* For public $\mathbf{P}_s \in \mathcal{R}_q^{n_{\mathsf{bin}} \times m_1}, \mathbf{P}_m \in \mathcal{R}_q^{n_{\mathsf{bin}} \times \ell}$ and $\mathbf{f} \in \mathcal{R}_q^{n_{\mathsf{bin}}}$, the following polynomial vector has binary coefficients

$$\mathbf{P}_s \mathbf{s}_1 + \mathbf{P}_m \mathbf{m} + \mathbf{f} \in \{0,1\}^{n_{\mathsf{bin}} \cdot d}. \tag{17}$$

4. *Shortness in the Euclidean norm.* For $i \in [Z]$, public bound $\mathcal{B}_i < \sqrt{q}$ and $\mathbf{E}_s^{(i)} \in \mathcal{R}_q^{n_i \times m_1}, \mathbf{E}_m^{(i)} \in \mathcal{R}_q^{n_i \times \ell}$ and $\mathbf{v}^{(i)} \in \mathcal{R}_q^{n_i}$, we have:

$$\|\mathbf{E}_s^{(i)} \mathbf{s}_1 + \mathbf{E}_m^{(i)} \mathbf{m} + \mathbf{v}^{(i)}\| \leqslant \mathcal{B}_i.$$

This is equivalent to additionally proving knowledge of the binary polynomial $\vartheta_i \in \mathcal{R}$ such that

$$\langle \mathsf{pow}(\mathcal{B}_i^2), \vartheta_i \rangle = \mathcal{B}_i^2 - \left\|\mathbf{E}_s^{(i)} \mathbf{s}_1 + \mathbf{E}_m^{(i)} \mathbf{m} + \mathbf{v}^{(i)}\right\|^2 \quad \text{over } \mathbb{Z} \tag{18}$$

where $\mathsf{pow}(n) := \sum_{i=0}^{\lfloor \log n \rfloor} (2X)^i \in \mathcal{R}$ for $n \leqslant 2^{d-1}$.

3   Shorter Proofs via Bimodal Gaussians

In order to provide zero-knowledge (or more precisely, simulatability) for proving relations in the ABDLOP committed messages $(\mathbf{s}_1, \mathbf{m})$ under the randomness $\mathbf{s}_2$, one applies the rejection sampling technique. In the original protocols presented in [LNP22], the standard rejection sampling [Lyu12] is used for $\mathbf{s}_1$ and the more recent one [LNS21a] for $\mathbf{s}_2$. In this section we describe how one can apply bimodal Gaussian rejection sampling [DDLL13] on both the message and randomness which significantly reduces the standard deviations, and consequently the proof size, compared to [LNP22].

3.1   Bimodal Gaussian Rejection Sampling on the Randomness

In our constructions, we apply a rejection sampling procedure to mask a secret vector $\vec{v}$ by first sampling $\vec{y}$ from a discrete Gaussian with standard deviation $\mathfrak{s}$, and then computing $\vec{z} := \vec{v} + \vec{y}$. By Lemma 5, if we additionally run $\mathsf{Rej}_1(\vec{z}, \vec{v}, \mathfrak{s})$, then the distribution of $\vec{z}$ is indistinguishable to the one where we simply sample $\vec{z}$ from a discrete Gaussian and output $\vec{z}$ with certain (known) probability. Here, it is important that one could generate $\vec{z}$ without having any information on $\vec{v}$.

Now, suppose that instead of Rej_1, we run Rej_2 which is used for bimodal Gaussian rejection sampling [DDLL13]. It is now a natural question to ask whether there is a way to simulate the $\vec{z}$ by having as little information on $\vec{v}$ as possible. We answer this question positively and show that this distribution is simulatable given only the inner product $\langle \vec{z}, \vec{v} \rangle$ of $\vec{z}$ and $\vec{v}$. We summarise our observation with the following lemma.

Lemma 7. *Let $\vec{v} \in \mathbb{Z}^m$ be a vector of norm T. Fix $\mathfrak{s} \geqslant \gamma T$ and $M = \exp\left(\frac{1}{2\gamma^2}\right)$. Then the distributions of the outputs of $\mathcal{A}(\vec{v})$ and $\mathcal{F}(\vec{v})$ defined in Fig. 5 are identical. Moreover, the probability that $\mathcal{A}$ outputs something is exactly $1/M$.*

$\mathcal{A}(\vec{v})$	$\mathcal{F}(\vec{v})$
01 $\vec{y} \leftarrow D_{\mathfrak{s}}^m$	01 $\vec{y} \leftarrow D_{\mathfrak{s}}^m$
02 $\vec{z} := \vec{y} + \vec{v}$	02 $(\vec{z}_+, \vec{z}_-) := (\text{sign}(\langle \vec{y}, \vec{v} \rangle) \cdot \vec{y}, -\text{sign}(\langle \vec{y}, \vec{v} \rangle) \cdot \vec{y})$
03 output $(\vec{z}, \vec{v})$ with prob. $\dfrac{\exp\left(\frac{\|\vec{v}\|^2}{2\mathfrak{s}^2}\right)}{M \cosh(\langle \vec{z}, \vec{v} \rangle / \mathfrak{s}^2)}$	03 $p := \dfrac{\exp\left(\frac{2|\langle \vec{y}, \vec{v} \rangle|}{\mathfrak{s}^2}\right)}{\exp\left(\frac{2|\langle \vec{y}, \vec{v} \rangle|}{\mathfrak{s}^2}\right) + 1}$
	04 $\vec{z} := \begin{cases} \vec{z}_+ \text{ with prob. } p \\ \vec{z}_- \text{ with prob. } 1-p \end{cases}$
	05 output $(\vec{z}, \vec{v})$ with prob. $\frac{1}{M}$

Fig. 5. Algorithms $\mathcal{A}$ and $\mathcal{F}$ for Lemma 7. We define $\text{sign}(x) = 1$ if $x \geqslant 0$ and -1 otherwise.

Proof. Fix $\vec{v} \in V$ and $\vec{z} \in \mathbb{Z}^m$ and let

$$p := \frac{\exp\left(\frac{2\langle \vec{z}, \vec{v} \rangle}{\mathfrak{s}^2}\right)}{\exp\left(\frac{2\langle \vec{z}, \vec{v} \rangle}{\mathfrak{s}^2}\right) + 1}.$$

By definition of $\mathcal{A}$, $\mathcal{A}(\vec{v}, \vec{z})$ is equal to

$$D_{\mathfrak{s}}^m(\vec{z} - \vec{v}) \cdot \frac{\exp\left(\frac{\|\vec{v}\|^2}{2\mathfrak{s}^2}\right)}{M \cosh\left(\frac{\langle \vec{z}, \vec{v} \rangle}{\mathfrak{s}^2}\right)} = D_{\mathfrak{s}}^m(\vec{z}) \cdot \frac{2\exp\left(\frac{2\langle \vec{z}, \vec{v} \rangle}{\mathfrak{s}^2}\right)}{M \left(\exp\left(\frac{2\langle \vec{z}, \vec{v} \rangle}{\mathfrak{s}^2}\right) + 1\right)} = D_{\mathfrak{s}}^m(\vec{z}) \cdot \frac{2p}{M}.$$

Now, we focus on $\mathcal{F}(\vec{v})$. We see that by construction, $\langle \vec{z}_+, \vec{v} \rangle \geqslant 0$ and $\langle \vec{z}_-, \vec{v} \rangle \leqslant 0$. Let us consider three separate cases. First, suppose $\vec{z}$ satisfies $\langle \vec{z}, \vec{v} \rangle > 0$. Informally, we want to compute the probability that $\vec{y} = \pm \vec{z}$ and $\mathcal{F}$ picks $\vec{z}_+$. Then,

$$\mathcal{F}(\vec{v}, \vec{z}) = 2D_{\mathfrak{s}}^m(\vec{z}) \cdot \frac{\exp\left(\frac{2\langle \vec{z}, \vec{v} \rangle}{\mathfrak{s}^2}\right)}{\exp\left(\frac{2\langle \vec{z}, \vec{v} \rangle}{\mathfrak{s}^2}\right) + 1} \cdot \frac{1}{M} = D_{\mathfrak{s}}^m(\vec{z}) \cdot \frac{2p}{M}.$$

Further, suppose $\langle \vec{z}, \vec{v} \rangle < 0$. Informally, we compute the probability that $\vec{y} = \pm \vec{z}$ and $\mathcal{F}$ picks $\vec{z}_-$. Then,

$$\mathcal{F}(\vec{v}, \vec{z}) = 2D_{\mathfrak{s}}^m(\vec{z}) \cdot \frac{1}{\exp\left(\frac{-2\langle \vec{z}, \vec{v} \rangle}{\mathfrak{s}^2}\right) + 1} \cdot \frac{1}{M} = D_{\mathfrak{s}}^m(\vec{z}) \cdot \frac{2p}{M}.$$

Finally, assume $\langle \vec{z}, \vec{v} \rangle = 0$ and thus $p = 1/2$. Then, $\mathcal{F}(\vec{v}, \vec{z})$ is simply the probability that $(\vec{y} = \vec{z} \wedge \mathcal{F}$ outputs $\vec{z}_+)$ or $(\vec{y} = -\vec{z} \wedge \mathcal{F}$ outputs $\vec{z}_-)$. Hence,

$$\mathcal{F}(\vec{v}, \vec{z}) = D_{\mathfrak{s}}^m(\vec{z}) \cdot \frac{1}{2M} + D_{\mathfrak{s}}^m(-\vec{z}) \cdot \frac{1}{2M} = D_{\mathfrak{s}}^m(\vec{z}) \cdot \frac{1}{M} = D_{\mathfrak{s}}^m(\vec{z}) \cdot \frac{2p}{M}.$$

Therefore, we proved that for every $\vec{z}$, $\mathcal{A}(\vec{v}, \vec{z}) = \mathcal{F}(\vec{v}, \vec{z})$.

Finally, the second part of the statement follows from a simple observation that $\mathcal{F}$ outputs something with probability exactly $1/M$. $\square$

Extended-MLWE Revisited. We observe that the only information about $\vec{v}$ needed in order to run the simulator $\mathcal{F}$ in the security proof is the value of $\langle \vec{y}, \vec{v} \rangle$. Hence, we reduce the simulatability property of our protocols to the hardness of the so-called Extended-MLWE. Here, as usual, an adversary needs to distinguish between the tuples $(\mathbf{B}, \mathbf{Bs})$ and $(\mathbf{B}, \mathbf{u})$, where $\mathbf{u}$ is a uniformly random vector but this time it is also given a "hint" of the form $(c, \mathbf{y}, \langle c\mathbf{s}, \mathbf{y} \rangle)$ where c and $\mathbf{y}$ are sampled from some known distributions. For simplicity, we will describe the problem in a "knapsack" form.

Definition 5 (Extended-MLWE). *The* Extended-MLWE *problem with parameters* n, m *and distribution* χ, ξ_c, ξ_y *over* $\mathcal{R}$ *asks the adversary* $\mathcal{A}$ *to distinguish between the two cases: 1)* $(\mathbf{B}, \mathbf{Bs}, c, \mathbf{y}, \langle c\mathbf{s}, \mathbf{y} \rangle)$ *and 2)* $(\mathbf{B}, \mathbf{u}, c, \mathbf{y}, \langle c\mathbf{s}, \mathbf{y} \rangle)$ *for* $\mathbf{B} \leftarrow \mathcal{R}_q^{m \times (n+m)}$, *a secret vector* $\mathbf{s} \leftarrow \chi^{n+m}$, *uniformly random vector* $\mathbf{u} \in \mathcal{R}_q^m$ *and* $(c, \mathbf{y}) \leftarrow \xi_c \times \xi_y^{n+m}$. *Then,* $\mathcal{A}$ *is said to have advantage* ϵ *in solving* Extended-$\mathsf{MLWE}_{n,m,\chi,\xi_c,\xi_y}$ *if*

$$\left| \Pr\left[b = 1 \,\middle|\, \mathbf{B} \leftarrow \mathcal{R}_q^{m \times (n+m)}; \mathbf{s} \leftarrow \chi^{n+m}; (c, \mathbf{y}) \leftarrow \xi_c \times \xi_y^{n+m}; b \leftarrow \mathcal{A}(\mathbf{B}, \mathbf{Bs}, c, \mathbf{y}, \langle c\mathbf{s}, \mathbf{y} \rangle) \right] \right.$$
$$\left. - \Pr\left[b = 1 \,\middle|\, \begin{array}{l} \mathbf{B} \leftarrow \mathcal{R}_q^{m \times (n+m)}; \mathbf{s} \leftarrow \chi^{n+m}; (c, \mathbf{y}) \leftarrow \xi_c \times \xi_y^{n+m}; \mathbf{u} \leftarrow \mathcal{R}_q^m; \\ b \leftarrow \mathcal{A}(\mathbf{B}, \mathbf{u}, c, \mathbf{y}, \langle c\mathbf{s}, \mathbf{y} \rangle) \end{array} \right] \right| \geqslant \epsilon.$$

We say that Extended-$\mathsf{MLWE}_{n,m,\chi,\xi_c,\xi_y}$ *is hard if for all PPT adversaries* $\mathcal{A}$*, the advantage in solving Extended-*$\mathsf{MLWE}_{n,m,\chi,\xi_c,\xi_y}$ *is negligible.*

We note that the (Module-)LWE problem with various side information has already been discussed in prior work e.g. [DGK+10,AP12,DDGR20]. As far as we are aware, this new variant of MLWE is the closest to the Extended Module-LWE problems defined by Lyubashevsky et al. [LNS21a], Alperin-Sheriff and Apon [ASA16], Alperin-Sheriff and Peikert [AP12] and Boudgoust et al. [BJRW21].

We observe that [ASA16] describes a similar problem with the two differences: (i) there is no c involved (assume that $c = 1$) and (ii) the hint is an arbitrary $\mathbb{Q}$-linear function on the "error" part $\mathbf{e}$ of the secret $\mathbf{s}$ (in particular it could be $\langle \mathbf{e}, \mathbf{y} \rangle \in \mathbb{Z}$ where $\mathbf{y} \leftarrow \xi_y^m$). Alperin-Sheriff and Apon show that their Extended-MLWE problem can be reduced to plain MLWE if the errors come from a discrete Gaussian with a large enough standard deviation. The proof strategy was later extended by Boudgoust et al. [BJRW21] who define another Extended-MLWE problem. This time, however, the hint becomes a whole polynomial $\langle \mathbf{e}, \mathbf{y} \rangle \in \mathcal{R}$. Finally, the only difference between our problem and the one in [LNS21a] is that the adversary is given the whole inner product $\langle c\mathbf{s}, \mathbf{y} \rangle$ instead of its sign.

If we consider our Extended-MLWE without any polynomial ring structure, then the problem becomes almost identical to the one introduced by Alperin-Sheriff and Peikert [AP12] (if we again assume $c = 1$). The authors additionally show that it is possible to reduce such a problem to plain LWE with the reduction loss $O(|\langle \vec{s}, \vec{y} \rangle|)$.

Applications. As an example, we show how to use the new rejection sampling strategy in the protocol for proving linear equations in the committed messages

[LNP22][Section 3], however this approach can also be applied in all the protocols from [LNP22]. Let $(\mathbf{t}_A, \mathbf{t}_B)$ be the ABDLOP commitment to the message pair $(\mathbf{s}_1, \mathbf{m}) \in \mathcal{R}_q^{m_1} \times \mathcal{R}_q^{\ell}$ under randomness $\mathbf{s}_2$, i.e.

$$
\begin{bmatrix} \mathbf{t}_A \\ \mathbf{t}_B \end{bmatrix} = \begin{bmatrix} \mathbf{A}_1 \\ \mathbf{0} \end{bmatrix} \cdot \mathbf{s}_1 + \begin{bmatrix} \mathbf{A}_2 \\ \mathbf{B} \end{bmatrix} \cdot \mathbf{s}_2 + \begin{bmatrix} \mathbf{0} \\ \mathbf{m} \end{bmatrix}. \tag{19}
$$

Suppose the prover wants to prove knowledge of the message $(\mathbf{s}_1, \mathbf{m})$ such that

$$
\mathbf{R}_1 \mathbf{s}_1 + \mathbf{R}_m \mathbf{m} = \mathbf{u}
$$

where $\mathbf{R}_1 \in \mathcal{R}_q^{N \times m_1}, \mathbf{R}_m \in \mathcal{R}_q^{N \times \ell}$ and $\mathbf{u} \in \mathcal{R}_q^N$.

We present the commit-and-prove protocol in Fig. 6 for proving linear relations. The only difference between this protocol and [LNP22, Fig. 4] is that for $\mathbf{z}_2$ we apply the new rejection sampling algorithm described above.

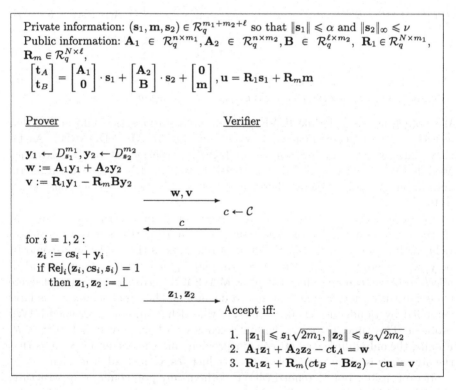

Fig. 6. Proof of knowledge $\Pi^{(1)}\left((\mathbf{s}_2, \mathbf{s}_1, \mathbf{m}), (f_1, f_2, \ldots, f_N)\right)$ of $(\mathbf{s}_1, \mathbf{s}_2, \bar{c}) \in \mathcal{R}_q^{m_1} \times \mathcal{R}_q^{m_2} \times \bar{\mathcal{C}}$ satisfying (i) $\mathbf{A}_1 \mathbf{s}_1 + \mathbf{A}_2 \mathbf{s}_2 = \mathbf{t}_A$, $\mathbf{B}\mathbf{s}_2 + \mathbf{m} = \mathbf{t}_B$ (ii) $\|\mathbf{s}_i \bar{c}\| \leqslant 2\mathfrak{s}_i \sqrt{2 m_i d}$ for $i = 1, 2$ and (iii) $\mathbf{R}_1 \mathbf{s}_1 + \mathbf{R}_m \mathbf{m} = \mathbf{u}$. Functions Rej_i are defined in Fig. 3.

3.2   Bimodal Gaussian Rejection Sampling on the Message

This subsection focuses on applying bimodal Gaussian rejection sampling on the message vector $\mathbf{s}_1$. First of all, we cannot apply Lemma 7 since it would potentially leak certain information about the message $\mathbf{s}_1$ which, unlike $\mathbf{s}_2$, is not freshly sampled every time a new proof is generated. Instead, we follow the original methodology from [DDLL13].

Concretely, let us focus on the protocol in Fig. 6. If one were to naively apply bimodal rejection sampling on $c\mathbf{s}_1$ then the masked opening of $c\mathbf{s}_1$ would become:

$$\mathbf{z}_1 := \mathbf{y}_1 + bc\mathbf{s}_1 \text{ where } b \leftarrow \{-1, 1\}.$$

As before, we set $\mathbf{z}_2 := \mathbf{y}_2 + c\mathbf{s}_2$. Hence, if we keep $\mathbf{w} := \mathbf{A}_1\mathbf{y}_1 + \mathbf{A}_2\mathbf{y}_2$ then by construction:

$$\mathbf{A}_1\mathbf{z}_1 + \mathbf{A}_2\mathbf{z}_2 = \mathbf{w} + c\left(\mathbf{A}_1 b\mathbf{s}_1 + \mathbf{A}_2\mathbf{s}_2\right).$$

Note that $\mathbf{A}_1 b\mathbf{s}_1 + \mathbf{A}_2\mathbf{s}_2$ is a top part of the ABDLOP commitment to $(b\mathbf{s}_1, \mathbf{m})$ under randomness $\mathbf{s}_2$. Thus, it is a natural approach to simply commit to $(b\mathbf{s}_1, \mathbf{m})$ and prove the quadratic equation. However, this comes with a big obstacle, i.e. we still need to prove the underlying relation in $\mathbf{s}_1, \mathbf{m}$ even though we committed to $b\mathbf{s}_1$ and $\mathbf{m}$. It might cause a problem even in the simple case of linear relations. Indeed, initially we want to prove that $\mathbf{R}_1\mathbf{s}_1 + \mathbf{R}_m\mathbf{m} = \mathbf{u}$. Since we committed to $b\mathbf{s}_1$ and not $\mathbf{s}_1$, it makes sense to try and prove the equivalent statement:

$$\mathbf{R}_1(b\mathbf{s}_1) + \mathbf{R}_m(b\mathbf{m}) = b\mathbf{u}. \tag{20}$$

This suggests that we should also commit to $b\mathbf{m}$ and not $\mathbf{m}$. However, it does not solve the issue completely since vector $\mathbf{u}$ is still multiplied by a (secret) sign b. Hence, the intuitive solution would be to also commit to b in the ABDLOP commitment, prove $b \in \{-1, 1\}$ and the linear relation (20) in $b\mathbf{s}_1, b\mathbf{m}$ and b. Therefore, the cost of such an approach is at least committing to an extra polynomial.

We show that for certain types of statements we can circumvent committing to b and still apply bimodal Gaussian rejection sampling. Namely, we focus on *sign-invariant* relations.

Definition 6. *Let $R \subseteq \{0, 1\}^* \times \mathcal{R}^{m_1+\ell}$ be a binary relation. We say that R is sign-invariant if for every pair $(u, \mathbf{w})$ we have: $R(u, \mathbf{w}) = 1 \iff R(u, -\mathbf{w}) = 1$.*

Suppose we want to prove knowledge of $(\mathbf{s}_1, \mathbf{m}) \in \mathcal{R}_q^{m_1+\ell}$ such that $(u, (\mathbf{s}_1, \mathbf{m})) \in R$ where R is a sign-invariant relation. Then, we can sample a fresh sign $b \leftarrow \{-1, 1\}$ and commit to $(b\mathbf{s}_1, b\mathbf{m})$ using the ABDLOP commitment. Further, we simply prove that $R(u, (b\mathbf{s}_1, b\mathbf{m})) = 1$ which implies that $R(u, (\mathbf{s}_1, \mathbf{m})) = 1$.

Concrete Instantiation. We demonstrate our intuition with the following example. Namely, we want to prove knowledge of $(\mathbf{s}_1, \mathbf{m})$ which satisfies:

$$\sigma(\mathbf{s}_1)^T\mathbf{s}_1 + \sigma(\mathbf{m})^T\mathbf{m} = 0.$$

Clearly, $(b\mathbf{s}_1, b\mathbf{m})$ satisfies the relation above for $b \in \{-1, 1\}$. As described before, we first sample a sign $b \leftarrow \{-1, 1\}$, randomness vector $\mathbf{s}_2 \leftarrow \chi$ and compute

$$\begin{bmatrix} \mathbf{t}_A \\ \mathbf{t}_B \end{bmatrix} = \begin{bmatrix} \mathbf{A}_1 \\ \mathbf{0} \end{bmatrix} \cdot b\mathbf{s}_1 + \begin{bmatrix} \mathbf{A}_2 \\ \mathbf{B} \end{bmatrix} \cdot \mathbf{s}_2 + \begin{bmatrix} \mathbf{0} \\ b\mathbf{m} \end{bmatrix}. \tag{21}$$

Then, we simply follow the multiplicative proof from [LNP22, Section 4] to prove that

$$\sigma(b\mathbf{s}_1)^T (b\mathbf{s}_1) + \sigma(b\mathbf{m})^T (b\mathbf{m}) = 0.$$

Concretely, consider the *masked opening* $\mathbf{z}_1 := \mathbf{y}_1 + bc\mathbf{s}_1$ of $\mathbf{s}_1$. Note that

$$\sigma(\mathbf{z}_1)^T \mathbf{z}_1 = c^2 \sigma(b\mathbf{s}_1)^T (b\mathbf{s}_1) + c \left(\sigma(\mathbf{y}_1)^T (b\mathbf{s}) + \mathbf{y}_1^T \sigma(b\mathbf{s}) \right) + \sigma(\mathbf{y}_1)^T \mathbf{y}_1$$

and hence the coefficient corresponding to the quadratic term c^2 is what we are interested in. Here, we used the property of the challenge space $\mathcal{C}$ that $c = \sigma(c)$ for $c \in \mathcal{C}$. We cannot do the same argument with $b\mathbf{m}$ since no masked opening of $b\mathbf{m}$ was sent. However, we observe that the verifier can compute $\mathbf{t}_B - \mathbf{B}\mathbf{z}_2 = -\mathbf{B}\mathbf{y}_2 + c(b\mathbf{m})$ which is of the similar form as the masked opening of $b\mathbf{s}_1$. Then

$$\sigma(\mathbf{t}_B - \mathbf{B}\mathbf{z}_2)^T (\mathbf{t}_B - \mathbf{B}\mathbf{z}_2)$$
$$= c^2 (b\mathbf{m})^T (b\mathbf{m}) - c \left(\sigma(\mathbf{B}\mathbf{y}_2)^T (b\mathbf{m}) + (\mathbf{B}\mathbf{y}_2)^T \sigma(b\mathbf{m}) \right) + \sigma(\mathbf{B}\mathbf{y}_2)^T \mathbf{B}\mathbf{y}_2.$$

Therefore, we want to prove that the term in front of c^2 in the following expression disappears, i.e.

$$\sigma(\mathbf{z}_1)^T \mathbf{z}_1 + \sigma(\mathbf{t}_B - \mathbf{B}\mathbf{z}_2)^T (\mathbf{t}_B - \mathbf{B}\mathbf{z}_2) = cg_1 + g_0$$

where

$$\begin{aligned} g_1 &:= \sigma(\mathbf{y}_1)^T (b\mathbf{s}) + \mathbf{y}_1^T \sigma(b\mathbf{s}) - \sigma(\mathbf{B}\mathbf{y}_2)^T (b\mathbf{m}) - (\mathbf{B}\mathbf{y}_2)^T \sigma(b\mathbf{m}) \\ g_0 &:= \sigma(\mathbf{y}_1)^T \mathbf{y}_1 + \sigma(\mathbf{B}\mathbf{y}_2)^T \mathbf{B}\mathbf{y}_2. \end{aligned} \tag{22}$$

The idea is then to additionally send a commitment $t = \mathbf{b}^T \mathbf{s}_2 + g_1$ to g_1 and send

$$v := g_0 + \mathbf{b}^T \mathbf{y}_2 = \sigma(\mathbf{y}_1)^T \mathbf{y}_1 + \sigma(\mathbf{B}\mathbf{y}_2)^T \mathbf{B}\mathbf{y}_2 + \mathbf{b}^T \mathbf{y}_2 \tag{23}$$

in the clear. Then, the verifier can check that:

$$v \overset{?}{=} \sigma(\mathbf{z}_1)^T \mathbf{z}_1 + \sigma(\mathbf{t}_B - \mathbf{B}\mathbf{z}_2)^T (\mathbf{t}_B - \mathbf{B}\mathbf{z}_2) + (\mathbf{b}^T \mathbf{z}_2 - ct). \tag{24}$$

We present the protocol for proving this relation in Fig. 7 and summarise its security properties in the full version of the paper.

Dealing with Relations Which Are Not Sign-Invariant. Typically, relations do not have the property that they are sign-invariant. In this case, to apply bimodal Gaussian rejection sampling on the message $\mathbf{s}_1$ one needs to be more careful. As hinted in the discussion above, one solution would be to commit to

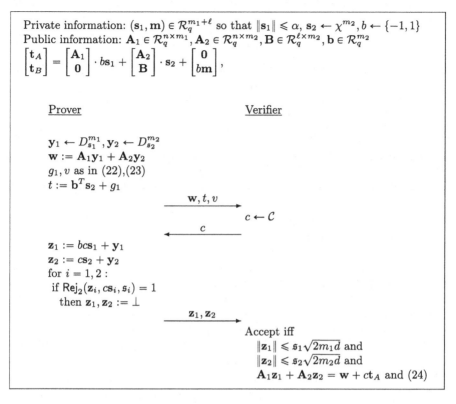

Private information: $(\mathbf{s}_1, \mathbf{m}) \in \mathcal{R}_q^{m_1+\ell}$ so that $\|\mathbf{s}_1\| \leqslant \alpha$, $\mathbf{s}_2 \leftarrow \chi^{m_2}, b \leftarrow \{-1,1\}$
Public information: $\mathbf{A}_1 \in \mathcal{R}_q^{n \times m_1}, \mathbf{A}_2 \in \mathcal{R}_q^{n \times m_2}, \mathbf{B} \in \mathcal{R}_q^{\ell \times m_2}, \mathbf{b} \in \mathcal{R}_q^{m_2}$

$$\begin{bmatrix} \mathbf{t}_A \\ \mathbf{t}_B \end{bmatrix} = \begin{bmatrix} \mathbf{A}_1 \\ \mathbf{0} \end{bmatrix} \cdot b\mathbf{s}_1 + \begin{bmatrix} \mathbf{A}_2 \\ \mathbf{B} \end{bmatrix} \cdot \mathbf{s}_2 + \begin{bmatrix} \mathbf{0} \\ b\mathbf{m} \end{bmatrix},$$

Prover   **Verifier**

$\mathbf{y}_1 \leftarrow D_{\mathfrak{s}_1}^{m_1}, \mathbf{y}_2 \leftarrow D_{\mathfrak{s}_2}^{m_2}$
$\mathbf{w} := \mathbf{A}_1\mathbf{y}_1 + \mathbf{A}_2\mathbf{y}_2$
g_1, v as in (22),(23)
$t := \mathbf{b}^T\mathbf{s}_2 + g_1$

$\xrightarrow{\quad \mathbf{w}, t, v \quad}$

$\qquad\qquad\qquad\qquad\qquad\qquad c \leftarrow \mathcal{C}$

$\xleftarrow{\quad c \quad}$

$\mathbf{z}_1 := bc\mathbf{s}_1 + \mathbf{y}_1$
$\mathbf{z}_2 := c\mathbf{s}_2 + \mathbf{y}_2$
for $i = 1, 2$:
$\quad$ if $\mathsf{Rej}_2(\mathbf{z}_i, c\mathbf{s}_i, \mathfrak{s}_i) = 1$
$\quad\quad$ then $\mathbf{z}_1, \mathbf{z}_2 := \perp$

$\xrightarrow{\quad \mathbf{z}_1, \mathbf{z}_2 \quad}$

$\qquad\qquad\qquad\qquad\qquad\qquad$ Accept iff
$\qquad\qquad\qquad\qquad\qquad\qquad \|\mathbf{z}_1\| \leqslant \mathfrak{s}_1\sqrt{2m_1 d}$ and
$\qquad\qquad\qquad\qquad\qquad\qquad \|\mathbf{z}_2\| \leqslant \mathfrak{s}_2\sqrt{2m_2 d}$ and
$\qquad\qquad\qquad\qquad\qquad\qquad \mathbf{A}_1\mathbf{z}_1 + \mathbf{A}_2\mathbf{z}_2 = \mathbf{w} + c\mathbf{t}_A$ and (24)

Fig. 7. Commit-and-prove protocol $\Pi_{\mathsf{quad}}(\mathbf{s}_2, \mathbf{s}_1, \mathbf{m})$ for messages $(\mathbf{s}_1, \mathbf{m}) \in \mathcal{R}_q^{m_1+\ell}$, randomness $\mathbf{s}_2 \in \mathcal{R}_q^{m_2}$ and $\bar{c} \in \bar{\mathcal{C}}$ which satisfy: $\mathbf{A}_1\mathbf{s}_1 + \mathbf{A}_2\mathbf{s}_2 = \mathbf{t}_A$, $\mathbf{Bs}_2 + \mathbf{m} = \mathbf{t}_B$ (ii) $\|\mathbf{s}_i\bar{c}\| \leqslant 2\mathfrak{s}_i\sqrt{2m_i d}$ for $i = 1, 2$ and (iii) $\sigma(\mathbf{s}_1)^T\mathbf{s}_1 + \sigma(\mathbf{m})^T\mathbf{m} = 0$.

the sign b (in the BDLOP part of the ABDLOP commitment) and prove that $b \in \{-1,1\}$[10]. Then, for example, to prove an arbitrary quadratic equation with automorphisms (15), we commit to $(b\mathbf{s}_1, b\mathbf{m} \parallel b)$ and equivalently prove:

$$\langle b\mathbf{s}_1 \parallel b\mathbf{m} \rangle_\sigma^T \mathbf{R}_{i,2} \langle b\mathbf{s}_1 \parallel b\mathbf{m} \rangle_\sigma + b\mathbf{r}_{i,1}^T \langle b\mathbf{s}_1 \parallel b\mathbf{m} \rangle_\sigma + r_{i,0} = 0$$

which is a quadratic equation in $b\mathbf{s}_1, b\mathbf{m}$ and b. Then, in the soundness argument of [LNP22] we would extract $\bar{\mathbf{s}}_1, \bar{\mathbf{m}}$ and $\bar{b} \in \{-1,1\}$ which satisfy

$$\langle \bar{\mathbf{s}}_1 \parallel \bar{\mathbf{m}} \rangle_\sigma^T \mathbf{R}_{i,2} \langle \bar{\mathbf{s}}_1 \parallel \bar{\mathbf{m}} \rangle_\sigma + \bar{b}\mathbf{r}_{i,1}^T \langle \bar{\mathbf{s}}_1 \parallel \bar{\mathbf{m}} \rangle_\sigma + r_{i,0} = 0.$$

Finally, since we proved that $\bar{b}$ is a sign, we define $(\mathbf{s}_1^*, \mathbf{m}^*) := (\bar{b}\bar{\mathbf{s}}_1, \bar{b}\bar{\mathbf{m}})$ and deduce that

$$\langle \mathbf{s}_1^* \parallel \mathbf{m}^* \rangle_\sigma^T \mathbf{R}_{i,2} \langle \mathbf{s}_1^* \parallel \mathbf{m}^* \rangle_\sigma + \mathbf{r}_{i,1}^T \langle \mathbf{s}_1^* \parallel \mathbf{m}^* \rangle_\sigma + r_{i,0} = 0$$

which is what we wanted to extract at the very beginning.

---

[10] Proving that b is a sign has already been covered in [LNP22, Section 5.1].

Similarly, to prove (17), we want to prove instead

$$\mathbf{P}_s(b\mathbf{s}_1) + \mathbf{P}_m(b\mathbf{m}) + b\mathbf{f} \in \{0, b\}^{n_{\mathsf{bin}}d}.$$

We observe that $x \in \{0, b\} = \{\frac{b-1}{2}, \frac{b+1}{2}\}$ if and only if $x - \frac{b-1}{2} \in \{0, 1\}$. Hence, the statement above is equivalent to:

$$\mathbf{P}_s(b\mathbf{s}_1) + \mathbf{P}_m(b\mathbf{m}) + b(\mathbf{f} - 2^{-1} \cdot \mathbf{1}) + 2^{-1} \cdot \mathbf{1} \in \{0, 1\}^{n_{\mathsf{bin}}d}$$

where $\mathbf{1} \in \mathcal{R}_q^{n_{\mathsf{bin}}}$ is the polynomial vector with the coefficient vector $\vec{1}$. Hence, we reduced our problem to proving that a linear combination of $b\mathbf{s}_1, b\mathbf{m}$ and b has binary coefficients. We conclude that using similar techniques, one can transform all the relations in $\mathbf{s}_1, \mathbf{m}$ described in Sect. 2.7 to equivalent ones in $b\mathbf{s}_1, b\mathbf{m}$ and $b \in \{-1, 1\}$.

4   Efficient One-out-of-Many Proofs

In this section we construct an efficient logarithmic-size one-out-of-many proof [GK15] with applications to lattice-based ring and group signatures using techniques from [LNP22] as the building block. In the full version of the paper we show how to further reduce the proof size using the techniques developed in Sect. 3, and eventually describe our ring signature construction.

The one-out-of-many proof considers the following problem. Informally, we want to prove knowledge of an opening to some commitment contained in a public set S without revealing any information about the commitment itself. In the lattice setting, we would like to prove knowledge of a short vector such that $\mathbf{As} \in S$, where S is a public set $S = \{\mathbf{t}_1, \ldots, \mathbf{t}_N\} \subseteq \mathcal{R}_q^n$ of size $N = d \cdot \mathfrak{d}^k$. In this section we assume that $\mathbf{s} \in \{0, 1\}^{md}$ has binary coefficients and $d = \mathfrak{l} \cdot \mathfrak{d}$ for $\mathfrak{l} \in \mathbb{N}$. For simplicity, we can already instantiate some of these parameters as $(d, \mathfrak{d}, \mathfrak{l}) = (64, 8, 16)$.

We now use the observation from [ESS+19, GK15, BCC+15] that $\mathbf{As} \in S$ if and only if there exists a binary vector $\vec{v} \in \{0, 1\}^N$ with exactly one 1, i.e. a unit vector, such that

$$\left[\vec{t}_1 \ \vec{t}_2 \ \cdots \ \vec{t}_N\right] \vec{v} = A\vec{s} \tag{25}$$

where $A = \mathsf{rot}(\mathbf{A}) \in \mathbb{Z}_q^{nd \times md}$ is the the rotation matrix of $\mathbf{A}$. One could then directly prove knowledge of $\vec{s}$ and $\vec{v}$ which satisfy conditions above using the protocol from Sect. 2.7. However, the proof size grows linearly in N since we would commit to the whole vector $\vec{v}$.

In order to circumvent this limitation, [GK15, BCC+15] observe that vector $\vec{v}$ can be uniquely decomposed into unit vectors $\vec{v}_1, \ldots, \vec{v}_k \in \{0, 1\}^{\mathfrak{d}}$ and $\vec{v}_{k+1} \in \{0, 1\}^d$ such that

$$\vec{v} = \vec{v}_1 \otimes \vec{v}_2 \otimes \cdots \otimes \vec{v}_{k+1} := \vec{v}_1 \otimes (\vec{v}_2 \otimes (\cdots \otimes (\vec{v}_k \otimes \vec{v}_{k+1}))). \tag{26}$$

For notational convenience, let us define the set of polynomials $\mathcal{X}$ in $\mathcal{R}_q$ with their coefficient vectors being a unit vector. Concretely, $\mathcal{X}$ is defined as follows:

$$\mathcal{X} := \{1, X, X^2, \ldots, X^{d-1}\}.$$

In the end, we want to commit to $\mathbf{s}$ and polynomials $u_1, \ldots, u_k, v_{k+1} \in \mathcal{X}$ such that $\vec{u}_i = \vec{v}_i \parallel 0^{d-\mathfrak{d}} \in \mathbb{Z}_q^{d11}$ for $i \in [k]$ and prove

$$T(\vec{v}_1 \otimes \cdots \otimes \vec{v}_{k+1}) = A\vec{s} \tag{27}$$

where $T \in \mathbb{Z}_q^{nd \times N}$ is the matrix on the left-hand side of (25). We formally define the corresponding relation:

$$R_{\mathsf{oom}} := \left\{ \begin{array}{c} ((T, A), (\mathbf{s}, u_1, \ldots, u_k, v_{k+1})) : \mathbf{s} \in \{0, 1\}^{md} \wedge T(\vec{v}_1 \otimes \cdots \otimes \vec{v}_{k+1}) = A\vec{s} \\ \wedge u_1, \ldots, u_k, v_{k+1} \in \mathcal{X} \text{ where } \vec{u}_i := \vec{v}_i \parallel 0^{d-\mathfrak{d}} \end{array} \right\}.$$

We now describe a commit-and-prove system for relation R_{oom} using the ABDLOP commitment. Suppose that $k \geq 1$, otherwise one can prove this relation directly using the framework from [LNP22].

First, note that proving $u_1, \ldots, u_k, v_{k+1} \in \mathcal{X}$ and $\mathbf{s} \in \{0, 1\}^{md}$ can be done directly using the techniques from Sect. 2.7 hence we focus first on (27). Our strategy to prove this equation with $k - 1$ tensor products would be somehow to reduce it to proving an equation of the same form with only $k - 2$ tensor products. Then, by recursion, we will end up with a system of linear equations with no tensor products involved and thus we can apply the methods presented in Sect. 2.7.

The key idea to reduce the number of tensor products is to ask the verifier for $\mathfrak{l}$ challenges $\vec{\varphi}_1, \ldots, \vec{\varphi}_{\mathfrak{l}} \in \mathbb{Z}_q^{nd}$ and then prove that:

$$\langle T(\vec{v}_1 \otimes \cdots \otimes \vec{v}_{k+1}) - A\vec{s}, \vec{\varphi}_i \rangle = 0 \quad \text{for } i = 1, 2, \ldots, \mathfrak{l}.$$

Note that if (27) was not true, then these $\mathfrak{l}$ equations above would hold with probability at most $q_1^{-\mathfrak{l}}$. Now, if we write

$$T := \begin{bmatrix} T_{0,1} & T_{0,2} & \cdots & T_{0,\mathfrak{d}} \end{bmatrix} \quad \text{where each } T_{0,i} \in \mathbb{Z}_q^{nd \times d\mathfrak{d}^{k-1}}$$

then by simple algebraic manipulation we obtain

$$\begin{aligned} \langle T(\vec{v}_1 \otimes \cdots \otimes \vec{v}_{k+1}) - A\vec{s}, \vec{\varphi}_i \rangle &= \langle \vec{v}_1 \otimes \cdots \otimes \vec{v}_{k+1}, \vec{\varphi}_i^T T \rangle - \langle \vec{s}, A^T \vec{\varphi}_i \rangle \\ &= \langle \vec{v}_1, T_{1,i}(\vec{v}_2 \otimes \cdots \otimes \vec{v}_{k+1}) \rangle - \langle \vec{s}, A^T \vec{\varphi}_i \rangle \end{aligned}$$

where

$$T_{1,i} := \begin{bmatrix} \vec{\varphi}_i^T T_{0,1} \\ \vdots \\ \vec{\varphi}_i^T T_{0,\mathfrak{d}} \end{bmatrix} \in \mathbb{Z}_q^{\mathfrak{d} \times d\mathfrak{d}^{k-1}}.$$

Now, let us define $\vec{w}_i := T_{1,i}(\vec{v}_2 \otimes \cdots \otimes \vec{v}_{k+1})$ and $w \in \mathcal{R}_q$ such that

$$\vec{w} = \vec{w}_1 \parallel \cdots \parallel \vec{w}_{\mathfrak{l}} \in \mathbb{Z}_q^d.$$

---

[11] Alternatively, $u_i \in \{1, X, X^2, \ldots, X^{\mathfrak{d}-1}\}$.

Next, we commit to w and show that for all i,

$$\langle \vec{v}_1, \vec{w}_i \rangle - \langle \vec{s}, A^T \vec{\varphi}_i \rangle = 0 \quad \text{and} \quad \vec{w}_i := T_{1,i}(\vec{v}_2 \otimes \cdots \otimes \vec{v}_{k+1}).$$

We observe that the first statement is equivalent to proving that the constant coefficient of

$$X^{(i-1)\mathfrak{d}} u_1 \sigma(w) - \sigma(\mathbf{a}_i)^T \mathbf{s}$$

is equal to zero where the coefficient vector of $\mathbf{a}_i \in \mathcal{R}_q^m$ is exactly $\vec{a}_i := A^T \vec{\varphi}_i$.

Lemma 8. *Let $i \in [\mathfrak{l}]$. Then, the constant coefficient of $X^{(i-1)\mathfrak{d}} u_1 \sigma(w) \in \mathcal{R}_q$ is equal to $\langle \vec{v}_1, \vec{w}_i \rangle$.*

Proof. First, we note that $\langle \vec{v}_1, \vec{w}_i \rangle = \langle X^{(i-1)\mathfrak{d}} u_1, w \rangle$. Here, we used the fact that the coefficient vector of u_1 is of the form $\vec{v}_1 \parallel 0^{d-\mathfrak{d}}$. Then, by Lemma 2, $\langle X^{(i-1)\mathfrak{d}} u_1, w \rangle$ is the constant coefficient of $X^{(i-1)\mathfrak{d}} u_1 \sigma(w)$.

On the other hand, the second statement can be combined for all i and written as:

$$\vec{w} = \begin{bmatrix} T_{1,1} \\ \vdots \\ T_{1,\mathfrak{l}} \end{bmatrix} (\vec{v}_2 \otimes \cdots \otimes \vec{v}_{k+1}). \tag{28}$$

Thus, we reduce the one-out-of-many problem to proving knowledge of a tuple $(\mathbf{s}, u_1, \ldots, u_k, v_{k+1}, w)$ which satisfies the following conditions: (i) $\mathbf{s} \in \{0,1\}^{md}$, (ii) $T_1(\vec{v}_2 \otimes \cdots \otimes \vec{v}_{k+1}) = \vec{w}$, (iii) for all $i \in [\mathfrak{l}]$, the constant coefficient of $X^{(i-1)\mathfrak{d}} u_1 \sigma(w) - \sigma(\mathbf{a}_i)^T \mathbf{s}$ is zero, and (iv) $u_1, \ldots, u_k, v_{k+1} \in \mathcal{X}$ where

$$\vec{u}_i := \vec{v}_i \parallel 0^{d-\mathfrak{d}} \text{ for } i \in [k] \quad \text{and} \quad T_1 := \begin{bmatrix} T_{1,1} \\ \vdots \\ T_{1,\mathfrak{l}} \end{bmatrix} \in \mathbb{Z}_q^{d \times d\mathfrak{d}^{k-1}}.$$

Note that the second statement only involves $k - 2$ tensor products.

We can define the correspond relation as:

$$R := \left\{ \begin{array}{l} ((T_1, (\mathbf{a}_i)_{i \in [\mathfrak{l}]}), (\mathbf{s}, u_1, \ldots, u_k, v_{k+1}, w)) : \mathbf{s} \in \{0,1\}^{md} \wedge T_1(\vec{v}_2 \otimes \cdots \otimes \vec{v}_{k+1}) = \vec{w} \\ \wedge \forall i \in [\mathfrak{l}], \text{ const coeff. of } X^{(i-1)\mathfrak{d}} u_1 \sigma(w) - \sigma(\mathbf{a}_i)^T \mathbf{s} \text{ is zero} \\ \wedge u_1, \ldots, u_k, v_{k+1} \in \mathcal{X} \text{ where } \vec{u}_i := \vec{v}_i \parallel 0^{d-\mathfrak{d}} \end{array} \right\}.$$

Intermediate Relations. We construct a commit-and-prove system for relation R using recursion. Namely, take $1 \leqslant j \leqslant k$ and consider the following generalised relation

$$R_j := \left\{ \begin{array}{l} \left((T_j \in \mathbb{Z}_q^{d \times d\mathfrak{d}^{k-j}}, (\mathbf{a}_i)_{i \in [\mathfrak{l}]}, (\varphi_{\iota,i})_{\iota \in [j-1], i \in [\mathfrak{l}]}), (\mathbf{s}, u_1, \ldots, u_k, v_{k+1}, w_1, \ldots, w_j) \right) : \\ \mathbf{s} \in \{0,1\}^{md} \wedge T_j(\vec{v}_{j+1} \otimes \cdots \otimes \vec{v}_{k+1}) = \vec{w}_j \\ \wedge \forall i \in [\mathfrak{l}], \text{ const coeff. of } X^{(i-1)\mathfrak{d}} u_1 \sigma(w_1) - \sigma(\mathbf{a}_i)^T \mathbf{s} \text{ is zero} \\ \wedge \forall \iota \in [j-1], i \in [\mathfrak{l}], \text{ const coeff. of } X^{(i-1)\mathfrak{d}} u_{\iota+1} \sigma(w_{\iota+1}) - \sigma(\varphi_{\iota,i}) w_\iota \text{ is zero} \\ \wedge u_1, \ldots, u_k, v_{k+1} \in \mathcal{X} \text{ where } \vec{u}_i := \vec{v}_i \parallel 0^{d-\mathfrak{d}} \end{array} \right\}. $$

$$\tag{29}$$

We highlight that in R_j elements $\varphi_{\iota,i}$ are polynomials in $\mathcal{R}_q$. Also, it is easy to see that $R_1 = R$.

Base Case. We first show how to prove R_k only using the methods described in Sect. 2.7. In the following, we say that a statement is of Type-n if it corresponds to the Statement n in Sect. 2.7.

To begin with, using the ABDLOP commitment we commit to

$$\mathbf{s}_1 := \mathbf{s} \parallel u_1 \parallel \cdots \parallel u_k \parallel v_{k+1} \in \mathcal{R}_q^{m+k+1}, \quad \mathbf{m} := (w_1, \ldots, w_k) \in \mathcal{R}_q^k.$$

Then, proving $\mathbf{s} \in \{0,1\}^{md}$ and $u_1, \ldots, u_k, v_{k+1} \in \{0,1\}^d$ is of Type-3. Next, by Lemma 2, proving $T_k \vec{v}_{k+1} = \vec{w}_k$ and $\langle \vec{1}, \vec{v}_i \rangle = 1$ for $i \in [k+1]$ is of Type-2. Further, it is easy to see that proving the constant coefficients of $X^{(i-1)\mathfrak{d}} u_1 \sigma(w_1) - \sigma(\mathbf{a}_i)^T \mathbf{s}$ and $X^{(i-1)\mathfrak{d}} u_{\iota+1} \sigma(w_{\iota+1}) - \sigma(\varphi_{\iota,i}) w_\iota$ vanish is of Type-2. Finally, proving that $\vec{u}_i = \vec{v}_i \parallel 0^{d-\mathfrak{d}}$ for $i \in [k]$ is equivalent to proving that the constant coefficient of $X^{-j} u_i$ is zero for $\mathfrak{d} \leqslant j \leqslant d$, which is of Type-2.

From now on, we will call the commit-and-prove protocol for relation R_k described above as Π_k.

Recursive Step. Let us assume we have a commit-and-prove system Π_{j+1} for relation R_{j+1} where $2 \leqslant j + 1 \leqslant k$. Now we want to use it to prove relation R_j. We observe that the only statement which is included in R_j but not in R_{j+1} is

$$T_j(\vec{v}_{j+1} \otimes \cdots \otimes \vec{v}_{k+1}) = \vec{w}_j. \tag{30}$$

We prove this equation as before. Namely, we ask the verifier for $\mathfrak{l}$ challenges $\vec{\varphi}_{j,1}, \ldots, \vec{\varphi}_{\mathfrak{l}} \in \mathbb{Z}_q^d$ and then prove that:

$$\langle T_j(\vec{v}_{j+1} \otimes \cdots \otimes \vec{v}_{k+1}) - \vec{w}_j, \vec{\varphi}_{j,i} \rangle = 0 \quad \text{for } i = 1, 2, \ldots, \mathfrak{l}.$$

Note that if (27) was not true, then these $\mathfrak{l}$ equations above would hold with probability at most $q_1^{-\mathfrak{l}}$. Now, if we write

$$T_j := \begin{bmatrix} T_{j,1} & T_{j,2} & \cdots & T_{j,\mathfrak{d}} \end{bmatrix} \quad \text{where each } T_{j,i} \in \mathbb{Z}_q^{d \times d\mathfrak{d}^{k-j-1}}$$

then we have

$$
\begin{aligned}
\langle T_j(\vec{v}_{j+1} \otimes \cdots \otimes \vec{v}_{k+1}) - \vec{w}_j, \vec{\varphi}_{j,i} \rangle &= \langle \vec{v}_{j+1} \otimes \cdots \otimes \vec{v}_{k+1}, \vec{\varphi}_{j,i}^T T_j \rangle - \langle \vec{w}_j, \vec{\varphi}_{j,i} \rangle \\
&= \langle \vec{v}_{j+1} \otimes \cdots \otimes \vec{v}_{k+1}, \vec{\varphi}_{j,i}^T T_j \rangle - \langle \vec{w}_j, \vec{\varphi}_{j,i} \rangle \\
&= \langle \vec{v}_{j+1}, T_{j+1,i}(\vec{v}_{j+2} \otimes \cdots \otimes \vec{v}_{k+1}) \rangle - \langle \vec{w}_j, \vec{\varphi}_{j,i} \rangle
\end{aligned}
$$

where

$$T_{j+1,i} := \begin{bmatrix} \vec{\varphi}_{j,i}^T T_{j,1} \\ \vdots \\ \vec{\varphi}_{j,i}^T T_{j,\mathfrak{d}} \end{bmatrix} \in \mathbb{Z}_q^{\mathfrak{d} \times \mathfrak{d}^{k-j-1}}.$$

Now, let us define $\vec{w}_{j+1,i} := T_{j+1,i}(\vec{v}_{j+2} \otimes \cdots \otimes \vec{v}_{k+1})$ and $w_{j+1} \in \mathcal{R}_q$ so that

$$\vec{w}_{j+1} = \vec{w}_{j+1,1} \parallel \cdots \parallel \vec{w}_{j+1,\mathfrak{l}} \in \mathbb{Z}_q^d.$$

Then, we need to show that for all i,

$$\langle \vec{v}_{j+1}, \vec{w}_{j+1,i} \rangle - \langle \vec{w}_j, \vec{\varphi}_{j,i} \rangle = 0 \quad \text{and} \quad \vec{w}_{j+1,i} = T_{j+1,i}(\vec{v}_{j+2} \otimes \cdots \otimes \vec{v}_{k+1}).$$

The first statement is equivalent to proving that the constant coefficient of

$$X^{(i-1)\mathfrak{d}} u_{j+1} \sigma(w_{j+1}) - \sigma(\varphi_{j,i}) w_j$$

is equal to zero. The second statement, however, can be combined for all i and written as:

$$\vec{w}_{j+1} = T_{j+1}(\vec{v}_{j+2} \otimes \cdots \otimes \vec{v}_{k+1}) \quad \text{where} \quad T_{j+1} := \begin{bmatrix} T_{j+1,1} \\ \vdots \\ T_{j+1,\mathfrak{l}} \end{bmatrix} \in \mathbb{Z}_q^{d \times \mathfrak{d}^{k-j-1}}. \quad (31)$$

Private information: $\mathbf{s}_1 := (\mathbf{s}, u_1, \ldots, u_k, v_{k+1}), \mathbf{m} := (w_1, \ldots, w_j), \mathbf{s}_2 \in \mathcal{R}_q^{m_2}$

Public information: $\mathbf{A}_1 \in \mathcal{R}_q^{n \times (m+k+1)}, \mathbf{A}_2 \in \mathcal{R}_q^{n \times m_2}, \mathbf{b}_1, \ldots, \mathbf{b}_j \in \mathcal{R}_q^{m_2},$

$T_j \in \mathbb{Z}_q^{d \times \mathfrak{d}^{k-j}}, (\mathbf{a}_i)_{i \in [\mathfrak{l}]}, (\varphi_{\iota,i})_{\iota \in [j-1], i \in [\mathfrak{l}]}$

$$\begin{bmatrix} t_A \\ t_1 \\ \vdots \\ t_j \end{bmatrix} = \begin{bmatrix} \mathbf{A}_1 \\ \mathbf{0} \end{bmatrix} \cdot \mathbf{s}_1 + \begin{bmatrix} \mathbf{A}_2 \\ \mathbf{b}_1^T \\ \vdots \\ \mathbf{b}_j^T \end{bmatrix} \cdot \mathbf{s}_2 + \begin{bmatrix} \mathbf{0} \\ w_1 \\ \vdots \\ w_j \end{bmatrix}$$

Prover   Verifier

$$\xleftarrow{\quad \vec{\varphi}_{j,i} \quad} \quad \vec{\varphi}_{j,1}, \ldots, \vec{\varphi}_{j,\mathfrak{l}} \leftarrow \mathbb{Z}_q^d$$

$T_j := \begin{bmatrix} T_{j,1} & T_{j,2} & \cdots & T_{j,\mathfrak{d}} \end{bmatrix}$

$T_{j+1,i} := \begin{bmatrix} \vec{\varphi}_{j,i}^T T_{j,1} \\ \vdots \\ \vec{\varphi}_{j,i}^T T_{j,\mathfrak{d}} \end{bmatrix}$ for $i \in [\mathfrak{l}]$

$T_{j+1} := \begin{bmatrix} T_{j+1,1} \\ \vdots \\ T_{j+1,\mathfrak{l}} \end{bmatrix} \in \mathbb{Z}_q^{d \times \mathfrak{d}^{k-j-1}}$

$\vec{w}_{j+1} := T_{j+1}(\vec{v}_{j+2} \otimes \cdots \otimes \vec{v}_{k+1})$

$t_{j+1} := \mathbf{b}_{j+1}^T \mathbf{s}_2 + w_{j+1}$ $\xrightarrow{\quad t_{j+1} \quad}$

Run Π_{j+1} Accept iff

                                                  Π_{j+1} accepts

Fig. 8. Commit-and-prove protocol Π_j for the relation R_j where $j < k$.

Therefore, we reduced proving (30) to proving that

- $X^{(i-1)\mathfrak{d}} u_{j+1} \sigma(w_{j+1}) - \sigma(\varphi_{j,i}) w_j$ is equal to zero
- $\vec{w}_{j+1} = T_{j+1}(\vec{v}_{j+2} \otimes \cdots \otimes \vec{v}_{k+1})$

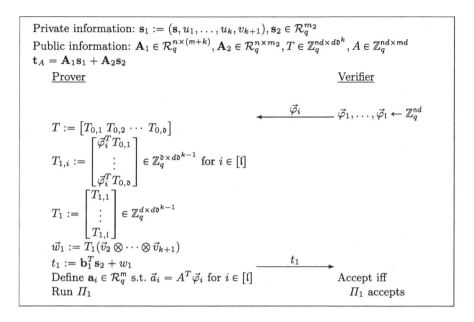

Fig. 9. Commit-and-prove protocol Π_{oom} for the relation R_{oom}.

which in combination with other relations in R_j, it directly reduces to proving relations in R_{j+1}.

In Fig. 8 we give a commit-and-prove protocol for relation R_j which uses Π_j as a black-box. One observes by discussion above that the correctness error for Π_j is the same as for Π_k (which can be calculated directly from [LNP22]). Simulatability follows from the fact that running Π_j, and thus Π_{j+1} up to Π_k as subroutines, involves only sending intermediate commitments t_i to w_i which can be simulated by the Extended-MLWE assumption. Finally, one can prove by induction that the knowledge soundness error for the protocol Π_j is $(k-j) \cdot q_1^{-l} + \varepsilon_k$ where ε_k is the knowledge soundness error for Π_k and is computed as in [LNP22]. The expected runtime of the extractor, that has black-box access to a (potentially malicious) prover which runs in time T, is $2^{k-j} \cdot \mathrm{poly}(T)$. Consequently, we can only consider values k which are logarithmic in the security parameter. Due to space constraints, we refer to the full version of the paper for more details.

Back to R_{oom}. At the very beginning of this section we showed how to reduce proving relation R_{oom} to proving R_1. Later on, we described a commit-and-prove protocol for R_1. Hence, we combine these two results to obtain a commit-and-prove protocol Π_{oom} in Fig. 9 for the one-out-of-many relation R_{oom}. Arguing similarly as above, the correctness error for Π_{oom} is the same as for Π_k and the soundness error is at most $k q_1^{-l} + \varepsilon_k$.

Acknowledgements. We would like to thank the anonymous reviewers for useful feedback. This work was conducted when the second author was at IBM Research Europe, and it was supported by the EU H2020 ERC Project 101002845 PLAZA.

References

[AFK21] Attema, T., Fehr, S., Klooß, M.: Fiat-Shamir transformation of multi-round interactive proofs. Cryptology ePrint Archive, Paper 2021/1377 (2021). https://eprint.iacr.org/2021/1377

[Ajt96] Ajtai, M.: Generating hard instances of lattice problems (extended abstract). In: STOC, pp. 99–108 (1996)

[ALS20] Attema, T., Lyubashevsky, V., Seiler, G.: Practical product proofs for lattice commitments. In: Micciancio, D., Ristenpart, T. (eds.) CRYPTO 2020. LNCS, vol. 12171, pp. 470–499. Springer, Cham (2020). https://doi.org/10.1007/978-3-030-56880-1_17

[AP12] Alperin-Sheriff, J., Peikert, C.: Circular and KDM security for identity-based encryption. In: Fischlin, M., Buchmann, J., Manulis, M. (eds.) PKC 2012. LNCS, vol. 7293, pp. 334–352. Springer, Heidelberg (2012). https://doi.org/10.1007/978-3-642-30057-8_20

[ASA16] Alperin-Sheriff, J., Apon, D.: Dimension-preserving reductions from LWE to LWR. Cryptology ePrint Archive, Report 2016/589 (2016). https://ia.cr/2016/589

[Ban93] Banaszczyk, W.: New bounds in some transference theorems in the geometry of numbers. Math. Ann. **296**(1), 625–635 (1993)

[BCC+15] Bootle, J., Cerulli, A., Chaidos, P., Ghadafi, E., Groth, J., Petit, C.: Short accountable ring signatures based on DDH. In: Pernul, G., Ryan, P.Y.A., Weippl, E. (eds.) ESORICS 2015. LNCS, vol. 9326, pp. 243–265. Springer, Cham (2015). https://doi.org/10.1007/978-3-319-24174-6_13

[BDE+22] Buser, M., et al.: A survey on exotic signatures for post-quantum blockchain: challenges & research directions. Cryptology ePrint Archive, Paper 2022/1151 (2022). https://eprint.iacr.org/2022/1151

[BDK+21] Beullens, W., Dobson, S., Katsumata, S., Lai, Y.-F., Pintore, F.: Group signatures and more from isogenies and lattices: generic, simple, and efficient. IACR Cryptology ePrint Archive, p. 1366 (2021)

[BDL+18] Baum, C., Damgård, I., Lyubashevsky, V., Oechsner, S., Peikert, C.: More efficient commitments from structured lattice assumptions. In: Catalano, D., De Prisco, R. (eds.) SCN 2018. LNCS, vol. 11035, pp. 368–385. Springer, Cham (2018). https://doi.org/10.1007/978-3-319-98113-0_20

[BJRW21] Boudgoust, K., Jeudy, C., Roux-Langlois, A., Wen, W.: On the hardness of module-LWE with binary secret. In: Paterson, K.G. (ed.) CT-RSA 2021. LNCS, vol. 12704, pp. 503–526. Springer, Cham (2021). https://doi.org/10.1007/978-3-030-75539-3_21

[BKP20] Beullens, W., Katsumata, S., Pintore, F.: Calamari and Falafl: logarithmic (linkable) ring signatures from isogenies and lattices. In: Moriai, S., Wang, H. (eds.) ASIACRYPT 2020. LNCS, vol. 12492, pp. 464–492. Springer, Cham (2020). https://doi.org/10.1007/978-3-030-64834-3_16

[BLS19] Bootle, J., Lyubashevsky, V., Seiler, G.: Algebraic techniques for short(er) exact lattice-based zero-knowledge proofs. In: Boldyreva, A., Micciancio, D. (eds.) CRYPTO 2019. LNCS, vol. 11692, pp. 176–202. Springer, Cham (2019). https://doi.org/10.1007/978-3-030-26948-7_7

[DDGR20] Dachman-Soled, D., Ducas, L., Gong, H., Rossi, M.: LWE with side information: attacks and concrete security estimation. In: Micciancio, D., Ristenpart, T. (eds.) CRYPTO 2020. LNCS, vol. 12171, pp. 329–358. Springer, Cham (2020). https://doi.org/10.1007/978-3-030-56880-1_12

[DDLL13] Ducas, L., Durmus, A., Lepoint, T., Lyubashevsky, V.: Lattice signatures and bimodal Gaussians. In: Canetti, R., Garay, J.A. (eds.) CRYPTO 2013. LNCS, vol. 8042, pp. 40–56. Springer, Heidelberg (2013). https://doi.org/10.1007/978-3-642-40041-4_3

[DGK+10] Dodis, Y., Goldwasser, S., Tauman Kalai, Y., Peikert, C., Vaikuntanathan, V.: Public-key encryption schemes with auxiliary inputs. In: Micciancio, D. (ed.) TCC 2010. LNCS, vol. 5978, pp. 361–381. Springer, Heidelberg (2010). https://doi.org/10.1007/978-3-642-11799-2_22

[DLP14] Ducas, L., Lyubashevsky, V., Prest, T.: Efficient identity-based encryption over NTRU lattices. In: Sarkar, P., Iwata, T. (eds.) ASIACRYPT 2014. LNCS, vol. 8874, pp. 22–41. Springer, Heidelberg (2014). https://doi.org/10.1007/978-3-662-45608-8_2

[DP16] Ducas, L., Prest, T.: Fast Fourier orthogonalization. In: ISSAC, pp. 191–198 (2016)

[ENS20] Esgin, M.F., Nguyen, N.K., Seiler, G.: Practical exact proofs from lattices: new techniques to exploit fully-splitting rings. In: Moriai, S., Wang, H. (eds.) ASIACRYPT 2020. LNCS, vol. 12492, pp. 259–288. Springer, Cham (2020). https://doi.org/10.1007/978-3-030-64834-3_9

[ESLL19] Esgin, M.F., Steinfeld, R., Liu, J.K., Liu, D.: Lattice-based zero-knowledge proofs: new techniques for shorter and faster constructions and applications. In: Boldyreva, A., Micciancio, D. (eds.) CRYPTO 2019. LNCS, vol. 11692, pp. 115–146. Springer, Cham (2019). https://doi.org/10.1007/978-3-030-26948-7_5

[ESS+19] Esgin, M.F., Steinfeld, R., Sakzad, A., Liu, J.K., Liu, D.: Short lattice-based one-out-of-many proofs and applications to ring signatures. In: Deng, R.H., Gauthier-Umaña, V., Ochoa, M., Yung, M. (eds.) ACNS 2019. LNCS, vol. 11464, pp. 67–88. Springer, Cham (2019). https://doi.org/10.1007/978-3-030-21568-2_4

[ESZ21] Esgin, M.F., Steinfeld, R., Zhao, R.K.: Matrict+: more efficient post-quantum private blockchain payments. IACR Cryptology ePrint Archive, p. 545 (2021)

[EZS+19] Esgin, M.F., Zhao, R.K., Steinfeld, R., Liu, J.K., Liu, D.: Matrict: efficient, scalable and post-quantum blockchain confidential transactions protocol. In: CCS, pp. 567–584. ACM (2019)

[FHK+20] Fouque, P.-A., et al.: Falcon: Fast-Fourier lattice-based compact signatures over NTRU. Technical report (2020). https://falcon-sign.info/falcon.pdf

[FS86] Fiat, A., Shamir, A.: How to prove yourself: practical solutions to identification and signature problems. In: Odlyzko, A.M. (ed.) CRYPTO 1986. LNCS, vol. 263, pp. 186–194. Springer, Heidelberg (1987). https://doi.org/10.1007/3-540-47721-7_12

[GK15] Groth, J., Kohlweiss, M.: One-out-of-many proofs: or how to leak a secret and spend a coin. In: Oswald, E., Fischlin, M. (eds.) EUROCRYPT 2015. LNCS, vol. 9057, pp. 253–280. Springer, Heidelberg (2015). https://doi.org/10.1007/978-3-662-46803-6_9

[GPV08] Gentry, C., Peikert, C., Vaikuntanathan, V.: Trapdoors for hard lattices and new cryptographic constructions. In: STOC, pp. 197–206 (2008)

[HHGP+03] Hoffstein, J., Howgrave-Graham, N., Pipher, J., Silverman, J.H., Whyte, W.: NTRUSign: digital signatures using the NTRU lattice. In: Joye, M. (ed.) CT-RSA 2003. LNCS, vol. 2612, pp. 122–140. Springer, Heidelberg (2003). https://doi.org/10.1007/3-540-36563-X_9

[LAZ19] Lu, X., Au, M.H., Zhang, Z.: Raptor: a practical lattice-based (linkable) ring signature. In: Deng, R.H., Gauthier-Umaña, V., Ochoa, M., Yung, M. (eds.) ACNS 2019. LNCS, vol. 11464, pp. 110–130. Springer, Cham (2019). https://doi.org/10.1007/978-3-030-21568-2_6

[LMPR08] Lyubashevsky, V., Micciancio, D., Peikert, C., Rosen, A.: SWIFFT: a modest proposal for FFT hashing. In: Nyberg, K. (ed.) FSE 2008. LNCS, vol. 5086, pp. 54–72. Springer, Heidelberg (2008). https://doi.org/10.1007/978-3-540-71039-4_4

[LNP22] Lyubashevsky, V., Nguyen, N.K., Plancon, M.: Lattice-based zero-knowledge proofs and applications: shorter, simpler, and more general. Cryptology ePrint Archive, Paper 2022/284 (2022). https://eprint.iacr.org/2022/284. To appear at CRYPTO 2022

[LNPS21] Lyubashevsky, V., Nguyen, N.K., Plancon, M., Seiler, G.: Shorter lattice-based group signatures via "almost free" encryption and other optimizations. In: Tibouchi, M., Wang, H. (eds.) ASIACRYPT 2021. LNCS, vol. 13093, pp. 218–248. Springer, Cham (2021). https://doi.org/10.1007/978-3-030-92068-5_8

[LNS20] Lyubashevsky, V., Nguyen, N.K., Seiler, G.: Practical lattice-based zero-knowledge proofs for integer relations. In: CCS, pp. 1051–1070. ACM (2020)

[LNS21a] Lyubashevsky, V., Nguyen, N.K., Seiler, G.: Shorter lattice-based zero-knowledge proofs via one-time commitments. In: Garay, J.A. (ed.) PKC 2021. LNCS, vol. 12710, pp. 215–241. Springer, Cham (2021). https://doi.org/10.1007/978-3-030-75245-3_9

[LNS21b] Lyubashevsky, V., Nguyen, N.K., Seiler, G.: SMILE: set membership from ideal lattices with applications to ring signatures and confidential transactions. In: Malkin, T., Peikert, C. (eds.) CRYPTO 2021. LNCS, vol. 12826, pp. 611–640. Springer, Cham (2021). https://doi.org/10.1007/978-3-030-84245-1_21

[LNSW13] Ling, S., Nguyen, K., Stehlé, D., Wang, H.: Improved zero-knowledge proofs of knowledge for the ISIS problem, and applications. In: Kurosawa, K., Hanaoka, G. (eds.) PKC 2013. LNCS, vol. 7778, pp. 107–124. Springer, Heidelberg (2013). https://doi.org/10.1007/978-3-642-36362-7_8

[LS15] Langlois, A., Stehlé, D.: Worst-case to average-case reductions for module lattices. Des. Codes Crypt. 75(3), 565–599 (2015)

[Lyu09] Lyubashevsky, V.: Fiat-Shamir with aborts: applications to lattice and factoring-based signatures. In: Matsui, M. (ed.) ASIACRYPT 2009. LNCS, vol. 5912, pp. 598–616. Springer, Heidelberg (2009). https://doi.org/10.1007/978-3-642-10366-7_35

[Lyu12] Lyubashevsky, V.: Lattice signatures without trapdoors. In: Pointcheval, D., Johansson, T. (eds.) EUROCRYPT 2012. LNCS, vol. 7237, pp. 738–755. Springer, Heidelberg (2012). https://doi.org/10.1007/978-3-642-29011-4_43

[NY90] Naor, M., Yung, M.: Public-key cryptosystems provably secure against chosen ciphertext attacks. In: STOC, pp. 427–437 (1990)

[TWZ20] Tao, Y., Wang, X., Zhang, R.: Short zero-knowledge proof of knowledge for lattice-based commitment. In: Ding, J., Tillich, J.-P. (eds.) PQCrypto

2020. LNCS, vol. 12100, pp. 268–283. Springer, Cham (2020). https://doi.org/10.1007/978-3-030-44223-1_15

[YAZ+19] Yang, R., Au, M.H., Zhang, Z., Xu, Q., Yu, Z., Whyte, W.: Efficient lattice-based zero-knowledge arguments with standard soundness: construction and applications. In: Boldyreva, A., Micciancio, D. (eds.) CRYPTO 2019. LNCS, vol. 11692, pp. 147–175. Springer, Cham (2019). https://doi.org/10.1007/978-3-030-26948-7_6

[YEL+21] Yuen, T.H., Esgin, M.F., Liu, J.K., Au, M.H., Ding, Z.: *DualRing*: generic construction of ring signatures with efficient instantiations. In: Malkin, T., Peikert, C. (eds.) CRYPTO 2021. LNCS, vol. 12825, pp. 251–281. Springer, Cham (2021). https://doi.org/10.1007/978-3-030-84242-0_10

Commitments

Commitments

GUC-Secure Commitments via Random Oracles: New Impossibility and Feasibility

Zhelei Zhou[1,2], Bingsheng Zhang[1,2(✉)], Hong-Sheng Zhou[3(✉)], and Kui Ren[1,2]

[1] Zhejiang University, Hangzhou, China
[2] ZJU-Hangzhou Global Scientific and Technological Innovation Center,
Hangzhou, China
{zl_zhou,bingsheng,kuiren}@zju.edu.cn
[3] Virginia Commonwealth University, Richmond, USA
hszhou@vcu.edu

Abstract. In the UC framework, protocols must be subroutine respecting; therefore, shared trusted setup might cause security issues. To address this drawback, Generalized UC (GUC) framework is introduced by Canetti *et al.* (TCC 2007). In this work, we investigate the impossibility and feasibility of GUC-secure commitments using global random oracles (GRO) as the trusted setup. In particular, we show that it is impossible to have a 2-round (1-round committing and 1-round opening) GUC-secure commitment in the global observable RO model by Canetti *et al.* (CCS 2014). We then give a new round-optimal GUC-secure commitment that uses only Minicrypt assumptions (i.e. the existence of one-way functions) in the global observable RO model. Furthermore, we also examine the complete picture on round complexity of the GUC-secure commitments in various global RO models.

1 Introduction

Secure multi-party computation (MPC) [26,39] is one of the most important cornerstone of modern cryptography. It enables n mutually distrustful players, $P_1, \ldots, P_n$ to securely evaluate any efficiently computable function f of their private inputs, $x_1, \ldots, x_n$. Since its introduction in the early 1980s, MPC has been extensively studied in the literature. Typically, the security properties of an MPC protocol are formalized using the well-known "simulation-paradigm" [26,27]. Roughly speaking, the idea is to require that any adversarial attacker $\mathcal{A}$ in the *real world* execution of the protocol, can be emulated by a so-called "simulator" $\mathcal{S}$ in an *ideal world* execution, where the players provide their inputs to a trusted third party who computes f for them and relays the result back to the players.

Z. Zhou and B. Zhang—Work supported by the National Key R&D Program of China (No. 2021YFB3101601), the National Natural Science Foundation of China (Grant No. 62072401), "Open Project Program of Key Laboratory of Blockchain and Cyberspace Governance of Zhejiang Province", and Input Output (iohk.io).
H.-S. Zhou—Work supported in part by NSF grant CNS-1801470, a Google Faculty Research Award and a research gift from Ergo Platform.

S. Agrawal and D. Lin (Eds.): ASIACRYPT 2022, LNCS 13794, pp. 129–158, 2022.
https://doi.org/10.1007/978-3-031-22972-5_5

From UC to GUC. To facilitate modular protocol design and analysis in the complex network environments, Canetti proposed the Universal Composibility (UC) framework [10], where, the notion of indistinguishability between the real and the ideal world is replaced by a notion of "interactive indistinguishability". More specifically, an interactive *environment*, which may communicate with both the honest players and the corrupted ones, should not be able to distinguish whether it is participating in the real execution or the ideal one. UC security guarantees the security of the MPC protocols under *concurrent executions*, and even other *arbitrary* protocols running in the same network cannot be adversarially affected—roughly speaking, the environment represents the collection of any other concurrent protocols. Additionally, this notion is closed under composition, enabling modular analysis of protocols.

However, protocols in the UC framework must be *subroutine respecting*, and shared setup cannot be directly modeled by the basic UC notion. To address this drawback, Canetti, Dodis, Pass and Walfish proposed the Generalized Universal Composibility (GUC) framework in 2007 [11]. Since then, many interesting and efficient protocols have been designed and analyzed under the GUC framework [9,14,15,20,37].

Random Oracles as a Global Setup: $\mathcal{G}_{sRO}$, $\mathcal{G}_{oRO}$, $\mathcal{G}_{pRO}$, *and* $\mathcal{G}_{poRO}$. It has been shown [11,12] that, to achieve secure multi-party computation for any nontrivial functionality in the UC and the GUC framework, certain trusted setups (e.g., CRS, PKI, etc.) are required. Random Oracle (RO) is a classic idealized setup that can be used to design UC-secure [28] and GUC-secure multi-party computation protocols [9,14].

Random oracle model [4] is a popular idealized model that has been widely used to justify the security of efficient cryptographic protocols. In spite of its known inability to provide provable guarantees when RO is instantiated with a real-world hash function [13], RO is still a promising setup without known real-world attacks. In fact, RO draws increasing attention along with recent advancement of the blockchain technology. It is generally viewed as a *transparent* setup that can be easily deployed with no reliance on any trusted party in the blockchain and other distributed system setting. Many RO-based non-interactive ZK systems, e.g., zk-STARK [5] and Fractal [17], are developed and deployed in real application scenarios. Note that, those RO-based protocols can achieve *post-quantum* security.

A natural formulation of a global RO, denoted as $\mathcal{G}_{sRO}$, has been defined in [11]: it is accessible to all parties both in the ideal world and the real world, but it offers neither "observability" nor "programmability". We emphasize that, it has been proven that it is impossible to achieve GUC-secure commitment in the $\mathcal{G}_{sRO}$ model [11]. Later, Canetti, Jain, and Scafuro [14] proposed a strengthened version of the global RO, denoted as $\mathcal{G}_{oRO}$, which allows the simulator to "observe" the queries made by the malicious parties, and GUC-secure commitment *can* be constructed in the $\mathcal{G}_{oRO}$ model. Camenisch *et al.* [9] further strengthened the $\mathcal{G}_{sRO}$ from a different direction: they designed a mechanism that allows the simulator to "program" the global RO without being detected by the adversary, and we denote this strengthened version of the global RO as $\mathcal{G}_{pRO}$. On top of both $\mathcal{G}_{oRO}$ and $\mathcal{G}_{pRO}$, Camensich *et al.* [9] then introduced an even stronger variant, called $\mathcal{G}_{poRO}$, and they constructed a round-optimal GUC-secure commitment in the $\mathcal{G}_{poRO}$ model [9]. Figure 3 depicts the relation of these global RO models.

Problem Statement. We study the round complexity of GUC-secure commitment in the global RO models. Clearly protocols relying on a *less idealized* setup and *weaker* computational assumptions will allow us to gain better confidence in the proved security statement. Note that, round-optimal GUC secure commitments can be constructed based on the strong global RO setup $\mathcal{G}_{poRO}$ [9]. On the other hand, in [11], it has been proven that constructing a GUC-secure commitment in the $\mathcal{G}_{sRO}$ model is impossible. Between these two extremes, in [14], Cannetti et al. have shown that it is feasible to construct a GUC-secure commitment in the $\mathcal{G}_{oRO}$ model; however, their construction relies on the discrete logarithm assumption, which cannot achieve (post-) quantum security. We are interested in GUC-secure commitment protocols using a global RO setup and Minicrypt [29] assumptions; these protocols can additionally achieve post-quantum security. This leads us to a natural research question:

What is the lower bounds of the round complexity[1] of a GUC-secure commitment in the $\mathcal{G}_{oRO}$ model?

If there exists such a lower bound on the round complexity of a GUC-secure commitment in the $\mathcal{G}_{oRO}$ model, we would like to find a round-optimal construction. We hereby ask:

If there exists such a lower bound, is that possible to construct round-optimal GUC-secure commitment in the $\mathcal{G}_{oRO}$ model, using only Minicrypt assumption?

1.1   Our Results

We give affirmative answers to the above research questions. Our findings can be summarized as follows.

A New Impossibility Result in the $\mathcal{G}_{oRO}$ Model. In this work, we show that 2-round (1-round for committing and 1-round for opening) GUC-secure commitment does not exist in the $\mathcal{G}_{oRO}$ model (cf. Sect. 3).

We prove this result by contradiction, and our main observation is as follows. Suppose such a 2-round GUC-secure commitment exists. First, it is easy to see that if the committing phase only takes one round, then there is only one message sent from the committer to the receiver; that is, the receiver does not send any message to the committer. Analogously, the receiver is also "silent" in the 1-round opening phase. Therefore, the potentially corrupted receiver can delay all its $\mathcal{G}_{oRO}$ queries until it receives the opening message from the committer.

Let us consider the case where the receiver is corrupted. During the simulation, the simulated committer needs to generate the commitment message

---

[1] Throughout this work, we do not consider the case of simultaneous rounds where two parties can send their messages to each other at the same round [24,36].

without the knowledge of the plaintext, and it later needs to generate the opening message for any given input (a.k.a. the plaintext). As discussed before, the corrupted receiver can choose not to query the $\mathcal{G}_{oRO}$ until the simulator has equivocated the commitment. Hence, the simulator cannot obtain any illegitimate queries from $\mathcal{G}_{oRO}$ for this corrupted receiver to facilitate this equivocation. Now, observe that this simulator has no extra power over a normal party; in particular, any committer can invoke such a simulator (algorithm) to violate the binding property of the commitment.

In the actual proof of our impossibility result, we let the corrupted committer to internally run the simulator algorithm to generate the commitment message, providing an empty list for the $\mathcal{G}_{oRO}$ illegitimate queries. Obviously, given this commitment message, the receiver/simulator cannot extract its plaintext; Therefore, with very high probability, the simulation would fail.

A New Round-Optimal Commitment Using $\mathcal{G}_{oRO}$. With respect to our impossibility result, a round-optimal commitment should takes at least 3 rounds. In this work, we show how to construct a round-optimal (2-round for committing and 1-round for opening) GUC-secure commitment only using Minicrypt assumptions in the $\mathcal{G}_{oRO}$ model (cf. Sect. 4).

A General Framework. A typical GUC-secure commitment requires both extractability and equivocality. The $\mathcal{G}_{oRO}$ model can directly provide the simulator with extractability; therefore, the challenge is to design an equivocation mechanism with round efficiency. A natural approach is to utilize a (property-based) perfect hiding non-interactive equivocal commitment: (i) in the 1st round, the receiver picks the commitment key and sends it to the committer; and (ii) in the 2nd round, the committer uses the equivocal commitment scheme to commit the message. To deploy this approach, the following questions need to be resolved:

– *How to instantiate such a perfect-hiding non-interactive equivocal commitment?*
– *How can the simulator obtain the equivocation trapdoor?*

In [14] and [37], the Pedersen commitment is used as a candidate of the equivocal commitment. It is well-known, the security of Pedersen commitment is based on the discrete logarithm assumption which is not (post-) quantum secure. In this work, we show how to construct a candidate of the equivocal commitment only using Minicrypt assumptions, i.e. the existence of one-way functions, in the $\mathcal{G}_{oRO}$ model.

To address the latter question, [14] introduced a 5-round mechanism that enables the simulator to obtain the equivocation trapdoor in the $\mathcal{G}_{oRO}$ model; whereas, [37] proposed a more round-efficient (3-round) mechanism to do so. More precisely, [37] let the receiver use a Non-Interactive Witness Indistinguishable (NIWI) argument to prove the knowledge of equivocation trapdoor w.r.t. the commitment key. The proof is sent together with the commitment key in the 1st round. Note that straight-line extractability is needed for this approach.

Following the technique proposed in [37], our framework adopts the Non-Interactive Witness Hiding (NIWH) argument with straight-line extractability [38] to prove the knowledge of equivocation trapdoor w.r.t. the commitment key. The straight-line extractable NIWH argument can be constructed under Minicrypt assumption in the $\mathcal{G}_{oRO}$ model. Putting things together, we can obtain a GUC-secure commitment using only Minicrypt assumptions. We present the technique roadmap of our framework in Fig. 1.

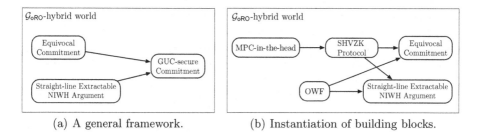

(a) A general framework.   (b) Instantiation of building blocks.

Fig. 1. Technique roadmap

Non-interactive Equivocal Commitment in Minicrypt. As shown in [18,35], it is possible to build a non-interactive equivocal commitment from a 3-round public-coin Special Honest Verifier Zero-Knowledge (SHVZK) protocol with 2-special soundness. In the SHVZK protocol, the prover sends the message flow a in the 1st round, and the receiver sends a public-coin randomness e as the challenge in the 2nd round. After receiving e, the prover computes and sends the response z in the last round. The technique of constructing non-interactive equivocal commitment can be summarized as follows. Let $\mathcal{R}_{\mathcal{L}}$ be an NP relation whose associate language is $\mathcal{L}$. The receiver randomly samples a pair $(x, w) \in \mathcal{R}_{\mathcal{L}}$ and sends x to the committer. To commit a message m, the committer invokes the SHVZK simulator for $x \in \mathcal{L}$, using m as the challenge. The simulator then outputs the simulated proof (a, z). The committer sends a to the receiver as its commitment message. To open the commitment, the committer can simply send m, z to the receiver, who will accept it if and only if (a, m, z) is an accepting SHVZK proof transcript. The equivocation trapdoor is w, which can be extracted from the straight-line extractor of NIWH as described above.

Since we aim to construct a commitment under Minicrypt assumptions, in our construction, $\mathcal{R}_{\mathcal{L}}$ is instantiated with a one-way function relation, i.e., $g(x) = y$ where g is a one-way function. Next, how to construct a 2-special sound SHVZK protocol under Minicrypt assumptions? One possible approach is to use the "MPC-in-the-head" paradigm proposed by Ishai et al. [30]. Roughly speaking, the main idea is for the prover to simulate the execution of an n-party computation protocol that checks if $(x, w) \in \mathcal{R}_{\mathcal{L}}$, where x is the public input and w is the witness. The prover then commits to all views of the parties and sends the commitments to the verifier. After that, the verifier chooses a random subset of the parties and asks the prover to open their corresponding views. The verifier accepts the proof if the revealed views are consistent. Unfortunately, to the best of our knowledge, none of the followups [1,16,19,25,31] since the initial work of [30] can lead to a 2-special sound SHVZK protocol merely under Minicrypt assumptions. To address this issue, we propose a new technique that can construct a 2-special sound protocol in the $\mathcal{G}_{oRO}$ model (cf. Sect. 4.2).

Towards a Complete Picture. In terms of the $\mathcal{G}_{oRO}$, our work gives a complete answer to our questions: we show there exists *no* 2-round GUC-secure commitment in the $\mathcal{G}_{oRO}$ model (cf. Sect. 3), and present a 3-round (round-optimal) GUC-secure commitment under only Minicrypt assumptions in the $\mathcal{G}_{oRO}$ model (cf. Sect. 4). Moreover, it is known that GUC-secure commitment does not exist in the $\mathcal{G}_{sRO}$ model [11], and round-optimal GUC-secure commitment can be constructed without further assumptions in the $\mathcal{G}_{poRO}$ model [9]. What about the $\mathcal{G}_{pRO}$? In this work, we also show some impossibility result: there exists *no* GUC-secure commitment with 1-round committing in the $\mathcal{G}_{pRO}$ model (see details in the full version of our paper). However, the feasibility of round-optimal GUC-secure commitment under Minicrypt assumptions in the $\mathcal{G}_{pRO}$ model remains an open question.

Further Investigation and Future Directions. We mainly focus on the commitment in this work. One may also wonder the lower bounds of the round complexity of other cryptographic primitives such as ZK, OT, etc. In fact, it is already known that there exists no NIZK in the observable RO model [38]. What about the ZK proofs in the $\mathcal{G}_{pRO}$ model? In this work, we show that our impossibility result can be extended to ZK proofs in the $\mathcal{G}_{pRO}$ model: there exists no non-trivial GUC-secure NIZK protocols in the $\mathcal{G}_{pRO}$ model (see details in the full version of our paper).

1.2   Related Work

In terms of UC security with local setups, non-interactive commitments (1-round for committing and 1-round for opening) can be constructed under various setup assumptions. For instance, Canetti and Fischlin gave a candidate in the CRS model [12]; Hofheinz and Müller-Quade suggested a candidate in the RO model [28]. As for UC security with global setups, it is still unclear if it is possible to construct a non-interactive GUC-secure commitment, and very few work, e.g., [20] is dedicated to this research area. In [11], Canetti *et al.* showed that it is impossible to construct a GUC-secure commitment merely relying on local CRS/RO functionalities; they further proposed a 7-round GUC-secure commitment protocol in the Agumented CRS (ACRS) model. Later, Dodis *et al.* proved that there exists *no* GUC-secure commitment with 1-round committing phase in the ACRS model against adaptive adversaries [20]. Note that their impossibility result can be extended to any other global setup whose output depends on the program ID (pid) of the querying party, but not the session ID (sid), such as the Key Registration of Knowledge (KRK) model [2]. To bypass this impossibility result, $\mathcal{G}_{oRO}$, $\mathcal{G}_{pRO}$ and $\mathcal{G}_{poRO}$ are proposed; note that the output of those setup functionalities depends on the session ID (sid).

Focusing on commitments in the $\mathcal{G}_{oRO}$, Canetti *et al.* proposed a 5-round GUC-secure commitment [14]. Later, Mohassel *et al.* gave a $(1+2)$-round GUC-secure commitment in the $\mathcal{G}_{oRO}$ model, where the committer and the receiver needs to have an additional 1-round setup phase followed by a 2-round commitment [37]. Note that their construction also employed Pedersen commitment, which cannot achieve (post-) quantum security. Byali *et al.* gave a 2-round GUC-secure commitment construction in the CRS and $\mathcal{G}_{oRO}$ hybrid model [8]. Following Byali *et al.* paradigm, GUC-secure ZK protocols [23,34] can also be constructed in the CRS and $\mathcal{G}_{oRO}$ hybrid model. With regard to post-quantum security, [7] gave a 5-round lattice-based GUC-secure commitment and [6] gave a 6-round code-based GUC-secure commitment in the $\mathcal{G}_{oRO}$ model.

In respect of the $\mathcal{G}_{pRO}$ and the $\mathcal{G}_{poRO}$, Camenisch *et al.* proposed a 3-round GUC-secure commitment from CDH assumption in the $\mathcal{G}_{pRO}$ model and an information-theoretical non-interactive GUC-secure commitment in the $\mathcal{G}_{poRO}$ model [9]. Recently, Canetti *et al.* proposed a 2-round OT adaptive-secure OT from DDH assumption in the $\mathcal{G}_{pRO}$ model [15], but their protocol is only UC-secure. Baum *et al.* constructed a GUC-secure commitment scheme that is additively homomorphic in the $\mathcal{G}_{poRO}$ model [3].

2   Preliminaries

2.1   Notations

Let $\lambda \in \mathbb{N}$ be the security parameter. We say that a function $\mathsf{negl} : \mathbb{N} \to \mathbb{N}$ is negligible if for every positive polynomial $p(\cdot)$ and all sufficiently large λ, it holds that $\mathsf{negl}(\lambda) < \frac{1}{p(\lambda)}$. We write $y := \mathsf{Alg}(x; r)$ when the algorithm Alg on input x and randomness r, outputs y. We write $y \leftarrow \mathsf{Alg}(x)$ for the process of sampling the randomness r and setting $y := \mathsf{Alg}(x; r)$. We also write $y \leftarrow S$ for sampling y uniformly at random from the set S. We use the abbreviation PPT to denote probabilistic polynomial-time. Let $[n]$ denote the set $\{1, 2, \ldots, n\}$ for some $n \in \mathbb{N}$. For an NP relation $\mathcal{R}$, we denote by $\mathcal{L}$ its associate language, i.e. $\mathcal{L} = \{x \mid \exists w \text{ s.t. } (x, w) \in \mathcal{R}\}$. We often write $\mathcal{R}_{\mathcal{L}}$ to denote the NP relation whose associate language is $\mathcal{L}$ for short. We also use $\mathcal{R}_{\mathcal{L}}(x, w) = 1$ to refer to $(x, w) \in \mathcal{R}_{\mathcal{L}}$. We say that two distribution ensembles $\mathcal{X} = \{\mathcal{X}_\lambda\}_{\lambda \in \mathbb{N}}$ and $\mathcal{Y} = \{\mathcal{Y}_\lambda\}_{\lambda \in \mathbb{N}}$ are identical (resp. computationally indistinguishable), denoted by $\mathcal{X} \equiv \mathcal{Y}$ (resp., $\mathcal{X} \stackrel{c}{\approx} \mathcal{Y}$), if for any unbounded (resp., PPT) distinguisher $\mathcal{D}$ there exists a negligible function $\mathsf{negl}(\cdot)$ such that $|\Pr[\mathcal{D}(\mathcal{X}_\lambda) = 1] - \Pr[\mathcal{D}(\mathcal{Y}_\lambda) = 1]| = 0$ (resp., $\mathsf{negl}(\lambda)$). When we define a protocol/scheme in form of $\Pi = \Pi.\{\mathsf{Alg}\text{-}1, \ldots, \mathsf{Alg}\text{-}n\}$, we use the notation $\Pi.\mathsf{Alg}\text{-}i$ to refer to the algorithm $\mathsf{Alg}\text{-}i$ of Π where $\mathsf{Alg}\text{-}i \in \{\mathsf{Alg}\text{-}1, \ldots, \mathsf{Alg}\text{-}n\}$.

2.2   Universal Composability

Canetti's UC Framework. The UC framework proposed by Canetti [10] lays down a solid foundation for designing and analyzing protocols secure against attacks in an arbitrary network execution environment. Roughly speaking, in the UC framework, a protocol Π is defined to be a computer program (or several programs) which is intended to be executed by multiple interconnected parties. Every party is identified by the unique pair (pid, sid), where pid is the Program ID (PID) and sid is the Session ID (SID). Let $\mathcal{A}$ be the adversary who can control the network and corrupt the parties. When a party is corrupted, the adversary $\mathcal{A}$ receives its private input and its internal state. We say a protocol is *terminating* if it can terminate in polynomial time, and we only consider terminating protocols in this work.

We call a protocol, the one for which we want to prove security, challenge protocol. A challenge protocol Π is a UC-secure realization of a functionality $\mathcal{F}$, if it satisfies that for every PPT adversary $\mathcal{A}$ attacking an execution of Π, there is another PPT adversary $\mathcal{S}$—known as the simulator—attacking the ideal process that interacts with $\mathcal{F}$ (by corrupting the same set of parties), such that the executions of Π with $\mathcal{A}$ and that of $\mathcal{F}$ with $\mathcal{S}$ makes no difference to any PPT network execution environment $\mathcal{Z}$.

The Ideal World Execution. In the ideal world, the set of parties $\mathcal{P} = \{P_1, \ldots, P_n\}$ only communicate with an ideal functionality $\mathcal{F}$ and the simulator $\mathcal{S}$. The corrupted parties are controlled by the simulator $\mathcal{S}$. The output of the environment $\mathcal{Z}$ in this execution is denoted by $\mathsf{EXEC}_{\mathcal{F},\mathcal{S},\mathcal{Z}}$.

The Real World Execution. In the real world, the set of parties $\mathcal{P} = \{P_1, \ldots, P_n\}$ communicate with each other and the adversary $\mathcal{A}$ to run the protocol Π. The corrupted parties are controlled by the adversary $\mathcal{A}$. The output of the environment $\mathcal{Z}$ in this execution is denoted by $\mathsf{EXEC}_{\Pi,\mathcal{A},\mathcal{Z}}$.

Definition 1. *We say a protocol Π UC-realizes functionality $\mathcal{F}$, if for any PPT environment $\mathcal{Z}$ and any PPT adversary $\mathcal{A}$ there exists a PPT simulator $\mathcal{S}$ s.t.* $\mathsf{EXEC}_{\Pi,\mathcal{A},\mathcal{Z}} \overset{c}{\approx} \mathsf{EXEC}_{\mathcal{F},\mathcal{S},\mathcal{Z}}$.

In order to conceptually modularize the design of the protocols, the notion of "hybrid world" is introduced. A protocol Π is said to be realized "in the $\mathcal{G}$ hybrid world" if Π invokes the ideal functionality $\mathcal{G}$ as a subroutine.

Definition 2. *We say protocol Π UC-realizes functionality $\mathcal{F}$ in the $\mathcal{G}$ hybrid world, if for any PPT environment $\mathcal{Z}$ and any PPT adversary $\mathcal{A}$ there exists a PPT simulator $\mathcal{S}$ s.t.* $\mathsf{EXEC}^{\mathcal{G}}_{\Pi,\mathcal{A},\mathcal{Z}} \overset{c}{\approx} \mathsf{EXEC}_{\mathcal{F},\mathcal{S},\mathcal{Z}}$.

Furthermore, in the UC framework, the environment $\mathcal{Z}$ cannot have the direct access to $\mathcal{G}$, but it can do so through the adversary. Namely, in the real world, the adversary $\mathcal{A}$ can access the ideal functionality $\mathcal{G}$ directly, and $\mathcal{A}$ queries $\mathcal{G}$ for $\mathcal{Z}$ and forwards the answers; analogously, in the ideal world, $\mathcal{Z}$ can query $\mathcal{G}$ through the simulator $\mathcal{S}$. This implicitly means that $\mathcal{G}$ is local to the challenge protocol instance. This allows the simulator $\mathcal{S}$ to simulate $\mathcal{G}$ in the ideal world as long as it "looks" indistinguishable from $\mathcal{G}$ hybrid world.

Canetti et al's GUC Framework. In Canetti's UC framework, the environment $\mathcal{Z}$ is constrained: it cannot have the direct access to the setup. It means that the setup is not global. This assumption might be impractical in real life applications where it is more plausible that there is a global setup published and used by many protocols.

Motivated by solving problems caused by modeling setup as a local subroutine, Canetti *et al.* introduced Generalized UC (GUC) which can be used for properly analyzing concurrent execution of protocols in the presence of global setup [11]. In the GUC framework, the environment $\mathcal{Z}$ is unconstrained: $\mathcal{Z}$ is allowed to access the setup directly without going through the simulator/adversary and invoke arbitrary protocols alongside the challenge protocol. Furthermore, the setup can be modeled as a *shared functionality* that can communicate with more than one protocol sessions. Let the output of the unconstrained PPT environment $\mathcal{Z}$ in the real world (resp. ideal world) execution be denoted by $\mathsf{GEXEC}_{\Pi,\mathcal{A},\mathcal{Z}}$ (resp. $\mathsf{GEXEC}_{\mathcal{F},\mathcal{S},\mathcal{Z}}$).

Definition 3. *We say a protocol Π GUC-realizes functionality $\mathcal{F}$, if for any unconstrained PPT environment $\mathcal{Z}$ and any PPT adversary $\mathcal{A}$ there exists a PPT simulator $\mathcal{S}$ s.t. $\mathsf{GEXEC}_{\Pi,\mathcal{A},\mathcal{Z}} \overset{c}{\approx} \mathsf{GEXEC}_{\mathcal{F},\mathcal{S},\mathcal{Z}}$.*

Since the unconstrained environment $\mathcal{Z}$ is given a high-level of flexibility: $\mathcal{Z}$ is allowed to invoke arbitrary protocols in parallel with the challenge protocol. This makes it extremely hard to prove the GUC security. Therefore, a simplified framework called Externalized UC (EUC) is introduced in [11]. In the EUC framework, the environment $\mathcal{Z}$ has direct access to the shared functionality $\mathcal{G}$ but does not initiate any new protocol sessions except the challenge protocol session. We call such an environment is $\mathcal{G}$-externalized constrained. We say a protocol Π is $\mathcal{G}$-subroutine respecting if it only shares state information via a single shared functionality $\mathcal{G}$. We take RO models as an example, and present the comparison of basic UC, GUC and EUC in Fig. 2.

Definition 4. *Let the protocol Π be $\mathcal{G}$-subroutine respecting. We say a protocol Π EUC-realizes functionality $\mathcal{F}$ with respect to shared functionality $\mathcal{G}$, if for any PPT $\mathcal{G}$-externalized constrained environment $\mathcal{Z}$ and any PPT adversary $\mathcal{A}$ there exists a PPT simulator $\mathcal{S}$ s.t. $\mathsf{EXEC}^{\mathcal{G}}_{\Pi,\mathcal{A},\mathcal{Z}} \overset{c}{\approx} \mathsf{EXEC}^{\mathcal{G}}_{\mathcal{F},\mathcal{S},\mathcal{Z}}$.*

In [11], Canetti *et al.* showed that for any $\mathcal{G}$-subroutine respecting protocol Π, proving Π EUC-realizes $\mathcal{F}$ with respect to $\mathcal{G}$ is equivalent to proving Π GUC-realizes $\mathcal{F}$. Therefore, when we want to prove the GUC security of a protocol, we always turn to EUC security for the sake of simplicity.

2.3 The Global Random Oracle Models

In this section, we review four well-known Global Random Oracle (GRO) models: (i) Global Strict Random Oracle (GSRO) model proposed by Canetti *et al.* in [14], which does not give any extra power to anyone; (ii) Global Observable Random Oracle (GORO) model[2] proposed by Canetti *et al.* in [14], which grants

---

[2] In [9], Camenisch *et al.* used the notations Restricted Observable Global Random oracles (GroRO), Restricted Programmable Global Random Oracles (GrpRO) and

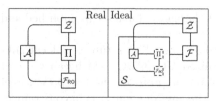
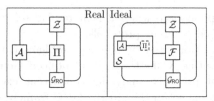

(a) Basic UC: the simulator $\mathcal{S}$ simulates the local $\mathcal{F}_{RO}$ and has full control.

(b) EUC: the global $\mathcal{G}_{RO}$ is external to the simulator, and the environment $\mathcal{Z}$ is $\mathcal{G}_{RO}$-externalized constrained.

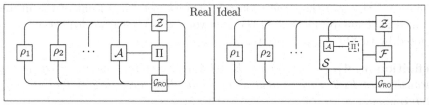

(c) GUC: the global $\mathcal{G}_{RO}$ is external to the simulator, and the environment $\mathcal{Z}$ not only has direct access to $\mathcal{G}_{RO}$, but also invokes arbitraty protocols $\rho_1, \rho_2, \cdots$ alongside the challenge protocol $\varPi$.

Fig. 2. Comparison of basic UC, GUC and EUC.

the ideal world simulator access to the list of illegitimate queries (to be defined later); (iii) Global Programmable Random Oracle (GPRO) model proposed by Camenisch *et al.* in [9], which allows the simulator to program on unqueried points without being detected; (iv) Global Programmable and Observable Random Oracle (GPORO) model proposed by Camenisch *et al.* in [9], which provides both programmability and observability. We present the relation of these models in Fig. 3, and the formal description of all the global random oracle models mentioned above in Fig. 4.

The GSRO Model. The GSRO model $\mathcal{G}_{sRO}$ is a natural extension of local RO model $\mathcal{F}_{RO}$: as depicted in Fig. 4(a), upon receiving (QUERY, sid, x) from any party, $\mathcal{G}_{sRO}$ first checks if the query (sid, x) has been queried before. If not, $\mathcal{G}_{sRO}$ answers with a random value of pre-specified length, that is $v \in \{0,1\}^{\ell_{out}(\lambda)}$, and records the tuple (sid, x, v); otherwise, the previously chosen value v is returned again even if the earlier query was made by another party. The sad truth is that Canetti *et al.* remarked that $\mathcal{G}_{sRO}$ does not suffice to GUC-realizes commitment functionality. Therefore, stronger variant global random oracle models are needed to realize non-trivial functionalities.

The GORO Model. Compared to $\mathcal{G}_{sRO}$, the GORO model $\mathcal{G}_{oRO}$ provides additionally observability. More precisely, some of the queries can be marked as "illegit-

---

Restricted Observable and Programmable Global Random Oracles (GrpoRO). Here we adopt the notations GORO, GPRO and GPORO which skips the "r" for the sake of the simplicity as in [15].

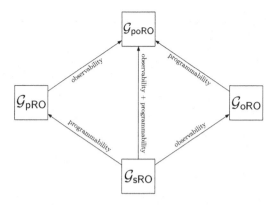

Fig. 3. Relation of the global random oracle models

imate" and potentially disclosed to the simulator. As depicted in Fig. 4(b), the GORO functionality $\mathcal{G}_{\mathsf{oRO}}$ interacts with a list of ideal functionality programs $\bar{\mathcal{F}} = \{\mathcal{F}_1, \ldots, \mathcal{F}_n\}$, where $\mathcal{F}_1, \ldots, \mathcal{F}_n$ are the protocol functionalities (e.g., commitment functionality, ZK functionality, etc.) that share the same global setup $\mathcal{G}_{\mathsf{oRO}}$. For any query (s, x) from any party $P = (\mathsf{pid}, \mathsf{sid})$ where s is the content of the SID field, if $s \neq \mathsf{sid}$, then this query is considered "illegitimate". After that, $\mathcal{G}_{\mathsf{oRO}}$ adds the tuple (s, x, v) to the list of illegitimate queries for SID s, which we denote as $\mathcal{Q}_s$. The illegitimate queries $\mathcal{Q}_s$ may be disclosed to the instance of ideal functionality whose SID is the one of the illegitimate queries. Then the ideal functionality instance leaks the illegitimate queries to the simulator.

The GPRO Model. Compared to $\mathcal{G}_{\mathsf{sRO}}$, the GPRO model $\mathcal{G}_{\mathsf{pRO}}$ additionally allows simulator/adversary to program the global random oracle on unqueried points. As depicted in Fig. 4(c), upon receiving (PROGRAM, sid, x, v) from the simulator/adversary, $\mathcal{G}_{\mathsf{pRO}}$ first checks if (sid, x) has been queried before. If not, $\mathcal{G}_{\mathsf{pRO}}$ stores (sid, x, v) in the query-answer lists. Any honest party can check whether a point has been programmed or not by sending the (ISPROGRAMED, sid, x) command to $\mathcal{G}_{\mathsf{pRO}}$. Thus, in the real world, the programmed points can always be detected. However, in the ideal world, the simulator $\mathcal{S}$ can successfully program the random oracle without being detected since it can always return (ISPROGRAMED, $\mathsf{sid}, 0$) when the adversary invokes (ISPROGRAMED, sid, x) to verify whether a point x has been programmed or not.

The GPORO Model. If we combine the GORO model and GPRO model together, we obtain the GPORO model $\mathcal{G}_{\mathsf{poRO}}$ which is depicted in Fig. 4(d). To the best of our knowledge, the GPORO model is the most powerful GRO model that enables efficient composable protocols in the GUC framework. For example, Camenisch *et al.* gave an efficient non-interactive GUC-secure commitment protocol in the GPORO model [9].

Remark 1. Camenisch et al. remarked that when one uses the (distinguishing) environment in a cryptographic reduction, one can have full control over the

---

Shared Functionality $\mathcal{G}_{\mathsf{sRO}}$

The functionality interacts with a set of parties $\mathcal{P} = \{P_1, \ldots, P_n\}$ and an adversary $\mathcal{S}$. It is parameterized by the input/output length $\ell_{\mathsf{in}}(\lambda)$ and $\ell_{\mathsf{out}}(\lambda)$. It maintains an initially empty list List.

- **Query.** Upon receiving (QUERY, s, x) from a party $P_i \in \mathcal{P}$ where $P_i = (\mathsf{pid}, \mathsf{sid})$, or the adversary $\mathcal{S}$:
  - Find v such that $(s, x, v) \in$ List. If there is no such v exists, select an uniformly random $v \in \{0,1\}^{\ell_{\mathsf{out}}(\lambda)}$ and record the tuple (s, x, v) in List.
  - Return (QUERYCONFIRM, s, v) to the requestor.

(a) The Global Strict Random Oracle Model $\mathcal{G}_{\mathsf{sRO}}$

Shared Functionality $\mathcal{G}_{\mathsf{oRO}}$

The functionality interacts with a set of parties $\mathcal{P} = \{P_1, \ldots, P_n\}$ and an adversary $\mathcal{S}$. It is parameterized by the input/output length $\ell_{\mathsf{in}}(\lambda)$ and $\ell_{\mathsf{out}}(\lambda)$, and a list of ideal functionality programs $\bar{\mathcal{F}}$. It maintains an initially empty list List.

- **Query.** Same as $\mathcal{G}_{\mathsf{sRO}}$ depicted in Figure 4(a), except when $\mathsf{sid} \neq s$, add the tuple (s, x, v) to the (initially empty) list of illegitimate queries for SID s, which we denote by $\mathcal{Q}_s$.
- **Observe.** Upon receiving a request from an instance of an ideal functionality in the list $\bar{\mathcal{F}}$, with SID s, return to this instance the list of illegitimate queries $\mathcal{Q}_s$ for SID s.

(b) The Global Observable Random Oracle Model $\mathcal{G}_{\mathsf{oRO}}$

Shared Functionality $\mathcal{G}_{\mathsf{pRO}}$

The functionality interacts with a set of parties $\mathcal{P} = \{P_1, \ldots, P_n\}$ and an adversary $\mathcal{S}$. It is parameterized by the input/output length $\ell_{\mathsf{in}}(\lambda)$ and $\ell_{\mathsf{out}}(\lambda)$. It maintains initially empty lists List, Prog.

- **Query.** Same as $\mathcal{G}_{\mathsf{sRO}}$ depicted in Figure 4(a).
- **Program.** Upon receiving (PROGRAM, sid, x, v) with $v \in \{0,1\}^{\ell_{\mathsf{out}}(\lambda)}$ from $\mathcal{S}$:
  - If $\exists v' \in \{0,1\}^{\ell_{\mathsf{out}}(\lambda)}$ such that $(\mathsf{sid}, x, v') \in$ List and $v \neq v'$, ignore this input.
  - Set List $:=$ List $\cup \{(\mathsf{sid}, x, v)\}$ and Prog $:=$ Prog $\cup \{(\mathsf{sid}, x)\}$.
  - Return (PROGRAMCONFIRM, sid) to $\mathcal{S}$.
- **IsProgramed.** Upon receiving (ISPROGRAMED, sid', x) from a party P_i or $\mathcal{S}$:
  - If the input was given by $P_i = (\mathsf{pid}, \mathsf{sid})$ and $\mathsf{sid} \neq \mathsf{sid}'$, ignore this input.
  - If $(\mathsf{sid}', x) \in$ Prog, set $b := 1$; otherwise, set $b := 0$.
  - Return (ISPROGRAMED, sid', b) to the requester.

(c) The Global Programmable Random Oracle Model $\mathcal{G}_{\mathsf{pRO}}$

Shared Functionality $\mathcal{G}_{\mathsf{poRO}}$

The functionality interacts with a set of parties $\mathcal{P} = \{P_1, \ldots, P_n\}$ and an adversary $\mathcal{S}$. It is parameterized by the input/output length $\ell_{\mathsf{in}}(\lambda)$ and $\ell_{\mathsf{out}}(\lambda)$, and a list of ideal functionality programs $\bar{\mathcal{F}}$. It maintains initially empty lists List, Prog.

- **Query/Observe.** Same as $\mathcal{G}_{\mathsf{oRO}}$ depicted in Figure 4(b).
- **Program/IsProgramed.** Same as $\mathcal{G}_{\mathsf{pRO}}$ depicted in Figure 4(c).

(d) The Global Programmable and Observable Random Oracle Model $\mathcal{G}_{\mathsf{poRO}}$

Fig. 4. The global random oracle models.

shared functionality [9]. More precisely, as depicted in Fig. 5, the reduction algorithm $\mathcal{B}$ simulates the complete view of the environment $\mathcal{Z}$ including the shared functionality $\mathcal{G}$, thus $\mathcal{B}$ has full control of $\mathcal{G}$.

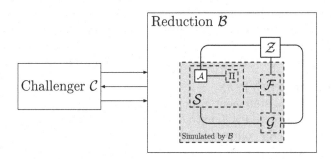

Fig. 5. In order to play against the external challenger $\mathcal{C}$, reduction algorithm $\mathcal{B}$ simulates everything (marked as gray) including the shared functionality $\mathcal{G}$, then starts the protocol Π with the real world adversary $\mathcal{A}$/environment $\mathcal{Z}$ by running $\mathcal{A}$/$\mathcal{Z}$ internally as black-box.

2.4 SHVZK Protocols

A 3-round public coin Special Honest Verifier Zero-Knowledge (SHVZK) protocol $\Pi = \Pi.\{\mathsf{Move1}, \mathsf{Move2}, \mathsf{Move3}, \mathsf{Verify}, \mathsf{Sim}\}$ allows a prover to convince a verifier that a statement x is true with the aid of the witness w. In the first round, the prover computes and sends the first flow message $a := \mathsf{Move1}(x, w; r)$ using the statement-witness pair (x, w) and some random coin r. In the second round, the verifier samples and sends a uniformly random public coin challenge $e \leftarrow \mathsf{Move2}(1^{\lambda})$. In the last round, the prover computes the response to the challenge $z := \mathsf{Move3}(x, w, e; r)$ using the statement-witness pair (x, w), challenge e and the random coin r. Finally the verifier accepts the statement x if and only if $\mathsf{Verify}(x, a, e, z) = 1$. We put the workflow of the SHVZK protocol in Fig. 6. We often call (a, e, z) the transcript between the prover and the verifier.

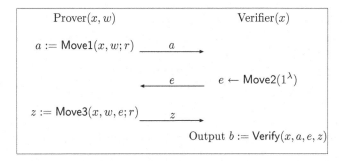

Fig. 6. The workflow of the SHVZK protocol

A SHVZK protocol should satisfy (i) perfect completeness, i.e. any honest prover who holds the witness w such that $(x, w) \in \mathcal{R}_{\mathcal{L}}$ can always make the verifier accept; (ii) k-special soundness, i.e. given any k distinct accepting transcripts, we can always extract the witness w; (iii) Special Honest Verifier Zero-Knowledge (SHVZK) property, i.e. given the challenge e ahead, there should be a PPT simulator algorithm Sim that takes the statement x, the challenge e and random coin r as input, and outputs the simulated (a, z) which is indistinguishable from the real one. The first property is easy to formalize. In order to formalize the k-special soundness and SHVZK, we consider the following experiments:

Experiment $\mathrm{EXPT}_{\mathcal{A},\Pi}^{\text{k-SS}}(\lambda)$:

1. $\mathcal{A}$ outputs a statement x along with k transcripts $\{(a, e_i, z_i)\}_{i \in [k]}$.
2. If $e_i \neq e_j$ where $i \neq j$: extract the witness w' from $\{(a, e_i, z_i)\}_{i \in [k]}$
3. If $(x, w') \in \mathcal{R}_{\mathcal{L}}$, output 1; otherwise, output 0.

Denote by $\mathbf{Adv}_{\mathcal{A},\Pi}^{\text{k-SS}}(\lambda) := \Pr[\mathrm{EXPT}_{\mathcal{A},\Pi}^{\text{k-SS}}(\lambda) = 1]$ the advantage of $\mathcal{A}$.

Experiment $\mathrm{EXPT}_{\mathcal{A},\Pi}^{\text{SHVZK}}(\lambda)$:

1. $\mathcal{A}$ outputs a statement-witness pair (x, w) along with a challenge e.
2. If $(x, w) \in \mathcal{R}_{\mathcal{L}}$: select a random string r and a random bit $b \in \{0, 1\}$, and compute the following:
   (a) If $b = 0$: $a := \mathsf{Move1}(x, w; r)$; $z := \mathsf{Move3}(x, w, e; r)$.
   (b) If $b = 1$: $(a, z) := \mathsf{Sim}(x, e; r)$.
3. $\mathcal{A}$ is given (a, z) as input, and it outputs a guess bit $b' \in \{0, 1\}$.
4. If $b = b'$, output 1; otherwise, output 0.

Denote by $\mathbf{Adv}_{\mathcal{A},\Pi}^{\text{SHVZK}}(\lambda) := \left| \Pr[\mathrm{EXPT}_{\mathcal{A},\Pi}^{\text{SHVZK}}(\lambda) = 1] - \frac{1}{2} \right|$ the advantage of $\mathcal{A}$.

Now we can formally define the SHVZK protocol.

Definition 5. *We say a protocol $\Pi = \Pi.\{\mathsf{Move1}, \mathsf{Move2}, \mathsf{Move3}, \mathsf{Verify}, \mathsf{Sim}\}$ is a SHVZK protocol if the following conditions hold:*

1. **(Perfect Completeness)** *For any $(x, w) \in \mathcal{R}_{\mathcal{L}}$, we say it is perfect complete if*

$$\Pr\left[\begin{array}{l} a := \mathsf{Move1}(x, w; r); e \leftarrow \mathsf{Move2}(1^\lambda); \\ z := \mathsf{Move3}(x, w, e; r) \end{array} : \mathsf{Verify}(x, a, e, z) = 1 \right] = 1$$

2. **(k-Special Soundness)** *For any PPT adversary $\mathcal{A}$, we say it has k-special soundness where $k \in \mathbb{N}$ and $k \geq 2$, if there exists a negligible function negl such that $\mathbf{Adv}_{\mathcal{A},\Pi}^{\text{k-SS}}(\lambda) \leq \mathsf{negl}(\lambda)$.*

3. **(Special Honest Verifier Zero-Knowledge)** *We say it has SHVZK if there exists a PPT simulator Sim such that for any PPT adversary $\mathcal{A}$, there exists a negligible function negl such that $\mathbf{Adv}_{\mathcal{A},\Pi}^{\text{SHVZK}}(\lambda) \leq \mathsf{negl}(\lambda)$.*

2.5 Straight-Line Extractable NIWH Argument in the RO Model

Witness Hiding (WH) interactive proofs were introduced by Feige and Shamir in [21], and the Non-Interactive Witness-Hiding (NIWH) argument in the plain model can be found in [33]. We here discuss the NIWH argument in the random oracle model. Note that, stronger security property such as *(straight-line) extractability* can now be achieved in the random oracle model: an extraction algorithm Ext could be constructed to extract the witness from a maliciously generated and accepting proof. More concretely, in an NIWH argument in the random oracle model $\Pi = \Pi.\{\mathsf{Prove}^{\mathcal{O}}, \mathsf{Verify}^{\mathcal{O}}, \mathsf{Ext}\}$, both the prover and the verifier are allowed to query the random oracle $\mathcal{O}$ at any moment, during the protocol execution. As in the plain model, the prover generates the proof π using the statement-witness pair (x, w) and a random string r and sends π to the verifier, and the verifier then verifies if the proof π is valid or not; the verifier outputs a bit b indicating the acceptance or rejection. Formally, the Prove and Verify algorithms in a NIWH argument in the RO model are described as follows:

- $\pi := \mathsf{Prove}^{\mathcal{O}}(x, w; r)$ takes input as a statement-witness pair (x, w) and a random string r, and it is allowed to query the random oracle $\mathcal{O}$. It outputs a proof π. When r is not important, we use $\mathsf{Prove}^{\mathcal{O}}(x, w)$ for simplicity.
- $b := \mathsf{Verify}^{\mathcal{O}}(x, \pi)$ takes input as a statement x and a proof π, and it is allowed to query the random oracle $\mathcal{O}$. It outputs a bit b indicating acceptance or rejection.

The straight-line extractable NIWH argument should satisfy the perfect completeness, computational soundness, witness hiding and straight-line extractability. The perfect completeness is trivial. The computational soundness means that any PPT prover cannot convince the verifier that a false statement is true with overwhelming probability. The last two properties are not to easy to formalize. We first talk about the witness hiding property: given the proof π generated by the prover, the verifier cannot compute any new witness that the verifier does not know before the interaction. In order to formally define the witness hiding property, we consider the following definition of hard instance ensembles [38].

Definition 6 (Hard Instance Ensembles). *Let $\mathcal{R}_{\mathcal{L}}$ be an NP relation, and $\mathcal{L}$ be its associate language, and $\mathcal{X} = \{\mathcal{X}_{\lambda}\}_{\lambda \in \mathbb{N}}$ be a probability ensemble s.t. $\mathcal{X}_{\lambda}$ ranges over $\mathcal{L} \cap \{0, 1\}^{\lambda}$. We say that $\mathcal{X}$ is hard for NP relation $\mathcal{R}_{\mathcal{L}}$ if for any PPT $\mathcal{A}$ and any $x \in \mathcal{X}$, there exists a negligible function negl s.t. $\Pr[(x, \mathcal{A}(x)) \in \mathcal{R}_{\mathcal{L}}] = \mathsf{negl}(\lambda)$.*

Then we should consider the following experiment:

    Experiment $\mathrm{EXPT}_{\mathcal{A}, \Pi}^{\mathrm{WH}}(\lambda)$:
      1. Select $(x, w) \in \mathcal{R}_{\mathcal{L}}$, and compute $\pi \leftarrow \mathsf{Prove}(x, w)$.
      2. $\mathcal{A}$ is given (x, π) as input, and it outputs w'.
      3. If $(x, w') \in \mathcal{R}_{\mathcal{L}}$, output 1; otherwise, output 0.
    Denote by $\mathbf{Adv}_{\mathcal{A}, \Pi}^{\mathrm{WH}}(\lambda) := \Pr[\mathrm{EXPT}_{\mathcal{A}, \Pi}^{\mathrm{WH}}(\lambda) = 1]$ the advantage of $\mathcal{A}$.

We now describe how to define the straight-line extractability property; note that our extractability definition is taken from that by Pass [38]. To enable the extractability, typically, the extraction algorithm Ext can be developed by simulating the random oracle for the prover and the verifier, and thus the algorithm

Ext has full control of the random oracle. In this paper, we consider a much more restricted random oracle, and the algorithm Ext is granted only with the *observability*; that is, Ext is allowed to see the query-answer list of the random oracle. For that reason, we write $\mathsf{Ext}^{\mathcal{O}}$ to indicate that, the extraction algorithm Ext does not have the full control of the random oracle, and is only granted to have the observability capability. With these notions above, we can formally define the straight-line extractable NIWH arguments in the RO model.

Definition 7. *Fix an NP relation $\mathcal{R}_{\mathcal{L}}$ whose associate language is $\mathcal{L}$. Consider a RO $\mathcal{O}$. We say a protocol $\Pi = \Pi.\{\mathsf{Prove},\mathsf{Verify}\}$ is a NIWH argument for $\mathcal{R}_{\mathcal{L}}$ in the RO model if the following condition holds:*

1. **(Perfect Completeness)** *For any $(x, w) \in \mathcal{R}_{\mathcal{L}}$, we say it is perfect complete if*
$$\Pr[\pi \leftarrow \mathsf{Prove}^{\mathcal{O}}(x, w) : \mathsf{Verify}^{\mathcal{O}}(x, \pi) = 1] = 1$$

2. **(Computational Soundness)** *For any $x \notin \mathcal{L}$, we say it is computational sound if for any PPT adversary $\mathcal{A}$, there exists a negligible function negl such that*
$$\Pr[\pi^* \leftarrow \mathcal{A}^{\mathcal{O}}(x) : \mathsf{Verify}^{\mathcal{O}}(x, \pi^*) = 1] \leq \mathsf{negl}(\lambda)$$

3. **(Witness Hiding)** *Let $\mathcal{X} = \{\mathcal{X}_\lambda\}_{\lambda \in \mathbb{N}}$ be a hard instance ensemble $\mathcal{R}_{\mathcal{L}}$. We say it is witness hiding for $\mathcal{R}_{\mathcal{L}}$ under the instance ensemble $\mathcal{X}$ if for any PPT adversary $\mathcal{A}$ and any $(x, w) \in \mathcal{R}_{\mathcal{L}}$ with $x \in \mathcal{X}$, there exists a negligible function negl s.t. $\mathbf{Adv}_{\mathcal{A}, \Pi}^{\mathrm{WH}}(\lambda) \leq \mathsf{negl}(\lambda)$. We say it is witness hiding for $\mathcal{R}_{\mathcal{L}}$ if it is witness hiding under all hard-instance ensembles $\mathcal{X}$ for $\mathcal{R}_{\mathcal{L}}$.*

4. **(Straight-line Extractability)** *For any $x \in \mathcal{L}$, we say it is straight-line extractable if for any PPT adversary $\mathcal{A}$,*
$$\Pr\left[\begin{matrix}\pi^* \leftarrow \mathcal{A}^{\mathcal{O}}(x); b := \mathsf{Verify}^{\mathcal{O}}(x, \pi^*); \\ w^* \leftarrow \mathsf{Ext}^{\mathcal{O}}(x, \pi^*)\end{matrix} : b = 1 \wedge (x, w^*) \in \mathcal{R}_{\mathcal{L}}\right] \geq 1 - \mathsf{negl}(\lambda)$$

2.6   Equivocal Commitment

Typically, an equivocal commitment scheme $\Pi = \Pi.\{\mathsf{KeyGen}, \mathsf{KeyVer}, \mathsf{Commit}, \mathsf{ComVer}, \mathsf{EquCom}, \mathsf{Equiv}\}$ allows the committer to generate the commitment c to any value m using the commitment key ck and the randomness r. Later, the committer can open c to m by sending the opening d to the receiver who verifies it. Furthermore, if the committer obtains the trapdoor td with respect to the ck, he can generate the equivocal commitment $\tilde{c}$, later open $\tilde{c}$ to any message $\tilde{m}$. Formally, the equivocal commitment has the following algorithms:

- $(\mathsf{ck}, \mathsf{td}) \leftarrow \mathsf{KeyGen}(1^\lambda)$ takes input as the security parameter λ, and outputs a commitment key ck and the trapdoor td.
- $b := \mathsf{KeyVer}(\mathsf{ck}, \mathsf{td})$ takes input as a commitment key ck and a trapdoor td. It outputs a bit b indicating acceptance or rejection.
- $(c, d) := \mathsf{Commit}(\mathsf{ck}, m; r)$ takes input as a commitment key ck, a message m and a randomness r. It outputs the commitment c and the opening d. We assume that there exists a deterministic algorithm that can extract m from d. When r is not important, we use $\mathsf{Commit}(\mathsf{ck}, m)$ for simplicity.

- $b := \mathsf{ComVer}(\mathsf{ck}, c, d)$ takes input as a commitment key ck, and a commitment-opening pair (c, d). It outputs a bit b indicating acceptance or rejection.
- $(\tilde{c}, \mathsf{st}) := \mathsf{EquCom}(\mathsf{ck}, \mathsf{td}; r)$ takes input as a commitment key ck, a trapdoor td, and a randomness r. It outputs a commitment $\tilde{c}$ and a state st. When r is not important, we use $\mathsf{EquCom}(\mathsf{ck}, \mathsf{td})$ for simplicity.
- $\tilde{d} := \mathsf{Equiv}(\mathsf{ck}, \mathsf{td}, \tilde{c}, \mathsf{st}, \tilde{m})$ takes input as a commitment key ck, a trapdoor td, a commitment $\tilde{c}$, a state st, and an arbitrary message $\tilde{m}$ for which equivocation is required. It outputs an opening $\tilde{d}$.

The equivocal commitment requires the following properties: perfect correctness, perfect hiding, computational binding and equivocation. Perfect correctness means that the honest committer can always make the receiver accept. Perfect hiding means that the commitment reveals nothing about the message.

Experiment $\mathrm{EXPT}_{\mathcal{A},\Pi}^{\text{hiding}}(\lambda)$:
1. Run $(\mathsf{ck}, \mathsf{td}) \leftarrow \mathsf{KeyGen}(1^\lambda)$.
2. $\mathcal{A}$ is given ck as input, and it outputs two distinct messages m_0, m_1.
3. Select a random bit $b \in \{0, 1\}$, and compute $c \leftarrow \mathsf{Commit}(\mathsf{ck}, m_b)$.
4. $\mathcal{A}$ is given m_b as input, and it outputs a bit b'.
5. If $b' = b$, output 1; otherwise, output 0.

Denote by $\mathbf{Adv}_{\mathcal{A},\Pi}^{\text{hiding}}(\lambda) := \left| \Pr[\mathrm{EXPT}_{\mathcal{A},\Pi}^{\text{hiding}}(\lambda) = 1] - \frac{1}{2} \right|$ the advantage of $\mathcal{A}$.

Computational binding means that it is infeasible for the PPT committer to output the commitment c that can be opened in two different ways.

Experiment $\mathrm{EXPT}_{\mathcal{A},\Pi}^{\text{binding}}(\lambda)$:
1. Run $(\mathsf{ck}, \mathsf{td}) \leftarrow \mathsf{KeyGen}(1^\lambda)$.
2. $\mathcal{A}$ is given ck as input, and it outputs (c, d_0, d_1).
3. If $d_0 \neq d_1$ and $\mathsf{ComVer}(\mathsf{ck}, c, d_0) = \mathsf{ComVer}(\mathsf{ck}, c, d_1) = 1$ holds, output 1; otherwise, output 0.

Denote by $\mathbf{Adv}_{\mathcal{A},\Pi}^{\text{binding}}(\lambda) := \Pr[\mathrm{EXPT}_{\mathcal{A},\Pi}^{\text{binding}}(\lambda) = 1]$ the advantage of $\mathcal{A}$.

Equivocation means that given the trapdoor td, one can open a previously constructed commitment c of message m to other message $\tilde{m} \neq m$.

Experiment $\mathrm{EXPT}_{\mathcal{A},\Pi}^{\text{equivocal}}(\lambda)$:
1. $\mathcal{A}$ is given 1^λ as input, and it outputs $(\mathsf{ck}, \mathsf{td}, m)$.
2. If $\mathsf{KeyVer}(\mathsf{ck}, \mathsf{td}) = 1$: select a random string r and a random bit $b \in \{0, 1\}$, and compute the following:
   (a) If $b = 0$: invoke $(c, d) := \mathsf{Commit}(\mathsf{ck}, m; r)$.
   (b) If $b = 1$: invoke $(c, \mathsf{st}) := \mathsf{EquCom}(\mathsf{ck}, \mathsf{td}; r)$; $d := \mathsf{Equiv}(\mathsf{ck}, \mathsf{td}, \tilde{c}, \mathsf{st}, m)$.
3. $\mathcal{A}$ is given (c, d) as input, and it outputs a bit b'.
4. If $b = b'$, output 1; otherwise, output 0.

Denote by $\mathbf{Adv}_{\mathcal{A},\Pi}^{\text{equivocal}}(\lambda) := \left| \Pr[\mathrm{EXPT}_{\mathcal{A},\Pi}^{\text{equivocal}}(\lambda) = 1] - \frac{1}{2} \right|$ the advantage of $\mathcal{A}$.

Now we can formally define the equivocal commitment, and it should satisfy the following definition:

Definition 8. *We say a scheme* $\Pi = \Pi.\{$KeyGen, KeyVer, Commit, ComVer, EquCom, Equiv$\}$ *is an equivocal commitment if the following conditions hold:*

1. *(Perfect Correctness) For any message* m, *we say it is perfect correct if*

$$\Pr[(\mathsf{ck},\mathsf{td}) \leftarrow \mathsf{KeyGen}(1^\lambda);(c,d) \leftarrow \mathsf{Commit}(\mathsf{ck},m):\mathsf{ComVer}(\mathsf{ck},c,d)=1]=1$$

2. *(Perfect Hiding) We say it is perfect hiding if for any adversary* $\mathcal{A}$ *s.t.* $\mathbf{Adv}_{\mathcal{A},\Pi}^{\text{hiding}}(\lambda)=0$.

3. *(Computational Binding) We say it is computational binding if for any PPT adversary* $\mathcal{A}$, *there exists a negligible function* negl *s.t.* $\mathbf{Adv}_{\mathcal{A},\Pi}^{\text{binding}}(\lambda) \leq$ negl(λ).

4. *(Equivocation) We say it is equivocal if for any PPT adversary* $\mathcal{A}$, *there exists a negligible function* negl *s.t.* $\mathbf{Adv}_{\mathcal{A},\Pi}^{\text{equivocal}}(\lambda) \leq$ negl(λ).

2.7 "MPC-in-the-Head" Paradigm

In [30], Ishai *et al.* proposed the famous "MPC-in-the-head" paradigm from which we can construct a SHVZK protocol using the MPC protocol. Before introducing the details of the paradigm, we have to define the MPC protocol.

Consider a function $f : (\{0,1\}^\lambda)^{n+1} \to \{0,1\}^\lambda$. We let $P_1,\dots,P_n$ be n parties modeled as PPT interactive machines. Assume that each party P_i holds a private input $w_i \in \{0,1\}^\lambda$ and a public input $x \in \{0,1\}^\lambda$, and wants to compute $y = f(x,w)$, where $w = (w_1,\dots,w_n)$. They communicate with each other using point-to-point secure channels (e.g. encrypted channels or OT channels) in the synchronous model. The parties jointly run a secure Multi-Party Computation (MPC) protocol Π_{MPC}. The protocol Π_{MPC} is specified via the next-message functions: there are multiple communication rounds, and in each round the party P_i sends into the channel a message that is computed as a deterministic function of the internal state of P_i (including private input w_i and random tape k_i) and the messages that P_i has received in the previous rounds. We denote by $\mathsf{view}_i(x,w_i)$ the view of P_i, which is the concatenation of the inputs x, w_i, the random tape k_i and all the messages received by P_i during the execution of Π_{MPC}. Each secure channel defines a relation of consistency between views. For instance, in the plain model, we say $\mathsf{view}_i(x,w_i)$ and $\mathsf{view}_j(x,w_j)$ are consistent if the outgoing messages in $\mathsf{view}_i(x,w_i)$ are identical to the incoming messages in $\mathsf{view}_j(x,w_j)$ and vice versa. Finally, all the views should yield the same output y, i.e. there are n functions $\Pi_{f,1},\dots,\Pi_{f,n}$ such that $y = \Pi_{f,i}(\mathsf{view}_i(x,w_i))$ for all $i \in [n]$. We note that, for our purpose of use, we require that every party P_i in the honest execution of Π_{MPC} has the same output y; while in the general case, the output of P_i can be different from each other.

In this work, we only consider security of MPC protocols in the semi-honest model. In the semi-honest model, the corrupted parties follow the instructions of the protocol, but are curious about the private information of other parties. Thus, the protocol needs to be designed in such a way that a corrupted P_i cannot infer information about w_j from its view $\mathsf{view}_i(x,w_i)$, where $j \neq i$.

We denote by $\mathsf{view}_T(x, w_1, \ldots, w_n)$ the joint view of players in set $T \subset [n]$ for the execution of Π_{MPC} on input $(x, w_1, \ldots, w_n)$. Consider a PPT simulator algorithm Sim that given the set $T \subset [n]$, the output of Π_{MPC} on input $(x, w_1, \ldots, w_n)$ (i.e. $f(x, w_1, \ldots, w_n)$), and the input of parties in T (i.e. $(x, (w_i)_{i \in T})$), it can output the simulated joint view of players in set T for the execution of Π_{MPC} on input $(x, w_1, \ldots, w_n)$ which we denote by $\mathsf{Sim}(T, x, (w_i)_{i \in T}, f(x, w_1, \ldots, w_n))$. With these notations, we have the following definition.

Definition 9. *We say an n-party protocol Π_{MPC} realizes f in the semi-honest model, if the following conditions hold:*

1. *(**Perfect Correctness**) For any inputs $x, w = (w_1, \ldots, w_n)$ and any random tape, we say Π_{MPC} realizes f with perfect correctness if $\forall i \in [n] : \Pr[y = \Pi_{f,i}(\mathsf{view}_i(x, w_i))] = 1$.*
2. *(**t-Privacy**) Let $1 \leq t < n$. We say Π_{MPC} realizes f with t-privacy if it is perfect correct and for every set of corrupted parties $T \subset [n]$ satisfying $|T| \leq t$, there exists a PPT simulator Sim such that*

$$\mathsf{view}_T(x, w_1, \ldots, w_n) = \mathsf{Sim}(T, x, (w_i)_{i \in T}, f(x, w_1, \ldots, w_n))$$

Now we can introduce the "MPC-in-the-head" paradigm. Let f be the following $(n + 1)$-argument function corresponding to an NP relation $\mathcal{R}_\mathcal{L}$, that is, $f(x, w_1, \ldots, w_n) = \mathcal{R}_\mathcal{L}(x, w_1 \oplus \cdots \oplus w_n)$. Here x is a public input known to all parties, w_i is the private input of party P_i, and the output is received by all parties. In a high-level description, the main idea is for the prover to simulate the execution of a t-private n-party MPC protocol that realizes f. Then the prover employs a statically binding commitment to commit to all views of the parties and sends them to the verifier. After that, the verifier chooses a random subset of the parties, where the size of the subset equals t, and asks the prover to open their corresponding views. Finally the verifier accepts the statement if and only if (i) the commitments are correctly opened and (ii) the opened views are consistent with each other. See more details in [30].

3   Impossibility in the GORO Model

In this section, we show that it is impossible to construct 2-round GUC-secure commitment protocols (one round for the committing phase and one round the for the opening phase) in the $\mathcal{G}_{\mathsf{oRO}}$ hybrid world against static adversaries. We first provide the formal description of transferable commitment functionality $\mathcal{F}_{\mathsf{tCOM}}$ from [14] in Fig. 7. The main difference with the traditional commitment functionality is that in $\mathcal{F}_{\mathsf{tCOM}}$, the simulator can request the list of the illegitimate queries from $\mathcal{F}_{\mathsf{tCOM}}$. If we use the traditional commitment functionality which has no such power in the $\mathcal{G}_{\mathsf{oRO}}$ hybrid world, the simulator will have no advantage over others at all. This is one of the reasons why transferable ideal functionalities were designed in the presence of the $\mathcal{G}_{\mathsf{oRO}}$ model, and we refer interesting readers to see more discussions in [14].

Functionality $\mathcal{F}_{\text{tCOM}}$

The functionality interacts with two parties C, R and an adversary $\mathcal{S}$.

- Upon receiving (COMMIT, sid, C, R, m) from C, do:
  - Record the tuple (sid, C, R, m), and send (RECEIPT, sid, C, R) to R and $\mathcal{S}$.
  - Ignore any subsequent COMMIT command.
- Upon receiving (DECOMMIT, sid, C, R) from C, do:
  - If there is a tuple (sid, C, R, m) recorded, send (DECOMMIT, sid, C, R, m) to R and $\mathcal{S}$, and halt.
  - Otherwise, ignore the message.
- When asked by the adversary $\mathcal{S}$, obtain from $\mathcal{G}_{\text{oRO}}$ the list of illegitimate queries $\mathcal{Q}_{\text{sid}}$ that pertain to SID sid, and send $\mathcal{Q}_{\text{sid}}$ to the adversary $\mathcal{S}$.

Fig. 7. The transferable functionality $\mathcal{F}_{\text{tCOM}}$ for commitment

We prove this impossibility by contradiction. Suppose that there exists such a 2-round GUC-secure protocol. Let us first consider the case where the receiver is corrupted, the simulator needs to produce an equivocal commitment without knowing the plaintext in the committing phase, and later open it to any given message (a.k.a. the plaintext) in the opening phase. We observe that the receiver does not need to send any message during the 2-round protocol execution, thus when the receiver is controlled by adversary, the corrupted receiver can delay all its $\mathcal{G}_{\text{oRO}}$ queries until it receives the opening message. In this case, the simulator cannot obtain the illegitimate queries of the corrupted receiver before producing the equivocal commitments, and thus has no advantages over the real world adversary. If the simulator still succeeds to produce the equivocal commitments even if it has no illegitimate queries, then distinctions will be revealed when the adversary performs the following attacks. The adversary corrupts the committer, and instructs the committer to run the simulator algorithm mentioned above to generate the commitment message. In this case, where the committer is corrupted, the receiver/simulator needs to extract the plaintext from this commitment message. However, the entire computation of the commitment message is totally independent of the plaintext, thus with high probability the simulation would fail. Formally, we prove this impossibility through Theorem 1.

Theorem 1. *There exists no terminating 2-round (one round for commitment phase and one round for decommitment phase) protocol Π that GUC-realizes $\mathcal{F}_{\text{tCOM}}$ depicted in Fig. 7 with static security, using only the shared functionality for global observable random oracle $\mathcal{G}_{\text{oRO}}$.*

Proof. Suppose there exists such a protocol Π that GUC-realizes $\mathcal{F}_{\text{tCOM}}$ in the $\mathcal{G}_{\text{oRO}}$ hybrid world. Then there must exist a PPT simulator $\mathcal{S}$ such that $\text{EXEC}^{\mathcal{G}_{\text{oRO}}}_{\mathcal{F}_{\text{tCOM}}, \mathcal{S}, \mathcal{Z}} \overset{c}{\approx} \text{EXEC}^{\mathcal{G}_{\text{oRO}}}_{\Pi, \mathcal{A}, \mathcal{Z}}$ for any PPT adversary $\mathcal{A}$ and any PPT $\mathcal{G}_{\text{oRO}}$-externally constrained environment $\mathcal{Z}$.

In particular, let us first consider the protocol session with SID sid_1, and let $\mathcal{A}$ be a dummy adversary that simply forwards protocol flows between corrupt parties and the environment $\mathcal{Z}$. Let $\mathcal{Z}$ corrupt the receiver R^* at first. Then $\mathcal{Z}$ chooses a random bit $b \in \{0, 1\}$ and gives it as the input to the honest committer

C. After that, $\mathcal{Z}$ waits for C to send the commitment ψ. Next, $\mathcal{Z}$ lets C reveal the committed value b'. If $b = b'$, $\mathcal{Z}$ outputs 1; otherwise, $\mathcal{Z}$ outputs 0.

In order to make the GUC experiments above remain indistinguishable, the simulator $\mathcal{S}$ needs to build an equivocal commitment $\tilde{\psi}$ without knowing b in the committing phase, where $\tilde{\psi}$ is computational indistinguishable from the real commitment ψ; later in the opening phase, $\mathcal{S}$ obtains b from $\mathcal{F}_{\text{tCOM}}$ and needs to open the previously sent commitment $\tilde{\psi}$ to b. For notation convenience, we write $\mathcal{S} = (\mathcal{S}_1, \mathcal{S}_2)$ to split the simulator algorithm in two phases: (i) $\mathcal{S}_1$ works in the committing phase, and it needs to output an equivocal commitment $\tilde{\psi}$ without knowing b; (ii) while $\mathcal{S}_2$ works in the opening phase, and upon receiving the message b from $\mathcal{F}_{\text{tCOM}}$, it needs to output the opening message r such that (b, r) correctly opens the previously sent commitment $\tilde{\psi}$.

We first describe the simulation strategy in the committing phase. Recall that, the main advantage of the simulator over the others is that it can obtain illegitimate queries of R^*. More precisely, $\mathcal{S}_1$ can request the illegitimate queries $\mathcal{Q}_{\text{sid}_1}$ from the commitment functionality $\mathcal{F}_{\text{tCOM}}$ who forwards this request to $\mathcal{G}_{\text{oRO}}$. The simulator $\mathcal{S}_1$ also can query $\mathcal{G}_{\text{oRO}}$ just like normal parties. In order to describe the process of querying to $\mathcal{G}_{\text{oRO}}$, we denote by $\mathcal{G}_{\text{oRO}}^*$ the simplified version of the $\mathcal{G}_{\text{oRO}}$, that is, the $\mathcal{G}_{\text{oRO}}$ with only the QUERY interface. We write $\mathcal{S}_1^{\mathcal{G}_{\text{oRO}}^*}$ to denote the event that $\mathcal{S}_1$ has the query access to $\mathcal{G}_{\text{oRO}}$ and can continuously query to $\mathcal{G}_{\text{oRO}}$. With above notations, we will write $\mathcal{S}_1^{\mathcal{G}_{\text{oRO}}^*}(\text{sid}_1, \mathcal{Q}_{\text{sid}_1})$ to denote the output (i.e., the equivocal commitment $\tilde{\psi}$ and the state st) produced by $\mathcal{S}_1$ after querying to $\mathcal{G}_{\text{oRO}}$, when running on the illegitimate queries $\mathcal{Q}_{\text{sid}_1}$ sent by R^*. We note that, $\mathcal{S}_1$ should be able to handle any PPT environment $\mathcal{Z}$. Consider such a case where $\mathcal{Z}$ instructs R^* to delay all its $\mathcal{G}_{\text{oRO}}$ queries until it receives the opening message. In this case, $\mathcal{S}_1$ finds nothing sent by R^* in $\mathcal{Q}_{\text{sid}_1}$, but should still be able to produce the equivocal commitment $\tilde{\psi}$. In other words, the algorithm $(\tilde{\psi}, \text{st}) \leftarrow \mathcal{S}_1^{\mathcal{G}_{\text{oRO}}^*}(\text{sid}_1, \mathcal{Q}_{\text{sid}_1})$ still works when $\mathcal{Q}_{\text{sid}_1} = \emptyset$, where $\emptyset$ is an empty set; otherwise, the environment $\mathcal{Z}$ will find the distinction. We note that, the algorithm $\mathcal{S}_1^{\mathcal{G}_{\text{oRO}}^*}(\text{sid}_1, \emptyset)$, i.e. we replace the $\mathcal{Q}_{\text{sid}_1}$ with the empty set $\emptyset$, can be run by any party, since the algorithm only makes use of the QUERY interface and anyone can query to $\mathcal{G}_{\text{oRO}}$. Now let us turn to the opening phase. Analogously, we can write $r \leftarrow \mathcal{S}_2^{\mathcal{G}_{\text{oRO}}^*}(\text{sid}_1, \tilde{\psi}, \text{st}, b, \emptyset)$ to denote the event where $\mathcal{S}_2$ can still open $\tilde{\psi}$ to the value b and the corresponding opening message r after querying to $\mathcal{G}_{\text{oRO}}$, even if there is noting sent by R^* in the list of the illegitimate queries (i.e. $\mathcal{Q}_{\text{sid}_1} = \emptyset$). We note that, even if we switch to a session with a different SID, both $\mathcal{S}_1^{\mathcal{G}_{\text{oRO}}^*}(\text{sid}_1, \emptyset)$ and $\mathcal{S}_2^{\mathcal{G}_{\text{oRO}}^*}(\text{sid}_1, \tilde{\psi}, \text{st}, b, \emptyset)$ still work as long as the appropriate inputs are provided.

In the following, we show that the existence of the simulator $\mathcal{S} = (\mathcal{S}_1, \mathcal{S}_2)$ above contradicts the security of Π against static corruptions, by creating a particular environment $\mathcal{Z}'$ which succeeds in distinguishing $\text{EXEC}_{\mathcal{F}_{\text{tCOM}}, \mathcal{S}', \mathcal{Z}'}^{\mathcal{G}_{\text{oRO}}}$ from $\text{EXEC}_{\Pi, \mathcal{A}', \mathcal{Z}'}^{\mathcal{G}_{\text{oRO}}}$ after a static corruption operation for any PPT simulator $\mathcal{S}'$. Let us consider the session with SID sid_2. Our $\mathcal{Z}'$ proceeds by corrupting the committer C^* at first, and then choosing a random bit $b \in \{0, 1\}$ which it gives as the input to C^*. Next $\mathcal{Z}'$ instructs C^* to run the algorithm $(\tilde{\psi}, \mathsf{st}) \leftarrow \mathcal{S}_1^{\mathcal{G}_{\mathsf{oRO}}^*}(\mathsf{sid}_2, \emptyset)$ and send $\tilde{\psi}$ to R. When R outputs $(\textsc{Receipt}, \mathsf{sid}_2, C, R)$, $\mathcal{Z}'$ instructs C^* to run the algorithm $r \leftarrow \mathcal{S}_2^{\mathcal{G}_{\mathsf{oRO}}^*}(\mathsf{sid}_2, \tilde{\psi}, \mathsf{st}, b, \emptyset)$ and send (b, r) to R. Finally $\mathcal{Z}'$ waits for R to output b'. In the real world, R always outputs $b' = b$. In the ideal world, $\mathcal{S}'$ should determine the committed value b' from $\tilde{\psi}$ in the committing phase. This means that in the ideal world, we must have that $b' = b$ with probability at most $\frac{1}{2}$, since the entire computation of $\tilde{\psi}$ is totally independent of b. Therefore, $\mathcal{Z}'$ can distinguish between the real world and the ideal world with probability at least $\frac{1}{2}$, contradicting our assumption that Π is GUC-secure.

4 Feasibility in the GORO Model

In this section, we propose a 3-round (2 rounds for the committing phase and 1 round for the opening phase) GUC-secure commitment protocol in the $\mathcal{G}_{\mathsf{oRO}}$ hybrid world, assuming the straight-line extractable NIWH arguments and perfect-hiding non-interactive equivocal commitment schemes exist. Then we instantiate the building blocks using only Minicrypt assumptions in the $\mathcal{G}_{\mathsf{oRO}}$ hybrid world. Therefore, our GUC-secure commitment protocol can be constructed via Minicrypt in the $\mathcal{G}_{\mathsf{oRO}}$ hybrid world. Since we prove that it is impossible to construct 2-round GUC-secure commitments in the $\mathcal{G}_{\mathsf{oRO}}$ hybrid world in Theorem 1, we stress that our construction is round-optimal.

4.1 Our GUC-Secure Commitment Construction

Recall that a GUC-secure commitment protocol requires two main properties: (i) *Equivocality:* when the receiver is corrupted, the simulator should be able to produce equivocal commitments that can open to any value later; (ii) *Extractability:* when the committer is corrupted, the simulator should be able to extract the committed value from the commitment.

The $\mathcal{G}_{\mathsf{oRO}}$ directly provides the desired extractability. Then we have to design a protocol that captures the equivocality. A natural approach is to employ the perfect-hiding non-interactive equivocal commitments. More precisely, we let the receiver generate the commitment key and send it to the committer in the first round; and then let the committer commit to the message using the equivocal commitment scheme. In order to provide extractability, we let the committer query the $\mathcal{G}_{\mathsf{oRO}}$ on the opening message of the commitment message above. Then we require the committer to commit to the answer of the $\mathcal{G}_{\mathsf{oRO}}$ via another instance of the equivocal commitment scheme. The committer sends all the commitment messages in the second round. The opening phase just takes one round, namely, the committer sends all the opening messages.

The only thing left is to provide the simulator with the advantage of getting the equivocation trapdoor over the others. Our solution is to let the receiver execute the straight-line extractable NIWH argument in the $\mathcal{G}_{\mathsf{oRO}}$ hybrid world which proves the knowledge of the equivocation trapdoor with respect to the commitment key. The receiver is required to send the proof along with the commitment key in the first round. Subsequently, the simulator can invoke the straight-line extractor to obtain the equivocation trapdoor.

We denote committer algorithm as C and receiver algorithm as R. We denote the event where queries $\mathcal{G}_{oRO}$ on input x and gets the answer y as $y := oRO(x)$. We assume ideal private and authenticated channels for all communications. Formally, we present our protocol Π_{tCOM} in Fig. 8 and prove the security through Theorem 2.

Protocol Π_{tCOM}

Primitives: Straight-line extractable NIWH argument in the $\mathcal{G}_{oRO}$ hybrid world $\Pi_{NIWH} = \Pi_{NIWH}.\{Prove^{\mathcal{G}_{oRO}}, Verify^{\mathcal{G}_{oRO}}, Ext^{\mathcal{G}_{oRO}}\}$, non-interactive equivocal commitment $\Pi_{ECom} = \Pi_{ECom}.\{KeyGen, KeyVer, Commit, ComVer, EquCom, Equiv\}$.
Inputs: C has a private input $m \in \{0,1\}^\lambda$. R has no input.

Committing Phase: This phase consists of 2 rounds.

- Round 1: R works as follows:
  - Generate the parameters of the commitment by invoking $(ck, td) \leftarrow \Pi_{ECom}.KeyGen(1^\lambda)$.
  - Compute the straight-line extractable NIWH proof by invoking $\pi \leftarrow \Pi_{NIWH}.Prove^{\mathcal{G}_{oRO}}(ck, td)$ for proving the knowledge of td. Send (ck, π) to C.
- Round 2: C works as follows:
  - Abort if $\Pi_{NIWH}.Verify^{\mathcal{G}_{oRO}}(ck, \pi) = 0$.
  - Commit to the message m by invoking $(c_1, d_1) \leftarrow \Pi_{ECom}.Commit(ck, m)$.
  - Compute $h := oRO(sid, 'C'||m||d_1||r)$ where $r \leftarrow \{0,1\}^\lambda$.
  - Commit to h by invoking $(c_2, d_2) \leftarrow \Pi_{ECom}.Commit(ck, h)$. Send (c_1, c_2) to R.

Opening Phase: This phase consists of 1 round.

- Round 3: C sends (m, d_1, d_2, r) to R.
- R computes $h := oRO(sid, 'C'||m||d_1||r)$, and accepts m if and only if $\Pi_{ECom}.ComVer(ck, c_1, d_1) = \Pi_{ECom}.ComVer(ck, c_2, d_2) = 1$ holds.

Fig. 8. Protocol Π_{tCOM} in the $\mathcal{G}_{oRO}$ hybrid world

Theorem 2. *Assume Π_{NIWH} is a straight-line extractable NIWH argument in the $\mathcal{G}_{oRO}$ hybrid world. Assume Π_{ECom} is an equivocal commitment scheme. Then the protocol Π_{tCOM} described in Fig. 8 GUC-realizes the functionality $\mathcal{F}_{tCOM}$ depicted in Fig. 7 in the $\mathcal{G}_{oRO}$ hybrid world against static malicious corruption.*

Proof. We leave the proof in the full version.

4.2 Instantiation of the Building Blocks

There are two building blocks, i.e. straight-line extractable NIWH arguments and perfect-hiding non-interactive equivocal commitment schemes, in our construction. In this section, we show how to instantiate them using only Minicrypt assumptions in the $\mathcal{G}_{oRO}$ hybrid world. We start by constructing a SHVZK protocol, since it is needed in both building blocks.

SHVZK Protocols from "MPC-in-the-Head". We here aim to construct a SHVZK protocol using only Minicrypt assumptions in the $\mathcal{G}_{oRO}$ hybrid world. Our starting point is the "MPC-in-the-head" paradigm introduced in Sect. 2.7.

Note that our construction requires an SHVZK protocol with 2-special soundness (, which we will explain the necessity later in Sect. 4.2); unfortunately, to the best of our knowledge, none of the followups [1, 16, 19, 25, 31] since the original work of [30], can lead to a 2-special sound protocol under only Minicrypt assumptions. Therefore, we need to design a new technique approach that transforms a MPC protocol into a SHVZK protocol with 2-special soundness.

Our Starting Point: [31]. We start with the 5-round SHVZK protocol proposed by Katz *et al.* in [31] which is based on only Minicrypt assumptions. In the high-level description, Katz *et al.* employed the $(n-1)$-private n-player MPC protocol in the preprocessing model and let the verifier provide its challenges in *two* phases: one for checking the correctness of the opened preprocessing executions, and the other for checking the consistency of the opened views. Roughly speaking, the 5-round protocol of Katz *et al.* works as follows:

- Round 1: The prover simulates m independent executions of the preprocessing phase, and commits to the states of the parties which can be obtained at the end of the preprocessing phase.
- Round 2: The verifier samples an uniform random challenge $c \in [m]$ and asks the prover to open the views of all the executions of the preprocessing phase except the c-th one.
- Round 3: The prover opens the states of all parties for each challenged execution of preprocessing phase. Beside that, the prover simulates the execution of Π_{MPC} that checks $\mathcal{R}_{\mathcal{L}}(x, w) = 1$ using the remaining unopened execution of the preprocessing phase. The prover then commits to each view of the parties.
- Round 4: The verifier samples an uniform random challenge $p \in [n]$ and asks the prover to open all the views of the parties except the p-th one.
- Round 5: The prover reveals the states of each challenged party following the preprocessing phase as well as its views in the execution of Π_{MPC}. The verifier checks that the opened views are consistent with each other and with an honest execution of Π_{MPC} (using the states from the preprocessing phase) that yields the output 1.

In [31], Katz *et al.* compressed the above 5-round protocol into a 3-round one by the following approach: (i) let the prover simulate the execution of Π_{MPC} for every emulation of the preprocessing phase and commit to all the resulting views as well as the states; (ii) let the verifier send its challenge (c, p), and asks the prover to open all the states except the c-th one of the preprocessing phase as well as all the views except the p-th one from the unopened preprocessing phase. We recall the formal 3-round SHVZK protocol of Katz *et al.* in the full version of our paper. We emphasize that the 3-round SHVZK protocol proposed by Katz *et al.* cannot be 2-special sound, and we argue this through Proposition 1.

Proposition 1. *Assume the n-party MPC protocol Π_{MPC} is $(n-1)$-private in the preprocessing model. Let m be the number of executions of preprocessing phase, where $m \geq 2$. The 3-round SHVZK protocol described in [31]:*

- *cannot achieve k-special soundness, for $k \leq m$.*
- *can achieve k-special soundness, for $k \geq m + 1$.*

Proof. We leave the proof in the full version.

Our Protocol Construction. Our key observation is that we can compress the above 5-round protocol into a 3-round one by applying the Fiat-Shamir transformation [22] to replace Round 2. Therefore, Round 1 and Round 3 can be merged, and we obtain a 3-round protocol with 2-special soundness. We can regard the first round of the resulting 3-round protocol as a "non-interactive proof" that proves the correctness of the execution of the preprocessing phase, but its soundness error is not negligible (i.e., $\frac{1}{m}$, where m is the number of the executions of preprocessing phase). This issue can be addressed by applying parallel repetition. Compared with the approach of [31], our approach needs additional RO assumptions but it is an SHVZK protocol with 2-special sound.

Protocol Π_{SHVZK}

Primitives: n-party MPC protocol Π_{MPC} which realizes f with $(n-1)$-privacy in the preprocessing model, where $f(x, w_1, \ldots, w_n) = \mathcal{R}_{\mathcal{L}}(x, w_1 \oplus \cdots \oplus w_n)$.
Random Oracles: $\mathsf{oRO}_1 : \{0,1\}^{\ell_{\mathsf{in}}(\lambda)} \to \{0,1\}^{\ell}$ and $\mathsf{oRO}_2 : \{0,1\}^{\ell_{\mathsf{in}}(\lambda)} \to (\mathbb{Z}_{m+1}^+)^{\lambda}$
Inputs: P, V have a common input x. P has a private input w s.t. $\mathcal{R}_{\mathcal{L}}(x, w) = 1$.

- Move1$(x, w; r)$:
  - For $i \in [\lambda], j \in [m]$:
    * Derive λ-bit random $\mathsf{seed}_{i,j}$ from randomness r and generate $\{\mathsf{state}_{i,j,k}\}_{k \in [n]} \leftarrow \mathsf{Preprocess}(\mathsf{seed}_{i,j})$.
    * For $k \in [n]$: select $r_{i,j,k} \leftarrow \{0,1\}^{\lambda}$ and commit to the states, i.e. compute state-commitments $\mathsf{com}_{i,j,k} := \mathsf{oRO}_1(\mathsf{sid}, \mathsf{state}_{i,j,k} || r_{i,j,k})$.
  - Compute $(c_1, \ldots, c_{\lambda}) := \mathsf{oRO}_2(\mathsf{sid}, \{\mathsf{com}_{i,j,k}\}_{i \in [\lambda], j \in [m], k \in [n]})$, where $c_i \in [m]$.
  - For $i \in [\lambda]$:
    * Simulate the execution of Π_{MPC} using (x, w) and the states generated by the c_i-th preprocessing phase (i.e., $\{\mathsf{state}_{i,c_i,k}\}_{k \in [n]}$), and output the views of the parties $\{\mathsf{view}_{i,k}(x, w_k)\}_{k \in [n]}$.
    * For $k \in [n]$: select $\tilde{r}_{i,k} \leftarrow \{0,1\}^{\lambda}$ and commit to the view of each party, i.e. compute view-commitments $\widetilde{\mathsf{com}}_{i,k} := \mathsf{oRO}_1(\mathsf{sid}, \mathsf{view}_{i,k}(x, w_k) || \tilde{r}_{i,k})$.
  - Send $a := (\{\mathsf{com}_{i,j,k}, \widetilde{\mathsf{com}}_{i,k}\}_{i \in [\lambda], j \in [m], k \in [n]}, \{\mathsf{state}_{i,j,k}, r_{i,j,k}\}_{i \in [\lambda], j \in [m] \setminus \{c_i\}, k \in [n]})$.
- Move2(1^{λ}): Send $e := (p_1, \ldots, p_{\lambda})$, where $p_i \in [n]$ and p_i is uniformly random.
- Move3$(x, w, e; r)$: Send $z := (\{\mathsf{view}_{i,k}(x, w_k), \tilde{r}_{i,k}, \mathsf{state}_{i,c_i,k}, r_{i,c_i,k}\}_{i \in [\lambda], k \in [n] \setminus \{p_i\}})$.
- Verify(x, a, e, z): Output 1 if and only if the following checks pass:
  - Check the commitments are opened correctly:
    * For $i \in [\lambda], j \in [m] \setminus \{c_i\}, k \in [n]$: check $\mathsf{com}_{i,j,k} = \mathsf{oRO}_1(\mathsf{sid}, \mathsf{state}_{i,j,k} || r_{i,j,k})$ holds.
    * For $i \in [\lambda], k \in [n] \setminus \{p_i\}$: check $\mathsf{com}_{i,c_i,k} = \mathsf{oRO}_1(\mathsf{sid}, \mathsf{state}_{i,c_i,k} || r_{i,c_i,k})$ and $\widetilde{\mathsf{com}}_{i,k} = \mathsf{oRO}_1(\mathsf{sid}, \mathsf{view}_{i,k}(x, w_k) || \tilde{r}_{i,k})$ hold.
  - Check the correctness of the executions of the preprocessing phase:
    * Compute $(c_1, \ldots, c_{\lambda}) := \mathsf{oRO}_2(\mathsf{sid}, \{\mathsf{com}_{i,j,k}\}_{i \in [\lambda], j \in [m], k \in [n]})$.
    * For $i \in [\lambda], j \in [m] \setminus \{c_i\}$: check $\{\mathsf{state}_{i,j,k}\}_{k \in [n]}$ are well-formed.
  - Check the consistency between the opened views:
    * For $i \in [\lambda], k \in [n] \setminus \{p_i\}$: check $\mathsf{view}_{i,k}(x, w_k)$ follows from the $\mathsf{state}_{i,c_i,k}$ correctly and $\mathsf{view}_{i,k}(x, w_k)$ yields output 1.
    * For $i \in [\lambda]$: check $\{\mathsf{view}_{i,k}(x, w_k)\}_{k \in [n] \setminus \{p_i\}}$ are consistent with each other.

Fig. 9. Protocol Π_{SHVZK} in the $\mathcal{G}_{\mathsf{oRO}}$ hybrid world

Let Π_{MPC} be the n-party MPC protocol which realizes f with $(n-1)$-privacy in the preprocessing model, where $f(x, w_1, \cdots, w_n) = \mathcal{R}_{\mathcal{L}}(x, w_1 \oplus \cdots \oplus w_n)$. Let Preprocess be the preprocessing algorithm that takes a λ-bit random string seed as input, and outputs the states $\{\text{state}\}_{i \in [n]}$ which are used for the computation later (cf. [31] for details). We use the $\mathcal{G}_{\text{oRO}}$ to instantiate the statically binding commitment (i.e., to commit msg with random string r, we use the answer of the $\mathcal{G}_{\text{oRO}}$ on input (msg, r) as the commitment and reveal (msg, r) as the opening). We denote the event where queries $\mathcal{G}_{\text{oRO}_i}$ on input x and gets the answer y as $y := \text{oRO}_i(x)$ for $i \in \{1, 2\}$ in the context, where $\text{oRO}_1 : \{0,1\}^{\ell_{\text{in}}(\lambda)} \to \{0,1\}^{\ell}$ and $\text{oRO}_2 : \{0,1\}^{\ell_{\text{in}}(\lambda)} \to (\mathbb{Z}_{m+1}^+)^{\lambda}$. We denote by m the number of the executions of the preprocessing phase. Formally, we present our protocol Π_{SHVZK} in Fig. 9 and prove the security through Theorem 3.

Theorem 3. *Assume Π_{MPC} is a secure n-party protocol that realizes $f_{\mathcal{R}}$ with perfect $(n-1)$-privacy, where $f(x, w_1, \cdots, w_n) = \mathcal{R}_{\mathcal{L}}(x, w_1 \oplus \cdots \oplus w_n)$. Then the protocol Π_{SHVZK} depicted in Fig. 9 is a SHVZK protocol that satisfies perfect completeness, 2-special soundness, perfect SHVZK.*

Proof. We leave the proof in the full version.

Perfect Hiding Non-interactive Equivocal Commitment. Given a SHVZK protocol, we can obtain a perfect-hiding non-interactive equivocal commitment. The intuition is as follows. Let $\mathcal{R}_{\mathcal{L}}$ be a hard NP relation. The receiver selects $(x, w) \in \mathcal{R}_{\mathcal{L}}$, and sets x as the commitment key and w as the equivocation trapdoor. The message m is used as the challenge on which to run the simulator for the SHVZK protocol with respect to x, producing the prover's first flow a and the response z. The first flow a is used as the commitment. The message m and response z are used as the opening. Equivocation is achieved by using the knowledge of w to execute the honest prover algorithm instead of the simulator algorithm. Similar ideas can be found in [18,35].

Let g be a one-way function; note that, due to the limit of space, we do not give the formal definition of one-way function, and we refer readers to see the definition in [32]. Formally, we present our non-interactive equivocal commitment in Fig. 10 and prove the security through Theorem 4. The proof of computational binding relies on the 2-special soundness, and this explains the reason why 2-special soundness is necessary in Sect. 4.2. We instantiate the NP relation with one-way function, i.e. $\mathcal{R}_1 = \{(y, \text{seed}) \mid y = g(\text{seed})\}$ where (y, seed) is the statement-witness pair and g is a one-way function. If we use our SHVZK protocol Π_{SHVZK} depicted in Fig. 9 as the building block, then we can obtain a perfect hiding non-interactive equivocal commitment scheme via only Minicrypt assumptions in the $\mathcal{G}_{\text{oRO}}$ hybrid world.

Theorem 4. *Assume Π_{SHVZK} is a 2-special sound SHVZK protocol. Assume g is a one-way function. Then Π_{ECom} depicted in Fig. 10 is an equivocal commitment that satisfies perfect correctness, perfect hiding, computational binding and perfect equivocation.*

Proof. We leave the proof in the full version.

Scheme Π_{ECom}

Primitives: SHVZK protocol $\Pi_{\text{SHVZK}} = \Pi_{\text{SHVZK}}.\{\text{Move1}, \text{Move2}, \text{Move3}, \text{Verify}, \text{Sim}\}$ and one-way function g.

- KeyGen(1^λ) : Select a random string $\text{seed} \leftarrow \{0,1\}^\lambda$, compute $y := g(\text{seed})$, and output $\text{ck} := y, \text{td} := \text{seed}$.
- KeyVer(ck, td) : Check if $\text{ck} = g(\text{td})$ holds. If so, output 1; otherwise, output 0.
- Commit(ck, m) : Select a random string $r \leftarrow \{0,1\}^\lambda$, invoke $(a, z) := \Pi_{\text{SHVZK}}.\text{Sim}(\text{ck}, m; r)$, and output $c := a, d := (m, z)$.
- ComVer(ck, c, d) : Check if $\Pi_{\text{SHVZK}}.\text{Verify}(\text{ck}, c, m, z) = 1$ holds. If so, output 1; otherwise, output 0.
- EquCom(ck, td) : Select a random string $s \leftarrow \{0,1\}^\lambda$, invoke $\tilde{a} := \Pi_{\text{SHVZK}}.\text{Move1}(\text{ck}, \text{td}; s)$, and output $\tilde{c} := \tilde{a}, \text{st} := s$.
- Equiv(ck, td, $\tilde{c}$, st, $\tilde{m}$) : Invoke $\tilde{z} := \Pi_{\text{SHVZK}}.\text{Move3}(\text{ck}, \text{td}, \tilde{m}; \text{st})$, and output $\tilde{d} := \tilde{z}$.

Fig. 10. Scheme Π_{ECom} based on one-way function

Straight-Line Extractable NIWH Argument. We construct the straight-line extractable NIWH argument in the $\mathcal{G}_{\text{oRO}}$ hybrid world using the technique described in [38]. We here describe the high-level description and the details can be found in the full version of our paper. Given a SHVZK protocol with 2-special soundness, we let the prover execute the honest prover algorithm to obtain the first flow message. Fixing this first flow message, we let the prover pick two distinct random challenges and compute the corresponding responses. Then the prover commits to the response by querying $\mathcal{G}_{\text{oRO}}$ and using the answer as the commitment. Next the prover sends the first flow message along with all the challenges and the commitments to the verifier. After that, the verifier asks the prover to open one commitment. Finally the verifier receives the response, and checks if the corresponding transcript is valid. The soundness error of the protocol described above is $\frac{1}{2}$, and it can be reduced by parallel repetitions. We also apply Fiat-Shamir transformation to remove the interaction [22]. The straight-line extractablity relies on the observability provided by $\mathcal{G}_{\text{oRO}}$ and 2-special soundness.

Theorem 5 ([38]). *Assume there is a 2-special sound SHVZK protocol, then there exists a straight-line extractable NIWH argument in the $\mathcal{G}_{\text{oRO}}$ hybrid world.*

5   Concluding Remarks: Towards a Complete Picture

In this work, we mainly focus on the lower bounds on round complexity for GUC-secure commitment protocols in the global random oracle models. We also wonder if such lower bounds exist, is it possible to construct round-optimal GUC-secure commitment protocols under Minicrypt assumptions?

In terms of the $\mathcal{G}_{\text{oRO}}$, our work gives a complete answer: we show it is impossible to construct 2-round GUC-secure commitment in the $\mathcal{G}_{\text{oRO}}$ hybrid world against static adversaries in Sect. 3, and construct a 3-round (round-optimal) GUC-secure commitment protocol under Minicrypt assumptions in the $\mathcal{G}_{\text{oRO}}$ hybrid world in Sect. 4. In the remaining, let us turn our attention on other global random oracle models.

As for the $\mathcal{G}_{\mathsf{sRO}}$, the results of [11] rules out the possibility of constructing any GUC-secure commitment protocol in the $\mathcal{G}_{\mathsf{sRO}}$ hybrid world. More precisely, they argued that no "public setup", namely no setup that provides only public information that is available to all parties, can suffice for realizing commitment protocols in the GUC framework. It is easy to see that this impossibility result holds in the $\mathcal{G}_{\mathsf{sRO}}$ hybrid world.

Regarding the $\mathcal{G}_{\mathsf{poRO}}$, non-interactive GUC-secure commitment protocol can be achieved. In fact, Camenisch et al. proposed a non-interactive GUC-secure commitment in the $\mathcal{G}_{\mathsf{poRO}}$ hybrid world without any further assumptions [9].

Among all the global random oracle models depicted in Fig. 4, only the $\mathcal{G}_{\mathsf{pRO}}$ has yet to be fully investigated. Actually, we already have some impossibility result: we find that there exists no GUC-secure commitment protocols with one-round committing phase in the $\mathcal{G}_{\mathsf{pRO}}$ hybrid world against static adversaries. Intuitively, we observe that the receiver does not have the chance to send any message in the committing phase in such commitment protocols. Note that, the $\mathcal{G}_{\mathsf{pRO}}$ only allows the simulator to program on the unqueried points without being detected, and the simulator benefits itself by letting the corrupted parties to work on its programmed points. Now let us consider the case where the committer is corrupted and the simulator acts as the receiver, the simulator needs to extract the committed value before the opening phase. In a commitment protocol where the committing phase only takes one round, the simulator (acting as the receiver) does not need to send any message, thus it cannot enforce the corrupted committer to produce its message on the programmed points. If the simulator still succeeds in extracting the committed value from the commitment message, then we can use such a simulator to break the hiding property of the commitment scheme since anyone can run this simulator without relying on the programmability of the $\mathcal{G}_{\mathsf{pRO}}$. In conclusion, the committing phase requires at least 2 rounds, plus (at least) 1 round of the opening phase, and the entire commitment protocol requires at least 3 rounds. We refer interesting readers to see the formal theorem and proof in the full version of our paper.

Given this lower bound in the $\mathcal{G}_{\mathsf{pRO}}$, we find that the 3-round (2 rounds for the committing phase, 1 round for the opening phase) GUC-secure commitment protocol proposed in [9] is round-optimal. But their construction relies on CDH assumption which lives in Cryptomania world. Unfortunately, we find it extremely hard to construct a round-optimal GUC-secure commitment protocol under only Minicrypt assumptions in the $\mathcal{G}_{\mathsf{pRO}}$ hybrid world, so we leave it as an open question.

References

1. Ames, S., Hazay, C., Ishai, Y., Venkitasubramaniam, M.: Ligero: lightweight sublinear arguments without a trusted setup. In: ACM CCS 2017, pp. 2087–2104. ACM Press (2017)
2. Barak, B., Canetti, R., Nielsen, J.B., Pass, R.: Universally composable protocols with relaxed set-up assumptions. In: FOCS 2004, pp. 186–195. IEEE Computer Society Press (2004)

3. Baum, C., David, B., Dowsley, R.: Insured MPC: efficient secure computation with financial penalties. In: Bonneau, J., Heninger, N. (eds.) FC 2020. LNCS, vol. 12059, pp. 404–420. Springer, Cham (2020). https://doi.org/10.1007/978-3-030-51280-4_22

4. Bellare, M., Rogaway, P.: Random oracles are practical: a paradigm for designing efficient protocols. In: ACM CCS 1993, pp. 62–73. ACM Press (1993)

5. Ben-Sasson, E., Bentov, I., Horesh, Y., Riabzev, M.: Scalable zero knowledge with no trusted setup. In: Boldyreva, A., Micciancio, D. (eds.) CRYPTO 2019. LNCS, vol. 11694, pp. 701–732. Springer, Cham (2019). https://doi.org/10.1007/978-3-030-26954-8_23

6. Branco, P.: A post-quantum UC-commitment scheme in the global random oracle model from code-based assumptions. Adv. Math. Commun. **15**(1), 113 (2021)

7. Branco, P., Goulão, M., Mateus, P.: UC-commitment schemes with phase-adaptive security from trapdoor functions. Cryptology ePrint Archive, Report 2019/529 (2019). https://eprint.iacr.org/2019/529

8. Byali, M., Patra, A., Ravi, D., Sarkar, P.: Fast and universally-composable oblivious transfer and commitment scheme with adaptive security. Cryptology ePrint Archive, Report 2017/1165 (2017). https://eprint.iacr.org/2017/1165

9. Camenisch, J., Drijvers, M., Gagliardoni, T., Lehmann, A., Neven, G.: The wonderful world of global random oracles. In: Nielsen, J.B., Rijmen, V. (eds.) EUROCRYPT 2018. LNCS, vol. 10820, pp. 280–312. Springer, Cham (2018). https://doi.org/10.1007/978-3-319-78381-9_11

10. Canetti, R.: Universally composable security: a new paradigm for cryptographic protocols. In: FOCS 2001, pp. 136–145. IEEE Computer Society Press (2001)

11. Canetti, R., Dodis, Y., Pass, R., Walfish, S.: Universally composable security with global setup. In: Vadhan, S.P. (ed.) TCC 2007. LNCS, vol. 4392, pp. 61–85. Springer, Heidelberg (2007). https://doi.org/10.1007/978-3-540-70936-7_4

12. Canetti, R., Fischlin, M.: Universally composable commitments. In: Kilian, J. (ed.) CRYPTO 2001. LNCS, vol. 2139, pp. 19–40. Springer, Heidelberg (2001). https://doi.org/10.1007/3-540-44647-8_2

13. Canetti, R., Goldreich, O., Halevi, S.: The random oracle methodology, revisited (preliminary version). In: ACM STOC 1998, pp. 209–218. ACM Press (1998)

14. Canetti, R., Jain, A., Scafuro, A.: Practical UC security with a global random oracle. In: ACM CCS 2014, pp. 597–608. ACM Press (2014)

15. Canetti, R., Sarkar, P., Wang, X.: Efficient and round-optimal oblivious transfer and commitment with adaptive security. In: Moriai, S., Wang, H. (eds.) ASIACRYPT 2020. LNCS, vol. 12493, pp. 277–308. Springer, Cham (2020). https://doi.org/10.1007/978-3-030-64840-4_10

16. Chase, M., et al.: Post-quantum zero-knowledge and signatures from symmetric-key primitives. In: ACM CCS 2017, pp. 1825–1842. ACM Press (2017)

17. Chiesa, A., Ojha, D., Spooner, N.: FRACTAL: post-quantum and transparent recursive proofs from holography. In: Canteaut, A., Ishai, Y. (eds.) EUROCRYPT 2020. LNCS, vol. 12105, pp. 769–793. Springer, Cham (2020). https://doi.org/10.1007/978-3-030-45721-1_27

18. Damgård, I.: On Σ-protocols. https://www.cs.au.dk/~ivan/Sigma.pdf

19. de Saint Guilhem, C.D., Orsini, E., Tanguy, T.: Limbo: efficient zero-knowledge MPCitH-based arguments. In: ACM CCS 2021, pp. 3022–3036. ACM Press (2021)

20. Dodis, Y., Shoup, V., Walfish, S.: Efficient constructions of composable commitments and zero-knowledge proofs. In: Wagner, D. (ed.) CRYPTO 2008. LNCS, vol. 5157, pp. 515–535. Springer, Heidelberg (2008). https://doi.org/10.1007/978-3-540-85174-5_29

21. Feige, U., Shamir, A.: Witness indistinguishable and witness hiding protocols. In: ACM STOC 1990, pp. 416–426. ACM Press (1990)
22. Fiat, A., Shamir, A.: How to prove yourself: practical solutions to identification and signature problems. In: Odlyzko, A.M. (ed.) CRYPTO 1986. LNCS, vol. 263, pp. 186–194. Springer, Heidelberg (1987). https://doi.org/10.1007/3-540-47721-7_12
23. Ganesh, C., Kondi, Y., Patra, A., Sarkar, P.: Efficient adaptively secure zero-knowledge from garbled circuits. In: Abdalla, M., Dahab, R. (eds.) PKC 2018. LNCS, vol. 10770, pp. 499–529. Springer, Cham (2018). https://doi.org/10.1007/978-3-319-76581-5_17
24. Garg, S., Ishai, Y., Srinivasan, A.: Two-round MPC: information-theoretic and black-box. In: Beimel, A., Dziembowski, S. (eds.) TCC 2018. LNCS, vol. 11239, pp. 123–151. Springer, Cham (2018). https://doi.org/10.1007/978-3-030-03807-6_5
25. Giacomelli, I., Madsen, J., Orlandi, C.: ZKBoo: faster zero-knowledge for Boolean circuits. In: USENIX Security 2016, pp. 1069–1083. USENIX Association (2016)
26. Goldreich, O., Micali, S., Wigderson, A.: How to play any mental game or a completeness theorem for protocols with honest majority. In: ACM STOC 1987, pp. 218–229. ACM Press (1987)
27. Goldwasser, S., Micali, S., Rackoff, C.: The knowledge complexity of interactive proof systems. SIAM J. Comput. **18**(1), 186–208 (1989)
28. Hofheinz, D., Müller-Quade, J.: Universally composable commitments using random oracles. In: Naor, M. (ed.) TCC 2004. LNCS, vol. 2951, pp. 58–76. Springer, Heidelberg (2004). https://doi.org/10.1007/978-3-540-24638-1_4
29. Impagliazzo, R.: A personal view of average-case complexity. In: SCT 1995, pp. 134–147. IEEE (1995)
30. Ishai, Y., Kushilevitz, E., Ostrovsky, R., Sahai, A.: Zero-knowledge from secure multiparty computation. In: ACM STOC 2007, pp. 21–30. ACM Press (2007)
31. Katz, J., Kolesnikov, V., Wang, X.: Improved non-interactive zero knowledge with applications to post-quantum signatures. In: ACM CCS 2018, pp. 525–537. ACM Press (2018)
32. Katz, J., Lindell, Y.: Introduction to Modern Cryptography. CRC Press, Boca Raton (2020)
33. Kuykendall, B., Zhandry, M.: Towards non-interactive witness hiding. In: Pass, R., Pietrzak, K. (eds.) TCC 2020. LNCS, vol. 12550, pp. 627–656. Springer, Cham (2020). https://doi.org/10.1007/978-3-030-64375-1_22
34. Lysyanskaya, A., Rosenbloom, L.N.: Universally composable sigma-protocols in the global random-oracle model. Cryptology ePrint Archive, Paper 2022/290 (2022). https://eprint.iacr.org/2022/290
35. MacKenzie, P., Yang, K.: On simulation-sound trapdoor commitments. In: Cachin, C., Camenisch, J.L. (eds.) EUROCRYPT 2004. LNCS, vol. 3027, pp. 382–400. Springer, Heidelberg (2004). https://doi.org/10.1007/978-3-540-24676-3_23
36. Masny, D., Rindal, P.: Endemic oblivious transfer. In: ACM CCS 2019, pp. 309–326. ACM Press (2019)
37. Mohassel, P., Rosulek, M., Scafuro, A.: Sublinear zero-knowledge arguments for RAM programs. In: Coron, J.-S., Nielsen, J.B. (eds.) EUROCRYPT 2017. LNCS, vol. 10210, pp. 501–531. Springer, Cham (2017). https://doi.org/10.1007/978-3-319-56620-7_18
38. Pass, R.: On deniability in the common reference string and random oracle model. In: Boneh, D. (ed.) CRYPTO 2003. LNCS, vol. 2729, pp. 316–337. Springer, Heidelberg (2003). https://doi.org/10.1007/978-3-540-45146-4_19
39. Yao, A.C.C.: Protocols for secure computations (extended abstract). In: FOCS 1982, pp. 160–164. IEEE Computer Society Press (1982)

Additive-Homomorphic Functional Commitments and Applications to Homomorphic Signatures

Dario Catalano[1], Dario Fiore[2($\boxtimes$)], and Ida Tucker[2]

[1] University of Catania, Catania, Italy
catalano@dmi.unict.it
[2] IMDEA Software Institute, Madrid, Spain
dario.fiore@imdea.org

Abstract. Functional Commitments (FC) allow one to reveal functions of committed data in a succinct and verifiable way. In this paper we put forward the notion of additive-homomorphic FC and show two efficient, pairing-based, realizations of this primitive supporting multivariate polynomials of constant degree and monotone span programs, respectively. We also show applications of the new primitive in the contexts of *homomorphic signatures*: we show that additive-homomorphic FCs can be used to realize homomorphic signatures (supporting the same class of functionalities as the underlying FC) in a simple and elegant way. Using our new FCs as underlying building blocks, this leads to the (seemingly) first expressive realizations of multi-input homomorphic signatures not relying on lattices or multilinear maps.

1 Introduction

Functional commitments (FC), put forth by Libert, Ramanna and Yung [22], allow a sender to commit to a vector x of length n and later to open the commitment to functions of the committed vector, namely to prove that $f(x) = y$. FCs are required to be *evaluation binding*, meaning that it is computationally hard to open a commitment at two distinct outputs $y \neq y'$ for the same function f. The distinguishing feature of FCs is that commitments and openings should be succinct, i.e., of size independent of n.

Functional commitments generalize the well known notions of vector commitments (VC) [4,5,23] and polynomial commitments (PC) [16]—two functionalities that, albeit specific, have nowadays a large number of applications. Besides VCs and PCs, state-of-the-art functional commitments capture linear forms [18,22] and semi-sparse polynomials [24].

An FC for an arbitrary computation f can be built via succinct commitments and SNARKs for NP: simply, use the latter to generate a succinct argument that "$y = f(x)$ and x opens the commitment". However, such an FC holds under *non-falsifiable assumptions* that are required to build SNARKs [12].

© International Association for Cryptologic Research 2022
S. Agrawal and D. Lin (Eds.): ASIACRYPT 2022, LNCS 13794, pp. 159–188, 2022.
https://doi.org/10.1007/978-3-031-22972-5_6

In contrast, due to the falsifiability of the evaluation binding notion and as confirmed by the existing constructions [22,24], functional commitments are realizable from falsifiable assumptions. Thanks to these two properties – succinctness and security under falsifiable assumptions – FCs can be seen as a simple form of succinct non-interactive arguments.[1] Whenever evaluation binding is sufficient, FCs are an attractive building block: they provide communication-efficiency through succinctness, without having to sacrifice assumptions (e.g., see the applications of vector/polynomial commitments, and FCs for inner products in [4,16,22]). For this reason we believe that advancing the understanding of FCs could help us better understand the fundamental problem of constructing succinct argument systems from minimal assumptions.

1.1   Our Results

In this work we make progress, along different fronts, in the study of functional commitments based on falsifiable assumptions.

We begin by exploring potential applications of FCs. While we know several applications of FCs for linear functionalities (and all the functionalities implied by them, such as vector and polynomial commitments), to the best of our knowledge, less is known about FCs for, say, multivariate polynomials or circuits.

We address this problem by showing a new application of FCs to building homomorphic signatures [1]. As it will be apparent later, this application becomes particularly interesting if the FC is *additively homomorphic*, namely if given two commitments to vectors x_1 and x_2, one can compute the commitment to the vector $x_1 + x_2$. This is a basic and useful property of commitment schemes. Yet we know of no FC that is additive-homomorphic and supports a rich class of computations; the only known additive-homomorphic FCs are the ones for linear forms of [18,22].

We bridge this gap by proposing the first additive-homomorphic FCs supporting the evaluation of functions beyond linear. Our techniques yield new homomorphic signatures that advance the state of the art, and a SNARG for a polynomial-time language from a falsifiable assumption.

Below we present our results in more detail, and in the next section we provide an overview of our techniques.

Additive-Homomorphic FC for Polynomials. We propose an additive-homomorphic FC scheme that allows one to commit to a vector x of length n and to open the commitment to $f(x)$ where f is a collection of m multivariate polynomials of bounded constant degree. Our scheme enjoys *compact* openings, i.e., a single proof, of size constant in both n and m, for all the m evaluations. We build this FC using bilinear groups and prove its security based on the Diffie-Hellman exponent assumption [2].

Compared to the FC for semi-sparse polynomials of [24] and an FC for polynomials obtained via linearization (cf. Sect. 1.2), the main novelty of ours is to

---

[1] Their functionality resembles commit-and-prove SNARKs except that FCs are evaluation binding rather than (knowledge) sound.

be additively homomorphic. Also, ours is the first FC with compact openings whose security is based on established assumptions: the scheme of [18] relies on the generic group model, and that of [24] uses a newly proposed assumption.

Additive-Homomorphic FC for Monotone Span Programs. Our second realization is an FC for a new polynomial time language, called *semi-quadratic arithmetic programs* (sQAPs, for short). In a nutshell, an sQAP is defined by a matrix $\mathbf{F}$ and accepts a pair of vectors $(\boldsymbol{z}, \boldsymbol{y})$ if there exists a solution $\boldsymbol{w}$ such that $\mathbf{F} \cdot (\boldsymbol{z} \circ \boldsymbol{w}) = \boldsymbol{y}$, where $\circ$ denotes entry-wise multiplication of vectors.[2] An FC for sQAPs allows one to commit to $(\boldsymbol{z}, \boldsymbol{y})$ and then open to $\mathbf{F}$, in the sense of proving that $\mathbf{F}$ accepts the pair of committed vectors. Our scheme is based on pairings, it is additively homomorphic and has constant size proofs consisting of three group elements. We prove its security based on a variant of the Diffie-Hellman exponent assumption that we justify in the generic group model.

We show that sQAPs are sufficiently expressive to capture the well known class of monotone span programs (MSPs) [15] and show how to turn our FC for sQAPs into one for MSPs. Also, via known transformations (see Footnote 8) it is possible to build a monotone span program that models the satisfiability of an NC^1 circuit, which therefore allows us to obtain *the first FC for* NC^1 *circuits*.

Applications to Homomorphic Signatures, and More. To motivate additive-homomorphic FCs we present a novel application of this primitive to build homomorphic signatures (HS) [1] (see Sect. 1.3 for an overview).

Notably, by plugging our new FCs in this transformation we obtain new HS that advance the state of the art as follows:

- Our FC for polynomials yields the first multi-input HS for polynomials based on pairings, and the first HS with "compact" signatures, where, again, by compact we mean that, for functions of the form $\boldsymbol{f} : \mathbb{F}^n \to \mathbb{F}^m$, the resulting signatures have size which is constant in both n and m. None of the previous schemes, e.g., [1,7,13] has compact signatures, as they need one signature for every output value.
- Through our FC for NC^1 we obtain the first *multi-input* HS based on pairings for NC^1 circuits. The most expressive HS based on pairings is that of Katsumata et al. [17] that also supports NC^1 circuits, but in the *single-input* model where the signer must sign the entire data vector at once. Prior multi-input HS for functions beyond linear instead need lattices [1,13] or multilinear maps [7]. Our result essentially shows that these powerful algebraic structures are not necessary to build such expressive HS.

In the full version we discuss further applications of additive-homomorphic FCs, such as updatable FCs and verifiable databases with expressive queries.

A SNARG for Linear Systems from Falsifiable Assumptions. In [18], Lai and Malavolta put forth a stronger security property for FC, that we call strong evaluation binding, which considers as an attack not only two inconsistent openings for the same function but also inconsistent openings for multiple

---

[2] sQAPs is in P as it can be decided via Gaussian elimination.

functions. Namely it must be computationally hard to produce a commitment and a collection of valid openings for function-output pairs $\{f_i, y_i\}_{i=1}^{Q}$ for which there exists no vector $\boldsymbol{x}$ such that $f_i(\boldsymbol{x}) = y_i$ for every $i = 1$ to Q. Lai and Malavolta only show how to realize a strong evaluation binding FC for linear maps by resorting to the generic group model. This is unsatisfactory as a generic group model proof essentially uses non-black-box extractability techniques, which cannot be considered falsifiable, and would defeat the main goal of this work which is constructing FCs from falsifiable assumptions.

In our construction of FC for sQAPs we show a new proof technique that allows us to reduce an adversary that produces a valid proof for an inconsistent system of equations to an adversary against a falsifiable assumption. Interestingly, we can apply the same technique to the linear map FC of [18] and prove its strong evaluation binding based on a falsifiable assumption, the parallel bilinear Diffie-Hellman exponent in [26].

This is to the best of our knowledge *the first strong evaluation binding and compact FC from a falsifiable assumption.* This result is interesting since, as one could observe, a strong evaluation binding FC with compact proofs for a language $\mathcal{L}$ yields *de facto* a SNARG for $\mathcal{L}$. Also, a strong evaluation binding FC with compact proofs for quadratic polynomials would yield a SNARG for NP, since a system of quadratic equations can model circuit satisfiability, e.g., through R1CS [10]. Therefore, due to the impossibility of Gentry and Wichs [12], our SNARG for linear maps from falsifiable assumptions can be seen as optimal, in the sense that it is unlikely to have an analogous result for quadratic functions.

1.2   Related Work

Libert et al. [22] introduce the notion of functional commitments and propose a construction for *linear forms* based on the Diffie-Hellman exponent assumption in bilinear groups. Lai and Malavolta [18] extend the scheme of [22] to support *linear maps* with *compact* openings, namely of size independent of both the input and the output lengths. Lipmaa and Pavlyk [24] propose an FC construction that supports, with compact proofs, a class of arithmetic circuits which roughly corresponds to semi-sparse polynomials. Their scheme is obtained by "scaling down" SNARK-based techniques and is proven secure from a newly proposed falsifiable assumption in bilinear groups. More generally, an FC for linear maps is sufficient to realize an FC for any *linearizable* function, that is a function f which can be implemented as $f(\boldsymbol{x}) = \langle \boldsymbol{p}(\boldsymbol{x}), \boldsymbol{\phi}_f \rangle$ where $\boldsymbol{p}(\cdot)$ is a vector of polynomial-time computable functions which do not depend on f and can be precomputed. Simply, the sender commits to the vector $\boldsymbol{p}(\boldsymbol{x})$ and then, for any f, opens the commitment to the linear form $\boldsymbol{\phi}_f$. Both the scheme of [24] and the one based on linearization are not additively homomorphic[3] and thus cannot be used in the applications discussed in this paper.

---

[3] Even if one starts from an additive-homomorphic FC for linear maps, one can notice that the transformation to FCs for linearizable functions does not preserve the additive-homomorphism.

In a recent work, Peikert et al. [25] propose the first construction of a vector commitment based on lattice assumptions and show an extension of it to a functional commitment for circuits. Their FC, however, works in a weaker model where a trusted authority uses secret information to generate an opening key for each function for which the prover wishes to generate an opening.

1.3 Technical Overview

FC for Polynomials. To illustrate the main ideas of our construction let us consider the simplified case where one opens the commitment to a single polynomial (i.e., no compactness) that is homogeneous. Note that a homogeneous polynomial of degree d, that we can write as $f(\boldsymbol{x}) = \sum_\ell f_\ell \cdot (x_1^{d_{\ell,1}} \cdots x_n^{d_{\ell,n}})$ with $\sum_j d_{\ell,j} = d$, can be linearized as an inner product between the vector of its coefficients and the vector of all degree-d terms. More precisely, assuming $d = 2^\delta$ a power of 2, given a homogeneous polynomial f we can build a vector $\hat{\boldsymbol{f}} \in \mathbb{F}^{n^d}$ such that for any $\boldsymbol{x} \in \mathbb{F}^n$ it holds $\langle \hat{\boldsymbol{f}}, \boldsymbol{x}^{(\delta)} \rangle = f(\boldsymbol{x})$, where $\boldsymbol{x}^{(\delta)}$ is the δ-fold Kronecker product of $\boldsymbol{x}$ with itself, i.e., $\boldsymbol{x}^{(1)} = \boldsymbol{x} \otimes \boldsymbol{x}$, $\boldsymbol{x}^{(2)} = \boldsymbol{x}^{(1)} \otimes \boldsymbol{x}^{(1)}$, etc.

Following this observation, one could use an FC for linear forms to commit to $\boldsymbol{x}^{(\delta)}$ and then open/verify the commitment using the appropriately computed linear form $\hat{\boldsymbol{f}}$. This idea however suffers the problem that the commitments would not be additively homomorphic.

Our approach to solve this problem is to generate a commitment C to $\boldsymbol{x}$ such that: (i) C is additively homomorphic, and (ii) the prover creates, at opening time, a linear-map commitment X_δ to $\boldsymbol{x}^{(\delta)}$ and convinces the verifier that the vector committed in X_δ is indeed the δ-fold Kronecker product of the vector committed in C. Once (ii) is achieved we could use the linear-map functionality to open X_δ to $\langle \hat{\boldsymbol{f}}, \boldsymbol{x}^{(\delta)} \rangle$. The challenge of achieving (ii) is to make this proof succinct without having to extract the committed vectors from the prover.

Our technique to solve this problem is algebraically involved. In what follows highlight the main ideas, without focusing too much on security.

For the X_δ produced in the opening we use the linear-map commitment of [18,22] in which the vector $\boldsymbol{x}^{(\delta)}$ is encoded in a group element

$$X_\delta = [p_{\boldsymbol{x}}^{(\delta)}(\alpha)]_1 = \sum_{j=1}^{n^d} x_j^{(\delta)} \cdot [\alpha^j]_1$$

where the elements $[\alpha^j]_1$ are part of the public parameters.[4] For the commitment to $\boldsymbol{x}$, assume for now that it includes $X_0 = [p_{\boldsymbol{x}}^{(0)}(\alpha)]_1 = \sum_{j=1}^n x_j \cdot [\alpha^j]_1$, and consider for simplicity the case of $\delta = 1$ (i.e., opening to a polynomial of degree

---

[4] We use the bracket notation for bilinear groups of [9].

$d = 2$). Then our first key observation is that

$$p_x^{(0)}(\alpha) \cdot (p_x^{(0)}(\alpha^n)/\alpha^n) = \left(\sum_{i=1}^{n} x_i \cdot \alpha^i\right) \left(\sum_{j=1}^{n} x_j \cdot \alpha^{n(j-1)}\right)$$

$$= \sum_{i,j=1}^{n} x_i x_j \cdot \alpha^{i+n(j-1)} = \sum_{k=1}^{n^2} x_k^{(1)} \cdot \alpha^k = p_x^{(1)}(\alpha)$$

Thus, if we include in the commitment the element $\hat{X}_0 = [\hat{p}_x^{(0)}(\alpha)]_2 = [p_x^{(0)}(\alpha^n)/\alpha^n]_2$, the verifier can test the correctness of X_1 via a pairing $e(X_1, [1]_2) = e(X_0, \hat{X}_0)$. Intuitively, this is secure because the pair $(X_0, \hat{X}_0)$ is part of the commitment and can be somehow considered "trusted"; so the pairing allows transferring this trust to X_1. To handle openings of polynomials of degree > 2, this is not sufficient though. Say that the prover includes in the opening the elements $X_2, X_1, \hat{X}_1$, and the verifier tests the correctness of X_2 via a "chain" of checks $e(X_1, [1]_2) \stackrel{?}{=} e(X_0, \hat{X}_0)$ and $e(X_2, [1]_2) \stackrel{?}{=} e(X_1, \hat{X}_1)$. The issue is that in the second check $(X_1, \hat{X}_1)$ is not "trusted"; in particular, while X_1 can be considered trusted due to the previous check, $\hat{X}_1$ is not, since it is generated by the prover and not tested.

Our second key idea is based on showing that the polynomial $\hat{p}_x^{(1)}(\alpha)$ in $\hat{X}_1$ can be expressed as the product of two polynomials $\phi_x^{(2)}(\alpha), \phi_x^{(3)}(\alpha)$, each of them a linear function of x. Precisely, it holds that (cf. Claim 2)

$$p_x^{(1)}(\alpha^n)/\alpha^n = \phi_x^{(2)}(\alpha) \cdot \phi_x^{(3)}(\alpha) = (p_x^{(0)}(\alpha^{n^2})/\alpha^{n^2}) \cdot (p_x^{(0)}(\alpha^{n^3})/\alpha^{n^3})$$

So, if we include in the commitment group elements Φ_2, Φ_3 encoding $\phi_x^{(2)}(\alpha)$ and $\phi_x^{(3)}(\alpha)$ respectively, the verifier will be able to use a pairing to test the correctness of the element $\hat{X}_1$ included in the opening, and mark X_1 as "trusted", as it can establish a correct link with the group elements in the commitment.

To summarize, in this example of a degree-4 homogeneous polynomial f, the commitment C of x includes $(X_0, \hat{X}_0, \Phi_2, \Phi_3)$, and the opening includes $(X_1, \hat{X}_1, X_2)$ and a linear-map opening proof generated using [18] to show that X_2 (seen as a commitment to $x^{(2)}$) opens to $\langle \hat{f}, x^{(2)} \rangle = f(x)$.

Importantly, all the group elements in the commitment can be expressed as a linear map of the vector x, thus making C additively homomorphic.

Going beyond degree 4 requires further extensions of our technique since a polynomial $\hat{p}_x^{(k)}(\alpha)$ factors into 2^k polynomials, which for $k > 1$ cannot be tested with a pairing. We bridge this gap by showing how to break each of these tests into a system of k quadratic equations using a tree-based encoding. This is our third key idea that allows us to generalize the techniques illustrated so far to handle degree-2^δ polynomials.

Eventually, we obtain an FC for arbitrary polynomials of constant degree d in which commitment and openings consist of exactly d group elements (notably, even if one opens m polynomials at the same time). Comparing to the techniques of prior FCs for linear maps [18,22], while our FC uses them in the final step of our opening algorithm, the remaining design ideas are novel and significantly different.

FC for Semi-quadratic Arithmetic Programs. We recall that in an FC for sQAPs one commits to a pair of vectors $x = (z, y)$ and then opens to $\mathbf{F}$ in the sense of proving that $\exists w : \mathbf{F} \cdot (z \circ w) = y$. Similarly to the FC for polynomials, we start from the idea of linearizing the computation in such a way that we can eventually resort to a linear-map FC (LMC). Specifically, we use the LMC of [18]. However, to do this linearization we cannot use the same technique of the previous scheme to produce a commitment to, e.g., $z \circ w$ or $z \otimes w$. Roughly speaking, the issue is that in sQAPs w is not committed ahead of time together with z; here w is a non-deterministic witness depending on each specific $\mathbf{F}$.

So we proceed differently. We let the prover compute a succinct encoding of the matrix $\mathbf{F}_z = \mathbf{F} \circ \mathbf{Z}$, where $\mathbf{Z} \in \mathbb{F}^{m \times n}$ is the matrix with $z^\top$ in every row, and we show how the verifier can check the validity of this encoding given $\mathbf{F}$ and a committed z. This way, we are left with the problem of proving that $(\mathbf{F}_z \mid y)$ is a satisfiable system of linear equations. To prove this, we let the prover generate a commitment W to the solution w and then generate an opening proof to argue that $y = \mathbf{F}_z \cdot w$ for the committed w. The generation of W and its opening to $\mathbf{F}_z$ rely on the LMC of [18].

Compared to [18], we introduce two technical novelties. The first one deals with enabling the verifier to check the opening by having only an encoding of $\mathbf{F}_z$, which can be linked to the public $\mathbf{F}$ and the commitment to z. The second and most important novelty concerns the security proof. The challenge is the presence of this non-deterministic component w which requires the prover to show the satisfiability of a system – a task that goes beyond what is captured by the notion of evaluation binding since we need that an efficient adversary cannot generate a valid opening if $(\mathbf{F}_z \mid y)$ is *not* satisfiable. This could be solved by resorting to the strong evaluation binding of the [18] LMC, but they only prove this property in the generic group model, essentially using a non-black-box extraction technique. In our paper we show a new proof technique for reducing an adversary producing a valid opening for an inconsistent system of equations into an adversary against a falsifiable assumption.

From FCs to Homomorphic Signatures. We present a novel approach to construct HS based on (additively homomorphic) FCs. The basic idea is that the signer generates a commitment C_x to the dataset x and a (standard) digital signature σ_{C_x} on the commitment. Given (C_x, σ_{C_x}), the server can compute a function f by giving to the verifier this pair (C_x, σ_{C_x}) (which is succinct) along with an opening of C_x to f (which is succinct as well). The resulting HS construction is clearly single-input since the signer must commit to the dataset all at once. We achieve a multi-input HS by exploiting FCs that are additively homomorphic. To sign the i-th element of the dataset, Alice commits to the sparse vector $x_i \cdot e_i$ with x_i in position i and 0 everywhere else; let C_i be the resulting commitment. If the server is given these commitments one by one, eventually it can reconstruct a commitment C to the currently available dataset by computing their sum homomorphically, and then proceed as in the single-input construction by opening C to the desired function f. This construction however is not secure as the verifier cannot be assured that C is validly obtained from commitments provided by Alice. Therefore we let Alice sign C_i using an homomorphic signature that only needs to support one functionality, the homomorphic sum in the commitment space. Interestingly, for pairing-based FCs, this HS can be implemented via well known linearly-homomorphic structure-preserving signatures [21][5]. Finally, we notice that for the sake of this application the FC only needs to satisfy a weaker notion of evaluation binding in which the adversary reveals the vector x committed in C, yet it manages to produce an opening to a function f and a result $y \neq f(x)$ that is accepted by the verification algorithm.

2   Preliminaries

Notation. We use $\lambda \in \mathbb{N}$ to denote the security parameter. If a function $\epsilon(\lambda) = O(\lambda^{-c})$ for every constant $c > 0$, then we say that ϵ is *negligible*, denoted $\epsilon(\lambda) = \mathsf{negl}(\lambda)$. A function $p(\lambda)$ is *polynomial* if $p(\lambda) = O(\lambda^c)$ for some constant $c > 0$. We say that an algorithm is *probabilistic polynomial time* (PPT) if its running time is bounded by some $p(\lambda) = \mathsf{poly}(\lambda)$. Given a finite set S, $x \leftarrow_\$ S$ denotes selecting x uniformly at random in S. For an algorithm A, we write $y \leftarrow A(x)$ for the output of A on input x. For a positive $n \in \mathbb{N}$, $[n]$ is the set $\{1, \ldots, n\}$. We denote vectors x and matrices $\mathbf{M}$ using bold fonts. For a ring $\mathcal{R}$, given two vectors $x, y \in \mathcal{R}^n$, $x \circ y$ denotes their entry-wise product, i.e., the vector with entries $(x_i y_i)_i$, while $z := (x \otimes y) \in \mathcal{R}^{n^2}$ denotes their Kronecker product (that is a vectorization of the outer product), i.e., $\forall i, j \in [n] : z_{i+(j-1)n} = x_i y_j$.

Bilinear Groups. Our FC constructions build on bilinear groups. A *bilinear group generator* $\mathcal{BG}(1^\lambda)$ outputs $\mathsf{bgp} := (q, \mathbb{G}_1, \mathbb{G}_2, \mathbb{G}_T, e, g_1, g_2)$, where $\mathbb{G}_1$, $\mathbb{G}_2$, $\mathbb{G}_T$ are groups of prime order q, $g_1 \in \mathbb{G}_1$ and $g_2 \in \mathbb{G}_2$ are two fixed generators, and $e : \mathbb{G}_1 \times \mathbb{G}_2 \to \mathbb{G}_T$ is an efficiently computable, non-degenerate, bilinear map. We present our results using Type-3 groups in which it is assumed that there is no efficiently computable isomorphisms between $\mathbb{G}_1$ and $\mathbb{G}_2$.

For group elements, we use the bracket notation of [9] in which, for $s \in \{1, 2, T\}$ and $x \in \mathbb{Z}_q$, $[x]_s$ denotes $g_s^x \in \mathbb{G}_s$. We use additive notation for $\mathbb{G}_1$ and $\mathbb{G}_2$ and multiplicative one for $\mathbb{G}_T$. For $s = 1, 2$, given an element $[x]_s \in \mathbb{G}_s$ and a scalar a, one can efficiently compute $a \cdot [x] = [ax] = g_s^{ax} \in \mathbb{G}_s$; given group elements $[a]_1 \in \mathbb{G}_1$ and $[b]_2 \in \mathbb{G}_2$, one can efficiently compute $[ab]_T = e([a]_1, [b]_2)$.

3   Functional Commitments

We recall the notion of functional commitments (FC) [22]. A crucial feature that makes this primitive interesting and nontrivial is that both commitment

---

[5] Strictly speaking the signature does not need to be structure preserving as long as it allows to (homomorphically) sign group elements.

and the openings are *succinct*, i.e., of size independent of the vector's length. In our work we also consider *compact* FCs, a notion introduced in [18], which requires openings size to be also independent of the function's output length.

Definition 1 (Functional Commitments). *A functional commitment scheme is a tuple of algorithms* FC = (Setup, Com, Open, Ver) *with the following syntax and that satisfies correctness and succinctness (or compactness).*

Setup$(1^\lambda, n, m) \to$ ck *on input the security parameter λ and the vector length n, outputs a commitment key* ck, *which defines the message space $\mathcal{X}$ and the class of admissible functions $\mathcal{F} \subseteq \{f : \mathcal{X}^n \to \mathcal{X}^m\}$ for some $n, m = $ poly(λ).*

Com$($ck$, \boldsymbol{x}; r) \to (C, aux)$ *on input a vector $\boldsymbol{x} \in \mathcal{X}^n$ and (possibly) randomness r, outputs a commitment C and related auxiliary information* aux. *We often omit r from the inputs, in which case we assume it is randomly sampled in the appropriate space.*

Open$($ck, aux$, f) \to \pi$ *on input an auxiliary information* aux *and a function $f \in \mathcal{F}$, outputs an opening proof π.*

Ver$($ck$, C, f, \boldsymbol{y}, \pi) \to b \in \{0,1\}$ *on input a commitment C, an opening proof π, a function $f \in \mathcal{F}$ and a value $y \in \mathcal{X}^m$, accepts ($b = 1$) or rejects ($b = 0$).*

Correctness. FC *is correct if for any $n, m \in \mathbb{N}$, all* ck $\leftarrow\$ $ Setup$(1^\lambda, n)$, *any $f : \mathcal{X}^n \to \mathcal{X}^m$ in the class $\mathcal{F}$, and any vector $\boldsymbol{x} \in \mathcal{X}^n$, if $(C, aux) \leftarrow$ Com$($ck$, \boldsymbol{x})$, then it holds* Ver$($ck$, C, f, f(\boldsymbol{x}), $Open$(ck, aux, f)) = 1$ *with probability 1.*

Succinctness/Compactness. *A functional commitment* FC *is succinct if there exists a fixed polynomial $p(\lambda) = $ poly(λ) such that that for any $n, m = $ poly(λ), any admissible function $f \in \mathcal{F}$ such that $f : \mathcal{X}^n \to \mathcal{X}^m$, honestly generated commitment key* ck $\leftarrow$ Setup$(1^\lambda, n, m)$, *vector $\boldsymbol{x} \in \mathcal{X}^n$, commitment $(C, aux) \in$ Com$($ck$)$ and opening $\pi \leftarrow$ Open$($ck, aux$, f)$, it holds that $|C| \leq p(\lambda)$ and $|\pi| \leq p(\lambda) \cdot m$. Furthermore, we say that* FC *is compact if $|\pi| \leq p(\lambda)$.*

3.1 Binding Notions of FCs

Intuitively, the security of FCs should model the hardness of computing openings for false statements that are accepted by the verification algorithm. The first definition in [22] is inspired by that of vector commitments [4]. It states that it should be computationally hard to open a commitment to two distinct outputs for the same function. Formally, it is defined as follows.

Definition 2 (Evaluation Binding). *For any PPT adversary $\mathcal{A}$,*

$$\mathbf{Adv}_{\mathcal{A}, \mathsf{FC}}^{\mathsf{EvBind}}(\lambda) = \Pr \left[\begin{array}{c} \mathsf{Ver}(\mathsf{ck}, C, f, \boldsymbol{y}, \pi) = 1 \\ \wedge \ \boldsymbol{y} \neq \boldsymbol{y}' \wedge \\ \mathsf{Ver}(\mathsf{ck}, C, f, \boldsymbol{y}', \pi') = 1 \end{array} : \begin{array}{c} \mathsf{ck} \leftarrow \mathsf{Setup}(1^\lambda, n) \\ (C, f, \boldsymbol{y}, \pi, \boldsymbol{y}', \pi') \leftarrow \mathcal{A}(\mathsf{ck}) \end{array} \right] = \mathsf{negl}(\lambda)$$

We define a weaker notion of evaluation binding in which the adversary is required to fully open the commitment (i.e., to show the vector x it contains) and to generate a valid opening for a false output, i.e., for some $y \neq f(x)$.[6] Intuitively, this is sufficient in applications where the verifier has either computed once the commitment or has received the commitment from a trusted party (e.g., the commitment comes with a valid signature of this party). We show in Sect. 6 that this notion is sufficient to construct homomorphic signatures from FCs.

Definition 3 (Weak Evaluation Binding). *For any PPT adversary* $\mathcal{A}$

$$
\mathbf{Adv}_{\mathcal{A},\mathsf{FC}}^{\mathsf{wEvBind}}(\lambda) = \Pr\left[
\begin{array}{c}
(C, \cdot) = \mathsf{Com}(\mathsf{ck}, x; r) \\
\wedge \; y \neq f(x) \; \wedge \\
\mathsf{Ver}(\mathsf{ck}, C, f, y, \pi) = 1
\end{array}
:
\begin{array}{c}
\mathsf{ck} \leftarrow \mathsf{Setup}(1^\lambda, n) \\
(x, r, f, y, \pi) \leftarrow \mathcal{A}(\mathsf{ck})
\end{array}
\right] = \mathsf{negl}(\lambda)
$$

One may observe that if an FC satisfies evaluation binding, then it also satisfies weak evaluation binding. For a formal proof, we refer to the full version.

Finally, we also mention a stronger version of evaluation binding, put forward by Lai and Malavolta [18]. Here, the adversary outputs a commitment, and a collection of openings to one or more functions. It is successful if all the claimed outputs define an inconsistent system of equations. Namely, it outputs $\{f_i, y_i\}$ for which there exists no x such that for all i $f_i(x) = y_i$.

Definition 4 (Strong Evaluation Binding). *For any PPT adversary* $\mathcal{A}$, *the advantage* $\mathbf{Adv}_{\mathcal{A},\mathsf{FC}}^{\mathsf{sEvBind}}(\lambda)$ *defined below is negligible.*

$$
\Pr\left[
\begin{array}{c}
\forall i \in [Q] : \mathsf{Ver}(\mathsf{ck}, C, f_i, y_i, \pi_1) = 1 \\
\wedge \; \nexists x \in \mathcal{X}^n : \forall i \in [Q] : f_i(x) = y_i
\end{array}
:
\begin{array}{c}
\mathsf{ck} \leftarrow \mathsf{Setup}(1^\lambda, n) \\
(C, \{f_i, y_i, \pi_i\}_{i=1}^Q) \leftarrow \mathcal{A}(\mathsf{ck})
\end{array}
\right]
$$

3.2 Additional Properties of FCs

In the full version we give the notions of hiding commitments and zero-knowledge openings. Here we define some extra properties of functional commitments that can be useful in applications and that are enjoyed by our constructions.

Additive-Homomorphic FCs. We consider additively homomorphic FCs in which, given two commitments C_1 and C_2 to vectors x_1 and x_2 respectively, one can compute a commitment to $x_1 + x_2$. Below, we formalize this property, considering also how to obtain the corresponding random coins and auxiliary information of the commitment.

Definition 5 (Additive-homomorphic FCs). *Let* FC *be a functional commitment scheme where* $\mathcal{X}$ *is a ring. Then* FC *is additive homomorphic if there exist deterministic algorithms* $\mathsf{FC.Add}(\mathsf{ck}, C_1, \ldots, C_n) \rightarrow C$, $\mathsf{FC.Add}_{\mathsf{aux}}(\mathsf{ck}, \mathsf{aux}_1, \ldots, \mathsf{aux}_n) \rightarrow \mathsf{aux}$ *and* $\mathsf{FC.Add}_r(\mathsf{ck}, r_1, \ldots, r_n) \rightarrow r$ *such that for any* $x_i \in \mathcal{X}$ *and* $(C_i, \mathsf{aux}_i) \leftarrow \mathsf{Com}(\mathsf{ck}, x_i; r_i)$, *if* $C \leftarrow \mathsf{FC.Add}(\mathsf{ck}, C_1, \ldots, C_n)$, $\mathsf{aux} \leftarrow \mathsf{FC.Add}_{\mathsf{aux}}(\mathsf{ck}, \mathsf{aux}_1, \ldots, \mathsf{aux}_n)$, *and* $r \leftarrow \mathsf{FC.Add}_r(\mathsf{ck}, r_1, \ldots, r_n)$, *then* $(C, \mathsf{aux}) = \mathsf{Com}(\mathsf{ck}, \sum_{i=1}^n x_i; r)$.

---

[6] This notion is similar in spirit to the basic security of accumulators [3].

Efficient Verification. In FCs the verification algorithm must read the function's description, which can be as large as its running time for certain computational models (e.g., linear forms, polynomials, circuits) and thus can make verifying and output of f as expensive as running f. To address this problem, we define a notion of amortized efficient verification for FCs. Similarly to homomorphic signatures [7] and preprocessing universal SNARKs [14], an FC has this property if the verifier can precompute a short verification key vk_f associated to f, and later can verify any opening for f by using only vk_f.

Definition 6 (Amortized efficient verification). *A functional commitment scheme* FC *has* amortized efficient verification *if there are two additional algorithms* $\mathsf{vk}_f \leftarrow \mathsf{VerPrep}(\mathsf{ck}, f)$ *and* $b \leftarrow \mathsf{EffVer}(\mathsf{vk}_f, C, \boldsymbol{y}, \pi)$ *such that for any honestly generated commitment key* $\mathsf{ck} \leftarrow \mathsf{Setup}(1^\lambda, n, m)$, *vector* $\boldsymbol{x} \in \mathcal{X}^n$, *commitment* $(C, \mathsf{aux}) \in \mathsf{Com}(\mathsf{ck})$ *and opening* $\pi \leftarrow \mathsf{Open}(\mathsf{ck}, \mathsf{aux}, f)$ *with* $f \in \mathcal{F}$, *it holds: (a)* $\mathsf{EffVer}(\mathsf{VerPrep}(\mathsf{ck}, f), C, \boldsymbol{y}, \pi) = \mathsf{Ver}(\mathsf{ck}, C, f, \boldsymbol{y}, \pi)$, *and (b)* EffVer *running time is a fixed polynomial* $p(\lambda, |\boldsymbol{y}|)$.

Aggregation. Intuitively, we say that FC has aggregatable openings if given several openings $\pi_1, \ldots, \pi_\ell$ such that each π_i verifies for the same commitment C and function-output pair $(f_i, \boldsymbol{y}_i)$, and given a function $g : \mathcal{X}^{m_1} \times \cdots \times \mathcal{X}^{m_\ell} \to \mathcal{X}^m$ one can compute an opening π that verifies for the composed function $g(f_1, \ldots, f_\ell)$ and the output $g(\boldsymbol{y}_1, \ldots, \boldsymbol{y}_\ell)$.

Definition 7. *A functional commitment scheme* FC *satisfies* aggregation *if there is an algorithm* $\pi \leftarrow \mathsf{Agg}(\mathsf{ck}, C, ((\pi_1, f_1, \boldsymbol{y}_1), \ldots, (\pi_\ell, f_\ell, \boldsymbol{y}_\ell)), g)$ *such that, for honestly generated commitment key* $\mathsf{ck} \leftarrow \mathsf{Setup}(1^\lambda, n, m)$, *commitment* C *and triples* $\{(\pi_i, f_i, \boldsymbol{y}_i)\}_{i=1}^\ell$ *such that for all* $i \in [\ell]$ *it holds* $\boldsymbol{y}_i \in \mathcal{X}^{m_i}$ *and* $\mathsf{Ver}(\mathsf{ck}, C, \pi_i, f_i, \boldsymbol{y}_i) = 1$, *then for any admissible function* $g : \mathcal{X}^{m_1} \times \cdots \times \mathcal{X}^{m_\ell} \to \mathcal{X}^m$,

$$\mathsf{Ver}(\mathsf{ck}, C, \mathsf{Agg}(\mathsf{ck}, C, ((\pi_1, f_1, \boldsymbol{y}_1), \ldots, (\pi_\ell, f_\ell, \boldsymbol{y}_\ell)), g), f^*, g(\boldsymbol{y}_1, \ldots, \boldsymbol{y}_\ell)) = 1$$

where f^* *is the composed function* $f^*(\boldsymbol{X}) = g(f_1(\boldsymbol{X}), \ldots, f_\ell(\boldsymbol{X}))$.

4   Additive-Homomorphic FC for Polynomials

In this section we propose our FC for polynomials, which supports the following features: additive-homomorphic, opening to multiple (multivariate) polynomials of the committed vector with a *compact* proof, efficient verification and linear aggregation. We build our scheme in bilinear groups and prove that it satisfies evaluation binding under the DHE assumption (Definition 8 [2]).

We build this FC in two steps. We begin by constructing an FC that only supports homogeneous multivariate polynomials whose degree is a power of two (see next section). Next, in Sect. 4.4 we show how an additive-homomorphic FC for homogeneous polynomials can be turned into one for all multivariate polynomials by letting one commit to vectors $(1, \boldsymbol{x})$.

4.1 Additive-Homomorphic FC for Homogeneous Polynomials

Below we describe our FC for homogeneous polynomials. See Sect. 1.3 for an intuition. To keep the exposition simpler we present a deterministic version of our FC which is not hiding, and refer to the full version for how to modify it in order to satisfy com-hiding and zero-knowledge openings.

$\underline{\mathsf{Setup}(1^\lambda, n, m, d)}$ Let $n, m, d \geq 1$ be three integers representing the length of the vectors to be committed, the number of the polynomials to be computed at opening time, and the degree of these polynomials, respectively. Define $N := n^d$, generate a bilinear group description $\mathsf{bgp} := (q, \mathbb{G}_1, \mathbb{G}_2, \mathbb{G}_T, e, g_1, g_2) \leftarrow \mathcal{BG}(1^\lambda)$, and let $\mathbb{F} := \mathbb{Z}_q$. Next, sample random $\alpha \leftarrow_\$ \mathbb{Z}_q$, $\boldsymbol{\beta} \leftarrow_\$ \mathbb{F}^m$ and output

$$\mathsf{ck} := \left(\begin{array}{c} \{[\alpha^j]_1, [\alpha^j]_2\}_{j\in[N]}, \{[\beta_i \cdot \alpha^j]_2\}_{i\in[m],j\in[N]} \\ \{[\alpha\beta_i]_1\}_{i\in[m]}, \{[\alpha^j\beta_i]_1\}_{i\in[m],j\in[2N]\setminus\{N+1\}} \end{array} \right)$$

$\underline{\mathsf{Com}(\mathsf{ck}, \boldsymbol{x})}$ We encode the vector $\boldsymbol{x}$ with the polynomial $p_{\boldsymbol{x}}(Z) := \sum_{j=1}^n x_j \cdot Z^j$. Also, for $\ell = 1, \ldots, d-1$, we define the polynomials

$$\phi_{\boldsymbol{x}}^{(\ell)}(Z) := p_{\boldsymbol{x}}(Z^{n^\ell})/Z^{n^\ell} = \sum_{j=1}^n x_j \cdot Z^{n^\ell(j-1)} \quad \text{of degree} \ \leq n^{\ell+1} - n^\ell$$

Next, we compute

$$X_0 := \sum_{j=1}^n x_j \cdot [\alpha^j]_1 = [p_{\boldsymbol{x}}(\alpha)]_1, \quad \hat{X}_0 := \sum_{j=1}^n x_j \cdot [\alpha^{n(j-1)}]_2 = [p_{\boldsymbol{x}}(\alpha^n)/\alpha^n]_2$$

$$\forall \ell = 2, \ldots, d-1 : \Phi_\ell := \begin{cases} \sum_{j=1}^n x_j \cdot [\alpha^{n^\ell(j-1)}]_1 = \left[\phi_{\boldsymbol{x}}^{(\ell)}(\alpha)\right]_1 & \text{if } \ell \text{ even} \\ \sum_{j=1}^n x_j \cdot [\alpha^{n^\ell(j-1)}]_2 = \left[\phi_{\boldsymbol{x}}^{(\ell)}(\alpha)\right]_2 & \text{if } \ell \text{ odd} \end{cases}$$

Output $C := (X_0, \hat{X}_0, \{\Phi_\ell\}_{\ell=2}^{d-1})$ and $\mathsf{aux} = \boldsymbol{x}$.

$\underline{\mathsf{Open}(\mathsf{ck}, \mathsf{aux}, \boldsymbol{f})}$ Let $\boldsymbol{f} = (f_1, \ldots, f_m)$ be a vector of m n-variate homogeneous polynomials of degree d, where $d = 2^\delta$ is a power of 2. We use a representation of each polynomial f_i via a linear form $\hat{\boldsymbol{f}}_i : \mathbb{F}^{n^d} \to \mathbb{F}$ such that $f_i(\boldsymbol{x}) = \hat{\boldsymbol{f}}_i^\top \cdot \boldsymbol{x}^{(\delta)}$, where $\boldsymbol{x}^{(\delta)} = (\boldsymbol{x} \otimes \cdots \otimes \boldsymbol{x})$ is the result of taking the Kronecker product of $\boldsymbol{x}$ with itself δ times.[7] Next, set $\boldsymbol{x}^{(0)} := \boldsymbol{x}$ and proceed as follows.

– For $k = 1, \ldots, \delta - 1$, compute

$$\boldsymbol{x}^{(k)} := \boldsymbol{x}^{(k-1)} \otimes \boldsymbol{x}^{(k-1)}, \quad X_k := \sum_{j=1}^{n^{2^k}} x_j^{(k)} \cdot [\alpha^j]_1, \quad \hat{X}_k := \sum_{j=1}^{n^{2^k}} x_j^{(k)} \cdot [\alpha^{n^{2^k}(j-1)}]_2$$

---

[7] Since $\boldsymbol{x}^{(\delta)}$ has several terms repeated multiple times (e.g., after one product, the resulting vector contains both x_ix_j and x_jx_i), we assume $\hat{\boldsymbol{f}}_i$ to always use the first of them, according to lexicographic order, and have 0 coefficients for the others.

Let us define the polynomials

$$p_{\boldsymbol{x}}^{(k)}(Z) := \sum_{j=1}^{n^{2^k}} x_j^{(k)} \cdot Z^j, \quad \hat{p}_{\boldsymbol{x}}^{(k)}(Z) := p_{\boldsymbol{x}}^{(k)}(Z^{n^{2^k}})/Z^{n^{2^k}} = \sum_{j=1}^{n^{2^k}} x_j^{(k)} \cdot Z^{n^{2^k}(j-1)}$$

and note that for every k the pair $(X_k, \hat{X}_k)$ is $([p_{\boldsymbol{x}}^{(k)}(\alpha)]_1, [\hat{p}_{\boldsymbol{x}}^{(k)}(\alpha)]_2)$.
$(X_k, \hat{X}_k)$ can be seen as a commitment to the vector $\boldsymbol{x}^{(k)} \in \mathbb{F}^{n^{2^k}}$.

- Compute the last vector $\boldsymbol{x}^{(\delta)} := \boldsymbol{x}^{(\delta-1)} \otimes \boldsymbol{x}^{(\delta-1)}$, and its commitment $X_\delta := \sum_{j=1}^{n^d} x_j^{(\delta)} \cdot [\alpha^j]_1 = [p_{\boldsymbol{x}}^{(\delta)}(\alpha)]_1$.
  For $k = 1$ to δ, one can verify the correctness of the element X_k based on the correctness of the previous pair $(X_{k-1}, \hat{X}_{k-1})$ (which eventually reduces to the correctness of the commitment pair $(X_0, \hat{X}_0)$) by testing $e(X_k, [1]_2) \stackrel{?}{=} e\left(X_{k-1}, \hat{X}_{k-1}\right)$. This equality holds based on the fact that, for every k, $p_{\boldsymbol{x}}^{(k)}(Z) = p_{\boldsymbol{x}}^{(k-1)}(Z) \cdot \hat{p}_{\boldsymbol{x}}^{(k-1)}(Z)$ (see Claim 2).
  The checks above can be seen as a way to progressively build trust in the elements $X_1, \ldots, X_\delta$. However for it to work we need that for a given k both elements of the previous pair $(X_{k-1}, \hat{X}_{k-1})$ are deemed correct.
- In this step we show how to enable the verification of the correctness of $\hat{X}_k$. This cannot be done via a quadratic equation, as we observed for X_k, but it is possible by letting the prover provide additional hints to the verifier.
  The main idea of this step is that, for $k = 1$ to $\delta - 1$, we can factor $\hat{p}_{\boldsymbol{x}}^{(k)}(Z)$ as the product of 2^k polynomials (implicitly) known to the verifier, namely

$$\hat{p}_{\boldsymbol{x}}^{(k)}(Z) = \prod_{\ell=2^k}^{2^{k+1}-1} \phi_{\boldsymbol{x}}^{(\ell)}(Z) \quad \text{(cf. Sect. 4.2, Claim 1)}$$

To let the verifier check this factorization with a pairing computation, we break the verification of this product into a set of $\approx 2^k$ quadratic equations. The idea is that, for every k, the prover builds a binary tree of height k in which the 2^k polynomials are the leaves and then are multiplied pair-wise in a bottom-up tree fashion, i.e., each node of the tree is the multiplication of its child nodes. More precisely, if we index the nodes of the k-th tree with an integer $1 \le \mu \le 2^{k+1} - 1$, then an internal node $\mu \in \{1, \ldots, 2^k - 1\}$ of the k-th tree is a group element $\Psi_{k,\mu}$, which encodes the product of the polynomials encoded in the two child nodes $\Psi_{k,2\mu}$ and $\Psi_{k,2\mu+1}$. Instead, the leaves are the elements $\{\Phi_\ell = [\phi_{\boldsymbol{x}}^{(\ell)}(\alpha)]_b\}_{\ell=2^k}^{2^{k+1}-1}$ (where $b = (\ell \bmod 2) + 1$) that are included in the commitment. In detail, the computation of all the internal nodes $\Psi_{k,\mu}$ proceed as follows.
For every $k = 2, \ldots, \delta - 1$ and $\mu = 2^k, \ldots, 2^{k+1} - 1$, initialize the polynomials $\psi_{k,\mu}(Z) := \phi_{\boldsymbol{x}}^{(\mu)}(Z)$. These are the leaves of the k-th tree. Next, for

$\mu = 2^k - 1, \ldots, 2$, compute

$$\Psi_{k,\mu} := \begin{cases} [\psi_{k,2\mu}(\alpha) \cdot \psi_{k,2\mu+1}(\alpha)]_1 & \text{if } \mu \text{ even} \\ [\psi_{k,2\mu}(\alpha) \cdot \psi_{k,2\mu+1}(\alpha)]_2 & \text{if } \mu \text{ odd} \end{cases}$$

Note that we do not compute the root node $\Psi_{k,1}$ but only stop at its children $\Psi_{k,2}, \Psi_{k,3}$. The root is indeed the element $\hat{X}_k$ already computed in the first step of this Open algorithm.

- Finally, we compute a linear-map evaluation proof for the commitment X_δ as follows. For every $i = 1$ to m, take the linear form $\hat{f}_i : \mathbb{F}^{n^d} \to \mathbb{F}$ such that $f_i(\boldsymbol{x}) = \hat{f}_i^{\top} \cdot \boldsymbol{x}^{(\delta)}$, and define the matrix $\mathbf{F} \in \mathbb{F}^{m \times N}$ that has $\hat{f}_i^{\top}$ in the i-th row. We generate a proof $\hat{\pi} \in \mathbb{G}_1$ for $\boldsymbol{y} = \mathbf{F} \cdot \boldsymbol{x}^{(\delta)}$ as

$$\hat{\pi} := \sum_{\substack{i \in [m] \\ j,k \in [N]:j \neq k}} F_{i,j} \cdot x_k^{(\delta)} \cdot [\alpha^{N+1-j+k}\beta_i]_1$$

- Return $\pi := (\{X_k\}_{k=1}^{\delta}, \{\hat{X}_k, \{\Psi_{k,\mu}\}_{\mu=2}^{2^k-1}\}_{k=1}^{\delta-1}, \hat{\pi})$.

$\underline{\mathsf{Ver}(ck, C, \pi, \boldsymbol{f}, \boldsymbol{y})}$ Parse the commitment as $C := (X_0, \hat{X}_0, \{\Phi_\ell\}_{\ell=2}^{d-1})$, and the proof $\pi := (\{X_k\}_{k=1}^{\delta}, \{\hat{X}_k, \{\Psi_{k,\mu}\}_{\mu=2}^{2^k-1}\}_{k=1}^{\delta-1}, \hat{\pi})$ as returned by Open. Output 1 if all the following checks pass and 0 otherwise:

- For $k = 1$ to $\delta - 1$ and $\mu \in [2^k, 2^{k+1} - 1]$ set $\Psi_{k,\mu} := \Phi_\mu$.
- For $k = 2$ to $\delta - 1$, check the validity of the k-th tree of elements $\{\Psi_{k,\mu}\}_{\mu=2}^{2^k-1}$. First, check all the internal nodes, bottom-up:

$$\textbf{for } k = 2 \ldots \delta - 1, \textbf{for } \mu = 2^k - 1 \ldots 2:$$

$$e(\Psi_{k,2\mu}, \Psi_{k,2\mu+1}) \stackrel{?}{=} \begin{cases} e(\Psi_{k,\mu}, [1]_2) & \text{if } \mu \text{ even} \\ e([1]_1, \Psi_{k,\mu}) & \text{if } \mu \text{ odd} \end{cases} \tag{1}$$

Second, check the roots of the trees:

$$\textbf{for } k = 1 \ldots \delta - 1 : e([1]_1, \hat{X}_k) \stackrel{?}{=} e(\Psi_{k,2}, \Psi_{k,3}) \tag{2}$$

- Check the validity of the chain of commitments:

$$\textbf{for } k = 1 \ldots \delta : e(X_k, [1]_2) \stackrel{?}{=} e(X_{k-1}, \hat{X}_{k-1}) \tag{3}$$

- Define the matrix $\mathbf{F}$ from $\boldsymbol{f}$ as in the Open algorithm, and check the proof for the linear map:

$$e\left(X_\delta, \sum_{\substack{i \in [m] \\ j \in [N]}} F_{i,j} \cdot [\alpha^{N+1-j}\beta_i]_2\right) \stackrel{?}{=} e(\hat{\pi}, [1]_2) \cdot e\left(\sum_{i=1}^m y_i \cdot [\alpha\beta_i]_1, [\alpha^N]_2\right) \tag{4}$$

It is easy to see that our commitments are additively homomorphic and that the scheme has efficient amortized verification as the verifier can precompute $\sum_{i\in[m],j\in[N]} F_{i,j} \cdot [\alpha^{N+1-j}\beta_i]_2$. We refer to the full version for further details about these properties as well as for a proof that the openings are linearly aggregatable in the sense of Definition 7.

Compactness. In our scheme, an opening consists of $2\delta + \sum_{k=2}^{\delta-1}(2^k - 2) = d$ group elements, and a commitment also comprises d elements. Since the degree is assumed to be a constant, $d = O(1)$, compactness follows.

Efficiency. It is easy to see that the complexity of Com is $O(nd)$, while Ver takes time $O(d+|\boldsymbol{y}|+|\boldsymbol{f}|)$ (and the $O(|\boldsymbol{f}|)$ part can be precomputed when using efficient verification). The most complex and computationally heavy procedure of our scheme is the Open algorithm, whose time complexity is $O(mdn^d \log n)$, which we justify as follows. Computing the commitments $(X_1, \ldots, X_\delta, \hat{X}_1, \ldots, \hat{X}_{\delta-1})$ in the first and second step takes time at most $\sum_{k=0}^{\delta} O(n^{2^k})$ which is $O(\delta n^d)$. Computing all the group elements $\Psi_{k,\mu}$ in the third step can take time at most $O(d^2 n^d \log n)$. This estimation is obtained by observing that: every $\psi_{k,\mu}(Z)$ has degree $< n^d$ (this is a non-tight worst case analysis, as many of them actually have much lower degree); for each node of the tree the polynomial $\psi_{k,\mu}(Z)$ can be computed via a multiplication of its children polynomials which, using FFT, takes time $O(dn^d \log n)$. So by summing over all the d elements $\{\psi_{k,\mu}\}_{k,\mu}$, we obtain the above estimation. Finally, the generation of $\hat{\pi}$ in the last step takes $O(mN \log N) = O(mdn^d \log n)$. This follows from an observation that, for every row $i = 1$ to m, the coefficients of the polynomial in α of degree $< 2N$ can be computed using an FFT-based multiplication instead of going over all the N^2 indices j, k.

4.2   Proof of Correctness

To prove correctness we proceed one by one on the equations of the verification algorithm. We begin recalling the definition of the polynomials

$$p_{\boldsymbol{x}}^{(k)}(Z) := \sum_{j=1}^{n^{2^k}} x_j^{(k)} \cdot Z^j, \quad \hat{p}_{\boldsymbol{x}}^{(k)}(Z) := p_{\boldsymbol{x}}^{(k)}(Z^{n^{2^k}})/Z^{n^{2^k}}, \quad \phi_{\boldsymbol{x}}^{(\ell)}(Z) := p_{\boldsymbol{x}}^{(0)}(Z^{n^\ell})/Z^{n^\ell}$$

Verification Eq. (1). For $2 \leq k \leq \delta - 1$ and $2^k \leq \mu \leq 2^{k+1} - 1$, the first step of the verification algorithm sets $\Psi_{k,\mu} = \Phi_\mu$, for $2 \leq k \leq \delta-1$ and $2^k \leq \mu \leq 2^{k+1}-1$, where each Φ_μ is defined in Com as

$$\Phi_\mu = \left[\phi_{\boldsymbol{x}}^{(\mu)}(\alpha)\right]_b = \left[p_{\boldsymbol{x}}(\alpha^{n^\mu})/\alpha^{n^\mu}\right]_b \quad : b = 1 \text{ if } \mu \text{ even}, b = 0 \text{ if } \mu \text{ odd}$$

On the other hand, Open initializes the polynomials $\psi_{k,\mu}(Z) := \phi_{\boldsymbol{x}}^{(\mu)}(Z)$ and then, for $2 \leq \mu \leq 2^k - 1$, it constructs $\Psi_{k,\mu} = [\psi_{k,2\mu}(\alpha) \cdot \psi_{k,2\mu+1}(\alpha)]_b$, with $b = 1$ if μ is even and $b = 2$ if μ is odd. By the construction of $\Psi_{k,\mu}$ for $2 \leq \mu \leq 2^k - 1$, and having observed that both algorithms start from the same leaves, it is therefore clear that each check of Eq. (1) is satisfied.

Verification Eq. (2). The intuition is that the check $e([1]_1, \hat{X}_k) \stackrel{?}{=} e(\Psi_{k,2}, \Psi_{k,3})$ is verifying whether the element $\hat{X}_k = \left[\hat{p}_{\boldsymbol{x}}^{(k)}(\alpha)\right]_2$ is the root of the k-th binary tree computed starting from the leaf nodes $\{\phi_{\boldsymbol{x}}^{(\mu)}(\alpha)\}_{\mu=2^k,\ldots,2^{k+1}-1}$, and where each node is the multiplication of its two children.

To show this, we observe that by the construction of the polynomials $\psi_{k,\mu}(Z)$ in Open as a multiplication tree, we have that

$$\psi_{k,2}(Z) \cdot \psi_{k,3}(Z) = \prod_{\ell=2^k}^{2^{k+1}-1} \phi_{\boldsymbol{x}}^{(\ell)}(Z)$$

The correctness of Eq. (2) then follows from the following Claim (whose proof appears in the full version), which shows that the polynomial $\hat{p}_{\boldsymbol{x}}^{(k)}(Z)$ encoded in $\hat{X}_k$ can be factored into the product $\prod_{\ell=2^k}^{2^{k+1}-1} \phi_{\boldsymbol{x}}^{(\ell)}(Z)$.

Claim 1. *Fix any vector $\boldsymbol{x}^{(0)} \in \mathbb{F}^n$ and for any $k \in [\delta-1]$, let $\boldsymbol{x}^{(k)} = \boldsymbol{x}^{(k-1)} \otimes \boldsymbol{x}^{(k-1)}$ and $\hat{p}_{\boldsymbol{x}}^{(k)}(Z) = \sum_{j=1}^{n^{2^k}} x_j^{(k)} \cdot Z^{n^{2^k}(j-1)}$. For $2 \le \ell \le d-1$, let $\phi_{\boldsymbol{x}}^{(\ell)}(Z) = \sum_{j=1}^{n} x_j^{(0)} \cdot Z^{n^\ell(j-1)}$. Then, it holds $\hat{p}_{\boldsymbol{x}}^{(k)}(Z) = \prod_{\ell=2^k}^{2^{k+1}-1} \phi_{\boldsymbol{x}}^{(\ell)}(Z)$.*

Verification Eq. (3). By construction of Open, we have

$$\forall k \in [\delta] : X_k = [p_{\boldsymbol{x}}^{(k)}(\alpha)]_1, \quad \forall k \in [\delta-1] : \hat{X}_k = [p_{\boldsymbol{x}}^{(k)}(\alpha^{n^{2^k}})/\alpha^{n^{2^k}}]_2$$

and by construction of Com, we have

$$X_0 = [p_{\boldsymbol{x}}^{(0)}(\alpha)]_1, \quad \hat{X}_0 = [p_{\boldsymbol{x}}^{(0)}(\alpha^n)/\alpha^n]_2$$

Let us state the following claim (whose proof appears in the full version).

Claim 2. *Fix any vector $\boldsymbol{x}^{(0)} \in \mathbb{F}^n$ and for any $k \in [\delta]$, let $\boldsymbol{x}^{(k)} = \boldsymbol{x}^{(k-1)} \otimes \boldsymbol{x}^{(k-1)}$ and $\hat{p}_{\boldsymbol{x}}^{(k)}(Z) = \sum_{j=1}^{n^{2^k}} x_j^{(k)} \cdot Z^{n^{2^k}(j-1)}$. Then for every $k \in [\delta]$ it holds $p_{\boldsymbol{x}}^{(k)}(Z) = p_{\boldsymbol{x}}^{(k-1)}(Z) \cdot \hat{p}_{\boldsymbol{x}}^{(k-1)}(Z)$.*

Then for every $1 \le k \le \delta$ it holds

$$e\left(X_{k-1}, \hat{X}_{k-1}\right) = \left[p_{\boldsymbol{x}}^{(k-1)}(\alpha) \cdot p_{\boldsymbol{x}}^{(k-1)}(\alpha^{n^{2^{k-1}}})/\alpha^{n^{2^{k-1}}}\right]_T = \left[p_{\boldsymbol{x}}^{(k)}(\alpha)\right]_T = e(X_k, [1]_2)$$

Verification Eq. (4). By construction of Open we have

$$\hat{\pi} = \sum_{\substack{i \in [m] \\ j,k \in [N]: j \neq k}} F_{i,j} \cdot x_k^{(\delta)} \cdot [\alpha^{N+1-j+k}\beta_i]_1$$

Thus, consider a correct output $y_i = f_i(\boldsymbol{x})$ which, by the definition of $\mathbf{F}$ in Open and Ver, is $y_i = \sum_{j \in [N]} F_{i,j} \cdot x_j^{(\delta)}$. Then it holds

$$
e \left(\sum_{\substack{i \in [m] \\ j,k \in [N]:j \neq k}} F_{i,j} \cdot x_k^{(\delta)} \cdot [\alpha^{N+1-j+k} \beta_i]_1, [1]_2 \right) \cdot e \left(\sum_{i=1}^m y_i \cdot [\alpha\beta_i]_1, [\alpha^N]_2 \right)
$$

$$
= \left[\sum_{\substack{i \in [m] \\ j,k \in [N]:j \neq k}} F_{i,j} \cdot x_k^{(\delta)} \cdot \alpha^{N+1-j+k} \beta_i + \sum_{i \in [m], j \in [N]} F_{i,j} \cdot x_j^{(\delta)} \cdot [\alpha^{N+1}\beta_i]_1 \right]_T
$$

$$
= \left[\left(\sum_{k \in [N]} x_k^{(\delta)} \cdot \alpha^k \right) \left(\sum_{\substack{i \in [m] \\ j \in [N]}} F_{i,j} \cdot \alpha^{N+1-j} \beta_i \right) \right]_T
$$

$$
= e \left(X_\delta, \sum_{i \in [m], j \in [N]} F_{i,j} \cdot [\alpha^{N+1-j} \beta_i]_2 \right)
$$

4.3 Proof of Security

We prove the evaluation binding of our FC based on the N-Diffie-Hellman-Exponent (N-DHE) assumption [2], which we recall below.

Definition 8 (N-DHE [2]). Let $\mathsf{bgp} = (q, \mathbb{G}_1, \mathbb{G}_2, \mathbb{G}_T, e, g_1, g_2)$ be a bilinear group setting. The N-DHE holds if for every PPT $\mathcal{A}$ the following advantage is negligible

$$
\mathbf{Adv}_{\mathcal{A}}^{N\text{-}DHE}(\lambda) = \Pr[\mathcal{A}(\mathsf{bgp}, \{[\alpha^i]_1, [\alpha^i]_2\}_{i \in [2N] \setminus \{N+1\}}) = [\alpha^{N+1}]_1]
$$

where the probability is over the random choice of $\alpha \leftarrow\!\!\$ \, \mathbb{Z}_q$ and $\mathcal{A}$'s random coins.

Theorem 1. If the n^d-DHE assumption holds, then the scheme FC of Sect. 4.1 satisfies evaluation binding.

Proof. Consider an adversary $\mathcal{A}$ who returns a tuple $(C, \boldsymbol{f}, \boldsymbol{y}, \pi, \boldsymbol{y}', \pi')$ that breaks evaluation binding. Parse

$$
\pi = (\{X_k\}_{k=1}^\delta, \{\hat{X}_k, \{\Psi_{k,\mu}\}_{\mu=2}^{2^k-1}\}_{k=1}^{\delta-1}, \hat{\pi}), \ \pi' = (\{X'_k\}_{k=1}^\delta, \{\hat{X}'_k, \{\Psi'_{k,\mu}\}_{\mu=2}^{2^k-1}\}_{j=1}^{\delta-1}, \hat{\pi}')
$$

and recall that by definition both proofs verify for the same commitment $C = (X_0, \hat{X}_0, \{\Phi_\ell\}_{\ell=2}^{d-1})$ and that $\boldsymbol{y} \neq \boldsymbol{y}'$. Let us call this event Win.

Let us define Coll as the event that $\mathcal{A}$'s output is such that $\boldsymbol{\beta}^\top \cdot (\boldsymbol{y} - \boldsymbol{y}') = 0$, where $\boldsymbol{\beta}$ is the vector sampled in ck.

We can partition adversaries in two classes: those that make Coll occur and those that do not. Clearly it holds.

$$\Pr[\mathsf{Win}] \leq \Pr[\mathsf{Win} \wedge \mathsf{Coll}] + \Pr[\mathsf{Win} \mid \overline{\mathsf{Coll}}]$$

To prove the theorem we show that under the n^d-DHE assumption both probabilities are negligible.

For the first probability, $\Pr[\mathsf{Win} \wedge \mathsf{Coll}]$, it is easy to see that we can reduce it to the discrete logarithm assumption (which is implied by n^d-DHE). The idea of the reduction is that, if $\boldsymbol{\beta}^\top \cdot (\boldsymbol{y} - \boldsymbol{y}') = 0$ occurs then one can recover the value of β_i such that $y_i - y_i' \neq 0$. Hence a discrete logarithm adversary that receives as input $[\eta]_1, [\eta]_2$ can choose a random index $i^* \leftarrow\!\!\!\$ [m]$, implicitly set $\beta_{i^*} = \eta$ and perfectly simulate all the group elements of ck. If $y_{i^*} \neq y_{i^*}'$ (which happens with probability $\geq 1/m$), then one can recover $\beta_{i^*} = \eta$. We don't formalize this reduction further as it is rather standard.

In the rest of the proof we focus on proving the remaining case, namely that $\Pr[\mathsf{Win} \mid \overline{\mathsf{Coll}}]$ is negligible. In particular, we show that for any PPT $\mathcal{A}$ there is a PPT $\mathcal{B}$ such that

$$\Pr[\mathsf{Win} \mid \overline{\mathsf{Coll}}] \leq \mathbf{Adv}_{\mathcal{B}}^{n^d\text{-}DHE}(\lambda)$$

$\mathcal{B}$ takes as input $\{[\alpha^i]_1, [\alpha^i]_2\}_{i \in [2N] \setminus \{N+1\}}$, samples $\boldsymbol{\beta} \leftarrow\!\!\!\$ \mathbb{F}^m$ and generates ck, which is distributed identically to that generated by Setup.

Next, $\mathcal{B}$ runs $(C, \boldsymbol{f}, \boldsymbol{y}, \pi, \boldsymbol{y}', \pi') \leftarrow \mathcal{A}(\mathsf{ck})$ and proceeds as follows.

It computes $z := \boldsymbol{\beta}^\top \cdot \boldsymbol{y}$ and $z' := \boldsymbol{\beta}^\top \cdot \boldsymbol{y}'$ (recall that conditioned on $\overline{\mathsf{Coll}}$, $z \neq z'$) and then outputs

$$(z' - z) \cdot (\hat{\pi} - \hat{\pi}').$$

Next, we claim that for a successful adversary $\mathcal{A}$, $\mathcal{B}$'s output is $[\alpha^{N+1}]_1$.

Consider the executions of the Ver algorithm for π and π'.

First, for $k = 1$ to $\delta - 1$ and $\mu \in [2^k, 2^{k+1} - 1]$, let $\Psi_{k,\mu}$ and $\Psi_{k,\mu}'$ be the internal variables set in the first step of the verification algorithm. We observe that $\Psi_{k,\mu} = \Psi_{k,\mu}'$ since in both cases (cf. the first step of Ver) they are built from the same set of values $\{\Phi_\ell\}_{\ell=2}^{d-1}$ included in C, which is common to both executions of Ver.

Second, we argue that by the validity of the verification Eq. (1) for both proofs (and by the non-degeneracy of the pairing function) we obtain that $\Psi_{k,\mu} = \Psi_{k,\mu}'$ for every $k = 2, \ldots, \delta - 1$ and $\mu = 2^j - 1, \ldots, 2$. We show this by induction. Let us consider the case of μ even (μ odd is analogous). For $\mu = 2^k - 1, \ldots, 2^{k-1}$, we are checking the parents of the leaves, and it holds $\Psi_{k,2\mu} = \Psi_{k,2\mu}' = \Phi_{2\mu}$, $\Psi_{k,2\mu+1} = \Psi_{k,2\mu+1}' = \Phi_{2\mu+1}$ since $2\mu \in [2^k, 2^{k+1}-2]$ and $2\mu+1 \in [2^k+1, 2^{k+1}-1]$. Therefore, by the non-degeneracy of the pairing function we have

$$\left.\begin{array}{r} e(\Phi_{2\mu}, \Phi_{2\mu+1}) = e(\Psi_{k,\mu}, [1]_2) \\ e(\Phi_{2\mu}, \Phi_{2\mu+1}) = e(\Psi_{k,\mu}', [1]_2) \end{array}\right\} \Rightarrow \Psi_{k,\mu} = \Psi_{k,\mu}'$$

Next, using the fact $\Psi_{k,\mu} = \Psi_{k,\mu}'$ for $\mu = 2^k - 1, \ldots, 2^{k-1}$, we can apply the same argument inductively to obtain that $\Psi_{k,\mu'} = \Psi_{k,\mu'}'$ for $\mu' = 2^{k-1} - 1, \ldots, 2^{k-2}$. Eventually, we obtain that for all k, $\Psi_{k,\mu} = \Psi_{k,\mu}'$ for $\mu = 2, 3$.

Third, notice that by the validity of verification Eqs. (3) and (2) for $k = 1$ (and by the non-degeneracy of the pairing function) we obtain that $X_1 = X_1'$ and $\hat{X}_1 = \hat{X}_1'$. Moving to $k > 1$, we can see that from the equalities $X_{k-1} = X_{k-1}'$ and $\hat{X}_{k-1} = \hat{X}_{k-1}'$, we can derive in a similar way $X_k = X_k'$ and $\hat{X}_k = \hat{X}_k'$. In particular for the latter we use the conclusion of the second claim. Notice that this argument leads to conclude that it must be the case that $X_\delta = X_\delta'$.

Finally, by the validity of the verification Eq. (4) for both proofs with the same X_δ, we have

$$e(\hat{\pi}, [1]_2)e([\alpha]_1, [\alpha^N]_2)^z = e(\hat{\pi}', [1]_2)e([\alpha]_1, [\alpha^N]_2)^{z'}$$
$$\Rightarrow \quad \hat{\pi} - \hat{\pi}' = (z - z') \cdot [\alpha^{N+1}]_1$$

$\square$

4.4 From Homogeneous to Generic Polynomials

We show how to go from an additive homomorphic FC scheme for homogenous polynomials to an FC that supports generic multivariate polynomials of the same degree. The basic idea is to extend vectors by prepending a 1 in the first position and then, instead of evaluating $f(x)$ one evaluates $\hat{f}(1, x)$ where $\hat{f}$ is the homogeneous polynomial in $n + 1$ variables defined as $\hat{f}(x_0, \ldots, x_n) :=$ $x_0^d \cdot f\left(\frac{x_1}{x_0}, \ldots, \frac{x_n}{x_0}\right)$, which is such that $\forall x : \hat{f}(1, x) = f(x)$.

In order to preserve the additive homomorphic property, we actually let one commit to vectors $(0, x)$. Then a commitment to $(1, x)$ is obtained by adding homomorphically $(1, 0)$ at verification time.

In terms of security, we show that the scheme from this transformation satisfies evaluation binding (and thus weak evaluation binding) provided that so does the FC we start from. See the full version for the transformation's details.

5 Additive-Homomorphic FC for Semi-quadratic Arithmetic Programs

In this section we propose our second FC scheme that supports a new language called *semi-quadratic arithmetic programs* (sQAP). As we show in Sect. 5.3, an FC for sQAPs is sufficiently powerful to build an FC for monotone span programs [15] and thus, using known transformations, an FC for NC^1 circuits.[8]

In a nutshell, an sQAP checks the satisfiability of a class of quadratic equations (from which the name). More in detail, an sQAP defined by a matrix $\mathbf{M}$ accepts a pair of vectors (z, y) if the linear system of equations $(\mathbf{M} \mid y)$ has a solution w' which is in multiplicative relation with the input z, i.e., $w' = w \circ z$ for some w. More formally:

---

[8] It is known that a circuit in the class NC^1 can be converted into a polynomial-size boolean formula, and the latter can be turned into a monotone span program of equivalent size, e.g. [20, Appendix G].

Definition 9 (Semi-Quadratic Arithmetic Programs). *A semi-quadratic arithmetic program (sQAP)* $f : \mathbb{F}^n \times \mathbb{F}^m \to \{\text{true}, \text{false}\}$ *over a finite field* $\mathbb{F}$ *is defined by a matrix* $\mathbf{F} \in \mathbb{F}^{m \times n}$. *On an input* $\boldsymbol{x} = (\boldsymbol{z}, \boldsymbol{y})$, f *accepts (i.e., outputs* true*) iff*

$$\exists \boldsymbol{w} \in \mathbb{F}^n : \mathbf{F} \cdot (\boldsymbol{w} \circ \boldsymbol{z}) = \boldsymbol{y}$$

We observe that sQAPs are a polynomial time language. Given $(\boldsymbol{z}, \boldsymbol{y})$, one can decide as follows. Define $\mathbf{F}'$ as the matrix of entries $F'_{i,j} = F_{i,j} \cdot z_j$ and output true if and only if $\exists \boldsymbol{w} \in \mathbb{F}^n : \mathbf{F}' \cdot \boldsymbol{w} = \boldsymbol{y}$ (e.g., using Gaussian elimination).

5.1   Our FC for sQAPs

We present our additive-homomorphic FC for sQAPs (see Sect. 1.3 for an overview).

Setup($1^\lambda, n, m$) Let $m, n \geq 1$ be two integers representing the size of the sQAPs
  supported by the scheme (i.e., matrices in $\mathbb{F}^{m \times n}$) and thus the length of
  the input vectors (pairs in $\mathbb{F}^n \times \mathbb{F}^m$). Generate a bilinear group description
  bgp $:= (q, \mathbb{G}_1, \mathbb{G}_2, \mathbb{G}_T, e, g_1, g_2) \leftarrow \mathcal{BG}(1^\lambda)$, and let $\mathbb{F} := \mathbb{Z}_q$. Next, sample
  random $\alpha, \gamma \leftarrow_\$ \mathbb{F}, \boldsymbol{\beta} \leftarrow_\$ \mathbb{F}^m$ and output

$$\text{ck} := \begin{pmatrix} \{[\alpha^j]_1, [\gamma^j]_1\}_{j \in [n]}, [(\alpha\gamma)^n]_2, \{[\alpha^j \beta_i \gamma^\ell]_2\}_{i \in [m], j \in [n], \ell \in [2n]}, \\ \{[\alpha^j \beta_i \gamma^{n+1}]_1\}_{i \in [m], j \in [2n] \setminus \{n+1\}}, \{[\alpha^j \beta_i \gamma^\ell]_1\}_{i \in [m], j, \ell \in [2n] : \ell \neq n+1} \end{pmatrix}$$

Com(ck, $\boldsymbol{x}$) Given an input $\boldsymbol{x} = (\boldsymbol{z}, \boldsymbol{y})$, we compute

$$C_z := \sum_{j \in [n]} z_j \cdot [\gamma^j]_1, \quad C_y := \sum_{i \in [m]} y_i \cdot [\alpha\gamma\beta_i]_1$$

Note, we encode $\boldsymbol{z}$ with the polynomial $p_z(X) = \sum_{j=1}^{m} z_j \cdot X^j$, and thus $C_z = [p_z(\gamma)]_1$. We output $C := (C_z, C_y)$ and aux $:= (\boldsymbol{z}, \boldsymbol{y})$.

Open(ck, aux, $\mathbf{F}$) Let $\mathbf{F} \in \mathbb{F}^{m \times n}$ be a sQAP which accepts the input $(\boldsymbol{z}, \boldsymbol{y})$ in
  aux. The opening algorithm performs the following steps:
  – Compute a witness $\boldsymbol{w} \in \mathbb{F}^n$ such that $\mathbf{F} \cdot (\boldsymbol{w} \circ \boldsymbol{z}) = \boldsymbol{y}$ and compute a
    commitment to it as $W := [p_w(\alpha)]_1 = \sum_{j \in [n]} w_j \cdot [\alpha^j]_1$.
  – Next, we compute an encoding Φ_z of the matrix $\mathbf{F} \circ \mathbf{Z}$ where $\mathbf{Z} \in \mathbb{F}^{m \times n}$
    is the matrix with $\boldsymbol{z}^\top$ in every row:

$$\Phi_z := \sum_{\substack{i \in [m] \\ j, \ell \in [n]}} F_{i,j} \cdot z_\ell \cdot [\alpha^{n+1-j} \beta_i \gamma^{n+1+\ell-j}]_2$$

Precisely, note that $\mathbf{F} \circ \mathbf{Z}$ is encoded in the terms including γ^{n+1} of the above polynomial, i.e., the (i, j)-th entry is in the term $F_{i,j} \cdot z_j \cdot [\alpha^{n+1-j} \gamma^{n+1} \beta_i]_2$.

– Finally, we compute an evaluation proof to show that the vector $\boldsymbol{w}$ committed in W is a solution to the linear system $((\mathbf{F} \circ \mathbf{Z}) \mid \boldsymbol{y})$, i.e., $(\mathbf{F} \circ \mathbf{Z}) \cdot \boldsymbol{w} = \mathbf{F} \cdot (\boldsymbol{w} \circ \boldsymbol{z}) = \boldsymbol{y}$:

$$\hat{\pi} := \sum_{\substack{i \in [m] \\ j,k \in [n]: j \neq k}} F_{i,j} \cdot z_j \cdot w_k \cdot [\alpha^{n+1-j+k} \beta_i \gamma^{n+1}]_1$$

$$+ \sum_{\substack{i \in [m] \\ j,k,\ell \in [n]: \ell \neq j}} F_{i,j} \cdot z_\ell \cdot w_k \cdot [\alpha^{n+1-j+k} \beta_i \gamma^{n+1-j+\ell}]_1$$

Output $\pi := (W, \varPhi_z, \hat{\pi})$.

$\mathsf{Ver}(\mathsf{ck}, C, \pi, \mathbf{F}, \mathsf{true})$ First, compute $\varPhi \leftarrow \sum_{i \in [m], j \in [m]} F_{i,j} \cdot [(\alpha\gamma)^{n+1-j} \beta_i]_2$ and then output 1 if all the following checks are satisfied.

$$e\left(C_z, \varPhi\right) \stackrel{?}{=} e\left([1]_1, \varPhi_z\right) \tag{5}$$

$$e\left(W, \varPhi_z\right) \stackrel{?}{=} e\left(\hat{\pi}, [1]_2\right) \cdot e\left(C_y, [(\alpha\gamma)^n]_2\right) \tag{6}$$

We refer to the full version for the correctness proof. Here we observe that: proofs are succinct (three group elements), and commitments are additively homomorphic. Also, it is easy to see that the scheme enjoys efficient amortized verification: $\mathsf{VerPrep}$ is the algorithm that on input $\mathbf{F}$ computes the element $\varPhi$, and EffVer performs the two checks described in Ver.

5.2   Proof of Security

We prove the weak evaluation binding of our FC for sQAPs based on the following assumption that we call *double parallel bilinear Diffie-Hellman exponent* (DP-BDHE) assumption, as it can be seen as a "double version" of the PBDHE assumption introduced by Waters in [26]. In the full version we justify (n, m)-DP-BDHE in the generic group model.

Definition 10 ((n, m)-DP-BDHE assumption). *Let* $\mathsf{bgp} = (q, \mathbb{G}_1, \mathbb{G}_2, \mathbb{G}_T, e, g_1, g_2)$ *be a bilinear group setting. The (n, m)-DP-BDHE holds if for every* $n, m = \mathsf{poly}(\lambda)$ *and any PPT* $\mathcal{A}$*, the following advantage is negligible*

$$\mathbf{Adv}_{\mathcal{A}}^{(n,m)\text{-}DP\text{-}BDHE}(\lambda) = \Pr[\mathcal{A}(\mathsf{bgp}, \varOmega) => \alpha^{n+1}\gamma^{n+1}\delta] \quad where$$

$$\varOmega := \begin{pmatrix} \left\{[\alpha^j]_1, [\gamma^j]_1\right\}_{j \in [n]}, \left\{[\alpha^j \beta_i \gamma^{n+1}]_1\right\}_{\substack{i \in [m], j \in [2n] \\ j \neq n+1}}, \left\{[\alpha^j \beta_i \gamma^\ell]_1\right\}_{\substack{i \in [m], j, \ell \in [2n] \\ \ell \neq n+1}} \\ [(\alpha\gamma)^n]_2, \left\{[\alpha^j \beta_i \gamma^\ell]_2\right\}_{i \in [m], j \in [n], \ell \in [2n]}, \\ \left\{\left[\frac{\delta}{\beta_k}\right]_2\right\}_{k \in [m]}, \left\{\left[\frac{\alpha^j \beta_i \gamma^{n+1}\delta}{\beta_k}\right]_2\right\}_{\substack{j \in [n], i, k \in [m] \\ i \neq k}}, \left\{\left[\frac{\alpha^j \beta_i \gamma^\ell \delta}{\beta_k}\right]_2\right\}_{\substack{i, k \in [m], j \in [n] \\ \ell \in [2n] \setminus \{n+1\}}} \end{pmatrix}$$

and the probability is over the random choices of $\alpha, \gamma, \delta \leftarrow_{\$} \mathbb{Z}_q$*,* $\boldsymbol{\beta} \leftarrow_{\$} \mathbb{Z}_q^m$ *and* $\mathcal{A}$*'s random coins.*

Theorem 2. *If the (n, m)-DP-BDHE assumption holds then the FC scheme of Sect. 5.1 satisfies weak evaluation binding.*

Proof. Let $\mathcal{A}$ be a PPT adversary against the weak evaluation binding of the FC scheme. We use $\mathcal{A}$ to build a PPT adversary $\mathcal{B}$ against the (n, m)-DP-BDHE assumption. $\mathcal{B}$ runs on input the bilinear group description and the list of group elements Ω.

$\mathcal{B}$ takes a subset of the elements in Ω, sets ck as below, and runs $\mathcal{A}(\mathsf{ck})$.

$$\mathsf{ck} := \left(\begin{array}{l} \{[\alpha^j]_1, [\gamma^j]_1\}_{j\in[n]}, [(\alpha\gamma)^n]_2, \{[\alpha^j\beta_i\gamma^\ell]_2\}_{i\in[m],j\in[n],\ell\in[2n]}, \\ \{[\alpha^j\beta_i\gamma^{n+1}]_1\}_{i\in[m],j\in[2n]\setminus\{n+1\}}, \{[\alpha^j\beta_i\gamma^\ell]_1\}_{i\in[m],j,\ell\in[2n]:\ell\neq n+1} \end{array} \right)$$

Let $\mathcal{A}$'s output be $((\boldsymbol{z}, \boldsymbol{y}), \mathbf{F}, \mathsf{true}, \pi)$. If $\mathcal{A}$ is successful we have that: (i) the proof is valid for the commitment $C = \mathsf{Com}(\mathsf{ck}, (\boldsymbol{z}, \boldsymbol{y}))$, and (ii) the sQAP does not accept $(\boldsymbol{z}, \boldsymbol{y})$. If we parse $\pi := (W, \Phi_z, \hat{\pi})$, condition (i) means

$$e([p_z(\gamma)]_1, \Phi) = e([1]_1, \Phi_z) \tag{7}$$

$$e(W, \Phi_z) = e(\hat{\pi}, [1]_2) \cdot e\left([\alpha\gamma\boldsymbol{\beta}^\top\boldsymbol{y}]_1, [(\alpha\gamma)^n]_2\right) \tag{8}$$

while condition (ii) means that for $\mathbf{F}' = (F_{i,j} \cdot z_j)_{i,j}$

$$\nexists \boldsymbol{w} \in \mathbb{F}^n : \mathbf{F}' \cdot \boldsymbol{w} = \boldsymbol{y} \tag{9}$$

As first step, for every $k \in [m]$, $\mathcal{B}$ computes $\pi'_k := e\left(\hat{\pi}, \left[\frac{\delta}{\beta_k}\right]_2\right)$. By the construction of Φ in the Ver algorithm and by Eq. (7) we have:

$$\begin{aligned}
\Phi_z &= \left[\left(\sum_{\ell\in[n]} z_\ell \cdot \gamma^\ell\right) \cdot \left(\sum_{i\in[m],j\in[n]} F_{i,j} \cdot (\alpha\gamma)^{n+1-j}\beta_i\right)\right]_2 \\
&= \sum_{\substack{i\in[m]\\j\in[n]}} F_{i,j} \cdot z_j \cdot [\alpha^{n+1-j}\beta_i\gamma^{n+1}]_2 + \sum_{\substack{i\in[m]\\j,\ell\in[n]:\ell\neq j}} F_{i,j} \cdot z_\ell \cdot [\alpha^{n+1-j}\beta_i\gamma^{n+1-j+\ell}]_2
\end{aligned}$$

Hence, by applying Eq. (8), for every $k \in [m]$, it holds

$$\begin{aligned}
\pi'_k &= e\left(W, \sum_{j\in[n]} F_{k,j} \cdot z_j \cdot \left[\alpha^{n+1-j}\gamma^{n+1}\delta\right]_2\right) \cdot \left[-y_k \cdot (\alpha\gamma)^{n+1}\delta\right]_T \cdot \\
&\quad e\left(W, \sum_{\substack{i\in[m]\setminus\{k\}\\j\in[n]}} F_{i,j} \cdot z_j \cdot \left[\frac{\alpha^{n+1-j}\beta_i\gamma^{n+1}\delta}{\beta_k}\right]_2\right) \cdot \\
&\quad e\left(W, \sum_{\substack{i\in[m]\\j,\ell\in[n]:\ell\neq j}} F_{i,j} \cdot z_\ell \cdot \left[\frac{\alpha^{n+1-j}\beta_i\gamma^{n+1-j+\ell}\delta}{\beta_k}\right]_2\right) \cdot \left[-\sum_{i\in[m]\setminus\{k\}} y_i \cdot \frac{(\alpha\gamma)^{n+1}\beta_i\delta}{\beta_k}\right]_T
\end{aligned}$$

As the second step, for every $k \in [m]$, $\mathcal{B}$ computes

$$\pi_k^* := \pi_k' \cdot e\left(W, -\sum_{\substack{i\in[m]\setminus\{k\} \\ j\in[n]}} F_{i,j} \cdot z_j \cdot \left[\frac{\alpha^{n+1-j}\beta_i\gamma^{n+1}\delta}{\beta_k}\right]_2\right) \cdot$$

$$e\left(W, -\sum_{\substack{i\in[m] \\ j,\ell\in[n]:\ell\neq j}} F_{i,j} \cdot z_\ell \cdot \left[\frac{\alpha^{n+1-j}\beta_i\gamma^{n+1-j+\ell}\delta}{\beta_k}\right]_2\right) \cdot$$

$$e\left([(\alpha\gamma)^n]_1, \sum_{i\in[m]\setminus\{k\}} y_i \cdot \left[\frac{\alpha\gamma\delta\beta_i}{\beta_k}\right]_2\right)$$

$$= e\left(W, \sum_{j\in[n]} F_{k,j} \cdot z_j \cdot \left[(\alpha\gamma)^{n+1-j}\delta\right]_2\right) \cdot \left[-y_k \cdot (\alpha\gamma)^{n+1}\delta\right]_T$$

Notice that the elements above can be efficiently computed by $\mathcal{B}$, given the group elements included in its input Ω. In particular, for every $j, \ell \in [n]$ such that $\ell \neq j$ (and any $i, k \in [m]$), notice that $\left[\frac{\alpha^{n+1-j}\beta_i\gamma^{n+1-j+\ell}\delta}{\beta_k}\right]_2$ is part of $\left\{\left[\frac{\alpha^{j'}\beta_i\gamma^{\ell'}\delta}{\beta_k}\right]_2\right\}_{j'\in[n],\ell\in[2n]\setminus\{n+1\}}$.

If the sQAP is not satisfied, i.e., condition (9) holds, it means that $(\mathbf{F}' \mid \boldsymbol{y})$ is an inconsistent system of equations, thus there exists a vector $\boldsymbol{c} \in \mathbb{F}^m$ such that $\boldsymbol{c}^\top \cdot \mathbf{F}' = \mathbf{0}^\top$ and $\boldsymbol{c}^\top \cdot \boldsymbol{y} = \tau \neq 0$. Let $V := \{v \cdot \boldsymbol{c} : v \in \mathbb{F}\}$. Then any vector $\boldsymbol{v} \in V$ is such that

$$\boldsymbol{v}^\top \cdot \mathbf{F}' = (0,\dots,0) \ \wedge \ \boldsymbol{v}^\top \cdot \boldsymbol{y} \neq 0$$

In particular, one of them, $\boldsymbol{u} = \tau^{-1} \cdot \boldsymbol{c}$, is such that $\boldsymbol{u}^\top \cdot \boldsymbol{y} = 1$. So, $\mathcal{B}$ finds $\boldsymbol{u}$ such that

$$\boldsymbol{u}^\top \cdot (\mathbf{F}' \mid \boldsymbol{y}) = (0, \cdots, 0, 1) \tag{10}$$

(e.g., by Gaussian elimination), and then $\mathcal{B}$ computes and returns

$$\Delta^* = \prod_{k\in[m]} (\pi_k^*)^{-u_k}$$

We show below that, conditioned on $\mathcal{A}$ being successful, $\Delta^* => (\alpha\gamma)^{n+1}\delta$, and thus $\mathcal{B}$ succeeds in breaking the (n, m)-DP-BDHE assumption.

Expanding each term $\pi_{\ell,k}^*$ we have

$$\Delta^* = e\left(W, -\sum_{j\in[n]} \left[(\alpha\gamma)^{n+1-j}\delta\right]_2 \sum_{k\in[m]} F_{k,j} \cdot z_j \cdot u_k\right) \cdot \left[(\alpha\gamma)^{n+1}\delta \sum_{k\in[m]} y_k u_k\right]_T$$

The equality $\Delta^* => (\alpha\gamma)^{n+1}\delta$ follows from the fact that, by Eq. (10), we have that for every $j \in [n]$, $\sum_{k\in[m]} u_k \cdot F_{k,j} \cdot z_j = \sum_{k\in[m]} u_k \cdot F_{k,j}' = 0$ and that $\sum_{k\in[m]} u_k \cdot y_k = 1$. $\qquad \square$

5.3   From FC for sQAPs to an FC for Monotone Span Programs

Here we show how to construct an FC for monotone span programs from an additive-homomorphic FC for sQAPs, which can be instantiated using the scheme presented in Sect. 5.1. We instantiate the same construction with vectors of length $n + 1$ so that the commitment to

We recall the notion of (monotone) span programs (MSP) of Karchmer and Wigderson [15].

Definition 11 (Monotone Span Programs [15]). *A (monotone) span program for attribute universe* $[n]$ *is a pair* $(\mathbf{M}, \rho)$ *where* $\mathbf{M} \in \mathbb{F}^{\ell \times m}$ *and* $\rho : [\ell] \to [n]$. *Given an input* $\boldsymbol{x} \in \{0, 1\}^n$, *we say that*

$$(\mathbf{M}, \rho) \text{ accepts } \boldsymbol{x} \text{ iff } (1, 0 \ldots, 0) \in \text{span}\langle \mathbf{M}_{\boldsymbol{x}} \rangle$$

where $\mathbf{M}_{\boldsymbol{x}}$ *denotes the matrix obtained from* $\mathbf{M}$ *by taking only the i-th rows* $\mathbf{M}_i$ *for which* $x_{\rho(j)} = 1$, *and* span *is the linear span of row vectors over* $\mathbb{F}$.

So, $(\mathbf{M}, \rho)$ accepts $\boldsymbol{x}$ iff there exist $\boldsymbol{w} \in \mathbb{F}^\ell$ such that

$$\sum_{i:x_{\rho(i)}=1} w_i \cdot \mathbf{M}_i = (1, 0, \ldots, 0)$$

Notice that the MSP can be evaluated in polynomial time by using Gaussian elimination to find $\boldsymbol{w}$.

As in other cryptographic works, e.g., [19], we work with a restricted version of MSPs in which each input x_i is read only once. Hence, $\ell = n$ and ρ is a permutation, which (up to a reordering of the rows of $\mathbf{M}$) can be assumed to be the identity function. Notice that the one-use restriction can be removed by working with larger input vectors of length $k \cdot n$ in which each entry x_i is repeated k times, if k is an upper bound on the input's fan out.

Therefore, in what follows we assume a monotone span program defined by a matrix $\mathbf{M} \in \mathbb{F}^{n \times m}$ and we say that

$$\mathbf{M} \text{ accepts } \boldsymbol{x} \quad \text{iff} \quad \exists \boldsymbol{w} \in \mathbb{F}^n : (\boldsymbol{w} \circ \boldsymbol{x})^\top \cdot \mathbf{M} = (1, 0 \ldots, 0)$$

It is easy to see that MSPs are an instance of the sQAPs of Definition 9. Given $\mathbf{M}$, set $\mathbf{F} := \mathbf{M}^\top$ and consider sQAP inputs $(\boldsymbol{z}, \boldsymbol{y}) := (\boldsymbol{x}, (1, 0 \ldots, 0)^\top)$. Then it is clear that the MSP $\mathbf{M}$ accepts $\boldsymbol{x}$ iff the sQAP $\mathbf{M}^\top$ accepts $(\boldsymbol{x}, (1, 0 \ldots, 0)^\top)$.

We can use this relation to build an FC for monotone span programs from an FC for sQAP. In particular, we can do it in such a way to preserve the additive-homomorphic property, which allows us to use this scheme in the application to homomorphic signatures of Sect. 6.

FC for MSPs from FC for sQAPs. Let FC$'$ be a functional commitment scheme for sQAPs. We build a scheme FC for monotone span programs as follows.

Setup($1^\lambda, n, m$) output ck $\leftarrow$ Setup$'(1^\lambda, n, m)$

$\underline{\mathsf{Com}(\mathsf{ck}, \boldsymbol{x})}$ Output $(C, \mathsf{aux}) \leftarrow \mathsf{Com}'(\mathsf{ck}, (\boldsymbol{x}, \mathbf{0}))$

$\underline{\mathsf{Open}(\mathsf{ck}, \mathsf{aux}, \mathbf{M})}$ Assume aux is the auxiliary information of a commitment to a pair of vectors $(\boldsymbol{x}, \mathbf{0})$. The opening proceeds as follows.

- Compute a commitment to the vector $(\mathbf{0}, (1, \mathbf{0}))$ without using random coins: $(C_1, \mathsf{aux}_1) \leftarrow \mathsf{Com}(\mathsf{ck}, (\mathbf{0}, (1, \mathbf{0})); \emptyset)$.
- Use the additive homomorphism to compute the auxiliary information corresponding to the commitment to $(\boldsymbol{x}, (1, \mathbf{0}))$: $\mathsf{a\hat{u}x} \leftarrow \mathsf{FC}'.\mathsf{Add}_{\mathsf{aux}}(\mathsf{ck}, \mathsf{aux}, \mathsf{aux}_1)$.
- Let $\mathbf{F} := \mathbf{M}^\top$ and run $\pi \leftarrow \mathsf{FC}'.\mathsf{Open}(\mathsf{ck}, \mathsf{a\hat{u}x}, \mathbf{F})$.

Return π.

$\underline{\mathsf{Ver}(\mathsf{ck}, C, \pi, \mathbf{M}, \mathsf{true})}$ Compute $(C_1, \mathsf{aux}_1) \leftarrow \mathsf{Com}(\mathsf{ck}, (\mathbf{0}, (1, \mathbf{0})); \emptyset)$ and $\hat{C} \leftarrow \mathsf{FC}'.\mathsf{Add}(\mathsf{ck}, C, C_1)$. Output $\mathsf{FC}'.\mathsf{Ver}(\mathsf{ck}, \hat{C}, \pi, \mathbf{M}^\top, \mathsf{true})$.

We state the following theorem. The proof easily follows from the characterization of MSPs from sQAP mentioned earlier.

Theorem 3. *If* FC' *is a weak evaluation binding* FC *for sQAP, then* FC *is a weak evaluation binding* FC *for MSPs.*

Remark 1. We note that our FCs for sQAPs and MSPs allow the prover to show that the program accepts, but not that it rejects. We believe that the schemes could be changed to achieve this property and we leave it for future work. However, we observe that proving only acceptance is sufficient when the MSP is used to express that a circuit C outputs 1, due to the following observation. If the claim is that C outputs 0, prover and verifier could switch to use $\bar{C}$ (that is C with a negated output), build an MSP for it, and show it accepts.

6 Homomorphic Signatures from Additive-Homomorphic Functional Commitments

Homomorphic Signatures. We recall the definition of homomorphic signatures (HS) of [1], extended to work with labeled programs [11], as used in several prior works, e.g., [6,7].

In an HS scheme, the signer can sign a set of messages $\{x_i\}$ so that anyone can later compute a function f on the signed messages and obtain a signature that certifies the correctness of the result. Each set of messages is grouped into a "dataset" which has an identifier Δ (e.g., the filename); inside such dataset each message x_i is assigned a "label" τ_i (e.g., its position). So, more precisely, in HS the signer signs a collection of messages (x_i) with respect to a dataset identifier Δ and a label τ. Evaluation instead consists in executing a function f on the messages associated to some labels $\tau_1, \ldots, \tau_n$ of a dataset Δ. A property that makes HS an interesting primitive is that the signatures resulted from the evaluation are succinct, i.e., of size at most logarithmic in the input size. In this paper we generalize HS to the case of functions with multiple outputs and define the notion of *compactness*, which says that signatures are succinct with respect to both input and output size. We provide below formal definitions.

Labeled Programs [11]. Let $\mathcal{L}$ be the label space (e.g., $\mathcal{L} = \{0,1\}^*$ or $\mathcal{L} = [n]$). A *labeled program* $\mathcal{P}$ is a tuple $(f, \tau_1, ..., \tau_n)$ where $f : \mathcal{X}^n \to \mathcal{X}^m$ and every $\tau_i \in \mathcal{L}$ is the label of the i-th input of f. Given a function $g : \mathcal{X}^\ell \to \mathcal{X}^m$, we can compose t labeled programs $\mathcal{P}_1, \ldots, \mathcal{P}_t$ with $m_1, \ldots, m_t$ outputs respectively, into $\mathcal{P}^*$. The latter, denoted as $\mathcal{P}^* = g(\mathcal{P}_1, \ldots, \mathcal{P}_t)$, is the program obtained by evaluating g on the $\ell = \sum_{i=1}^t m_i$ outputs of $\mathcal{P}_1, \ldots, \mathcal{P}_t$. The labeled inputs of $\mathcal{P}^*$ are the distinct labeled inputs of $\mathcal{P}_1, \ldots, \mathcal{P}_t$ (all inputs with the same label are merged into a single input of $\mathcal{P}^*$). If $f_{id} : \mathcal{X} \to \mathcal{X}$ denotes the identity function and $\tau \in \mathcal{L}$, $\mathcal{I}_\tau = (f_{id}, \tau)$ is the identity program with label τ.

Definition 12 (Homomorphic Signature). *A homomorphic signature scheme* HS *is a tuple of PPT algorithms* (KeyGen, Sign, Ver, Eval) *that work as follows and satisfy* authentication correctness, evaluation correctness *and* succinctness.

KeyGen$(1^\lambda, \mathcal{L}) \to$ (sk, pk) *Given the security parameter λ and the label space $\mathcal{L}$, outputs a public key* pk *and a secret key* sk. *The public key* pk *defines the message space $\mathcal{X}$ and the set $\mathcal{F}$ of admissible functions.*

Sign$(\mathsf{sk}, \Delta, \tau, x) \to \sigma$ *On input the secret key* sk, *a dataset identifier $\Delta \in \{0,1\}^*$, a label $\tau \in \mathcal{L}$, and a message $x \in \mathcal{X}$, outputs a signature σ.*

Eval$(\mathsf{pk}, f, \sigma_1, \ldots, \sigma_n) \to \sigma$ *On input the public key* pk, *a function $f : \mathcal{X}^n \to \mathcal{X}^m$ in the class $\mathcal{F}$ and a tuple of signatures $(\sigma_i)_{i=1}^n$, outputs a new signature σ.*

Ver$(\mathsf{pk}, \mathcal{P}, \Delta, \boldsymbol{y}, \sigma) \to \{0,1\}$ *On input the public key* pk, *a labeled program $\mathcal{P} = (f, \tau_1, \ldots, \tau_n)$ with $f : \mathcal{X}^n \to \mathcal{X}^m$, a dataset identifier Δ, a value $\boldsymbol{y} \in \mathcal{X}^m$, and a signature σ, outputs either 0 (reject) or 1 (accept).*

Authentication Correctness. *Informally, authentication correctness means that a "fresh" signature generated by* Sign *on message x and label τ verifies correctly for x as output of the identity program $\mathcal{I}_\tau$. More formally, a scheme* HS *satisfies authentication correctness if for a given label space $\mathcal{L}$, all key pairs* (sk, pk) $\leftarrow$ KeyGen$(1^\lambda, \mathcal{L})$, *any label $\tau \in \mathcal{L}$, dataset identifier $\Delta \in \{0,1\}^*$, and any signature $\sigma \leftarrow$* Sign$(\mathsf{sk}, \Delta, \tau, x)$, Ver$(\mathsf{pk}, \mathcal{I}_\tau, \Delta, x, \sigma) = 1$ *holds with all but negligible probability.*

Evaluation Correctness. *Informally, this property means that executing* Eval *with a function g on signatures $(\sigma_1, \ldots, \sigma_t)$, where σ_i verifies for x_i as output of $\mathcal{P}_i$, produces a signature σ that verifies for $g(x_1, \ldots, x_t)$ as output of the composed program $g(\mathcal{P}_1, \ldots, \mathcal{P}_t)$. More formally, fix a key pair* (pk, sk) $\leftarrow$ KeyGen$(1^\lambda, \mathcal{L})$, *a function $g : \mathcal{X}^\ell \to \mathcal{X}^m$, and a set of program/message/signature triples $\{(\mathcal{P}_i, \boldsymbol{x}_i, \sigma_i)\}_{i=1}^t$ such that* Ver$(\mathsf{pk}, \mathcal{P}_i, \Delta, \boldsymbol{x}_i, \sigma_i) = 1$. *If $\boldsymbol{x}^* = g(\boldsymbol{x}_1, \ldots, \boldsymbol{x}_t)$, $\mathcal{P}^* = g(\mathcal{P}_1, \ldots, \mathcal{P}_t)$, and $\sigma^* =$* Eval$(\mathsf{pk}, g, \sigma_1, \ldots, \sigma_t)$, *then* Ver$(\mathsf{pk}, \mathcal{P}^*, \Delta, \boldsymbol{x}^*, \sigma^*) = 1$ *holds with all but negligible probability.*

Succinctness/Compactness. *An HS scheme* HS *is succinct (resp. compact) if there exists a universal polynomial $p(\lambda)$ such that for any keys* (pk, sk) $\leftarrow$ KeyGen$(1^\lambda, \mathcal{L})$, *integer $n = $ poly(λ) and function $f : \mathcal{X}^n \to \mathcal{X}$ in $\mathcal{F}$ (resp. integers $n, m = $ poly(λ) and function $f : \mathcal{X}^n \to \mathcal{X}^m$ in $\mathcal{F}$), messages $(x_1, \ldots, x_n) \in \mathcal{X}^n$,* labels $(\tau_1, \ldots, \tau_n) \in \mathcal{L}^n$, and dataset $\Delta \in \{0,1\}^*$, if $\sigma_i \leftarrow \mathsf{Sign}(\mathsf{sk}, \Delta, \tau_i, x_i)$ and $\sigma \leftarrow \mathsf{Eval}(\mathsf{pk}, f, \sigma_1, \ldots, \sigma_n)$, then $|\sigma| \leq p(\lambda) \cdot \log n$ (resp. $|\sigma| \leq p(\lambda) \cdot \log n \cdot \log m$).

$\mathbf{Exp}_{\mathcal{A},\mathsf{HS}}^{\mathsf{strong\text{-}Ad\text{-}UF}}(\lambda)$	Oracle $\mathcal{O}_{\mathsf{Sign}}(\Delta, \tau, m)$
$T \leftarrow \emptyset$; $(\mathsf{pk},\mathsf{sk}) \leftarrow\!\!\$\, \mathsf{KeyGen}(1^\lambda, \mathcal{L})$	**if** $(\Delta, \tau, \cdot, \cdot) \notin T$ **then**
$(\mathcal{P}^*, \Delta^*, x^*, \sigma^*) \leftarrow \mathcal{A}^{\mathcal{O}_{\mathsf{Sign}}(\cdot)}(\mathsf{pk})$ // signing query phase	$\sigma \leftarrow \mathsf{Sign}(\mathsf{sk}, \Delta, \tau, x)$
$b_{\mathsf{Ver}} \leftarrow \mathsf{Ver}(\mathsf{pk}, \mathcal{P}^*, \Delta^*, m^*, \sigma^*)$ // the signature verifies	$T \leftarrow T \cup \{(\Delta, \tau, x, \sigma)\}$
$b_1 \leftarrow \exists j : (\Delta^*, \tau_j^*, \cdot, \cdot) \notin T$ // type-1: new dataset/label	**return** σ
$b_2 \leftarrow x^* \neq f^*(x_1, \ldots, x_n)$ // type-2: all inputs queried	**else return** $\bot$
where $\forall i : (\Delta^*, \tau_i^*, x_i, \cdot) \in T$ // but wrong result	
return $b_{\mathsf{Ver}} \wedge (b_1 \vee b_2)$	

Fig. 1. Strong adaptive security experiment for homomorphic signatures.

Remark 2 (Single-input vs. multi-input HS). The HS notion presented here allows one to sign the messages of a dataset one by one. We call such a scheme a *multi-input* HS. In contrast, *single-input* HS are HS schemes where Sign only works on input *all* the messages of the dataset.

Security. Informally, an HS is secure if an adversary, without knowledge of the secret key, can only produce signatures that are either the ones obtained from the signer, or they are signatures obtained through the Eval algorithm on signatures obtained from the signer. The formalization of this intuition can have different strengths according to how a forgery is defined. We refer to [6] for a discussion on different notions of unforgeability. In this work we adopt the simplest and strongest notion from [6], called strong-adaptive security.

Definition 13 (Strong Adaptive Security). *Let* $\mathbf{Exp}_{\mathcal{A},\mathsf{HS}}^{\mathsf{strong\text{-}Ad\text{-}UF}}(\lambda)$ *be the security experiment of Fig. 1, and let* $\mathbf{Adv}_{\mathcal{A},\mathsf{HS}}^{\mathsf{strong\text{-}Ad\text{-}UF}}(\lambda) = \Pr[\mathbf{Exp}_{\mathcal{A},\mathsf{HS}}^{\mathsf{strong\text{-}Ad\text{-}UF}}(\lambda) = 1]$ *be the advantage of* $\mathcal{A}$ *against the strong adaptive security of scheme* HS. *We say that* HS *is* strong adaptive secure *if for every PPT adversary* $\mathcal{A}$ *there exists a negligible function* $\epsilon(\lambda)$ *such that* $\mathbf{Adv}_{\mathcal{A},\mathsf{HS}}^{\mathsf{strong\text{-}Ad\text{-}UF}}(\lambda) \leq \epsilon(\lambda)$.

HS can also satisfy a privacy property, called context hiding [1], which informally says that signatures on outputs do not leak information about the inputs. An HS can have efficient amortized verification [7]; in brief this means that given f one can precompute a function-specific verification key which can be used later to verify any signature for f's outputs in at most polylogarithmic time. We give formal definitions of these properties in the full version.

6.1   From FCs to HS

Let FC be an additively homomorphic functional commitment scheme for a class of functions $\mathcal{F}$, such that the commitments are in $\mathcal{C}$ and $\mathsf{FC.Add} : \mathcal{C}^n \to \mathcal{C}$ is its homomorphic addition algorithm. Let LHS be an HS with message space $\mathcal{C}$ and that supports the evaluation of FC.Add. We use these two schemes to build an HS scheme HS for functions in $\mathcal{F}$. The scheme is described in Fig. 2. We refer to the introduction for an intuitive explanation of the construction.

Below, given a labeled program $(f, \boldsymbol{i})$ with $f : \mathcal{X}^t \to \mathcal{X}^m$ and $\boldsymbol{i} = (i_1, \dots, i_t) \in [n]^t$, we define $\hat{f}_{\boldsymbol{i}} : \mathcal{X}^n \to \mathcal{X}^m$ as the n-input function that, ignoring inputs at positions $j \notin \boldsymbol{i}$, works identically as f.

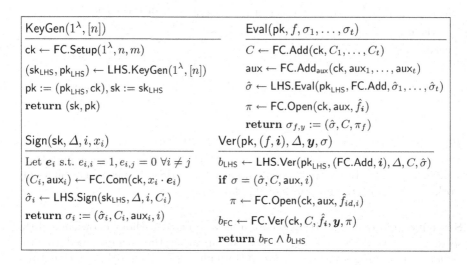

Fig. 2. HS from additive FC and LHS for FC.Add.

The correctness of the scheme can be checked by inspection. In the following theorem we prove its security. For lack of space, we defer to the full version for the proof, further propertied of this construction, and a discussion on how to instantiate the LHS scheme based on [8].

Theorem 4. *If* LHS *is strongly-adaptive secure and* FC *is weak evaluation binding, then* HS *is strongly-adaptive secure.*

Acknowledgements. We would like to thank Pierre Bourse for initial discussions that inspired this work, and Ignacio Cascudo for a useful discussion. This work has received funding in part from the European Research Council (ERC) under the European Union's Horizon 2020 research and innovation program under project PICOCRYPT (grant agreement No. 101001283), by the Spanish Government under projects SCUM (ref. RTI2018-102043-B-I00), and RED2018-102321-T, by the Madrid Regional Government under project BLOQUES (ref. S2018/TCS-4339), by a research grant from Nomadic Labs and the Tezos Foundation, and by the Programma ricerca di ateneo UNICT 35 2020-22 linea 2 and by research gifts from Protocol Labs.

References

1. Boneh, D., Freeman, D.M.: Homomorphic signatures for polynomial functions. In: Paterson, K.G. (ed.) EUROCRYPT 2011. LNCS, vol. 6632, pp. 149–168. Springer, Heidelberg (2011). https://doi.org/10.1007/978-3-642-20465-4_10

2. Boneh, D., Gentry, C., Waters, B.: Collusion resistant broadcast encryption with short ciphertexts and private keys. In: Shoup, V. (ed.) CRYPTO 2005. LNCS, vol. 3621, pp. 258–275. Springer, Heidelberg (2005). https://doi.org/10.1007/11535218_16

3. Camenisch, J., Lysyanskaya, A.: Dynamic accumulators and application to efficient revocation of anonymous credentials. In: Yung, M. (ed.) CRYPTO 2002. LNCS, vol. 2442, pp. 61–76. Springer, Heidelberg (2002). https://doi.org/10.1007/3-540-45708-9_5

4. Catalano, D., Fiore, D.: Vector commitments and their applications. In: Kurosawa, K., Hanaoka, G. (eds.) PKC 2013. LNCS, vol. 7778, pp. 55–72. Springer, Heidelberg (2013). https://doi.org/10.1007/978-3-642-36362-7_5

5. Catalano, D., Fiore, D., Messina, M.: Zero-knowledge sets with short proofs. In: Smart, N. (ed.) EUROCRYPT 2008. LNCS, vol. 4965, pp. 433–450. Springer, Heidelberg (2008). https://doi.org/10.1007/978-3-540-78967-3_25

6. Catalano, D., Fiore, D., Nizzardo, L.: On the security notions for homomorphic signatures. In: Preneel, B., Vercauteren, F. (eds.) ACNS 2018. LNCS, vol. 10892, pp. 183–201. Springer, Cham (2018). https://doi.org/10.1007/978-3-319-93387-0_10

7. Catalano, D., Fiore, D., Warinschi, B.: Homomorphic signatures with efficient verification for polynomial functions. In: Garay, J.A., Gennaro, R. (eds.) CRYPTO 2014, Part I. LNCS, vol. 8616, pp. 371–389. Springer, Heidelberg (2014). https://doi.org/10.1007/978-3-662-44371-2_21

8. Catalano, D., Marcedone, A., Puglisi, O.: Authenticating computation on groups: new homomorphic primitives and applications. In: Sarkar, P., Iwata, T. (eds.) ASIACRYPT 2014, Part II. LNCS, vol. 8874, pp. 193–212. Springer, Heidelberg (2014). https://doi.org/10.1007/978-3-662-45608-8_11

9. Escala, A., Herold, G., Kiltz, E., Ràfols, C., Villar, J.: An algebraic framework for Diffie-Hellman assumptions. In: Canetti, R., Garay, J.A. (eds.) CRYPTO 2013, Part II. LNCS, vol. 8043, pp. 129–147. Springer, Heidelberg (2013). https://doi.org/10.1007/978-3-642-40084-1_8

10. Gennaro, R., Gentry, C., Parno, B., Raykova, M.: Quadratic span programs and succinct NIZKs without PCPs. In: Johansson, T., Nguyen, P.Q. (eds.) EUROCRYPT 2013. LNCS, vol. 7881, pp. 626–645. Springer, Heidelberg (2013). https://doi.org/10.1007/978-3-642-38348-9_37

11. Gennaro, R., Wichs, D.: Fully homomorphic message authenticators. In: Sako, K., Sarkar, P. (eds.) ASIACRYPT 2013, Part II. LNCS, vol. 8270, pp. 301–320. Springer, Heidelberg (2013). https://doi.org/10.1007/978-3-642-42045-0_16

12. Gentry, C., Wichs, D.: Separating succinct non-interactive arguments from all falsifiable assumptions. In: Fortnow, L., Vadhan, S.P. (eds.) 43rd ACM STOC, pp. 99–108. ACM Press (2011). https://doi.org/10.1145/1993636.1993651

13. Gorbunov, S., Vaikuntanathan, V., Wichs, D.: Leveled fully homomorphic signatures from standard lattices. In: Servedio, R.A., Rubinfeld, R. (eds.) 47th ACM STOC, pp. 469–477. ACM Press (2015). https://doi.org/10.1145/2746539.2746576

14. Groth, J., Kohlweiss, M., Maller, M., Meiklejohn, S., Miers, I.: Updatable and universal common reference strings with applications to zk-SNARKs. In: Shacham, H., Boldyreva, A. (eds.) CRYPTO 2018, Part III. LNCS, vol. 10993, pp. 698–728. Springer, Cham (2018). https://doi.org/10.1007/978-3-319-96878-0_24

15. Karchmer, M., Wigderson, A.: On span programs. In: Proceedings of the Eighth Annual Structure in Complexity Theory Conference, pp. 102–111 (1993)

16. Kate, A., Zaverucha, G.M., Goldberg, I.: Constant-size commitments to polynomials and their applications. In: Abe, M. (ed.) ASIACRYPT 2010. LNCS, vol. 6477, pp. 177–194. Springer, Heidelberg (2010). https://doi.org/10.1007/978-3-642-17373-8_11

17. Katsumata, S., Nishimaki, R., Yamada, S., Yamakawa, T.: Designated verifier/prover and preprocessing NIZKs from Diffie-Hellman assumptions. In: Ishai, Y., Rijmen, V. (eds.) EUROCRYPT 2019, Part II. LNCS, vol. 11477, pp. 622–651. Springer, Cham (2019). https://doi.org/10.1007/978-3-030-17656-3_22

18. Lai, R.W.F., Malavolta, G.: Subvector commitments with application to succinct arguments. In: Boldyreva, A., Micciancio, D. (eds.) CRYPTO 2019, Part I. LNCS, vol. 11692, pp. 530–560. Springer, Cham (2019). https://doi.org/10.1007/978-3-030-26948-7_19

19. Lewko, A., Okamoto, T., Sahai, A., Takashima, K., Waters, B.: Fully secure functional encryption: attribute-based encryption and (hierarchical) inner product encryption. In: Gilbert, H. (ed.) EUROCRYPT 2010. LNCS, vol. 6110, pp. 62–91. Springer, Heidelberg (2010). https://doi.org/10.1007/978-3-642-13190-5_4

20. Lewko, A., Waters, B.: Unbounded HIBE and attribute-based encryption. In: Paterson, K.G. (ed.) EUROCRYPT 2011. LNCS, vol. 6632, pp. 547–567. Springer, Heidelberg (2011). https://doi.org/10.1007/978-3-642-20465-4_30

21. Libert, B., Peters, T., Joye, M., Yung, M.: Linearly homomorphic structure-preserving signatures and their applications. In: Canetti, R., Garay, J.A. (eds.) CRYPTO 2013, Part II. LNCS, vol. 8043, pp. 289–307. Springer, Heidelberg (2013). https://doi.org/10.1007/978-3-642-40084-1_17

22. Libert, B., Ramanna, S.C., Yung, M.: Functional commitment schemes: from polynomial commitments to pairing-based accumulators from simple assumptions. In: Chatzigiannakis, I., Mitzenmacher, M., Rabani, Y., Sangiorgi, D. (eds.) ICALP 2016. LIPIcs, vol. 55, pp. 30:1–30:14. Schloss Dagstuhl (2016). https://doi.org/10.4230/LIPIcs.ICALP.2016.30

23. Libert, B., Yung, M.: Concise mercurial vector commitments and independent zero-knowledge sets with short proofs. In: Micciancio, D. (ed.) TCC 2010. LNCS, vol. 5978, pp. 499–517. Springer, Heidelberg (2010). https://doi.org/10.1007/978-3-642-11799-2_30

24. Lipmaa, H., Pavlyk, K.: Succinct functional commitment for a large class of arithmetic circuits. In: Moriai, S., Wang, H. (eds.) ASIACRYPT 2020, Part III. LNCS, vol. 12493, pp. 686–716. Springer, Cham (2020). https://doi.org/10.1007/978-3-030-64840-4_23

25. Peikert, C., Pepin, Z., Sharp, C.: Vector and functional commitments from lattices. In: Nissim, K., Waters, B. (eds.) TCC 2021, Part III. LNCS, vol. 13044, pp. 480–511. Springer, Cham (2021). https://doi.org/10.1007/978-3-030-90456-2_16

26. Waters, B.: Ciphertext-policy attribute-based encryption: an expressive, efficient, and provably secure realization. In: Catalano, D., Fazio, N., Gennaro, R., Nicolosi, A. (eds.) PKC 2011. LNCS, vol. 6571, pp. 53–70. Springer, Heidelberg (2011). https://doi.org/10.1007/978-3-642-19379-8_4

Linear-Map Vector Commitments and Their Practical Applications

Matteo Campanelli[1]([✉]), Anca Nitulescu[1], Carla Ràfols[2],
Alexandros Zacharakis[2], and Arantxa Zapico[2]

[1] Protocol Labs, San Francisco, USA
{matteo,anca}@protocol.ai
[2] Universitat Pompeu Fabra, Barcelona, Spain
{carla.rafols,alexandros.zacharakis,arantxa.zapico}@upf.edu

Abstract. Vector commitments (VC) are a cryptographic primitive that allows one to commit to a vector and then "open" some of its positions efficiently. Vector commitments are increasingly recognized as a central tool to scale highly decentralized networks of large size and whose content is dynamic. In this work, we examine the demands on the properties that a vector commitment should satisfy in the light of the emerging plethora of practical applications and propose new constructions that improve the state-of-the-art in several dimensions and offer new tradeoffs. We also propose a unifying framework that captures several constructions and we show how to generically achieve some properties from more basic ones. On the practical side, we focus on building efficient schemes that do not require a new trusted setup (we can reuse existing ceremonies for other pairing-based schemes, such as "powers of tau" run by real-world systems such as Zcash or Filecoin).

1 Introduction

Vector commitment schemes [9,22] (or VC) allow a party to commit to a vector $\mathbf{v}$ through a short digest and then open some of its elements guaranteeing *position binding*[1] (one should not be able to open a commitment at position i to two different values $v_i \neq v_i'$). For this primitive to be interesting the proof of opening—or just "opening"—should be of size sublinear in m, the size of the committed vector. A vector commitment with *subvector opening* also supports a short opening for arbitrary *subsets* of positions I (rather than individual ones only). More specifically this opening should be of size independent, not only of m, but of $|I|$. We denote commitment schemes with such property as SVC [20] (also called VC with batch opening in [4]).

---

[1] For the applications considered in this work, hiding properties are not necessary. In particular, our commitments are deterministic.

Arantxa Zapico has been funded by a Protocol Labs PhD Fellowship PL-RGP1-2021-062. Alexandros Zacharakis has been partially funded by Protocol Labs Research Grant PL-RGP1-2021-048.

S. Agrawal and D. Lin (Eds.): ASIACRYPT 2022, LNCS 13794, pp. 189–219, 2022.
https://doi.org/10.1007/978-3-031-22972-5_7

Functional Vector Commitments, first introduced by Libert, Ramanna and Yung in [21], capture the ability to compute commitments to vectors and later perform openings of linear functions (inner-products) $f : \mathbb{F}^m \to \mathbb{F}^n$ of these vectors, for some field $\mathbb{F}$.

Both vector commitments with subvector openings and functional commitments for inner-products can be captured as vector commitments with openings for a more general class of function families, linear maps. Lai and Malavolta [20] were the first to introduce Linear Map Commitments (LMC). In such a scheme, the prover is able to open the commitment to some vector $\mathbf{v}$ to the output of multiple linear functions or, equivalently, to the output of one linear-map $f : \mathbb{F}^m \to \mathbb{F}^n$, by producing a single short proof. In this work, we revisit Lai and Malavolta [20] LMC notion and augment it to a full-featured vector commitment generic definition that recovers all previously-defined schemes and more. We call our primitive Linear Map Vector Commitment and use LVC for short[2].

1.1 Motivation for Better Vector Commitments

Vector commitments are very useful to scale highly decentralized networks of large size and whose content is dynamic [4,7,10,15] (such dynamic content can be the state of a blockchain, amount stored on a wallet, the value of a file in a decentralized storage network, etc.). Beyond the basic requirement that openings should be efficient, in this work we also discuss how to achieve some additional properties of LVC. We discuss some of the most prominent applications of LVC to motivate and justify the importance of these properties in practice.

Verifiable Databases. One of the applications that can be significantly improved by Vector Commitments is Verifiable Databases (VDB). In this setting, a client outsources the storage of a database to a server while keeping the ability to access and change some of its records, i.e. query functions of the data and update some of the data and ensure the server does not tamper with the data. Solutions using (binding) commitment schemes provide security but not efficiency in such a setting. A popular instantiation that achieves both of them is a Merkle tree [23], but this is not expressive enough to allow for functional openings.

For a VC scheme to be the ideal solution for VDB application, we require it to additionally support efficient updates and expressive openings. For example, an LVC scheme that allows the client to update records of the database in sublinear time and to verify linear-map queries at almost the same cost as simple position openings is a great improvement over current solutions.

Stateless Cryptocurrency. A recent application that motivated more efficient constructions of VC schemes is *stateless cryptocurrency*, i.e. a payment system based on a distributed ledger where neither validators of transactions nor system users need to store the full ledger state. The ideal vector commitment scheme

---

[2] We prefer LVC rather than LMC to emphasize the Vector Commitment aspect of our notion.

that provides the best trade-off between storage, bandwidth, and computation in this setting should have all of the following properties: it must have a small commitment size, short proofs, efficient computation for openings and it should allow for proof updates and for aggregation to minimise communication in the transactions and *maintainability* for the proofs, that allows updating all pre-stored proofs in sublinear time.

Proof of Space. Proof of Space (PoS) is a protocol that allows miners (storage providers) to convince the network that they are dedicating physical storage over time in an efficient way. In a nutshell, a miner commits to a file (data) that uses a specified amount of disk space and then the miner proves that it continues to store the data by answering to recurring audits that consist of random spot-checks. A PoS construction based on vector commitments, as described in [13], requires short opening proofs for subvectors to be stored in a blockchain, cross-commitments aggregation techniques and the possibility to implement space-time tradeoffs to reduce the proving time for the miner (ideally sublinear in the size of the vector).

"Caching" Optimizations. In some applications, e.g. when performing HTTP queries, clients use the so-called *prefetching*[3] and receive from a server not only the values of interest but other related values that could potentially be queried in the near future (e.g., values in a neighboring range of the queried values). Vector commitments with efficient proofs for special ("caching") subset openings allow to add verifiability to such queries in a way that does not affect the speed of the server since the proving procedure for a bigger subset is close or the same as for individual positions.

1.2 Desired Properties and Limitations

At the very least a basic LVC should be *efficient* (small proof size and low opening/verifying computational needs). Obviously, the same design goals as with other cryptographic protocols apply, i.e. ideally one would like to prove security under as standard assumptions as possible.

Reusable setup refers to the common reference string that many pairing-based schemes use as public parameters. Ideally, one would like to have a transparent setup (consisting of uniformly distributed elements) that does not rely on any trusted parameter generation. It is common to sacrifice this goal for efficiency and settle for a trusted setup (producing a SRS, or structured reference string) that can be generated in a ceremony. But such ceremonies are complicated to implement[4], so it is interesting to design LVC that do not have special SRS distributions and can reuse existing setups for other primitives.

---

[3] https://developer.mozilla.org/en-US/docs/Web/HTTP/Link_prefetching_FAQ.

[4] This remains true even if many setups are updatable [18] and they can be generated and updated non-interactively in a secure way as long as one party is honest. There might be issues if not enough parties participate in generating the SRS or updates are not properly validated.

Expressivity refers to the opening possibilities. One would like VC to be as expressive as possible, meaning that it should be possible to open to functions of the vector as general as possible (subvector openings, linear or arbitrary functions).

Proof Aggregation captures the ability to "pack" two or more proofs together obtaining a new proof for their combined claims (e.g. $\mathbf{f}(\mathbf{v}) = y$ and $\mathbf{f}'(\mathbf{v}) = y'$). This should be done without knowledge of the opening of the vector and aggregation cost should be sublinear in the vector length. Importantly, the resulting proof should not significantly grow each time we perform an aggregation. *Onehop* aggregation allows only to aggregate fresh proofs. Ideally, one would also want to aggregate already aggregated proofs.

Updatability allows to efficiently update opening proofs: if C is a commitment to $\mathbf{v}$ and a position needs to be updated resulting in a new commitment C', an updatable VC must provide a method to update an opening π_f for a function f that is valid for C into a new opening for the same function that is valid for the new commitment C'. The new opening should be computed by only knowing the portion of the vector that is supposed to change and in time faster than recomputing the opening from scratch.

Maintainability aims at amortizing the proving costs in systems where committed values have a long life span and evolve over time. This is achieved by means of dedicated memory to reduce the computation time needed to open proofs. Concretely, the property requires that (1) one can efficiently store some values to reduce the cost of computing any individual openings (2) after updating a single position of the committed vector, it should be possible to update all proofs in time sublinear in the size of the vector (less than computing a single proof from scratch in some cases).

Homomorphic properties apply to commitments as well as to proofs. An LVC has homomorphic commitments if it is possible to meaningfully combine commitments *without knowing their openings*: that is, from commitments C_1 and C_2 to $\mathbf{v}_1$ and $\mathbf{v}_2$, any party must be able to compute a commitment to $\alpha \mathbf{v}_1 + \beta \mathbf{v}_2$ for any $\alpha, \beta \in \mathbb{F}$. The scheme has homomorphic openings if it is possible to derive a proof that $f(\mathbf{v}_1 + \mathbf{v}_2) = \mathbf{y}_1 + \mathbf{y}_2$ from proofs for the claims $f(\mathbf{v}_1) = \mathbf{y}_1$ and $f(\mathbf{v}_2) = \mathbf{y}_2$. Finally, a vector commitment scheme has homomorphic proofs when it is possible to combine proofs of statements for different functions but same vector. As we will see, this property is interesting for its implications.

1.3   Our Contributions

Theoretical Advances. On the theoretical frontier, we unify previous definitions and augment them with additional properties. The basic notion we use is Linear Map Vector Commitments (LVC) and is inspired by the work of Lai and Malavolta [20]. We then define additional properties on top of this definition and explore their relations. Specifically, we augment this notion with *updatability* and aggregation properties, including a novel notion -*unbounded aggregation*-capturing the ability to aggregate already aggregated proofs but relaxing incremental aggregation [7] in the sense that the verifier is allowed to do work linear in the number of aggregation hops (i.e. aggregation is "history" dependent), also, disaggregation is not possible. We show that having additional homomorphic properties is highly desirable, by arguing that any LVC that satisfies them: (1) can be augmented with unbounded aggregation as well as updatability; (2) can support general linear map openings (i.e. for any $f : \mathbb{F}^m \to \mathbb{F}^n$) as long as it supports inner product openings (i.e. for $f' : \mathbb{F}^m \to \mathbb{F}$). This allows us to focus on efficient constructions for inner products with homomorphic properties.

VC Constructions. First, we present two pairing-based LVC constructions for inner products based on the properties of monomial and Lagrange polynomial basis and prove that they satisfy all the relevant homomorphic properties to obtain unbounded aggregation and support general linear maps. In terms of expressivity, these constructions generalize previous work [26,27] by supporting linear functions instead of only position or subvector openings. VC for this class of functions are core components of important primitives such as arguments of knowledge for Inner Product (IP) relations or aggregation arguments [11].

Second, we present two novel maintainable constructions by exploiting the tensor structure of multivariate and univariate polynomials. These constructions allow a stronger, more flexible form of maintainability: they support an arbitrary memory/time trade-off for openings, meaning that one can decide how much memory it wants to use to reduce the opening time.

The multivariate case is a generalization of Hyperproofs [26] in several dimensions. Roughly speaking maintanability is achieved in Hyperproofs by constructing a binary tree of proofs where at the leaves there are the values of individual positions. We present a single construction that can be instantiated in several ways (recovering Hyperproofs as a special case) with these features: (i) the tree can be of any arity, so proofs are shorter[5]; (ii) the leaves can be commitments for any LVC and not only individual openings, to achieve a fully flexible trade-off. As a result of (ii), the scheme is more expressive (as it can support openings to linear functions/subvector openins at leaf level if the underlying commitment supports it).

The univariate construction presents a similar generalization of previous work by [28] but it has the additional feature that the setup is independent of the trade-off, and can be decided by the prover on the fly.

Practical Improvements. As in some applications like Proof of Space, the subset of opened positions is not very meaningful and its distribution is expected to be known in advance, we study how to improve verification efficiency for certain special subsets I openings in our inner-product constructions. For some structured sets I, we achieve a verifier that performs half of the work it does for arbitrary sets J of the same size in the Lagrange construction, and only a constant number of group operations in the one that uses the monomial basis.

---

[5] If one uses the Inner Pairing Product argument of Bünz et al. [6] on top of PST commitments as suggested in Hyperproofs the difference in proof size is not so relevant, but IPP will be much cheaper to run.

Table 1. Comparison of our LVCs with other aggregatable VC schemes (aggSVC) designed for Stateless Cryptocurrencies and Proof of Space applications. All schemes have $O(1)$-sized proofs that verify in $O(1)$ time and can update commitments in $O(1)$ time.

VC Scheme	Setup	Aggregation	Updates	Assumption	Functional Opening	Special Sets Opening (size n)
PoS aggSVC [7]	Trusted	Incremental Same-Com	hint	RSA	SVC	$O(n)$
Pointproofs [15]	Trusted	One-hop Cross-Com	key	pairings	×	$O(n)$
Stateless aggSVC [27]	Trusted	One-hop Same-Com	key	pairings	SVC	$O(1)$
Our Lagrange LVC	Reusable	UnboundedCross-Com	key	AGM	LVC	$O(1)$
Our Monomial LVC	Reusable	UnboundedCross-Com	keyless	AGM	LVC	$O(1)$

Table 2. Comparison of our schemes with other maintainable VC. We consider vectors of dimension $m = k \cdot m'$ where m' is the amount of memory dedicated for storing proofs. All schemes are aggregatable using generic techniques, SNARKs or Inner Pairing Products [6]. All times/sizes omit the dependence on the security parameter λ. We omit constant additive terms from proof sizes. In the multivariate construction, ℓ refers to a constant parameter.

VC Scheme	Setup	Homomorphic	Aggregation	$|\pi|$	Prove	OpenAll	UpdateAll
Merkle Trees	Transparent	×	SNARK	$\log m$	$O(k)$	$O(m)$	$O(k + \log m')$
Hyperproofs [26]	Trusted	✓	IPP	$\log m$	$O(k)$	$O(m \log m')$	$O(\log m')$
Our Multivariate LVC	Trusted	✓	IPP	$\log_\ell m'$	$O(k)$	$O(m \log m')$	$O(\log m')$
Our Univariate LVC	Reusable	✓	IPP	$\log m'$	$O(k)$	$O(m \log m')$	$O(\log m')$

Second, we mitigate the challenges of deploying these constructions due to their need of a trusted setup. With the exception of the multivariate variant of the maintainable construction, all our constructions can reuse trusted setups such as "powers of tau" that were run for pairing-based SNARK schemes used in real-world applications[6], as opposed to for example [15], in which a certain middle power of τ needs to be missing in the SRS (Tables 1 and 2).

In the full version of this work we demonstrate the practical benefits of our special subset construction by providing an implementation and comparisons with current solutions.

1.4 Related Work

Vector commitments were fully formalized in [9] and two first constructions were proposed under standard, constant-size, assumptions: CDH in bilinear groups and RSA respectively. Many follow-up works built on these constructions to obtain better efficiency and more properties such as subvector openings, functional openings, aggregation, updates and variants of these. A number of constructions [4,7] use the properties of hidden order groups to achieve constructions with attractive features such as constant size parameters or incremental aggregation but are concretely less efficient than pairing-based constructions.

---

[6] E.g., the one used by ZCash. https://z.cash or and Filecoin [12].

Merkle trees are quite efficient and only need a transparent setup. They also offer natural time-memory tradeoffs due to their tree structure. Nevertheless, VC schemes based on bilinear groups are more expressive in terms of openings, have homomorphic properties, allow for efficient updates for the proofs and aggregation mechanisms, so they are becoming an interesting alternative.

Expressivity. VC were generalized by Libert et al. [21], who formalize the notion of functional commitments (FC). They construct vector commitments with openings to linear-forms of the vector based on the Diffie-Hellman exponent assumption over pairing groups. Later, Lai and Malavolta [20] introduce subvector openings and show applications to building succinct-arguments of knowledge (similar applications were shown by [4]) in the bilinear group setting. They also generalize the notion of SVCs to allow the prover to reveal arbitrary linear maps computed over the committed vector. Previously, only Functional VC for single-output linear functions were proposed which did not account for provers that want to reveal multiple locations or function outputs of the committed vector in a concise way.

Updatability. Vector commitments that allow for updates are useful in applications such as stateless cryptocurrencies. A weak variant of updatability requires the algorithms that update the commitment and the opening to take as input an opening for the position in which the vector update occurs called *hints*. Recent RSA-based constructions are hint-updatable [4,7]. Compared to hint updates, key-updates only need fixed update keys corresponding to the updated positions. Schemes based on bilinear groups require such fixed keys, and no extra information about the change made in the vector in order to update.

Aggregation. Vector Commitments with an additional aggregation property are very appealing for blockchain applications for their even shorter proofs of opening. Campanelli et al. [7] showed two constructions of incrementally aggregatable SVCs, that have constant-size parameters and work over groups of unknown order. Unfortunately, the practical efficiency of these constructions is still not suffiecient for their deployment in real-world systems.

Gorbunov et al. [15] show how to extend the VC scheme of [22] to allow for cross-commitment aggregation. Like our constructions, they assume the Algebraic Group Model (AGM) [14] in bilinear groups and a random oracle. Their final SVC requires public parameters whose size is linear in the size of the committed vector, while cross-commitment aggregation allow for splitting up a long vector into shorter ones and simply aggregate the proofs. However, this approach allows only for one-hop aggregation, meaning that already aggregated proofs cannot be reused in further aggregations by external nodes.

Tomescu et al. [27] showed how to realize an *updatable* SVC with one-hop aggregation from bilinear groups. Their scheme has linear-sized public parameters, and it supports commitment updates, proof updates from a static linear-sized update key tied only to the updated position, in contrast with the dynamic update *hints* required by related works.

Maintainability. Apart from Merkle tree based Vector Commitments which are known to be maintainable, Srinivasan et al. [26] show that the multilinear PST polynomial commitment [24] can be turned to a maintainable VC construction. Pre-computing all (single-position) opening proofs is done in quasilinear time (contrary to the trivial quadratic time) and updating all proofs after a (single position) vector update needs only logarithmic time. Contrary to Merkle tree based approaches, the scheme has *homomorphic* properties. Furthermore, due to its algebraic structure, it supports one-hop aggregation through generic means, namely, Inner Pairing Product Arguments [6], albeit with a concretely expensive proving computation. Tomescu et al. [28] add the same attribute to KZG polynomial commitment schemes, resulting in an univariate construction with the same properties.

2   Preliminaries

Bilinear Groups. A bilinear group is given by a description $\mathsf{gk} = (p, \mathbb{G}_1, \mathbb{G}_2, \mathbb{G}_T, e)$ with additive notation such that p is prime, so $\mathbb{F} = \mathbb{F}_p$ is a field. $\mathbb{G}_1, \mathbb{G}_2$ are cyclic (additive) groups of prime order p. We use the notation $[a]_1, [b]_2, [c]_t$ for elements in $\mathbb{G}_1, \mathbb{G}_2$ and $\mathbb{G}_T$ respectively. $e : \mathbb{G}_1 \times \mathbb{G}_2 \to \mathbb{G}_T$ is a bilinear asymmetric map (pairing), which means that $\forall a, b \in \mathbb{Z}_p, e([a]_1, [b]_2) := [ab]_t$. We implicitly have that $[1]_t := e([1]_1, [1]_2)$ generates $\mathbb{G}_T$. We use $[a]_{1,2}$ to refer to 2 group elements $[a]_1 \in \mathbb{G}_1, [a]_2 \in \mathbb{G}_2$. In our constructions, we denote by $\mathcal{G}(p)$ the algorithm that, given as input the prime value p, outputs a description $\mathsf{gk} = (p, \mathbb{G}_1, \mathbb{G}_2, \mathbb{G}_T, e)$.

Algebraic Group Model (AGM). The algebraic group model [14] lies between the standard model and the stronger generic group model. In AGM, we consider only so-called algebraic adversaries. Such adversaries have direct access to group elements and, in particular, can use their bit representation, like in the standard model. However, these adversaries are assumed to output new group elements only by applying the group operation to received group elements (like in the generic group model). This requirement is formalized as follows: Suppose an adversary $\mathcal{A}$ is given some group elements $[x_1]_1 \ldots [x_m]_1 \in \mathbb{G}_1$. Then, for every new group element $[z]_1 \in \mathbb{G}_1$ that the adversary outputs, it must also output $z_1 \ldots z_m \in \mathbb{F}$ such that $[z]_1 = \sum_{i=1}^m [z_i x_i]_1$.

3   Definitions: Linear-Map Vector Commitments

In the following, we define what we call Linear-map Vector Commitments (LVC) schemes. Notably, this definition has been introduced by Lai and Malavolta in [20] (except that there the name is *Linear Map Commitments*) to capture further functionalities of vector commitments, whose definition before only account for proofs of *position openings* (Vector Commitments) or more generally *subvector openings* (Sub-vector commitments). We introduce the definition and security properties of LVC. Importantly, we do not consider the hiding property as for our applications all vectors are public.

Linear-Map Vector Commitment. A linear-map vector commitment scheme for function families $\mathcal{F} \subset \{f : \mathcal{M}^m \to \mathcal{M}^n\}$ is a tuple of PPT algorithms (LVC.KeyGen, LVC.Commit, LVC.Open, LVC, Vf) that work as follows:

LVC.KeyGen$(1^\lambda, \mathcal{F}) \to$ (prk, vrk): The setup algorithm takes the security parameter λ, a family of functions $\mathcal{F}$ implicitly defining the message space $\mathcal{M}$, and the maximum vector length $m = \mathrm{poly}(\lambda)$, and outputs a pair of keys (prk, vrk).

LVC.Commit(prk, $\mathbf{v}$) $\to$ (C, aux): On input the proving key prk, and a vector $\mathbf{v} = (v_1, v_2 \ldots, v_m) \in \mathcal{M}^m$, returns a commitment C and auxiliary information aux. This algorithm is *deterministic*.

LVC.Open(prk, aux, f, $\mathbf{y}$) $\to \pi_f$: Takes as input prk, the auxiliary information aux, a function $f \in \mathcal{F}$, and a claimed result $\mathbf{y} \in \mathcal{M}^n$. It outputs a proof π_f that $f(\mathbf{v}) = \mathbf{y}$.

LVC.Vf(vrk, C, f, $\mathbf{y}$, π_f) $\to 0/1$: Takes as input the verification key vrk, C, function f, $\mathbf{y} \in \mathcal{M}^n$, and proof π_f. It accepts or rejects.

A LVC scheme must satisfy the following properties:

Definition 1 (LVC correctness). *An* LVC *scheme is* perfectly correct *if for all $\lambda \in \mathbb{N}$, for any family of functions $\mathcal{F} \subset \{f : \mathcal{M}^m \to \mathcal{M}^n\}$ and any $\mathbf{v} \in \mathcal{M}^m$,*

$$\Pr\left[\mathrm{LVC.Vf}(\mathrm{vrk}, C, f, \mathbf{y}, \pi_f) = 1 \,\middle|\, \begin{array}{l} (\mathrm{prk}, \mathrm{vrk}) \leftarrow \mathrm{LVC.KeyGen}(1^\lambda, \mathcal{F}) \\ (C, \mathrm{aux}) \leftarrow \mathrm{LVC.Commit}(\mathrm{prk}, \mathbf{v}) \\ \pi_f \leftarrow \mathrm{LVC.Open}(\mathrm{prk}, \mathrm{aux}, f, \mathbf{y}) \end{array}\right] = 1.$$

Definition 2 (LVC (strong) function binding). *A linear map commitment* LVC *satisfies strong function binding if, for any* PPT *adversary $\mathcal{A}$, for all $\lambda \in \mathbb{N}$, for all integers $K \in \mathrm{poly}(\lambda)$, and for any family of functions $\mathcal{F}$, the following probability is negligible in λ:*

$$\Pr\left[\begin{array}{c} \forall k \in [K]: \\ \mathrm{LVC.Vf}(\mathrm{vrk}, C, f_k, \mathbf{y}_k, \pi_{f_k}) = 1 \\ \land \ \nexists\, \mathbf{v} \in \mathcal{M}^m \ s.\ t. \\ \forall k \in [K]: \ f_k(\mathbf{v}) = \mathbf{y}_k \end{array} \,\middle|\, \begin{array}{c} (\mathrm{prk}, \mathrm{vrk}) \leftarrow \mathrm{LVC.KeyGen}(1^\lambda, \mathcal{F}) \\ \left(C, \{f_k, \mathbf{y}_k, \pi_{f_k}\}_{k \in [K]}\right) \leftarrow \mathcal{A}(\mathrm{prk}, \mathrm{vrk}) \end{array}\right]$$

The definition above can be relaxed to hold only for *honestly-generated* commitments C, raising to the *weak function binding* notion. In the weak definition, the adversary $\mathcal{A}$ returns a vector $\mathbf{v}$ while the commitment C is computed via LVC.Commit. In this work, constructions are proven strong function binding.

3.1 Homomorphic Properties for LVC

Homomorphic Commitments. Linear-map vector commitment schemes that satisfy homomorphic commitments allow to combine commitments of two vectors into a single one of their sum (or any linear combination). Namely, for all λ, and $(\mathsf{vrk}, \mathsf{prk}) \leftarrow \mathsf{LVC.KeyGen}(1^\lambda, \mathcal{F})$, if $(\mathsf{C}_1, \mathsf{aux}_1) \leftarrow \mathsf{LVC.Commit}(\mathsf{prk}, \mathbf{v}_1)$ and $(\mathsf{C}_2, \mathsf{aux}_2) \leftarrow \mathsf{LVC.Commit}(\mathsf{prk}, \mathbf{v}_2)$, then $\tilde{\mathsf{C}} = (\alpha \mathsf{C}_1 + \beta \mathsf{C}_2)$ is a valid commitment to $\tilde{\mathbf{v}} = (\alpha \mathbf{v}_1 + \beta \mathbf{v}_2)$ for any $\alpha, \beta \in \mathcal{M}$.

In this work, we are particularly interested in LVC that also have *homomorphic proofs* for different functions applied to a committed vector and *homomorphic openings* for the same function applied to different initial vectors.

Homomorphic Proofs. An LVC scheme has *homomorphic proofs* if it allows recombine two proofs π_1, π_2 corresponding to linear maps f_1, f_2 into a new proof $\tilde{\pi}$ that opens to a linear combination of f_1 and f_2 applied to the same committed vector. Namely, for all λ, $\mathcal{F} \subset \{f : \mathcal{M}^m \to \mathcal{M}^n\}$ and all vectors $\mathbf{v} \in \mathcal{M}^m$, and $(\mathsf{vrk}, \mathsf{prk}) \leftarrow \mathsf{LVC.KeyGen}(1^\lambda, \mathcal{F})$, $(\mathsf{C}, \mathsf{aux}) \leftarrow \mathsf{LVC.Commit}(\mathsf{prk}, \mathbf{v})$, if $\pi_1 \leftarrow \mathsf{LVC.Open}(\mathsf{prk}, \mathsf{aux}, f_1, \mathbf{y}_1)$ and $\pi_2 \leftarrow \mathsf{LVC.Open}(\mathsf{prk}, \mathsf{aux}, f_2, \mathbf{y}_2)$, then for all $\alpha, \beta \in \mathcal{M}$:

$$\tilde{\pi} = (\alpha \pi_1 + \beta \pi_2) \text{ verifies } \mathsf{LVC.Vf}(\mathsf{vrk}, \mathsf{C}, \tilde{f} = (\alpha f_1 + \beta f_2), \tilde{\mathbf{y}} = (\alpha \mathbf{y}_1 + \beta \mathbf{y}_2), \tilde{\pi}) = 1.$$

Homomorphic Openings. An LVC scheme has *homomorphic openings* if we can combine opening proofs for the same linear-map f applied to two different vectors $\mathbf{v}_1$ and $\mathbf{v}_2$ to obtain a new proof of opening $\tilde{\pi}$ that verifies with respect to the linear combination $\tilde{\mathsf{C}}$ of the two initial commitments $\mathsf{C}_1, \mathsf{C}_2$ and show the result of $\mathbf{f}$ applied to the linear combination of the vectors $\mathbf{v}_1$ and $\mathbf{v}_2$.

More formally, for all λ, $\mathcal{F} \subset \{f : \mathcal{M}^m \to \mathcal{M}^n\}$, vectors $\mathbf{v}_1, \mathbf{v}_2 \in \mathcal{M}^m$, and $(\mathsf{vrk}, \mathsf{prk}) \leftarrow \mathsf{LVC.KeyGen}(1^\lambda, \mathcal{F})$, if $\pi_1 \leftarrow \mathsf{LVC.Open}(\mathsf{prk}, \mathsf{aux}_1, f, \mathbf{y}_1)$ and $\pi_2 \leftarrow \mathsf{LVC.Open}(\mathsf{prk}, \mathsf{aux}_2, f, \mathbf{y}_2)$, where $(\mathsf{C}_1, \mathsf{aux}_2) \leftarrow \mathsf{LVC.Commit}(\mathsf{prk}, \mathbf{v}_1)$ and $(\mathsf{C}_2, \mathsf{aux}_2) \leftarrow \mathsf{LVC.Commit}(\mathsf{prk}, \mathbf{v}_2)$, then for all $\alpha, \beta \in \mathcal{M}$:

$$\tilde{\pi} = (\alpha \pi_1 + \beta \pi_2) \text{ verifies } \mathsf{LVC.Vf}(\mathsf{vrk}, \tilde{\mathsf{C}} = (\alpha \mathsf{C}_1 + \beta \mathsf{C}_2), f, \tilde{\mathbf{y}} = (\alpha \mathbf{y}_1 + \beta \mathbf{y}_2), \tilde{\pi}) = 1.$$

4   Generic Constructions from Homomorphic Proofs

Many natural schemes (such as [15,27], PST commitments or our constructions in Sect. 5) have homomorphic proofs or openings. This motivates us to consider generic constructions that enhance any LVC scheme with homomorphic properties. We start by defining the notions of unbounded aggregation for same and cross-commitments and then we show how to add such properties to LVC schemes that have homomorphic proofs for the former and, additionally, homomorphic commitments for the latter.

4.1   New Notion: Unbounded Aggregation

The intuition for our definition is that, given t proofs, commitments or openings, we can aggregate them by performing a linear combination with random coefficients. Importantly, these coefficients have to be chosen after the claims are fixed and for that we rely on the RO model, as it is often the case for aggregation in the literature.

In our work, we go a step further and show how this procedure can be done over already aggregated proofs. Actually, aggregating *already aggregated* proofs consists off just sampling new coefficients and using them for fresh linear combinations. Importantly, the verifier needs to have access to the aggregation history: it has to recompute the coefficient corresponding to each initial proof π, which is the product of all the coefficients used in the aggregations it was involved in. Note that this also adds a small overhead to the verifier: it makes a linear (in the number of aggregation "hops") number of hash computations.

Example for Same-Commitment Aggregation: Consider vector $\mathbf{v}$ committed in C, functions f_1, f_2 and f_3; let π_1, π_2 and π_3 be proofs that $f_1(\mathbf{v}) = \mathbf{y}_1$, $f_2(\mathbf{v}) = \mathbf{y}_2$ and $f_3(\mathbf{v}) = \mathbf{y}_3$. An aggregated proof for $f_2(\mathbf{v}) = \mathbf{y}_2$, $f_3(\mathbf{v}) = \mathbf{y}_3$, would be $\pi_1^* = \pi_2 + \gamma_1\pi_3$, for $\gamma_1 = \mathsf{H}(C, \{(f_2, \mathbf{y}_2), (f_3, \mathbf{y}_3)\})$. In a second step, we can aggregate a proof that $f_1(\mathbf{v}) = \mathbf{y}_1$, by performing $\pi_2^* = \pi_1 + \gamma_2\pi_1^*$, for $\gamma_2 = \mathsf{H}(C, (f_1, \mathbf{y}_1), \gamma_1)$. At the verification step, the verifier would reconstruct the coefficients of each initial proof in π_2^*. For instance, $\delta_1 = 1$, $\delta_2 = \gamma_1\gamma_2$, $\delta_3 = \gamma_2$. Then, the verifier can run the LVC.Vf algorithm to check whether $\pi_2^* = \pi_1 + \gamma_2\pi_1^* = \pi_1 + \gamma_1\gamma_2\pi_2 + \gamma_2\pi_3$ is a valid proof that function $f = f_1 + \gamma_1\gamma_2 f_2 + \gamma_2 f_3$ evaluated at the vector committed in C opens to $y = y_1 + \gamma_1\gamma_2 y_2 + \gamma_2 y_3$. For this last step to work we need the homomorphic proof property and the verifier to have access to the aggregation "history".

To describe our history of claims we move to *trees* of statements $\{f_j, \mathbf{y}_j\}_{j=1}^t$. In these trees, leaves are pairs of function–output $(f, \mathbf{y})$. As in the usual case internal nodes are defined as an ordered list of subtrees. An empty history/tree is referred to as null. We denote trees using the syntax $T_{f,\mathbf{y}}$ and the operation that "merges" two subtrees in order adding a new root as "$\because$". The following definition formalizes the above and will be useful in our construction. We remark that we include the commitment in each of the leaves of the trees $T_{f,\mathbf{y}}$. This does not increase the input size for cross-commitment aggregation where this information is necessary (for same-commitment aggregation the commitment is not necessary). This also allows to model more closely the "claims" for the cross-commitment case where each proof is for a statement $(C, f, \mathbf{y})$.

Definition 3. *Given a tree T we associate to each of its internal nodes a hash label h defined so that $h(L \because R) := \mathsf{H}(C, L, R)$. We then associate to each of the leaves in the tree a label*

$$\delta(\mathsf{leaf}) := \prod_{i=1,\ldots,t} h(x_i)^{r(x_i,\,\mathsf{leaf})}$$

where the x_i-s are the internal nodes along the path from leaf to the root (root included and starting from the bottom), the predicate $r(x, \mathsf{leaf})$ is 1 if leaf is a right child of x and 0 otherwise.

Remark 1 (Unbounded vs One-hop vs Incremental). Previous works have defined other types of aggregation. In one-hop aggregation (or batching) [4] aggregated proofs cannot be aggregated further. Incremental aggregation [7] does not have this limitation. The difference between the latter and our notion is that incremental aggregation does not require to keep track of the order in which the aggregation has been applied (for verification or further aggregation). On the other hand, we do require to track order, but we argue that this is not an overhead in many settings. In particular, even incremental aggregators and verifiers need to know the claims related to the proofs being aggregated, albeit in no order. Adding a structure to the claims roughly adds a number of bits linear in the length of the opening for additional separators (see also examples on tree histories above).

When we consider unbounded-aggregatable LVC, we assume KeyGen outputs additional parameters for aggregations in pp. The aggregation algorithm will follow this syntax[7]:

$$\text{LVC.Agg}(\text{pp}, T_{f,\mathbf{y}}, \pi, T_{f',\mathbf{y}'}, \pi') \rightarrow \pi^*$$

We subsequently modify the syntax for the verification algorithm in an (unbounded) aggregatable LVC as follows:

$$\text{LVC.Vf}(\text{vrk}, \mathsf{C}, T_{f,\mathbf{y}} \therefore T'_{f,\mathbf{y}}, \pi^*) \rightarrow b \in \{0,1\}$$

with $T_{f,\mathbf{y}}$ replacing $f, \mathbf{y}$.

We require the following correctness property and that function binding still holds.

Definition 4 (Unbounded Aggregation Correctness). *For any* $T_{f,\mathbf{y}}$, $T_{f',\mathbf{y}'}$ *and any* π, π':

$$\Pr\left[\begin{array}{l} (\text{LVC.Vf}(\text{vrk}, \mathsf{C}, T_{f,\mathbf{y}}, \pi) = 1 \wedge \\ \text{LVC.Vf}(\text{vrk}, \mathsf{C}, T'_{f,\mathbf{y}}, \pi') = 1) \Rightarrow \\ \text{LVC.Vf}(\text{vrk}, \mathsf{C}, T_{f,\mathbf{y}} \therefore T'_{f,\mathbf{y}}, \pi^*) = 1 \end{array} \middle| \begin{array}{l} (\text{prk}, \text{vrk}, \text{pp}) \leftarrow \text{LVC.KeyGen}(1^\lambda, \mathcal{F}) \\ (\mathsf{C}, \text{aux}) \leftarrow \text{LVC.Commit}(\text{prk}, \mathbf{v}) \\ \pi^* \leftarrow \text{LVC.Agg}(\text{pp}, T_{f,\mathbf{y}}, \pi, T_{f',\mathbf{y}'}, \pi') \end{array}\right] = 1$$

Definition 5 (Unbounded Aggregation Function Binding). *For any* $T_{f,\mathbf{y}}$, $T_{f',\mathbf{y}'}$ *the following probability is negligible in* λ:

$$\Pr\left[\begin{array}{l} \text{LVC.Vf}(\text{vrk}, \mathsf{C}, T_{f,\mathbf{y}} \therefore T'_{f,\mathbf{y}}, \pi^*) = 1 \\ \wedge \nexists \mathbf{a} \text{ s.t. } f(\mathbf{a}) = \mathbf{y} \wedge f'(\mathbf{a}) = \mathbf{y}' \end{array} \middle| \begin{array}{l} (\text{prk}, \text{vrk}, \text{pp}) \leftarrow \text{LVC.KeyGen}(1^\lambda, \mathcal{F}) \\ (\mathsf{C}, \pi^*, T_{f,\mathbf{y}}, T'_{f,\mathbf{y}}) \leftarrow \mathcal{A}(\text{pp}, \text{prk}, \text{vrk}) \end{array}\right]$$

Definition: Cross-Commitment Aggregation. Unbounded aggregation can be performed across different commitments as well. This property is called *Cross-commitment Aggregation* and makes sense when we have a set of commitments $\mathsf{C}'_1, \ldots, \mathsf{C}'_t$ that we want to open at one or more maps f, as it allows to compute a succinct proof of opening for linear-maps from different vectors committed

---

[7] The algorithms can be generalized for more proofs. Proof size remains the same, also for cross-commitment aggregation.

separately. Below we show our syntax which directly expands on our same-commitment aggregation described above. Function binding and correctness are also straightforward to expand. We let $T_{f,\mathbf{y}}$ include our commitments in the leaves (see also next section).

Cross-commitment aggregation: LVC.CrossAgg$(\mathsf{pp}, T_{f,\mathbf{y}}, \pi, T_{f',\mathbf{y}'}, \pi') \to \pi^*$

Cross-commitment verification: LVC.CrossVfy$\big(\mathsf{vrk}, \big(\mathsf{C}'_j\big)_j, T_{f,\mathbf{y}}, \pi^*\big) \to 0/1$

4.2 Unbounded Aggregation for LVC

We now describe unbounded aggregation algorithms for *any* LVC scheme that satisfies the homomorphic properties of Sect. 3.1.

LVC.KeyGen$(1^\lambda, \mathcal{F}) \to (\mathsf{prk}, \mathsf{vrk}, \mathsf{pp}, \{\mathsf{upk}_j\}_{j=1}^m)$:   Additionally generate the description of a hash function $\mathsf{H}(\cdot)$ and set it as pp.

LVC.Agg$(\mathsf{pp}, T_{f,\mathbf{y}}, \pi, T_{f',\mathbf{y}'}, \pi') \to \pi^*$:
    Compute $\gamma = \mathsf{H}(\mathsf{C}, T_{f,\mathbf{y}}, T_{f',\mathbf{y}'})$ and output $\pi^* = \pi + \gamma\pi'$.

LVC.Vf$(\mathsf{vrk}, \mathsf{C}, T_{f,\mathbf{y}} \therefore T_{f',\mathbf{y}'}, \pi^*) \to b$
    Return $b \leftarrow$ LVC.Vf$\big(\mathsf{vrk}, \mathsf{C}, f^*, y^*, \pi^*\big)$ where:
    – let $\{\mathsf{leaf}_i = (\mathsf{C}, f_i, \mathbf{y}_i)\}_{i=1}^\ell$ be all the leaves in $T_{f,\mathbf{y}} \therefore T_{f',\mathbf{y}'}$.
    – For each i let $\delta_i := \delta(\mathsf{leaf}_i)$ be the value defined as in Definition 3.

$$f^* := \sum_i \delta_i f_i \qquad y^* := \sum_i \delta_i \mathbf{y}_i$$

Theorem 1. *When applied to a function binding LVC scheme with homomorphic proofs,* (LVC.Agg, LVC.Vf) *satisfies Unbounded Aggregation Correctness (as in Definition 4) and Function Binding (Definition 5) in the ROM.*

Proof. Correctness follows by inspection, using the fact that the LVC satisfies homomorphic proof, so we omit it.

For function binding, let $\big(\mathsf{C}, \pi^*, T_{f,\mathbf{y}}, T_{f',\mathbf{y}'}\big)$ be an output of $\mathcal{A}$ such that LVC.Vf$(\mathsf{vrk}, \mathsf{C}, T_{f,\mathbf{y}} \therefore T_{f',\mathbf{y}'}, \pi^*) = 1$. By construction this implies IP.Vf$\big(\mathsf{vrk}, \mathsf{C}, \sum_i \delta_i f_i, \sum_i \delta_i \mathbf{y}_i, \pi^*\big) = 1$. Because IP is function binding, except with negligible probability, there exists a vector $\mathbf{a}$ such that $f(\mathbf{a}) = \mathbf{y}$, for $\mathbf{y} = \sum_i \delta_i \mathbf{y}_i$, $f(\mathbf{X}) = \sum_i \delta_i f_i(\mathbf{X})$ then there exists $\mathbf{a}$ such that $\sum_{i=1}^t \delta_i f_i(\mathbf{a}) = \sum_{i=1}^t \delta_i \mathbf{y}_i$.

Since H is a random oracle, the coefficients δ_i do not depend on $\mathbf{y}_i, f_i$. And by the Schwartz-Zippel lemma, except with probability $r/\mathbb{F}$, $f_i(\mathbf{a}) = \mathbf{y}_i$ for all i, which concludes the proof. □

Cross-Commitment Aggregation for LVC. For the case of cross-commitment aggregation, we proceed similarly but we also need to homomorphically operate on the commitments (recall that hashing on trees implicitly hashes the commitments too since we include them there).

LVC.CrossAgg$(\mathsf{pp}, T_{f,\mathbf{y}}, \pi, T_{f',\mathbf{y}'}, \pi') \to \pi^*$:
    Compute $\gamma = \mathsf{H}(T_{f,\mathbf{y}}, T_{f',\mathbf{y}'})$
    Output $\pi^* = \pi + \gamma\pi'$

LVC.CrossVfy$(\text{vrk}, (C, C', T_{f,\mathbf{y}} \therefore T_{f',\mathbf{y}'}, \pi^*)) \to b$
-   let $\text{leaf}_1, \dots, \text{leaf}_\ell$ be all the leaves in $T_{f,\mathbf{y}} \therefore T_{f',\mathbf{y}'}$. We add to each leaf leaf_i and additional subindex j that refers to which commitment the proof in leaf_{ij} corresponds to. Note that we still consider ℓ leaves.
-   each leaf_{ij} is of the form $(C_j, f_i, \mathbf{y}_i)$
-   For each i let $\delta_{ij} := \delta(\text{leaf}_{ij})$ be the value defined as in Definition 3.
-   Compute

$$f_j^* := \sum_i \delta_{ij} f_i \qquad y_j^* := \sum_i \delta_{ij} \mathbf{y}_i$$

-   Return 1 iff $b_j = 1$ for all $b_j \leftarrow$ LVC.Vf$(\text{vrk}, C_j, f_j^*, y_j^*, \pi^*)$.

Efficiency. For our constructions, the verification equations for computing $b_i =$ IP.Vf$(\text{vrk}, C^*, f^*, y^*, \pi^*)$ are two pairing equations where the elements in the right side can be aggregated, and thus the verifier performs only $\ell + 1$ pairings.

Security. The security of this augmented construction follows analogously to that for same-commitment aggregation, with the additional requirement for the LVC scheme to have homomorphic commitments and openings.

4.3   From Inner-Products to Arbitrary Linear-Maps

In this section we show we can obtain LVC schemes for any family of functions $\mathcal{F} \subset \{f : \mathbb{F}^m \to \mathbb{F}^n\}$ starting from simpler constructions that have homomorphic proofs and openings.

Our starting point are LVC schemes for $\mathcal{F}_{\mathsf{IP}} = \{f : \mathbb{F}^m \to \mathbb{F}\}$, or inner-product VC schemes, that we will denote as IP $=$ (IP.KeyGen, IP.Commit, IP.Open, IP.Vf). All this algorithms work as the ones for LVC, except that instead of $f \in \mathcal{F}_{\mathsf{IP}_{m,p}}$, they use the vector $\mathbf{f} \in \mathbb{F}^m$ so that $f(\mathbf{v}) = \mathbf{f} \cdot \mathbf{v}$.

We can write the linear-map $f : \mathbb{F}^m \to \mathbb{F}^n$ as $f = (f_1, f_2, \dots f_n)$, where each f_i is an inner product function. If the IP scheme has homomorphic proofs, and we set π_i to be the proof that $f_i(\mathbf{v}) = \mathbf{f}_i \cdot \mathbf{v} = y_i$, an aggregation of $\{\pi_i\}_{i=1}^n$ is a proof of the statement $f(\mathbf{v}) = \mathbf{y}$. Later, in the following section, we show two possible constructions of IP vector commitments schemes that can be used to instantiate the framework in this section.

An IP aggregation algorithm for one-hop aggregation[8] of proofs works as follows:

IP.Agg$(\text{pp}, \{\mathbf{f}_i, y_i\}_{i=1}^n, \pi = (\pi_i)_{i=1}^n) \to \pi'$:
    Parse $\text{pp} = H$, where H is a hash function, compute $\gamma = \mathsf{H}(C, \{\mathbf{f}_i, y_i\}_{i=1}^n)$
    Output $\pi' = \sum_{i=1}^n \gamma^{i-1} \pi_i$
IP.VfAgg$(\text{vrk}, C, \{\mathbf{f}_i, y_i\}_{i=1}^n, \pi') \to b$:
    Compute $\gamma = \mathsf{H}(C, \{\mathbf{f}_i, y_i\}_{i=1}^n)$, $\quad \mathbf{f}' = \sum_{i=1}^n \gamma^{i-1} \mathbf{f}_i, \quad y' = \sum_{i=1}^n \gamma^{i-1} y_i$
    Output $b \leftarrow$ IP.Vf$(\text{vrk}, C, \mathbf{f}', y', \pi')$.

---

[8] Naturally, this can be seen as a particular case of unbounded aggregation.

Using IP.Agg, we present an alternative way of computing concise proofs of LVC for more general functions $f : \mathbb{F}^m \to \mathbb{F}^n$, based on aggregation.

LVC.KeyGen$(1^\lambda, \mathcal{F}) \to$ (prk, vrk, pp):
- Run (prk, vrk) $\leftarrow$ IP.KeyGen$(1^\lambda, \mathcal{F}_{\mathsf{IP}})$ and generate aggregation parameters pp $=$ H (a hash function). Output (prk, vrk, pp).

LVC.Commit(prk, $\mathbf{v}) \to$ (C, aux):
- Run (C, aux) $\leftarrow$ IP.Commit(prk, $\mathbf{v}$) and output (C, aux).

LVC.Open(prk, pp, aux, f, $\mathbf{y}) \to \pi$:
- Parse $f = (f_1, f_2, \ldots f_n)$ and $\mathbf{y} = (y_1, \ldots y_n)$. Consider $\mathbf{f}_i$ as the vector representing inner-product function f_i. Run $\pi_i \leftarrow$ IP.Open(prk, aux, $\mathbf{f}_i, y_i$) for $i \in [n]$ and output $\pi \leftarrow$ IP.Agg(pp, $\{\mathbf{f}_i, y_i\}_{i=1}^n, (\pi_i)_{i=1}^n$).

LVC.VfAgg(vrk, pp, C, f, $\mathbf{y}, \pi) \to b$:
- Parse $f = (f_1, f_2, \ldots f_n)$ and $\mathbf{y} = (y_1, \ldots y_n)$. Consider $\mathbf{f}_i$ as the vector representing function f_i. Output $b \leftarrow$ IP.VfAgg(vrk, C, $\{\mathbf{f}_i, y_i\}_{i=1}^n, \pi$)

4.4 Updability for LVC

We consider updatability as an extra property of the LVC scheme. The KeyGen algorithm additionally computes the update keys, while two extra algorithms are defined as follows:

LVC.UpdCom(upk, C, j, $\delta) \to$ C$'$: takes as input C, a position $j \in [m]$, update key upk, and a constant $\delta \in \mathcal{M}$. It outputs C$'$ as a commitment for $\mathbf{v}' = \mathbf{v} + \delta \mathbf{e}_j$[9].

LVC.UpdOpen(upk, j, δ, f, $\mathbf{y}, \pi) \to \pi'$: Takes as input upk, j, δ, a function f, a valid opening pair $(\mathbf{y}, \pi)$ for f and outputs a proof π' for the new opening $\mathbf{y}' = f(\mathbf{v} + \delta \mathbf{e}_j)$.

Update Correctness. Let (prk, vrk, upk) $\leftarrow$ LVC.KeyGen$(1^\lambda, \mathcal{F})$, and let $(C, j, f, \mathbf{y}, \pi)$ be a tuple such that LVC.Vf(vrk, C, f, $\mathbf{y}, \pi$) $= 1$. Then LVC satisfies update correctness if for any $\delta \in \mathcal{M}$,

$$\Pr\left[\begin{array}{c} \mathsf{LVC.Vf(vrk, C', f, y', \pi') = 1} \\ \wedge\ \mathbf{y}' = \mathbf{y} + \delta f(\mathbf{e}_j) \end{array} \middle| \begin{array}{c} \mathsf{C'} \leftarrow \mathsf{LVC.UpdCom(upk}_j, \mathsf{C}, j, \delta) \\ \pi' \leftarrow \mathsf{LVC.UpdOpen(upk}_j, j, \delta, f, \mathbf{y}, \pi) \end{array}\right] = 1.$$

Updates for IP. We present a generic construction of the updatability algorithms for inner-product schemes. We state that even though algorithms can be generalized to LVC for arbitrary functions, for ease of exposition we only present it for inner-product openings, rather than generic linear-maps.

It is easy to see that commitments can be updated when one value of the vector changes by simply applying the linear-homomorphic property of the underlying IP scheme. Given C such that (C, aux) $\leftarrow$ LVC.Commit(prk, $\mathbf{v}$), when position t of the vector changes, i.e. $\mathbf{v}' = \mathbf{v} + \delta \mathbf{e}_t$ we can compute a commitment to the

---

[9] This notion can be generalized to more than one position.

new vector $\mathbf{v}'$ as $C' = (C + \hat{C})$ where $(\hat{C}, a\hat{u}x) \leftarrow$ LVC.Commit$(prk, \mathbf{e}_t)$ is given as an update key.

Moreover, it is possible to update existing proofs using the homomorphic openings property of the IP scheme: when position t of the vector changes as above, to update a prior proof we simply add to π a proof $\hat{\pi}$ corresponding to the opening of $f(\delta \mathbf{e}_t)$. The resulting $\pi' = \pi + \hat{\pi}$ corresponds to the opening of the sum $f(\mathbf{v}') = f(\mathbf{v}) + \delta f(\mathbf{e}_t)$ with respect to the updated commitment $C' = C + \hat{C}$.

We extend IP arguments to satisfy updatability by asking the IP.KeyGen algorithm to additionally generate updatable keys and introduce IP.UpdCom and IP.UpdOpen that work the following way;

IP.KeyGen$(1^\lambda, \mathcal{F}_{IP}) \rightarrow (prk, vrk, \{upk_j\}_{j=1}^m)$:

- Additionally generate public update keys upk: Set $\pi_{u_{ij}} \leftarrow$ IP.Open$(prk,$ $aux_j, \mathbf{e}_i, u_{ij} = \mathbf{e}_i \cdot \mathbf{e}_j)$, $\forall i, j \in [m]$, Define $upk_j = \{\pi_{u_{ij}}\}_{i=1}^m$ for all $j \in [m]$, and output $(prk, vrk, \{upk_i\}_{i=1}^m)$.

IP.UpdCom$(prk, C, t, \delta) \rightarrow C'$:

- Set $\hat{C} \leftarrow$ IP.Commit$(prk, \mathbf{e}_t)$, and output $C' = C + \delta \hat{C}$.

IP.UpdOpen$(upk_t, t, \delta, C, \mathbf{f}, y, \pi) \rightarrow \pi'$:

- Parse $upk_t = \{\pi_{u_{it}}\}_{i=1}^m$ and compute $\hat{\pi} = \sum_{i=1}^m f_i \pi_{u_{it}}$.
- Set $\pi' = \pi + \delta \hat{\pi}$ as proof for $y' = y + \mathbf{f} \cdot \delta \mathbf{e}_t$ and output π'.

Theorem 2. *If* IP *satisfies function binding and has homomorphic commitments and openings, the extension above satisfies update correctness.*

Proof. The proof follows directly by the definition of homomorphic proof and IP.UpdCom, IP.UpdOpen.

5   Constructions for Inner-Pairing VC

In this section, we present two constructions of LVC for inner products, that is, for functions $f \subset \mathcal{F}_{IP} = \{f : \mathbb{F}^m \rightarrow \mathbb{F}\}$. We denote as IP = (IP.KeyGen, IP.Commit, IP.Open, IP.Vf) a vector commitment scheme with inner product openings. All the algorithms work as the ones for LVC, except that they take as inputs the vector of coefficients of the linear function $f \in \mathcal{F}_{IP}$, $f(\mathbf{v}) = \mathbf{f} \cdot \mathbf{v}$, i.e. use the vector $\mathbf{f} \in \mathbb{F}_p^m$.

The first one is in the monomial basis and the other based on the univariate sumcheck of [2, 25] that considers vectors encoded as polynomials in the Lagrange basis. We prove they are indeed linear vector commitment arguments with homomorphic proofs and openings. Therefore, they can be used as a starting point to obtain further aggregation properties as shown in Sect. 4.1 and, in particular, lead to two different more generic linear-map vector commitment schemes.

5.1 Monomial Basis

For the first scheme, we consider vectors $\mathbf{a} \in \mathbb{F}^m$ encoded as a polynomial in the monomial basis, that is as $a(X) = \sum_{i=1}^{m} a_i X^{i-1}$.

IP.KeyGen($1^\lambda, \mathcal{F}_{\mathsf{IP}}$) $\to$ (prk, vrk):
　Generate group description $\mathsf{gk} = (p, \mathbb{G}_1, \mathbb{G}_2, \mathbb{G}_T, e) \leftarrow \mathcal{G}(p)$
　Sample $\tau \leftarrow \mathbb{F}$
　Output prk $= (\{[\tau^i]_{1,2}\}_{i=0}^{m-1})$, vrk $= ([\tau^{m-1}]_1, \{[\tau^i]_2\}_{i=0}^{m})$.
IP.Commit(prk, $\mathbf{a}$) $\to$ (C_a, aux): Compute $\mathsf{C}_a = \sum_{i=1}^{m} a_i [\tau^{i-1}]_1$ and output (C_a, $\mathbf{a}$).
IP.Open(prk, aux, $\mathbf{b}, y$) $\to \pi$:
　Find $R(X), H(X)$ such that $\deg(R) < m - 1$ and

$$\left(\sum_{i=1}^{m} a_i X^{i-1} \right) \left(\sum_{i=1}^{m} b_i X^{m-i} \right) - y X^{m-1} = R(X) + X^m H(X).$$

　Define $\hat{R}(X) = X R(X)$
　Output $\pi = ([R(\tau)]_1, [H(\tau)]_1, [\hat{R}(\tau)]_1)$.
IP.Vf(vrk, $\mathsf{C}_a, \mathbf{b}, y, \pi$) $\to$ 0/1: Compute $\mathsf{C}_b = \sum_{i=1}^{m} b_i [\tau^{m-i}]_1$, parse $\pi = ([R]_1, [H]_1, [\hat{R}]_1)$ and output 1 if and only if

$$e(\mathsf{C}_a, \mathsf{C}_b) - e(y[\tau^{m-1}]_1, [1]_2) = e([R]_1, [1]_2) + e([H]_1, [\tau^m]_2) \text{ and}$$

$$e([R]_1, [\tau]_2) = e([\hat{R}]_1, [1]_2).$$

Remark 2. The second verification equation is meant to ensure that $[R]_1$ is the evaluation at τ of a polynomial of degree at most $m-2$. Note that it is important for security that only $m - 1$ powers of τ are available to the adversary in $\mathbb{G}_1$, otherwise the second equation does not guarantee that the degree is at most $m - 2$. Importantly, even though we present our construction using a srs with powers of τ up to $m - 1$ in $\mathbb{G}_1$ and m in $\mathbb{G}_2$, it can easily be adapted for a bigger srs and, in particular, existing trusted setups where the same powers of τ are available in both groups are enough. For the second check, if $m + k$ powers of τ are given in $\mathbb{G}_1$, $\hat{R}(X)$ should be defined as $X^{k+2} R(X)$.

We implement this construction for single positions and compare it with individual position openings in Merkle tree-based vector commitments in the full version of the paper. Below, we state the theorems for security guarantees, and refer the reader to the full version for the formal proofs.

Theorem 3. *The construction above satisfies Completeness, Homomorphic Proofs and Homomorphic Openings.*

Theorem 4. *The construction above satisfies Strong Function Binding in the AGM under the $(m - 1, m)$-BSDH Assumption [3].*

Intuition. Without loss of generalization, we consider an adversary that provides two proofs π_1, π_2 with IP.Vf($\mathsf{vrk}, \mathsf{C}_a, \mathbf{b}_k, y_k, \pi_{b_k}) = 1$ for $k = 1, 2$ and there is no $\mathbf{a} \in \mathbb{F}^m$ s. t. $\mathbf{a} \cdot \mathbf{b}_k = y_k$.

For commitment C_a and proofs $\pi_k = ([R_k]_1, [H_k]_1, [\hat{R}_k]_1)$ under the AGM we can extract polynomials $a(X), H_k(X), R_k(X), \hat{R}_k(X)$ of degree up to $m - 1$ such that the proof elements are their evaluations in $\mathbb{G}_1$ at secret point τ. On the other hand, the second verification equation in our IP scheme assures that $R_k(X)X = \hat{R}_k(X)$. Because $\deg(\hat{R}_k) \leq m - 1$ $\deg(R_1), \deg(R_2) \leq m - 2$.

Consider $\mathbf{a} \in \mathbb{F}^m$ the vector of the coefficients of $a(X) = \sum_{i=1}^{m} a_i X^{i-1}$. Then, from the first verification equation in both of the proofs we have that $p_1(X), p_2(X)$ have a common root in τ, where for $k = 1, 2$:

$$P_k(X) = \left(\sum_{i=1}^{m} a_i X^{i-1} \right)\left(\sum_{i=1}^{m} b_{ki} X^{m-i} \right) - y_k X^{m-1} - R_k(X) + X^m H_k(X).$$

If for some k, $p_k(X)$ is not the zero polynoial, since τ is one of its roots, we can solve the discrete logarithm problem and extract τ from $[P_k(\tau)]_1$. Thus, it must be the case that $p_k(X) \equiv 0$ for $k = 1, 2$. Because $\deg(R_b), \deg(R_c) < m - 1$ and $\deg(X^m H_b(X)), \deg(X^m H_c(X)) > m - 1$, we have that the coefficient for X^{m-1} in polynomial $P_k(X)$ is $\sum_{i=1}^{m} a_i b_{ki} - y_k = 0$. Indeed, there exists a vector $\mathbf{a}$ such that $\mathbf{a} \cdot \mathbf{b}_k = y_k$, contradicting the initial assumption that the adversary $\mathcal{A}$ breaks the strong functional binding.

Updates Without Keys. We remark that we do not need any additional update keys added to the setup. Indeed, the update key is made by proofs of inner products between cannonic vectors $\mathbf{e}_i \cdot \mathbf{e}_i = 1$ or $\mathbf{e}_i \cdot \mathbf{e}_j = 0$. In our construction for encodings in the monomial basis, a proof that $\mathbf{e}_i \cdot \mathbf{e}_i = 1$ consists on $R(X) = H(X) = 0$. On the other hand, to prove that $\mathbf{e}_i \cdot \mathbf{e}_j = 0$ for $i \neq j$ the proof is (the evaluation in the group of) either $R(X) = X^{m+i-j}$ if $j > i$, or $H(X) = X^{i-j}$ if $i > j$. As such powers of τ are already included in prk, $\mathsf{upk} = \emptyset$.

5.2   Lagrange Basis

In this second scheme, for a Lagrange basis $\{\lambda_i(X)\}_{i=1}^{m}$ over a multiplicative group $\mathbb{H} = \{h_1, \ldots, h_m\}$ of size m in $\mathbb{F}$ we encode a vector $\mathbf{a} \in \mathbb{F}^m$ as a polynomial $a(X) = \sum_{i=1}^{m} a_i \lambda_i(X)$. Recall that when $\mathbb{H}$ is a multiplicative subgroup, $\lambda_i(0) = m^{-1}$ for all $i \in [m]$. Moreover, if we set $t(X) = \prod_{i=1}^{m}(X - h_i)$ we have that $\lambda_i(X)\lambda_j(X) \equiv 0 \mod t(X)$, and $\lambda_i(X)^2 \equiv \lambda_i(X) \mod t(X)$. The construction below, presented in [25], exploits these properties in the proof of openings for inner-products:

IP.KeyGen($1^\lambda, \mathcal{F}_{\mathsf{IP}_m}) \rightarrow (\mathsf{prk}, \mathsf{vrk})$:
        Generate group description $\mathsf{gk} = (p, \mathbb{G}_1, \mathbb{G}_2, \mathbb{G}_T, e) \leftarrow \mathcal{G}(p)$, define multiplicative group $\mathbb{H} = \{h_1, \ldots, h_m\}$ in $\mathbb{F}$, and compute Lagrange polynomials $\{\lambda_j(X)\}_{j=1}^{m}$ over $\mathbb{H}$.

Sample $\tau \leftarrow \mathbb{F}$ and output $\mathsf{prk} = \left(\{[\tau^i]_{1,2}\}_{i=1}^m, \{[\lambda_i(\tau)]_1\}_{i=1}^{m-1}, [\tau^m]_2\right)$ and $\mathsf{vrk} = \left([1]_{1,2}, \{[\tau^i]_2, [\lambda_i(\tau)]_2\}_{i=1}^m\right)$.

IP.Commit$(\mathsf{prk}, \mathbf{a}) \to (\mathsf{C}_a, \mathsf{aux})$: Compute $\mathsf{C}_a = \sum_{i=1}^m a_i[\lambda_i(\tau)]_1$ and output $(\mathsf{C}_a, \mathbf{a})$.

IP.Open$(\mathsf{prk}, \mathsf{aux}, \mathbf{b}, y) \to \pi$:

Find $R(X), H(X)$ such that $\deg(R) < m - 1$ and

$$\left(\sum_{i=1}^m a_i\lambda_i(X)\right)\left(\sum_{i=1}^m b_i\lambda_i(X)\right) - m^{-1}y = XR(X) + t(X)H(X)$$

Define $\hat{R}(X) = XR(X)$ and output $\pi = ([R(\tau)]_1, [H(\tau)]_1, [\hat{R}(\tau)]_1)$.

IP.Vf$(\mathsf{vrk}, \mathsf{C}_a, \mathbf{b}, y, \pi) \to 0/1$: Calculate $\mathsf{C}_b = \sum_{i=1}^m b_i[\lambda_i(\tau)]_2$

Parse $\pi = ([R]_1, [H]_1, [\hat{R}]_1)$ and output 1 if and only if

$$e(\mathsf{C}_a, \mathsf{C}_b) - e(m^{-1}y[1]_1, [1]_2) = e([R]_1, [1]_2) + e([H]_1, [t(\tau)]_2), \text{ and}$$

$$e([R]_1, [\tau]_2) = e([\hat{R}]_1, [1]_2).$$

The proof of completeness can be found in [25]. Below, we state the theorems for Strong Function Binding and homomorphic proofs and openings, and refer the reader to the full version of this paper for the formal proofs.

Theorem 5. *The construction above has Homomorphic Proofs and Openings.*

Theorem 6. *The construction above satisfies Strong Function Binding in the AGM under the $(m-1, m)$-BSDH Assumption [3].*

Intuition. The proof goes as the one for Theorem 4 except that

$$p_k(X) = \left(\sum_{i=1}^m a_i\lambda_i(X)\right)\left(\sum_{i=1}^m b_{ki}\lambda_i(X)\right) - m^{-1}y_k - XR_k(X) + t(X)H_k(X).$$

Once more, if one of the polynomials $p_k(X)$ is not the zero polynomial, since τ is one of its roots, we can solve the discrete logarithm problem and extract τ from $[P_k(\tau)]_1$.

Then, $P_k(X) \equiv 0$, for both $k = 1, 2$. Because $\deg(R_k) < m - 1$ and

$$\left(\sum_{i=1}^m a_i\lambda_i(X)\right)\left(\sum_{i=1}^m b_{ki}\lambda_i(X)\right) \equiv \sum_{i=1}^m a_i b_{ki}\lambda_i(X) \mod t(X),$$

$\sum_{i=1}^m a_i b_{ki}\lambda_i(X) - m^{-1}y_k = XR_k(X)$, which implies $\sum_{i=1}^m a_i b_{ki}\lambda_i(0) - m^{-1}y_k = 0$. As $\mathbb{H}$ is a multiplicative subgroup, $\lambda_i(0) = m^{-1}$ for all $i \in [m]$ and thus $\sum_{i=1}^m a_i b_{ki} = y_k$. Then, there exists $\mathbf{a}$ such that $\mathbf{a} \cdot \mathbf{b}_k = y_k$ for $k = 1, 2$, contradicting the initial claim that adversary $\mathcal{A}$ is successful.

Updatability with Short Keys. In this construction, a proof that $\mathbf{e}_i \cdot \mathbf{e}_i = 1$ is the encoding in a group of the polynomial $R_i(\tau)$, for $R_i(X) = (\lambda_i(X) - 1)/X$. On the other hand, the proof that $\mathbf{e}_i \cdot \mathbf{e}_j = 0$ for $i \neq j$ is $[H(\tau)]_1$, for $H(X) = ((\lambda_i(X)\lambda_j(X))/t(X)$. Including the evaluation of all these polynomials in upk would require a srs of quadratic size. Still, as noted in [27], these keys can be computed in constant time from a linear-size update key.

6   Subvector Openings

In this section, we present schemes for VC with Subvector Openings (SVC), starting from the constructions of Sect. 5. We will consider SVC as a special case of LVC. The class of functions that open a set of positions $I = \{i_1, \ldots, i_n\}$ of a committed vector $\mathbf{v} \in \mathbb{F}^m$ is given by the linear-map f_I with

$$f_I : \mathbb{F}^m \to \mathbb{F}^n, \qquad f_I(\mathbf{v}) = (\mathbf{e}_{i_1} \cdot \mathbf{v}, \ldots \mathbf{e}_{i_n} \cdot \mathbf{v})$$

where for each $k \in [n]$, e_{i_k} is the i_kth vector of the canonical basis $\mathbb{F}^m$.

Naturally, for a vector $\mathbf{v} \in \mathbb{F}^m$, we can construct proofs of openings of subvectors $\mathbf{v}_I = (v_i)_{i \in I}$ by aggregating different inner product proofs for vectors $\mathbf{e}_{i_k}$ for $i_k \in I$ using the techniques in Sect. 4.1. We refer to these aggregated proofs as *non-native* subvector openings, given that they require a random oracle and in particular, are no longer algebraic and homomorphic. As opposed to them, we call *native* subvector opening, a scheme that is algebraic and homomorphic.

In what follows, we improve on Subvector Openings in some special scenarios, achieving native aggregation for new schemes and reducing the verifier complexity in existing ones.

6.1   Native SV Openings for the Monomial Basis

For the construction of Sect. 5.1, we introduce native subvector openings for subsets with consecutive position $I = \{i, i+1, \ldots, i+k\}$. That is, for $\tilde{\mathbf{c}} = (c_i)_{i \in I}$ such that there exist $\mathbf{u}_1, \mathbf{u}_2$ with $\mathbf{c} = (\mathbf{u}_1, \tilde{\mathbf{c}}, \mathbf{u}_2)$. To prove an opening of $\tilde{\mathbf{c}}$, we only need commitments to $R(X) = \sum_{s=1}^{i-1} c_i X^{m-i+s-1}$ and $H(X) = \sum_{i=i+k+1}^{m} c_{m-i+s+1} X^{s-1}$, which are shifted-encodings of $\mathbf{u}_1, \mathbf{u}_2$. The verifier checks that $\deg(R) < m-1$, computes $\tilde{C}(X) = \sum_{s=i}^{i+k} \tilde{c}_s X^{s-i}$ and $\tilde{C} = [\tilde{C}(\tau)]_1$ and checks whether $e(\mathsf{C} - \tilde{\mathsf{C}}, [\tau^{m-i}]_1) = e([R]_1, [1]_2) + e([H]_1, [\tau^{m+k}]_2)$.

Note that, given individual proofs of openings as in Sect. 5.1, that is, $[R_s(\tau)]_1, [H_s(\tau)]_1$ such that $C(X)X^{m-s} - c_s X^{m-1} = R_s(X) + X^m H_s(X)$ and $\deg(R_s) < m-1$, for the commitments defined above we have $[R]_1 = [R_i(\tau)]_1$ and $[H]_1 = [H_{i+k}(\tau)]_1$, that is, proofs can be aggregated at no cost for the prover.

6.2   Non-native SV Openings for the Monomial Basis

For the LVC scheme of Sect. 5.1, the techniques of Sect. 4.1 allow us to redefine the Open and Vf algorithms to work for an arbitrary subset of positions $I \subset$

$[m]$. More specifically, the prover will simply run IP.Open$(\text{prk}, \text{aux}, \mathbf{e}_{i_k}, \mathbf{v})$ for $k = 1, \ldots, n$ to obtain (v_{i_k}, π_{i_k}) and π_{i_k} a proof of correct computation of v_{i_k}. Then, use the random oracle to sample a randomness $\gamma \in \mathbb{F}$ and output $\pi_I = \sum_{k=1}^n \gamma^{k-1} \pi_{i_k}$.

The verifier will receive $\pi_I = ([R]_1, [H]_1, [\hat{R}]_1)$, compute $y = \sum_{k=1}^n \gamma^{k-1} v_{i_k}$, and check as before $e([R]_1, [\tau]_2) = e([\hat{R}]_1, [1]_2)$ and

$$e\left(\mathsf{C}, \sum_{k=1}^n \gamma^{k-1}[\tau^{m-i_k}]_2\right) - e\left(y[\tau^{m-1}]_1, [1]_2\right) = e\left([R]_1, [1]_2\right) + e\left([H]_1, [\tau^m]_2\right).$$

Note that verifier's work is dominated by the computation of $\sum_{k=1}^n \gamma^{k-1} [\tau^{m-i_k}]_2$, so we analyze for which sets $I \subset [m]$ this computation can be cheaper than $|I|$ $\mathbb{G}_2$-exponentiations. Without loss of generality, we can re-assign $\gamma^{k-1} \to \gamma^{m-i_k}$, and thus our verifier now needs to compute $\sum_{k=1}^n [(\gamma X)^{m-i_k}]_2 = \sum_{i \in I} [(\gamma X)^{m-i}]_2$.

Now, note that if $I_{k,s,n} \subset [m]$ is an arithmetic progression, i.e. it is such that for a given ratio s, a starting power k and a number n of desired elements, $I_{k,s,n} = \{k, s + k, \ldots, (n-1)s + k\}$, then

$$\sum_{i \in I_{k,s,n}} (\gamma X)^{m-i} = (\gamma X)^k \frac{1 - (\gamma X)^n}{1 - (\gamma X)^s}.$$

This reduces the work of the verifier to compute $\sum_{i \in I_{k,s,n}} (\gamma X)^{m-i}$ to constant. Note that the verifier cannot compute $(1 - (\gamma X)^s)^{-1}$, so we multiply all the terms of the equation by $1 - (\gamma X)^s$. I.e, the verifier computes $y = \sum_{i \in I_{k,s,n}} \gamma^{m-i} y_i$ and checks whether

$$e\left([C]_1, \gamma^k[\tau^k]_2 - \gamma^{k+n}[\tau^{k+n}]_2\right) - e\left([\tau^{m-1}]_1 y - [\tau^{n+s-1}]_1 \gamma^s y, [1]_2\right)$$
$$= e\left([R]_1, 1 - \gamma^s[\tau^s]_2)\right) + e\left([H]_1, [\tau^n]_2 - \gamma^s[\tau^{n+s}]_2\right).$$

6.3 Lagrange Basis

Native. In the Lagrange Basis, one can use the native subset openings of [27]. There, the verifier needs to compute computation the vanishing polynomial $t_I(X) = \prod_{i \in I}(X - \mathsf{h}_i)$. To reduce verifier's work we focus on those subsets $I \subset [m]$ such that $t_I(X)$ can be calculated in less than $|I|$ computations. One answer to this question comes from cosets. That is, given $\mathbb{H} = \{1, \omega, \omega^2, \ldots, \omega^{m-1}\}$ group of roots of unity where $m = 2^n$, let $\mathbb{H}_k$ be the subgroup of order 2^k of $\mathbb{H}$, where k goes from 0 to n. Then, for each $0 \leq s < 2^{n/k}$ we can construct the coset $I = \omega^s \mathbb{H}_k$, whose vanishing polynomial is $t_I(X) = X^{2^k} - (\omega^s)^{2^k}$. Verifier accepts if and only if $e\left(\mathsf{C} - \tilde{\mathsf{C}}, [1]_2\right) = e\left([H]_1, [x^{2^k}]_2 - \omega^{s2^k}\right)$.

Non-native. Given that the native subvector opening procedure above works for arbitrary subsets $I \subset [m]$, we don't consider aggregation of individual positions. The latter makes sense only when applying a linear function to the new subset. That is, when the verifier is given $C_{f,I}$, claimed to be a commitment to $\mathbf{f} \cdot \mathbf{c}_I$, for some linear function $\mathbf{f}$ applied to the vector $\mathbf{c}_I = (c_i)_{i \in I}$.

7 Maintainable Vector Commitment Schemes

7.1 Multivariate Case

One of the key points of vector commitment schemes that allow to speedup subvector openings is the ability to pre-compute and store individual openings and later aggregate them to create subvector openings without incurring linear amount of computations each time.

In constructions such as the ones presented in Sect. 5, the proof of opening of one position involves *all* other elements in the vector. That is, the polynomials committed to create the proof have coefficients that involve all the values of the committed vector $\mathbf{v} \in \mathbb{F}^m$. As a consequence, prover work is linear in the size of $\mathbf{v}$ (as it has to evaluate polynomials of degree m). To alleviate this, Shrinivasan et al. [26] utilize a tree-like structure for computing/communicating proofs which allows pre-computation in quasi-linear (instead of quadratic) time and efficient updates at the cost of a proof of size $\log m$.

In this section, we extend the techniques of [26] to achieve trade-offs and efficiency improvements. Roughly speaking, we present a way to "compose" the tree-based commitments of [26] with constant size ones. We achieve this by considering trees that themselves have commitments for leaves instead of openings. The intuition is the following: we divide the vector $\mathbf{v}$ in small chunks $\{\mathbf{v}_j\} \in \mathbb{F}^k$. We then arrange these chunks in a tree as follows: each chunk corresponds to a leaf of the tree and each node is a succinct representation of its children. The root of the tree is the commitment to the vector. An opening proof only involves the elements in the path of the root to the leaf containing the position to be opened. That is, if we want to open value a in position i of $\mathbf{v} \in \mathbb{F}^{k \cdot m'}$, we prove that (1) c_j is the leaf that contains the commitment to the j chunk containing i and (2) c_j opens to a in the position corresponding to i. The former part can be pre-computed and efficiently maintained while the latter is computed on the fly.

This results in a construction with the following memory/time trade-off: for any $k, m' \in \mathbb{N}$ with $m = k \cdot m'$, any opening can be computed in time *independent of m'* after pre-computing and storing $O_\lambda(m')$ values (independent of k). Furthermore, a relaxed *maintainability* notion is satisfied: all stored values can be pre-computed efficiently in $O_\lambda(m \cdot \log m')$ time and updated in $O(\log m')$ time.

Additionally, we show how to use a higher arity tree (any constant ℓ contrary to the binary ones used in [26]) to further reduce the proof size by a constant factor, namely $O_\lambda(\log_\ell m')$ (assuming a constant size commitment for the leaf part), at the expense of a slightly worse prover time. We note that–apart from the evident advantage of shorter proofs–this results in smaller aggregation time for the prover and verifier when using inner pairing products.

Our starting point is the PST polynomial commitment [24]. The PST polynomial commitment is a natural generalization of the KGZ polynomial commitment [19] for multivariate polynomials, that is, it allows to commit to ν-variate polynomials of individual degrees less than ℓ. The core idea of the construction lies in the fact that for every $p(\mathbf{X}) \in \mathbb{F}[X_\nu, \ldots, X_1]$ and $\mathbf{x} = (x_\nu, \ldots, x_1) \in \mathbb{F}^\nu$, $p(\mathbf{x}) = y$ if and only if there exist polynomials $H_\nu(\mathbf{X}), \ldots, H_1(\mathbf{X})$ such that

$$p(\mathbf{X}) - y = \sum_{j=1}^{\nu} H_j(\mathbf{X}) \cdot (X_j - x_j)$$

where the proof polynomials $H_j(\mathbf{X})$ are efficiently computable.

Using standard techniques to encode monomials in a cryptographically secure bilinear group (encode setting $\mathbf{X} = \boldsymbol{\tau}$ and publishing all the monomials $[\tau_\nu^{d_\nu} \cdots \tau_1^{d_1}]_1$ and $[\boldsymbol{\tau}]_2$) results in a polynomial commitment with proof of size roughly ν group elements.

Tree Structure. To achieve the flexible memory/time trade-off, instead of having the vector values in the leaves of the tree, we replace them with elements $[\mathbf{r}]_1 \cdot \mathbf{v}_j$ where $[\mathbf{r}] \in \mathbb{G}_1^k$ is the commitment key of an arbitrary algebraic vector commitment scheme LVC. To open a position of $\mathbf{v}$, we use the PST approach to reach corresponding leaf j, and then the opening algorithm of LVC on $\mathbf{v}_j$.

One subtlety of replacing leaves with commitments is that a standalone PST proof is no longer binding, that is, the prover can undetectably claim arbitrary values that supposedly correspond to a leaf. We overcome this by using a low degree test to ensure that the claimed value for the leaf is uniquely defined.

Note that the root of the tree depends on the elements $\boldsymbol{\tau}, \mathbf{r}$. Viewing both $\boldsymbol{\tau} = (\tau_\nu, \ldots, \tau_1)$ and $\mathbf{r} = (r_k, \ldots, r_1)$ as formal variables $\mathbf{X}, \mathbf{R}$, we can treat the root node (the commitment) as an evaluation of a polynomial. Now, note that this polynomial corresponds to the interpolation of the elements of the leaves in Σ^ν. Thus, the aforementioned polynomial is

$$p(\mathbf{X}, \mathbf{R}) = \boldsymbol{\lambda}(\mathbf{X}) \cdot (\mathbf{R} \cdot \mathbf{v}_1, \ldots, \mathbf{R} \cdot \mathbf{v}_{\ell^\nu}) = (\boldsymbol{\lambda}(\mathbf{X}) \otimes \mathbf{R}) \cdot \mathbf{v}$$

The prover can still evaluate one by one the variables $X_\nu, \ldots, X_1$ at $\sigma_\nu, \ldots, \sigma_1$ -as it would do in the simple PST case- and end up with a polynomial $q(\mathbf{R}) = p(\boldsymbol{\sigma}, \mathbf{R}) = \mathbf{R} \cdot \mathbf{v}_j$. To ensure that q does not contain any X_j variable, we also include a low degree test in the proof. The evaluation of the latter polynomial at $[\mathbf{r}]_1$ corresponds to the leaf commitment at position $\boldsymbol{\sigma}$ and can be opened by employing the Open algorithm of the leaf commitment scheme with key $[\mathbf{r}]_1$.

Construction. First, we introduce some notation. Let $\Sigma \subseteq \mathbb{F}$ denote an interpolating set of size ℓ. Given $\boldsymbol{\sigma} = (\sigma_\nu, \ldots, \sigma_1) \in \Sigma^\nu$, we denote $\boldsymbol{\sigma}_{|i} = (\sigma_\nu, \ldots, \sigma_i) \in \Sigma^{\nu-i+1}$. For $\mathbf{v} = (\mathbf{v}_\sigma)_{\sigma \in \Sigma^\nu}$ with $\mathbf{v}_\sigma \in \mathbb{F}^k$ and $\boldsymbol{\sigma}_1 \in \Sigma^i$ we denote with $\mathbf{v}_{k,\sigma_1}$ the vector $(\mathbf{v}_{\sigma_1,\sigma_2})_{\sigma_2 \in \Sigma^{\nu-i}}$, that is, the concatenation of vectors $\mathbf{v}_j$ whose ℓ-ary representation of the index j is prefixed with $\boldsymbol{\sigma}_1$. Finally, we denote with $\boldsymbol{\tau}_{\nu,\ell}$ the ν-variate monomial basis of individual degree less than ℓ evaluated at $\tau_\nu, \ldots, \tau_1$. In all cases, we omit the subscript when it is clear from the context.

We present the construction next. While our aim is individual position open-ings, the construction supports a bigger family of functions: linear forms[10] applied to one of the k-sized chunks of the vector. Concretely, let $\mathcal{F}_{p,k} \subseteq \{f : \mathbb{F}^k \to \mathbb{F}\}$ be the family of linear forms supported by the leaf commitment scheme. We define the ℓ, ν-extended family as

$$\mathsf{Ext}_{\ell,\nu}\text{-}\mathcal{F}_{p,k} = \{f : \mathbb{F}^{k \cdot \ell^\nu} \to \mathbb{F} \mid \exists f' \in \mathcal{F}_{p,k}, i \in \{1, \ldots, \ell^\nu\} \text{ s.t.}$$

$$\forall \mathbf{v}_1, \ldots, \mathbf{v}_{\ell^\nu} \in \mathbb{F}^k : f(\mathbf{v}_1, \ldots, \mathbf{v}_{\ell^\nu}) = f'(\mathbf{v}_i)\}$$

Our construction is a linear vector commitment MVTree for the family $\mathsf{Ext}_{\ell^\nu}\text{-}\mathcal{F}_{p,k}$, that uses as a black box an algebraic linear vector commitment scheme LVC$'$ for the family $\mathcal{F}_{p,k}$.

MVTree.KeyGen$(1^\lambda, \mathsf{Ext}_{\ell^\nu}\text{-}\mathcal{F}_{p,k}) \to (\mathsf{prk}, \mathsf{vrk})$:
- $(\mathsf{prk}' = [\mathbf{r}]_1, \mathsf{vrk}') \leftarrow \mathsf{LVC}'.\mathsf{KeyGen}(1^\lambda, \mathcal{F}_{p,k})$
- Let $\boldsymbol{\lambda}(X)$ be the vector of Lagrange polynomials associated to Σ.
- Sample $\tau_\nu, \ldots, \tau_1 \leftarrow \mathbb{F}$ and output $\mathsf{prk} = (\mathsf{prk}', [\boldsymbol{\lambda}]_1 = [\boldsymbol{\lambda}(\tau_\nu) \otimes \cdots \otimes \boldsymbol{\lambda}(\tau_1) \otimes \mathbf{r}]_1, [\boldsymbol{\tau} \otimes \mathbf{r}]_1)$, $\quad \mathsf{vrk} = (\mathsf{vrk}', [\tau_\nu]_2, \ldots, [\tau_1]_2, [\tau_\nu^{\ell-1} \cdots \tau_1^{\ell-1}]_2)$, $\mathsf{upk} = (\{[\boldsymbol{\lambda}(\tau_j) \otimes \cdots \otimes \boldsymbol{\lambda}(\tau_1) \otimes \mathbf{r}]_1\}_{j=\nu-1}^{1})$,

MVTree.Commit$(\mathsf{prk}, \mathbf{v}) \to (\mathsf{C}, \mathsf{aux})$:
- For all $\sigma \in \Sigma^\nu$: compute $(C_\sigma, \mathsf{aux}_\sigma) \leftarrow \mathsf{LVC}'.\mathsf{Commit}(\mathsf{prk}', \mathbf{v}_\sigma)$. Compute $\mathsf{C} = [p(\boldsymbol{\tau}, \mathbf{r})]_1 = [\boldsymbol{\lambda}]_1 \cdot \mathbf{v}$ and output $\mathsf{C}, \mathsf{aux} = (\{\mathsf{aux}_\sigma\}_{\sigma \in \Sigma^\nu}, \mathbf{v})$

MVTree.Open$(\mathsf{prk}, \mathsf{aux}, f, \mathbf{y}) \to \pi$:
- Let $f(\mathbf{v}_1, \ldots, \mathbf{v}_{\ell^\nu}) = f'(\mathbf{v}_i)$ for $f' \in \mathcal{F}_{p,k}$ and $i = (\sigma)_\ell$ in ℓ-ary.
- Consider $\boldsymbol{\tau}, \mathbf{r}$ as formal variables $\mathbf{X} = (X_\nu, \ldots, X_1), \mathbf{R} = (R_k, \ldots, R_1)$.
- Denote $p_{\nu+1}(\mathbf{X}, \mathbf{R}) = p(\mathbf{X}, \mathbf{R}) = (\boldsymbol{\lambda}(\mathbf{X}) \otimes \mathbf{R}) \cdot \mathbf{v}$
- For all $\nu \geq j \geq 1$:
    Compute $p_j(X_{j-1}, \ldots, X_1, \mathbf{R}) = \boldsymbol{\lambda}(X_{j-1}, \ldots, X_1, \mathbf{R}) \cdot \mathbf{v}_{\sigma_{|j}}$
    Compute $H_j(X_j, \ldots, X_1, \mathbf{R})$ as

$$H_j(X_j, \ldots, X_1, \mathbf{R}) = \frac{p_{j+1}(X_j, \ldots, X_1, \mathbf{R}) - p_j(X_{j-1}, \ldots, X_1, \mathbf{R})}{(X_j - \sigma_j)}$$

    and group element $[H_j]_1 = [H_j(\tau_j, \ldots, \tau_1, \mathbf{r})]_1$
- Compute $\hat{\mathsf{C}}_\sigma = [\tau_\nu^{\ell-1} \cdots \tau_1^{\ell-1} \cdot \mathbf{r}]_1 \cdot \mathbf{v}_\sigma$, $\pi' \leftarrow \mathsf{LVC}'.\mathsf{Open}(\mathsf{prk}', \mathsf{aux}_\sigma, f', \mathbf{y})$ and output $\pi = ([H_\nu]_1, \ldots, [H_1]_1, C_\sigma, \hat{\mathsf{C}}_\sigma, \pi')$.

MVTree.Vf$(\mathsf{vrk}, \mathsf{C}, f, \mathbf{y}, \pi) \to 0/1$:
- Let $f(\mathbf{v}_1, \ldots, \mathbf{v}_{\ell^\nu}) = f'(\mathbf{v}_i)$ for $f' \in \mathcal{F}_{p,k}$ and $i = (\sigma)_\ell$ in ℓ-ary.
- $b_{\mathsf{Path}} \leftarrow e(\mathsf{C} - C_\sigma, [1]_2) = \sum_{j=1}^\nu e([H_j]_1, [\tau_j - \sigma_j]_2)$
- $b_{\mathsf{LD\text{-}Test}} \leftarrow e(C_\sigma, [\tau_\nu^{\ell-1} \cdots \tau_1^{\ell-1}]_2) = e(\hat{\mathsf{C}}_\sigma, [1]_2)$
- $b_{\mathsf{Leaf}} \leftarrow \mathsf{LVC}'.\mathsf{Vf}(\mathsf{vrk}', C_\sigma, f', \mathbf{y}, \pi')$
- Output $b_{\mathsf{Path}} \wedge b_{\mathsf{LD\text{-}Test}} \wedge b_{\mathsf{Leaf}}$

---

[10] We use linear forms for simplicity, one could also consider general linear functions.

We omit explicitly describing the update algorithm. Instead, we demonstrate in Theorem 8 how to efficiently update all proofs after modifying a position in the committed vector.

We summarize the properties of the construction in the following theorems. Due to space limitations, we omit their proofs and refer the interested reader to the full version of this paper.

Theorem 7. *Let* LVC′ *be an algebraic vector commitment scheme that satisfies completeness, homomorphic openings and weak function binding for a function family* $\mathcal{F}_{p,k}$. *Then,* MVTree *satisfies (1) completeness, (2) Homomorphic Openings and (3) strong function binding for* Ext_{ℓ^ν}-$\mathcal{F}_{p,k}$ *in the AGM under the* $(\ell - 1) \cdot \nu$-BSDH *assumption [3].*

Theorem 8. *Consider construction* MVTree *and let* $\pi^\sigma = ([H_\nu^\sigma]_1, \ldots, [H_1^\sigma]_1,$ $\mathsf{C}_\sigma, \hat{\mathsf{C}}_\sigma, \pi_\sigma')$ *be some proof of opening for a leaf commitment in position* σ *written in* ℓ-*ary.*

Then, computing all partial proofs $\left\{([H_\nu^\sigma]_2, \ldots, [H_1^\sigma]_1, \mathsf{C}_\sigma, \hat{\mathsf{C}}_\sigma)\right\}_{\sigma \in \Sigma^\nu}$ *can be done in* $O_\lambda(k \cdot \nu \cdot \ell^\nu) = O_\lambda(\nu \cdot m)$ *time and storing them needs* $O_\lambda(\ell^\nu) = O_\lambda(m/k)$ *space. Furthermore, if we update* C *by adding* δ *in some position* i^*, *we can update all partial proofs in time* $O_\lambda(\nu)$.

Efficiency of the Multivariate Construction. We only consider the case where $\ell = O(1)$. First, let's focus on the time needed to compute $[H_j]_1$. One can simply write the polynomial $p_j - p_{j-1}$ as a polynomial in $1, X_j, \ldots, X_j^{\ell-1}$ with polynomial coefficients in the other variables. Then, we can use standard (univariate) polynomial division to divide each term with $X_j - \sigma_j$ in constant time. To encode it in the group, it is enough to note that the total degree of each term is $k \cdot \ell^{j-1}$, so we need to perform ℓ multi-exponentiations of this size totaling in $O(k \cdot \ell^j)$ operations.

That said, we demonstrate the efficiency of the construction. The commitment key consists of linear in m group elements. Opening needs $O(k \cdot \ell^j)$ operations for each iteration, totaling in $O(k \cdot \ell^\nu)$ time. By inspection of the construction, proofs size is $\log_\ell(m/k) + 2 + |\pi'|$, where π' is the size of an opening of the leaf commitment. Finally, verification consists of (1) a $\log_\ell(m/k)$-size pairing product equation, (2) a low degree test involving constant operations and (3) a verification of an opening of a leaf commitment.

Remark 3 (On aggregation). The first two verification tests are pairing product equations. Assuming the leaf commitment verification is also a pairing product equation, one can use inner pairing products [6] to aggregate many such equations as done in [26] and, thus, achieve one-hop cross commitment aggregation. While the aggregated proof size decreases exponentially, this comes at the cost of a significant overhead for the prover due to the need to work in the target group. Reducing the proof size from $\log_2 m$ to roughly $\log_\ell(m/k)$ (assuming constant size/verification for leaf commitment opening) can make aggregation significantly cheaper for the prover.

7.2   Univariate Maintainable Vector Commitments

In this section, we give an optimized construction that achieves the same memory-time tradeoffs for the prover that the scheme in Sect. 7.1, but for univariate polynomials. For that, we rely on the q-BSDH assumption for $q = m - 1$ [3], while we only needed $q = \log m$ plus the assumption that the leaf commitment is sound in the multivariate case.

Our work generalizes a previous univariate construction of [28] in a similar way as it generalizes hyperproofs. Namely, our construction truncates the tree at some level so that leaves are commitments and not individual positions.

For vectors of size m, we offer the following trade-off: for any ν, κ, such that $m = 2^{\nu+\kappa+1}$, one can derive openings of size $\nu + 5$ group elements. The prover can pre-compute and store $2^\nu - 1$ proofs, and then compute proofs by performing $O(\kappa 2^\kappa)$ group operations. We show also how to compute all proofs with $O(\nu m)$ group operations (plus $O(m(\nu + \kappa))$ field operations). The proofs are maintainable, as an update in a position requires recomputing $O(\nu)$ proofs. One interesting feature is that the trusted setup depends only on m (the powers of τ) and not on ν, κ, so the right tradeoff can be decided on the fly.

Overview. Our construction builds a tree of commitments to a vector $\mathbf{v} \in \mathbb{F}^m$ build as follows. The root of the tree is a commitment $\mathsf{C} = [\boldsymbol{\lambda}]_1 \mathbf{v}$, where $\boldsymbol{\lambda} = ([\lambda_1(\tau)]_1, \dots, [\lambda_m(\tau)]_1)$, for $\{\lambda_j(X)\}$ the Lagrange interpolation polynomials for $\mathbb{H}$. The two children will be $\mathsf{C}_0 = [\boldsymbol{\lambda}_0]_1 \mathbf{v}_0$ and $\mathsf{C}_1 = [\boldsymbol{\lambda}_1]_1 \mathbf{v}_1$, which are commitments to $\mathbf{v}_0$ and $\mathbf{v}_1$ with keys $\boldsymbol{\lambda}_0$ and $\boldsymbol{\lambda}_1$ of half the size to be specified next. The two children of C_0 will be $\mathsf{C}_{00} = [\boldsymbol{\lambda}_{10}]_1 \mathbf{v}_{10}, \mathsf{C}_{10} = [\boldsymbol{\lambda}_{10}]_1 \mathbf{v}_{10}$ and so on. The leaves are commitments $\mathsf{C}_\mathbf{b}$, $\mathbf{b} = (b_\nu, \dots, b_0) \in \{0,1\}^{\nu+1}$ to vectors of size 2^κ. For any leaf index $\mathbf{b} = (b_\nu, \dots, b_0)$, we denote $\mathbf{b}_{|j} = (b_j \dots b_0)$ the suffix[11] of size j. Note that $\mathsf{C}_{\mathbf{b}_{|j}}$ for $j = 0, \dots, \nu - 1$ denotes all the commitments from the root to the leaf $\mathsf{C}_\mathbf{b}$.

The division into vectors of half the size is done in bit reverse order according to the least significant bit of the binary representation of the index, b_0. At the first level, there will be two vectors $\mathbf{v}_0, \mathbf{v}_1$ of size $m/2$ containing all positions of $\mathbf{v}$ with suffix b_0. At the next level, there will be four vectors $\mathbf{v}_{00}, \mathbf{v}_{01}, \mathbf{v}_{10}, \mathbf{v}_{11}$ of size $m/4$, and $\mathbf{v}_{b_1 b_0}$ indicates all the positions of $\mathbf{v}$ (in the natural order) that have as suffix $b_1 b_0$ and so on.

The division into commitment keys of half the size will follow a similar pattern. At level 1, the group of roots of unity $\mathbb{H}$ will be split into $\mathbb{H}^0$ and $\mathbb{H}^1$, according to the least significant bit of the binary representation of the index of the root, i.e. $\mathbb{H}^0$ consists of all even and $\mathbb{H}^1$ all odd powers of ω. In particular, $\mathbb{H}^0$ are the roots of unity of size $m/2$, and $\mathbb{H}^1 = \omega \mathbb{H}^0$ is a coset. At level 2, the commitment keys will be associated to $\mathbb{H}^{00}, \mathbb{H}^{01}, \mathbb{H}^{10}, \mathbb{H}^{11}$ and by the same reasoning, $\mathbb{H}^{00}$ are the roots of unity of size $m/4$, $\mathbb{H}^{10} = \omega^2 \mathbb{H}^{00}$, $\mathbb{H}^{01} = \omega \mathbb{H}^{00}$ and $\mathbb{H}^{11} = \omega^3 \mathbb{H}^{00}$. More generally, we note that for any $0 \le j \le \nu$ and any string $(b_j, \dots, b_0) \in \{0,1\}^{j+1}$,

---

[11] Note that this notation is different than the one we used in the multivariate case. In the latter case, this notation denoted prefixes while here it denotes suffixes. We do this because in each case the corresponding notation makes presentation easier.

$\mathbb{H}^{\mathbf{b}_{|j}} = \omega^s \mathbb{H}_r$, for $s = \sum_{i=0}^{j} b_i 2^i$ and $r = \frac{m}{2^{j+1}}$. The vanishing polynomial associated to $\mathbb{H}^{\mathbf{b}_{|j}}$ will be denoted $t_{\mathbf{b}_{|j}}(X) = X^r - (\omega^s)^r = X^{\frac{m}{2^{j+1}}} - \omega^{\frac{m \sum_{i=0}^{j} b_i 2^i}{2^{j+1}}}$. The Lagrange polynomials associated to the interpolation set $\mathbb{H}^{\mathbf{b}_{|j}}$ with the natural order will be written as $\boldsymbol{\lambda}^{\mathbf{b}_{|j}}(X) = (\lambda_1^{\mathbf{b}_{|j}}(X), \ldots, \lambda_r^{\mathbf{b}_{|j}}(X))$ and the commitment key for node $\mathbf{b}_{|j}$ is $\boldsymbol{\lambda}^{\mathbf{b}_{|j}} = [\boldsymbol{\lambda}^{\mathbf{b}_{|j}}(\tau)]_1$.

As in the multivariate case, the idea to open the commitment to some function f that is a linear function of some chunk $\mathbf{v}_i$ is to (1) open the root commitment to the leaf and (2) open the commitment to the leaf using the IP argument for the Lagrange basis of Sect. 5 or the construction of Tomescu et al. [27]. For (2), since at the leaf level the commitment is w.r.t to the key $\boldsymbol{\lambda}^{\mathbf{b}}$ for some $\mathbf{b} = (b_\nu, \ldots, b_0)$, we prove the following lemma, that shows that the construction for inner products of Sect. 5 works for any coset of roots of unity.

Theorem 9. *Let $\mathbb{H} \subset \mathbb{F}$ be a subset of roots of unity of size $m = 2^{\nu+\kappa+1}$, for some $\kappa, \nu \geq 0$. Given some $\mathbf{b} \in \{0,1\}^{\nu+1}$, define $s = \sum_{i=0}^{\nu} b_i 2^i$, $r = 2^\kappa$, $\mathbb{H}_r \subset \mathbb{H}$ the subgroup of roots of unity of size r, and $\mathbb{H}^{\mathbf{b}} = \omega^s \mathbb{H}_r$. Let $t_{\mathbf{b}}(X)$ be the vanishing polynomial at $\mathbb{H}^{\mathbf{b}}$ and $\boldsymbol{\lambda}^{\mathbf{b}}(X)$ the associated Lagrange basis polynomials. Then, if $A(X) = \boldsymbol{\lambda}^{\mathbf{b}}(X) \cdot \mathbf{a}$ and $B(X) = \boldsymbol{\lambda}^{\mathbf{b}}(X) \cdot \mathbf{b}$, it holds that $\mathbf{a} \cdot \mathbf{b} = y$ if and only if there exist polynomials $H(X), R(X)$ with $\deg(R) < r - 2$ such that*

$$A(X)B(X) - r^{-1}y = XR(X) + t_{\mathbf{b}}(X)H(X).$$

Therefore, at any leaf $\mathbf{b}$ we can open the commitment to any linear relation and verify with the same equation. To open C to a certain leaf commitment C_i, the idea is to implicitly show from root to leaf that $\mathsf{C}_{\mathbf{b}_{|j}}$, $\mathsf{C}_{\mathbf{b}_{|j+1}}$ agree in $\mathbb{H}^{\mathbf{b}_{|j+1}}$. This is proven by showing that their difference is divisible by $t_{(1-b_{j+1})\mathbf{b}_{|j}}(X)$. More specifically, we prove the following lemma, that shows how the parent and the children nodes ate each level relate through a simple equation:

Lemma 1. *Consider two cosets $\mathbb{H}_{0\mathbf{b}_{|j}}$ and $\mathbb{H}_{1\mathbf{b}_{|j}}$. Let $C_{\mathbf{b}_{|j}}(X)$ be an encoding of vector $\mathbf{v}^{\mathbf{b}_{|j}}$, and $C_{0\mathbf{b}_{|j}}(X), C_{1\mathbf{b}_{|j}}(X)$ those of vectors $\mathbf{v}^{0\mathbf{b}_{|j}}$ and $\mathbf{v}^{1\mathbf{b}_{|j}}$. For all $j = 0, \ldots, \nu$ it is true that*

$$C_{\mathbf{b}_{|j}}(X) = t_{1\mathbf{b}_{|j}}(X) \frac{C_{0\mathbf{b}_{|j}}(X) - C_{1\mathbf{b}_{|j}}(X)}{2\omega^{sj}} + C_{1\mathbf{b}_{|j}}(X)$$

$$C_{\mathbf{b}_{|j}}(X) = t_{0\mathbf{b}_{|j}}(X) \frac{C_{0\mathbf{b}_{|j}}(X) - C_{1\mathbf{b}_{|j}}(X)}{-2\omega^{sj}} + C_{0\mathbf{b}_{|j}}(X)$$

Scheme Description. Formally, we present an LVC commitment scheme that works for the function family:

$$\mathsf{Ext}_\nu\text{-}\mathcal{F}_{p,2^\kappa} = \{f : \mathbb{F}^m \to \mathbb{F}, m = 2^{\kappa+\nu+1} \mid \exists \mathbf{f} \in \mathbb{F}^{2^\kappa}, i \in 2^\nu \text{ s.t.}$$
$$\forall \mathbf{v}_1, \ldots, \mathbf{v}_{2^\nu} \in \mathbb{F}^{2^\kappa} : f(\mathbf{v}_1, \ldots, \mathbf{v}_{2^\nu}) = \mathbf{v}_i \cdot \mathbf{f}\}$$

Algorithms LVC.KeyGen and LVC.Commit are the same as the Lagrange basis construction of Sect. 5 and are omitted. The commitment to $\mathbf{v}$ is $\mathsf{C} = [\boldsymbol{\lambda}^\top]_1 \mathbf{v}$

together with the auxiliary input information aux. Note that step 4. of the open algorithm is IP.Open from Sect. 5.2.

UVTree.Open$(\mathsf{pk}, \mathbf{b}, \mathsf{aux}, f, \mathbf{y}) \rightarrow \pi$:

1. Let $f(\mathbf{v}_{0...0}, \ldots, \mathbf{v}_{1...1}) = \mathbf{v_b} \cdot \mathbf{f}$ for $\mathbf{f} \in \mathbb{F}^{2^\kappa}$ and some $\mathbf{b} = (b_\nu, \ldots, b_0)$.
2. For any $0 \leq j \leq \nu$, compute $\mathsf{C}_{\mathbf{b}_{|j}} = [\boldsymbol{\lambda}^{\mathbf{b}_{|j}}]_1 \mathbf{v}_{\mathbf{b}_{|j}}$.
3. Compute $[H]_1 = (\mathsf{C}_0 - \mathsf{C}_1)/2$, and for any $0 \leq j \leq \nu - 1$, compute $K_{b_{|j}} = (-1)^j (2\omega^{s_j})^{-1}$. Then define $[H_{\mathbf{b}_{|j}}]_1 = K_{b_{|j}} (\mathsf{C}_{0b_j...b_0} - \mathsf{C}_{1b_j...b_0})$.
4. Find $R(X), H_{\mathbf{b}}(X)$ such that if

$$(\boldsymbol{\lambda}^{\mathbf{b}}(X) \; \mathbf{v_b}) \left(\sum_{i=1}^{2^\kappa} f_i \lambda_i^{\mathbf{b}}(X) \right) - y 2^{-\kappa} = X R(X) + H_{\mathbf{b}}(X) t_{\mathbf{b}}(X).$$

Define $\hat{R}(X) = X^{m+1-2^\kappa} R(X)$.[12] Define $\hat{\mathsf{C}}_{\mathbf{b}} = \tau^{m-2^\kappa} \mathsf{C}_{\mathbf{b}}$.

5. Output $\pi = ([H_{b_0}]_1, \ldots, [H_{\mathbf{b}_{|\nu-1}}]_1, [H_{\mathbf{b}}(\tau)]_1, [R(\tau)]_1, [\hat{R}(\tau)]_1, \mathsf{C}_{\mathbf{b}}, \hat{\mathsf{C}}_{\mathbf{b}})$.

UVTree.Vf$(\mathsf{vk}, \mathsf{C}, f, \mathbf{y}, \pi) \rightarrow 0/1$:

1. Use the vector representation $\mathbf{f}$ of f and compute $\mathsf{C}_f = \sum_{i=1}^{2^\kappa} f_i [\lambda_i^{\mathbf{b}}(\tau)]_2$.
2. Check that

$$e(\mathsf{C} - \mathsf{C}_{\mathbf{b}}, 1) = e([H]_1, [t_{b_0}(\tau)]_2) + \sum_{j=0}^{\nu-1} e([H_{\mathbf{b}_{|j}}]_1, [t_{\mathbf{b}_{|j+1}}(\tau)]_2) \quad (1)$$

$$e(\mathsf{C}_{\mathbf{b}}, \mathsf{C}_f) - e(m^{-1} y[1]_1, [1]_2) = e([R]_1, [1]_2) + e([H_{\mathbf{b}}]_1, [t_{\mathbf{b}}(\tau)]_2) \quad (2)$$

$$e([R]_1, [\tau^{m+1-2^\kappa}]_2) = e([\hat{R}]_1, [1]_2) \quad (3)$$

$$e(\mathsf{C}_{\mathbf{b}}, [\tau^{m-2^\kappa}]_2) = e(\hat{\mathsf{C}}_{\mathbf{b}}, [1]_2) \quad (4)$$

Maintainability. The cost of computing all proofs is $O(\nu m)$. For each piece $\mathbf{v}_i$ with $O(\kappa 2^\kappa)$ operations one can compute the coefficients in the monomial basis. Following Lemma 1, the parent node can be computed in cost dominated by $2^\kappa = \frac{m}{2^{\nu+1}}$ exponentiations from the expression of children nodes, and since there are 2^ν parent nodes the cost is dominated by $\frac{m}{2}$ exponentiations. Going one level up, the vector size doubles but the number of nodes is halved. We conclude that to compute all proofs one needs $O(\kappa 2^\kappa + \nu \frac{m}{2})$. The number of proofs to store (including leaf commitments) is $2^{\nu+1} - 1$.

Theorem 10. *When instantiated with a function binding argument for inner product relations* IP, *the scheme above is a function binding LVC argument under the AGM if the* $(m-1, m)$-*DLOG assumption holds.*

---

[12] We assume as in Sect. 5 that at most $m-1$ powers of τ are in the SRS in group $\mathbb{G}_1$. The degree check is meant to ensure that $R(X)$ is of degree at most $2^\kappa - 2$.

Proof. Let $\mathcal{A}$ be an adversary against the function binding game as in Definition 3. We will see, through game reductions, that the advantage of $\mathcal{A}$ in strong function binding is negligible even for $k = 2$, that is, for two non-compatible functions f_1, f_2. Note that for two functions to be non compatible they must be defined on the same block $\mathbf{b}$.

$\mathcal{A}$ plays Game_0, the strong function binding game as in Definition 3, and outputs $(\mathsf{C}, \{f_k, y_k, \pi_k\}_{k=1,2})$, where $\pi_1 = (\{[H_{\mathbf{b}|j}]_1,\}_{j=0}^{\nu-1}, [H_{\mathbf{b}}]_1, [R]_1, [\hat{R}]_1, \mathsf{C}_{\mathbf{b}}, \hat{\mathsf{C}}_{\mathbf{b}})$, $\pi_2 = (\{[H'_{\mathbf{b}|j}]_1\}_{j=0}^{\nu-1}, [H'_{\mathbf{b}}]_1, [R']_1, [\hat{R}']_1, \mathsf{C}'_{\mathbf{b}}, \hat{\mathsf{C}}'_{\mathbf{b}})$, s.t. $\mathsf{LVC.Verify}(\mathsf{vk}, \mathsf{C}, f_1, y_1, \pi_1) = 1$, $\mathsf{LVC.Verify}(\mathsf{vk}, \mathsf{C}, f_2, y_2, \pi_2) = 1$, and wins if there exists no $\mathbf{v} \in \mathbb{F}^m$ such that $f_1(\mathbf{v}) = y_1$ and $f_2(\mathbf{v}) = y_2$.

Recall $\mathcal{A}$ is algebraic and thus we assume one can extract polynomials $C_{\mathbf{b}}(X), C'_{\mathbf{b}}(X), \hat{C}_{\mathbf{b}}(X), \hat{C}'_{\mathbf{b}}(X)$ which are, algebraic representations of $\mathsf{C}_{\mathbf{b}}, \mathsf{C}'_{\mathbf{b}}$ and $H_{\mathbf{b}}(X), H'_{\mathbf{b}}(X), \{H_{\mathbf{b}|j}(X), H'_{\mathbf{b}|j}(X)\}_{j=0}^{\nu-1}$ the ones for $[H_{\mathbf{b}}]_1, [H'_{\mathbf{b}}]_1, \{[H_{\mathbf{b}|j}]_1, [H'_{\mathbf{b}|j}]_1\}_{j=0}^{\nu-1}$, respectively.

Let Game_1 be exactly as Game_0 but the game aborts if $C_{\mathbf{b}}(X)$ or $C'_{\mathbf{b}}(X)$ are polynomials of degree more than $2^\kappa - 1$. If this is not the case, it is easy to find τ by observing that in this case either $C_{\mathbf{b}}(X)X^{m-2^\kappa} - \hat{C}(X)$ or $C'_{\mathbf{b}}(X)X^{m-2^\kappa} - \hat{C}'(X)$ is a non-zero polynomial with a root in τ so the difference between both games is bounded by the advantage of any adversary against the $(m-1, m)$-DLOG problem.

Let Game_2 be exactly as Game_1 but upon receiving π_1, π_2, it checks if $\mathsf{C}_{\mathbf{b}}$ and $\mathsf{C}'_{\mathbf{b}}$ are equal and aborts otherwise. We next bound the probability of abort.

Define the polynomial $p(X) = C_{\mathbf{b}}(X) - C'_{\mathbf{b}}(X) - (H(X) - H'(X))t_{b_0}(X) + \sum_{j=0}^{\nu-1}(H_{\mathbf{b}|j}(X) - H_{\mathbf{b}|j+1}(X))t_{\mathbf{b}|j}(X)$, which is the difference of verification Eq. (1) for each commitment. If $p(X) \neq 0$, the output of the adversary can be used to construct an adversary against the $(m-1, m)$-DLOG assumption, since τ is a root of $p(X)$. On the other hand, if $p(X) = 0$, $C_{\mathbf{b}}(X) - C'_{\mathbf{b}}(X)$ can be written as a sum of terms that are multiples of $t_{\mathbf{b}|j}(X)$ for $j = 0, \dots, \nu$. But all of these vanishing polynomials evaluate to 0 in $\mathsf{h} \in \mathbb{H}^{\mathbf{b}}$, since $t_{\mathbf{b}}(X) | t_{\mathbf{b}|j}(X)$ for $j = 0, \dots, \nu$. Therefore, $C_{\mathbf{b}}(X) - C'_{\mathbf{b}}(X)$ is also 0 when evaluated at the coset. But since this polynomial is of degree at most 2^k, $C_{\mathbf{b}}(X) = C'_{\mathbf{b}}(X)$ which implies that necessarily $\mathsf{C}_{\mathbf{b}} = \mathsf{C}'_{\mathbf{b}}$.

Therefore, in Game_2, except with negligible probability the leaf commitment is the same and the probability that the adversary wins is the same as in the strong function binding game of the inner product commitment. $\square$

References

1. Aranha, D.F., Pagnin, E., Rodríguez-Henríquez, F.: LOVE a pairing. In: Longa, P., Ràfols, C. (eds.) LATINCRYPT 2021. LNCS, vol. 12912, pp. 320–340. Springer, Cham (2021). https://doi.org/10.1007/978-3-030-88238-9_16

2. Ben-Sasson, E., Chiesa, A., Riabzev, M., Spooner, N., Virza, M., Ward, N.P.: Aurora: transparent succinct arguments for R1CS. In: Ishai, Y., Rijmen, V. (eds.) EUROCRYPT 2019, Part I. LNCS, vol. 11476, pp. 103–128. Springer, Cham (2019). https://doi.org/10.1007/978-3-030-17653-2_4

3. Boneh, D., Boyen, X.: Efficient selective identity-based encryption without random oracles. J. Cryptol. **24**(4), 659–693 (2011). https://doi.org/10.1007/s00145-010-9078-6

4. Boneh, D., Bünz, B., Fisch, B.: Batching techniques for accumulators with applications to IOPs and stateless blockchains. In: Boldyreva, A., Micciancio, D. (eds.) CRYPTO 2019, Part I. LNCS, vol. 11692, pp. 561–586. Springer, Cham (2019). https://doi.org/10.1007/978-3-030-26948-7_20

5. Bowe, S.: BLS12-381: New zk-SNARK elliptic curve construction. Zcash Company Blog (2017). https://z.cash/blog/new-snark-curve

6. Bünz, B., Maller, M., Mishra, P., Tyagi, N., Vesely, P.: Proofs for Inner Pairing Products and Applications. In: Tibouchi, M., Wang, H. (eds.) ASIACRYPT 2021, Part III. LNCS, vol. 13092, pp. 65–97. Springer, Cham (2021). https://doi.org/10.1007/978-3-030-92078-4_3

7. Campanelli, M., Fiore, D., Greco, N., Kolonelos, D., Nizzardo, L.: Incrementally Aggregatable Vector Commitments and Applications to Verifiable Decentralized Storage. In: Moriai, S., Wang, H. (eds.) ASIACRYPT 2020, Part II. LNCS, vol. 12492, pp. 3–35. Springer, Cham (2020). https://doi.org/10.1007/978-3-030-64834-3_1

8. Campanelli, M., Fiore, D., Han, S., Kim, J., Kolonelos, D., Oh, H.: Succinct zero-knowledge batch proofs for set accumulators. Cryptology ePrint Archive (2021)

9. Catalano, D., Fiore, D.: Vector commitments and their applications. In: Kurosawa, K., Hanaoka, G. (eds.) PKC 2013. LNCS, vol. 7778, pp. 55–72. Springer, Heidelberg (2013). https://doi.org/10.1007/978-3-642-36362-7_5

10. Chepurnoy, A., Papamanthou, C., Zhang, Y.: EDRAX: a cryptocurrency with stateless transaction validation. Cryptology ePrint Archive, Report 2018/968 (2018). https://eprint.iacr.org/2018/968

11. Daza, V., Ràfols, C., Zacharakis, A.: Updateable inner product argument with logarithmic verifier and applications. In: Kiayias, A., Kohlweiss, M., Wallden, P., Zikas, V. (eds.) PKC 2020, Part I. LNCS, vol. 12110, pp. 527–557. Springer, Cham (2020). https://doi.org/10.1007/978-3-030-45374-9_18

12. Filecoin: Filecoin powers of tau ceremony attestations (2020). https://github.com/arielgabizon/perpetualpowersoftau

13. Fisch, B.: PoReps: Proofs of space on useful data. Cryptology ePrint Archive, Report 2018/678 (2018). https://eprint.iacr.org/2018/678

14. Fuchsbauer, G., Kiltz, E., Loss, J.: The Algebraic Group Model and its Applications. In: Shacham, H., Boldyreva, A. (eds.) CRYPTO 2018, Part II. LNCS, vol. 10992, pp. 33–62. Springer, Cham (2018). https://doi.org/10.1007/978-3-319-96881-0_2

15. Gorbunov, S., Reyzin, L., Wee, H., Zhang, Z.: Pointproofs: aggregating proofs for multiple vector commitments. In: Ligatti, J., Ou, X., Katz, J., Vigna, G. (eds.) ACM CCS 2020, pp. 2007–2023. ACM Press, November 2020

16. Grassi, L., Khovratovich, D., Rechberger, C., Roy, A., Schofnegger, M.: Poseidon: a new hash function for {Zero-Knowledge} proof systems. In: 30th USENIX Security Symposium (USENIX Security 2021), pp. 519–535 (2021)

17. Groth, J.: On the Size of Pairing-Based Non-interactive Arguments. In: Fischlin, M., Coron, J.-S. (eds.) EUROCRYPT 2016, Part II. LNCS, vol. 9666, pp. 305–326. Springer, Heidelberg (2016). https://doi.org/10.1007/978-3-662-49896-5_11

18. Groth, J., Kohlweiss, M., Maller, M., Meiklejohn, S., Miers, I.: Updatable and universal common reference strings with applications to zk-SNARKs. In: Shacham, H., Boldyreva, A. (eds.) CRYPTO 2018, Part III. LNCS, vol. 10993, pp. 698–728. Springer, Cham (2018). https://doi.org/10.1007/978-3-319-96878-0_24

19. Kate, A., Zaverucha, G.M., Goldberg, I.: Constant-size commitments to polynomials and their applications. In: Abe, M. (ed.) ASIACRYPT 2010. LNCS, vol. 6477, pp. 177–194. Springer, Heidelberg (2010). https://doi.org/10.1007/978-3-642-17373-8_11

20. Lai, R.W.F., Malavolta, G.: Subvector Commitments with Application to Succinct Arguments. In: Boldyreva, A., Micciancio, D. (eds.) CRYPTO 2019, Part I. LNCS, vol. 11692, pp. 530–560. Springer, Cham (2019). https://doi.org/10.1007/978-3-030-26948-7_19

21. Libert, B., Ramanna, S.C., Yung, M.: Functional commitment schemes: from polynomial commitments to pairing-based accumulators from simple assumptions. In: Chatzigiannakis, I., Mitzenmacher, M., Rabani, Y., Sangiorgi, D. (eds.) ICALP 2016, Volume 55 of LIPIcs, pp. 30:1–30:14. Schloss Dagstuhl, July 2016

22. Libert, B., Yung, M.: Concise mercurial vector commitments and independent zero-knowledge sets with short proofs. In: Micciancio, D. (ed.) TCC 2010. LNCS, vol. 5978, pp. 499–517. Springer, Heidelberg (2010). https://doi.org/10.1007/978-3-642-11799-2_30

23. Merkle, R.C.: A digital signature based on a conventional encryption function. In: Pomerance, C. (ed.) CRYPTO 1987. LNCS, vol. 293, pp. 369–378. Springer, Heidelberg (1988). https://doi.org/10.1007/3-540-48184-2_32

24. Papamanthou, C., Shi, E., Tamassia, R.: Signatures of correct computation. In: Sahai, A. (ed.) TCC 2013. LNCS, vol. 7785, pp. 222–242. Springer, Heidelberg (2013). https://doi.org/10.1007/978-3-642-36594-2_13

25. Ràfols, C., Zapico, A.: An algebraic framework for universal and updatable SNARKs. In: Malkin, T., Peikert, C. (eds.) CRYPTO 2021, Part I. LNCS, vol. 12825, pp. 774–804. Springer, Cham (2021). https://doi.org/10.1007/978-3-030-84242-0_27

26. Srinivasan, S., Chepurnoy, A., Papamanthou, C., Tomescu, A., Zhang, Y.: Hyperproofs: aggregating and maintaining proofs in vector commitments. In: 31st USENIX Security Symposium (USENIX Security 2022), Boston, MA. USENIX Association, August 2022

27. Tomescu, A., Abraham, I., Buterin, V., Drake, J., Feist, D., Khovratovich, D.: Aggregatable subvector commitments for stateless cryptocurrencies. In: Galdi, C., Kolesnikov, V. (eds.) SCN 2020. LNCS, vol. 12238, pp. 45–64. Springer, Cham (2020). https://doi.org/10.1007/978-3-030-57990-6_3

28. Tomescu, A., et al.: Towards scalable threshold cryptosystems. In: 2020 IEEE Symposium on Security and Privacy, pp. 877–893. IEEE Computer Society Press, May 2020

PointProofs, Revisited

Benoît Libert[1,2], Alain Passelègue[2,3], and Mahshid Riahinia[2(✉)]

[1] CNRS, Laboratoire LIP, Lyon, France
[2] ENS de Lyon, Laboratoire LIP (U. Lyon, CNRS, ENSL, Inria, UCBL),
Lyon, France
{benoit.libert,mahshid.riahinia}@ens-lyon.fr
[3] Inria, Lyon, France
alain.passelegue@inria.fr

Abstract. Vector commitments allow a user to commit to a vector of length n using a constant-size commitment while being able to locally open the commitment to individual vector coordinates. Importantly, the size of position-wise openings should be independent of the dimension n. Gorbunov, Reyzin, Wee, and Zhang recently proposed PointProofs (CCS 2020), a vector commitment scheme that supports non-interactive aggregation of proofs across multiple commitments, allowing to drastically reduce the cost of block propagation in blockchain smart contracts. Gorbunov *et al.* provide a security analysis combining the algebraic group model and the random oracle model, under the weak n-bilinear Diffie-Hellman Exponent assumption (n-wBDHE) assumption. In this work, we propose a novel analysis that does not rely on the algebraic group model. We prove the security in the random oracle model under the n-Diffie-Hellman Exponent (n-DHE) assumption, which is implied by the n-wBDHE assumption considered by Gorbunov *et al.* We further note that we do not modify their scheme (and thus preserve its efficiency) nor introduce any additional assumption. Instead, we prove the security of the scheme as it is via a strictly improved analysis.

Keywords: Vector commitments · Aggregation · Provable security

1 Introduction

As introduced in [12,22], vector commitments (VCs) allow a user to commit to a vector of messages by generating a short commitment string. Later, the committer should be able to concisely reveal individual coordinates of the message vector. Here, "concisely" means that the partial opening information (called "proof" hereafter) should have constant size – no matter how large the committed vector is – and still convince the verifier that the opened coordinate is correct. As in standard commitments, a vector commitment scheme should satisfy two security properties: (1) A *binding* property which asserts that no efficient adversary should be able to generate a commitment of a vector that can be opened to

© International Association for Cryptologic Research 2022
S. Agrawal and D. Lin (Eds.): ASIACRYPT 2022, LNCS 13794, pp. 220–246, 2022.
https://doi.org/10.1007/978-3-031-22972-5_8

two different values at the same position, and (2) a *hiding* property which guarantees that revealing a subset of components should not reveal any information about messages at non-revealed positions. Vector commitments enable significant savings in terms of storage, by storing only a constant-size commitment to a vector instead of commitments to individual coordinates, and bandwidth, thanks to the ability to provably and succinctly open individual positions.

In 2020, Gorbunov, Reyzin, Wee, and Zhang [16] introduced a vector commitment scheme, called PointProofs, which additionally supports non-interactive aggregation of proofs across multiple commitments. Two types of aggregation are supported:

- *Same-commitment aggregation* allows anyone to publicly aggregate single-position proofs for the same vector commitment into a single proof;
- *Cross-commitment aggregation* allows anyone to further aggregate same-commitment-aggregated proofs for distinct commitments (and possibly distinct subsets of positions) and fold them into a single constant-size proof.

Supporting proof aggregations is particularly useful for optimizing distributed applications, such as blockchain propagation. In this context, a third party (the validator) validates blocks by performing operations that depend on data owned by several distinct users. Vector commitments that support proof aggregation make it possible to drastically reduce storage: Instead of storing all users' data, each user can commit to their data individually so that a validator stores only their respective (concise) commitments. When needed, a user can compute proofs for opening positions relevant to the block validation, and aggregate these proofs into a single proof using same-commitment aggregation. Cross-commitment aggregation further allows a validator to aggregate all proofs from distinct users into a single proof that can be included in a block, letting other validators verify the block using a single proof. We also note that PointProofs supports updates of commitments, allowing a user who has already committed to a vector to update some components of this vector without having to compute a new vector commitment from scratch.

In [16], Gorbunov *et al.* consider the use case of blockchain smart contracts. They show that using their scheme instead of former state-of-the-art vector commitments allows a 60%-reduction of bandwidth overheads for propagating a block of transactions. In this work, we focus on improving the security analysis of the scheme without modifying it. We thus refer to [16] for further applications as well as for a detailed efficiency analysis of PointProofs in terms of space and time.

The security requirements of vector commitments with aggregation are easily defined by extending the standard hiding and binding requirements. Specifically, the hiding property requires that (possibly aggregated) proofs for opened positions do not reveal any information about unopened messages. The *binding* property is extended as follows: For same-commitment (resp. cross-commitment) aggregation, binding requires that no efficient adversary be able to come up with a vector commitment C (resp. a set of vector commitments $C_1, \ldots, C_\ell$) together with two conflicting aggregated proofs, which open a position of an output vector commitment to two distinct values. While the PointProofs commitment is perfectly hiding (like its underlying vector commitment scheme [22]), its computational binding property is argued in the algebraic group model, as well as in the random oracle model (ROM), under the n-wBDHE assumption in bilinear groups.

Recall that the algebraic group model (AGM) is an intermediate idealized model, introduced in [15], that stands between the generic group model and the standard model. As a reminder, in the generic group model, adversaries do not have access to the bit representation of group elements: From the adversary's standpoint, each group element is represented by a unique uniformly random bit-string, and group operations are performed by querying an oracle that returns the representation of the resulting group element (to ensure uniqueness, the oracle keeps track of all group elements known to the adversary). In the generic group model, computational problems and their decisional variants are equivalent, and the Discrete Logarithm problem is provably intractable, as shown by Shoup in [30]. This illustrates why proofs in the generic group model are more often considered as sanity checks rather than proofs of security.

The algebraic group model is a security model weaker than the generic group model, in which one only considers *algebraic adversaries*. Unlike the generic group model, no restriction is made regarding access to the group elements in the AGM: Algebraic adversaries have the same access to group elements as in the standard model. Yet, adversaries are restricted to only handle group elements that are computed by applying group operations to known group elements, similarly as in the generic group model. That is, given elements $g_1, \ldots, g_\ell$ from a multiplicative group $\mathbb{G}$, an algebraic adversary can only access elements of the form $\prod_{i=1}^{\ell} g_i^{\lambda_i}$ for coefficients λ_i's of its choice. Hence, the main difference between the generic group model and the algebraic group model is that the latter allows using coefficients λ_i that depend on the actual bit representation of elements g_i's, while the former forbids it. Despite this minor relaxation, the algebraic group model is still considered as being very idealistic and to be avoided when it is possible.

Our Contribution. In this work, we provide a different security analysis of PointProofs, which relies on the *Generalized Forking Lemma* [1] and the *Local Forking Lemma* [2]. Using these tools, we prove the scheme to be binding in the random oracle model, under the n-Diffie-Hellman Exponent (n-DHE) assumption in groups equipped with a bilinear map. As opposed to the original proof of Gorbunov *et al.* [16], we circumvent the use of algebraic group model, and rely on a weaker assumption; the n-DHE assumption being implied by the aforementioned n-wBDHE assumption. In the ROM, we thus prove the binding property under the same assumption as the one used in the underlying vector commitment scheme due to Libert and Yung [22].

We believe this result to be important in the context of vector commitments as it proves the security of PointProofs as a vector commitment scheme supporting cross-commitment aggregation with constant-size openings under a falsifiable assumption [26] without restricting oneself to algebraic adversaries. Moreover, PointProofs is extremely efficient [32] and, among known candidates supporting cross-commitment aggregation [5,16,31], it is the only one that simultaneously provides optimal proof length and linear-size public parameters. Even if we only consider same-commitment aggregation, it implies one of the most efficient schemes with sub-vector openings among those [13,16,17,32] that simultaneously feature linear-size public parameters and optimal-size proofs (recall that elements of a pairing-friendly group usually have a shorter representation than those of hidden-order groups).

We insist that we do not introduce any additional assumptions in Point-Proofs, neither do we alter the efficiency of the scheme in the process. Our approach thus provides a strict improvement over the prior analysis. Before outlining our security proof, we first briefly recall the PointProofs construction.

Construction. PointProofs builds on the vector commitment of [22] and can also be seen as an application of the inner product functional commitment scheme of [21], which are both inspired by the broadcast encryption scheme of Boneh, Gentry and Waters [8]. Let n denote the dimension of committed vectors, and consider cyclic groups $\mathbb{G} = \langle g \rangle$ and $\hat{\mathbb{G}} = \langle \hat{g} \rangle$ of prime order p equipped with an asymmetric bilinear map $e : \mathbb{G} \times \hat{\mathbb{G}} \to \mathbb{G}_T$. Let $g_T = e(g, \hat{g})$ be the generator of $\mathbb{G}_T$. The scheme uses public parameters $\left(g, \hat{g}, \{g_i\}_{i \in [2n] \setminus \{n+1\}}, \{\hat{g}_i\}_{i \in [n]}, H\right)$, with $g_i = g^{(\alpha)^i}$ and $\hat{g}_i = \hat{g}^{(\alpha)^i}$, where α is chosen uniformly at random from $\mathbb{Z}_p$, and $H : \{0,1\}^* \to \mathbb{Z}_p$ is a hash function modeled as a random oracle.

To commit to a vector $\mathbf{m} = (m_1, \ldots, m_n) \in \mathbb{Z}_p^n$, one chooses $\gamma \leftarrow U(\mathbb{Z}_p)$ uniformly and computes a multi-base Pedersen commitment [27] of the form

$$C = g^\gamma \cdot \prod_{j=1}^{n} g_j^{m_j} = g^{\gamma + \sum_{j=1}^{n} m_i \cdot \alpha^j} \quad ,$$

which can be seen as raising g to the evaluation of a polynomial defined by the coefficients contained in $\mathbf{m}$. To open a position $i \in [n]$ of $\mathbf{m}$ to m_i, the committer reveals a proof

$$\pi_i = g_{n+1-i}^\gamma \cdot \prod_{j=1,j\neq i}^{n} g_{n+1-i+j}^{m_j} = \left(C / g^{m_i \cdot \alpha^i}\right)^{\alpha^{n+1-i}} \quad ,$$

which is an element of $\mathbb{G}$ whose discrete logarithm is the same polynomial evaluation as in C, except that the coefficient m_i is lacking, and the polynomial is multiplied by α^{n-i+1}, so that π_i does not depend on the monomial α^{n+1}. This proof can be easily verified by checking that

$$e(C, \hat{g}^{\alpha^{n+1-i}}) = e(\pi_i, \hat{g}) \cdot g_T^{m_i \cdot \alpha^{n+1}} \quad ,$$

where $g_T^{\alpha^{n+1}} = e(g_1, \hat{g}_n)$ is computable from the public parameters.

In order to aggregate multiple proofs $(\pi_i)_{i \in S}$ involving the same commitment C, where $S \subseteq [n]$, anyone can derive randomness for each proof π_i from the random oracle as $t_i \leftarrow H(i, C, S, \mathbf{m}[S])$, with $\mathbf{m}[S]$ being the sub-vector $(m_i)_{i \in S}$, and define the aggregated proof as $\pi_S = \prod_{i \in S} \pi_i^{t_i}$. Verification is achieved in a similar way to the single position case, by additionally verifying the linear combination for coefficients provided by the random oracle evaluations. That is, the verifier checks that

$$e(C, \hat{g}^{\sum_{i \in S} \alpha^{n+1-i} \cdot t_i}) = e(\pi_S, \hat{g}) \cdot g_T^{\alpha^{n+1} \sum_{i \in S} m_i \cdot t_i}.$$

Finally, the cross-commitment aggregation of proofs $(\pi_{S^{(j)}})_{j \in [\ell]}$ (which might result from the same-commitment-aggregation process) proceeds in a similar way. Again, some randomness $t'_j \leftarrow H'(j, \{C^{(j)}, S^{(j)}, \mathbf{m}^{(j)}[S^{(j)}]\}_{j \in [d]})$ is first derived from random oracle evaluations (of a second random oracle H'), and the cross-commitment aggregated proof is defined to be $\pi = \prod_{j=1}^{\ell} (\pi_{S^{(j)}})^{t'_j}$. Verification is performed in a similar way to the same-commitment-aggregated case: The verifier first derives all random coefficients (the $t_i^{(j)}$ for $i \in S^{(j)}$ for each underlying same-commitment-aggregated proof, as well as the t'_j) before verifying that

$$\prod_{j \in [\ell]} \left(e(C^{(j)}, \hat{g}^{\sum_{i \in S^{(j)}} \alpha^{n+1-i} \cdot t_i^{(j)}}) \right)^{t'_j} = e(\pi, \hat{g}) \cdot \prod_{j \in [\ell]} \left(g_T^{\alpha^{n+1} \cdot \sum_{i \in S^{(j)}} m_i^{(j)} \cdot t_i^{(j)}} \right)^{t'_j}.$$

$$(1)$$

Technical Overview. As already mentioned, our proof strategy relies on the Local [2] and Generalized [1] Forking Lemmas. We first briefly remind the intuition behind these lemmas. The standard Forking Lemma [29] considers the setting in which a probabilistic polynomial time adversary $\mathcal{A}$, given access to a random oracle H, succeeds with non-negligible probability in some experiment which consists of outputting a pair (y, aux), where y lies in the domain of H and aux is some auxiliary information, such that the triplet $(y, H(y), \mathsf{aux})$ satisfies a target condition. Let us denote by $x_1, \ldots, x_q$ the q queries made by $\mathcal{A}$ to the random oracle, and let us assume that y is the j-th query for some $j \in [q]$.[1]

The Forking Lemma states that running $\mathcal{A}$ again with the same coins but replacing H with another random oracle H' which satisfies $H'(x_i) = H(x_i)$ for $i < j$, results in $\mathcal{A}$ succeeding again with some non-negligible probability with output $(y, H'(y), \mathsf{aux}')$. The important bit here is that $\mathcal{A}$'s output involves the same y, but now $H'(y)$ differs (with overwhelming probability) from $H(y)$. This new triplet $(y, H'(y), \mathsf{aux}')$ is called a fork. This lemma has notably been used in the context of signature schemes based on applying the Fiat-Shamir paradigm to 3-round identification protocols [14] with special-soundness, where the triplet $(y, H(y), \mathsf{aux})$ is a transcript and the target condition is for it to be valid.

On one hand, the Local Forking Lemma [2] is a refinement of the standard Forking Lemma, which states that one is able to create a fork by replacing H by a random oracle H' that only differs from H on the specific input y.

---

[1] Typically, the target condition is sparse and the range of H is exponentially large, therefore $\mathcal{A}$ must query $H(x)$ to succeed with non-negligible probability.

On the other hand, the Generalized Forking Lemma [1] is an extension to the setting where multiple y's are generated by the adversary. That is, the output of $\mathcal{A}$ is of the form $(y_1, H(y_1), \ldots, y_\ell, H(y_\ell), \mathsf{aux})$ and allows to create forks for different y_i's, e.g., a first fork $(y_1, H'(y_1), \ldots, y'_{\ell'}, H'(y'_{\ell'}), \mathsf{aux}')$ and a second fork $(y_1, H(y_1), \ldots, y_\ell, H''(y_\ell), \mathsf{aux}'')$. Each fork is obtained by using a different random oracle that outputs the same values as H for all the queries preceding the forking point, and whose values are sampled uniformly at random and independently of H as soon as the forking point is hit. In the previous example, y_1 is the forking point of the first tuple and y_ℓ is that of the second one.

We start by explaining how we reduce binding in the case of same-commitment aggregation to the hardness of the n-DHE problem. First, we recall that the n-DHE problem asks to compute g_{n+1} given $\left(g, \hat{g}, \{g_i\}_{i \in [2n] \setminus \{n+1\}}, \{\hat{g}_i\}_{i \in [n]}\right)$ (borrowing the notation from the construction described in the previous part). Consider an adversary $\mathcal{A}$ that manages to break the binding property with non-negligible probability. Our n-DHE solver sets the public parameters to be the n-DHE instance and uses $\mathcal{A}$ as follows.

$\mathcal{A}$ is able to generate a tuple $(C, S_0, S_1, \mathbf{m}_0[S_0], \mathbf{m}_1[S_1], \pi_0, \pi_1)$ containing a commitment C as well as two sets $S_0, S_1 \subseteq [n]$ such that $S_0 \cap S_1 \neq \emptyset$ and valid proofs π_0, π_1 with respect to sub-vectors $\mathbf{m}_0[S_0] \in \mathbb{Z}_p^{|S_0|}$, $\mathbf{m}_1[S_1] \in \mathbb{Z}_p^{|S_1|}$ such that $\mathbf{m}_0[i^*] \neq \mathbf{m}_1[i^*]$ for some $i^* \in S_0 \cap S_1$. The following holds for this output:

$$e(C, \hat{g}^{\alpha^{n+1-i}})^{\sum_{i \in S_b} t_i^{(b)}} = e(\pi_b, \hat{g}) \cdot g_T^{\alpha^{n+1} \sum_{i \in S_b} m_i \cdot t_i^{(b)}}, \tag{2}$$

where $t_i^{(b)} = H(i, C, S_b, \mathbf{m}_b)$, for both $b = 0$ and $b = 1$.

Random oracle queries made by $\mathcal{A}$ are of the form $(i, C, S, \mathbf{m}[S])$, and both $(i^*, C, S_0, \mathbf{m}_0[S_0])$ and $(i^*, C, S_1, \mathbf{m}_1[S_1])$ must have been queried for Eq. 2 to hold. One can then apply the Generalized Forking Lemma in order to create forks. In our case, the auxiliary information aux is the pair of proofs. We aim to obtain two forks: a first one of the form $(C, S_0, S'_1, \mathbf{m}_0[S_0], \mathbf{m}'_1[S'_1], \pi'_0, \pi'_1)$, related to a random oracle H' such that $H(i^*, C, S_0, \mathbf{m}_0[S_0]) \neq H'(i^*, C, S_0, \mathbf{m}_0[S_0])$, and a second one of the form $(C, S''_0, S_1, \mathbf{m}''_0[S''_0], \mathbf{m}_1[S_1], \pi''_0, \pi''_1)$, related to H'' and such that $H(i^*, C, S_1, \mathbf{m}_1[S_1]) \neq H''(i^*, C, S_1, \mathbf{m}_1[S_1])$. In addition, we need that for all $i \in S_0 \setminus \{i^*\}$, $H(i, C, S_0, \mathbf{m}_0[S_0]) = H'(i, C, S_0, \mathbf{m}_0[S_0])$ and that for all $i \in S_1 \setminus \{i^*\}$, $H(i, C, S_1, \mathbf{m}_1[S_1]) = H''(i, C, S_1, \mathbf{m}_1[S_1])$.

Such forks are obtained by applying the Generalized Forking Lemma as follows: to ensure that the mentioned conditions about the values of H, H', H'' are satisfied, we design the reduction algorithm to simulate the random oracle such that all hash values for inputs $(i, C, S_0, \mathbf{m}_0[S_0])$ where $i \in S_0 \setminus \{i^*\}$ (resp. $(i^*, C, S_1, \mathbf{m}_1[S_1])$ where $i \in S_1 \setminus \{i^*\}$) are set before setting the hash values for $(i^*, C, S_0, \mathbf{m}_0[S_0])$ (resp. $(i^*, C, S_1, \mathbf{m}_1[S_1])$). More precisely, our reduction first makes a random guess about the value of i^*, which is a correct guess with probability $1/n$. Then, on receiving a query $(i, C, S, \mathbf{m}[S])$, it checks whether $i^* \in S$. If so, it first defines the hash values for inputs $(i, C, S, \mathbf{m}[S])$ for all $i \neq i^*$, and finally sets the value of $H(i^*, C, S, \mathbf{m}[S])$ at the end. Doing so, the conditions on the values of H, H', H'' are satisfied, and the Generalized Forking Lemma guarantees that the two desired forks can be obtained.

To conclude the proof, one simply re-writes Eq. (2) with each fork using $b = 0$ and $b = 1$, respectively. The first fork leads to equation:

$$e(C, \hat{g}^{\alpha^{n+1-i}})^{\sum_{i \in S_0} t_i'} = e(\pi_0', \hat{g}) \cdot g_T^{\alpha^{n+1} \sum_{i \in S_0} m_i \cdot t_i'} \quad,$$

where $t_i' = H'(i, C, S_0, \mathbf{m}_0)$. A similar equation is obtained for the second fork. Thanks to the conditions satisfied by H, H', H'' values, it follows that for all $i \neq i^*$, we have $t_i^{(0)} = t_i'$ and $t_i^{(1)} = t_i''$, where $t_i'' = H''(i, C, S_1, \mathbf{m}_1)$.

Finally, combining these equations allows to recover an equation that depends only on terms $e(g_{n+1}, \hat{g})$, $e(\pi_1, \hat{g})$, $e(\pi_1'', \hat{g})$, $e(\pi_0, \hat{g})$, $e(\pi_0', \hat{g})$. Setting aside the term $e(g_{n+1}, \hat{g})$ and focusing on the $\mathbb{G}$-component, the reduction manages to compute g_{n+1} as a combination of $\pi_1, \pi_1'', \pi_0, \pi_0'$, which is the solution to the n-DHE problem.

In the supplementary material, we also propose a different proof which relies on the Local Forking Lemma, and compare this approach to the above one. These two proofs provide different bounds for the advantage and run-time of the reduction, and we believe that, in the context of PointProofs, the proof based on the Generalized Forking Lemma provides a tighter reduction.

The case of cross-commitment aggregation follows a similar strategy, but this time we reduce the binding property of the cross-commitment aggregations to that of the same-commitment aggregations. This proof is also in the random oracle model. Given an adversary $\mathcal{A}$ against the binding property of the cross-commitment scheme, we construct an adversary $\mathcal{B}$ against the binding property of the same-commitment scheme as follows: $\mathcal{B}$ splits the random oracles queries made by $\mathcal{A}$ into two categories: those corresponding to same commitment evaluations (the $t_i^{(j)}$'s in the above description), which are redirected by $\mathcal{B}$ to the random oracle to which it has access, and those corresponding to cross-commitment evaluations (the t_j''s). $\mathcal{B}$ simulates the response to the queries of the second category. It first runs $\mathcal{A}$ which outputs two tuples of the form

$$\left(\pi_0, \{C_0^{(j)}, S_0^{(j)}, \mathbf{m}_0^{(j)}[S_0^{(j)}]\}_{j \in [d_0]}\right), \qquad \left(\pi_1, \{C_1^{(j)}, S_1^{(j)}, \mathbf{m}_1^{(j)}[S_1^{(j)}]\}_{j \in [d_1]}\right) \quad,$$

that breaks the binding property. In other words, there exist $j_0 \in [d_0]$, $j_1 \in [d_1]$ such that $C_0^{(j_0)} = C_1^{(j_1)}$ and $\mathbf{m}_0^{(j_0)}[i^*] \neq \mathbf{m}_1^{(j_1)}[i^*]$ for some $i^* \in S_0^{(j_0)} \cap S_1^{(j_1)}$.

$\mathcal{B}$ then uses the Local Forking Lemma twice. In the first fork, it redefines the hash value of the query $(j_0, \{C_0^{(j)}, S_0^{(j)}, \mathbf{m}_0^{(j)}[S_0^{(j)}]\}_{j \in [d_0]})$. The output of $\mathcal{A}$ in this fork involves the same first collection of commitments $\{C_0^{(j)}, S_0^{(j)}, \mathbf{m}_0^{(j)}[S_0^{(j)}]\}_{j \in [d_0]}$ as in the initial execution, together with a proof π_0'. The equation obtained by running the verification algorithm (Eq. 1) on this collection of commitments is such that the value of all t_j''s are the same as $\mathcal{A}$'s first run except if $j = j_0$. By forking a second time on query $(j_1, \{C_1^{(j)}, S_1^{(j)}, \mathbf{m}_1^{(j)}[S_1^{(j)}]\}_{j \in [d_1]})$ and repeating the same arguments, $\mathcal{B}$ obtains two pairs of equations, that can be combined using a similar gymnastic as in the same-commitment proof to recover a valid attack against the binding property of the same-commitment aggregations.

We emphasize that using the Generalized Forking Lemma instead of the Local Forking Lemma does not seem to be an option in this case. Indeed, focusing on the first fork, our proof relies on the capacity to create a fork for the query $(j_0, \{C_0^{(j)}, S_0^{(j)}, \mathbf{m}_0^{(j)}[S_0^{(j)}]\}_{j \in [d_0]})$ without changing every other hash values $H(j, \{C_0^{(j)}, S_0^{(j)}, \mathbf{m}_0^{(j)}[S_0^{(j)}]\}_{j \in [d_0]})$, for $j \in [d_0] \backslash \{j_0\}$. Using the Generalized Forking Lemma would require to set all the latter hash values before the value for $(j_0, \{C_0^{(j)}, S_0^{(j)}, \mathbf{m}_0^{(j)}[S_0^{(j)}]\}_{j \in [d_0]})$, but contrary to the previous case, one cannot simply guess j_0 as it lies in an arbitrary range. For this reason, we rely on the Local Forking Lemma for proving the binding property in this case.

Related Work. Historically, vector commitments with logarithmic-size openings have been known for 3 decades, with the folklore construction based on Merkle trees [23]. In 2008, Catalano *et al.* [11] called for constructions with constant-size openings with the motivation of compressing proofs in zero-knowledge databases [24]. Vector commitments with $O(1)$-size openings appeared later on [12,22], with a first realization based on a q-type assumption put forth by Libert and Yung [22]. Catalano and Fiore [12] obtained constructions from the standard RSA assumption and the Computational Diffie-Hellman assumption in pairing-friendly groups. Peikert *et al.* [28] recently came up with the first candidate under standard lattice assumptions. Meanwhile, applications of vector commitments were considered in the context of zero-knowledge databases [22], verifiable data streaming [18], authenticated dictionaries [20,34], de-centralized storage [10], succinct arguments [3,19], cryptocurrencies [13,32] and blockchain transactions [3,16], or certificates of collective knowledge [25].

Back in 2010, Kate, Zaverucha and Goldberg [17] introduced the related notion of polynomial commitments, which allows committing to a polynomial in such a way that the committer can later prove that the committed polynomial evaluates to specific values on certain inputs. They showed that their scheme enables batch openings, where a constant-size proof convinces the verifier about multiple polynomial evaluations at once. Libert, Ramanna and Yung [21] suggested inner product functional commitments, which imply both vector commitments and polynomial commitments.

Lai and Malavolta [19] and Boneh *et al.* [3] independently generalized VCs by introducing the notion of sub-vector commitments, where the sender can generate a short proof π_S that opens a sub-vector $\mathbf{m}[S]$ of $\mathbf{m}$, for some subset $S \subseteq [n]$. Lai and Malavolta [19] provided instantiations in hidden order groups and also showed that a variant of the Catalano-Fiore commitment [12] allows sub-vector openings under a constant-size assumption (namely, the cube-CDH assumption) in pairing-friendly groups. We remark that sub-vector commitments can also be realized from polynomial commitments with batch openings, as shown by Camenisch *et al.* [9, Section 3.1]. However, their construction intentionally prevents proof aggregation.

The property of proof aggregation was considered in [3,10,16,31,34]. Boneh, Bünz and Fisch [3] and Tomescu *et al.* [32] independently considered same-commitment aggregation in hidden-order groups and under q-type assumptions in pairing-friendly groups, respectively. Campanelli *et al.* [10] defined incrementally aggregatable VCs, where different sub-vector openings can be merged into a constant-size opening for the union of their sub-vectors. Moreover, aggregated proofs support further aggregation. They showed how to realize incrementally aggregatable VCs in hidden-order groups.

Gorbunov et al. [16] proposed PointProofs as the first construction enabling cross-commitment aggregation. They also showed [16, Appendix A] that a variant of the Lai-Malavolta commitment [19] supports same-commitment aggregation, but still at the cost of quadratic-size public parameters. As underlined in [16], same-commitment aggregation implies sub-vector openings by having the committer aggregate same-commitment proofs.

In [16, Appendix B], Gorbunov et al. also showed that the restriction to algebraic adversaries is unnecessary if one just aims at a relaxed binding property – which may be sufficient in certain blockchain applications – which assumes honestly generated commitments. Here, we remove the restriction to algebraic adversaries even when commitments are adversarially generated.

The recent Hyperproofs construction of Srinivasan et al. [31] also allows cross-commitment aggregation and makes it possible to update all proofs in sub-linear time when the vector changes. On the downside, it loses the conciseness of PointProofs as its proofs have size $O(\log n)$. Besides [16,31], we are only aware of one alternative VC scheme supporting cross-commitment aggregation, which was proposed by Boneh et al. [5]. However, it is only known to be secure in the combined AGM+ROM setting.

2   Preliminaries

We use λ to denote the security parameter. For a natural integer $n \in \mathbb{N}$, the set $\{1, 2, \cdots, n\}$ is denoted by $[n]$. We denote by $\mathsf{negl}(\lambda)$ a negligible function in λ, and PPT stands for probabilistic polynomial-time. For a finite set S, we write $x \overset{R}{\leftarrow} S$ to denote that x is sampled uniformly at random from S. We denote vectors by bold characters e.g. $\mathbf{m}$. For a vector $\mathbf{m} = (m_1, \ldots, m_n)$ and a subset of indices $S \subseteq [n]$, we denote by $\mathbf{m}[S]$ the sub-vector $(m_{i_1}, \ldots, m_{i_{|S|}})$, where $S = \{i_1, \ldots, i_{|S|}\}$ with $i_j < i_{j+1}$ for each $j \in \{1, \ldots, |S| - 1\}$. For a single index $i \in [n]$, we sometimes denote m_i by $\mathbf{m}[i]$.

2.1   Bilinear Maps and Complexity Assumptions

Let $(\mathbb{G}, \hat{\mathbb{G}}, \mathbb{G}_T)$ be cyclic groups of prime order p that are equipped with a bilinear map $e : \mathbb{G} \times \hat{\mathbb{G}} \to \mathbb{G}_T$. We rely on a parameterized assumption which was introduced by Boneh, Gentry and Waters [8]. While this assumption was originally defined using symmetric pairings [4,8], we consider a natural extension to asymmetric pairings, which were used in PointProofs.

Definition 1. *Let $(\mathbb{G}, \hat{\mathbb{G}}, \mathbb{G}_T)$ be asymmetric bilinear groups of prime order p. The n-**Diffie-Hellman Exponent** (n-DHE) problem is, given*

$$(g, g^\alpha, g^{(\alpha^2)}, \ldots, g^{(\alpha^n)}, g^{(\alpha^{n+2})}, \ldots, g^{(\alpha^{2n})}, \hat{g}, \hat{g}^\alpha, \hat{g}^{(\alpha^2)}, \ldots, \hat{g}^{(\alpha^n)})$$

where $\alpha \overset{R}{\leftarrow} \mathbb{Z}_p$, $g \overset{R}{\leftarrow} \mathbb{G}$, $\hat{g} \overset{R}{\leftarrow} \hat{\mathbb{G}}$, to compute $g^{(\alpha^{n+1})}$.

We note that this assumption is the same as the one underlying the binding property of the vector commitment scheme of Libert and Yung [22]. As an artifact of the algebraic group model, Gorbunov *et al.* [16] considered a stronger version of the above assumption where $g^{(\alpha^{2n+1})}, \ldots, g^{(\alpha^{3n})}$ are also given.

2.2   Generalized Forking Lemma

Here, we recall the Generalized Forking Lemma as stated in [1] which is later used in one of our proofs.

Game $G_{\mathcal{A},\pi}$

$$f = (\rho, h_1, \ldots, h_Q) \xleftarrow{R} \mathcal{F}$$
$$(L, \{out_\ell\}_{\ell \in L}) \leftarrow \mathcal{A}(\pi, f)$$

If $L = \emptyset$ output 0.

Else, let $L = (\ell_1, \ldots, \ell_m)$ such that $\ell_1 \leq \cdots \leq \ell_m$

For $i = 1, \ldots, m$ do

    Set $succ_i \leftarrow 0$, $k_i \leftarrow 0$, $k_{max} \leftarrow 8mQ/\epsilon \cdot \ln(8m/\epsilon)$

    While $succ_i = 0$ and $k_i < k_{max}$ do

        $f' \xleftarrow{R} \mathcal{F}$ such that $f'_{|\ell_i} = f_{|\ell_i}$

        Let $f' = (\rho, h_1, \ldots, h_{\ell_i - 1}, h'_{\ell_i}, \ldots, h'_Q)$

        $(L', \{out'_\ell\}_{\ell \in L'}) \leftarrow \mathcal{A}(\pi, f')$

        If $h'_{\ell_i} \neq h_{\ell_i}$ and $L' \neq \emptyset$ and $\ell_i \in L'$ then

            keep out'_{ℓ_i} and set $succ_i \leftarrow 1$

        Else

            set $k_i \leftarrow k_i + 1$

If $succ_i = 1$ for all $i \in [m]$, then

    output $(L, \{out_\ell\}_{\ell \in L}, \{out'_\ell\}_{\ell \in L})$

Else output 0

Fig. 1. Game $G_{\pi,\mathcal{A}}$ where an algorithm is forked in the Generalized Forking Lemma.

Let SAMP() be a probabilistic algorithm that returns a value π which we think of as parameters. Also, consider an algorithm $\mathcal{A}$ that takes as input the parameters π and uses some randomness $f = (\rho, h_1, \ldots, h_Q)$, where ρ is value of the random tape of $\mathcal{A}$ and $h_1, \ldots, h_Q$ are responses received by querying a random oracle $H : \{0,1\}^* \rightarrow \mathbb{Z}_p$, and Q is the maximal number of the hash queries. We denote by $\mathcal{F}$ the space of all such randomness. Also, for any $f \in \mathcal{F}$ and $i \in [Q]$, we denote by $f_{|i}$ the sub-vector $(\rho, h_1, \ldots, h_{i-1})$. Algorithm $\mathcal{A}$ outputs a pair $(L, \{out_\ell\}_{\ell \in L})$, where L is a subset of $[Q]$, and each out_ℓ is a string, for $\ell \in L$. We consider $L = \emptyset$ as failure, and $L \neq \emptyset$ as success. Let ϵ be the probability that the output of $\mathcal{A}(\pi, f)$ is successful. We define the game $G_{\pi,\mathcal{A}}$ as in Fig. 1 parameterized by π and $\mathcal{A}$, where $\pi \xleftarrow{R} \mathsf{SAMP}()$. We now state the lemma as proven by Bagherzandi *et al.* [1] and used in [7].

Lemma 1 (Generalized Forking Lemma [1]). *Let* SAMP, $\mathcal{A}$, *and* $H :$ $\{0,1\}^* \rightarrow \mathbb{Z}_p$ *be as described, where* $\mathcal{A}$ *runs in time* τ *and succeeds with probability* ϵ. *If* $p > 8mQ/\epsilon$, *then the game* $G_{\pi,\mathcal{A}}$ *runs in time at most* $\tau \cdot 8m^2 Q/\epsilon \cdot \ln(8m/\epsilon)$, *and is successful with probability at least* $\epsilon/8$.

2.3   Local Forking Lemma

We also recall the Local Forking Lemma of Bellare *et al.* [2], which will be used in our proof for the cross-commitment case. The difference with the classical Forking Lemma is that the random oracle is only reprogrammed on the forking point, instead of all points from the forking point onwards.

Let $\mathsf{SAMP}()$ be a probabilistic algorithm that returns a value π which we think of as parameters. We also consider a deterministic algorithm $\mathcal{A}$, that given $\pi \xleftarrow{R} \mathsf{SAMP}()$, and having access to a random oracle $H \in \mathcal{H}$, outputs an integer $\alpha \geq 0$, and a string x. We consider $\alpha = 0$ as failure, and $\alpha \geq 1$ as success. If $\alpha \geq 1$, we require x to be the α-th query that $\mathcal{A}$ has issued to the oracle H. We consider the two following games parameterized by π and $\mathcal{A}$, where $\pi \xleftarrow{R} \mathsf{SAMP}()$:

Game $G_{\pi,\mathcal{A}}^{\mathsf{single}}$	Game $G_{\pi,\mathcal{A}}^{\mathsf{double}}$
$H \xleftarrow{R} \mathcal{H}$ $(\alpha, x) \leftarrow \mathcal{A}^H(\pi)$ $\quad$ If $\alpha \geq 1$ $\quad\quad$ Return 1 $\quad$ Otherwise $\quad\quad$ Return 0	$H \xleftarrow{R} \mathcal{H}$ $(\alpha, x) \leftarrow \mathcal{A}^H(\pi)$ $\quad$ $H' \leftarrow H$ $H'[x] \xleftarrow{R} \{0,1\}^*$ $(\alpha', x') \leftarrow \mathcal{A}^{H'}(\pi)$ $\quad$ If $(\alpha = \alpha') \wedge (\alpha' \geq 1)$ $\quad\quad$ Return 1 $\quad$ Otherwise $\quad\quad$ Return 0

Fig. 2. Game $G_{\pi,\mathcal{A}}^{\mathsf{single}}$, and Game $G_{\pi,\mathcal{A}}^{\mathsf{double}}$, where the local forking happens in the latter.

We now recall the statement of the lemma.

Lemma 2 (Local Forking Lemma, [2]). *Let* SAMP *and* $\mathcal{A}$ *be as described, and let* q *be the number of* H-*queries issued by* $\mathcal{A}$. *It holds that:*

$$\Pr[G_{\pi,\mathcal{A}}^{\mathsf{double}} = 1] \geq 1/q \cdot \Pr[G_{\pi,\mathcal{A}}^{\mathsf{single}} = 1]^2.$$

2.4   Vector Commitments with Aggregation

We recall the formal definition of vector commitments with aggregation introduced in [16]. As in [16], we divide the definition into two parts; the case of same-commitment aggregation, and the case of cross-commitment aggregation.

2.4.1   Same-Commitment Aggregation

Definition 2 (Vector Commitment with Same-Commitment Aggregation [16]). A vector commitment with same-commitment aggregation for message space $\mathcal{M}$ consists of six algorithms Setup, Commit, UpdateCommit, Prove, Aggregate, Verify as follows:

Setup$(1^\lambda, 1^n) \rightarrow$ pp : On input the security parameter λ and a number n which is the length of underlying vector of a commitment in the scheme, it outputs public parameters pp that is used by all other algorithms.

Commit$_{pp}(\mathbf{m}; \text{aux}) \rightarrow C$: On input a message vector $\mathbf{m} = (m_1, \ldots, m_n)$ of length n, uses some auxiliary information (i.e. randomness) aux to output a commitment C.

UpdateCommit$_{pp}(C, S, \mathbf{m}[S], \mathbf{m}'[S], \text{aux}) \rightarrow C'$: Takes as input a commitment C, a subset $S \subseteq [n]$, and $\mathbf{m}[S] = (m_i)_{i \in S}$ as the underlying message vector of C, and uses some auxiliary information aux to change $\mathbf{m}[S]$ to $\mathbf{m}'[S] = (m_i')_{i \in S}$ and outputs a new commitment C' for this new vector of messages.

Prove$_{pp}(i, m_i, \text{aux}) \rightarrow \pi_i$: On input an index $i \in [n]$ and a message bit $m_i \in \mathcal{M}$, uses the auxiliary information aux that was used in the algorithm Commit to output a proof π_i for this message bit.

Aggregate$_{pp}(C, S, \mathbf{m}[S], \{\pi_i\}_{i \in S}) \rightarrow \pi_S$: Takes as input a commitment C, a subset $S \subseteq [n]$, a subset of message bits $\mathbf{m}[S] = (m_i)_{i \in S}$, and a set of proofs $\{\pi_i\}_{i \in S}$ where each π_i for $i \in S$ is the proof generated for m_i using the algorithm Prove. It outputs an aggregated proof π_S.

Verify$_{pp}(C, S, \mathbf{m}[S], \pi_S) \rightarrow b$: On input a commitment C, a subset $S \subseteq [n]$, a sub-vector of messages $\mathbf{m}[S]$, and an aggregated proof π_S, and outputs a bit $b \in \{0, 1\}$.

We require a vector commitment scheme with same-commitment aggregation to satisfy the following properties:

Correctness of Opening. For all λ, n, $\mathbf{m} = (m_1, \ldots, m_n) \in \mathcal{M}^n$, and $S \subseteq [n]$,

$$\Pr\left[\text{Verify}(C, S, \mathbf{m}[S], \pi_S) = 1 : \begin{array}{l} \text{pp} \leftarrow \text{Setup}(1^\lambda, 1^n) \\ C \leftarrow \text{Commit}_{pp}(\mathbf{m}; \text{aux}) \\ \{\pi_i \leftarrow \text{Prove}_{pp}(i, m_i, \text{aux})\}_{i \in S} \\ \pi_S \leftarrow \text{Aggregate}(C, S, \mathbf{m}[S], \{\pi_i\}_{i \in S}) \end{array}\right] = 1.$$

Correctness of Updates. For all parameters λ, n, message vectors $\mathbf{m} = (m_1, \ldots, m_n), \mathbf{m}' = (m_1', \ldots, m_n') \in \mathcal{M}^n$, subset $S \subseteq [n]$, and aux such that $m_i = m_i'$ for all $i \in [n] \backslash S$, we have

$$\mathsf{UpdateCommit}_{\mathsf{pp}}(C, S, \mathbf{m}[S], \mathbf{m}'[S], \mathsf{aux}) = \mathsf{Commit}_{\mathsf{pp}}(\mathbf{m}'; \mathsf{aux}),$$

where $C \leftarrow \mathsf{Commit}_{\mathsf{pp}}(\mathbf{m}; \mathsf{aux})$, and $\mathsf{pp} \leftarrow \mathsf{Setup}(1^\lambda, 1^n)$.

Binding. For all λ, n, and any PPT adversary $\mathcal{A}$, the probability of finding a tuple $(C, S_0, S_1, \mathbf{m}_0[S_0], \mathbf{m}_1[S_1], \pi_0, \pi_1)$, such that

$$\mathsf{Verify}(C, S_0, \mathbf{m}_0[S_0], \pi_0) = \mathsf{Verify}(C, S_1, \mathbf{m}_1[S_1], \pi_1) = 1$$

and $\mathbf{m}_0[i] \neq \mathbf{m}_1[i]$ for some $i \in S_0 \cap S_1$, is negligible in λ.

2.4.2 Cross-Commitment Aggregation

Definition 3 (Vector Commitment with Cross-Commitment Aggregation [16]). A vector commitment with cross-commitment aggregation for message space $\mathcal{M}$ consists of the six algorithms Setup, Commit, UpdateCommit, Prove, Aggregate, Verify as in the same-commitment case, and two additional algorithms AggregateAcross, and VerifyAcross that are as follows:

AggregateAcross$_{\mathsf{pp}}$ $(\{C_j, S_j, \mathbf{m}_j[S_j], \pi_j\}_{j \in [d]}) \to \pi$: Takes as input a collection of commitments C_j together with each of their aggregated proofs π_j with respect to subset S_j and message sub-vector $\mathbf{m}_j[S_j]$, and outputs a cross-aggregated proof π.

VerifyAcross$_{\mathsf{pp}}$ $(\pi, \{C_j, S_j, \mathbf{m}_j[S_j], \pi_j\}_{j \in [d]}) \to b$: Given a cross-aggregated proof π, and a collection of underlying commitments, subsets, and message sub-vectors $\{C_j, S_j, \mathbf{m}_j[S_j], \pi_j\}_{j \in [d]}$, this algorithm outputs a bit $b \in \{0, 1\}$.

We require a vector commitment scheme with cross-commitment aggregation to satisfy the correctness of opening as in Definition 2 extended to cross-commitment aggregations. Also, it should satisfy an extension of binding property as follows:

Binding (for cross-commitments). For all λ, n, and any PPT adversary $\mathcal{A}$, the probability of finding the two following tuples with the following described properties is negligible in λ:

$$(\pi_0, \{C_0^{(j)}, S_0^{(j)}, \mathbf{m}_0^{(j)}[S_0^{(j)}]\}_{j \in [\ell_0]}), \text{ and } (\pi_1, \{C_1^{(j)}, S_1^{(j)}, \mathbf{m}_1^{(j)}[S_1^{(j)}]\}_{j \in [\ell_1]}),$$

such that

$$\mathsf{VerifyAcross}(\pi_0, \{C_0^{(j)}, S_0^{(j)}, \mathbf{m}_0^{(j)}[S_0^{(j)}]\}_{j \in [\ell_0]})$$
$$= \mathsf{VerifyAcross}(\pi_1, \{C_1^{(j)}, S_1^{(j)}, \mathbf{m}_1^{(j)}[S_1^{(j)}]\}_{j \in [\ell_1]}) = 1$$

and there exist $j_0 \in [\ell_0]$, and $j_1 \in [\ell_1]$, for which it holds that $C_0^{(j_0)} = C_1^{(j_1)}$, and $\mathbf{m}_0^{(j_0)}[i] \neq \mathbf{m}_1^{(j_1)}[i]$, for some $i \in S_0^{(j_0)} \cap S_1^{(j_1)}$.

2.4.3 Statistical Hiding

As stated in [16], one can optionally require a vector commitment scheme to generate commitments that are hiding. Intuitively, this property requires that any commitment C that is generated in the scheme must reveal no information about its underlying message vector $\mathbf{m}$. Also, any proof π_i generated with respect to the i-th element m_i of a message vector $\mathbf{m} = (m_1, \ldots, m_n)$ should not reveal any information about any other element m_j of the message, where $j \neq i$.

Since PointProofs were already proven to be *statistically hiding* in [16], we rather focus only on the binding property and do not further detail hiding. We refer the reader to [16] for a details regarding the hiding property.

3   The Case of Same-Commitment Aggregation

We first consider the simpler variant of PointProofs [16] which only allows aggregating proofs for sub-vectors contained in the same commitment. This construction implicitly uses the functional commitment scheme of [21] to aggregate proofs using randomizers derived from a random oracle. Its description is as follows.

Setup$(1^\lambda, 1^n)$: To generate public parameters, do the following:
1. Choose bilinear groups $(\mathbb{G}, \hat{\mathbb{G}}, \mathbb{G}_T)$ of prime order $p > 2^\lambda$ and $g \xleftarrow{R} \mathbb{G}$, $\hat{g} \xleftarrow{R} \hat{\mathbb{G}}$.
2. Pick a random $\alpha \xleftarrow{R} \mathbb{Z}_p^*$ and compute $g_1, \ldots, g_n, g_{n+2}, \ldots, g_{2n} \in \mathbb{G}$ as well as $\hat{g}_1, \ldots, \hat{g}_n \in \hat{\mathbb{G}}$, where $g_i = g^{(\alpha^i)}$ for each $i \in [2n] \setminus \{n+1\}$ and $\hat{g}_i = \hat{g}^{(\alpha^i)}$ for each $i \in [n]$.
3. Choose a hash function $H : \{0,1\}^* \to \mathbb{Z}_p$ that will be modeled as a random oracle in the analysis.

The public parameters are defined to be

$$\mathsf{pp} = \big(g, \hat{g}, \{g_i\}_{i \in [2n] \setminus \{n+1\}}, \{\hat{g}_i\}_{i \in [n]}, H\big)$$

and the trapdoor is $tk = g_{n+1} = g^{(\alpha^{n+1})}$.[2]

Commit$_{\mathsf{pp}}(m_1, \ldots, m_n; \mathsf{aux})$: To commit to a vector $(m_1, \ldots, m_n) \in \mathbb{Z}_p^n$, choose $\gamma \xleftarrow{R} \mathbb{Z}_p$ and compute

$$C = g^\gamma \cdot \prod_{j=1}^n g_j^{m_j}.$$

The output is C and the auxiliary information is $\mathsf{aux} = (m_1, \ldots, m_n, \gamma)$.

UpdateCommit$_{\mathsf{pp}}(C, S, \mathbf{m}[S], \mathbf{m}'[S], \mathsf{aux})$: Given $C \in \mathbb{G}$ and the state information $\mathsf{aux} = (m_1, \ldots, m_n, \gamma)$, choose $\gamma' \xleftarrow{R} \mathbb{Z}_p$ and compute

$$C' = g^{\gamma'} \cdot C \cdot \prod_{j \in S} g_j^{\mathbf{m}'[j] - \mathbf{m}[j]}$$

together with $\mathsf{aux}' = (\bar{m}_1, \ldots, \bar{m}_n, \gamma + \gamma')$, where $\bar{m}_i = m_i'$ if $i \in S$ and $\bar{m}_i = m_i$ if $i \notin S$.

---

[2] The trapdoor is only used to prove the hiding property.

Prove$_{pp}(m_i, i, \text{aux})$: Parse aux as $(m_1, \ldots, m_n, \gamma)$ and compute

$$\pi_i = g_{n+1-i}^{\gamma} \cdot \prod_{j=1, j \neq i}^{n} g_{n+1-i+j}^{m_j}. \tag{3}$$

The opening of C at position i consists of $\pi_i \in \mathbb{G}$.

Aggregate$_{pp}(C, S, \mathbf{m}[S], \{\pi_i\}_{i \in S})$: Given a commitment $C \in \mathbb{G}$, a sub-vector $\mathbf{m}[S]$ with $S \subseteq [q]$, and the corresponding proofs $\{\pi_i\}_{i \in S}$, compute

$$\pi_S = \prod_{i \in S} \pi_i^{t_i}$$

where $t_i = H(i, C, S, \mathbf{m}[S])$.

Verify$_{pp}(C, S, \mathbf{m}[S], \pi_S)$: Given $\pi_S \in \mathbb{G}$ return 1 if $C \in \mathbb{G}$ and

$$e(C, \prod_{i \in S} \hat{g}_{n+1-i}^{t_i}) = e(\pi_S, \hat{g}) \cdot e(g_1, \hat{g}_n)^{\sum_{i \in S} m[i] \cdot t_i} \tag{4}$$

where $t_i = H(i, C, S, \mathbf{m}[S])$ for each $i \in S$. Otherwise, it returns 0.

In [16], the scheme was proven binding in the algebraic group model and in the random oracle model. We now show that, using the Forking Lemma [29] (more precisely, its generalization used in [1,7]), we can prove its security in the random oracle model (i.e., without using the algebraic group model) under the n-DHE assumption, which already underlies the binding property of the vector commitment scheme in [22].

In Supplementary Material A, we provide an alternative proof using the Local Forking Lemma [2] and give a comparison between the advantage/running-time ratios of the two reductions.

We note that the security analysis of [16] highlighted the necessity of including S and $\mathbf{m}[S]$ among the inputs of the hash function when the coefficient $\{t_i\}_{i \in S}$ are computed in the aggregation algorithm. Consistently with this observation, the proof of Theorem 1 crucially relies on the fact that $(S, \mathbf{m}[S])$ are hashed along with (i, C).

In order to rely on the General Forking Lemma, we need to answer random oracle queries in a careful way, by adapting a technique used by Boneh et al. [7] in the context of multi-signatures supporting key aggregation.

Theorem 1. *The above commitment is binding in the random oracle model if the n-DHE assumption holds.*

Proof. Suppose that the adversary $\mathcal{A}$ is able to generate a commitment C as well as two sets $S_0, S_1 \subset [n]$ such that $S_0 \cap S_1 \neq \emptyset$ and convincing proofs π_0, π_1 respectively for sub-vectors $\mathbf{m}_0[S_0] \in \mathbb{Z}_p^{|S_0|}$, $\mathbf{m}_1[S_1] \in \mathbb{Z}_p^{|S_1|}$ such that $\mathbf{m}_0[i] \neq \mathbf{m}_1[i]$ for some $i \in S_0 \cap S_1$. Let $\Pr[\neg \text{Bind}]$ be the probability of $\mathcal{A}$ generating such tuple. In the random oracle model, we build an algorithm $\mathcal{C}$ that uses $\mathcal{A}$ to solve the n-DHE problem. Let q_H be the maximum number of queries that $\mathcal{A}$ can issue to the random oracle H.

Consider an algorithm SAMP that generates an n-DHE instance $\pi = (g, \hat{g}, \{g_i\}_{i \in [2n] \setminus \{n+1\}}, \{\hat{g}_i\}_{i \in [n]})$, and an algorithm $\mathcal{B}$ that on input π and randomness $f = (\rho, h_1, \ldots, h_Q)$, where $Q = n \cdot q_H$, does as follows.

$\mathcal{B}$ begins by drawing a random index $i^\dagger \xleftarrow{R} U([n])$. It runs $\mathcal{A}$ on input $(g, \hat{g}, \{g_i\}_{i \in [2n] \setminus \{n+1\}}, \{\hat{g}_i\}_{i \in [n]})$ and randomness ρ. First, $\mathcal{B}$ initializes a counter $\ell = 0$, which it increments every time it sets a new hash value. When $\mathcal{A}$ makes a H-query $(i, C, S, \mathbf{m}[S])$, $\mathcal{B}$ uses the values in $(h_1, \ldots, h_Q)$ to respond as follows:

- If the input $(i, C, S, \mathbf{m}[S])$ is such that the hash value $H(i, C, S, \mathbf{m}[S])$ was previously defined, $\mathcal{B}$ returns the previously-defined value.
- If $(i, C, S, \mathbf{m}[S])$ is such that $i^\dagger \in S$, then $\mathcal{B}$ does the following: For each index $i' \in S \setminus \{i^\dagger\}$, it increments ℓ and sets $H(i', C, S, \mathbf{m}[S]) \leftarrow h_\ell$. Finally, it increments ℓ and sets $H(i^\dagger, C, S, \mathbf{m}[S]) \leftarrow h_\ell$. Note that $\mathcal{B}$ programs H on $|S|$ inputs at once for such hash queries and that $H(i^\dagger, C, S, \mathbf{m}[S])$ is set after all other inputs for indices $i' \in S \setminus \{i^\dagger\}$. Then, $\mathcal{B}$ returns the corresponding value of $H(i, C, S, \mathbf{m}[S])$ to $\mathcal{A}$.
- Else, $\mathcal{B}$ increments ℓ and returns h_ℓ as the value for $H(i, C, S, \mathbf{m}[S])$.

Since $\mathcal{A}$ makes at most q_H and $\mathcal{B}$ sets at most n hash values at each query, at most $Q = n \cdot q_H$ values are set in the process.

With probability $\epsilon := \Pr[\neg \mathsf{Bind}]$, $\mathcal{A}$ outputs

$$(C, S_0, S_1, \mathbf{m}_0[S_0], \mathbf{m}_1[S_1], \pi_0, \pi_1)$$

such that

$$e(C, \prod_{i \in S_0} \hat{g}_{n+1-i}^{t_i^{(0)}}) = e(\pi_0, \hat{g}) \cdot e(g_1, \hat{g}_n)^{\sum_{i \in S_0} \mathbf{m}_0[i] \cdot t_i^{(0)}} \tag{5}$$

$$e(C, \prod_{i \in S_1} \hat{g}_{n+1-i}^{t_i^{(1)}}) = e(\pi_1, \hat{g}) \cdot e(g_1, \hat{g}_n)^{\sum_{i \in S_1} \mathbf{m}_1[i] \cdot t_i^{(1)}} \tag{6}$$

where $t_i^{(b)} = H(i, C, S_b, \mathbf{m}_b[S_b])$ for each $i \in S_b$ and $b \in \{0, 1\}$. Then, $\mathcal{B}$ determines the smallest $i^\star \in S_0 \cap S_1$ such that $\mathbf{m}_0[i^\star] \neq \mathbf{m}_1[i^\star]$. If $i^\star \neq i^\dagger$, it aborts and outputs $(\emptyset, \emptyset)$. Otherwise, if $i^\star = i^\dagger$ (which is the case with probability $1/n$ since $i^\dagger$ is drawn uniformly and independently of $\mathcal{A}$'s view), let $\ell_0 \in [Q]$ be the index of the random oracle query $H(i^\star, C, S_0, \mathbf{m}_0[S_0])$ and let $\ell_1 \in [Q]$ be the index of the random oracle query $H(i^\star, C, S_1, \mathbf{m}_1[S_1])$. Let $h_{\ell_0}, h_{\ell_1} \in \mathbb{Z}_p$ be the corresponding responses. Note that, due to the way $\mathcal{B}$ sets the responses to random oracle queries, any value $H(i, C, S_b, \mathbf{m}_b[S_b])$ for an index $i \in S_b \setminus \{i^\star\}$ is set before $H(i^\star, C, S_b, \mathbf{m}_b[S_b]) = h_{\ell_b}$, for $b \in \{0, 1\}$. Finally, $\mathcal{B}$ outputs $(L = \{\ell_0, \ell_1\}, \{out_{\ell_0}, out_{\ell_1}\})$, where

$$out_{\ell_0} = out_{\ell_1} = (C, S_0, S_1, \mathbf{m}_0[S_0], \mathbf{m}_1[S_1], \pi_0, \pi_1, h_{\ell_0}, h_{\ell_1}) \tag{7}$$

Note that $\mathcal{B}$ outputs a-non empty subset $L = \{\ell_0, \ell_1\}$ successfully with probability at least ϵ/n.

Now, we describe a reduction C that solves an n-DHE instance $(g, \hat{g}, \{g_i\}_{i \in [2n] \setminus \{n+1\}}, \{\hat{g}_i\}_{i \in [n]})$ using A. Algorithm C runs the game $G_{\mathcal{B}, \pi}$ defined in Fig. 1, where π is the given n-DHE instance, and $\mathcal{B}$ is the algorithm that uses the adversary A as described above. If the game outputs 0, then C aborts. By Lemma 1, with probability at least $(\epsilon/n)/8$, $G_{\mathcal{B}, \pi}$ outputs $(L = \{\ell_0, \ell_1\}, \{out_{\ell_0}, out_{\ell_1}\}, \{out'_{\ell_0}, out'_{\ell_1}\})$ after having forked twice. Then, C parses out_{ℓ_0} and out_{ℓ_1} as in (7) and obtains C and $(S_b, \mathbf{m}_b[S_b], \pi_b)$ for $b \in \{0, 1\}$ satisfying Eqs. (5)–(6). It also parses out'_{ℓ_0} and out'_{ℓ_1} as described hereunder and performs the following computations:

- For the first forking, it parses

$$out'_{\ell_0} = (C, S_0, S'_1, \mathbf{m}_0[S_0], \mathbf{m}'_1[S'_1], \pi'_0, \pi'_1, h'_{\ell_0}, h'_{\ell_1}),$$

where Verify outputs 1 on both $(C, S_0, \mathbf{m}_0[S_0], \pi'_0)$, and $(C, S'_1, \mathbf{m}'_1[S'_1], \pi'_1)$. Note that $(S'_1, \mathbf{m}'_1[S'_1])$ may differ from their counterparts $(S_1, \mathbf{m}_1[S_1])$ of the first execution but it does not matter. What matters is that the second run involves the same $(S_0, \mathbf{m}_0[S_0])$ as in the first execution and the hash query $H(i^*, C, S_0, \mathbf{m}_0[S_0])$ is also the ℓ_0-th hash query in the second execution, where it obtains a different response h'_{ℓ_0}. This holds since the forking occurs at the ℓ_0-th oracle query and the executions are identical up to that point. Hence, the ℓ_0-th query is indeed issued on the input $(i^*, C, S_0, \mathbf{m}_0[S_0])$ during the forking. Now, since the index $i^* \in S_0 \cap S_1$ determined in the first run belongs to S_0, we know that

$$t_{i^*}^{(0)} = H(i^*, C, S_0, \mathbf{m}_0[S_0]) = h'_{\ell_0} \neq h_{\ell_0},$$

but other hash values of the form $H(i, C, S_0, \mathbf{m}_0[S_0])$ for $i \neq i^*$ are the same as in the initial execution because $\mathcal{B}$ assigned the values of $H(i, C, S_0, \mathbf{m}_0[S_0])$ for $i \neq i^*$ before the forking point. Let us now consider the proofs π_0, π'_0 obtained in the first run of $\mathcal{B}$ and the first forking, respectively. By dividing out the Eqs. (5) of both runs, we have

$$e(C, \hat{g}_{n+1-i^*}^{\Delta t_{i^*}^{(0)}}) = e(\pi_0/\pi'_0, \hat{g}) \cdot e(g_1, \hat{g}_n)^{\mathbf{m}_0[i^*] \cdot \Delta t_{i^*}^{(0)}}, \tag{8}$$

where $\Delta t_{i^*}^{(0)} \triangleq h_{\ell_0} - h'_{\ell_0} \neq 0$.

- For the second forking, the reduction C parses out'_{ℓ_1} as

$$out'_{\ell_1} = (C, S''_0, S_1, \mathbf{m}''_0[S''_0], \mathbf{m}_1[S_1], \pi''_0, \pi''_1, h''_{\ell_0}, h''_{\ell_1}).$$

Here, $(S''_0, \mathbf{m}''_0[S''_0])$ may differ from the pair $(S_0, \mathbf{m}_0[S_0])$ extracted from out_{ℓ_1} at the very first execution, but it does not matter. The forking point being the ℓ_1-th hash query, we know that the first and third executions are identical up to that point. Consequently, the ℓ_1-th query is issued on the input $(i^*, C, S_1, \mathbf{m}_1[S_1])$ in this forking, where it obtains a different response h''_{ℓ_1}

than in the very first run. With non-negligible probability, Lemma 1 ensures that $\mathcal{B}$'s output in this forking involves the same $(S_1, \mathbf{m}_1[S_1])$ as in the first run and the hash query $H(i^\star, C, S_1, \mathbf{m}_1[S_1])$ is also the ℓ_1-th hash query. Since $i^\star \in S_1$, we can repeat the same arguments as in the first fork and, by dividing out the verification equations (6) of the first and third runs, $\mathcal{B}$ obtains

$$e(C, \hat{g}_{n+1-i^\star}^{\Delta t_{i^\star}^{(1)}}) = e(\pi_1/\pi_1'', \hat{g}) \cdot e(g_1, \hat{g}_n)^{\mathbf{m}_1[i^\star] \cdot \Delta t_{i^\star}^{(1)}}, \tag{9}$$

where $\Delta t_{i^\star}^{(1)} \triangleq h_{\ell_1} - h_{\ell_1}'' \neq 0$.

Then, raising both members of (9) to the power $\omega \triangleq \Delta t_{i^\star}^{(0)}/\Delta t_{i^\star}^{(1)}$ yields

$$e(C, \hat{g}_{n+1-i^\star}^{\Delta t_{i^\star}^{(0)}}) = e((\pi_1/\pi_1'')^\omega, \hat{g}) \cdot e(g_1, \hat{g}_n)^{\mathbf{m}_1[i^\star] \cdot \Delta t_{i^\star}^{(0)}}. \tag{10}$$

If we now use the hypothesis that $\mathbf{m}_0[i^\star] \neq \mathbf{m}_1[i^\star]$, the combination of (10) and (8) implies

$$e(\pi_0/\pi_0', \hat{g}) \cdot e(g_1, \hat{g}_n)^{\mathbf{m}_0[i^\star] \cdot \Delta t_{i^\star}^{(0)}} = e((\pi_1/\pi_1'')^\omega, \hat{g}) \cdot e(g_1, \hat{g}_n)^{\mathbf{m}_1[i^\star] \cdot \Delta t_{i^\star}^{(0)}}.$$

Now, since $e(g_1, \hat{g}_n) = e(g_{n+1}, \hat{g})$, we have:

$$e(g_{n+1}, \hat{g})^{\Delta t_{i^\star}^{(0)} \cdot (\mathbf{m}_0[i^\star] - \mathbf{m}_1[i^\star])} = e((\pi_1/\pi_1'')^\omega, \hat{g})/e(\pi_0/\pi_0', \hat{g}),$$

which then allows $\mathcal{B}$ to compute the sought-after n-DHE solution, by looking only at the $\mathbb{G}$-components, as

$$g_{n+1} \triangleq \left(\frac{(\pi_1/\pi_1'')^\omega}{\pi_0/\pi_0'} \right)^{1/\left(\Delta t_{i^\star}^{(0)} \cdot (\mathbf{m}_0[i^\star] - \mathbf{m}_1[i^\star]) \right)}. \tag{11}$$

By Lemma 1, with probability at least $(\epsilon/n)/8$, the reduction $\mathcal{C}$ succeeds in solving the n-DHE problem. $\qquad\square$

4   The Case of Cross-Commitment Aggregation

Let $H' : \{0,1\}^* \to \mathbb{Z}_p$ be a hash function modeled as a random oracle. Algorithms AggregateAcross and VerifyAcross are as follows:

AggregateAcross$_{\mathsf{pp}}$ $(\{C^{(j)}, S^{(j)}, \mathbf{m}^{(j)}[S^{(j)}], \pi_j\}_{j \in [d]})$: Given a collection of $(\{C^{(j)}, S^{(j)}, \mathbf{m}^{(j)}[S^{(j)}], \pi_j\}_{j \in [d]})$, where each π_j is the same-commitment-aggregated proof of $C^{(j)}$ with respect to the sub-vector of message $\mathbf{m}^{(j)}$ limited to indices in $S^{(j)}$, compute and output

$$\pi = \prod_{j=1}^d (\pi_j)^{t_j'},$$

where $t_j' = H'(j, \{C^{(j)}, S^{(j)}, \mathbf{m}^{(j)}[S^{(j)}]\}_{j \in [d]})$.

VerifyAcross$(\pi, \{C^{(j)}, S^{(j)}, \mathbf{m}^{(j)}[S^{(j)}], \pi_j\}_{j\in[d]})$: Given $\pi \in \mathbb{G}$, return 1 if $C^{(j)} \in \mathbb{G}$ for all $j \in [d]$, and

$$\prod_{j=1}^{d} e\left(C^{(j)}, \prod_{i\in S^{(j)}} \hat{g}_{n+1-i}^{t_{j,i}}\right)^{t'_j} = e(\pi, \hat{g}) \cdot e(g_1, \hat{g}_n)^{\sum_{j\in[d], i\in S^{(j)}} \mathbf{m}^{(j)}[i]\cdot t_{j,i}\cdot t'_j}$$

where

$$t_{j,i} = H(i, C^{(j)}, S^{(j)}, \mathbf{m}^{(j)}[S^{(j)}]), \qquad t'_j = H'(j, \{C^{(j)}, S^{(j)}, \mathbf{m}^{(j)}[S^{(j)}]\}_{j\in[d]}).$$

We now prove the cross-commitment binding property under the n-DHE assumption in the ROM, without restricting ourselves to algebraic adversaries.

Here, we rely on the Local Forking Lemma instead of the Generalized Forking Lemma. The reason is that the proof of Theorem 2 proceeds with a reduction from the same-commitment case. In the process, it has to fork on the hash function H'. For this purpose, if we were to use the Generalized Forking Lemma as in the proof of Theorem 1, we would have no way to guess which hash query should be defined after other hash queries involving related inputs. Therefore we need the Local Forking Lemma to force *all but one* of the cross-commitment aggregation coefficients $\{t'_j\}_{j\in[d]}$ to be identical in two adversarial runs.

Theorem 2. *The above cross-commitment scheme is binding in the random oracle model assuming the hardness of the n-DHE problem.*

Proof. For the sake of contradiction, let us assume that an adversary $\mathcal{A}$ has non-negligible probability ϵ of contradicting the binding property of the cross-commitment aggregation in PointProofs. Namely, with probability ϵ, $\mathcal{A}$ can generate two tuples

$$\left(\pi_0, \{C_0^{(j)}, S_0^{(j)}, \mathbf{m}_0^{(j)}[S_0^{(j)}]\}_{j\in[d_0]}\right), \qquad \left(\pi_1, \{C_1^{(j)}, S_1^{(j)}, \mathbf{m}_1^{(j)}[S_1^{(j)}]\}_{j\in[d_1]}\right),$$

such that VerifyAcross accepts $(\pi_b, \{C_b^{(j)}, S_b^{(j)}, \mathbf{m}_b^{(j)}[S_b^{(j)}]\}_{j\in[d_b]})$ for each value of $b \in \{0,1\}$, and there exist indices $j_0 \in [d_0]$ and $j_1 \in [d_1]$ for which $C_0^{(j_0)} = C_1^{(j_1)}$ and $\mathbf{m}_0^{(j_0)}[i] \neq \mathbf{m}_1^{(j_1)}[i]$, for some $i \in S_0^{(j_0)} \cap S_1^{(j_1)}$. In the random oracle model, we give a reduction $\mathcal{B}$ that uses $\mathcal{A}$ to break the binding property of the *same-commitment* aggregation of PointProofs.

$\mathcal{B}$ receives public parameters $\mathsf{pp} = (g, \hat{g}, \{g_i\}_{i\in[2n]\setminus\{n+1\}}, \{\hat{g}_i\}_{i\in[n]})$ from its own challenger in the same-commitment aggregation game and runs $\mathcal{A}$ on pp. Note that $\mathcal{B}$, which is attacking the binding property of the same-commitment aggregation of PointProofs, has oracle access to H, but $\mathcal{A}$ has also oracle access to H'. Algorithm $\mathcal{B}$ responds to $\mathcal{A}$'s oracle queries to H by redirecting the query to H (so, it does not simulate H itself for $\mathcal{A}$). It responds to $\mathcal{A}$'s queries to the second random oracle H' in the following way. In a first execution, it answers H'-queries with values $h_1, h_2, \ldots, h_Q \in \mathbb{Z}_p$, where Q denotes the total number of queries made by $\mathcal{A}$ to H'. We assume w.l.o.g. that all these queries are distinct. With probability ϵ, $\mathcal{A}$ outputs

$$\left(\pi_0, \{C_0^{(j)}, S_0^{(j)}, \mathbf{m}_0^{(j)}[S_0^{(j)}]\}_{j\in[d_0]}\right), \quad \left(\pi_1, \{C_1^{(j)}, S_1^{(j)}, \mathbf{m}_1^{(j)}[S_1^{(j)}]\}_{j\in[d_1]}\right),$$

such that the aggregated verification algorithm returns 1 running on both tuples. Namely,

$$\prod_{j=1}^{d_0} e\left(C_0^{(j)}, \prod_{i\in S_0^{(j)}} \hat{g}_{n+1-i}^{t_{j,i}^{(0)}}\right)^{t_j'^{(0)}} = e(\pi_0, \hat{g}) \cdot e(g_1, \hat{g}_n)^{\sum_{j\in[d_0],i\in S_0^{(j)}} \mathbf{m}_0^{(j)}[i]\cdot t_{j,i}^{(0)}\cdot t_j'^{(0)}}$$

(12)

$$\prod_{j=1}^{d_1} e\left(C_1^{(j)}, \prod_{i\in S_1^{(j)}} \hat{g}_{n+1-i}^{t_{j,i}^{(1)}}\right)^{t_j'^{(1)}} = e(\pi_1, \hat{g}) \cdot e(g_1, \hat{g}_n)^{\sum_{j\in[d_1],i\in S_1^{(j)}} \mathbf{m}_1^{(j)}[i]\cdot t_{j,i}^{(1)}\cdot t_j'^{(1)}}$$

(13)

where $t_{j,i}^{(b)} = H(i, C_b^{(j)}, S_b^{(j)}, \mathbf{m}_b^{(j)}[S_b^{(j)}])$, for each $j \in [d_b]$, $i \in S_b^{(j)}$, and $b \in \{0,1\}$, and $t_j'^{(b)} = H'(j, \{C_b^{(j)}, S_b^{(j)}, \mathbf{m}_b^{(j)}[S_b^{(j)}]\}_{j\in[d_b]})$, for each $j \in [d_b]$ and $b \in \{0,1\}$.

Then, $\mathcal{B}$ determines the two indices $j_0 \in [d_0]$, $j_1 \in [d_1]$, for which the binding property is contradicted, i.e., $C_0^{(j_0)} = C_1^{(j_1)}$, and $\mathbf{m}_0^{(j_0)}[i] \neq \mathbf{m}_1^{(j_1)}[i]$, for some $i \in S_0^{(j_0)} \cap S_1^{(j_1)}$. Let $\ell_b \in [Q]$ be the index of the query

$$H'(j_b, \{C_b^{(j)}, S_b^{(j)}, \mathbf{m}_b^{(j)}[S_b^{(j)}]\}_{j\in[d_b]}),$$

for $b \in \{0,1\}$. Let $h_{\ell_0}, h_{\ell_1} \in \mathbb{Z}_p$ be the corresponding responses.

The reduction $\mathcal{B}$ then locally forks the adversary twice. It first runs $\mathcal{A}$ a second time with the same random tape and answers all random oracle queries using the outputs $h_1, \ldots, h_{\ell_0-1}, h'_{\ell_0}, h_{\ell_0+1}, \ldots, h_Q \in \mathbb{Z}_p$, where $h'_{\ell_0} \xleftarrow{R} \mathbb{Z}_p$ is chosen afresh and all other outputs h_ℓ for $\ell \neq \ell_0$ are identical to those of the first execution. The Local Forking Lemma (Lemma 2) ensures that with probability at least equal to $1/Q \cdot \epsilon^2$, $\mathcal{A}$'s second run outputs

$$\left(\pi_0', \{C_0^{(j)}, S_0^{(j)}, \mathbf{m}_0^{(j)}[S_0^{(j)}]\}_{j\in[d_0]}, \pi_1', \{C_1'^{(j)}, S_1'^{(j)}, \mathbf{m}_1'^{(j)}[S_1'^{(j)}]\}_{j\in[d_1']}\right).$$

Note that the second collection $\{C_1'^{(j)}, S_1'^{(j)}, \mathbf{m}_1'^{(j)}[S_1'^{(j)}]\}_{j\in[d_1']}$ might be different from its counterpart $\{C_1^{(j)}, S_1^{(j)}, \mathbf{m}_1^{(j)}[S_1^{(j)}]\}_{j\in[d_1]}$ of the first run, but what matters is that this run involves the same collection $\{C_0^{(j)}, S_0^{(j)}, \mathbf{m}_0^{(j)}[S_0^{(j)}]\}_{j\in[d_0]}$ as the first execution of $\mathcal{A}$ and the hash query $H'(j_0, \{C_0^{(j)}, S_0^{(j)}, \mathbf{m}_0^{(j)}[S_0^{(j)}]\}_{j\in[d_0]})$

is also the ℓ_0-th query issued by $\mathcal{A}$ where it receives a different response h'_{ℓ_0}. Since $j_0 \in d_0$, we know that

$$t'^{(0)}_{j_0} = H'(j_0, \{C^{(j)}_0, S^{(j)}_0, \mathbf{m}^{(j)}_0[S^{(j)}_0]\}_{j \in [d_0]}) = h_{\ell_0} \neq h'_{\ell_0},$$

but other hash values $t'^{(0)}_j$ for $j \in [d_0] \backslash \{j_0\}$ are the same as in the initial execution because of the *local* forking. If we now consider the two proofs π_0, π'_0 obtained in the two runs, by dividing out the Eqs. (12) of both runs, we have

$$e\left(C^{(j_0)}_0, \prod_{i \in S^{(j_0)}_0} \hat{g}^{t^{(0)}_{j_0,i}}_{n+1-i*}\right)^{\Delta t'^{(0)}_{j_0}} = e(\pi_0/\pi'_0, \hat{g}) \cdot e(g_1, \hat{g}_n)^{\sum\limits_{i \in S^{(j_0)}_0} \mathbf{m}^{(j_0)}_0[i] \cdot t^{(0)}_{j_0,i} \cdot \Delta t'^{(0)}_{j_0}} \tag{14}$$

where $\Delta t'^{(0)}_{j_0} = h_{\ell_0} - h'_{\ell_0} \neq 0$. Raising both sides of Eq. (14) to the power $\omega_0 \triangleq 1/(\Delta t'^{(0)}_{j_0})$ yields

$$e\left(C^{(j_0)}_0, \prod_{i \in S^{(j_0)}_0} \hat{g}^{t^{(0)}_{j_0,i}}_{n+1-i*}\right) = e((\pi_0/\pi'_0)^{\omega_0}, \hat{g}) \cdot e(g_1, \hat{g}_n)^{\sum\limits_{i \in S^{(j_0)}_0} \mathbf{m}^{(j_0)}_0[i] \cdot t^{(0)}_{j_0,i}} \tag{15}$$

Then, $\mathcal{B}$ locally forks $\mathcal{A}$ a second time on the hash query $H'(j_1, \{C^{(j)}_1, S^{(j)}_1, \mathbf{m}^{(j)}_1[S^{(j)}_1]\}_{j \in [d_1]})$, which was the ℓ_1-th H'-query in the first execution. Namely, it runs $\mathcal{A}$ a second time with the same random tape as in the first run and now answers $\mathcal{A}$'s random oracle queries to H' using the outputs $h_1, \ldots, h_{\ell_1-1}, h''_{\ell_1}, h_{\ell_1+1}, \ldots, h_Q \in \mathbb{Z}_p$, where $h''_{\ell_1} \xleftarrow{R} \mathbb{Z}_p$ is freshly sampled and all other outputs h_ℓ for $\ell \neq \ell_1$ are the same as in the first execution. By the Local Forking Lemma, with probability at least equal to $1/Q \cdot \epsilon^2$, $\mathcal{A}$'s third run outputs

$$\left(\pi''_0, \{C''^{(j)}_0, S''^{(j)}_0, \mathbf{m}''^{(j)}_0[S''^{(j)}_0]\}_{j \in [d''_0]}, \pi''_1, \{C^{(j)}_1, S^{(j)}_1, \mathbf{m}^{(j)}_1[S^{(j)}_1]\}_{j \in [d_1]}\right).$$

Again, the collection $\{C''^{(j)}_0, S''^{(j)}_0, \mathbf{m}''^{(j)}_0[S''^{(j)}_0]\}_{j \in [d''_0]}$ might differ from its counterpart $\{C_0^{(j)}, S_0^{(j)}, \mathbf{m}_0^{(j)}[S_0^{(j)}]\}_{j \in [d_0]}$ of the first execution of $\mathcal{A}$, yet, this run involves the same collection $\{C^{(j)}_1, S^{(j)}_1, \mathbf{m}^{(j)}_1[S^{(j)}_1]\}_{j \in [d_1]}$ as in the first run and the hash query $H'(j_1, \{C^{(j)}_1, S^{(j)}_1, \mathbf{m}^{(j)}_1[S^{(j)}_1]\}_{j \in [d_1]})$ is also the ℓ_1-th query to H' where $\mathcal{A}$ receives a different response h''_{ℓ_1}. Since $j_1 \in d_1$, we can repeat the same arguments as in the first fork and, by dividing out the verification equations (13), $\mathcal{B}$ obtains

$$e\left(C^{(j_1)}_1, \prod_{i \in S^{(j_1)}_1} \hat{g}^{t^{(1)}_{j_1,i}}_{n+1-i*}\right)^{\Delta t'^{(1)}_{j_1}} = e(\pi_1/\pi''_1, \hat{g}) \cdot e(g_1, \hat{g}_n)^{\sum\limits_{i \in S^{(j_1)}_1} \mathbf{m}^{(j_1)}_1[i] \cdot t^{(0)}_{j_1,i} \cdot \Delta t'^{(1)}_{j_1}} \tag{16}$$

where $\Delta t_{j_1}^{'(1)} = h_{\ell_1} - h_{\ell_1}'' \neq 0$. Again, by raising both members of Eq. (14) to the power $\omega_1 \triangleq 1/(\Delta t_{j_1}^{'(1)})$ we have

$$e\left(C_1^{(j_1)}, \prod_{i \in S_1^{(j_1)}} \hat{g}_{n+1-i^\star}^{t_{j_1,i}^{(1)}}\right) = e((\pi_1/\pi_1'')^{\omega_1}, \hat{g}) \cdot e(g_1, \hat{g}_n)^{\sum_{i \in S_1^{(j_1)}} \mathbf{m}_1^{(j_1)}[i] \cdot t_{j_1,i}^{(0)}} \tag{17}$$

Finally, $\mathcal{B}$ outputs the tuple

$$\left(C, S_0^{(j_0)}, S_1^{(j_1)}, \mathbf{m}_0^{(j_0)}[S_0^{(j_0)}], \mathbf{m}_1^{(j_1)}[S_1^{(j_1)}], (\pi_0/\pi_0')^{\omega_0}, (\pi_1/\pi_1'')^{\omega_1}\right),$$

where $C = C_0^{(j_0)} = C_1^{(j_1)}$. Regarding Eqs. (15) and (17), Verify accepts both

$$\left((\pi_0/\pi_0')^{\omega_0}, C, S_0^{(j_0)}, \mathbf{m}_0^{(j_0)}[S_0^{(j_0)}]\right), \qquad \left((\pi_1/\pi_1'')^{\omega_1}, C, S_1^{(j_1)}, \mathbf{m}_1^{(j_1)}[S_1^{(j_1)}]\right),$$

and there exists an index $i \in S_0^{(j_0)} \cap S_1^{(j_1)}$ for which $\mathbf{m}_0^{(j_0)}[i] \neq \mathbf{m}_1^{(j_1)}[i]$. With non-negligible probability $(1/Q \cdot \epsilon^2)^2$, $\mathcal{B}$ thus breaks the binding property of the same-commitment aggregation construction from Sect. 3, which contradicts the statement of Theorem 1. □

Acknowledgements. The second and third authors were supported by the French ANR RAGE project (ANR-20-CE48-0011) and the PEPR Cyber France 2030 programme (ANR-22-PECY-0003).

A   Proof via Local Forking Lemma

In this section, in order to compare with the reduction obtained from the Generalized Forking Lemma, we prove the binding property of same-commitment aggregation of PointProofs [16] in the random oracle model via Local Forking Lemma [2].

A.1   The Case of Same-Commitment Aggregation

Theorem 3. *The vector commitment scheme described in Description 3 is binding in the random oracle model if the n-DHE assumption holds.*

Proof. Suppose there exists an adversary $\mathcal{A}$, that with a non-negligible probability ϵ generates a commitment C as well as two sets $S_0, S_1 \subset [n]$, such that $S_0 \cap S_1 \neq \emptyset$, together with convincing proofs π_0, π_1 for sub-vectors $\mathbf{m}_0[S_0] \in \mathbb{Z}_p^{|S_0|}$, $\mathbf{m}_1[S_1] \in \mathbb{Z}_p^{|S_1|}$ such that $\mathbf{m}_0[i] \neq \mathbf{m}_1[i]$ for some $i \in S_0 \cap S_1$. We build an algorithm $\mathcal{B}$ in the random oracle model that uses $\mathcal{A}$ to solve the n-DHE problem.

$\mathcal{B}$ first runs $\mathcal{A}$ on input of an n-DHE instance $(g, \hat{g}, \{g_i\}_{i \in [2n] \setminus \{n+1\}}, \{\hat{g}_i\}_{i \in [n]})$ set as the public parameters pp of the vector commitment scheme. In a first execution, it answers random oracle queries with values $h_1, \ldots, h_Q \in \mathbb{Z}_p$, where Q

denotes the total number of H-queries made by $\mathcal{A}$. We assume w.l.o.g. that all random oracle queries are distinct. With probability ϵ, $\mathcal{A}$ outputs a tuple

$$(C, S_0, S_1, \mathbf{m}_0[S_0], \mathbf{m}_1[S_1], \pi_0, \pi_1)$$

such that

$$e(C, \prod_{i \in S_0} \hat{g}_{n+1-i}^{t_i^{(0)}}) = e(\pi_0, \hat{g}) \cdot e(g_1, \hat{g}_n)^{\sum_{i \in S_0} \mathbf{m}_0[i] \cdot t_i^{(0)}} \tag{18}$$

$$e(C, \prod_{i \in S_1} \hat{g}_{n+1-i}^{t_i^{(1)}}) = e(\pi_1, \hat{g}) \cdot e(g_1, \hat{g}_n)^{\sum_{i \in S_1} \mathbf{m}_1[i] \cdot t_i^{(1)}} \tag{19}$$

where $t_i^{(b)} = H(i, C, S_b, \mathbf{m}_b[S_b])$ for each $i \in S_b$ and $b \in \{0, 1\}$. Then, algorithm $\mathcal{B}$ determines the smallest $i^\star \in S_0 \cap S_1$ such that $\mathbf{m}_0[i^\star] \neq \mathbf{m}_1[i^\star]$. Let $\ell_0 \in [Q]$ be the index of the random oracle query $H(i^\star, C, S_0, \mathbf{m}_0[S_0])$ and let $\ell_1 \in [Q]$ be the index of the random oracle query $H(i^\star, C, S_1, \mathbf{m}_1[S_1])$. Let $h_{\ell_0}, h_{\ell_1} \in \mathbb{Z}_p$ be the corresponding responses.

The reduction then locally forks the adversary twice. It first runs $\mathcal{A}$ a second time with the same random tape and answers all random oracle queries using the outputs $h_1, \ldots, h_{\ell_0-1}, h'_{\ell_0}, h_{\ell_0+1}, \ldots, h_Q \in \mathbb{Z}_p$, where $h'_{\ell_0} \xleftarrow{R} \mathbb{Z}_p$ is chosen afresh and all other outputs h_ℓ for $\ell \neq \ell_0$ are identical to those of the first execution. The Local Forking Lemma (Lemma 2) ensures that with probability at least equal to $1/Q \cdot \epsilon^2$, $\mathcal{A}$'s second run outputs $(C, S_0, S'_1, \mathbf{m}_0[S_0], \mathbf{m}'_1[S'_1], \pi'_0, \pi'_1)$. Note that $(S'_1, \mathbf{m}'_1[S'_1])$ may differ from their counterparts $(S_1, \mathbf{m}_1[S_1])$ of the first execution but this run involves the same $(S_0, \mathbf{m}_0[S_0])$ as in the first execution and the hash query $H(i^\star, C, S_0, \mathbf{m}_0[S_0])$ is also the ℓ_0-th hash query in this execution, where $\mathcal{A}$ receives a different response h'_{ℓ_0}. Since $i^\star \in S_0$, we know that

$$t_{i^\star}^{(0)} = H(i^\star, C, S_0, \mathbf{m}_0[S_0]) = h_{\ell_0} \neq h'_{\ell_0}$$

with overwhelming probability $1 - 1/p$, but other hash values $t_i^{(0)}$ for $i \in S_0 \setminus \{i^\star\}$ are the same as in the initial execution because of the *local* forking. If we now consider the two proofs π_0, π'_0 obtained in the two runs, by dividing out the equations (18) of both runs, we have

$$e(C, \hat{g}_{n+1-i^\star}^{\Delta t_{i^\star}^{(0)}}) = e(\pi_0/\pi'_0, \hat{g}) \cdot e(g_1, \hat{g}_n)^{\mathbf{m}_0[i^\star] \cdot \Delta t_{i^\star}^{(0)}}, \tag{20}$$

where $\Delta t_{i^\star}^{(0)} \triangleq h_{\ell_0} - h'_{\ell_0} \neq 0$ except with probability $1/p$.

Then, $\mathcal{B}$ locally forks $\mathcal{A}$ a second time on the hash query $H(i^\star, C, S_1, \mathbf{m}_1[S_1])$, which was the ℓ_1-th hash query in the first execution. Namely, it runs $\mathcal{A}$ a second time with the same random tape as in the first run and now answers all random oracle queries using the outputs $h_1, \ldots, h_{\ell_1-1}, h''_{\ell_1}, h_{\ell_1+1}, \ldots, h_Q \in \mathbb{Z}_p$, where $h''_{\ell_1} \xleftarrow{R} \mathbb{Z}_p$ is freshly sampled and all other outputs h_ℓ for $\ell \neq \ell_1$ are the same as in the first execution. Here again, regarding the Local Forking Lemma, with probability at least equal to $1/Q \cdot \epsilon^2$, $\mathcal{A}$'s third run outputs $(C, S_0'', S_1, \mathbf{m}_0''[S_0''], \mathbf{m}_1[S_1], \pi_0'', \pi_1'')$. Note that $(S_0'', \mathbf{m}_0''[S_0''])$ may differ from the pair $(S_0, \mathbf{m}_0[S_0])$ of the first execution but this run involves the same $(S_1, \mathbf{m}_1[S_1])$ as in the first execution of $\mathcal{A}$ and the hash query $H(i^\star, C, S_1, \mathbf{m}_1[S_1])$ is also the ℓ_1-th query in the this run, where $\mathcal{A}$ receives a different response h_{ℓ_1}''. Since $i^\star \in S_1$, we can repeat the same arguments as in the first fork and, by dividing out the verification equations (19) of the first and third runs, $\mathcal{B}$ obtains

$$e(C, \hat{g}_{n+1-i^\star}^{\Delta t_{i^\star}^{(1)}}) = e(\pi_1/\pi_1'', \hat{g}) \cdot e(g_1, \hat{g}_n)^{\mathbf{m}_1[i^\star] \cdot \Delta t_{i^\star}^{(1)}}, \tag{21}$$

where $\Delta t_{i^\star}^{(1)} \triangleq h_{\ell_1} - h_{\ell_1}'' \neq 0$ except with probability $1/p$. Then, raising both sides of (21) to the power $\omega \triangleq \Delta t_{i^\star}^{(0)}/\Delta t_{i^\star}^{(1)}$ yields

$$e(C, \hat{g}_{n+1-i^\star}^{\Delta t_{i^\star}^{(0)}}) = e((\pi_1/\pi_1'')^\omega, \hat{g}) \cdot e(g_1, \hat{g}_n)^{\mathbf{m}_1[i^\star] \cdot \Delta t_{i^\star}^{(0)}}. \tag{22}$$

If we now use the hypothesis that $m_{i^\star} \neq m_{i^\star}'$, the combination of (22) and (8) implies

$$e(\pi_0/\pi_0', \hat{g}) \cdot e(g_1, \hat{g}_n)^{\mathbf{m}_0[i^\star] \cdot \Delta t_{i^\star}^{(0)}} = e((\pi_1/\pi_1'')^\omega, \hat{g}) \cdot e(g_1, \hat{g}_n)^{\mathbf{m}_1[i^\star] \cdot \Delta t_{i^\star}^{(0)}},$$

which allows $\mathcal{B}$ to compute and output

$$g_{n+1} \triangleq \left(\frac{(\pi_1/\pi_1'')^\omega}{\pi_0/\pi_0'} \right)^{1/\left(\Delta t_{i^\star}^{(0)} \cdot (\mathbf{m}_0[i^\star] - \mathbf{m}_1[i^\star]) \right)}. \tag{23}$$

Thus, with probability at least equal to $\left((1/Q) \cdot \epsilon^2\right)^2$, the reduction $\mathcal{B}$ succeeds in solving the n-DHE problem. □

A.2   Local vs Generalized Forking Lemma

We provided two proofs for the binding property of same-commitment aggregation of the vector commitment scheme proposed in [16] as PointProofs. In one technique, we used the Generalized Forking Lemma (Lemma 1) to prove the binding property (Theorem 1), and in the other technique, we used the Local Forking Lemma (Lemma 2) to prove the same (Theorem 3). Here, we compare the two techniques in terms of the advantage/run-time ratio of the reduction in each case.

Let ϵ, t be respectively the winning probability and run-time of $\mathcal{A}$ which is the adversary of PointProofs' binding property. Furthermore, let q be the number of oracle queries that $\mathcal{A}$ issues to H. We denote by m the number of forkings (i.e. the number of times an n-DHE adversary re-runs $\mathcal{A}$) which is equal to 2 in both of our proofs. The advantage/run-time ratio in each case is as follows:

- Using Local Forking Lemma

$$\frac{\mathsf{Adv}}{t} = \frac{(1/q \cdot \epsilon^2)^m}{t} = \frac{\epsilon^4}{t \cdot q^2}$$

- Using Generalized Forking Lemma

$$\frac{\mathsf{Adv}}{t} = \frac{\epsilon/8}{t \cdot 8 \cdot m^2 \cdot q \cdot 1/\epsilon \cdot \ln(8m/\epsilon)} = \frac{\epsilon^2}{t \cdot 256 \cdot q \cdot \ln(16/\epsilon)},$$

Since we can consider $\epsilon \geq 1/2$, we have $\ln(16/\epsilon) = \ln(16) - \ln(\epsilon) \leq \ln(16) - \ln(1/2) \approx 3.4$. So, for the Generalized Forking Lemma case, we have

$$\frac{\mathsf{Adv}}{t} \geq \frac{\epsilon^2}{t \cdot 256 \cdot q \cdot 3.4} \geq \frac{\epsilon^2}{870 \cdot t \cdot q}$$

Since q, the number of oracle queries, can be potentially very large, using Generalized Forking Lemma seems to give a tighter reduction in the case of PointProofs.

References

1. Bagherzandi, A., Cheon, J. H., Jarecki, S.: Multisignatures secure under the discrete logarithm assumption and a generalized forking lemma. In: ACM-CCS (2008)
2. Bellare, M., Dai, W., Li, L.: The local forking lemma and its application to deterministic encryption. In: Galbraith, S.D., Moriai, S. (eds.) ASIACRYPT 2019. LNCS, vol. 11923, pp. 607–636. Springer, Cham (2019). https://doi.org/10.1007/978-3-030-34618-8_21
3. Boneh, D., Bünz, B., Fisch, B.: Batching techniques for accumulators with applications to IOPs and stateless blockchains. In: Boldyreva, A., Micciancio, D. (eds.) CRYPTO 2019. LNCS, vol. 11692, pp. 561–586. Springer, Cham (2019). https://doi.org/10.1007/978-3-030-26948-7_20
4. Boneh, D., Boyen, X., Goh, E.-J.: Hierarchical identity based encryption with constant size ciphertext. In: Cramer, R. (ed.) EUROCRYPT 2005. LNCS, vol. 3494, pp. 440–456. Springer, Heidelberg (2005). https://doi.org/10.1007/11426639_26
5. Boneh, D., Drake, J., Fisch, B., Gabizon, A.: Efficient polynomial commitment schemes for multiple points and polynomials. Cryptology ePrint Archive Report 2020/81
6. Boneh, D., Drake, J., Fisch, B., Gabizon, A.: Halo Infinite: proof-carrying data from additive polynomial commitments. In: Malkin, T., Peikert, C. (eds.) CRYPTO 2021. LNCS, vol. 12825, pp. 649–680. Springer, Cham (2021). https://doi.org/10.1007/978-3-030-84242-0_23
7. Boneh, D., Drijvers, M., Neven, G.: Compact multi-signatures for smaller blockchains. In: Peyrin, T., Galbraith, S. (eds.) ASIACRYPT 2018. LNCS, vol. 11273, pp. 435–464. Springer, Cham (2018). https://doi.org/10.1007/978-3-030-03329-3_15
8. Boneh, D., Gentry, C., Waters, B.: Collusion resistant broadcast encryption with short ciphertexts and private keys. In: Shoup, V. (ed.) CRYPTO 2005. LNCS, vol. 3621, pp. 258–275. Springer, Heidelberg (2005). https://doi.org/10.1007/11535218_16

9. Camenisch, J., Dubovitskaya, M., Haralambiev, K., Kohlweiss, M.: Composable and modular anonymous credentials: definitions and practical constructions. In: Iwata, T., Cheon, J.H. (eds.) ASIACRYPT 2015. LNCS, vol. 9453, pp. 262–288. Springer, Heidelberg (2015). https://doi.org/10.1007/978-3-662-48800-3_11

10. Campanelli, M., Fiore, D., Greco, N., Kolonelos, D., Nizzardo, L.: Incrementally aggregatable vector commitments and applications to verifiable decentralized storage. In: Moriai, S., Wang, H. (eds.) ASIACRYPT 2020. LNCS, vol. 12492, pp. 3–35. Springer, Cham (2020). https://doi.org/10.1007/978-3-030-64834-3_1

11. Catalano, D., Fiore, D., Messina, M.: Zero-knowledge sets with short proofs. In: Smart, N. (ed.) EUROCRYPT 2008. LNCS, vol. 4965, pp. 433–450. Springer, Heidelberg (2008). https://doi.org/10.1007/978-3-540-78967-3_25

12. Catalano, D., Fiore, D.: Vector commitments and their applications. In: Kurosawa, K., Hanaoka, G. (eds.) PKC 2013. LNCS, vol. 7778, pp. 55–72. Springer, Heidelberg (2013). https://doi.org/10.1007/978-3-642-36362-7_5

13. Chepurnoy, A., Papamanthou, C., Srinivasan, S., Zhang, Y.: Edrax: a cryptocurrency with stateless transaction validation. Cryptology ePrint Archive Report 2018/968

14. Fiat, A., Shamir, A.: How to prove yourself: practical solutions to identification and signature problems. In: Odlyzko, A.M. (ed.) CRYPTO 1986. LNCS, vol. 263, pp. 186–194. Springer, Heidelberg (1987). https://doi.org/10.1007/3-540-47721-7_12

15. Fuchsbauer, G., Kiltz, E., Loss, J.: The algebraic group model and its applications. In: Shacham, H., Boldyreva, A. (eds.) CRYPTO 2018. LNCS, vol. 10992, pp. 33–62. Springer, Cham (2018). https://doi.org/10.1007/978-3-319-96881-0_2

16. Gorbunov, S., Reyzin, L., Wee, H., Zhang, Z.: PointProofs: aggregating proofs for multiple vector commitments In: ACM-CCS (2020)

17. Kate, A., Zaverucha, G.M., Goldberg, I.: Constant-size commitments to polynomials and their applications. In: Abe, M. (ed.) ASIACRYPT 2010. LNCS, vol. 6477, pp. 177–194. Springer, Heidelberg (2010). https://doi.org/10.1007/978-3-642-17373-8_11

18. Krupp, J., Schröder, D., Simkin, M., Fiore, D., Ateniese, G., Nuernberger, S.: Nearly optimal verifiable data streaming. In: Cheng, C.-M., Chung, K.-M., Persiano, G., Yang, B.-Y. (eds.) PKC 2016. LNCS, vol. 9614, pp. 417–445. Springer, Heidelberg (2016). https://doi.org/10.1007/978-3-662-49384-7_16

19. Lai, R.W.F., Malavolta, G.: Subvector commitments with application to succinct arguments. In: Boldyreva, A., Micciancio, D. (eds.) CRYPTO 2019. LNCS, vol. 11692, pp. 530–560. Springer, Cham (2019). https://doi.org/10.1007/978-3-030-26948-7_19

20. Leung, D., Gilad, Y., Gorbunov, S., Reyzin, L., Zeldovich, N.: Aardvark: a concurrent authenticated dictionary with short proofs. Cryptology ePrint Archive Report 2020/975 (2020)

21. Libert, B., Ramanna, S., Yung, M.: Functional commitment schemes: from polynomial commitments to pairing-based accumulators from simple assumptions. In: ICALP (2016)

22. Libert, B., Yung, M.: Concise mercurial vector commitments and independent zero-knowledge sets with short proofs. In: Micciancio, D. (ed.) TCC 2010. LNCS, vol. 5978, pp. 499–517. Springer, Heidelberg (2010). https://doi.org/10.1007/978-3-642-11799-2_30

23. Merkle, R.C.: A certified digital signature. In: Brassard, G. (ed.) CRYPTO 1989. LNCS, vol. 435, pp. 218–238. Springer, New York (1990). https://doi.org/10.1007/0-387-34805-0_21

24. Micali, S., Rabin, M.-O., Kilian, J.: Zero-knowledge Sets. In: FOCS (2003)
25. Micali, S., Reyzin, L., Vlachos, G., Wahby, R., Zeldovich, N.: Compact certificates of collective knowledge. In: IEEE S & P (2021)
26. Naor, M.: On cryptographic assumptions and challenges. In: Boneh, D. (ed.) CRYPTO 2003. LNCS, vol. 2729, pp. 96–109. Springer, Heidelberg (2003). https://doi.org/10.1007/978-3-540-45146-4_6
27. Pedersen, T.P.: Non-interactive and information-theoretic secure verifiable secret sharing. In: Feigenbaum, J. (ed.) CRYPTO 1991. LNCS, vol. 576, pp. 129–140. Springer, Heidelberg (1992). https://doi.org/10.1007/3-540-46766-1_9
28. Peikert, C., Pepin, Z., Sharp, C.: Vector and functional commitments from lattices. In: Nissim, K., Waters, B. (eds.) TCC 2021. LNCS, vol. 13044, pp. 480–511. Springer, Cham (2021). https://doi.org/10.1007/978-3-030-90456-2_16
29. Pointcheval, D., Stern, J.: Security arguments for digital signatures and blind signatures. J. Cryptology **13**, 361–396 (2000). https://doi.org/10.1007/s001450010003
30. Shoup, V.: Lower bounds for discrete logarithms and related problems. In: Fumy, W. (ed.) EUROCRYPT 1997. LNCS, vol. 1233, pp. 256–266. Springer, Heidelberg (1997). https://doi.org/10.1007/3-540-69053-0_18
31. Srinivasan, S., Chepurnoy, A., Papamanthou, C., Tomescu, A., Zhang, Y.: Hyperproofs: aggregating and maintaining proofs in vector commitments. In: USENIX Security (2022)
32. Tomescu, A., Abraham, I., Buterin, V., Drake, J., Feist, D., Khovratovich, D.: Aggregatable subvector commitments for stateless cryptocurrencies. In: Galdi, C., Kolesnikov, V. (eds.) SCN 2020. LNCS, vol. 12238, pp. 45–64. Springer, Cham (2020). https://doi.org/10.1007/978-3-030-57990-6_3
33. Tomescu, A.: How to compute all Pointproofs. Cryptology ePrint Archive Report 2020/1516
34. Tomescu, A., Xia, Y., Newman, Z.: Authenticated dictionaries with cross-incremental proof (dis)aggregation. Cryptology ePrint Archive Report 2020/1239

Theory

Universal Ring Signatures
in the Standard Model

Pedro Branco[1(✉)], Nico Döttling[2], and Stella Wohnig[2,3]

[1] Johns Hopkins University, Baltimore, USA
`pedrodemelobranco@gmail.com`
[2] Helmholtz Center for Information Security (CISPA), Saarbrücken, Germany
[3] Universität des Saarlandes, Saarbrücken, Germany

Abstract. Ring signatures allow a user to sign messages on behalf of an *ad hoc* set of users - a ring - while hiding her identity. The original motivation for ring signatures was whistleblowing [Rivest et al. ASIACRYPT'01]: a high government employee can anonymously leak sensitive information while certifying that it comes from a reliable source, namely by signing the leak. However, essentially all known ring signature schemes require the members of the ring to publish a structured verification key that is compatible with the scheme. This creates somewhat of a paradox since, if a user does not want to be framed for whistleblowing, they will stay clear of signature schemes that support ring signatures.

In this work, we formalize the concept of universal ring signatures (URS). A URS enables a user to issue a ring signature with respect to a ring of users, independently of the signature schemes they are using. In particular, none of the verification keys in the ring need to come from the same scheme. Thus, in principle, URS presents an effective solution for whistleblowing.

The main goal of this work is to study the feasibility of URS, especially in the standard model (i.e. no random oracles or common reference strings). We present several constructions of URS, offering different trade-offs between assumptions required, the level of security achieved, and the size of signatures:

- Our first construction is based on superpolynomial hardness assumptions of standard primitives. It achieves compact signatures. That means the size of a signature depends only logarithmically on the size of the ring and on the number of signature schemes involved.
- We then proceed to study the feasibility of constructing URS from standard polynomially-hard assumptions only. We construct a non-compact URS from witness encryption and additional standard assumptions.
- Finally, we show how to modify the non-compact construction into a compact one by relying on indistinguishability obfuscation.

Keywords: Ring signatures · Whistleblowing

© International Association for Cryptologic Research 2022
S. Agrawal and D. Lin (Eds.): ASIACRYPT 2022, LNCS 13794, pp. 249–278, 2022.
https://doi.org/10.1007/978-3-031-22972-5_9

1   Introduction

Ring Signatures. Ring signatures, introduced in [33], allow for a user to create a signature σ for a message m with respect to an ad-hoc group of users R, called a ring. A ring signature should be: i) unforgeable, meaning that, given a valid signature σ for a ring R, it must have been created by one of the users in R; and ii) anonymous, meaning that it should be infeasible for someone, even if they have access to every signing key corresponding to the verification keys in the ring R, to identify which user created the signature.

Ring signatures have recently found wide-spread application in the context of cryptocurrencies. However in this work we revisit the original motivation of ring signatures: *whistleblowing* [33]. Using a ring signature scheme, a whistleblower in a high government office with access to some classified information can leak this information e.g. to the media, in a way that convinces them that this information comes from a reliable source, namely by signing the leak. At the same time, the identity of the whistleblower remains hidden in the ring of insiders. A critical aspect in this scenario is that *the whistleblower can issue such a signature without the consent of the other parties in the ring.*

Rivest, Shamir and Tauman-Kalai [33] showed that signature schemes with RSA verification keys can be used to issue ring signatures. If RSA signatures were the universally agreed-upon standard for digital signatures, this would be great for whistleblowers! Yet, currently there is a plethora of competing schemes and standards for digital signatures.

Support for ring signatures might however even deter users from adopting some signature scheme: Knowing that a certain signature scheme supports ring signatures, why should loyal government officials even use such a scheme and potentially be framed for being a whistleblower? Furthermore, wouldn't it even be in the interest of a government to mandate their officials to use signature schemes which do not allow to issue ring signatures? Can the kind of whistle-blowing envisioned by [33] be prohibited by such measures? Are there effective countermeasures which protect users against being abused as a crowd in which a whistleblower seeks anonymity? Concretely, can we construct signature schemes which protect their users from being involuntarily forced into a ring?

Universal Ring Signatures. Formalizing the idea of a ring signature compatible with *all* digital signature schemes, we define the notion of *Universal Ring Signatures* (URS)[1]. URS allow users to create a ring signature for a ring composed of verification keys $R = (\mathsf{vk}_1, \ldots, \mathsf{vk}_\ell)$ *independently* of the structure of each vk_i and even the signature schemes which were used to create these keys. In other words, each vk_i can be a verification key from a *(possibly different) signature scheme.*[2] Most importantly, *none of the verification keys is required to be compatible with known ring signature schemes.*

---

[1] The term universal ring signatures was also used in [36] to refer to a completely different property of ring signatures.

[2] For example, one of the verification keys can be from an SIS-based signature scheme and another from a group-based signature scheme.

Thus, URS allow users to conceal their identity inside a ring in a *non-cooperative way*: The user can create a signature with respect to a ring of verification keys, even if they were specifically chosen to be incompatible with specific ring signature schemes. This is in stark contrast to standard ring signatures, where the parties *cooperate* by issuing verification keys that are compatible with a ring signature scheme, thus intentionally providing anonymity to one another (which is what happens in a cryptocurrency setting).

A URS provides a way out of the whistleblower problem described above. Equipped with a URS scheme, a whistleblower just needs to somehow specify (implicitly or explicitly) the verification keys of the users in the ring. However, unlike for all known ring signature schemes, these verification keys do not need to obey any particular structure.

Ring Signatures via Non-interactive Zero-Knowledge Proofs. Non-interactive zero-knowledge (NIZK) proofs [8] are a powerful and quite general tool to make protocols secure against malicious adversaries. In the context of ring signatures, the slightly stronger notion of non-interactive zero-knowledge proofs of knowledge (NIZKPoK) provide a stronger soundness guarantee, in the sense that any (efficient) prover providing a valid proof of some statement x must *know* corresponding witness w of x.

NIZKPoK proofs provide a direct approach to construct ring signatures: For a ring R, a message m and a commit c one provides a proof π which certifies that c commits to a signature σ such that the pair (σ, m) verifies under some verification key vk in the ring R.

This construction does not require that the verification keys in the ring R come from one and the same signature scheme. Thus, NIZKPoK proofs in fact imply universal ring signatures. Yet, NIZK (and thus also NIZKPoK) are known to be impossible in the standard model [23], that is without a common reference string and without making use of the random oracle heuristic [4]. We will later discuss the ramifications of relying on either the random oracle model or the random oracle heuristic in the construction of URS.

1.1 Our Results

The main problem we address in this work is the question of whether universal ring signatures exist in the standard model, and if so under which assumptions.

Before we tackle the problem of constructing universal ring signatures, we first provide definitions that formalize the requirements informally laid out above.

We present three standard model URS construction, offering different trade-offs between compactness, security and primitives/assumptions needed to construct them. Our schemes are *fully* universal, in the sense that no assumptions on the structure of verification keys are made.

Our first construction is a URS scheme with compact signatures, i.e., the signature size depends only logarithmically on the number of users in the ring and on the number of signature schemes. This scheme relies on superpolynomial hardness of standard assumptions. Specifically, we rely on a superpolynomially secure signature scheme, a (polynomially secure) perfectly binding commitment scheme, perfectly sound non-interactive witness-indistinguishability (NIWI) proof systems for NP and somewhere perfectly binding (SPB) hashing scheme [3]. All of these primitives can be instantiated using standard hardness assumptions.

We get the following theorem.

Theorem 1 (Informal). *Assuming the existence of perfectly binding commitment schemes, perfectly sound NIWI proof systems for NP and SPB hashing schemes (all three with polynomial security), there exists a universal ring signature scheme in the standard model with compact signatures under the condition that the underlying signature schemes are superpolynomially secure.*

While this construction provides the baseline for our investigation, it raises the question whether superpolynomial hardness is necessary to construct standard model universal ring signatures. Compared with 2-move blind signatures, we do know standard model constructions (again, no CRS or RO) from superpolynomial hardness assumptions [19,20], yet we don't know of any such construction from polynomial hardness assumptions and in fact, it is known that no such construction is achievable via a black-box reduction [16]. Thus, it is conceivable that something similar might be the case for universal ring signatures.

Perhaps somewhat surprisingly, our second construction shows that this is not the case for URS: We provide a construction that enjoys a security reduction to polynomial and falsifiable hardness assumptions. Concretely, we rely on the existence of a witness encryption (WE) scheme for NP, a perfectly sound NIWI proof system for NP, an SPB hashing scheme, and a pseudorandom function (PRF). In terms of compactness, the size of the signatures of this scheme depends linearly on the number of users in the ring. Further, this scheme fulfills a slightly relaxed notion of anonymity, which we call t-anonymity, which requires that there need to be at least t honestly generated verification keys in the ring. The standard notion of anonymity corresponds to 2-anonymity.

Theorem 2 (Informal). *Assuming the existence of a WE for NP, a perfectly sound NIWI proof system for NP, an SPB hashing scheme, and a PRF, there exists a (non-compact) universal ring signature scheme in the standard model with t-anonymity, where t is a parameter depending on the signature schemes involved.*

For all conceivable purposes, the parameter t here is a small constant. Concretely, t depends on the entropy κ of the honest verification keys involved. Asymptotically, any such key must have entropy at least $\kappa = \omega(\log(\lambda))$. Otherwise, it would be trivially insecure. Our only requirement on t will be that $t \cdot \kappa \geq \lambda$. In terms of concrete parameters, κ would have to be at least 50 bits (or else the underlying scheme would be trivially insecure). Setting $t = 3$ or $t = 4$ will be sufficient for this parameter choice.

This leaves open the question of compactness. Is perhaps any standard model URS necessarily non-compact?

We can also resolve this question negatively, yet under still a (potentially) stronger assumption: We provide a construction of a compact WE scheme from polynomial hardness assumptions for a special type of languages that we call (t, N) threshold conjunction languages, which together with Theorem 2 will imply a compact URS scheme from polynomial hardness assumptions.

A (t, N) threshold conjunction language is the set of statements $(x_1, \ldots, x_N)$ for which there are at least t valid statements x_i among them. The size of the ciphertexts we receive when encrypting under such a statement is compact in the sense that it only depends logarithmically on N. Our WE construction requires indistinguishability obfuscation ($i\mathcal{O}$), puncturable pseudorandom functions (PPRF) [10], somewhere statistically binding (SSB) hashing schemes [27,30] and (t, N)-linear secret sharing (LSS). We obtain the following theorem.

Theorem 3 (Informal). *Assuming the existence of an $i\mathcal{O}$ for all circuits, a (non-compact) WE for NP, a PPRF, an SSB hashing scheme, and a (t, N)-LSS, there exists a compact WE scheme for (t, N) threshold conjunction languages, when $N - t \in \mathcal{O}(\log N)$.*

Combining the two previous theorems, we obtain our final URS construction. This URS construction achieves compact signatures.

Theorem 4 (Informal). *Assuming the existence of a compact WE for $(N - 1, N)$ threshold conjunction languages, a perfectly sound NIWI proof system for NP, an SPB hashing scheme and a PRF, there exists a compact universal ring signature scheme in the standard model with t-anonymity.*

1.2   Discussion and Interpretation of Our Results

Returning to our main motivation, a URS enables whistleblowing since a whistleblower can *force* any honest users into a ring, regardless of which signature scheme they use. In this sense, one can view the process of signing a message using a URS as an *adversarial act*: even if a set of honest users do not want to hide the whistleblower, there are no effective measures on the level of signature schemes which could protect users from being included in an anonymity set.

Bearing this in mind, we interpret our results, which establish the feasibility of URS, as demonstrating the impossibility of designing signature schemes that resist coercion into rings. Needless to say, the rather heavy components involved in our constructions do not lead to practically useful protocols.

Above we briefly discussed that universal ring signatures can be constructed from NIZKPoK proofs and by now there is a plethora of constructions of NIZKPoK proofs from standard assumptions in the common reference string (CRS) model [8,12,15,25,28,32], or alternatively in the random oracle model [4]. If the goal was to construct a practically useful URS to provide support across different, seemingly incompatible but *common* signature schemes, then a protocol relying on succinct NIZKPoK arguments would be preferable. In such a setting, one would expect the users of these schemes to collaborate in the sense that they are willing to provide anonymity to one another, i.e. one could assume that all users trust a common reference string as well as all the signature schemes involved.

Yet, the scenario we are interested in is different, in the sense that the "users" have no reason to trust one another, as they were potentially forced into a ring against their will. In this sense, a universal ring signature scheme in the CRS could give users who have been forced into a ring against their will a means of plausible deniability, e.g. by claiming that they do not trust the CRS that was used to generate a universal ring signature, as the party who generated such a CRS may also forge such a signature.

On the other hand, if we consider URS in the random oracle model, then the unsoundness of the ROM could cause issues. When protocols in the ROM are instantiated, we replace the random oracle with a concrete hash function H. As shown by Goldwasser and Kalai [24], this heuristic can lead to unsound proof systems if the underlying language already depends on this (concrete) hash function H.

This issue also comes up in the context of universal ring signatures, as one of the signature schemes could be chosen *depending on the hash function H*. Somewhat more concretely, assume we wanted to build a signature scheme Σ^* which makes a URS relying on a random oracle unsound, in the sense that if any verification key of Σ^* is used in a ring R, then universal ring signatures can be forged, while Σ^* is still EUF-CMA secure. We could achieve this by taking any EUF-CMA secure signature scheme Σ and modifying it to Σ^* by additionally including into the verification keys vk^* of Σ^* an obfuscated program $\mathcal{O}$ which lets anyone publicly generate URS of rings involving vk^*. Note that this obfuscated program $\mathcal{O}$ needs to *know* a succinct description of the hash function H, but this is feasible as we assume H to be *instantiated*, rather than a random oracle. The same can in fact be argued for any fixed static common reference string CRS, i.e. CRS can be hardwired into $\mathcal{O}$. Note that while for such a scheme the size of the verification key would increase, both generation and verification would remain essentially unchanged.

Looking ahead, if such a transformation from Σ to Σ^* was done starting relative to one of our standard-model secure URS, then Σ^* would be necessarily insecure. But for a URS whose unforgeability rests on the CRS model or the random oracle model, we would generally expect such a Σ^* to be unforgeable (once the CRS or the RO has been instantiated).

The bottom line of this discussion is that it seems hard to argue that URS constructions in the CRS model or the ROM would be robust against signature schemes which undermine the unforgeability of the URS by depending on the concrete CRS which is used or the concrete hash function which instantiates the Fiat-Shamir paradigm.

1.3   Previous Works

Ring signatures have been extensively studied in the last two decades. Constructions in the random oracle model (ROM) include [1,9,14,29,33]. Ring signatures in the CRS model were studied in [11,35], where [11] solves the interesting but orthogonal problem of how to include users in a ring whose public keys are not posted publicly by using a PKI structure. We can also find standard model constructions for ring signatures in e.g. [3,5,31].

All works presented above assume some form of structure on the verification keys. For example, the work of [33] assumes that ring verification keys are RSA keys or the work of [5] assumes that ring verification keys are composed by a standard verification key and a uniformly random string.

The only exceptions we are aware of are the works [1,22]. In these works, ring signatures that support different signature schemes are presented. However, these works are only *somewhat universal* in the sense that there are signature schemes that are not compatible with their schemes.[3] Moreover, these schemes are only secure in the ROM whereas we work in the standard model. In essence, the focus of these works is different from ours as they sacrifice universality for efficiency. In this work, we take the opposite direction.

A construction of a universal primitive from $i\mathcal{O}$ has previously been given for a notion called signature aggregators in [26]. This allows to combine signatures from different users using arbitrary signature schemes into one signature to succinctly store and verify. The application and techniques used are however different and can not be transferred to ring signatures trivially.

2   Technical Overview

Before presenting our constructions of URS, we briefly recall the ring signature scheme of Backes *et al.* [3]

In the scheme of [3] (which is itself based on [5]), verification keys are composed by $VK_i = (vk_i, pk_i)$ where vk_i is a verification key of a standard signature scheme Sig and pk_i is a public key of a public-key encryption (PKE) scheme that has pseudorandom ciphertexts[4].

To sign a message m with respect to a ring $R = \{VK_i\}_{i \in [\ell]}$, the signer i first generates a signature $\sigma \leftarrow \mathsf{Sig.Sign}(sk_i, m)$ and then encrypts σ it using pk_i, that is, $ct_0 \leftarrow \mathsf{PKE.Enc}(pk_i, \sigma)$. The signer then samples $ct_1 \leftarrow_\$ \{0,1\}^\lambda$. One crucial point is that, if the underlying PKE has pseudorandom ciphertexts, then we cannot distinguish well-formed ciphertexts from uniformly random strings. In particular, this means that ct_0 contains (computationally) no information about the public key under which it was encrypted.

The signer now proves that either ct_0 or ct_1 encrypts a valid signature under one of the verification keys in the ring using a non-interactive witness-indistinguishable (NIWI) proof system. If off-the-shelf NIWIs were used in this construction, the size of the proof would scale linearly with the size of the ring. This would lead to signatures of size $\mathcal{O}(|R| \cdot \mathsf{poly}(\lambda))$, where λ is the security parameter. To circumvent this problem, [3] employed a new strategy.

---

[3] More precisely, the scheme of [1] is compatible with *trapdoor-one-way* and *three-move* signature schemes. The scheme of [22] is compatible with certain sigma protocols. Any scheme outside of these classes is not compatible with their ring signature schemes.

[4] Examples of such PKE schemes exist from the LWE or DDH assumption.

Compact NIWI Proofs. The main ingredient to compress the size of the NIWI proof is a somewhere perfectly binding (SPB) hashing scheme. An SPB hashing scheme allows one to hash a database such that the hash perfectly binds to the database item an index i, while the hashing key hides the index i. [3,27,30].

Given ct_0, ct_1, the signer can now use a NIWI proof system together with a somewhere perfectly binding (SPB) hashing scheme to create a compact proof π that either ct_0 or ct_1 encrypts a valid signature under one of the keys in the ring. The basic idea here is that instead of proving a statement over all verification keys in the ring, it is sufficient to prove a statement about just two SPB hashes. More concretely, to compute the proof π, the signer first generates an SPB pair of hashing key/secret key $(hk_j, shk_j) \leftarrow$ SPB.KeyGen$(1^\lambda, i)$ that binds to position i, for $j \in \{0, 1\}$. Then, it hashes R into a digest $h_j \leftarrow$ SPB.Hash(hk_j, R) for $j \in \{0, 1\}$. Finally, the signer proves that there exists an index i such that one of the two statements is true:

1. ct_0 encrypts a valid signature under vk_i and hk_0 binds to i;
2. ct_1 encrypts a valid signature under vk_i and hk_1 binds to i.

The signature is composed by $(ct_0, ct_1, hk_0, hk_1, \pi)$. Thus, by the efficiency requirements of SPB, the signature has size $\mathcal{O}(\log |R| \cdot \mathsf{poly}(\lambda))$.

Finally, to verify that a signature is valid, one just needs to recompute h_j as the hash of R under hk_j, for $j \in \{0, 1\}$, and check that π is a valid proof.

Security. Unforgeability and anonymity are roughly argued as follows in [3]. To argue unforgeability, the security of the scheme is reduced to the security of the underlying signature scheme. To do this, the reduction receives a verification key vk_{i^*} from the challenger, creates the remaining verification keys vk_i, for $i \neq i^*$, and also the public keys pk_i for all $i \in [\ell]$. Importantly, the public keys pk_i are created such that the reduction knows the corresponding secret keys.

Upon receiving a (ring signature) forge from the adversary, the reduction proceeds as follows:

1. Decrypt both ct_0 and ct_1, to obtain σ_0 and σ_1, respectively;
2. Check if any of σ_0, σ_1 is a valid signature under vk_{i^*}. If one of them is valid, the reduction outputs it as the forge.

By the perfect correctness of the SPB hashing and perfect soundness of the NIWI, the reduction outputs a valid forge with non-negligible probability.

To prove anonymity, one relies on the witness-indistinguishability of the NIWI and the fact that the underlying PKE has pseudorandom ciphertexts. Concretely, given two honestly generated verification keys vk_{i_0} and vk_{i_1}, build a sequence of hybrids to prove that a signature created under vk_{i_0} is indistinguishable from a signature created under vk_{i_1}. The sequence of hybrids starts by replacing ct_1 with an encryption of a valid signature under vk_{i_1}, and this change goes unnoticed since the PKE has pseudorandom ciphertexts. Next, change the index in the witness used to create the proof π from i_0 to i_1 using the witness-indistinguishability of the NIWI scheme.

2.1 Compact Universal Ring Signatures from Signatures with Superpolynomial Security

The construction of the Backes et al. scheme [3] serves as the starting point of our first construction. Observe that the ring signature verification keys of the Backes et al. scheme have a special format: each verification key VK_i is composed of a standard verification key vk_i and a public key pk_i.

The public key pk_i, which can be chosen by the unforgeability reduction, is what enables this reduction to extract a valid forge. In a URS, however, verification keys are not required to have any particular format. In particular, they are not required to include an independently chosen public key of a PKE. How can we facilitate the extraction of a forge by an unforgeability reduction in the setting of URS?

Commitments Instead of Ciphertexts. Our first observation is that the cipher-texts in the scheme of Backes et al. [3] are never decrypted *in the actual scheme.* So, ciphertexts in this scheme actually serve as extractable commitments. Thus, a natural approach is to rely on commitments instead of ciphertexts in this construction. The main reason for using commitments instead of ciphertexts is that we can choose a *keyless* commitment scheme.

Using a commitment scheme, we can build a URS as follows: To sign a message m under a ring of users $R = \{\mathsf{vk}_1, \ldots, \mathsf{vk}_\ell\}$ (where each vk_i is from a possibly different signature scheme), a signer first creates a signature $\sigma \leftarrow \mathsf{Sig.Sign}_i(\mathsf{sk}_i, m)$ using its signature scheme Sig_i. Then, it commits to $(\mathsf{com}_0, \gamma_0) \leftarrow \mathsf{CS.Commit}(1^\lambda, \sigma)$ and to $(\mathsf{com}_1, \gamma_1) \leftarrow \mathsf{CS.Commit}(1^\lambda, 0)$ (where γ_b is the opening information). Using SPB and NIWI exactly as before, the signer can create a compact proof π that one of the commitments hides a valid signature under one of the keys in R.

Anonymity follows by essentially the same argument as before, where the hiding property of the underlying commitment is used instead of the ciphertext pseudorandomness of the PKE in [3].

Unforgeability from Superpolynomial Hardness. We now show how the unforgeability reduction can extract a valid forge from the adversary. Assume that the hiding property of the commitment scheme CS holds against *polynomial-time* adversaries but that CS can be extracted in *superpolynomial-time.* We can then use *complexity leveraging* to prove the unforgeability of the scheme, given that the underlying signature schemes are unforgeable against superpolynomial-time adversaries.

Concretely, given a PPT adversary $\mathcal{A}$ that breaks the unforgeability of our URS, we can construct a superpolynomial-time reduction against the unforgeability of one of the Sig_i. The reduction, after receiving a forge $\Sigma^* = (\mathsf{com}_0^*, \mathsf{com}_1^*, \mathsf{hk}_0^*, \mathsf{hk}_1^*, \pi^*)$ by $\mathcal{A}$, opens both com_0 and com_1 by brute force to recover σ_0^* and σ_1^* respectively. Note that, since CS can be extracted in superpolynomial time, the reduction succeeds in recovering σ_0^* and σ_1^*. Now, as before, the reduction tests if there is a $b \in \{0, 1\}$ such that $1 \leftarrow \mathsf{Sig.Verify}_i(\mathsf{vk}_i, m, \sigma_b^*)$ and outputs σ_b^* if it is the case.

2.2 Non-compact Universal Ring Signatures from Witness Encryption

Considering both the construction of Backes et al. [3] and our construction in the last paragraph, the question emerges of how one could possibly *efficiently* extract a signature, even if we cannot shoehorn an extraction trapdoor into the protocol utilizing a CRS or augmenting the verification keys. Somewhat more abstractly:

Is it possible to extract a secret from a protocol when the protocol constraints don't allow us to embed an extraction gadget into the protocol?

Extracting via Witness Encryption. Our way out of this dilemma starts with the observation that by relying on a sufficiently strong tool, namely standard witness encryption (WE) [18], we can repurpose any *sufficiently cryptographic* object as a public key. In our case, these objects will be the verification keys of the honest parties.

Recall that a WE for an NP language $\mathcal{L}$ (with relation $\mathcal{R}$) allows an encrypter to encrypt a message m with respect to a statement x. If $x \in \mathcal{L}$, then a party in possession of a witness w such that $\mathcal{R}(x, w) = 1$ can recover the encrypted m. But, if $x \notin \mathcal{L}$, then indistinguishability of encryptions holds. Currently, we have constructions of WE from indistinguishability obfuscation $(i\mathcal{O})$ [17] or multilinear maps [18], but WE is potentially a weaker assumption than either of these.

To use the security of WE, we need to craft a language $\mathcal{L}$ with distinct true and false statements, such that witnesses of true statements allow for decryption, whereas ciphertexts under false statements hide the encrypted message. Ideally, true and false statements should be indistinguishable. Our design-choice of true and false statements will be informed by the following consideration: Consider two distributions of (honest) verification keys, one where each honest vk is generated using truly random coins, and another one where each honest ṽk is generated using (possibly correlated) pseudorandom coins. While these distributions are clearly computationally indistinguishable, under the right circumstances we can also make them *statistically far*, meaning that one of them can serve as a distribution of true statements, while the other one will be the distribution of false statements.

More concretely, let PRG be a pseudorandom generator (PRG). We say that a verification key vk is *malformed* if it is created using random coins coming from a PRG, instead of using truly random coins. That is, for some seed s

$$(\mathsf{vk}, \mathsf{sk}) \leftarrow \mathsf{Sig.KeyGen}(1^\lambda; \mathsf{PRG}(s)).$$

Similarly, a *well-formed* key vk is created using truly random coins.

Now, consider the language $\mathcal{L}$ parameterized by ℓ different verification keys $\{\mathsf{vk}_i\}_{i \in [\ell]}$. The *yes* instances of $\mathcal{L}$ are the instances $\{\mathsf{vk}_i\}_{i \in [\ell]}$ where *all but one of the verification keys are malformed*. In other words, there exist $\{s_i\}_{i \in [\ell] \setminus \{i^*\}}$ with $i^* \in [\ell]$ such that for all $i \in [\ell] \setminus \{i^*\}$

$$(\mathsf{vk}_i, \mathsf{sk}_i) \leftarrow \mathsf{Sig.KeyGen}_i(1^\lambda; \mathsf{PRG}(s_i)).$$

Looking ahead, the dichotomy between *all but one key are malformed* vs *at least two keys are well-formed* is what will allow us to prove unforgeability and anonymity respectively. In the former case, the statement under which the WE ciphertext is created is true and, thus, we will be able to decrypt it. In the latter case, the statement is false. Therefore, we can use the security of the WE scheme.

At first glance, this approach seems to work. However, there is a caveat: when the reduction wants verification keys to be well-formed, it might accidentally end up creating them malformed. As an example, consider a signature scheme Sig whose verification keys have less min-entropy than the underlying PRG. Say the key generation algorithm $\mathsf{Sig.Gen}(1^\lambda, r)$ only uses the first $\lambda/3$ bits of r whereas the PRG seed has $\lambda/2$ bits of entropy. In other words, the distributions of well-formed keys and malformed keys might not be sufficiently statistically far. Then, there is a non-negligible probability that a key chosen from the well-formed distribution is actually malformed. We could assume that the underlying signature schemes have exponential security (e.g., verification keys have λ bits of min-entropy) but this would to some degree defeat the purpose of URS.

Replacing the PRG by a PRF. The solution for this problem is to use a pseudo-random function (PRF) instead of a PRG to sample malformed keys. Instead of generating malformed keys individually, we now generate them in a correlated fashion: A set of keys $\{\mathsf{vk}_i\}$ is malformed iff a PRF key K exists such that

$$(\mathsf{vk}_i, \mathsf{sk}_i) \leftarrow \mathsf{Sig.KeyGen}_i(1^\lambda; \mathsf{PRF}(K, i)).$$

Note that now, all malformed keys are correlated via the PRF key. This implies that the distribution of t malformed keys has λ bits of min-entropy because as soon as we choose the PRF key, all malformed keys are fixed. On the other hand, when sampling t well-formed keys independently, the resulting distribution will have $t\kappa$ bits of min-entropy where κ is the min-entropy of each verification key. Setting $t\kappa > \lambda$ we conclude that the distributions of well-formed and malformed keys are statistically far apart.

This fact will allow us to prove t-anonymity by *making the number of honest keys in the ring just large enough.*

Given this, we redefine the language $\mathcal{L}$ in the following way: *yes* instances of $\mathcal{L}$ are the instances $\{\mathsf{vk}_i\}_{i \in [\ell]}$ where *all but one of the verification keys are malformed.* In other words, there exists $K \in \{0,1\}^\lambda$ such that for all $i \in [\ell] \setminus \{i^*\}$

$$(\mathsf{vk}_i, \mathsf{sk}_i) \leftarrow \mathsf{Sig.KeyGen}_i(1^\lambda; \mathsf{PRF}(K, i)).$$

The Scheme. Armed with a WE scheme WE for the language $\mathcal{L}$ described above, we now outline how we can construct a URS scheme.

The scheme is essentially the same as above except that we use the WE scheme for language $\mathcal{L}$ as a drop-in replacement for the commitment scheme.

To sign a message m with respect to the ring R, the signer encrypts a valid signature σ created using its own signing key. Then, it encrypts σ using WE under the statement $x = R$, that is, $\mathsf{ct}_0 \leftarrow \mathsf{WE.Enc}(1^\lambda, x, \sigma)$. Additionally, it creates the ciphertext $\mathsf{ct}_1 \leftarrow \mathsf{WE.Enc}(1^\lambda, x, 0)$. Finally, the signer can again use NIWI and SPB to prove compactly that one of the ciphertexts encrypts a valid signature.

We first analyze the size of the signature. Note that, for all known WE schemes, the ciphertext size is proportional to the size of the verification circuit for the language $\mathcal{L}$. Since the statement is of size $\mathcal{O}(|R| \cdot \mathsf{poly}(\lambda))$, then the ciphertexts output by WE are of size $\mathcal{O}(|R| \cdot \mathsf{poly}(\lambda))$. This implies that the signature is of size $\mathcal{O}(|R| \cdot \mathsf{poly}(\lambda))$.

Security. We now sketch how we prove the security of the scheme. As mentioned before, we will set all but one key to be malformed in order to prove unforgeability. Whereas in the t-anonymity proof, we set none of the keys to be malformed (recall that t-anonymity requires that the challenge ring as at least t honestly generated verification keys).

To prove unforgeability, we design a reduction that sets all verification keys, but the challenge key vk_{i^*} to be malformed. That is, $\{\mathsf{vk}_i\}_{i\in[\ell]\setminus\{i^*\}}$ are malformedly created using a PRF key K. By the security of the PRF, the adversary is not able to distinguish the case where the verification keys $\{\mathsf{vk}_i\}_{i\in[\ell]\setminus\{i^*\}}$ are well-formed from the case when they are malformed.

The crucial observation now is that the reduction has a valid witness $w = K$ for the statement $x = R$ under which WE ciphertexts are encrypted. This means that, upon receiving a URS forge

$$\Sigma^* = (\mathsf{ct}_0^*, \mathsf{ct}_1^*, \mathsf{hk}_0^*, \mathsf{hk}_1^*, \pi^*)$$

by the adversary, the reduction can use w to decrypt both ct_0^* and ct_1^*. An analysis identical as for the previous scheme shows us that, if Σ^* is a valid URS signature, then there is a non-negligible probability that one of ct_0^* and ct_1^* decrypts to a valid signature σ^* under vk_{i^*}.

In the t-anonymity proof, we set *none* of the verification keys to be malformed, from which the adversary chooses t of them, say, $\mathsf{vk}_{i_0}, \ldots, \mathsf{vk}_{i_{t-1}}$. If the parameters of the PRF are chosen properly, then there is a negligible probability that $x \in \mathcal{L}$. As explained above, since all t verification keys are sampled independently, it is unlikely that $t-1$ share correlations via a PRF key K. This is because the distribution of $t-1$ honestly generated keys has much more min-entropy than $t-1$ malformed keys. Thus, there will be *at least two well formed* verification keys in the challenge ring R^* with overwhelming probability. We conclude that WE encryptions of σ are indistinguishable from WE encryptions of 0 by the security of the WE.

Given this, we can easily build a sequence of hybrids in a similar fashion as for the previous schemes. That is, given two honestly generated verification keys $\mathsf{vk}_{i_0}, \mathsf{vk}_{i_1}$ and a signature $\Sigma^* = (\mathsf{ct}_0^*, \mathsf{ct}_1^*, \mathsf{hk}_0^*, \mathsf{hk}_1^*, \pi^*)$ for a message m^* with respect to the ring R^* where $\mathsf{vk}_{i_0}, \mathsf{vk}_{i_1} \in R^*$:

1. We first replace ct_1^* by an encryption of a valid signature σ' under vk_{i_1}. By the security of the underlying WE, this change is undetected by the adversary.
2. We switch witnesses from i_0 to i_1, using the witness-indistinguishability of the NIWI scheme.

2.3   Compact Universal Ring Signatures from Indistinguishability Obfuscation

At first glance, the techniques that we employed in the previous construction seem hopeless in our ultimate goal of building a compact URS from falsifiable hardness assumptions. On the one hand, for all known WE schemes that we know of, the size of the ciphertexts grows with the size of the statement. On the other hand, if we try to reduce the size of the statement of the language $\mathcal{L}$, we immediately run into trouble.

The reason for this is that to be able to extract a valid forge, the reduction needs to set up all verification keys but the challenge one in a *special mode*.[5] If the reduction sets just a few of them in this special mode, anonymity does not hold anymore: An adversary breaking anonymity could just use the same strategy as the unforgeability reduction to extract a signature from the challenge URS signature since, in the anonymity game, all but two verification keys may be adversarially chosen.

Given this state of affairs, it seems implausible (or even impossible!) that we can achieve a compact URS scheme just from WE.

Our final contribution is to build a WE scheme for a special type of NP languages that we call *threshold conjunction languages*. A threshold conjunction language $\mathcal{L}'$ is a language of the form

$$\mathcal{L}' = \{(x_1, \ldots, x_N) : \exists (x_{i_1}, \ldots, x_{i_{N-1}}) \text{ s.t. } x_{i_1} \in \mathcal{L} \wedge \cdots \wedge x_{i_{N-1}} \in \mathcal{L}\}.$$

In other words, given an instance $x = (x_1, \ldots, x_N)$, x is a yes instance of $\mathcal{L}'$ if *all but one* of the x_i are instances of $\mathcal{L}$.

Compact URS from Compact WE. Assume for now that we have a *compact* WE scheme for threshold conjunction languages. That is ciphertexts of such a scheme scale only logarithmically with N. Then, plugging this WE scheme into our construction from the previous section immediately yields a compact URS.

Compact Witness Encryption for Threshold Conjunction Languages. It remains to show how we can obtain such a scheme. For simplicity, we focus on the case where we have N instances $x = (x_1, \ldots, x_N)$ and $x \in \mathcal{L}'$ iff $x_i \in \mathcal{L}$ for all $i \in [N]$. The case where all but one of the statements x_i must be true can be easily obtained by additionally using a secret sharing scheme.

The high-level idea of the construction is as follows: We build an obfuscated circuit $\bar{\mathcal{C}}$ that receives an index $i \in [N]$ and outputs non-compact WE ciphertexts $\mathsf{WE.Enc}(1^\lambda, x_i, r_i)$ for uniform $r_i \leftarrow_\$ \{0,1\}$.[6] The ciphertext of our new WE scheme for a message $m \in \{0,1\}$ is composed by $\bar{\mathcal{C}}$ and $c = m + \sum r_i$.

If one is in possession of witnesses for all statements x_i, then by the correctness of the underlying non-compact WE scheme, one can recover all r_i. On the

---

[5] In our case, the special mode is when keys are malformed.

[6] To make the circuit size independent of N, we use a pseudorandom function (PRF) to succinctly describe all the r_i. This PRF has to be puncturable in order to use the *puncturing technique* of [34].

other hand, if one of the statements x_{i*} is false, then we can build a sequence of hybrids where we replace $\mathsf{WE.Enc}(1^\lambda, x_i, r_i)$ by an encryption of 0 and then replace c by a uniform value.

Although the idea seems to work at first glance, there is a critical issue: The scheme is not compact. The reason for this is that we have to hardwire all the statements in $\bar{\mathcal{C}}$, otherwise how does the circuit know under which statements it must encrypt each r_i? To circumvent this problem we use (again!) a somewhere statistically binding (SSB) hashing scheme in a similar way as [27].[7] That is, the circuit only has a hash value $h \leftarrow \mathsf{SSB.Hash}(\mathsf{hk}, \{x_1, \ldots, x_N\})$ hardwired. Now, when it receives (i, x_i, γ_i), it first checks if γ_i is a valid opening with respect to x_i, h. Since $\{x_1, \ldots, x_N\}$ is public, anyone can compute a valid opening

$$\gamma_i \leftarrow \mathsf{SSB.Open}(\mathsf{hk}, \{x_1, \ldots, x_N\}, i)$$

for every $i \in [N]$.

Recall that the verification algorithm of an SSB hashing scheme can be implemented in size $\mathcal{O}(\log N \cdot \mathsf{poly}(\lambda))$. Hence, the efficiency requirements are met and the circuit is now of size $\mathcal{O}(\log N \cdot \mathsf{poly}(\lambda))$.

We thus obtain a WE scheme that outputs ciphertexts that depend only logarithmically on N.

How to Avoid the Exponential Security Loss of Current $i\mathcal{O}$ Schemes. We stress that, although the scheme presented above enjoys a polynomial reduction to the underlying cryptographic primitives, current $i\mathcal{O}$ schemes incur a security loss - compared to the underlying hardness assumptions - which is proportional to the size of the domain of the circuit being obfuscated (e.g., [2,6,7]). This implies that the construction presented above suffers from an exponential security loss when we instantiate the $i\mathcal{O}$ scheme by any known construction since the circuit being obfuscated has an exponentially-sized domain.[8]

Intending to avoid this exponential security loss, we present an alternative construction of compact WE for threshold languages where we just obfuscate a program with a polynomial-size domain. Note that, if the domain of the obfuscated program has only polynomial size, then the security reduction from $i\mathcal{O}$ to the underlying hardness assumptions loses only a polynomial factor.

As explained above, the statements cannot be hardwired in the circuit, otherwise, the size of the obfuscated circuit is not compact. To avoid this conundrum, we utilize the $i\mathcal{O}$ for Turing machines (TM) scheme of [21].

We note that, in the scheme of [21], a TM is modeled as a sequence of circuits. The input is written on a tape and the obfuscated TM accesses the input via a laconic oblivious transfer (LOT) [13]. We can consider a second tape which includes the statements $(x_1, \ldots, x_N)$ and from which the TM reads from using a LOT in a similar way as in [21]. Note that since $(x_1, \ldots, x_N)$ is public knowledge, this tape can be created by any party and does not have to be part

---

[7] This time we use SSB in its *statistically binding* form.

[8] Observe that the obfuscated circuit receives as input an index i, a statement x_i and an SSB proof γ_i.

of the description of the obfuscated TM. Instead, only the LOT hash needs to be hardwired in the TM. The size of the resulting obfuscated TM depends only logarithmically on the size of this tape.

Given this, to encrypt a message m, one obfuscates a TM $\mathcal{M}$ that receives an index $i \in [N]$ as input, retrieves x_i from the public tape and outputs $\mathsf{WE.Enc}(1^\lambda, x_i, r_i)$.[9] A ciphertext is composed by $\bar{\mathcal{M}}$ (which is the result of obfuscating $\mathcal{M}$) and $c = m + \sum r_i$. Decryption works exactly as before.

As mentioned before, the size of $\bar{\mathcal{M}}$ depends only logarithmically on N and, hence, the size of the ciphertext is $\mathcal{O}(\log N \cdot \mathsf{poly}(\lambda))$.

Furthermore, since the obfuscated TM $\bar{\mathcal{M}}$ has a polynomial-size domain, its security proof incurs only a polynomial security loss compared to the underlying hardness assumption.

3 Preliminaries

Throughout this work, λ denotes the security parameter and PPT stands for "probabilistic polynomial-time". A negligible function $\mathsf{negl}(n)$ in n is a function that vanishes faster than the inverse of any polynomial in n.

For $n \in \mathbb{N}$, $[n]$ denotes the set $\{1, \ldots, n\}$. If S is a (finite) set, we denote by $x \leftarrow_{\$} S$ an element $x \in S$ sampled according to a uniform distribution. If D is a distribution over S, $x \leftarrow_{\$} D$ denotes an element $x \in S$ sampled according to D. If $\mathcal{A}$ is an algorithm, $y \leftarrow \mathcal{A}(x)$ denotes the output y after running $\mathcal{A}$ on input x. If $\mathcal{A}$ and $\mathcal{O}$ are algorithms, $\mathcal{A}^{\mathcal{O}}$ means that $\mathcal{A}$ has oracle access to $\mathcal{O}$.

Additionally, we assume familiarity with the following notions from standard literature: Signature Schemes, Non-Interactive Witness-Indistinguishable Proof Systems, Commitment Schemes, Somewhere Statistically Binding and Somewhere Perfectly Binding Hashing Schemes, Pseudorandom Generators, Witness Encryption Schemes, Indistinguishability Obfuscation, and Puncturable Pseudorandom Functions. For completeness, a full collection of definitions of these notions and possible instantiations can be found in the full version of the paper. We also require Linear Secret Sharing with a slightly modified definition given below.

Linear Secret Sharing. Linear secret sharing (LSS) is used to divide a secret into shares such that if one is in possession of an authorized set of shares, then one can reconstruct the secret. In this work, we use threshold LSS (which, for simplicity, we simply refer to as LSS).

Definition 5 (Linear Secret Sharing). *Let $t \leq N$. A (t, N)-linear secret sharing (LSS)* LSS *scheme is composed of the following algorithms:*

- $(s_1, \ldots, s_N) \leftarrow \mathsf{Share}(m)$ *takes as input a message m. It outputs N shares* $(s_1, \ldots, s_N)$.

---

[9] We remark that the underlying WE also has a domain of polynomial size hence it only looses a polynomial factor in security if it is based on $i\mathcal{O}$ [17,21].

- $m \leftarrow \mathsf{Reconstruct}(s_{i_1}, \ldots, s_{i_t})$ *takes as input* t *shares* $(s_{i_1}, \ldots, s_{i_t})$. *It outputs a message* m.

A (t, N)-*LSS scheme, which is generated by a generating matrix in the systematic form, has the following additional algorithm:*

- $(s_{i_{z+1}}, \ldots, s_{i_N}) \leftarrow \mathsf{RemainShare}(m, s_{i_1}, \ldots, s_{i_z})$ *that takes as input a message* m *and uniformly chosen shares* $s_{i_j} \leftarrow_\$ \{0,1\}^\lambda$ *for* $j \in [z]$ *with* $z < t$, *and outputs* $N - z$ *remaining shares* $(s_{i_{z+1}}, \ldots, s_{i_N})$.

Definition 6 (Correctness). *A LSS scheme* LSS *is said to be correct if for all messages* m, *all subsets* $\{i_1, \ldots, i_t\} \subseteq [N]$ *and any* $z < t$ *it holds that:*

$$\Pr\left[m = \mathsf{Reconstruct}(s_{i_1}, \ldots, s_{i_t}) : (s_1, \ldots, s_N) \leftarrow \mathsf{Share}(m)\right] = 1.$$

$$\text{and } \Pr\left[\begin{array}{c} m = \mathsf{Reconstruct}(s_{i_1}, \ldots, s_{i_t}) : \\ s_{i_j} \leftarrow_\$ \{0,1\}^\lambda \text{ for } j \in [z] \\ (s_{i_{z+1}}, \ldots, s_{i_N}) \leftarrow \mathsf{RemainShare}(m, s_{i_1}, \ldots, s_{i_z}) \end{array}\right] = 1.$$

Definition 7 (Privacy). *We say that a* (t, N)-*LSS scheme* LSS *is private if for all subsets* $\{i_{i_1}, \ldots, i_{i_z}\} \subset [N]$ *where* $z < t$, *all pairs of messages* (m_0, m_1) *and all PPT adversaries* $\mathcal{A}$ *we have that*

$$\left| \begin{array}{l} \Pr\left[1 \leftarrow \mathcal{A}(s_{0,i_1}, \ldots, s_{0,i_z}) : (s_{0,1}, \ldots, s_{0,N}) \leftarrow \mathsf{Share}(m_0)\right] - \\ \Pr\left[1 \leftarrow \mathcal{A}(s_{1,i_1}, \ldots, s_{1,i_z}) : (s_{1,1}, \ldots, s_{1,N}) \leftarrow \mathsf{Share}(m_1)\right] \end{array} \right| \leq \mathsf{negl}(\lambda).$$

4   Universal Ring Signatures

In this section we present the definition of URS. A URS is composed of a signing and a verification algorithm.

Definition 8 (Universal Ring Signature). *A universal ring signature (URS) scheme* URS *is composed of the following algorithms:*

- $\Sigma \leftarrow \mathsf{Sign}(1^\lambda, \mathsf{sk}_i, m, R, i, S)$ *takes as input a security parameter* 1^λ, *a signing key* sk_i, *a message* m, *a ring of keys* $R = (\mathsf{vk}_1, \ldots, \mathsf{vk}_\ell)$ *an index* $i \in [\ell]$ *and a list of signature schemes* $S = \{\mathsf{Sig}_i = (\mathsf{Sig.KeyGen}_i, \mathsf{Sig.Sign}_i, \mathsf{Sig.Verify}_i)\}_{i \in [M]}$, *where each* vk_j *is a public verification key under exactly one[10] of the schemes* Sig_i. *It outputs a signature* Σ.
- $b \leftarrow \mathsf{Verify}(\Sigma, m, R, S)$ *takes as input a signature* σ, *a message* m, *a ring of keys* R *and a list of signature schemes* S. *It outputs a bit* $b \in \{0,1\}$.

We want a URS to fulfill correctness, unforgeability and anonymity.

---

[10] In practice, keys/certificates are usually annotated with their respective schemes and we assume such a labelling here.

Definition 9 (Correctness). *We say that a URS* URS = (Sign, Verify) *is correct if for all* $\lambda \in \mathbb{N}$, *all* $\ell, M = \text{poly}(\lambda)$, *all correct signature schemes* Sig', *all* $j \in [\ell]$, *all messages* m *and all* $(\text{vk}, \text{sk}) \leftarrow \text{Sig}'.\text{KeyGen}(1^\lambda)$, *we have that*

$$\Pr\left[1 \leftarrow \text{Verify}\left(\text{Sign}(1^\lambda, \text{sk}, m, R, j, S), m, R, S\right)\right] = 1$$

for any $R = (\text{vk}_1, \ldots, \text{vk}_\ell)$ *such that* $\text{vk}_j = \text{vk}$ *and any* $S = \{\text{Sig}_i\}_{i \in [M]}$ *such that* Sig' $\in S$. *That is, the remaining elements in* R, S *may be arbitrarily chosen.*

We now define the unforgeability of a URS. A URS scheme should be compatible with any signature scheme. Hence, we would like to let the adversary choose signature schemes for the URS scheme. However, the adversary could choose an insecure signature scheme and, in this case, we cannot guarantee unforgeability. Hence, the experiment should provide a list of secure signature schemes and verification keys at the beginning of the experiment. The forge given by the adversary must be with respect to these verification keys.[11] Our definition is similar to the one of *unforgeability with respect to insider corruption* for standard ring signatures [5], which is the strongest unforgeability definition.

Definition 10 (Unforgeability). *Let* $\mathcal{A}$ *be an adversary. We denote by* Ls *a list of challenge signature schemes*

$$\text{Ls} = \{\text{Sig}_i = (\text{Sig.KeyGen}_i, \text{Sig.Sign}_i, \text{Sig.Verify}_i)\}_{i \in [M]}.$$

Consider the following experiment, denoted by $\text{Exp}_{\text{Unf}}^{\text{URS}}(\text{Ls}, \mathcal{A}, 1^\lambda)$:

1. *The experiment provides* Ls *to* $\mathcal{A}$.
2. *The adversary outputs a list of indices* $\{\text{ind}_i\}_{i \in [\ell]}$.
3. *For all* $i \in [\ell]$, *the experiment computes* $(\text{vk}_i, \text{sk}_i) \leftarrow \text{Sig.KeyGen}_{\text{ind}_i}(1^\lambda)$ *and outputs* $R = (\text{vk}_1, \ldots, \text{vk}_\ell)$ *to the adversary. Also it initialises a set* $\mathcal{K} = \emptyset$ *and remembers the indices* ind_i.
4. *The adversary may now make three types of requests*[12]:
   - Corrupt(i), *which the experiment answers with the secret key* sk_i. *Also it adds* vk_i *to* $\mathcal{K}$.
   - URSSign($m, \bar{R}, i, \bar{S}$) *takes as input an index* $i \in [\ell]$, *a message* m, *a ring of keys* $\bar{R}$ *(not necessarily contained in R) and a list of signature schemes* $\bar{S}$. *If* $\text{vk}_i \in \bar{R}$, *we denote its position as* i^*. *If additionally* $\text{Sig}_{\text{ind}_i} \in \bar{S}$, *the experiment answers with* $\Sigma \leftarrow \text{URS.Sign}(1^\lambda, \text{sk}_i, m, \bar{R}, i^*, \bar{S})$.
   - Sign(m, i) *takes as input an index* $i \in [\ell]$ *and a message* m. *The experiment answers with* $\Sigma \leftarrow \text{Sig.Sign}_{\text{ind}_i}(1^\lambda, \text{sk}_i, m)$.

---

[11] Note that, in the unforgeability definition for standard ring signatures in [5] a similar situation happens: The forge of the adversary must be with respect to verification keys created honestly and not with respect to maliciously chosen verification keys.

[12] Note that as the key generation algorithms are publicly available, the adversary may honestly generate key pairs itself. The corruption oracle simply serves to corrupt the initial honest keys. Arbitrary additional adversarially chosen keys can be included in ring signature queries, as we do not require $\bar{R} \subseteq R$.

5. $\mathcal{A}$ outputs $(\Sigma^*, m^*, R^*, S^*)$.
6. If $1 \leftarrow \mathsf{Verify}(\Sigma^*, m^*, R^*, S^*)$, $R^* \subseteq R \setminus \mathcal{K}$, $S^* \subseteq \mathsf{Ls}$ and the message m^* was never queried in a $\mathsf{URSSign}$ or Sign request, the experiment outputs 1.[13] Else, it outputs 0.

We say that a URS $\mathsf{URS} = (\mathsf{Sign}, \mathsf{Verify})$ is unforgeable, if for all $\lambda \in \mathbb{N}$, $M = \mathsf{poly}(\lambda)$, all lists of EUF-CMA secure signature schemes $\mathsf{Ls} = \{\mathsf{Sig}_i\}_{i \in [M]}$ and all PPT adversaries $\mathcal{A}$ we have that

$$\Pr\left[1 \leftarrow \mathsf{Exp}_{\mathsf{Unf}}^{\mathsf{URS}}(\mathsf{Ls}, \mathcal{A}, 1^\lambda)\right] = \mathsf{negl}(\lambda).$$

In the anonymity experiment, the goal of the adversary is to guess which user created a given signature. We give a general definition called t-anonymity, which mandates that at least t honest keys in the anonymity set must be honestly chosen for anonymity to hold. The adversary may include at least t honest and additional maliciously chosen verification keys (potentially from insecure signature schemes) in a challenge ring. It should still be unable to determine which of the honest parties signed a given URS under that ring.

The case of 2-anonymity coincides with the definition of *anonymity against full key exposure* of [5]. This is the strongest anonymity definition for ring signatures and is even known to imply unrepudiability, meaning that a member in the ring cannot prove that they did not sign the message [31]. As it is the standard case, we will refer to 2-anonymity as *anonymity* throughout this work.

Definition 11 (t-Anonymity). *Let* $\mathcal{A} = (\mathcal{A}_1, \mathcal{A}_2, \mathcal{A}_3)$ *be an adversary. We denote a list of challenge signature schemes by* $\mathsf{Ls} = \{\mathsf{Sig}_i = (\mathsf{Sig.KeyGen}_i,$ $\mathsf{Sig.Sign}_i, \mathsf{Sig.Verify}_i)\}_{i \in [M]}$. *We define the t-anonymity experiment* $\mathsf{Exp}_{\mathsf{Anon}_t}^{\mathsf{URS}}(\mathsf{Ls}, \mathcal{A}, 1^\lambda)$ *as follows:*

1. $(\{\mathsf{ind}_i\}_{i \in [\ell]}, \mathsf{aux}_1) \leftarrow \mathcal{A}_1(1^\lambda, \mathsf{Ls})$.
2. *For all* $i \in [\ell]$, *the experiment computes* $(\mathsf{vk}_i, \mathsf{sk}_i) \leftarrow \mathsf{Sig.KeyGen}_{\mathsf{ind}_i}(1^\lambda; r_i)$ *with random coins* r_i *and sets* $K = (\mathsf{vk}_1, \ldots, \mathsf{vk}_\ell)$.
3. $(m^*, R^* = (\mathsf{vk}_1', \ldots, \mathsf{vk}_p'), S^* = (\mathsf{Sig}_1', \ldots, \mathsf{Sig}_q'), (j_k)_{k \in [t]}, \mathsf{aux}_2) \leftarrow \mathcal{A}_2(K,$ $(r_1, \ldots, r_\ell), \mathsf{aux}_1)$ *where* $\mathsf{vk}_{j_k}' \in K$ *for* $k \in [t]$ *with indices* l_k *in* K *(i.e.* $\mathsf{vk}_{j_k}' = \mathsf{vk}_{l_k})$. *Additionally, the signature schemes corresponding to these public keys,* $\mathsf{Sig}_{\mathsf{ind}_{l_k}}$, *must be in the set* S^*. *If these conditions are violated, the experiment aborts.*
4. $\Sigma^* \leftarrow \mathsf{URS.Sign}(1^\lambda, \mathsf{sk}_{l_k}, m^*, R^*, j_k, S^*)$ *where* $k \leftarrow_\$ [t]$.
5. $k' \leftarrow \mathcal{A}_3(\Sigma^*, \mathsf{aux}_2)$.
6. *If* $k = k'$, *then output 1. Else, output 0.*

---

[13] We can consider the stronger notion, where a forge is valid, if no query of the form $\mathsf{URSSign}(m^*, R^*, \cdot, \cdot)$ or $\mathsf{Sign}(m^* \| R^*, i)$ for $\mathsf{vk}_i \in R^*$ was made. This can be achieved by the standard trick of signing the message $(m^* \| R^*)$ instead of m^* or a hash $H(m^* \| R^*)$ thereof for compactness.

We say that a URS URS = (Sign, Verify) is t-anonymous, if for all $\lambda \in \mathbb{N}$, all sizes $M = \mathsf{poly}(\lambda)$, all lists of signature schemes $\mathsf{Ls} = \{\mathsf{Sig}_i\}_{i \in [M]}$ and all PPT adversaries $\mathcal{A} = (\mathcal{A}_1, \mathcal{A}_2, \mathcal{A}_3)$ we have that

$$\left| \Pr\left[1 \leftarrow \mathsf{Exp}^{\mathsf{URS}}_{\mathsf{Anon}_t}(\mathsf{Ls}, \mathcal{A}, 1^\lambda) \right] - \frac{1}{t} \right| = \mathsf{negl}(\lambda).$$

Efficiency of URS. We remark that URS inherits the efficiency of the most inefficient signature scheme in the ring. For this reason, it is unlikely that we can construct a URS with good and practical parameters and efficiency.

5 Universal Ring Signature from Signature Schemes with Superpolynomial Security

In this section, we present a construction of URS that is based on signature schemes that are superpolynomially hard to forge. From this hardness, we can prove security of the URS scheme using complexity leveraging.

5.1 Construction

We start by presenting the construction of this URS scheme.

For simplicity, we assume, that there is an upper bound on the size of all descriptions of signature verification circuits. Also, for public keys $\mathsf{vk} \leftarrow \mathsf{Sig.KeyGen}(1^\lambda)$, we assume that they are labeled with their respective schemes. That is, there is a function $\mathsf{tag}(.,.)$ which takes vk and a signature scheme Sig and outputs 1, iff the key vk was made under Sig, but 0 for any other signature verification scheme as input. $\mathsf{Sig.Verify}$ should only accept keys vk with the corresponding tag to Sig, that is $\mathsf{tag}(\mathsf{vk}, \mathsf{Sig}) = 1$.

In the scheme below, we assume that all used signature schemes are unforgeable against superpolynomial adversaries running in $\mathcal{O}(T'(\lambda) \cdot \mathsf{poly}(\lambda))$. We then use a commitment scheme whose hiding property holds against PPT adversaries but can be broken in time $T'(\lambda) \in \omega(\mathsf{poly}(\lambda))$. A signature of our URS for a message m includes a commitment to a signature of m in one of the underlying signature schemes. This will give our reduction, which runs in superpolynomial time, an advantage in the unforgeability experiment, where it may extract the commitments and provide a forge against the underlying signature scheme. However, this opening strategy cannot be used by an adversary against anonymity, as they are running in polynomial time.

Construction 1. *Let:*

- CS *be a commitment scheme such that the hiding property holds against polynomial-time adversaries but can be broken in time $T'(\lambda) \in \omega(\mathsf{poly}(\lambda))$, which is super-polynomial.*
- SPB *be a SPB hashing scheme;*

- $\mathcal{L}$ be a language such that

$$\mathcal{L} = \left\{ \begin{array}{c} (m, \mathsf{com}, \mathsf{hk}, h, \mathsf{rhk}, rh) : \exists (\mathsf{vk}, i, \mathsf{Sig.Verify}, \mathsf{ind}, \tau, \rho, \sigma, \gamma) \ s.t. \\ 1 \leftarrow \mathsf{SPB.Verify}(\mathsf{hk}, h, i, \mathsf{vk}, \tau) \\ 1 \leftarrow \mathsf{SPB.Verify}(\mathsf{rhk}, rh, \mathsf{ind}, \mathsf{Sig.Verify}, \rho) \\ 1 \leftarrow \mathsf{CS.Verify}(\mathsf{com}, \sigma, \gamma) \\ 1 \leftarrow \mathsf{Sig.Verify}(\mathsf{vk}, m, \sigma) \end{array} \right\};$$

where Sig.Verify is a description of the verification algorithm of a signature scheme Sig.[14]
- NIWI be a NIWI scheme for the language

$$\mathcal{L}_{\mathsf{OR}} = \left\{ \begin{array}{c} (m, \mathsf{com}_0, \mathsf{com}_1, \mathsf{hk}_0, \mathsf{hk}_1, h_0, h_1, \mathsf{rhk}_0, \mathsf{rhk}_1, rh_0, rh_1) : \\ \exists b \in \{0,1\} \ s.t. \ (m, \mathsf{com}_b, \mathsf{hk}_b, h_b, \mathsf{rhk}_b, rh_b) \in \mathcal{L} \end{array} \right\}.$$

We now describe our scheme in full detail.
$\mathsf{Sign}(1^\lambda, \mathsf{sk}_i, m, R = (\mathsf{vk}_1, \dots, \mathsf{vk}_\ell), i, S = \{\mathsf{Sig}_i\}_{i \in [M]})$

- Determine an index ind such that $\mathsf{tag}(\mathsf{vk}_i, \mathsf{Sig}_{\mathsf{ind}})$. Parse $\mathsf{Sig}_{\mathsf{ind}} = (\mathsf{Sig.KeyGen}, \mathsf{Sig.Sign}, \mathsf{Sig.Verify})$. Set $S' = \{\mathsf{Sig.Verify}_i\}_{i \in [M]}$ to be the list of verification algorithms in S.
- Compute $\sigma \leftarrow \mathsf{Sig.Sign}(\mathsf{sk}_i, m)$.
- Compute $(\mathsf{hk}_j, \mathsf{shk}_j) \leftarrow \mathsf{SPB.Gen}(1^\lambda, \ell, i)$ and $h_j \leftarrow \mathsf{SPB.Hash}(\mathsf{hk}_j, R)$ for $j \in \{0,1\}$. Also, compute the proof $\tau \leftarrow \mathsf{SPB.Open}(\mathsf{hk}_0, \mathsf{shk}_0, R, i)$.
- Compute $(\mathsf{rhk}_j, \mathsf{rshk}_j) \leftarrow \mathsf{SPB.Gen}(1^\lambda, M, \mathsf{ind})$ and $rh_j \leftarrow \mathsf{SPB.Hash}(\mathsf{rhk}_j, S')$ for $j \in \{0,1\}$. Also, compute the proof $\rho \leftarrow \mathsf{SPB.Open}(\mathsf{rhk}_0, \mathsf{rshk}_0, S', \mathsf{ind})$.
- Compute $(\mathsf{com}_0, \gamma_0) \leftarrow \mathsf{CS.Commit}(1^\lambda, \sigma)$ and $(\mathsf{com}_1, \gamma_1) \leftarrow \mathsf{CS.Commit}(1^\lambda, 0)$.
- Set $x = (m, \mathsf{com}_0, \mathsf{com}_1, \mathsf{hk}_0, \mathsf{hk}_1, h_0, h_1, \mathsf{rhk}_0, \mathsf{rhk}_1, rh_0, rh_1)$.
- Set $w = (\mathsf{vk}, i, \mathsf{Sig.Verify}_{\mathsf{ind}}, \mathsf{ind}, \tau, \rho, \sigma, \gamma_0)$.
- Compute the proof $\pi \leftarrow \mathsf{NIWI.Prove}(x, w)$.
- Output $\Sigma = (\mathsf{com}_0, \mathsf{com}_1, \mathsf{hk}_0, \mathsf{hk}_1, \mathsf{rhk}_0, \mathsf{rhk}_1, \pi)$.

$\mathsf{Verify}(\Sigma, m, R, S = \{\mathsf{Sig}_i\}_{i \in [M]})$:

- Parse Σ as $(\mathsf{com}_0, \mathsf{com}_1, \mathsf{hk}_0, \mathsf{hk}_1, \mathsf{rhk}_0, \mathsf{rhk}_1, \pi)$. Set $S' = \{\mathsf{Sig.Verify}_i\}_{i \in [M]}$ to be the list of verification algorithms in S.
- Compute $h_j \leftarrow \mathsf{SPB.Hash}(\mathsf{hk}_j, R)$ for $j \in \{0,1\}$.
- Compute $rh_j \leftarrow \mathsf{SPB.Hash}(\mathsf{rhk}_j, S')$ for $j \in \{0,1\}$.
- Set $x = (m, \mathsf{com}_0, \mathsf{com}_1, \mathsf{hk}_0, \mathsf{hk}_1, h_0, h_1, \mathsf{rhk}_0, \mathsf{rhk}_1, rh_0, rh_1)$.
- If $1 \leftarrow \mathsf{NIWI.Verify}(x, \pi)$, output 1. Else, output 0.

We remark, that we only require the verification algorithms of the underlying signature schemes to verify a URS signature. Therefore, we only include these algorithms in S', which is hashed down by SPB and provided to NIWI. This is to reduce size. Essentially, our verification algorithm URS.Verify could only take the list of signature verification algorithms S' as an input, but we state the full list of signature schemes to fit our more general definition.

---

[14] We assume that for all schemes, |Sig.Verify| is bounded by a polynomial $\beta(\lambda)$.

Signature Size. A signature for a message m with respect to a ring R (of size ℓ) and a list of schemes S (of size M) is composed of $\Sigma = (\mathsf{com}_0, \mathsf{com}_1, \mathsf{hk}_0,$ $\mathsf{hk}_1, \mathsf{rhk}_0, \mathsf{rhk}_1, \pi)$. Both $\mathsf{com}_0, \mathsf{com}_1$ are of size $\mathcal{O}(\mathsf{poly}(\lambda))$ and independent of ℓ and M. The size of the hashing keys $\mathsf{hk}_0, \mathsf{hk}_1$, the proof τ and the circuit $\mathsf{SPB.Verify}(\mathsf{hk}, h, i, \mathsf{vk}, \tau)$ can be bounded by $\mathcal{O}(\log(\ell) \cdot \mathsf{poly}(\lambda))$. Analogously, $\mathsf{rhk}_0, \mathsf{rhk}_1$, ρ and the runtime of $\mathsf{SPB.Verify}(\mathsf{rhk}, rh, \mathsf{ind}, \mathsf{Sig.Verify}, \rho)$ are bounded by $\mathcal{O}(\log(M) \cdot \mathsf{poly}(\lambda))$.[15]

Given that, we conclude that the circuit that verifies the relation of language $\mathcal{L}$ has size at most $\mathcal{O}((\log(M) + \log(\ell)) \cdot \mathsf{poly}(\lambda))$. Hence, the proof π has size $\mathcal{O}((\log(M) + \log(\ell)) \cdot \mathsf{poly}(\lambda))$. We conclude that the total size of the signature is $\mathcal{O}((\log(M) + \log(\ell)) \cdot \mathsf{poly}(\lambda))$. Thus, it grows only logarithmic in the number of users in the ring and logarithmic in the number of signature schemes.

5.2   Proofs

We now show that the construction presented above fulfills the required properties for a URS. We start by showing correctness. Then we proceed to prove unforgeability and anonymity. Our proof of unforgeability uses a superpolynomial-time reduction.

Theorem 12 (Correctness). *The scheme presented in Construction 1 is correct, given that* NIWI *is perfectly complete and* SPB *and* CS *are correct.*

Theorem 13 (Unforgeability). *We assume the challenge signature schemes* $\mathsf{LS} = \{\mathsf{Sig}_i\}_{i \in [M]}$ *to be unforgeable against adversaries running in superpolynomial time* $T'(\lambda) \cdot \mathsf{poly}(\lambda)$ *for* $T'(\lambda) \in \omega(\mathsf{poly}(\lambda))$. *We assume, that our commitment scheme allows extraction in time* $T'(\lambda)$, *but is secure against PPT adversaries. Then the scheme presented in Construction 1 is unforgeable against PPT adversaries, given that* NIWI *is perfectly sound and* SPB *is somewhere perfectly binding.*

At a high level, we will build a superpolynomial-time reduction that breaks unforgeability for the underlying signature scheme. The reduction, upon receiving the challenge URS signature $\Sigma^* = (\mathsf{com}_0^*, \mathsf{com}_1^*, \mathsf{hk}_0^*, \mathsf{hk}_1^*, \mathsf{rhk}_0^*, \mathsf{rhk}_1^*, \pi^*)$ from the adversary, opens the commitments com_0^* and com_1^* using brute force. Note that, since we allow the reduction to run in superpolynomial time, it will succeed in breaking the hiding property of the commitment scheme. Then, by the perfect soundness of the NIWI scheme, the reduction can extract a valid signature from either com_0 or com_1 with non-negligible probability and, thus, break the unforgeability of the signature scheme.

Theorem 14 (Anonymity). *Assume that* SPB *is index hiding,* NIWI *is witness-indistinguishable and* CS *is hiding. Then the scheme presented in Construction 1 is anonymous.*

---

[15] This holds, as we assumed, that we can bound $|\mathsf{Sig.Verify}|$ by a polynomial $\beta(\lambda)$ for all signature schemes Sig.

To prove the theorem above, we build a sequence of hybrids starting from the 2-anonymity game where $k = 1$ and ending at a hybrid describing the game for $k = 2$. Let vk'_{j_1} and vk'_{j_2} be the challenge verification keys in the anonymity game and let $\Sigma = (m^*, \mathsf{com}_0, \mathsf{com}_1, \mathsf{hk}_0, \mathsf{hk}_1, \mathsf{rhk}_0, \mathsf{rhk}_1, \pi)$ be the challenge signature build using vk'_{j_1}. First note that the length of π does not reveal information even if the keys $\mathsf{vk}'_{j_1}, \mathsf{vk}'_{j_2}$ or signature verification circuits are of different length. This is due to the Or-statement in $\mathcal{L}_{\mathsf{OR}}$. In the first hybrid, we change hk_1 and rhk_1 to be SPB hashing keys binding to index j_1. Next, we replace com_1 by a commitment of a valid signature under vk'_{j_2}. In the next hybrid, we can replace the proof π by a new one computed using the new signature under vk'_{j_2} (this change goes unnoticed by the witness indistinguishability of the NIWI). We can now replace com_0 by a commitment of a valid signature under vk'_{j_2}. In the next step, we replace hk_0 and rhk_0 to be SPB hashing keys binding to index j_2 and, finally, compute π as the proof that com_0 is a commitment to a valid signature under vk'_{j_2} for which hk_0 and rhk_0 bind to.

6   Non-compact Universal Ring Signature from Witness Encryption

In this section we present a URS scheme from falsifiable assumptions. The resulting URS has a signature size that scales with the size of the ring. We first present the construction. Then, we proceed to the analysis of the scheme.

6.1   Construction

We now present our construction for URS from WE.

Construction 2. *Let*

- $\mathsf{PRF} : \mathcal{K} \times [\ell] \to \{0,1\}^\lambda$ *be a PRF.*
- $\mathcal{L}'$ *be a language such that*

$$\mathcal{L}' = \left\{ \begin{array}{l} (\{\mathsf{vk}_i\}_{i \in [\ell]} : \exists \left(\{\mathsf{Sig}_{i_j}\}_{j \in [\ell-1]}, K \right) \ s.t. \\ \qquad r_{i_j} \leftarrow \mathsf{PRF}(K, i_j) \\ \qquad (\mathsf{vk}_{i_j}, \mathsf{sk}_{i_j}) \leftarrow \mathsf{Sig.KeyGen}_{i_j}(1^\lambda; r_{i_j}) \end{array} \right\}.$$

- WE *be a witness encryption scheme for language $\mathcal{L}'$.*
- SPB *be a SPB hashing scheme;*
- $\mathcal{L}$ *be a language such that*

$$\mathcal{L} = \left\{ \begin{array}{l} (m, \mathsf{ct}, \mathsf{hk}, h, \mathsf{rhk}, rh, x) : \exists (\mathsf{vk}, i, \mathsf{Sig.Verify}, \mathsf{ind}, \tau, \rho, \sigma, r_{\mathsf{ct}}) \ s.t. \\ \qquad 1 \leftarrow \mathsf{SPB.Verify}(\mathsf{hk}, h, i, \mathsf{vk}, \tau) \\ \qquad 1 \leftarrow \mathsf{SPB.Verify}(\mathsf{rhk}, rh, \mathsf{ind}, \mathsf{Sig.Verify}, \rho) \\ \qquad \mathsf{ct} \leftarrow \mathsf{WE.Enc}(1^\lambda, x, \sigma; r_{\mathsf{ct}}) \\ \qquad 1 \leftarrow \mathsf{Sig.Verify}(\mathsf{vk}, m, \sigma) \end{array} \right\};$$

where Sig.Verify *is a description of the verification algorithm of a signature scheme* Sig.[16]

- NIWI *be a NIWI scheme for the language*

$$\mathcal{L}_{\mathsf{OR}} = \left\{ \begin{array}{c} (m, \mathsf{ct}_0, \mathsf{ct}_1, \mathsf{hk}_0, \mathsf{hk}_1, h_0, h_1, \mathsf{rhk}_0, \mathsf{rhk}_1, rh_0, rh_1, x) : \\ \exists b \in \{0,1\} \ s.t. \ (m, \mathsf{ct}_b, \mathsf{hk}_b, h_b, \mathsf{rhk}_b, rh_b, x) \in \mathcal{L} \end{array} \right\}.$$

We now describe the scheme in full detail.

$\mathsf{Sign}(1^\lambda, \mathsf{sk}_i, m, R = (\mathsf{vk}_1, \ldots, \mathsf{vk}_\ell), i, S = \{\mathsf{Sig}_i\}_{i \in [M]})$:

- *Determine an index* ind *with* $\mathsf{tag}(\mathsf{vk}_i, \mathsf{Sig}_{\mathsf{ind}})$. *Parse* $\mathsf{Sig}_{\mathsf{ind}} = (\mathsf{Sig.KeyGen}, \mathsf{Sig.Sign}, \mathsf{Sig.Verify})$. *Set* $S' = \{\mathsf{Sig.Verify}_i\}_{i \in [M]}$ *to be the list of verification algorithms in* S.
- *Compute* $\sigma \leftarrow \mathsf{Sig.Sign}(\mathsf{sk}_i, m)$.
- *Compute* $(\mathsf{hk}_j, \mathsf{shk}_j) \leftarrow \mathsf{SPB.Gen}(1^\lambda, \ell, i)$ *and* $h_j \leftarrow \mathsf{SPB.Hash}(\mathsf{hk}_j, R)$ *for* $j \in \{0,1\}$. *Also, compute the proof* $\tau \leftarrow \mathsf{SPB.Open}(\mathsf{hk}_0, \mathsf{shk}_0, R, i)$.
- *Compute* $(\mathsf{rhk}_j, \mathsf{rshk}_j) \leftarrow \mathsf{SPB.Gen}(1^\lambda, M, \mathsf{ind})$ *and* $rh_j \leftarrow \mathsf{SPB.Hash}(\mathsf{rhk}_j, S')$ *for* $j \in \{0,1\}$. *Also, compute the proof* $\rho \leftarrow \mathsf{SPB.Open}(\mathsf{rhk}_0, \mathsf{rshk}_0, S', \mathsf{ind})$.
- *Encrypt* $\mathsf{ct}_0 \leftarrow \mathsf{WE.Enc}(1^\lambda, x', \sigma; r_{\mathsf{ct}})$ *and* $\mathsf{ct}_1 \leftarrow \mathsf{WE.Enc}(1^\lambda, x', 0)$, *where* $x' = R$.
- *Set* $x = (m, \mathsf{ct}_0, \mathsf{ct}_1, \mathsf{hk}_0, \mathsf{hk}_1, h_0, h_1, \mathsf{rhk}_0, \mathsf{rhk}_1, rh_0, rh_1, x')$.
- *Set* $w = (\mathsf{vk}, i, \mathsf{Sig.Verify}_{\mathsf{ind}}, \mathsf{ind}, \tau, \rho, \sigma, r_{\mathsf{ct}})$.
- *Compute the proof* $\pi \leftarrow \mathsf{NIWI.Prove}(x, w)$.
- *Output* $\Sigma \leftarrow (\mathsf{ct}_0, \mathsf{ct}_1, \mathsf{hk}_0, \mathsf{hk}_1, \mathsf{rhk}_0, \mathsf{rhk}_1, \pi)$.

$\mathsf{Verify}(\Sigma, m, R, S)$:

- *Parse* $\Sigma = (\mathsf{ct}_0, \mathsf{ct}_1, \mathsf{hk}_0, \mathsf{hk}_1, \mathsf{rhk}_0, \mathsf{rhk}_1, \pi)$. *Set* $S' = \{\mathsf{Sig.Verify}_i\}_{i \in [M]}$ *to be the list of verification algorithms in* S.
- *Compute* $h_j \leftarrow \mathsf{SPB.Hash}(\mathsf{hk}_j, R)$ *for* $j \in \{0,1\}$.
- *Compute* $rh_j \leftarrow \mathsf{SPB.Hash}(\mathsf{rhk}_j, S')$ *for* $j \in \{0,1\}$.
- *Set* $x = (m, \mathsf{ct}_0, \mathsf{ct}_1, \mathsf{hk}_0, \mathsf{hk}_1, h_0, h_1, \mathsf{rhk}_0, \mathsf{rhk}_1, rh_0, rh_1, R)$.
- *If* $1 \leftarrow \mathsf{NIWI.Verify}(x, \pi)$, *output* 1. *Else, output* 0.

Signature Size. A signature for a message m under a ring R (of size ℓ) and a list of schemes S (of size M) is of the form $\Sigma = (\mathsf{ct}_0, \mathsf{ct}_1, \mathsf{hk}_0, \mathsf{hk}_1, \mathsf{rhk}_0, \mathsf{rhk}_1, \pi)$. We first analyze the size of the ciphertexts $\mathsf{ct}_0, \mathsf{ct}_1$. The circuit that verifies the relation $\mathcal{R}'$ of language $\mathcal{L}'$ needs to have size at least $\mathcal{O}(\ell \cdot \mathsf{poly}(\lambda))$ since witnesses for this language are of that size. It is clear that the conditions can be checked in a circuit of this size.

Moreover, a similar analysis as the one made for Construction 1 shows that the total size of $(\mathsf{hk}_0, \mathsf{hk}_1, \mathsf{rhk}_0, \mathsf{rhk}_1, \pi)$ is $\mathcal{O}((\log \ell + \log M) \cdot \mathsf{poly}(\lambda))$. We may assume, that $M \leq \ell$ because signature schemes that no corresponding key exists for in R may be omitted without altering functionality.

We conclude that the signatures in this scheme have size $\mathcal{O}(\ell \cdot \mathsf{poly}(\lambda))$.

---

[16] We assume again, that for all schemes, $|\mathsf{Sig.Verify}|$ is bounded by a polynomial $b(\lambda)$.

6.2   Proofs

We now give the proofs of the security of the proposed scheme.

Theorem 15 (Correctness). *The scheme presented in Construction 2 is correct, given that* NIWI *is perfectly complete.*

Theorem 16 (Unforgeability). *Assume that* Sig_i *is EUF-CMA,* PRF *is a pseudorandom function,* NIWI *is perfectly sound and* WE *is correct. Then, the scheme presented in Construction 2 is unforgeable.*

To prove unforgeability, we first build a hybrid where the experiment computes all verification keys, except for vk_{i^*}, using randomness from a PRF (instead of using truly random coins). Note that this change goes unnoticed given that PRF is a PRF. Next, we build a reduction to the unforgeability of the underlying signature scheme. The idea is similar to the proof of Theorem 13. Namely, the goal of the reduction is to extract a valid signature from either ct_0 or ct_1. To do this, note that the reduction is in possession of the key K such that vk_i is created using random coins $\text{PRF}(K, i)$, for all $i \neq i^*$ where vk_{i^*} is the challenge verification key. Then, by the correctness of the WE and the perfect soundness of the NIWI, the reduction can use K to decrypt both ct_0 and ct_1. In the end, there is a non-negligible probability that the reduction can extract a valid signature under vk_{i^*}, thus breaking the unforgeability of the signature scheme.

Theorem 17 (*t*-Anonymity). *Assume that* NIWI *is witness-indistinguishable,* SPB *is index hiding and* WE *is soundness secure. Then the scheme presented in Construction 2 is t-anonymous where $t = (\lambda - \omega(\log \lambda))/q$ and q is a lower bound of the min-entropy of verification keys in the ring.*

The proof of the theorem is similar to the proof of Theorem 14. However, now we would like to use the security of the WE to replace ct_1 by an encryption of a valid signature under one key (and then replace back by an encryption of 0). To do this, we note that (unlike the unforgeability security proof described above) all verification keys in K are computed using truly random coins. The challenge ring given by the adversary must include at least t of these keys. A simple information-theoretical argument states that there is only a negligible probability that there is a PRF key K such that $t - 1$ of these honestly generated verification keys are malformed. This is because they are sampled independently and thus it is unlikely that they are correlated via a PRF key. Hence, we can conclude that $\ell - 1$ verification keys in the adversary's ring are not created using random coins $\text{PRF}(K, i)$, except with negligible probability. In other words, there is a negligible probability that $x' \in \mathcal{L}'$. We can thus use the security of the WE to safely replace encryptions of signatures and encryptions of 0. That is, we switch out the encrypted signature in ct_0 from one under one challenge key to a signature under another one.

7 Compact Witness Encryption for Threshold Conjunction Languages

In this section we present a WE scheme that is compact for threshold conjunction languages. We first define the notion of threshold conjunction languages.

Definition 18 (Threshold Conjunction Languages) *Let $\mathcal{L}$ be an NP language with relation $\mathcal{R}$. We define a (t, N)-threshold conjunction language $\mathcal{L}'$ as:*

$$\mathcal{L}' = \left\{ (x_1, \ldots, x_N) : \exists \{i_j\}_{j \in [t]} \in [N] \text{ s.t. } x_{i_j} \in \mathcal{L} \right\}.$$

In other words, an accepting instance $(x_1, \ldots, x_N)$ of $\mathcal{L}'$ is one such that there are at least t accepting instances x_{i_j}.

7.1 Construction from Indistinguishability Obfuscation

We now describe our WE scheme for any (t, N)-threshold conjunction language $\mathcal{L}'$. The protocol achieves compact ciphertexts, i.e., of size $\mathcal{O}(\log N)$, when $N - t \in \mathcal{O}(\log N)$.

Construction 3. *Let $N \in \mathsf{poly}(\lambda)$ and t be such that $N - t \in \mathcal{O}(\log N)$ and $\mathcal{L}$ be an NP language. Let*

- LSS *be a (t, N)-LSS scheme. In the following, we assume that shares can be written as strings in $\{0, 1\}^\lambda$.*
- WE *be a (non-compact) WE scheme for language $\mathcal{L}$.*
- iO *be an obfuscator for all circuits.*
- PPRF *be a puncturable PRF.*
- SSB *be an SSB hashing scheme.*

Additionally, consider the following circuit $\mathcal{C}[\lambda, \mathsf{hk}, h, k_0, k_1, t, N]$ which has the values λ, hk, h, k_0, k_1, t and N hardwired.

$\mathcal{C}[\lambda, \mathsf{hk}, h, k_0, k_1, t, N](i, \tau_i, x_i)$:

- *If $0 \leftarrow \mathsf{SSB.Verify}(\mathsf{hk}, h, i, x_i, \tau_i)$ or $i \geq t$, return $\bot$.*
- *Compute $s_i \leftarrow \mathsf{PPRF.Eval}(k_0, i)$ and random coins $r_i \leftarrow \mathsf{PPRF.Eval}(k_1, i)$.*
- *Compute $\mathsf{ct}_i \leftarrow \mathsf{WE.Enc}(1^\lambda, x_i, s_i; r_i)$. Output ct_i.*

We now define the WE scheme for the (t, N)-conjunction language $\mathcal{L}'$.

$\mathsf{Enc}(1^\lambda, x, m)$:

- *Parse $x = (x_1, \ldots, x_N)$.*
- *Create PPRF keys $k_0 \leftarrow \mathsf{PPRF.KeyGen}(1^\lambda)$ and $k_1 \leftarrow \mathsf{PPRF.KeyGen}(1^\lambda)$.*
- *For $i \in [t-1]$, compute pseudorandom shares $s_i \leftarrow \mathsf{PPRF}(k_0, i)$. Compute the remaining shares $(s_t, \ldots, s_N) \leftarrow \mathsf{LSS.RemainShare}(m, s_1, \ldots, s_{t-1})$.*
- *Compute $\mathsf{hk} \leftarrow \mathsf{SSB.Gen}(1^\lambda, t-1, j)$ for $j \leftarrow_{\$} [t-1]$. Moreover, compute $h \leftarrow \mathsf{SSB.Hash}(\mathsf{hk}, \{x_1, \ldots, x_{t-1}\})$.*
- *Consider the circuit $\mathcal{C} = \mathcal{C}[\lambda, \mathsf{hk}, h, k_0, k_1, t, N]$. Compute $\bar{\mathcal{C}} \leftarrow \mathsf{iO}(1^\lambda, \mathcal{C})$.*

- *For $i \in \{t, \ldots, N\}$, compute encryptions $\mathsf{ct}_i \leftarrow \mathsf{WE.Enc}(1^\lambda, x_i, s_i)$.*
- *Output $\mathsf{ct} = (\{\mathsf{ct}_i\}_{i \in \{t, \ldots, N\}}, \bar{\mathcal{C}}, \mathsf{hk})$.*

$\mathsf{Dec}(w, \mathsf{ct})$:

- *Parse $w = (w_{i_1}, \ldots, w_{i_t})$ and ct as $(\{\mathsf{ct}_i\}_{i \in \{t, \ldots, N\}}, \bar{\mathcal{C}}, \mathsf{hk})$*
- *For $i \in [t-1]$, compute $\tau_i \leftarrow \mathsf{SSB.Open}(\mathsf{hk}, \{x_1, \ldots, x_{t-1}\}, i)$ and run $\mathsf{ct}_i \leftarrow \bar{\mathcal{C}}(i, \tau_i, x_i)$.*
- *For $j \in [t]$, decrypt $s_{i_j} \leftarrow \mathsf{WE.Dec}(w_{i_j}, \mathsf{ct}_{i_j})$.*
- *Reconstruct $m \leftarrow \mathsf{LSS.Reconstruct}(s_{i_1}, \ldots, s_{i_t})$. Output m.*

Ciphertext Size. The ciphertext is of the form $(\{\mathsf{ct}_i\}_{i \in \{t, \ldots, N\}}, \bar{\mathcal{C}}, \mathsf{hk})$. Assume that the language $\mathcal{L}$ has a verification circuit $\mathcal{C}_\mathcal{L}$. The ciphertexts ct_i for $i \in \{t, \ldots, N\}$ have size $\mathcal{O}(|\mathcal{C}_\mathcal{L}| \cdot \mathsf{poly}(\lambda))$. Since $N - t \in \mathcal{O}(\log(N))$, the size of $\{\mathsf{ct}_i\}_{i \in \{t, \ldots, N\}}$ is $\mathcal{O}(\log(N) \cdot |\mathcal{C}_\mathcal{L}| \cdot \mathsf{poly}(\lambda))$. The obfuscated circuit $\mathcal{C}$ implements the $\mathsf{SSB.Verify}$ algorithm which is of size $\mathcal{O}(\log(N))$. Moreover, all other operations in $\mathcal{C}$ are independent of N and depend only on $|\mathcal{C}_\mathcal{L}|$. Hence, $|\mathcal{C}| \in \mathcal{O}(\log(N) \cdot |\mathcal{C}_\mathcal{L}| \cdot \mathsf{poly}(\lambda))$. Finally, the hashing key hk is of size $\mathcal{O}(\log(N))$ by the efficiency requirements of SSB.

We conclude that the scheme presented above outputs ciphertexts of size $\mathcal{O}(\log(N) \cdot |\mathcal{C}_\mathcal{L}| \cdot \mathsf{poly}(\lambda))$.

7.2   Proofs

We now prove that the scheme is correct and soundness secure.

Theorem 19 (Correctness). *The scheme presented in Construction 3 is correct, given that LSS, SSB and WE are correct.*

Theorem 20 (Soundness security). *The scheme presented in Construction 3 is soundness secure given that SSB is index hiding and somewhere statistically binding, iO is a secure $i\mathcal{O}$ obfuscator, PPRF is pseudorandom at punctured points, WE is soundness secure and LSS is private.*

Before presenting the formal proof, we give a brief outline. The proof follows a sequence of hybrids, where the last one can be reduced to the privacy of the LSS. First, note that if $x \notin \mathcal{L}'$, then there do not exist t instances $x_i \in \mathcal{L}$. Assume, for simplicity that $t = N$, then there exists an index i^* such that $x_{i^*} \notin \mathcal{L}$. We start with a hybrid that is identical to the real soundness security game.

Then, we use the index hiding of the SSB hashing scheme to replace hk by a hashing key that is binding to index i^*. We then use the *puncturing* technique of [34]. That is, we create punctured PRF keys k_0' and k_1' (by puncturing the PPRF keys k_0 and k_1 respectively) at the point i^*. At the same time, we embed into the obfuscated circuit the ciphertext $\mathsf{ct}_{i^*} \leftarrow \mathsf{WE.Enc}(1^\lambda, x_{i^*}, s_{i^*}; r_{i^*})$ where $s_{i^*} \leftarrow \mathsf{PPRF.Eval}(k_0, i^*)$ and $r_{i^*} \leftarrow \mathsf{PPRF.Eval}(k_1, i^*)$. Given that the SSB is somewhere statistically binding at the point i^*, the circuits are functionally equivalent and we can use the security of the $i\mathcal{O}$ obfuscator to argue indistinguishability. We can now replace the values s_{i^*}, r_{i^*} by uniform ones since the PPRF is pseudorandom at punctured points. Finally, we replace ct_{i^*} by an encryption of 0. To conclude the proof, we can easily build a reduction to the security of the LSS.

In the more general case, some WE encryptions with respect to false statements are computed using the obfuscated program and some are given in the plain. For the former ones, we simply repeat the process above. For the latter ones, we use security of WE to replace these encryptions by encryptions of 0.

In the full version of the paper we present a variant of this protocol that does not incur in exponential loss of security in the reduction.

7.3 Compact Universal Ring Signature from Compact WE for Threshold Conjunction Languages

Consider again the URS construction of Sect. 6. One of the requirements of this URS scheme is a (non-compact) WE for a language $\mathcal{L}'$ which is itself a $(N-1, N)$-threshold conjunction language. When we plug the WE scheme for (t, N)-threshold conjunction languages as a drop-in replacement for non-compact WE, we obtain a compact URS scheme.

Specifically, the following theorem is a direct consequence of plugging the compact WE scheme for (t, N)-threshold conjunction languages described above with the URS signature from Sect. 6.

Theorem 21. *Let*

- $\mathsf{PRG} : \{0,1\}^{\lambda/2} \to \{0,1\}^\lambda$ *be a PRG.*
- $\mathcal{L}'$ *be the $(\ell-1, \ell)$ threshold conjunction language defined in Construction 2.*
- WE *be a compact witness encryption scheme for the $(\ell-1, \ell)$ threshold conjunction language $\mathcal{L}'$. As we have just established, this primitive can be built from secure $i\mathcal{O}$, $(\ell-1, \ell)$-LSS, (non-compact) WE for NP, PPRF and SSB.*
- SPB *be a SPB hashing scheme;*
- $\mathcal{L}$ *and $\mathcal{L}_{\mathsf{OR}}$ be the languages defined in Construction 2.*
- NIWI *be a NIWI scheme for $\mathcal{L}_{\mathsf{OR}}$.*

Then there exists a URS scheme that satisfies correctness, anonymity and unforgeability. Moreover, a signature Σ with respect to a ring of users R and a ring of signature schemes S has size $|\Sigma| \in \mathcal{O}((\log \ell + \log M)\mathsf{poly}(\lambda))$ where $\ell = |R|$ and $M = |S|$.

Acknowledgments. Nico Döttling: Funded by the European Union. Views and opinions expressed are however those of the author(s) only and do not necessarily reflect those of the European Union or the European Research Council. Neither the European Union nor the granting authority can be held responsible for them (ERC-2021-STG 101041207 LACONIC).

References

1. Abe, M., Ohkubo, M., Suzuki, K.: 1-out-of-n signatures from a variety of keys. In: Zheng, Y. (ed.) ASIACRYPT 2002. LNCS, vol. 2501, pp. 415–432. Springer, Heidelberg (2002). https://doi.org/10.1007/3-540-36178-2_26
2. Ananth, P., Jain, A.: Indistinguishability obfuscation from compact functional encryption. In: Gennaro, R., Robshaw, M. (eds.) CRYPTO 2015. LNCS, vol. 9215, pp. 308–326. Springer, Heidelberg (2015). https://doi.org/10.1007/978-3-662-47989-6_15
3. Backes, M., Döttling, N., Hanzlik, L., Kluczniak, K., Schneider, J.: Ring signatures: logarithmic-size, no setup—from standard assumptions. In: Ishai, Y., Rijmen, V. (eds.) EUROCRYPT 2019, Part III. LNCS, vol. 11478, pp. 281–311. Springer, Cham (2019). https://doi.org/10.1007/978-3-030-17659-4_10
4. Bellare, M., Rogaway, P.: Random oracles are practical: a paradigm for designing efficient protocols. In: Denning, D.E., Pyle, R., Ganesan, R., Sandhu, R.S., Ashby, V. (eds.) ACM CCS 93: 1st Conference on Computer and Communications Security, pp. 62–73. ACM Press, Fairfax (1993)
5. Bender, A., Katz, J., Morselli, R.: Ring signatures: stronger definitions, and constructions without random oracles. In: Halevi, S., Rabin, T. (eds.) TCC 2006. LNCS, vol. 3876, pp. 60–79. Springer, Heidelberg (2006). https://doi.org/10.1007/11681878_4
6. Bitansky, N., Garg, S., Lin, H., Pass, R., Telang, S.: Succinct randomized encodings and their applications. In: Servedio, R.A., Rubinfeld, R. (eds.) 47th Annual ACM Symposium on Theory of Computing, pp. 439–448. ACM Press, Portland (2015)
7. Bitansky, N., Vaikuntanathan, V.: Indistinguishability obfuscation from functional encryption. In: Guruswami, V. (ed.) 56th Annual Symposium on Foundations of Computer Science, pp. 171–190. IEEE Computer Society Press, Berkeley (2015)
8. Blum, M., Feldman, P., Micali, S.: Non-interactive zero-knowledge and its applications (extended abstract). In: 20th Annual ACM Symposium on Theory of Computing, pp. 103–112. ACM Press, Chicago (1988)
9. Boneh, D., Gentry, C., Lynn, B., Shacham, H.: Aggregate and verifiably encrypted signatures from bilinear maps. In: Biham, E. (ed.) EUROCRYPT 2003. LNCS, vol. 2656, pp. 416–432. Springer, Heidelberg (2003). https://doi.org/10.1007/3-540-39200-9_26
10. Boneh, D., Waters, B.: Constrained pseudorandom functions and their applications. In: Sako, K., Sarkar, P. (eds.) ASIACRYPT 2013, Part II. LNCS, vol. 8270, pp. 280–300. Springer, Heidelberg (2013). https://doi.org/10.1007/978-3-642-42045-0_15
11. Boyen, X.: Mesh signatures. In: Naor, M. (ed.) EUROCRYPT 2007. LNCS, vol. 4515, pp. 210–227. Springer, Heidelberg (2007). https://doi.org/10.1007/978-3-540-72540-4_12
12. Brakerski, Z., Koppula, V., Mour, T.: NIZK from LPN and trapdoor hash via correlation intractability for approximable relations. In: Micciancio, D., Ristenpart, T. (eds.) CRYPTO 2020. LNCS, vol. 12172, pp. 738–767. Springer, Cham (2020). https://doi.org/10.1007/978-3-030-56877-1_26
13. Cho, C., Döttling, N., Garg, S., Gupta, D., Miao, P., Polychroniadou, A.: Laconic oblivious transfer and its applications. In: Katz, J., Shacham, H. (eds.) CRYPTO 2017, Part II. LNCS, vol. 10402, pp. 33–65. Springer, Cham (2017). https://doi.org/10.1007/978-3-319-63715-0_2

14. Dodis, Y., Kiayias, A., Nicolosi, A., Shoup, V.: Anonymous identification in *ad hoc* groups. In: Cachin, C., Camenisch, J.L. (eds.) EUROCRYPT 2004. LNCS, vol. 3027, pp. 609–626. Springer, Heidelberg (2004). https://doi.org/10.1007/978-3-540-24676-3_36
15. Feige, U., Lapidot, D., Shamir, A.: Multiple non-interactive zero knowledge proofs based on a single random string (extended abstract). In: 31st Annual Symposium on Foundations of Computer Science, pp. 308–317. IEEE Computer Society Press, St. Louis (1990)
16. Fischlin, M., Schröder, D.: On the impossibility of three-move blind signature schemes. In: Gilbert, H. (ed.) EUROCRYPT 2010. LNCS, vol. 6110, pp. 197–215. Springer, Heidelberg (2010). https://doi.org/10.1007/978-3-642-13190-5_10
17. Garg, S., Gentry, C., Halevi, S., Raykova, M., Sahai, A., Waters, B.: Candidate indistinguishability obfuscation and functional encryption for all circuits. In: 54th Annual Symposium on Foundations of Computer Science, pp. 40–49. IEEE Computer Society Press, Berkeley (2013)
18. Garg, S., Gentry, C., Sahai, A., Waters, B.: Witness encryption and its applications. In: Boneh, D., Roughgarden, T., Feigenbaum, J. (eds.) 45th Annual ACM Symposium on Theory of Computing, pp. 467–476. ACM Press, Palo Alto (2013)
19. Garg, S., Gupta, D.: Efficient round optimal blind signatures. In: Nguyen, P.Q., Oswald, E. (eds.) EUROCRYPT 2014. LNCS, vol. 8441, pp. 477–495. Springer, Heidelberg (2014). https://doi.org/10.1007/978-3-642-55220-5_27
20. Garg, S., Rao, V., Sahai, A., Schröder, D., Unruh, D.: Round optimal blind signatures. In: Rogaway, P. (ed.) CRYPTO 2011. LNCS, vol. 6841, pp. 630–648. Springer, Heidelberg (2011). https://doi.org/10.1007/978-3-642-22792-9_36
21. Garg, S., Srinivasan, A.: A Simple Construction of iO for Turing Machines. In: Beimel, A., Dziembowski, S. (eds.) TCC 2018, Part II. LNCS, vol. 11240, pp. 425–454. Springer, Cham (2018). https://doi.org/10.1007/978-3-030-03810-6_16
22. Goel, A., Green, M., Hall-Andersen, M., Kaptchuk, G.: Stacking sigmas: a framework to compose σ-protocols for disjunctions. Cryptology ePrint Archive, Report 2021/422 (2021). https://ia.cr/2021/422
23. Goldreich, O., Oren, Y.: Definitions and properties of zero-knowledge proof systems. J. Cryptol. **7**(1), 1–32 (1994)
24. Goldwasser, S., Kalai, Y.T.: On the (in)security of the Fiat-Shamir paradigm. In: 44th Annual Symposium on Foundations of Computer Science, pp. 102–115. IEEE Computer Society Press, Cambridge (2003)
25. Groth, J., Ostrovsky, R., Sahai, A.: Perfect non-interactive zero knowledge for NP. In: Vaudenay, S. (ed.) EUROCRYPT 2006. LNCS, vol. 4004, pp. 339–358. Springer, Heidelberg (2006). https://doi.org/10.1007/11761679_21
26. Hohenberger, S., Koppula, V., Waters, B.: Universal signature aggregators. In: Oswald, E., Fischlin, M. (eds.) EUROCRYPT 2015, Part II. LNCS, vol. 9057, pp. 3–34. Springer, Heidelberg (2015). https://doi.org/10.1007/978-3-662-46803-6_1
27. Hubacek, P., Wichs, D.: On the communication complexity of secure function evaluation with long output. In: Roughgarden, T. (ed.) ITCS 2015: 6th Conference on Innovations in Theoretical Computer Science, pp. 163–172. Association for Computing Machinery, Rehovot (2015)
28. Jain, A., Jin, Z.: Non-interactive Zero Knowledge from Sub-exponential DDH. In: Canteaut, A., Standaert, F.-X. (eds.) EUROCRYPT 2021. LNCS, vol. 12696, pp. 3–32. Springer, Cham (2021). https://doi.org/10.1007/978-3-030-77870-5_1

29. Libert, B., Peters, T., Qian, C.: Logarithmic-size ring signatures with tight security from the DDH assumption. In: Lopez, J., Zhou, J., Soriano, M. (eds.) ESORICS 2018, Part II. LNCS, vol. 11099, pp. 288–308. Springer, Cham (2018). https://doi.org/10.1007/978-3-319-98989-1_15

30. Okamoto, T., Pietrzak, K., Waters, B., Wichs, D.: New realizations of somewhere statistically binding hashing and positional accumulators. In: Iwata, T., Cheon, J.H. (eds.) ASIACRYPT 2015, Part I. LNCS, vol. 9452, pp. 121–145. Springer, Heidelberg (2015). https://doi.org/10.1007/978-3-662-48797-6_6

31. Park, S., Sealfon, A.: It wasn't me! - repudiability and claimability of ring signatures. In: Boldyreva, A., Micciancio, D. (eds.) CRYPTO 2019, Part III. LNCS, vol. 11694, pp. 159–190. Springer, Cham (2019). https://doi.org/10.1007/978-3-030-26954-8_6

32. Peikert, C., Shiehian, S.: Noninteractive zero knowledge for np from (plain) learning with errors. In: Boldyreva, A., Micciancio, D. (eds.) CRYPTO 2019, Part I. LNCS, vol. 11692, pp. 89–114. Springer, Cham (2019). https://doi.org/10.1007/978-3-030-26948-7_4

33. Rivest, R.L., Shamir, A., Tauman, Y.: How to leak a secret. In: Boyd, C. (ed.) ASIACRYPT 2001. LNCS, vol. 2248, pp. 552–565. Springer, Heidelberg (2001). https://doi.org/10.1007/3-540-45682-1_32

34. Sahai, A., Waters, B.: How to use indistinguishability obfuscation: deniable encryption, and more. In: Shmoys, D.B. (ed.) 46th Annual ACM Symposium on Theory of Computing, pp. 475–484. ACM Press, New York (2014)

35. Shacham, H., Waters, B.: Efficient ring signatures without random oracles. In: Okamoto, T., Wang, X. (eds.) PKC 2007. LNCS, vol. 4450, pp. 166–180. Springer, Heidelberg (2007). https://doi.org/10.1007/978-3-540-71677-8_12

36. Tso, R.: A new way to generate a ring: Universal ring signature. Comput. Math. Appl. **65**(9), 1350–1359 (2013). https://www.sciencedirect.com/science/article/pii/S0898122112000491. Advanced Information Security

The Abe-Okamoto Partially Blind Signature Scheme Revisited

Julia Kastner[1]([⊠])(ID), Julian Loss[2], and Jiayu Xu[3](ID)

[1] Department of Computer Science, ETH Zurich, Zurich, Switzerland
julia.kastner@inf.ethz.ch
[2] CISPA Helmholtz Center for Information Security, Saarbrücken, Germany
loss@cispa.de
[3] School of Electrical Engineering and Computer Science, Oregon State University,
Corvallis, OR, USA
xujiay@oregonstate.edu

Abstract. Partially blind signatures, an extension of ordinary blind signatures, are a primitive with wide applications in e-cash and electronic voting. One of the most efficient schemes to date is the one by Abe and Okamoto (CRYPTO 2000), whose underlying idea—the OR-proof technique—has served as the basis for several works.

We point out several subtle flaws in the original proof of security, and provide a new detailed and rigorous proof, achieving similar bounds as the original work. We believe our insights on the proof strategy will find useful in the security analyses of other OR-proof-based schemes.

1 Introduction

Blind signatures, first introduced by Chaum [11], are a fundamental cryptographic primitive. They allow two parties, a *signer* who holds the secret key and a *user* who holds the message, to jointly generate a signature. Roughly speaking, security requires that the signer learns nothing about the message nor the signature (*blindness*), and the user cannot forge a signature that does not result from its interaction with the signer (*one-more unforgeability*). Blind signatures have found extensive applications in settings where anonymity is of great concern, such as e-cash [11,13,19,37] and electronic voting [12,18].

However, in a blind signature scheme, the signer has absolutely no control over the message it signs. This leads to various shortcomings in practice. First, in an e-cash system where a bank uses blind signatures to issue its coins, to avoid the double spending problem, the bank has to keep record of all coins that have been spent; to prevent the ledger from growing unlimitedly, old coins need to expire after a period of time, so that the corresponding entries in the ledger can be deleted. Second, there is no way to inscribe the value or expiration date of a

J. Kastner—Work done while supported by ERC Project PREP-CRYPTO 724307.
J. Loss—Work done while at University of Maryland.
J. Xu—Work done while at George Mason University.

S. Agrawal and D. Lin (Eds.): ASIACRYPT 2022, LNCS 13794, pp. 279–309, 2022.
https://doi.org/10.1007/978-3-031-22972-5_10

coin. Thus, the bank has to use a different public key for each value/expiration date, and anyone who spends or receives these coins has to maintain a list of all public keys, which has to evolve over time when old coins expire and are replaced by new ones. Similarly, in electronic voting, voters have to download a new public key for each election.

To address these issues, Abe & Fujisaki [2] proposed an extension called *partially* blind signatures, which allow a signer to explicitly include some common information (called the *tag*) in the signature. The tag is agreed upon by the signer and the user in advance and remains unblinded throughout the signing procedure; for example, it can be the date of issue or the value of the electronic coin. Setting the tag to the empty string yields an ordinary blind signature scheme. Informally, a partially blind signature scheme is secure if it satisfies (1) *partial blindness*: for multiple signatures that use the same tag, an adversarial signer cannot link these signatures to the signing sessions they originate from; and (2) *one-more-unforgeability*, or *OMUF security*: an adversarial user that interacts with the signer in at most ℓ many sessions, cannot output more than ℓ valid message-signature pairs.

Despite 25 years of research, there have been very few partially blind signature schemes ever proposed. The most efficient scheme up to date is the one proposed by Abe and Okamoto (AO) [4], which involves only 2 group (multi-)exponentiations for the signer and 4 (multi-)exponentiations for the user. The scheme is based on the classical OR-proof technique for obtaining witness indistinguishable protocols by Cramer *et al.* [15], and its security proof involves an intricate rewinding argument. The ideas behind both the scheme and its security proof repeatedly appear in blind signatures [1,5,6,35].

Unfortunately, close scrutiny shows that there are a number of critical issues with the proof of one-more-unforgeability in AO and in some other subsequent works. In particular, the analysis of the reduction's success probability is based on a problematic counting argument. In this paper, we revisit the AO partially blind signature scheme and present a new comprehensive analysis of its one-more-unforgeability, which addresses *all issues in the original security proof.* (The proof of partial blindness in AO is correct and is not the focus of this paper). The contributions of this paper are two-fold. First, we identify the flaws in the proof of AO, which we elaborate on in Sect. 1.1. Second, we overcome these issues by resorting to a more involved and rigorous counting argument. Our insights lead to new proof techniques and a much better understanding of AO's ideas. While we focus on the AO partially blind signature scheme, we believe that our techniques are applicable to other blind signature schemes based on the OR-proof technique.

1.1 Technical Overview

In this section we provide an overview of our security proof of the AO partially blind signature scheme, and explain the issues in the original work [4]. Similar to AO, our proof is done in two steps. First we consider the simplified case where there is only a single tag. This is the most technically involved part of the entire security analysis, and contains essential modifications to the proof in AO. Then we generalize it to the multi-tag case. This part of the proof is straightforward and mostly follows [4]. For simplicity, we only discuss the case of a single tag in this technical overview.

Forking: A Recap. The reduction in our security proof uses the forking technique to rewind the adversary and solve the discrete logarithm problem [31]. As is standard in a forking argument, we first define what we call a *deterministic wrapper* which provides a simplified, non-interactive interface to the reduction. More precisely, the wrapper takes as input an *instance* $\mathbf{I}$ (containing a public key and the internal values used to generate the signer's first messages of all signing sessions), a *random tape* rand (containing the random tape of the actual adversary), and a random *hash vector* $\overrightarrow{h}$ (to be used as outputs of random oracle queries). The reduction forks the wrapper instead of forking the adversary directly. In more concrete terms, this means that the reduction runs the wrapper once on inputs $\mathbf{I}, \text{rand}, \overrightarrow{h}$ and obtains an output which implicitly defines an index $J \in [|\overrightarrow{h}|]$. It then generates a vector $\overrightarrow{h}'$ by resampling the vector $\overrightarrow{h}$ uniformly at random from position J, and keeping the first $J - 1$ entries the same. It reruns the wrapper on inputs $\mathbf{I}, \text{rand}, \overrightarrow{h}'$, which will generate a run that is identical up the point where the reduction answers the J-th random oracle query. In particular, the input to this query remains identical in both runs. The goal of the reduction is to infer some equality from these relations so as to solve a discrete logarithm instance that it suitably embeds in its interaction with the adversary (see below).

Dealing with OR-Proofs in Forking. The AO scheme uses the classical OR-proof strategy of [15] to combine two Schnorr-style signatures into one. The witness for one branch of the proof is the actual secret key x of the scheme; the other branch corresponds to the *tag key* $\mathbf{z}$ which is obtained through hashing the tag info. On the signer's side, the protocol is a witness indistinguishable (WI) proof of knowledge of at least one witness, either the secret key x or the discrete logarithm of the tag key dlog $\mathbf{z}$. This gives rise to the following proof strategy, which was also used in [6]: The reduction can choose these tag keys such that it knows a witness and sign without knowing the secret key (so it can embed a discrete logarithm challenge in the public key), or it can embed its discrete logarithm challenge in a tag key and sign using the actual secret key. The intuitive idea here is that for each run of the protocol, the witness used internally by the reduction is perfectly hidden from the adversary (due to WI). Thus, the probability that the reduction is able to extract the "opposing" witness (i.e., the one it is not using itself for answering signing queries) from two forking runs of the adversary should be high.

Unfortunately, this intuition proves incorrect upon closer inspection. While WI perfectly hides the witness during any *single* run of the protocol, the transcripts of two executions of the protocol with the adversary (as performed by the reduction) can depend on the witness internally used by the reduction. Therefore, arguing that the reduction indeed extracts the opposing witness from two runs of the adversary turns out to be highly non-trivial.

Partnering Runs. We now describe the general idea for proving that the reduction has a significant probability to extract the witness it needs. For now we fix an instance $\mathbf{I}$ and a random tape rand, and consider the hash vector $\overrightarrow{h}$ as the only varying parameter of the reduction. Using a simple counting argument, one can show that for a significant portion of pairs $\mathbf{I}$, rand, there must exist two hash vectors $\overrightarrow{h}$, $\overrightarrow{h}'$ that lead to the same transcript between the wrapper and the adversary when the wrapper is run on $(\mathbf{I}, \text{rand}, \overrightarrow{h})$ or $(\mathbf{I}, \text{rand}, \overrightarrow{h}')$, respectively. Borrowing the terminology from [4], we refer to such triples $(\mathbf{I}, \text{rand}, \overrightarrow{h})$, $(\mathbf{I}, \text{rand}, \overrightarrow{h}')$ as *partners*. The key observation is that the witness extracted from partnering runs is independent of which witness was used by the reduction as part of the instance $\mathbf{I}$, and thus the reduction has a significant probability of extracting the desired witness (i.e., the witness not used by the reduction).[1] Unfortunately, given $\mathbf{I}$, rand, finding a pair of partners $(\mathbf{I}, \text{rand}, \overrightarrow{h})$ and $(\mathbf{I}, \text{rand}, \overrightarrow{h}')$ might not be efficiently possible, as in general, only few of them may exist. Hence it requires an additional argument to ensure that the reduction produces forks from which the desired witness can be efficiently extracted.

From Partners to Triangles. The next step in our chain of reasoning is to apply the strategy of AO for "amplifying" the number of forking runs from which the desired witness can be extracted. Thus, analogous to AO, we define *triangles* as follows. The corners of a triangle will be three triples $(\mathbf{I}, \text{rand}, \overrightarrow{h})$, $(\mathbf{I}, \text{rand}, \overrightarrow{h}')$, $(\mathbf{I}, \text{rand}, \overrightarrow{h}'')$, which produce successful runs for the wrapper. In addition, $\overrightarrow{h}$, $\overrightarrow{h}'$, $\overrightarrow{h}''$ all share a common prefix of some $i - 1$ entries and start to fork from each other at the i-th entry. The most important property of a triangle, however, is that $(\mathbf{I}, \text{rand}, \overrightarrow{h})$ and $(\mathbf{I}, \text{rand}, \overrightarrow{h}')$ be partnering runs, i.e., produce the same transcript for the wrapper. (AO refer to the pair of partnering runs as the "triangle base" and to the remaining pairs of triples as the "triangle sides"). We illustrate this in Fig. 1. As observed by AO, if the forked runs corresponding to $(\mathbf{I}, \text{rand}, \overrightarrow{h})$ and $(\mathbf{I}, \text{rand}, \overrightarrow{h}')$ yield the desired witness (i.e., the one not stored inside $\mathbf{I}$), then either of the forked runs $(\mathbf{I}, \text{rand}, \overrightarrow{h})$, $(\mathbf{I}, \text{rand}, \overrightarrow{h}'')$ or $(\mathbf{I}, \text{rand}, \overrightarrow{h}')$, $(\mathbf{I}, \text{rand}, \overrightarrow{h}'')$ yield the same witness. Their key insight is that the number of triangles should be far greater than the number of triangle bases formed by partnering runs $(\mathbf{I}, \text{rand}, \overrightarrow{h})$ and $(\mathbf{I}, \text{rand}, \overrightarrow{h}')$. Intuitively, this is the case because a *single pair* of triples $(\mathbf{I}, \text{rand}, \overrightarrow{h})$, $(\mathbf{I}, \text{rand}, \overrightarrow{h}')$ can serve as the base in *many different* triangles.

A Gap in AO. The next step in the analysis of AO is to count the number of triangles for which at least one side yields the desired witness. (We call such

---

[1] Due to the WI property of the scheme, for any $(\mathbf{I}, \text{rand}, \overrightarrow{h})$, there exists a corresponding triple $(\mathbf{I}', \text{rand}, \overrightarrow{h})$ that contains the other witness and produces the same transcript as $(\mathbf{I}, \text{rand}, \overrightarrow{h})$. This means that the same witness w could have been extracted from a pair of partnering runs $(\mathbf{I}, \text{rand}, \overrightarrow{h})$, $(\mathbf{I}, \text{rand}, \overrightarrow{h}')$, or from $(\mathbf{I}', \text{rand}, \overrightarrow{h})$, $(\mathbf{I}', \text{rand}, \overrightarrow{h}')$, where one of $\mathbf{I}$ and $\mathbf{I}'$ contains w, and the other instance does not.

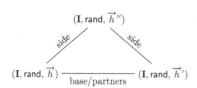

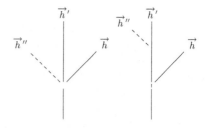

(a) A triangle consists of a pair of partners (the base) and one additional tuple (the top). A pair consisting of the top and one of the base corners is called a side.

(b) Left: forking as in a triangle (solid lines are the base, dashed lines are the top); right: not a triangle (forking at wrong point).

Fig. 1. Triangles

triangle sides "successful"). Recall that we keep $\mathbf{I}$, rand fixed throughout this counting argument, and argue only about the number of successful hash vectors associated with runs using $\mathbf{I}$, rand. If we can show that there are enough of triangles with a successful side, we might hope that when sampling a random pair $(\mathbf{I}, \text{rand}, \overrightarrow{h}), (\mathbf{I}, \text{rand}, \overrightarrow{h}'')$ during forking, the reduction will hit a successful triangle side, from which the desired witness can be extracted.

This is the point where our analysis diverges significantly from [4]. As noted above, many triangles may share a base; that is, for any given base, there exist many possible triangle tops. This makes it possible to "amplify" the extractability of the desired witness from a single base to extracting it from many possible triangle sides which are adjacent to this base in some triangle. (Recall that if a triangle base is successful, then at least one of the two sides must also be successful). However, we observe that *many triangles may also share a side*. If many triangles overlap on successful sides (but not on unsuccessful sides), it might happen that the total number of successful sides is *much smaller* than the total number of unsuccessful sides.[2]

Indeed, this is where the most crucial gap occurs in [4]. First, for each triangle base corner $(\mathbf{I}, \text{rand}, \overrightarrow{h})$, they assign this corner a partner $(\mathbf{I}, \text{rand}, \overrightarrow{h}')$ using the mapping Prt (so $(\mathbf{I}, \text{rand}, \overrightarrow{h}') = Prt(\mathbf{I}, \text{rand}, \overrightarrow{h})$ forms a triangle base together with $(\mathbf{I}, \text{rand}, \overrightarrow{h})$; see [4, p. 284]). It is, however, unclear if this is intended to be

---

[2] We stress that simply replacing a triple $(\mathbf{I}, \text{rand}, \overrightarrow{h})$ with an indistinguishable triple $(\mathbf{I}', \text{rand}, \overrightarrow{h})$ is not sufficient to solve this problem. Indeed, one might hope that since the adversary can not detect this change, an unsuccessful side may become successful when switching from $\mathbf{I}$ to $\mathbf{I}'$, as the desired witness would flip. However, a successful forking pair $((\mathbf{I}', \text{rand}, \overrightarrow{h}), (\mathbf{I}', \text{rand}, \overrightarrow{h}'))$ need only exist if $((\mathbf{I}, \text{rand}, \overrightarrow{h}), (\mathbf{I}, \text{rand}, \overrightarrow{h}'))$ is a base. The same is not true, in general, for sides, as their endpoints may not (and generally do not) yield the same transcript. Because of this, an unsuccessful side $((\mathbf{I}, \text{rand}, \overrightarrow{h}), (\mathbf{I}, \text{rand}, \overrightarrow{h}'))$ might not even be part of a triangle side when switching witnesses from $\mathbf{I}$ to $\mathbf{I}'$.

an injective assignment (i.e., no two base corners can share the same partner). If so, there is a gap as to why this assignment is possible, i.e., why there are enough such partners for each of the base corners to find a *different* partner. In fact, we provide an argument in our analysis for why such partners—which we call *opposing base corners*—are *not much fewer* than original base corners, but they do not necessarily need to be equal in size.

On the other hand, if the assignment Prt is not injective, then different triangles may share the same side. This is also problematic, as we explain now. [4] proceeds to claim that if (for a fixed pair $\mathbf{I}, \mathsf{rand}$) at least $\frac{4}{5}$ of triangle sides are unsuccessful, then at least $\frac{3}{5}$ of triangle bases are also unsuccessful, i.e., they yield the undesired witness that is used by the reduction. (See the proof of the last claim on [4, p. 284]). Although this claim is not explicitly argued, the underlying reasoning seems to be as follows: since every triangle has two sides and one base, if $\frac{4}{5}$ of all sides are unsuccessful, then at least $\frac{4}{5} + \frac{4}{5} - 1 = \frac{3}{5}$ fraction of triangles have two unsuccessful sides, which implies that their bases must also be unsuccessful. However, this argument *implicitly assumes that no triangles ever share a base or a side*, which, as we have mentioned, is not necessarily the case.

Concrete Counterexamples and Additional Issues. We now provide concrete counterexamples to show why the claim above is false if triangles may share sides, or even just bases. For triangles sharing sides, consider the example in the middle of Fig. 2, where 8 out of the 10 triangle sides are unsuccessful, yet only 2 out of the 6 triangle bases are unsuccessful. For triangles sharing only bases (recall that in this case there is already a gap as to why there exists an assignment Prt such that triangles do not share sides), the claim is also untrue: see the rightmost part of Fig. 2 for an example where 5 out of the 6 triangle sides are unsuccessful, yet only 1 out of the 2 triangle bases are unsuccessful.

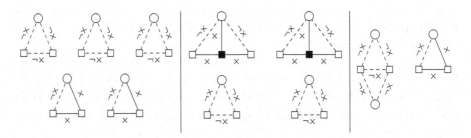

Fig. 2. Claim in [4] that if at least $\frac{4}{5}$ of triangle sides are unsuccessful (i.e., yield the undesirable witness $\neg\times$), then at least $\frac{2}{3}$ of bases (incident to two square nodes) also yield this witness. This holds for non-overlapping triangles (left), but not for triangles overlapping in sides (middle) or in bases (right).

We further note that there are some relatively minor gaps that are easier to fix. In particular, it is incorrect to assert that the probability to extract either witness from a triangle base is close to $\frac{1}{2}$—we refer here to the last sentence in the proof of the last claim on [4, p. 284]:

> Since the information of a base, $(\overrightarrow{\varepsilon}, \overrightarrow{\varepsilon}')[(\overrightarrow{h}, \overrightarrow{h}')]$, is independent of the witness the simulator already has as a part of Ω [**I**, rand], this contradicts that a biased result should occur with probability (over Ω [**I**, rand]) less than $1/2 + 1/\mathsf{poly}(n)$ for any polynomial poly.

(The expressions in brackets are a translation to our notation).

To see why this claim is incorrect, imagine a computationally unbounded adversary that finds the secret key $x = \mathrm{dlog}\ \mathbf{y}$ by brute force, and wins the OMUF game by running the real signer's code. Then the signatures produced by this adversary—including pairs of signatures obtained from triangle bases—will always yield the same witness (the secret key x), rather than yielding either witness with probability close to $\frac{1}{2}$. Our approach to deal with this issue is to define a "majority witness" $\times$ which can be extracted from many triangle bases (for a suitable definition of many). We then show that it is possible to extract $\times$, using a suitable counting argument.

Resolving the Issues from Earlier Works. We now provide an overview of our strategy to bridge the gaps in [4], achieving the same result. We first recall that for any triple $(\mathbf{I}, \mathsf{rand}, \overrightarrow{h})$, there is a corresponding instance $\mathbf{I}'$ that contains the other branch of witness, such that $(\mathbf{I}, \mathsf{rand}, \overrightarrow{h})$ and $(\mathbf{I}', \mathsf{rand}, \overrightarrow{h})$ yield the same transcript. This naturally leads to the concept of *both-sided triangle bases*, namely triangle bases $((\mathbf{I}, \mathsf{rand}, \overrightarrow{h}), (\mathbf{I}, \mathsf{rand}, \overrightarrow{h}'))$ that are also the base of some triangle when $\mathbf{I}$ is replaced by $\mathbf{I}'$. Using several counting arguments, we show that the set of both-sided base corners must be large. While our counting arguments are more detailed and rigorous, they are in the same spirit as those of [4].

We now bridge the gap in [4], by showing that there cannot be too large of an overlap between triangle sides such that the absolute amount of successful triangle sides would get small. We define *good base corners* as triples that are incident to many successful both-sided triangle bases, as well as many successful triangle sides. We further require that these triangle sides and bases must exist at the good base corner's *maximum branching index*—the index at which the largest number of partners fork from it. Similarly, we define *good opposing corners* that are incident to a successful both-sided triangle base and many successful sides, but the triangle base and sides are located at the maximum branching index of the triple *at the other end of the base*.

Our crucial observation is that *if there are not too many good base corners, then there must be many good opposing corners*. To see this, consider a base corner $(\mathbf{I}, \mathsf{rand}, \overrightarrow{h}')$ that is not good, and consider all triples $(\mathbf{I}, \mathsf{rand}, \overrightarrow{h})$ that are partners of $(\mathbf{I}, \mathsf{rand}, \overrightarrow{h}')$. Let i denote the maximum branching index of $(\mathbf{I}, \mathsf{rand}, \overrightarrow{h}')$; by definition, a significant portion of these partners $(\mathbf{I}, \mathsf{rand}, \overrightarrow{h})$ fork with $(\mathbf{I}, \mathsf{rand}, \overrightarrow{h}')$ at index i. Recall that if a triangle base is successful, then at least one of its sides must also be successful. Since most of the triangle sides involving $(\mathbf{I}, \mathsf{rand}, \overrightarrow{h}')$ are unsuccessful at index i, this means that many of the *other* triangle sides, i.e., those involving the partners $(\mathbf{I}, \mathrm{rand}, \overrightarrow{h}\,)$, are successful at index i. In other words, a significant portion of a non-good base corner $(\mathbf{I}, \mathrm{rand}, \overrightarrow{h}')$'s partners, are good opposing corners. (In the formal proof, we will also rule out the possibility that different non-good base corners' corresponding good opposing corners overlap too much).

The above conclusion means that, when the reduction samples the triple for the first forking run, with significant probability the triple is either a good base corner or a good opposing corner. Then, due to the definitions of these good triangle corners, it is not hard to show that with significant probability the reduction hits a successful triangle side while sampling the second triple—that is, the desired witness can be extracted from the two forking runs.

Finally, we remark that our reduction guesses in advance which hash values the adversary will actually use to produce its signatures. This introduces a loss of $\binom{Q_h}{\ell+1}$ in the reduction's advantage, where Q_h is the number of the adversary's hash queries and ℓ is the number of signing sessions closed. This step is necessary in our analysis as we need all possible forking indices to have a signature attached to them in order to lower-bound the set of good opposing base corners. (See Remark 2 in Sect. 4.4). We notice that a loss in this order of magnitude seems inherent due to the recent polynomial-time ROS-attack [7], and that we achieve comparable bounds to the original work of Abe & Okamoto [4].[3]

1.2 Related Work

Partially blind signatures were introduced in [2], which also presented a scheme based on a non-standard RSA-type assumption. Cao *et al.* [10] proposed another construction based on the RSA assumption, but their scheme was cryptoanalyzed in [27]. Zhang *et al.* [38], as well as Chow *et al.* [14], proposed schemes based on bilinear pairings, and Papachristoudis *et al.* [29] proposed a scheme based on lattice assumptions. Okamoto [28] proposed a theoretical construction that does not rely on the random oracle model. Finally, Maitland & Boyd [26] considered a *restrictive* partially blind signature scheme, where the user's choice of messages must follow certain rules.

There is a rich literature on (ordinary) blind signatures and their applications. Its security notion was formalized by Pointcheval & Stern [30] and Juels *et al.* [22], and later strengthened by Schröder & Unruh [34]. Fischlin [16] and Abe & Ohkubo [3] considered security definitions in the universal composability (UC) framework. Camenisch *et al.* [9] and Fischlin & Schröder [17] considered a stronger notion of blindness called *selective-failure blindness*. There are a large number of blind signature schemes based on various assumptions and in various models; a very incomplete list includes [1,8,20,21,25,28,30,32,33].

We notice that the security analyses of (partially) blind signature schemes are usually extremely involved, with the original security proofs sometimes being

---

[3] See the top of [4, p. 285], where the reduction's advantage includes a term η_1^2, where $\eta_1 = \eta/2Q_h^{\ell+1}$ and η is the adversary's advantage.

flawed. Apart from the schemes already discussed, we give two additional examples here. The security of the Schnorr blind signature [33] relies on the hardness of the ROS problem, which was recently shown to be easy [7]; a new security proof in the weaker sequential setting appears in [23]. For partially blind signature schemes, the aforementioned Zhang *et al.* scheme [38] has an issue in its security proof, and the full analysis came much later [36]. This paper can be seen as yet another attempt of spotting and fixing issues in previous works; however, we stress that the underlying OR-proof technique of the Abe-Okamoto scheme is widely used in blind signatures, and we believe that our techniques will find applications in the security analyses of other schemes as well.

2 Preliminaries

2.1 Notation

We denote by $[\ell] := \{1, \ldots, \ell\}$. For a vector $\overrightarrow{h}$, its i-th entry is denoted by h_i, and the vector of its first i entries is denoted by $\overrightarrow{h}_{[i]}$. We denote by $x \overset{\$}{\leftarrow} X$ that x is sampled uniformly at random from set X. For a vector $\overrightarrow{x} \in X^n$, we denote by $\overrightarrow{x}' \overset{\$}{\leftarrow} X^n_{|\overrightarrow{x}_{[i]}}$ that $\overrightarrow{x}'$ is sampled uniformly at random from $\{\overrightarrow{x}' \in X^n | \overrightarrow{x}'_{[i]} = \overrightarrow{x}_{[i]}\}$. For an algorithm A, we use t_A to denote its running time.

2.2 Computational Problems

Definition 1 (Discrete Logarithm Problem). *For public parameters* $pp = (\mathbb{G}, q, \mathbf{g})$ *for a group* $\mathbb{G}$ *with order* q *and generator* $\mathbf{g}$*, we describe the discrete logarithm game* $\mathbf{DLOG}_{\mathbb{G}}$ *with adversary* A *as follows:*

Setup. *Sample* $x \overset{\$}{\leftarrow} \mathbb{Z}_q$ *and set* $\mathbf{y} := \mathbf{g}^x$*. Output* $(pp, \mathbf{y})$ *to* A*.*
Output Determination. *When* A *outputs* $x' \subset \mathbb{Z}_q$*, return 1 if* $g^{x'} = \mathbf{y}$ *and 0 otherwise.*

We define the advantage of A *as*

$$\text{adv}_A^{\mathbf{DLOG}_{\mathbb{G}}} := \Pr[\mathbf{DLOG}_{\mathbb{G}}^A = 1]$$

where the probability goes over the randomness of the game as well as the randomness of the adversary A*. We say that the discrete logarithm problem is* (t, ϵ)*-hard in* $\mathbb{G}$ *if for any adversary* A *that runs in time at most* t*, it holds that*

$$\text{adv}_A^{\mathbf{DLOG}_{\mathbb{G}}} \leq \epsilon.$$

(When it is clear from context, we may omit $\mathbb{G}$ *and only write* $\mathbf{DLOG}$ *for the game).*

2.3 Partially Blind Signatures

The definitions in this section mostly follow [4].

Definition 2 (Partially Blind Signature scheme). *A* three-move *partially blind signature scheme* $\mathsf{PBS} = (\mathsf{KeyGen}, \mathsf{Sign} = (\mathsf{Sign}_1, \mathsf{Sign}_2), \mathsf{User} = (\mathsf{User}_1, \mathsf{User}_2), \mathsf{Verify})$ *consists of the following* PPT *algorithms:*

Key Generation. *On input public parameters* pp, *the probabilistic algorithm* KeyGen *outputs a public key* pk *and a secret key* sk. *Henceforth we assume that* pp *is provided to all parties (including the adversary) as an input, and do not explicitly write it.*

Signer: *The interactive signer* $\mathsf{Sign} = (\mathsf{Sign}_1, \mathsf{Sign}_2)$ *has two phases:*

Sign_1: *On input a tag* info *and a secret key* sk, *the probabilistic algorithm* Sign_1 *outputs an internal signer state* $\mathsf{st}_{\mathsf{Sign}}$, *and a response* R.

Sign_2: *On input the secret key* sk, *a challenge value* e, *and the corresponding internal state* $\mathsf{st}_{\mathsf{Sign}}$, *the deterministic algorithm* Sign_2 *outputs a response* S.

User. *The interactive user* $\mathsf{User} = (\mathsf{User}_1, \mathsf{User}_2)$ *has two phases:*

User_1: *On input a public key* pk, *a tag* info, *a message* m, *and a* Sign_1 *response* R, *the probabilistic algorithm* User_1 *outputs a challenge value* e *and an internal user state* $\mathsf{st}_{\mathsf{User}}$.

User_2: *On input a public key* pk, *a* Sign_2 *response* S, *and the corresponding internal user state* $\mathsf{st}_{\mathsf{User}}$, *the deterministic algorithm* User_2 *outputs a signature* sig *on message* m *along with the tag* info.

Verification. *On input a public key* pk, *a message* m, *a signature* sig, *and a tag* info, *the deterministic algorithm* Verify *outputs either* 1 *or* 0, *where* 1 *indicates that the signature is valid, and* 0 *that it is not.*

We say a partially blind signature scheme PBS *is* (perfectly) *correct if for all* pk, m, sig, info *that result from an honest interaction between signer and user,* $\mathsf{Verify}(\mathsf{pk}, m, \mathsf{sig}, \mathsf{info}) = 1$.

We now define the one-more-unforgeability of a partially blind signature scheme. We do not focus on partial blindness in this paper; we include the definition in in the full version [24] for completeness, and for a proof that the Abe-Okamoto scheme is partially blind, see the original paper [4].

Definition 3 (One-more-unforgeability). *For a three-move partially blind signature scheme* PBS, *we define the* ℓ-one more unforgeability *(ℓ-OMUF) game* $\ell\text{-}\mathbf{OMUF}_{\mathsf{PBS}}$ *with an adversary* U *(in the role of the user) as follows:*

Setup. *Sample a pair of keys* $(\mathsf{pk}, \mathsf{sk}) \xleftarrow{\$} \mathsf{PBS.KeyGen}(\mathsf{pp})$. *Initialize* $\ell_{\mathsf{closed}} := 0$ *and run* U *on input* pk.

Online Phase. U *is given access to oracles* sign_1 *and* sign_2, *which behave as follows.*

Oracle sign_1: *On input* info, *the oracle samples a fresh session identifier* sid. *It sets* $\mathsf{open}_{\mathsf{sid}} := \mathtt{true}$ *and generates* $(R_{\mathsf{sid}}, \mathsf{st}_{\mathsf{sid}}) \xleftarrow{\$} \mathsf{PBS.Sign}_1(\mathsf{sk}, \mathsf{info})$. *Then it returns the response* R_{sid} *together with* sid *to* U.

Oracle sign$_2$: *If $\ell_{\text{closed}} < \ell$, the oracle takes as input a challenge e and a session identifier sid. If $\text{open}_{\text{sid}} = \text{false}$, it returns $\bot$. Otherwise, it sets $\ell_{\text{closed}}{+}{+}$ and $\text{open}_{\text{sid}} := \text{false}$. Then it computes the response $S \xleftarrow{\$} \text{PBS.Sign}_2(\text{sk}, \text{st}_{\text{sid}}, e)$ and returns S to U.*

Output Determination. *When U outputs distinct tuples $(m_1, \text{sig}_1, \text{info}_1), \ldots, (m_k, \text{sig}_k, \text{info}_k)$, return 1 if $k \geq \ell_{\text{closed}} + 1$ and for all $i \in [k]$: $\text{PBS.Verify}(\text{pk}, \sigma_i, m_i, \text{info}_i) = 1$. Otherwise, return 0.*

We define the advantage of U as

$$\text{adv}_{\mathsf{U}}^{\ell\text{-OMUF}_{\text{PBS}}} = \Pr\left[\ell\text{-OMUF}_{\text{PBS}}^{\mathsf{U}} = 1\right]$$

where the probability goes over the randomness of the game as well as the randomness of the adversary U. We say the scheme PBS is (t, ϵ, ℓ)-one-more unforgeable if for any adversary U that runs in time at most t and makes at most ℓ queries to sign$_2$,

$$\text{adv}_{\mathsf{U}}^{\ell\text{-OMUF}_{\text{PBS}}} \leq \epsilon.$$

If U always queries the same tag to oracle sign$_1$, we denote the game as ℓ-1-info-OMUF$_{\text{PBS}}$ and say that PBS is (t, ϵ, ℓ)-single-tag one-more unforgeable.

3   The Abe-Okamoto Partially Blind Signature Scheme

In this section we describe the partially blind signature scheme by Abe & Okamoto [4]. The idea of the scheme relies on the OR-Proof technique by Cramer *et al.* [15]. It runs a proof of knowledge that the signer knows either the secret key x or the discrete logarithm of the so-called *tag key* $\mathbf{z}$, which is obtained through hashing the tag info. In this way we obtain a *witness indistinguishable* scheme: an honest signer does not know dlog $\mathbf{z}$ and is forced to use x for issuing signatures; while the reduction may program the random oracle so that it knows the dlog $\mathbf{z}$ and can then simulate the signer without knowing the secret key x.

Key Generation. On input public parameters $\text{pp} = (\mathbb{G}, \mathbf{g}, q, \mathsf{H}^*, \mathsf{H})$ (where H^* and H are random oracles with ranges $\mathbb{G}$ and $\mathbb{Z}_q$, respectively), KeyGen samples $x \xleftarrow{\$} \mathbb{Z}_q$ and sets $\mathbf{y} := \mathbf{g}^x$. It then outputs $(\text{pk}, \text{sk}) := (\mathbf{y}, x)$.

Signer. $\text{Sign} = (\text{Sign}_1, \text{Sign}_2)$ behaves as follows:

Sign_1: On input info and sk, Sign_1 computes the tag key $\mathbf{z} := \mathsf{H}^*(\text{info})$ and samples $u, s, d \xleftarrow{\$} \mathbb{Z}_q$. It then computes the *commitments* $\mathbf{a} := \mathbf{g}^u, \mathbf{b} := \mathbf{g}^s \cdot \mathbf{z}^d$. It outputs the response $(\mathbf{a}, \mathbf{b})$ to the user and an internal state $\text{st}_{\text{Sign}} := (u, s, d)$.

Sign_2: On input $e \in \mathbb{Z}_q, \text{st}_{\text{Sign}} = (u, s, d), \text{sk} = x$, Sign_2 computes $c := e - d$ and $r := u - cx$. It outputs the response (r, c, s, d) to the user.

User. $\text{User} = (\text{User}_1, \text{User}_2)$ behaves as follows:

User_1: On input $\text{pk}, m, \text{info}, \mathbf{a}, \mathbf{b}$, User_1 computes the tag key $\mathbf{z} := \mathsf{H}^*(\text{info})$ and samples $t_1, t_2, t_3, t_4 \xleftarrow{\$} \mathbb{Z}_q$. It then computes $\boldsymbol{\alpha} := \mathbf{g}^{t_1} \cdot \mathbf{y}^{t_2} \cdot \mathbf{a}$ and $\boldsymbol{\beta} := \mathbf{g}^{t_3} \cdot \mathbf{z}^{t_4} \cdot \mathbf{b}$, queries $h := \mathsf{H}(\boldsymbol{\alpha}, \boldsymbol{\beta}, \mathbf{z}, m)$ for the message m it wants to sign, and computes the blinded challenge $e := h - t_2 - t_4$. It outputs e to the signer and an internal state $\text{st}_{\text{User}} := (t_1, t_2, t_3, t_4)$.

User$_2$: On input pk, (r, c, s, d), st$_{\mathsf{User}} = (t_1, t_2, t_3, t_4)$, User$_1$ computes $\rho :=$ $r + t_1$, $\omega := c + t_2$, $\sigma := s + t_3$, and $\delta := d + t_4$. It then verifies that $\omega + \delta = \mathsf{H}(\mathbf{g}^\rho \cdot \mathbf{y}^\omega, \mathbf{g}^\sigma \cdot \mathbf{z}^\delta, \mathbf{z}, m)$; if so, it outputs the signature $(\rho, \omega, \sigma, \delta)$. (Otherwise, it outputs $\perp$).

Verification. On input $\mathbf{y}, m,$ info, $(\rho, \omega, \sigma, \delta)$, Verify computes $\mathbf{z} := \mathsf{H}^*(\text{info})$. It outputs 1 if $\omega + \delta = \mathsf{H}(\mathbf{g}^\rho \cdot \mathbf{y}^\omega, \mathbf{g}^\sigma \cdot \mathbf{z}^\delta, \mathbf{z}, m)$ and 0 otherwise.

For a graphic illustration of the scheme, see see the full version [24].

4 Computing the Probability for Extracting the "Good" Witness

As mentioned in the introduction, our analysis of the Abe-Okamoto scheme is done in two steps. In this section, we deal with the case that the adversary U only uses a *single* tag, i.e., U plays the ℓ-1-info-**OMUF**$_{\mathsf{AO}}$ game.

4.1 The Deterministic OMUF Wrapper

Restricting the Adversary to Making $\ell + 1$ Hash Queries. Suppose that the adversary U makes ℓ queries to sign$_2$ (henceforth "signing queries") and Q_h queries to H (henceforth "hash queries"), and uses a single tag $\overline{\text{info}}$. Below we assume w.l.o.g. that U never makes the same query to H twice.

We say that a message-signature pair $(m, (\rho, \omega, \sigma, \delta))$ *corresponds to* an index $i \in [Q_h]$, or corresponds to the adversary U's i-th hash query, if this query was $\mathsf{H}(\mathbf{y}^\omega \mathbf{g}^\rho, \mathbf{z}^\delta \mathbf{g}^\sigma, \mathbf{z}, m)$. (When the message m is clear from context, we may say that the signature $(\rho, \omega, \sigma, \delta)$ corresponds to index i.) We remark that we can further assume w.l.o.g. that there exist $\ell + 1$ hash queries of U, each of which corresponds to a distinct message-signature pair in the output of U (in particular, $Q_h \geq \ell + 1$). This is because otherwise one of the following must hold (assuming that U succeeds):

- There exists a pair $(m, (\omega, \rho, \delta, \sigma))$ that does not correspond to any hash query, i.e., $\mathsf{H}(\mathbf{y}^\omega \mathbf{g}^\rho, \mathbf{z}^\delta \mathbf{g}^\sigma, \mathbf{z}, m)$ has never been queried. In this case, U can be turned into another adversary U' that runs the code of U and additionally makes such a hash query; obviously U and U' have the same advantage.
- There exist two distinct pairs $(m_1, (\omega_1, \rho_1, \delta_1, \sigma_1)), (m_2, (\omega_2, \rho_2, \delta_2, \sigma_2))$ that correspond to the same hash query. In this case, we have that $m_1 = m_2$, $\mathbf{y}^{\omega_1} \mathbf{g}^{\rho_1} = \mathbf{y}^{\omega_2} \mathbf{g}^{\rho_2}$, and $\mathbf{z}^{\delta_1} \mathbf{g}^{\sigma_1} = \mathbf{z}^{\delta_2} \mathbf{g}^{\sigma_2}$. Then a reduction to the discrete logarithm problem can easily compute both x and w as $x = (\omega_1 - \omega_2)^{-1} \cdot (\rho_2 - \rho_2)$ and $w = (\delta_1 - \delta_2)^{-1} \cdot (\sigma_2 - \sigma_1)$.

It is not hard to see that any adversary U can be turned into another adversary that makes *exactly* $\ell + 1$ hash queries, with a factor of $\binom{Q_h}{\ell+1}$ loss in advantage. Formally, we define an adversary $\mathsf{M} := \mathsf{M}^{\mathsf{U}}$ that works as follows. M, on input of a public key pk, chooses a random subset I of $[Q_h]$ with $|I| = \ell + 1$, and invokes

U(pk). For U's i-th query to H, if $i \notin I$, M responds with a random integer in $\mathbb{Z}_q$. For any other query (including queries to signing oracles, queries to H*, and the i-th query to H for $i \in I$), M forwards it to the corresponding oracle of M's own challenger, and forwards the response back to U. When U outputs a set of $\ell + 1$ message-signature pairs, M checks if every pair $(m, (\rho, \omega, \sigma, \delta))$ corresponds to some index $i \in I$, that is, U's i-th hash query was $H(\mathbf{y}^\omega \mathbf{g}^\rho, \mathbf{z}^\delta \mathbf{g}^\sigma, \mathbf{z}, m)$. If so, M copies U's output (and outputs $\perp$ otherwise).

Lemma 1. *For* M *described above, we have that*

$$\mathrm{adv}_{\mathsf{M}}^{\ell\text{-}1\text{-info-}\mathbf{OMUF}_{\mathsf{AO}}} \geq \frac{\mathrm{adv}_{\mathsf{U}}^{\ell\text{-}1\text{-info-}\mathbf{OMUF}_{\mathsf{AO}}}}{\binom{Q_h}{\ell+1}}.$$

Proof. It is straightforward that M simulates the OMUF game to U perfectly. Assume that U succeeds. By our assumption on U, there is a set of indices $I^* \subset [Q_h]$ corresponding to the message-signature pairs in U's output, with $|I^*| = \ell + 1$. If $I^* = I$, then M also succeeds. Since I is a random subset of size $\ell + 1$ of $[Q_h]$, the probability that $I^* = I$ is $\frac{1}{\binom{Q_h}{\ell+1}}$. The lemma follows. □

The lemma above implies that it is sufficient to consider an adversary that makes exactly $\ell + 1$ (distinct) hash queries, since an upper bound of the adversary's advantage in this specific case immediately translates to such an upper bound in the general case. Below we simply assume that the adversary makes $\ell + 1$ hash queries.

The Deterministic Wrapper. For any adversary M that makes exactly $\ell + 1$ distinct hash queries, we define a deterministic *wrapper* A that, given the witness and random coin tosses for one side, simulates the view of M. The wrapper uses either the **y**-side witness (i.e., the secret key) x or the **z**-side witness $w = \mathrm{dlog}\,\mathbf{z}$ to respond to sign_2 queries, and simulates the other side of the OR-proof using fixed values. We begin with the formal definition of an instance:

Definition 4 (Instances). *For the deterministic wrapper simulating the OMUF-game to the adversary we define two types of* instances **I**. *A* **y**-*side (a.k.a. honest) instance consists of the following components:*

$b = 0$: *bit indicating that the secret key x will be used for simulation*
x: *the secret key, also referred to as the* **y**-*side witness*
$\mathbf{z}$: *the tag key, to be returned by oracle* H* *for requested* $\overline{\mathrm{info}}$
d_i, s_i: *simulator choices for* **z**-*side part corresponding to the i-th signing session*
u_i: *discrete logarithm of the* **y**-*side commitment* $\mathbf{a}_i$ *in the i-th signing session.*

A **z**-*side instance consists of the following components:*

$b = 1$: *bit indicating that the tag witness w will be used for simulation*
y: *the public key*
w: *the discrete logarithm of the tag key* **z** *as above*
c_i, r_i: *simulator choices for* **y**-*side part corresponding to the i-th signing session*

v_i: *discrete logarithm of the* **z**-*side commitment* $\mathbf{b}_i$ *in the i-th signing session.*

Let $\overrightarrow{h}$ be the vector of responses returned by random oracle H (so $\left|\overrightarrow{h}\right|$ = $\ell + 1$), rand be the randomness used by the adversary M, and $\overline{\mathsf{info}}$ be the tag used in the OMUF game. We define a deterministic wrapper $\mathsf{A} := \mathsf{A}_{\overline{\mathsf{info}}}^{\mathsf{M}}$ that runs on $(\mathbf{I}, \mathsf{rand}, \overrightarrow{h})$ as shown in Fig. 3. The wrapper allows us to argue about which $(\mathbf{I}, \mathsf{rand}, \overrightarrow{h})$ tuples cause the adversary to succeed.

A has two simulation modes. For $b = 0$, it runs the honest signer's algorithm to simulate both sign_1 and sign_2 oracle queries; for H^* queries, it responds with $\mathbf{z}$ if the input is $\overline{\mathsf{info}}$ and $\perp$ for all other inputs. In mode $b = 1$, A knows w and not x. It therefore runs the so-called $\mathbf{z}$-side signer (see the full version [24]), which is the honest signer's algorithm except that w is treated as the secret key. A responds to queries to H^* with $\mathbf{g}^w$ for $\overline{\mathsf{info}}$ and $\perp$ otherwise. In both modes, A responds to queries to H using entries in the hash vector $\overrightarrow{h}$. Finally, upon receiving M's output message-signature pairs, A checks if they are all valid, and if so, A copies M's output (and outputs $\perp$ otherwise).

It is easy to see that

$$t_{\mathsf{A}} = t_{\mathsf{M}} + \mathrm{O}(\ell) = t_{\mathsf{U}} + \mathrm{O}(\ell) + \mathrm{O}(Q_h{}^2) = t_{\mathsf{U}} + \mathrm{O}(\ell) + \mathrm{O}(Q_h{}^2),$$

where the term $\mathrm{O}(\ell)$ comes from verifying $\ell + 1$ signatures, and $\mathrm{O}(Q_h{}^2)$ comes from identifying the hash indices that correspond to signatures.

$\mathsf{A}(\mathbf{I}, \mathsf{rand}, \overrightarrow{h})$	$\mathsf{sign}_1(\mathsf{info})$
00 parse b from $\mathbf{I}$	20 if $\mathsf{info} = \overline{\mathsf{info}}$
01 if $b = 0$	21 $\mathsf{sid}{+}{+}$
02 parse $(b, x, \mathbf{z}, \overrightarrow{d}, \overrightarrow{s}, \overrightarrow{u}) := \mathbf{I}$	22 $\mathsf{open}(\mathsf{sid}) := \mathbf{true}$
03 $\mathsf{pk} := \mathbf{g}^x$	23 if $b = 0$
04 else	24 $\mathbf{a}_{\mathsf{sid}} := \mathbf{g}^{u_{\mathsf{sid}}}$
05 parse $(b, \mathbf{y}, w, \overrightarrow{c}, \overrightarrow{r}, \overrightarrow{v}) := \mathbf{I}$	25 $\mathbf{b}_{\mathsf{sid}} := \mathbf{g}^{s_{\mathsf{sid}}} \cdot \mathbf{z}^{d_{\mathsf{sid}}}$
06 $\mathsf{pk} := \mathbf{y}$	26 else
07 $\mathsf{sid} := 0$	27 $\mathbf{a}_{\mathsf{sid}} := \mathbf{g}^{r_{\mathsf{sid}}} \cdot \mathbf{y}^{c_{\mathsf{sid}}}$
08 $j := 0$	28 $\mathbf{b}_{\mathsf{sid}} := \mathbf{g}^{v_{\mathsf{sid}}}$
09 $(m_i, (\rho_i, \omega_i, \sigma_i, \delta_i))_{i=1}^{\ell+1} := \mathsf{M}^{\mathsf{sign}_1, \mathsf{sign}_2, \mathsf{H}, \mathsf{H}^*}(\mathsf{pk}; \mathsf{rand})$	29 return $(\mathsf{sid}, \mathbf{a}_{\mathsf{sid}}, \mathbf{b}_{\mathsf{sid}})$
10 if $\forall i$: $\mathsf{Verify}(\mathsf{pk}, m_i, (\rho_i, \omega_i, \sigma_i, \delta_i))$	30 else return $\perp$
11 return $(m_i, (\rho_i, \omega_i, \sigma_i, \delta_i))_{i=1}^{\ell+1}$	$\mathsf{sign}_2(\mathsf{sid}, e_{\mathsf{sid}})$
12 else	31 if $\mathsf{open}(\mathsf{sid})$
13 return $\perp$	32 if $b = 0$
$\mathsf{H}(\xi)$	33 $c_{\mathsf{sid}} := e_{\mathsf{sid}} - d_{\mathsf{sid}}$
14 $j{+}{+}$	34 $r_{\mathsf{sid}} := u_{\mathsf{sid}} - c_{\mathsf{sid}} \cdot x$
15 return h_j	35 else
	36 $d_{\mathsf{sid}} := e_{\mathsf{sid}} - c_{\mathsf{sid}}$
$\mathsf{H}^*(\mathsf{info})$	37 $s_{\mathsf{sid}} := v_{\mathsf{sid}} - d_{\mathsf{sid}} \cdot w$
16 if $\mathsf{info} = \overline{\mathsf{info}}$	38 else
17 if $b = 0$ return $\mathbf{z}$	39 return $\perp$
18 else return $\mathbf{g}^w$	40 $\mathsf{open}(\mathsf{sid}) := \mathbf{false}$
19 else return $\perp$	41 return $(c_{\mathsf{sid}}, r_{\mathsf{sid}}, d_{\mathsf{sid}}, s_{\mathsf{sid}})$

Fig. 3. Wrapper A that simulates the OMUF game to the adversary M

The Set of Successful Tuples. Let

$$\mathsf{Succ} := \{(\mathbf{I}, \mathsf{rand}, \overrightarrow{h})|\mathsf{A}(\mathbf{I}, \mathsf{rand}, \overrightarrow{h}) \neq \perp\}$$

be the set of all "successful" input tuples to the wrapper A. For a pair of instance and randomness $\mathbf{I}, \mathsf{rand}$, it is also useful to define $\mathsf{Succ}_{\mathbf{I},\mathsf{rand}}$ as the set of successful input tuples with instance $\mathbf{I}$ and randomness rand, i.e.,

$$\mathsf{Succ}_{\mathbf{I},\mathsf{rand}} := \left\{(\mathbf{I}', \mathsf{rand}', \overrightarrow{h}) \in \mathsf{Succ} \left| \begin{array}{l} \mathbf{I}' = \mathbf{I} \\ \mathsf{rand}' = \mathsf{rand} \end{array} \right. \right\}.$$

In the following we further denote by $\mathcal{I}$ the set of all possible instances, by $\mathcal{R}$ the set of all possible randomness of A, and by ϵ the success probability of A, i.e.,

$$\epsilon := \frac{|\mathsf{Succ}|}{|\mathcal{I} \times \mathcal{R} \times \mathbb{Z}_q^{\ell+1}|}$$

We show in Lemma 2 below (in Sect. 4.3) that the simulation using the $\mathbf{z}$-side witness is perfectly indistinguishable from the real execution where the $\mathbf{y}$-side witness is used (this is called the *witness indistinguishability* of the scheme), i.e., A simulates the OMUF game to M perfectly. Furthermore, if M succeeds, then so does A, since A copies M's output in this case (see lines 10–11 of Fig. 3). Therefore,

$$\epsilon = \mathrm{adv}_{\mathsf{M}}^{\ell\text{-1-info-OMUF}_{\mathsf{AO}}}.$$

4.2   Basic Definitions

We first define some concepts related to the wrapper A's input tuple $(\mathbf{I}, \mathsf{rand}, \overrightarrow{h})$, that will be used throughout the security proof.

Transcripts. We begin with the definition of the *query transcript*, which consists of the adversary's signing queries:

Definition 5 (Query Transcript). *Consider the wrapper A running on input tuple $(\mathbf{I}, \mathsf{rand}, \overrightarrow{h})$. The query transcript, denoted $\overrightarrow{e}(\mathbf{I}, \mathsf{rand}, \overrightarrow{h})$, is the vector of queries e_{sid} made to the sign_2 oracle (simulated by A) by the adversary M, ordered by sid.*

Next, we define (full) interaction *transcripts* between adversary M and wrapper A. These contain, in addition to $\overrightarrow{e}(\mathbf{I}, \mathsf{rand}, \overrightarrow{h})$, also M's sign_1 queries and the signatures from the output of M. This will be useful to argue about A's behavior on different inputs $(\mathbf{I}, \mathsf{rand}, \overrightarrow{h})$. Looking ahead, we will see that it is possible to deterministically transform $(\mathbf{I}, \mathsf{rand}, \overrightarrow{h})$ into a dual input $\Phi_{\mathsf{rand}, \overrightarrow{h}}(\mathbf{I}, \mathsf{rand}, \overrightarrow{h})$ that results in the same behavior as $(\mathbf{I}, \mathsf{rand}, \overrightarrow{h})$ (i.e., produces the same full transcript as $(\mathbf{I}, \mathsf{rand}, \overrightarrow{h})$), but inverts the type of the witness $\mathbf{I}$ from $\mathbf{y}$-side to $\mathbf{z}$-side (or vice-versa).

Definition 6 (Full Transcripts). *Consider the wrapper* A *running on input tuple* $(\mathbf{I}, \mathrm{rand}, \overrightarrow{h})$. *We denote by* $\mathrm{tr}(\mathbf{I}, \mathrm{rand}, \overrightarrow{h})$ *the transcript produced between* A *and the adversary* M, *i.e., all messages sent between the user (played by* M*) and the signer (played by* A*). Concretely,*

$$\mathrm{tr}(\mathbf{I}, \mathrm{rand}, \overrightarrow{h}) = \left(\mathsf{info}, (\overrightarrow{\mathbf{a}}, \overrightarrow{\mathbf{b}}), \overrightarrow{e}, (\overrightarrow{c}, \overrightarrow{r}, \overrightarrow{d}, \overrightarrow{s}), \mathsf{sig}_1, \dots \mathsf{sig}_{\ell+1} \right),$$

where $\mathsf{sig}_1, \dots, \mathsf{sig}_{\ell+1}$ *are the signatures output by* M. *(If* M *aborts at any point during the protocol or outputs fewer than* $\ell + 1$ *signatures, we consider any undefined entry to be* $\perp$*).*

Forking, Partners, and Triangles. We next define what it means for two input tuples to *fork* successfully—this corresponds to all cases where the reduction would be able to compute at least one of the two witnesses from the resulting signatures. However, without further work, the witness that can be computed might be the one that the reduction already knows.

Definition 7 (Successful forking). *We say two successful input tuples* $(\mathbf{I}, \mathrm{rand}, \overrightarrow{h}), (\mathbf{I}, \mathrm{rand}, \overrightarrow{h}') \in \mathsf{Succ}$ *fork from each other at index* $i \in [\ell+1]$ *if* $\overrightarrow{h}_{[i-1]} = \overrightarrow{h}'_{[i-1]}$ *but* $h_i \neq h_i$. *We denote the set of hash vector pairs* $(\overrightarrow{h}, \overrightarrow{h}')$ *such that* $(\mathbf{I}, \mathrm{rand}, \overrightarrow{h}), (\mathbf{I}, \mathrm{rand}, \overrightarrow{h}')$ *fork at index* i *as* $F_i(\mathbf{I}, \mathrm{rand})$.

We now define *partners*, which will play a key role in our analysis. Informally, two tuples $(\mathbf{I}, \mathrm{rand}, \overrightarrow{h})$ and $(\mathbf{I}, \mathrm{rand}, \overrightarrow{h}')$ are partners at some index i if they fork from this index and produce the same query transcript (but not necessarily the same full transcript).

Definition 8 (Partners). *We say two (successful) tuples* $(\mathbf{I}, \mathrm{rand}, \overrightarrow{h}), (\mathbf{I}, \mathrm{rand}, \overrightarrow{h}')$ *are partners at index* $i \in [\ell + 1]$ *if the followings hold:*

- $(\mathbf{I}, \mathrm{rand}, \overrightarrow{h})$ *and* $(\mathbf{I}, \mathrm{rand}, \overrightarrow{h}')$ *fork at index* i
- $\overrightarrow{e}(\mathbf{I}, \mathrm{rand}, \overrightarrow{h}) = \overrightarrow{e}(\mathbf{I}, \mathrm{rand}, \overrightarrow{h}')$

We denote the set of $(\overrightarrow{h}, \overrightarrow{h}')$ *such that* $(\mathbf{I}, \mathrm{rand}, \overrightarrow{h})$ *and* $(\mathbf{I}, \mathrm{rand}, \overrightarrow{h}')$ *are partners at index* i *by* $\mathrm{prt}_i(\mathbf{I}, \mathrm{rand})$. *We further denote by* $P_{\mathbf{I},\mathrm{rand}}$ *the following set:*

$$P_{\mathbf{I},\mathrm{rand}} = \left\{ (\mathbf{I}, \mathrm{rand}, \overrightarrow{h}) \in \mathsf{Succ}_{\mathbf{I},\mathrm{rand}} \middle| \exists \overrightarrow{h}', i \in [\ell+1] : (\overrightarrow{h}, \overrightarrow{h}') \in \mathrm{prt}_i(\mathbf{I}, \mathrm{rand}) \right\}$$

We define *triangles* in order to extend the nice properties of partners to more general forking tuples. Informally, a triangle consists of three vectors $\overrightarrow{h}, \overrightarrow{h}', \overrightarrow{h}''$ which all fork from each other at the same index, and also have the property that $\overrightarrow{h}$ and $\overrightarrow{h}'$ are partners at this index. This way, it is natural to view these vectors as corners of the triangle and any pair of two vectors as the sides.

Definition 9 (Triangles). *A triangle at index $i \in [\ell+1]$ with respect to* $\mathbf{I}, \mathsf{rand}$ *is a tuple of three (successful) tuples in the following set:*

$$
\triangle_i(\mathbf{I}, \mathsf{rand}) = \left\{
\begin{array}{l}
((\mathbf{I}, \mathsf{rand}, \overrightarrow{h}), \\
(\mathbf{I}, \mathsf{rand}, \overrightarrow{h}'), \\
(\mathbf{I}, \mathsf{rand}, \overrightarrow{h}''))
\end{array}
\left|
\begin{array}{l}
(\overrightarrow{h}, \overrightarrow{h}') \in \mathrm{prt}_i(\mathbf{I}, \mathsf{rand}) \\
(\overrightarrow{h}, \overrightarrow{h}'') \in F_i(\mathbf{I}, \mathsf{rand}) \\
(\overrightarrow{h}', \overrightarrow{h}'') \in F_i(\mathbf{I}, \mathsf{rand})
\end{array}
\right.
\right\}
$$

For a triangle $((\mathbf{I}, \mathsf{rand}, \overrightarrow{h}), (\mathbf{I}, \mathsf{rand}, \overrightarrow{h}'), (\mathbf{I}, \mathsf{rand}, \overrightarrow{h}'')) \in \triangle_i(\mathbf{I}, \mathsf{rand})$, *we call the pair of tuples* $((\mathbf{I}, \mathsf{rand}, \overrightarrow{h}), (\mathbf{I}, \mathsf{rand}, \overrightarrow{h}'))$ *the* base, *and* $((\mathbf{I}, \mathsf{rand}, \overrightarrow{h}), (\mathbf{I}, \mathsf{rand}, \overrightarrow{h}''))$ *and* $((\mathbf{I}, \mathsf{rand}, \overrightarrow{h}'), (\mathbf{I}, \mathsf{rand}, \overrightarrow{h}''))$ *the* sides. *We further refer to the tuples* $(\mathbf{I}, \mathsf{rand}, \overrightarrow{h})$, $(\mathbf{I}, \mathsf{rand}, \overrightarrow{h}')$, $(\mathbf{I}, \mathsf{rand}, \overrightarrow{h}'')$ *as* corners, *where the two corners incident to the base are called* base corners, *and the third corner is called the* top. *We will sometimes write* $(\overrightarrow{h}, \overrightarrow{h}', \overrightarrow{h}'') \in \triangle_i(\mathbf{I}, \mathsf{rand})$ *for compactness.*

Maximum Branching Index and Set. In the following we define two important characteristics of partner tuples. We begin by defining the *maximum branching index*, which is the index at which a partner tuple $(\mathbf{I}, \mathsf{rand}, \overrightarrow{h}) \in P_{\mathbf{I},\mathsf{rand}}$ has *the most partners*.

Definition 10 (Maximum Branching Index). *Fix a pair* $\mathbf{I}, \mathsf{rand}$. *The maximum branching index of a partner tuple* $(\mathbf{I}, \mathsf{rand}, \overrightarrow{h}) \in P_{\mathbf{I},\mathsf{rand}}$ *is the index at which* $(\mathbf{I}, \mathsf{rand}, \overrightarrow{h})$ *has the most partners, i.e.,*

$$
\mathrm{Br}_{\max}(\mathbf{I}, \mathsf{rand}, \overrightarrow{h}) = \mathrm{argmax}_{i \in [\ell+1]} \left| \left\{ \overrightarrow{h}' \middle| (\overrightarrow{h}, \overrightarrow{h}') \in \mathrm{prt}_i(\mathbf{I}, \mathsf{rand}) \right\} \right|.
$$

In case of ties, we pick the lowest such index.

The maximum branching index naturally defines a partition of any non-empty set of partnered tuples $P_{\mathbf{I},\mathsf{rand}}$, where the i-th set of the partition contains all tuples with maximum branching index i. We define the *maximum branching set* as the largest part of this partition, i.e., the largest subset of tuples that share a common maximum branching index.

Definition 11 (Maximum Branching Set). *For a pair* $\mathbf{I}, \mathsf{rand}$, *consider the partition of partner tuples according to their maximal branching indices:*

$$
B_i(\mathbf{I}, \mathsf{rand}) = \left\{ (\mathbf{I}, \mathsf{rand}, \overrightarrow{h}) \middle| \mathrm{Br}_{\max}(\mathbf{I}, \mathsf{rand}, \overrightarrow{h}) = i \right\}.
$$

The maximum branching set *of* $\mathbf{I}, \mathsf{rand}$ *is defined as the largest set among them, i.e.,*

$$
B_{max}(\mathbf{I}, \mathsf{rand}) = B_{i_{max}(\mathbf{I}, \mathsf{rand})}(\mathbf{I}, \mathsf{rand}),
$$

where

$$
i_{max}(\mathbf{I}, \mathsf{rand}) = \mathrm{argmax}_{i \in [\ell+1]} |B_i(\mathbf{I}, \mathsf{rand})|.
$$

In case of ties, we pick the lowest such index.

Note in particular that $B_{\mathrm{Br}_{\max}(\mathbf{I},\mathsf{rand},\overrightarrow{h})}(\mathbf{I}, \mathsf{rand})$ (henceforth $B_{\mathrm{Br}_{\max}}(\mathbf{I}, \mathsf{rand}, \overrightarrow{h})$ for simplicity) is the set of all tuples $(\mathbf{I}, \mathsf{rand}, \overrightarrow{h}')$ which have the same maximum branching index as $(\mathbf{I}, \mathsf{rand}, \overrightarrow{h})$ (so $(\mathbf{I}, \mathsf{rand}, \overrightarrow{h}) \in B_{\mathrm{Br}_{\max}}(\mathbf{I}, \mathsf{rand}, \overrightarrow{h})$).

4.3   The Mapping Φ

For any successful tuple $(\mathbf{I}, \mathsf{rand}, \overrightarrow{h})$, we now define the mapping $\Phi_{\mathsf{rand},\overrightarrow{h}}$ and prove its transcript preserving properties in Lemma 2. We remark that this mapping is not efficiently computable and will merely serve as a technical tool in our analysis.

Definition 12 (Mapping instances via transcript). *For* $(\mathbf{I}, \mathsf{rand}, \overrightarrow{h}) \in$ Succ*, we define* $\Phi_{\mathsf{rand},\overrightarrow{h}}(\mathbf{I})$ *as follows. For a* **y***-side instance* $\mathbf{I} = (1, w, \mathbf{y}, \overrightarrow{c}, \overrightarrow{r}, \overrightarrow{u})$, $\Phi_{\mathsf{rand},\overrightarrow{h}}(\mathbf{I})$ *is a* **z***-side instance that consists of*

$$b = 0 \qquad x = \mathrm{dlog}\, \mathbf{y} \qquad \mathbf{z} = \mathbf{g}^w \qquad \forall i \in [\ell]: d_i = e_i - c_i$$
$$\forall i \in [\ell]: s_i = u_i - d_i \cdot w \qquad \forall i \in [\ell]: v_i = c_i \cdot x + r_i$$

For a **z***-side instance* $\mathbf{I} = (0, x, \mathbf{z}, d, s, v)$, $\Phi_{\mathsf{rand},\overrightarrow{h}}(\mathbf{I})$ *is a* **y***-side instance that consists of*

$$b = 1 \qquad w = \mathrm{dlog}\, \mathbf{z} \qquad \mathbf{y} = \mathbf{g}^x \qquad \forall i \in [\ell]: c_i = e_i - d_i$$
$$\forall i \in [\ell]: r_i = v_i - c_i \cdot x \qquad \forall i \in [\ell]: u_i = d_i \cdot w + s_i$$

(where $\overrightarrow{e}$ *is the query vector produced by* $\mathsf{rand}, \overrightarrow{h}$ *using instance* $\mathbf{I}$*). We will sometimes use the notation* $\Phi_{\overrightarrow{e}}$ *instead of* $\Phi_{\mathsf{rand},\overrightarrow{h}}$ *for a given* $(\mathbf{I}, \mathsf{rand}, \overrightarrow{h})$*. We also define* $\Phi(\mathbf{I}, \mathsf{rand}, \overrightarrow{h}) = (\Phi_{\mathsf{rand},\overrightarrow{h}}(\mathbf{I}), \mathsf{rand}, \overrightarrow{h})$.

Lemma 2 ($\Phi_{\mathsf{rand},\overrightarrow{h}}$ **is a bijection that preserves transcripts**)**.** *Fix* $\mathsf{rand}, \overrightarrow{h}$. *For all tuples* $(\mathbf{I}, \mathsf{rand}, \overrightarrow{h}) \in$ Succ*,* $\Phi_{\mathsf{rand},\overrightarrow{h}}$ *is a self-inverse bijection and*

$$\mathsf{tr}(\mathbf{I}, \mathsf{rand}, \overrightarrow{h}) = \mathsf{tr}(\Phi_{\mathsf{rand},\overrightarrow{h}}(\mathbf{I}), \mathsf{rand}, \overrightarrow{h})$$

The proof is deferred to to the full version [24].

The lemma above shows that the Abe-Okamoto scheme is *witness indistinguishable*, i.e., a simulator that uses the **z**-side witness to sign (see see the full version [24]) creates a view identical to the real view to the adversary. In particular, this implies that the wrapper A simulates the ℓ-OMUF game to the adversary M perfectly.

Corollary 1. $(\mathbf{I}, \mathsf{rand}, \overrightarrow{h}) \in$ Succ $\Leftrightarrow (\Phi_{\mathsf{rand},\overrightarrow{h}}(\mathbf{I}), \mathsf{rand}, \overrightarrow{h}) \in$ Succ.

We look into the effect of the transcript mapping function on partner tuples. We have proven that $\Phi_{\mathsf{rand},\overrightarrow{h}}$ preserves the transcript (and hence success) of $(\mathbf{I}, \mathsf{rand}, \overrightarrow{h})$. However, note that this does not (by itself) imply that partnering tuples $(\mathbf{I}, \mathsf{rand}, \overrightarrow{h})$ and $(\mathbf{I}, \mathsf{rand}, \overrightarrow{h}')$ result in partnering tuples $(\Phi_{\mathsf{rand},\overrightarrow{h}}(\mathbf{I}), \mathsf{rand}, \overrightarrow{h})$ and $(\Phi_{\mathsf{rand},\overrightarrow{h}}(\mathbf{I}), \mathsf{rand}, \overrightarrow{h}')$, or $(\Phi_{\mathsf{rand},\overrightarrow{h}'}(\mathbf{I}), \mathsf{rand}, \overrightarrow{h})$ and $(\Phi_{\mathsf{rand},\overrightarrow{h}'}(\mathbf{I}), \mathsf{rand}, \overrightarrow{h}')$, respectively. Lemma 3 asserts that this is indeed the case.

Lemma 3 (Partners stay partners through Φ). *For all* $\mathbf{I}$, rand, *and vectors* $\overrightarrow{h}$, $\overrightarrow{h}'$,

$$(\overrightarrow{h}, \overrightarrow{h}') \in \mathrm{prt}_i(\mathbf{I}, \mathsf{rand}) \Leftrightarrow (\overrightarrow{h}, \overrightarrow{h}') \in \mathrm{prt}_i(\Phi_{\mathsf{rand}, \overrightarrow{h}}(\mathbf{I}), \mathsf{rand})$$

$$\Leftrightarrow (\overrightarrow{h}, \overrightarrow{h}') \in \mathrm{prt}_i(\Phi_{\mathsf{rand}, \overrightarrow{h}'}(\mathbf{I}), \mathsf{rand})$$

We refer the reader to the full version for the proof.

Corollary 2. $\mathrm{Br}_{\max}(\mathbf{I}, \mathsf{rand}, \overrightarrow{h}) = \mathrm{Br}_{\max}(\Phi_{\mathsf{rand}, \overrightarrow{h}}(\mathbf{I}), \mathsf{rand}, \overrightarrow{h})$.

4.4   Extracting a Witness from a Fork

Witness Extraction. We briefly recall how the reduction can compute a witness from two signatures from forking runs of the wrapper A. We say a signature $(\rho, \omega, \sigma, \delta)$ on a message m in the output of A on input $(\mathbf{I}, \mathsf{rand}, \overrightarrow{h})$ *corresponds to* a hash value h_i, if $\mathsf{H}(\mathbf{g}^\rho \mathbf{y}^\omega, \mathbf{g}^\sigma \mathbf{z}^\delta, \mathbf{z}, m)$ was the i-th hash query made to the random oracle H in this run of A. Informally we say that a witness *can be extracted* from $\mathbf{I}$, rand, and a pair of forking hash vectors $(\overrightarrow{h}, \overrightarrow{h}') \in F_i(\mathbf{I}, \mathsf{rand})$, if it can be efficiently computed from the two signatures corresponding to h_i and h'_i. We make this formal in the following definition.

Definition 13 (Witness Extraction). *Fix* $\mathbf{I}$, rand *and let* $(\overrightarrow{h}, \overrightarrow{h}') \in F_i(\mathbf{I},$ rand) *for some* $i \in [\ell + 1]$. *Moreover, denote* $\mathsf{sig}_i, \mathsf{sig}'_i$ *the signatures that correspond to* h_i *and* h'_i, *respectively. Consider the two witness extraction algorithms* $\mathsf{E_y}, \mathsf{E_z}$ *as described in Fig. 4. For* $\times \in \{\mathbf{y}, \mathbf{z}\}$, *we say that the* $\times$-side *witness can be extracted from* $(\mathbf{I}, \mathsf{rand}, \overrightarrow{h})$ *and* $(\mathbf{I}, \mathsf{rand}, \overrightarrow{h}')$ *at index* i *if* $\mathsf{E}_\times$ *on input* $(\mathsf{sig}_i, \mathsf{sig}'_i)$ *does not return* $\perp$.

Lemma 4. *Let* $\mathbf{I}, \mathsf{rand}, i, (\overrightarrow{h}, \overrightarrow{h}') \in F_i(\mathbf{I}, \mathsf{rand}), \mathsf{sig}_i, \mathsf{sig}'_i$, *and algorithms* $\mathsf{E_y}, \mathsf{E_z}$ *be as in Definition 13. Then at least one of* $\mathsf{E_y}$ *and* $\mathsf{E_z}$ *outputs a correct witness on input the two signatures* $\mathsf{sig}_i = (\rho_i, \omega_i, \sigma_i, \delta_i)$ *and* $\mathsf{sig}'_i = (\rho'_i, \omega'_i, \sigma'_i, \delta'_i)$ *corresponding to* h_i *and* h'_i. *More specifically,* $\mathsf{E_y}$ *outputs the* $\mathbf{y}$-side *witness if and only if* $\omega_i \neq \omega'_i$, *otherwise* $\mathsf{E_z}$ *outputs the* $\mathbf{z}$-side *witness.*

The proof is a standard forking argument and is deferred to to the full version [24].

Remark 1. We note that the witness may be contained in the instance $\mathbf{I}$, in which case the witness can be trivially extracted. For the purposes of the lemma we only consider the more interesting case that the witness can be computed from the two signatures directly, regardless of which witness was used for simulating the signing oracles.

$E_y((\rho_i, \omega_i, \sigma_i, \delta_i), (\rho_i', \omega_i', \sigma_i', \delta_i'))$	$E_z((\rho_i, \omega_i, \sigma_i, \delta_i), (\rho_i', \omega_i', \sigma_i', \delta_i'))$
42 if $(\omega_i \neq \omega_i')$	46 if $(\delta_i \neq \delta_i')$
43 return $x := \frac{\rho_i - \rho_i'}{\omega_i' - \omega_i}$	47 return $w := \frac{\sigma_i - \sigma_i'}{\delta_i' - \delta_i}$
44 else	48 else
45 return $\perp$	49 return $\perp$

Fig. 4. The two witness extraction algorithms from Definition 13

Witnesses in Triangles. We now show that if a witness can be extracted from the base of a triangle, it can also be extracted from at least one of the sides. This was previously shown in [4].

Corollary 3. *Fix* $\mathbf{I}, \mathsf{rand}$ *and let* $(\overrightarrow{h}, \overrightarrow{h}', \overrightarrow{h}'') \in \triangle_i(\mathbf{I}, \mathsf{rand})$ *for some* $i \in [\ell + 1]$. *Moreover, suppose that the* **y**-*side witness can be extracted from the base* $(\mathbf{I}, \mathsf{rand}, \overrightarrow{h}), (\mathbf{I}, \mathsf{rand}, \overrightarrow{h}')$ *of the triangle at index* i. *Then the* **y**-*side witness can also be extracted from at least one of the sides* $(\mathbf{I}, \mathsf{rand}, \overrightarrow{h}), (\mathbf{I}, \mathsf{rand}, \overrightarrow{h}'')$ *or* $(\mathbf{I}, \mathsf{rand}, \overrightarrow{h}'), (\mathbf{I}, \mathsf{rand}, \overrightarrow{h}'')$ *at index* i. *An analogous statement holds for the* **z**-*side witness.*

Proof. Toward a contradiction, suppose that the **y**-side witness can be extracted from the base $(\mathbf{I}, \mathsf{rand}, \overrightarrow{h}), (\mathbf{I}, \mathsf{rand}, \overrightarrow{h}')$ at index i, but can not be extracted at index i for either of the sides $(\mathbf{I}, \mathsf{rand}, \overrightarrow{h}), (\mathbf{I}, \mathsf{rand}, \overrightarrow{h}'')$ or $(\mathbf{I}, \mathsf{rand}, \overrightarrow{h}'), (\mathbf{I}, \mathsf{rand}, \overrightarrow{h}'')$. Then, by Lemma 4, $\omega_i = \omega_i''$ and $\omega_i' = \omega_i''$, so $\omega_i = \omega_i'$. By Lemma 4 again, the **y**-side witness can not be extracted from $(\mathbf{I}, \mathsf{rand}, \overrightarrow{h}), (\mathbf{I}, \mathsf{rand}, \overrightarrow{h}')$, a contradiction. An analogous argument can be made for the **z**-side. $\square$

We now define *both-sided triangle base corners* as triangle base corners $(\mathbf{I}, \mathsf{rand}, \overrightarrow{h})$ which remain base corners of some triangle at their maximal branching index when mapped via $\Phi_{\mathsf{rand}, \overrightarrow{h}}$. (Recall that by Corollary 2, the maximal branching index is preserved under Φ). On top of this, if $(\mathbf{I}, \mathsf{rand}, \overrightarrow{h})$ is a both-sided triangle base corner, and forms a triangle base with $(\mathbf{I}, \mathsf{rand}, \overrightarrow{h}')$ at index $\mathsf{Br}_{\max}(\mathbf{I}, \mathsf{rand}, \overrightarrow{h})$, then $(\Phi_{\mathsf{rand}, \overrightarrow{h}}(\mathbf{I}), \mathsf{rand}, \overrightarrow{h})$ and $(\Phi_{\mathsf{rand}, \overrightarrow{h}}, \mathsf{rand}, \overrightarrow{h}')$ also form a triangle base.

For every such tuple $(\mathbf{I}, \mathsf{rand}, \overrightarrow{h})$, we further define the set $D_i^{\mathbf{y}}(\mathbf{I}, \mathsf{rand}, \overrightarrow{h})$ of tuples that form a both-sided triangle base with $(\mathbf{I}, \mathsf{rand}, \overrightarrow{h})$ at index i from which the **y**-side witness can be extracted, and an analogous set $D_i^{\mathbf{z}}(\mathbf{I}, \mathsf{rand}, \overrightarrow{h})$ for the **z**-side witness. This allows us to then define sets $B_T^{\mathbf{y}}$ and $B_T^{\mathbf{z}}$ that contain tuples where the majority of both-sided triangle bases incident to the tuple allow for extraction of the **y**-side or **z**-side witness, respectively.

Definition 14 (Both-sided Triangle Base Corners). *We call elements of the set*

$$B_T := \left\{ (\mathbf{I}, \mathrm{rand}, \overrightarrow{h}) \,\middle|\, \begin{array}{c} \exists \overrightarrow{h}', \\ \overrightarrow{h}'', \overrightarrow{h}''' \end{array} : \begin{array}{c} (\overrightarrow{h}, \overrightarrow{h}', \overrightarrow{h}'') \in \triangle_{\mathrm{Br}_{\max}(\mathbf{I}, \mathrm{rand}, \overrightarrow{h})}(\mathbf{I}, \mathrm{rand}) \\ (\overrightarrow{h}, \overrightarrow{h}', \overrightarrow{h}''') \in \triangle_{\mathrm{Br}_{\max}(\mathbf{I}, \mathrm{rand}, \overrightarrow{h})}(\varPhi_{\mathrm{rand}, \overrightarrow{h}}(\mathbf{I}), \mathrm{rand}) \end{array} \right\}$$

both-sided triangle base corners. For any index $i \in [\ell + 1]$, we define sets

$$D_i^{\mathbf{y}}(\mathbf{I}, \mathrm{rand}, \overrightarrow{h}) := \left\{ (\mathbf{I}, \mathrm{rand}, \overrightarrow{h}') \,\middle|\, \begin{array}{c} \exists \overrightarrow{h}'', \\ \overrightarrow{h}''' \end{array} : \begin{array}{c} (\overrightarrow{h}, \overrightarrow{h}', \overrightarrow{h}'') \in \triangle_i(\mathbf{I}, \mathrm{rand}) \\ (\overrightarrow{h}, \overrightarrow{h}', \overrightarrow{h}''') \in \triangle_i(\varPhi_{\mathrm{rand}, \overrightarrow{h}}(\mathbf{I}), \mathrm{rand}) \\ \text{The } \mathbf{y}\text{-side witness can be} \\ \text{extracted from } (\mathbf{I}, \mathrm{rand}, \overrightarrow{h}), \\ (\mathbf{I}, \mathrm{rand}, \overrightarrow{h}') \text{ at index } i \end{array} \right\}$$

and $B_T^{\mathbf{y}} \subset B_T$ as

$$B_T^{\mathbf{y}} := \left\{ (\mathbf{I}, \mathrm{rand}, \overrightarrow{h}) \,\middle|\, \begin{array}{c} D^{\mathbf{y}}_{\mathrm{Br}_{\max}(\mathbf{I}, \mathrm{rand}, \overrightarrow{h})}(\mathbf{I}, \mathrm{rand}, \overrightarrow{h}) \neq \emptyset \\ \left| D^{\mathbf{y}}_{\mathrm{Br}_{\max}(\mathbf{I}, \mathrm{rand}, \overrightarrow{h})}(\mathbf{I}, \mathrm{rand}, \overrightarrow{h}) \right| \\ \geq \left| D^{\mathbf{z}}_{\mathrm{Br}_{\max}(\mathbf{I}, \mathrm{rand}, \overrightarrow{h})}(\mathbf{I}, \mathrm{rand}, \overrightarrow{h}) \right| \end{array} \right\}$$

We define sets $D_i^{\mathbf{z}}(\mathbf{I}, \mathrm{rand}, \overrightarrow{h})$ and $B_T^{\mathbf{z}}$ analogously.

Lemma 5 (Both-sided triangle bases produce the same witness on both sides).

1. $\varPhi(B_T^{\mathbf{y}}) = B_T^{\mathbf{y}}$ and $\varPhi(B_T^{\mathbf{z}}) = B_T^{\mathbf{z}}$;
2. $B_T^{\mathbf{y}} \cup B_T^{\mathbf{z}} = B_T$.

We defer the proof to to the full version [24].

We define $B_T^{\times}$ as the larger set of $B_T^{\mathbf{y}}$ and $B_T^{\mathbf{z}}$. By the second item of Lemma 5, $|B_T^{\times}| \geq \frac{1}{2}|B_T|$.

Let $B_{T,\mathbf{y}}^{\times}$ (resp. $B_{T,\mathbf{z}}^{\times}$) be the subset of $B_T^{\times}$ with $\mathbf{y}$-side instances (resp. $\mathbf{z}$-side instances). We stress that $B_T^{\mathbf{y}}$ and $B_{T,\mathbf{y}}^{\times}$ are two different sets: $(\mathbf{I}, \mathrm{rand}, \overrightarrow{h}) \in B_T^{\mathbf{y}}$ means that more both-sided triangle bases (with $(\mathbf{I}, \mathrm{rand}, \overrightarrow{h})$ as one of its corners) allow for extracting the $\mathbf{y}$-side witness than the $\mathbf{z}$-side witness; whereas $(\mathbf{I}, \mathrm{rand}, \overrightarrow{h}) \in B_{T,\mathbf{y}}^{\times}$ means that $(\mathbf{I}, \mathrm{rand}, \overrightarrow{h}) \in B_T^{\times}$ and $\mathbf{I}$ is a $\mathbf{y}$-side witness.

Lemma 6. $\left| B_{T,\mathbf{y}}^{\times} \right| = \left| B_{T,\mathbf{z}}^{\times} \right| = \frac{1}{2}\left| B_T^{\times} \right|$.

Proof. By the first item of Lemma 5, $\varPhi$ is a bijection within $B_T^{\times}$, and since $\varPhi$ maps a tuple with a $\mathbf{y}$-side instance to a tuple with a $\mathbf{z}$-side instance (and vice versa), we know that $\varPhi$ is a bijection between $B_{T,\mathbf{y}}^{\times}$ and $B_{T,\mathbf{z}}^{\times}$; therefore, $\left| B_{T,\mathbf{y}}^{\times} \right| = \left| B_{T,\mathbf{z}}^{\times} \right|$. Since $B_{T,\mathbf{y}}^{\times}$ and $B_{T,\mathbf{z}}^{\times}$ form a partition of $B_T^{\times}$, we know that $\left| B_{T,\mathbf{y}}^{\times} \right| + \left| B_{T,\mathbf{z}}^{\times} \right| = \left| B_T^{\times} \right|$, and the lemma follows. □

We now give a lower bound of the size of $B_T^\times$. Let $\epsilon_{B_T^\times}$ be the probability of getting a tuple in $B_T^\times$ while sampling uniformly at random, i.e.,

$$\epsilon_{B_T^\times} := \frac{|B_T^\times|}{\left|\mathcal{I} \times \mathcal{R} \times \mathbb{Z}_q^{\ell+1}\right|}.$$

Lemma 7 (Lower-bounding the size of $B_T^\times$). *Assume* $\epsilon \geq \dfrac{432\left(1-\frac{1}{(\ell+1)^2}\right)}{q}.$ *Then*

$$\epsilon_{B_T^\times} \geq \frac{\epsilon}{96}.$$

We defer the proof to the full version [24].

Finding Triangle Tops. In order for our security proof to go through, a key step is to compute the probability that the reduction hits a triangle side from which the $\times$-side witness can be extracted when forking the wrapper, independently of the witness that is being used by the reduction. This event is crucial in our proof because, assuming that the reduction samples one of these sides, it is likely that it did so with the witness opposite of $\times$, meaning that it extracts the witness $\times$ it *does not already know* with significant probability, hence solving the discrete logarithm problem. In order to lower bound the probability of the event above, we first define *relevant triangle tops* for a both-sided triangle base corner $(\mathbf{I}, \mathrm{rand}, \overrightarrow{h}) \in B_T^\times$. These are all the tuples $(\mathbf{I}, \mathrm{rand}, \overrightarrow{h}'')$ such that $(\overrightarrow{h}, \overrightarrow{h}', \overrightarrow{h}'')$ forms triangles at index i (where $\overrightarrow{h}'$ is as in the definition of both-sided triangle tops (Definition 14)).

Definition 15 (Relevant triangle tops). *For a tuple* $(\mathbf{I}, \mathrm{rand}, \overrightarrow{h})$, *define its relevant triangle tops at index i as tuples in the following set:*

$$T_{T,i}^\times(\mathbf{I}, \mathrm{rand}, \overrightarrow{h}) := \left\{ (\mathbf{I}, \mathrm{rand}, \overrightarrow{h}'') \left| \exists \overrightarrow{h}' : \begin{array}{c} (\overrightarrow{h}, \overrightarrow{h}', \overrightarrow{h}'') \in \triangle_i(\mathbf{I}, \mathrm{rand}) \\ \text{The } \times\text{-side witness} \\ \text{can be extracted from } (\mathbf{I}, \mathrm{rand}, \overrightarrow{h}), \\ (\mathbf{I}, \mathrm{rand}, \overrightarrow{h}') \text{ at } i \end{array} \right. \right\}$$

We will mostly consider relevant triangle tops at the maximum branching index $\mathrm{Br}_{\max}(\mathbf{I}, \mathrm{rand}, \overrightarrow{h})$ and we thus define $T_T^\times(\mathbf{I}, \mathrm{rand}, \overrightarrow{h}) := T_{T,\mathrm{Br}_{\max}(\mathbf{I}, \mathrm{rand}, \overrightarrow{h})}^\times(\mathbf{I}, \mathrm{rand}, \overrightarrow{h})$.

What remains to be shown is that many elements of $B_T^\times$ actually have many relevant triangle tops, regardless of whether they reside in $B_{T,\mathbf{y}}^\times$ or $B_{T,\mathbf{z}}^\times$, i.e., independently of the witness that they store. This ensures that when the reduction samples and then (partially) resamples the vectors during the forking process, it will hit a side from which the desired witness can be extracted with significant probability, as explained above.

Lemma 8 (There are enough relevant triangle tops). *There exists a subset $G_{\mathbf{y}} \subset B_{T,\mathbf{y}}^{\times}$ with $|G_{\mathbf{y}}| \geq \frac{3}{8}\left|B_{T,\mathbf{y}}^{\times}\right|$ such that for each $(\mathbf{I}, \text{rand}, \overrightarrow{h}) \in G_{\mathbf{y}}$,*

$$\left|T_T^{\times}(\mathbf{I}, \text{rand}, \overrightarrow{h})\right| \geq \frac{\epsilon_{B_T^{\times}}}{16(\ell+1)} \cdot q^{\ell-\text{Br}_{\max}(\mathbf{I}, \text{rand}, \overrightarrow{h})+2} - 2q^{\ell-\text{Br}_{\max}(\mathbf{I}, \text{rand}, \overrightarrow{h})+1}.$$

An analogous statement holds for $B_{T,\mathbf{z}}^{\times}$.

The proof is deferred to the full version [24].

Corollary 4. *Let $G_{\mathbf{y}}$ be as in Lemma 8. Then*

$$\Pr_{\substack{(\mathbf{I}, \text{rand}, \overrightarrow{h}) \xleftarrow{\$} \mathcal{I} \times \mathcal{R} \times \mathbb{Z}_q^{\ell+1} \\ i \xleftarrow{\$} [\ell+1], \overrightarrow{h}' \xleftarrow{\$} \mathbb{Z}_q^{\ell+1}{}_{|\overrightarrow{h}_{[i-1]}}}} \left[(\mathbf{I}, \text{rand}, \overrightarrow{h}') \in T_T^{\times}(\mathbf{I}, \text{rand}, \overrightarrow{h}) \,\middle|\, \begin{array}{l} (\mathbf{I}, \text{rand}, \overrightarrow{h}) \in G_{\mathbf{y}} \\ \text{Br}_{\max}(\mathbf{I}, \text{rand}, \overrightarrow{h}) = i \end{array} \right]$$

$$\geq \frac{\epsilon_{B_T^{\times}}}{16(\ell+1)} - \frac{2}{q}.$$

An analogous statement holds for $G_{\mathbf{z}}$.

Proof. Suppose $(\mathbf{I}, \text{rand}, \overrightarrow{h}) \in G_{\mathbf{y}}$ and $\text{Br}_{\max}(\mathbf{I}, \text{rand}, \overrightarrow{h}) = i$. Note that $\left|\mathbb{Z}_q^{\ell+1}{}_{|\overrightarrow{h}_{[i-1]}}\right| = q^{\ell-i+2}$. Therefore, the probability of sampling an $\overrightarrow{h}'$ such that $(\mathbf{I}, \text{rand}, \overrightarrow{h}') \in T_T^{\times}(\mathbf{I}, \text{rand}, \overrightarrow{h})$ is

$$\frac{\left|T_T^{\times}(\mathbf{I}, \text{rand}, \overrightarrow{h})\right|}{q^{\ell-i+2}} \geq \frac{\frac{\epsilon_{B_T^{\times}}}{16(\ell+1)} \cdot q^{\ell-i+2} - 2q^{\ell-i+1}}{q^{\ell-i+2}} = \frac{\epsilon_{B_T^{\times}}}{16(\ell+1)} - \frac{2}{q}.$$

$\square$

Opposing Base Corners. By Corollary 3 we know that each triangle with a relevant base has at least one relevant side. We now want to consider the probability of finding such a relevant side in the forking proof.

To this end, we consider *opposing base corners*—corners of relevant bases whose partners are in $G_{\mathbf{y}}$ or $G_{\mathbf{z}}$. See See the full version [24] for a graphic illustration. (Keep in mind that the sets $G_{\mathbf{y}}$ and $G_{\mathbf{z}}$ are the sets of both sided triangle base corners for which there exist many triangle tops).

Definition 16 (Opposing base corners).

$$O_T^{\times} := \left\{ (\mathbf{I}, \text{rand}, \overrightarrow{h}) \,\middle|\, \exists \overrightarrow{h}': \begin{array}{l} (\mathbf{I}, \text{rand}, \overrightarrow{h}') \in G_{\mathbf{y}} \cup G_{\mathbf{z}} \\ (\overrightarrow{h}, \overrightarrow{h}') \in \text{prt}_{\text{Br}_{\max}(\mathbf{I}, \text{rand}, \overrightarrow{h}')}(\mathbf{I}, \text{rand}) \\ \text{the } \times\text{-side witness can be} \\ \text{extracted from } (\mathbf{I}, \text{rand}, \overrightarrow{h}), \\ (\mathbf{I}, \text{rand}, \overrightarrow{h}') \text{ at } \text{Br}_{\max}(\mathbf{I}, \text{rand}, \overrightarrow{h}') \end{array} \right\}$$

Good Corners with Useful Tops. For each tuple $(\mathbf{I}, \mathrm{rand}, \overrightarrow{h})$ in $O_T^\times$ or $B_T^\times$ we define *useful triangle tops*—triangle tops that allow for extraction of the $\times$-side witness when combined with the base corner $(\mathbf{I}, \mathrm{rand}, \overrightarrow{h})$ (see the full version [24] for a graphic illustration):

Definition 17 (Useful triangle tops). *For any* $(\mathbf{I}, \mathrm{rand}, \overrightarrow{h}) \in O_T^\times \cup B_T^\times$, *define*

$$A_{T,i}^\times(\mathbf{I}, \mathrm{rand}, \overrightarrow{h}) := \left\{ \begin{array}{l} (\mathbf{I}, \mathrm{rand}, \overrightarrow{h}'') \\ \in T_{T,i}^\times(\mathbf{I}, \mathrm{rand}, \overrightarrow{h}) \end{array} \middle| \begin{array}{l} \text{the } \times \text{-side witness can be} \\ \text{extracted from } (\mathbf{I}, \mathrm{rand}, \overrightarrow{h}), \\ (\mathbf{I}, \mathrm{rand}, \overrightarrow{h}'') \text{ at index } i \end{array} \right\}$$

Recall that relevant base corners—those in $G_\mathbf{y}$ or $G_\mathbf{z}$—are tuples in $B_T^\times$ for which many triangle tops are relevant (i.e., the corresponding $T_T^\times$ set is large). We now consider a subset of these relevant base corners for which a lot of the relevant triangle tops are useful (i.e., the corresponding $A_T^\times$ set is large). We call these base corners *good*.

Definition 18 (Good base corners). *We say that a base corner in* $G_\mathbf{y} \cup G_\mathbf{z}$ *is good if it lies within the following set:*

$$\widehat{B_T^\times} := \left\{ (\mathbf{I}, \mathrm{rand}, \overrightarrow{h}) \in G_\mathbf{y} \cup G_\mathbf{z} \middle| \begin{array}{l} \left| A_T^\times(\mathbf{I}, \mathrm{rand}, \overrightarrow{h}) \right| \\ \geq \frac{1}{2} \left| T_T^\times(\mathbf{I}, \mathrm{rand}, \overrightarrow{h}) \right| \\ -q^{\ell - \mathrm{Br}_{\max}(\mathbf{I}, \mathrm{rand}, \overrightarrow{h}) + 1} \end{array} \right\}$$

We now want to show that if the set of good base corners is small, then there exist a lot of opposing base corners—which we call *good opposing base corners*—that fulfill a property analogous to good base corners.

Definition 19 (Good opposing base corners).

$$\widehat{O_T^\times} := \left\{ (\mathbf{I}, \mathrm{rand}, \overrightarrow{h}) \middle| \exists \overrightarrow{h}' : \begin{array}{l} (\mathbf{I}, \mathrm{rand}, \overrightarrow{h}') \in G_\mathbf{y} \cup G_\mathbf{z} \\ (\overrightarrow{h}, \overrightarrow{h}') \in \mathrm{prt}_{\mathrm{Br}_{\max}(\mathbf{I}, \mathrm{rand}, \overrightarrow{h}')}(\mathbf{I}, \mathrm{rand}) \\ \text{the } \times \text{-side witness can be} \\ \text{extracted from } (\mathbf{I}, \mathrm{rand}, \overrightarrow{h}), \\ (\mathbf{I}, \mathrm{rand}, \overrightarrow{h}') \text{ at } \mathrm{Br}_{\max}(\mathbf{I}, \mathrm{rand}, \overrightarrow{h}') \\ \left| A_{T, \mathrm{Br}_{\max}(\mathbf{I}, \mathrm{rand}, \overrightarrow{h}')}^\times(\mathbf{I}, \mathrm{rand}, \overrightarrow{h}) \right| \\ \geq \frac{1}{2} \left| T_{T, \mathrm{Br}_{\max}(\mathbf{I}, \mathrm{rand}, \overrightarrow{h}')}^\times(\mathbf{I}, \mathrm{rand}, \overrightarrow{h}) \right| \\ -q^{\ell - \mathrm{Br}_{\max}(\mathbf{I}, \mathrm{rand}, \overrightarrow{h}') + 1} \end{array} \right\}$$

Let $\widehat{B_{T,\mathbf{y}}^\times} \subset \widehat{B_T^\times}$ and $\widehat{O_{T,\mathbf{y}}^\times} \subset \widehat{O_T^\times}$ be analogous to $B_{T,\mathbf{y}}^\times \subset B_T^\times$, i.e., the subset of tuples with $\mathbf{y}$-side instances. We define $\widehat{B_{T,\mathbf{z}}^\times}$ and $\widehat{O_{T,\mathbf{z}}^\times}$ similarly.

Lemma 9. *If* $\left| \widehat{B_{T,\mathbf{y}}^\times} \right| < \frac{1}{2} |G_\mathbf{y}|$, *then* $\left| \widehat{O_{T,\mathbf{y}}^\times} \right| \geq \frac{1}{8(\ell+1)} |G_\mathbf{y}|$. *An analogous statement holds for* $\mathbf{z}$.

Proof. Let $F = G_\mathbf{y} \setminus \widehat{B^\times_{T,\mathbf{y}}}$ (so $|F| \geq \frac{1}{2}|G_\mathbf{y}|$). Consider any $(\mathbf{I}, \mathsf{rand}, \overrightarrow{h}') \in F$, and let $i = \mathrm{Br}_{\max}(\mathbf{I}, \mathsf{rand}, \overrightarrow{h}')$. Then

$$\left| A^\times_{T,i}(\mathbf{I}, \mathsf{rand}, \overrightarrow{h}') \right| < \frac{1}{2} \left| T^\times_{T,i}(\mathbf{I}, \mathsf{rand}, \overrightarrow{h}') \right| - q^{\ell-i+1}.$$

By Corollary 3, for any $(\overrightarrow{h}, \overrightarrow{h}', \overrightarrow{h}'') \in \triangle_i(\mathbf{I}, \mathsf{rand})$ such that the $\times$-side witness can be extracted from the base $(\mathbf{I}, \mathsf{rand}, \overrightarrow{h})$, $(\mathbf{I}, \mathsf{rand}, \overrightarrow{h}')$, if the $\times$-side witness cannot be extracted from $(\mathbf{I}, \mathsf{rand}, \overrightarrow{h}')$, $(\mathbf{I}, \mathsf{rand}, \overrightarrow{h}'')$, then it can be extracted from $(\mathbf{I}, \mathsf{rand}, \overrightarrow{h})$, $(\mathbf{I}, \mathsf{rand}, \overrightarrow{h}'')$. (All extractions mentioned above are at index i). Therefore,

$$\left| A^\times_{T,i}(\mathbf{I}, \mathsf{rand}, \overrightarrow{h}) \right| + \left| A^\times_{T,i}(\mathbf{I}, \mathsf{rand}, \overrightarrow{h}') \right| \geq \left| T^\times_{T,i}(\mathbf{I}, \mathsf{rand}, \overrightarrow{h}') \right|.$$

We note that all but $q^{\ell-i+1}$ elements of $T^\times_{T,i}(\mathbf{I}, \mathsf{rand}, \overrightarrow{h})$ are also elements of $T^\times_{T,i}(\mathbf{I}, \mathsf{rand}, \overrightarrow{h}')$. This is because $(\mathbf{I}, \mathsf{rand}, \overrightarrow{h}^*) \in T^\times_{T,i}(\mathbf{I}, \mathsf{rand}, \overrightarrow{h}) \setminus T^\times_{T,i}(\mathbf{I}, \mathsf{rand}, \overrightarrow{h}')$ implies that $(\overrightarrow{h}, \overrightarrow{h}^*) \in F_i(\mathbf{I}, \mathsf{rand})$ but $(\overrightarrow{h}', \overrightarrow{h}^*) \notin F_i(\mathbf{I}, \mathsf{rand})$, which means that $\overrightarrow{h}^*$ must share its first i entries with $\overrightarrow{h}'$ (recall that $\overrightarrow{h}$ and $\overrightarrow{h}'$ share the first $i-1$ entries), so there are at most $q^{\ell-i+1}$ such vectors. We get that

$$\left| T^\times_{T,i}(\mathbf{I}, \mathsf{rand}, \overrightarrow{h}') \right| \geq \left| T^\times_{T,i}(\mathbf{I}, \mathsf{rand}, \overrightarrow{h}) \right| - q^{\ell-i+1}.$$

Combining all inequalities above, we get

$$\begin{aligned}
\left| A^\times_{T,i}(\mathbf{I}, \mathsf{rand}, \overrightarrow{h}) \right| &\geq \left| T^\times_{T,i}(\mathbf{I}, \mathsf{rand}, \overrightarrow{h}') \right| - \left| A^\times_{T,i}(\mathbf{I}, \mathsf{rand}, \overrightarrow{h}') \right| \\
&> \left| T^\times_{T,i}(\mathbf{I}, \mathsf{rand}, \overrightarrow{h}') \right| - \left(\frac{1}{2} \left| T^\times_{T,i}(\mathbf{I}, \mathsf{rand}, \overrightarrow{h}') \right| - q^{\ell-i+1} \right) \\
&= \frac{1}{2} \left| T^\times_{T,i}(\mathbf{I}, \mathsf{rand}, \overrightarrow{h}') \right| + q^{\ell-i+1} \\
&\geq \frac{1}{2} \left(\left| T^\times_{T,i}(\mathbf{I}, \mathsf{rand}, \overrightarrow{h}) \right| - q^{\ell-i+1} \right) + q^{\ell-i+1} \\
&> \frac{1}{2} \left| T^\times_{T,i}(\mathbf{I}, \mathsf{rand}, \overrightarrow{h}) \right| - q^{\ell-i+1}
\end{aligned}$$

I.e., if $(\mathbf{I}, \mathsf{rand}, \overrightarrow{h}') \in F$, then all of its partners $(\mathbf{I}, \mathsf{rand}, \overrightarrow{h})$ at index i with which it forms triangle bases from which the $\times$-side witness can be extracted, are in $\widehat{O^\times_{T,\mathbf{y}}}$.

We now lower-bound the number of such partners $(\mathbf{I}, \mathsf{rand}, \overrightarrow{h})$. Define the set of tuples that yield the same query transcript with $(\mathbf{I}, \mathsf{rand}, \overrightarrow{h}')$ as

$$E(\mathbf{I}, \mathsf{rand}, \overrightarrow{h}') = \{(\mathbf{I}, \mathsf{rand}, \overrightarrow{h}^*) | \overrightarrow{e}(\mathbf{I}, \mathsf{rand}, \overrightarrow{h}^*) = \overrightarrow{e}(\mathbf{I}, \mathsf{rand}, \overrightarrow{h}')\}.$$

Note that $E(\mathbf{I}, \mathsf{rand}, \overrightarrow{h}')$ is the set of partners of $(\mathbf{I}, \mathsf{rand}, \overrightarrow{h})$ at any index. Consider a subset $E_i(\mathbf{I}, \mathsf{rand}, \overrightarrow{h}')$ of all tuples that fork from $(\mathbf{I}, \mathsf{rand}, \overrightarrow{h}')$ at index

i, i.e., $E_i(\mathbf{I}, \text{rand}, \overrightarrow{h}') = \{(\mathbf{I}, \text{rand}, \overrightarrow{h}^\star) | (\overrightarrow{h}^\star, \overrightarrow{h}') \in \text{prt}_i(\mathbf{I}, \text{rand})\}$. Recall that $i = \text{Br}_{\max}(\mathbf{I}, \text{rand}, \overrightarrow{h}')$. By the definition of maximum branching index, we have

$$\left|E_i(\mathbf{I}, \text{rand}, \overrightarrow{h}')\right| \geq \frac{1}{\ell+1}\left(\left|E(\mathbf{I}, \text{rand}, \overrightarrow{h}')\right| - 1\right) \geq \frac{1}{2(\ell+1)}\left|E(\mathbf{I}, \text{rand}, \overrightarrow{h}')\right|$$

(where the -1 comes from excluding $(\mathbf{I}, \text{rand}, \overrightarrow{h}')$ itself). As $(\mathbf{I}, \text{rand}, \overrightarrow{h}') \in B_T^\times$, it holds that at least half of the tuples in $E_i(\mathbf{I}, \text{rand}, \overrightarrow{h}')$, together with $(\mathbf{I}, \text{rand}, \overrightarrow{h}')$, allow for the extraction of the $\times$-side witness. This means that at least half of the tuples in $E_i(\mathbf{I}, \text{rand}, \overrightarrow{h}')$ are in $\widehat{O_{T,\mathbf{y}}^\times}$.

We have shown that for any $(\mathbf{I}, \text{rand}, \overrightarrow{h}') \in F$, at least $\frac{1}{4(\ell+1)}$ of tuples in $E(\mathbf{I}, \text{rand}, \overrightarrow{h}')$ are in $\widehat{O_{T,\mathbf{y}}^\times}$. Further note that for any $(\mathbf{I}_1, \text{rand}_1, \overrightarrow{h}_1)$ and $(\mathbf{I}_2, \text{rand}_2, \overrightarrow{h}_2)$, either $E(\mathbf{I}_1, \text{rand}_1, \overrightarrow{h}_1) = E(\mathbf{I}_2, \text{rand}_2, \overrightarrow{h}_2)$ or $E(\mathbf{I}_1, \text{rand}_1, \overrightarrow{h}_1) \cap E(\mathbf{I}_2, \text{rand}_2, \overrightarrow{h}_2) = \emptyset$.[4] Summing over all $E(\mathbf{I}, \text{rand}, \overrightarrow{h}')$ for some $(\mathbf{I}, \text{rand}, \overrightarrow{h}') \in F$, we get

$$|O_T^\times| \geq \frac{1}{4(\ell+1)} \sum_{\substack{E \text{ s.t. } E=E(\mathbf{I},\text{rand},\overrightarrow{h}') \\ \text{for some } (\mathbf{I},\text{rand},\overrightarrow{h}') \in F}} |E| \geq \frac{1}{4(\ell+1)} \sum_{\substack{E \text{ s.t. } E=E(\mathbf{I},\text{rand},\overrightarrow{h}') \\ \text{for some } (\mathbf{I},\text{rand},\overrightarrow{h}') \in F}} |E \cap F|$$

$$= \frac{1}{4(\ell+1)} \left| \bigcup_{\substack{E \text{ s.t. } E=E(\mathbf{I},\text{rand},\overrightarrow{h}') \\ \text{for some } (\mathbf{I},\text{rand},\overrightarrow{h}') \in F}} (E \cap F) \right|$$

$$= \frac{1}{4(\ell+1)} |F| \geq \frac{1}{8(\ell+1)} |G_\mathbf{y}|.$$

$\square$

Remark 2. We point out that it is at this point that we need to require the adversary to make *exactly* $\ell + 1$ hash queries (and thus lose a $\binom{Q_h}{\ell+1}$ factor in advantage). The proof of Lemma 9 would not go through with $Q_h > \ell + 1$ hash queries, as hash vectors in this case may fork at arbitrary indices that do not have a corresponding signature. Therefore, not every tuple in an E-set would also be a partner of every other tuple in the same E-set (with the definition of partners adapted to this setting, i.e., two tuples can only be partners if they both have a signature at their forking index).

In the following, we want to avoid the case distinction of whether triangle corners come from the B-sets or the O-sets. We therefore define *good triangle corners*:

---

[4] This is because $E(\mathbf{I}_1, \text{rand}_1, \overrightarrow{h}_1) \cap E(\mathbf{I}_2, \text{rand}_2, \overrightarrow{h}_2) \neq \emptyset$ implies that $\mathbf{I}_1 = \mathbf{I}_2$, $\text{rand}_1 = \text{rand}_2$, and $\overrightarrow{e}(\mathbf{I}_1, \text{rand}_1, \overrightarrow{h}_1) = \overrightarrow{e}(\mathbf{I}_2, \text{rand}_2, \overrightarrow{h}_2)$, which in turn implies that $E(\mathbf{I}_1, \text{rand}_1, \overrightarrow{h}_1) = E(\mathbf{I}_2, \text{rand}_2, \overrightarrow{h}_2)$.

Definition 20. *Let $\widehat{G_{\mathbf{y}}}$ be the larger set of $\widehat{B_{T,\mathbf{y}}^{\times}}$ and $\widehat{O_{T,\mathbf{y}}^{\times}}$. Furthermore, for a tuple $(\mathbf{I}, \mathrm{rand}, \overrightarrow{h}) \in \widehat{G_{\mathbf{y}}}$, let $t(\mathbf{I}, \mathrm{rand}, \overrightarrow{h})$ be an index at which many relevant triangle tops exist, i.e.,*

$$
t(\mathbf{I}, \mathrm{rand}, \overrightarrow{h}) = \begin{cases} \mathrm{Br}_{\max}(\mathbf{I}, \mathrm{rand}, \overrightarrow{h}) & (if \widehat{G_{\mathbf{y}}} = \widehat{B_{T,\mathbf{y}}^{\times}}) \\ \mathrm{Br}_{\max}(\mathbf{I}, \mathrm{rand}, \overrightarrow{h'}) & (if \widehat{G_{\mathbf{y}}} = \widehat{O_{T,\mathbf{y}}^{\times}}) \end{cases}
$$

(where $\overrightarrow{h}'$ is as in the definition of $\widehat{O_{T,\mathbf{y}}^{\times}}$). If multiple such $\overrightarrow{h}'$ (and thus multiple choices for t) exist, choose one that results in the smallest value of t. Define set $\widehat{G_{\mathbf{z}}}$ analogously, and for a tuple $(\mathbf{I}, \mathrm{rand}, \overrightarrow{h}) \in \widehat{G_{\mathbf{z}}}$, define $t(\mathbf{I}, \mathrm{rand}, \overrightarrow{h})$ analogously.

It is easy to see that for a good opposing base corner, the number of triangle tops is the same as for the corresponding tuple from $G_{\mathbf{y}} \cup G_{\mathbf{z}}$. We state this as a lemma.

Lemma 10.

$$
\Pr_{\substack{b \xleftarrow{\$} \{0,1\} \\ (\mathbf{I},\mathrm{rand},\overrightarrow{h}) \xleftarrow{\$} \mathcal{I}_b \times \mathcal{R} \times \mathbb{Z}_q{}^{\ell+1} \\ i \xleftarrow{\$} [\ell+1], \overrightarrow{h}' \xleftarrow{\$} \mathbb{Z}_q{}^{\ell+1}_{|\overrightarrow{h}_{[i-1]}}}} \left[\overrightarrow{h}' \in T_{T,i}^{\times}(\mathbf{I}, \mathrm{rand}, \overrightarrow{h}) \,\middle|\, \begin{array}{c} (\mathbf{I}, \mathrm{rand}, \overrightarrow{h}) \in \widehat{G_{\mathbf{y}}} \\ t(\mathbf{I}, \mathrm{rand}, \overrightarrow{h}) = i \end{array} \right] \geq \frac{\epsilon_{B_T^{\times}}}{16(\ell+1)} - \frac{2}{q}
$$

An analogous statement holds for $\widehat{G_{\mathbf{z}}}$.

Proof. If $\widehat{G_{\mathbf{y}}} = \widehat{B_{T,\mathbf{y}}^{\times}}$, then the lower bound is implied by Corollary 4. If $\widehat{G_{\mathbf{y}}} = \widehat{O_{T,\mathbf{y}}^{\times}}$, setting the partner from the proof of Lemma 8 to the triangle corner from $\widehat{O_{T,\mathbf{y}}^{\times}}$ yields this lower bound. $\square$

We furthermore note the following regarding the probability of sampling a tuple in $\widehat{G_{\mathbf{y}}}$ and $\widehat{G_{\mathbf{z}}}$:

Lemma 11.

$$
\Pr_{\substack{b \xleftarrow{\$} \{0,1\} \\ (\mathbf{I},\mathrm{rand},\overrightarrow{h}) \xleftarrow{\$} \mathcal{I}_b \times \mathcal{R} \times \mathbb{Z}_q{}^{\ell+1} \\ i \xleftarrow{\$} [\ell+1], \overrightarrow{h}' \xleftarrow{\$} \mathbb{Z}_q{}^{\ell+1}_{|\overrightarrow{h}_{[i-1]}}}} \Pr \left[(\mathbf{I}, \mathrm{rand}, \overrightarrow{h}) \in \widehat{G_{\mathbf{y}}} \right] \geq \frac{3}{128(\ell+1)} \epsilon_{B_T^{\times}}
$$

The same holds for $\widehat{G_{\mathbf{z}}}$.

We defer the proof to the [24]. We will use the sets $\widehat{G_{\mathbf{y}}}$ and $\widehat{G_{\mathbf{z}}}$ for simplicity in the forking proof to avoid case distinctions over whether $\widehat{B_{T,\mathbf{y}}^{\times}}$ or $\widehat{O_{T,\mathbf{y}}^{\times}}$ (or $\widehat{B_{T,\mathbf{z}}^{\times}}$ or $\widehat{O_{T,\mathbf{z}}^{\times}}$) are larger.

4.5   Forking Proof for Concurrent OMUF

In this section, we show that the Abe-Okamoto partially blind signature scheme AO is single-tag one-more unforgeable. We extend the proof to multiple tags in Sect. 4.6.

Theorem 1 (OMUF security for single-tag adversaries). *For all $\ell \in \mathbb{N}$, if there exists an adversary U that makes Q_h hash queries to random oracle H and (t_U, ϵ_U, ℓ)-breaks* 1-info-**OMUF**$_{AO}$ *with* $\epsilon_U \geq \dfrac{432\left(1-\frac{1}{(\ell+1)^2}\right)}{q} \cdot \binom{Q_h}{\ell+1}$, *then there exists an algorithm* B *that* $\left(t_B = 2t_U + O(Q_h{}^2), \epsilon_B \approx \dfrac{3\epsilon_U^2}{75423744 \cdot \binom{Q_h}{\ell+1}^2 \cdot (\ell+1)^3}\right)$- *breaks* **DLOG**.

Proof. We use the wrapper A as described in Fig. 3. We now construct a reduction B that plays the **DLOG** game as follows.

After B receives its discrete logarithm challenge **U**, it samples a bit $b \xleftarrow{\$} \{0,1\}$. It then samples an instance **I** of type b where it sets $\mathbf{z} := \mathbf{U}$ if $b = 0$ and $\mathbf{y} := \mathbf{U}$ if $b = 1$, and all other items uniformly at random from $\mathbb{Z}_q$. Furthermore, B samples a random tape rand for A and a random hash vector $\overrightarrow{h}$. After that, B runs A on $(\mathbf{I}, \mathsf{rand}, \overrightarrow{h})$. If A returns a set of $\ell + 1$ valid message-signature pairs, B chooses a random index $i \xleftarrow{\$} [\ell + 1]$. B then re-samples the vector $\overrightarrow{h}' \xleftarrow{\$} \mathbb{Z}_q{}^{\ell+1}_{|\overrightarrow{h}[i-1]}$ and runs A on $(\mathbf{I}, \mathsf{rand}, \overrightarrow{h}')$. If A outputs a second set of $\ell + 1$ valid message-signature pairs, B identifies the signature matching the hash value h_i and h_i' respectively in both pair (it aborts if there exists no such signature for h_i'). Denote the corresponding signature components to the ith hash query by $\rho_i, \rho_i', \omega_i, \omega_i', \sigma_i, \sigma_i', \delta_i, \delta_i'$ (see the full version [24]).

If $\omega_i \neq \omega_i'$ and $b = 1$, B computes

$$x := (\omega_i - \omega_i')^{-1} \cdot (\rho_i' - \rho_i)$$

as its output; if $\delta_i \neq \delta_i'$ and $b = 0$, B computes

$$w := (\delta_i - \delta_i')^{-1} \cdot (\sigma_i' - \sigma_i)$$

as its output. Otherwise B aborts. (If A fails to return a set of $\ell + 1$ valid message-signature pairs either time, B also aborts).

B runs A twice, and performs $\Theta(\ell)$ additional computation (in particular, B verifies up to $2(\ell + 1)$ signatures). Plugging in $t_A = t_U + O(Q_h{}^2)$, we get that

$$t_B = 2t_U + O(Q_h{}^2).$$

We now analyze the advantage of reduction B. Let ϵ_U be the advantage of U in the OMUF game, and ϵ be the probability that A outputs $\ell + 1$ valid message-signature pairs. By Lemma 1 and subsequent analysis in Sect. 4.1,

$$\epsilon \geq \frac{\epsilon_U}{\binom{Q_h}{\ell+1}}.$$

We can see that B internally runs the witness extracting algorithm E_y or E_z in Definition 13. Forking over the set $\widehat{G}$ of good base corners yields the theorem statement. We provide a detailed computation of the probability in the full version [24]. □

4.6 Extension to Multiple Tags

Theorem 2. *Let* U *be an adversary against* ℓ-**OMUF**$_{AO}$ *that runs in time* t_U, *closes at most* ℓ_{info} *signing sessions per tag* info, *closes at most* ℓ *signing sessions in total, and queries at most* Q_{info} *tags* info *to oracle* H^*. *Let* $adv_{Q_{info},\ell_{info},U}^{OMUF_{AO}}$ *be* U*'s advantage. Then there exists a reduction* B *against* 1-info-**OMUF**$_{AO}$ *that runs in time* $t_B \approx t_U$ *and makes at most* ℓ_{info} *signing queries and has advantage*

$$adv_B^{\ell_{info}\text{-}1\text{-}info\text{-}OMUF_{AO}} \geq \frac{adv_{Q_{info},\ell_{info},A}^{\ell-OMUF_{AO}} - \frac{\ell}{q}}{Q_{info}}.$$

The proof of this theorem mostly follows that in [4]. We provide it in the full version [24] for completeness.

References

1. Abe, M.: A secure three-move blind signature scheme for polynomially many signatures. In: Pfitzmann, B. (ed.) EUROCRYPT 2001. LNCS, vol. 2045, pp. 136–151. Springer, Heidelberg (2001). https://doi.org/10.1007/3-540-44987-6_9
2. Abe, M., Fujisaki, E.: How to date blind signatures. In: Kim, K., Matsumoto, T. (eds.) ASIACRYPT 1996. LNCS, vol. 1163, pp. 244–251. Springer, Heidelberg (1996). https://doi.org/10.1007/BFb0034851
3. Abe, M., Ohkubo, M.: A framework for universally composable non-committing blind signatures. In: Matsui, M. (ed.) ASIACRYPT 2009. LNCS, vol. 5912, pp. 435–450. Springer, Heidelberg (2009). https://doi.org/10.1007/978-3-642-10366-7_26
4. Abe, M., Okamoto, T.: Provably secure partially blind signatures. In: Bellare, M. (ed.) CRYPTO 2000. LNCS, vol. 1880, pp. 271–286. Springer, Heidelberg (2000). https://doi.org/10.1007/3-540-44598-6_17
5. Alkeilani Alkadri, N., Harasser, P., Janson, C.: BlindOR: an efficient lattice-based blind signature scheme from OR-proofs. In: Conti, M., Stevens, M., Krenn, S. (eds.) CANS 2021. LNCS, vol. 13099, pp. 95–115. Springer, Cham (2021). https://doi.org/10.1007/978-3-030-92548-2_6
6. Baldimtsi, F., Lysyanskaya, A.: Anonymous credentials light. In: ACM CCS 2013 (2013)
7. Benhamouda, F., Lepoint, T., Loss, J., Orrù, M., Raykova, M.: On the (in)security of ROS. In: Canteaut, A., Standaert, F.-X. (eds.) EUROCRYPT 2021, Part I. LNCS, vol. 12696, pp. 33–53. Springer, Cham (2021). https://doi.org/10.1007/978-3-030-77870-5_2
8. Camenisch, J.L., Piveteau, J.-M., Stadler, M.A.: Blind signatures based on the discrete logarithm problem (rump session). In: De Santis, A. (ed.) EUROCRYPT 1994. LNCS, vol. 950, pp. 428–432. Springer, Heidelberg (1995). https://doi.org/10.1007/BFb0053458

9. Camenisch, J., Neven, G., Shelat, A.: Simulatable adaptive oblivious transfer. In: Naor, M. (ed.) EUROCRYPT 2007. LNCS, vol. 4515, pp. 573–590. Springer, Heidelberg (2007). https://doi.org/10.1007/978-3-540-72540-4_33

10. Cao, T., Lin, D., Xue, R.: A randomized RSA-based partially blind signature scheme for electronic cash. Comput. Secur. **24**, 44–49 (2005)

11. Chaum, D.: Blind signatures for untraceable payments. In: Chaum, D., Rivest, R.L., Sherman, A.T. (eds.) Advances in Cryptology, pp. 199–203. Springer, Boston (1983). https://doi.org/10.1007/978-1-4757-0602-4_18

12. Chaum, D.: Elections with unconditionally-secret ballots and disruption equivalent to breaking RSA. In: Barstow, D., et al. (eds.) EUROCRYPT 1988. LNCS, vol. 330, pp. 177–182. Springer, Heidelberg (1988). https://doi.org/10.1007/3-540-45961-8_15

13. Chaum, D., Fiat, A., Naor, M.: Untraceable electronic cash. In: Goldwasser, S. (ed.) CRYPTO 1988. LNCS, vol. 403, pp. 319–327. Springer, New York (1990). https://doi.org/10.1007/0-387-34799-2_25

14. Chow, S.S.M., Hui, L.C.K., Yiu, S.M., Chow, K.P.: Two improved partially blind signature schemes from bilinear pairings. In: Boyd, C., González Nieto, J.M. (eds.) ACISP 2005. LNCS, vol. 3574, pp. 316–328. Springer, Heidelberg (2005). https://doi.org/10.1007/11506157_27

15. Cramer, R., Damgård, I., Schoenmakers, B.: Proofs of partial knowledge and simplified design of witness hiding protocols. In: Desmedt, Y.G. (ed.) CRYPTO 1994. LNCS, vol. 839, pp. 174–187. Springer, Heidelberg (1994). https://doi.org/10.1007/3-540-48658-5_19

16. Fischlin, M.: Round-optimal composable blind signatures in the common reference string model. In: Dwork, C. (ed.) CRYPTO 2006. LNCS, vol. 4117, pp. 60–77. Springer, Heidelberg (2006). https://doi.org/10.1007/11818175_4

17. Fischlin, M., Schröder, D.: Security of blind signatures under aborts. In: Jarecki, S., Tsudik, G. (eds.) PKC 2009. LNCS, vol. 5443, pp. 297–316. Springer, Heidelberg (2009). https://doi.org/10.1007/978-3-642-00468-1_17

18. Fujioka, A., Okamoto, T., Ohta, K.: A practical secret voting scheme for large scale elections. In: Seberry, J., Zheng, Y. (eds.) AUSCRYPT 1992. LNCS, vol. 718, pp. 244–251. Springer, Heidelberg (1993). https://doi.org/10.1007/3-540-57220-1_66

19. Hanatani, Y., Komano, Y., Ohta, K., Kunihiro, N.: Provably secure electronic cash based on blind multisignature schemes. In: Di Crescenzo, G., Rubin, A. (eds.) FC 2006. LNCS, vol. 4107, pp. 236–250. Springer, Heidelberg (2006). https://doi.org/10.1007/11889663_20

20. Hauck, E., Kiltz, E., Loss, J., Nguyen, N.K.: Lattice-based blind signatures, revisited. In: Micciancio, D., Ristenpart, T. (eds.) CRYPTO 2020, Part II. LNCS, vol. 12171, pp. 500–529. Springer, Cham (2020). https://doi.org/10.1007/978-3-030-56880-1_18

21. Hazay, C., Katz, J., Koo, C.-Y., Lindell, Y.: Concurrently-secure blind signatures without random oracles or setup assumptions. In: Vadhan, S.P. (ed.) TCC 2007. LNCS, vol. 4392, pp. 323–341. Springer, Heidelberg (2007). https://doi.org/10.1007/978-3-540-70936-7_18

22. Juels, A., Luby, M., Ostrovsky, R.: Security of blind digital signatures (extended abstract). In: Kaliski, B.S. (ed.) CRYPTO 1997. LNCS, vol. 1294, pp. 150–164. Springer, Heidelberg (1997). https://doi.org/10.1007/BFb0052233

23. Kastner, J., Loss, J., Xu, J.: On pairing-free blind signature schemes in the algebraic group model. In: Hanaoka, G., Shikata, J., Watanabe, Y. (eds.) PKC 2022. LNCS, vol. 13178, pp. 468–497. Springer, Cham (2022). https://doi.org/10.1007/978-3-030-97131-1_16

24. Kastner, J., Loss, J., Xu, J.: The Abe-Okamoto partially blind signature scheme revisited cryptology. ePrint Archive, Paper 2022/1232 (2022)
25. Katsumata, S., Nishimaki, R., Yamada, S., Yamakawa, T.: Round-optimal blind signatures in the plain model from classical and quantum standard assumptions. In: Canteaut, A., Standaert, F.-X. (eds.) EUROCRYPT 2021, Part I. LNCS, vol. 12696, pp. 404–434. Springer, Cham (2021). https://doi.org/10.1007/978-3-030-77870-5_15
26. Maitland, G., Boyd, C.: A provably secure restrictive partially blind signature scheme. In: Naccache, D., Paillier, P. (eds.) PKC 2002. LNCS, vol. 2274, pp. 99–114. Springer, Heidelberg (2002). https://doi.org/10.1007/3-540-45664-3_7
27. Martinet, G., Poupard, G., Sola, P.: Cryptanalysis of a partially blind signature scheme or *how to make* $100 *bills with* $1 *and* $2 *ones*. In: Di Crescenzo, G., Rubin, A. (eds.) FC 2006. LNCS, vol. 4107, pp. 171–176. Springer, Heidelberg (2006). https://doi.org/10.1007/11889663_15
28. Okamoto, T.: Efficient blind and partially blind signatures without random oracles. In: Halevi, S., Rabin, T. (eds.) TCC 2006. LNCS, vol. 3876, pp. 80–99. Springer, Heidelberg (2006). https://doi.org/10.1007/11681878_5
29. Papachristoudis, D., Hristu-Varsakelis, D., Baldimtsi, F., Stephanides, G.: Leakage-resilient lattice-based partially blind signatures (2019)
30. Pointcheval, D., Stern, J.: Provably secure blind signature schemes. In: Kim, K., Matsumoto, T. (eds.) ASIACRYPT 1996. LNCS, vol. 1163, pp. 252–265. Springer, Heidelberg (1996). https://doi.org/10.1007/BFb0034852
31. Pointcheval, D., Stern, J.: Security arguments for digital signatures and blind signatures. J. Cryptol. **13**, 361–396 (2000)
32. Rückert, M.: Lattice-based blind signatures. In: Abe, M. (ed.) ASIACRYPT 2010. LNCS, vol. 6477, pp. 413–430. Springer, Heidelberg (2010). https://doi.org/10.1007/978-3-642-17373-8_24
33. Schnorr, C.P.: Security of blind discrete log signatures against interactive attacks. In: Qing, S., Okamoto, T., Zhou, J. (eds.) ICICS 2001. LNCS, vol. 2229, pp. 1–12. Springer, Heidelberg (2001). https://doi.org/10.1007/3-540-45600-7_1
34. Schröder, D., Unruh, D.: Security of blind signatures revisited. In: Fischlin, M., Buchmann, J., Manulis, M. (eds.) PKC 2012. LNCS, vol. 7293, pp. 662–679. Springer, Heidelberg (2012). https://doi.org/10.1007/978-3-642-30057-8_39
35. Tessaro, S., Zhu, C.: Short Pairing-free blind signatures with exponential security. Cryptology ePrint Archive, Report 2022/047 (2022)
36. Tyagi, N., et al.: A fast and simple partially oblivious PRF, with applications. Cryptology ePrint Archive, Report 2021/864 (2021)
37. Yi, X., Lam, K.-Y.: A new blind ECDSA scheme for bitcoin transaction anonymity. In: ASIACCS 2019 (2019)
38. Zhang, F., Safavi-Naini, R., Susilo, W.: Efficient verifiably encrypted signature and partially blind signature from bilinear pairings. In: Johansson, T., Maitra, S. (eds.) INDOCRYPT 2003. LNCS, vol. 2904, pp. 191–204. Springer, Heidelberg (2003). https://doi.org/10.1007/978-3-540-24582-7_14

An Analysis of the Algebraic Group Model

Cong Zhang[1,4], Hong-Sheng Zhou[2(✉)], and Jonathan Katz[3]

[1] Zhejiang University, Hangzhou, China
[2] Virginia Commonwealth University, Richmond, USA
hszhou@vcu.edu
[3] University of Maryland, College Park, USA
[4] ZJU-Hangzhou Global Scientific and Technological Innovation Center,
Hangzhou, China

Abstract. The algebraic group model (AGM), formalized by Fuchs-bauer, Kiltz, and Loss, has recently received significant attention. One of the appealing properties of the AGM is that it is viewed as being (strictly) weaker than the generic group model (GGM), in the sense that hardness results for algebraic algorithms imply hardness results for generic algorithms, and generic reductions in the AGM (namely, between the algebraic formulations of two problems) imply generic reductions in the GGM. We highlight that as the GGM and AGM are currently formalized, this is not true: hardness in the AGM may not imply hardness in the GGM, and a generic reduction in the AGM may not imply a similar reduction in the GGM.

1 Introduction

Computational Assumptions in Groups. Since the work of Diffie and Hellman [DH76], there have been many elegant cryptographic schemes and protocols whose security can be based on the conjectured hardness of certain computational problems in (cyclic) groups. To prove security in this setting, we begin by formulating an appropriate hardness assumption relative to a group $\mathbb{G}$. It is important to stress that such assumptions are always relative to some *specific encoding* of the elements of $\mathbb{G}$, even though this is not always made explicit. For example, let $\mathbb{G}$ denote the cyclic group of order p, for some large prime p such that $q = 2p + 1$ is also prime. One way to encode elements of $\mathbb{G}$ is to represent them as integers in the order-p subgroup of $\mathbb{Z}_q^*$, with the group operation corresponding to multiplication modulo q. Another way to encode elements of $\mathbb{G}$

The authorship order is randomized, and all authors contributed equally.

C. Zhang—Work supported in part by Zhejiang University Education Foundation Qizhen Scholar Foundation. Portions of this work were done while at the University of Maryland.

H.-S. Zhou—Work supported in part by NSF grant CNS-1801470, a Google Faculty Research Award, and a research gift from Ergo Platform.

S. Agrawal and D. Lin (Eds.): ASIACRYPT 2022, LNCS 13794, pp. 310–322, 2022.
https://doi.org/10.1007/978-3-031-22972-5_11

is to represent them as integers in $\mathbb{Z}_p$ with the group operation corresponding to addition modulo p. Even though these are both encodings of the same group (or, put differently, these two encodings are isomorphic), it is reasonable to conjecture that the discrete-logarithm problem is hard in the first case even though it is trivial to solve in the second case. Encodings matter.

Beyond understanding the hardness of specific problems in groups, it is also interesting to understand relations between different problems. Here, too, the specific encoding may affect the relations that can be shown.

Unfortunately, the current state-of-the-art in complexity theory does not allow us to prove any unconditional hardness results relative to any concrete group encoding; namely, we do not know how to prove lower bounds on the probability with which arbitrary algorithms can solve some problem relative to any specific encoding of group elements. (On the other hand, we can in some cases show unconditional relations between certain problems, e.g., that—for any encoding—hardness of the decisional Diffie-Hellman assumption implies hardness of the discrete-logarithm problem.) This has motivated researchers to investigate the possibility of proving hardness results for *specific* (restricted) classes of algorithms. Two examples we study in this work are the class of *generic* algorithms, and the class of *algebraic* algorithms. We discuss these in more detail below.

Generic Algorithms and the Generic Group Model. Roughly speaking, generic algorithms operate independently of any particular group encoding. That is, they ignore the specific encoding of group elements but instead treat group elements "generically." Studying this class of algorithms is well motivated, since several well-known algorithms such as the baby-step/giant-step algorithm [PH78] and Pollard's rho algorithm [Pol78] are generic in this sense. A generic algorithm has the advantage that it works for *any* encoding of group elements; it cares only about the mathematical structure of the underlying group, but not its encoding. Researchers have proposed different variants of the so-called *generic group model* (GGM) [Nec94, Sho97, Mau05, MPZ20] in an effort to formally define the notion of a generic algorithm. We describe these in Sect. 2.1.

It is possible to prove unconditional hardness results in the generic group model. While the implications of such results for hardness relative to any specific encoding are unclear, at a minimum a proof of hardness in the GGM serves as a "sanity check" that some assumption is reasonable. Indeed, the GGM is now a canonical tool to establish (some level of) confidence for new hardness assumptions or even security of cryptographic schemes. Moreover, for some specific group encodings (e.g., appropriately defined elliptic-curve groups) and certain problems, the best known algorithms are indeed generic.

Algebraic Algorithms and the Algebraic Group Model. Other work [BV98, PV05] has proposed a class of so-called *algebraic* algorithms. Roughly speaking, algebraic algorithms are allowed to exploit the concrete encoding of group elements, but they are restricted to only being able to derive (new) group elements via group operations involving elements they have been provided with as input. Fuchsbauer, Kiltz, and Loss [FKL18] recently formalized this idea as the *algebraic group model* (AGM), and showed a number of results in that model. A number of papers have since extended those results [MTT19, KLX20,BFL20,ABK+21,GT21], and have used the AGM to prove security of cryptographic constructions [MBKM19,RS20,KLX22,FPS20,ABB+20,RZ21].

The utility of studying the AGM is not immediately clear, and we are not aware of any natural group-theoretic algorithms that are algebraic but not generic.[1] We are also not aware of any unconditional hardness results for problems of cryptographic interest in the AGM. (Though lower bounds for some problems are possible in an extension of the AGM [KLX20].) Nevertheless, Fuchsbauer, Kiltz, and Loss argue that the AGM can be useful for studying *reductions* between problems. As an example, for many group encodings the best-known algorithm for solving the computational Diffie-Hellman problem is to first solve the discrete-logarithm problem. In the AGM, one can prove that this is inherent, in the sense that hardness of the latter implies hardness of the former. Such a result is not known to hold in general.

To justify the usefulness of studying reductions in the AGM, Fuchsbauer et al. [FKL18, Lemma 2.2] claim that a generic reduction between two problems in the AGM implies a generic reduction between those problems in the GGM. That is, if there is a generic reduction R showing that the hardness of (algebraic) security game **H** implies hardness of (algebraic) security game **G**, and if **H** can be proven unconditionally hard for generic algorithms, then **G** is also hard in the GGM. Their proof of this claim uses the following natural steps:

Step 1: Assume toward a contradiction that **G** is not hard in the GGM, so there is a generic algorithm A_{gen}^G that succeeds in game **G** with high probability.

Step 2: Since any generic algorithm is also algebraic, the reduction R can be applied to A_{gen}^G to obtain an algebraic algorithm $A_{alg}^H := R^{A_{gen}^G}$ that succeeds with high probability in **H**.

Step 3: Since R is generic, A_{alg}^H is in fact a generic algorithm. But this contradicts the fact that **H** is unconditionally hard for generic algorithms.

While the above is appealing, some steps are not entirely clear. In particular, it is not obvious that the intuitive conversion of a generic algorithm to an algebraic algorithm (cf. step 2) is applicable in all contexts. And even if it is possible to transform the generic algorithm A_{gen}^G to an "equivalent" algebraic algorithm A_{alg}^G, it is then not clear that the resulting algebraic algorithm $R^{A_{alg}^G}$ can be meaningfully transformed back into a generic algorithm (cf. step 3).

1.1   Our Results

Seeking to better understand the algebraic group model and its relationship to the generic group model, we provide self-contained descriptions of both and then

---

[1] Fuchsbauer et al. claim that index-calculus algorithms are algebraic, but without any further explanation. It is not clear to us what they mean by this.

explore their relationship. We first observe that the formal definition of algebraic algorithms proposed by Fuchsbauer et al. may not match the intended intuition. Specifically, Fuchsbauer et al. define an algorithm to be algebraic if it provides a *representation* of any group elements it outputs. (See more details in Sect. 3.) This is supposed to ensure that "the only way for an algebraic algorithm to output a new group element is to derive it via group multiplication from known group elements" [FKL18]. However, we show in Sect. 3 an algorithm that obtains a new group element using non-group operations but can still output a valid representation of that element.

More importantly, we show that a generic algorithm need not be algebraic, and that it might be hard to convert a generic algorithm to an algebraic one with the same behavior. In particular, we show a counterexample to the claim of Fuchsbauer et al. as described above by showing a security game called the "binary encoding game (**beg**)" and describing a generic reduction from the discrete-logarithm problem to this game. (Note that the discrete-logarithm problem is unconditionally hard in the GGM, and is conjectured to be hard for certain encodings.) But we show that **beg** is easy in the GGM. Thus:

Theorem 1 (Informal). *A generic reduction in the AGM does not imply a generic reduction in the GGM.*

Concurrent Work. In concurrent and independent work, Zhandry [Zha22] studies the GGM and the AGM and gives a new definition of the AGM. We consider the AGM as originally defined by Fuchsbauer et al. [FKL18]. Zhandry does not address the relationship between generic reductions in the AGM vs. the GGM, and does not show any analogue of our theorem stated above.

Discussion. Our counterexample to [FKL18, Lemma 2.2] is admittedly contrived, and an important next step is to understand whether there is some subclass of security games for which a version of their lemma might still apply. Any such subclass should of course be broad enough to include security games of cryptographic relevance. More generally, we believe that a more-formal treatment of the GGM and AGM, and the relationship between them, is warranted.

2 Preliminaries

In this section, we provide the required background and preliminaries.

Algorithms. We denote by $s \leftarrow S$ uniform sampling of variable s from the finite set S. Algorithms are written using uppercase letters (e.g., A, B). To indicate that a probabilistic algorithm A runs on some inputs $(x_1, \ldots, x_n)$ and returns y, we write $y \leftarrow A(x_1, \ldots, x_n)$. If A has oracle access to an algorithm B during its execution, we write $y \leftarrow A^B(x_1, \ldots, x_n)$.

Group Encodings. Throughout this work, we restrict attention to the cyclic group $\mathbb{G}$ of prime order p. For concreteness, we often identify $\mathbb{G}$ with the additive group $\mathbb{Z}_p$. As highlighted in the Introduction, however, we explicitly focus on *encodings* of this group and its impact on algorithms for various problems.

Fix some $\ell \geq \lceil \log p \rceil$. An encoding $\sigma : \mathbb{Z}_p \to \{0,1\}^\ell$ is simply an injective map from $\mathbb{Z}_p$ to $\{0,1\}^\ell$. We let id be the "trivial" encoding in which each element of $\mathbb{Z}_p$ is encoded as a binary integer in the range $\{0, \ldots, p-1\}$ using $\lceil \log p \rceil$ bits and then padded to the left with 0s to a string of length ℓ, and the group operation is addition modulo p. We often use boldface capital letters (e.g., $\mathbf{X}, \mathbf{Y}$) for encodings of group elements.

As notational shorthand, we will often use standard multiplicative notation for group operations on (encodings of) group elements. Thus, $\sigma(x)\sigma(y)$ refers to computing the group operation on the group elements $\sigma(x), \sigma(y)$; note that $\sigma(x)\sigma(y) = \sigma(x+y \bmod p)$. Similarly, for r an integer, $\sigma(x)^r$ refers to computing the r-fold group operation on $\sigma(x)$; of course, $\sigma(x)^r = \sigma(xr \bmod p)$.

---

dlog$_\sigma^\mathsf{A}$

01 $z \leftarrow \mathbb{Z}_p$
02 $z' \leftarrow \mathsf{A}(\sigma(1), \sigma(z))$
03 Return 1 iff $z' = z$

Fig. 1. The discrete-logarithm game **dlog**.

Security Games. We use a variant of code-based security games [BR06]. A game $\mathbf{G}_\sigma$, parameterized by an encoding σ, has a main procedure and (possibly zero) oracle procedures that describe how oracle queries are answered. Figure 1 shows an example of the discrete-logarithm game. We let $\mathbf{G}_\sigma^\mathsf{A}$ be a random variable denoting the boolean output of game $\mathbf{G}_\sigma$ played by algorithm A. Algorithm A is said to *succeed* when $\mathbf{G}_\sigma^\mathsf{A} = 1$, and the success probability of A in $\mathbf{G}_\sigma$ is $\mathbf{Succ}_{\mathbf{G}_\sigma}^\mathsf{A} \stackrel{\text{def}}{=} \Pr[\mathbf{G}_\sigma^\mathsf{A} = 1]$. $\mathbf{Time}_{\mathbf{G}_\sigma}^\mathsf{A}$ denotes the running time of $\mathbf{G}_\sigma^\mathsf{A}$.

Security Reductions. Let $\mathbf{G}_\sigma, \mathbf{H}_\sigma$ be security games. We write $\mathbf{H}_\sigma \xrightarrow{(\Delta_t, \Delta_\epsilon)} \mathbf{G}_\sigma$ if there is an algorithm R (a *reduction*) such that for all algorithms A, algorithm $\mathsf{B} := \mathsf{R}^\mathsf{A}$ satisfies

$$\mathbf{Succ}_{\mathbf{H}_\sigma}^\mathsf{B} \geq \frac{1}{\Delta_\epsilon} \cdot \mathbf{Succ}_{\mathbf{G}_\sigma}^\mathsf{A}, \quad \mathbf{Time}_{\mathbf{H}_\sigma}^\mathsf{B} \leq \Delta_t \cdot \mathbf{Time}_{\mathbf{G}_\sigma}^\mathsf{A}.$$

Note that the reduction may depend on the encoding, and a reduction with some parameters may exist for certain encodings and not others. (For examples of reductions that depend on the encoding, see [Gal12, Section 21.4].)

2.1   Generic Algorithms

In general, an algorithm A in a game $\mathbf{G}_\sigma$ may depend on σ. A *generic* algorithm, however, should be "oblivious" to the encoding used. At least two ways of formalizing this have been considered, one due to Shoup [Sho97] and another due to Maurer [Mau05].

Shoup's approach can be summarized as requiring a generic algorithm A to work for all encodings. Since A cannot depend on the encoding, however, it must be provided with some way to perform group operations. We can provide such capabilities (both to A and possibly the game itself) by giving access to two oracles that we collectively call *encoding oracles*:

- a *labeling oracle* that takes as input $x \in \mathbb{Z}_p$ and returns $\sigma(x)$, and
- a *group-operation oracle* that takes as input strings s_1, s_2 and does the following: if $s_1 = \sigma(x)$ and $s_2 = \sigma(y)$, return $\sigma(x + y \bmod p)$; otherwise, return $\bot$.

Calls to these oracles take unit time by definition. We denote by $\widehat{\mathbf{G}}_\sigma$ the modification of a game $\mathbf{G}_\sigma$ to include the above oracles. We define[2] $\mathbf{Succ}_{\mathbf{G}}^{\mathsf{A}} = \min_\sigma\{\mathbf{Succ}_{\widehat{\mathbf{G}}_\sigma}^{\mathsf{A}}\}$ and $\mathbf{Time}_{\mathbf{G}}^{\mathsf{A}} = \max_\sigma\{\mathbf{Time}_{\widehat{\mathbf{G}}_\sigma}^{\mathsf{A}}\}$.

Maurer's approach to defining the generic group model is similar in spirit, but technically different. Here, roughly speaking, a generic algorithm does not have access to any encodings of group elements at all; instead, the algorithm is able to access group elements only via abstract "handles." One way to formalize this is by initializing a counter ctr to 1, and a table T to empty, at the beginning of an algorithm's execution. The algorithm now has access to three encoding oracles that take the following form:

- the labeling oracle takes as input $x \in \mathbb{Z}_p$. It stores (ctr, x) in T and increments ctr. (It does not return anything.)
- the group-operation oracle takes as input positive integers $i, j < \mathsf{ctr}$. It finds (i, x) and (j, y) in T, stores $(\mathsf{ctr}, x + y \bmod p)$ in T, and increments ctr. (It does not return anything.)
- an *equality oracle* takes as input positive integers $i, j < \mathsf{ctr}$. It finds (i, x) and (j, y) in T and returns 1 if $x = y$ and 0 otherwise.

Note that ctr can also be incremented, and T populated, by actions that occur as part of the game itself rather than due to actions of the algorithm. For example, the discrete-logarithm game of Fig. 1 would be modified to store $(1, x)$ in T and increment ctr as part of step 1; it would also provide no input to A in step 2. Moreover, if A is supposed to output a group element in some game, then it should instead output a positive integer $i < \mathsf{ctr}$; this will correspond to an output of $\sigma(x)$, where (i, x) is the record stored in T. If we let $\widetilde{\mathbf{G}}$ denote the appropriate modification of a game $\mathbf{G}$, then we again define $\mathbf{Succ}_{\mathbf{G}}^{\mathsf{A}} = \min_\sigma\{\mathbf{Succ}_{\widetilde{\mathbf{G}}_\sigma}^{\mathsf{A}}\}$ and $\mathbf{Time}_{\mathbf{G}}^{\mathsf{A}} = \max_\sigma\{\mathbf{Time}_{\widetilde{\mathbf{G}}_\sigma}^{\mathsf{A}}\}$.

---

[2] While one might expect $\mathbf{Succ}_{\widehat{\mathbf{G}}_\sigma}^{\mathsf{A}}$ and $\mathbf{Time}_{\widehat{\mathbf{G}}_\sigma}^{\mathsf{A}}$ to be independent of σ (and that is the case for "natural" generic algorithms), that may not be the case in general.

We refer to *Shoup-generic* and *Maurer-generic* algorithms depending on the model under consideration. With respect to either model, we say a game $\mathbf{G}$ is (t, ϵ)-hard in the generic group model if for every generic algorithm A it holds that $\mathbf{Time}_{\mathbf{G}}^{\mathsf{A}} \leq t \Rightarrow \mathbf{Succ}_{\mathbf{G}}^{\mathsf{A}} \leq \epsilon$.

A generic algorithm A (in either model) with success probability $\epsilon = \mathbf{Succ}_{\mathbf{G}}^{\mathsf{A}}$ may fail to run in a "standard" game $\mathbf{G}_{\sigma}$ where the encoding oracles are not present. However, for any σ it is possible to modify a generic algorithm A (of either type) in a black-box way (by simulating the encoding oracles) to obtain an algorithm A_{σ} where $\mathbf{Succ}_{\mathbf{G}_{\sigma}}^{\mathsf{A}_{\sigma}} = \epsilon$ and the time complexity of A_{σ} relative to A reflects only the time required to perform group operations for the encoding σ.

$$\boxed{\begin{array}{l} \mathbf{S}_{\sigma}^{\mathsf{A}} \\ \\ 01 \;\; b_1 \cdots b_\ell := \sigma(1) \\ 02 \;\; b \leftarrow \mathsf{A} \\ 03 \;\; \text{Return 1 iff } b = b_1 \end{array}}$$

Fig. 2. Game $\mathbf{S}$.

For completeness, we remark that there can be games where the optimal success probabilities for generic algorithms differ depending on which generic group model is used. Consider, for example, game $\mathbf{S}$ in Fig. 2. With respect to Shoup's notion of generic algorithms, there exists a trivial algorithm A that has success probability 1 for any encoding. (A simply asks its encoding oracle for $\sigma(1)$ and outputs the first bit.) On the other hand, with respect to Maurer's notion of generic algorithms it is not possible to have an algorithm that achieves success probability better than $1/2$ for all encodings.

Generic Reductions. For games $\mathbf{G}$, $\mathbf{H}$, we write $\mathbf{H} \xmapsto{(\Delta_t, \Delta_\epsilon)}_{\text{S-GGM}} \mathbf{G}$ if there is a generic *reduction* R (where generic is defined relative to Shoup's model) such that for all generic algorithms A, algorithm $\mathsf{B} := \mathsf{R}^{\mathsf{A}}$ (which is generic) satisfies

$$\mathbf{Succ}_{\mathbf{H}}^{\mathsf{B}} \geq \frac{1}{\Delta_\epsilon} \cdot \mathbf{Succ}_{\mathbf{G}}^{\mathsf{A}}, \quad \mathbf{Time}_{\mathbf{H}}^{\mathsf{B}} \leq \Delta_t \cdot \mathbf{Time}_{\mathbf{G}}^{\mathsf{A}}.$$

We define $\mathbf{H} \xmapsto{(\Delta_\epsilon, \Delta_t)}_{\text{M-GGM}} \mathbf{G}$ analogously with respect to Maurer's model.

3 Algebraic Algorithms

Algebraic algorithms are another example of a class of algorithms that has been considered in the context of group-theoretic problems. The main idea, which seems to have originated in work of Paillier and Vergnaud [PV05], is to try to capture the notion of an algorithm that, on the one hand, only performs group operations on group elements (as in the generic group model) but, on the other hand, can depend on a specific encoding σ rather than being "encoding-agnostic." As one might expect, formalizing this intuition is not straightforward. The main difficulty is that, with an encoding σ fixed, it is no longer clear how to differentiate between arbitrary computations on group elements done by an algorithm and group operations on group elements (that may depend on σ).

Fuchsbauer et al. [FKL18] suggest one way to resolve the above dilemma. Roughly speaking, they do not attempt to place any restrictions on intermediate computations done by an algorithm, but instead require that any group elements output by an algorithm must[3] be accompanied by a *representation* relative to the ordered set S of group elements (the *base set*) provided to that algorithm as input. (A representation of a group element $\sigma(y)$ relative to an ordered set of group elements $S = (\sigma(x_1), \ldots, \sigma(x_k))$ is a vector $\boldsymbol{r} = (r_1, \ldots, r_k) \in \mathbb{Z}_p^k$ such that $\sigma(y) = \prod_i \sigma(x_i)^{r_i}$. Note this implies $y = \sum_i r_i x_i \bmod p$.) To ensure nontriviality, we assume the set S always includes $\sigma(1)$ (i.e., $\sigma(1)$ is always provided to the algorithm as input). To be clear: (1) group elements received by the algorithm as a result of an oracle call are added to the base set (in particular, the base set can expand during the course of executing the algorithm; a valid representation must always be relative to the current set), and (2) an algebraic algorithm must also provide a representation for any group elements it provides as input to some oracle call. This is intended to capture the intuitive idea that the only way for an algebraic algorithm to generate a new group element is to derive it via group operations from known group elements.

$$\boxed{\begin{array}{l} \mathsf{A}(1) \\ \hline 01\ r_1, r_2 \leftarrow \mathbb{Z}_p \\ 02\ s \leftarrow r_1 \cdot r_2 \bmod p \\ 03\ \text{Output } (s, s) \end{array}}$$

Fig. 3. Algorithm A with respect to the identity encoding id.

We note a number of unsatisfactory aspects of this definition:

1. The definition does not constrain algorithms that do not output group elements. In particular, for the discrete-logarithm game the class of algebraic algorithms is the class of all algorithms. Thus, the AGM is useless for analyzing games where the algorithm's output is not a group element.
2. The formalization considers some algorithms to be algebraic even though they may not match one's intuition regarding what operations an algebraic algorithm should be allowed to perform. For example, consider algorithm A

---

[3] Formally, if an algorithm violates these requirements in some game, then by definition it does not succeed.

in Fig. 3 with respect to the identity encoding $\sigma = \mathsf{id}$. This algorithm samples two group elements r_1, r_2 and then *multiplies* them modulo p. The group operation here, however, is *addition* modulo p. Nevertheless, A is able to output a representation of the resulting group element s with respect to its base set $\{1\}$. More generally, whenever the encoding is such that the discrete-logarithm problem can be solved efficiently relative to that encoding, any algorithm can be made algebraic by simply computing a representation of any group elements it outputs.

3. Perhaps more problematic is that, once a particular encoding σ is fixed, it is not immediately well-defined what it means for an algorithm to "be provided with a group element as input" or to "output a group element." To get a sense of the problem, consider a game involving an oracle that, on input i, returns the ith bit of $\sigma(x)$. At no point in time does an algorithm in that game ever receive a group element from an oracle; nevertheless, it is clearly trivial to construct an algorithm that outputs the group element $\sigma(x)$. Fuchsbauer et al. attempt to address this issue by requiring that "other elements" (i.e., non-group elements) "must not depend on any group elements," but it is not clear how such a requirement can be formalized.

It seems intuitive, and one would like to claim, that algebraic algorithms are at least as strong as generic algorithms, in the sense that for any game G, any generic algorithm A with $\epsilon = \mathbf{Succ}_{\mathsf{G}}^{\mathsf{A}}$, and any encoding σ, it is possible to construct an algebraic algorithm A_σ achieving the same success probability by simply simulating the encoding oracles for A and keeping track of the representations of any group elements generated during the execution of A. As already noted by Fuchsbauer et al., however, thus is not necessarily true (at least for Shoup's version of the GGM). Specifically, in Shoup's GGM it may be possible to obliviously sample group elements (i.e., without knowledge of their discrete logarithm), something that is ruled out by definition in the AGM.

We show in Sect. 4, in the context of reductions, that it is also not the case that all generic algorithms can be made algebraic.

Although Fuchsbauer et al. conjecture that any Maurer-generic algorithm can be made algebraic, we are not aware of a proof of that conjecture.

Generic Reductions for Algebraic Adversaries. Fuchsbauer et al. [FKL18] consider generic reductions for algebraic adversaries; we map their definition to our syntax. For games G, H, write $\mathsf{H} \xRightarrow{(\Delta_t, \Delta_\epsilon)}_{\mathsf{alg}} \mathsf{G}$ if there is a generic reduction R such that for all algebraic algorithms A and encodings σ, algorithm $\mathsf{B} := \mathsf{R}^{\mathsf{A}}$ satisfies

$$\mathbf{Succ}_{\mathsf{H}_\sigma}^{\mathsf{B}} \geq \frac{1}{\Delta_\epsilon} \cdot \mathbf{Succ}_{\mathsf{G}_\sigma}^{\mathsf{A}}, \quad \mathbf{Time}_{\mathsf{H}_\sigma}^{\mathsf{B}} \leq \Delta_t \cdot \mathbf{Time}_{\mathsf{G}_\sigma}^{\mathsf{A}}. \tag{1}$$

The reduction is deliberately restricted to be generic (rather than algebraic) so that, as explained by Fuchsbauer et al., if A is algebraic then B will be algebraic, and if A is generic then B will be generic. We remark that the above notion seems to be useful only for Shoup-generic reductions; it is not clear how a Maurer-generic reduction would be able to provide A with encodings of group elements that A expects.

We observe several technical issues with the above definition:

– It is not true that when R is generic and A is algebraic, the composed algorithm $B = R^A$ is algebraic. Indeed, a simple counterexample is a generic algorithm R that obliviously samples a group element and outputs it.
– Even if (1) holds for all algebraic algorithms A, it is not clear whether it holds for all generic algorithms A. Again, this is because a generic algorithm is not necessarily algebraic (nor is it necessarily possible to construct an algebraic algorithm with the same behavior).

4   A Counterexample

In this section, we give an example showing that a generic reduction in the AGM does not imply a reduction in the GGM. Concretely, we show two games **G** and **H** such that: (1) there is a Shoup-generic reduction from **H** to **G**; (2) **H** is hard for Shoup-generic algorithms; but (3) **G** is easy for Shoup-generic algorithms. Formally,

Theorem 2. *There are security games* **G** *and* **H** *such that*

– $\mathbf{H} \xrightarrow{(2,1)}_{\text{alg}} \mathbf{G}$;
– **H** *is* $(t, O(t^2/p))$-*hard with respect to Shoup-generic algorithms;*
– *There is a Shoup-generic algorithm* A *running in time* $O(\ell)$ *with* $\mathbf{Succ}^A_{\mathbf{G}} = 1$.

$\mathbf{beg}^A_\sigma$

01 $z \leftarrow \mathbb{Z}_p$
02 parse $\mathbf{Z} = \sigma(z)$ as the bitstring $z_1 \cdots z_\ell$
03 $(\mathbf{X}, \mathbf{U}_1, \ldots, \mathbf{U}_\ell) := (\sigma(1), \sigma(z_1), \ldots, \sigma(z_\ell))$
04 $\mathbf{Z}' \leftarrow A(\mathbf{X}, \mathbf{U}_1, \ldots, \mathbf{U}_\ell)$
05 Return 1 iff $(\mathbf{Z}' = \mathbf{Z})$

Fig. 4. The binary encoding game.

Proof. Take **H** as the discrete-logarithm game from Fig. 1. Security game **G** is one we introduce called the *binary encoding game* (**beg**); see Fig. 4. Hardness of **H** for Shoup-generic algorithms was shown in [Sho97]. It is easy to see that there is a Shoup-generic algorithm A with $\mathbf{Succ}^A_{\mathbf{beg}} = 1$: for each i, the algorithm sets $z'_i := 1$ iff $\mathbf{U}_i = \mathbf{X}$ and then outputs $\mathbf{Z}' := z'_1 \cdots z'_\ell$. Thus, it only remains to prove that $\mathbf{dlog} \xrightarrow{(2,1)}_{\text{alg}} \mathbf{beg}$.

Fix an encoding σ. Generic reduction R is given $(\mathbf{X}, \mathbf{Z}) := (\sigma(1), \sigma(z))$ as input along with oracle access to an algebraic algorithm A; it proceeds as follows:

1. Parse $\mathbf{Z}$ as the bitstring $z_1 \cdots z_\ell$. Set $z_0 := 1$.
2. Request $\mathbf{I} = \sigma(0)$ from the labeling oracle.
3. For $i = 1, \ldots, \ell$ do: if $z_i = 0$ then set $\mathbf{U}_i := \mathbf{I}$; else set $\mathbf{U}_i := \mathbf{X}$.
4. Run $\mathsf{A}(\mathbf{X}, \mathbf{U}_1, \ldots, \mathbf{U}_\ell)$ to obtain output $\mathbf{Z}'$ along with a representation $(x_0, x_1, \ldots, x_\ell)$ such that $\mathbf{Z}' = \mathbf{X}^{x_0} \cdot \mathbf{U}_1^{x_1} \cdots \mathbf{U}_\ell^{x_\ell}$.
5. Output $\sum_{i=0}^{\ell} z_i \cdot x_i \bmod p$.

We now analyze the behavior of R. Let A be an algebraic adversary with $\epsilon = \mathbf{Succ}_{\mathbf{beg}_\sigma}^{\mathsf{A}}$. Observe that when A is run as a subroutine by R in game $\mathbf{dlog}_\sigma$, the input provided to A is distributed identically as in $\mathbf{beg}_\sigma$. Moreover, whenever A succeeds it holds that (1) $\mathbf{Z}' = \mathbf{Z}$ and (2) $z = \sum z_i \cdot x_i \bmod p$. It follows that $\mathbf{Succ}_{\mathbf{dlog}_\sigma}^{\mathsf{R}^\mathsf{A}} = \epsilon$. This completes the proof.

In light of our counterexample, we highlight where the proof of the result by Fuchsbauer et al. [FKL18, Lemma 2.2] fails. Note that the generic algorithm A with $\mathbf{Succ}_{\mathbf{beg}}^{\mathsf{A}} = 1$ that we construct as part of the proof cannot be converted to an algebraic algorithm. (More formally: the "trivial" attempt to convert A to an algebraic algorithm by monitoring its encoding oracles does not work, nor do we see another way to convert A to an algebraic algorithm. Moreover, as long as the discrete-logarithm problem is hard for some particular encoding σ, there is no efficient way to convert A into an algebraic algorithm with similar behavior relative to that encoding.)

5   Concluding Thoughts

Our work raises several issues related to the AGM. For starters, it is unclear whether the AGM is a meaningful class of algorithms to study; on the one hand because we are not aware of any (natural) algebraic algorithms that are not generic, and on the other hand because it is not clear whether the class of algebraic algorithms contains the class of generic algorithms. This may be related to the issue of whether the current formalization of the AGM adequately captures one's intuition about what "algebraic" algorithms can do, as well as whether it is possible to formally define what it means for certain objects not to "depend on" encodings of group elements. One argument in favor of the AGM is that it provides a meaningful way to analyze reductions; our work shows, however, that the main justification for studying reductions in the AGM does not hold in certain settings.

Our work raises several interesting directions for future work, including the question of developing other formalism for the algebraic group model, as well as formally resolving the question as to whether the class of algebraic algorithms strictly includes the class of Maurer-generic algorithms.

Acknowledgments. We thank Steven Galbraith for interesting discussions about the AGM and helpful comments on an earlier draft of this work.

References

[ABB+20] Abdalla, M., Barbosa, M., Bradley, T., Jarecki, S., Katz, J., Xu, J.: Universally composable relaxed password authenticated key exchange. In: Micciancio, D., Ristenpart, T. (eds.) CRYPTO 2020. LNCS, vol. 12170, pp. 278–307. Springer, Cham (2020). https://doi.org/10.1007/978-3-030-56784-2_10

[ABK+21] Abdalla, M., Barbosa, M., Katz, J., Loss, J., Xu, J.: Algebraic adversaries in the universal composability framework. In: Tibouchi, M., Wang, H. (eds.) ASIACRYPT 2021. LNCS, vol. 13092, pp. 311–341. Springer, Cham (2021). https://doi.org/10.1007/978-3-030-92078-4_11

[BFL20] Bauer, B., Fuchsbauer, G., Loss, J.: A classification of computational assumptions in the algebraic group model. In: Micciancio, D., Ristenpart, T. (eds.) CRYPTO 2020. LNCS, vol. 12171, pp. 121–151. Springer, Cham (2020). https://doi.org/10.1007/978-3-030-56880-1_5

[BR06] Bellare, M., Rogaway, P.: The security of triple encryption and a framework for code-based game-playing proofs. In: Vaudenay, S. (ed.) EUROCRYPT 2006. LNCS, vol. 4004, pp. 409–426. Springer, Heidelberg (2006). https://doi.org/10.1007/11761679_25

[BV98] Boneh, D., Venkatesan, R.: Breaking RSA may not be equivalent to factoring. In: Nyberg, K. (ed.) EUROCRYPT 1998. LNCS, vol. 1403, pp. 59–71. Springer, Heidelberg (1998). https://doi.org/10.1007/BFb0054117

[DH76] Diffie, W., Hellman, M.E.: New directions in cryptography. IEEE Trans. Inf. Theory 22(6), 644–654 (1976)

[FKL18] Fuchsbauer, G., Kiltz, E., Loss, J.: The algebraic group model and its applications. In: Shacham, H., Boldyreva, A. (eds.) CRYPTO 2018. LNCS, vol. 10992, pp. 33–62. Springer, Cham (2018). https://doi.org/10.1007/978-3-319-96881-0_2

[FPS20] Fuchsbauer, G., Plouviez, A., Seurin, Y.: Blind Schnorr signatures and signed ElGamal encryption in the algebraic group model. In: Canteaut, A., Ishai, Y. (eds.) EUROCRYPT 2020. LNCS, vol. 12106, pp. 63–95. Springer, Cham (2020). https://doi.org/10.1007/978-3-030-45724-2_3

[Gal12] Galbraith, S.D.: Mathematics of Public Key Cryptography. Cambridge University Press, Cambridge (2012)

[GT21] Ghoshal, A., Tessaro, S.: Tight state-restoration soundness in the algebraic group model. In: Malkin, T., Peikert, C. (eds.) CRYPTO 2021. LNCS, vol. 12827, pp. 64–93. Springer, Cham (2021). https://doi.org/10.1007/978-3-030-84252-9_3

[KLX20] Katz, J., Loss, J., Xu, J.: On the Security of Time-Lock Puzzles and Timed Commitments. In: Pass, R., Pietrzak, K. (eds.) TCC 2020. LNCS, vol. 12552, pp. 390–413. Springer, Cham (2020). https://doi.org/10.1007/978-3-030-64381-2_14

[KLX22] Kastner, J., Loss, J., Xu, J.: On pairing-free blind signature schemes in the algebraic group model. In: Hanaoka, G., Shikata, J., Watanabe, Y. (eds.) PKC 2022. Lecture Notes in Computer Science(), vol. 13178, pp. 468–497. Springer, Cham (2022). https://doi.org/10.1007/978-3-030-97131-1_16

[Mau05] Maurer, U.: Abstract models of computation in cryptography. In: Smart, N.P. (ed.) Cryptography and Coding 2005. LNCS, vol. 3796, pp. 1–12. Springer, Heidelberg (2005). https://doi.org/10.1007/11586821_1

[MBKM19] Maller, M., Bowe, S., Kohlweiss, M., Meiklejohn, S.: Sonic: zero-knowledge snarks from linear-size universal and updatable structured reference strings. In: Cavallaro, L., Kinder, J., Wang, X.F., Katz, J. (eds) ACM CCS 2019, pp. 2111–2128. ACM Press, November 2019

[MPZ20] Maurer, U., Portmann, C., Zhu, J.: Unifying generic group models. Cryptology ePrint Archive, Report 2020/996 (2020). https://eprint.iacr.org/2020/996

[MTT19] Mizuide, T., Takayasu, A., Takagi, T.: Tight Reductions for Diffie-Hellman Variants in the Algebraic Group Model. In: Matsui, M. (ed.) CT-RSA 2019. LNCS, vol. 11405, pp. 169–188. Springer, Cham (2019). https://doi.org/10.1007/978-3-030-12612-4_9

[Nec94] Nechaev, V.I.: Complexity of a determinate algorithm for the discrete logarithm. Math. Notes **55**(2), 165–172 (1994). https://doi.org/10.1007/BF02113297

[PH78] Pohlig, S., Hellman, M.: An improved algorithm for computing logarithms over GF(p) and its cryptographic significance. IEEE Trans. Inf. Theory **24**(1), 106–110 (1978)

[Pol78] Pollard, J.M.: Monte Carlo methods for index computation (mod p). Math. Comput. **32**(143), 918–924 (1978)

[PV05] Paillier, P., Vergnaud, D.: Discrete-log-based signatures may not be equivalent to discrete log. In: Roy, B. (ed.) ASIACRYPT 2005. LNCS, vol. 3788, pp. 1–20. Springer, Heidelberg (2005). https://doi.org/10.1007/11593447_1

[RS20] Rotem, L., Segev, G.: Algebraic distinguishers: from discrete logarithms to decisional Uber assumptions. In: Pass, R., Pietrzak, K. (eds.) TCC 2020. LNCS, vol. 12552, pp. 366–389. Springer, Cham (2020). https://doi.org/10.1007/978-3-030-64381-2_13

[RZ21] Ràfols, C., Zapico, A.: An algebraic framework for universal and updatable SNARKs. In: Malkin, T., Peikert, C. (eds.) CRYPTO 2021. LNCS, vol. 12825, pp. 774–804. Springer, Cham (2021). https://doi.org/10.1007/978-3-030-84242-0_27

[Sho97] Shoup, V.: Lower bounds for discrete logarithms and related problems. In: Fumy, W. (ed.) EUROCRYPT 1997. LNCS, vol. 1233, pp. 256–266. Springer, Heidelberg (1997). https://doi.org/10.1007/3-540-69053-0_18

[Zha22] Zhandry, M.: To label, or not to label (in generic groups). To appear at *Crypto 2022* (2022). https://eprint.iacr.org/2022/226

Instantiability of Classical Random-Oracle-Model Encryption Transforms

Alice Murphy[1]([✉]), Adam O'Neill[2], and Mohammad Zaheri[3]

[1] Department of Computer Science, University of Waterloo, Waterloo, Canada
anlmurph@uwaterloo.ca
[2] Manning CICS, University of Massachusetts Amherst, Amherst, USA
adamo@cs.umass.edu
[3] Snap Inc., Santa Monica, USA

Abstract. Extending work leveraging program obfuscation to instantiate random-oracle-based transforms (*e.g.*, Hohenberger *et al.*, EUROCRYPT 2014, Kalai *el al.*, CRYPTO 2017), we show that, using obfuscation and other assumptions, there exist standard-model hash functions that suffice to instantiate the classical RO-model encryption transforms OAEP (Bellare and Rogaway, EURO-CRYPT 1994) and Fujisaki-Okamoto (CRYPTO 1999, J. Cryptology 2013) for specific public-key encryption (PKE) schemes to achieve IND-CCA security. Our result for Fujisaki-Okamoto employs a simple modification to the scheme.

Our instantiations do not require much stronger assumptions on the base schemes compared to their corresponding RO-model proofs. For example, to instantiate low-exponent RSA-OAEP, the assumption we need on RSA is sub-exponential partial one-wayness, matching the assumption (partial one-wayness) on RSA needed by Fujisaki *et al.* (J. Cryptology 2004) in the RO model up to sub-exponentiality. For the part of Fujisaki-Okamoto that upgrades public-key encryption satisfying indistinguishability against plaintext checking attack to IND-CCA, we again do not require much stronger assumptions up to sub-exponentiality.

We obtain our hash functions in a unified way, extending a technique of Brzuska and Mittelbach (ASIACRYPT 2014). We incorporate into their technique: (1) extremely lossy functions (ELFs), a notion by Zhandry (CRYPTO 2016), and (2) *multi-bit* auxiliary-input point function obfuscation (MB-AIPO). While MB-AIPO is impossible in general (Brzuska and Mittelbach, ASIACRYPT 2014), we give plausible constructions for the special cases we need, which may be of independent interest.

Keywords: Fujisaki-Okamoto · RSA-OAEP · Random oracle · Standard model · Chosen-ciphertext security · Extremely lossy functions

1 Introduction

1.1 Background and Goal

THE RANDOM ORACLE MODEL AND UNINSTANTIABILITY. The random oracle (RO) model [10] is a popular paradigm for designing practical cryptographic schemes. The

S. Agrawal and D. Lin (Eds.): ASIACRYPT 2022, LNCS 13794, pp. 323–352, 2022.
https://doi.org/10.1007/978-3-031-22972-5_12

idea is that in the design and analysis of a scheme all parties are assumed to have access to one or more oracles that implement independent random functions (called ROs). The hope is that when the scheme is implemented in practice, using cryptographic hashing in place of the ROs, then the scheme retains security. (Replacing the ROs with some functions is said to "instantiate" the scheme via these functions.) Unfortunately, this paradigm has been shown to be false in a strong sense, starting with the work of Canetti, Goldreich, and Halevi [28]. They exhibit schemes that are secure in the RO model but are insecure when instantiated with *any* efficient function, let alone cryptographic hashing. Such unfortunate schemes are called *uninstantiable*. Thus, it is crucial to demonstrate *instantiatiability* of popular RO model schemes by giving efficient functions that can provably replace their ROs. This not only gives us better evidence of their security, but also provides insights into their security that were previously obscured in the ROM. This insight can lead to tweaks that increase their security and new design goals for cryptographic hashing.

Before proceeding, it should be clarified that our hash functions made to replace ROs are not practically efficient. Thus, we do not propose that our hash functions are actually used. Rather, their *existence* makes it more plausible that the schemes we instantiate meet their goals when using cryptographic hashing.

RO MODEL TRANSFORMS. A particularly vexing case of uninstantiability concerns *transforms* in the RO model; in other words, compilers that take one or more "base schemes" (that may or may not use ROs) and output a "target scheme" that uses ROs. We say that the transform "works" if for any secure base schemes the output target scheme is secure (under the appropriate security notions). The instantiated scheme should have the same security property, so we refer to the transform as uninstantiable if for any standard-model hash functions replacing the ROs, there exist secure base schemes such that the corresponding target scheme is insecure. This means the transform cannot "work" in the standard model in general.

OUR FOCUS: CLASSICAL ENCRYPTION TRANSFORMS. We are concerned with instantiability of two highly influential RO model transforms that output a (public-key) encryption scheme, the Optimal Asymmetric Encryption Padding (OAEP) trapdoor permutation-based transform [11] and the Fujisaki-Okamoto (FO) hybrid-encryption transform [37]. These are considered two of the "crown jewels" of the RO model, but their instantiability has not been established. In fact, there exist *uninstantiability* results to some extent. Accordingly, the main question we study is:

Do there exist standard-model hash functions that suffice to instantiate IND-CCA2 secure OAEP and FO?

We briefly recall how these transforms work. OAEP takes a trapdoor permutation (TDP) $\mathcal{F}$ (typically RSA) and produces a public-key encryption scheme whose public key is an instance f of the TDP. It uses two ROs $\mathcal{G}, \mathcal{H}$ and the encryption algorithm has the form:

$$\mathcal{E}_f^{\mathsf{OAEP}}(m; r) = f(s\|t) \text{ where } s = \mathcal{G}(r) \oplus m\|0^\zeta \text{ and } t = \mathcal{H}(s) \oplus r,$$

where $\zeta \in \mathbb{N}$ is a redundancy parameter.

FO uses a public-key encryption scheme and a symmetric-key encryption scheme to produce a new public-key encryption scheme. We modify the original encryption algorithm [37] by incorporating changes from Hofheinz, Hövelmanns, and Kiltz [49] to obtain the form:

$$\mathcal{E}_{pk}^{hy}(m; r) = \mathcal{E}_{pk}^{asy}(r; \mathcal{H}(r)) \| \mathcal{E}_K^{sy}(m) \quad \text{where} \quad K = \mathcal{G}(r \| c_1), c_1 = \mathcal{E}_{pk}^{asy}(r; \mathcal{H}(r)) ,$$

where $\mathcal{E}^{asy}$ denotes the encryption algorithm of the starting public-key scheme and $\mathcal{E}^{sy}$ denotes the encryption algorithm of the starting symmetric-key scheme.

Instantiability results for OAEP and FO are challenging because there are negative results known. Notably, Kiltz and Pietrzak [61] show a black-box separation for OAEP in the ideal TDP model, and Brzuska et al. [23] show the FO transform to be uninstantiable, even assuming IND-CPA security of the base PKE scheme. Further results about the schemes are discussed below.

1.2 Further Related Work and Open Questions

ATTEMPTS AT INSTANTIABILITY OF OAEP AND FO. The question of instantiability of OAEP and FO was posed by Canetti [26] and Boldyreva and Fischlin [18, 19]. The latter gave partial instantiations of variants of the transforms, where only *one* of the ROs is instantiated. Kiltz et al. [60] showed IND-CPA security of RSA-OAEP using lossiness of RSA, while Bellare, Hoang, and Keelveedhi [7] showed RSA-OAEP is the same for public-key-independent messages assuming the round functions meet their UCE notion. Cao et al. [29] gave partial instantiations of RSA-OAEP, as well as full instantiations for some variants of it.

On the negative side, Brown [22] and Paillier and Villar [64] showed negative results for proving RSA-OAEP is IND-CCA secure in restricted models, and Kiltz and Pietrzak [61] showed a general black-box impossibility result. Their results do not contradict ours because we use non-blackbox assumptions. Furthermore, they do not apply to TDP's satisfying properties common-inputs extractability (CIE) and second-inputs extractability (SIE). Shoup [70] exhibited a black-box separation showing that a form of *non-malleability* for the TDP is necessary. On the other hand, Fujisaki et al. [39] show that the seemingly stronger assumption of *partial one-wayness* (POW) on the TDP is sufficient.

FO has evaded any positive results in the standard model, despite its growing importance. The assumptions needed by Brzuska et al. [23] were later relaxed by Goyal et al. [46]. We evade these results by exploiting the fact that they do not apply when the PKE scheme is OW-PCA or lossy. Brzuska et al. [23] actually show uninstantiability of the underlying "Encrypt-with-Hash" (EwH) [6] portion of the transform, namely $\mathcal{E}_{pk}^{asy}(r; \mathcal{H}(r))$. Thus, our main focus is on the "hybrid encryption" part of the transform $\mathcal{E}_{pk}^{asy}(r) \| \mathcal{E}_K^{sy}(m)$ where $K = \mathcal{G}(r \| c_1), c_1 = \mathcal{E}_{pk}^{asy}(r; \mathcal{H}(r))$. We also consider the first part by making other assumptions on the base scheme. Concurrently, Zhandry [73] introduced a negative result for the FO transform when using *random oracles* in his augmented random oracle model (AROM). We use structured hash functions instead.

We have previously seen success in instantiating classical RO-based transforms outside the encryption domain, such as the full-domain hash (FDH) signature scheme [50, 72] and Fiat-Shamir (*e.g.*, [58]). In particular, we have seen such lines of work first use obfuscation and later drop it (*e.g.*, by Zhandry [72] in the case of FDH); we are hopeful the same pattern will emerge for our results.

RESULTS IN THE (Q)ROM. Results about the security of RSA-OAEP in the RO model were shown in [11,39,70]. Ultimately, these works showed RSA-OAEP is IND-CCA2 secure in the RO model assuming only one-wayness of RSA, but with a loose security reduction.

The original security bound for FO is lossy. With the recent interest in post-quantum cryptography and FO's applications to it, there has been work on getting tight reductions for FO and variants in the quantum RO model, *e.g.* [49,51,55,56,69], all of which are set in the ROM. Our security bound for the instantiated FO is also lossy.[1] An interesting question is whether "implicit rejection" can help with this, as it does in the RO case.

1.3 Our Results

A UNIFIED PARADIGM. Our standard-model hash functions for OAEP and FO are obtained via a unified paradigm that uses indistinguishability obfuscation (iO) [3,41] to obfuscate the composition of a punctured pseudorandom function (PPRF) [21,59,68] and extremely lossy function (ELF) [72]. In our proofs, we extend an idea of Brzuska and Mittelbach [25] to construct universal computational extractors [7]. In our extension, we utilize *multi-bit* auxiliary-input point function obfuscation (MB-AIPO) [27], as well as ELFs.

ELFs AND THEIR APPLICABILITY. To explain ELFs [72], we first recall the notion of a lossy function, a trapdoor-less version of lossy trapdoor functions [65]. A lossy function key can be generated in one of two modes, the injective or the lossy mode, where the first induces an injective function and the second induces a highly non-injective one. Furthermore, keys generated via these two modes are indistinguishable to any efficient adversary. Note that the lossy function image cannot be *too* small, else there would be a trivial distinguisher. ELFs achieve *much more lossiness* by reversing the order of quantifiers. Namely, for an ELF, for every adversary there exists an (adversary-dependent) indistinguishable lossy key-generation mode. The induced function can even have an appropriate *polynomial*-size image. Zhandry [72] constructs ELFs based on exponential DDH, where the lossy mode depends on the run-time of the adversary.

We observe ELFs seem useful for "answering decryption queries" in a proof of IND-CCA security. Indeed, a high-level strategy in the reduction could be, on answering a decryption query, to iterate over all possible ELF outputs in the lossy mode to see which one permits correct decryption. But there is a problem: the ELF output used in

---

[1] Looking ahead, we do not obtain a *post-quantum* secure instantiation of FO in this work based on known realizations of our hash functions. Yet, clearly a classically secure one is a step forward.

the challenge ciphertext would not look random to a reduction running the IND-CCA adversary and simulating the decryption oracle this way. This is because the reduction must be able to enumerate the entire lossy ELF image. To solve this problem, we wrap the ELF into a higher-level program that we obfuscate. This program outputs a special, truly random point on the input used in forming the challenge ciphertext, and otherwise evaluates the ELF.

RESULTS ON OAEP. For simplicity, consider the case of public-key-independent messages; we later explain how to deal with the public-key-dependent case. We show that low-exponent RSA-OAEP is fully instantiable under the same assumption on the base scheme (RSA) used by Fujisaki *et al.* [38] in the RO model, namely partial one-wayness. Here we instantiate $\mathcal{G}$ in OAEP as $\mathsf{iO}(\mathsf{ELF}(\mathsf{PRF}_K(\cdot)))$ where iO is an indistinguishability obfuscator [3,41], ELF is an injective-mode ELF, and PRF is a puncturable pseudorandom function [21,59,68]. The PRF key and ELF function are hardcoded into the obfuscated program. To instantiate $\mathcal{H}$ we use a one-wayness extractor [52] with polynomial-length output (see below). In the proof (and not in the construction), multi-bit point function obfuscation with auxiliary input (MB-AIPO) is used.

RESULTS ON FUJISAKI-OKAMOTO. We focus on the part of the transform from OW-PCA to IND-CCA2 (cf. transform 3.2.2 of Hofheinz *et al.* [49]), which is *not* subject to uninstantiability results. Moreover, we propose a modified version of this part of the FO transform:

$$\mathcal{E}^{\mathsf{hy}}_{pk}(m; r) = \mathcal{E}^{\mathsf{asy}}_{pk}(r; z) \| \mathcal{E}^{\mathsf{sy}}_K(m\|r) \quad \text{where} \quad K = \mathcal{G}(r\|\mathcal{E}^{\mathsf{asy}}_{pk}(r; z)) .$$

Decryption recovers r from the asymmetric ciphertext, computes the symmetric key with the hash function, and then decrypts the symmetric ciphertext $m\|r'$, m is returned iff $r = r'$. Moreover, if the symmetric-key encryption is already *randomized* and *randomness-recovering*, then r can safely be used as its coins as there is no additional overhead (c.f. Remark 4.2 in the full version of the paper).

We show this modified part of the FO transform is fully instantiable under suitable assumptions. To describe the assumptions, we introduce a new notion of cryptography with "adaptive" auxiliary input. This refers to an adversary being given auxiliary input that includes access to an oracle. Specifically, for our instantiation we require MB-AIPO with adaptive auxiliary input where the input point has the form $r^*\|c_1^*$, the output point is K^*, and the auxiliary input has the form (t, d, c^*, pk', m) where $c^* = c_1^*\|c_2^*$ is an encryption of m. Furthermore, the oracle provided to the adversary is either a public-key ciphertext validity checker or, as a separate assumption, a symmetric-key ciphertext validity checker. Beyond this, we need that the public-key encryption scheme is sub-exponentially OW-PCA and the symmetric-key encryption scheme is sub-exponentially secure authenticated encryption [9]. Notably, we later show that our new ELF-based MB-AIPO is secure for the adaptive auxiliary input needed, albeit for public-key-independent messages.

NEW MB-AIPOS. We wish to justify the existence of MB-AIPOs for the distributions needed in the OAEP and FO instantiation proofs. This is challenging because in general MB-AIPO for computationally unpredictable auxiliary input is likely impossible [24].

To circumvent this result for OAEP, we provide a new and simple RSA-based MB-AIPO. The auxiliary input contains an RSA ciphertext, and it is plausible this combination is secure. For FO, we show a new MB-AIPO for *statistically unpredictable* auxiliary input (which is not subject to the [24] result) based on ELFs that we further prove is sufficient for us when the PKE scheme is *lossy* [8] and the one-time AE scheme is *information-theoretic* and *leakage-resilient* in the sense of [2]. Of course, one can simply assume security of our MB-AIPO wrt. the *specific* computationally unpredictable auxiliary input needed. Then information-theoretic security of the AE and lossiness of the PKE can be removed, which yields a more practical result.

LEVERAGING SUB-EXPONENTIAL SECURITY ASSUMPTIONS. Finally, we leverage sub-exponential security assumptions to handle public-key-dependent messages. To see the reason, consider that the auxiliary information given to an MB-AIPO adversary in our proofs should contain an encryption of the challenge message. However, the challenge message depends on the obfuscation itself, the latter being in the public key. Thus, we have to *guess* the message in the auxiliary information. A generic argument to this effect would require sub-exponential security assumptions on *all* of the primitives, whereas for us it is crucial to avoid this assumption on ELFs, for which we do not know sub-exponentially secure instantiations. Thus, we use a tailored argument at this step of the proof. While we do not view sub-exponential assumptions as too devastating, it is an important open problem to handle public-key-dependent messages without them. Current techniques to remove sub-exponential iO [1] do not seem applicable to our case, because the message is not hashed or fed through an obfuscation.

ON THE ASSUMPTIONS. Arguably, our assumptions are strong, but not unreasonably so. We note that new constructions of iO have recently emerged [43,53,54,71] under safer assumptions. ELFs have been built from exponential DDH [72], which is a common assumption on elliptic curves. To construct a sub-exponential one-wayness extractor with polynomial output length, we can use diO with short auxiliary input as per [13], which is stronger than iO but is plausibly satisfied by the same constructions.[2] (diO with short auxiliary input is weaker than full-fledged diO, which is implausible [42].) Perhaps the most exotic assumption we need are MB-AIPOs for specific auxiliary input distributions. However, we lend plausibility by suggesting specific constructions.

2   Preliminaries

We overview notations and definitions used; some of which are taken from the prior work of Cao *et al.* [29].

---

[2] Unfortunately, for another construction of a one-wayness extractor with polynomial-length output from ELFs due to Zhandry [72], it does not seem possible to set parameters to get sub-exponential security.

2.1 Notation and Conventions

For a probabilistic algorithm A, by $y \leftarrow_\$ A(x)$ we mean that A is executed on input x and the output is assigned to y. We sometimes use $y \leftarrow A(x; r)$ to make A's random coins explicit. We denote by $\Pr[A(x) = y : x \leftarrow_\$ X]$ the probability that A outputs y on input x when x is sampled according to X. We denote by $[A(x)]$ the set of possible outputs of A when run on input x. The security parameter is denoted $k \in \mathbb{N}$ and 1^k denotes the unary encoding of the security parameter. Integer parameters often implicitly depend on k.

Unless otherwise specified, all algorithms must run in probabilistic polynomial time (PPT) in k, and an algorithm's run time includes that of any overlying experiment as well as the size of its code.

The length of a string s is denoted $|s|$. We denote by $s|_i^j$ the substring of s from the i-th least significant bit (LSB) to the j-th most significant bit (MSB) of s (inclusive), where $1 \leq i \leq j \leq |s|$. For convenience, we denote by $s|_\ell = s|_1^\ell$ the ℓ LSBs of s and $s|^\ell = s|_{|s|-\ell}^{|s|}$ the ℓ MSBs of s, for $1 \leq \ell \leq |s|$. Vectors are denoted in boldface, for example $\mathbf{x}$. If $\mathbf{x}$ is a vector then $|\mathbf{x}|$ denotes the number of components of $\mathbf{x}$ and $\mathbf{x}[i]$ denotes its i-th component, for $1 \leq i \leq |\mathbf{x}|$. Note that we begin indexing at 1, not 0. For convenience, we extend algorithmic notation to operate on each vector of inputs component-wise. For example, if A is an algorithm and $\mathbf{x}, \mathbf{y}$ are vectors then $\mathbf{z} \leftarrow_\$ A(\mathbf{x}, \mathbf{y})$ denotes that $\mathbf{z}[i] \leftarrow_\$ A(\mathbf{x}[i], \mathbf{y}[i])$ for all $1 \leq i \leq |\mathbf{x}|$. Unless otherwise specified, ε denotes the empty string. A function $f \colon \mathbb{N} \to [0, 1]$ is *negligible* if for every constant c and all but finitely many $k \in \mathbb{N}$ we have $f(k) < 1/k^c$.

Many games return a value like $(b' = b)$. This means that the boolean truth value of the statement $b' = b$ is returned. Define the *left-or-right selector function* as $\mathsf{LR}(x_0, x_1, b) = x_b$ for $x_0, x_1 \in \{0, 1\}^*$ and $b \in \{0, 1\}$.

INDISTINGUISHABILITY. Let $\mathcal{X} = \{X_k\}_{k \in \mathbb{N}}$ and $\mathcal{Y} = \{Y_k\}_{k \in \mathbb{N}}$ be distribution ensembles. We say that $\mathcal{X}$ is *computationally indistinguishable* from $\mathcal{Y}$, denoted $\mathcal{X} \approx_c \mathcal{Y}$, if for all PPT distinguishers D

$$|\Pr[D(x_k) \Rightarrow 1] - \Pr[D(Y_k) \Rightarrow 1]| \leq \mathsf{negl}(k)$$

We say that $\mathcal{X}$ is *statistically indistinguishable* from $\mathcal{Y}$, denoted $\mathcal{X} \approx_s \mathcal{Y}$, if for all (even bounded) distinguishers D

$$|\Pr[D(x_k) \Rightarrow 1] - \Pr[D(Y_k) \Rightarrow 1]| \leq \mathsf{negl}(k) .$$

2.2 Encryption Schemes and Their Security

SYMMETRIC-KEY ENCRYPTION. A *symmetric-key (or private key) encryption scheme* SE with message space Msg is a tuple of algorithms $(\mathcal{K}, \mathcal{E}, \mathcal{D})$. The key-generation algorithm $\mathcal{K}$ on input 1^k outputs a private key K. The encryption algorithm $\mathcal{E}$ on inputs K and a message $m \in \mathsf{Msg}(1^k)$ outputs a ciphertext c. The deterministic decryption algorithm $\mathcal{D}$ on inputs K and ciphertext c outputs a message m or $\bot$. We require that for all $K \in [\mathcal{K}(1^k)]$ and all $m \in \mathsf{Msg}(1^k)$, $\mathcal{D}_K(\mathcal{E}_K(m)) = m$ with probability 1.

Game $\mathcal{AE}_{\mathsf{SE}}^{A,1}(k)$	Game $\mathcal{AE}_{\mathsf{SE}}^{A,0}(k)$
$K \leftarrow_\$ \mathcal{K}(1^k)$	$K \leftarrow_\$ \mathcal{K}(1^k)$
$b' \leftarrow_\$ A^{\mathcal{E}_K(\cdot), \mathcal{V}_K(\cdot)}(1^k)$	$b' \leftarrow_\$ A^{\$(\cdot), \perp(\cdot)}(1^k)$
Return b'	Return b'
Oracle $\mathcal{E}_K(m)$	**Oracle** $\$(m)$
$c \leftarrow_\$ \mathcal{E}_K(m)$	$c \leftarrow_\$ \mathcal{E}_K(m)$
Return c	$u \leftarrow_\$ \{0,1\}^{|c|}$
Oracle $\mathcal{V}_K(c)$	Return u
$m \leftarrow \mathcal{D}_K(c)$	**Oracle** $\perp(c)$
If $m = \perp$ return 0	Return $\perp$
Return 1	

Fig. 1. Games to define $\mathcal{AE}$ for private-key encryption.

AUTHENTICATED ENCRYPTION. Let $\mathsf{SE} = (\mathcal{K}, \mathcal{E}, \mathcal{D})$ be a symmetric key encryption scheme. To define authenticated encryption [9], we give a combined definition of privacy and authenticity following Rogaway and Shrimpton [67]. Let A be an adversary. For every $k \in \mathbb{N}$, the experiments in Fig. 1 define the AE game. Define the *AE-advantage* of A against SE as

$$\mathbf{Adv}_{\mathsf{SE},A}^{\mathrm{ae}}(k) = \left| \Pr\left[\mathcal{AE}_{\mathsf{SE}}^{A,1}(k) \Rightarrow 1 \right] - \Pr\left[\mathcal{AE}_{\mathsf{SE}}^{A,0}(k) \Rightarrow 1 \right] \right| .$$

We say that SE is AE-secure if $\mathbf{Adv}_{\mathsf{SE},A}^{\mathrm{ae}}(k)$ is negligible in k for all PPT A.

PUBLIC-KEY ENCRYPTION. A *public-key encryption scheme* PKE is a tuple of algorithms $(\mathsf{Kg}, \mathsf{Enc}, \mathsf{Dec})$, with message space Msg and coin space Coins. The key-generation algorithm Kg on input 1^k outputs a public key pk and matching secret key sk. The encryption algorithm Enc on inputs pk and a message $m \in \mathsf{Msg}(1^k)$ outputs a ciphertext c. The deterministic decryption algorithm Dec on inputs sk and ciphertext c outputs a message m or $\perp$. We require that for all $(pk, sk) \in [\mathsf{Kg}(1^k)]$ and all $m \in \mathsf{Msg}(1^k)$, $\mathsf{Dec}(sk, (\mathsf{Enc}(pk, m)) = m$ with probability 1. When multiple primitives are being used, algorithms of PKE will be denoted PKE.Kg, PKE.Enc, etc. to avoid confusion.

PRIVACY OF PUBLIC-KEY ENCRYPTION [45,66]. Let $\mathsf{PKE} = (\mathsf{Kg}, \mathsf{Enc}, \mathsf{Dec})$ be a public key encryption scheme and let $A = (A_1, A_2)$ be an adversary. Let $\mathcal{M}$ be a PPT algorithm that takes inputs 1^k and a public key pk to return a message $m \in \mathsf{Msg}(1^k)$. For all $k \in \mathbb{N}$ and ATK $\in \{\mathrm{CPA}, \mathrm{CCA1}, \mathrm{CCA2}\}$, the experiment in Fig. 2 (left) defines the IND-ATK security game. The *ind-atk advantage* of A against PKE is defined as

$$\mathbf{Adv}_{\mathsf{PKE},A}^{\mathrm{ind\text{-}atk}}(k) = 2 \cdot \Pr\left[\mathrm{IND\text{-}ATK}_{\mathsf{PKE}}^{A}(k) \Rightarrow 1 \right] - 1 .$$

Game IND-ATK$_{PKE}^{A}(k)$	**Game** OW-PCA$_{PKE}^{A}(k)$
$b \leftarrow_\$ \{0,1\}$; $(pk, sk) \leftarrow_\$ \mathsf{Kg}(1^k)$	$(pk, sk) \leftarrow_\$ \mathsf{Kg}(1^k)$
$(st, m_0, m_1) \leftarrow_\$ A_1^{\mathcal{O}_1(\cdot)}(1^k, pk)$	$m \leftarrow_\$ \mathsf{Msg}(1^k)$; $r \leftarrow_\$ \mathsf{Coins}(1^k)$
$c \leftarrow_\$ \mathsf{Enc}(pk, m_b)$	$c \leftarrow \mathsf{Enc}(pk, m; r)$
$b' \leftarrow_\$ A_2^{\mathcal{O}_2(\cdot)}(st, pk, c)$	$m' \leftarrow_\$ A^{\mathsf{PCO}_{sk}(\cdot,\cdot)}(pk, c)$
Return $(b = b')$	If $m = m'$ then return 1
	Else return 0

Fig. 2. Games to define IND-ATK (left) and OW-PCA (right) security for public-key encryption.

If atk = cpa, then $\mathcal{O}_1(\cdot) = \varepsilon$ and $\mathcal{O}_2(\cdot) = \varepsilon$. In this case, we say PKE is *secure against chosen-plaintext attack* (IND-CPA) if $\mathbf{Adv}_{PKE,A}^{ind\text{-}cpa}(k)$ is negligible in k for all PPT A. Similarly, if atk = cca1, then $\mathcal{O}_1(\cdot) = \mathsf{Dec}(sk, \cdot)$, and $\mathcal{O}_2(\cdot) = \varepsilon$; if atk = cca2, then $\mathcal{O}_1(\cdot) = \mathsf{Dec}(sk, \cdot)$, and $\mathcal{O}_2(\cdot) = \mathsf{Dec}(sk, \cdot)$. In the case of cca2, A_2 is not allowed to ask $\mathcal{O}_2$ to decrypt c. We say that PKE is secure against non-adaptive chosen-ciphertext attack or IND-CCA1 (resp. adaptive chosen-ciphertext attack or IND-CCA2), if $\mathbf{Adv}_{PKE,A}^{ind\text{-}cca1}(k)$ (resp. $\mathbf{Adv}_{PKE,A}^{ind\text{-}cca2}(k)$) is negligible in k for all PPT A.

ONE-WAYNESS UNDER PLAINTEXT CHECKING ATTACK. Let PKE $= (\mathsf{Kg}, \mathsf{Enc}, \mathsf{Dec})$ be a public key encryption scheme. For every $k \in \mathbb{N}$, the experiment in Fig. 2 (right) defines the OW-PCA security game. We say PKE is OW-PCA secure if for any PPT adversary A

$$\mathbf{Adv}_{PKE,A}^{ow\text{-}pca}(k) = \Pr\left[\,\mathrm{OW\text{-}PCA}_{PKE}^{A}(k) \Rightarrow 1\,\right] ,$$

is negligible in k. Here $\mathsf{PCO}_{sk}(\cdot, \cdot)$ is the plaintext-checking oracle that on input (c, m) outputs 1 iff $\mathsf{Dec}(sk, c) = m$. We say that PKE is *sub-exponentially* OW-PCA if for every PPT A we have $\mathbf{Adv}_{PKE,A}^{ow\text{-}pca}(k) = O(2^{-k^\alpha})$ for a constant $0 \leq \alpha \leq 1$.

2.3 Trapdoor Permutations and Their Security

TRAPDOOR PERMUTATIONS. A trapdoor permutation (TDP) family with domain T.Dom is a tuple of algorithms $\mathcal{F} = (\mathsf{Kg}, \mathsf{Eval}, \mathsf{Inv})$. Algorithm Kg on input 1^k outputs a pair (F, F^{-1}), where $F \colon \mathsf{T.Dom}(k) \to \mathsf{T.Dom}(k)$. Algorithm Eval on inputs a function F and $x \in \mathsf{T.Dom}(k)$ outputs $y \in \mathsf{T.Dom}(k)$. We often write $F(x)$ instead of $\mathsf{Eval}(F, x)$. Algorithm Inv on inputs a function F^{-1} and $y \in \mathsf{T.Dom}(k)$ outputs $x \in \mathsf{T.Dom}(k)$. We often write $F^{-1}(y)$ instead of $\mathsf{Inv}(F^{-1}, y)$. We require that for any $(F, F^{-1}) \in [\mathsf{Kg}(1^k)]$ and any $x \in \mathsf{T.Dom}(k)$, $F^{-1}(F(x)) = x$.

ONE-WAYNESS. Let $\mathcal{F} = (\mathsf{Kg}, \mathsf{Eval}, \mathsf{Inv})$ be a trapdoor permutation family with domain T.Dom. We say $\mathcal{F}$ is *one-way* if for every PPT inverter I

$$\mathbf{Adv}_{\mathcal{F},I}^{owf}(k) = \Pr_{\substack{(F, F^{-1}) \leftarrow_\$ \mathsf{Kg}(1^k) \\ x \leftarrow_\$ \mathsf{T.Dom}(k)}}\left[\begin{array}{c} x' \leftarrow I(F, F(x)) \\ x' = x \end{array}\right] \leq \mathsf{negl}(k) .$$

PARTIAL ONE-WAYNESS [38]. Let $\mathcal{F} = (\mathsf{Kg}, \mathsf{Eval}, \mathsf{Inv})$ be a trapdoor permutation family with domain T.Dom. We say $\mathcal{F}$ is $(\mu, \mu + \zeta)$-*partial one way* $((\mu, \mu + \zeta)$-POW) if for every PPT inverter I

$$\mathbf{Adv}^{\text{pow}}_{\mathcal{F},I}(k) = \Pr_{\substack{(F,F^{-1}) \,\leftarrow\!\!\$\, \mathsf{Kg}(1^k) \\ x \,\leftarrow\!\!\$\, \mathsf{T.Dom}(k)}} \left[\begin{array}{c} x' \leftarrow I(F, F(x)) \\ x' = x|^{\mu + \zeta}_{\mu} \end{array} \right] \leq \mathsf{negl}(k) \ .$$

We additionally say that $\mathcal{F}$ is sub-exponentially $(\mu, \mu + \zeta)$-POW if for all PPT inverters I and all $k \in \mathbb{N}$, there exists some constant $0 < \alpha < 1$ such that the advantage of I is bounded by $O(2^{-k^\alpha})$. Fujisaki *et al.* [38] show that in the case of RSA one-wayness implies partial one-wayness.

2.4 Algebraic Properties of RSA

We recall algebraic properties of RSA that hold in the low-exponent regime for appropriate parameters. For generality of our results, we state them for abstract TDPs. We adapt them from Cao *et al.* [29].

SECOND-INPUT EXTRACTABILITY. Informally, a TDP is SIE if there is an efficient extractor that given a TDP function F, an image $F(x)$, and some portion of the preimage, can return the entire preimage. Formally: Let $\mathcal{F} = (\mathsf{Kg}, \mathsf{Eval}, \mathsf{Inv})$ be a trapdoor permutation family with domain $\{0, 1\}^n$. For $1 \leq i \leq j \leq n$, we say $\mathcal{F}$ is (i, j)-*second-input-extractable* $((i, j)$-SIE) if there exists an efficient extractor $\mathcal{E}$ such that for every $k \in \mathbb{N}$, every $F \in [\mathsf{Kg}(1^k)]$, and every $x \in \{0, 1\}^n$, extractor $\mathcal{E}$ on inputs $F, F(x), x|^j_{i+1}$ outputs x. We often write ζ-SIE instead of $(n - \zeta, n)$-SIE.

COMMON-INPUTS EXTRACTABILITY. Informally, a TDP is CIE if there is an efficient extractor that on inputs an instance of the TDP family F, two image points $F(x_1), F(x_2)$, returns the preimages x_1, x_2 if a run of bits of both preimages are equal. Formally: Let $\mathcal{F} = (\mathsf{Kg}, \mathsf{Eval}, \mathsf{Inv})$ be a trapdoor permutation family with domain T.Dom. For $1 \leq i \leq j \leq n$, we say $\mathcal{F}$ is (i, j)-*common-input-extractable* $((i, j)$-CIE) if there exists an efficient extractor $\mathcal{E}$ such that for every $k \in \mathbb{N}$, every $F \in [\mathsf{Kg}(1^k)]$, and every $x_1, x_2 \in \mathsf{T.Dom}$, extractor $\mathcal{E}$ on inputs $F, F(x_1), F(x_2)$ outputs (x_1, x_2) if $x_1|^j_{i+1} = x_2|^j_{i+1}$. We often write ζ-CIE instead of $(n - \zeta, n)$-CIE.

PARAMETERS. Barthe *et al.* [4] show via the univariate Coppersmith algorithm [31] that RSA is ζ-SIE and ζ-CIE for sufficiently large ζ. Specifically, they show RSA is ζ_1-SIE for $\zeta_1 > n(e - 1)/e$, and ζ_2-CIE for $\zeta_2 > n(e^2 - 1)/e^2$. Cao *et al.* [29] show a generalization to runs of arbitrary consecutive bits using the (heuristic) *bivariate* Coppersmith algorithm [17,31,32]. Specifically, they show that RSA is (i, j)-SIE for $(j - i) > n(e - 1)/e$, and (i, j)-CIE for $(j - i) > n(e^2 - 1)/e^2$, assuming the bivariate Coppersmith algorithm is efficient. Although its efficiency is heuristic, it works well in practice [16,20,35,57].

2.5 Function Families and Associated Security Notions

FUNCTION FAMILIES. A function family with domain F.Dom and range F.Rng is a tuple of algorithms $\mathcal{F} = (\mathcal{K}_F, F)$ that work as follows. Algorithm $\mathcal{K}_F$ on input a unary encoding of the security parameter 1^k outputs a key K_F. Deterministic algorithm F on inputs K_F and $x \in$ F.Dom(k) outputs $y \in$ F.Rng(k). We alternatively write $\mathcal{F}$ as a function $\mathcal{F}: K_F \times$ F.Dom $\to$ F.Rng.

ONE-WAYNESS EXTRACTORS. Let $\mathcal{F}: K_F \times$ F.Dom $\to$ F.Rng be a function family. We say $\mathcal{F}$ is a *one-wayness extractor* [52] if for any PPT adversary A and any unpredictable distribution D we have

$$\mathbf{Adv}^{\mathsf{cdist}}_{\mathcal{F},A,D} = \mid \Pr\left[\, A(K_F, z, F(K_F, x)) = 1 \,\right] - \Pr\left[\, A(K_F, z, R) = 1 \,\right] \mid ,$$

is negligible in k, where $K_F \leftarrow_\$ K_F(1^k)$, $(z, x) \leftarrow_\$ D_k$, and $R \leftarrow_\$$ F.Rng(k).

We additionally say that $\mathcal{F}$ is a sub-exponential one-wayness extractor if for any PPT adversary A, any sub-exponentially unpredictable distribution D and all $k \in \mathbb{N}$, there exists some constant $0 < \alpha < 1$ such that the advantage of A is bounded by $O(2^{-k^\alpha})$.

We explain how to build a sub-exponential one-wayness extractor, which is essentially a sub-exponentially secure universal hardcore function. The construction due to Bellare *et al.* [13] from diO + PPRFs has polynomial output length as desired. The form of diO needed has short auxiliary input, evading impossibility results of [42]. Moreover, the construction is sub-exponentially secure if the underlying primitives are also. It is not clear how to make an alternative construction from ELFs [72] sub-exponentially secure. However, it suffices for public-key-independent messages in our results.

2.6   The OAEP Transform

PADDING SCHEME. We define a general notion of a padding scheme following [11, 61]. For $\nu, \rho, \mu \in \mathbb{N}$, the associated *padding scheme* is a triple of algorithms PAD $=$ $(\Pi, \mathsf{PAD}, \mathsf{PAD}^{-1})$ defined as follows. Algorithm Π on input 1^k outputs a pair $(\pi, \hat{\pi})$ where $\pi : \{0,1\}^{\mu+\rho} \to \{0,1\}^\nu$ and $\hat{\pi} : \{0,1\}^\nu \to \{0,1\}^\mu \cup \{\bot\}$ such that π is injective and for all $m \in \{0,1\}^\mu$ and $r \in \{0,1\}^\rho$ we have $\hat{\pi}(\pi(m\|r)) = m$. Algorithm PAD on inputs π and $m \in \{0,1\}^\mu$ outputs $y \in \{0,1\}^\nu$. Algorithm PAD^{-1} on inputs a mapping $\hat{\pi}$ and $y \in \{0,1\}^\nu$ outputs $m \in \{0,1\}^\mu$ or $\bot$.

PADDING-BASED ENCRYPTION. Let PAD be a padding transform from domain $\{0,1\}^{\mu+\rho}$ to range $\{0,1\}^\nu$. Let $\mathcal{F}$ be a TDP with domain $\{0,1\}^\nu$. The associated *padding-based encryption scheme* is a triple of algorithms $\mathsf{PAD}[\mathcal{F}] = (\mathsf{Kg}, \mathsf{Enc}, \mathsf{Dec})$ defined in Fig. 3.

$\mathsf{Kg}(1^k)$	$\mathsf{Enc}(pk, m\|r)$	$\mathsf{Dec}(sk, c)$
$(\pi, \hat{\pi}) \leftarrow_\$ \Pi$	$(\pi, F) \leftarrow pk$	$(\hat{\pi}, F^{-1}) \leftarrow sk$
$(F, F^{-1}) \leftarrow_\$ \mathsf{Kg}(1^k)$	$y \leftarrow \pi(m\|r)$	$y \leftarrow F^{-1}(c)$
$pk \leftarrow (\pi, F)$	$c \leftarrow F(y)$	$m \leftarrow \hat{\pi}(y)$
$sk \leftarrow (\hat{\pi}, F^{-1})$	Return c	Return m
Return (pk, sk)		

Fig. 3. Padding based encryption scheme $\mathsf{PAD}[\mathcal{F}] = (\mathsf{Kg}, \mathsf{Enc}, \mathsf{Dec})$.

Algorithm $\mathsf{OAEP}_{(K_G,K_H)}(m\|r)$	Algorithm $\mathsf{OAEP}^{-1}_{(K_G,K_H)}(x)$
$s \leftarrow (m\|0^\zeta) \oplus G(K_G, r)$	$s\|t \leftarrow x$; $r \leftarrow t \oplus H(K_H, s)$
$t \leftarrow r \oplus H(K_H, s)$	$m' \leftarrow s \oplus G(K_G, r)$
$x \leftarrow s\|t$	If $m'|_\zeta = 0^\zeta$ then return $m'|^\mu$
Return x	Return $\perp$

Fig. 4. OAEP padding scheme $\mathsf{OAEP}[\mathcal{G}, \mathcal{H}]$.

OAEP PADDING SCHEME. We recall the OAEP padding scheme [11]. Let message length μ, randomness length ρ, and redundancy length ζ be integer parameters, and $\nu = \mu + \rho + \zeta$. Let $\mathcal{G} \colon \mathcal{K}_G \times \{0,1\}^\rho \to \{0,1\}^{\mu+\zeta}$ and $\mathcal{H} \colon \mathcal{K}_H \times \{0,1\}^{\mu+\zeta} \to \{0,1\}^\rho$ be function families. The associated *OAEP padding scheme* is a triple of algorithms $\mathsf{OAEP}[\mathcal{G}, \mathcal{H}] = (\mathcal{K}_{\mathsf{OAEP}}, \mathsf{OAEP}, \mathsf{OAEP}^{-1})$ defined as follows. On input 1^k, $\mathcal{K}_{\mathsf{OAEP}}$ returns (K_G, K_H) where $K_G \leftarrow_\$ \mathcal{K}_G(1^k)$ and $K_H \leftarrow_\$ \mathcal{K}_H(1^k)$, and $\mathsf{OAEP}, \mathsf{OAEP}^{-1}$ are as defined in Fig. 4.

OAEP ENCRYPTION SCHEME. As in Fig. 3, we denote by $\mathsf{OAEP}[\mathcal{G}, \mathcal{H}, \mathcal{F}] = (\mathsf{OAEP.Kg}, \mathsf{OAEP.Enc}, \mathsf{OAEP.Dec})$ the OAEP-based encryption scheme $\mathcal{F}$-OAEP with $n = \nu$. We typically think of $\mathcal{F}$ as RSA, and all our results apply to this case under suitable assumptions.

2.7 The Fujisaki-Okamoto Transform

The Fujisaki-Okamoto (FO) transformation [36,37] is a technique to convert weak public-key encryption schemes into strong ones which resist chosen-ciphertext attack (i.e., are IND-CCA2 secure). Let $\mathsf{SE} = (\mathcal{K}, \mathcal{E}, \mathcal{D})$ be a private-key encryption scheme and let $\mathsf{PKE} = (\mathsf{Kg}, \mathsf{Enc}, \mathsf{Dec})$ be a public-key encryption scheme. Assume $\mathcal{K}(1^k)$ outputs a key $K \in \{0,1\}^k$ and $\mathsf{PKE.Coins} \subseteq \mathsf{PKE.Msg}$. Moreover, let $\mathcal{H} \colon \mathcal{K}_H \times \mathsf{H.Dom} \to \mathsf{H.Rng}$ and $\mathcal{G} \colon \mathcal{K}_G \times \mathsf{PKE.Coins} \to \{0,1\}^k$ be hash function families. The FO transform $\mathsf{FO}[\mathcal{H}, \mathcal{G}, \mathsf{PKE}, \mathsf{SE}] = (\mathsf{FO.Kg}, \mathsf{FO.Enc}, \mathsf{FO.Dec})$ is defined in Fig. 5.

$\mathsf{FO.Kg}(1^k)$	$\mathsf{FO.Enc}(pk, m; r)$	$\mathsf{FO.Dec}(sk, c)$
$(pk', sk') \leftarrow_\$ \mathsf{PKE.Kg}(1^k)$	$(pk', K_H, K_G) \leftarrow pk$	$(sk', K_H, K_G) \leftarrow sk$
$K_H \leftarrow_\$ \mathcal{K}_H(1^k)$	$y \leftarrow H(K_H, r)$	$r \leftarrow \mathsf{PKE.Dec}(sk', c_1)$
$K_G \leftarrow_\$ \mathcal{K}_G(1^k)$	$c_1 \leftarrow \mathsf{PKE.Enc}(pk', r; y)$	If $r = \perp$ then return $\perp$
$pk \leftarrow (pk', K_H, K_G)$	$K \leftarrow G(K_G, r)$	$c_1' \leftarrow \mathsf{PKE.Enc}(pk', r; H(K_H, r))$
$sk \leftarrow (sk', K_H, K_G)$	$c_2 \leftarrow_\$ \mathcal{E}_K^{\mathsf{sy}}(m)$	If $c_1' \neq c_1$ then return $\perp$
Return (pk, sk)	$c \leftarrow (c_1, c_2)$	$K \leftarrow G(K_G, r)$
	Return c	$m \leftarrow \mathcal{D}_K^{\mathsf{sy}}(c_2)$
		Return m

Fig. 5. FO transform $\mathsf{FO}[\mathcal{H}, \mathcal{G}, \mathsf{PKE}, \mathsf{SE}] = (\mathsf{FO.Kg}, \mathsf{FO.Enc}, \mathsf{FO.Dec})$.

2.8 Program Obfuscation

Here we present three different types of obfuscation used in this paper. We start by recalling the definition of indistinguishability obfuscation from [3,41].

INDISTINGUISHABILITY OBFUSCATION. A PPT algorithm iO is called an indistinguishability obfuscator for a circuit ensemble $\mathcal{C} = \{\mathcal{C}_k\}_{k \in \mathbb{N}}$ if the following conditions hold:

- **Correctness:** For all security parameters $k \in \mathbb{N}$, for all $C \in \mathcal{C}_k$, and for all inputs x, we have that

$$\Pr\left[C'(x) = C(x) : C' \leftarrow_{\$} iO(1^k, C)\right] = 1 \ .$$

- **Security:** For any PPT distinguisher D, for all pairs of circuits $C_0, C_1 \in \mathcal{C}_k$ such that $|C_0| = |C_1|$ and $C_0(x) = C_1(x)$ on all inputs x, we have that

$$\mathbf{Adv}_{iO,D,\mathcal{C}}^{io}(k) = |\Pr\left[D(1^k, iO(1^k, C_0)) = 1\right] - \Pr\left[D(1^k, iO(1^k, C_1)) = 1\right]|$$
$$\leq \mathsf{negl}(k) \ .$$

One can also represent security as a game that picks a random bit b and gives the adversary, who can make exactly one query, oracle access to $iO(\mathsf{LR}(\cdot, \cdot, b))$. Both circuits in the query must be the same size and functionally equivalent.

We additionally say that iO is a sub-exponentially indistinguishability obfuscator for a circuit ensemble $\mathcal{C} = \{\mathcal{C}_k\}_{k \in \mathbb{N}}$ if for every PPT distinguisher D, for all $k \in \mathbb{N}$ and for all pairs of functionally equivalent circuits $C_0, C_1 \in \mathcal{C}_k$, there exists some constant $0 < \alpha < 1$ such that the advantage of D is bounded by $O(2^{-k^\alpha})$.

We now formalize the definition of unpredictable distributions which are used to define obfuscators for point functions.

COMPUTATIONALLY UNPREDICTABLE DISTRIBUTION. We call distribution ensemble $\mathcal{D} = \{D_k = (Z_k, X_k)\}_{k \in \mathbb{N}}$, on tuples of strings, computationally unpredictable (cup) if for every PPT algorithm A, we have

$$\Pr\left[A(1^k, z) \Rightarrow x : (z, x) \leftarrow_{\$} D_k\right] \leq \mathsf{negl}(k) \ .$$

We call it *sub-exponentially unpredictable* if there exists some constant $0 < \alpha < 1$ such that the above probability is bounded by $O(2^{-k^\alpha})$.

STATISTICALLY UNPREDICTABLE DISTRIBUTIONS. We call distribution ensemble $\mathcal{D} = \{D_k = (Z_k, X_k)\}_{k \in \mathbb{N}}$, on tuples of strings, statistically unpredictable (sup) if for every (even unbounded) algorithm A, we have that

$$\Pr\left[A(1^k, z) \Rightarrow x : (z, x) \leftarrow_{\$} D_k\right] \leq \mathsf{negl}(k) \ .$$

POINT OBFUSCATION WITH AUXILIARY INFORMATION. Although indistinguishability obfuscation applies to general circuits, we can also study obfuscation schemes for particular classes of functions, such as point functions. A point function p_x for some value x is defined as follows: $p_x(\tilde{x}) = 1$ iff $\tilde{x} = x$ and equals $\perp$ otherwise.

We now give the definition of point function obfuscation following [15]. A PPT algorithm AIPO is a point function obfuscator for the class of distributions $\mathcal{D} = \{D_k = (Z_k, X_k)\}_{k \in \mathbb{N}}$, where X_k is the input point distribution and Z_k is the auxiliary information distribution, if the following conditions hold:

- **Correctness:** For all security parameters $k \in \mathbb{N}$, for all $(z, x) \leftarrow_\$ D_k$, AIPO on input x outputs a polynomial-size circuit p_x that returns 1 on x and $\perp$ everywhere else.
- **Security:** To distinguisher A we associate the experiment in Fig. 6, for every $k \in \mathbb{N}$. We require that for every PPT distinguisher A

$$\mathbf{Adv}^{\text{aipo}}_{\text{AIPO}, A, D}(k) = 2 \cdot \Pr\left[\text{AIPO}^{D, A}_{\text{AIPO}}(k) \Rightarrow 1 \right] - 1 \le \text{negl}(k) \ .$$

SUB-EXPONENTIAL SECURITY. We additionally say AIPO is a *sub-exponentially secure* point obfuscator if for any sub-exponentially unpredictable distribution ensemble $\{D_k = (Z_k, X_k)\}_{k \in \mathbb{N}}$ there exists some constant $\alpha > 0$ such that for every PPT A, and for all $k \in \mathbb{N}$, the advantage of every PPT adversary A is bounded by $O(2^{-k^\alpha})$.

AUXILIARY-INPUT POINT OBFUSCATION WITH MULTI-BIT OUTPUT. A multi-bit point function $p_{x,y}$ is similar to a regular point function p_x in that $\perp$ is returned for all inputs $x' \ne x$. But unlike p_x, which just returns a single bit 1 input x, $p_{x,y}$ returns the multi-bit string y.

A PPT algorithm MB-AIPO is a multi-bit point obfuscator for the distribution ensemble $\mathcal{D} = \{D_k = (Z_k, X_k, Y_k)\}_{k \in \mathbb{N}}$, on triples of strings, if the following conditions hold:

- **Correctness:** For all security parameters $k \in \mathbb{N}$, for all $(z, x, y) \leftarrow_\$ D_k$, MB-AIPO on input x, y outputs a polynomial-size circuit that returns y on x and $\perp$ on all other inputs.
- **Security:** To distinguisher A, we associate the experiment in Fig. 6, for every $k \in \mathbb{N}$. We require that for every PPT distinguisher A,

$$\mathbf{Adv}^{\text{mb-aipo}}_{\text{MB-AIPO}, A, \mathcal{D}}(k) = 2 \cdot \Pr\left[\text{MB-AIPO}^{\mathcal{D}, A}_{\text{MB-AIPO}}(k) \Rightarrow 1 \right] - 1 \le \text{negl}(k) \ .$$

Game $\text{AIPO}^{\mathcal{D}, A}_{\text{AIPO}}(k)$	**Game** $\text{MB-AIPO}^{\mathcal{D}, A}_{\text{MB-AIPO}}(k)$
$b \leftarrow_\$ \{0, 1\}$; $(z, x_0) \leftarrow_\$ D_k$	$b \leftarrow_\$ \{0, 1\}$; $(z, x, y_0) \leftarrow_\$ D_k$
$x_1 \leftarrow_\$ \{0, 1\}^{|x_0|}$	$y_1 \leftarrow_\$ \{0, 1\}^{|y_0|}$
$p \leftarrow_\$ \text{AIPO}(x_b)$	$p \leftarrow_\$ \text{MB-AIPO}(x, y_b)$
$b' \leftarrow_\$ A(1^k, z, p)$	$b' \leftarrow_\$ A(1^k, z, p)$
Return $(b = b')$	Return $(b = b')$

Fig. 6. Games to define AIPO (left) and MB-AIPO (right) security.

$$\boxed{\begin{array}{l} \textbf{Game } \text{PRF-DIST}^A_{\text{PRF}}(k) \\[4pt] b \leftarrow_\$ \{0,1\} \; ; \; (S, st) \leftarrow_\$ A_1(1^k) \\ K \leftarrow_\$ \text{PRF.Kg}(1^k) \\ K_S \leftarrow_\$ \text{PRF.Punct}(K, S) \\ \mathbf{y}_0 \leftarrow \text{PRF.Eval}(K, S) \\ \mathbf{y}_1 \leftarrow_\$ \text{PRF.Rng}(k)^{\times|S|} \\ b' \leftarrow_\$ A_2(st, S, K_S, \mathbf{y}_b) \\ \text{Return } (b = b') \end{array}}$$

Fig. 7. Game to define PRF-DIST security.

We omit definitions of unpredictability and sub-exponential security in the context of MB-AIPOs since they extend naturally from their AIPO counterparts. Although we will note that in the case of MB-AIPO the unpredictable sampling distribution has the form $\mathcal{D} = \{D_k = (Z_x, X_k, Y_k)\}_{k \in \mathbb{N}}$ where Y_k represents the multi-bit output point. Unpredictability is defined the same way as above, in particular, the attacker is not given the point sampled from Y_k, nor are they required to predict it. MB-AIPO for computationally unpredictable auxiliary inputs is likely impossible in general [24]. Our choice is therefore to use statistical unpredictability or assume MB-AIPO for a *specific* computationally unpredictable auxiliary input.

2.9 Puncturable PRFs

A family of puncturable pseudorandom functions (PPRFs) [21,59,68] with domain PRF.Dom and range PRF.Rng is a tuple of algorithms PRF $=$ (PRF.Kg, PRF.Punct, PRF.Eval) that work as follows. Algorithm PRF.Kg on input 1^k outputs a key K. Algorithm PRF.Eval takes as inputs a key K and $x \in \text{PRF.Dom}(k)$ and outputs $y \in \text{PRF.Rng}(k)$. We often write $\text{PRF}_K(x)$ instead of $\text{PRF.Eval}(K, x)$. Additionally, there is a PPT puncturing algorithm PRF.Punct which on inputs a key K and a polynomial-size set $S \subseteq \text{PRF.Dom}(k)$, outputs a special, punctured key K_S. We say PRF is puncturable PRF if the following two properties hold:

- **Functionality preserved under puncturing:** For every PPT adversary $A = (A_1, A_2)$ such that adversary $A_1(1^k)$ outputs a polynomial-size set $S \subseteq \text{PRF.Dom}(k)$, it holds for all $x \in \text{PRF.Dom}(k)$ where $x \notin S$ that

$$Pr[\text{PRF.Eval}(K, x) = \text{PRF.Eval}(K_S, x) :$$
$$K \leftarrow_\$ \text{PRF.Kg}(1^k), \; K_S \leftarrow_\$ \text{PRF.Punct}(K, S)] = 1 \; .$$

- **Pseudorandom at punctured points:** To attacker $A = (A_1, A_2)$, we associate the experiment in Fig. 7 for every $k \in \mathbb{N}$. We require that for every PPT adversary $A = (A_1, A_2)$,

$$\mathbf{Adv}^{\text{pprf}}_{\text{PRF},A}(k) = 2 \cdot Pr\left[\text{PRF-DIST}^A_{\text{PRF}}(k) \Rightarrow 1\right] - 1 \leq \text{negl}(k) \; .$$

The works [21,59,68] construct PPRFs from one-way functions.

2.10 Extremely Lossy Functions

A family of extremely lossy functions (ELFs) ELF with domain ELF.Dom and range ELF.Rng is a tuple of algorithms $\mathsf{ELF} = (\mathsf{ELF.IKg}, \mathsf{ELF.LKg}, \mathsf{ELF.Eval})$ that work as follows. Algorithm ELF.IKg on input 1^k outputs the description of a function $f: \mathsf{ELF.Dom}(k) \to \mathsf{ELF.Rng}(k)$. Algorithm ELF.LKg on inputs 1^k and polynomial r outputs the description of a function $f: \mathsf{ELF.Dom}(k) \to \mathsf{ELF.Rng}(k)$. Algorithm ELF.Eval on inputs a function f and $x \in \mathsf{ELF.Dom}(k)$ outputs $y \in \mathsf{ELF.Rng}(k)$. We often write $f(x)$ instead of $\mathsf{ELF.Eval}(f, x)$. An ELF has the following properties:

- **Correctness:** For f output by (1^k), the function f is injective.
- **Key-indistinguishability:** For any polynomial p and inverse polynomial function δ, there is a polynomial q such that, for any adversary A running in time at most p, and any $r \geq q$, we have that
- **Lossiness:** for all polynomials r, over $f \leftarrow\!\!\text{\$}\ \mathsf{ELF.LKg}(1^k, r)$ the function f has image of at most r.
- **Efficiently enumerable image:** For any polynomial r, let f be an output of $\mathsf{ELF.LKg}(1^k, r)$. Then on inputs f, r and in time $\mathrm{poly}(|\mathsf{ELF.Dom}|, r)$, $f([\mathsf{ELF.Dom}])$ can be output.

Zhandry gives a construction from the exponential DDH assumption.

3 Low-Exponent RSA-OAEP Instantiation

In this section, we show low-exponent (*e.g.*, $e = 3$) RSA-OAEP is fully instantiable using its algebraic properties described in Sect. 2.4. We leave the instantiability of high-exponent RSA-OAEP for future work.

$\underline{\mathsf{ELF'.IKg}(1^k)}$	$\underline{\mathsf{ELF'.LKg}(1^k, r)}$	$\underline{\mathsf{ELF'.Eval}(K, f, x)}$
$f \leftarrow\!\!\text{\$}\ \mathsf{ELF.IKg}(1^k)$	$f \leftarrow\!\!\text{\$}\ \mathsf{ELF.LKg}(1^k, r)$	$y \leftarrow \mathsf{ELF.Eval}(f, x)$
$K \leftarrow\!\!\text{\$}\ \mathcal{K}_{\mathsf{PI}}(1^k)$	$K \leftarrow\!\!\text{\$}\ \mathcal{K}_{\mathsf{PI}}(1^k)$	Return $\mathsf{PRG}(\mathsf{PI}_K(y))$
Return (K, f)	Return (K, f)	

Fig. 8. Augmented ELF construction $\mathsf{ELF'}[\mathsf{PRG}, \mathsf{PI}, \mathsf{ELF}] = (\mathsf{ELF'.IKg}, \mathsf{ELF'.LKg}, \mathsf{ELF'.Eval})$.

Procedure $\mathcal{K}_G(1^k)$	**Procedure** $G(K_G, x)$
$K \leftarrow\!\!\text{\$}\ \mathsf{PRF.Kg}(1^k)$	$C_G \leftarrow\!\!\text{\$}\ K_G(1^k)$
$f \leftarrow\!\!\text{\$}\ \mathsf{ELF.IKg}(1^k)$	Return $C_G(x)$
$K_G \leftarrow\!\!\text{\$}\ \mathsf{iO}(pad(s(k), f(\mathsf{PRF}_K(\cdot))))$	
Return K_G	

Fig. 9. The hash function family $\mathcal{G}$.

3.1 Augmented ELFs

For convenience, we define a notion of *augmented* ELFs to make the evaluation of the ELF in injective mode on a uniform input to be uniform on an appropriate *binary* range. We will need this below. The idea is to compose the ELF, f, with a pairwise-independent hash and pseudorandom generator, *i.e.* $\mathsf{PRG}(\mathsf{PI}_K(f(\cdot)))$. Namely, let $\mathsf{ELF} = (\mathsf{ELF}.\mathsf{IKg}, \mathsf{ELF}.\mathsf{LKg}, \mathsf{ELF}.\mathsf{Eval})$ be an ELF, $\mathsf{PI}\colon \mathcal{K}_{\mathsf{PI}} \times \{0,1\}^n \to \{0,1\}^m$ be a function family such that $m \leq |\mathsf{ELF}.\mathsf{Dom}| - 2\log(1/\epsilon) + 1$ for negligible ϵ, and $\mathsf{PRG}\colon \{0,1\}^m \to \{0,1\}^r$ be a function. Define the associated *augmented* ELF $\mathsf{ELF}'[\mathsf{PRG}, \mathsf{PI}, \mathsf{ELF}] = (\mathsf{ELF}'.\mathsf{IKg}, \mathsf{ELF}'.\mathsf{LKg}, \mathsf{ELF}'.\mathsf{Eval})$ as in Fig. 8.

Proposition 1. *Suppose* ELF *is a secure ELF,* PI *is pairwise-independent hash, and* PRG *is a secure PRG. Then the associated augmented ELF* $\mathsf{ELF}'[\mathsf{PRG}, \mathsf{PI}, \mathsf{ELF}]$, *as defined in Fig. 8, is such that the output of the following experiment is computationally indistinguishable from* (f', z) *where* $z \in \{0,1\}^r$ *is independent and uniform:*

$$f' \leftarrow\!\!\!{}_\$ \mathsf{ELF}'.\mathsf{IKg}(1^k) \,;\ x \leftarrow\!\!\!{}_\$ \mathsf{ELF}.\mathsf{Dom}(x) \,;\ Return\ (f', f'(x))\ .$$

This follows by first applying the Leftover Hash Lemma [47] and then the security of the PRG.

3.2 The Result

We will need MB-AIPO for the following distribution ensemble. We suggest using our new RSA-based construction in the full version of Sect. 5; in particular, this RSA-based obfuscator "plays well" with the auxiliary input in this case. Define the distribution ensemble $\mathcal{D}^{\mathcal{OAEP}} = \{D_k^{\mathcal{OAEP}}\}_{k\in\mathbb{N}}$ be as follows:

Distribution $D_k^{\mathcal{OAEP}}$

$r^* \leftarrow\!\!\!{}_\$ \{0,1\}^\rho \,;\ z^* \leftarrow\!\!\!{}_\$ \{0,1\}^{\mu+\zeta}$

$K_H \leftarrow\!\!\!{}_\$ \mathcal{K}_H(1^k) \,;\ (F, F^{-1}) \leftarrow\!\!\!{}_\$ \mathsf{Kg}(1^k)$

$m \leftarrow\!\!\!{}_\$ \{0,1\}^\mu$

$s^* \leftarrow z^* \oplus (m\|0^\zeta) \,;\ y^* \leftarrow H(K_H, s^*)$

$t^* \leftarrow r^* \oplus y^* \,;\ c^* \leftarrow F(s^*\|t^*)$

$L \leftarrow (c^*, K_H, F, m)$

Return(L, r^*, z^*)

OAEP.Kg(1^k)	OAEP.Enc(pk, m)	OAEP.Dec(sk, c)
$K_G \leftarrow_\$ \mathcal{K}_G(1^k)$	$(F, K_G, K_H) \leftarrow pk$	$(F^{-1}, K_G, K_H) \leftarrow sk$
$K_H \leftarrow_\$ \mathcal{K}_H(1^k)$	$r \leftarrow_\$ \{0,1\}^\rho$	$s\|t \leftarrow F^{-1}(c)$
$(F, F^{-1}) \leftarrow_\$ \mathsf{Kg}(1^k)$	$z \leftarrow G(K_G, r)$	$r \leftarrow t \oplus H(K_H, s)$
$pk \leftarrow (F, K_G, K_H)$	$s \leftarrow z \oplus (m\|0^\varsigma)$	$m' \leftarrow s \oplus G(K_G, r)$
$sk \leftarrow (F^{-1}, K_G, K_H)$	$t \leftarrow r \oplus H(K_H, s)$	If $m'|_\varsigma = 0^\varsigma$ then return $m'|^\mu$
Return (pk, sk)	$c \leftarrow F(s\|t)$	Return $\perp$
	Return c	

Fig. 10. OAEP$[\mathcal{G}, \mathcal{H}, \mathcal{F}] = ($OAEP.Kg, OAEP.Enc, OAEP.Dec$)$ where $\mathcal{G}$ is defined in Fig. 9.

Theorem 1. *Let* n, μ, ς, ρ *be integer parameters. Let* $\mathcal{F}$ *be a family of trapdoor permutations with domain* $\{0,1\}^n$, *where* $n = \mu + \varsigma + \rho$. *Assume* $\mathcal{F}$ *is sub-exponentially OW,* $(\mu, \mu + \varsigma)$-*SIE, and* $(\mu, \mu + \varsigma)$-*CIE. Assume* ELF *is a secure augmented ELF with* ELF.Rng $= \{0,1\}^{\mu+\varsigma}$, PRF *is a secure puncturable PRF with* PRF.Dom $= \{0,1\}^\rho$ *, iO is a sub-exponentially secure iO for* $\mathcal{P}/poly$, *and sub-exponential MB-AIPO for the distribution ensemble* $\mathcal{D}^{\mathcal{OAEP}}$ *exists. Let* $\mathcal{G} : \mathcal{K}_G \times \{0,1\}^\rho \rightarrow \{0,1\}^{\mu+\varsigma}$ *and* $\mathcal{H} : \mathcal{K}_H \times \{0,1\}^{\mu+\varsigma} \rightarrow \{0,1\}^\rho$ *be hash function families, where* $\mathcal{G}$ *is in Fig. 9*[3] *and* $\mathcal{H}$ *is a sub-exponentially secure one-wayness extractor. Then* OAEP$[\mathcal{G}, \mathcal{H}, \mathcal{F}] = ($OAEP.Kg, OAEP.Enc, OAEP.Dec$)$, *as defined in Fig. 10, is IND-CCA2 secure.*

The full proof can be found in the full version of the paper; below we present a proof sketch. At a high-level, the idea is to change ELF to lossy mode so that a simulator can answer decryption queries by exhaustively searching the lossy image and using algebraic properties of RSA.

Game G_1: This is the standard IND-CCA2 security game, shown in Fig. 11. $\mathcal{G}$ is computed by the circuit $\mathcal{C}_1[K, f] = f(\mathsf{PRF}_K(\cdot))$ where f is in injective mode and the PRF key K is not punctured. Note that in G_1, $z^* = G(K_G, r^*)$.

Game G_2: The PRF key K is replaced with a key K^* which is punctured at r^* and the circuit $\mathcal{C}_1$ is switched to $\mathcal{C}_2$. $\mathcal{C}_2$ depends on an MB-AIPO of the point function p_{r^*, z^*} so that on inputs not equal to r^*, $f(\mathsf{PRF}_{K^*}(\cdot))$ is evaluated and on input r^*, the obfuscated point function p_{r^*, z^*} is evaluated (and $p_{r^*, z^*}(r^*) = z^*$). The input-output behavior of the circuits in G_1 and G_2 are identical and they are the same size (using padding), only their descriptions differ. Since the adversary gets obfuscated versions of these circuits, games G_1 and G_2 are indistinguishable by the security of iO.

Game G_3: Previously, z^* was given by $f(\mathsf{PRF}_K(r^*))$. In G_3, r^* is defined as $f(x^*)$ where x^* is sampled randomly from the PRF range. This change is indistinguishable by the pseudorandomness at punctured points of the puncturable PRF.

---

[3] Here the function $pad(\cdot \cdot)$ pads the circuit specified by the second argument to the length specified by the first argument. Here we implicitly set $s(k)$ to what is needed in the proof; cf. [24].

Game $G_1(k)$

$b \leftarrow\!\!\$ \{0,1\}$; $K \leftarrow\!\!\$ \mathsf{PRF.Kg}(1^k)$

$r^* \leftarrow\!\!\$ \{0,1\}^\rho$; $f \leftarrow\!\!\$ \mathsf{ELF.IKg}(1^k)$

$x^* \leftarrow \mathsf{PRF}_K(r^*)$; $z^* \leftarrow f(x^*)$

$K_G \leftarrow\!\!\$ \mathsf{iO}(pad(\mathcal{C}_1[K,f]))$

$K_H \leftarrow\!\!\$ \mathcal{K}_H(1^k)$; $(F, F^{-1}) \leftarrow\!\!\$ \mathsf{Kg}(1^k)$

$pk \leftarrow (F, K_H, K_G)$; $sk \leftarrow (F^{-1}, K_H, K_G)$

$(st, m_0, m_1) \leftarrow\!\!\$ A_1^{\mathsf{Dec}(\cdot)}(1^k, pk)$

$s^* \leftarrow z^* \oplus (m_b \| 0^\varsigma)$; $y^* \leftarrow H(K_H, s^*)$

$t^* \leftarrow r^* \oplus y^*$; $c^* \leftarrow F(s^* \| t^*)$

$b' \leftarrow\!\!\$ A_2^{\mathsf{Dec}(\cdot)}(st, pk, c^*)$

Return $(b = b')$

Fig. 11. IND-CCA2 security game for OAEP with adversary $A = (A_1, A_2)$.

Game G_4: In G_3 we had $z^* = f(x^*)$, where x^* was random. In this game, z^* is changed to a randomly sampled string from the range of G. This game is indistinguishable from the previous because f is a secure augmented ELF.

Game G_5: The circuit $\mathcal{C}_2$ now uses the un-punctured PRF key K instead of K^*, the key punctured at r^*. Like the transition to G_2, this update to $\mathcal{C}_2$ does not change its input-output behavior and is therefore undetected due to iO security.

Game G_6: By considering the running time of the IND-CCA adversary A, the ELF is switched to lossy mode. This reduces the range of $f(\mathsf{PRF}_K(\cdot))$ to polynomial size. This game also updates A_1's decryption oracle to include a "bad" flag which is silently set to true if A_1 makes a decryption query $\overline{c} = F(\overline{s} \| (\overline{r} \oplus H(K_H, \overline{s})))$, where $\overline{s} = \overline{z} \oplus (\overline{m} \| 0^\varsigma)$, in which the last ς bits of $\overline{z}$ are equal to the last ς bits of z^*. So the bad flag condition can be written as $\overline{z}|_\varsigma = z^*|_\varsigma$.

This flag does not change the input-output behavior of the decryption oracle. Thus to bound the probability the switch from G_5 to G_6 is detected, we only need to invoke indistinguishability of the ELF injective and lossy modes.

Game G_7: We further update A_1's decryption oracle to return $\bot$ if the bad flag introduced in G_6 is true. Hence G_6 and G_7 follow the "identical-until-bad" of [12], allowing the game transition to be bounded by the probability bad is set.

Let us consider what it means for bad to be set to true. As stated in G_6, this occurs when A_1 queries their decryption oracle with a ciphertext $\overline{c} = F(\overline{s} \| (\overline{r} \oplus H(K_H, \overline{s})))$, where $\overline{s} = \overline{z} \oplus (\overline{m} \| 0^\varsigma)$, such that $\overline{z}|_\varsigma = z^*|_\varsigma$. A_1 gets as input the function F, the hash keys K_H and K_G. At this point, K_G is the circuit described in G_3 under iO. The last ς bits of z^* are encoded in this circuit as the last ς bits of the MB-AIPO output point (since the output point is z^*). Hence the only way A_1 can obtain z^* (with non-negligible probability) is by breaking MB-AIPO security. So, the security of the MB-AIPO is used to bound the probability the switch from G_6 to G_7 is detected.

Game G_8: In this game both A_1 and A_2's decryption oracles are changed to decrypt using only the public key (F, K_H, K_G) and no secret keys. These decryption oracles have the same input-output behavior as the oracles in G_7, and hence their change is undetectable to the adversary. Decryption without the private key is achieved by exploiting three properties: the polynomial-sized ELF range, second-input extractability (SIE), common-inputs extractability (CIE), which are algebraic properties of RSA defined by Barthe *et al.* [4] that hold due to the Coppersmith algorithm [31]; we actually use generalizations due to Cao *et al.* [29] that hold due to the bivariate Coppersmith algorithm [17,31,32].

First, note the polynomial ELF range allows $\overline{z} = f(\mathsf{PRF}_K(\overline{r}))$ to be found via exhaustive search instead of by using F^{-1}, *unless $\overline{z} = z^*$, the challenge point.* In G_7, all valid ciphertexts were decrypted by A_1's oracles except for those with $\overline{z}|_\varsigma = z^*|_\varsigma$. In G_8, with overwhelming probability, z^* will not be in the lossy ELF range and hence will not be found through exhaustively searching the range. So if A_1 makes a decryption query in G_8 that cannot be decrypted using exhaustive search, $\perp$ is returned. But if A_2 makes a valid query $\overline{c}$ in G_7 with $\overline{z}|_\varsigma = z^*|_\varsigma$, then their decryption oracle will decrypt. So to achieve this behavior in G_8 we run a CIE extractor on inputs $F, \overline{c}, c^*$. The extractor returns $\overline{s}\|\overline{t}$ and $s^*\|t^*$ if $\overline{z}|_\varsigma = z^*|_\varsigma$ and $\perp$ otherwise. If $\perp$ is returned then the query was not a valid ciphertext and $\perp$ is returned by the oracle. If $\overline{s}\|\overline{t}$ is returned then decryption can be completed using the hash keys.

Game G_9: In this final game the MB-AIPO output point in the circuit $\mathcal{C}_2$ is switched from z^* to random $\overline{z}$ (while z^* is still used in the formation of s^*). Since $\overline{z}$ is the MB-AIPO output point and z^* was the output point in G_8, the security of MB-AIPO is used to bound the probability the adversary detects this transition.

A_2's challenge ciphertext is $c^* = F(s^*\|(r^* \oplus H(K_H, s^*)))$ where $s^* = z^* \oplus (m_b \|0^\varsigma)$. At this point, z^* is randomly sampled and is independent of r^*. Moreover, K_G given to A is independent of z^*. So m_b is hidden in c^* by z^* acting as a one-time-pad. So the challenge bit b is hidden and hence c^* looks random to A_2, concluding the proof sketch.

4 Fujisaki-Okamoto Instantiation

Inspired by Hofheinz, Hövelmanns, and Kiltz [49], we take a modular approach to instantiating FO. Our main contribution is to instantiate the part of the PKE transform from OW-PCA to IND-CCA. Here we need to assume the SE is information-theoretic and leakage-resilient AE. Then we observe how to instantiate a transform from OW-CPA to OW-PCA based on prior work assuming the PKE is lossy. Composing these transforms provides an instantiation of FO under the foregoing assumptions. As a point of comparison, Matsuda and Hanaoka [62] also construct IND-CCA encryption from lossy encryption, but their construction follows a different blueprint than FO.

4.1 Cryptography with Adaptive Auxiliary Input

We define primitives in a setting where the adversary gets auxiliary information depending on the secrets. Such a setting was considered by Dodis *et al.* [33]. We further extend it to consider what we call *adaptive* auxiliary input, where the adversary is given an oracle that depends on the secrets.

ADAPTIVE DISTRIBUTION ENSEMBLES. An *adaptive distribution ensemble* is a pair $(\mathcal{O}, \mathcal{D})$ where $\mathcal{O}$ is an oracle and $\mathcal{D} = \{D_k = (Z_k, X_k)\}_{k \in \mathbb{N}}$ is a distribution ensemble. We call $(\mathcal{O}, \mathcal{D})$ *adaptive computationally unpredictable* (acup) if for every PPT algorithm A,

$$\Pr\left[A^{\mathcal{O}(z,x,\cdot)}(1^k, z) \Rightarrow x : (z, x) \leftarrow_\$ D_k \right] \leq \mathsf{negl}(k) \ .$$

We call it *sub-exponentially unpredictable* if there exists some constant $0 < \alpha < 1$ such that the above probability is bounded by $O(2^{-k^\alpha})$. Adaptive statistically unpredictable (asup) is defined similarly.

AE WITH ADAPTIVE AUXILIARY INPUT. Let $\mathsf{SE} = (\mathcal{K}, \mathcal{E}, \mathcal{D})$ be a private-key encryption scheme and let A be an adversary. Let $(\mathcal{O}, \mathcal{D})$ be an adaptive distribution ensemble where $\mathcal{O}$ is an oracle and distribution ensemble $\mathcal{D} = \{D_k = (Z_k, K_k)\}_{k \in \mathbb{N}}$ is such that K_k is uniform on $\mathcal{K}(1^k)$. For every $k \in \mathbb{N}$, the experiments in Fig. 12 define the AE-AUX game (where the code of $\mathcal{O}$ is elided). Define the *AE-AUX advantage* of A against SE wrt. $(\mathcal{O}, \mathcal{D})$ as

$$\mathbf{Adv}^{\mathrm{ae\text{-}aux}}_{\mathsf{SE},A,\mathcal{O},D}(k) = \left| \Pr\left[\mathrm{AE\text{-}AUX}^{A,1}_{\mathsf{SE},\mathcal{O},D}(k) \Rightarrow 1 \right] - \Pr\left[\mathrm{AE\text{-}AUX}^{A,0}_{\mathsf{SE},\mathcal{O},D}(k) \Rightarrow 1 \right] \right| \ .$$

We say that SE is secure under AE-AUX wrt. $(\mathcal{O}, \mathcal{D})$ if $\mathbf{Adv}^{\mathrm{ae\text{-}aux}}_{\mathsf{SE},A,\mathcal{O},D}(k)$ is negligible in k for all PPT A.

LEAKAGE-RESILIENT AE. Leakage resilience [2] corresponds to the case in which the oracle is empty ($\mathcal{O} = \varepsilon$) and $\mathcal{D}$ is statistically unpredictable. We are not aware if such a definition has appeared in the literature before. Leakage-resilient AE has been studied, *e.g.*, by Bartwell *et al.* [5], but they use the weaker "only computation leaks" paradigm of Micali and Reyzin [63].

MB-AIPO WITH ADAPTIVE AUXILIARY INPUT. MB-AIPOs with adaptive auxiliary input are similarly defined wrt. adaptive distribution ensembles, meaning that in the MB-AIPO experiment (Fig. 6), A gets oracle $\mathcal{O}$. We believe this to be a natural progression of the notion, capturing the intuition that if the input point is unpredictable relative to an oracle, the MB-AIPO is secure relative to the same oracle. The notions of acup-MB-AIPO and asup-MB-AIPO are defined naturally. Note that in this work we only consider MB-AIPOs with adaptive auxiliary input relative to *specific* adaptive distribution ensembles.

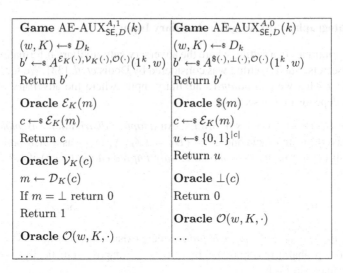

Fig. 12. Games to define AE-AUX for private-key encryption.

4.2 From OW-PCA to IND-CCA

Here we consider instantiability of the part of the Fujisaki-Okamoto (FO) transform that upgrades OW-PCA to IND-CCA, as in Sect. 3.2.2 of [49]. In the full version, we also consider insantiability of the part of the FO transform that upgrades OW-CPA to OW-PCA, showing a positive result by making the stronger assumption of lossiness [8] (compared to OW-CPA) on the base PKE scheme. In fact, we show that by assuming lossiness of the base PKE scheme, we can also construct an MB-AIPO from ELFs (mentioned in Sect. 5) that is secure wrt. each of the three (adaptive) distribution ensembles required in Theorem 2.

We slightly tweak the part of the Fujisaki-Okamoto (FO) transform that upgrades OW-PCA to IND-CCA, as in Sect. 3.2.2 of [49]. Note that this part is not subject to an uninstantiability result. Here we encrypt $m\|r$ instead of m under the symmetric encryption scheme. Our version of this part of FO, which we call $\overline{\mathsf{FO}}$, also differs from the original in that the symmetric key is set to be the hash of $r\|c_1$ (where c_1 is the asymmetric ciphertext), instead of just the hash of r, which is also done in [49]. Let $\mathsf{SE} = (\mathcal{K}^{\mathsf{sy}}, \mathcal{E}^{\mathsf{sy}}, \mathcal{D}^{\mathsf{sy}})$ and $\mathsf{PKE} = (\mathsf{PKE.Kg}, \mathsf{PKE.Enc}, \mathsf{PKE.Dec})$ be private and public-key encryption schemes, respectively. Let $\{0,1\}^k$ and $\{0,1\}^\mu$ be the SE key-space and message-space, respectively. Let $\mathcal{G}: K_G \times (\mathsf{PKE.Msg} \times \mathsf{PKE.Ctxt}) \to \{0,1\}^k$ be the hash function family as constructed in Fig. 14. $\overline{\mathsf{FO}}[\mathcal{G}, \mathsf{PKE}, \mathsf{SE}] = (\overline{\mathsf{FO}}.\mathsf{Kg}, \overline{\mathsf{FO}}.\mathsf{Enc}, \overline{\mathsf{FO}}.\mathsf{Dec})$ is defined in Fig. 13.

$\overline{\mathsf{FO}}.\mathsf{Kg}(1^k)$	$\overline{\mathsf{FO}}.\mathsf{Enc}(pk, m; r)$	$\overline{\mathsf{FO}}.\mathsf{Dec}(sk, c)$
$(pk', sk') \leftarrow\!\!{}^\$ \mathsf{PKE}.\mathsf{Kg}(1^k)$	$(pk', K_G) \leftarrow pk$	$(c_1, c_2) \leftarrow c;\ (sk', K_G) \leftarrow sk$
$K_G \leftarrow\!\!{}^\$ \mathcal{K}_G(1^k)$	$z \leftarrow\!\!{}^\$ \mathsf{PKE}.\mathsf{Coins}(1^k)$	$r \leftarrow \mathsf{PKE}.\mathsf{Dec}(sk', c_1)$
$pk \leftarrow (pk', K_G)$	$c_1 \leftarrow \mathsf{PKE}.\mathsf{Enc}(pk', r; z)$	If $r = \bot$ then return $\bot$
$sk \leftarrow (sk', K_G)$	$K \leftarrow G(K_G, r\|c_1)$	$K \leftarrow G(K_G, r\|c_1)$
Return (pk, sk)	$c_2 \leftarrow \mathcal{E}^{\mathsf{sy}}_K(m\|r)$	$m\|r' \leftarrow \mathcal{D}^{\mathsf{sy}}_K(c_2)$
	$c \leftarrow (c_1, c_2)$	If $r = r'$ then return m
	Return c	Return

Fig. 13. Modified part of FO transform $\overline{\mathsf{FO}}[\mathcal{G}, \mathsf{PKE}, \mathsf{SE}] = (\overline{\mathsf{FO}}.\mathsf{Kg}, \overline{\mathsf{FO}}.\mathsf{Enc}, \overline{\mathsf{FO}}.\mathsf{Dec})$.

Procedure $\mathcal{K}_G(1^k)$	**Procedure** $G(K_G, x)$
$K_{\mathsf{PRF}} \leftarrow\!\!{}^\$ \mathsf{PRF}.\mathsf{Kg}(1^k)$	$C_G \leftarrow\!\!{}^\$ K_G(1^k)$
$f \leftarrow\!\!{}^\$ \mathsf{ELF}.\mathsf{IKg}(1^k)$	Return $C_G(x)$
$K_G \leftarrow\!\!{}^\$ \mathsf{iO}(pad(s(k), f(\mathsf{PRF}_{K_{\mathsf{PRF}}}(\cdot))))$	
Return K_G	

Fig. 14. The hash function family $\mathcal{G}$.

Theorem 2. *Assume that* ELF *is a secure augmented ELF,* PRF *is a secure puncturable PRF and* iO *is a sub-exponentially secure indistinguishability obfuscator. Assume sub-exponentially secure MB-AIPO (1) for the adaptive distribution ensemble* $(\mathsf{PCO}_{sk'}(\cdot, \cdot), \mathcal{D}^{\mathcal{FO}}_1)$, *(2) for adaptive distribution ensemble* $(\mathcal{V}_{K^*}(\cdot), \mathcal{D}^{\mathcal{FO}}_1)$, *and (3) for the distribution* $\mathcal{D}_7$ *(Fig. 21 of the full version). Moreover, assume* PKE *is sub-exponentially OW-PCA and* SE *is sub-exponentially secure one-time AE. Then if* $\mathcal{G}$ *is instantiated as in Fig. 14[4],* $\overline{\mathsf{FO}}$ *as defined in Fig. 13 is IND-CCA2 secure.*

The full proof can be found in the full version of the paper; below we present a proof sketch.

Game G_1: We start with the standard IND-CCA2 security game with PPT adversary $A = (A_1, A_2)$, shown in Fig. 15, in which the hash function G is given by $\mathsf{iO}(\mathcal{C}_1[K, f])$. Our goal in this game chain is to show that ciphertext $c^*_2 = \mathcal{E}^{\mathsf{sy}}_{K^*}(m\|r^*)$ looks uniformly random to any efficient adversary given the corresponding public-key ciphertext c^*_1 and K_G. To do so, we again use our new approach, incorporating an ELF and MB-AIPO into the technique of [25].

Game G_2: First, we change $\mathcal{C}_1$ to $\mathcal{C}_2$ in a manner that does not change the input/output behavior. The PRF key K_{PRF} is replaced with a key K^*_{PRF} which is punctured at $r^*\|c^*_1$. $\mathcal{C}_2$ depends on an MB-AIPO of the point function with input point $r^*\|c^*_1$ and output point K^*. On inputs $x \neq r^*\|c^*_1$, $G(K_G, x)$ is evaluated as $f(\mathsf{PRF}_{K^*_{\mathsf{PRF}}}(x))$. On inputs $x = r^*\|c^*_1$, $G(K_G, x)$ is evaluated as the MB-AIPO and hence outputs K^*. Therefore, this game is functionally equivalent to the previous game and the circuits in G_1 and G_2 are indistinguishable by the security of iO.

---

[4] Here the function $pad(\cdot.\cdot)$ pads the circuit specified by the second argument to the length specified by the first argument. We implicitly set $s(k)$ to what is needed in the proof; cf. [24].

Game $G_1(k)$

$K_{\mathsf{PRF}} \leftarrow_\$ \mathsf{PRF.Kg}(1^k)$; $f \leftarrow_\$ \mathsf{ELF.IKg}(1^k)$

$r^* \leftarrow_\$ \mathsf{G.Dom}(k)$; $z^* \leftarrow_\$ \mathsf{PKE.Coins}(1^k)$

$(pk', sk') \leftarrow_\$ \mathsf{PKE.Kg}(1^k)$

$c_1^* \leftarrow \mathsf{PKE.Enc}(pk', r^*; z^*)$

$t^* \leftarrow \mathsf{PRF}_{K_{\mathsf{PRF}}}(r^* \| c_1^*)$; $K^* \leftarrow f(t^*)$

$K_G \leftarrow_\$ \mathsf{iO}(pad(\mathcal{C}_1[K_{\mathsf{PRF}}, f]))$

$pk \leftarrow (pk', K_G)$; $sk \leftarrow (sk', K_G)$

$b \leftarrow_\$ \{0,1\}$; $(st, m_0, m_1) \leftarrow_\$ A_1^{\mathsf{Dec}(\cdot)}(1^k, pk)$

$c_2^* \leftarrow \mathcal{E}_{K^*}^{\mathsf{sy}}(m_b \| r^*)$; $c^* \leftarrow (c_1^*, c_2^*)$

$b' \leftarrow_\$ A_2^{\mathsf{Dec}(\cdot)}(st, pk, c^*)$

Return $(b = b')$

Fig. 15. IND-CCA2 security game for FO with adversary $A = (A_1, A_2)$.

Game G_3: The symmetric encryption key and MB-AIPO output point is K^*, where, previously, $f(\mathsf{PRF}_{K_{\mathsf{PRF}}}(r^* \| c_1^*)) = K^*$. In the third game, K^* becomes $K^* = f(t^*)$ where t^* is sampled uniformly at random from the PRF range. This change is indistinguishable by the security of the PRF at punctured points.

Game G_4: Next, K^*, the symmetric encryption key and MB-AIPO output point, is switched to random. This game is indistinguishable from the previous because f is a secure augmented ELF.

Game G_5: In this game the PRF key used in the obfuscated circuit $\mathcal{C}_2$ is switched from K_{PRF}^* (punctured at $r^* \| c_1^*$) to K_{PRF} which is unpunctured. In the previous game when evaluated at $r^* \| c_1^*$, $\mathcal{C}_2$ would return the output of the MB-AIPO at this point, not the ELF PRF composition. As in the transition from G_2 to G_3, the circuit input-output behavior in G_5 is identical to that of G_4. The difference in circuit descriptions is indistinguishable by the security property of iO.

Game G_6: By considering the running time of the IND-CCA adversary A, the ELF is switched to lossy mode, shrinking the range of $f(\mathsf{PRF}_{K_{\mathsf{PRF}}}(\cdot))$ down to polynomial size. Previously in G_5, the symmetric encryption key K^* was sampled randomly from the *injective* ELF range, so in G_6 when K^* is sampled from this same range, with overwhelming probability this value of K^* will not be in the image of $f(\mathsf{PRF}_{K_{\mathsf{PRF}}}(\cdot))$.

At this point we introduce three flags to the FO decryption oracle to track A's nefarious activities. In G_6 these flags, bad_0, bad_1, and bad_2, are all "silent," meaning their states do not affect the behavior of the oracles. Using three game transitions, we show that the probability of each flag being set to true is negligible. Since the transitions from G_i to G_{i+1} for $i \in \{6, 7, 8\}$ follow the "identical-until-bad$_{\{0,1,2\}}$" model of [12], the game transitions can be bounded by the probability $\mathsf{bad}_{\{0,1,2\}}$ is set.

Game G_7: In the first of these three transitions, A_1's decryption oracle is changed so that it returns $\bot$ when bad_0 is true, which occurs when A_1 makes a decryption query $\bar{c} = (\bar{c}_1, \bar{c}_2)$ where the symmetric key computed in the decryption procedure,

$\overline{K} = G(K_G, \overline{r} \| \overline{c}_1)$, is such that $\overline{K} = K^*$. Recall from G_6 that f is in lossy mode and thus with high probability the only way the current hash circuit could output the key K^* is if the MB-AIPO input point $r^* \| c_1^*$ was used as input. In other words, if bad_0 is set to true, then $\overline{r} \| \overline{c}_1 = r^* \| c_1^*$. Thus, the probability bad_0 is set to true is bounded by the security of MB-AIPO.

Game G_8: This game continues from G_7 and differs in A_2's decryption oracle, which returns $\bot$ when bad_1 is set to true. This occurs when A_2 makes a query $\overline{c} = (\overline{c}_1, \overline{c}_2)$ where $\overline{K} = K^*$ (as in G_7) and $\overline{c}_1 \neq c_1^*$. This can only happen if K^* is in the image of f, which is in lossy mode. In this game K^* is randomly sampled from the injective ELF range and so with high probability will not be in the polynomial-sized lossy ELF range, and hence w.h.p. bad_1 will not be set to true.

Game G_9: This game continues from G_8 and differs in A_2's decryption oracle, which returns $\bot$ when bad_2 is set to true. This occurs when A_2 makes a query $\overline{c} = (\overline{c}_1, \overline{c}_2)$ where $\overline{K} = K^*$ (as in G_7), $\overline{c}_1 = c_1^*$, $\overline{c}_2 \neq c_2^*$, and $\overline{c}_2$ is a valid symmetric ciphertext. If bad_2 is set to true, then A_2 has found a valid symmetric ciphertext different from their challenge ($\overline{c}_2 \neq c_2^*$). To set bad_2, A_2 must find a valid symmetric ciphertext under the same key as the challenge key, K^*, hence we bound the probability bad_2 is true with an AE-AUX adversary.

Game G_{10}: In this final game, the output point of the MB-AIPO in K_G is switched from the symmetric key K^* to a uniformly random string $\overline{K}$. The challenge ciphertext is still formed using K^* but the obfuscated output point in the hash circuit $\overline{K}$ is now independent of the challenge ciphertext given to A. The probability that A detects the transition from G_9 to G_{10} is bounded by the security of MB-AIPO.

Now that the K^* is uniformly random and independent of the public key, c_2^* looks uniformly random by virtue of the symmetric-key encryption scheme being IND-CPA secure concluding the proof sketch.

5 New Auxiliary-Input Multi-Bit Point Function Obfuscators and Applications

Recall that in both our OAEP and FO instantiations we need a point function obfuscation with multi-bit output (MB-AIPO), for uniformly random input and output points, that is secure wrt. certain auxiliary inputs, even though MB-AIPO is impossible in general [24]. We first show how to obtain an MB-AIPO for statistically unpredictable inputs (albeit only polynomially secure), as needed for our FO instantiation, from ELFs. We then show that the MB-AIPO required for the RSA-OAEP instantiation can be built from RSA itself under a strong yet reasonable assumption on RSA. As far as we are aware, before our work there was only one candidate MB-AIPO, due to Bitansky and Canetti [14].

The full section can be found in the full version of the paper.

Acknowledgements. We thank Dakshita Khurana for collaboration in the early stages of this work. Furthermore, we are indebted to Pooya Farshim for helpful insights. A.O. was supported in part by a gift from Cisco Systems. Most of this work was done while M.Z. was at Georgetown University.

References

1. Agrikola, T., Couteau, G., Hofheinz, D.: The usefulness of sparsifiable inputs: how to avoid subexponential iO. In: Kiayias, A., Kohlweiss, M., Wallden, P., Zikas, V. (eds.) PKC 2020, Part I. LNCS, vol. 12110, pp. 187–219. Springer, Cham (2020). https://doi.org/10.1007/978-3-030-45374-9_7

2. Akavia, A., Goldwasser, S., Vaikuntanathan, V.: Simultaneous hardcore bits and cryptography against memory attacks. In: Reingold, O. (ed.) TCC 2009. LNCS, vol. 5444, pp. 474–495. Springer, Heidelberg (2009). https://doi.org/10.1007/978-3-642-00457-5_28

3. Barak, B., et al.: On the (im)possibility of obfuscating programs. In: Kilian, J. (ed.) CRYPTO 2001. LNCS, vol. 2139, pp. 1–18. Springer, Heidelberg (2001). https://doi.org/10.1007/3-540-44647-8_1

4. Barthe, G., Pointcheval, D., Zanella-Béguelin, S.: Verified security of redundancy-free encryption from rabin and RSA. Cryptology ePrint Archive, Report 2012/308 (2012). http://eprint.iacr.org/2012/308

5. Barwell, G., Martin, D.P., Oswald, E., Stam, M.: Authenticated encryption in the face of protocol and side channel leakage. In: Takagi, T., Peyrin, T. (eds.) ASIACRYPT 2017, Part I. LNCS, vol. 10624, pp. 693–723. Springer, Cham (2017). https://doi.org/10.1007/978-3-319-70694-8_24

6. Bellare, M., Boldyreva, A., O'Neill, A.: Deterministic and efficiently searchable encryption. In: Menezes, A. (ed.) CRYPTO 2007. LNCS, vol. 4622, pp. 535–552. Springer, Heidelberg (2007). https://doi.org/10.1007/978-3-540-74143-5_30

7. Bellare, M., Hoang, V.T., Keelveedhi, S.: Instantiating random oracles via UCEs. In: Canetti, R., Garay, J.A. (eds.) CRYPTO 2013, Part II. LNCS, vol. 8043, pp. 398–415. Springer, Heidelberg (2013). https://doi.org/10.1007/978-3-642-40084-1_23

8. Bellare, M., Hofheinz, D., Yilek, S.: Possibility and impossibility results for encryption and commitment secure under selective opening. In: Joux, A. (ed.) EUROCRYPT 2009. LNCS, vol. 5479, pp. 1–35. Springer, Heidelberg (2009). https://doi.org/10.1007/978-3-642-01001-9_1

9. Bellare, M., Namprempre, C.: Authenticated encryption: relations among notions and analysis of the generic composition paradigm. In: Okamoto, T. (ed.) ASIACRYPT 2000. LNCS, vol. 1976, pp. 531–545. Springer, Heidelberg (2000). https://doi.org/10.1007/3-540-44448-3_41

10. Bellare, M., Rogaway, P.: Random oracles are practical: a paradigm for designing efficient protocols. In: Denning, D.E., Pyle, R., Ganesan, R., Sandhu, R.S., Ashby, V. (eds.) ACM CCS 1993, pp. 62–73. ACM Press (1993)

11. Bellare, M., Rogaway, P.: Optimal asymmetric encryption. In: De Santis, A. (ed.) EUROCRYPT 1994. LNCS, vol. 950, pp. 92–111. Springer, Heidelberg (1995). https://doi.org/10.1007/BFb0053428

12. Bellare, M., Rogaway, P.: The security of triple encryption and a framework for code-based game-playing proofs. In: Vaudenay, S. (ed.) EUROCRYPT 2006. LNCS, vol. 4004, pp. 409–426. Springer, Heidelberg (2006). https://doi.org/10.1007/11761679_25

13. Bellare, M., Stepanovs, I., Tessaro, S.: Poly-many hardcore bits for any one-way function and a framework for differing-inputs obfuscation. In: Sarkar, P., Iwata, T. (eds.) ASIACRYPT 2014, Part II. LNCS, vol. 8874, pp. 102–121. Springer, Heidelberg (2014). https://doi.org/10.1007/978-3-662-45608-8_6

14. Bitansky, N., Canetti, R.: On strong simulation and composable point obfuscation. In: Rabin, T. (ed.) CRYPTO 2010. LNCS, vol. 6223, pp. 520–537. Springer, Heidelberg (2010). https://doi.org/10.1007/978-3-642-14623-7_28

15. Bitansky, N., Paneth, O.: Point obfuscation and 3-round zero-knowledge. In: Cramer, R. (ed.) TCC 2012. LNCS, vol. 7194, pp. 190–208. Springer, Heidelberg (2012). https://doi.org/10.1007/978-3-642-28914-9_11

16. Bleichenbacher, D.: On the security of the KMOV public key cryptosystem. In: Kaliski, B.S. (ed.) CRYPTO 1997. LNCS, vol. 1294, pp. 235–248. Springer, Heidelberg (1997). https://doi.org/10.1007/BFb0052239

17. Blömer, J., May, A.: A tool kit for finding small roots of bivariate polynomials over the integers. In: Cramer, R. (ed.) EUROCRYPT 2005. LNCS, vol. 3494, pp. 251–267. Springer, Heidelberg (2005). https://doi.org/10.1007/11426639_15

18. Boldyreva, A., Fischlin, M.: Analysis of random oracle instantiation scenarios for OAEP and other practical schemes. In: Shoup, V. (ed.) CRYPTO 2005. LNCS, vol. 3621, pp. 412–429. Springer, Heidelberg (2005). https://doi.org/10.1007/11535218_25

19. Boldyreva, A., Fischlin, M.: On the security of OAEP. In: Lai, X., Chen, K. (eds.) ASIACRYPT 2006. LNCS, vol. 4284, pp. 210–225. Springer, Heidelberg (2006). https://doi.org/10.1007/11935230_14

20. Boneh, D., Durfee, G.: Cryptanalysis of RSA with private key d less than $N^{0.292}$. In: Stern, J. (ed.) EUROCRYPT 1999. LNCS, vol. 1592, pp. 1–11. Springer, Heidelberg (1999). https://doi.org/10.1007/3-540-48910-X_1

21. Boyle, E., Gilboa, N., Ishai, Y.: Function secret sharing. In: Oswald, E., Fischlin, M. (eds.) EUROCRYPT 2015, Part II. LNCS, vol. 9057, pp. 337–367. Springer, Heidelberg (2015). https://doi.org/10.1007/978-3-662-46803-6_12

22. Brown, D.R.L.: A weak-randomizer attack on RSA-OAEP with e = 3. Cryptology ePrint Archive, Report 2005/189 (2005). http://eprint.iacr.org/2005/189

23. Brzuska, C., Farshim, P., Mittelbach, A.: Random-oracle uninstantiability from indistinguishability obfuscation. In: Dodis, Y., Nielsen, J.B. (eds.) TCC 2015, Part II. LNCS, vol. 9015, pp. 428–455. Springer, Heidelberg (2015). https://doi.org/10.1007/978-3-662-46497-7_17

24. Brzuska, C., Mittelbach, A.: Indistinguishability obfuscation versus multi-bit point obfuscation with auxiliary input. In: Sarkar, P., Iwata, T. (eds.) ASIACRYPT 2014, Part II. LNCS, vol. 8874, pp. 142–161. Springer, Heidelberg (2014). https://doi.org/10.1007/978-3-662-45608-8_8

25. Brzuska, C., Mittelbach, A.: Using indistinguishability obfuscation via UCEs. In: Sarkar, P., Iwata, T. (eds.) ASIACRYPT 2014, Part II. LNCS, vol. 8874, pp. 122–141. Springer, Heidelberg (2014). https://doi.org/10.1007/978-3-662-45608-8_7

26. Canetti, R.: Towards realizing random oracles: hash functions that hide all partial information. In: Kaliski, B.S. (ed.) CRYPTO 1997. LNCS, vol. 1294, pp. 455–469. Springer, Heidelberg (1997). https://doi.org/10.1007/BFb0052255

27. Canetti, R., Dakdouk, R.R.: Obfuscating point functions with multibit output. In: Smart, N. (ed.) EUROCRYPT 2008. LNCS, vol. 4965, pp. 489–508. Springer, Heidelberg (2008). https://doi.org/10.1007/978-3-540-78967-3_28

28. Canetti, R., Goldreich, O., Halevi, S.: The random oracle methodology, revisited. J. ACM 51(4), 557–594 (2004)

29. Cao, N., O'Neill, A., Zaheri, M.: Toward RSA-OAEP without random oracles. In: Kiayias, A., Kohlweiss, M., Wallden, P., Zikas, V. (eds.) PKC 2020, Part I. LNCS, vol. 12110, pp. 279–308. Springer, Cham (2020). https://doi.org/10.1007/978-3-030-45374-9_10

30. Coppersmith, D.: Finding a small root of a bivariate integer equation; factoring with high bits known. In: Maurer, U. (ed.) EUROCRYPT 1996. LNCS, vol. 1070, pp. 178–189. Springer, Heidelberg (1996). https://doi.org/10.1007/3-540-68339-9_16

31. Coppersmith, D.: Finding a small root of a univariate modular equation. In: Maurer, U. (ed.) EUROCRYPT 1996. LNCS, vol. 1070, pp. 155–165. Springer, Heidelberg (1996). https://doi.org/10.1007/3-540-68339-9_14

32. Coron, J.-S., Kirichenko, A., Tibouchi, M.: A note on the bivariate Coppersmith theorem. J. Cryptol. **26**(2), 246–250 (2013)
33. Dodis, Y., Kalai, Y.T., Lovett, S.: On cryptography with auxiliary input. In: Mitzenmacher, M. (ed.) Proceedings of the 41st Annual ACM Symposium on Theory of Computing, STOC 2009, Bethesda, MD, USA, 31 May–2 June 2009, pp. 621–630. ACM (2009)
34. Dodis, Y., Smith, A.: Entropic security and the encryption of high entropy messages. In: Kilian, J. (ed.) TCC 2005. LNCS, vol. 3378, pp. 556–577. Springer, Heidelberg (2005). https://doi.org/10.1007/978-3-540-30576-7_30
35. Durfee, G., Nguyen, P.Q.: Cryptanalysis of the RSA schemes with short secret exponent from Asiacrypt '99. In: Okamoto, T. (ed.) ASIACRYPT 2000. LNCS, vol. 1976, pp. 14–29. Springer, Heidelberg (2000). https://doi.org/10.1007/3-540-44448-3_2
36. Fujisaki, E., Okamoto, T.: Secure integration of asymmetric and symmetric encryption schemes. In: Wiener, M. (ed.) CRYPTO 1999. LNCS, vol. 1666, pp. 537–554. Springer, Heidelberg (1999). https://doi.org/10.1007/3-540-48405-1_34
37. Fujisaki, E., Okamoto, T.: Secure integration of asymmetric and symmetric encryption schemes. J. Cryptol. **26**(1), 80–101 (2013)
38. Fujisaki, E., Okamoto, T., Pointcheval, D., Stern, J.: RSA-OAEP is secure under the RSA assumption. In: Kilian, J. (ed.) CRYPTO 2001. LNCS, vol. 2139, pp. 260–274. Springer, Heidelberg (2001). https://doi.org/10.1007/3-540-44647-8_16
39. Fujisaki, E., Okamoto, T., Pointcheval, D., Stern, J.: RSA-OAEP is secure under the RSA assumption. J. Cryptol. **17**(2), 81–104 (2004)
40. Fuller, B., O'Neill, A., Reyzin, L.: A unified approach to deterministic encryption: new constructions and a connection to computational entropy. In: Cramer, R. (ed.) TCC 2012. LNCS, vol. 7194, pp. 582–599. Springer, Heidelberg (2012). https://doi.org/10.1007/978-3-642-28914-9_33
41. Garg, S., Gentry, C., Halevi, S., Raykova, M., Sahai, A., Waters, B.: Candidate indistinguishability obfuscation and functional encryption for all circuits. SIAM J. Comput. **45**(3), 882–929 (2016)
42. Garg, S., Gentry, C., Halevi, S., Wichs, D.: On the implausibility of differing-inputs obfuscation and extractable witness encryption with auxiliary input. In: Garay, J.A., Gennaro, R. (eds.) CRYPTO 2014, Part I. LNCS, vol. 8616, pp. 518–535. Springer, Heidelberg (2014). https://doi.org/10.1007/978-3-662-44371-2_29
43. Gay, R., Pass, R.: Indistinguishability obfuscation from circular security. In: Khuller, S., Williams, V.V. (eds.) STOC 2021: 53rd Annual ACM SIGACT Symposium on Theory of Computing, Virtual Event, Italy, 21–25 June 2021, pp. 736–749. ACM (2021)
44. Goldreich, O., Levin, L.A.: A hard-core predicate for all one-way functions. In: Johnson, D.S. (ed.) Proceedings of the 21st Annual ACM Symposium on Theory of Computing, 14–17 May 1989, Seattle, Washington, USA, pp. 25–32. ACM (1989)
45. Goldwasser, S., Micali, S.: Probabilistic encryption. J. Comput. Syst. Sci. **28**(2), 270–299 (1984)
46. Goyal, R., Koppula, V., Waters, B.: Lockable obfuscation. In: Umans, C. (ed.) 58th FOCS, pp. 612–621. IEEE Computer Society Press (2017)
47. Håstad, J., Impagliazzo, R., Levin, L.A., Luby, M.: A pseudorandom generator from any one-way function. SIAM J. Comput. **28**(4), 1364–1396 (1999)
48. Hemenway, B., Ostrovsky, R.: Building lossy trapdoor functions from lossy encryption. In: Sako, K., Sarkar, P. (eds.) ASIACRYPT 2013, Part II. LNCS, vol. 8270, pp. 241–260. Springer, Heidelberg (2013). https://doi.org/10.1007/978-3-642-42045-0_13
49. Hofheinz, D., Hövelmanns, K., Kiltz, E.: A modular analysis of the Fujisaki-Okamoto transformation. In: Kalai, Y., Reyzin, L. (eds.) TCC 2017, Part I. LNCS, vol. 10677, pp. 341–371. Springer, Cham (2017). https://doi.org/10.1007/978-3-319-70500-2_12

50. Hohenberger, S., Sahai, A., Waters, B.: Replacing a random oracle: full domain hash from indistinguishability obfuscation. In: Nguyen, P.Q., Oswald, E. (eds.) EUROCRYPT 2014. LNCS, vol. 8441, pp. 201–220. Springer, Heidelberg (2014). https://doi.org/10.1007/978-3-642-55220-5_12

51. Hövelmanns, K., Kiltz, E., Schäge, S., Unruh, D.: Generic authenticated key exchange in the quantum random oracle model. In: Kiayias, A., Kohlweiss, M., Wallden, P., Zikas, V. (eds.) PKC 2020, Part II. LNCS, vol. 12111, pp. 389–422. Springer, Cham (2020). https://doi.org/10.1007/978-3-030-45388-6_14

52. Hsiao, C.-Y., Lu, C.-J., Reyzin, L.: Conditional computational entropy, or toward separating pseudoentropy from compressibility. In: Naor, M. (ed.) EUROCRYPT 2007. LNCS, vol. 4515, pp. 169–186. Springer, Heidelberg (2007). https://doi.org/10.1007/978-3-540-72540-4_10

53. Jain, A., Lin, H., Sahai, A.: Simplifying constructions and assumptions for $i\mathcal{O}$. Cryptology ePrint Archive, Report 2019/1252 (2019). https://eprint.iacr.org/2019/1252

54. Jain, A., Lin, H., Sahai, A.: Indistinguishability obfuscation from well-founded assumptions. In: Khuller, S., Williams, V.V. (eds.) STOC 2021: 53rd Annual ACM SIGACT Symposium on Theory of Computing, Virtual Event, Italy, 21–25 June 2021, pp. 60–73. ACM (2021)

55. Jiang, H., Zhang, Z., Chen, L., Wang, H., Ma, Z.: IND-CCA-secure key encapsulation mechanism in the quantum random oracle model, revisited. In: Shacham, H., Boldyreva, A. (eds.) CRYPTO 2018, Part III. LNCS, vol. 10993, pp. 96–125. Springer, Cham (2018). https://doi.org/10.1007/978-3-319-96878-0_4

56. Jiang, H., Zhang, Z., Ma, Z.: Tighter security proofs for generic key encapsulation mechanism in the quantum random oracle model. In: Ding, J., Steinwandt, R. (eds.) PQCrypto 2019. LNCS, vol. 11505, pp. 227–248. Springer, Cham (2019). https://doi.org/10.1007/978-3-030-25510-7_13

57. Jutla, C.S.: On finding small solutions of modular multivariate polynomial equations. In: Nyberg, K. (ed.) EUROCRYPT 1998. LNCS, vol. 1403, pp. 158–170. Springer, Heidelberg (1998). https://doi.org/10.1007/BFb0054124

58. Kalai, Y.T., Rothblum, G.N., Rothblum, R.D.: From obfuscation to the security of Fiat-Shamir for proofs. In: Katz, J., Shacham, H. (eds.) CRYPTO 2017, Part II. LNCS, vol. 10402, pp. 224–251. Springer, Cham (2017). https://doi.org/10.1007/978-3-319-63715-0_8

59. Kiayias, A., Papadopoulos, S., Triandopoulos, N., Zacharias, T.: Delegatable pseudorandom functions and applications. In: Sadeghi, A.-R., Gligor, V.D., Yung, M. (eds.) ACM CCS 2013, pp. 669–684. ACM Press (2013)

60. Kiltz, E., O'Neill, A., Smith, A.: Instantiability of RSA-OAEP under chosen-plaintext attack. In: Rabin, T. (ed.) CRYPTO 2010. LNCS, vol. 6223, pp. 295–313. Springer, Heidelberg (2010). https://doi.org/10.1007/978-3-642-14623-7_16

61. Kiltz, E., Pietrzak, K.: On the security of padding-based encryption schemes – or – why we cannot prove OAEP secure in the standard model. In: Joux, A. (ed.) EUROCRYPT 2009. LNCS, vol. 5479, pp. 389–406. Springer, Heidelberg (2009). https://doi.org/10.1007/978-3-642-01001-9_23

62. Matsuda, T., Hanaoka, G.: Chosen ciphertext security via point obfuscation. In: Lindell, Y. (ed.) TCC 2014. LNCS, vol. 8349, pp. 95–120. Springer, Heidelberg (2014). https://doi.org/10.1007/978-3-642-54242-8_5

63. Micali, S., Reyzin, L.: Physically observable cryptography. In: Naor, M. (ed.) TCC 2004. LNCS, vol. 2951, pp. 278–296. Springer, Heidelberg (2004). https://doi.org/10.1007/978-3-540-24638-1_16

64. Paillier, P., Villar, J.L.: Trading one-wayness against chosen-ciphertext security in factoring-based encryption. In: Lai, X., Chen, K. (eds.) ASIACRYPT 2006. LNCS, vol. 4284, pp. 252–266. Springer, Heidelberg (2006). https://doi.org/10.1007/11935230_17

65. Peikert, C., Waters, B.: Lossy trapdoor functions and their applications. SIAM J. Comput. **40**(6), 1803–1844 (2011)
66. Rackoff, C., Simon, D.R.: Cryptographic defense against traffic analysis. In: 25th ACM STOC, pp. 672–681. ACM Press (1993)
67. Rogaway, P., Shrimpton, T.: A provable-security treatment of the key-wrap problem. In: Vaudenay, S. (ed.) EUROCRYPT 2006. LNCS, vol. 4004, pp. 373–390. Springer, Heidelberg (2006). https://doi.org/10.1007/11761679_23
68. Sahai, A., Waters, B.: How to use indistinguishability obfuscation: deniable encryption, and more. In: Shmoys, D.B. (ed.) 46th ACM STOC, pp. 475–484. ACM Press (2014)
69. Saito, T., Xagawa, K., Yamakawa, T.: Tightly-secure key-encapsulation mechanism in the quantum random oracle model. In: Nielsen, J.B., Rijmen, V. (eds.) EUROCRYPT 2018, Part III. LNCS, vol. 10822, pp. 520–551. Springer, Cham (2018). https://doi.org/10.1007/978-3-319-78372-7_17
70. Shoup, V.: OAEP reconsidered. J. Cryptol. **15**(4), 223–249 (2002)
71. Wee, H., Wichs, D.: Candidate obfuscation via oblivious LWE sampling. In: Canteaut, A., Standaert, F.-X. (eds.) EUROCRYPT 2021, Part III. LNCS, vol. 12698, pp. 127–156. Springer, Cham (2021). https://doi.org/10.1007/978-3-030-77883-5_5
72. Zhandry, M.: The magic of ELFs. In: Robshaw, M., Katz, J. (eds.) CRYPTO 2016, Part I. LNCS, vol. 9814, pp. 479–508. Springer, Heidelberg (2016). https://doi.org/10.1007/978-3-662-53018-4_18
73. Zhandry, M.: Augmented random oracles. Cryptology ePrint Archive, Paper 2022/783 (2022). https://eprint.iacr.org/2022/783

Nonmalleable Digital Lockers and Robust Fuzzy Extractors in the Plain Model

Daniel Apon[1]($\boxtimes$), Chloe Cachet[2]($\boxtimes$), Benjamin Fuller[2], Peter Hall[3], and Feng-Hao Liu[4]

[1] MITRE, McLean, VA, USA
dapon.crypto@gmail.com
[2] University of Connecticut, Mansfield, CT, USA
{chloe.cachet,benjamin.fuller}@uconn.edu
[3] New York University, New York, USA
pf2184@nyu.edu
[4] Florida Atlantic University, Boca Raton, FL, USA
liuf@fau.edu

Abstract. We give the first constructions in the plain model of 1) nonmalleable digital lockers (Canetti and Varia, TCC 2009) and 2) robust fuzzy extractors (Boyen et al., Eurocrypt 2005) that secure sources with entropy below $1/2$ of their length. Constructions were previously only known for both primitives assuming random oracles or a common reference string (CRS).

Along the way, we define a new primitive called a nonmalleable point function obfuscation with associated data. The associated data is public but protected from all tampering. We use the same paradigm to then extend this to digital lockers. Our constructions achieve nonmalleability over the output point by placing a CRS into the associated data and using an appropriate non-interactive zero-knowledge proof. Tampering is protected against the input point over low-degree polynomials and over any tampering to the output point and associated data. Our constructions achieve virtual black box security.

These constructions are then used to create robust fuzzy extractors that can support low-entropy sources in the plain model. By using the geometric structure of a syndrome secure sketch (Dodis et al., SIAM Journal on Computing 2008), the adversary's tampering function can always be expressed as a low-degree polynomial; thus, the protection provided by the constructed nonmalleable objects suffices.

Keywords: Point obfuscation · Digital lockers · Nonmalleability · Virtual black box obfuscation · Fuzzy extractors

1 Introduction

The random oracle (RO) paradigm [9] allows one to analyze cryptographic primitives/protocols with an idealized random function, significantly simplifying the

© International Association for Cryptologic Research 2022
S. Agrawal and D. Lin (Eds.): ASIACRYPT 2022, LNCS 13794, pp. 353–383, 2022.
https://doi.org/10.1007/978-3-031-22972-5_13

designs and analyses. Since instantiating RO with a real-life object is impossible for the general case [23], it is important to identify useful RO properties that are achievable under specific hard problems.

Initial Efforts – Point Obfuscation. Canetti [20] initiated a study on an important property of random oracles called *oracle hashing*—or *point obfuscation*—and realized it in the plain model. More specifically, a point function I_{val} is indexed by a string val and acts as follows:

$$I_{\mathsf{val}}(\mathsf{val}') = \begin{cases} 1 & \mathsf{val} = \mathsf{val}' \\ 0 & \text{otherwise} \end{cases}.$$

An obfuscated point function should reveal nothing beyond the input/output behavior of the function $I_{\mathsf{val}}(\cdot)$. This security notion is called virtual black-box (VBB) security. Constructions are known from multiple assumptions [4,20,27,46].

VBB secure obfuscation of point functions captures the idea that the output of the RO is independent of its input, and that one can verify whether the output (for now, up to one bit) of an RO is correctly generated from a specific input. While VBB security is impossible for general functions [6], VBB secure obfuscation appears possible for point functions. (Similar techniques are used to obfuscate wildcards, conjunctions, and hyperplanes [7,12,18,24,31,39].)

Next Step – Nonmalleability. However, there are many other properties of the RO that make it a desirable object. For example, given an RO output value on input x, it should be infeasible to obtain another output of RO on any related input point (e.g., $x+1$). Applied to our setting, this is known as *nonmalleable point obfuscation*. The nonmalleability of random oracles enables many other objects that resist active attack. For example, this work considers robust fuzzy extractors [16] as an application, which were first constructed from random oracles.

Canetti and Varia [25] defined a nonmalleable point function and realized it in the common reference string (CRS) model. However, as one of the most valuable properties of the RO is that no trusted setup is required, an ideal instantiation would not require a CRS.

To tackle this, Komargodski and Yogev [44] proposed a construction of a nonmalleable point obfuscation in the plain model.[1] Prior work in plain model point obfuscation considers a limiting tampering class of low-degree polynomials where the degree relates to the hardness of the underlying number-theoretic assumption.

Another Step Forward – Digital Lockers. An obfuscated point function only outputs one bit. However, we are generally interested in the RO outputting a random string for a given input. To emulate this functionality, a natural

---

[1] Unfortunately, their underlying cryptographic assumption was broken by Bartusek, Ma, and Zhandry [8]. An alternative assumption was posed in [45], but this did not suffice to show security. Fortunately, Bartusek, Ma, and Zhandry introduced their own assumption and accompanying construction, showing their assumption holds in a strong variant of the generic group model [8].

extension is the *multi-bit* point function, where each function $I_{\mathsf{val},\mathsf{key}}$ is indexed by a pair of strings $(\mathsf{val}, \mathsf{key})$ and works as follows:

$$I_{\mathsf{val},\mathsf{key}}(\mathsf{val}') = \begin{cases} \mathsf{key} & \mathsf{val} = \mathsf{val}' \\ \bot & \text{otherwise} \end{cases}.$$

An obfuscation of a function of this class is called a *digital locker*, which is useful in password [20] and biometric authentication [1,22].

Though we know how to build digital lockers in the plain model [21], the only existing nonmalleable constructions require a CRS. Fenteany and Fuller [38] achieved half of the goal, constructing a digital locker that nonmalleabile against tampering only on val in the standard model. However, while the work [38] pointed out a technique to additionally protect key, it required a CRS, similarly to the original work [25]. As an ideal instantiation of RO does not require a trusted setup, this naturally motivates our main question:

Can one build a nonmalleable digital locker in the plain model without setup?

Our Technical Contributions We answer the main question in the affirmative, constructing a nonmalleable digital locker in the plain model. We present the following contributions:

1. **Point Obfuscation with Associated Data** We define a new primitive called a *nonmalleable point obfuscator with associated data*. We then instantiate this object using group assumptions introduced by Bartusek, Ma, and Zhandry [8].
2. **Creating a Multibit Output** We then integrate this construction with the real or random construction [21], yielding a nonmalleable digital locker that prevents tampering on the input and associated data only. This step is not black box in the point obfuscations. Instead, it is created from scratch using similar techniques from the same group assumptions as the constructed point obfuscation.
3. **Protecting the Multibit Output** By putting the CRS of a true simulation extractable non-interactive zero-knowledge proof (NIZK) [32] into the associated data, we can protect the output of the digital locker. Conceptually, our new tool protects the NIZK crs, which (if intact) can be used to derive nonmalleability for the other parts of the construction. This step is black box from an appropriate variant of a digital locker.

In all of the above steps, the prevented tampering class for the input point, val is low-degree polynomials, rather than the desired complete tamper resistance. However, this class is still meaningful in many applications where a RO was previously used.

1.1   Low Entropy Robust Fuzzy Extractors in the Plain Model

Despite a limited tampering class, our nonmalleable objects suffice to construct the first plain model robust fuzzy extractors [16] that support sources whose entropy is less than half their length $1/2$, a known barrier for information-theoretically secure constructions [35]. We notice that all prior computationally secure constructions relied on some form of a CRS, and our work shows that this component is not required.

A fuzzy extractor is a pair of algorithms (Gen, Rep) with two properties:

Correctness. Let w, w' be values that are close in some distance metric, and define (key, pub) $\leftarrow$ Gen(w). Then it is true that Rep(w', pub) = key.

Security. The value key is computationally indistinguishable from a uniform value given pub.

Digital lockers have been used to construct reusable fuzzy extractors, as in [50] [1,22], i.e., one can derive multiple keys from the same entropy source. An additional desirable property is robustness [33], which prevents an adversary from modifying pub in an attempt to force Rep to produce a different key.

Robust fuzzy extractors are notoriously difficult to construct – we show various limitations of the prior constructions in Table 1. Dodis and Wichs [35] showed that it is only possible information-theoretically if the entropy of w is at least half its length. Feng and Tang [37] showed this barrier exists in the CRS model, as well. Feng and Tang construct a robust fuzzy extractor with computational security for entropy sources that can depend on the CRS.

We construct the first robust fuzzy extractor in the plain model that supports entropy for w that is less than half its length. We combine our nonmalleable digital locker with a specific error-correction component, the syndrome construction [11,30,34]. The syndrome construction allows the reduction to extract a low-degree polynomial that is consistent with the adversary's tampering. Similar techniques were used to construct CRS model robust fuzzy extractors from algebraic-manipulation detection codes [29]. We present a second construction directly from the nonmalleable point function from associated data which is able to extract a limited length key.[2]

To the best of our knowledge, our work and that of Cramer et al. [29] are the only two approaches to building a robust fuzzy extractor that do not build a robust extractor first. This is because our nonmalleable tools only prevent limited tampering classes; both works use the secure sketch component to guarantee the adversary's tampering is in this low complexity class.

1.2 Technical Overview

In this section, we present an overview of our techniques. In the CRS model, nonmalleability of point functions can be achieved as [25], by using a nonmalleable NIZK system – in addition to generating a regular $C \leftarrow \mathsf{DL}(I_{\mathsf{val,key}})$, one also appends a zero-knowledge proof π to the output showing knowledge of the pair (val, key) inside C. However, any non-trivial nonmalleable NIZK system would require a trusted (nontamperable) CRS for security of the proof system, so the

---

[2] We also show that a nonmalleable point function (without associated data) suffices to construct a robust secure sketch [34].

Table 1. Comparison of Robust Fuzzy Extractors. The CRS* model means that the distribution of W can depend on the CRS, however, the CRS is still assumed not to be modified. For a distribution W, $H_\infty(W)$ represents min-entropy (see Sect. 2) and $|W|$ represents its length. IT corresponds to information-theoretic security and Comp. represents security against computationally bounded adversaries. Syn. is the syndrome or null space of an appropriate error correcting code. The column of SS errors indicates the error tolerance of the underlying secure sketch. This parameter is related to the information leakage of the secure sketch. This work and prior computational works require a secure sketch that corrects $2t$ errors, which leads to more leakage.

Scheme	Model	Security	SS errors	$H_\infty(W) < |W|/2$?
[14,15]	RO	IT	t	✓
[33]	Plain	IT	t	X
[29]	CRS	IT	t	X
[53–55]	CRS	Comp	$2t$	✓
[37]	CRS*	Comp	$2t$	✓
Syn. + NM Point Obf w/Assoc. Data	Plain	Comp	$2t$	✓
Syn. + NM Digital Locker	Plain	Comp	$2t$	✓

overall obfuscation would be (crs, C, π). Without trusted setup, an adversary may simply replace the crs, rendering the NIZK ineffective and breaking non-malleability. So, this trusted setup required immediately fails at achieving our goal.

Point Obfuscation with Associated Data To achieve our goal, we formalize a notion that blends any public string with point obfuscation in a meaningful way, called *point obfuscation with associated data*. More specifically, the obfuscator $\mathsf{Obf}(I_{\mathsf{val}}, \mathsf{ad})$ takes as input the point function I_{val} and an additional public string ad (e.g., crs) and then outputs an obfuscated program C along with ad. The output program C should be VBB secure, and ad is treated as public information.

We formulate nonmalleability properties that treat the two inputs quite differently. The adversary outputs (C', ad', f) and wins if C' is consistent with the values $f(\mathsf{val})$ and ad', and one of the following hold:

1. The function belongs to some targeted function class, i.e., $f \in \mathcal{F}$, or
2. The function f is the identity and $\mathsf{ad}' \neq \mathsf{ad}$.

Nonmalleability requires that the adversary has only a negligible winning probability, meaning that they cannot replace ad by any other string, nor tamper val consistently by any function in the class $\mathcal{F}$.

Remark 1. It is undesirable that in the definition the adversary output their tampering function. The desired notion is that the adversary cannot output (C', ad') that is consistent with any f. This notion is impossible to achieve in the plain model if f contains linear shifts. Essentially, given an obfuscation of point x, an adversary not required to output their mauling function may simply create an obfuscation of independent point y. It is clear that if the function $f(z) = z - x + y$ is in $\mathcal{F}$, this would be a valid tampering, but it is impossible to prevent without requiring the adversary shows some awareness of its specific tampering. The definition where the adversary chooses and outputs f after seeing C does imply that all fixed functions f are prevented [45]. See the full version for more details [3, Appendix A].

How to Construct this Object. Before instantiating such an object, we recall some notations and related constructions of nonmalleable point obfuscations in prior work [8,38,44]. We note that all of these constructions rely on groups that only efficiently admit linear operations.

Suppose that g is a generator of a prime order group whose order is p. Throughout this paper, $[x]_g$ will be used to represent g^x (called implicit notation in [36]) so as to highlight the behavior in the exponent. We treat val as an element in $\mathbb{Z}_p$. Let the class of tampering functions $\mathcal{F}$ correspond to low degree polynomials over $\mathbb{Z}_p$. Previous constructions [8] use a set of polynomial encodings, denoted as $\mathcal{P}$, and compute the following for $\mathsf{Obf}(I_{\mathsf{val}})$:

1. Sample some $P \leftarrow \mathcal{P}$,
2. Output $P, [P(\mathsf{val})]_g$.

The intuition for security[3] is twofold: 1) that $\mathcal{P}$ is sufficiently randomized to argue virtual black box security [6], and that 2) for all instances of $P \in \mathcal{P}$ no fixed affine functions of P - i.e., $\alpha P(\mathsf{val}) + \beta$ - correspond to any $P'(f(\mathsf{val}))$ for $P' \in \mathcal{P}$ and low degree polynomial f. Prior work achieves these two properties jointly by randomizing the low degree coefficients of P and fixing some higher powers to have a coefficient of 1. For example, Bartusek et al. [8] consider $P_a(x) = ax + x^2 + x^3 + x^4 + x^5$.

Our construction builds such a function class $\mathcal{P}$, parameterizing $P \in \mathcal{P}$ by both a random a and ad, so that ad and val can be blended in a secure way. Let $\rho := |\mathsf{ad}|$. Then, we have:

$$P_{a,\mathsf{ad}}(x) \stackrel{\text{def}}{=} ax + \sum_{i=2}^{\rho+1} \mathsf{ad}_i x^i + \sum_{i=\rho+2}^{\rho+6} x^i.$$

In the above, the random a corresponds to the lowest degree coefficient of P and the bits of ad set intermediate coefficients of the polynomial P. We can prove security using the same group assumption used in prior nonmalleable point obfuscation works [8,38].

While the construction has a similar structure to prior work, analysis of nonmalleability is significantly more complicated by the fact that the adversary

---

[3] The actual constructions are more complicated to ensure correctness holds, using other points of randomness and group elements to check correctness. These are not used in arguing nonmalleability. For simplicity, we do not discuss correctness in this section.

Algorithm 1: Augmented real-or-random construction that provides non-malleability over input point and associated data. Obf is an obfuscator and NMObf is a nonmalleable obfuscator.

Input $(\mathsf{val}, \mathsf{key}, \mathsf{ad})$.

Sample random z.

for *each bit i of* key **do**

    if $\mathsf{key}_i = 1$ **then**

        | $C_i \leftarrow \mathsf{Obf}(I_{\mathsf{val}})$

    else

        | $C_i \leftarrow \mathsf{Obf}(I_z)$

    end

end

Let $C_0 \leftarrow \mathsf{NMObf}(I_{\mathsf{val},\mathsf{ad}})$. `// To distinguish an all-zero key and provide`
`nonmalleability`

Output $C = (C_0, C_1, \ldots, C_{|\mathsf{key}|}, \mathsf{ad})$.

---

1) knows ad, 2) can output any value for ad', and 3) doesn't have to explain how ad' arose from ad. This gives the adversary more flexibility, and proving nonmalleability becomes a careful multi-step procedure.

To give some intuition for the algebraic structure, it is important that the powers multiplied by the bits of ad are below the powers with coefficients 1. If these were switched, one could apply a polynomial tampering function to x and change the associated data to compensate for the resulting changes in the higher powers.

Extending to the Multibit Setting. Next, we integrate the above with the real-or-random approach of Canetti and Dakdouk [21]. The modified algorithm is summarized in Algorithm 1.

On the technical side, this approach requires the polynomials in the group to have more randomized powers, similar to the prior work of Fenteany and Fuller [38]. However, unlike their work, we only use one nonmalleable point obfuscation, the rest simply provide privacy. That is, only C_0 in Algorithm 1 is nonmalleable. As we show, this is sufficient to ensure nonmalleability over the resultant digital locker.

Protecting the Multibit Output. The above instantiation of the real-or-random construction prevents tampering of the input point and associated data but provides no protection over key. Our protection of the associated data allows us to upgrade the NIZK construction of [25] to the plain model. Our technique protects the associated data, which is set as `crs`, and the security of NIZK protects everything else, so long as `crs` cannot be tampered with. As we discuss in Sect. 5.3, we are also able to use a weaker NIZK system, specifically true simulation extractable NIZKs, which may be instantiable in pairing-free groups.

1.3 Discussion and Open Questions

This work presents the first constructions in the plain model of nonmalleable digital lockers and low-entropy robust fuzzy extractors. The integration of the nonmalleable point function with associated data with the real-or-random construction is technical and non-black box. Ideally, one would be able to define some necessary condition such that general black box composition of our point obfuscation with associated data and any other point obfuscation or digital locker is possible. One can view our construction as evidence that our particular nonmalleable point obfuscator with associated data is safe under composition with a specific point function.

There are known barriers to constructing digital lockers secure against auxiliary data that is hard to invert (such as a point function) if indistinguishability obfuscation exists [10,19]. Security in the presence of auxiliary data is the standard method for arguing composition.

In this work, we focus on nonmalleability of digital lockers. Obfuscating wildcards, conjunctions, and hyperplanes use similar techniques [7,12,18,24,31,39], so our techniques may apply. We note that some of these objects directly yield non-robust fuzzy extractors [31,39], so it may be possible to provide robustness by making the obfuscation nonmalleable. It seems less likely the techniques can be used to protect obfuscation of general evasive functions [5], compute-and-compare programs [17,43,56] and general obfuscation [2,40–42,48,49].

We generically use (true simulation extractible) NIZKs. Optimizing this construction is important, since this object will likely represent the dominant computational cost.

2 Preliminaries

Logarithms are base 2. Let $X_i \in \mathcal{Z}$ be random variables. We denote by $X = X_1, ..., X_n$ the tuple $(X_1, ..., X_n)$. For a discrete random variable X, the *min-entropy* of X is $H_\infty(X) = -\log(\max_x \Pr[X = x])$. For a pair of discrete random variables X, Y, the average min-entropy of $X|Y$ is

$$\tilde{H}_\infty(X|Y) = -\log\left(\mathop{\mathbb{E}}_{y \in Y}\left(2^{-H_\infty(X|Y)}\right)\right).$$

The notation id is used to denote the identity function: $\forall x, \mathrm{id}(x) = x$. Capitalized letters are used for random variables and lowercase letters for samples. Let $\{D_\lambda\}$ be an ensemble of sets. Two circuits, C and C', with inputs in D^λ are *functionally equivalent*, denoted $C \equiv C'$, if $\forall x \in D^\lambda, C(x) = C'(x)$. For a matrix $\mathbf{A}$, let $\mathbf{A}_i$ denote the ith row and $\mathbf{A}_{i,j}$ to denote the entry in the i row and jth column.

Definition 1. *An ensemble of distributions* $\mathcal{X} = \{X_\lambda\}_{\lambda \in \mathbb{N}}$, *where* $\mathcal{X}_\lambda$ *is over* D^λ, *is* well-spread *if the function* $H_\infty(X_\lambda)$ *mapping* λ *to non negative reals grows faster than* $\omega(\log \lambda)$. *That is,* $H_\infty(X_\lambda) = \omega(\log \lambda)$.

Definition 2. *An ensemble of distributions* $\mathcal{X} = \{X_\lambda\}_{\lambda \in \mathbb{N}}$, *where* $\mathcal{X}_\lambda$ *is over* D^λ, *is* efficiently sampleable *if exists a PPT algorithm given* 1^λ *as input whose output is identically distributed as* X_λ.

Throughout this work, we will use λ to represent the security parameter, ρ to represent the length of the associated data, ℓ to represent the length of the output key, and τ to represent the maximum degree of the polynomial the adversary uses for mauling.

3 Obfuscation Definitions

All obfuscation definitions include require only polynomial slowdown, which is easily verifiable for all presented constructions. The main object we introduce in this work is a nonmalleable point function with associated data. A traditional point function $I_{\mathsf{val}} : \mathbb{Z}_p \mapsto \{0,1\}$ takes a single input $\mathsf{val} \in \mathbb{Z}_p$ and returns 1 if and only if the input x to the function is val. An obfuscator is designed to preserve this functionality while hiding val. The definition of a nonmalleable point function with associated data adds a second input to I denoted as $\mathsf{ad} \in \{0,1\}^\rho$. This input does not need to be hidden by the obfuscator but should be nonmalleable. So the raw functionality is just a point function of the pair $\mathsf{val}, \mathsf{ad}$. That is,

$$I_{\mathsf{val},\mathsf{ad}}(x,y) = \begin{cases} 1 & x = \mathsf{val} \wedge y = \mathsf{ad} \\ 0 & \text{otherwise.} \end{cases}$$

Note that, since in our use cases ad is public, an honest user may just use the given ad in using the obfuscated point function. In our further sections, we use $\mathsf{lockPoint}(\cdot)$ to denote point obfuscation algorithm and $\mathsf{unlockPoint}$ as the obfuscated program. As prior work [25,38,44], we first present the notion of an obfuscation verifier:

Definition 3 (Obfuscation Verifier). *Let* $\lambda \in \mathbb{N}$ *be a security parameter and let* $\mathcal{O}$ *input* $x \in \mathsf{D}^\lambda$ *and output a program* $\mathcal{P}$. *An algorithm* $\mathsf{V}_{\mathsf{obf}}$ *is a value verifier if* $\forall x \in \mathsf{D}^\lambda$ *it is true that* $\mathrm{Pr}_{\mathsf{V}_{\mathsf{obf}},\mathcal{O}}[\mathsf{V}_{\mathsf{obf}}(\mathcal{P}) = 1 | \mathcal{P} \leftarrow \mathcal{O}(x)] = 1.$

Definition 4 (Nonmalleable Point Function with Associated Data). *For security parameter* $\lambda \in \mathbb{N}$ *parameter* $\rho \in \mathbb{N}$, *let* D_λ *be a sequence of input domains and* $\mathcal{F} : \mathsf{D}_\lambda \rightarrow \mathsf{D}_\lambda$ *be a family of functions. Let* $\mathcal{X}$ *be a family of distributions over* D_λ. *A* $(\mathcal{F}, \mathcal{X}, \rho)$-*nonmalleable point function obfuscation with associated data* $\mathsf{lockPoint}$ *is a PPT algorithm that inputs a point* $\mathsf{val} \in \mathsf{D}_\lambda$ *and* $\mathsf{ad} \in \{0,1\}^\rho$, *and outputs a circuit* $\mathsf{unlockPoint}$. *Let* $\mathsf{V}_{\mathsf{obf}}$ *be an obfuscation verifier for* $\mathsf{lockPoint}$ *as defined in Definition 3. The following properties must hold:*

1. **Completeness:** *For all* $\mathsf{val} \in \mathsf{D}^\lambda, \mathsf{ad} \in \{0,1\}^\rho$, *it holds that*

$$\mathrm{Pr}[\mathsf{unlockPoint}(\cdot,\cdot) \equiv I_{\mathsf{val},\mathsf{ad}}(\cdot,\cdot) | \mathsf{unlockPoint} \leftarrow \mathsf{lockPoint}(\mathsf{val},\mathsf{ad})] \geq 1 - \mathtt{ngl}(\lambda),$$

where the probability is over the randomness of $\mathsf{lockPoint}$.

2. **Virtual Black Box Security:** *For every PPT $\mathcal{A}$ and any polynomial function p, there exists a simulator $\mathcal{S}$ and a polynomial function $q(\cdot)$ such that, for all large enough $\lambda \in \mathbb{N}$, all $\mathsf{val} \in \mathsf{D}^\lambda, \mathsf{ad} \in \{0,1\}^\rho$ and for any predicate $\mathcal{P} : \mathsf{D}^\lambda \times \{0,1\}^\rho \mapsto \{0,1\}$,*

$$| \Pr[\mathcal{A}(\mathsf{unlockPoint}, \mathsf{ad}) = \mathcal{P}(\mathsf{val}, \mathsf{ad}) | \mathsf{unlockPoint} \leftarrow \mathsf{lockPoint}(\mathsf{val}, \mathsf{ad})]$$

$$- \Pr[\mathcal{S}^{I_{\mathsf{val},\mathsf{ad}}(\cdot)}(1^\lambda, \mathsf{ad}) = \mathcal{P}(\mathsf{val}, \mathsf{ad})] | \leq \frac{1}{p(\lambda)},$$

where $\mathcal{S}$ is allowed $q(\lambda)$ oracle queries total to $I_{\mathsf{val},\mathsf{ad}}$ and the probabilities are over the internal randomness of $\mathcal{A}$ and $\mathsf{lockPoint}$, and of $\mathcal{S}$, respectively. Here $I_{\mathsf{val},\mathsf{ad}}(\cdot)$ is an oracle that returns 1 when provided input $(\mathsf{val}, \mathsf{ad})$ and 0 otherwise.

3. **Nonmalleability:** *For any $X \in \mathcal{X}$, for all $\mathsf{ad} \in \{0,1\}^\rho$, for any PPT $\mathcal{A}$, there exists $\epsilon = \mathtt{ngl}(\lambda)$, such that defining*

$$\mathsf{unlockPoint} \leftarrow \mathsf{lockPoint}(\mathsf{val}, \mathsf{ad}),$$

$$(C, f, \mathsf{ad}^*) \leftarrow \mathcal{A}(\mathsf{unlockPoint}, \mathsf{ad})$$

it is true that :

$$\Pr_{\mathsf{val}\leftarrow X} \begin{bmatrix} \mathsf{V_{obf}}(C) = 1, (I_{f(\mathsf{val}),\mathsf{ad}^*} \equiv C) \\ f \in \mathcal{F} \ \vee (f = \mathsf{id} \wedge \mathsf{ad}^* \neq \mathsf{ad}) \end{bmatrix} \leq \epsilon.$$

3.1   Nonmalleable Digital Locker

We recall the definition of a nonmalleable digital locker. To distinguish this from the case of point obfuscation, we use $\mathsf{lock}()$ to denote the multi-bit point obfuscation algorithm and unlock as the (obfuscated) digital locker. In our construction, all tampering of the output key is prevented, so we remove the notion of a key verifier that was used in [38].

Definition 5 (Nonmalleable Digital Locker). *For security parameter $\lambda \in \mathbb{N}$, let D_λ be a sequence of domains, let*

1. *$\mathcal{F} : \mathsf{D}_\lambda \to \mathsf{D}_\lambda$ be a function family,*
2. *$\mathcal{X}$ be a family of distributions over D^λ,*
3. *lock be a PPT algorithm that maps points $\mathsf{val} \in \mathsf{D}^\lambda, \mathsf{key} \in \{0,1\}^n$ to a circuit unlock, and*
4. *$\mathsf{V_{obf}}$ be an obfuscation verifier.*

The algorithm lock is a $(\mathcal{F}, \mathcal{X}, n)$-nonmalleable digital locker if all of the below are satisfied:

1. **Completeness** *For all $\mathsf{val} \in \mathsf{D}^\lambda, \mathsf{key} \in \{0,1\}^n$ it holds that*

$$\Pr[\mathsf{unlock}(\cdot) \equiv I_{\mathsf{val},\mathsf{key}}(\cdot) | \mathsf{unlock} \leftarrow \mathsf{lock}(\mathsf{val}, \mathsf{key})] \geq 1 - \mathtt{ngl}(\lambda),$$

where the probability is over the randomness of lock. Here $I_{\mathsf{val},\mathsf{key}}$ is a function that returns key when provided input val, otherwise $I_{\mathsf{val},\mathsf{key}}$ returns $\perp$.

2. **Virtual Black Box Security:** *For all PPT $\mathcal{A}$ and $p = \text{poly}(\lambda)$, $\exists \mathcal{S}$ and $q(\lambda) = \text{poly}(\lambda)$ such that for all large enough $\lambda \in \mathbb{N}$, $\forall \text{val} \in D_\lambda, \text{key} \in \{0,1\}^n, \mathcal{P} : D_\lambda \times \{0,1\}^n \mapsto \{0,1\}$,*

$$\left| \Pr[\mathcal{A}(\text{lock}(\text{val}, \text{key})) = \mathcal{P}(\text{val}, \text{key})] - \Pr[\mathcal{S}^{I_{\text{val},\text{key}}}(1^\lambda) = \mathcal{P}(\text{val}, \text{key})] \right| \leq \frac{1}{p(\lambda)},$$

where $\mathcal{S}$ is allowed $q(\lambda)$ oracle queries to $I_{\text{val},\text{key}}$ and the probabilities are over the internal randomness of $\mathcal{A}$ and lock, *and of $\mathcal{S}$, respectively.*

3. **Nonmalleability** $\forall X \in \mathcal{X}, PPT$ $\mathcal{A}, \text{key} \in \{0,1\}^n$, *there exists $\epsilon = \text{ngl}(\lambda)$ such that:*

$$\Pr_{\text{val} \leftarrow X} \left[\left(\begin{array}{c} V_{\text{obf}}(C) = 1, \\ (f \in \mathcal{F} \wedge \text{key}' \neq \perp) \vee \\ (\text{key}' \notin \{\perp, \text{key}\} \wedge f = \text{id}) \end{array} \right) \left| \begin{array}{c} \text{unlock}_{\text{val},\text{key}} \leftarrow \text{lock}(\text{val}, \text{key}) \\ (C, f) \leftarrow \mathcal{A}(\text{unlock}_{\text{val},\text{key}}) \\ \text{key}' \leftarrow C(f(\text{val})) \end{array} \right. \right] \leq \epsilon.$$

recall id *is the identity function.*

Remark 2. As mentioned in the Introduction, there are alternative notions of nonmalleability. We formally define fixed nonmalleability, a weaker definition which was used in [25], and oblivious nonmalleability, which does not require the adversary to output the targeted function f in the full version [3, Appendix A]. There we show that oblivious nonmalleability is impossible in general. One can bypass this result by using cryptographic tools that extract the tampering function, such as a random oracle or non-falsifiable assumptions.

3.2   Same Point Definitional Equivalences

The soundness in Definitions 4 and 5 are virtual black box security [6]. In the majority of this work, we will be using distributional indistinguishability, which says that obfuscations of all well spread distributions X are indistinguishable from obfuscations of random points. Bitanski and Canetti [13] showed that this definition is equivalent to virtual black box obfuscation for point functions (see also [20,52]). Furthermore, they showed this equivalence holds when given a constant number of obfuscations on related points. Fenteany and Fuller [38] show that this equivalence holds if given a polynomial number of copies $\text{unlockPoint}_1 \leftarrow \text{lockPoint}(X), ..., \text{unlockPoint}_\ell \leftarrow \text{lockPoint}(X)$ as long as the same value is locked in each call to lockPoint. In the full version [3], we generalize these results showing that a vector of obfuscations that have output on a single input point are secure when composed with associated data. That is, define the circuit class

$$\mathbf{Point}_{\text{val},\text{key},\text{ad}}(\text{val}', \text{ad}') = \begin{cases} \text{key} & \text{val}' = \text{val} \wedge \text{ad}' = \text{ad} \\ \perp & \text{otherwise} \end{cases}.$$

Note that point functions and digital lockers both with and without associated data variants fall into this class by adjusting whether ad and key are of length 0. These proofs are straightforward extensions of the proofs in [38]. There are presented for completeness in the full version of this work [3].

Definition 6 (Distributional Indistinguishability). *A* **Point** *obfuscator is called a good distributional indistinguishable (DI) obfuscator if for any PPT $\mathcal{A}$ with binary output and any well-spread distribution $\mathcal{X}$ over points in D^λ, for all vectors* $\vec{\mathsf{key}}, \vec{\mathsf{ad}}$ *then there exists some negligible function ϵ such that*

$$\left| \Pr_{\mathsf{val}\leftarrow\mathcal{X}}[\mathcal{A}(\{C_i, \vec{\mathsf{ad}}_i\}_{i=1}^\ell) = 1 | \{C_i \leftarrow \mathbf{Point}(\mathsf{val}, \vec{\mathsf{ad}}_i, \vec{\mathsf{key}}_i)\}_{i=1}^\ell] \right.$$
$$\left. - \Pr_{u\xleftarrow{\$}\mathsf{D}^\lambda}[\mathcal{A}(\{C_i, \vec{\mathsf{ad}}_i\}_{i=1}^\ell) = 1 | \{C_i \leftarrow \mathbf{Point}(u, \vec{\mathsf{ad}}_i, \vec{\mathsf{key}}_i)\}_{i=1}^\ell] \right| \leq \epsilon.$$

Theorem 1. *For the class* **Point** *under $\ell = \mathsf{poly}(\lambda)$ composition where the same* val *is used in each obfuscation, distributional indistinguishability and virtual black box security (in Definition 4) are equivalent.*

3.3 Group Theoretic Assumptions

We present our underlying group-theoretic assumptions here. As a reminder, we use the implicit notation [36] to denote encoding in a group with generator g (where $[x]_g$ denotes g^x).

Assumption 1 [8, Assumption 3]. *Fix some $\psi \in \mathbb{Z}^+$. Let $\mathcal{G} = \{\mathbb{G}_\lambda\}_{\lambda\in\mathbb{N}}$ be a group ensemble with efficient representation and operations where each $\mathbb{G}_\lambda$ is a group of prime order $p(\lambda) \in (2^\lambda, 2^{\lambda+1})$. Let $\{\mathcal{X}_\lambda\}$ be a family of well-spread distributions over $\mathsf{D}^\lambda = \mathbb{Z}_{p(\lambda)}$. Then for any PPT $\mathcal{A}$:*

$$\left| \Pr[\mathcal{A}(\{k_i, [k_i x + x^i]_g\}_{i\in[2,\ldots,\psi]}) = 1] - \Pr[\mathcal{A}(\{k_i, [k_i r + r^i]_g\}_{i\in[2,\ldots,\psi]})] \right| = \mathsf{ngl}(\lambda).$$

where $x \leftarrow \mathcal{X}_\lambda, r \leftarrow \mathbb{Z}_{p(\lambda)}, k_i \leftarrow \mathbb{Z}_{p(\lambda)}$.

Bartusek, Ma, and Zhandry [8] justified Assumption 1 by showing it holds in the generic group model even if $\mathcal{X}_\lambda$ depends on g. This model of allowing a distribution to depend on g is related to the non-uniform generic group model [26]. Such an assumption is crucial to arguing plain model security (rather than treating $\mathcal{X}_\lambda$ as independent of g). The second assumption can be proved from Assumption 1, see [8, Lemma 8], and is useful for arguing nonmalleability:

Assumption 2 [8, Assumption 4]. *Fix some $\psi \in \mathbb{Z}^+$. Let $\mathcal{G}$ and $\mathcal{X}_\lambda$ be defined as in Assumption 1. For any PPT $\mathcal{A}$,*

$$\Pr[[x]_g \leftarrow \mathcal{A}(\{k_i, [k_i x + x^i]_g\}_{i\in[2,..,\psi]})] = \mathsf{ngl}(\lambda).$$

where $x \leftarrow \mathcal{X}_\lambda$ and $k_i \leftarrow \mathbb{Z}_{p(\lambda)}$.

4 Nonmalleable Point Functions with Associated Data

We begin by instantiating a nonmalleable point obfuscation satisfying Definition 4.

Construction 1. *Let $\lambda \in \mathbb{N}$ be a security parameter, let $\rho \in \mathbb{N}$ be a parameter. Let $\mathcal{G} = \{\mathbb{G}_\lambda\}_{\lambda \in \mathbb{N}}$ be a group ensemble with efficient representation and operations where each $\mathbb{G}_\lambda$ is a group of prime order $p(\lambda) \in (2^\lambda, 2^{\lambda+1})$. Define five polynomials $p_1, ..., p_5$ as follows:*

$$p_{1,\mathsf{ad},c_1}(\mathsf{val}) = c_1\mathsf{val} + \sum_{i=1}^{\rho} \mathsf{ad}_i\mathsf{val}^{i+1} + \sum_{i=\rho+2}^{\rho+6} \mathsf{val}^i,$$

$$p_{2,c_2}(\mathsf{val}) = c_2\mathsf{val} + \mathsf{val}^{\rho+7},$$

$$p_{3,c_3}(\mathsf{val}) = c_3\mathsf{val} + \mathsf{val}^{\rho+8},$$

$$p_{4,c_4}(\mathsf{val}) = c_4\mathsf{val} + \mathsf{val}^{\rho+9},$$

$$p_{5,c_5}(\mathsf{val}) = c_5\mathsf{val} + \mathsf{val}^{\rho+10}.$$

In the above, all calculations are conducted modulo $\mathbb{Z}_{p(\lambda)}$.

Let g be a generator of the group $\mathbb{G}_\lambda$. Let $c_1, c_2, c_3, c_4, c_5 \overset{\$}{\leftarrow} \mathbb{Z}_{p(\lambda)}$ be input randomness. Let $\rho \overset{def}{=} |\mathsf{ad}|$. Consider the following construction:

$$\mathsf{lockPoint}(\mathsf{val}, \mathsf{ad}; a, b, c) \overset{def}{=} \begin{pmatrix} c_1, & [p_{1,\mathsf{ad},c_1}(\mathsf{val})]_g \\ c_2, & [p_{2,c_2}(\mathsf{val})]_g \\ c_3, & [p_{3,c_3}(\mathsf{val})]_g \\ c_4, & [p_{4,c_4}(\mathsf{val})]_g \\ c_5, & [p_{5,c_5}(\mathsf{val})]_g \end{pmatrix}$$

$\mathsf{V_{obf}}$ *is the circuit that checks that* $\mathsf{unlockPoint}$ *consists of the appropriate number of values and group elements. If not, it outputs 0. Given a program* $\mathsf{unlockPoint}$ *consisting of five pairs $\{(c_i', g_i')\}_{i=1}^5$[4] and inputs $\mathsf{val}', \mathsf{ad}'$ compute:*

$$\left[p_{1,\mathsf{ad}',c_1'}(\mathsf{val}')\right]_g \overset{?}{=} g_1',$$

$$\left\{\left[p_{i,c_i'}(\mathsf{val}')\right]_g \overset{?}{=} g_i'\right\}_{i=2}^5.$$

If all of these checks pass, output 1. Otherwise, output 0.

Theorem 2. *Let all parameters be as in Construction 1, let $\rho \in \mathbb{N}$ be a parameter. Define $\mathcal{F} : \mathbb{Z}_{p(\lambda)} \to \mathbb{Z}_{p(\lambda)}$ as the set of non-constant, non-identity polynomials of maximum power τ. Suppose that*

1. *Assumption 1 holds for $\psi = \max\{\tau(\rho+6), \rho+10\}$ and*
2. *$(\rho+6)2^{2\rho}/p(\lambda)^3 = \mathtt{ngl}(\lambda)$.*

Then, Construction 1 is a $(\mathcal{F}, \mathcal{X}, \rho)$-nonmalleable point function obfuscation with associated data.

---

[4] g is a generator that is a global system parameter along with the group description. Note that it is efficiently checkable 1) whether the order of a group is prime and 2) whether an element g is a generator of the known order group.

Remark 3. In the above, the size of associated data is limited to be $\rho \approx \log(p(\lambda))$, which is linear in the security parameter λ. Our primary application has the associated data as the CRS of some NIZK. Such strings can be quite long. In Sect. 5.4, we show that it suffices to include a short value in the associated data whose size is $\Theta(\log \lambda)$.

In order to prove that Construction 1 satisfies Definition 4, we must prove correctness, virtual black box security, and nonmalleability.

Correctness: We present the following lemma proving correctness. Its proof is deferred to the full version [3].

Lemma 1. *For any ρ such that $(\rho + 6)2^{2\rho}/p(\lambda)^3 + \rho/p(\lambda) = \mathtt{ngl}(\lambda)$, Construction 1 satisfies completeness.*

Security: We present the following theorem proving security. Its proof is deferred to the full version [3]. Within the proof, Lemma 2 presents a general approach to creating valid point obfuscations from Assumption 1, which will be used in later constructions, as well.

Theorem 3. *Let ρ be the length of ad. Suppose that Assumption 1 holds for highest power $\psi = \rho + 10$. Then, Construction 1 satisfies virtual black box security.*

Nonmalleability: Finally, we must prove nonmalleability. We give the main theorem below. The proof strategy for it is as follows:

1. **Lemma 2.** We first prove that any method of incorporating associated data suffices for keeping val from being changed as long as there are enough large powers of val that are not affected by associated data. We show this holds even for adversaries that may arbitrarily tamper with the associated data.
2. **Lemma 3.** We then prove that, if the value val is not tampered, then for Construction 1 it is difficult to change $\mathsf{ad} \in \{0,1\}^\rho$ to any distinct $\mathsf{ad}' \in \{0,1\}^\rho$.

The aggregate of both of these results yields the desired nonmalleabillity property. We include the statements of Lemma 2 and Lemma 3 below, as well. Their proofs are deferred to the full version [3].

Theorem 4. *Let λ be a security parameter. Let $\{\mathcal{X}_\lambda\}$ be a well-spread distribution ensemble and let $\tau, \rho \in \mathbb{Z}^+$ be parameters that are both $\mathtt{poly}(\lambda)$. Let $\mathcal{F}_{poly}$ be the ensemble of functions f_λ where f_λ is the set of non-constant, non-identity polynomials in $\mathbb{Z}_{p(\lambda)}[x]$ with degree at most τ. Suppose that Assumption 1 holds for $\psi = \max\{\rho + 10, \tau(\rho + 6)\}$. Then, the obfuscator in Construction 1 is nonmalleable over $\mathcal{F}_{poly}$ with distribution ensemble $\{\mathcal{X}_\lambda\}$, and $\mathcal{AD} = \{0,1\}^\rho$.*

Lemma 2. *Let λ be a security parameter. Let $\{\mathcal{X}_\lambda\}$ be a well-spread distribution ensemble and let $\tau, \ell \in \mathbb{Z}^+$ be $\mathrm{poly}(\lambda)$. Let $\mathcal{F}_{poly}$ be the ensemble of functions f_λ where f_λ is the set of non-constant, non-identity polynomials in $\mathbb{Z}_{p(\lambda)}[x]$ with degree at most τ.*

Let $P(x) = r_1 x + \ldots + r_{\rho-1} x^{\rho-1} + r_\rho x^\rho$ with $r_i \in \mathbb{Z}_{p(\lambda)}$, and let $\vec{P} = \{r_1, \ldots, r_\rho\}$ where any or all of the r_i may be 0. Suppose that Assumption 1 holds for $\psi = \max\{\rho + 10, \tau(\rho + 6)\}$. Define as obfuscation (with c_1, c_2, c_3, c_4, c_5 uniformly distributed in $\mathbb{Z}_{p(\lambda)}$)

$$\mathsf{lockPoint}_P(\mathsf{val}, \vec{P}; c_1, c_2, c_3, c_4, c_5) \stackrel{def}{=} \vec{P}, \begin{bmatrix} c_1, & \left[c_1\mathsf{val} + \mathsf{val}P(\mathsf{val}) + \sum_{i=\rho+2}^{\rho+6} \mathsf{val}^i\right]_g \\ c_2, & \left[c_2\mathsf{val} + \mathsf{val}^{\rho+7}\right]_g \\ c_3, & \left[c_3\mathsf{val} + \mathsf{val}^{\rho+8}\right]_g \\ c_4, & \left[c_4\mathsf{val} + \mathsf{val}^{\rho+9}\right]_g \\ c_5, & \left[c_5\mathsf{val} + \mathsf{val}^{\rho+10}\right]_g \end{bmatrix}.$$

Consider $\mathcal{F}_{poly}$ and distribution ensemble $\{\mathcal{X}_\lambda\}$. For any nonmalleability PPT adversary $\mathcal{A}$ in Definition 4, $\mathcal{A}$ outputs a valid $f, P', \mathsf{unlockPoint}_{P'}$ with negligible probability.

Lemma 3. *Let λ be a security parameter. Let $\{\mathcal{X}_\lambda\}$ be a well-spread distribution ensemble and let $\tau, \rho \in \mathbb{Z}^+$ be $\mathrm{poly}(\lambda)$. Let $\mathcal{F}_{poly}$ be the ensemble of functions f_λ where f_λ is the set of non-constant, non-identity polynomials in $\mathbb{Z}_{p(\lambda)}[x]$ with degree at most τ.*

Let $P_{\vec{b}}(x) = b_\rho x^\rho + b_{\rho-1} x^{\rho-1} + \ldots + b_1 x$ where $b_i \in \{0, 1\}$. Suppose that Assumption 2 holds for $\psi = \max\{\rho + 10, \tau(\rho + 6)\}$. Define as an obfuscation (with c_1, c_2, c_3, c_4, c_5 uniformly distributed in $p(\lambda)$):

$$\mathsf{lockPoint}(\mathsf{val}, \vec{b}; c_1, c_2, c_3, c_4, c_5) \stackrel{def}{=} \vec{b}, \begin{bmatrix} c_1, & \left[c_1\mathsf{val} + \mathsf{val}P_{\vec{b}}(\mathsf{val}) + \sum_{i=\rho+2}^{\rho+6} \mathsf{val}^i\right]_g \\ c_2, & \left[c_2\mathsf{val} + \mathsf{val}^{\rho+7}\right]_g \\ c_3, & \left[c_3\mathsf{val} + \mathsf{val}^{\rho+8}\right]_g \\ c_4, & \left[c_4\mathsf{val} + \mathsf{val}^{\rho+9}\right]_g \\ c_5, & \left[c_5\mathsf{val} + \mathsf{val}^{\rho+10}\right]_g \end{bmatrix}.$$

Consider $\mathcal{F}_{poly}$ and distribution ensemble $\{\mathcal{X}_\lambda\}$. The probability that any PPT algorithm outputs a valid obfuscation with the identity function f and some $P_{\vec{b}'}$ with $\vec{b}' \in \{0, 1\}^\rho, \vec{b}' \neq \vec{b}$ is negligible.

5 Standard Model Digital Lockers

We will now construct a nonmalleable digital locker in two steps.

- In Sect. 5.1 we amend our previous construction of a $\mathsf{NMPO}_{\mathsf{ad}}$ to instead output a predetermined key rather than a single bit. Nonmalleability of the input val and ad must still be preserved, but *no* nonmalleability is guaranteed for key.

– In Sect. 5.2, we use this intermediate digital locker with a non-interactive zero
knowledge proof, to guarantee complete nonmalleability over key.

Of course, correctness and security must hold for val, key as well. The end result
of these efforts (Construction 3) will be a digital locker with: 1) input val non-
malleable over low-degree polynomials, 2) public helper string ad nonmalleable
over any tampering, and 3) output key nonmalleable over any tampering. As we
will see in Sect. 6, these tampering classes have meaningful applications.

5.1   Digital Lockers Nonmalleable Over Val and Ad

We integrate our $\mathtt{NMPO_{ad}}$ with the real-or-random construction [21] in Fig. 1. The
essential idea is that we may encode each bit of key as a real (encoding val) or
random (encoding a random point) point obfuscation, with an additional obfuscation of val to ensure that is the point being tested. We encode the attestation
of ad in this additional obfuscation.

In order to adapt our techniques to a real-or-random digital locker with
$|\mathsf{key}| = \ell$, then, it is clear that we must ensure that each point obfuscation
retains security in the presence of up to ℓ other copies of the same point (i.e.,
if $\mathsf{key} = 1^\ell$). The previous construction is clearly not sufficient, providing two
copies of the obfuscation breaks security (see discussion in [38]), but we may use
similar techniques as so. We begin by defining the intermediate cryptographic
object.

**Definition 7 (Input Nonmalleable Digital Locker with Associated
Data).** *For security parameter $\lambda \in \mathbb{N}$, let $\{D^\lambda\}$ be an ensemble of finite sets,
let $\rho \in \mathbb{N}$ be a parameter. Let*

1. *$\mathcal{F} : D^\lambda \to D^\lambda$ be a function family,*
2. *$\mathcal{X}$ be a family of distributions over D^λ,*
3. *iLock be a PPT algorithm that maps points $\mathsf{val} \in D^\lambda$, $\mathsf{ad} \in \{0,1\}^\rho$, $\mathsf{key} \in
   \{0,1\}^n$ to a circuit iUnlock, and*
4. *$\mathsf{V_{obf}}$ be an obfuscation verifier.*

*The algorithm iLock is a $(\mathcal{F}, \mathcal{X}, \rho, n)$-input nonmalleable digital locker with asso-
ciated data if all of the below are satisfied:*

1. ***Completeness*** *For all $\mathsf{val} \in D^\lambda$, $\mathsf{ad} \in \{0,1\}^\rho$, $\mathsf{key} \in \{0,1\}^n$ it holds that*

   $$\Pr[\mathsf{iUnlock}(\cdot) \equiv I_{\mathsf{val},\mathsf{ad},\mathsf{key}}(\cdot) | \mathsf{iUnlock} \leftarrow \mathsf{iLock}(\mathsf{val}, \mathsf{ad}, \mathsf{key})] \geq 1 - \mathrm{ngl}(\lambda),$$

   *where the probability is over the randomness of iLock. Here $I_{\mathsf{val},\mathsf{ad},\mathsf{key}}$ is a
   function that returns key when provided input $(\mathsf{val}, \mathsf{ad})$, otherwise $I_{\mathsf{val},\mathsf{ad},\mathsf{key}}$
   returns $\bot$.*
2. ***Virtual Black Box Security:*** *For all PPT $\mathcal{A}$ and $p(\lambda) = \mathtt{poly}(\lambda)$, $\exists S$
   and $q(\lambda) = \mathtt{poly}(\lambda)$ such that for all large enough $\lambda \in \mathbb{N}$, $\forall \mathsf{val} \in D^\lambda$, $\mathsf{ad} \in$*

$\{0,1\}^\rho, \mathsf{key} \in \{0,1\}^n, \mathcal{P} : \mathsf{D}^\lambda \times \{0,1\}^{\rho+n} \mapsto \{0,1\},$

$$\Big| \Pr[\mathcal{A}(\mathsf{iLock}(\mathsf{val}, \mathsf{ad}, \mathsf{key}), \mathsf{ad}) = \mathcal{P}(\mathsf{val}, \mathsf{ad}, \mathsf{key})]$$
$$- \Pr[\mathcal{S}^{I_{\mathsf{val}, \mathsf{ad}, \mathsf{key}}}(1^\lambda, \mathsf{ad}) = \mathcal{P}(\mathsf{val}, \mathsf{ad}, \mathsf{key})]\Big| \leq \frac{1}{p(\lambda)},$$

where S is allowed $q(\lambda)$ oracle queries to $I_{\mathsf{val}, \mathsf{ad}, \mathsf{key}}$ and the probabilities are over the internal randomness of $\mathcal{A}$ and lock, and of $\mathcal{S}$, respectively.

3. **Input Nonmalleability** For all $X \in \mathcal{X}, PPT \mathcal{A}, \mathsf{ad} \in \{0,1\}^\rho, \mathsf{key} \in \{0,1\}^n,$ there exists $\epsilon = \mathtt{ngl}(\lambda)$ such that:

$$\Pr_{\mathsf{val} \leftarrow X} \left[\begin{array}{c|c} \mathsf{V}_{\mathrm{obf}}(C) = 1, & \\ f \in \mathcal{F} \vee (f = \mathsf{id} \wedge \mathsf{ad}' \neq \mathsf{ad}) & \mathsf{unlock}_{\mathsf{val}, \mathsf{key}} \leftarrow \mathsf{iLock}(\mathsf{val}, \mathsf{ad}, \mathsf{key}) \\ C(f(\mathsf{val}), \mathsf{ad}') \neq \bot & (C, f, \mathsf{ad}') \leftarrow \mathcal{A}(\mathsf{unlock}_{\mathsf{val}, \mathsf{key}}, \mathsf{ad}) \end{array} \right] \leq \epsilon.$$

Remark 4. Note that input nonmalleability does not protect against key tampering. In fact, an adversary that arbitrarily mauls key to $\mathsf{key}' \in \{0,1\}^n$ is allowed for this object, so long as val and ad are not tampered.

Before introducing the construction, we define some polynomials that will be used in the construction as follows:

$$p_{0, \mathsf{ad}, \vec{c_0}}(\mathsf{val}) = c_{0,1}\mathsf{val} + \sum_{i=1}^{\ell} c_{0,i+1}\mathsf{val}^{i+1} + \sum_{i=1}^{\rho} \mathsf{ad}_i \mathsf{val}^{\ell+1+i} + \sum_{i=1}^{5} \mathsf{val}^{\ell+\rho+1+i}, \tag{1}$$

$$p_{0,1,c_{0,\ell+2}}(\mathsf{val}) = c_{0,\ell+2}\mathsf{val} + \mathsf{val}^{\ell+\rho+7}, \tag{2}$$

$$p_{0,2,c_{0,\ell+3}}(\mathsf{val}) = c_{0,\ell+3}\mathsf{val} + \mathsf{val}^{\ell+\rho+8}, \tag{3}$$

$$p_{0,3,c_{0,\ell+4}}(\mathsf{val}) = c_{0,\ell+4}\mathsf{val} + \mathsf{val}^{\ell+\rho+9}, \tag{4}$$

$$p_{0,4,c_{0,\ell+5}}(\mathsf{val}) = c_{0,\ell+5}\mathsf{val} + \mathsf{val}^{\ell+\rho+10}, \tag{5}$$

$$p_{\vec{c}}^*(\mathsf{val}) = c_{j,1}\mathsf{val} + \sum_{i=1}^{\ell} c_{j,i+1}\mathsf{val}^{i+1}. \tag{6}$$

Construction 2. *Let $\lambda \in \mathbb{N}$ be a security parameter, let $\rho, \ell \in \mathbb{N}$ be parameters. Let $\mathcal{G} = \{\mathbb{G}_\lambda\}$ be a group ensemble with efficient representation and operations where each $\mathbb{G}_\lambda$ is a group of prime order $p(\lambda) \in (2^\lambda, 2^{\lambda+1})$. Let $\mathsf{D}^\lambda = \mathbb{Z}_{p(\lambda)}$. Let g be a generator of $\mathbb{G}_\lambda$. Let $\rho, \ell \in \mathbb{Z}^+$ such that $\rho = O(\log \lambda)$ and $\ell = \mathtt{poly}(\lambda)$. Define the Construction of $(\mathsf{iLock}, \mathsf{iUnlock})$ as in Fig. 1.*

Theorem 5. *Let all parameters be as in Construction 2. Let $\tau \in \mathbb{N}$ and $\rho \in \mathbb{N}$ be parameters.*

1. *Suppose that Assumption 1 holds for maximum power $\max\{\ell + \rho + 10, \tau(\ell + \rho + 6)\}$,*

iLock(val, ad, key) :

1. Define $\ell = |\text{key}|$,
2. Sample $z \leftarrow \mathbb{Z}_{p(\lambda)}$,
3. Sample $\mathbf{C} \leftarrow \mathbb{Z}_{p(\lambda)}^{(\ell+1)\times(\ell+1)}$,
   $c_{0,\ell+2}, c_{0,\ell+3}, c_{0,\ell+4}, c_{0,\ell+5} \leftarrow \mathbb{Z}_{p(\lambda)}$,
4. Compute $\text{unlockPoint}_{\text{ad}} =$

$$\begin{bmatrix} \left[p_{0,\text{ad},\mathbf{C}_0}(\text{val})\right]_g \\ c_{0,\ell+2}, \left[p_{0,1,c_{0,\ell+2}}(\text{val})\right]_g \\ c_{0,\ell+3}, \left[p_{0,2,c_{0,\ell+3}}(\text{val})\right]_g \\ c_{0,\ell+4}, \left[p_{0,3,c_{0,\ell+4}}(\text{val})\right]_g \\ c_{0,\ell+5}, \left[p_{0,4,c_{0,\ell+5}}(\text{val})\right]_g \end{bmatrix}$$

5. For $i = 1$ to ℓ:

$$\text{unlockPoint}_i = \begin{cases} \left[p^*_{\mathbf{C}_i}(\text{val})\right]_g & \text{key}_i = 1 \\ \left[p^*_{\mathbf{C}_i}(z)\right]_g & \text{key}_i = 0 \end{cases}.$$

6. Output $\mathbf{C}, \text{unlockPoint}_{\text{ad}}, \{\text{unlockPoint}_i\}_{i=1}^{\ell}$.

iUnlock($\mathbf{C}'$, unlockPoint$'_{\text{ad}}$, $\{\text{unlockPoint}'_i\}_{i=1}^{\ell}$, val$'$, ad$'$):

1. Parse unlockPoint$'_{\text{ad}}$ as
   $c'_{0,\ell+2}, c'_{0,\ell+3}, c'_{0,\ell+4}, c'_{0,\ell+5}$,
   $g'_{0,1}, g'_{0,2}, g'_{0,3}, g'_{0,4}, g'_{0,5}$.
2. Verify

$$\left[p_{1,\text{ad}',\mathbf{C}'_0}(\text{val}')\right]_g = g'_{0,1},$$

$$\left\{\left[p_{i,c'_{0,i}}(\text{val}')\right]_g = g'_{0,i}\right\}_{i=2}^{5}.$$

   If one checks does not output $\bot$.
3. Initialize key $= \vec{0}^{\ell}$.
4. For $i = 1$ to ℓ:
   (a) If $[p^*_{\mathbf{C}'_i}(\text{val}')]_g =$ unlockPoint$'_i$ set key$_i = 1$.
5. Output key.

Fig. 1. Real-or random-instantiation of input nonmalleable digital locker with associated data.

2. Let $\mathcal{F}_{\text{poly}}$ be the family of polynomials over $\mathbb{Z}_{p(\lambda)}$ with maximum degree τ, and
3. $(\ell + \rho + 10)2^{2\rho}/p(\lambda)^3 = \text{ngl}(\lambda)$.

Then, Construction 2 is a $(\mathcal{F}_{\text{poly}}, \mathcal{X}, \rho, \ell)$-input nonmalleable digital locker with associated data.

The proof of this statement is deferred to the full version [3]. The technical details behind Theorem 5 follow the same structure as Theorem 2 — we prove correctness, virtual black box security, and input nonmalleability separately, each following a similar proof structure as the respective property of Construction 1.

5.2   Adding Key Nonmalleability

We now show that the input nonmalleable digital locker with associated data suffices to build a fully nonmalleable digital locker for the same function class. Let iLock be such an object and $\Pi = (\text{Setup}, P, V)$ be some appropriate non-interactive proof system (described in Sect. 5.3) using a crs of length ρ for the following language that proves well-formness of iLock:

$$\mathcal{L} = \{\text{iUnlock} : \exists(\text{val}, \text{crs}, \text{key}, r) \text{ such that iUnlock} = \text{iLock}(\text{val}, \text{crs}, \text{key}; r)\}$$

```
lock(val, key) :                                    V_obf(iUnlock, π, crs):

  1. Sample (crs = (crs₁, crs₂), TK, EK) ← Setup(1^λ).    1. If V_obf Input(iUnlock) = 0 output 0.
  2. Compute iUnlock ← iLock(val, crs₁, key; r).          2. If crs = 0⃗ output 0.
  3. Compute π ← P(unlock'; val, key, r, crs).            3. if V(π, unlock', crs) = 0 output 0.
  4. Output (iUnlock, π, crs).                            4. Output 1.

unlock(val, iUnlock, π, crs = (crs₁, crs₂)): Output iUnlock(val, crs₁)
```

Fig. 2. Digital locker construction.

Construction 3. *For security parameter $\lambda \in \mathbb{N}$, let $\mathcal{F} : \mathsf{D}^\lambda \to \mathsf{D}^\lambda$ be a family of functions, let $\rho, \ell \in \mathbb{N}$ be parameters, $\mathcal{X}$ be a family of distributions over D^λ. Suppose that*

1. *iLock is a $(\mathcal{F}_{\mathsf{poly}}, \mathcal{X}, \rho, \ell)$-input-nonmalleable digital locker with associated data with associated obfuscation verifier $\mathsf{V}_{\mathsf{obf\,Input}}$, and*
2. *$\Pi = (\mathsf{Setup}, P, V)$ is an NIZK system for the language $\mathcal{L}$ with short non-tamperable CRS.[5] We formally define this property and show a generic construction in Sect. 5.3.*

Then define $(\mathsf{lock}, \mathsf{unlock}, \mathsf{V}_{\mathsf{obf}})$ as in Fig. 2.

Theorem 6. *Let notation be as in Construction 3. Suppose that*

1. *iLock is a $(\mathcal{F}_{\mathsf{poly}}, \mathcal{X}, \rho, \ell)$-input-nonmalleable digital locker with associated data with associated obfuscation verifier $\mathsf{V}_{\mathsf{obf\,Input}}$, and*
2. *$\Pi = (\mathsf{Setup}, P, V)$ is a true simulation extractable non-interactive zero knowledge proof system as described in Sect. 5.3,*
3. *That every function $f \in \mathcal{F}$ is entropy preserving; i.e., for any well-spread X, $f(X)$ is also well-spread.*

Then $\mathsf{lock}, \mathsf{unlock}$ is a $(\mathcal{F}, \mathcal{X}, n)$-nonmalleable digital locker.

Proof (Proof of Theorem 6). Following Definition 5, we need to prove completeness, soundness, and nonmalleability. Completeness can be easily verified, so we just focus on the non-trivial parts, i.e., proof of soundness and nonmalleability.

Soundness. To prove soundness, we first observe that according to Theorem 1, for this class of circuits being obfuscated DI is equivalent to VBB, so for the rest of the proof, we focus on proving the DI. We prove soundness by contradiction. Suppose there exists a PPT adversary $\mathcal{A}$, a key $\mathsf{key} \in \{0,1\}^\ell$, and a well-spread distribution X such that

$$| \Pr_{\mathsf{val} \leftarrow \mathcal{X}}[\mathcal{A}(\mathsf{lock}(\mathsf{val}, \mathsf{key})) = 1] - \Pr_{r \xleftarrow{\$} \mathsf{D}^\lambda}[\mathcal{A}(\mathsf{lock}(r, \mathsf{key})) = 1] > \epsilon$$

---

[5] That is, crs can be split into $(\mathsf{crs}_1, \mathsf{crs}_2)$ where crs_1 has length independent of the language, i.e., $O(\lambda)$, and only crs_1 is required to be non-tamperable. crs_2 cannot be modified (computationally infeasible) given the original crs_1.

for some non-negligible ϵ, then there exists an adversary $\mathcal{B}$ that breaks the DI security of the input-nonmalleable digital locker. This reaches a contradiction.

$\mathcal{B}$ receives the distribution X samples $(\mathsf{crs}_1, \mathsf{crs}_2, \mathsf{TK}, \mathsf{EK}) \leftarrow \mathsf{Setup}(1^\lambda)$ for the proof system, and sets associated data as crs_1. $\mathcal{B}$ sends this distribution to the reduction for iLock with the input distribution the same X, and associated data, crs_1. The reduction samples some $\mathsf{val} \leftarrow X$ or uniform r. $\mathcal{B}$ receives iUnlock. Next $\mathcal{B}$ creates a simulated π. It sends iUnlock, π, crs to $\mathcal{A}$ and outputs $\mathcal{A}$'s decision.

Clearly, if val is from the distribution X, then the reduction has simulated an indistinguishable $\mathsf{lock}(\mathsf{val}, \mathsf{key})$ (assuming the simulated proof π is indistinguishable), or otherwise, $\mathsf{lock}(r, \mathsf{key})$. That is, in both cases, the obfuscation is properly prepared assuming the indistinguishability of the simulated proof. Thus, the advantage of the adversary $\mathcal{A}$ translates to the advantage of $\mathcal{B}$ in breaking the DI of the nonmalleable point obfuscation. By the equivalence of DI and VBB of point obfuscation, this breaks the soundness of the nonmalleable point obfuscation.

Nonmalleability. Now we prove nonmalleability. As before, we prove by contradiction. Suppose there exists a PPT adversary $\mathcal{A}$ and $\mathsf{key} \in \{0,1\}^\ell$, a well-spread distribution X such that $\mathcal{A}$ breaks the nonmalleability experiment with non-negligible probability ϵ. Then there exists an adversary $\mathcal{B}$ that breaks the nonmalleability of the underlying $\mathsf{iLock}(\cdot)$.

$\mathcal{B}$ follows exactly the same procedure in preparing the input to the adversary $\mathcal{A}$ as in soundness proof above. Now $\mathcal{A}$ would return a triple $(C, f, \mathsf{crs}^* = (\mathsf{crs}_1^*, \mathsf{crs}_2^*))$ that passes the checking conditions with a non-negligible probability ϵ. Assume C is different from the original obfuscation given to $\mathcal{A}$ (as we don't allow identity tampering). $\mathcal{B}$ does the following:

- If the crs_1 is modified to a different crs_1^*, then the reduction just outputs the C, f, crs_1^* which correspond to a tamper according to nonmalleability of $\mathsf{iLock}(\cdot)$.
- If the crs_1 is kept intact but crs_2 is modified to a different crs_2^*, then this breaks the underlying NIZK as it is computationally infeasible to obtain a consistent but different crs_2^*.
- If the $\mathsf{crs} = \mathsf{crs}^*$ in C is intact yet the statement-proof pair is modified, then $\mathcal{B}$ runs the witness extractor to extract a valid witness, i.e., val' used to generate C. As the input obfuscated circuits received by $\mathcal{B}$ are properly prepared by the challenger, the simulated proof given to the adversary $\mathcal{A}$ is with respect to a true statement. In this case, the notion of true simulation extractability allows $\mathcal{B}$ to extract a valid witness by running the extractor. Thus, given $\mathsf{val}' = f(\mathsf{val})$. $\mathcal{B}$ can prepare an obfuscation (with an arbitrary associated data of val'), breaking the nonmalleability of $\mathsf{iLock}(\cdot)$.

Since $\mathcal{A}$ wins the nonmalleable experiment with a non-negligible probability, one of the above case must happen with a non-negligible probability. This would imply the contradiction we expect. The above two arguments complete the proof of Theorem 6.

5.3   The Building Block – True Simulation Extractable NIZK

In this section, we present the building block used in Construction 3 – true simulation extractable NIZK. The notion was introduced by Dodis et al. [32] as a relaxation of *all* simulation extractable NIZK. We describe the notion in what follows.

Definition 8. *Let R be an NP relation on pairs (x, w) with corresponding language $L_R = \{x : \exists w$ such that $(x, w) \in R\}$. A true-simulation extractable non-interactive zero-knowledge (NIZK) argument for a relation R consists of three algorithms* (Setup, Prove, Verify) *with the following syntax:*

- (crs, TK, EK) $\leftarrow$ Setup(1^λ): *creates a common reference string* crs, *a trapdoor* TK, *and an extraction key* EK.
- $\pi \leftarrow$ Prove(crs, x, w): *creates an argument π that $R(x, w) = 1$.*
- $0/1 \leftarrow$ Verify(crs, x, π): *verifies whether or not the argument π is correct.*

For presentation simplicity, we omit crs *in the* Prove *and* Verify. *We require that the following three basic properties hold:*

- ***Completeness.*** *For any $(x, w) \in R$, if* (crs, TK, EK) $\leftarrow$ Setup(1^λ), $\pi \leftarrow$ Prove(x, w), *then* Verify(x, π) $= 1$.
- ***Soundness.*** *For any PPT adversary $\mathcal{A}$, the following probability is negligible: for* (crs, TK, EK) $\leftarrow$ Setup(1^λ), $(x^*, \pi^*) \leftarrow \mathcal{A}$(crs) *such that $x^* \notin L_R$ but* Verify(x^*, π^*) $= 1$.
- ***Composable Zero-knowledge.*** *There exists a PPT simulator $\mathcal{S}$ such that for any PPT $\mathcal{A}$, the advantage (the probability $\mathcal{A}$ wins minus one half) is negligible in the following game.*
  - *The challenger samples* (crs, TK, EK) $\leftarrow$ Setup(1^λ) *and sends* (crs, TK) *to $\mathcal{A}$*
  - *$\mathcal{A}$ chooses $(x, w) \in R$ and sends to the challenger.*
  - *The challenger generates $\pi_0 \leftarrow$ Prove(x, w), $\pi_1 \leftarrow$ Sim(x, TK), and then samples a random bit $b \leftarrow \{0, 1\}$. Then he sends π_b to $\mathcal{A}$.*
  - *$\mathcal{A}$ outputs a guess bit b', and wins if $b' = b$.*
- ***Extractibility.*** *Additionally, true simulation extractability requires that there exists a PPT extractor* Ext *such that for any PPT adversary $\mathcal{A}$, the probability $\mathcal{A}$ wins is negligible in the following game:*
  - *The challenger samples* (crs, TK, EK) $\leftarrow$ Setup(1^λ) *and sends* crs *to $\mathcal{A}$.*
  - *$\mathcal{A}$ is allowed to make oracle queries to the simulation algorithm* Sim$'((x, w),$ TK) *adaptively.* Sim$'$ *first checks if $(x, w) \in R$ and returns* Sim(x, TK) *if that is the case.*
  - *$\mathcal{A}$ outputs a tuple x^*, L^*, π^*.*
  - *The challenger runs the extractor $w^* \leftarrow$ Ext($L^*, (x^*, \pi^*),$ EK).*
  - *$\mathcal{A}$ wins if (1) the pair (x^*, L^*) was not part of the simulator query, (2) the proof π^* verifies, and (3) $R(x^*, w^*) = 0$.*

Briefly speaking, a true simulation extractable NIZK requires that the adversary can only query the simulation oracle only on true statements, whereas all simulation extractability allows the adversary to query on any (perhaps false) statement. As shown by the work [32], the true simulation extractable NIZK can be constructed in a fairly simple way as summarized by the following theorem.

Theorem 7 ([32]). *Assume that there exists a CCA2 encryption and a regular NIZK argument for NP languages, then there exists a true simulation extractable NIZK for NP languages.*

The work [32] showed how to instantiate the building blocks under the SXDH assumption over bilinear groups. There is plausible evidence that the regular NIZK can be constructed without the need of pairing groups, c.f. [28], under some non-standard assumptions.

5.4 NIZK with Short Non-tamperable CRS

The generic use of the NIZK from Dodis et al. [32] requires long CRS that would depend on the language being proved, and this is a general fact for NIZKs. In our application, however, this poses a challenge when we combine this with our non-malleable obfuscation with associate data. Particularly, the correctness of Theorem 2 requires a group that has a length larger than that of associated data. We notice that the language $\mathcal{L}$ used in Construction 3 requires a long CRS, as the statement and the witness are long. So, putting CRS as the associated data in the non-malleable digital locker would require a significantly larger group, which is undesirable.

To handle this technical subtlety, we present a simple transformation from any NIZK into one whose CRS has the following structure: $crs = (crs_1, crs_2)$, where only crs_1 is short and non-tamperable, crs_2 can be arbitrarily long but cannot be tampered consistently (computationally infeasible) as long as crs_1 is kept intact. In this way, we can put crs_1 as the associated data into our non-malleable digital locker, and keep crs_2 public, as we presented in the prior section. Thus, the underlying group of the non-malleable obfuscation can be significantly smaller.

To achieve this, given any crs' from the underlying NIZK, we define a new NIZK which is essentially the same as the original one, except in the CRS generation: first it samples a collision resistant hash function h and computes $z = h(crs)$. It outputs $crs = (crs_1 = (h, z), crs_2 = crs')$ as the new CRS. The verifier will always check whether $h(crs_2) = z$ and rejects immediately if it does not hold. The security (zero-knowledge, soundness) is not affected by crs_1, as it can be generated just given crs'.

6 Application to Fuzzy Extractors

In this section, we show that a nonmalleable digital locker suffices to build a robust fuzzy extractor [14–16,33] when combined with a standard secure sketch.

We note information-theoretic robust fuzzy extractor in the plain model or CRS models requires the source to have an entropy of at least half its length [35]. In this work, we consider computational robust fuzzy extractors in the plain model. We begin with a few definitions.

Definition 9 (Secure Sketch). *Let λ be a security parameter. Let $\mathcal{W} = \mathcal{W}_\lambda$ be a family of random variables over metric space $(\mathcal{M}, \mathsf{dis}) = (\mathcal{M}_\lambda, \mathsf{dis}_\lambda)$. Then* SS, Rec *is a $(\mathcal{M}, \mathcal{W}, t, \delta)$-secure sketch if the following hold:*

Correctness. *For all $w, w' \in \mathcal{M}$ such that $\mathsf{dis}(w, w') \leq t$, $\Pr[\mathsf{Rec}(w', \mathsf{SS}(w)) = w] \geq 1 - \delta$.*
Security. *For all distributions $W \in \mathcal{W}$ it is true that $\tilde{\mathsf{H}}_\infty(W|\mathsf{SS}(W)) \geq \omega(\log \lambda)$.*

Definition 10 (Robust Fuzzy extractor). *An $(\mathcal{M}, \mathcal{W}, \ell, t)$-computationally robust fuzzy extractor is a pair of PPT algorithms* (Gen, Rep) *where for all $w, w' \in \mathcal{M}$,*

- (key, pub) $\leftarrow$ Gen(w), *where* key $\in \{0,1\}^\ell$ *and* pub $\in \{0,1\}^*$
- key$'$ $\leftarrow$ Rep(pub, w')

such that the following properties are true:

- **Correctness :** *For all $w, w' \in \mathcal{M}$ such that $\mathsf{dist}(w, w') \leq t$,*

$$\Pr\left[\mathsf{key}' = \mathsf{key} \mid (\mathsf{key}, \mathsf{pub}) \leftarrow \mathsf{Gen}(w), \mathsf{key}' \leftarrow \mathsf{Rep}(\mathsf{pub}, w')\right] \geq 1 - \mathtt{ngl}(\lambda).$$

- **Security :** *For any distribution $W \in \mathcal{W}$, and for* (key, pub) $\leftarrow$ Gen(W), *for all PPT $\mathcal{A}$ there exists some $\mathtt{ngl}(\lambda)$ function such that*

$$|\Pr[\mathcal{A}(\mathsf{key}, \mathsf{pub}) = 1] - \Pr[\mathcal{A}(U_\ell, \mathsf{pub}) = 1]| \leq \mathtt{ngl}(\lambda).$$

where U_ℓ is a uniformly distributed random variable on $\{0,1\}^\ell$.
- **Robustness:** *Let $W, W' \in \mathcal{M}$ be (correlated) distributions such that*

$$\Pr_{(w,w')\leftarrow(W,W')}[\mathsf{dis}(w, w') \leq t] = 1$$

and $W, W' \in \mathcal{W}$. For all $W, W' \in \mathcal{W}$ and for all adversaries $\mathcal{A}$, the advantage of $\mathcal{A}$ in the following experiment is at most $\mathtt{ngl}(\lambda)$:
1. *Sample $(w, w') \leftarrow (W, W')$.*
2. *Compute* (key, pub) $\leftarrow$ FE.Gen(w) *and send it to $\mathcal{A}$.*
3. *$\mathcal{A}$ outputs* pub$'$ *and wins if* pub$' \neq$ pub *and* FE.Rep(pub$'$, w') $\notin \{\bot, \mathsf{key}\}$.

Before introducing a common secure sketch which uses code syndromes we introduce the notation of $\mathsf{Wgt}(x) = \mathsf{dis}(x, 0)$ as the Hamming weight of x.

Gen(w) :	Rep(w', ss', unlock'):
1. Compute $ss \leftarrow$ SS(w).	1. If V_{key}(unlock') = 0 output $\bot$.
2. Sample random key $\in \{0,1\}^\ell$.	2. Let $w^* \leftarrow$ Rec(w', ss')
3. Obfuscate unlock$_{w,key} \leftarrow$ lock(w, key).	3. If dis(w', w^*) > t or $w^* \notin \mathbb{F}_q^n$ output $\bot$.
4. Output key, pub = (ss, unlock$_{w,key}$).	4. Output unlock'(w^*).

Fig. 3. Robust Fuzzy Extractor from nonmalleable digital locker and syndrome secure sketch.

Definition 11 (Syndrome). *Let* $\mathbf{A} : \mathbb{F}_q^k \to \mathbb{F}_q^n$ *be a* $(n, k, d = 2t + 1)$*-linear error code, then there exists a matrix* Syn $: \mathbb{F}_q^n \to \mathbb{F}_q^{n-k}$ *with two properties:*

1. *For all values* x *where* Wgt(x) $\le t$ *the value* Syn(x) *is unique.*
2. *There is an efficient mapping from* $s \in \mathbb{F}_q^{n-k}$ *to the value* x *of weight at most* t *if one exists. Let* Invert *denote this mapping. If no such value exists then the output of* Invert *is* $\bot$.
3. *For any two values* s, s' *where* Wgt(s), Wgt(s'), Wgt($s - s'$) $\le t$ *it is true that*

$$\text{Invert(Syn}(s - s')) = \text{Invert(Syn}(s) - \text{Syn}(s'))$$
$$= \text{Invert(Syn}(s)) - \text{Invert(Syn}(s')) = s - s'.$$

Definition 12 (Syndrome Secure Sketch [11,30,34]). *Let* $\mathcal{W} \in \mathbb{F}_q^n$ *be the set of all distributions* W *where* $\text{H}_\infty(W) = (n - k) \log q + \omega(\log \lambda)$. *Let* Syn *be the Syndrome of an* $(n, k, d = 2t+1)$*-error correcting code. Then define* SS(w) = Syn(w) *and* Rec(w', s) = $w' -$ Invert(Syn(w') $- s$) = $w' -$ Invert(Syn($w' - w$)) = w. *Then* (SS, Rec) *is a* $(\mathbb{F}_q^n, \mathcal{W}, t, 0)$*-secure sketch.*

Theorem 8. *Assume the following:*

1. (SS, Rec) *be a syndrome secure sketch for distance* $2t$, *that is,* $d = 4t + 1$,
2. $\mathcal{W}$ *is the set of all efficiently sampleable distributions* W *where*

$$\tilde{\text{H}}_\infty(W|\text{SS}(W)) \ge \omega(\log \lambda),$$

3. (lock, unlock, V_{key}) *is a nonmalleable digital locker for* $(\mathcal{F}, \mathcal{X})$ *where* $\mathcal{F}$ *includes all functions* $f : \mathbb{F}_q^n \to \mathbb{F}_q^n$ *of the form* $f(x) = x + a$ *and where* $\mathcal{X}$ *is the set of all distributions* X *where* $\text{H}_\infty(X) = \omega(\log \lambda)$.

Then (Gen, Rep) *described in Fig. 3 is a* $(\mathcal{M}, \mathcal{W}, \ell, t)$*-robust fuzzy extractor (Definition 10).*

See the full version [3] for the full proof. The intuition behind the robustness proof is that the adversary will be able to extract the function f from the robust fuzzy extractor adversary's output by computing Invert($ss' - ss$).

Aligning Tampering Functions. There is a subtlety when we instantiate the fuzzy extractor of Theorem 8 – the digital locker in Theorem 8 requires a function class of the domain $\mathbb{F}_q^n$, whereas the digital locker constructed in Fig. 2 works in $\mathbb{Z}_{p(\lambda)}$. It is unclear whether there is an additively homomorphic mapping between these spaces for arbitrary p, q, n. Therefore, a trivial plug-in of the digital locker of Fig. 2 does not work. In Sect. 6.1, we show that that how to align readings in a simple way at the cost of increased leakage of the secure sketch.

An Alternative to Efficiently Sampleable W. Theorem 8 required W to be efficiently sampleable. This is because in the proof the reduction samples a $w \leftarrow W$ to compute a secure sketch ss and create the conditional distribution $W|\mathsf{SS}(w)$. An alternative approach is to define all of the objects throughout our main technical sections to be nonmalleable in the presence of auxiliary information Z such that $\mathrm{H}_\infty(W|Z) \geq \omega(\log \lambda)$. In this case, $\mathcal{A}'$ can receive ss as auxiliary information and directly forward it to $\mathcal{A}$.

All of the proofs contained in this work naturally extend to the setting of auxiliary information. The major work needed to have confidence in the auxiliary input approach is to show that [8, Assumption 3] holds in the non-uniform generic group model [26] in the presence of auxiliary information. Importantly, the distribution W has average min-entropy conditioned on $\mathsf{SS}(W)$. There are strong impossibility results on digital lockers that are secure against hard to invert auxiliary information [19].

Applications of Nonmalleable Point Function Obfuscation. Nonmalleable point obfuscation and nonmalleable point obfuscation with associated data (Definition 4) can be used to build robust secure sketches and robust fuzzy extractors, respectively.

- **Robust secure sketch:** Robustness for secure sketches is defined in a similar fashion as for fuzzy extractors. For correlated distributions W, W', the adversary receives $\mathsf{SS}(w)$ from the challenger and outputs SS'. The adversary wins the robustness game if he succeeds in finding a value SS' such that $\mathsf{Rec}(\mathsf{SS}', w') \notin \{\bot, w\}$. Informally, suppose (lockPoint, unlockPoint) is a nonmalleable point obfuscation and $(\mathsf{SS}, \mathsf{Rec})$ is a syndrome-based secure sketch. Then Fig. 4 describes a robust secure sketch. The formal theorem and proof can be found in the full version [3].
- **Robust fuzzy extractor:** Let (lockPoint, unlockPoint) be a nonmalleable point obfuscation with associated data, $(\mathsf{SS}, \mathsf{Rec})$ be a syndrome-based secure sketch and ext be a randomness extractor. Then Fig. 5 describes a robust fuzzy extractor. We stress that this construction requires the remaining entropy of W to be high conditioned on both the produced key which is produced using a randomness extractor [47,51] and $\mathsf{SS}(w)$. There is no limitation on the key length in the robust fuzzy extractor from the nonmalleable digital locker (in Theorem 8). The formal theorem and proof can be found in the full version [3].

SS'(w) :

1. Compute $ss \leftarrow$ SS(w).
2. Obfuscate
   unlockPoint$_w \leftarrow$ lockPoint(w).
3. Output (ss, unlock_w).

Rec'(w', ss', unlockPoint'):

1. If V_{obf}(unlockPoint') = 0 output $\perp$.
2. Compute $w^* \leftarrow$ Rec(w', ss')
3. If dis(w', w^*) > t or $w^* \notin \mathbb{F}_q^n$ output $\perp$.
4. Else if unlockPoint'(w^*) = 0 output $\perp$.
5. Else output w^*.

Fig. 4. Robust Secure Sketch from nonmalleable point obfuscation and syndrome secure sketch.

Gen(w) :

1. Sample random seed $\in \{0, 1\}^\rho$.
2. Generate key $\leftarrow$ ext(w; seed).
3. Compute $ss \leftarrow$ SS(w).
4. Obfuscate
   unlockPoint$_{w,\text{seed}} \leftarrow$ lockPoint(w, seed).
5. Output key and
   pub = $(ss, \text{unlockPoint}_{w,\text{seed}}, \text{seed})$.

Rep(w', ss', unlockPoint', seed'):

1. If V_{key}(unlockPoint') = 0 output $\perp$.
2. Compute $w^* \leftarrow$ Rec(w', ss')
3. If dis(w', w^*) > t or $w^* \notin \mathbb{F}_q^n$ output $\perp$.
4. if unlockPoint'(w^*, seed') = 0 output $\perp$.
5. Output key $\leftarrow$ ext(w^*; seed').

Fig. 5. Robust Fuzzy Extractor from nonmalleable point obfuscation with associated data, syndrome secure sketch and randomness extractor.

6.1 Instantiations – Aligning the Tampering Function Classes

In this section, we show how to align the tampering function classes required by the fuzzy extractor of Theorem 8 and the construction of Fig. 2. This deals with the mismatch in input domain for the syndrome (which takes inputs in $\mathbb{F}_q^n$) and the nonmalleable digital locker (which takes inputs in $\mathbb{Z}_p$).

Assume that the input readings w, w' are q-ary strings of length n. Instead of using a q-ary error correcting code ($\mathbf{A} \in \mathbb{F}_q^{n \times k}$ and Syn : $\mathbb{F}_q^{n \times (n-k)}$), we consider an error correcting code with entries in $\mathbb{F}_{q'}$ for some prime $q' \geq 2(q-1)+1$. That is, let $\mathbf{A}' \in \mathbb{F}_q^{n \times k}$ be a $(n, k, d = 4t + 1)$ linear error correcting code, and let Syn' be the corresponding syndrome. Furthermore, we make the restriction $p \geq q^n$, where $\mathbb{Z}_p$ is the input domain of the digital locker of Fig. 2. In the construction of Rep, note there is a check if the recovered value, w^*, is not q-ary, in which case we output $\perp$. Thus, for the adversary to successfully break robustness they must produce a q-ary output.

Now we encode every string $x \in \mathbb{F}_q^n$ as the natural q-ary representation, i.e., $x \mapsto \sum_{i \in [n]} x_i q^{i-1} \in \mathbb{Z}_p$, denoted as Enc(x). Moreover, the digital locker takes input an encoded version of w, i.e.,

$$\text{lockPoint}(\text{Enc}(w), \text{seed}) \text{ and } \text{unlockPoint}(\text{Enc}(w^*), \text{seed}').$$

By setting things up in this way, Theorem 8 holds even if the underlying digital locker is non-malleable for shift functions in $\mathbb{Z}_p$.

In Theorem 8 the reduction extracts a tampering function $f : \mathbb{F}_q^n \to \mathbb{F}_q^n$ where $f(w) = w + \text{Invert}(ss' - ss)$. With the modified syndrome construction, the function $f : \mathbb{F}_q^n \to \mathbb{F}_q^n$, as above, the reduction can extract a function $f(w) = w + \mathsf{Invert}(ss' - ss)$. By the check of $w^* \in \mathbb{F}_q^n$ and the initial condition that $w \in \mathbb{F}_q^n$, this implies that $w_i + \mathsf{Invert}(ss' - ss)_i \in \mathbb{F}_q$, we can first conclude that $\mathsf{Invert}(ss - ss')$ can be represented in $\{-(q-1), ..., (q-1)\}^n$. Under this representation, we conclude that for each i, $w_i + \mathsf{Invert}(ss' - ss)_i \in \mathbb{F}_q$ using standard integer addition. So, for each i, we are guaranteed an element in $\mathbb{F}_q$ (i.e., $\mathsf{Enc}(w^*) = \mathsf{Enc}(w) + \mathsf{Enc}(\mathsf{Invert}(ss' - ss)))$, which corresponds exactly to a shift tampering function in $\mathbb{Z}_p$, and thus the reduction can break the underlying non-malleable digital locker.

The effect of this transform is to increase the required entropy on the distribution W. The standard analysis of the secure sketch assumes that $\mathsf{SS}(W)$ leaks $(n-k)\log q$ bits of information about W. By increasing the syndrome from q to q' this increases the leakage of the secure sketch by $(n-k)\log(q'/q) \approx (n-k)\log 2$. This transform applies to the constructions in Figs. 4 and 5 as well. We do not include it in our proofs to show the general connection between syndrome secure sketches and nonmalleable point obfuscation variants.

Acknowledgements. The authors thank the reviewers for their helpful comments and suggestions. The authors wish to thank Leonid Reyzin for important discussions. The work of D.A. was done while at NIST. C.C. is supported by NSF Awards #1849904 and 2141033 and a fellowship from Synchrony Inc. B.F. is supported by NSF Awards #1849904, and 2141033. The work of F.L. is supported by the NSF Award #1942400.

This research is based upon work supported in part by the Office of the Director of National Intelligence (ODNI), Intelligence Advanced Research Projects Activity (IARPA), via Contract No. 2019-19020700008. This material is based upon work supported by the Defense Advanced Research Projects Agency under Air Force Contract No. FA8702-15-D-0001. Any opinions, findings, conclusions or recommendations expressed in this material are those of the author(s) and do not necessarily reflect the views of DARPA, ODNI, IARPA, or the U.S. Government. The U.S. Government is authorized to reproduce and distribute reprints for governmental purposes notwithstanding any copyright annotation therein.

References

1. Alamélou, Q., et al.: Pseudoentropic isometries: a new framework for fuzzy extractor reusability. In: AsiaCCS (2018)
2. Ananth, P., Jain, A.: Indistinguishability obfuscation from compact functional encryption. In: Gennaro, R., Robshaw, M. (eds.) CRYPTO 2015. LNCS, vol. 9215, pp. 308–326. Springer, Heidelberg (2015). https://doi.org/10.1007/978-3-662-47989-6_15
3. Apon, D., Cachet, C., Fenteany, P., Fuller, B., Liu, F.-H.: Nonmalleable digital lockers and robust fuzzy extractors in the plain model. Cryptology ePrint Archive, Report (2022). https://eprint.iacr.org/2022/1108
4. Bahler, L., Di Crescenzo, G., Polyakov, Y., Rohloff, K., Cousins, D.B.: Practical implementation of lattice-based program obfuscators for point functions. In: 2017 International Conference on High Performance Computing & Simulation (HPCS), pp. 761–768. IEEE (2017)

5. Barak, B., Bitansky, N., Canetti, R., Kalai, Y.T., Paneth, O., Sahai, A.: Obfuscation for evasive functions. In: Lindell, Y. (ed.) TCC 2014. LNCS, vol. 8349, pp. 26–51. Springer, Heidelberg (2014). https://doi.org/10.1007/978-3-642-54242-8_2

6. Barak, B., et al.: On the (im) possibility of obfuscating programs. J. ACM (JACM) **59**(2), 6 (2012)

7. Bartusek, J., Lepoint, T., Ma, F., Zhandry, M.: New techniques for obfuscating conjunctions. In: Ishai, Y., Rijmen, V. (eds.) EUROCRYPT 2019. LNCS, vol. 11478, pp. 636–666. Springer, Cham (2019). https://doi.org/10.1007/978-3-030-17659-4_22

8. Bartusek, J., Ma, F., Zhandry, M.: The distinction between fixed and random generators in group-based assumptions. In: Boldyreva, A., Micciancio, D. (eds.) CRYPTO 2019. LNCS, vol. 11693, pp. 801–830. Springer, Cham (2019). https://doi.org/10.1007/978-3-030-26951-7_27

9. Bellare, M., Rogaway, P.: Random oracles are practical: a paradigm for designing efficient protocols. In: CCS 1993 - Proceedings of the First ACM Conference on Computer and Communications Security (1993)

10. Bellare, M., Stepanovs, I., Tessaro, S.: Contention in cryptoland: obfuscation, leakage and UCE. In: Kushilevitz, E., Malkin, T. (eds.) TCC 2016. LNCS, vol. 9563, pp. 542–564. Springer, Heidelberg (2016). https://doi.org/10.1007/978-3-662-49099-0_20

11. Bennett, C.H., Brassard, G., Crépeau, C., Skubiszewska, M.-H.: Practical quantum oblivious transfer. In: Feigenbaum, J. (ed.) CRYPTO 1991. LNCS, vol. 576, pp. 351–366. Springer, Heidelberg (1992). https://doi.org/10.1007/3-540-46766-1_29

12. Bishop, A., Kowalczyk, L., Malkin, T., Pastro, V., Raykova, M., Shi, K.: A simple obfuscation scheme for pattern-matching with wildcards. In: Shacham, H., Boldyreva, A. (eds.) CRYPTO 2018. LNCS, vol. 10993, pp. 731–752. Springer, Cham (2018). https://doi.org/10.1007/978-3-319-96878-0_25

13. Bitansky, N., Canetti, R.: On strong simulation and composable point obfuscation. In: Rabin, T. (ed.) CRYPTO 2010. LNCS, vol. 6223, pp. 520–537. Springer, Heidelberg (2010). https://doi.org/10.1007/978-3-642-14623-7_28

14. Boyen, X.: Reusable cryptographic fuzzy extractors. In: Proceedings of the 11th ACM Conference on Computer and Communications Security, pp. 82–91 (2004)

15. Boyen, X.: Robust and reusable fuzzy extractors. In: Security with Noisy Data, pp. 101–112. Springer, Heidelberg (2007). https://doi.org/10.1007/978-1-84628-984-2_6

16. Boyen, X., Dodis, Y., Katz, J., Ostrovsky, R., Smith, A.: Secure remote authentication using biometric data. In: Cramer, R. (ed.) EUROCRYPT 2005. LNCS, vol. 3494, pp. 147–163. Springer, Heidelberg (2005). https://doi.org/10.1007/11426639_9

17. Brakerski, Z., Rothblum, G.N.: Obfuscating conjunctions. J. Cryptol. **30**(1), 289–320 (2017)

18. Brakerski, Z., Vaikuntanathan, V., Wee, H., Wichs, D.: Obfuscating conjunctions under entropic ring LWE. In: Proceedings of the 2016 ACM Conference on Innovations in Theoretical Computer Science, pp. 147–156 (2016)

19. Brzuska, C., Farshim, P., Mittelbach, A.: Indistinguishability obfuscation and UCEs: the case of computationally unpredictable sources. In: Garay, J.A., Gennaro, R. (eds.) CRYPTO 2014. LNCS, vol. 8616, pp. 188–205. Springer, Heidelberg (2014). https://doi.org/10.1007/978-3-662-44371-2_11

20. Canetti, R.: Towards realizing random oracles: hash functions that hide all partial information. In: Kaliski, B.S. (ed.) CRYPTO 1997. LNCS, vol. 1294, pp. 455–469. Springer, Heidelberg (1997). https://doi.org/10.1007/BFb0052255

21. Canetti, R., Dakdouk, R.R.: Obfuscating point functions with multibit output. In: Smart, N. (ed.) EUROCRYPT 2008. LNCS, vol. 4965, pp. 489–508. Springer, Heidelberg (2008). https://doi.org/10.1007/978-3-540-78967-3_28
22. Canetti, R., Fuller, B., Paneth, O., Reyzin, L., Smith, A.: Reusable fuzzy extractors for low-entropy distributions. J. Cryptol. **34**(1), 1–33 (2021)
23. Canetti, R., Goldreich, O., Halevi, S.: The random oracle methodology, revisited. J. ACM **51**(4), 557–594 (2004)
24. Canetti, R., Rothblum, G.N., Varia, M.: Obfuscation of hyperplane membership. In: Micciancio, D. (ed.) TCC 2010. LNCS, vol. 5978, pp. 72–89. Springer, Heidelberg (2010). https://doi.org/10.1007/978-3-642-11799-2_5
25. Canetti, R., Varia, M.: Non-malleable obfuscation. In: Reingold, O. (ed.) TCC 2009. LNCS, vol. 5444, pp. 73–90. Springer, Heidelberg (2009). https://doi.org/10.1007/978-3-642-00457-5_6
26. Coretti, S., Dodis, Y., Guo, S.: Non-uniform bounds in the random-permutation, ideal-cipher, and generic-group models. In: Shacham, H., Boldyreva, A. (eds.) CRYPTO 2018. LNCS, vol. 10991, pp. 693–721. Springer, Cham (2018). https://doi.org/10.1007/978-3-319-96884-1_23
27. Cousins, D.B., et al.: Implementing conjunction obfuscation under entropic ring LWE. In: 2018 IEEE Symposium on Security and Privacy (SP), pp. 354–371. IEEE (2018)
28. Couteau, G., Katsumata, S., Ursu, B.: Non-interactive zero-knowledge in pairing-free groups from weaker assumptions. In: Canteaut, A., Ishai, Y. (eds.) EUROCRYPT 2020. LNCS, vol. 12107, pp. 442–471. Springer, Cham (2020). https://doi.org/10.1007/978-3-030-45727-3_15
29. Cramer, R., Dodis, Y., Fehr, S., Padró, C., Wichs, D.: Detection of algebraic manipulation with applications to robust secret sharing and fuzzy extractors. In: Smart, N. (ed.) EUROCRYPT 2008. LNCS, vol. 4965, pp. 471–488. Springer, Heidelberg (2008). https://doi.org/10.1007/978-3-540-78967-3_27
30. Crépeau, C.: Efficient cryptographic protocols based on noisy channels. In: Fumy, W. (ed.) EUROCRYPT 1997. LNCS, vol. 1233, pp. 306–317. Springer, Heidelberg (1997). https://doi.org/10.1007/3-540-69053-0_21
31. Demarest, L., Fuller, B., Russell, A.: Code offset in the exponent. In: 2nd Conference on Information-Theoretic Cryptography (ITC 2021). Schloss Dagstuhl-Leibniz-Zentrum für Informatik (2021)
32. Dodis, Y., Haralambiev, K., López-Alt, A., Wichs, D.: Efficient public-key cryptography in the presence of key leakage. In: Abe, M. (ed.) ASIACRYPT 2010. LNCS, vol. 6477, pp. 613–631. Springer, Heidelberg (2010). https://doi.org/10.1007/978-3-642-17373-8_35
33. Dodis, Y., Kanukurthi, B., Katz, J., Reyzin, L., Smith, A.: Robust fuzzy extractors and authenticated key agreement from close secrets. IEEE Trans. Inf. Theory **58**(9), 6207–6222 (2012)
34. Dodis, Y., Ostrovsky, R., Reyzin, L., Smith, A.: Fuzzy extractors: how to generate strong keys from biometrics and other noisy data. SIAM J. Comput. **38**(1), 97–139 (2008)
35. Dodis, Y., Wichs, D.: Non-malleable extractors and symmetric key cryptography from weak secrets. In: Proceedings of the Forty-First Annual ACM Symposium on Theory of Computing, pp. 601–610. ACM (2009)
36. Escala, A., Herold, G., Kiltz, E., Ràfols, C., Villar, J.: An algebraic framework for Diffie-Hellman assumptions. J. Cryptol. **30**(1), 242–288 (2017)

37. Feng, H., Tang, Q.: Computational robust (fuzzy) extractors for CRS-dependent sources with minimal min-entropy. In: Nissim, K., Waters, B. (eds.) TCC 2021. LNCS, vol. 13043, pp. 689–717. Springer, Cham (2021). https://doi.org/10.1007/978-3-030-90453-1_24

38. Fenteany, P., Fuller, B.: Same point composable and nonmalleable obfuscated point functions. In: Conti, M., Zhou, J., Casalicchio, E., Spognardi, A. (eds.) ACNS 2020. LNCS, vol. 12147, pp. 124–144. Springer, Cham (2020). https://doi.org/10.1007/978-3-030-57878-7_7

39. Galbraith, S.D., Zobernig, L.: Obfuscated fuzzy hamming distance and conjunctions from subset product problems. In: Hofheinz, D., Rosen, A. (eds.) TCC 2019. LNCS, vol. 11891, pp. 81–110. Springer, Cham (2019). https://doi.org/10.1007/978-3-030-36030-6_4

40. Garg, S., Gentry, C., Halevi, S., Raykova, M., Sahai, A., Waters, B.: Candidate indistinguishability obfuscation and functional encryption for all circuits. In: 2013 IEEE 54th Annual Symposium on Foundations of Computer Science, pp. 40–49. IEEE (2013)

41. Garg, S., Gentry, C., Halevi, S., Raykova, M., Sahai, A., Waters, B.: Candidate indistinguishability obfuscation and functional encryption for all circuits. SIAM J. Comput. **45**(3), 882–929 (2016)

42. Gentry, C., Lewko, A.B., Sahai, A., Waters, B.: Indistinguishability obfuscation from the multilinear subgroup elimination assumption. In: 2015 IEEE 56th Annual Symposium on Foundations of Computer Science (FOCS), pp. 151–170. IEEE (2015)

43. Goyal, R., Koppula, V., Waters, B.: Lockable obfuscation. In: 2017 IEEE 58th Annual Symposium on Foundations of Computer Science (FOCS), pp. 612–621. IEEE (2017)

44. Komargodski, I., Yogev, E.: Another step towards realizing random oracles: nonmalleable point obfuscation. In: Nielsen, J.B., Rijmen, V. (eds.) EUROCRYPT 2018. LNCS, vol. 10820, pp. 259–279. Springer, Cham (2018). https://doi.org/10.1007/978-3-319-78381-9_10

45. Komargodski, I., Yogev, E.: Another step towards realizing random oracles: Nonmalleable point obfuscation. Cryptology ePrint Archive, Report 2018/149 (2018). Version 20190226:074205, https://eprint.iacr.org/2018/149

46. Lynn, B., Prabhakaran, M., Sahai, A.: Positive results and techniques for obfuscation. In: Cachin, C., Camenisch, J.L. (eds.) EUROCRYPT 2004. LNCS, vol. 3027, pp. 20–39. Springer, Heidelberg (2004). https://doi.org/10.1007/978-3-540-24676-3_2

47. Nisan, N., Zuckerman, D.: Randomness is linear in space. J. Comput. Syst. Sci. **52**(1), 43–52 (1996)

48. Pass, R., Seth, K., Telang, S.: Indistinguishability obfuscation from semantically-secure multilinear encodings. In: Garay, J.A., Gennaro, R. (eds.) CRYPTO 2014. LNCS, vol. 8616, pp. 500–517. Springer, Heidelberg (2014). https://doi.org/10.1007/978-3-662-44371-2_28

49. Sahai, A., Waters, B.: How to use indistinguishability obfuscation: deniable encryption, and more. In: Proceedings of the Forty-Sixth Annual ACM Symposium on Theory of Computing, pp. 475–484. ACM (2014)

50. Simhadri, S., Steel, J., Fuller, B.: Cryptographic authentication from the iris. In: Lin, Z., Papamanthou, C., Polychronakis, M. (eds.) ISC 2019. LNCS, vol. 11723, pp. 465–485. Springer, Cham (2019). https://doi.org/10.1007/978-3-030-30215-3_23

51. Vadhan, S.P., et al.: Pseudorandomness, vol. 7. Now Delft (2012)
52. Varia, M.H.: Studies in program obfuscation. PhD thesis, Massachusetts Institute of Technology (2010)
53. Wen, Y., Liu, S.: Robustly reusable fuzzy extractor from standard assumptions. In: Peyrin, T., Galbraith, S. (eds.) ASIACRYPT 2018. LNCS, vol. 11274, pp. 459–489. Springer, Cham (2018). https://doi.org/10.1007/978-3-030-03332-3_17
54. Wen, Y., Liu, S., Gu, D.: Generic constructions of robustly reusable fuzzy extractor. In: Lin, D., Sako, K. (eds.) PKC 2019. LNCS, vol. 11443, pp. 349–378. Springer, Cham (2019). https://doi.org/10.1007/978-3-030-17259-6_12
55. Wen, Y., Liu, S., Hu, Z., Han, S.: Computational robust fuzzy extractor. Comput. J. **61**(12), 1794–1805 (2018)
56. Wichs, D., Zirdelis, G.: Obfuscating compute-and-compare programs under LWE. In: 2017 IEEE 58th Annual Symposium on Foundations of Computer Science (FOCS), pp. 600–611. IEEE (2017)

Continuously Non-malleable Codes Against Bounded-Depth Tampering

Gianluca Brian[1](✉)(iD), Sebastian Faust[2](iD), Elena Micheli[2],
and Daniele Venturi[1,2](iD)

[1] Sapienza University of Rome, Rome, Italy
{brian,venturi}@di.uniroma1.it
[2] Technische Universität Darmstadt, Darmstadt, Germany
{sebastian.faust,elena.micheli}@tu-darmstadt.de

Abstract. Non-malleable codes (Dziembowski, Pietrzak and Wichs, ICS 2010 & JACM 2018) allow protecting arbitrary cryptographic primitives against related-key attacks (RKAs). Even when using codes that are guaranteed to be non-malleable against a *single* tampering attempt, one obtains RKA security against poly-many tampering attacks at the price of assuming perfect memory erasures. In contrast, *continuously* non-malleable codes (Faust, Mukherjee, Nielsen and Venturi, TCC 2014) do not suffer from this limitation, as the non-malleability guarantee holds against *poly-many* tampering attempts. Unfortunately, there are only a handful of constructions of continuously non-malleable codes, while standard non-malleable codes are known for a large variety of tampering families including, e.g., NC0 and decision-tree tampering, AC0, and recently even bounded polynomial-depth tampering. We change this state of affairs by providing the first constructions of continuously non-malleable codes in the following natural settings:

– Against decision-tree tampering, where, in each tampering attempt, every bit of the tampered codeword can be set arbitrarily after adaptively reading up to d locations within the input codeword. Our scheme is in the plain model, can be instantiated assuming the existence of one-way functions, and tolerates tampering by decision trees of depth $d = O(n^{1/8})$, where n is the length of the codeword. Notably, this class includes NC0.

G. Brian—Supported by grant SPECTRA from Sapienza University of Rome. This work was partly done while G. Brian was visiting the University of Warsaw, Poland, supported by the Copernicus Award (agreement no. COP/01/2020) from the Foundation for Polish Science and by the Premia na Horyzoncie grant (agreement no. 512681/PnH2/2021) from the Polish Ministry of Education and Science.

S. Faust and E. Micheli—This work has been funded by the German Research Foundation (DFG) CRC 1119 CROSSING (project S7), by the German Federal Ministry of Education and Research and the Hessen State Ministry for Higher Education, Research and the Arts within their joint support of the National Research Center for Applied Cybersecurity ATHENE.

D. Venturi—Supported by grant SPECTRA from Sapienza University of Rome.

© International Association for Cryptologic Research 2022
S. Agrawal and D. Lin (Eds.): ASIACRYPT 2022, LNCS 13794, pp. 384–413, 2022.
https://doi.org/10.1007/978-3-031-22972-5_14

- Against bounded polynomial-depth tampering, where in each tampering attempt the adversary can select any tampering function that can be computed by a circuit of bounded polynomial depth (and unbounded polynomial size). Our scheme is in the common reference string model, and can be instantiated assuming the existence of time-lock puzzles and simulation-extractable (succinct) non-interactive zero-knowledge proofs.

1   Introduction

Related-key attacks (RKAs) allow an adversary to break security of a cryptographic primitive by invoking it under one or more keys that satisfy known relations. Such attacks were first introduced as a tool for the cryptanalysis of blockciphers [20,52], but can also be mounted in practice thanks to the ability of attackers to influence secret keys via tampering attacks [21,22,45].

Theoretically, we can model $\mathcal{F}$-RKA security of a given cryptographic primitive as follows: The attacker can choose multiple tampering functions $f_1, f_2, \ldots$ within a family of allowed manipulations $\mathcal{F}$ of the secret key, and later observe the effect of such changes at the output by invoking the primitive on chosen inputs. An elegant solution to the problem of constructing $\mathcal{F}$-RKA-secure cryptoschemes is provided by *non-malleable codes* [40]. Intuitively, an $\mathcal{F}$-non-malleable code allows us to encode a message so that a modified codeword via a function $f \in \mathcal{F}$ either decodes to the same message or to a completely unrelated value. In the application to RKA security, we simply encode the secret key κ and store the corresponding codeword γ in memory. A RKA changes the memory content to $\tilde{\gamma} = f(\gamma)$ for some function $f \in \mathcal{F}$. Hence, at each invocation, we decode the codeword stored in memory and run the corresponding cryptographic primitive using the obtained key. Since the decoded key is either equal to the original or unrelated to it, we obtain $\mathcal{F}$-RKA security.

Unfortunately, there are two important caveats to the above general solution: (i) Since non-malleable codes are only secure against a *single* tampering attempt $f \in \mathcal{F}$, at each invocation we must completely erase the memory and re-encode the key; (ii) In case the modified codeword is invalid, and thus cannot be decoded, we must self-destruct and stop using the underlying primitive. It turns out that limitation (ii) is inherent, in that Gennaro, Lysyanskaya, Malkin, Micali and Rabin [45] established that RKA security is impossible without self-destruct.[1] On the other hand, it would be desirable to remove limitation (i) as perfect erasures of the memory are notoriously hard to implement in practice [26]. Another drawback of limitation (i) is that it makes the cryptoscheme stateful (even if it was stateless to start with) and requires fresh randomness for re-encoding the key.

---

[1] Their attack is simple: The j-th tampering function tries to set the j-th bit of the secret key to 0: If the device returns an invalid output, the next function f_{j+1} additionally sets the j-th bit of the key to 1 and otherwise sets it to 0.

The stronger notion of *continuously* non-malleable codes [43] allows us to overcome limitation (i): Since such codes guarantee $\mathcal{F}$-non-malleability even against poly-many tampering attempts, one immediately obtains $\mathcal{F}$-RKA security without assuming perfect erasures.

1.1 Our Contribution

A nice feature of the above compiler is its generality: In order to achieve $\mathcal{F}$-RKA security all we need to do is to design an $\mathcal{F}$-non-malleable code. In recent years, there has been a tremendous progress in the design of non-malleable codes for several tampering families $\mathcal{F}$ of practical interest, including: bit-wise independent and split-state tampering [2,4,6,29,40,50,51,53–55], space-bounded tampering [42], small-locality and small-depth circuits [7,10,12,48], decision-tree and AC0 tampering [13,15], and very recently even bounded polynomial-depth tampering [11,14,35]. In contrast, continuous non-malleability is only known for bit-wise independent tampering [32,34], tampering functions with few fixed points and high entropy [49], constant-state tampering [3], split-state tampering [5,36,43,56] and space-bounded tampering [30], leaving open the following intriguing question:

> *Can we construct* continuously *non-malleable codes against natural non-compartmentalized tampering families, such as decision trees, AC0 or even bounded polynomial-depth circuits?*

We answer the above question in the affirmative:

- In the setting of decision-tree tampering, we construct a code which resists continuous tampering attacks from the family of functions that modify every bit of the tampered codeword arbitrarily after adaptively reading up to d locations from the input codeword. Our scheme is in the plain model, assumes the existence of one-way functions, and tolerates tampering by decision trees of depth $d = O(n^{1/8})$, where n is the length of the codeword. Notably, this class includes NC0.
- In the setting of bounded polynomial-depth tampering, we construct a code that resists continuous tampering attacks, where the adversary can select any tampering function that can be computed by a circuit of bounded polynomial depth (and unbounded polynomial size). Notably, this class includes non-uniform NC. Our scheme is in the common reference string (CRS) model, and assumes the existence of time-lock puzzles and simulation-extractable (succinct) non-interactive zero-knowledge (NIZK) proofs.

We remark that both our constructions rely on computational assumptions. Although we don't know whether they are necessary for decision-tree or bounded-depth continuous tampering, achieving information-theoretic guarantees in the continuous scenario turned out to be challenging for even more well-studied families [3,5,28,30,32–34,39,42,49]. We leave this problem open for future work.

1.2   Technical Overview

Due to space constraints, most proofs have been deferred to the full version of this paper [25]. Let us start by reviewing different flavors of *one-time* non-malleability (see Sect. 3 for formal definitions).

- *Non-malleability w.r.t. message/codeword:* A code is non-malleable *w.r.t.* *message* (resp. *w.r.t. codeword*) if a tampered codeword either decodes to the original message (resp. is identical to the original codeword) or decodes to a completely unrelated value.
- *Super non-malleability:* A code is *super non-malleable* [43,44] if the tampered codeword itself (when valid) is unrelated to the original message. Note that the distinction between w.r.t. message and w.r.t. codeword also applies here.

Persistent Tampering. The above flavors can be naturally extended to the setting of continuous non-malleability. Our first observation is that, in the setting of non-compartmentalized tampering, continuous non-malleability is only achievable in the case of *persistent* tampering, where the j-th tampering function f_j is applied to the output of the previous function f_{j-1}.

The latter can be seen as follows. Consider an adversary that computes offline a valid encoding of two different messages, for simplicity say $\mu_0 = 0^k$ and $\mu_1 = 1^k$. Call γ_0 and γ_1 the corresponding codewords. Next, the attacker prepares a tampering query that hard-wires γ_0, γ_1 and proceeds as follows: It reads the first bit $\gamma[1]$ of the target codeword; if $\gamma[1] = 0$ it overwrites the target codeword with γ_0, while if $\gamma[1] = 1$ it overwrites the target codeword with γ_1. As a result, the adversary learns the first bit of the target codeword. Now, if tampering is non-persistent, the attacker can repeat this procedure to efficiently recover the entire codeword, which clearly violates continuous non-malleability.[2]

In light of the above attack, in what follows, and without loss of generality, when we refer to continuous non-malleability, we implicitly refer to the case of persistent tampering.

Decision-Tree Tampering. To show our first result, we revisit the recent construction of non-malleable codes against decision-tree tampering by Ball, Guo and Wichs [15]. On a high-level, this construction first encodes the message μ using a *leakage-resilient* non-malleable code in the split-state model, resulting in a codeword (γ_L, γ_R) consisting of a right and a left part. Then, each part γ_i for $i \in \{L, R\}$ is encoded independently as follows: we sample a random small set (whose size is that of the underlying codeword) in a much larger array, plant the input in these locations and zero everything else out. Finally, we use a ramp secret sharing with relatively large secrecy threshold to encode a description of the small set (which can be represented by a seed ζ_i). To decode, we can simply

---

[2] To the best of our knowledge, this observation is new. Previous work in the setting of non-compartmentalized tampering implicitly circumvented the above attack by requiring each tampering function to have high min-entropy and few fixed points, or by assuming that the number of tampering queries is a-priori bounded [49].

extract the seed and output what is in the corresponding locations of the array. This allows us to recover both parts γ_L, γ_R and thus obtain the initial message.

Ball, Guo and Wichs [15] show how to simulate the decoded message corresponding to one decision-tree tampering query using bounded split-state leakage and one split-state tampering query on the underlying non-malleable code. Although our construction is similar to theirs, proving continuous non-malleability is non-trivial and requires significant new ideas. We discuss some of them below.

First, in the original construction, the positions of the codeword that are not indexed by ζ_i are ignored, since they are not useful for the reconstruction. In our case, however, an attacker could copy the original codeword into the zero bits and overwrite the rest with a valid encoding of an unrelated message, which would allow it to retrieve the original encoding, thus breaking continuous non-malleability. We avoid this by requiring such positions to be 0 for the codeword to be valid. Second, we must ensure that the adversary cannot modify the other parts of the outer codeword without touching the inner codeword: this is because otherwise the adversary could use some tampering queries to save a state inside the codeword, and then use another tampering query to actually tamper with the codeword using more information than he should. We avoid this attack, by relying on computational assumptions. The idea is to sample verification keys vk_L, vk_R for a one-time signature scheme, generate (γ_L, γ_R) as an encoding of the string $\mu \| vk_L \| vk_R$, and finally append signatures σ_L, σ_R to the left and right part of the above described final encoding. In Sect. 3.3, we also show that this trick works generically to compile any super non-malleable code w.r.t. message into a super non-malleable code w.r.t. codeword, so long as the tampering family $\mathcal{F}$ allows us to evaluate the signing algorithm of the signature scheme. Intuitively, our code against decision-tree tampering removes this assumption thanks to the fact that the split-state model allows us to run arbitrary polynomial-time functions (independently on the two parts of the codeword).

In a nutshell, our scheme uses as building blocks a split-state nmc, a signature scheme and a simple procedure transforming states into their sparse versions. The latter takes as input a length-c-string γ, samples a random set $\mathcal{I}$ of c indices in $[n]$ with $n > c$, and outputs the sparse codeword $\gamma^* = (\gamma_1^*, \gamma_2^*)$, where γ_1^* is a RSS encoding of $\mathcal{I}$, and γ_2^* is a length-n-string that has γ in the positions indexed by $\mathcal{I}$, and zeros elsewhere. To extract the original string from the sparse one, it suffices to use the RSS decoding algorithm on the first part, and return the corresponding bits of the second part.

The design of our scheme follows.

Algorithm Enc*(μ). Proceed as follows:
1. Sample two pairs of keys $(sk_L, vk_L), (sk_R, vk_R)$ for the signature scheme
2. Compute the split-state codeword (γ_L, γ_R) for the message $(\mu \| vk_L \| vk_R)$
3. Compute the sparse strings γ_L^* and γ_R^* for γ_L and γ_R.
4. Sign γ_L^* and γ_R^* with, respectively, sk_L and sk_R, to get σ_L and σ_R.
5. The final codeword is $(\sigma_L, \gamma_L^*, \sigma_R, \gamma_R^*)$.

The decoding algorithm extracts γ_L and γ_R from their sparse versions γ_L^* and γ_R^* and checks that in the remaining positions there are only zeros, decodes the split-state codeword (γ_L, γ_R) to get $\mu||vk_L||vk_R$, verifies the signatures and outputs $\perp$ if verification fails, μ otherwise.

Unfortunately, even with the above modifications, it is unclear how to extend the original proof of security to the setting of continuous tampering, even if one assumes the underlying split-state non-malleable code to be continuously non-malleable. The reason is that the reduction needs to leak some bits from the codeword for each tampering query, therefore having a large number of tampering queries would lead to leaking too much information from the split-state codeword. Instead, we exploit the power of *super* non-malleability: Assume the underlying split-state code is super non-malleable w.r.t. codeword.[3] Then, the reduction only needs to know the index q^* of the first tampering query which actually modifies the inner codeword. In case the tampered inner codeword $(\tilde{\gamma}_L, \tilde{\gamma}_R)$ is invalid, the experiment stops and we are done. Otherwise, if $(\tilde{\gamma}_L, \tilde{\gamma}_R)$ is valid, the reduction obtains it in full. At this point, the reduction is able to simulate the answer to all subsequent tampering queries on its own, as tampering is persistent, which allows us to conclude continuous non-malleability.[4]

It remains to be seen how the reduction can obtain the index q^*. A possible strategy would be to simulate the outcome of all the tampering queries inside the leakage oracle, and then return the index of the first tampering query which actually modifies the codeword; however, each bit of a tampering query can depend on bits of both the left and right part of the inner codeword, while a split-state leakage query is only allowed to see one of these parts. Our strategy is to guess the index q^*, and then check at the end of the experiment if the guess was correct or wrong. Here, we additionally exploit the fact that the underlying split-state super non-malleable code is information-theoretically secure, which essentially allows the reduction to run many instances of the experiment inside the leakage oracle, and check that the adversary does not try to cancel its advantage (due to a wrong simulation). A similar strategy was already used in [23,24,56]. The formal proof appears in Sect. 4.1.

Bounded Polynomial-Depth Tampering. Our second construction exploits the observation that, for certain tampering families, continuous non-malleability w.r.t. codeword can be reduced to one-time super non-malleability w.r.t. codeword plus logarithmic (in the security parameter) leakage on the codeword. Indeed, this is the case as long as the leakage family allows us to run polynomially-many tampering functions in parallel, and return the index of the first query that actually modifies the codeword (if any). We formalize this observation in Sect. 3.3 (see Theorem 3). Note that the latter clearly holds true in the setting of bounded polynomial-depth leakage and tampering.[5]

In light of the above, it suffices to construct a one-time super non-malleable code w.r.t. codeword against bounded polynomial-depth tampering. We do so, by

---

[3] We can take, e.g., the non-malleable code of [5] for a concrete instantiation.

[4] As a bonus, we actually prove continuous *super* non-malleability.

[5] The same observation holds true for the setting of AC0 tampering, but not for decision-tree tampering.

looking at a slightly more general question. Namely, in Sect. 4.2, we show how to compile a *leakage-resilient* non-malleable code into a super non-malleable code in the CRS model, using simulation-extractable NIZK proofs. The idea is to encode a message μ using the underlying code, and then append to the resulting encoding γ a NIZK proof of knowledge π of the randomness ρ used by the encoder. The decoder outputs $\perp$ if the NIZK proof does not verify correctly.

In the reduction, we can simulate the NIZK proof π and then use a leakage query in order to obtain the tampered proof $\tilde{\pi}$ (so long as the proof $\tilde{\pi}$ is valid), along with the extracted witness $\tilde{\rho}$ corresponding to a tampered codeword $(\tilde{\gamma}, \tilde{\pi}) = f(\gamma, \pi)$ in the experiment defining super non-malleability. Unfortunately, the randomness $\tilde{\rho}$ is too long[6] for being obtained via a leakage query. However, this issue can be resolved by generating ρ using a pseudorandom generator G and letting the corresponding λ-bit seed σ be the witness. This allows the overall leakage to depend only on the security parameter, either assuming simulation-extractable SNARKs [9] (which inherently require non-falsifiable assumptions [47]), or by making the size of the proof depend only on the size of the witness (which can be achieved using fully-homomorphic encryption [46]).

More in detail, our compiler builds on a leakage-resilient one-time non-malleable code $(\mathsf{Enc}, \mathsf{Dec})$, a pseudorandom generator G, and a simulation-extractable proof system. The relation $\mathcal{R}$ for the proof system is satisfied by every couple statement-witness (γ, σ) where $\gamma = \mathsf{Enc}(\mu; \mathsf{G}(\sigma))$ for some message μ. Our encoding (and decoding) algorithm takes as input a CRS ω for the underlying proof system, and is described below.

Algorithm $\mathsf{Enc}^*(\omega, \mu)$: Proceed as follows:
1. Generate a random seed σ for the PRG.
2. Use the underlying non-malleable encoding algorithm Enc with randomness $\mathsf{G}(\sigma)$ to compute a codeword γ for μ
3. Generate a proof π for the couple (γ, σ)
4. Output (γ, π).

The decoding algorithm verifies the proof, returns $\perp$ if verification fails, and the message μ underlying γ otherwise.

A subtlety in the above proof sketch is that the leakage family supported by the underlying code must allow simulating the proof π, applying the tampering function f on (γ, π), verifying the tampered proof $\tilde{\pi}$, and extracting the corresponding tampered seed $\tilde{\sigma}$. Similarly, the tampering family supported by the underlying code must allow simulating the proof π and applying the tampering function f on (γ, π). Hence, this compiler does not work for all tampering families. Fortunately, it clearly works for the setting of bounded polynomial-depth tampering.

Our final result is then achieved by adapting a recent construction of Dachman-Soled, Komargodski and Pass [35], who showed how to obtain one-time non-malleability w.r.t. message against bounded polynomial-depth tampering

---

[6] Note that we cannot extract the proof outside the leakage function, as the corresponding statement is the tampered modified codeword $\tilde{\gamma}$ inside the leakage oracle.

assuming the existence of key-less hash functions and time-lock puzzles (along with other standard assumptions); in the CRS model, we show that their construction can be simplified and proven leakage-resilient one-time non-malleable assuming the existence of time-lock puzzles and simulation-extractable NIZKs. We refer the reader to Sect. 4.2 and the full version for more details.

Necessity of Super Non-malleability for the Inner Split-State Code. In our construction against decision-tree tampering, we require the inner split-state encoding to be a super non-malleable code, thus allowing for the simulation of the whole codeword. We argue that this is not an artifact of our proof, but rather a necessity for our construction to achieve security. Indeed, by using a contrived instance of a non-malleable code which is not super non-malleable, and contrived instances of the ramp secret sharing and the signature scheme, we are able to instantiate our scheme so that the adversary becomes able to retrieve the message in full. We consider here a simplified version of our scheme in which we remove the signature scheme, and we point the reader to [25] for the detailed explanation and for how to reintroduce back the signatures.

First of all, we need a split-state non-malleable code which has a good amount of spare bits, initially set to 0, and a secondary mode of operation which uses the spare bits to reconstruct the message instead of the actual relevant bits. Then, we need a malleable RSS encoding which allows to only replace a part of the encoded value leaving everything else intact.

The attack then proceeds as follows: the adversary is now able to tamper with the RSS encoding so that the spare bits of the split-state codeword are in a known location (while keeping the other positions untouched), and he is also able to replace those spare bits with some encoding of either 0 or 1 depending on some bit that the adversary wants to leak, leaving everything else untouched. Finally, the adversary uses multiple queries to leak every bit he left untouched, thus recovering all the bits that are necessary to reconstruct the original message.

Application to RKA Security Without Erasures. It is well known that a continuously $\mathcal{F}$-non-malleable code allows us to obtain a natural notions of $\mathcal{F}$-RKA security for arbitrary cryptographic primitives. This was proven by Faust, Mukherjee, Nielsen, and Venturi [43] for the case of non-persistent tampering. In [25], we show that the same works for the case of persistent tampering.

1.3 Related Work

In recent work, Freitag *et al.* [41] investigate non-malleable time-lock puzzles in the concurrent setting. Their definition generalizes continuous non-persistent non-malleable codes against bounded depth tampering, but requires that the adaptive choice of tampering functions runs in bounded depth too. They provide an impossibility result for the latter, which we extend to all the continuous non-persistent non-malleable codes against global tampering. Given that, they introduce the weaker notion of functional concurrent non-malleable time-lock puzzles, present a construction assuming the existence of (plain) time-lock puzzles in the auxiliary-input random oracle model, and provide interesting applications in coin tossing and electronic auctions.

Dachman-Soled and Kulkarni [36] show that *continuous* super non-malleability in the split-state model inherently requires setup. This impossibility, instead, does not hold for continuous super non-malleability against *persistent* tampering attacks, which can be achieved information-theoretically in the split-state model.

Leakage-Resilient Locally Decodable and Updatable Non-Malleable Codes [38] are a fine-grained tool for protecting RAM machines against leakage and tampering. In literature, there are constructions in the split-state and continuous setting [38], with information theoretic security [27], as well as tight upper and lower bounds [37].

An alternative approach for obtaining generic RKA-security is to rely on non-malleable key derivation [31,44,57]. The difference with non-malleable codes is that in this case one stores a uniformly random string in memory which is used to derive a key for the underlying cryptoscheme at each invocation. Continuously non-malleable key derivation can essentially be achieved only for tampering via polynomials or functions with high entropy.

Another line of research seeks direct constructions of RKA-secure cryptographic primitives, including, e.g., pseudorandom functions [1,16,18] public-key encryption [8,58], identity-based encryption and signatures [19]. RKA security has become a de-facto standard for block-ciphers, and systems are often designed while implicitly relying on the RKA-security of the underlying block-cipher (see, e.g., [17] and references therein).

2   Preliminaries

We start by setting up some basic notation and by recalling the notion of coding schemes. For space reasons, the definition of other standard cryptographic primitives is deferred to the full version [25].

2.1   Notation

We denote by $[n]$ the set $\{1, \ldots, n\}$. For a string $x \in \{0,1\}^*$, we denote its length by $|x|$; if $i \in [|x|]$ and $\mathcal{I} \subseteq [|x|]$, we denote by $x[i]$ the i-th bit of x and by $x[\mathcal{I}]$ the substring of x obtained by only considering the bits indexed by $\mathcal{I}$.

If $\mathcal{X}$ is a set, $|\mathcal{X}|$ represents the number of elements in $\mathcal{X}$. When x is chosen randomly in $\mathcal{X}$, we write $x \leftarrow_\$ \mathcal{X}$. When A is a randomized algorithm, we write $y \leftarrow_\$ \mathsf{A}(x)$ to denote a run of A on input x (and implicit random coins ρ) and output y; the value y is a random variable and $\mathsf{A}(x; \rho)$ denotes a run of A on input x and randomness ρ. An algorithm A is *probabilistic polynomial-time* (PPT for short) if A is randomized and for any input $x, \rho \in \{0,1\}^*$, the computation of $\mathsf{A}(x; \rho)$ terminates in a polynomial number of steps (in the size of the input).

Asymptotics. We denote by $\lambda \in \mathbb{N}$ the security parameter. A function p is *polynomial* (in the security parameter), if $p(\lambda) = O(\lambda^c)$ for some constant $c > 0$. A function $\nu : \mathbb{N} \to [0,1]$ is *negligible* (in the security parameter) if it vanishes faster than the inverse of any polynomial in λ, i.e. $\nu(\lambda) = O(1/p(\lambda))$ for all positive polynomials $p(\lambda)$. Unless stated otherwise, we implicitly assume that the security parameter is given as input (in unary) to all algorithms.

Random Variables. For a random variable $\mathbf{X}$, we write $\mathbb{P}[\mathbf{X} = x]$ for the probability that $\mathbf{X}$ takes on a particular value $x \in \mathcal{X}$, with $\mathcal{X}$ being the set over which $\mathbf{X}$ is defined. The statistical distance between two random variables $\mathbf{X}$ and $\mathbf{Y}$ over $\mathcal{X}$ is defined as $\Delta(\mathbf{X}; \mathbf{Y}) := \frac{1}{2} \sum_{x \in \mathcal{X}} |\mathbb{P}[\mathbf{X} = x] - \mathbb{P}[\mathbf{Y} = x]|$. Given two ensembles $\mathbf{X} = \{\mathbf{X}_\lambda\}_{\lambda \in \mathbb{N}}$ and $\mathbf{Y} = \{\mathbf{Y}_\lambda\}_{\lambda \in \mathbb{N}}$, we write $\mathbf{X} \equiv \mathbf{Y}$ to denote that $\mathbf{X}_\lambda$ and $\mathbf{Y}_\lambda$ are identically distributed, $\mathbf{X} \stackrel{s}{\approx} \mathbf{Y}$ to denote that they are *statistically close*, i.e. $\Delta(\mathbf{X}_\lambda; \mathbf{Y}_\lambda) \leq \nu(\lambda)$ for some negligible function $\nu : \mathbb{N} \to [0,1]$, and $\mathbf{X} \stackrel{c}{\approx} \mathbf{Y}$ to denote that they are *computationally indistinguishable*, i.e. for all PPT distinguishers D there is a negligible function $\nu : \mathbb{N} \to [0,1]$ such that:

$$\Delta_\mathsf{D}(\mathbf{X}_\lambda; \mathbf{Y}_\lambda) := |\mathbb{P}[\mathsf{D}(X_\lambda) = 1] - \mathbb{P}[\mathsf{D}(Y_\lambda) = 1]| \leq \nu(\lambda).$$

The notion of computational/statistical indistinguishability generalizes immediately to ensembles of interactive experiments $\{\mathbf{G}_\mathsf{A}(\lambda)\}_{\lambda \in \mathbb{N}}$ where the adversary A outputs a bit at the end of the interaction.

2.2 Coding Schemes

A (k, n)-code is a pair of algorithms $\Gamma = (\mathsf{Init}, \mathsf{Enc}, \mathsf{Dec})$ specified as follows.

Initialization: The initialization algorithm Init is a randomized algorithm that takes as input the security parameter $\lambda \in \mathbb{N}$ (in unary) and outputs a CRS $\omega \in \{0,1\}^*$.

Encoding: The encoding algorithm Enc is a randomized algorithm that takes as input a CRS $\omega \in \{0,1\}^*$, a message $\mu \in \{0,1\}^k$ and outputs a codeword $\gamma \in \{0,1\}^n$.

Decoding: The decoding algorithm Dec is a deterministic algorithm that takes as input a CRS $\omega \in \{0,1\}^*$, a codeword $\gamma \in \{0,1\}^n$ and outputs either a value in $\{0,1\}^k$ or $\perp$ (denoting an invalid codeword).

We say that Γ satisfies correctness if for all $\omega \in \mathsf{Init}(1^\lambda)$ and all messages $\mu \in \{0,1\}^k$ it holds that $\mathbb{P}[\mathsf{Dec}(\omega, \mathsf{Enc}(\omega, \mu)) = \mu] = 1$, where the probability is over the randomness of the encoding algorithm.

Remark 1 (Coding schemes in the plain model). A code in the plain model can be obtained by restricting Init to output the empty string. In that case, we simply write $\Gamma = (\mathsf{Enc}, \mathsf{Dec})$ and omit the string ω as an input of the encoding and decoding algorithm.

Ramp Secret Sharing. A ramp secret sharing is a coding scheme satisfying the additional property that any subset of the bits of a codeword with size at most $\lfloor t \cdot n \rfloor$, for some $t \in (0,1)$, reveals nothing about the message.

Definition 1 (Ramp secret sharing). *We say that Γ is a binary (k, n, t)-ramp secret sharing if Γ is a (k, n)-code satisfying the following property: For every $\mu \in \{0, 1\}^k$, and for every non-empty subset $\mathcal{I} \subseteq \{0, 1\}^n$ of size at most $\lfloor t \cdot n \rfloor$, we have that $\mathsf{Enc}(\mu)|_{\mathcal{I}}$ is identically distributed to the uniform distribution over $\{0, 1\}^{|\mathcal{I}|}$.*

As shown by Ball *et al.* [10], any binary linear error correcting code is a binary ramp secret sharing with suitable secrecy. In particular, every binary linear error correcting code correcting at most d errors is a binary ramp secret sharing with secrecy $(d - 1)/n$.

Lemma 1 ([10]). *For any message length $k \in \mathbb{N}$ there exist parameters $n \in \mathbb{N}$ and $t \in (0, 1)$ such that there is a binary (k, n, t)-ramp secret sharing.*

3   Non-malleable Codes

In this section, we revisit the definition of non-malleable codes and establish relations among different flavors of non-malleability.

3.1   Non-malleability

Let Γ be a (k, n)-code, and $\mathcal{F} = \{f : \{0, 1\}^n \to \{0, 1\}^n\}$ be a family of functions. Informally, Γ is non-malleable against tampering in $\mathcal{F}$ if decoding a codeword tampered via functions in $\mathcal{F}$ yields either the *original message* or a completely unrelated value. In this paper, we refer to the above flavor of security as *non-malleability w.r.t. message*. Instead, when a tampered codeword (always via functions in $\mathcal{F}$) is either identical to the *original codeword* or decodes to a completely unrelated value, we speak of *non-malleability w.r.t. codeword*.[7]

A stronger (as the name suggests) flavor of non-malleability is the so-called *super non-malleability*, introduced implicitly in [43] (and explicitly in [44]). This property requires that not only the output of the decoding, but *the codeword itself*, is independent of the message, as long as the tampered codeword is valid and either different from the original codeword (yielding super non-malleability w.r.t. codeword) or decoding to something different than the original message (yielding super non-malleability w.r.t. message).

The definition below formalizes continuous (super) non-malleability w.r.t. message/codeword. For readability, it will be useful to introduce the following predicates depending on a code Γ, a CRS ω, two messages μ_0, μ_1, two codewords $\gamma, \tilde{\gamma}$ and a tampering function $f \in \mathcal{F}$:

- $\mathsf{msg}(\omega, \mu_0, \mu_1, \gamma, \tilde{\gamma})$: outputs 1 if and only if $\mathsf{Dec}(\omega, \tilde{\gamma}) \in \{\mu_0, \mu_1\}$;
- $\mathsf{cdw}(\omega, \mu_0, \mu_1, \gamma, \tilde{\gamma})$: outputs 1 if and only if $\tilde{\gamma} = \gamma$;

---

[7] In the literature, the latter flavor of non-malleability is sometimes known as *strong non-malleability* whereas the former flavor is also known as *weak non-malleability*. However, we find this terminology rather confusing due to the fact that a code can be at the same time weakly non-malleable and super non-malleable (as defined below).

$$\boxed{\begin{array}{l} \mathbf{CNM}_{\Gamma,\mathsf{A},\mathcal{F},\mathcal{G}}^{\mathsf{same},\mathsf{output}}(\lambda, b) \\[4pt] \hline 1:\ \omega \leftarrow\!\!{\scriptstyle\$}\ \mathsf{Init}(1^\lambda) \\ 2:\ (\mu_0, \mu_1, \alpha_0) \leftarrow\!\!{\scriptstyle\$}\ \mathsf{A}_0(\omega) \\ 3:\ \gamma \leftarrow\!\!{\scriptstyle\$}\ \mathsf{Enc}(\omega, \mu_b) \\ 4:\ \mathbf{return}\ \mathsf{A}_1^{\mathcal{O}^{\mathsf{tamper}}(\gamma, \cdot), \mathcal{O}_\ell^{\mathsf{leak}}(\gamma, \cdot)}(\alpha_0) \end{array}}$$

Fig. 1. Experiment defining leakage-resilient (super) non-malleable codes, with an adversary A consisting of subroutines $(\mathsf{A}_0, \mathsf{A}_1)$.

- standard$(\tilde{\mu}, \tilde{\gamma})$: outputs $\tilde{\mu}$;
- super$(\tilde{\mu}, \tilde{\gamma})$: outputs $\tilde{\mu}$ if $\tilde{\mu} \in \{\diamond, \bot\}$, and $\tilde{\gamma}$ otherwise.

The above algorithms are called inside the tampering oracle $\mathcal{O}^{\mathsf{tamper}}(\gamma, \cdot)$, which initializes[8] $\hat{\gamma} = \gamma$ and self-destruct parameter $\delta = 0$, and behaves as follows:

1. if $\delta = 1$, output $\bot$;
2. compute $\tilde{\gamma} = f(\hat{\gamma})$ and $\tilde{\mu} = \mathsf{Dec}(\omega, \tilde{\gamma})$;
3. if same$(\omega, \mu_0, \mu_1, \hat{\gamma}, \tilde{\gamma}) = 1$, set $\tilde{\mu} = \diamond$;
4. if $\tilde{\mu} = \bot$, set $\delta = 1$;
5. set $\hat{\gamma} = \tilde{\gamma}$ and return output$(\tilde{\mu}, \tilde{\gamma})$;

We model leakage resilience by an oracle $\mathcal{O}_\ell^{\mathsf{leak}}(\gamma, \cdot)$ that accepts as input functions $g \in \mathcal{G}$ and returns $g(\gamma)$ (or $\bot$ if $\delta = 1$), for a total of at most ℓ bits.

Definition 2 (Continuously non-malleable codes). *Let Γ be a (k, n)-code, and $\mathcal{F} \subseteq \{f : \{0,1\}^n \to \{0,1\}^n\}$ and $\mathcal{G} \subseteq \{g : \{0,1\}^n \to \{0,1\}^*\}$ be family of functions. For flags* same $\in \{\mathsf{msg}, \mathsf{cdw}\}$ *and* output $\in \{\mathsf{standard}, \mathsf{super}\}$ *we say that Γ is a $(\mathcal{G}, \ell)$-leakage-resilient persistent continuously $\mathcal{F}$-non-malleable code if the following holds for the experiments defined in Fig. 1:*

$$\left\{\mathbf{CNM}_{\Gamma,\mathsf{A},\mathcal{F},\mathcal{G}}^{\mathsf{same},\mathsf{output}}(\lambda, 0)\right\}_{\lambda \in \mathbb{N}} \overset{\mathrm{c}}{\approx} \left\{\mathbf{CNM}_{\Gamma,\mathsf{A},\mathcal{F},\mathcal{G}}^{\mathsf{same},\mathsf{output}}(\lambda, 1)\right\}_{\lambda \in \mathbb{N}}. \tag{1}$$

In particular:

- *When Eq. (1) holds for* same $= \mathsf{msg}$ *(resp.* same $= \mathsf{cdw}$*) we speak of persistent continuous non-malleability w.r.t. message (resp. w.r.t. codeword);*
- *When Eq. (1) holds for* output $= \mathsf{super}$*, we refer to persistent continuous super non-malleability w.r.t. message/codeword. When* output $= \mathsf{standard}$*, we speak of persistent continuous non-malleability w.r.t. message/codeword.*
- *When Eq. (1) holds in the information-theoretic setting with statistical distance at most $\epsilon \in [0, 1]$, we say that Γ is leakage-resilient persistent continuously super non-malleable with statistical security ϵ.*

---

[8] The oracle additionally takes as input all the values that are required to evaluate the above predicates. We omit them for clarity.

One-Time Non-malleability. When we restrict the adversary by only allowing one tampering query, we obtain the weaker notion of *one-time non-malleability*. To formalize the latter, it suffices to replace Item 4 with an instruction which sets $\delta = 1$ regardless of the value of $\tilde{\mu}$. We denote the resulting experiment as $\mathbf{1NM}^{\text{same,output}}_{\Gamma,\mathsf{A},\mathcal{F},\mathcal{G}}(\lambda, b)$, and in Definition 2 it only suffices to replace Eq. (1) with

$$\left\{ \mathbf{1NM}^{\text{same,output}}_{\Gamma,\mathsf{A},\mathcal{F},\mathcal{G}}(\lambda, 0) \right\}_{\lambda \in \mathbb{N}} \overset{c}{\approx} \left\{ \mathbf{1NM}^{\text{same,output}}_{\Gamma,\mathsf{A},\mathcal{F},\mathcal{G}}(\lambda, 1) \right\}_{\lambda \in \mathbb{N}} \tag{2}$$

to obtain the new notion.

3.2   Families of Tampering Functions

Below, we define a few tampering families of interest for this paper.

Split-State Tampering. Let Γ be a $(k, n_\mathsf{L} + n_\mathsf{R})$-code. In the split-state model, we think of a codeword $\gamma \in \{0,1\}^n$ as consisting of two parts $\gamma_\mathsf{L} \in \{0,1\}^{n_\mathsf{L}}, \gamma_\mathsf{R} \in \{0,1\}^{n_\mathsf{R}}$. Hence, we consider the following families of tampering and leakage functions:

$$\mathcal{F}_{\text{split}}(n_\mathsf{L}, n_\mathsf{R}) := \{ f = (f_\mathsf{L}, f_\mathsf{R}) : f_\mathsf{L} : \{0,1\}^{n_\mathsf{L}} \rightarrow \{0,1\}^{n_\mathsf{L}}, f_\mathsf{R}\{0,1\}^{n_\mathsf{R}} \rightarrow \{0,1\}^{n_\mathsf{R}} \}$$

$$\mathcal{G}_{\text{split}}(n_\mathsf{L}, n_\mathsf{R}) := \{ g = (g_\mathsf{L}, g_\mathsf{R}) : g_\mathsf{L} : \{0,1\}^{n_\mathsf{L}} \rightarrow \{0,1\}^{\ell}, g_\mathsf{R} : \{0,1\}^{n_\mathsf{R}} \rightarrow \{0,1\}^{\ell} \}.$$

In this case, we simply say that Γ is ℓ-leakage-resilient super non-malleable w.r.t. message/codeword in the split-state model.

Decision Trees. Let Γ be a (k, n)-code and $d \in \mathbb{N}$. Consider a binary tree of depth d whose internal nodes are labelled by numbers in $[n]$ and whose leaves contain values in $\{0,1\}$. Given a binary tree as above, we define a decision tree of depth d for $\{0,1\}^n$ as a Boolean function that takes as input a string $\gamma \in \{0,1\}^n$ and is described as follows:

- it starts from the root;
- it reads the label $i \in [n]$ of the node, and observes the i-th bit of the codeword $\gamma_i \in \{0,1\}$: if $\gamma_i = 0$, it descends to the left subtree, while if $\gamma_i = 1$, it moves to the right subtree;
- it outputs the value of the leaf at the end of the path.

We denote with $\mathcal{DT}^d(n)$ the set of all decision trees for $\{0,1\}^n$ with depth at most d. Hence, we consider the tampering family:

$$\mathcal{F}^d_{\text{dtree}}(n) := \left\{ f := (f_1, \ldots, f_n) : \forall i \in [n], f_i \in \mathcal{DT}^d(n) \right\},$$

and the leakage family $\mathcal{G}^d_{\text{dtree}}(n) := \mathcal{DT}^d(n)$. In this case, we simply say that Γ is ℓ-leakage-resilient super non-malleable w.r.t. message/codeword against depth-d decision-tree tampering and leakage.

Bounded Polynomial-Time Tampering. Let $S(\lambda), T(\lambda)$ be polynomials in the security parameter. A non-uniform algorithm A is described by a family of algorithms $\{A_\lambda\}_{\lambda \in \mathbb{N}}$ (i.e., a different algorithm for each choice of the security parameter). Each A_λ corresponds to an algorithm whose input size is $n(\lambda)$, where $n : \mathbb{N} \to \mathbb{N}$. We say that a non-uniform algorithm A is S-size T-time if, for every input of size $n(\lambda)$ for some $\lambda \in \mathbb{N}$, the total work of the algorithm is at most $S(\lambda)$ and its parallel running time is upper bounded by $T(\lambda)$. We denote the family of non-uniform S-size T-time algorithms as $\mathcal{F}^{S,T}_{\text{non-uni}}(n)$, and let

$$\mathcal{F}^{T}_{\text{non-uni}}(n) := \bigcup_{S \in poly(\lambda)} \mathcal{F}^{S,T}_{\text{non-uni}}(n).$$

3.3 Simple Facts

It is not hard to show that (super) non-malleability w.r.t. message is strictly weaker than (super) non-malleability w.r.t. codeword (e.g., consider a contrived code where we append a dummy bit to each codeword which is ignored by the decoding algorithm). It is also easy to see that non-malleability w.r.t. message/codeword is strictly weaker than super non-malleability w.r.t. message/codeword (e.g., consider a contrived code where we encode the message twice and where the decoding algorithm ignores the second copy of the codeword).

Below, we formalize three simple observations. (i) Assuming one-way functions, one can transform any (super) non-malleable code w.r.t. message into one w.r.t. codeword. (ii) For any (super) non-malleable code w.r.t. message/codeword there is a natural tradeoff between security and leakage resilience. (iii) In some cases, one-time super non-malleability w.r.t. codeword, along with leakage resilience, are sufficient to imply continuous non-malleability (in the setting of persistent tampering). All the above statements hold as long as the tampering family $\mathcal{F}$ and the leakage family $\mathcal{G}$ supported by the code are large enough (as detailed below). For simplicity, we stick to the plain model (but similar statements hold true in the CRS model).

Adding Super Non-malleability w.r.t. Codeword. Let $\Gamma = (\mathsf{Enc}, \mathsf{Dec})$ be a code and $\Sigma = (\mathsf{Gen}, \mathsf{Sign}, \mathsf{SigVer})$ be a signature scheme. Consider the following derived code $\Gamma^* = (\mathsf{Enc}^*, \mathsf{Dec}^*)$.

Encoding: The encoding algorithm Enc^* takes as input a message $\mu \in \{0,1\}^k$, samples $(sk, vk) \leftarrow\!\!\$ \, \mathsf{Gen}(1^\lambda)$, computes $\gamma \leftarrow\!\!\$ \, \mathsf{Enc}(vk \| \mu)$ and $\sigma \leftarrow\!\!\$ \, \mathsf{Sign}(sk, \gamma)$, and outputs $\gamma^* = (\gamma, \sigma)$.

Decoding: The decoding algorithm Dec^* takes as input a codeword $\gamma^* = (\gamma, \sigma)$, and computes $\mu^* = vk \| \mu = \mathsf{Dec}(\gamma)$. If either $\mu^* = \bot$ or $\mathsf{SigVer}(vk, \gamma, \sigma) = 0$, output $\bot$. Else output μ.

Let $\mathcal{F} \subseteq \{f : \{0,1\}^{n+s} \to \{0,1\}^{n+s}\}$, $\mathcal{G} \subseteq \{g : \{0,1\}^{n+s} \to \{0,1\}^*$ be families of functions. In the theorem below, for any function $f \in \mathcal{F}$, and any $\gamma \in \{0,1\}^n$ and $\sigma \in \{0,1\}^s$, we write $f(\gamma, \sigma)_1$ (resp. $f(\gamma, \sigma)_2$) for the function that outputs the first n bits (resp. the last s bits) of $f(\gamma, \sigma)$.

Theorem 1. *Assume that Σ is a strongly one-time unforgeable signature scheme with $\mathcal{M} = \{0,1\}^n$, $\mathcal{S} = \{0,1\}^s$ and $\mathcal{V} = \{0,1\}^v$, and that Γ is a $(\mathcal{G}(n), \ell + s)$-leakage-resilient persistent continuously $\mathcal{F}(n)$-super-non-malleable $(k + v, n)$-code w.r.t. message. Then, the above defined $(k, n + s)$-code Γ^* is $(\mathcal{G}(n + s), \ell)$-leakage-resilient persistent continuously $\mathcal{F}(n + s)$-super-non-malleable w.r.t. codeword, so long as for all $g \in \mathcal{G}(n + s)$, all $f \in \mathcal{F}(n + s)$, and all $(sk, vk) \in \mathsf{Gen}(1^\lambda)$ and $\rho \in \{0,1\}^*$, it holds that*

$$\mathcal{G}(n) \supseteq \{g(\cdot, \mathsf{Sign}(sk, \cdot; \rho)), f(\cdot, \mathsf{Sign}(sk, \cdot; \rho))_2, \} \tag{3}$$

$$\mathcal{F}(n) \supseteq \{f(\cdot, \mathsf{Sign}(sk, \cdot; \rho))_1, \mathsf{SigVer}(vk, f(\cdot, \mathsf{Sign}(sk, \cdot; \rho)))\}. \tag{4}$$

Intuitively, if the signature scheme is strongly unforgeable, then a tampering attacker cannot maul γ^* while preserving vk. On the other hand, the security of the underlying non-malleable code guarantees that every change to vk makes the mauled message independent.

Remark 2 (On compartmentalized tampering). Note that Theorem 1 does not immediately apply in the split-state setting where $\mathcal{F} = \mathcal{F}_{\mathsf{split}}(n, n)$ and $\mathcal{G} = \mathcal{G}_{\mathsf{split}}(n, n)$, because the conditions of Eq. (3) and Eq. (4) are not satisfied in general. However, we can slightly modify the code Γ^* by signing the left part γ_L and the right part γ_R of a codeword $\gamma = (\gamma_L, \gamma_R) \in \{0,1\}^{2n}$ separately, yielding signatures σ_L and σ_R, and letting $\gamma^* = ((\gamma_L, \sigma_L), (\gamma_R, \sigma_R))$ to obtain the above result for the families $\mathcal{G}_{\mathsf{split}}(n + s, n + s)$ and $\mathcal{F}_{\mathsf{split}}(n + s, n + s)$.

Adding Leakage Resilience. Next, we show how to use complexity leveraging in order to add leakage resilience to any strong-enough non-malleable code. The latter was already shown by Brian *et al.* [23] for the case of split-state tampering, who proved how leakage can be simulated by guessing and later verifying the accuracy of the guess. In particular, the security loss is exponential in the number of bits leaked, as the reduction correctly simulates the leakage only when the guess is exact. We observe that this can be generalized to the case where tampering via $\mathcal{F}$ can reveal whether the answer to a leakage query in $\mathcal{G}$ is correct. We call this property $\mathcal{G}$-friendliness.

Definition 3 (Leakage-friendly tampering). *Let $\mathcal{F} \subseteq \{f : \{0,1\}^n \to \{0,1\}^n\}$ and $\mathcal{G} \subseteq \{g : \{0,1\}^n \to \{0,1\}^\ell\}$ be families of functions. We say that $\mathcal{F}$ is $\mathcal{G}$-leakage friendly if for all $g \in \mathcal{G}$, all $f \in \mathcal{F}$, and all strings $y \in \{0,1\}^\ell$ it holds that $\hat{f} \in \mathcal{F}$ where $\hat{f}$ is the function that upon input $\gamma \in \{0,1\}^n$ outputs $f(\gamma)$ if and only if $y = g(\gamma)$ (and outputs $\bot$ otherwise).*

Theorem 2. *Let $\mathcal{F} \subseteq \{f : \{0,1\}^n \to \{0,1\}^n\}$ and $\mathcal{G} \subseteq \{g : \{0,1\}^n \to \{0,1\}^\ell\}$ be families of functions such that $\mathcal{F}$ is $\mathcal{G}$-leakage friendly. Assume that Γ is persistent continuously $\mathcal{F}$-(super)-non-malleable w.r.t. message/codeword, with statistical security $\epsilon \in (0,1)$. Then, Γ is $\mathcal{G}$-leakage-resilient persistent continuously $\mathcal{F}$-(super)-non-malleable w.r.t. message/codeword, with statistical security $2^\ell \cdot \epsilon$, assuming that all the leakage is done before the first tampering query.*

Remark 3 (On computational security). Theorem 2 also holds in the computational setting, so long as $\ell = O(\log \lambda)$. In fact, it even holds for $\ell = \omega(\log \lambda)$ assuming Γ has sub-exponential security.

Remark 4 (On adaptive leakage). We can extend Theorem 2 to leakage families $\mathcal{G} \subseteq \{g : \{0,1\}^n \to \{0,1\}^*\}$, so long as the notion of leakage friendliness holds for up to q leakage functions. In this case, leakage resilience holds against adversaries making at most[9] q leakage queries.

Achieving Persistent Continuous Super Non-malleability. Finally, we establish a connection between one-time super non-malleability and persistent continuous super non-malleability. Intuitively, one can simulate continuous tampering by leaking the index of the first tampering query that modifies the codeword and then obtaining the corresponding mauled codeword via a single tampering query. This connection was first outlined in [49], and later proven formally in [5] in the split-state setting. We generalize this observation to general tampering families.

Theorem 3. *Let Γ be a $(\mathcal{G}(n), \ell+1)$-leakage-resilient $\mathcal{F}(n)$-super-non-malleable (k, n)-code w.r.t. codeword. Assume that for every $q(\lambda) \in poly(\lambda)$, and every tuple of tampering functions $f^{(1)}, \ldots, f^{(q)} \in \mathcal{F}(n)$, the leakage family $\mathcal{G}(n)$ contains the function $\hat{g}(\gamma)$ that computes $(f^{(1)}(\gamma), \ldots, f^{(q)}(\gamma)))$ and returns 1 if and only if $f^{(1)}(\gamma) = \cdots f^{(q-1)}(\gamma) = \gamma$, but $f^{(q)}(\gamma) \neq \gamma$. Then, Γ is also a $(\mathcal{G}(n), \ell)$-leakage-resilient persistent continuously $\mathcal{F}(n)$-super-non-malleable (k, n)-code w.r.t. codeword.*

Remark 5 (On super non-malleability w.r.t. codeword). Theorem 3 holds even starting with a super non-malleable code w.r.t. message, so long as the family $\mathcal{F}$ is closed under composition of poly-many functions (i.e., for all $q(\lambda) \in poly(\lambda)$ and all $f^{(1)}, \ldots, f^{(q)} \in \mathcal{F}$ the function $f^{(q)} \circ f^{(q-1)} \circ \cdots \circ f^{(1)}$ is contained in $\mathcal{F}$).

4 Our Constructions

4.1 Decision-Tree Tampering

Our construction is inspired by [15], with a few modifications that are necessary in order to prove persistent continuous super non-malleability w.r.t. codeword. To facilitate the description, let us introduce the following auxiliary function. For $n, c \in \mathbb{N}$, let $\phi : \{0,1\}^{c \log n} \to \mathcal{P}([n])$ be the function that, upon input a string $\zeta \in \{0,1\}^{c \log n}$ corresponding to c binary representations of distinct numbers in $[n]$, outputs the corresponding set of indices $\mathcal{I} \subseteq [n]$.

Our scheme is made of two layers, where the outer layer takes as input a split-state encoding of the message. Let $n, c, t \in \mathbb{N}$ be such that $t \geq c \log n$. Let $(\mathsf{Enc}_{\mathsf{RSS}}, \mathsf{Dec}_{\mathsf{RSS}})$ be a binary ramp secret sharing with messages in $\{0,1\}^t$. Consider the coding scheme $(\mathsf{Enc}^*_{n,c,t}, \mathsf{Dec}^*_{n,c,t})$ described below.

---

[9] Note that, e.g., $\mathcal{F}_{\mathsf{split}}$ is $\mathcal{G}_{\mathsf{split}}$-leakage friendly for any $q \in poly(\lambda)$.

Algorithm $\mathsf{Enc}^*_{n,c,t}(\gamma)$. Upon input $\gamma \in \{0,1\}^c$:

1. Sample a random string ζ over the set of all strings of length $c \log n$ corresponding to c binary representations of distinct numbers in $[n]$.
2. Let $\mathcal{I} = \phi(\zeta)$ and let $\overline{\mathcal{I}} = [n] \setminus \mathcal{I}$.
3. Let γ^* be such that $\gamma^*[\mathcal{I}] = \gamma$ and $\gamma^*[\overline{\mathcal{I}}] = 0^{n-c}$.
4. Output $(\mathsf{Enc}_{\mathsf{RSS}}(\zeta), \gamma^*)$.

Algorithm $\mathsf{Dec}^*_{n,c,t}(\gamma_{\mathsf{RSS}}, \gamma^*)$. Proceed as follows:

1. Decode $\zeta = \mathsf{Dec}_{\mathsf{RSS}}(\gamma_{\mathsf{RSS}})$ and let $\mathcal{I} = \phi(\zeta)$.
2. If there exists $i \in [n] \setminus \mathcal{I}$ such that $\gamma^*[i] = 1$, return $\perp$.
3. Let $\gamma := \gamma^*[\mathcal{I}]$.
4. Output γ (or (γ, ζ) when ζ is explicitly needed).

We observe that the only difference between our version of the $\mathsf{Dec}^*_{n,c,t}$ algorithm and the one in [15] is the check we perform in Item 2. This modification is required in order to obtain super non-malleability because, otherwise, an attacker could copy the original codeword into the 0 bits and then overwrite it with a constant valid codeword, and this would allow for the retrieval of the original encoding, and thus of the underlying message, in full.

We are now ready to define the final encoding scheme $\Gamma^* = (\mathsf{Enc}^*, \mathsf{Dec}^*)$ with security against decision-tree leakage and tampering. Let $m, n_\mathsf{L}, n_\mathsf{R}, c, t_\mathsf{L}, t_\mathsf{R}, s, v \in \mathbb{N}$ be parameters. Let $\Sigma = (\mathsf{Gen}, \mathsf{Sign}, \mathsf{SigVer})$ be a signature scheme with message space $\mathcal{M} = \{0,1\}^*$, signature space $\mathcal{S} = \{0,1\}^s$ and verification keys in $\mathcal{V} = \{0,1\}^v$. Let $\Gamma = (\mathsf{NMEnc}, \mathsf{NMDec})$ be a $(m+2v, 2c)$-code. Let $\mathsf{Enc}_\mathsf{L} := \mathsf{Enc}^*_{n_\mathsf{L},c,t_\mathsf{L}}$, $\mathsf{Enc}_\mathsf{R} := \mathsf{Enc}^*_{n_\mathsf{R},c,t_\mathsf{R}}$, $\mathsf{Dec}_\mathsf{L} := \mathsf{Dec}^*_{n_\mathsf{L},c,t_\mathsf{L}}$, $\mathsf{Dec}_\mathsf{R} := \mathsf{Dec}^*_{n_\mathsf{R},c,t_\mathsf{R}}$.

Algorithm $\mathsf{Enc}^*(\mu)$. Upon input $\mu \in \{0,1\}^m$:

1. Sample $(sk_\mathsf{L}, vk_\mathsf{L}) \leftarrow_\$ \mathsf{Gen}(1^\lambda)$ and $(sk_\mathsf{R}, vk_\mathsf{R}) \leftarrow_\$ \mathsf{Gen}(1^\lambda)$.
2. Run $(\gamma_\mathsf{L}, \gamma_\mathsf{R}) \leftarrow_\$ \mathsf{NMEnc}(\mu \| vk_\mathsf{L} \| vk_\mathsf{R})$.
3. Run $\gamma_\mathsf{L}^* \leftarrow_\$ \mathsf{Enc}_\mathsf{L}(\gamma_\mathsf{L})$ and $\gamma_\mathsf{R}^* \leftarrow_\$ \mathsf{Enc}_\mathsf{R}(\gamma_\mathsf{R})$.
4. Compute $\sigma_\mathsf{L} \leftarrow_\$ \mathsf{Sign}(sk_\mathsf{L}, \gamma_\mathsf{L}^*)$ and $\sigma_\mathsf{R} \leftarrow_\$ \mathsf{Sign}(sk_\mathsf{R}, \gamma_\mathsf{R}^*)$.
5. Output $\gamma^* := (\sigma_\mathsf{L}, \gamma_\mathsf{L}^*, \sigma_\mathsf{R}, \gamma_\mathsf{R}^*)$.

Algorithm $\mathsf{Dec}^*(\gamma^*)$. Proceed as follows:

1. Parse $\gamma^* = (\sigma_\mathsf{L}, \gamma_\mathsf{L}^*, \sigma_\mathsf{R}, \gamma_\mathsf{R}^*)$
2. Run $\gamma_\mathsf{L} = \mathsf{Dec}_\mathsf{L}(\gamma_\mathsf{L}^*)$ and $\gamma_\mathsf{R} = \mathsf{Dec}_\mathsf{R}(\gamma_\mathsf{R}^*)$.
3. Run $\mu \| vk_\mathsf{L} \| vk_\mathsf{R} = \mathsf{NMDec}(\gamma_\mathsf{L}, \gamma_\mathsf{R})$.
4. Check that $\mathsf{SigVer}(vk_\mathsf{L}, \gamma_\mathsf{L}^*, \sigma_\mathsf{L}) = 1$ and $\mathsf{SigVer}(vk_\mathsf{R}, \gamma_\mathsf{R}^*, \sigma_\mathsf{R}) = 1$
5. Output μ, or $\perp$ if the above check fails.

We establish the following theorem.

Theorem 4. *Let Σ, Γ, and Γ^* be as above. Assume that Σ is a strongly one-time unforgeable signature scheme with signature length $s = \beta c$ for some $\beta \in (0,1)$, that Γ is an αc-leakage-resilient super non-malleable $(k + 2v, 2c)$-code w.r.t. codeword in the split-state model for some constant $\alpha < 1$, and that the privacy thresholds $t_\mathsf{L}, t_\mathsf{R}$ of the ramp secret sharing satisfy $t_\mathsf{L} \geq d$ and $t_\mathsf{R} \geq (4t_\mathsf{L} + c)d$. Then, the code Γ^* described above is a persistent continuously super non-malleable (m,n)-code against depth-d decision-tree tampering for $d = O(c^{1/4})$ and $n = O(c^2)$.*

Remark 6 (On simulating persistent continuous tampering). The definition of persistent continuous tampering states that the adversary A has unlimited access to the tampering oracle, unless A fails to produce a valid codeword, thus receiving $\perp$ in all subsequent tampering queries. However, we observe that this is equivalent to asking that A cannot send any more queries to the tampering oracle after receiving, as a result to a tampering query, a codeword $\tilde{\gamma} \in \{0,1\}^n \cup \{\perp\}$ which is different from $\diamond$. This is because, once obtained a tampered codeword which is either $\perp$ or a valid codeword, the adversary can simulate all the other queries on its own. Notice that this only holds in the case of super non-malleability, since A needs the tampered codeword in order to simulate the subsequent queries.

The remainder of the section is dedicated to the proof of Theorem 4.

Establishing Useful Notation and Procedures. For ease of notation, let $\mathcal{F}^d_{\text{dtree}}(n) :=$ $\mathcal{F}^d_{\text{dtree}}, \mathcal{F}_{\text{split}}(c,c) := \mathcal{F}_{\text{split}}, \mathcal{G}_{\text{split}}(c,c) := \mathcal{G}_{\text{split}}, \mathbf{G}^*_{\mathsf{A}}(\lambda, b) := \mathbf{CNM}^{\text{cdw,super}}_{\Gamma^*, \mathsf{A}, \mathcal{F}^d_{\text{dtree}}, \emptyset}(\lambda, b)$ and $\mathbf{G}_{\mathsf{A}}(\lambda, b) := \mathbf{1NM}^{\text{cdw,super}}_{\Gamma, \mathsf{A}, \mathcal{F}_{\text{split}}}(\lambda, b)$. For all adversaries A against $\mathbf{G}^*_{\mathsf{A}}(\lambda, b)$, we can assume, without loss of generality, that A performs at most $p = poly(\lambda)$ tampering queries. Finally, let $\mathsf{Enc}^{\mathsf{L}}_{\mathsf{RSS}}$ be the instantiantion of $\mathsf{Enc}_{\mathsf{RSS}}$ used in $\mathsf{Enc}_{\mathsf{L}}$ and let $\mathsf{Enc}^{\mathsf{R}}_{\mathsf{RSS}}$ be the instantiation of $\mathsf{Enc}_{\mathsf{RSS}}$ used in $\mathsf{Enc}_{\mathsf{R}}$.

The proof is by reduction. In order to simplify the exposition, we define a template procedure ObtainBits which we will invoke several times in the actual proof. Informally, ObtainBits tries to evaluate the decision trees corresponding to the positions in $\mathcal{I}$ of the codeword tampered via f using the information $\mathcal{L}$ already known to the reduction itself; if some information is missing, it leaks it from the codeword. Since the reduction uses ObtainBits both inside and outside the leakage oracle, different sub-procedures are needed to leak these bits, depending on when ObtainBits is invoked. The formal definition follows.

Procedure ObtainBits$_{\text{Bit,Return}}(f, \mathcal{I}, \mathcal{L})$:
- **Instantiation:** A sub-procedure Bit taking as input an index $i \in [n]$ and returning a bit $b_i \in \{0,1\}$, and a sub-procedure Return taking as input the set $\mathcal{L}$ and a string $x \in \{0,1\}^*$ and returning some value.
- **Input:** A collection of decision trees f, a set of indices $\mathcal{I} \subseteq [n]$, a set $\mathcal{L} = \{(i,b) : i \in [n], b \in \{0,1\}\}$ such that if $(i_1, b_1), (i_2, b_2) \in \mathcal{L}$ and $i_1 = i_2$ then $b_1 = b_2$. Informally, $\mathcal{I}$ is the set of decision trees the procedure should compute and $\mathcal{L}$ is the prior knowledge of the algorithm invoking the procedure.
1. Let x be an initially empty string.
2. For all $i \in \mathcal{I}$, let initially $\mathsf{T} = f[i]$ and compute T as follows.
   (a) Let r be the label on the root of T.
   (b) If r is a leaf (i.e. $\mathsf{T} = r$), then append r to x and step to the next index $i \in \mathcal{I}$ (or break the loop if all decision trees have been computed).
   (c) If there exists $(r, b) \in \mathcal{L}$ for a $b \in \{0,1\}$, let $b^* = b$; otherwise, run $b^* \leftarrow \mathsf{Bit}(r)$ and replace $\mathcal{L} \leftarrow \mathcal{L} \cup \{(r, b^*)\}$.

(d) Replace T with its left subtree if $b^* = 0$ and with its right subtree if $b^* = 1$.

(e) Go to Item 2a.

3. Run $y \leftarrow \mathsf{Return}(\mathcal{L}, x)$ and output y.

As for the sub-procedures, we define the following possibilities for the template argument Bit.

- **Procedure** $\mathsf{Leak}(i)$: Use the leakage oracle to leak the bit i from the split-state codeword.
- **Procedure** $\mathsf{Await}(i)$: Abort the procedure $\mathsf{ObtainBits}$, returning (await, i).

Finally, we define the following possibilities for the template argument Return.

- **Procedure** $\mathsf{Ready}(\mathcal{L}, x)$: Return (ready).
- **Procedure** $\mathsf{Check}(\mathcal{L}, x)$: Return 1 if x is the all 0 string and return 0 if x contains at least one 1.
- **Procedure** $\mathsf{Update}(\mathcal{L}, x)$: Return the updated set $\mathcal{L}$.

Notice that, when using the sub-procedure Leak, algorithm $\mathsf{ObtainBits}$ presents an undefined behaviour whenever there exists $(i, b) \notin \mathcal{L}$ such that i does not refer to any position on the split-state codeword; however, our reduction only invokes $\mathsf{ObtainBits}$ with sets $\mathcal{L}$ such that the only missing indices are indices which belong to the split-state codeword.

Ruling Out Signature Forgeries. For any adversary A against $\mathbf{G}_\mathsf{A}^*(\lambda, b)$, $q \in [p], j \in \{\mathsf{L}, \mathsf{R}\}$, let $\mathbf{W}_j^{(q)}$ be the event in which the first $q - 1$ tampering queries from A do not modify the codeword and the q-th tampering query $f^{(q)}$ is such that $f^{(q)}(\gamma^*) = (\tilde{\sigma}_\mathsf{L}, \tilde{\gamma}_\mathsf{L}^*, \tilde{\sigma}_\mathsf{R}, \tilde{\gamma}_\mathsf{R}^*)$ satisfies (i) $\mathsf{NMDec}(\mathsf{Dec}_\mathsf{L}(\tilde{\gamma}_\mathsf{L}^*), \mathsf{Dec}_\mathsf{R}(\tilde{\gamma}_\mathsf{R}^*)) = \tilde{\mu} \| \tilde{vk}_\mathsf{L} \| \tilde{vk}_\mathsf{R}$ with $\tilde{vk}_j = vk_j$ and (ii) $\mathsf{SigVer}(vk_j, \tilde{\gamma}_j^*, \tilde{\sigma}_j) = 1$ and $(\tilde{\gamma}_j^*, \tilde{\sigma}_j) \neq (\gamma_j^*, \sigma_j)$. Let $\mathbf{W} := \mathbf{W}_\mathsf{L} \cup \mathbf{W}_\mathsf{R}$, where $\mathbf{W}_\mathsf{L} := \bigcup_{q \in [p]} \mathbf{W}_\mathsf{L}^{(q)}$ and $\mathbf{W}_\mathsf{R} := \bigcup_{q \in [p]} \mathbf{W}_\mathsf{R}^{(q)}$. Informally, $\mathbf{W}$ is the event in which the adversary A against $\mathbf{G}_\mathsf{A}^*(\lambda, b)$ modifies the message but not the codeword, thus successfully forging a signature.

For $b \in \{0, 1\}$, let $\mathbf{H}_\mathsf{A}^*(\lambda, b)$ be the experiment $\mathbf{G}_\mathsf{A}^*(\lambda, b)$ in which the challenger aborts whenever $\mathbf{W}$ happens. Clearly, the two experiments $\mathbf{G}^*$ and $\mathbf{H}^*$ are only distinguishable when $\mathbf{W}$ happens, therefore, if we show that $\mathbf{W}$ happens with negligible probability, it follows that $\mathbf{G}^*(\lambda, b)$ and $\mathbf{H}^*(\lambda, b)$ are statistically close.

Lemma 2. *For all PPT adversaries A there is a negligible function $\nu : \mathbb{N} \to [0, 1]$ such that $\Pr[\mathbf{W}] \leq \nu(\lambda)$.*

Reducing to Split-State Non-malleability with Augmented Adversaries. Now we want to perform the reduction to the split-state super non-malleable code. Unfortunately, we cannot convert each decision-tree tampering query to a split-state tampering query because each conversion needs some leakage and we would end up leaking too many bits. However, the reduction only needs to simulate the first tampering query which actually modifies the codeword, because the answer to all previous queries is $\diamond$.

In order to apply this idea, we first define an experiment $\mathbf{H}^{\mathsf{aug}}$ which, informally, is the same of $\mathbf{G}$ except that the adversary is given one-time oracle access to the needed information, i.e. the index of the first tampering query actually modifying the codeword. The only remaining problem is that the reduction $\hat{\mathsf{A}}^{\mathsf{aug}}$ still performs too much leakage to verify whether the tampered codeword is valid or not; this is because the reduction should check that the padding string inside the codeword γ^* does not contain any 1. The solution is to give the reduction $\hat{\mathsf{A}}^{\mathsf{aug}}$ oracle access to this information too, so that now $\hat{\mathsf{A}}^{\mathsf{aug}}$ is able to simulate the experiment to the adversary A without performing too much leakage.

More formally, let A be an adversary telling apart $\mathbf{H}^*(\lambda, 0)$ and $\mathbf{H}^*(\lambda, 1)$ with non-negligible advantage and let $\mathsf{RunInfo}_{\mathsf{A}}(\tau)$ be a function which takes as input the transcript τ of the execution of $\mathsf{A}(1^\lambda; \rho_{\mathsf{A}})$ when the codeword is γ^* and outputs the index $q_\diamond$ of the first tampering query that is not answered $\diamond$ and a bit $b_\perp$ which is 1 if the output of such tampering query is $\perp$ and 0 otherwise. Notice that τ is uniquely determined by the random coins ρ_{A} of A and the decision-tree codeword $\gamma^* = \mathsf{comp}(\gamma)$ which is compiled by some deterministic compilation instructions comp from the split-state codeword γ. Therefore, we can define the oracle $\mathcal{O}_{\mathsf{A}}^{\mathsf{aug}}(\gamma, \mathsf{comp}, \rho_{\mathsf{A}})$ which is initialized with the split-state codeword γ and, upon receiving the query containing the instructions comp and the random coins ρ_{A}, computes τ and outputs $\mathsf{RunInfo}_{\mathsf{A}}(\tau)$. Consider the experiment $\mathbf{H}_{\hat{\mathsf{A}},\mathsf{A}}^{\mathsf{aug}}(\lambda, b)$ which is exactly the same as $\mathbf{G}_{\hat{\mathsf{A}}}$ except that $\hat{\mathsf{A}}$ is given one-time oracle access to $\mathcal{O}_{\mathsf{A}}^{\mathsf{aug}}(\gamma, \cdot, \cdot)$ before the tampering query.

Let $\mathcal{I}_{\mathsf{L}}^{\mathsf{sgn}}, \mathcal{I}_{\mathsf{L}}^{\mathsf{rss}}, \mathcal{I}_{\mathsf{L}}^{\mathsf{str}}, \mathcal{I}_{\mathsf{R}}^{\mathsf{sgn}}, \mathcal{I}_{\mathsf{R}}^{\mathsf{rss}}, \mathcal{I}_{\mathsf{R}}^{\mathsf{str}}$ be a partition of $[n]$ such that, given an encoding γ^*, $\mathcal{I}_{\mathsf{L}}^{\mathsf{sgn}}$ (resp. $\mathcal{I}_{\mathsf{R}}^{\mathsf{sgn}}$) contains the positions of γ^* in which is stored the left (resp. right) signature, $\mathcal{I}_{\mathsf{L}}^{\mathsf{rss}}$ (resp. $\mathcal{I}_{\mathsf{R}}^{\mathsf{rss}}$) contains the positions of γ^* in which is stored the left (resp. right) ramp secret sharing and $\mathcal{I}_{\mathsf{L}}^{\mathsf{str}}$ (resp. $\mathcal{I}_{\mathsf{R}}^{\mathsf{str}}$) contains the positions of γ^* in which is stored the string containing the left (resp. right) part of the codeword and the left (resp. right) zeroes. For $j \in \{\mathsf{L}, \mathsf{R}\}$, let $\mathcal{I}_j = \mathcal{I}_j^{\mathsf{sgn}} \cup \mathcal{I}_j^{\mathsf{rss}} \cup \mathcal{I}_j^{\mathsf{str}}$. We now show a reduction $\hat{\mathsf{A}}^{\mathsf{aug}}$ which is able to tell apart $\mathbf{H}_{\hat{\mathsf{A}}^{\mathsf{aug}},\mathsf{A}}^{\mathsf{aug}}(\lambda, 0)$ and $\mathbf{H}_{\hat{\mathsf{A}}^{\mathsf{aug}},\mathsf{A}}^{\mathsf{aug}}(\lambda, 1)$ with non-negligible advantage.

1. Sample random coins $\rho_{\mathsf{A}}, \rho_{\mathsf{L}}^{\mathsf{enc}}, \rho_{\mathsf{R}}^{\mathsf{enc}}, \rho_{\mathsf{L}}^{\mathsf{sgn}}, \rho_{\mathsf{R}}^{\mathsf{sgn}}$ and random strings $\zeta_{\mathsf{L}}, \zeta_{\mathsf{R}}$.
2. For $j \in \{\mathsf{L}, \mathsf{R}\}$, let $\mathcal{I}_j^{\mathsf{cdw}} = \phi(\zeta_j)$ and $\mathcal{I}_j^{\mathsf{zero}} = \mathcal{I}_j^{\mathsf{str}} \setminus \mathcal{I}_j^{\mathsf{cdw}}$.
3. Compute $\omega_{\mathsf{L}} = \mathsf{Enc}_{\mathsf{RSS}}^{\mathsf{L}}(\zeta_{\mathsf{L}}; \rho_{\mathsf{L}}^{\mathsf{enc}})$ and $\omega_{\mathsf{R}} = \mathsf{Enc}_{\mathsf{RSS}}^{\mathsf{R}}(\zeta_{\mathsf{R}}; \rho_{\mathsf{R}}^{\mathsf{enc}})$.
4. Sample $(sk_{\mathsf{L}}, vk_{\mathsf{L}}) \leftarrow\!\!\!{}_{\$}\ \mathsf{Gen}(1^\lambda)$ and $(sk_{\mathsf{R}}, vk_{\mathsf{R}}) \leftarrow\!\!\!{}_{\$}\ \mathsf{Gen}(1^\lambda)$.
5. Run $\mathsf{A}(1^\lambda; \rho_{\mathsf{A}})$, obtaining the challenge messages μ_0, μ_1; then construct the challenge messages $\mu_0^* := \mu_0 || vk_{\mathsf{L}} || vk_{\mathsf{R}}$ and $\mu_1^* := \mu_1 || vk_{\mathsf{L}} || vk_{\mathsf{R}}$ and send μ_0^*, μ_1^* to the challenger.
6. For $j \in \{\mathsf{L}, \mathsf{R}\}$, construct the leakage function g_j^{sgn} which hard-wires the values $\rho_j^{\mathsf{enc}}, \rho_j^{\mathsf{sgn}}, \zeta_j, \omega_j, sk_j$ and, upon input the codeword part γ_j, computes $\gamma_j^* = \mathsf{Enc}_j(\gamma_j; \rho_j^{\mathsf{enc}}, \zeta_j)$ and $\sigma_j = \mathsf{Sign}(sk_j, \gamma_j^*; \rho_j^{\mathsf{sgn}})$ and outputs σ_j.
7. Send $(g_{\mathsf{L}}^{\mathsf{sgn}}, g_{\mathsf{R}}^{\mathsf{sgn}})$ to the leakage oracle, thus obtaining the signatures $(\sigma_{\mathsf{L}}, \sigma_{\mathsf{R}})$.
8. Let $\mathcal{L}$ be a set which, initially, contains all the pairs (i, b) such that $i \in [n] \setminus \mathcal{I}_{\mathsf{L}}^{\mathsf{cdw}} \cup \mathcal{I}_{\mathsf{R}}^{\mathsf{cdw}}$ and $b = \gamma^*[i]$. Notice that the only bits unknown to $\hat{\mathsf{A}}$ are

the ones belonging to the split-state codeword, namely, the ones in $\mathcal{I}_L^{cdw}$ and in $\mathcal{I}_R^{cdw}$; therefore, $\hat{A}$ is able to construct the set $\mathcal{L}$.

9. Using the information in $\mathcal{L}$, construct the compilation information comp which is used to compile the split-state codeword γ into the decision-tree codeword $\gamma^* = \text{comp}(\gamma)$.

10. Send (comp, ρ_A) to the augmented oracle $\mathcal{O}_A^{aug}$, thus receiving a pair $(q_\diamond, b_\perp)$.

11. Upon receiving the q-th tampering query $f^{(q)} \in \mathcal{F}_{dtree}^d$ from A, return $\diamond$ if $q < q_\diamond$; otherwise let $f = f^{(q)}$ and do the following.

(a) *Obtaining the necessary bits:* run the procedure

$$\mathcal{L} \leftarrow \text{ObtainBits}_{\text{Leak,Update}}(f, \mathcal{I}_L^{sgn} \cup \mathcal{I}_L^{rss} \cup \mathcal{I}_R^{sgn} \cup \mathcal{I}_R^{rss}, \mathcal{L}),$$

then use the set $\mathcal{L}$ to compute the tampered signatures $\tilde{\sigma}_L, \tilde{\sigma}_R$ and the tampered encodings $\tilde{\omega}_L, \tilde{\omega}_R$.

(b) *Obtaining the new positions:* for $j \in \{L, R\}$, compute $\tilde{\zeta}_j = \text{Dec}_{\text{RSS}}(\tilde{\omega}_j)$ and let $\tilde{\mathcal{I}}_j^{cdw} = \phi(\tilde{\zeta}_j)$ and $\tilde{\mathcal{I}}_j^{zero} = \tilde{\mathcal{I}}_j^{str} \setminus \tilde{\mathcal{I}}_j^{cdw}$.

(c) *Leaking the remaining bits for the left part:* construct the leakage function $\hat{g}_L^{\mathcal{L}}$ which hard-wires (a description of) the tampering function f, the sets $\mathcal{I}_L^{cdw}$ and $\tilde{\mathcal{I}}_L^{cdw}$ and the set $\mathcal{L}$ and, upon input the left part γ_L of the codeword, constructs the set $\mathcal{L}_L = \{(i, \gamma^*[i]) : i \in \mathcal{I}_L^{cdw}\}$, runs the procedure

$$y \leftarrow \text{ObtainBits}_{\text{Await,Ready}}(f, \tilde{\mathcal{I}}_L^{cdw}, \mathcal{L} \cup \mathcal{L}_L) \tag{5}$$

and returns y. Then, send $(\hat{g}_L^{\mathcal{L}}, \epsilon)$ to the leakage oracle, thus obtaining a value y. If $y = (\text{await}, i)$ for some $i \in \mathcal{I}_R^{cdw}$, leak $\gamma^*[i]$ from the right part of the codeword, update $\mathcal{L} \leftarrow \mathcal{L} \cup \{(i, \gamma^*[i])\}$ and repeat this step.

(d) *Leaking the remaining bits for the right part:* construct the leakage function $\hat{g}_R^{\mathcal{L}}$ which hard-wires (a description of) the tampering function f, the sets $\mathcal{I}_R^{cdw}$ and $\tilde{\mathcal{I}}_R^{cdw} \cup \tilde{\mathcal{I}}_R^{zero}$ and the set $\mathcal{L}$ and, upon input the right part γ_R of the codeword, constructs the set $\mathcal{L}_R = \{(i, \gamma^*[i]) : i \in \mathcal{I}_R^{cdw}\}$, runs the procedure

$$y \leftarrow \text{ObtainBits}_{\text{Await,Ready}}(f, \tilde{\mathcal{I}}_R^{cdw} \cup \tilde{\mathcal{I}}_R^{zero}, \mathcal{L} \cup \mathcal{L}_R)$$

and returns y. Then, send $(\epsilon, \hat{g}_R^{\mathcal{L}})$ to the leakage oracle, thus obtaining a value y. If $y = (\text{await}, i)$ for some $i \in \mathcal{I}_L^{cdw}$, leak $\gamma^*[i]$ from the left part of the codeword, update $\mathcal{L} \leftarrow \mathcal{L} \cup \{(i, \gamma^*[i])\}$ and repeat this step.

(e) *Validating the right part:* construct the leakage function $\hat{h}_R^{chk}$ which hard-wires (a description of) the tampering function f, the sets $\mathcal{I}_R^{cdw}$ and $\tilde{\mathcal{I}}_R^{cdw} \cup \tilde{\mathcal{I}}_R^{zero}$ and the set $\mathcal{L}$ and, upon input the right part γ_R of the codeword, constructs the set $\mathcal{L}_R = \{(i, \gamma^*[i]) : i \in \mathcal{I}_R^{cdw}\}$, runs the procedure

$$b_{\text{valid}} \leftarrow \text{ObtainBits}_{\text{Await,Check}}(f, \tilde{\mathcal{I}}_R^{cdw} \cup \tilde{\mathcal{I}}_R^{zero}, \mathcal{L} \cup \mathcal{L}_R)$$

and returns b_{valid}. Then, send $(\epsilon, \hat{h}_R^{chk})$ to the leakage oracle, thus obtaining the bit b_{valid}. If $b_{\text{valid}} = 0$, abort the simulation and return a random guess.

(f) *Tampering with the codeword:* for $j \in \{L, R\}$, construct the tampering function $\hat{f}_j$ which hard-wires the strings $\sigma_L, \sigma_R, \omega_L, \omega_R$, the sets $\mathcal{I}_L^{\text{cdw}}, \mathcal{I}_R^{\text{cdw}}$, $\mathcal{L}$ and (a description of) the tampering query f and, upon input the codeword part γ_j, computes the tampered codeword part $\tilde{\gamma}_j$ by using the additional bits given by $\mathcal{L}$ and then returns $\tilde{\gamma}_j$. Send the query $(\hat{f}_L, \hat{f}_R)$ to the tampering oracle, thus obtaining a codeword $\tilde{\gamma} \in \{0,1\}^{2c} \cup \{\diamond, \bot\}$. If $\tilde{\gamma} \in \{\diamond, \bot\}$, abort the simulation and return a random guess. Otherwise, let $\tilde{\gamma} = (\tilde{\gamma}_L, \tilde{\gamma}_R)$, reconstruct $\tilde{\gamma}_L^*$ (resp. $\tilde{\gamma}_R^*$) using the value $\tilde{\gamma}_L$ and the set $\mathcal{I}_L^{\text{cdw}}$ (resp. the value $\tilde{\gamma}_R$ and the set $\mathcal{I}_R^{\text{cdw}}$) and set $\tilde{\gamma}^* = (\tilde{\sigma}_L, \tilde{\gamma}_L^*, \tilde{\sigma}_R, \tilde{\gamma}_R^*)$.

(g) *Checking the signature:* reconstruct the tampered message $\tilde{\mu} || \tilde{vk}_L || \tilde{vk}_R$. Then, check that $\tilde{vk}_L \neq vk_L$ and $\tilde{vk}_R \neq vk_R$, compute $b_L = \text{SigVer}(\tilde{vk}_L, \tilde{\sigma}_L, \tilde{\gamma}_L^*)$ and $b_R = \text{SigVer}(\tilde{vk}_R, \tilde{\sigma}_R, \tilde{\gamma}_R^*)$, check that $b_L = b_R = 1$ and abort the simulation returning a random guess if one of the previous checks fails.

Finally, set $\tilde{\gamma}^* = \bot$ if $b_\bot = 1$, return $\tilde{\gamma}^*$ to A and output the same distinguishing bit as A.

For the analysis, notice that the reduction $\hat{\mathsf{A}}^{\text{aug}}$ perfectly simulates $\mathbf{H}^*(\lambda, b)$ to A unless the leakage performed exceeds the admissible leakage $\alpha c - 1$; therefore, when the leakage is within the bounds, $\hat{\mathsf{A}}^{\text{aug}}$ has the same advantage of A.

The following lemma allows us to conclude that $\mathbf{G}_{\hat{\mathsf{A}}}(\lambda, 0)$ and $\mathbf{G}_{\hat{\mathsf{A}}}(\lambda, 1)$ are computationally close.

Lemma 3. *If there exists an adversary $\hat{\mathsf{A}}^{\text{aug}}$ which is able to distinguish between $\mathbf{H}_{\hat{\mathsf{A}}^{\text{aug}}, \mathsf{A}}^{\text{aug}}(\lambda, 0)$ and $\mathbf{H}_{\hat{\mathsf{A}}^{\text{aug}}, \mathsf{A}}^{\text{aug}}(\lambda, 1)$ with non-negligible advantage, then there exists an adversary $\hat{\mathsf{A}}$ which is able to distinguish between $\mathbf{G}_{\hat{\mathsf{A}}}(\lambda, 0)$ and $\mathbf{G}_{\hat{\mathsf{A}}}(\lambda, 1)$ with non-negligible advantage.*

Bounding the Leakage. It remains to bound the leakage made by the reduction.

Proposition 1 ([15, **Proposition 1**]). *Let $n, c, t \in \mathbb{N}$ such that $t \geq c \log n$. Let A be an arbitrary algorithm that reads adaptively at most t bits of $(\text{Enc}_{\text{RSS}}(\zeta), \phi(\zeta))$. Let $\mathbf{Y}$ denote the number of distinct 1's in $\phi(\zeta)$ which are read by A. Then, over the randomness of ζ and Enc_{RSS},*

$$\Pr\left[\mathbf{Y} \geq \frac{2tc}{n}\right] \leq \exp\left(-\frac{tc}{3n}\right).$$

Lemma 4. *Suppose $t_R \geq (4t_L + c + 2s)d$. Let ℓ_R^{bit} be the amount of positions b leaked from γ_R. Then, for any $\gamma \in \{0,1\}^{2c}$, the event that $\ell_R^{\text{bit}} \geq 2(4t_R + 4t_L + c + 2s)dc/n_R$ happens with probability at most $(4d + 1) \exp(-t_R c/3n_R)$.*

Lemma 5. *Suppose $t_L \geq d$. Let ℓ_L^{bit} be the amount of positions b leaked from γ_L. Then, for any $\gamma \in \{0,1\}^{2c}$, the event that $\ell_L^{\text{bit}} \geq 2(4t_L + 4t_R + n_R + 2s)dc/n_L$ happens with probability at most $(4t_L + 4t_R + n_R + 2s)d/t_L \exp(-t_L c/3n_L)$.*

Let

$$\ell^{\mathsf{tamp}} = \left(\ell_L^{\mathsf{bit}} + \ell_R^{\mathsf{bit}}\right)(1 + \log(c))$$
$$= 2dc\left(\frac{4t_L + 4t_R + n_R + 2s}{n_L} + \frac{4t_R + 4t_L + c + 2s}{n_R}\right)(1 + \log(c)).$$

By the above lemmas, the event that the amount of leakage performed by $\hat{A}$ exceeds $\ell^{\mathsf{tamp}} + 2s + 2$ (recall that the reduction also leaks $2s$ bits for the signatures and 2 bits for checking the simulation) happens with probability at most

$$(4d+1)\exp(-t_R c/3n_R) + (4t_L + 4t_R + n_R + 2s)d/t_L \exp(-t_L c/3n_L). \quad (6)$$

Lemma 6. *Fix $\alpha \in (0,1)$. Then, there exist constants $\eta_1, \eta_2, \eta_3, \eta_4$ (only dependent on α) such that, if $t_L = \eta_1 c \log n$, $t_R = \eta_2 dc \log n \log c$, $n_L = \eta_3 d^3 c \log n \log^3 c$, $n_R = \eta_4 d^2 c \log n \log^2 c$, then $\ell^{\mathsf{tamp}} \leq \alpha c$ with overwhelming probability.*

By choosing the parameters as in Lemma 6, the length of the final codeword satisfies

$$n = 2s + 4t_L + 4t_R + n_L + n_R = O(d^3 c \log n \log^3 c),$$

which can be rewritten as $n/\log n = O(c^{7/4} \log^3 c)$, thus making $n = O(c^2)$ a good approximation, and the total amount of leakage is $\ell = \ell^{\mathsf{tamp}} + 2\beta c + 2$, which, with a good choice of the parameters $\eta_1, \ldots, \eta_4$ and α, β, can simply be rewritten as $\ell \leq \alpha c$. This concludes the proof of Theorem 4.   □

4.2   Bounded Polynomial-Depth Tampering

Our construction for bounded polynomial-depth tampering, works in three steps.

(i) First, we show a compiler for turning any *leakage-resilient* non-malleable code into a leakage-resilient *super* non-malleable code; the compiler is non-black-box, as it relies on NIZK proofs, and thus yields a code in the CRS model (even if the initial code is in the plain model).

(ii) Second, we show how to instantiate the above compiler by simplifying the non-malleable code for bounded polynomial-depth tampering of Dachman-Soled et al. [35] (thanks to the fact that we rely on trusted setup).

(iii) Third, we argue that the family of bounded polynomial-depth tampering satisfies the conditions of Theorem 3, so that persistent continuous non-malleability follows by steps (i) and (ii).

Let $\Gamma = (\mathsf{Enc}, \mathsf{Dec})$ be a (k, n)-code with randomness space $\{0,1\}^r$, let $G : \{0,1\}^s \to \{0,1\}^r$ be a PRG, and let $\Pi = (\mathsf{CRSGen}, \mathsf{Prove}, \mathsf{ProofVer})$ be a non-interactive argument system with proof space $\mathcal{P} = \{0,1\}^m$ for the relation:

$$\mathcal{R} = \left\{(\gamma, \sigma) \in \{0,1\}^n \times \{0,1\}^s : \exists \mu \in \{0,1\}^k \text{ s.t. } \gamma = \mathsf{Enc}(\mu; G(\sigma))\right\}. \quad (7)$$

Consider the following $(k, n+m)$-code $\Gamma^* = (\mathsf{Init}^*, \mathsf{Enc}^*, \mathsf{Dec}^*)$ in the CRS model.

Initialization: The initialization algorithm Init^* outputs $\omega \leftarrow_{\$} \mathsf{CRSGen}(1^\lambda)$.

Encoding: The encoding algorithm Enc^* proceeds as follows:
- sample a uniformly random seed $\sigma \leftarrow_{\$} \{0,1\}^s$ and compute $\rho = \mathsf{G}(\sigma)$;
- let $\gamma = \mathsf{Enc}(\mu; \rho)$;
- run $\pi \leftarrow_{\$} \mathsf{Prove}(\omega, \gamma, \sigma)$;
- return $\gamma^* = (\gamma, \pi)$.

Decoding: The decoding algorithm Dec^*, upon input a codeword $\gamma^* = (\gamma, \pi)$, proceeds as follows:
- run $\mathsf{ProofVer}(\omega, \gamma, \pi)$, and output $\bot$ if the verification fails;
- compute $\mu = \mathsf{Dec}(\gamma)$, and output $\bot$ if the decoding fails;
- else, return μ.

Let $\mathcal{F} \subseteq \{f : \{0,1\}^{n+m} \to \{0,1\}^{n+m}\}$ be a family of functions. In the theorem below, for any function $f \in \mathcal{F}$, and any $\gamma \in \{0,1\}^n$ and $\pi \in \{0,1\}^m$, we write $f(\gamma, \pi)_1$ (resp. $f(\gamma, \pi)_2$) for the function that outputs the first n bits (resp. the last m bits) of $f(\gamma, \pi)$.

Theorem 5. *Assume that Π is a one-time simulation extractable non-interactive zero-knowledge argument system for the relation of Eq. (7), with proof space $\mathcal{P} = \{0,1\}^m$, with zero-knowledge simulator $\mathsf{S} = (\mathsf{S}_0, \mathsf{S}_1)$ and with extractor K. Let Γ be a $(\mathcal{G}(n), \ell + s + m)$-leakage-resilient $\mathcal{F}(n)$-non-malleable (k, n)-code w.r.t. message/codeword.*

Then, the above defined $(k, n + m)$-code Γ^* is $(\mathcal{G}(n + m), \ell)$-leakage-resilient $\mathcal{F}(n + m)$-super-non-malleable w.r.t. message/codeword, so long as for every $g \in \mathcal{G}(n + m)$ and every $f \in \mathcal{F}(n + m)$, all $\gamma \in \{0,1\}^n$, all $\pi \in \{0,1\}^m$, and all $(\omega, \zeta, \xi) \in \mathsf{S}_0(1^\lambda)$, it holds that:

$$\mathcal{G} \supseteq \{g(\cdot, \mathsf{S}_1(\zeta, \cdot))_1, \mathsf{ProofVer}(\omega, f(\cdot, \mathsf{S}_1(\zeta, \cdot))), \mathsf{K}(\xi, f(\cdot, \mathsf{S}_1(\zeta, \cdot)))\} \tag{8}$$

$$\mathcal{F} \ni f(\cdot, \mathsf{S}_1(\zeta, \cdot))_1. \tag{9}$$

Instantiating the Proof System. Since the underlying code Γ needs to tolerate at least m bits of leakage, where m is the size of a proof under Π, Theorem 5 implicitly requires proofs that are sub-linear in the size of the statement (which is a codeword), but not of the witness (which is a seed for the PRG). In the literature, such proofs are referred as Succinct Non-interactive Arguments of Knowledge (SNARKs). In [9], the authors present a simulation-extractable SNARK whose proofs consist of 4 group elements. The security proof relies on both the generic group model (GGM) and the random oracle model (ROM).

Alternatively, we can use [46], where fully-homomorphic encryption (FHE) and NIZK argument systems are used to achieve succinct-proof NIZK argument systems for all of NP. The succinct proof for an NP relation $\mathcal{R}$ is built as follows:

- The witness x is encrypted with key σ into a ciphertext u of the same length by means of a symmetric-key encryption scheme (namely, one-time pad with a pseudorandom key generated from σ via a PRG G).

- The key generation algorithm of the FHE is called with randomness ρ to get (pk, sk). Next, the FHE scheme is used with keys (pk, sk) and randomness τ to encrypt the symmetric key σ into a ciphertext z. Then, the FHE evaluation algorithm takes as input the ciphertext z, and the NP relation $\mathcal{R}$ over statement y and witness $u \oplus \mathsf{G}(\cdot)$, and returns a ciphertext v.
- The underlying prover provides an argument π for the statement (pk, z, v) and witness (ρ, σ, τ), proving that (pk, sk) are generated according to ρ, that z is an encryption of σ according to pk, τ and that v decrypts to 1.
- The succinct proof is given by (pk, z, u, π).

Since $|u| = |x|$ and (pk, z, π) are polynomial in the security parameter, the proof size is $|x| + poly(\lambda)$. Also note that (pk, z, u, π) is sufficient to verify the proof, as one can obtain v and then call the underlying verification algorithm.

In their work, Gentry et al. [46] show that this transformation preserves the soundness and the zero-knowledge property of the underlying NIZK argument system. However, their result also applies to simulation extractability. For a high-level idea, call A an adversary against the simulation-extractability of the succinct-proof scheme. Assume that, given a simulated proof (pk, z, u, π) for a statement y of its choice, A manages to produce an accepting and fresh pair $(\tilde{y}, (\tilde{pk}, \tilde{u}, \tilde{z}, \tilde{\pi}))$. Consider the extractor that takes as input $(\tilde{y}, (\tilde{pk}, \tilde{u}, \tilde{z}, \tilde{\pi}))$ and as trapdoor (pk, sk), and does the following. If $\tilde{pk} \neq pk$, it computes the homomorphic evaluation $\tilde{v}$ of the circuit $\mathcal{R}(\tilde{y}, \tilde{u} \oplus \mathsf{G}(\cdot))$ on ciphertext $\tilde{z}$ with $\tilde{pk}$. Then, it runs the underlying extractor over $((\tilde{pk}, \tilde{z}, \tilde{v}), \tilde{\pi})$ to get $(\tilde{\rho}, \tilde{\sigma}, \tilde{\tau})$. If $\tilde{pk} = pk$, the extractor only needs to decrypt $\tilde{z}$ to get $\tilde{\sigma}$. In both cases, it outputs $\tilde{x} = \tilde{u} \oplus \mathsf{G}(\tilde{\sigma})$.

Instantiating the Underlying Code. To instantiate the underlying code, we start from the construction of Dachman-Soled et al. [35] which is in the plain model and relies on key-less hash functions, time-lock puzzles, as well as other standard assumptions. In the CRS model, their construction can be simplified as follows: The encoding of a message μ consists of a time-lock puzzle ζ computed using μ (with some fixed difficulty parameter) and a simulation-extractable NIZK proof of knowledge π of the message μ inside the puzzle. We refer the reader to [25] for the formal description and the security analysis in the CRS model.

Proving Continuous Non-malleability. Finally, we invoke Theorem 3 to conclude persistent continuous non-malleability. To do that, we need to check that the leakage family of bounded polynomial-depth circuits contains the function $\hat{g}$ in the statement of the theorem. In our case, it suffices to consider leakage resilience against circuits of depth $\leq T + c$ for a small constant c, and compute the leakage function $\hat{g}$ as follows. Upon input the codeword γ, consider q parallel sub-circuits, where the i-th circuit computes $f^{(i)}(\gamma)$, and outputs $b_i = 1$ if $f^{(i)}(\gamma) = \gamma$, $b_i = 0$ otherwise. The circuit will then output 1 if $b_1 = \cdots = b_{q-1} = 0$ and $b_q = 1$, and 0 otherwise. By inspection, every sub-circuit has depth $\leq T + c$, as it computes a tampering function and a bit-wise comparison (feasible in constant depth). To check if $b_1 = \cdots = b_{q-1} = 0$, it suffices to compute $b = \mathbf{OR}(b_1, \ldots, b_{q-1})$. The leakage function finally outputs $\mathbf{AND}(\mathbf{NOT}(b), b_q)$.

5 Conclusions

We have shown how to achieve continuous non-malleability in two natural settings: (i) decision-tree tampering, and (ii) bounded polynomial-depth tampering. The first result is in the plain model; the second result requires trusted setup. Both constructions rely on computational assumptions (one-way functions in (i), and time-lock puzzles and simulation-extractable succinct-proof NIZKs in (ii)). Natural open problems include: removing computational assumptions from our construction in (i), and weakening the assumptions from our construction in (ii). We leave these as interesting directions for future research.

Our paper provides the first crucial insights for constructing continuously non-malleable codes against non-compartmentalized tampering. In particular:

- We prove for the first time that security against non-persistent global tampering is impossible in the continuous setting.
- We prove for the first time that, when the target tampering family is powerful enough, continuous non-malleability follows from one-time super non-malleability with log bits of leakage resilience. The latter, in particular, is true for bounded-depth tampering and for AC0 tampering.
- We show a generic transform to reduce one-time *super* non-malleability to one-time non-malleability using NIZK proofs; this transform requires the underlying tampering family to satisfy certain properties, which are met in the setting of bounded polynomial-depth tampering.

We believe the above observations are important, and will turn useful for future constructions of continuously non-malleable codes against other non-compartmentalized tampering families (e.g., AC0 tampering), possibly under weaker assumptions.

References

1. Abdalla, M., Benhamouda, F., Passelègue, A., Paterson, K.G.: Related-key security for pseudorandom functions beyond the linear barrier. In: Garay, J.A., Gennaro, R. (eds.) CRYPTO 2014. LNCS, vol. 8616, pp. 77–94. Springer, Heidelberg (2014). https://doi.org/10.1007/978-3-662-44371-2_5
2. Aggarwal, D., Dodis, Y., Lovett, S.: Non-malleable codes from additive combinatorics. In: Shmoys, D.B. (ed.) 46th ACM STOC, pp. 774–783. ACM Press, May/June 2014
3. Aggarwal, D., Döttling, N., Nielsen, J.B., Obremski, M., Purwanto, E.: Continuous non-malleable codes in the 8-split-state model. In: Ishai, Y., Rijmen, V. (eds.) EUROCRYPT 2019. LNCS, vol. 11476, pp. 531–561. Springer, Cham (2019). https://doi.org/10.1007/978-3-030-17653-2_18
4. Aggarwal, D., Kanukurthi, B., Obbattu, S.L.B., Obremski, M., Sekar, S.: Rate one-third non-malleable codes. Cryptology ePrint Archive, Report 2021/1042 (2021). https://eprint.iacr.org/2021/1042
5. Aggarwal, D., Kazana, T., Obremski, M.: Inception makes non-malleable codes stronger. In: Kalai, Y., Reyzin, L. (eds.) TCC 2017. LNCS, vol. 10678, pp. 319–343. Springer, Cham (2017). https://doi.org/10.1007/978-3-319-70503-3_10

6. Aggarwal, D., Obremski, M.: A constant rate non-malleable code in the split-state model. In: 61st FOCS, pp. 1285–1294. IEEE Computer Society Press, November 2020

7. Agrawal, S., Gupta, D., Maji, H.K., Pandey, O., Prabhakaran, M.: Explicit non-malleable codes against bit-wise tampering and permutations. In: Gennaro, R., Robshaw, M. (eds.) CRYPTO 2015. LNCS, vol. 9215, pp. 538–557. Springer, Heidelberg (2015). https://doi.org/10.1007/978-3-662-47989-6_26

8. Applebaum, B., Harnik, D., Ishai, Y.: Semantic security under related-key attacks and applications. In: Chazelle, B. (ed.) ICS 2011, pp. 45–60. Tsinghua University Press, January 2011

9. Baghery, K., Pindado, Z., Ràfols, C.: Simulation extractable versions of Groth's zk-SNARK revisited. In: Krenn, S., Shulman, H., Vaudenay, S. (eds.) CANS 2020. LNCS, vol. 12579, pp. 453–461. Springer, Cham (2020). https://doi.org/10.1007/978-3-030-65411-5_22

10. Ball, M., Dachman-Soled, D., Guo, S., Malkin, T., Tan, L.-Y.: Non-malleable codes for small-depth circuits. In: Thorup, M. (ed.) 59th FOCS, pp. 826–837. IEEE Computer Society Press, October 2018

11. Ball, M., Dachman-Soled, D., Kulkarni, M., Lin, H., Malkin, T.: Non-malleable codes against bounded polynomial time tampering. In: Ishai, Y., Rijmen, V. (eds.) EUROCRYPT 2019. LNCS, vol. 11476, pp. 501–530. Springer, Cham (2019). https://doi.org/10.1007/978-3-030-17653-2_17

12. Ball, M., Dachman-Soled, D., Kulkarni, M., Malkin, T.: Non-malleable codes for bounded depth, bounded fan-in circuits. In: Fischlin, M., Coron, J.-S. (eds.) EUROCRYPT 2016. LNCS, vol. 9666, pp. 881–908. Springer, Heidelberg (2016). https://doi.org/10.1007/978-3-662-49896-5_31

13. Ball, M., Dachman-Soled, D., Kulkarni, M., Malkin, T.: Non-malleable codes from average-case hardness: AC^0 Decision Trees, and Streaming Space-Bounded Tampering. In: Nielsen, J., Rijmen, V. (eds.) EUROCRYPT 2018. LNCS, vol. 10822, pp. 618–650. Springer, Cham. https://doi.org/10.1007/978-3-319-78372-7_20

14. Ball, M., Dachman-Soled, D., Loss, J.: (Nondeterministic) hardness vs. non-malleability. Cryptology ePrint Archive, Report 2022/070 (2022). https://eprint.iacr.org/2022/070

15. Ball, M., Guo, S., Wichs, D.: Non-malleable codes for decision trees. In: Boldyreva, A., Micciancio, D. (eds.) CRYPTO 2019. LNCS, vol. 11692, pp. 413–434. Springer, Cham (2019). https://doi.org/10.1007/978-3-030-26948-7_15

16. Bellare, M., Cash, D.: Pseudorandom functions and permutations provably secure against related-key attacks. In: Rabin, T. (ed.) CRYPTO 2010. LNCS, vol. 6223, pp. 666–684. Springer, Heidelberg (2010). https://doi.org/10.1007/978-3-642-14623-7_36

17. Bellare, M., Cash, D., Miller, R.: Cryptography secure against related-key attacks and tampering. In: Lee, D.H., Wang, X. (eds.) ASIACRYPT 2011. LNCS, vol. 7073, pp. 486–503. Springer, Heidelberg (2011). https://doi.org/10.1007/978-3-642-25385-0_26

18. Bellare, M., Kohno, T.: A theoretical treatment of related-key attacks: RKA-PRPs, RKA-PRFs, and applications. In: Biham, E. (ed.) EUROCRYPT 2003. LNCS, vol. 2656, pp. 491–506. Springer, Heidelberg (2003). https://doi.org/10.1007/3-540-39200-9_31

19. Bellare, M., Paterson, K.G., Thomson, S.: RKA security beyond the linear barrier: IBE, encryption and signatures. In: Wang, X., Sako, K. (eds.) ASIACRYPT 2012. LNCS, vol. 7658, pp. 331–348. Springer, Heidelberg (2012). https://doi.org/10.1007/978-3-642-34961-4_21

20. Biham, E.: New types of cryptanalytic attacks using related keys (extended abstract). In: Helleseth, T. (ed.) EUROCRYPT 1993. LNCS, vol. 765, pp. 398–409. Springer, Heidelberg (1994). https://doi.org/10.1007/3-540-48285-7_34
21. Biham, E., Shamir, A.: Differential fault analysis of secret key cryptosystems. In: Kaliski, B.S. (ed.) CRYPTO 1997. LNCS, vol. 1294, pp. 513–525. Springer, Heidelberg (1997). https://doi.org/10.1007/BFb0052259
22. Boneh, D., DeMillo, R.A., Lipton, R.J.: On the importance of checking cryptographic protocols for faults (extended abstract). In: Fumy, W. (ed.) EUROCRYPT 1997. LNCS, vol. 1233, pp. 37–51. Springer, Heidelberg (1997). https://doi.org/10.1007/3-540-69053-0_4
23. Brian, G., Faonio, A., Obremski, M., Simkin, M., Venturi, D.: Non-malleable secret sharing against bounded joint-tampering attacks in the plain model. In: Micciancio, D., Ristenpart, T. (eds.) CRYPTO 2020. LNCS, vol. 12172, pp. 127–155. Springer, Cham (2020). https://doi.org/10.1007/978-3-030-56877-1_5
24. Brian, G., Faonio, A., Venturi, D.: Continuously non-malleable secret sharing: joint tampering, plain model and capacity. In: Nissim, K., Waters, B. (eds.) TCC 2021. LNCS, vol. 13043, pp. 333–364. Springer, Cham (2021). https://doi.org/10.1007/978-3-030-90453-1_12
25. Brian, G., Faust, S., Micheli, E., Venturi, D.: Continuously non-malleable codes against bounded-depth tampering. Cryptology ePrint Archive, Paper 2022/1231 (2022). https://eprint.iacr.org/2022/1231
26. Canetti, R., Eiger, D., Goldwasser, S., Lim, D.-Y.: How to protect yourself without perfect shredding. In: Aceto, L., Damgård, I., Goldberg, L.A., Halldórsson, M.M., Ingólfsdóttir, A., Walukiewicz, I. (eds.) ICALP 2008. LNCS, vol. 5126, pp. 511–523. Springer, Heidelberg (2008). https://doi.org/10.1007/978-3-540-70583-3_42
27. Chandran, N., Kanukurthi, B., Raghuraman, S.: Information-theoretic local non-malleable codes and their applications. In: Kushilevitz, E., Malkin, T. (eds.) TCC 2016. LNCS, vol. 9563, pp. 367–392. Springer, Heidelberg (2016). https://doi.org/10.1007/978-3-662-49099-0_14
28. Chattopadhyay, E., Goyal, V., Li, X.: Non-malleable extractors and codes, with their many tampered extensions. In: Wichs, D., Mansour, Y. (eds.) 48th ACM STOC, pp. 285–298. ACM Press, June 2016
29. Chattopadhyay, E., Zuckerman, D.: Non-malleable codes against constant split-state tampering. In: 55th FOCS, pp. 306–315. IEEE Computer Society Press, October 2014
30. Chen, B., Chen, Y., Hostáková, K., Mukherjee, P.: Continuous space-bounded non-malleable codes from stronger proofs-of-space. In: Boldyreva, A., Micciancio, D. (eds.) CRYPTO 2019. LNCS, vol. 11692, pp. 467–495. Springer, Cham (2019). https://doi.org/10.1007/978-3-030-26948-7_17
31. Chen, Yu., Qin, B., Zhang, J., Deng, Y., Chow, S.S.M.: Non-malleable functions and their applications. In: Cheng, C.-M., Chung, K.-M., Persiano, G., Yang, B.-Y. (eds.) PKC 2016. LNCS, vol. 9615, pp. 386–416. Springer, Heidelberg (2016). https://doi.org/10.1007/978-3-662-49387-8_15
32. Coretti, S., Dodis, Y., Tackmann, B., Venturi, D.: Non-malleable encryption: simpler, shorter, stronger. In: Kushilevitz, E., Malkin, T. (eds.) TCC 2016. LNCS, vol. 9562, pp. 306–335. Springer, Heidelberg (2016). https://doi.org/10.1007/978-3-662-49096-9_13
33. Coretti, S., Faonio, A., Venturi, D.: Rate-optimizing compilers for continuously non-malleable codes. In: Deng, R.H., Gauthier-Umaña, V., Ochoa, M., Yung, M. (eds.) ACNS 2019. LNCS, vol. 11464, pp. 3–23. Springer, Cham (2019). https://doi.org/10.1007/978-3-030-21568-2_1

412   G. Brian et al.

34. Coretti, S., Maurer, U., Tackmann, B., Venturi, D.: From single-bit to multi-bit public-key encryption via non-malleable codes. In: Dodis, Y., Nielsen, J.B. (eds.) TCC 2015. LNCS, vol. 9014, pp. 532–560. Springer, Heidelberg (2015). https://doi.org/10.1007/978-3-662-46494-6_22

35. Dachman-Soled, D., Komargodski, I., Pass, R.: Non-malleable codes for bounded parallel-time tampering. In: Malkin, T., Peikert, C. (eds.) CRYPTO 2021. LNCS, vol. 12827, pp. 535–565. Springer, Cham (2021). https://doi.org/10.1007/978-3-030-84252-9_18

36. Dachman-Soled, D., Kulkarni, M.: Upper and lower bounds for continuous non-malleable codes. In: Lin, D., Sako, K. (eds.) PKC 2019. LNCS, vol. 11442, pp. 519–548. Springer, Cham (2019). https://doi.org/10.1007/978-3-030-17253-4_18

37. Dachman-Soled, D., Kulkarni, M., Shahverdi, A.: Tight upper and lower bounds for leakage-resilient, locally decodable and updatable non-malleable codes. In: Fehr, S. (ed.) PKC 2017. LNCS, vol. 10174, pp. 310–332. Springer, Heidelberg (2017). https://doi.org/10.1007/978-3-662-54365-8_13

38. Dachman-Soled, D., Liu, F.-H., Shi, E., Zhou, H.-S.: Locally decodable and updatable non-malleable codes and their applications. In: Dodis, Y., Nielsen, J.B. (eds.) TCC 2015. LNCS, vol. 9014, pp. 427–450. Springer, Heidelberg (2015). https://doi.org/10.1007/978-3-662-46494-6_18

39. Damgård, I., Kazana, T., Obremski, M., Raj, V., Siniscalchi, L.: Continuous NMC secure against permutations and overwrites, with applications to CCA secure commitments. In: Beimel, A., Dziembowski, S. (eds.) TCC 2018. LNCS, vol. 11240, pp. 225–254. Springer, Cham (2018). https://doi.org/10.1007/978-3-030-03810-6_9

40. Dziembowski, S., Pietrzak, K., Wichs, D.: Non-malleable codes. In: Yao, A.C.-C. (ed.) ICS 2010, pp. 434–452. Tsinghua University Press, January 2010

41. Ephraim, N., Freitag, C., Komargodski, I., Pass, R.: Non-malleable time-lock puzzles and applications. Cryptology ePrint Archive, Report 2020/779 (2020). https://eprint.iacr.org/2020/779

42. Faust, S., Hostáková, K., Mukherjee, P., Venturi, D.: Non-malleable codes for space-bounded tampering. In: Katz, J., Shacham, H. (eds.) CRYPTO 2017. LNCS, vol. 10402, pp. 95–126. Springer, Cham (2017). https://doi.org/10.1007/978-3-319-63715-0_4

43. Faust, S., Mukherjee, P., Nielsen, J.B., Venturi, D.: Continuous non-malleable codes. In: Lindell, Y. (ed.) TCC 2014. LNCS, vol. 8349, pp. 465–488. Springer, Heidelberg (2014). https://doi.org/10.1007/978-3-642-54242-8_20

44. Faust, S., Mukherjee, P., Venturi, D., Wichs, D.: Efficient non-malleable codes and key-derivation for poly-size tampering circuits. In: Nguyen, P.Q., Oswald, E. (eds.) EUROCRYPT 2014. LNCS, vol. 8441, pp. 111–128. Springer, Heidelberg (2014). https://doi.org/10.1007/978-3-642-55220-5_7

45. Gennaro, R., Lysyanskaya, A., Malkin, T., Micali, S., Rabin, T.: Algorithmic tamper-proof (ATP) security: theoretical foundations for security against hardware tampering. In: Naor, M. (ed.) TCC 2004. LNCS, vol. 2951, pp. 258–277. Springer, Heidelberg (2004). https://doi.org/10.1007/978-3-540-24638-1_15

46. Gentry, C., Groth, J., Ishai, Y., Peikert, C., Sahai, A., Smith, A.D.: Using fully homomorphic hybrid encryption to minimize non-interactive zero-knowledge proofs. J. Cryptol. 28(4), 820–843 (2015)

47. Gentry, C., Wichs, D.: Separating succinct non-interactive arguments from all falsifiable assumptions. In: Fortnow, L., Vadhan, S.P. (eds.) 43rd ACM STOC, pp. 99–108. ACM Press, June 2011

48. Gupta, D., Maji, H.K., Wang, M.: Explicit rate-1 non-malleable codes for local tampering. In: Boldyreva, A., Micciancio, D. (eds.) CRYPTO 2019. LNCS, vol. 11692, pp. 435–466. Springer, Cham (2019). https://doi.org/10.1007/978-3-030-26948-7_16

49. Jafargholi, Z., Wichs, D.: Tamper detection and continuous non-malleable codes. In: Dodis, Y., Nielsen, J.B. (eds.) TCC 2015. LNCS, vol. 9014, pp. 451–480. Springer, Heidelberg (2015). https://doi.org/10.1007/978-3-662-46494-6_19

50. Kanukurthi, B., Obbattu, S.L.B., Sekar, S.: Four-state non-malleable codes with explicit constant rate. In: Kalai, Y., Reyzin, L. (eds.) TCC 2017. LNCS, vol. 10678, pp. 344–375. Springer, Cham (2017). https://doi.org/10.1007/978-3-319-70503-3_11

51. Kanukurthi, B., Obbattu, S.L.B., Sekar, S.: Non-malleable randomness encoders and their applications. In: Nielsen, J.B., Rijmen, V. (eds.) EUROCRYPT 2018. LNCS, vol. 10822, pp. 589–617. Springer, Cham (2018). https://doi.org/10.1007/978-3-319-78372-7_19

52. Knudsen, L.R.: Cryptanalysis of LOKI 91. In: Seberry, J., Zheng, Y. (eds.) AUSCRYPT 1992. LNCS, vol. 718, pp. 196–208. Springer, Heidelberg (1993). https://doi.org/10.1007/3-540-57220-1_62

53. Li, X.: Improved non-malleable extractors, non-malleable codes and independent source extractors. In: Hatami, H., McKenzie, P., King, V. (eds.) 49th ACM STOC, pp. 1144–1156. ACM Press, June 2017

54. Li, X.: Non-malleable extractors and non-malleable codes: Partially optimal constructions. Cryptology ePrint Archive, Report 2018/353 (2018). https://eprint.iacr.org/2018/353

55. Liu, F.-H., Lysyanskaya, A.: Tamper and leakage resilience in the split-state model. In: Safavi-Naini, R., Canetti, R. (eds.) CRYPTO 2012. LNCS, vol. 7417, pp. 517–532. Springer, Heidelberg (2012). https://doi.org/10.1007/978-3-642-32009-5_30

56. Ostrovsky, R., Persiano, G., Venturi, D., Visconti, I.: Continuously non-malleable codes in the split-state model from minimal assumptions. In: Shacham, H., Boldyreva, A. (eds.) CRYPTO 2018. LNCS, vol. 10993, pp. 608–639. Springer, Cham (2018). https://doi.org/10.1007/978-3-319-96878-0_21

57. Qin, B., Liu, S., Yuen, T.H., Deng, R.H., Chen, K.: Continuous non-malleable key derivation and its application to related-key security. In: Katz, J. (ed.) PKC 2015. LNCS, vol. 9020, pp. 557–578. Springer, Heidelberg (2015). https://doi.org/10.1007/978-3-662-46447-2_25

58. Wee, H.: Public key encryption against related key attacks. In: Fischlin, M., Buchmann, J., Manulis, M. (eds.) PKC 2012. LNCS, vol. 7293, pp. 262–279. Springer, Heidelberg (2012). https://doi.org/10.1007/978-3-642-30057-8_16

Failing Gracefully: Decryption Failures and the Fujisaki-Okamoto Transform

Kathrin Hövelmanns[1]($\boxtimes$), Andreas Hülsing[1]($\boxtimes$), and Christian Majenz[2]($\boxtimes$)

[1] Eindhoven University of Technology, Eindhoven, The Netherlands
`authors-fo-failure@huelsing.net`
[2] Department of Applied Mathematics and Computer Science,
Technical University of Denmark, Lyngby, Denmark

Abstract. In known security reductions for the Fujisaki-Okamoto transformation, decryption failures are handled via a reduction solving the rather unnatural task of finding failing plaintexts *given the private key*, resulting in a Grover search bound. Moreover, they require an implicit rejection mechanism for invalid ciphertexts to achieve a reasonable security bound in the QROM. We present a reduction that has neither of these deficiencies: We introduce two security games related to finding decryption failures, one capturing the *computationally hard* task of *using the public key* to find a decryption failure, and one capturing the *statistically hard* task of searching the random oracle for *key-independent* failures like, e.g., large randomness. As a result, our security bounds in the QROM are tighter than previous ones with respect to the generic random oracle search attacks: The attacker can only partially compute the search predicate, namely for said key-independent failures. In addition, our entire reduction works for the explicit-reject variant of the transformation and improves significantly over all of its known reductions. Besides being the more natural variant of the transformation, security of the explicit reject mechanism is also relevant for side channel attack resilience of the implicit-rejection variant. Along the way, we prove several technical results characterizing preimage extraction and certain search tasks in the QROM that might be of independent interest.

Keywords: Public-key encryption · post-quantum security · QROM · Fuji-saki-Okamoto transformation · decryption failures · NIST

1 Introduction

The Fujisaki-Okamoto (FO) transform [FO99, FO13] is a well known transformation that combines a weakly secure public-key encryption scheme and a weakly secure secret-key encryption scheme into an IND-CCA secure public-key encryption scheme in the random oracle model. Dent [Den03, Table 5] gave an adoption

---

A.H. was supported by an NWO VIDI grant (Project No. VI.Vidi.193.066). C.M. was supported by a NWO VENI grant (Project No. VI.Veni.192.159).

S. Agrawal and D. Lin (Eds.): ASIACRYPT 2022, LNCS 13794, pp. 414–443, 2022.
https://doi.org/10.1007/978-3-031-22972-5_15

for the setting of key-encapsulation. This adoption for key encapsulation mechanisms (KEM) is now the de-facto standard to build secure KEMs. In particular, it was used in virtually all KEM submissions to the NIST PQC standardisation process [NIS17]. In the context of post-quantum security, however, two novel issues surfaced: First, many of the PKE schemes being transformed into KEM are not perfectly correct, i.e., they sometimes fail to decrypt a ciphertext to its plaintext. Second, security proofs have to be done in the quantum-accessible random oracle model (QROM) to be applicable to quantum attackers.

Both problems were tackled in [HHK17] and a long sequence of follow-up works (among others [SXY18, JZC+18, BHH+19, HKSU20, KSS+20]). While these works made great progress towards achieving tighter reductions in the QROM, the treatment of decryption failures did not improve significantly. In this work, we make significant progress on the treatment of decryption failures. Along the way, we obtain several additional results relevant on their own.

An additional quirk of existing QROM reductions for the FO transform is that they require an *implicit rejection* variant, where pseudorandom session keys are returned instead of reporting decapsulation errors, to avoid extreme reduction losses. (The only known concrete bound [DFMS21] for Dent's variant is much weaker then those known for the implicit rejection variant.)

The Fujisaki-Okamoto transformation. We recall the FO transformation for KEM as introduced in [Den03, Table 5] and revisited by [HHK17], there called $FO_m^\perp$. $FO_m^\perp$ constructs a KEM from a public-key encryption scheme PKE, and the overall transformation $FO_m^\perp$ can be described by first modifying PKE to obtain a deterministic scheme PKE^G, and then applying a PKE-to-KEM transformation (called $U_m^\perp$ in [HHK17]) to PKE^G:

MODIFIED SCHEME PKE^G. Starting from PKE and a hash function G, deterministic encryption scheme PKE^G is built by letting Enc^G encrypt messages m according to the encryption algorithm Enc of PKE, but using the hash value $G(m)$ as the random coins for Enc: $Enc^G(pk, m) := Enc(pk, m; G(m))$. Dec^G uses the decryption algorithm Dec of PKE to decrypt a ciphertext c to obtain m', and rejects by returning $\perp$ if c fails to decrypt or m' fails to encrypt back to c.

PKE-TO-KEM TRANSFORMATION $U_m^\perp$. Starting from a deterministic encryption scheme PKE' and a hash function H, key encapsulation algorithm $KEM_m^\perp :=$ $U_m^\perp[PKE', H]$ is built by letting $Encaps(pk) := (c := Enc'(pk, m), K := H(m))$, where m is picked at random from the message space. Decapsulation will return $K := H(m)$ unless c fails to decrypt, in which case it returns failure symbol $\perp$.

COMBINED PKE-TO-KEM TRANSFORMATION $FO_m^\perp$. The 'full FO' transformation $FO_m^\perp$ is defined by taking PKE and hash functions G and H, and defining $FO_m^\perp[PKE, G, H] := U_m^\perp[PKE^G, H]$. While there exists a plethora of variants that differ from $FO_m^\perp$, it was proven [BHH+19] that security of these variants is either equivalent to or implied by security of $FO_m^\perp$.

The role of correctness errors in security proofs for FO. Correctness errors play a role during the proof that an FO-transformed KEM is IND-CCA secure: To tackle the CCA part, it is necessary to simulate the decapsulation oracle ODECAPS without the secret key, meaning the plaintext has to be obtained via strategies different from decrypting. While different strategies for this exist in both ROM and QROM, they all have in common that the obtained plaintext is rather a plaintext that encrypts to the queried ciphertext (a "ciphertext preimage") than the decryption. Consequently, the simulation fails to recognise *failing ciphertexts*, i.e., ciphertexts for which decryption results in a plaintext different from the ciphertext preimage (or even in $\perp$), and will in this case behave differently from ODECAPS. Hence, the simulations are distinguishable from ODECAPS if the attacker can craft such failing ciphertexts.

The approach chosen by [HHK17] was to show that the distinguishing advantage between the two cases can be bounded by the advantage in a game COR. Game COR (defined in [HHK17]) provides an adversary with a key pair (including the secret key) and asks to return a *failing message*, i.e., a message that encrypts to a failing ciphertext, for the derandomized scheme PKE^G. [HHK17] further bounded the maximal advantage in game COR for PKE^G in terms of a statistical worst-case quantity δ_{wc} of PKE, which is the expected maximum probability for plaintexts to cause a decryption failure, with the expectation being taken over the key pair. This results in a typical search bound as the adversary can use the secret key to check if a ciphertext fails. In the QROM, the resulting bound is therefore $8q^2\delta_{\mathrm{wc}}$, q being the number of queries to G.[1]

Intuitively, this notion suffers from two related unnatural features:

– First, it is unnatural to provide adversaries with the secret key, as long as the scheme has at least some basic security.[2] In particular, this observation applies to adversaries tasked with finding failing plaintexts, which is not a mere issue of aesthetics: If the secret key is given to the adversary, an analysis of this bound can't make use of computational assumptions without becoming heuristic.[3]

– Second, it is unnatural that the bound contains a Grover-like search term with regard to δ_{wc}: As IND-CCA adversaries don't have access to the secret key, they can only check if ciphertexts fail via their *classical* CCA oracle, which should render a Grover search impossible. Furthermore, in ROM and QROM, it should be the (usually much smaller) number of CCA queries that limits the adversary's ability to search, not the number of random oracle queries. Hence this bound seems overly conservative.

While follow-up works have used different games in place of COR to deal with decryption errors, all result in the same quantum search bound in terms of δ_{wc}.

---

[1] Some publications (e.g., [JZC+18]) use the bound $2q \cdot \sqrt{\delta_{\mathrm{wc}}}$, it is however straightforward to verify that the bound above can be achieved by using [HKSU20, Lemma 2.9] as a drop-in replacement. Note that this is indeed a quadratic improvement unless $4q \cdot \sqrt{\delta_{\mathrm{wc}}} > 1$, in which case the IND-CCA bound is meaningless, anyways.

[2] Schemes that allow for a key recovery attack serve as pathological examples why this argument does not hold in generality.

[3] An example we happen to be aware of is the analysis of the correctness error bound of Kyber [BDK+18].

Main contribution. Our main contribution is a new security reduction for the FO transformation that improves over existing ones in two ways.

DECRYPTION FAILURES. We introduce a family of new security games, the _Find Failing Plaintext_ (FFP) games. These provide a much more natural framework for dealing with decryption errors in the FO transformation, and it is the novel structure of our reduction that allows their usage. Two important members of the FFP family are as follows: The first one, _Find Failing Plaintext that is Non-Generic_ (FFP-NG), gives a public key to the adversary and asks it to find a message that triggers a decryption failure more likely with respect to this key pair than with respect to an independent key pair. The second one, _Find Failing Plaintext with No Key_ (FFP-NK), tasks an adversary with producing a message that triggers a decryption failure with respect to an independently sampled key pair, without providing any key to the adversary. As summarised in Fig. 1, we provide a reduction from FFP-NG and passive security of PKE together with FFP-NK for PKE^G to IND-CCA security of the FO-transformed of PKE. This new reduction structure avoids both unnatural features mentioned above:

– None of the two failure-related games FFP-NG and FFP-NK provide the adversary with the secret key. In particular, we show how to bound an adversary's advantage in game FFP-NK in terms of δ_{ik}, the worst-case decryption error rate when the message is picked _independently of the key_, and additional related statistical parameters . We give two concrete example bounds, one involving the variance based on Chebyshev's inequality and one based on a Gaussian-shaped tail bound. We expect that these "independent-key" statistical parameters can be estimated more conveniently and _without heuristics_, by exploiting the computational assumptions of the PKE scheme at hand.

– Game FFP-NK still allows for a Grover search advantage, but only when searching for messages that are more likely to cause a failure _on average over the key_. This game corresponds, e.g., to the first attempt at finding a failure in attacks like [DVV18,BS20,DRV20]. In the context of the entire security reduction for FO, the advantage in this game is multiplied with the number of decapsulation queries a CCA attacker makes, correctly reflecting the fact that the ability of _identifying_ a decryption failure should depend on the CCA oracle and is thus limited. Game FFP-NG defines a property of the underlying PKE scheme, it thus allows to analyze the hardness of finding meaningful decryption failures independently from the hardness of searching a random oracle for them. FFP-NG seems thus more amenable to both security reductions and cryptanalysis.

As a consequence of these features, we expect our reduction to yield much better security bounds that provide non-trivial provable security for real-world parameters.

FO WITH EXPLICIT REJECTION. Our reduction employs a technique for generalized _preimage extraction_ in the QROM that was recently introduced in [DFMS21]. As shown by [DFMS21], this technique is well-suited for proving FO$_m^\perp$ secure. We furthermore generalize the one-way to hiding (OWTH) lemma [AHU19] such that it is compatible with the technique from [DFMS21]. OWTH was used to derive the state-of-the-art bounds for implicitly rejecting variants, and combining the two techniques, we obtain a security bound for $FO_m^\perp$ that is competitive with said state-of-the-art bounds.

QROM TOOLS. To facilitate the above-described reduction, we provide two technical tools that might be of independent interest: Firstly, we generalize the OWTH framework from [AHU19] such that it can be combined with the extractable quantum random oracle simulation from [DFMS21], rendering the two techniques compatible with being used together in the same security reduction. We make crucial use of this possibility to avoid the additional reduction losses that [DFMS21] need to accept to be able to use the plain one-way to hiding framework in juxtaposition with the extractable simulator.

Secondly, we prove query lower bounds for tasks where an algorithm has access to a QRO (or even an extractable simulator thereof) and has to output an input value x which, together with the corresponding oracle output $RO(x)$, achieves a large value under some figure-of-merit function. We use this technical result to provide the aforementioned bounds for the adversarial advantage in the FFP-NK game, but they might prove of independent interest.

TL;DR for scheme designers. Section 6 provides concrete bounds for the IND-CCA security of $FO_m^\perp[PKE, G, H]$. Besides having to analyze the conjectured passive security of PKE, applying the bounds to a concrete scheme PKE requires to analyze the following computational and statistical properties:
- γ, the spreadness of PKE.
- An upper bound for FFP-NG against PKE.
- Either an upper bound for FFP-NK for PKE^G, in our extended oracle model that allows preimage extractions, or, two statistical values: δ_{ik}, the worst-case decryption error rate when the message is picked *independently of the key*, and $\sigma_{\delta_{ik}}$, the maximal variance of δ_{ik}.

Acknowledgements. We would like to thank Dominique Unruh for valuable discussions about the semi-classical one-way to hiding lemma and Manuel Barbosa for pointing out the use of heuristics in bounds for delta.

2 ROM Reduction

This section substantiates the upper half of Fig. 1 in the ROM. The first step of common security reductions for the FO transformation consists of simulating the decapsulation oracle without using the secret key. This simulation allows transforming an IND-CCA-KEM-adversary $\mathcal{A}$ against $KEM_m^\perp := FO_m^\perp[PKE, G, H]$ into an IND-CPA-KEM-adversary $\tilde{\mathcal{A}}$ against the same $KEM_m^\perp$. The oracle simulation, however, will not accurately simulate the behaviour of Decaps for ciphertexts that trigger decryption errors. We will show that from an adversary capable of distinguishing between the real decapsulation oracle and its simulation, we can construct an adversary $\mathcal{B}$ that is able to extract failing plaintexts for the derandomised version PKE^G of PKE. In more detail, we formalise extraction of failing plaintexts as the winning condition of two Find Failing Plaintext (FFP) games,

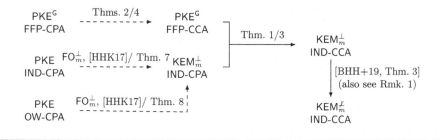

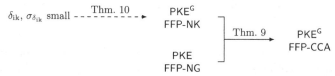

Fig. 1. Summary of our results. Top: "Ths. X/Y" indicates that we provide a ROM Thm. X (in Sect. 2) and a QROM Thm. Y (Sect. 4). Bottom: Breaking down FFP-CPA security of PKE^G (Sect. 5). Solid (dashed) arrows indicate tight (non-tight) reductions in the QROM. Theorems 2 and 4 have comparably mild tightness loss: It is linear in the number of decryption queries. Theorems 7 and 8 are as lossy as previously known ones.

which we formally define in Definition 1 (also see Fig. 2). For ATK $\in \{$CPA, CCA$\}$, an adversary $\mathcal{B}$ playing the FFP-ATK game for a deterministic encryption scheme PKE gets access to the same oracles as in the respective IND-ATK game, outputs a message m, and wins if $\mathsf{Dec}(\mathsf{Enc}(m)) \neq m$. (Here, and in the following, we sometimes omit the arguments pk and sk, respectively.) For such messages m we say that m is a *failing plaintext*, or shorter, that m *fails*. The final bounds we obtain are essentially similar to the ones in [HHK17] except for involving a different correctness definition, see the discussion after Remark 1. Game FFP-CCA was already introduced in [BS20], there called COR-ad-CCA.

Definition 1 (FFP-ATK). *Let* PKE $= ($KG, Enc, Dec$)$ *be a deterministic public-key encryption scheme. For* ATK $\in \{$CPA, CCA$\}$, *we define* FFP-ATK *games as in Fig. 2, where* $\mathsf{O}_{\mathsf{ATK}}$ *is trivial if* ATK $=$ CPA *and*

$$\mathsf{O}_{\mathsf{ATK}} := \text{oDecrypt} \quad \textit{if } \mathsf{ATK} = \mathsf{CCA}.$$

We define the FFP-ATK *advantage function of an adversary* $\mathcal{A}$ *against* PKE *as*

$$\mathrm{Adv}_{\mathsf{PKE}}^{\mathsf{FFP\text{-}ATK}}(\mathcal{A}) := \Pr[\mathsf{FFP\text{-}ATK}_{\mathsf{PKE}}^{\mathcal{A}} \Rightarrow 1] .$$

Note that in neither FFP-ATK game, the adversary has access to the secret key. In particular, the FFP-CPA game only differs from the correctness game COR defined in [HHK17] in exactly this fact, as game COR additionally provides the secret key. We note that an adversary winning either FFP-ATK game for a deterministic scheme PKE can be used to win in game COR.

We start by introducing two simulations of the Decaps oracle, oDecaps' and a variant oDecaps'' of oDecaps'. oDecaps'' extracts failing plaintexts from

Game FFP-ATK	oDecrypt(c)
01 $(pk, sk) \leftarrow$ KG	06 $m := \mathsf{Dec}(sk, c)$
02 $m \leftarrow \mathcal{A}^{\text{O}_{\mathsf{ATK}}, \mathsf{G}}(pk)$	07 **return** m
03 $c := \mathsf{Enc}(pk, m)$	
04 $m' := \mathsf{Dec}(sk, c)$	
05 **return** $[\![m' \neq m]\!]$	

Fig. 2. Games FFP-ATK for a deterministic PKE, where ATK $\in \{\mathsf{CPA}, \mathsf{CCA}\}$. O_{ATK} is the decryption oracle present in the respective IND-ATK-KEM game (see Definition 1) and G is a random oracle, provided if it is used in the definition of PKE.

adversarial decapsulation queries, and is simulatable by FFP adversaries with access to the decryption oracle oDecrypt for PKE$^\mathsf{G}$. Both simulations of the Decaps oracle make use of a list $\mathcal{L}$ of previous queries to G and their respective encryptions. For this to work, we replace G with a modification G$'$ that keeps track of all issued queries and compiles $\mathcal{L}$. The original Decaps oracle and its simulations are defined in Fig. 3, using the following conventions. For a set of pairs $\mathcal{L} \subset \mathcal{X} \times \mathcal{Y}$, we assume that a total order is chosen on $\mathcal{X}$ and $\mathcal{Y}$. We denote by $\mathcal{L}^{-1}(y)$ the first preimage of y. Formally, we define $\mathcal{L}^{-1}(y)$ by setting

$$
\mathcal{L}^{-1}(y) := \begin{cases} x & \text{if } (x, y) \in \mathcal{L} \text{ and } x \leq x' \text{ for all } x' \text{ s. th. } (x', y) \in \mathcal{L} \\ \bot & \nexists\, x \text{ s. th. } (x, y) \in \mathcal{L}. \end{cases} \quad (1)
$$

The simulation oDecaps$'$ can, however, only *reverse* encryptions that were already computed by the adversary (with a query to oracle G$'$) *before* their query to oracle oDecaps$'$, which is where the spreadness of PKE comes into play: If γ is large, it becomes unlikely that the attacker can guess an encryption $c = \mathsf{Enc}(pk, m; \mathsf{G}(m))$ without a respective query to G. oDecaps$'$ will furthermore answer inconsistently if the reversion (in other words, the preimage) of c differs from its decryption, meaning that c belongs to a failing plaintext that can be recognized by the failure-extracting variant oDecaps$''$.

Theorem 1. *Let* PKE *be a (randomised)* PKE *scheme that is γ-spread, and let* $\mathsf{KEM}^\perp_m := \mathsf{FO}^\perp_m[\mathsf{PKE}, \mathsf{G}, \mathsf{H}]$. *Let* $\mathcal{A}$ *be an* IND-CCA-KEM-*adversary (in the ROM) against* $\mathsf{KEM}^\perp_m$, *making at most* q_D *many queries to its decapsulation oracle* oDecaps. *Then there exist an* IND-CPA-KEM *adversary* $\tilde{\mathcal{A}}$ *and an* FFP-CCA *adversary* $\mathcal{B}$ *against* PKE$^\mathsf{G}$ *such that*

$$
\mathsf{Adv}^{\mathsf{IND\text{-}CCA\text{-}KEM}}_{\mathsf{KEM}^\perp_m}(\mathcal{A}) \leq \mathsf{Adv}^{\mathsf{IND\text{-}CPA\text{-}KEM}}_{\mathsf{KEM}^\perp_m}(\tilde{\mathcal{A}}) + \mathsf{Adv}^{\mathsf{FFP\text{-}CCA}}_{\mathsf{PKE}^\mathsf{G}}(\mathcal{B}) + q_\mathsf{D} \cdot 2^{-\gamma}. \quad (2)
$$

$\tilde{\mathcal{A}}$ *makes* q_G *queries to* G *and* $q_\mathsf{H} + q_\mathsf{D}$ *queries to* H, $\mathcal{B}$ *makes* q_G *queries to* G *and* q_D *decryption queries, and both adversaries run in about the time of* $\mathcal{A}$.

Proof. Let $\mathcal{A}$ be an adversary against $\mathsf{KEM}^\perp_m$. We define $\tilde{\mathcal{A}}$ as the IND-CPA-KEM adversary against $\mathsf{KEM}^\perp_m$ that runs $b' \leftarrow \mathcal{A}^{\mathsf{G}', \mathsf{H}, \text{oDecaps}'}$ and returns b'. We furthermore define our FFP-CCA adversary $\mathcal{B}$ against PKE$^\mathsf{G}$ as follows: $\mathcal{B}$ runs

oDECAPS(c)	oDECAPS$'(c \neq c^*)$	oDECAPS$''(c \neq c^*)$
01 $m' := \mathsf{Dec}(sk, c)$	12 $m := \mathcal{L}_G^{-1}(c)$	23 $m := \mathcal{L}_G^{-1}(c)$
02 if $m' = \bot$	13 if $m = \bot$	24 $m' := \text{oDECRYPT}(c)$
03 return $K:=\bot$	14 return $K:=\bot$	25 if $m \neq \bot$ and $m \neq m'$
04 else	15 else return $K := \mathsf{H}(m)$	26 $\mathcal{L}_{\text{FAIL}} := \mathcal{L}_{\text{FAIL}} \cup \{m\}$
05 $c' := \mathsf{Enc}(pk, m'; \mathsf{G}(m'))$	oDECRYPT$(c \neq c^*)$	27 if $m = \bot$
06 if $c \neq c'$ return $\bot$	16 $m' := \mathsf{Dec}(sk, c)$	28 return $K:=\bot$
07 else return $\mathsf{H}(m')$	17 if $m' = \bot$	29 else
$\mathsf{G}'(m)$	18 return $\bot$	30 return $K := \mathsf{H}(m)$
08 $r := \mathsf{G}(m)$	19 else	
09 $c := \mathsf{Enc}(pk, m; r)$	20 if $\mathsf{Enc}(pk, m'; \mathsf{G}(m')) \neq c$	
10 $\mathcal{L}_G := \mathcal{L}_G \cup \{(m, c)\}$	21 return $\bot$	
11 return r	22 else return m'	

Fig. 3.   Simulation oDECAPS$'$ of oracle oDECAPS for $\mathsf{KEM}_m^\bot$, failing-plaintext-extracting version oDECAPS$''$ of oDECAPS$'$, and decryption oracle oDECRYPT for PKE^G. Oracles oDECAPS$'$ and oDECAPS$''$ use in lines 12 and 23 the notation introduced in Eq. (1). G' only differs from G by compiling list $\mathcal{L}_G$ (which was initialized to $\emptyset$).

$\mathcal{A}^{G',H,\text{oDECAPS}''}$, using its own FFP-CCA oracle oDECRYPT to simulate oDECAPS$''$. As soon as oDECAPS$''$ adds a plaintext m to $\mathcal{L}_{\text{FAIL}}$, $\mathcal{B}$ aborts $\mathcal{A}$ and returns m. If $\mathcal{A}$ finishes and $\mathcal{L}_{\text{FAIL}}$ is still empty, $\mathcal{B}$ returns $\bot$.

First, we will relate $\mathcal{A}$'s success probability to the one of $\tilde{\mathcal{A}}$. Note that unless $\tilde{\mathcal{A}}$'s simulation oDECAPS$'$ of the decapsulation oracle fails, $\tilde{\mathcal{A}}$ perfectly simulates the game to $\mathcal{A}$ and wins if $\mathcal{A}$ wins. Let DIFF be the event that $\mathcal{A}$ makes a decryption query c such that $\mathsf{Decaps}(sk, c) \neq \text{oDECAPS}'(c)$. We bound

$$\frac{1}{2} + \text{Adv}_{\mathsf{KEM}_m^\bot}^{\text{IND-CCA-KEM}}(\mathcal{A}) = \Pr[\mathcal{A} \text{ wins}] = \Pr[\mathcal{A} \text{ wins} \wedge \neg\mathsf{DIFF}] + \Pr[\mathcal{A} \text{ wins} \wedge \mathsf{DIFF}]$$

$$= \Pr[\tilde{\mathcal{A}} \text{ wins} \wedge \neg\mathsf{DIFF}] + \Pr[\mathcal{A} \text{ wins} \wedge \mathsf{DIFF}] \leq \Pr[\tilde{\mathcal{A}} \text{ wins}] + \Pr[\mathsf{DIFF}]$$

$$= \frac{1}{2} + \text{Adv}_{\mathsf{KEM}_m^\bot}^{\text{IND-CPA-KEM}}(\tilde{\mathcal{A}}) + \Pr[\mathsf{DIFF}].$$

To analyze the probability of event DIFF, we note that it covers several cases:

- Original oracle oDECAPS(c) rejects, whereas simulation oDECAPS$'(c)$ does not, meaning that c is an encryption belonging to a previous query m to G', but fails the reencryption check performed by oDECAPS(c). Since the latter means that either $m' := \mathsf{Dec}(sk, c) = \bot$ or that $\mathsf{Enc}(pk, m'; \mathsf{G}(m')) \neq c = \mathsf{Enc}(pk, m; \mathsf{G}(m))$, this case only occurs if $\mathsf{Dec}(sk, c) \neq m$, meaning m fails.
- Neither oracle rejects, but the return values differ, i.e., c is an encryption belonging to a previous query m to G', but decrypts to some message $m' \neq m$.
- oDECAPS$'(c)$ rejects, whereas oDECAPS(c) does not, i.e., while c would pass the reencryption check, its decryption m has not yet been queried to G'.

In either of the former two cases, G' has been queried on a failing plaintext m and the decapsulation oracle has been queried on its encryption c, meaning that the failing plaintext can be found and recognized by $\mathcal{B}$ since $\mathcal{B}$ can use its own FFP-CCA oracle oDECRYPT to simulate oDECAPS''. We will denote the last case by GUESS since $\mathcal{A}$ has to find a guess for a ciphertext c that passes the reencryption check, meaning it is indeed of the form $c = \text{Enc}(pk, m; \text{G}'(m))$ for $m := \text{Dec}(sk, c)$, while not having queried G' on m yet. Whenever DIFF occurs, $\mathcal{B}$ succeeds unless GUESS occurs. In formulae,

$$\Pr[\text{DIFF}] = \Pr[\text{DIFF} \wedge \neg\text{GUESS}] + \Pr[\text{DIFF} \wedge \text{GUESS}]$$
$$\leq \text{Adv}_{\text{PKE}^\text{G}}^{\text{FFP-CCA}}(\mathcal{B}) + \Pr[\text{GUESS}].$$

Together with Lemma 1 below, this yields the desired bound. $\square$

We continue by bounding the probability of event GUESS. We will also need to analyze a very similar event in Theorem 2, in which we revisit the FFP-CCA attacker $\mathcal{B}$ against PKE^G, and where we will simulate $\mathcal{B}$'s oracle oDECRYPT via an oracle oDECRYPT' (see Fig. 4). Therefore, we generalize the definition of event GUESS accordingly. Since GUESS means that $\mathcal{A}$ computed a ciphertext $c = \text{Enc}(pk, m; \text{G}(m))$ *before* querying G on m, the probability can be upper bounded in terms of the maximal probability of any ciphertext being hit by $\text{Enc}(pk, -; -)$. For completeness, we prove Lemma 1 in the full version.

Lemma 1. *Let* PKE *be γ-spread, and let $\mathcal{A}$ be an adversary expecting oracles* G, H *as well as either a decapsulation oracle* oDECAPS *for* $\text{KEM}_m^{\perp}$ *or a decryption oracle* oDECRYPT *for* PKE^G, *issuing at most q_D queries to the latter. When run with* G' *and simulated oracle* oDECAPS' *(or* oDECRYPT', *respectively), there is only a small probability that original oracle* oDECAPS *(oDECRYPT) would not have rejected, but simulation* oDECAPS' *(oDECRYPT') does. Concretely, we have*

$$\Pr[\text{GUESS}] \leq q_D \cdot 2^{-\gamma}. \tag{3}$$

So far, we have shown that whenever an IND-CCA adversary $\mathcal{A}$'s behaviour is significantly changed by being run with simulation oDECAPS' instead of the real oracle oDECAPS, we can use $\mathcal{A}$ to find a failing plaintext, assuming access to the FFP-CCA decryption oracle oDECRYPT for PKE^G. We now show that oDECRYPT can be simulated via oracle oDECRYPT' (see Fig. 4) without the secret key, thereby being able to construct an FFP-CPA adversary from any FFP-CCA adversary that succeeds with the same probability up to (at most) a multiplicative factor equal to the number of decryption queries the FFP-CCA adversary makes.

Theorem 2. *Let* PKE *be -γ-spread, and let $\mathcal{B}$ be an* FFP-CCA *adversary against* PKE^G, *issuing at most q_D many decryption queries. Then there exists an* FFP-CPA *adversary $\tilde{\mathcal{B}}$ such that*

$$\text{Adv}_{\text{PKE}^\text{G}}^{\text{FFP-CCA}}(\mathcal{B}) \leq (q_D + 1) \cdot \text{Adv}_{\text{PKE}^\text{G}}^{\text{FFP-CPA}}(\tilde{\mathcal{B}}) + q_D \cdot 2^{-\gamma}. \tag{4}$$

Adversary $\tilde{\mathcal{B}}$ makes at most the same number of queries to G *as $\mathcal{B}$ and runs in about the time of $\mathcal{B}$.*

oDecrypt$'(c)$	$\tilde{\mathcal{B}}^{\mathsf{G}}$
01 $m := \mathcal{L}_{\mathsf{G}}^{-1}(c)$	06 $i \leftarrow_\$ \{1, ..., q_{\mathsf{D}} + 1\}$
02 **return** m	07 **if** $i < q_{\mathsf{D}} + 1$
G$'(m)$	08 Run $\mathcal{B}^{\mathsf{G}',\text{oDecrypt}'}(pk)$ until i-th query c_i to oDecrypt$'$
03 $c := \mathsf{Enc}(m; \mathsf{G}(m))$	09 $m := \mathcal{L}_{\mathsf{G}}^{-1}(c_i)$
04 $\mathcal{L}_{\mathsf{G}} := \mathcal{L}_{\mathsf{G}} \cup \{(m, c)\}$	10 **else**
05 **return** $\mathsf{G}(m)$	11 $m \leftarrow \mathcal{B}^{\mathsf{G}',\text{oDecrypt}'}(pk)$
	12 **return** m

Fig. 4. Simulation oDecrypt$'$ of oracle oDecrypt for PKE^{G}, which is defined analogously to oDecaps$'$ (see Fig. 3), and FFP-CPA adversary $\tilde{\mathcal{B}}$. For the reader's convenience, we repeat the definition of G$'$.

Proof. To simulate oDecrypt, we use a similar strategy as in the proof of Theorem 1. We define the events DIFF and GUESS in the same way as in the proof of Theorem 1, except now with respect to the adversary $\mathcal{B}$ and oracles oDecrypt (oDecrypt$'$) instead of oDecaps (oDecaps$'$). If our simulation does not fail, then a reduction can simulate the FFP-CCA game to $\mathcal{B}$ and use $\mathcal{B}$'s output to win its own FFP-CPA game. The simulation will fail if either GUESS happens (with probability at most $q_D \cdot 2^{-\gamma}$ due to Lemma 1), or DIFF, while GUESS does not, meaning that the failing message triggering DIFF can be extracted from $\mathcal{L}_{\mathsf{G}}$. Our reduction $\tilde{\mathcal{B}}$ combines both approaches (using $\mathcal{B}$'s output and $\mathcal{L}_{\mathsf{G}}$). Since $\tilde{\mathcal{B}}$ has no knowledge of the secret key, it cannot determine which message will let it succeed and hence has to guess.

Assume without loss of generality that $\mathcal{B}$ makes exactly q_D many queries to oracle oDecrypt. Consider the adversary $\tilde{\mathcal{B}}^{\mathsf{G}}$ in Fig. 4. $\tilde{\mathcal{B}}$ samples $i \leftarrow \{1, ..., q_{\mathsf{D}} + 1\}$ and either runs $\mathcal{B}^{\mathsf{G}',\text{oDecrypt}'}$ until its i-th query to oDecrypt$'$ or until the end if $i = q_{\mathsf{D}} + 1$. To implement G$'$, $\tilde{\mathcal{B}}$ uses its oracle G. Simulation oDecrypt$'$ is defined in Fig. 4 and works analogous to oDecaps$'$ in the previous proof. Finally, $\tilde{\mathcal{B}}$ outputs query preimage $\mathcal{L}_{\mathsf{G}}^{-1}(c_i)$, where c_i is $\mathcal{B}$'s i-th query to decryption oracle oDecrypt$'$, unless $i = q_{\mathsf{D}} + 1$, in which case $\tilde{\mathcal{B}}$ outputs the output of $\mathcal{B}$.

Using the same chain of inequalities as in the proof of Theorem 1, and again using Lemma 1, we obtain

$$\text{Adv}_{\mathsf{PKE}^{\mathsf{G}}}^{\mathsf{FFP\text{-}CCA}}(\mathcal{B}) \leq \Pr[\mathcal{B} \text{ wins } \wedge \neg\mathsf{DIFF}] + \Pr[\mathsf{DIFF} \wedge \neg\mathsf{GUESS}] + q_{\mathsf{D}} \cdot 2^{-\gamma}. \quad (5)$$

Adversary $\tilde{\mathcal{B}}$ perfectly simulates game FFP-CCA unless DIFF occurs, and wins with probability $1/q_{\mathsf{D}}+1$ if $\mathcal{B}$ wins by returning a failing plaintext or if $\mathcal{B}$ issues a decryption query that triggers DIFF but not GUESS.

$$\text{Adv}_{\mathsf{PKE}^{\mathsf{G}}}^{\mathsf{FFP\text{-}CPA}}(\tilde{\mathcal{B}}) = \frac{1}{q_{\mathsf{D}} + 1} \cdot (\Pr[\mathcal{B} \text{ wins } \wedge \neg\mathsf{DIFF}] + \Pr[\mathsf{DIFF} \wedge \neg\mathsf{GUESS}]) \quad (6)$$

Combining Eqs. (5) and (6) yields the desired bound. $\square$

Next, we observe that IND-CPA security of KEM$_m^{\perp}$ can be based on passive security of PKE. This result is implicitly contained in [HHK17] since [HHK17] proved such a result for IND-CCA security of $\text{KEM}_m^{\perp}$. Combining Theorems 1 and 2 with the result from [HHK17], we obtain the following

Corollary 1. *Let* PKE *and* $\mathcal{A}$ *be as in Theorem 1. Then there exist a* OW-CPA *adversary* $\mathcal{B}_{\text{OW-CPA}}$ *and an* IND-CPA *adversary* $\mathcal{B}_{\text{IND-CPA}}$ *such that*

$$\text{Adv}_{\text{KEM}_m^{\perp}}^{\text{IND-CCA-KEM}}(\mathcal{A}) \le (q_{\text{RO}} + q_{\text{D}} + 1) \cdot \text{Adv}_{\text{PKE}}^{\text{OW}}(\mathcal{B}_{\text{OW-CPA}})$$
$$+ (q_{\text{D}} + 1) \cdot \text{Adv}_{\text{PKE}^{\text{G}}}^{\text{FFP-CPA}}(\mathcal{C}) + 2q_{\text{D}} \cdot 2^{-\gamma}$$

and

$$\text{Adv}_{\text{KEM}_m^{\perp}}^{\text{IND-CCA-KEM}}(\mathcal{A}) \le 3 \cdot \text{Adv}_{\text{PKE}}^{\text{IND-CPA}}(\mathcal{B}_{\text{IND-CPA}}) + \frac{2 \cdot (q_{\text{RO}} + q_{\text{D}}) + 1}{|\mathcal{M}|}$$
$$+ (q_{\text{D}} + 1) \cdot \text{Adv}_{\text{PKE}^{\text{G}}}^{\text{FFP-CPA}}(\mathcal{B}) + 2q_{\text{D}} \cdot 2^{-\gamma}.$$

$\mathcal{C}$ *makes* q_{G} *queries to* G, *and all adversaries run in about the time of* $\mathcal{A}$.

We remark that the factor 2 in front of the additive term $q_{\text{D}} \cdot 2^{-\gamma}$ is an artefact of our modular proof (in terms of Theorems 1 and 2). It is straightforward to show that the bound of Corollary 1 can be proven without the factor of 2, when directly analyzing the composition of the reductions from Theorems 1 and 2.

When comparing our bounds with the respective bounds from [HHK17], we note that our bounds are still in the same asymptotic ball park and differ from the bounds in [HHK17] essentially by replacing the worst-case correctness term δ_{wc} (there denoted by δ) present in [HHK17] by $\text{Adv}_{\text{PKE}^{\text{G}}}^{\text{FFP-CPA}}(\mathcal{B})$, and having an additional term in γ even for $\text{KEM}_m^{\not\perp}$. We believe that the additional γ-term could be removed by doing a direct proof for $\text{KEM}_m^{\not\perp}$, but redoing the whole proof for this variant was outside the scope of this work. We will further analyze $\text{Adv}_{\text{PKE}^{\text{G}}}^{\text{FFP-CPA}}(\mathcal{B})$ in Sect. 5.

Remark 1 (Obtaining the results for $\text{FO}_m^{\not\perp}[\text{PKE}]$*).* We can use the results from [BHH+19] to furthermore show that the bounds given in Corollary 1 also hold if $\text{KEM}_m^{\perp} := \text{FO}_m^{\perp}[\text{PKE}, \text{G}, \text{H}]$ is replaced with $\text{KEM}_m^{\not\perp} := \text{FO}_m^{\perp}[\text{PKE}, \text{G}, \text{H}]$: In more detail, it follows directly from [BHH+19, Theorem 3] that for any IND-CCA-KEM attacker $\mathcal{A}$ against $\text{KEM}_m^{\not\perp}$, there exists an IND-CCA-KEM attacker $\mathcal{B}$ against $\text{KEM}_m^{\perp}$ such that $\text{Adv}_{\text{KEM}_m^{\not\perp}}^{\text{IND-CCA-KEM}}(\mathcal{A}) \le \text{Adv}_{\text{KEM}_m^{\perp}}^{\text{IND-CCA-KEM}}(\mathcal{B})$ and Corollary 1 does not contain any terms relative to $\text{KEM}_m^{\perp}$ itself, it only contains terms relative to the underlying schemes PKE and PKE^{G}.

3   Compressed Oracles and Extraction

We want to generalize the ROM results obtained in Sect. 2 to the QROM. To this end, we will use an extension of the compressed oracle technique [Zha19] that was introduced in [DFMS21]. It was shown in [Zha19] how a quantum-accessible random oracle $\text{O} : X \to Y$ can be simulated by preparing a database D with an entry D_x for each input value x, with each D_x being initialized as a uniform superposition of all elements of Y, and omitting the "oracle-generating" measurements until after the algorithm accessing O has finished. In [DFMS21], this oracle simulation was generalized to obtain an *extractable* oracle simulator eCO (for extractable Compressed Oracle) that has two interfaces, the random oracle interface eCO.RO and an extraction interface eCO.E$_f$, defined relative to a function $f : X \times Y \to T$. Whenever it is clear from context which function f is used, we simply write eCO.E instead of eCO.E$_f$.

In general, eCO.E$_f$ can extract preimage entries from the "database" D during the runtime of an adversary instead of only after the adversary terminated. This allows for adaptive behaviour of a reduction, based on an adversary's queries. In [DFMS21], it was already used for the same purpose we need it for – the simulation of a decapsulation oracle, by having eCO.E extract a preimage plaintext from the ciphertext on which the decapsulation oracle was queried. We will denote oracles modelled as extractable quantum-accessible ROs by eQRO$_f$, and a proof that uses an eQRO$_f$ will be called *a proof in the eQROM$_f$*.

We will now make this description more formal, closely following notation and conventions from [DFMS21]. Like in [DFMS21], we describe an inefficient variant of the oracle that is not (yet) "compressed". Efficient simulation is possible via a standard sparse encoding, see [DFMS21, Appendix A]. The simulator eCO for a random function $O : \{0,1\}^m \to \{0,1\}^n$ is a stateful oracle with a state stored in a quantum register $D = D_{0^m} \dots D_{1^m}$, where for each $x \in \{0,1\}^m$, register D_x has $n + 1$ qubits used to store superpositions of n-bit output strings y, encoded as $0y$, and an additional symbol $\perp$, encoded as 10^n. We adopt the convention that an operator expecting n input qubits acts on the last n qubits when applied to D_x. The compressed oracle has the following three components.

- The initial state of the oracle, $|\phi\rangle = |\perp\rangle^{2^m}$
- A quantum query with query input register X and output register Y is answered using the oracle unitary O_{XYD} defined by

$$O_{XYD}|x\rangle_X = |x\rangle_X \otimes \left(F_{D_x} \mathsf{CNOT}_{D_x:Y}^{\otimes n} F_{D_x} \right), \tag{7}$$

where $F|\perp\rangle = |\phi_0\rangle$, $F|\phi_0\rangle = |\perp\rangle$ and $F|\psi\rangle = |\psi\rangle$ for all $|\psi\rangle$ such that $\langle\psi|\perp\rangle = \langle\psi|\phi_0\rangle = 0$, with $|\phi_0\rangle = |+\rangle^{\otimes n}$ being the uniform superposition. The CNOT operator here is responsible for XORing the function value (stored in D_x, now in superposition) into the query algorithm's output register.
- A *recovery algorithm* that recovers a standard QRO O: apply $F^{\otimes 2^m}$ to D and measure it to obtain the function table of O.

We now make our description of the extraction interface eCO.E formal: Given a random oracle $O : \{0,1\}^m \to \{0,1\}^n$, let $f : \{0,1\}^m \times \{0,1\}^n \to \{0,1\}^\ell$ be a function. We define a family of measurements $(\mathcal{M}^t)_{t\in\{0,1\}^\ell}$. The measurement $\mathcal{M}^t$ has measurement projectors $\{\Sigma^{t,x}\}_{x\in\{0,1\}^m\cup\{\emptyset\}}$ defined as follows. For $x \in \{0,1\}^m$, the projector selects the case where D_x is the first (in lexicographical order) register that contains y such that $f(x,y) = t$, i.e.

$$\Sigma^{t,x} = \bigotimes_{x'<x} \bar{\Pi}_{D_{x'}}^{t,x'} \otimes \Pi_{D_x}^{t,x}, \quad \text{with} \quad \Pi^{t,x} = \sum_{\substack{y\in\{0,1\}^n:\\f(x,y)=t}} |y\rangle\langle y| \tag{8}$$

and $\bar{\Pi} = \mathbb{1} - \Pi$. $\Sigma^{t,\emptyset}$ covers the case where no register contains such a y, i.e.

$$\Sigma^{t,\emptyset} = \bigotimes_{x' \in \{0,1\}^m} \bar{\Pi}_{D'_x}^{t,x'}. \tag{9}$$

As an example, say we model a random oracle H as such an $eQRO_f$. Using $f(x,y) := [\![H(x) = y]\!]$, $\mathcal{M}^1$ allows us to extract a preimage of y.

eCO is initialized with the initial state of the compressed oracle. eCO.RO is quantum-accessible and applies the compressed oracle query unitary O_{XYD}. eCO.E is classically-accessible. On input t, it applies $\mathcal{M}^t$ to eCO's internal state and returns the result. eCO has useful properties that were characterized in [DFMS21, Theorem 3.4]. These characterisations are in terms of the quantity

$$\Gamma(f) = \max_t \Gamma_{R_{f,t}}, \text{ with}$$

$$R_{f,t}(x,y) :\Leftrightarrow f(x,y) = t \text{ and}$$

$$\Gamma_R := \max_x |\{y \mid R(x,y)\}|. \tag{10}$$

For $f = \mathsf{Enc}(\cdot; \cdot)$, the encryption function of a PKE that takes as inputs a message m and an encryption randomness r, we have $\Gamma(f) = 2^{-\gamma} |\mathcal{R}|$ if PKE is γ-spread. In this case, eCO.E(c) outputs a plaintext m such that $\mathsf{Enc}(m, \mathsf{eCO.RO}(m)) = c$, or $\perp$ if the ciphertext c has not been computed using eCO.RO before.

4   QROM Reduction

In this section, we generalize the reductions from Sect. 2 to the QROM. To do so, we give in Fig. 6 the quantum analogues of the simulated decapsulation oracles oDECAPS$'$ and oDECAPS$''$ from Fig. 3, which were (essentially) developed in [DFMS21]. We have to adapt our simulations since the ROM simulations from Fig. 3 use book-keeping techniques and therefore cannot be easily implemented in the standard QROM. Instead, we use the formalism described in Sect. 3, i.e., we use a simulation of a quantum-accessible random oracle and *make use of the additional extraction interface* eCO.E: While the simulations in Fig. 3 had access to a list $\mathcal{L}_\mathsf{G}$ that could be used to extract potential ciphertext preimages, the simulations in Fig. 6 can now extract them by accessing extractor eCO.E (see lines 12 and 24). The rest of the simulation is exactly as before. Using the notation from Sect. 3, we denote the modelling of the ROM as extractable by $eQROM_{\mathsf{Enc}}$, as we extract preimages relative to function $f = \mathsf{Enc}(pk, \cdot, \cdot)$, with the message being f's first and the randomness being f's second input.

We split this section as follows: Sect. 4.1 ends with IND-CPA security of $\mathsf{KEM}_m^\perp$ and FFP-CPA security of PKE^G, in the $eQROM_{\mathsf{Enc}}$. We give the $eQROM_f$ definition of FFP-ATK in Fig. 5. Section 4.2 develops the necessary $eQROM_{\mathsf{Enc}}$ tools to further analyze IND-CPA security of $\mathsf{KEM}_m^\perp$. Concretely, Sect. 4.2 provides an $eQROM_{\mathsf{Enc}}$-compatible variant of the one-way to hiding (OWTH) lemma for semi-classical oracles as introduced in [AHU19]. Equipped with the results from Sect. 4.2, we show in Sect. 4.3 that *also in the* $eQROM_{\mathsf{Enc}}$, IND-CPA security of $\mathsf{FO}_m^\perp[\mathsf{PKE}, \mathsf{G}, \mathsf{H}]$ can be based on passive security of PKE.

Game FFP-ATK	oDECRYPT(c)
01 $(pk, sk) \leftarrow$ KG	05 $m := $ Dec(sk, c)
02 $m \leftarrow \mathcal{A}^{\text{O}_{\text{ATK}}, \text{eCO}}(pk)$	06 **return** m
03 $c := $ Enc(pk, m)	
04 **return** $[\![$Dec($sk, c) \neq m]\!]$	

Fig. 5. Games FFP-ATK for a deterministic PKE, where ATK $\in \{$CPA, CCA$\}$, in the eQROM$_f$. Like in its classical counterpart (see Fig. 2, page 420), O$_{\text{ATK}}$ is the decryption oracle present in the respective IND-ATK-KEM game . The only difference is that random oracle G is now modelled as an extractable superposition oracle eCO.

4.1 From IND-CPA$_{\text{FO[PKE]}}$ and FFP-CCA$^{\text{G}}_{\text{PKE}}$ to IND-CCA$_{\text{FO[PKE]}}$

We begin by proving a quantum analogue of Theorem 1.

Theorem 3. *Let* PKE *be a (randomized)* PKE *that is γ-spread, and* KEM$^{\perp}_m :=$ FO$^{\perp}_m$[PKE, G, H]. *Let $\mathcal{A}$ be an* IND-CCA-KEM-*adversary (in the QROM) against* KEM$^{\perp}_m$, *making at most q_{D}, q_{G} and q_{H} queries to* oDECAPS, G *and* H, *respectively. Let furthermore d and w be the combined query depth and query width of $\mathcal{A}$'s random oracle queries. Then there exist an* IND-CPA-KEM *adversary $\tilde{\mathcal{A}}$ and an* FFP-CCA *adversary $\mathcal{B}$ against* PKE^{G}, *both in the eQROM$_{\text{Enc}}$, such that*

$$\text{Adv}^{\text{IND-CCA-KEM}}_{\text{KEM}^{\perp}_m}(\mathcal{A}) \leq \text{Adv}^{\text{IND-CPA-KEM}}_{\text{KEM}^{\perp}_m}(\tilde{\mathcal{A}}) + \text{Adv}^{\text{FFP-CCA}}_{\text{PKE}^{\text{G}}}(\mathcal{B}) + 12q_{\text{D}}(q_{\text{G}} + 4q_{\text{D}}) \cdot 2^{-\gamma/2}.$$

The adversary $\tilde{\mathcal{A}}$ makes $q_{\text{G}} + q_{\text{H}} + q_{\text{D}}$ queries to eCO.RO *with a combined depth of $d + q_{\text{D}}$ and a combined width of w, and q_{D} queries to* eCO.E. *Here,* eCO.RO *simulates* G $\times$ H. *The adversary $\mathcal{B}$ makes q_{D} many queries to* oDECRYPT *and* eCO.E *and q_{G} queries to* eCO.RO, *and neither $\tilde{\mathcal{A}}$ nor $\mathcal{B}$ query* eCO.E *on the challenge ciphertext. The running times of the adversaries $\tilde{\mathcal{A}}$ and $\mathcal{B}$ are bounded as* Time($\tilde{\mathcal{A}}$) = Time($\mathcal{A}$) + $O(q_{\text{D}})$ *and* Time(B) = Time($\mathcal{A}$) + $O(q_{\text{D}})$.

Before proving the theorem, we point out similarities and differences to the ROM counterpart, Theorem 1. First note that the bounds look very similar. The only difference lies in the additive error term that depends on the spreadness parameter γ. In the above theorem, this additive error term $O(q_{\text{D}}q_{\text{G}}2^{-\gamma/2})$ is much larger than the term $O(q_{\text{D}}2^{-\gamma})$ present in Theorem 1. It originates from dealing with the fact that the extraction technique used to simulate the Decaps oracle inflicts an error onto the simulation of the QRO. We expect that for many real-world schemes, the additive security loss of $O(q_{\text{D}}q_{\text{G}}2^{-\gamma/2})$ is still small enough to be neglected. Another important difference between Theorem 3 and Theorem 1 is of course that the adversaries $\tilde{\mathcal{A}}$ and $\mathcal{B}$ are now in the non-standard eQROM$_{\text{Enc}}$. Looking ahead, we provide further reductions culminating in Corollary 6 which gives a standard-QROM bound for KEM$^{\perp}_m$ in terms of (standard model) security properties of PKE.

Proof. We prove this theorem via a number of hybrid games, drawing some inspiration from the reduction for the entire FO transformation given in [DFMS21].

$\text{oDecaps}(c \neq c^*)$	$\text{oDecaps}'(c \neq c^*)$	$\text{oDecaps}''(c \neq c^*)$
01 $m' := \text{Dec}(sk, c)$	12 $m \leftarrow \text{eCO.E}(c)$	24 $m \leftarrow \text{eCO.E}(c)$
02 if $m' = \bot$	13 if $m = \bot$	25 $m' := \text{oDecrypt}(c)$
03 return $K := \bot$	14 return $\bot$	26 if $m \neq \bot$ and $m \neq m'$
04 else	15 else	27 $\mathcal{L}_{\text{FAIL}} := \mathcal{L}_{\text{FAIL}} \cup \{m\}$
05 $c' := \text{Enc}(pk, m'; G(m'))$	16 return $H(m)$	28 if $m = \bot$
06 if $c \neq c'$		29 return $\bot$
07 return $\bot$		30 else
08 else	$\text{oDecrypt}(c)$	31 return $H(m)$
09 return $H(m')$	17 $m' := \text{Dec}(sk, c)$	
	18 if $m' = \bot$	
	19 return $\bot$	
G', input registers X, Y	20 else if	
10 Apply eCO.RO_{XYD}	$\text{Enc}(pk, m'; G(m')) \neq c$	
11 return registers XY	21 return $\bot$	
	22 else	
	23 return m'	

Fig. 6. Simulated and failing-plaintext-extracting versions of the decapsulation oracle oDecaps for $\text{FO}_m^{\bot}[\text{PKE}, G, H]$, using the extractable QRO simulator eCO from [DFMS21] (see Sect. 3). The simulations of oDecaps are exactly like the ROM ones in Fig. 3 except for how they extract ciphertext preimages (lines 12, 24). eCO is assumed to be freshly initialized before $\text{oDecaps}'$ or $\text{oDecaps}''$ is used for the first time, and extraction interface eCO.E is defined with respect to function $f = \text{Enc}(pk, \cdot; \cdot)$.

Game G_0 is $\text{IND-CCA-KEM}_{\text{KEM}_m^{\bot}}(\mathcal{A})$.

Game G_1 is like **Game G_0**, except for two modifications: The quantum-accessible random oracle G is replaced by G' as defined in Fig. 6, and after the adversary has finished, we compute $\hat{m}_i := \text{eCO.E}(c_i)$ for all $i = 1, ..., q_D$, where c_i is the input to the adversary's ith decapsulation query. By property 1 in [DFMS21, Lem. 3.4], G' perfectly simulates G until the first eCO.E-query, and since the first eCO.E-query occurs only after $\mathcal{A}$ finishes, we have

$$\text{Adv}_{\text{KEM}_m^{\bot}}^{\text{IND-CCA-KEM}}(\mathcal{A}) = \text{Adv}^{\textbf{Game } G_0} = \text{Adv}^{\textbf{Game } G_1}. \tag{11}$$

Game G_2 is like **Game G_1**, except that $\hat{m}_i := \text{eCO.E}(c_i)$ is computed right after $\mathcal{A}$ submits c_i instead of computing it in the end. Note that **Game G_2** can be obtained from **Game G_1** by first swapping the eCO.E call that produces $\hat{m}_1$ with all eCO.RO calls that happen after the adversary submits c_1, including the calls inside oDecaps, then continuing with the eCO.E-call that produces $\hat{m}_2$, etc. By property 2.c of [DFMS21, Lem. 3.4] and since $\Gamma(\text{Enc}(\cdot; \cdot)) = 2^{-\gamma}|\mathcal{R}|$ for γ-spread PKE schemes, we have that

$$\left| \text{Adv}^{\textbf{Game } G_1} - \text{Adv}^{\textbf{Game } G_2} \right| \leq 8\sqrt{2}q_D(q_G + q_D) \cdot 2^{-\gamma/2}. \tag{12}$$

Game G_3 is the same as **Game G_2**, except that $\mathcal{A}$ in run with access to the oracle $\text{oDecaps}'$ instead of oDecaps, meaning that upon a decapsulation query on c_i, $\mathcal{A}$ receives $\text{oDecaps}'(c_i) = H(\hat{m}_i)$ instead of $\text{oDecaps}(c_i) =$

$\text{Decaps}(sk, c_i)$ (using the convention $H(\bot) := \bot$). We still let the game also compute $o\text{DECAPS}(c_i)$, as $o\text{DECAPS}$ makes queries to eCO.RO which can influence the behavior of eCO.E in subsequent queries. (Note that the reencryption step of $o\text{DECAPS}$ triggers a call to G', which in turn uses eCO.RO.) We define $\mathcal{B}$ exactly as in the proof of Theorem 1, except that it uses the oracles G' and $o\text{DECAPS}''$ defined in Fig. 6: $\mathcal{B}$ runs $\mathcal{A}^{G',H,o\text{DECAPS}''}$, using its own FFP-CCA oracle $o\text{DECRYPT}$ to simulate $o\text{DECAPS}''$ and answering H queries by simulating a fresh compressed oracle.[4] As soon as $o\text{DECAPS}''$ adds a plaintext m to $\mathcal{L}_{\text{FAIL}}$, $\mathcal{B}$ aborts $\mathcal{A}$ and returns m. If $\mathcal{A}$ finishes and $\mathcal{L}_{\text{FAIL}}$ is still empty, $\mathcal{B}$ returns $\bot$.

Let DIFF be the event that $\mathcal{A}$ makes a decryption query c in **Game G_2** such that $o\text{DECAPS}(c) \neq o\text{DECAPS}'(c)$. Like in Theorem 1, we bound

$$\frac{1}{2} + \text{Adv}^{\textbf{Game } G_2} = \Pr\left[\mathcal{A} \text{ wins in } \textbf{Game } G_2\right]$$

$$= \Pr\left[\mathcal{A} \text{ wins in } \textbf{Game } G_2 \wedge \neg\text{DIFF}\right] + \Pr\left[\mathcal{A} \text{ wins in } \textbf{Game } G_2 \wedge \text{DIFF}\right]$$

$$= \Pr\left[\mathcal{A} \text{ wins in } \textbf{Game } G_3 \wedge \neg\text{DIFF}\right] + \Pr\left[\mathcal{A} \text{ wins in } \textbf{Game } G_2 \wedge \text{DIFF}\right]$$

$$\leq \Pr\left[\mathcal{A} \text{ wins in } \textbf{Game } G_3\right] + \Pr\left[\text{DIFF}\right] = \frac{1}{2} + \text{Adv}^{\textbf{Game } G_3} + \Pr\left[\text{DIFF}\right] .$$

Again, event DIFF encompasses three cases: For some decapsulation query c,

- the original decapsulation oracle $o\text{DECAPS}(c)$ rejects, but the simulation $o\text{DECAPS}'(c) = H(\hat{m})$ does not. By construction of the oracles, this implies that $\text{Dec}(sk, \text{Enc}(pk, \hat{m}, \text{eCO.RO}(\hat{m}))) \neq \hat{m}$ if the eCO.RO call in the previous equation is performed right after the considered $o\text{DECAPS}''$ call.
- Neither oracle rejects, but the return values differ, i.e., calling eCO.E(c) in line 12 yielded something different than $\text{Dec}(sk, c)$. Like above, this implies that preimage $\hat{m} := \text{eCO.E}(c)$ fails
- $o\text{DECAPS}(c)$ does not reject, while $o\text{DECAPS}'(c)$ does, i.e., $\hat{m} := \text{eCO.E}(c)$ in line 12 yielded $\bot$, but the re-encryption check inside the $o\text{DECAPS}$ call in line 25 checked out, meaning that $\text{Enc}(pk, m, \text{eCO.RO}(m)) = c$ for $m := \text{Dec}(sk, c)$. (Equivalently, the latter means that $o\text{DECRYPT}(c) = m$.)

In the above, any statements about eCO calls that are not actually performed by the adversary or an oracle are assumed to be made right after the query c and do not cause any measurement disturbance in that case.

We will again denote the last case by GUESS. Whenever DIFF occurs, $\mathcal{B}$ succeeds unless only case GUESS occurs: If $\text{DIFF} \wedge \neg\text{GUESS}$ occurs, then a failing plaintext is extractable from the ciphertext that triggered $\text{DIFF} \wedge \neg\text{GUESS}$ (this time due to access to eCO.E), and the plaintext is recognisable as failing by $\mathcal{B}$ due to its FFP-CCA oracle $o\text{DECRYPT}$. In formulae,

$$\Pr[\text{DIFF}] = \Pr[\text{DIFF} \wedge \neg\text{GUESS}] + \Pr[\text{DIFF} \wedge \text{GUESS}] \leq \text{Adv}_{\text{PKE}^G}^{\text{FFP-CCA}}[\mathcal{B}] + \Pr[\text{GUESS}].$$

---

[4] We remark that a t-wise independent function for sufficiently large $t = O(q_H + q_D)$ also suffices, which is more efficient as it doesn't require (nearly as much) quantum memory.

In summary, we can bound the difference in advantages between **Game G_2** and **Game G_3** as

$$\left|\text{Adv}^{\textbf{Game } G_2} - \text{Adv}^{\textbf{Game } G_3}\right| \leq \text{Adv}_{\text{PKE}^G}^{\text{FFP-CCA}}(\mathcal{B}) + \Pr[\text{GUESS}].$$

The following two steps are in a certain sense symmetric to the steps for **Games 0–2**: $\mathcal{A}$ playing **Game G_3** can almost be simulated without using the oDECAPS oracle, except that oDECAPS is still invoked before each call to the oracle oDECAPS$'$, without the result ever being used. This is an artifact from **Game G_2**. Omitting the oDECAPS invocations might introduce changes in $\mathcal{A}$'s view, as these invocations might influence the behavior of eCO.E in subsequent queries. We therefore define **Game G_4** like **Game G_3**, except that the oDECAPS invocations are postponed until after $\mathcal{A}$ finishes. By a similar argument as for the transition from **Game G_1** to **Game G_2**, we obtain

$$\left|\text{Adv}^{\textbf{Game } G_3} - \text{Adv}^{\textbf{Game } G_4}\right| \leq 8\sqrt{2}q_D^2 2^{-\gamma/2}.$$

Finally, **Game G_5** is like **Game G_4**, but the computations of oDECAPS(c_i) are omitted entirely. In game 4, all invocations of oDECAPS already happened after the execution of $\mathcal{A}$, hence this omission does not influence $\mathcal{A}$'s success probability.

Let $\tilde{\mathcal{A}}$ be an IND-CPA-KEM adversary against KEM$_m^\perp$ in the eQROM$_{\text{Enc}}$, simulating **Game G_5** to $\mathcal{A}$: $\tilde{\mathcal{A}}$ has access to a single extractable oracle whose oracle interface eCO.RO simulates the combination of G and H, i.e., eCO.RO simulates G $\times$ H. (We decided to combine G and H into one oracle to simplify the subsequent analysis of the IND-CPA advantage against KEM$_m^\perp$ that will be carried out in Sect. 4.3.) $\tilde{\mathcal{A}}$ runs $b' \leftarrow \mathcal{A}^{\text{G}',\text{H},\text{oDECAPS}'}$ and returns b'. The simulation of $\mathcal{A}$'s oracles using eCO.RO is straightforward (preparing the redundant register in uniform superposition, querying the combined oracle, and uncomputing the redundant register).

We now have

$$\text{Adv}^{\textbf{Game } G_4} = \text{Adv}^{\textbf{Game } G_5} = \text{Adv}_{\text{KEM}_m^\perp}^{\text{IND-CPA-KEM}}(\tilde{\mathcal{A}}). \tag{13}$$

Collecting the terms from the hybrid transitions, using Lemma 2 below, and bounding $q_D 2^{-\gamma} \leq q_D^2 2^{-\gamma/2}$ yields the desired bound. The statements about query numbers, width and depth, as well as the runtime, are straightforward. $\qquad\square$

Like in Sect. 2, we continue by bounding the probability of event GUESS, and Lemma 2 below is the eQROM$_{\text{Enc}}$ analogue of Lemma 1. Again, we will soon revisit FFP-CCA attacker $\mathcal{B}$ against PKE^G, and we will simulate $\mathcal{B}$'s oracle oDECRYPT via an oracle oDECRYPT$'$ (see Fig. 7) that differs from oDECRYPT if an event equivalent to GUESS occurs. Therefore, we again generalize the definition of event GUESS accordingly.

Lemma 2. *Let* PKE *and* $\mathcal{A}$ *be like in Lemma 1 (see page 422), except that* $\mathcal{A}$ *is now considered in the* eQROM$_{\text{Enc}}$. *Let* $\mathcal{A}$ *be run with* G$'$ *and* oDECAPS *or* oDECAPS$'$ *(*oDECRYPT *or* oDECRYPT$'$*), but for each query* c_i, *both* $\hat{m}_i =$

oDecrypt$'(c)$	G$'$, input registers X, Y
01 $m \leftarrow$ eCO.E(c)	03 Apply eCO.RO$_{XYD}$
02 **return** m	04 **return** registers XY

Fig. 7. Simulation oDecrypt$'$ of oracle oDecrypt for PKE^G. For the reader's convenience, we repeat the definition of G$'$.

oDecrypt$'(c_i)$ and $m_i =$ oDecrypt(c_i) are computed in that order, regardless of which of the two oracles oDecaps and oDecaps$'$ (oDecrypt and oDecrypt$'$) $\mathcal{A}$ has access to. Then GUESS, the event that $\hat{m}_i = \bot$ while $m_i \neq \bot$, is very unlikely. Concretely,

$$\Pr[\text{GUESS}] \leq 2q_D \cdot 2^{-\gamma}. \tag{14}$$

Proof. We begin by bounding the probability that for some fixed $i \in \{1, ..., q_D\}$ we have $\hat{m}_i = \bot$ but $m_i \neq \bot$. From the definitions of oDecaps and oDecaps$'$, as well as the definitions of the interfaces eCO.RO and eCO.E, we obtain

$$\sqrt{\Pr[\hat{m}_i = \bot \wedge m_i \neq \bot]} = \sqrt{\Pr[\hat{m}_i = \bot \wedge \text{Enc}(m_i, \text{eCO.RO}(m_i)) = c_i]}$$
$$= \left\| \Pi_Y^{c,x} O_{XYF} \Sigma_F^{c,\emptyset} |m_i\rangle_X |0\rangle_Y |\psi_i\rangle_{FE} \right\| \tag{15}$$

Here, $|\psi_i\rangle$ is the adversary-oracle state before $\mathcal{A}$ submits the query c_i and the projectors $\Pi_Y^{c,x}$ and $\Sigma^{c,\emptyset}$ are with respect to $f = \text{Enc}$ (see Eq. (8)). We begin by simplifying the expression on the right hand side. We have $O_{XYF}|m_i\rangle_X = F_{F_{m_i}} \text{CNOT}_{F_{m_i}:Y}^{\otimes n} F_{F_{m_i}} \otimes |m_i\rangle_X$ and $\Pi_Y \text{CNOT}_{F_{m_i}:Y}^{\otimes n} |0\rangle_Y = \text{CNOT}_{F_{m_i}:Y}^{\otimes n} \Pi_{F_{m_i}} |0\rangle_Y$ for any projector Π that is diagonal in the computational basis. We can thus simplify

$$\left\| \Pi_Y^{c,x} O_{XYF} \Sigma_F^{c,\emptyset} |m_i\rangle_X |0\rangle_Y |\psi_i\rangle_{FE} \right\| = \left\| \Pi_{F_{m_i}}^{c,x} F_{F_{m_i}} \Sigma_F^{c,\emptyset} |m_i\rangle_X |0\rangle_Y |\psi_i\rangle_{FE} \right\|$$
$$\leq \left\| F_{F_{m_i}} \Pi_{F_{m_i}}^{c,x} \Sigma_F^{c,\emptyset} |m_i\rangle_X |0\rangle_Y |\psi_i\rangle_{FE} \right\| + \left\| [\Pi^{c,x}, F] \right\|$$
$$\leq \left\| F_{F_{m_i}} \Pi_{F_{m_i}}^{c,x} \Sigma_F^{c,\emptyset} |m_i\rangle_X |0\rangle_Y |\psi_i\rangle_{FE} \right\| + \sqrt{2} \cdot 2^{-\gamma/2} \tag{16}$$

where we have applied the two observations and omitted any final unitary operators in the first equality, and the last inequality is due to Lemma 3.3 in [DFMS21]. But the remaining norm term vanishes as

$$\Pi_{F_{m_i}}^{c,x} \Sigma_F^{c,\emptyset} = (\Pi^{c,x} \bar{\Pi}^{c,x})_{F_{m_i}} \otimes (\bar{\Pi}^{c,x})_{F_{\mathcal{M} \setminus \{m_i\}}}^{\otimes |\mathcal{M}|-1} = 0. \tag{17}$$

Combining Eqs. (15) to (17) and squaring the resulting inequality yields

$$\Pr[\hat{m}_i = \bot \wedge m_i \neq \bot] \leq 2 \cdot 2^{-\gamma}. \tag{18}$$

Collecting the terms and applying a union bound over the q_D decapsulation queries yields the desired bound. $\square$

So far, we have shown that whenever an IND-CCA adversary $\mathcal{A}$'s behaviour is significantly changed by being run with simulation oDECAPS' instead of the real oracle oDECAPS, we can use $\mathcal{A}$ to find a failing plaintext, assuming access to the decryption oracle oDECRYPT provided in the FFP-CCA game. We continue by proving an eQROM$_{\mathsf{Enc}}$-analogue of Theorem 2, i.e., we show that oDECRYPT can be simulated via oracle oDECRYPT' (see Fig. 7) without the secret key, thereby being able to construct an FFP-CPA adversary from any FFP-CCA adversary (both in the eQROM$_{\mathsf{Enc}}$).

Theorem 4. *Let* PKE *and* $\mathcal{B}$ *be like in Theorem 2 (see page 422), except that* $\mathcal{B}$ *is now considered in the* eQROM$_{\mathsf{Enc}}$*, issuing at most* $q_{\mathsf{eCO.RO}}/q_{\mathsf{eCO.E}}$ *many queries to its respective oracle* eCO.RO/eCO.E*. Then there exist an* FFP-CPA *adversary* $\tilde{\mathcal{B}}$ *in the* eQROM$_{\mathsf{Enc}}$ *such that*

$$\mathrm{Adv}_{\mathsf{PKE}^{\mathsf{G}}}^{\mathsf{FFP\text{-}CCA}}(\mathcal{B}) \leq (q_{\mathsf{D}} + 1)\mathrm{Adv}_{\mathsf{PKE}^{\mathsf{G}}}^{\mathsf{FFP\text{-}CPA}}(\tilde{\mathcal{B}}) + 12q_{\mathsf{D}}(q_{\mathsf{G}} + 4q_{\mathsf{D}})2^{-\gamma/2} \qquad (19)$$

The adversary $\tilde{\mathcal{B}}$ *makes* $q_{\mathsf{eCO.RO}}$ *queries to* eCO.RO *and* $q_{\mathsf{eCO.E}} + q_{\mathsf{D}}$ *queries to* eCO.E*, and its runtime satisfies* $\mathrm{Time}(\tilde{\mathcal{B}}) = \mathrm{Time}(\mathcal{B}) + O(q_{\mathsf{D}})$*.*

Proof. On a high level, the proof works as follows. Analogous to Theorem 3, we simulate oDECRYPT by oDECRYPT'. As we wish to remove the usage of oDECRYPT entirely, however, we cannot use it to determine at which oDECRYPT' query a failure occurs. We thus resort to guessing that information. On a technical level this proof follows the proof of Theorem 3 with deviations similar as in the proof of Theorem 2. Let oDECRYPT' be the simulation defined in Fig. 7. Let **Game G_0** be the FFP-CCA-game, and let **Games $G_1 - G_5$** be defined based on **Game G_0** like in the proof of Theorem 3. Like in the proof of Theorem 3, we have

$$\mathrm{Adv}^{\mathbf{Game\ G_0}} \leq \mathrm{Adv}^{\mathbf{Game\ G_5}} + 12q_{\mathsf{D}}(q_{\mathsf{G}} + 2q_{\mathsf{D}})2^{-\gamma/2} + \Pr[\mathsf{DIFF}]$$

$$\leq \mathrm{Adv}^{\mathbf{Game\ G_5}} + 12q_{\mathsf{D}}(q_{\mathsf{G}} + 2q_{\mathsf{D}})2^{-\gamma/2} + \Pr[\mathsf{DIFF} \wedge \neg\mathsf{GUESS}] + \Pr[\mathsf{GUESS}]. \qquad (20)$$

Assume without loss of generality that $\mathcal{B}$ makes exactly q_{D} many queries to the oracle for $\mathsf{Dec}^{\mathsf{G}}$ (if it does not, we modify $\mathcal{B}$ by adding a number of useless decryption queries in the end). We define an FFP-CPA adversary $\tilde{\mathcal{B}}^{\mathsf{eCO}}$ defined exactly like the classical one in Fig. 4 (except that it has quantum access to its oracles), i.e., $\tilde{\mathcal{B}}$ samples $i \leftarrow \{1, ..., q_{\mathsf{D}} + 1\}$ and runs $\mathcal{B}^{\mathsf{G}', \mathrm{oDECRYPT}'}$ until the i-th query, or until the end if $i = q_{\mathsf{D}} + 1$. Finally, $\tilde{\mathcal{B}}$ outputs m_i, the output of $\mathcal{B}^{\mathsf{G}', \mathrm{oDECRYPT}'}$'s i-th decryption query, unless $i = q_{\mathsf{D}} + 1$, in which case $\tilde{\mathcal{B}}$ outputs the output of $\mathcal{B}^{\mathsf{G}', \mathrm{oDECRYPT}'}$. By construction,

$$\mathrm{Adv}_{\mathsf{PKE}^{\mathsf{G}}}^{\mathsf{FFP\text{-}CPA}}(\tilde{\mathcal{B}}) \geq \left(\mathrm{Adv}^{\mathbf{Game\ G_5}} + \Pr[\mathsf{DIFF} \wedge \neg\mathsf{GUESS}]\right)/(q_{\mathsf{D}} + 1) \qquad (21)$$

(note that all instances of $\mathrm{Adv}^{\mathbf{Game\ i}}$ are for $\mathcal{B}$ playing **Game i**.) Combining Eqs. (20) and (21) and Lemma 2 yields the desired bound. The statement about $\tilde{\mathcal{B}}$'s running time and number of queries is straightforward. □

Combining Theorems 3 and 4, we obtain the following

Corollary 2. *Let* PKE *and* $\mathcal{A}$ *be as in Theorem 3. Then there exist an* IND-CPA-KEM *adversary* $\tilde{\mathcal{A}}$ *and an* FFP-CPA *adversary* $\mathcal{B}$, *both in the* eQROM$_{\mathsf{Enc}}$, *such that*

$$\mathrm{Adv}^{\mathsf{IND\text{-}CCA\text{-}KEM}}_{\mathsf{KEM}^{\perp}_m}(\mathcal{A}) \leq \mathrm{Adv}^{\mathsf{IND\text{-}CPA\text{-}KEM}}_{\mathsf{KEM}^{\perp}_m}(\tilde{\mathcal{A}}) + (q_{\mathsf{D}} + 1)\mathrm{Adv}^{\mathsf{FFP\text{-}CPA}}_{\mathsf{PKE}^{\mathsf{G}}}(\mathcal{B})$$
$$+ 24q_{\mathsf{D}}(q_{\mathsf{G}} + 4q_{\mathsf{D}})2^{-\gamma/2} \tag{22}$$

Both $\tilde{\mathcal{A}}$ *and* $\mathcal{B}$ *make* $q_{\mathsf{G}} + q_{\mathsf{H}} + q_{\mathsf{D}}$ *queries to* eCO.RO, *with a combined depth (width) of* $d + q_{\mathsf{D}}$ *(w), and* q_{D} *queries to* eCO.E. *The running times of* $\tilde{\mathcal{A}}$ *and* $\mathcal{B}$ *satisfy* $\mathrm{Time}(\tilde{\mathcal{A}}) = \mathrm{Time}(\mathcal{A}) + O(q_{\mathsf{D}})$ *and* $\mathrm{Time}(\mathcal{B}) = \mathrm{Time}(\mathcal{A}) + O(q_{\mathsf{D}})$.

Again, the additive error terms are a factor of 2 larger due to our modular proof (in terms of Theorems 3 and 4), which can be avoided with a direct proof.

While the additive error term depending on γ improves by roughly a power 2 over the corresponding term in the security bound of [DFMS21], the only known concrete bound for FO$^{\perp}_m$, we remark that we do not expect it to be tight. It turns out, however, that many relevant schemes have abundantly randomized ciphertexts.

4.2   Semi-classical OWTH in the eQROM$_f$

To analyze IND-CPA-KEM security of KEM$^{\perp}_m$ in the eQROM$_{\mathsf{Enc}}$, we want to apply an eQROM$_{\mathsf{Enc}}$ argument to show that keys encapsulated by FO$^{\perp}_m$[PKE, G, H] are random-looking unless the adversary can be used to attack the underlying scheme PKE. We will need to argue that the challenge key $K^* := \mathsf{H}(m^*)$ and the encryption randomness $\mathsf{G}(m^*)$ used for challenge ciphertext c^* can be replaced with fresh random values, in the eQROM$_{\mathsf{Enc}}$. To that end, we develop eQROM$_f$ generalizations of the semi-classical OWTH theorems from [AHU19].

We will first describe how we model this 'replacing with fresh randomness' on a subset $\mathcal{S} \subset \mathcal{X}$ for superposition oracle, and how our approach generalizes previous approaches. Previous work (like [AHU19]) used two oracles O_0 and O_1 that only differ on some set $\mathcal{S}$, while algorithm $\mathcal{A}$'s input is always defined relative to oracle O_0. In the case where $\mathcal{A}$'s oracle is O_1, the input uses fresh randomness from the adversary's point of view. Here we meet the first eQROM$_{\mathsf{Enc}}$-related roadblock: Superposition oracles have the property that initially, each value eCO.RO(x) is in *quantum superposition*, which complicates equating two oracles everywhere but on $\mathcal{S}$. As it suffices for our purpose, we define the 'resampling' set $\mathcal{S}$ as follows: We assume $\mathcal{A}$'s input inp to be classical, generated by an algorithm GenInp with classical access to eCO^0. We can then define $\mathcal{S}$ as the set of all inputs x queried by GenInp, e.g., for input $(c^*, K^*) := (\mathsf{Enc}(pk, m^*; \mathsf{G}(m^*)), \mathsf{H}(m^*))$, $\mathcal{S}$ is $\{m^*\}$.) Apart from how we model $\mathcal{S}$, we proceed as in [AHU19]: Use eCO^0 to generate $\mathcal{A}$'s input and replace $\mathcal{A}$'s access to eCO^0 with access to an independent extractable compressed oracle eCO^1.

Clearly, if GenInp does not query eCO^0, the two oracles eCO^0 and eCO^1 are perfectly indistinguishable to $\mathcal{A}$. But what if $\mathcal{A}$'s input depends on eCO^0? [AHU19] related $\mathcal{A}$'s distinguishing advantage to the probability of "FIND", the event that an element of $\mathcal{S}$ is detected in $\mathcal{A}$'s queries to the QRO via a quantum measurement. This result, however, is in the (plain) QROM, and FIND is not the only distinction opportunity in the eQROM$_f$ as there are now two oracle interfaces, eCO.RO and eCO.E. As an example, let $\mathcal{A}$ have input $(x, t := f(x, eCO^0.RO(x)))$ for some oracle input value x. *Without any* eCO.RO *query*, $\mathcal{A}$ can tell the two cases apart by querying eCO.E on t: Querying eCO^0.E on t results in output x with overwhelming probability, while querying eCO^1.E on t yields output $\perp$. Extraction queries hence have to be taken into account.

Before stating this section's main theorems, we will describe our approach more formally. Borrowing the notation from [AHU19], we define *'punctured' versions* eCO$\backslash\mathcal{S}$ of eCO: During each eCO.RO query, we first apply a *'semi-classical'* oracle $O_{\mathcal{S}}^{\mathsf{SC}}$, and then oracle unitary O_{XYD}. Intuitively, $O_{\mathcal{S}}^{\mathsf{SC}}$ marks if an element of $\mathcal{S}$ was found in one of the query registers. Formally, $O_{\mathcal{S}}^{\mathsf{SC}}$ acts on the query input registers $X_1, \cdots X_w$ and a 'flag' register F that holds one qubit per oracle query, by first mapping $|x_1, \cdots x_w, b\rangle$ to $|x_1, \cdots x_w, b \oplus [\![x_1 \in \mathcal{S} \vee \cdots \vee x_w \in \mathcal{S}]\!]\rangle$, and then measuring register F in the computational basis.

Like in [AHU19], we denote the event that any measurement of F returns 1 by FIND. In that case, the query has collapsed to a superposition of states where at least one input register only contains elements of $\mathcal{S}$. If FIND does not occur, then all oracle queries collapsed to states not containing any elements of $\mathcal{S}$, and in consequence, set $\mathcal{S}$ defining $\mathcal{A}$'s input is effectively removed from the query input domain. In this case, the only way to distinguish between eCO^0 and eCO^1 is to perform an extraction query where eCO^0.E might return an element of $\mathcal{S}$. We will call this event EXT. If neither FIND nor EXT occur, the two scenarios are indistinguishable to $\mathcal{A}$.

The following helper lemma formalizes the above reasoning and extends it to some other probability distances: Eq. (23) formalizes that if $\mathcal{A}$ neither triggers FIND nor EXT, its behaviour in the two cases is the same: arbitrary events will be equally likely in both cases. Equations (24) and (25) have a similar interpretation. The proof of Lemma 3 is mostly reworking the probabilities by reasoning about the cases and eliminating the case where neither FIND nor EXT occurs. It is given in the full version.

Lemma 3. *Let* eCO^0 *and* eCO^1 *be two extractable superposition oracles from* $\mathcal{X}$ *to* $\mathcal{Y}$ *for some function* $f : \mathcal{X} \times \mathcal{Y} \to \mathcal{T}$, *and let* GenInp *be an algorithm with classical output* inp, *having access to* eCO^0. *Let* S *be the set of elements* $x \in \mathcal{X}$ *whose oracle values are needed to compute* inp, *and let* $\mathcal{T}_S := \{t \mid \exists x \in S$ *s.th.* $t = f(x, eCO^0(x))\}$. *Let* FIND *be the event that flag register* F *is ever measured to be in state 1 during a call to* $\mathcal{A}$'s *punctured oracle, and let* EXT *be the event that* $\mathcal{A}$ *performs an extraction query on any* $t \in \mathcal{T}_S$. *Let* E *be an arbitrary (classical) event. Then*

$$\Pr[\mathsf{E} \wedge \neg\mathsf{FIND} \wedge \neg\mathsf{EXT} : \mathcal{A}^{eCO^0\backslash\mathcal{S}}] = \Pr[\mathsf{E} \wedge \neg\mathsf{FIND} \wedge \neg\mathsf{EXT} : \mathcal{A}^{eCO^1\backslash\mathcal{S}}], \quad (23)$$

$$|\Pr[\mathsf{E} \wedge \neg\mathsf{FIND} : \mathcal{A}^{eCO^0\backslash\mathcal{S}}] - \Pr[\mathsf{E} \wedge \neg\mathsf{FIND} : \mathcal{A}^{eCO^1\backslash\mathcal{S}}]| \leq \Pr[\mathsf{EXT} : \mathcal{A}^{eCO^0\backslash\mathcal{S}}], \quad (24)$$

$$|\Pr[\mathsf{FIND} : \mathcal{A}^{eCO^0\backslash\mathcal{S}}] - \Pr[\mathsf{FIND} : \mathcal{A}^{eCO^1\backslash\mathcal{S}}]| \leq \Pr[\mathsf{EXT} : \mathcal{A}^{eCO^0\backslash\mathcal{S}}] \quad (25)$$

where all probabilities are taken over the coins of GenInp *and the internal randomness of* $\mathcal{A}$ *and we used* $\mathcal{A}^{\mathcal{O}_0}$ *as a shorthand for* $\mathcal{A}^{\mathcal{O}_0}(inp)$.

The following theorem relates the distinguishing advantage between eCO^0 and eCO^1 to the probability that FIND or EXT occur. Intuitively, the theorem states that no algorithm $\mathcal{A}$ will recognize the reprogramming unless $\mathcal{A}$ makes a random oracle or an extraction query related to its input. Theorem 5 is the eQROM_f counterpart of [AHU19, Th. 1, 'Semi-classical O2H']. Its proof is given in the full version. In the special case where EXT never happens, e.g., when extraction queries are triggered by an oracle simulation like $\mathrm{oDecaps}'$ that forbids critical inputs, we obtain the same bound as [AHU19, Th. 1], but in the eQROM_f.

Theorem 5 (eQROM_f-OWTH: Distinguishing to Finding). *Let* eCO^0, eCO^1, GenInp, $\mathcal{S}$, FIND *and* EXT *be like in Lemma 3. We define the* OWTH *distinguishing advantage function of* $\mathcal{A}$ *as*

$$\mathrm{Adv}^{\mathsf{OWTH}}_{\mathsf{eQRO}_f}(\mathcal{A}) := |\Pr[1 \leftarrow \mathcal{A}^{\mathsf{eCO}^0}(inp)] - \Pr[1 \leftarrow \mathcal{A}^{\mathsf{eCO}^1}(inp)]| ,$$

where the probabilities are over the coins of GenInp *and the randomness of* $\mathcal{A}$. *For any algorithm* $\mathcal{A}$ *of query depth* d *with respect to* $\mathsf{eCO.RO}$, *we have that*

$$\mathrm{Adv}^{\mathsf{OWTH}}_{\mathsf{eQRO}_f}(\mathcal{A}) \leq 4 \cdot \sqrt{d \cdot \Pr[\mathsf{FIND} : \mathcal{A}^{\mathsf{eCO}^1 \backslash \mathcal{S}}]}$$
$$+ 2 \cdot (\sqrt{d} + 1) \cdot \sqrt{\Pr[\mathsf{EXT} : \mathcal{A}^{\mathsf{eCO}^0}]} + \Pr[\mathsf{EXT} : \mathcal{A}^{\mathsf{eCO}^1}]. \quad (26)$$

If additionally $\Pr[\mathsf{EXT} : \mathcal{A}^{\mathsf{eCO}^0 \backslash \mathcal{S}}] = \Pr[\mathsf{EXT} : \mathcal{A}^{\mathsf{eCO}^1 \backslash \mathcal{S}}] = 0$, *we obtain*

$$\mathrm{Adv}^{\mathsf{OWTH}}_{\mathsf{eQRO}_f}(\mathcal{A}) \leq 4 \cdot \sqrt{d \cdot \Pr[\mathsf{FIND} : \mathcal{A}^{\mathsf{eCO}^1 \backslash \mathcal{S}}]}. \quad (27)$$

In many cases, a desired reduction will not know the 'resampled' set $\mathcal{S}$. Theorem 6 relates the probability of FIND to the advantage of a preimage extractor ExtractSet that extracts an element of $\mathcal{S}$ without knowing $\mathcal{S}$: ExtractSet will run $\mathcal{A}$ with the unpunctured oracle eCO and measure one of its queries to generate its output. In one of our proofs, we additionally need to puncture on a set different from $\mathcal{S}$. We therefore prove Theorem 6 for *arbitrary* sets $\mathcal{S}''$.

Theorem 6 (eQROM_f-OWTH: Finding to Extracting). *Let* $\mathcal{A}$ *be an algorithm with access to an extractable superposition oracle* eCO *from* $\mathcal{X}$ *to* $\mathcal{Y}$ *for some function* $f : \mathcal{X} \times \mathcal{Y} \rightarrow \mathcal{T}$, *with query depth* d *with respect to* $\mathsf{eCO.RO}$, *and let* GenInp *be like in Lemma 3. Let* FIND *be the event that flag register* F *is ever measured to be in state 1 during a call to* $\mathcal{A}$'s *punctured oracle, where the puncturing happens on a set* $\mathcal{S}''$.

Let ExtractSet *be the algorithm that on input inp chooses* $i \leftarrow_\$ \{1, \cdots d\}$, *runs* $\mathcal{A}^{\mathsf{eCO}}(inp)$ *until the* i-th *query to* $\mathsf{eCO.RO}$; *then measures all query input registers in the computational basis and outputs the set* $\mathcal{S}'$ *of measurement outcomes. Then*

$$\Pr[\mathsf{FIND} : \mathcal{A}^{\mathsf{eCO} \backslash \mathcal{S}''}] \leq 4d \cdot \Pr[\mathcal{S}'' \cap \mathcal{S}' \neq \emptyset : \mathcal{S}' \leftarrow \mathsf{ExtractSet}] . \quad (28)$$

The proof (given in the full version directly follows from [AHU19, Th. 2, 'Search in semi-classical oracle'] since [AHU19, Th. 2] gives the bound of Theorem 6 for algorithms $\mathcal{B}$ accessing a semi-classical oracle $O_{\mathcal{S}''}^{SC}$ itself (rather than some oracle punctured on $\mathcal{S}''$). An algorithm $\mathcal{B}^{O_{\mathcal{S}''}^{SC}}$ hence can perfectly simulate eCO\$\mathcal{S}''$ to $\mathcal{A}$ by simulating eCO and having the puncturing done by its own oracle $O_{\mathcal{S}''}^{SC}$.

If the input inp of $\mathcal{A}$ is independent of $\mathcal{S}''$, we also get an extraction bound, an eQROM$_f$ counterpart of [AHU19, Cor. 1], which is proven in the same way.

Corollary 3 (eQROM$_f$-OWTH: **Extracting independent values**). *If $\mathcal{S}$ and inp are independent, then for any algorithm $\mathcal{A}^{eCO}$ issuing q many queries to eCO.RO in total,*

$$\Pr[\text{FIND} : \mathcal{A}^{eCO\backslash\mathcal{S}''}] \leq 4q \cdot p_{max} ,$$

where $p_{max} := \max_{x \in X} \Pr_{\mathcal{S}''}[x \in S]$. As a special case, we obtain that

$$\Pr[\text{FIND} : \mathcal{A}^{eCO\backslash\{x\}}] \leq 4q|X|^{-1} , \tag{29}$$

for $\mathcal{S}'' = \{x\}$ with uniformly chosen $x \in X$, assuming that x was not needed to generate the input to $\mathcal{A}$.

4.3   From IND-CPA$_{PKE}$ or OW-CPA$_{PKE}$ to IND-CPA$_{FO[PKE]}$

We will now use the OWTH results from Sect. 4.2 to show that the IND-CPA security of $FO_m^\perp[PKE, G, H]$ can be based on the passive security of PKE. In Theorem 7, we base IND-CPA security of $FO_m^\perp[PKE, G, H]$ on the IND-CPA security of PKE, and we base it on OW-CPA security of PKE in Theorem 8. The obtained bounds are the same as their known plain QROM counterparts.

Theorem 7. *Let $\mathcal{A}$ be an IND-CPA adversary against KEM$_m^\perp$ in the eQROM$_{Enc}$, issuing q many queries to eCO.RO in total, with a query depth of d, and q_E many queries to eCO.E, where none of them is with its challenge ciphertext. Then there exists an IND-CPA adversary $\mathcal{B}_{IND\text{-}CPA}$ against PKE such that*

$$\text{Adv}_{KEM_m^\perp}^{IND\text{-}CPA\text{-}KEM}(\mathcal{A}) \leq 4 \cdot \sqrt{d \cdot \text{Adv}_{PKE}^{IND\text{-}CPA}(\mathcal{B}_{IND\text{-}CPA})} + 8q|\mathcal{M}|^{-1/2},$$

with $\text{Time}(\mathcal{B}_{IND\text{-}CPA}) = \text{Time}(\mathcal{A}) + \text{Time}(eCO, q, q_E)$ and $\text{QMem}(\mathcal{B}_{IND\text{-}CPA}) = \text{QMem}(\mathcal{A}) + \text{QMem}(eCO, q, q_E)$.

Note that forbidding extraction queries to eCO.E on c^* is no limitation in our context: eCO.E queries are only triggered by an IND-CCA adversary querying its simulated oracle oDECAPS', and oDECAPS' rejects queries on c^*.

A full proof is given in the full version. To summarise the proof, we first define a Game G_1 like the IND-CPA-KEM game, except that encryption randomness $r^* := G(m^*)$ and honest KEM key $K_0 := H(m^*)$ are replaced with fresh uniform randomness. In Game G_1, the forwarded KEM key is a uniformly random key either way, the advantage of $\mathcal{A}$ in Game G_1 hence is 0. It remains to bound the distinguishing advantage between the IND-CPA-KEM game and Game G_1.

We apply Theorem 5 which bounds this distinguishing advantage in terms of the probability of event FIND_{m^*}, the event that m^* is detected in the adversary's random oracle queries. To further bound $\Pr[\mathsf{FIND}_{m^*}]$, we use IND-CPA security of PKE to replace $\mathcal{A}$'s ciphertext input c^* with an encryption of an independent message. As m^* now is independent of $\mathcal{A}$'s input, FIND_{m^*} is highly unlikely for large enough message spaces. (This uses Corollary 3 .)

Theorem 8. *For any* IND-CPA *adversary* $\mathcal{A}$ *like in Theorem 7, with a query width of* w*, there furthermore exists an* OW-CPA *adversary* $\mathcal{B}_{\mathsf{OW\text{-}CPA}}$ *such that*

$$\mathsf{Adv}^{\mathsf{IND\text{-}CPA}}_{\mathsf{KEM}^{\perp}_m}(\mathcal{A}) \leq 8d \cdot \sqrt{w \cdot \mathsf{Adv}^{\mathsf{OW}}_{\mathsf{PKE}}(\mathcal{B}_{\mathsf{OW\text{-}CPA}})},$$

with $\mathrm{Time}(\mathcal{B}_{\mathsf{OW\text{-}CPA}}) = \mathrm{Time}(\mathcal{A}) + \mathrm{Time}(\mathsf{eCO}, q, q_E)$ *and* $\mathrm{QMem}(\mathcal{B}_{\mathsf{OW\text{-}CPA}}) = \mathrm{Time}(\mathcal{A}) + \mathrm{QMem}(\mathsf{eCO}, q, q_E)$.

Again, a full proof is given in the full version. The proof does exactly the same steps as the one of Theorem 7, up to the point where we bound $\Pr[\mathsf{FIND}_{m^*}]$. To bound $\Pr[\mathsf{FIND}_{m^*}]$, we use Theorem 6 to relate $\Pr[\mathsf{FIND}_{m^*}]$ to the OW-CPA advantage of an algorithm that extracts m^* from $\mathcal{A}$'s oracle queries.

5   Characterizing FFP-CPA$_{\mathsf{PKE}^{\mathsf{G}}}$

While it may very well be that the maximal success probability in game FFP-CPA for $\mathsf{PKE}^{\mathsf{G}}$ can already be bounded for particular instantiations of $\mathsf{PKE}^{\mathsf{G}}$ without too much technical overhead, even in the eQROM$_{\mathsf{Enc}}$, this section offers an alternative way to bound this probability: In Theorem 9, we relate the success probability in game FFP-CPA for $\mathsf{PKE}^{\mathsf{G}}$ to two failure-related success probabilities that are easier to analyze. This reduction separates the *computationally hard* problem of exploiting knowledge of the public key to find failing ciphertexts for PKE, from the *statistically hard* problem of searching the QRO G for failing plaintexts m for $\mathsf{PKE}^{\mathsf{G}}$ *without knowledge of the key.*

We begin by defining these two new notions related to decryption failures: In Fig. 8 we define a new variant of the FFP game that differs from game FFP-CPA by providing $\mathcal{A}$ not even with the public key. Since the adversary obtains <u>N</u>o <u>K</u>ey whatsoever, the game is called FFP-NK, and we define the advantage of an FFP-NK adversary $\mathcal{A}$ against PKE as

$$\mathsf{Adv}^{\mathsf{FFP\text{-}NK}}_{\mathsf{PKE}}(\mathcal{A}) := \Pr[\mathsf{FFP\text{-}NK}^{\mathcal{A}}_{\mathsf{PKE}} \Rightarrow 1].$$

Furthermore, we define a <u>F</u>ind <u>n</u>on-<u>g</u>enerically <u>F</u>ailing <u>P</u>laintext (FFP-NG) game, also in Fig. 8. In this game, the adversary gets a public key pk_0 as input and is allowed to issue a single message-randomness pair to a <u>F</u>ailure <u>C</u>hecking <u>O</u>racle FCO that is defined either relative to (sk_0, pk_0), the key pair whose public key constitutes $\mathcal{A}$'s input, or relative to a key pair (sk_1, pk_1) which is an independent key pair. We define the advantage of an FFP-NG adversary $\mathcal{A}$ against PKE as

$$\mathsf{Adv}^{\mathsf{FFP\text{-}NG}}_{\mathsf{PKE}}(\mathcal{A}) := \left| \Pr[\mathsf{FFP\text{-}NG}^{\mathcal{A}}_{\mathsf{PKE},0} \Rightarrow 1] - \Pr[\mathsf{FFP\text{-}NG}^{\mathcal{A}}_{\mathsf{PKE},1} \Rightarrow 1] \right|.$$

Game FFP-NK	**Game FFP-NG$_b$**	$\text{FCO}_b(m; r)$ //one query
01 $m \leftarrow \mathcal{A}$	05 $(sk_0, pk_0) \leftarrow \text{KG}$	09 $c \leftarrow \text{Enc}(pk_b, m; r)$
02 $(pk, sk) \leftarrow \text{KG}$	06 $(sk_1, pk_1) \leftarrow \text{KG}$	10 $m' := \text{Dec}(sk_b, c)$
03 $c := \text{Enc}(pk, m)$	07 $b' \leftarrow \mathcal{A}^{\text{FCO}_b}(pk_0)$	11 **return** $[\![m \neq m']\!]$
04 **return** $[\![\text{Dec}(sk, c) \neq m]\!]$	08 **return** $[\![b = b']\!]$	

Fig. 8. Key-independent game FFP-NK for deterministic schemes PKE, and the find non-generically failing ciphertexts games FFP-NG (with $b \in \{0, 1\}$). $\mathcal{A}$ can make at most one query to FCO_b.

While the game is formalized as an oracle distinguishing game, $\mathcal{A}$ can only win the game with an advantage over random guessing if it queries oracle FCO on a message-randomness pair that fails with a different probability with respect to key pair (sk_0, pk_0) than with respect to key pair (sk_1, pk_1), a key pair about which $\mathcal{B}$ can only gather information by its query to FCO. We expect this game to be a more palatable target for both provable security and cryptanalysis compared to FFP-CPA$_{\text{PKE}^\text{G}}$ or correctness-related games from the existing literature.

Theorem 9. *Let* PKE *be a public-key encryption scheme. For any* FFP-CPA *adversary* $\mathcal{A}$ *in the* eQROM$_{\text{Enc}}$ *against* PKE$^\text{G}$ *making* q_R *and* q_E *queries to* eCO.RO *and* eCO.E, *respectively, there exist an* FFP-NK *adversary* $\mathcal{C}$ *in the* eQROM$_{\text{Enc}}$ *against* PKE$^\text{G}$ *and an* FFP-NG *adversary* $\mathcal{B}$ *against* PKE *with*

$$\text{Adv}^{\text{FFP-CPA}}_{\text{PKE}^\text{G}}(\mathcal{A}) \leq \text{Adv}^{\text{FFP-NG}}_{\text{PKE}}(\mathcal{B}) + \text{Adv}^{\text{FFP-NK}}_{\text{PKE}^\text{G}}(\mathcal{C}).$$

The running time of $\mathcal{C}$ *is about that of* $\mathcal{A}$, *that of* $\mathcal{B}$ *is* $\text{Time}(\mathcal{B}) = \text{Time}(A) + \text{Time}(\text{eCO}, q_{RO}, q_E)$ *and* $\text{QMem}(\mathcal{B}) = \text{QMem}(A) + \text{QMem}(\text{eCO}, q_{RO}, q_E)$.

The proof consists of the following two steps: Apply the FFP-NG definition to argue that the FFP-CPA game's key pair can be replaced with an independent one whose public key is not given to $\mathcal{A}$. After this change, winning means solving FFP-NK for PKE$^\text{G}$. The full proof is given in the full version.

5.1 Characterizing FFP-NK$_{\text{PKE}^\text{G}}$

In the last section, we have related the success probability of an adversary in game FFP-CPA for PKE$^\text{G}$ to the success property of an adversary in game FFP-NK for PKE$^\text{G}$, in the eQROM$_{\text{Enc}}$. Intuitively, an adversary in game FFP-NK will succeed if it can find oracle inputs m such that m and $r := \text{eCO.RO}(m)$ satisfy the predicate that (m, r) fails with respect to pk. To prove the upper bound we provide in Theorem 10, we therefore generically bound the success probability for a certain search problem in Sect. 5.2. While we note that the search bound might be of independent interest, it in particular allows us to characterize the maximal advantage in game FFP-NK in terms of two statistical values for the underlying randomised scheme PKE. We begin with the definitions of δ_{ik} and $\sigma_{\delta_{\text{ik}}}$: Below, we define the worst-case decryption error rate δ_{ik} *under independent keys*, and the maximal variance of the decryption error rate $\sigma_{\delta_{\text{ik}}}$.

Definition 2 (worst-case independent-key decryption error rate, maximal decryption error variance). *We define the* worst-case decryption error rate under independent keys δ_{ik} *and the* maximal decryption error variance under independent keys $\sigma_{\delta_{ik}}$ *of a public-key encryption scheme* PKE *as*

$$\delta_{ik} := \max_{m \in \mathcal{M}} \left[\Pr_{(sk,pk),r} [(m,r)\ fails] \right] = \max_{m \in \mathcal{M}} \mathbb{E}_r \left[\Pr_{(sk,pk)} [(m,r)\ fails] \right] , \ and$$

$$\sigma_{\delta_{ik}}^2 := \max_{m \in \mathcal{M}} \mathbb{V}_r \left[\Pr_{(sk,pk)} [(m,r)\ fails] \right] \ both\ for\ uniformly\ random\ r.$$

We want to stress that δ_{ik} *differs from the worst-case term* δ_{wc} that was introduced in [HHK17] (there denoted by δ) since δ_{wc} is defined by

$$\delta_{wc} := \mathbb{E}_{KG} \max_{m \in \mathcal{M}} \Pr_{r \leftarrow_\$ \mathcal{R}} [(m,r)\ fails].$$

Intuitively, δ_{wc} is the best possible advantage of an adversary, trying to find the message most likely to fail for a given key pair, while for δ_{ik}, the key pair will be randomly sampled *after* the adversary had made its choice m. On a formal level, it is easy to verify that δ_{wc} serves as an upper bound for δ_{ik}.

Theorem 10. *Let* PKE *be a public-key encryption scheme with worst-case independent-key decryption error rate* δ_{ik} *and decryption error rate variance* $\sigma_{\delta_{ik}}$. *For any* FFP-NK *adversary* $\mathcal{A}$ *in the* eQROM$_{\mathsf{Enc}}$ *against* PKE^{G}, *setting* $C = 304$, *we have that*

$$\mathrm{Adv}_{\mathsf{PKE}^{\mathsf{G}}}^{\mathsf{FFP\text{-}NK}}(\mathcal{A}) \leq \delta_{ik} + 3\sqrt{C}q\sigma_{\delta_{ik}} + 2Cq^2\sigma_{\delta_{ik}}^2 \delta_{ik}(-\log \sqrt{C}q\sigma_{\delta_{ik}}),$$

The proof is given in the full version.

In the full version, we also give an alternative bound that grows with the logarithm of the number of RO queries, assuming a *Gaussian tail bound* for the decryption error distribution.

5.2 Finding Large Values of a Function in the eQROM$_f$

In this section, we provide the technical results for the eQROM$_f$ that we need to prove Theorem 10. Throughout this section, f is a fixed function such that eQROM$_f$ is well-defined. We begin by providing a bound for the success probability of an algorithm in the eQROM$_f$ that searches for a value x that, together with its oracle value eCO.RO(x), satisfies a relation R. In the lemma below, we will use the quantity Γ_R that was defined in Eq. (10) (see page 426).

Lemma 4. *Let* $R \subset \mathcal{X} \times \mathcal{Y}$ *be a relation and* $\mathcal{A}^{\mathsf{eCO}}$ *an algorithm with access to* eQRO$_f$ *from* $\mathcal{X}$ *to* $\mathcal{Y}$ *for some function* $f : \mathcal{X} \times \mathcal{Y} \to \mathcal{T}$, *making* q *queries to* eCO.RO. *Then*

$$\Pr_{x \leftarrow \mathcal{A}^{\mathsf{eCO}}}[R(x, \mathsf{eCO.RO}(x))] \leq 152(q+1)^2 \Gamma_R |\mathcal{Y}|^{-1}, \tag{30}$$

independently of the number of queries $\mathcal{A}$ *makes to* eCO.E. *Here it is understood that* eCO.RO *is queried once in the very end to determine* eCO.RO(x).

Proof. The only difference between [DFMS21, Proposition 3.5] and Lemma 4 is that $\mathcal{A}$ now additionally has access to eCO.E. The proof is thus the same as for [DFMS21, Proposition 3.5], with the additional observation that queries to eCO.E commute with the progress measure operator $\mathcal{M}$ for any relation R. This is because i) both $\mathcal{M}$ and the operator applied upon an eCO.E query are controlled unitaries controlling on the database register of the compressed oracle database of the eQRO$_f$, and ii) the target registers of $\mathcal{M}$ and eCO.E are disjoint.   □

According to Lemma 4, it is hard to search a random oracle, even given extraction access. We will now use Lemma 4 to show that it is also hard to produce an input to the oracle so that the resulting input-output pair has a large value under a function F, in expectation . To state a theorem making this intuition precise and quantitative, let $F : X \times Y \to I \subset [0,1]$, and let I be ordered as $I = \{t_1, ..., t_R\}$ with $t_i > t_{i-1}$. The hardness of the task of finding large values is related to a "tail bound" $G(t)$ for the probability of $F(x,r)$ being larger than t .

Theorem 11. *Let F and I be as above. Let further $G : [0,1] \to [0,1]$ be non-increasing such that $G(t) \geq \Pr_{r \leftarrow Y}[F(x,r) \geq t]$ for all x. Let $C := 304$, $\Delta G(i) := G(t_i) - G(t_{i+1})$ (setting formally $G(t_{R+1}) = 0$), and let $\kappa_q := \min\{i | Cq^2 G(t_i) \leq 1\}$. Then for any algorithm $\mathcal{A}^{eCO}$ making at most $q \geq 1$ queries to eCO.RO,*

$$\mathbb{E}_{x \leftarrow \mathcal{A}^{eCO}}[F(x, eCO.RO(x))] \leq t_{\kappa_q} + Cq^2 \sum_{i=\kappa_q+1}^{R} t_i \Delta G(i) . \tag{31}$$

eCO.RO is queried once in the end to determine eCO.RO(x).

Proof. Let $x \leftarrow \mathcal{A}^{eCO}$. We bound

$$\mathbb{E}\left[F(x, eCO.RO(x))\right] = \sum_{i=1}^{R} t_i \Pr[F(x, eCO.RO(x)) = t_i]$$

$$= \sum_{i=1}^{R} t_i \left(\Pr[F(x, eCO.RO(x)) \geq t_i] - \Pr[F(x, eCO.RO(x)) \geq t_{i+1}]\right)$$

$$= t_1 + \sum_{i=2}^{R} \Pr[F(x, eCO.RO(x)) \geq t_i](t_i - t_{i-1})$$

$$\leq t_1 + \sum_{i=2}^{R} \min(1, Cq^2 G(t_i))(t_i - t_{i-1}) = t_{\kappa_q} + Cq^2 \sum_{i=\kappa_q+1}^{R} G(t_i)(t_i - t_{i-1}),$$

where we have used Lemma 4 with the relation $R_{f,\geq t_i}$ defined by $R_{f,\geq t_i}(x,y) :\Leftrightarrow f(x,y) \geq t_i$ in the second-to-last line. We further bound

$$\sum_{i=\kappa_q+1}^{R} G(t_i)(t_i - t_{i-1}) = -G(t_{\kappa_q+1})t_{\kappa_q} + \sum_{i=\kappa_q+1}^{R} t_i \Delta G(i) \leq \sum_{i=\kappa_q+1}^{R} t_i \Delta G(i).$$

□

We provide a corollary for the case where G is given by Chebyshev's inequality.

Corollary 4. *Let F, I, and C be as in Theorem 11, and let the expectation values and variances of $F(x,r)$ for random $r \leftarrow \mathcal{Y}$ be bounded as $\mathbb{E}_r[F(x,r)] \leq \mu$ and $\mathbb{V}_r[F(x,r)] \leq \sigma^2$, respectively. Then, for an algorithm $\mathcal{A}^{\mathrm{eCO}}$ making at most $q \geq 1$ quantum queries to eCO.RO,*

$$\mathbb{E}_{x \leftarrow \mathcal{A}^{\mathrm{eCO}}}[F(x, \mathrm{eCO.RO}(x))] \leq \mu + 3\sqrt{C}q\sigma + 2Cq^2\sigma^2\mu(-\log(\sqrt{C}q\sigma)). \tag{32}$$

Proof. By Chebyshev's inequality, we can set $G(t) = \sigma^2(t-\mu)^{-2}$. We thus obtain $t_{\kappa_q} \leq \sqrt{C}q\sigma + \mu$. We bound

$$\sum_{i=\kappa_q+1}^{R} t_i \Delta G(i) = -\sum_{i=\kappa_q+1}^{R} t_i \int_{t_i}^{t_{i+1}} G'(t)\mathrm{d}t \leq -\int_{t_{\kappa_q}}^{1} tG'(t)\mathrm{d}t \tag{33}$$

$$= 2\sigma^2 \int_{t_{\kappa_q}}^{1} \frac{t}{t-\mu}\mathrm{d}t = 2\sigma^2 \int_{t_{\kappa_q}-\mu}^{1-\mu} \frac{u+\mu}{u}\mathrm{d}u = 2\sigma^2\left(1 - t_{\kappa_q} + \mu\log\frac{1-\mu}{t_{\kappa_q}-\mu}\right). \tag{34}$$

We arrive at the bound

$$\mathbb{E}_{x \leftarrow \mathcal{A}^{\mathrm{eCO}}}[F(x, \mathrm{eCO.RO}(x))] \leq \mu + \sqrt{C}q\sigma + 2Cq^2\sigma^2(1 + \mu(\log(1-\mu) - \log(\sqrt{C}q\sigma))).$$

If $\sqrt{C}q\sigma \geq 1$, the claimed bound trivially holds, else $\sqrt{C}q\sigma \geq Cq^2\sigma^2$ and thus

$$\mathbb{E}_{x \leftarrow \mathcal{A}^{\mathrm{eCO}}}[F(x, \mathrm{eCO.RO}(x))] \leq \mu + 3\sqrt{C}q\sigma + 2Cq^2\sigma^2\mu\log(\log(1-\mu) - \log(\sqrt{C}q\sigma)).$$

$\square$

6 Tying Everything Together

Combining the reductions from Sect. 4.1 and 4.3, we obtain a first corollary that still relies on FFP-CPA of PKE^G. Corollary 6 states our main result.

Corollary 5. *Let PKE and IND-CCA-KEM $\mathcal{A}$ against $\mathrm{KEM}_m^\perp$ be like in Theorem 3 (on page 427). Then there exist an IND-CPA adversary $\mathcal{B}_{\mathrm{IND}}$, a OW-CPA adversary $\mathcal{B}_{\mathrm{OW}}$ and an FFP-CPA adversary $\mathcal{C}$ against PKE^G in the $\mathrm{eQROM}_{\mathrm{Enc}}$ such that*

$$\mathrm{Adv}_{\mathrm{KEM}_m^\perp}^{\mathrm{IND\text{-}CCA\text{-}KEM}}(\mathcal{A}) \leq \widetilde{\mathrm{Adv}}_{\mathrm{PKE}} + (q_\mathsf{D}+1)\mathrm{Adv}_{\mathrm{PKE}}^{\mathrm{FFP\text{-}CPA}}(\mathcal{C}) + \varepsilon_\gamma, \quad with \tag{35}$$

$$\widetilde{\mathrm{Adv}}_{\mathrm{PKE}} = \begin{cases} 4 \cdot \sqrt{(d+q_\mathsf{D}) \cdot \mathrm{Adv}_{\mathrm{PKE}}^{\mathrm{IND\text{-}CPA}}(\mathcal{B}_{\mathrm{IND}})} + \frac{8(q+q_\mathsf{D})}{\sqrt{|\mathcal{M}|}} & or \\ 8(d+q_\mathsf{D}) \cdot \sqrt{w \cdot \mathrm{Adv}_{\mathrm{PKE}}^{\mathrm{OW}}(\mathcal{B}_{\mathrm{OW}})}. \end{cases} \tag{36}$$

The additive error term is given by $\varepsilon_\gamma = 24q_\mathsf{D}(q_\mathsf{G}+4q_\mathsf{D})2^{-\gamma/2}$, $\mathcal{C}$ makes $q_\mathsf{G}+q_\mathsf{H}+q_\mathsf{D}$ queries to eCO.RO and q_D to eCO.E. $\mathcal{B}_{\mathrm{IND}}$'s, $\mathcal{B}_{\mathrm{OW}}$'s and $\mathcal{C}$'s running time are bounded as $\mathrm{Time}(\mathcal{B}_{\mathrm{IND/OW}}) = \mathrm{Time}(\mathcal{A}) + \mathrm{Time}(\mathrm{eCO}, q_\mathsf{G} + q_\mathsf{H} + q_\mathsf{D}) + O(q_\mathsf{D})$ and $\mathrm{Time}(\mathcal{C}) = \mathrm{Time}(\mathcal{A}) + O(q_\mathsf{D})$.

Corollary 6. *Let* PKE *and* $\mathcal{A}$ *be like in Theorem 3, and let* PKE *furthermore have worst-case random-key decryption error rate* δ_{ik}, *decryption error rate variance* $\sigma_{\delta_{ik}}$ *and decryption error tail envelope* τ. *Set* $C = 304$ *and assume* $\sqrt{C}q_G\sigma_{\delta_{ik}} \leq 1/2$. *Then there exists an* FFP-NG *adversary* $\mathcal{C}$ *against* PKE *such that*

$$\text{Adv}^{\text{IND-CCA-KEM}}_{\text{KEM}^\perp_m}(\mathcal{A}) \leq \widetilde{\text{Adv}}_{\text{PKE}} + (q_D + 1)(\text{Adv}^{\text{FFP-NG}}_{\text{PKE}}(\mathcal{C}) + \varepsilon_{\delta_{ik}}) + \varepsilon_\gamma \qquad (37)$$

with $\widetilde{\text{Adv}}_{\text{PKE}}$ *and* ε_γ *like in Corollary 5. The additive error term* $\varepsilon_{\delta_{ik}}$ *is given by* $\varepsilon_{\delta_{ik}} \leq \delta_{ik} + (3 + 2\delta_{ik})\sqrt{C}q_G\sigma_{\delta_{ik}}$. $\mathcal{C}$'s *running time is bounded by* $\text{Time}(\mathcal{A}) + \text{Time}(\text{eCO}, q_G + q_H + q_D) + O(q_D)$.

In the full version, we give an alternative corollary with an $\varepsilon_{\delta_{ik}}$ that only grows logarithmically with the number of RO queries, assuming a *Gaussian-shaped tail bound* for the decryption error probability distribution.

Proof. Corollary 6 follows by combining Corollary 5 with Theorems 9 and 10 from Sect. 5. We simplified error term $\varepsilon_{\delta_{ik}}$ from Theorem 10 by using the inequality $x^2/\log(x) \leq x$ for $x \leq 1/2$ for $x = \sqrt{C}q_G\sigma_{\delta_{ik}}$, exploiting the mild condition $\sqrt{C}q_G\sigma_{\delta_{ik}} \leq 1/2^5$. □

The above result has two main advantages over previous ones: i) The additive loss can be much smaller than the additive loss of roughly $q_G^2\delta_{wc}$ present in all previous bounds. ii) It holds for the explicit rejection variant of the transformation, with bounds that are competitive with previous ones that were limited to implicitly rejecting variants.

References

[AHU19] Ambainis, A., Hamburg, M., Unruh, D.: Quantum security proofs using semi-classical oracles. In: Boldyreva, A., Micciancio, D. (eds.) CRYPTO 2019. LNCS, vol. 11693, pp. 269–295. Springer, Cham (2019). https://doi.org/10.1007/978-3-030-26951-7_10

[BDK+18] Bos, J., et al.: CRYSTALS - Kyber: a CCA-secure module-lattice-based KEM. In: IEEE EuroS&P 2018, pp. 353–367 (2018)

[BHH+19] Bindel, N., Hamburg, M., Hövelmanns, K., Hülsing, A., Persichetti, E.: Tighter proofs of CCA security in the quantum random oracle model. In: Hofheinz, D., Rosen, A. (eds.) TCC 2019. LNCS, vol. 11892, pp. 61–90. Springer, Cham (2019). https://doi.org/10.1007/978-3-030-36033-7_3

[BS20]   Bindel, N., Schanck, J.M.: Decryption failure is more likely after success. In: Ding, J., Tillich, J.-P. (eds.) PQCrypto 2020. LNCS, vol. 12100, pp. 206–225. Springer, Cham (2020). https://doi.org/10.1007/978-3-030-44223-1_12

[Den03] Dent, A.W.: A designer's guide to KEMs. In: Paterson, K.G. (ed.) Cryptography and Coding 2003. LNCS, vol. 2898, pp. 133–151. Springer, Heidelberg (2003). https://doi.org/10.1007/978-3-540-40974-8_12

---

[5] Without it the bound involving $\sigma_{\delta_{ik}}$ from Theorem 10 is almost trivial.

[DFMS21] Don, J., Fehr, S., Majenz, C., Schaffner, C.: Online-extractability in the quantum random-oracle model. Cryptology ePrint Archive, Report 2021/280 (2021)

[DRV20] D'Anvers, J.-P., Rossi, M., Virdia, F.: *(One) failure is not an option*: bootstrapping the search for failures in lattice-based encryption schemes. In: Canteaut, A., Ishai, Y. (eds.) EUROCRYPT 2020. LNCS, vol. 12107, pp. 3–33. Springer, Cham (2020). https://doi.org/10.1007/978-3-030-45727-3_1

[DVV18] D'Anvers, J.-P., Vercauteren, F., Verbauwhede, I.: On the impact of decryption failures on the security of LWE/LWR based schemes. Cryptology ePrint Archive, Report 2018/1089 (2018)

[FO99] Fujisaki, E., Okamoto, T.: Secure integration of asymmetric and symmetric encryption schemes. In: Wiener, M. (ed.) CRYPTO 1999. LNCS, vol. 1666, pp. 537–554. Springer, Heidelberg (1999). https://doi.org/10.1007/3-540-48405-1_34

[FO13] Fujisaki, E., Okamoto, T.: Secure integration of asymmetric and symmetric encryption schemes. J. Cryptol. **26**(1), 80–101 (2013)

[HHK17] Hofheinz, D., Hövelmanns, K., Kiltz, E.: A modular analysis of the Fujisaki-Okamoto transformation. In: Kalai, Y., Reyzin, L. (eds.) TCC 2017. LNCS, vol. 10677, pp. 341–371. Springer, Cham (2017). https://doi.org/10.1007/978-3-319-70500-2_12

[HKSU20] Hövelmanns, K., Kiltz, E., Schäge, S., Unruh, D.: Generic authenticated key exchange in the quantum random oracle model. In: Kiayias, A., Kohlweiss, M., Wallden, P., Zikas, V. (eds.) PKC 2020. LNCS, vol. 12111, pp. 389–422. Springer, Cham (2020). https://doi.org/10.1007/978-3-030-45388-6_14

[JZC+18] Jiang, H., Zhang, Z., Chen, L., Wang, H., Ma, Z.: IND-CCA-secure key encapsulation mechanism in the quantum random oracle model, revisited. In: Shacham, H., Boldyreva, A. (eds.) CRYPTO 2018. LNCS, vol. 10993, pp. 96–125. Springer, Cham (2018). https://doi.org/10.1007/978-3-319-96878-0_4

[KSS+20] Kuchta, V., Sakzad, A., Stehlé, D., Steinfeld, R., Sun, S.-F.: Measure-rewind-measure: tighter quantum random oracle model proofs for one-way to hiding and CCA security. In: Canteaut, A., Ishai, Y. (eds.) EUROCRYPT 2020. LNCS, vol. 12107, pp. 703–728. Springer, Cham (2020). https://doi.org/10.1007/978-3-030-45727-3_24

[NIS17] NIST: National institute for standards and technology. Post-quantum crypto project (2017). http://csrc.nist.gov/groups/ST/post-quantum-crypto/

[SXY18] Saito, T., Xagawa, K., Yamakawa, T.: Tightly-secure key-encapsulation mechanism in the quantum random oracle model. In: Nielsen, J.B., Rijmen, V. (eds.) EUROCRYPT 2018. LNCS, vol. 10822, pp. 520–551. Springer, Cham (2018). https://doi.org/10.1007/978-3-319-78372-7_17

[Zha19] Zhandry, M.: How to record quantum queries, and applications to quantum indifferentiability. In: Boldyreva, A., Micciancio, D. (eds.) CRYPTO 2019. LNCS, vol. 11693, pp. 239–268. Springer, Cham (2019). https://doi.org/10.1007/978-3-030-26951-7_9

Cryptanalysis

Optimising Linear Key Recovery Attacks with Affine Walsh Transform Pruning

Antonio Flórez-Gutiérrez$^{(\boxtimes)}$ [iD]

Inria, Paris, France
antonio.florez_gutierrez@inria.fr

Abstract. Linear cryptanalysis [25] is one of the main families of key-recovery attacks on block ciphers. Several publications [16,19] have drawn attention towards the possibility of reducing their time complexity using the fast Walsh transform. These previous contributions ignore the structure of the key recovery rounds, which are treated as arbitrary boolean functions. In this paper, we optimise the time and memory complexities of these algorithms by exploiting zeroes in the Walsh spectra of these functions using a novel affine pruning technique for the Walsh Transform. These new optimisation strategies are then showcased with two application examples: an improved attack on the DES [1] and the first known attack on 29-round PRESENT-128 [9].

Keywords: Linear cryptanalysis · Key recovery attacks · FFT · Walsh transform · Pruning · DES · PRESENT

1 Introduction

General Background

Linear Cryptanalysis. Matsui's linear cryptanalysis [25] is a widely studied family of statistical cryptanalysis against block ciphers and other symmetric constructions, and any new proposals are expected to justify their resilience against it. Linear attacks are commonly turned into key recovery attacks, in which a linear distinguisher is extended by one or more rounds by incorporating a key guess. If the attack requires a data complexity of N and l bits of the key are guessed, the time complexity of a standard linear key recovery attack is $\mathcal{O}(N) + \mathcal{O}(2^{2l})$ [26].

Fast Key Recovery Algorithms. In the paper by Collard et al. [16], a new key recovery algorithm based on the fast Walsh transform[1] was presented which can sometimes reduce the time complexity of attacks on key-alternating ciphers to $\mathcal{O}(N) + \mathcal{O}(l2^l)$. However, this technique has several limitations, as it complicates common optimisations of previous attacks, most notably key schedule-induced relations. The technique was generalised to multiple rounds by Flórez-Gutiérrez et al. [19], however, many limitations to the algorithm remained.

---

[1] Called fast Fourier transform/FFT in the paper.

Supplementary Information The online version contains supplementary material available at https://doi.org/10.1007/978-3-031-22972-5_16.

© International Association for Cryptologic Research 2022
S. Agrawal and D. Lin (Eds.): ASIACRYPT 2022, LNCS 13794, pp. 447–476, 2022.
https://doi.org/10.1007/978-3-031-22972-5_16

Our Contribution

New Pruned Walsh Transform Algorithm. We describe a new pruning technique for the fast Walsh transform which is effective when the nonzero inputs and the desired outputs lie in (unions of) affine subspaces of $\mathbb{F}_2^n$. The algorithm reduces the computation of the desired outputs to a Walsh transform of smaller size than that of the full transform, thus achieving a large reduction in time complexity.

Reduced Attack Complexity. We next show how this pruned algorithm can be used to optimise linear key recovery attacks. Previous techniques based on the Walsh transform treated the key recovery map as a black box, which meant that the size of the input to this map often became the bottleneck of the algorithm. In our new approach, we see that in some common cases the cipher construction leads to the presence of a lot of zeros in the Walsh spectrum which can be used to improve the key recovery. This, together with information about the key schedule, can greatly reduce the time complexity. We also show how additional zeros can be created by rejecting a small fraction of the data.

Applications

Cryptanalysis of the DES. The first application is a variant of Matsui's attack on the DES [26] in which the last round of the linear approximation has been removed, and is treated as a key recovery round. We improve the data complexity by a factor of $2^{0.5}$ with respect to the best previous result of Biham and Perle [4], but the memory complexity grows due to the larger key guess.

Cryptanalysis of Reduced-Round PRESENT. We add a key recovery round to the 28-round attack on PRESENT by Flórez-Gutiérrez et al. [19] with the new pruning techniques, giving the first known attack on 29-round PRESENT-128.

Paper Structure. Section 2 covers some techniques and notations which are used in the rest of the paper, as well as the specifications of the applications' target ciphers. Section 3 describes the affine pruning algorithm for the fast Walsh transform from a theoretical perspective. Section 4 provides tools which help the cryptanalyst identify zeroes in the Walsh spectra of the maps which appear in key recovery attacks. Chapter 5 combines the results of the previous two sections by optimising linear key recovery attacks to make use of the cipher structure. Sections 6 and 7 describe the applications to the DES and PRESENT.

2   Preliminaries

2.1   Linear Key Recovery Attacks

Linear Approximation. Let $E : \mathbb{F}_2^n \times \mathbb{F}_2^\kappa \longrightarrow \mathbb{F}_2^n$ be a block cipher. A linear approximation of E is an expression of the form $\langle \alpha, x \rangle + \langle \beta, y \rangle$, where $\langle \cdot, \cdot \rangle$

denotes the dot product in $\mathbb{F}_2^n$. The correlation of the approximation is

$$\text{cor}(\alpha, \beta) = \frac{1}{2^{n+\kappa}} \sum_{K \in \mathbb{F}_2^\kappa} \sum_{x \in \mathbb{F}_2^n} (-1)^{\langle \alpha, x \rangle + \langle \beta, E_K(x) \rangle}. \tag{1}$$

Linear attacks make use of biased linear approximations, that is, of approximations whose correlation is different from zero.

Key Recovery Attack. We consider a cipher of the form $E' = F \circ E$, and a biased linear approximation $\langle \alpha, x \rangle + \langle \beta, y \rangle$ of E. In a key recovery attack, we guess a part k of K so that the value of the linear approximation can be computed for each pair $(x, y = E'_K(x))$ in a collection $\mathcal{D}$ of N known plaintext-ciphertext pairs. We compute an experimental estimation[2] of the correlation for each guess:

$$\widehat{\text{cor}}(k) = \frac{1}{N} \sum_{(x,y) \in \mathcal{D}} (-1)^{\langle \alpha, x \rangle + \langle \beta, F_k^{-1}(y) \rangle}. \tag{2}$$

If the value of k corresponding to the correct key K appears within the largest $2^{|k|-a}$ in the list[3], we say that the attack achieves an advantage of a [28]. As a rule of thumb, the attack requires $\mathcal{O}\left(\text{cor}(\alpha, \beta)^{-2}\right)$ data pairs to succeed. In this paper we use the more precise model of Blondeau and Nyberg [8].

Multiple Linear Approximations. It is common for linear attacks to make use of more than one linear approximation [6,21]. In the PRESENT attack we use the χ^2 multiple linear cryptanalysis statistic:

$$Q(k) = \sum_{i=1}^{M} \widehat{\text{cor}}_i(k)^2, \tag{3}$$

where $\widehat{\text{cor}}_i(k)$ denotes the experimental correlation for the i-th approximation. In a multiple linear attack, the data complexity is determined by the capacity $C = \sum_{i=1}^{M} \text{cor}(\alpha_i, \beta_i)^2$. Detailed models were given by Blondeau and Nyberg [8].

2.2 The Walsh Transform

Definition 1. *Let $f : \mathbb{F}_2^n \longrightarrow \mathbb{C}$ be a complex-valued function on $\mathbb{F}_2^n$. We refer to the space of functions of this kind as $\mathbb{CF}_2^n$, which is isomorphic to $\mathbb{C}^{2^n}$. The Hadamard or Walsh transform of f is another map $\widehat{f} : \mathbb{F}_2^n \longrightarrow \mathbb{C}$ given by[4]*

$$\widehat{f}(u) = \sum_{x \in \mathbb{F}_2^n} (-1)^{\langle u, x \rangle} f(x). \tag{4}$$

---

[2] The notation $\widehat{\text{cor}}$ should not be confused with the Walsh transform $\widehat{f}$.

[3] $|x|$ will denote the number of bits of a binary vector x.

[4] It is common to use the *normalised* Hadamard transform, which is divided by $\sqrt{2^n}$, but for the purposes of this paper we will not use this factor in the definition.

The transform of any vector in $\mathbb{CF}_2^n$ can be computed efficiently using:

$$
\begin{aligned}
\widehat{f}(u) = {} & \sum_{x_{n-2}\in\mathbb{F}_2} \cdots \sum_{x_0\in\mathbb{F}_2} (-1)^{u_{n-2}x_{n-2}+\cdots+u_0x_0} f(0, x_{l-2}, \ldots, x_0) \\
& + (-1)^{u_{n-1}} \sum_{x_{n-2}\in\mathbb{F}_2} \cdots \sum_{x_0\in\mathbb{F}_2} (-1)^{u_{n-2}x_{n-2}+\cdots+u_0x_0} f(1, x_{l-2}, \ldots, x_0).
\end{aligned}
\tag{5}
$$

This formula, in a divide-and-conquer approach, leads to the fast Walsh transform algorithm [18], which has a time complexity of $n2^n$ additions/subtractions. An associated transformation can be defined for (vectorial) boolean functions:

Definition 2. *Let $g : \mathbb{F}_2^n \longrightarrow \mathbb{F}_2^m$ be any vectorial boolean function. We define its Walsh transform as the map $\widehat{g} : \mathbb{F}_2^n \times \mathbb{F}_2^m \longrightarrow \mathbb{C}$ given by the formula*

$$
\widehat{g}(u, v) = \sum_{x\in\mathbb{F}_2^n} (-1)^{\langle u,x\rangle\oplus\langle v,g(x)\rangle}.
\tag{6}
$$

The coefficients of this map $\widehat{g}$ are often called the Walsh spectrum of g. It is a complex matrix whose columns are the Walsh transforms of $\mathrm{ind}_{g,v} : x \mapsto (-1)^{\langle v,g(x)\rangle}$, complex representations of its linear components $x \mapsto \langle v, g(x)\rangle$. When m=1 we can ignore the second input and assume $v = (1)$ to define $\widehat{g}(u)$. We will also use the Walsh spectrum restricted to a subset X:

Definition 3. *Let $g : \mathbb{F}_2^n \longrightarrow \mathbb{F}_2^m$ be a vectorial boolean function, and $X \subseteq \mathbb{F}_2^n$ a subset of its domain. The Walsh transform of g restricted to X is defined as*

$$
\widehat{g_{x\in X}}(u, v) = \sum_{x\in X} (-1)^{\langle u,x\rangle\oplus\langle v,g(x)\rangle}.
\tag{7}
$$

We define the transform restricted to $Y \subseteq \mathbb{F}_2^m$ as $\widehat{g_{g(x)\in Y}} = \widehat{g_{x\in g^{-1}(Y)}}$.

2.3   Walsh Transform-Accelerated Linear Cryptanalysis

FFT-accelerated linear cryptanalysis was introduced by Collard et al. [16]. Flórez-Gutiérrez et al. [19] provided a two-matrix description for instances in which the linear approximation can be separated into two independent parts, such as when key recovery is considered on both the plaintext and the ciphertext sides. We now show a small generalisation of this approach using d-dimensional arrays.

We consider a linear approximation whose value can be expressed as

$$
f_0(x) \oplus \underbrace{f_1(x_1 \oplus k_1^O, k_1^I) \oplus \cdots \oplus f_d(x_d \oplus k_d^O, k_d^I)}_{F(X\oplus K^O, K^I)},
\tag{8}
$$

where $(x_1, \ldots, x_d) = X$ are separate parts of the plaintext-ciphertext pair x (we denote this by $x \mapsto X$). $(k_1^O, \ldots, k_d^O) = K^O$ is *outer* key material which is xored directly to x, and $(k_1^I, \ldots, k_d^I) = K^I$ is additional *inner* key material. Our aim is to compute all values of the experimental correlations $\widehat{\mathrm{cor}}(K^O, K^I)$:

$$N \cdot \widehat{\mathrm{cor}}(K^O, K^I) = \sum_{x \in \mathcal{D}} (-1)^{f_0(x) \oplus f_1(x_1 \oplus k_1^O, k_1^I) \oplus \ldots \oplus f_d(x_d \oplus k_d^O, k_d^I)}$$

$$= \sum_X (-1)^{F(X \oplus K^O, K^I)} \underbrace{\sum_{\substack{x \in \mathcal{D} \\ x \mapsto X}} (-1)^{f_0(x)}}_{A[X]}$$

$$(9)$$

$$= \frac{1}{2^{|X|}} \sum_Y (-1)^{\langle K^O, Y \rangle} \left[\sum_Z (-1)^{\langle Y, Z \rangle} (-1)^{F(Z, K^I)} \right] \sum_X (-1)^{\langle Y, X \rangle} A[X]$$

$$= \frac{1}{2^{|X|}} \sum_Y (-1)^{\langle K^O, Y \rangle} \left(\prod_{i=0}^d \widehat{f}_i(y_i, k_i^I) \right) \widehat{A}[Y],$$

using the convolution theorem. The attack can be performed as follows:

1. For each f_i, precompute $2^{|k_i^I|}$ tables of size $2^{|k_i^O|}$ containing $\widehat{f}_i(\cdot, k_i^I)$.
2. *Distillation phase:* Construct the $2^{|x_1|} \times \cdots \times 2^{|x_d|}$-dimensional array A.
3. *Analysis phase:*
   (a) Apply the FWT on the array A to obtain $\widehat{A}$. We can consider A is a one-dimensional array of $2^{|X|}$ elements.
   (b) For each value of K^I:
      i. Multiply each entry $\widehat{A}[Y]$ of $\widehat{A}$ by $\prod_{i=0}^d \widehat{f}_i(y_i, k_i^I)$.
      ii. Apply another FWT to obtain an array containing $\widehat{\mathrm{cor}}[\cdot, K^I]$.
4. *Search phase:* Exhaustive search over the rest of the key for the guesses with the largest values of $2^{|X|} N \widehat{\mathrm{cor}}[K^O, K^I]$.

The memory complexity of this algorithm mainly consists $2^{|X|}$ memory registers to store $\widehat{A}$. The time complexity of the distillation phase is $\mathcal{O}(N)$, as each plaintext-ciphertext pair is checked once and discarded. The time complexity of the analysis phase is dominated by the loop on K^I, and consists of $d2^{|K^I|+|K^O|}$ multiplications and $|K^O| 2^{|K^I|+|K^O|}$ additions/subtractions. The time complexity of the search phase is given by models such as [8].

Other improvements to this algorithm were proposed by Flórez-Gutiérrez et al. [19], most notably in the case of multiple linear cryptanalysis. By separating the key guesses into groups, it is possible to perform a "complete" key guess k_T (accounting for any dependencies which are induced by the key schedule) while still using the FFT algorithm on different parts of the key guess for each individual approximation. The authors also introduced some Walsh transform pruning techniques for cases in which some external keybits can be deduced from the internal keybits. This paper builds on that improvement.

2.4   DES Specification

The Data Encryption Standard [1] is one of the most widely analysed block ciphers due to its use in the industry. It has a block length of 64 bits and a key

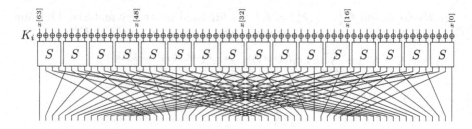

Fig. 1. A round of PRESENT.

size of 56 bits, and is a 16-round Feistel network. Each state (L, R) consists of two (left and right) 32-bit parts. The cipher operates as follows:

$(L_0, R_0) \leftarrow IP(P);$
for $i \leftarrow 1$ **to** 16 **do**
$\quad L_i \leftarrow R_{i-1};$
$\quad R_i \leftarrow L_{i-1} \oplus f(R_{i-1}, K_i);$
end
$C \leftarrow IP^{-1}(R_{16}, L_{16});$

where IP is a fixed initial permutation and each K_i is a 48-bit round subkey.

The Round Function f. First, an expansion function E is applied on the 32-bit input to obtain a 48-bit string. This string is xored with the round subkey, and eight different 6-to-4-bit Sboxes $S_1, \ldots, S_8$ are applied to obtain a 32-bit string. Finally, an output permutation P is applied.

The Key Schedule. It extracts sixteen 48-bit subkeys $K_1, \ldots, K_{16}$ from the key:

$(C_0, D_0) \leftarrow PC_1(P);$
for $i \leftarrow 1$ **to** 16 **do**
$\quad C_i \leftarrow LS_{p(i)}(C_{i-1});$
$\quad D_i \leftarrow LS_{p(i)}(D_{i-1});$
$\quad K_i \leftarrow PC_2(C_i, D_i);$
end

where C_i and D_i are 28 bits long, PC_1 and PC_2 are two permutated choices, LS_j is a j bit rotation to the left, and $p(i)$ is either 1 or 2.

Notation. In this paper, $X[j]$ will denote the j-th rightmost (least significant) bit of X, starting from 0. We will also ignore IP, IP^{-1} and PC_1 and denote $P = (L_0, R_0)$, $C = (R_{16}, L_{16})$, $K = (C_0, D_0)$ instead.

2.5 PRESENT Specification

PRESENT [9] is a lightweight block cipher which has received substantial attention from cryptanalysts since its introduction, and is a popular target for linear cryptanalysis. PRESENT has a block size of 64 and can operate with keys of either 80 or 128 bits. It is a substitution permutation network with 31 rounds (Fig. 1):

$X \leftarrow P$;
for $i \leftarrow 1$ **to** 31 **do**
$\quad X \leftarrow$ addRoundKey(X, K_i);
$\quad X \leftarrow$ sBoxLayer(X);
$\quad X \leftarrow$ pLayer(X);
end
$C \leftarrow$ addRoundKey(X, K_{32});

Sbox Layer. The nonlinear operation consists of the parallel application of 16 identical 4-bit Sboxes on all the nibbles of the state.

Permutation Layer. The linear transformation is a bit permutation, which sends the bit in position i to the position $P(i) = 16i \bmod 63, i \neq 63, P(63) = 63$. For its inverse we do the same with $P^{-1}(j) = 4j \bmod 63, j \neq 63, P^{-1}(63) = 63$.

Key Schedule. A 64-bit round subkey K_i is xored to the state in each round. These are obtained from the master key K. For 128 bits:

for $i \leftarrow 1$ **to** 31 **do**
$\quad K_i \leftarrow K[127, \ldots, 64]$;
$\quad K \leftarrow LS_{61}(K)$;
$\quad K[127, 126, 125, 124] \leftarrow S(K[127, 126, 125, 124])$;
$\quad K[123, 122, 121, 120] \leftarrow S(K[123, 122, 121, 120])$;
$\quad K[66, \ldots, 62] \leftarrow K[66, \ldots, 62] \oplus RC_i$;
end
$K_{32} \leftarrow K[127, \ldots, 64]$;

Notation. We denote the i-th rightmost bit of X starting from 0 by $X[i]$.

3   Affine Pruned Walsh Transform Algorithm

In order to remove unnecessary computations from the algorithm of Sect. 2.3, we must efficiently compute the Walsh transform when the non-zero inputs or desired outputs are limited to previously-known fixed subsets of $\mathbb{F}_2^n$. An algorithm which obtains the desired outputs with less computations than the "full" fast transform will be called a *pruned* fast Walsh transform algorithm. The case of fixed values for some output position bits was already considered by Flórez-Gutiérrez et al. in [19]. Our algorithms generalise this result.

Definition 4 (Problem statement). *Let* $f : \mathbb{F}_2^n \longrightarrow \mathbb{C}$ *be any vector in* $\mathbb{CF}_2^n$. *We assume that lists* $L, M \subseteq \mathbb{F}_2^n$ *are given, and that* $f(x) = 0$ *for all* $x \in \mathbb{F}_2^n \setminus L$. *The aim is to compute* $\widehat{f}(y)$ *for all* $y \in M$ *with as few operations as possible.*

3.1 Overview of Previous Results for the One-Dimensional DFT

The pruning problem has already been studied for the one-dimensional discrete Fourier transform (DFT), as it arises naturally in some applications. Markel [24] prunes the decimation-in-frequency algorithm for the case in which L consists of the first 2^r, $r < s$ points of the input. Similarly, Skinner [30] prunes the decimation-in-time algorithm for the case in which L consists of the first 2^r points in bit-reversed order. An algorithm limiting both inputs and outputs at the same time was introduced by Sreenivas and Rao [32]. A pruned decimation-in-time algorithm which can compute the outputs in a consecutive (but possibly shifted) frequency window was presented by Nagai [27]. Sorensen and Burrus [31] proposed an alternative *transform decomposition* technique, which maps the nonzero inputs to a series of smaller DFTs, and then combines the results. All these algorithms exhibit similar complexities: evaluating 2^r points of a 2^n point transform costs $\mathcal{O}(r2^n)$. However, an interesting phenomenon was observed by Shousheng and Torkelson [20]: when the subset of outputs M is a *comb* of equidistant points, a smaller complexity of $\mathcal{O}(2^n + r2^r)$ can be achieved.

Alves et al. [2] introduced the first *traceback* pruning method for arbitrary input or output sets. Hu and Wan [22] showed a similar technique and found the average complexity as a function of $n, |L|$ and $|M|$. The overhead computations were reduced by Singh and Srinivasan [29]. Pruning has been recently generalised to mixed-radix and composite length DFTs in works such as [14,33].

We consider the pruning problem for the Walsh transform or $(2, \ldots, 2)$-dimensional DFT, specifically the case when L and M lie in affine subspaces of $\mathbb{F}_2^n$. Our algorithm takes a different approach to the works mentioned above: we reduce the Walsh transform to one of significantly smaller dimension.

3.2 Walsh Transform Pruning for Affine Sets

We now describe a pruned algorithm which can be used when both the input and output sets of the Walsh transform lie in affine subspaces of $\mathbb{F}_2^n$.

Definition 5 (Affine pruning problem). *Let $f : \mathbb{F}_2^n \longrightarrow \mathbb{C}$ be a vector. We are given lists $L, M \subseteq \mathbb{F}_2^n$, vector subspaces $X, U \subseteq \mathbb{F}_2^n$ and vectors $x_0, u_0 \in \mathbb{F}_2^n$ so that $L \subseteq x_0 + X, M \subseteq u_0 + U$, and $f(x) = 0$ for all $x \notin L$. The aim is to compute $\widehat{f}(y)$ for all $y \in M$ with as few operations as possible.*

Example. Consider the Walsh transform of size $16 = 2^4$. The fast transform requires $4 \cdot 2^4 = 64$ additions. Let the lists $L = x_0 + X$ and $M = u_0 + U$ be

$$x_0 = (0,0,1,0), \quad X = \mathrm{span}\,\{(0,0,0,1),(0,1,1,0),(1,0,1,0)\},$$
$$u_0 = (0,1,0,0), \quad U = \mathrm{span}\,\{(0,0,0,1),(0,0,1,0),(1,1,0,0)\}.$$

A traceback-based pruning approach as done in [2,20,22,24,27,30,32] is shown in Fig. 2. By removing unnecesary computations from the fast Walsh transform, we obtain the desired outputs with 32 additions and subtractions.

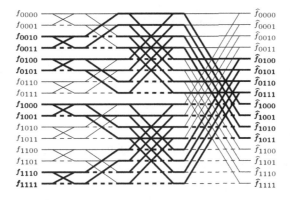

Fig. 2. Using traceback techniques, we can reduce the cost of this Walsh Transform of length 16 from 64 to 32 operations.

Let us examine the expressions for each of the outputs:

$$\widehat{f}_{0100} = + f_{0010} + f_{0011} - f_{0100} - f_{0101} + f_{1000} + f_{1001} - f_{1110} - f_{1111}$$
$$\widehat{f}_{0101} = + f_{0010} - f_{0011} - f_{0100} + f_{0101} + f_{1000} - f_{1001} - f_{1110} + f_{1111}$$
$$\widehat{f}_{0110} = - f_{0010} - f_{0011} - f_{0100} - f_{0101} + f_{1000} + f_{1001} + f_{1110} + f_{1111}$$
$$\widehat{f}_{0111} = - f_{0010} + f_{0011} - f_{0100} + f_{0101} + f_{1000} - f_{1001} + f_{1110} - f_{1111}$$
$$\widehat{f}_{1000} = + f_{0010} + f_{0011} + f_{0100} + f_{0101} - f_{1000} - f_{1001} - f_{1110} - f_{1111}$$
$$\widehat{f}_{1001} = + f_{0010} - f_{0011} + f_{0100} - f_{0101} - f_{1000} + f_{1001} - f_{1110} + f_{1111}$$
$$\widehat{f}_{1010} = - f_{0010} - f_{0011} + f_{0100} + f_{0101} - f_{1000} - f_{1001} + f_{1110} + f_{1111}$$
$$\widehat{f}_{1011} = - f_{0010} + f_{0011} + f_{0100} - f_{0101} - f_{1000} + f_{1001} + f_{1110} - f_{1111}$$

We observe the following properties:

$$\widehat{f}_{0100} = -\widehat{f}_{1010}, \ \widehat{f}_{0101} = -\widehat{f}_{1011}, \ \widehat{f}_{0110} = -\widehat{f}_{1000}, \ \widehat{f}_{0111} = -\widehat{f}_{1001}$$

The difference in the indices in each of these pairs is $(1,1,1,0)$, which is orthogonal to X. There are also pairs of inputs which always appear with opposite signs: (f_{0010}, f_{1110}), (f_{0011}, f_{1111}), (f_{0100}, f_{1000}), and (f_{0101}, f_{1001}). In this case, the difference between the indices is $(1,1,0,0)$, which is orthogonal to U.

This suggests an algorithm which subtracts the input pairs from each other at the beginning and duplicates the output pairs at the end, such as the one in Fig. 3. With the appropriate intermediate values, the size 2^4 transform is reduced to a size 2^2 transform. The total cost is 24 additions and subtractions.

We now proceed to formalise the "trick", starting with the following lemma:

Lemma 6. *Let $X, U \subseteq \mathbb{F}_2^n$ be vector subspaces of $\mathbb{F}_2^n$. We can define t as*

$$t := \dim\left(\frac{X}{X \cap U^\perp}\right) = \dim\left(\frac{U}{U \cap X^\perp}\right). \tag{10}$$

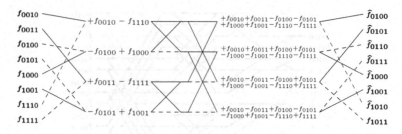

Fig. 3. Organising the inputs and outputs carefully allows us to reduce the cost of the transform to just 24 operations.

There exist isomorphisms $\phi : X/(X \cap U^\perp) \xrightarrow{\cong} \mathbb{F}_2^t$ and $\psi : U/(U \cap X^\perp) \xrightarrow{\cong} \mathbb{F}_2^t$ which preserve the inner product:

$$\langle y, v \rangle = \langle \phi(y), \psi(v) \rangle \text{ for all } y \in \frac{X}{X \cap U^\perp}, v \in \frac{U}{U \cap X^\perp}. \tag{11}$$

Proof. The equality of the dimensions is a consequence of the dimension formula and the properties of orthogonal spaces. It is also easy to show that the inner product $\langle y, v \rangle$ is well-defined for any $y \in X/(X \cap U^\perp)$ and $v \in U/(U \cap X^\perp)$.

We will construct a pair of "orthonormal" bases starting from two arbitrary bases $\{y_1, \dots, y_t\}$ and $\{v_1, \dots, v_t\}$. We will first ensure $\langle y_1, v_j \rangle = \delta_{1j}$ for all j and $\langle y_i, v_1 \rangle = \delta_{i1}$ for all i, and then work recursively. There is at least one j so that $\langle y_1, v_j \rangle = 1$ (if $y_1 \perp v_j$ for all j, we'd have $y_1 \perp U$, $y_1 = 0$). We swap the v_j so that $\langle y_1, v_1 \rangle = 1$. We then modify both bases as follows:

$$y_1^{new} = y_1 \qquad y_i^{new} = y_i + \langle y_i, v_1 \rangle y_1 \text{ for all } i \neq 1$$
$$v_1^{new} = v_1 \qquad v_j^{new} = v_j + \langle y_1, v_j \rangle v_1 \text{ for all } j \neq 1$$

These new bases have the following properties:

$$\langle y_1^{new}, v_1^{new} \rangle = \langle y_1, v_1 \rangle \qquad\qquad\qquad = 1$$
$$\langle y_1^{new}, v_j^{new} \rangle = \langle y_1, v_j \rangle + \langle y_1, v_j \rangle \langle y_1, v_1 \rangle = 0 \text{ for all } j \neq 1$$
$$\langle y_i^{new}, v_1^{new} \rangle = \langle y_i, v_1 \rangle + \langle y_i, v_1 \rangle \langle y_1, v_1 \rangle = 0 \text{ for all } i \neq 1$$

This process can be iterated on the rest of the elements until we obtain a pair of bases $\{y_1, \dots, y_t\}$ and $\{v_1, \dots, v_t\}$ which verify $\langle y_i, v_j \rangle = \delta_{ij}$. We obtain ϕ and ψ by mapping these bases to the standard basis of $\mathbb{F}_2^t$. $\quad\square$

This lemma provides the basis for the following result and Algorithm 1:

Proposition 7. *Let $\widehat{f}$ be the Walsh transform of $f \in \mathbb{CF}_2^n$. We are given lists $L \subseteq x_0 + X \subseteq \mathbb{F}_2^n$ and $M \subseteq u_0 + U \subseteq \mathbb{F}_2^n$, where $x_0 + X$ and $u_0 + U$ are affine subspaces, and assume $f(x) = 0$ for all $x \notin L$. Let $t = \dim\left(X/(X \cap U^\perp)\right) = \dim\left(U/(U \cap X^\perp)\right)$. There is an algorithm which computes $\widehat{f}(u)$ for all $u \in M$ with $|L| + t2^t + |M|$ additions using 2^t memory registers.*

Algorithm 1: Fast Walsh transform pruned to affine subspaces

Parameters: $L \subseteq x_0 + X \subseteq \mathbb{F}_2^n, M \subseteq u_0 + U \subseteq \mathbb{F}_2^n, (X, U$ subspaces).
Input: $f : L \longrightarrow \mathbb{C}$
Output: $\widehat{f} : M \longrightarrow \mathbb{C}$
$\mathcal{B}_X = \{y_1, \ldots, y_t\} \leftarrow \text{GetBasis}(X/(X \cap U^\perp))$;
$\mathcal{B}_U = \{v_1, \ldots, v_t\} \leftarrow \text{GetBasis}(U/(U \cap X^\perp))$;
for $k \leftarrow 1$ **to** $t - 1$ **do**   // Generate "good" bases
$\quad$ **while** $\langle y_k, v_k \rangle = 0$ **do** $(v_k, v_{k+1}, \ldots, v_{t-1}, v_t) \leftarrow (v_{k+1}, v_{k+2}, \ldots, v_t, v_k)$;
$\quad$ **for** $i \leftarrow k + 1$ **to** t **do** $y_i \leftarrow y_i + \langle y_i, v_k \rangle y_k$;
$\quad$ **for** $j \leftarrow k + 1$ **to** t **do** $v_j \leftarrow v_j + \langle y_k, v_j \rangle v_k$;
end
let $g : \mathbb{F}_2^t \longrightarrow \mathbb{C}, g(y) = 0 \; \forall y \in \mathbb{F}_2^t$;
foreach $x \in L$ **do**   // Absorb the nonzero inputs
$\quad (i_1, \ldots, i_t) \leftarrow \text{GetCoordinates}(\overline{x - x_0}, \mathcal{B}_X)$;
$\quad g(i_1, \ldots, i_t) \leftarrow g(i_1, \ldots, i_t) + (-1)^{\langle x - x_0, u_0 \rangle} f(x)$;
end
$g \leftarrow \text{FWT}(g)$;   // Fast Walsh transform of size 2^t
foreach $u \in M$ **do**   // Generate the desired outputs
$\quad (j_1, \ldots, j_t) \leftarrow \text{GetCoordinates}(\overline{u - u_0}, \mathcal{B}_U)$;
$\quad \widehat{f}(u) \leftarrow (-1)^{\langle x_0, u \rangle} g(j_1, \ldots, j_t)$;
end
return $\widehat{f}$

Proof. Let $u = u_0 + u'$, $u' \in U$ be one of the desired outputs.

$$\widehat{f}(u) = \sum_{x \in \mathbb{F}_2^n} (-1)^{\langle u, x \rangle} f(x) = \sum_{x' \in X} (-1)^{\langle u, x_0 \rangle + \langle u', x' \rangle + \langle u_0, x' \rangle} f(x_0 + x')$$

$$= (-1)^{\langle u, x_0 \rangle} \sum_{y \in X/(X \cap U^\perp)} (-1)^{\langle u', y \rangle} \sum_{x' \in y} (-1)^{\langle u_0, x' \rangle} f(x_0 + x'),$$

where $x \in y'$ means that x is a representative of the class y, in other words, $y = x' + (X \cap U^\perp)$. This suggests the following algorithm:

1. For each $y \in X/(X \cap U^\perp)$, compute $g(y) = \sum_{x' \in y} (-1)^{\langle u_0, x' \rangle} f(x_0 + x')$, forming an array g of length 2^t. We go over all $x \in L$, compute $x' = x - x_0$, and add $f(x)$ to the bin corresponding to the class of x'. This costs at most $|L|$ additions. We do not need to store any entries of f in memory.
2. We apply the fast Walsh transform on g with $t2^t$ additions. The result is a vector $\widehat{g}$ which contains, for each $v \in V \in U/(U \cap X^\perp)$:

$$\widehat{g}(v) = \sum_{y \in X/(X \cap U^\perp)} (-1)^{\langle v, y \rangle} \sum_{x' \in y} (-1)^{\langle u_0, x' \rangle} f(x_0 + x').$$

Lemma 6 justifies the validity of this step.
3. For each output $u \in M$, separate $u = u_0 + u'$, and sign-swap the entry of $\widehat{g}$ indexed under the class of u' according to $\langle x_0, u \rangle$ to obtain $\widehat{f}(u)$. The total

cost is at most $|M|$. Each output can be queried individually, and we can even store the vector $\widehat{g}$ and query any output in $\mathcal{O}\left(1\right)$ afterwards.

Example. We return to the example to illustrate how the algorithm of Fig. 3 is justified by Proposition 7. Indeed, $U \cap X^{\perp} = X^{\perp} = \text{span}\left\{(1,1,1,0)\right\}$ and $X \cap U^{\perp} = U^{\perp} = \text{span}\left\{(1,1,0,0)\right\}$, so $t = 2$ and the transform reduces to one of size 2^2. The inputs and outputs of the reduced transform correspond to the bases $(\overline{(0,1,1,0)}, \overline{(0,0,0,1)})$ of $X/(X \cap U^{\perp})$ and $(\overline{(0,0,1,0)}, \overline{(0,0,0,1)})$ of $U/(U \cap X^{\perp})$.

3.3 A Small Generalisation

We have described a pruned fast Walsh transform algorithm which is effective when the inputs and/or outputs are restricted to affine subspaces of small dimension. We have also shown that the time complexity doesn't just depend on the dimensions of these subspaces, but also on their orthogonality. The next natural step is to look into algorithms for arbitrary subsets of $\mathbb{F}_2^n$.

We can find the smallest subspaces which cover all inputs and outputs by choosing random $x_0 \in L$ and $u_0 \in M$ and picking $X = \text{span}\left(\{x - x_0\}_{x \in L}\right)$ and $U = \text{span}\left(\{u - u_0\}_{u \in M}\right)$. However, if $|L|, |M| \gg n$ it is very likely that $X = U = \mathbb{F}_2^n$, and we just obtain the traditional fast Walsh transform algorithm. This is the case in the applications later in the paper.

In these applications, however, the nonzero coefficients can be covered by a small amount of low dimension subspaces. We assume that we separate the lists L and M as disjoint unions $L = L_1 \cup \cdots \cup L_p$ and $M = M_1 \cup \cdots \cup M_q$. Let's also assume that there exist $x_0^1, \ldots, x_0^p$ and $u_0^1, \ldots, u_0^q$, as well as $X_1, \ldots, X_p$ and $U_1, \ldots, U_q$ so that $L_i \subseteq x_0^i + X_i$ and $M_j \subseteq u_0^j + U_j$. Although the list families $\{L_i\}$ and $\{M_j\}$ are disjoint, the affine subspace families $\{x_0^i + X_i\}$ and $\{u_0^j + U_j\}$ need not be disjoint. Because of the linearity of the Walsh transform, we can compute the transform for each pair (L_i, M_j) separately, and combine the results at the end. Let $t_{ij} := \dim\left(X_i/(X_i \cap U_j^{\perp})\right)$. The time complexity is:

$$q|L| + \sum_{i=1}^{p} \sum_{j=1}^{q} t_{ij} \cdot 2^{t_{ij}} + p|M| \text{ additions/subtractions.} \qquad (12)$$

4 Zeros in the Walsh Spectra of SPN Constructions

This section adapts some previously-known results on the Walsh transform (see [13]) to quickly identify zeroes in the Walsh spectra of block cipher constructions which alternate a bricklayer nonlinear map and a linear transformation, such as Substitution Permutation Networks. We also illustrate how in some cases slightly modifying to the key recovery map so that it rejects some plaintexts can drastically reduce the number of nonzero coefficients.

Lemma 8. *Let* $f : \mathbb{F}_2^n \longrightarrow \mathbb{F}_2^m$, $f(x) = Lx \oplus c$, *where* $L \in GL(\mathbb{F}_2^n, \mathbb{F}_2^m)$ *is a linear map and* $c \in \mathbb{F}_2^m$ *is a constant. Then*

$$\widehat{f}(u, v) = \begin{cases} 0 & \text{if } u \neq L^T v \\ (-1)^{\langle v, c \rangle} 2^n & \text{if } u = L^T v \end{cases} \quad \text{for all } u \in \mathbb{F}_2^n, v \in \mathbb{F}_2^m. \quad (13)$$

Lemma 9. *Let* $f_i : \mathbb{F}_2^{n_i} \longrightarrow \mathbb{F}_2^{m_i}$, $i = 1, \ldots, d$ *be* d *vectorial boolean functions. We consider the* bricklayer *map* $\mathbf{F} : \mathbb{F}_2^{\sum_i n_i} \longrightarrow \mathbb{F}_2^{\sum_i m_i}$, *which is obtained by concatenation,* $\mathbf{F}(x_1, \ldots, x_d) = (f_1(x_1), \ldots, f_d(x_d))$. *Then, for any* $(u_1, \ldots, u_d) \in \mathbb{F}_2^{n_1} \times \ldots \times \mathbb{F}_2^{n_d}$ *and* $(v_1, \ldots, v_d) \in \mathbb{F}_2^{m_1} \times \ldots \times \mathbb{F}_2^{m_d}$, *we have*

$$\widehat{\mathbf{F}}((u_1, \ldots, u_d), (v_1, \ldots, v_d)) = \prod_{i=1}^{d} \widehat{f}_i(u_i, v_i). \quad (14)$$

Note that if $m_i = 1$ *and* f_i *is balanced, then* $\widehat{f}_i(u_i, v_i) = \begin{cases} \widehat{f}_i(u_i) & \text{if } v_i = 1 \\ 0 & \text{if } u_i \neq 0, v_i = 0 \\ 2^{n_i} & \text{if } u_i = 0, v_i = 0 \end{cases}$.

Lemma 10. *Let* $f : \mathbb{F}_2^n \longrightarrow \mathbb{F}_2^l$ *and* $g : \mathbb{F}_2^l \longrightarrow \mathbb{F}_2^m$ *be vectorial boolean functions. Let* $X \subseteq \mathbb{F}_2^n$, $Z \subseteq \mathbb{F}_2^l$ *and* $Y \subseteq \mathbb{F}_2^m$ *be subsets. We have*

$$2^l \widehat{g \circ f}(u, v) = \sum_{w \in \mathbb{F}_2^l} \widehat{f}(u, w) \cdot \widehat{g}(w, v) \quad (15)$$

$$2^l \widehat{g \circ f_{x \in X}}(u, v) = \sum_{w \in \mathbb{F}_2^l} \widehat{f_{x \in X}}(u, w) \cdot \widehat{g}(w, v) \quad (16)$$

$$2^l \widehat{g \circ f_{g \circ f(x) \in Y}}(u, v) = \sum_{w \in \mathbb{F}_2^l} \widehat{f}(u, w) \cdot \widehat{g_{g(z) \in Y}}(w, v) \quad (17)$$

$$2^l \widehat{g \circ f_{f(x) \in Z}}(u, v) = \sum_{w \in \mathbb{F}_2^l} \widehat{f_{f(x) \in Z}}(u, w) \widehat{g}(w, v) = \sum_{w \in \mathbb{F}_2^l} \widehat{f}(u, w) \widehat{g_{z \in Z}}(w, v) \quad (18)$$

Using these results, we can often obtain compact formulas for the Walsh coefficients of some key recovery maps, such as the following:

Proposition 11. *Let* $f_i : \mathbb{F}_2^n \longrightarrow \mathbb{F}_2^{l_i}$ *be* d *balanced vectorial boolean functions, let* $L : \mathbb{F}_2^{\sum_i l_i} \longrightarrow \mathbb{F}_2^l$ *be a linear map, and let* $g : \mathbb{F}_2^l \longrightarrow \mathbb{F}_2$ *be a boolean function. In the applications, the* f_i *will be some Sboxes with possibly truncated outputs,* L *will be a truncation of the linear layer, and* g *will be a linear combination of outputs of an Sbox layer. We also consider a subset* $Z \subseteq \mathbb{F}_2^l$. *We consider the composition* $h = g \circ L \circ \mathbf{F}$, *where* $\mathbf{F}$ *is the bricklayer function* $\mathbf{F}(x_1, \ldots, x_d) = (f_1(x_1), \ldots, f_d(x_d))$. *The Walsh coefficients of* h *can be obtained through the* *following formula:*

$$\widehat{h}_{L(\mathbf{F}(x))\in Z}(u_1,\ldots,u_d) = \frac{1}{2^l} \underbrace{\sum_{w_1\in\mathbb{F}_2^{l_1}} \cdots \sum_{w_d\in\mathbb{F}_2^{l_d}} \sum_{v\in\mathbb{F}_2^l} \prod_{i=1}^d \widehat{f}_i(u_i,w_i)\widehat{g_{z\in Z}}(v)}_{\substack{w_i=0 \ if \ u_i=0 \\ (w_1,\ldots,w_d)=L^t v}}. \quad (19)$$

Proof. We use Lemma 10 to write the Walsh coefficients of h as

$$\widehat{h}_{L(\mathbf{F}(x))\in Z}(u_1,\ldots,u_d) = \frac{1}{2^{\sum_i l_i+l}} \sum_{w\in\mathbb{F}_2^{\sum_i l_i}} \sum_{v\in\mathbb{F}_2^l} \widehat{\mathbf{F}}(u,w)\widehat{L}(w,v)\widehat{g_{z\in Z}}(v).$$

According to Lemma 8, $\widehat{L}(w,v) \neq 0$ if and only if $w = L^t v$, in which case $\widehat{L}(w,v) = 2^{\sum_i l_i}$. This means we only have to consider the sums over the w_i for which an appropriate v exists, and vice versa. Furthermore, we can write $\widehat{\mathbf{F}}(u,w) = \prod_{i=1}^d \widehat{f}_i(u_i,w_i)$ according to Lemma 9. Since $\widehat{f}_i(0,w_i) = 0$ if $w_i \neq 0$, we can assume $w_i = 0$ for the i for which $u_i = 0$.

In particular, for the case in which all $l_i = 1$:

Corollary 12. *Let $f_i : \mathbb{F}_2^{n_i} \longrightarrow \mathbb{F}_2$ be l boolean functions and $g : \mathbb{F}_2^l \longrightarrow \mathbb{F}_2$. We consider $h(x_1,\ldots,x_l) = g(f_1(x_1),\ldots,f_d(x_l))$ and the subset $Z \subseteq \mathbb{F}_2^d$. Then*

$$\widehat{h_{\mathbf{F}(x)\in Z}}(u_1,\ldots,u_l) = \frac{2^{\sum_{i,u_i=0} n_i}}{2^l} \widehat{g_{z\in Z}}(w(u_1,\ldots,u_l)) \prod_{i,u_i\neq 0} \widehat{f}_i(u_i),$$

where $w(u_1,\ldots,u_l)_i = \begin{cases} 0 & \text{if } u_i = 0 \\ 1 & \text{if } u_i \neq 0 \end{cases}$.

We'll show how the previous result describes $\widehat{h_{f(x)\in Z}}$ and its zeroes in a compact manner. We first look at $\widehat{g_{z\in Z}}$. Given any $w \in \mathbb{F}_2^l$ so that $\widehat{g_{z\in Z}}(w) = 0$, we can deduce that $\widehat{h_{\mathbf{F}(x)\in Z}}(u_1,\ldots,u_l) = 0$ for all $(u_1,\ldots,u_l)$ so that $w = w(u_1,\ldots,u_l)$. Furthermore, for the $(u_1,\ldots,u_l)$ for which $\widehat{g_{z\in Z}}(w(u_1,\ldots,u_l)) \neq 0$, the Walsh coefficient $\widehat{h_{\mathbf{F}(x)\in Z}}(u_1,\ldots,u_l)$ can be written as the product of $\widehat{g_{z\in Z}}(w(u_1,\ldots,u_l))$ and the $\widehat{f}_i(u_i)$ corresponding to each $u_i \neq 0$.

An interesting situation appears when $\widehat{g_{z\in Z}}(1,\ldots,1) = 0$. Given $(u_1,\ldots,u_l)$ so that $u_i \neq 0$ for all i, we know that $\widehat{h_{\mathbf{F}(x)\in Z}}(u_1,\ldots,u_l) = 0$, and any nonzero Walsh coefficient must verify $u_i = 0$ for at least one i. As a result, the nonzero Walsh coefficients can be separated into l vector subspaces U_i of dimensions $\sum_{j\neq i} n_j - n_i$. Each U_i is determined by the n_i linear equations $u_i = 0$.

When $\widehat{g}(1\ldots1) = 0$, we obtain this decomposition without any modifications to the key recovery map. When $\widehat{g}(1\ldots1) \neq 0$, we would like to choose some large $Z \subseteq \mathbb{F}_2^d$ so that $\widehat{g_{z\in Z}}(1,\ldots,1) = 0$. We can use the following result:

Proposition 13. *Let* $g : \mathbb{F}_2^l \longrightarrow \mathbb{F}_2$ *be a map for which* $\widehat{g}(1 \ldots 1) = a \neq 0$. *There exists* $Z \subseteq \mathbb{F}_2^l$ *with* $|Z| = 2^l - |a|$ *so that* $\widehat{g_{z \in Z}}(1 \ldots 1) = 0$.

We have substituted the key recovery map, which normally takes values ± 1 depending on the linear approximation, for a modified map which is zero when $\mathbf{F}(x) \notin Z$. From the perspective of the attack, we are rejecting the plaintext-ciphertext pairs for which the input of g is not in Z. Assuming independence, the resulting attack has the same parameters except for the data complexity, which increases by a factor of $2^l/|Z|$ to compensate the rejected plaintexts.

These results describe *static* key recovery maps $F(X \oplus K^O)$ without inner key guesses. We must also consider maps of the form $F(X \oplus K^O, K^I)$. When all $l_i = 1$, the xoring of a round subkey between rounds only changes the Walsh coefficient signs, and the positions of the zero coefficients remain unaltered:

Corollary 14. *Let* $f_i : \mathbb{F}_2^{n_i} \longrightarrow \mathbb{F}_2$ *be* l *boolean functions,* $g : \mathbb{F}_2^l \longrightarrow \mathbb{F}_2$, *and let* $k \in \mathbb{F}_2^l$ *be a fixed parameter. We consider the parametric function* $h(x_1, \ldots, x_l; k) = g((f_1(x_1), \ldots, f_l(x_l)) \oplus k)$ *and the subset* $Z \subseteq \mathbb{F}_2^l$. *Then*

$$\widehat{h(\cdot, k)}_{\mathbf{F}(x) \oplus k \in Z}(u_1, \ldots, u_l) = (-1)^{\langle k, w(u_1, \ldots, u_l) \rangle} \widehat{h(\cdot, 0)}_{\mathbf{F}(x) \in Z}(u_1, \ldots, u_l).$$

5 Optimised Attack Algorithm

We now provide a linear key recovery algorithm which makes use of the affine pruned Walsh transform. We assume that the target linear approximation is of the form $f_0(x) + f(X \oplus K^O, K^I)$, but it also applies to key recovery maps with several parts. We will also make some redundancy assumptions:

- The parts of the plaintext-ciphertext pair X which are xored with the outer key guess K^O lie in an affine subspace of the form $x_0 + Y \subseteq \mathbb{F}_2^{|K^O|}$.
- The nonzero Walsh coefficients of $F(\cdot, 0)$ lie in the union of l affine subspaces $u_0^i + U_i \subseteq \mathbb{F}_2^{|K^O|}$. We denote the number of nonzero coefficients in $u_0^i + U_i$ by $|L_i|$. We also assume that the nonzero Walsh coefficients of $F(\cdot, K^I)$ occupy the same subspaces. If the latter is not true, each value of K^I must be treated separately, and the cost of the analysis phase is multiplied by $2^{|K^I|}$.
- Given the key schedule of the cipher, for a given guess of K^I, the possible values of K^O lie within an affine subspace of the form $v_0^{K^I} + V_{K^I} \subseteq \mathbb{F}_2^{|K^O|}$.

We denote the dimensions of the relevant quotient spaces for the first Walsh transform as $t_i = \dim\left(Y/(Y \cap U_i^\perp)\right)$. For the last set of Walsh transforms, we assume that these dimensions are constant for all the K^I, that is $r_i = \dim\left(U_i/(U_i \cap V_{K^I}^\perp)\right)$ for all $K^I \in \mathbb{F}_2^{|K^I|}$. This assumption is not necessary but it simplifies the complexity calculation.

The broad idea of the attack procedure is to compute $\widehat{\mathrm{cor}}(\cdot, K^I)$ as the sum of l linear transformations of A. Each linear operation corresponds to the part of the Walsh spectrum of F which lies in the affine subspace $u_0^i + U_i \subseteq \mathbb{F}_2^{|K^O|}$. The full attack algorithm is the following:

1. *Distillation phase:* We can merge the first step of the first pruned Walsh transform into the distillation phase to save time and memory. Depending on the relative sizes of N and $2^{\dim(Y)}$, we have two options:
   - Perform the distillation phase as usual (compute A in full) and compute the first step of the pruned Walsh transform algorithm for each of the l pruned Walsh transforms separately to obtain l tables g_i of lengths 2^{t_i}. We note that we only need $2^{\dim(Y)}$ counters to store A. The cost of this operation is $N + l \cdot 2^{\dim(Y)}$ additions.
   - We can instead construct l distilled tables g_i directly, without building the intermediate array A. The cost of this operation is $l \cdot N$ additions.
   Both options require $\sum_{i=1}^{l} 2^{t_i}$ registers to store the resulting distilled data.
2. *Analysis phase:* We also save time and memory by mixing the last step of the first Walsh transform, the eigenvalue multiplication step, and the first step of the second set of Walsh transforms.
   (a) *First Walsh transform:* Perform the (standard) fast Walsh transform on each of the arrays g_i to obtain l arrays $\widehat{g}_i$. The time complexity of this operation is $\sum_{i=1}^{l} t_i 2^{t_i}$ additions.
   (b) *Walsh spectrum multiplication:* This step and the next are repeated for each guess of K^I. Inside each subspace $u_0^i + U_i$, we go over all the nonzero Walsh coefficients. For the nonzero coefficients which belong to more than one subspace, we must only consider them in one of these subspaces. For each coefficient, we fetch the appropriate entry of $\widehat{g}_i$ and multiply it by the coefficient $\hat{F}(u_0^i + u', K^I)$. The result is then added to the appropriate coordinate of an array h of length 2^{r_i}. This step uses $2^{|K^I|} \sum_{i=1}^{l} |L_i|$ products and additions and requires $\sum_{i=1}^{l} 2^{r_i}$ additional memory registers (assuming we can reuse the same memory from one K^I to the next). If Corollary 14 applies, it is possible to achieve further savings by performing the multiplication step a single time.
   (c) *Second set of Walsh transforms:* We perform the fast Walsh transform on each of the h_i to obtain $\widehat{h}_i$, at a cost of $\sum_{i=1}^{l} r_i 2^{r_i}$ additions.
   (d) *Unfolding step:* For each guess of K^O, we compute $\widehat{\mathrm{cor}}(K^O, K^I)$ by adding l values (with appropriate signs), one from each of the $\widehat{h}_i$. This costs $l 2^{|K^I|} 2^{\dim(V)}$ additions.

By adding up the cost of each step we find that the total time and memory complexity of the algorithm is, after removing terms of lower order:

$$\underbrace{2^{|K^I|} N l}_{*} + \underbrace{2^{|K^I|} \sum_{i=1}^{l} t_i 2^{t_i}}_{*} + \underbrace{2^{|K^I|} \sum_{i=1}^{l} L_i}_{**} + 2^{|K^I|} \sum_{i=1}^{l} r_i 2^{r_i} \text{ additions,} \tag{20}$$

$$\underbrace{2^{|K^I|} \sum_{i=1}^{l} L_i}_{**} \text{ products, and} \tag{21}$$

$$\sum_{i=1}^{l} 2^{t_i} + \sum_{i=1}^{l} 2^{r_i} \text{ registers,} \tag{22}$$

where the factors indicated by ∗ can be removed when the nonzero Walsh coefficients of $F(\cdot, K^I)$ occupy the same subspaces $u_0^i + U_i$ independently from K^I, and the factors with ∗∗ can be removed when the Walsh coefficients of the different $\widehat{F}(\cdot, K^I)$ only differ by sign as in Corollary 14.

6   Application to the DES

As an application example, we present a variant of Matsui's linear attack [25, 26] on the DES [1]. This variant has lower data complexity ($2^{41.5}$ vs. 2^{43}), but has a larger memory complexity ($2^{38.75}$ vs. $2^{26.00}$) due to the larger key guess.

We use a 13-round linear approximation identical to the 14-round linear approximation used in [26], but with the last round removed. This increases the correlation from $-2^{-19.75}$ to $2^{-19.07}$. The input mask is $(00000000, 01040080)$ at (L_1, R_1) and the output mask is $(21040080, 00000000)$ at (L_{14}, R_{14}).

Figure 4 indicates the active keybits in the key recovery in rounds 1, 15, and 16. There are 40 active keybits in total: 3 are active in round 1, one is active in round 15, 28 are active in round 16, 3 are active in both rounds 1 and 16, and 5 are active in both rounds 15 and 16. All active keybits are represented as part of K, after applying the appropriate bit rotation. There are 43 active plaintext/ciphertext bits (four of which are duplicated before the key addition because of the expansion map) and 40 active keybits (eight of which are used twice). An attack using the same version of Algorithm 2 as [26] would have a time complexity of $O(N) + 2^{43+40} \simeq 2^{83}$ operations. An attack based on the FFT without any kind of optimisation [17] would require $O(N) + 48 \cdot 2^{48}$ operations.

6.1   The Walsh Spectrum of the Key Recovery Map

Figure 5 shows the full key recovery map for the attack, including all the key material. In other words, it shows how the linear approximation is computed from the plaintext, ciphertext, and key. Our aim is to identify the zeroes in this function's Walsh spectrum. We note that all key material is xored to the plaintext/ciphertext, and that there are seven plaintext/ciphertext bits which are xored at the end and can be considered separately as the term f_0. The rest of the map consists of two independent parts if we ignore the key schedule: one corresponds to the first round and the other corresponds to the last two rounds.

In the case of the map for the first round, which we will denote by f_1, we can see that it consists of the application of S_5 and the xoring of three of its output bits. If we look at the Walsh spectrum of S_5, we can see that for the output $y_1 \oplus y_2 \oplus y_3$ we have 50 nonzero coefficients out of the total 64.

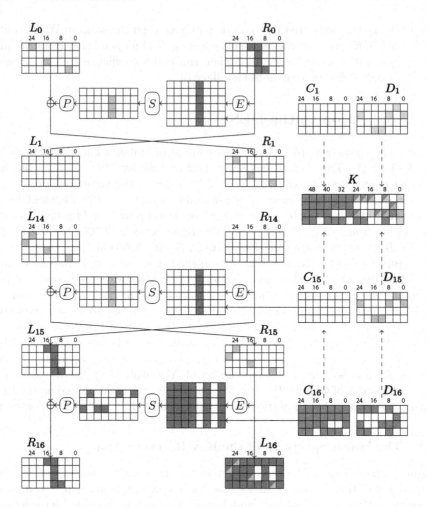

Fig. 4. Key recovery in rounds 1, 15 and 16 of the DES. States are represented as divided into nibbles, except for those before the S-box layer which are divided in groups of 6 bits. The least significant bit is the one on the upper right. ☐ represents a bit which appears linearly in the linear approximation, while ■ represents any other active (nonlinear) bit. ☐, ☐, and ■ represent keybits which are active in rounds 1, 15 and 16, respectively. (Color figure online)

The map for the last two rounds f_2 is a little more complex. It is the composition of three maps: the first is an $\mathbb{F}_2^{42} \to \mathbb{F}_2^{12}$ map consisting of the application of the six active Sboxes in round 16 (selecting a single output bit for each), as well as the identity on the six active bits on the left part of the ciphertext. We then apply a linear $\mathbb{F}_2^{12} \to \mathbb{F}_2^6$ map which xors the outputs of the six sboxes into the ciphertext material. Finally, we apply S_5 and xor the four outputs. If we look at the Walsh spectrum of S_5 with output mask F (Table 1), we note that there are 32 zeros, one of them corresponding to the input mask 3F.

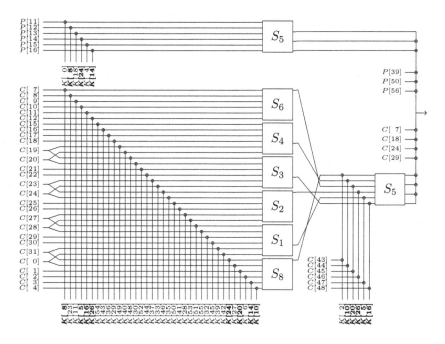

Fig. 5. Schematic of the key recovery map for the DES attack.

Table 1. Part of the Walsh spectrum of S_5: $\widehat{S_5}(\cdot, \mathbf{F})$.

00	0	08	8	10	-40	18	-8	20	0	28	0	30	8	38	0
01	0	09	-8	11	8	19	-8	21	0	29	0	31	8	39	0
02	-8	0A	0	12	0	1A	0	22	-24	2A	8	32	0	3A	-8
03	-8	0B	0	13	0	1B	0	23	-8	2B	8	33	0	3B	8
04	0	0C	-8	14	0	1C	0	24	0	2C	0	34	0	3C	8
05	8	0D	0	15	8	1D	8	25	-8	2D	-8	35	8	3D	0
06	0	0E	-8	16	0	1E	0	26	0	2E	0	36	0	3E	8
07	-8	0F	0	17	8	1F	-8	27	-8	2F	-8	37	-8	3F	0

We consider the coefficients $\widehat{f}_2(u_0, \ldots, u_5, u_6)$, where u_6 corresponds to the six active bits in the left half of the ciphertext. The mask u_6 will be determined by the rest of parts of the mask, as from Corollary 12 we can deduce that

$$\widehat{f}_2(u_0, \ldots, u_5, u_6) \neq 0 \implies (u_6[i] = 1 \longleftrightarrow u_i \neq 0 \text{ for all } i). \tag{23}$$

Furthermore, the following expression for the Walsh coefficient can be deduced:

$$\widehat{f}_2(u_0, \ldots, u_5, \text{ind}(u_0, \ldots, u_5)) = \\
\widehat{S_8}(u_0, 1)\widehat{S_4}(u_1, 4)\widehat{S_6}(u_2, 1)\widehat{S_2}(u_3, 1)\widehat{S_1}(u_4, 4)\widehat{S_3}(u_5, 4)\widehat{S_5}(\text{ind}(u_0, \ldots, u_5), \mathbf{F}), \tag{24}$$

where $\mathrm{ind}(u_0, \ldots, u_5)[i] = 1 \iff u_i \neq 0$. We also collect the following information about the Walsh spectra of the active Sboxes in the last round:

- $\widehat{S_8}(\cdot, 1)$ has 15 zeros.   – $\widehat{S_6}(\cdot, 1)$ has 17 zeros.   – $\widehat{S_1}(\cdot, 4)$ has 14 zeros.
- $\widehat{S_4}(\cdot, 4)$ has 12 zeros.   – $\widehat{S_2}(\cdot, 1)$ has 20 zeros.   – $\widehat{S_3}(\cdot, 4)$ has 18 zeros.

By adding the number of nonzero coefficients associated to each value in Table 1, we conclude that despite being a map defined in $\mathbb{F}_2^{42}$, the Walsh spectrum of f_2 only has around $2^{30.31}$ nonzero coefficients. Furthermore, since $\widehat{S_5}(3\mathrm{F}, \mathrm{F}) = 0$, $u_0, \ldots, u_5$ cannot all be nonzero at the same time. All nonzero coefficients belong to at least one of six vector subspaces of dimension 35. Each subspace $\widetilde{U_i}$ is determined by fixing one $u_i = 0$, which is a six bit condition, as well as the bit condition $u_6[i] = 0$. Since $\widehat{S_5}(3\mathrm{D}, \mathrm{F}) = 0$, we can ignore the subspace $\widetilde{U_1}$.

6.2   Attack Algorithm and Complexity

Based on the observations we have made on the key recovery map for the attack, we propose the following attack algorithm. We have provided a more thorough description of the subspaces Y, V and U_i as supplementary material.

Distillation phase and first set of Walsh transforms. The nonzero Walsh coefficients of the key recovery map form five affine subspaces which are handled separately. The first step in the analysis phase consists of five pruned transforms whose inputs are restricted to a subspace Y of dimension 40 (due to the duplicate input bits in the key recovery map) and whose outputs are restricted to subspaces $U_i = \mathbb{F}_2^6 \times \widetilde{U_i}$ of dimension 41. We can show that $\dim(Y/(Y \cap U_2^{\perp})) = 33$, $\dim(Y/(Y \cap U_0^{\perp})) = 35$, and $\dim(Y/(Y \cap U_i^{\perp})) = 37$ for $i = 3, 4, 5$.

1. Initialise three arrays g_3, g_4, g_5 of length 2^{37}, one array g_0 of length 2^{35} and one array g_2 of length 2^{33}.
2. For each pair (x, y), increment or decrement one position in each of the g_i according to the values of the appropriate parts of the plaintext and ciphertext and to $P[39] + P[50] + P[56] + C[7] + C[18] + C[24] + C[29]$.
3. Apply the fast Walsh transform on each of the g_i.

The time complexity of these steps is around $6N$ memory accesses and $3 \cdot 37 \cdot 2^{37} + 35 \cdot 2^{35} + 33 \cdot 2^{33} \simeq 2^{43.93}$ additions and subtractions.

Multiplying by the Walsh coefficients. The key recovery map has $50 \cdot 2^{30.31} \simeq 2^{35.95}$ nonzero Walsh coefficients. They can be enumerated by separating them into 32 sets, one for each $\widehat{S5}(\cdot, \mathrm{F}) \neq 0$, and looking at the nonzero positions in the LATs of (up to) 7 other active Sboxes.

1. Initialise one array h_2 of length 2^{38}, one array h_0 of length 2^{37}, and three arrays h_3, h_4, h_5 of length 2^{34}.

2. For each of the nonzero Walsh coefficients, retrieve the associated output of the first Walsh transform from one of the g_i (if the coefficient lies in more than one of the U_i, we can choose any), multiply it by the coefficient and add or subtract the result to the appropriate position of the array h_i.

The time complexity of this step is $7 \cdot 2^{35.95} \simeq 2^{38.76}$ products.

Second set of Walsh transforms and exhaustive search. The Walsh transforms in the second set are pruned at the inputs according to the subspaces U_i, and at the outputs according to a subspace V of dimension 40 given by the key schedule. We can show that $\dim(V/(V \cap U_2^{\perp})) = 38$, $\dim(V/(V \cap U_0^{\perp})) = 37$, and $\dim(V/(V \cap U_i^{\perp})) = 34$ for $i = 3, 4, 5$.

1. Perform the standard Walsh transform on the five arrays h_0, h_2, h_3, h_4, h_5.
2. For each of the 2^{40} possible key guesses, we add one coordinate from of each of the five arrays to obtain the experimental correlations. We keep the 2^{24} guesses with the highest correlation, as we aim for an advantage of 16 bits.
3. For each one of the 40-bit partial key guesses, we try all possibilities of the 16 other keybits exhaustively until either the key is found or the attack fails.

The time complexity of these steps is $38 \cdot 2^{38} + 37 \cdot 2^{37} + 3 \cdot 34 \cdot 2^{34} + 5 \cdot 2^{40} \simeq 2^{44.41}$ additions/subtractions and 2^{40} trial encryptions.

Attack Complexity. The data complexity of the attack was determined using the model of Blondeau and Nyberg [8]. We obtain a 16 bit advantage with 70% probability with $N = 2^{41.5}$ data. The memory complexity is dominated by the ten arrays, which require $2^{39.74}$ memory registers of 64 bits. This can be reduced to around $2^{38.75}$ by performing the multiplication step in a way in which the g_i and the h_i do not have to be allocated at the same time.

For the time complexity, we consider that on a modern processor a DES encryption takes 16 clock cycles, a product takes 6 clock cycles, and a memory access or an addition take 1 clock cycle. We obtain

$$\frac{1}{16} \cdot 6 \cdot 2^{41.5} + \frac{1}{16} \left(2^{43.93} + 2^{44.41} \right) + \frac{6}{16} \cdot 2^{38.76} + 2^{40} \simeq 2^{42.13} \text{ DES encryptions.}$$

This attack is, to the best of our knowledge, the best in terms of data complexity. However, it has rather high time (if we exclude data generation) and especially memory complexities when compared to previous attacks (Table 2).

7   Application to PRESENT-128

In this section we introduce the first, to the best of the authors' knowledge, attack on 29-round PRESENT-128. It is based on a previous attack on PRESENT-80 [19] and adds an additional key recovery round. The attack uses the full codebook and has a time complexity of $2^{124.06}$ 29-round PRESENT encryptions.

Table 2. Comparison of selected attacks on the Data Encryption Standard.

Type	Complexity			P_S	Source
	Data	Time	Memory		
Differential cryptanalysis	$2^{47.00}$ CP	$2^{37.00}$	$\mathcal{O}(1)$	58%	[5]
Linear cryptanalysis	$2^{43.00}$ KP	$2^{39.00}$	$2^{26.00}$	50%	[26]
Multiple linear cryptanalysis	$2^{42.78}$ KP	$2^{38.86}$	$2^{30.00}$	85%	[11]
Conditional linear cryptanalysis	$2^{42.00}$ KP	$2^{42.00}$	$2^{28.00}$	90%	[4]
Linear cryptanalysis	$2^{41.50}$ KP	$2^{42.13}$	$2^{38.75}$	70%	Section 6

Table 3. The linear approximations of 24-round PRESENT which conform set II of [19], and which are also used in our attack.

Group ([19])	Input mask	Input S-box	Output mask	Output S-box	Qty.	24R ELP
A	A	5,6,9,10	2,8	5,7,13,15	32	$2^{-65.1}$
B	C	5,6,9,10	2,8	5,7,13,15	32	$2^{-65.6}$
C	A	5,6,9,10	2,8	6,14	16	$2^{-65.8}$
	A	13,14	2,8	5,7,13,15	16	
D	2,4	5,6,9,10	2,8	5,7,13,15	64	$2^{-66.0}$
E	C	5,6,9,10	2,8	6,14	16	$2^{-66.3}$
	C	13,14	2,8	5,7,13,15	16	
F	A	13,14	2,8	6,14	8	$2^{-66.5}$
G	2,4	5,6,9,10	2,8	6,14	32	$2^{-66.7}$
	8	5,6,9,10	2,8	5,7,13,15	32	
	2,4	13,14	2,8	5,7,13,15	32	
Total					296	$2^{-57.8}$

The attack uses one of the three sets of linear approximations which were defined in [19] and provide a trade-off between capacity and key recovery complexity. We will use set II, which has 296 approximations and a total capacity of $2^{-57.8}$. Table 3 shows all the approximations which conform this distinguisher in a compact form. All of them have a single active Sbox in the first round and a single active Sbox in the last round, and the input mask always has Hamming weight 1 or 2 while the output mask always has Hamming weight 1.

7.1 Key Recovery Example for a Single Approximation

As an example, we consider the 24-round linear approximation with input mask 0000000000A00000 and output mask 0000000000200000, between the 3rd and the 26th rounds. We add two rounds of key recovery at the input side and three rounds at the output side. We will apply the pruned Walsh transform-based attack algorithm to compute its experimental correlation for all key guesses.

For comparison purposes, we consider the cost when using the Walsh transform without pruning. There are 32 active bits in K_1, 8 active bits in K_2, 4 active bits in K_{28}, 16 active bits in K_{29}, and 64 active bits in K_{30} (crossed-out in Fig. 6). They add up to 28 bits of inner key guess K^I and 96 bits of outer key guess K^O. We thus require 2^{96} memory registers, and the time complexity is in the order of $96 \cdot 2^{96+28} \simeq 2^{130.6}$ additions, which leaves little margin to repeat it for several approximations using less than 2^{128} equivalent encryptions.

In order to reduce this cost as much as possible, we consider both the structure of the key recovery map and the key schedule in order to prune both stages of Walsh transforms. The key recovery map consists of three independent parts corresponding to each of the three active bits in the input and output masks.

Both parts corresponding to the input mask are essentially identical. If we denote by S_1 the second component of S (that is, the second output bit), then these $\mathbb{F}_2^{16} \longrightarrow \mathbb{F}_2$ maps are of the form $S_1(S_1(x_3), S_1(x_2), S_1(x_1), S_1(x_0) \oplus k^I)$. Using Corollary 14, each of their Walsh coefficient is the product of up to five coefficients of the Walsh spectrum of S_1, which we note has six zeros.

We next look at the remaining part, which has a similar structure but over three rounds. In round 27, we consider $\widehat{S^{-1}}(\mathsf{F}, 2) = \widehat{S}(2, \mathsf{F}) = 4$. By rejecting the ciphertexts which lead to an input 3, 5, B or D to this Sbox, this coefficient becomes zero. We can split all nonzero Walsh coefficients into two affine subspaces of dimension 48 corresponding to the nonzero Walsh coefficients $\widehat{S^{-1}}_{x \in \mathbb{F}_2^4 \setminus x}(\mathsf{B}, 2)$ and $\widehat{S^{-1}}_{x \in \mathbb{F}_2^4 \setminus x}(\mathsf{D}, 2)$. The "inactive" bits in each of these subspaces have been surrounded by a thicker outline in Fig. 6. The cost of this modification is a reduction of the available data by a factor of $3/4 = 2^{-0.42}$.

We now consider the key schedule. When pruning the Walsh transforms, we prefer relationships which are linear or which describe outer active keybits in terms of inner active keybits. We first guess the 28 inner keybits, painted (dark) red in the figure. The outer bits which can be deduced from these are colored (light) green. The other outer bits are guessed individually. There are three bits of K_{30} which can be deduced from the guess for K_{28}.

Let us compute the time complexity of obtaining all the $\widehat{\mathrm{cor}}(K^O, K^I)$. We start with two Walsh transforms whose outputs are restricted to subspaces of dimension $48 + 32 = 80$. The distillation phase costs $2N$ operations and requires $2 \cdot 2^{80}$ memory registers. The cost of the Walsh transforms themselves is $2 \cdot 80 \cdot 2^{80} \simeq 2^{87.32}$ additions. The cost of the Walsh coefficients multiplication is at most $\left(\frac{10}{16}\right)^{20} \cdot 2 \cdot 2^{80} \simeq 2^{67.44}$ products.

The second pair of Walsh transforms is repeated once for each of the 2^{28} guesses of K^I. In every case, the Walsh transforms have inputs restricted to subspaces of dimension 80 and outputs restricted to subspaces of dimension 93. The dimension of $X/(X \cap U^{\perp})$ is minimal and equal to 77. The total cost of these transforms is thus $2^{28} \cdot 2 \cdot 77 \cdot 2^{77} \simeq 2^{112.27}$ additions. The cost of combining the resulting arrays would be 2^{120} additions. However, 25 bits of the key guess at

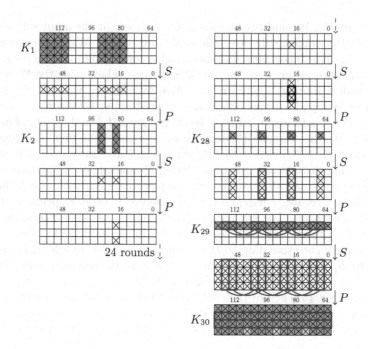

Fig. 6. Key recovery for one approximation.

Table 4. Restricted Walsh spectra used in the PRESENT-128 attack.

	v	0	1	2	3	4	5	6	7	8	9	A	B	C	D	E	F
$\widehat{S}_{S(x)\in\mathbb{F}_2^4\backslash\mathcal{X}}(2,\cdot)$	$\mathcal{X} = \varnothing$	0	0	4	4	-4	-4	0	0	4	-4	0	8	0	8	-4	4
	$\mathcal{X} = \{3,5,\text{B},\text{D}\}$	0	0	4	4	-4	-4	0	0	0	0	0	8	0	8	0	0
	v	0	1	2	3	4	5	6	7	8	9	A	B	C	D	E	F
$\widehat{S}_{S(x)\in\mathbb{F}_2^4\backslash\mathcal{X}}(4,\cdot)$	$\mathcal{X} = \varnothing$	0	0	-4	4	-4	-4	0	8	-4	-4	0	-8	0	0	-4	4
	$\mathcal{X} = \{1,3,\text{D},\text{F}\}$	0	0	0	0	-4	-4	0	8	-4	-4	0	-8	0	0	0	0
	v	0	1	2	3	4	5	6	7	8	9	A	B	C	D	E	F
$\widehat{S}_{S(x)\in\mathbb{F}_2^4\backslash\mathcal{X}}(8,\cdot)$	$\mathcal{X} = \varnothing$	0	0	4	-4	0	0	-4	4	-4	4	0	0	-4	4	8	8
	$\mathcal{X} = \{0,1,2,4,$ $5,7,9,\text{C}\}$	0	0	0	-4	0	0	-4	0	0	4	0	0	-4	0	8	0

K_1 and three bits of the guess at K_{28} can be deduced from the guess at K_{30}, and the calculation can be performed with 2^{92} additions.

We note that we have decreased the time complexity by a factor of almost 2^{16} by increasing the data complexity by a factor of $4/3 \simeq 2^{0.42}$, illustrating that a carefully picked filtering of the data can lead to significant time gains.

7.2   Overview of the Complete Attack

We divide the 296 linear approximations into two groups depending on the Hamming weight of the input mask and their time complexity contribution:

Type I (Groups D,G). These are the 160 approximations with input masks of Hamming weight 1. For these approximations, there are 16 active bits in K_1, 4 in K_2, 4 in K_{28}, 16 in K_{29} and 64 in K_{30}. We can compute $\widehat{cor}$ for these approximations with around $160 \cdot 2^{24} \cdot 80 \cdot 2^{80} \simeq 2^{117.64}$ additions without pruning.

Type II (Groups A,B,C,E,F). These are the 136 approximations with input masks of Hamming weight 2. There are 32 active bits in K_1, 8 in K_2, 4 in K_{28}, 16 in K_{29}, and 64 bits in K_{30}. We treat these approximations as in the example: we study the Walsh spectrum of the active Sbox in round 27 (see Table 4). For 48 approximations, we are interested in $\widehat{S}(2, \cdot)$, and we can split the Walsh spectrum of the key recovery map into two affine subspaces of dimension 80 by discarding $1/4$ of the data. For 40 approximations, the coefficient is $\widehat{S}(4, \cdot)$, and we can split the spectrum into 2 spaces of dimension 80 by discarding $1/4$ of the data. For the other 48 approximations, the coefficient is $\widehat{S}(4, \cdot)$, in which case the spectrum lies on a subspace of dimension 80 after discarding $1/2$ of the data. Given these restrictions, we can compute $\widehat{cor}$ with either $2 \cdot 2^{28} \cdot 80 \cdot 2^{80} \simeq 2^{115.32}$ or $2^{28} \cdot 80 \cdot 2^{80} \simeq 2^{114.32}$ additions. Further reductions are possible if we used the key schedule, but they are different for each approximation. Ignoring these, $2^{123.08}$ additions are required in total. We also have to combine both arrays corresponding to each approximation, which requires at most 2^{92} additions per approximation if we consider the key schedule.

Computing the Multiple Linear Cryptanalysis Statistic: First Step. We must also consider the cost of computing the multiple linear cryptanalysis statistic. Using the notation of [19], the approximations form $M_2 = 32$ groups (8 groups for type I and 24 groups for type II) which share the same key guesses K^O and K^I. We can compute the sum of squares within each group and combine them in the next step. Considering the key schedule, for the Type II approximations we need to guess at most 92 bits, and for Type I at most 88 bits. This step can thus be performed with $136 \cdot 2^{92} + 160 \cdot 2^{88} \simeq 2^{99.2}$ products and additions.

Computing the Multiple Linear Cryptanalysis Statistic: Second Step. The combined tables of the previous step are used to compute Q_{k_T} for each value of a global key guess k_T. Figure 7 shows a guess of 123 keybits from which all the key guesses can be deduced. For each guess of k_T, we must add 32 values, one from each of the tables constructed in the previous step, at a cost of $32 \cdot 2^{123} = 2^{128}$ additions. After this we can find the five remaining keybits with an exhaustive search costing 2^{123} encryptions if we aim for a five-bit advantage.

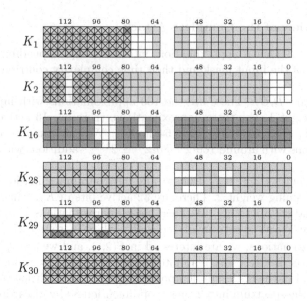

Fig. 7. Determining all the active keybits for all approximations (crossed out in the figure) with as few guesses as possible. We can deduce the (light) green bits if we know the 123 keybits highlighted in (dark) red. (Color figure online)

Data Complexity. We once again use the model from [8], with careful consideration that the number of available plaintexts depends on the approximation. We find that if the whole codebook is used (2^{64} distinct known plaintexts), a 5 bit advantage is achieved with 67% probability.

Memory Complexity. There are two main steps which contribute to the memory complexity. The distillation phase requires $160 \cdot 2^{16+64} + 136 \cdot 2 \cdot 2^{32+48} \simeq 2^{88.75}$ registers. The 32 intermediate multiple linear cryptanalysis statistic tables use $2^{99.2}$ memory registers, which dominate the memory complexity of the attack.

Time Complexity. The dominant parts of the time complexity are the computation of the multiple linear cryptanalysis statistic and the final exhaustive key search. The latter takes 2^{123} PRESENT encryptions, while the former requires 2^{128} additions. If we assume that a sum requires at most 128 bit operations and a 29-round PRESENT encryption requires at least 3776 (64 for each subkey addition and Sbox layer), these will be equivalent to at most $2^{123.12}$ encryptions. The total time complexity is thus $2^{124.06}$ encryptions (Table 5).

Table 5. Comparison of linear attacks on reduced-round PRESENT. Attacks on PRESENT-80 are also included for the sake of completeness. KP = Known Plaintext. DKP = Distinct Known Plaintext.

Key	Rds.	Complexity			P_S	Source
		Data	Time	Memory		
80	26	$2^{63.8}$ KP	$2^{72.0}$	$2^{32.0}$	51%	[7,15]
		$2^{63.0}$ KP	$2^{68.6}$	$2^{48.0}$	95%	[10]
		$2^{61.1}$ KP	$2^{68.2}$	$2^{44.0}$	95%	[19]
		$2^{60.8}$ KP	$2^{71.8}$	$2^{44.0}$	95%	[19]
	27	$2^{64.0}$ KP	$2^{74.0}$	$2^{67.0}$	95%	[34]
		$2^{63.8}$ DKP	$2^{77.3}$	$2^{48.0}$	95%	[10]
		$2^{63.4}$ DKP	$2^{72.0}$	$2^{44.0}$	95%	[19]
	28	$2^{64.0}$ DKP	$2^{77.4}$	$2^{51.0}$	95%	[19]
128	28	$2^{64.0}$ DKP	2^{122}	$2^{84.6}$	95%	[19]
	29	$2^{64.0}$ DKP	$2^{124.06}$	$2^{99.2}$	67%	Sect. 7

8   Conclusion

Summary of Results. We have introduced a new framework for pruning of the fast Walsh transform to affine subspaces and used it as part of an optimised version of the attack algorithms of [16,19], whose time complexity can be significantly lowered with respect to previous iterations.

In general terms, the time complexity of a key recovery attack using the fast Walsh transform largely depends on three factors: the number of active bits in the plaintext/ciphertext, the number of active keybits, and the number of input bits to the key recovery map which combines the two to evaluate the linear approximation. Previous versions of the Walsh-based attack algorithm often ran into a bottleneck imposed by the latter, in the sense that any additional redundancy in the key or the data would not reduce the time complexity or only reduce it by a logarithmic factor. Our improved algorithm can effectively exploit the construction of the map. In the application examples, the number of independent active keybits becomes the bottleneck of the attack.

We have showcased the usability of this improved version of the algorithm by describing two attacks which are only possible (in the sense of having a smaller time complexity than exhaustive search) thanks to it. We have provided the best known attack on the DES with regards to data complexity as well as the first attack on 29-round PRESENT-128 in the literature.

Further Research. The first continuation to this work would be application to other ciphers. This technique might prove particularly useful in differential-linear cryptanalysis [3,23], as using the same key guess for both ciphertexts in a pair introduces a lot of redundancy. We also think that, since applying the framework to an attack is a fairly technically involved task, an automatic tool which computes an optimal key recovery algorithm given a linear distinguisher of a block cipher could be of great use to the community.

The results shown in this paper are most effective in the case of specific cipher constructions, such as ciphers which use a bit permutation as the linear layer, a case in which the Walsh spectrum can be described in a sufficient way. It would be of interest to try to generalise these results to other common constructions. In the applications, we also find that the attacks become limited by the number of active keybits. For this reason, another open question would be whether it is possible to adapt conditional guessing techniques such as [12] to Walsh transform-based linear key recovery attacks. A broader open problem would be to find interesting applications of pruned fast Walsh transform algorithms to other problems in symmetric cryptology.

Acknowledgements. This project has received funding from the European Research Council (ERC) under the European Union's Horizon 2020 research and innovation programme (grant agreement no. 714294 - acronym QUASYModo).

References

1. Data Encryption Standard (DES): Federal Information Processing Standards Publication 46–3, U.S. Department of Commerce, National Institute of Standards and Technology (1977, reaffirmed 1988 1993, 1999, withdrawn 2005)
2. Alves, R., Osorio, P., Swamy, M.: General FFT pruning algorithm. In: Proceedings of the 43rd IEEE Midwest Symposium on Circuits and Systems (Cat.No.CH37144), vol. 3, pp. 1192–1195 (2000)
3. Biham, E., Dunkelman, O., Keller, N.: Differential-linear cryptanalysis of serpent. In: Johansson, T. (ed.) FSE 2003. LNCS, vol. 2887, pp. 9–21. Springer, Heidelberg (2003). https://doi.org/10.1007/978-3-540-39887-5_2
4. Biham, E., Perle, S.: Conditional linear cryptanalysis - cryptanalysis of DES with less than 2^{42} complexity. IACR Trans. Symmetric Cryptol. **2018**(3), 215–264 (2018)
5. Biham, E., Shamir, A.: Differential cryptanalysis of the full 16-round DES. In: Brickell, E.F. (ed.) CRYPTO 1992. LNCS, vol. 740, pp. 487–496. Springer, Heidelberg (1993). https://doi.org/10.1007/3-540-48071-4_34
6. Biryukov, A., De Cannière, C., Quisquater, M.: On multiple linear approximations. In: Franklin, M. (ed.) CRYPTO 2004. LNCS, vol. 3152, pp. 1–22. Springer, Heidelberg (2004). https://doi.org/10.1007/978-3-540-28628-8_1
7. Blondeau, C., Nyberg, K.: Improved parameter estimates for correlation and capacity deviates in linear cryptanalysis. IACR Trans. Symmetric Cryptol. **2016**(2), 162–191 (2016)
8. Blondeau, C., Nyberg, K.: Joint data and key distribution of simple, multiple, and multidimensional linear cryptanalysis test statistic and its impact to data complexity. Des. Codes Cryptogr. **82**(1–2), 319–349 (2017)
9. Bogdanov, A., et al.: PRESENT: an ultra-lightweight block cipher. In: Paillier, P., Verbauwhede, I. (eds.) CHES 2007. LNCS, vol. 4727, pp. 450–466. Springer, Heidelberg (2007). https://doi.org/10.1007/978-3-540-74735-2_31

10. Bogdanov, A., Tischhauser, E., Vejre, P.S.: Multivariate profiling of hulls for linear cryptanalysis. IACR Trans. Symmetric Cryptol. **2018**(1), 101–125 (2018)
11. Bogdanov, A., Vejre, P.S.: Linear cryptanalysis of DES with asymmetries. In: Takagi, T., Peyrin, T. (eds.) ASIACRYPT 2017. LNCS, vol. 10624, pp. 187–216. Springer, Cham (2017). https://doi.org/10.1007/978-3-319-70694-8_7
12. Broll, M., Canale, F., Flórez-Gutiérrez, A., Leander, G., Naya-Plasencia, M.: Generic framework for key-guessing improvements. In: Tibouchi, M., Wang, H. (eds.) ASIACRYPT 2021. LNCS, vol. 13090, pp. 453–483. Springer, Cham (2021). https://doi.org/10.1007/978-3-030-92062-3_16
13. Carlet, C.: Boolean Functions for Cryptography and Coding Theory. Cambridge University Press, Cambridge (2021)
14. Castro-Palazuelos, D., Medina-Melendrez, M., Torres-Roman, D., Yuriy, S.: Unified commutation-pruning technique for efficient computation of composite DFTs. EURASIP J. Adv. Sig. Process. 11-2015 (2015)
15. Cho, J.Y.: Linear cryptanalysis of reduced-round PRESENT. In: Pieprzyk, J. (ed.) CT-RSA 2010. LNCS, vol. 5985, pp. 302–317. Springer, Heidelberg (2010). https://doi.org/10.1007/978-3-642-11925-5_21
16. Collard, B., Standaert, F.-X., Quisquater, J.-J.: Improving the time complexity of Matsui's linear cryptanalysis. In: Nam, K.-H., Rhee, G. (eds.) ICISC 2007. LNCS, vol. 4817, pp. 77–88. Springer, Heidelberg (2007). https://doi.org/10.1007/978-3-540-76788-6_7
17. Collard, B., Standaert, F.-X., Quisquater, J.-J.: Experiments on the multiple linear cryptanalysis of reduced round serpent. In: Nyberg, K. (ed.) FSE 2008. LNCS, vol. 5086, pp. 382–397. Springer, Heidelberg (2008). https://doi.org/10.1007/978-3-540-71039-4_24
18. Cooley, J., Tukey, J.: An algorithm for the machine calculation of complex Fourier series. Math. Comput. **19**, 297–301 (1965)
19. Flórez-Gutiérrez, A., Naya-Plasencia, M.: Improving key-recovery in linear attacks: application to 28-round PRESENT. In: Canteaut, A., Ishai, Y. (eds.) EUROCRYPT 2020. LNCS, vol. 12105, pp. 221–249. Springer, Cham (2020). https://doi.org/10.1007/978-3-030-45721-1_9
20. He, S., Torkelson, M.: Computing partial DFT for comb spectrum evaluation. IEEE Sig. Process. Lett. **3**(6), 173–175 (1996)
21. Hermelin, M., Cho, J.Y., Nyberg, K.: Multidimensional linear cryptanalysis. J. Cryptol. **32**(1), 1–34 (2019)
22. Hu, Z., Wan, H.: A novel generic fast Fourier transform pruning technique and complexity analysis. IEEE Trans. Sig. Process. **53**(1), 274–282 (2005)
23. Langford, S.K., Hellman, M.E.: Differential-linear cryptanalysis. In: Desmedt, Y.G. (ed.) CRYPTO 1994. LNCS, vol. 839, pp. 17–25. Springer, Heidelberg (1994). https://doi.org/10.1007/3-540-48658-5_3
24. Markel, J.: FFT pruning. IEEE Trans. Audio Electroacoust. (1971)
25. Matsui, M.: Linear cryptanalysis method for DES cipher. In: Helleseth, T. (ed.) EUROCRYPT 1993. LNCS, vol. 765, pp. 386–397. Springer, Heidelberg (1994). https://doi.org/10.1007/3-540-48285-7_33
26. Matsui, M.: The first experimental cryptanalysis of the data encryption standard. In: Desmedt, Y.G. (ed.) CRYPTO 1994. LNCS, vol. 839, pp. 1–11. Springer, Heidelberg (1994). https://doi.org/10.1007/3-540-48658-5_1
27. Nagai, K.: Pruning the decimation-in-time FFT algorithm with frequency shift. IEEE Trans. Acoust. Speech Sig. Process.' **34**(4), 1008–1010 (1986)
28. Selçuk, A.A.: On probability of success in linear and differential cryptanalysis. J. Cryptol. **21**(1), 131–147 (2008)

29. Singh, S., Srinivasan, S.: Architecturally efficient FFT pruning algorithm. Electron. Lett. **41**(23), 1–2 (2005)

30. Skinner, D.: Pruning the decimation in-time FFT algorithm. IEEE Trans. Acoust. Speech Sig. Process. **24**(2), 193–194 (1976)

31. Sorensen, H., Burrus, C.: Efficient computation of the DFT with only a subset of input or output points. IEEE Trans. Sig. Process. **41**(3), 1184–1200 (1993)

32. Sreenivas, T., Rao, P.: FFT algorithm for both input and output pruning. IEEE Trans. Acoust. Speech Sig. Process. **27**(3), 291–292 (1979)

33. Wang, L., Zhou, X., Sobelman, G.E., Liu, R.: Generic mixed-radix FFT pruning. IEEE Sig. Process. Lett. **19**(3), 167–170 (2012)

34. Zheng, L., Zhang, S.: FFT-based multidimensional linear attack on PRESENT using the 2-bit-fixed characteristic. Secur. Commun. Netw. **8**(18), 3535–3545 (2015)

Statistical Decoding 2.0: Reducing Decoding to LPN

Kévin Carrier[1]([✉]), Thomas Debris-Alazard[2], Charles Meyer-Hilfiger[3], and Jean-Pierre Tillich[3]

[1] ETIS Laboratory, CY Cergy-Paris University, Cergy-Pontoise, France
`kevin.carrier@ensea.fr`
[2] Project GRACE, Inria Saclay-Ile de France, Palaiseau, France
`thomas.debris@inria.fr`
[3] Project COSMIQ, Inria de Paris, Paris, France
`{charles.meyer-hilfiger,jean-pierre.tillich}@inria.fr`

Abstract. The security of code-based cryptography relies primarily on the hardness of generic decoding with linear codes. The best generic decoding algorithms are all improvements of an old algorithm due to Prange: they are known under the name of information set decoders (ISD). A while ago, a generic decoding algorithm which does not belong to this family was proposed: statistical decoding. It is a randomized algorithm that requires the computation of a large set of parity-checks of moderate weight, and uses some kind of majority voting on these equations to recover the error. This algorithm was long forgotten because even the best variants of it performed poorly when compared to the simplest ISD algorithm. We revisit this old algorithm by using parity-check equations in a more general way. Here the parity-checks are used to get LPN samples with a secret which is part of the error and the LPN noise is related to the weight of the parity-checks we produce. The corresponding LPN problem is then solved by standard Fourier techniques. By properly choosing the method of producing these low weight equations and the size of the LPN problem, we are able to outperform in this way significantly information set decoders at code rates smaller than 0.3. It gives for the first time after 60 years, a better decoding algorithm for a significant range which does not belong to the ISD family.

1 Introduction

1.1 The Decoding Problem and Code-based Cryptography

Code-based cryptography relies crucially on the hardness of decoding generic linear codes which can be expressed as follows in the binary case

Problem 1.1 (decoding a linear code). *Let $\mathscr{C}$ be a binary linear code over $\mathbb{F}_2$ of dimension k and length n, i.e. a subspace of $\mathbb{F}_2^n$ of dimension k. We are given $\mathbf{y} \in \mathbb{F}_2^n$, an integer t and want to find a codeword $\mathbf{c} \in \mathscr{C}$ and an error vector $\mathbf{e} \in \mathbb{F}_2^n$ of Hamming weight $|\mathbf{e}| = t$ for which $\mathbf{y} = \mathbf{c} + \mathbf{e}$.*

S. Agrawal and D. Lin (Eds.): ASIACRYPT 2022, LNCS 13794, pp. 477–507, 2022.
https://doi.org/10.1007/978-3-031-22972-5_17

This terminology stems from information theory, $\mathbf{y}$ is a noisy version of a codeword $\mathbf{c}$: $\mathbf{y} = \mathbf{c} + \mathbf{e}$ where $\mathbf{e}$ is a vector of weight t and we want to recover the original codeword $\mathbf{c}$. It can also be viewed as solving an underdetermined linear system with a weight constraint. Indeed, we can associate to a subspace $\mathscr{C}$ of dimension k of $\mathbb{F}_2^n$ a binary $(n-k) \times n$ matrix $\mathbf{H}$ (also called a *parity-check* matrix of the code) whose kernel defines $\mathscr{C}$, namely $\mathscr{C} = \{\mathbf{x} \in \mathbb{F}_2^n : \mathbf{H}\mathbf{x}^\mathsf{T} = \mathbf{0}\}$. The decoding problem is equivalent to find an $\mathbf{e}$ of Hamming weight t such that $\mathbf{H}\mathbf{e}^\mathsf{T} = \mathbf{s}^\mathsf{T}$ where $\mathbf{s}$ is the *syndrome* of $\mathbf{y}$ with respect to $\mathbf{H}$, *i.e.* $\mathbf{s}^\mathsf{T} = \mathbf{H}\mathbf{y}^\mathsf{T}$. This can be verified by observing that if there exists $\mathbf{c} \in \mathscr{C}$ and $\mathbf{e}$ such that $\mathbf{y} = \mathbf{c} + \mathbf{e}$ then $\mathbf{H}\mathbf{y}^\mathsf{T} = \mathbf{H}(\mathbf{c}+\mathbf{e})^\mathsf{T} = \mathbf{H}\mathbf{c}^\mathsf{T} + \mathbf{H}\mathbf{e}^\mathsf{T} = \mathbf{H}\mathbf{e}^\mathsf{T}$.

The decoding problem has been studied for a long time and despite many efforts on this issue [2–4,12,14,19,20,24,26] the best algorithms [3,5,6,20] are exponential in the number of errors that have to be corrected: correcting t errors in a binary linear code of length n with the aforementioned algorithms has a cost of $2^{\alpha n(1+o(1))}$ where $\alpha = \alpha(R, \tau)$ is a constant depending of the code rate $R \overset{\triangle}{=} \frac{k}{n}$, the error rate $\tau \overset{\triangle}{=} \frac{t}{n}$ and the algorithm which is used. All the efforts that have been spent on this problem have only managed to decrease slightly this exponent α. Let us emphasize that this exponent is the key for estimating the security level of any code-based cryptosystem. We expect that this problem is the hardest at the Gilbert-Varshamov relative distance $\tau = \delta_{\mathrm{GV}}$ where $\delta_{\mathrm{GV}} \overset{\triangle}{=} h^{-1}(1-R)$, with h being the binary entropy function $h(x) \overset{\triangle}{=} -x\log_2 x - (1-x)\log_2(1-x)$ and $h^{-1}(x)$ its inverse ranging over $[0, \frac{1}{2}]$. This corresponds in the case of random linear codes to the largest relative weight below which there is typically just one solution of the decoding problem assuming that there is one. Above this bound, the number of solutions becomes exponential (at least as long as $\tau < 1-\delta_{\mathrm{GV}}$) and this helps to devise more efficient decoders. Furthermore, all the aforementioned algorithms become polynomial in the regime $\frac{1-R}{2} \le \tau \le \frac{1+R}{2}$ (see an illustration of this behavior in Fig. 1).

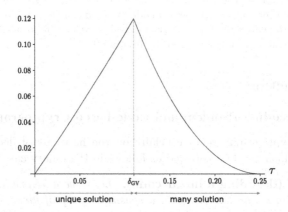

Fig. 1. Complexity exponent α of the Prange ISD algorithm [24] as a function of the error ratio $\tau \overset{\triangle}{=} \frac{t}{n}$ at rate $R = \frac{1}{2}$. The peak corresponds to the normalized Gilbert-Varshamov distance $\delta_{\mathrm{GV}} = h^{-1}(1-R)$.

There are code-based cryptographic primitives whose security relies precisely on the difficulty of decoding at the Gilbert-Varshamov relative distance (something which is also called *full distance decoding* [5,6,20]), for instance the Stern code-based identification schemes or associated signatures schemes [1,13,16,27]. In the light of the upcoming NIST second call for new quantum resistant signature algorithms, it is even more important to have a stable and precise assessment of what we may expect about the complexity of solving this problem. For much smaller distances, say sub-linear, which is relevant for cryptosystems like [21,22], the situation seems much more stable/well understood, since the complexity exponent of all the above-mentioned algorithms is the same in this regime [7].

1.2   ISD Algorithms and Beyond: Statistical Decoding

All the aforementioned algorithms can be viewed as a refinement of the original Prange algorithm [24] and are actually all referred to as Information Set Decoding (ISD) algorithms. Basically, they all use a common principle, namely making the bet that in a certain set of about k positions (the "information set") there are only very few errors and using this bet to speed-up decoding. The parameters of virtually all code-based cryptographic algorithms (for the Hamming metric) have been chosen according to the running time of this family of algorithms. Apart from these algorithms, there is one algorithm which is worth mentioning, namely statistical decoding. It was first proposed by Al Jabri in [17] and improved a little bit by Overbeck in [23]. Later on, [15] proposed an iterative version of this algorithm.

It is essentially a two-stage algorithm, the first step consisting in computing an exponentially large number of parity-check equations of the smallest possible weight w, and then from these parity-check equations the error is recovered by some kind of majority voting based on these equations. This majority voting is based on the following principle, take a parity-check equation $\mathbf{h}$ for the code $\mathscr{C}$ we want to decode, *i.e.* a binary vector $\mathbf{h} = (h_i)_{1 \leq i \leq n}$ such that $\langle \mathbf{h}, \mathbf{c} \rangle = 0$ for every $\mathbf{c}$ in $\mathscr{C}$. Assume that the i-th bit of the parity-check is 1, then since $\langle \mathbf{h}, \mathbf{y} \rangle = \langle \mathbf{h}, \mathbf{e} \rangle = e_i + \sum_{j \neq i} h_j e_j$, the i-th bit e_i of the error $\mathbf{e}$ we want to recover satisfies

$$e_i + \sum_{j \neq i} h_j e_j = \langle \mathbf{h}, \mathbf{y} \rangle . \tag{1.1}$$

The sum $\sum_{j \neq i} h_j e_j$ is biased, say it is equal to 1 with probability $\frac{1-\varepsilon}{2}$ with a bias ε which is (essentially) a decreasing function of the weight w of the parity-check $\mathbf{h}$. This allows to recover e_i with about $\Theta\left(1/\varepsilon^2\right)$ parity-checks. However the bias is exponentially small in the minimum weight of $\mathbf{h}$ and $\mathbf{e}$ and the complexity of such an algorithm is exponential in the codelength. An asymptotic analysis of this algorithm was performed in [9] and it turns out that even if we had a way to obtain freely the parity-check equations we need, this kind of algorithm could not even outperform the simplest ISD algorithm: the Prange algorithm. This is done in [9] by showing that there is no loss in generality if we just care about getting the best exponent to restrict ourselves to a single parity-check weight w

(see Sect. 5 in [9]) and then analyse the complexity of such a putative algorithm for a single weight by using the knowledge of the typical number of parity-check equations of a given weight in a random linear code. The complexity exponent we get is a lower bound on the complexity of statistical decoding. We call such a putative statistical decoding algorithm, *genie-aided statistical decoding*: we are assisted by a genie which gives for free all the parity-check equations we require (but of course we can only get as much parity-check equations of some weight w as there exists in the code we want to decode). The analysis of the exponent we obtain with such genie-aided statistical decoding is given in [9, §7] and shows that it is outperformed very significantly by the Prange algorithm (see [9, §7.2]).

1.3   Contributions

In this work, we modify statistical decoding so that each parity-check yields now an LPN sample which is a noisy linear combination involving part of the error vector. This improves significantly statistical decoding, since the new decoding algorithm outperforms significantly all ISD's for code rates smaller than 0.3. It gives for the first time after 60 years, a better decoding algorithm that does not belong to the ISD family, and this for a very significant range of rates. The only other example where ISD algorithms have been beaten was in 1986, when Dumer introduced his collision technique. This improved the Prange decoder only for rates in the interval $[0.98, 1]$ and interestingly enough it gave birth to all the modern improvements of ISD algorithms starting from Stern's algorithm [26].

A New Approach: Using Parity-Checks to Reduce Decoding to LPN. Our approach for solving the decoding problem reduces it to the so-called Learning Parity with Noise Problem (LPN).

Problem 1.2 (LPN). *Let $\mathcal{O}_{\mathbf{s},\tau}(\cdot)$ be an oracle parametrized by $\mathbf{s} \in \mathbb{F}_2^s$ and $\tau \in [0, 1]$ such that on a call it outputs $(\mathbf{a}, \langle \mathbf{s}, \mathbf{a} \rangle + e)$ where $\mathbf{a} \in \mathbb{F}_2^s$ is uniformly distributed and e is distributed according to a Bernoulli of parameter τ. We have access to $\mathcal{O}_{\mathbf{s},\tau}(\cdot)$ and want to find $\mathbf{s}$.*

(1.1) can be interpreted as an LPN sample with an $\mathbf{s}$ of size 1, namely e_i. However, if instead of splitting the support of the parity-check with one bit on one side and the other ones on the other side, but choose say s positions on the first part (say the s first ones) and $n - s$ on the other, we can write

$$\langle \mathbf{h}, \mathbf{y} \rangle = \underbrace{\sum_{i=1}^{s} h_i e_i}_{\text{linear comb.}} + \underbrace{\sum_{j>s} h_j e_j}_{\text{LPN noise}} .$$

We may interpret such a scalar product as an LPN sample where the secret is $(e_1, \cdots, e_s)$; *i.e.* we have a noisy information on a linear combination $\sum_{i=1}^{s} h_i e_i$ on the s first bits of the error where the noise is given by the term $\sum_{j>s} h_j e_j$

and the information is of the form $\sum_{i=1}^{s} h_i e_i + \text{noise} = \langle \mathbf{h}, \mathbf{y} \rangle$. Again the second linear combination is biased, say $\mathbb{P}\left(\sum_{j>s} h_j e_j = 1\right) = \frac{1-\varepsilon}{2}$ and information theoretic arguments show that again $\Theta\left(1/\varepsilon^2\right)$ samples are enough to determine $(e_1, \cdots, e_s)$. It seemed that we gained nothing here since we still need as many samples as before and it seems that now recovering $(e_1, \cdots, e_s)$ is much more complicated than performing majority voting.

However with this new approach, we just need parity-check equations of low weight on $n - s$ positions (those that determine the LPN noise) whereas in statistical decoding algorithm we have to compute parity-check equations of low weight on $n - 1$ positions. This brings us to the main advantage of our new method: the parity-checks we produce have much lower weight on those $n - s$ positions than those we produce for statistical decoding. This implies that the bias ε in the LPN noise is much bigger with the new method and the number $N = \Theta\left(1/\varepsilon^2\right)$ of parity-check equations much lower. Secondly, by using the fast Fourier transform, we can recover $(e_1, \cdots, e_s)$ in time $O\left(s2^s\right)$. Therefore, as long as the number of parity-checks we need is of order $\Omega\left(2^s\right)$, there is no exponential extra cost of having to recover $(e_1, \cdots, e_s)$. This new approach will be called from now on *Reduction to LPN* decoding (RLPN).

Subset Sum Techniques and Bet on the Error Distribution. As just outlined, our RLPN decoder needs an exponential number $N = \Theta\left(1/\varepsilon^2\right)$ of parity-checks of small weight on $n - s$ positions. This can be achieved efficiently by using collision/subset techniques used in the inner loop of ISD's. Recall that all ISD's proceed in two steps, (i) first they pick an augmented information set and (ii) then have an inner loop computing low weight codewords of some sort. Step (ii) uses advanced techniques to solve subset-sum problems like birthday paradox [10,12], Wagner algorithm [28] or representations techniques [3,19]. All these techniques can also be used in a natural way in our RLPN decoder to compute the low weight parity-checks we need.

Furthermore, another idea of ISD's can be used in our RLPN decoder. All ISD's are making, in a fundamental way, a bet on the error weight distribution in several zones related to the information set picked up in (i). There are two zones: the potentially augmented information set and the rest of the positions. ISD algorithms assume that the (augmented) information set contains only very few errors. A similar bet can be made in our case. We have two different zones: on one hand the s positions determining s error bits and on the other $n - s$ bits which determine the LPN noise. It is clearly favorable to have an error ratio which is smaller on the second part. The probability that this unlikely event happens is largely outweighed by the gain in the bias of the LPN noise.

Our Results. Using all the aforementioned ingredients results in dramatically improving statistical decoding (see Fig. 2), especially in the low rate regime ($R \leq \frac{1}{2}$) where ISD algorithms are known to perform slightly worse than in the high rate regime ($R > \frac{1}{2}$). Indeed, the complexity exponent $\alpha(R) \stackrel{\triangle}{=} \alpha(R, \delta_{\text{GV}}(R))$ of

ISD's for full decoding (*a.k.a.* the GV bound decoding) which could be expected to be symmetric in R is actually bigger in the low rate regime than in the high rate regime: $\alpha(R) > \alpha(1 - R)$ for $0 < R < \frac{1}{2}$. This results in an exponent curve which is slightly tilted towards the left, the maximum exponent being always obtained for $R < \frac{1}{2}$. Even worse, the behavior for very small rates (*i.e.* $R \to 0^+$) is fundamentally different in the very high rate regime ($R \to 1^-$). The complexity curve behaves like $\alpha(R) \approx R$ in the first case and like $\alpha(R) \approx \frac{1-R}{2}$ in the second (at least for all later improvements of the Prange decoder incorporating collision techniques). This behavior at 0 for full distance decoding has never been changed by *any* decoder. It should be noted that $\alpha(R) = R(1+o(1))$ around 0 means that the complexity behaves like $2^{\alpha(R)n} = 2^{R(1+o(1))n} = 2^{k(1+o(1))}$, so in essence ISD's are not performing really better than trivial enumeration on all codewords. This fundamental barrier is still unbroken by our RLPN decoder, but it turns out that $\alpha(R)$ approaches R much more slowly with RLPN. For instance, for $R = 0.02$ we have $\alpha(R) \approx \frac{R}{2}$. This behavior in the very low regime is instrumental for the improvement we obtain on ISD's. In essence, this improvement is due in this regime to the conjunction of RLPN decoding with a collision search of low weight parity-checks. This method can be viewed as the dual (*i.e.* operating on the dual code) of the collision search performed in advanced ISD's which are successful for lowering the complexity exponent down to $\alpha(R) \approx \frac{1-R}{2}$ in the high rate regime. In some sense, the RLPN strategy allows us to *dualize* advanced ISD techniques for working in the low rate regime.

All in all, using [3] (one of the most advanced ISD techniques) to compute low weight codewords of some shape we are able to outperform significantly even the latest improvements of ISD algorithms for code rates R smaller than 0.3 as shown in Fig. 2. This is a breakthrough in this area, given the dominant role that ISD algorithms have played during all those years for assessing the complexity of decoding a linear code. Note however that the correctness of this algorithm relies on the LPN error model (Assumption 3.7) for which some recent experiments have found out not to be completely accurate (see https://github.com/tillich/RLPNdecoding/tree/master/verification_heuristic/histogram). However, experimental results seem to indicate that this LPN modeling can be replaced by the weaker Conjecture 3.11 which is compatible with the experiments we have made and for which there is a clear path to demonstrate its validity (see Subsect. 3.4).

Proving the Standard Assumption of Statistical Decoding. In analyzing the new decoding algorithm, we also put statistical decoding on a much more rigorous foundation. We show that the basic condition that has to be met for both statistical decoding and RLPN decoding, namely that the number N of parity-check equations that are available is at least of order $\Omega\left(1/\varepsilon^2\right)$ in the case of statistical decoding and $\Omega\left(s/\varepsilon^2\right)$ in the case of RLPN decoding where ε is the bias of the LPN noise, is also essentially the condition which ensures that the bias is well approximated by the standard assumption made for statistical decoding which assumes that

$$\mathrm{bias}\left(\langle \mathbf{e}_{\mathscr{N}}, \mathbf{h}_{\mathscr{N}} \rangle\right) \approx \mathrm{bias}\left(\langle \mathbf{e}_{\mathscr{N}}, \mathbf{h}'_{\mathscr{N}} \rangle\right), \tag{1.2}$$

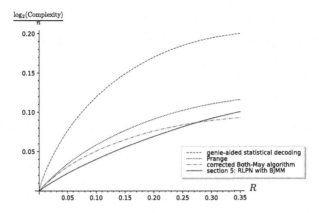

Fig. 2. Complexity exponent for full distance decoding of genie-aided statistical decoding [9, §7] (recall that this is a *lower bound* on the complexity exponent of statistical decoding), the basic Prange ISD algorithm [24], the best state-of-the-art algorithm of [6] (with a correction in the exponent, see the full version of this paper [8, Ap. B]) and our RLPN decoder as a function of R.

where bias(X) is defined for a binary random variable as bias$(X) \overset{\triangle}{=} \mathbb{P}(X = 0) - \mathbb{P}(X = 1)$, $\mathcal{N}$ is a subset of $n - s$ positions (those which are involved in the LPN noise), $\mathbf{h}$ is chosen uniformly at random among the parity-checks of weight w on $\mathcal{N}$ of the code $\mathscr{C}$ we decode whereas $\mathbf{h}'$ is chosen uniformly at random among the words of weight w on $\mathcal{N}$. We will namely prove that as soon as the parameters are chosen such that $N = \omega \left(1/\text{bias} \left(\langle \mathbf{e}_{\mathcal{N}}, \mathbf{h}'_{\mathcal{N}} \rangle \right)^2 \right)$, we have that for all but a proportion $o(1)$ of codes $\mathscr{C}$ (as proved in Proposition 3.1 in Subsect. 3.1): bias$\left(\langle \mathbf{e}_{\mathcal{N}}, \mathbf{h}_{\mathcal{N}} \rangle \right) = (1 + o(1))\text{bias} \left(\langle \mathbf{e}_{\mathcal{N}}, \mathbf{h}'_{\mathcal{N}} \rangle \right)$.

2   Notation and Coding Theory Background

Vectors and Matrices. Vectors and matrices are respectively denoted in bold letters and bold capital letters such as $\mathbf{a}$ and $\mathbf{A}$. The entry at index i of the vector $\mathbf{x}$ is denoted by x_i. The canonical scalar product $\sum_{i=1}^{n} x_i y_i$ between two vectors $\mathbf{x}$ and $\mathbf{y}$ of $\mathbb{F}_2^n$ is denoted by $\langle \mathbf{x}, \mathbf{y} \rangle$. Let $\mathscr{I}$ be a list of indexes. We denote by $\mathbf{x}_{\mathscr{I}}$ the vector $(x_i)_{i \in \mathscr{I}}$. In the same way, we denote by $\mathbf{A}_{\mathscr{I}}$ the sub-matrix made of the columns of $\mathbf{A}$ which are indexed by $\mathscr{I}$. The concatenation of two vectors $\mathbf{x}$ and $\mathbf{y}$ is denoted by $\mathbf{x}||\mathbf{y}$. The Hamming weight of a vector $\mathbf{x} \in \mathbb{F}_2^n$ is defined as the number of its non-zero coordinates, namely $|\mathbf{x}| \overset{\triangle}{=} \# \{i \in [\![1, n]\!] : x_i \neq 0\}$ where $\#\mathscr{A}$ stands for the cardinality of a finite set $\mathscr{A}$ and $[\![a, b]\!]$ stands for the set of the integers between a and b.

Probabilistic Notation. For a finite set $\mathcal{S}$, we write $X \xleftarrow{\$} \mathcal{S}$ when X is an element of $\mathcal{S}$ drawn uniformly at random in it. For a Bernoulli random variable X, denote by bias(X) the quantity bias$(X) \overset{\triangle}{=} \mathbb{P}(X = 0) - \mathbb{P}(X = 1)$. For a Bernoulli random variable X of parameter $p = \frac{1-\varepsilon}{2}$, i.e. $\mathbb{P}(X = 1) = \frac{1-\varepsilon}{2}$, we have bias$(X) = \varepsilon$.

Soft-O Notation. For real valued functions defined over $\mathbb{R}$ or $\mathbb{N}$ we define $o()$, $O\,()$, $\Omega\,()$, $\Theta\,()$, in the usual way and also use the less common notation $\widetilde{O}\,()$ and $\widetilde{\Omega}\,()$, where $f = \widetilde{O}\,(g)$ means that $f(x) = O\left(g(x)\log^k g(x)\right)$ and $f = \widetilde{\Omega}\,(g)$ means that $f(x) = \Omega\left(g(x)\log^k g(x)\right)$ for some k. We will use this for functions which have an exponential behavior, say $g(x) = e^{\alpha x}$, in which case $f(x) = \widetilde{O}\,(g(x))$ means that $f(x) = O\,(P(x)g(x))$ where P is a polynomial in x. We also use $f = \omega(g)$ when f dominates g asymptotically; that is when $\lim\limits_{x \to \infty} \frac{|f(x)|}{g(x)} = \infty$.

Coding Theory. A binary linear code $\mathscr{C}$ of length n and dimension k is a subspace of the vector space $\mathbb{F}_2^n$ of dimension k. We say that it has parameters $[n, k]$ or that it is an $[n, k]$-code. Its *rate* R is defined as $R \overset{\triangle}{=} \frac{k}{n}$. A generator matrix $\mathbf{G}$ for $\mathscr{C}$ is a full rank $k \times n$ matrix over $\mathbb{F}_2$ such that $\mathscr{C} = \{\mathbf{uG} : \mathbf{u} \in \mathbb{F}_2^k\}$. In other words, the rows of $\mathbf{G}$ form a basis of $\mathscr{C}$. A parity-check matrix $\mathbf{H}$ for $\mathscr{C}$ is a full-rank $(n - k) \times n$ matrix over $\mathbb{F}_2$ such that $\mathscr{C} = \{\mathbf{c} \in \mathbb{F}_2^n : \mathbf{Hc^{\mathsf{T}}} = \mathbf{0}\}$. In other words, $\mathscr{C}$ is the null space of $\mathbf{H}$. The code whose generator matrix is the parity-check matrix of $\mathscr{C}$ is called the dual code of $\mathscr{C}$. It might be seen as the subspace of parity-checks of $\mathscr{C}$ and is defined equivalently as

Definition 2.1 (dual code). *The* dual code $\mathscr{C}^{\perp}$ *of an* $[n, k]$-code $\mathscr{C}$ *is an* $[n, n - k]$-code which is defined by $\mathscr{C}^{\perp} \overset{\triangle}{=} \{\mathbf{h} \in \mathbb{F}_2^n : \forall \mathbf{c} \in \mathscr{C},\ \langle \mathbf{c}, \mathbf{h} \rangle = 0\}$.

It will also be very convenient to consider the operation of puncturing a code, *i.e.* keeping only a subset of entries in a codeword.

Definition 2.2 (punctured code). *For a code $\mathscr{C}$ and a subset $\mathscr{I}$ of code positions, we denote by $\mathscr{C}_{\mathscr{I}}$ the punctured code obtained from $\mathscr{C}$ by keeping only the positions in $\mathscr{I}$, i.e. $\mathscr{C}_{\mathscr{I}} = \{\mathbf{c}_{\mathscr{I}} : \mathbf{c} \in \mathscr{C}\}$.*

We will also use several times that random binary linear codes can be decoded successfully, with a probability of error going to 0, as the codelength goes to infinity as long as the code rate is below the capacity, and this of any binary input symmetric channel whose definition is

Definition 2.3 (binary input memoryless symmetric channel). *A binary input memoryless symmetric channel (BIMS) with output a finite alphabet $\mathscr{Y}$, is an error model on $\{0,1\}^*$ assuming that when a bit $b \in \{0,1\}$ is sent, it gets mapped to $y \in \mathscr{Y}$ with probability denoted by $p(y|b)$ (these are the transition probabilities of the channel). Being symmetric means that there is an involution f such that $p(y|0) = p(f(y)|1)$. Being memoryless means that the outputs of the channel are independent conditioned on the inputs: when $b_1 \cdots b_n \in \{0,1\}^n$ is sent, the probability that the output is $y_1 \cdots y_n$ is given by $p(y_1|b_1) \cdots p(y_n|b_n)$.*

We use here this rather general formulation to analyze what is going on when we have several different LPN samples corresponding to the same parity-check **h**. The error model that we have in this case will be more complicated than the standard binary symmetric channel (see Definition 2.6 below). The capacity of such a channel is given by

Definition 2.4 (capacity of a BIMS channel). *The capacity[1] C of a BIMS channel with transition probabilities $(p(y|b))_{\substack{y \in \mathscr{Y} \\ b \in \{0,1\}}}$ is given by*

$$C \triangleq \sum_{y \in \mathscr{Y}} \sum_{b \in \{0,1\}} \frac{p(y|b)}{2} \log_2 \frac{p(y|b)}{\frac{1}{2}p(y|0) + \frac{1}{2}p(y|1)}.$$

LPN samples correspond to the binary symmetric channel (BSC) given by

Definition 2.5 (binary symmetric channel). *BSC(p) is a BIMS channel with output alphabet $\mathscr{Y} = \{0,1\}$ and transition probabilities $p(0|0) = p(1|1) = 1 - p$, $p(1|0) = p(0|1) = p$, where p is the crossover probability of the channel.*

In other words, this means that a bit b is transformed into its opposite $1 - b$ with probability p when sent through the channel. It is readily verified that

Definition 2.6 (binary symmetric channel). *The capacity C of BSC(p) is given by $C = 1 - h(p)$.*

We will also talk about maximum likelihood decoding a code (under the assumption that the input codeword is chosen uniformly at random) for a given channel, meaning the following

Definition 2.7 (maximum likelihood decoding). *Maximum likelihood decoding of a binary code $\mathscr{C} \subset \{0,1\}^n$ over a BIMS channel with transitions probabilities $(p(y|b))_{\substack{y \in \mathscr{Y} \\ b \in \{0,1\}}}$ corresponds, given a received word $\mathbf{y} \in \mathscr{Y}^n$, to output the (or one of them if there are several equally likely candidates) codeword $\mathbf{x}$ which maximizes $p(\mathbf{y}|\mathbf{x})$. Here $p(\mathbf{y}|\mathbf{x}) \triangleq p(y_i|x_i) \cdots p(y_n|x_n)$ denotes the probability of receiving $\mathbf{y}$ given that $\mathbf{x}$ was sent.*

In a sense, this is the best possible decoding algorithm for a given channel model. There is a variation of Shannon's theorem (see for instance [25, Th. 4.68 p. 203]) which says that a family of random binary linear codes $(\mathscr{C}_n)_n$ attain the capacity of a BIMS channel.

Theorem 2.8. *Consider a BIMS channel of capacity C. Let $\delta > 0$ and consider a family of random binary linear codes $\mathscr{C}_n$ of length n and rate smaller than $(1 - \delta)C$ obtained by choosing their generator matrix uniformly at random. Then under maximum likelihood decoding, the probability of error after decoding goes to 0 as n tends to infinity.*

---

[1] The formula given here is strictly speaking the symmetric capacity of a channel, but these two notions coincide in the case of a BIMS channel.

3   Reduction to LPN and the Associated Algorithm

The purpose of this section is (i) to explain in detail the reduction to LPN, (ii) to give a high level description of the algorithm which does not specify the method for finding the dual codewords we need, and then (iii) to give its complexity. We assume from now on that we are given $\mathbf{y}$ which is equal to a sum of a codeword $\mathbf{c}$ of the code $\mathscr{C}$ we want to decode plus an error vector $\mathbf{e}$ of Hamming weight t:

$$\mathbf{y} = \mathbf{c} + \mathbf{e}, \quad \mathbf{c} \in \mathscr{C}, \quad |\mathbf{e}| = t.$$

We will start this section by explaining how we reduce decoding to an LPN problem and also show how the LPN noise can be estimated accurately.

3.1   Reduction to LPN

Recall that in RLPN decoding we first randomly select a subset $\mathscr{P}$ of s positions

$$\mathscr{P} \subseteq [\![1, n]\!] \quad \text{such that} \quad \#\mathscr{P} = s$$

where s is a parameter that will be chosen later. $\mathscr{P}$ corresponds to the entries of $\mathbf{e}$ we aim to recover and is the secret in the LPN problem. We denote by $\mathscr{N} \overset{\triangle}{=} [\![1, n]\!] \setminus \mathscr{P}$ the complementary set, with a choice of the letter $\mathscr{N}$ standing for "noise" for reasons that will be clear soon. Given $\mathbf{h} \in \mathscr{C}^\perp$, we compute,

$$\langle \mathbf{y}, \mathbf{h} \rangle = \langle \mathbf{e}, \mathbf{h} \rangle = \sum_{j \in \mathscr{P}} h_j e_j + \sum_{j \in \mathscr{N}} h_j e_j = \langle \mathbf{e}_\mathscr{P}, \mathbf{h}_\mathscr{P} \rangle + \langle \mathbf{e}_\mathscr{N}, \mathbf{h}_\mathscr{N} \rangle$$

It gives access to the following LPN sample:

$$(\mathbf{a}, \langle \mathbf{s}, \mathbf{a} \rangle + e) \quad \text{where} \quad \mathbf{s} \overset{\triangle}{=} \mathbf{e}_\mathscr{P}, \ \mathbf{a} \overset{\triangle}{=} \mathbf{h}_\mathscr{P} \ \text{and} \ e \overset{\triangle}{=} \langle \mathbf{e}_\mathscr{N}, \mathbf{h}_\mathscr{N} \rangle.$$

Here e follows a Bernoulli distribution that is a function of n, s and u (*resp.* w) the weight of $\mathbf{e}$ (*resp.* $\mathbf{h}$) restricted to $\mathscr{N}$, namely

$$u \overset{\triangle}{=} |\mathbf{e}_\mathscr{N}| \quad \text{and} \quad w \overset{\triangle}{=} |\mathbf{h}_\mathscr{N}|.$$

The probability that e is equal to 1 is estimated through the following proposition which gives for the first time a rigorous statement for the standard assumption (1.2) made for statistical decoding.

Proposition 3.1. *Assume that the code $\mathscr{C}$ is chosen by picking for it an $(n - k) \times n$ binary parity-check matrix uniformly at random. Let $\mathscr{N}$ be a fixed set of $n - s$ positions in $[\![1, n]\!]$ and $\mathbf{e}$ be some error of weight u on $\mathscr{N}$. Choose $\mathbf{h}$ uniformly at random among the parity-checks of $\mathscr{C}$ of weight w on $\mathscr{N}$ and $\mathbf{h}'$ uniformly at random among the words of weight w on $\mathscr{N}$. Let $\delta \overset{\triangle}{=} \mathrm{bias}\left(\langle \mathbf{e}, \mathbf{h}' \rangle\right)$. If the parameters k, s, u, w are chosen as functions on n so that for n going to infinity, the expected number N of parity-checks of $\mathscr{C}$ of weight w on $\mathscr{N}$ satisfies $N = \omega\left(1/\delta^2\right)$ then for all but a proportion $o(1)$ of codes we have*

$$\mathrm{bias}\left(\langle \mathbf{e}_\mathscr{N}, \mathbf{h}_\mathscr{N} \rangle\right) = (1 + o(1))\delta.$$

Proof. Let us define for $b \in \{0,1\}$:

$$E_b \overset{\triangle}{=} \#\{\mathbf{h} \in \mathscr{C}^{\perp} : |\mathbf{h}_{\mathscr{N}}| = w, \langle \mathbf{e}_{\mathscr{N}}, \mathbf{h}_{\mathscr{N}} \rangle = b\} \qquad (3.1)$$

$$E'_b \overset{\triangle}{=} \#\{\mathbf{h}' \in \mathbb{F}_2^n : |\mathbf{h}'_{\mathscr{N}}| = w, \langle \mathbf{e}_{\mathscr{N}}, \mathbf{h}'_{\mathscr{N}} \rangle = b\} \qquad (3.2)$$

By using [2, Lemma 1.1 p.10][2], we obtain

$$\mathbb{E}(E_b) = \frac{E'_b}{2^k} \quad \text{and} \quad \mathbf{Var}(E_b) \le \frac{E'_b}{2^k}.$$

By using now the Bienaymé-Tchebychev inequality, we obtain for any function f mapping the positive integers to positive real numbers:

$$\mathbb{P}_{\mathscr{C}}\left(|E_b - \mathbb{E}(E_b)| \ge \sqrt{f(n)\mathbb{E}(E_b)}\right) \le \frac{1}{f(n)}. \qquad (3.3)$$

Since bias $(\langle \mathbf{e}_{\mathscr{N}}, \mathbf{h}_{\mathscr{N}} \rangle) = \frac{E_0 - E_1}{E_0 + E_1}$ we have with probability greater than $1 - \frac{2}{f(n)}$

$$\frac{\mu_0 - \mu_1 - \sqrt{2f(n)}\sqrt{\mu_0 + \mu_1}}{\mu_0 + \mu_1 + \sqrt{2f(n)}\sqrt{\mu_0 + \mu_1}} \le \text{bias}(\langle \mathbf{e}_{\mathscr{N}}, \mathbf{h}_{\mathscr{N}} \rangle) \le \frac{\mu_0 - \mu_1 + \sqrt{2f(n)}\sqrt{\mu_0 + \mu_1}}{\mu_0 + \mu_1 - \sqrt{2f(n)}\sqrt{\mu_0 + \mu_1}} \qquad (3.4)$$

where $\mu_i \overset{\triangle}{=} \mathbb{E}(E_i)$ and where we used that for all positive x and y, $\sqrt{x} + \sqrt{y} \le \sqrt{2(x+y)}$. We let $f(n) = \delta\sqrt{N}/2$. Since $N = \mu_0 + \mu_1$ this implies $f(n) = \delta\sqrt{\mu_0 + \mu_1}/2$. By the assumptions made in the proposition, note that $f(n)$ tends to infinity as n tends to infinity. We notice that

$$\sqrt{2f(n)}\sqrt{\mu_0 + \mu_1} = \delta^{1/2}(\mu_0 + \mu_1)^{3/4} = o\left(\delta(\mu_0 + \mu_1)\right) \qquad (3.5)$$

because

$$\frac{\delta^{1/2}(\mu_0 + \mu_1)^{3/4}}{\delta(\mu_0 + \mu_1)} = \frac{1}{\sqrt{\delta\sqrt{\mu_0 + \mu_1}}} = \frac{1}{\sqrt{2f(n)}} \to 0 \text{ as } n \to \infty.$$

Equation (3.4) can now be rewritten as

$$\frac{\mu_0 - \mu_1 - o\left(\delta(\mu_0 + \mu_1)\right)}{\mu_0 + \mu_1 + o\left(\delta(\mu_0 + \mu_1)\right)} \le \text{bias}(\langle \mathbf{e}_{\mathscr{N}}, \mathbf{h}_{\mathscr{N}} \rangle) \le \frac{\mu_0 - \mu_1 + o\left(\delta(\mu_0 + \mu_1)\right)}{\mu_0 + \mu_1 - o\left(\delta(\mu_0 + \mu_1)\right)} \qquad (3.6)$$

Now, on the other hand

$$\delta = \text{bias}(\langle \mathbf{e}_{\mathscr{N}}, \mathbf{h}'_{\mathscr{N}} \rangle) = \frac{E'_0 - E'_1}{E'_0 + E'_1} = \frac{\frac{E'_0}{2^k} - \frac{E'_1}{2^k}}{\frac{E'_0}{2^k} + \frac{E'_1}{2^k}} = \frac{\mu_0 - \mu_1}{\mu_0 + \mu_1} \quad \text{(by (3.1))}.$$

From this it follows that we can rewrite (3.6) as

$$\frac{\delta}{1 + o(\delta)} - o(\delta) \le \text{bias}(\langle \mathbf{e}_{\mathscr{N}}, \mathbf{h}_{\mathscr{N}} \rangle) \le \frac{\delta}{1 - o(\delta)} + o(\delta) \qquad (3.7)$$

from which it follows immediately that bias $(\langle \mathbf{e}_{\mathscr{N}}, \mathbf{h}_{\mathscr{N}} \rangle) = \delta(1 + o(1))$. $\qquad \square$

---

[2] Note that there is an additional condition "Suppose Lq^{-r} grows exponentially in n" in the statement of this lemma, but it is readily seen that this condition is neither necessary nor used in the proof.

Remark 3.2. Note that the condition $N = \Omega\left(1/\delta^2\right)$, respectively $N = \Omega\left(s/\delta^2\right)$ is the condition we need in order that statistical decoding, respectively RLPN decoding succeed. This means that if we just have slightly more equations than the ratio $\frac{1}{\delta^2}$, then the standard assumption (1.2) made for statistical decoding holds. The point of this assumption is that it allows easily to estimate the bias as the following lemma shows.

Lemma 3.3. *Under the same assumptions made in Proposition 3.1, we have that for all but a proportion $o(1)$ of codes,*

$$\mathrm{bias}(\langle \mathbf{e}_{\mathcal{N}}, \mathbf{h}_{\mathcal{N}} \rangle) = \delta(1 + o(1)) \quad \text{with} \quad \delta \triangleq \frac{K_w^{n-s}(u)}{\binom{n-s}{w}}$$

where $u \triangleq |\mathbf{e}_{\mathcal{N}}|$ and K_w^n stands for the Krawtchouk polynomial of order n and degree $w \in [\![0, n]\!]$ which is defined as:

$$K_w^n(X) \triangleq \sum_{j=0}^{w} (-1)^j \binom{X}{j}\binom{n-X}{w-j}.$$

Proof. By using Proposition 3.1 (and the same notation as the one used there) we have that for all but a proportion $o(1)$ of codes $\mathrm{bias}(\langle \mathbf{e}_{\mathcal{N}}, \mathbf{h}_{\mathcal{N}} \rangle) = (1 + o(1))\mathrm{bias}\left(\langle \mathbf{e}_{\mathcal{N}}, \mathbf{h}'_{\mathcal{N}} \rangle\right)$. Now by definition of u, we have

$$\mathrm{bias}\left(\langle \mathbf{e}_{\mathcal{N}}, \mathbf{h}'_{\mathcal{N}} \rangle\right) = \frac{1}{\binom{n-s}{w}} \sum_{j \text{ even}} \binom{u}{j}\binom{n-s-u}{w-j} - \frac{1}{\binom{n-s}{w}} \sum_{j \text{ odd}} \binom{u}{j}\binom{n-s-u}{w-j}$$

$$= \frac{1}{\binom{n-s}{w}} \sum_{j} (-1)^j \binom{u}{j}\binom{n-s-u}{w-j}$$

$$= \frac{K_w^{n-s}(u)}{\binom{n-s}{w}}.$$

$\square$

We will now repeatedly denote by *bias* of the LPN sample the quantity ε appearing in the previous lemma and the *estimated bias* the quantity namely

Definition 3.4 (bias of the LPN samples). *The* bias ε *of the LPN samples is defined by*

$$\varepsilon \triangleq \mathrm{bias}(\langle \mathbf{e}_{\mathcal{N}}, \mathbf{h}_{\mathcal{N}} \rangle)$$

when $\mathbf{e}_{\mathcal{N}}$ has Hamming weight u and $\mathbf{h}$ is drawn uniformly at random among the parity-check equations of weight w restricted on $\mathcal{N}$. The estimated bias is the quantity δ defined by

$$\delta \triangleq \mathrm{bias}(\langle \mathbf{e}_{\mathcal{N}}, \mathbf{h}'_{\mathcal{N}} \rangle)$$

when $\mathbf{e}_{\mathcal{N}}$ has Hamming weight u and $\mathbf{h}'$ is drawn uniformly at random among the binary words of weight w restricted on $\mathcal{N}$. This quantity is equal to

$$\delta = \frac{K_w^{n-s}(u)}{\binom{n-s}{w}}.$$

The point of introducing Krawtchouk polynomials is that we can bring in asymptotic expansions of Krawtchouk polynomials. Most of the relevant properties we need about Krawtchouk polynomials are given in [18, §II.B]. They can be summarized by

Proposition 3.5. *1. Value at 0. For all $0 \leq w \leq n$, $K_w^n(0) = \binom{n}{w}$.*
2. Reciprocity. For all $0 \leq t, w \leq n$, $\binom{n}{t}K_w^n(t) = \binom{n}{w}K_t^n(w)$.
3. Roots. The polynomials K_w^n have w distinct roots which lie in the interval

$$[\![n/2 - \sqrt{w(n-w)}, n/2 + \sqrt{w(n-w)}]\!].$$

The distance between roots is at least 2 and at most $o(n)$.

4. Magnitude outside the root region. *We set $\tau \triangleq \frac{t}{n}$, $\omega \triangleq \frac{w}{n}$. We assume $w \leq n/2$ and $t \leq n/2 - \sqrt{w(n-w)}$. Let $z \triangleq \frac{1-2\tau-\sqrt{D}}{2(1-\omega)}$ where $D \triangleq (1-2\tau)^2 - 4\omega(1-\omega)$. We have*

$$K_w^n(t) = 2^{n(\tau \log_2(1-z) + (1-\tau)\log_2(1+z) - \omega \log_2 z + o(1))}. \tag{3.8}$$

5. Magnitude in the root region. Between any two consecutive roots of K_w^n, where $1 \leq w \leq \frac{n}{2}$, there exists t such that:

$$K_w^n(t) = 2^{n\left(\frac{1+h(\omega)-h(\tau)}{2}+o(1)\right)} \quad \text{where } \omega \triangleq \frac{w}{n} \text{ and } \tau \triangleq \frac{t}{n}. \tag{3.9}$$

By using this proposition, we readily obtain

Proposition 3.6 (exponential behavior of δ^2). *Let τ and ω be two reals in the interval $\left[0, \frac{1}{2}\right]$. Let $\omega^\perp \triangleq \frac{1}{2} - \sqrt{\omega(1-\omega)}$ and $z \triangleq \frac{1-2\tau-\sqrt{D}}{2(1-\omega)}$ where $D \triangleq (1-2\tau)^2 - 4\omega(1-\omega)$. There exists a sequence of positive integers $(t_n)_{n\in\mathbb{N}}$ and $(w_n)_{n\in\mathbb{N}}$, such that $\frac{t_n}{n} \underset{n\to\infty}{\longrightarrow} \tau$, $\frac{w_n}{n} \underset{n\to\infty}{\longrightarrow} \omega$ and $\frac{\log_2(K_{w_n}^n(t_n)^2/\binom{n}{w_n}^2)}{n}$ has a limit which we denote $\tilde{\delta}(\tau, \omega)$ with*

$$\tilde{\delta}(\tau, \omega) = \begin{cases} 2\left(\tau \log_2(1-z) + (1-\tau)\log_2(1+z) - \omega \log_2 z - h(\omega)\right) & \text{if } \tau \in [0, \omega^\perp] \\ 1 - h(\tau) - h(\omega) & \text{otherwise.} \end{cases}$$

Proof. In the case $\tau \in [0, \omega^\perp]$ we just let $t_n = \lceil \tau n \rceil$, $w_n = \lceil \omega n \rceil$ and use directly the asymptotic expansion (3.8). In the case $\tau \in \left[\omega^\perp, \frac{1}{2}\right]$ we still define w_n with $w_n \triangleq \lceil \omega n \rceil$ but define t_n differently. For n large enough, we know from Proposition 3.5 that $\lceil \tau n \rceil$ lies between two zeros of the Krawtchouk polynomial and that there exists an integer t_n in this interval such that $\frac{\log_2(K_{w_n}^n(t_n))}{n} = \frac{1+h(\omega)-h(\tau_n)}{2} + o(1)$ where $\tau_n = \frac{t_n}{n}$. Now since the size of this interval is an $o(n)$ we necessarily have $\tau_n = \tau + o(1)$ and therefore $\frac{\log_2(K_{w_n}^n(t_n))}{n} = \frac{1+h(\omega)-h(\tau)}{2} + o(1)$. $\quad\square$

The point of this proposition is that the term $2\log_2(K_w^{n-s}(u)/\binom{n-s}{w})$ quantifies the exponential behaviour of the square ε^2 of the bias ε (see Lemma 3.3) and $1/\varepsilon^2$ is up to polynomial terms the number of parity-checks we need for having enough information to solve the LPN problem as will be seen. This is because the capacity of the BSC($\frac{1-\varepsilon}{2}$) is $1 - h\left(\frac{1-\varepsilon}{2}\right) = \theta(\varepsilon^2)$ and that solving an LPN-problem with a secret of size s and N samples amounts to be able to decode a random linear code of rate $\frac{s}{N}$ over the BSC($\frac{1-\varepsilon}{2}$). It is therefore doable as soon as the rate is below the capacity (see Theorem 2.8). The reason why the Shannon capacity appears here is because of the following heuristic/assumption we will make here:

Assumption 3.7 (LPN modelling). *We will assume that the $\langle \mathbf{e}_\mathcal{N}, \mathbf{h}_\mathcal{N} \rangle$ are i.i.d Bernoulli random variables of parameter $\frac{1-\varepsilon}{2}$.*

Strictly speaking, the corresponding random variables are not independent. However, note that similar heuristics are also used to analyze a related lattice decoder making use of short dual lattice vectors (they are called dual attacks in the literature). We will discuss this assumption in more depth in Subsect. 3.4. Assumption 3.7 models the LPN noise as a binary symmetric channel BSC($\frac{1-\varepsilon}{2}$) of crossover probability $\frac{1-\varepsilon}{2}$. A straightforward application of Theorem 2.8 together with the fact that the capacity of a binary symmetric BSC($\frac{1-\varepsilon}{2}$) is $1 - h\left(\frac{1-\varepsilon}{2}\right) = \Omega(\varepsilon^2)$ implies

Fact 3.8. *With Assumption 3.7, the number N of LPN samples is such that $s/N = O(\varepsilon^2)$ for a small enough constant in the O, performing maximum-likelihood decoding of the corresponding $[N, s]$ binary code recovers the secret $\mathbf{e}_\mathcal{P}$ with probability $1 - o(1)$.*

Performing maximum likelihood decoding of the corresponding code can be achieved by a fast Fourier transform on a relevant vector. Indeed, for a given received word $\mathbf{y}$ and a set $\mathcal{H}$ of N parity-checks so that their restriction to $\mathcal{P}$ leads to a set $\mathcal{H}$ of N different vectors of $\mathbb{F}_2^s$, we let for $\mathbf{a} \in \mathcal{H}$, $\widetilde{\mathbf{a}}$ be the unique parity-check in $\widetilde{\mathcal{H}}$ such that $\widetilde{\mathbf{a}}_\mathcal{P} = \mathbf{a}$ and define $f_{\mathbf{y},\mathcal{H}}$ as

$$f_{\mathbf{y},\mathcal{H}} : \mathbf{a} \in \mathbb{F}_2^s \mapsto \begin{cases} (-1)^{\langle \mathbf{y}, \widetilde{\mathbf{a}} \rangle} & \text{if } \mathbf{a} \in \mathcal{H} \\ 0 & \text{otherwise} \end{cases} \tag{3.10}$$

We   define
the Fourier transform of such a function by $\widehat{f}(\mathbf{x}) \triangleq \sum_{\mathbf{u} \in \mathbb{F}_2^s} f(\mathbf{u})(-1)^{\langle \mathbf{x}, \mathbf{u} \rangle}$. The code $\mathcal{D}$ we want to decode (obtained via our LPN samples) is described as

$$\mathcal{D} \triangleq \{\mathbf{c_x}, \ \mathbf{x} \in \mathbb{F}_2^s\} \text{ where } \mathbf{c_x} \triangleq (\langle \mathbf{x}, \mathbf{a} \rangle)_{\mathbf{a} \in \mathcal{H}}, \tag{3.11}$$

and the word $\mathbf{u}_{\mathbf{y},\mathcal{H}}$ we want to decode is given by $\mathbf{u}_{\mathbf{y},\mathcal{H}} = (\langle \mathbf{y}, \widetilde{\mathbf{a}} \rangle)_{\mathbf{a} \in \mathcal{H}}$. It is readily seen that

$$\widehat{f_{\mathbf{y},\mathcal{H}}}(\mathbf{x}) = \sum_{\mathbf{a} \in \mathbb{F}_2^s} f(\mathbf{a})(-1)^{\langle \mathbf{x}, \mathbf{a} \rangle} = \sum_{\mathbf{a} \in \mathcal{H}} (-1)^{\langle \mathbf{x}, \mathbf{a} \rangle + \langle \mathbf{y}, \widetilde{\mathbf{a}} \rangle} = \#\mathcal{H} - 2|\mathbf{u}_{\mathbf{y},\mathcal{H}} - \mathbf{c_x}|.$$

In other words, finding the closest codeword to $\mathbf{u}_{\mathbf{y},\mathcal{H}}$ is nothing but finding the $\mathbf{x}$ which maximizes $\widehat{f_{\mathbf{y},\mathcal{H}}}(\mathbf{x})$. This is achieved in time $O\left(s2^s\right)$ by performing a fast Fourier transform. Notice that an exhaustive search would cost $O\left(2^{2s}\right)$.

3.2   Sketch of the Whole Algorithm

Algorithm 3.1. RLPN decoder

Input: $\mathbf{y}$, t, $\mathscr{C}$ an $[n, k]$-code
Output: $\mathbf{e}$ such that $|\mathbf{e}| = t$ and $\mathbf{y} - \mathbf{e} \in \mathscr{C}$.
function RLPNDECODE($\mathbf{y}$, $\mathscr{C}$, t)
$\quad s, u \leftarrow$ OPTIM(t, k, n)
$\qquad\qquad$ ▷ s and u in order to minimize the complexity of the following procedure.
$\quad$**for** i from 1 to N_{iter} **do** $\qquad\qquad$ ▷ N_{iter} is a certain function of n, s, t and u.
$\qquad \mathscr{P} \xleftarrow{\$} \{\mathscr{I} \subseteq [\![1, n]\!] \ : \ \#\mathscr{I} = s\}$
$\qquad \mathscr{N} \leftarrow [\![1, n]\!] \setminus \mathscr{P}$
$\qquad \mathscr{H} \leftarrow$ CREATE($N, w, \mathscr{P}$)
$\qquad \widehat{f_{\mathbf{y}, \mathscr{H}}} \leftarrow$ FFT($f_{\mathbf{y}, \mathscr{H}}$)
$\qquad \mathbf{x}_0 \leftarrow \arg\max \widehat{f_{\mathbf{y}, \mathscr{H}}}$
$\qquad$**if** $\widehat{f_{\mathbf{y}, \mathscr{H}}}(\mathbf{x}_0) \geq \frac{\delta N}{2}$ **then** $\qquad\qquad$ ▷ $\delta \overset{\triangle}{=} K_w^{n-s}(u)/\binom{n-s}{w}$.
$\qquad\quad|\quad$**return** $\mathbf{e}$ such that $\mathbf{e}_{\mathscr{P}} = \mathbf{x}_0$ and $\mathbf{e}_{\mathscr{N}} =$ RLPNDECODE($\mathbf{y}_{\mathscr{N}}, \mathscr{C}_{\mathscr{N}}, t - |\mathbf{x}_0|$))
$\qquad$**end if**
$\quad$**end for**
end function

Besides, the fast Fourier transform solving the LPN problem, Algorithm 3.1 uses two other ingredients:

- A routine CREATE($N, w, \mathscr{P}$) creating a set $\mathscr{H}$ of N parity-check equations $\mathbf{h}$ such that $|\mathbf{h}_{\mathscr{N}}| = w$ where $\mathscr{N} \overset{\triangle}{=} [\![1, n]\!] \setminus \mathscr{P}$. We will not specify how this function is realized here: this is done in the following sections. This procedure together with an FFT for decoding the code associated to the parity-check equations in $\mathscr{H}$ (see Eq. (3.11)) form the inner loop of our algorithm.
- An outer loop making a certain number N_{iter} of calls to the inner procedure, checking each time a new set $\mathscr{P}$ of s positions with the hope of finding an $\mathscr{N}$ containing an unusually low number u of errors in it. The point is that with a right u, the number of times we will have to check a new $\mathscr{P}$ is outweighed by the decrease in N because the bias δ is much higher for such a u.

3.3   Analysis of the RLPN Decoder

We need to show now that our RLPN decoder returns what we expect. It is what the following proposition shows (a proof can be found in the full paper [8]).

Proposition 3.9 (acceptation criteria). *Under Assumption 3.7, by choosing* $N_{\text{iter}} = \omega\left(\frac{1}{P_{succ}}\right)$ *(where P_{succ} is the probability over the choice of $\mathscr{N}$ that there are exactly u errors in $\mathscr{N}$), $s = \omega(1)$ and $N = \omega\left(\frac{n}{\delta^2}\right)$, we have with probability* $1 - o(1)$ *that at least one iteration is such that $\mathbf{e}_{\mathscr{P}}$ meets the acceptation criteria*

$\widehat{f_{\mathbf{y},\mathscr{H}}}(\mathbf{e}_{\mathscr{P}}) \geq \frac{\delta N}{2}$. *Moreover, the probability that there exists* $\mathbf{x} \neq \mathbf{e}_{\mathscr{P}}$ *which meets this acceptation criteria is* $o(1)$.

The space and time complexity of this method are given by

Proposition 3.10. *Assume that* CREATE$(N, w, \mathscr{P})$ *produces* N *parity-check equations in space* S_{eq} *and time* T_{eq}. *The probability* P_{succ} *(over the choice of* $\mathscr{N}$) *that there are exactly* u *errors in* $\mathscr{N}$ *is given by* $P_{succ} = \frac{\binom{s}{t-u}\binom{n-s}{u}}{\binom{n}{t}}$. *The space complexity* S *and the time complexity* T *of the RLPN-decoder are given by*

$$\textbf{Space}: \ S = O\left(S_{eq} + 2^s\right), \quad \textbf{Time}: \ T = \tilde{O}\left(\frac{T_{eq} + 2^s}{P_{succ}}\right).$$

The parameters s, u *and* w *have to meet the following constraints*

$$N \leq 2^s \tag{3.12}$$

$$N \leq \frac{\binom{n-s}{w}}{2^{k-s}}. \tag{3.13}$$

Under Assumption 3.7 the algorithm outputs the correct $\mathbf{e}_{\mathscr{P}}$ *with probability* $1 - o(1)$ *if in addition we choose* N *and* N_{iter} *such that*

$$N = \omega\left(n\left(\frac{\binom{n-s}{w}}{K_w^{n-s}(u)}\right)^2\right) \tag{3.14}$$

$$N_{iter} = \omega\left(\frac{1}{P_{succ}}\right). \tag{3.15}$$

Proof. All the points are straightforward here, with the exception of the constraints. The first constraint is that the number of parity-checks should not be bigger than the total number of different LPN samples we can possibly produce. The second one is that the number of parity-checks needed is smaller than the number of available parity-checks. The conditions ensuring the correctness of the algorithm follow immediately from Proposition 3.9. □

3.4   On the Validity of Assumption 3.7

The proof of the correctness of the algorithm relies on the validity of the LPN modelling (Assumption 3.7). We have programmed this algorithm and have verified that for several parameters it gives the correct answer. The corresponding experiments with the programs that have been used for running them can be found on https://github.com/tillich/RLPNdecoding. However, we have also found out (see https://github.com/tillich/RLPNdecoding/tree/master/ verification_heuristic/histogram) that the second largest Fourier coefficient (the one which corresponds to the second nearest codeword, besides $\mathbf{e}_{\mathscr{P}}$) does not behave in the same way in the LPN model as in practice with the noise given by the $\langle \mathbf{h}_{\mathscr{N}}, \mathbf{e}_{\mathscr{N}} \rangle$'s. This can be traced back to the fact that $\langle \mathbf{h}_{\mathscr{N}}, \mathbf{e}_{\mathscr{N}} \rangle$ and $\langle \mathbf{h}'_{\mathscr{N}}, \mathbf{e}_{\mathscr{N}} \rangle$

are positively correlated when $\mathbf{h}_{\mathcal{N}}$ and $\mathbf{h}'_{\mathcal{N}}$ are close to each other in Hamming distance. Actually these correlations have an effect on the tails of the largest Fourier coefficients as demonstrated in Fig. 3 which display longer tails corresponding to the largest Fourier coefficients in the case of a noise produced by $\langle \mathbf{h}_{\mathcal{N}}, \mathbf{e}_{\mathcal{N}} \rangle$'s (called parity-checks in the figure) instead of Fourier coefficients produced by decoding a code with a $\mathrm{BSC}(\frac{1-\varepsilon}{2})$ noise (called BSC in the figure). This phenomenon vanishes when k gets larger as can be verified in Fig. 3 or on https://github.com/tillich/ RLPNdecoding/tree/master/verification_heuristic/histogram. From our experiments (see more details on https://github.com/tillich/RLPNdecoding) this phenomenon is not severe enough to prevent Algorithm 3.1 from working but needs some adjustments about how larger N has to be in terms of $\frac{1}{\delta^2}$. This experimental evidence leads us to conjecture

Conjecture 3.11. Algorithm 3.1 is successful if we replace in Proposition 3.10 the condition $N = \omega \left(n \left(\frac{\binom{n-s}{w}}{K_w^{n-s}(u)} \right)^2 \right)$ by the slightly stronger condition $N = \omega \left(n^\alpha \left(\frac{\binom{n-s}{w}}{K_w^{n-s}(u)} \right)^2 \right)$ for a certain $\alpha \geq 1$.

If this conjecture is true, then obviously the asymptotic exponent of the complexity is unchanged if we replace Assumption 3.7 by Conjecture 3.11. A semi-heuristic way to verify this conjecture could be to proceed as follows

1. Let W be the weight of the vector $\left(\left\langle \widetilde{\mathbf{h}}_{\mathcal{N}}, \mathbf{e}_{\mathcal{N}} \right\rangle \right)_{\mathbf{h} \in \mathcal{H}}$. Compute $\mathbf{Var}(W)$ and prove that $\mathbf{Var}(W)$ is of order $O\left(n^\beta N\right)$ where β is some constant.
2. Use this computation to bound heuristically the tails of the Fourier coefficients and use this computation of $\mathbf{Var}(W)$ to give an estimation for the second largest Fourier coefficient when decoding the $[N, s]$-code which agrees with the experimental evidence.
3. Use this to prove that the second largest Fourier coefficient is typically far away enough from the first one to prove the validity of Conjecture 3.11.

4   Collision Techniques for Finding Low Weight Parity-Checks

4.1   Using the [10] Method

A way for creating parity-checks with a low weight on $\mathcal{N}$ is simply to use subset-sum/collision techniques [10,11,26]. We start here with the simplest method for performing such a task pioneered by Dumer in [10]. Consider a parity-check matrix $\mathbf{H}$ for the code $\mathscr{C}$ we want to decode and keep only the columns belonging to $\mathcal{N}$ to obtain an $(n-k) \times (n-s)$ matrix $\mathbf{H}_{\mathcal{N}}$. The row-space of $\mathbf{H}_{\mathcal{N}}$ generates the restrictions $\mathbf{h}_{\mathcal{N}}$ to $\mathcal{N}$ of the parity-checks $\mathbf{h}$ of $\mathscr{C}$. This row-space is nothing but the dual code $\mathscr{C}^\perp$ punctured in $\mathscr{P}$, i.e. we keep only the positions in $\mathcal{N}$.

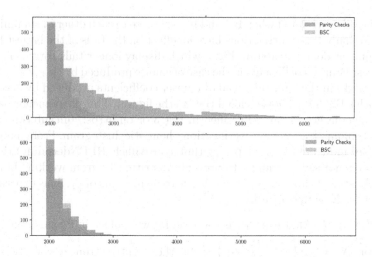

Fig. 3. Tails of the largest Fourier coefficients when decoding the $[N, s]$-code either with the noise produced by the $\langle \mathbf{h}_{\mathcal{N}}, \mathbf{e}_{\mathcal{N}} \rangle$'s or by the ideal LPN noise model (the $\mathrm{BSC}(\frac{1-\varepsilon}{2})$ noise model). Both figures correspond to parity-checks $\mathbf{h}_{\mathcal{N}}$ of weight 6 and to $s = 19$. However they differ in the value for k. k equals 26 in the first figure and displays rather heavy tails for the largest Fourier coefficients corresponding to the parity-checks $\mathbf{h}_{\mathcal{N}}$ whereas $k = 40$ corresponds to rather similar tails in both cases. This is a general trend that can be verified on https://github.com/tillich/RLPNdecoding/tree/master/ verification_heuristic/histogram, when k gets larger, the heavy tail phenomenon vanishes.

With our notation, this is $\mathscr{C}_{\mathcal{N}}^{\perp}$ and is an $[n - s, n - k]$-code. Therefore if we want to find parity-checks $\mathbf{h}$ of $\mathscr{C}$ such that $|\mathbf{h}_{\mathcal{N}}| = w$, this amounts to find codewords of $\mathscr{C}_{\mathcal{N}}^{\perp}$ of weight w. For this, we compute a parity-check matrix $\mathbf{H}'$ of $\mathscr{C}_{\mathcal{N}}^{\perp}$ *i.e.* a $(k - s) \times (n - s)$ matrix such that $\mathscr{C}_{\mathcal{N}}^{\perp} = \{\mathbf{c} \in \mathbb{F}_2^{n-s} : \mathbf{H}'\mathbf{c}^{\mathsf{T}} = 0\}$. We split such a matrix in two parts randomly chosen and of the same size $\mathbf{H}' = (\mathbf{H}_1\ \mathbf{H}_2)$. We obtain an algorithm of time and space complexity, T and S respectively, producing N codewords of weight w, with $N = \dfrac{\left(\frac{n-s}{2}\right)^2}{2^{k-s}}(1 + o(1))$ and S = T $= O\left(\left(\frac{\frac{n-s}{2}}{\frac{w}{2}}\right) + N\right)$. The algorithm for producing such codewords is to set up two lists,

$$\mathscr{L}_1 \stackrel{\triangle}{=} \left\{(\mathbf{H}_1\mathbf{h}_1^{\mathsf{T}}, \mathbf{h}_1) : |\mathbf{h}_1| = \frac{w}{2}\right\} \quad \text{and} \quad \mathscr{L}_2 \stackrel{\triangle}{=} \left\{(\mathbf{H}_2\mathbf{h}_2^{\mathsf{T}}, \mathbf{h}_2) : |\mathbf{h}_2| = \frac{w}{2}\right\}$$

and looking for collisions $\mathbf{H}_1\mathbf{h}_1^{\mathsf{T}} = \mathbf{H}_2\mathbf{h}_2^{\mathsf{T}}$ in the lists. It yields vectors $\mathbf{h}' = \mathbf{h}_1 \| \mathbf{h}_2$ of weight w which are in $\mathscr{C}_{\mathcal{N}}^{\perp}$ since $\mathbf{H}'\mathbf{h}'^{\mathsf{T}} = \mathbf{H}_1\mathbf{h}_1^{\mathsf{T}} + \mathbf{H}_2\mathbf{h}_2^{\mathsf{T}} = 0$. These vectors in $\mathbb{F}_2^{n-s}$ can be completed to give vectors $\mathbf{h} \in \mathbb{F}_2^n$ such that $\mathbf{h}_{\mathcal{N}} = \mathbf{h}'$. The number of collisions is expected to be of order $\left(\frac{\frac{n-s}{2}}{\frac{w}{2}}\right)^2 / 2^{k-s}$ since $2^{-(k-s)}$ is the collision probability of two vectors in $\mathbb{F}_2^{k-s}$. The algorithm for performing this task is given by Algorithm 4.1.

Algorithm 4.1. Creating low weight parity-checks by collisions

Input $\mathscr{C}$, w, $\mathscr{P}$

Output a list of parity-check equations **h** of $\mathscr{C}$ such that $|\mathbf{h}_{\mathscr{N}}| = w$ where $\mathscr{N} \triangleq [\![1, n]\!] \setminus \mathscr{P}$.

function CREATE($\mathscr{C}$, w, $\mathscr{P}$)

$\quad$ **H** $\leftarrow$ PARITY-CHECK-MATRIX($\mathscr{C}^{\perp}$, $\mathscr{P}$)

$\qquad$ ▷ returns a parity-check matrix for $\mathscr{C}^{\perp}$ with an identity corresponding to

$\quad$ the positions in $\mathscr{P}$: $\mathbf{H} = \begin{pmatrix} \mathbf{I} & \mathbf{P} \\ \mathbf{0} & \mathbf{H}' \end{pmatrix}$ where we assume that the first block corresponds

$\quad$ to the positions of $\mathscr{P}$.

$\quad \mathscr{L}_1 \leftarrow \{ (\mathbf{H}_1 \mathbf{h}_1^{\mathsf{T}}, \mathbf{h}_1) : |\mathbf{h}_1| = w/2, \mathbf{h}_1 \in \mathbb{F}_2^{\frac{n-s}{2}} \}$

$\quad \mathscr{L}_2 \leftarrow \{ (\mathbf{H}_2 \mathbf{h}_2^{\mathsf{T}}, \mathbf{h}_2) : |\mathbf{h}_2| = w/2, \mathbf{h}_2 \in \mathbb{F}_2^{\frac{n-s}{2}} \}$

$\qquad$ ▷ We assume $\mathbf{H}' = (\mathbf{H}_1 \ \mathbf{H}_2)$, with $\mathbf{H}_1$ and $\mathbf{H}_2$ of the same size.

$\quad \mathscr{L} \leftarrow \{ \mathbf{h}_1 || \mathbf{h}_2 \in \mathscr{L}_1 \times \mathscr{L}_2 : \mathbf{H}_1 \mathbf{h}_1^{\mathsf{T}} = \mathbf{H}_2 \mathbf{h}_2^{\mathsf{T}} \}$

$\quad$ **return** $\{ \mathbf{h}' \mathbf{P}^{\mathsf{T}} || \mathbf{h}' : \mathbf{h}' \in \mathscr{L} \}$

$\qquad$ ▷ It is straightforward to check that $\mathbf{h}' \mathbf{P}^{\mathsf{T}} || \mathbf{h}'$ belongs to $\mathscr{C}^{\perp}$.

end function

We have represented in Fig. 4 the form of the parity-checks output by this method, together with the bet we make on the error.

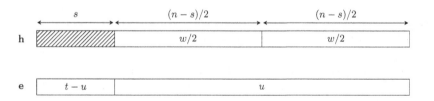

Fig. 4. The form of the parity-checks produced by this method, *vs.* the bet made on the error. The hatched rectangle of size s for **h** indicates that the weight is arbitrary on this part.

The amortized cost for producing a parity-check equation of weight w is $O(1)$ as long as $N \geq \Omega \left(\binom{\frac{n-s}{2}}{\frac{w}{2}} \right)$. It is insightful to consider the smallest value of w for which $\binom{\frac{n-s}{2}}{\frac{w}{2}} \leq \binom{\frac{n-s}{2}}{\frac{w}{2}}^2 / 2^{k-s}$. This is roughly speaking the smallest value (up to negligible terms) of w for which the amortized cost for producing parity-check equations of weight w is $O(1)$ per equation. In such a case, we roughly have $N \approx \binom{\frac{n-s}{2}}{\frac{w}{2}} \approx \frac{\binom{\frac{n-s}{2}}{\frac{w}{2}}^2}{2^{k-s}} \approx 2^{k-s}$. In other words with this choice we have $T_{\text{eq}} = O\left(2^{k-s}\right)$. Let us choose now u as the "typical error weight" when restricted to $\mathscr{N}$, namely $u \approx t\frac{n-s}{n}$ and s such that the decoding complexity of the $[N, s]$-code is also of order the codelength, *i.e.* $N = \widetilde{\Theta}\left(2^s\right)$. This would imply $2^s \approx 2^{k-s}$, which means that we are going to choose $s = \frac{k}{2}$. By using Proposition 3.10, all these choices would yield a time complexity $\mathrm{T}_{\mathrm{Dumer86}}$ for decoding $\mathscr{C}$ which would be of order

$$\mathrm{T}_{\mathrm{Dumer86}} = \widetilde{O}\left(2^{k/2}\right), \tag{4.1}$$

if the constraint $N = \widetilde{\Omega}\left(\left(\frac{\binom{n-s}{w}}{K_w^{n-s}(u)}\right)^2\right)$ for successful decoding the $[N, s]$-code is

met. This amounts to $2^{Rn/2} = \widetilde{\Omega}\left(\left(\frac{\binom{n(1-R/2)}{w}}{K_w^{n(1-R/2)}(t(1-R/2))}\right)^2\right)$, where R is the code

rate, $i.e.$ $R = \frac{k}{n}$. By using Proposition 3.1, we can give an asymptotic formula for this constraint. It translates into $R/2 \geq 2(1 - R/2)\,\widetilde{\delta}\,(\tau, \omega/(1 - R/2))$, where $\widetilde{\delta}$ is the function defined in Proposition 3.6. Amazingly enough this constraint is met up to very small values of R, it is only below $R \approx 0.02$ that this condition is not met anymore. This innocent looking remark has actually very concrete consequences. This means that above the range $R \gtrsim 0.02$ the asymptotic complexity exponent, $i.e.$ $\alpha_{\mathrm{Dumer86}} \triangleq \limsup_n \log_2 \mathrm{T}_{\mathrm{Dumer86}}/n$ where $\mathrm{T}_{\mathrm{Dumer86}}$ is the time complexity, satisfies

$$\alpha_{\mathrm{Dumer86}} \leq \frac{R}{2}. \tag{4.2}$$

This is very surprising, since in the vicinity of $R \approx 0$ the asymptotic time complexity of *all known* decoding methods approach quickly R. In other words, in this regime, the complexity is of order $\mathrm{T} \approx 2^{Rn} = 2^k$ for full distance (*a.k.a.* GV) decoding, meaning that they are not better than exhaustive search. Unfortunately this is also the case for our method. It can namely be proved that even by optimizing on the value of s, w and u we can not do better than this with our method, since $\alpha_{\mathrm{Dumer86}}(R) \sim R$ as R approaches 0. However, as can be guessed from the fact that $\alpha_{\mathrm{Dumer86}} \leq \frac{R}{2}$ for $R \gtrsim 0.02$, the behaviour of the complexity is much better for our RLPN decoder. This can be verified in Fig. 5.

It is worthwhile to recall that ISD algorithms in the regime of the rate *close to* 1 precisely use this collision method to find low weight codewords in order to reduce significantly the complexity of decoding. In a sense, we have a dual version of the birthday/collision decoder of [10] with reduced complexity for rates close to 0.

4.2   Improving [10] by Puncturing as in [11]

There is a simple way of improving the generation of dual codewords of low weight on $\mathscr{N}$. It consists in partitioning $\mathscr{N}$ in two sets $\mathscr{N}_1$ and $\mathscr{N}_2$ with $\mathscr{N}_2$ being a subset of positions of size just a little bit above $n - k$ (which is the dimension of the dual code $\mathscr{C}^{\perp}$), say $n - k + \ell$ and then to use the collision method to get dual codewords of weight w_2 on $\mathscr{N}_2$. The same method is used in the improvement

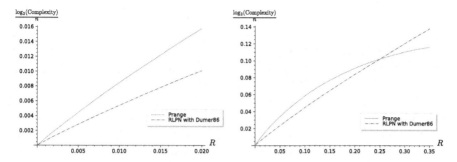

Fig. 5. The complexity of the RLPN-decoder for very small rates *vs.* the simplest information set decoder, namely the ISD Prange decoder [24]. For small R, there is no much difference between the ISD Prange decoder and much more evolved decoders like [3,5,6,20]. The RLPN-decoder with the very simple [10] technique performs much better for small rates than ISD decoders. It is only outperformed by the Prange decoder for rates above 0.25 approximately.

[11] of the simple collision decoder [10] or in a slightly less efficient way in [26]. It just consists in finding codewords in $\mathscr{C}^{\perp}$ which have weight w_1 on $\mathcal{N}_1$ and w_2 on $\mathcal{N}_2$ instead of simply weight w on $\mathcal{N}$. We have represented in Fig. 6 the form of the parity-checks we produce with this method. Note that the weight w_1 is expected to be half the size $k - \ell - s$ of $\mathcal{N}_1$.

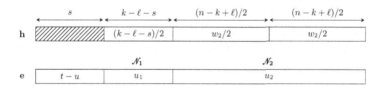

Fig. 6. The form of the parity-checks produced by this method, *vs.* the bet made on the error. The hatched rectangle of size s for **h** indicates that the weight is arbitrary on this part.

To understand the bias we get in this case, the proof of Proposition 3.1 can be readily adapted to yield

Proposition 4.1. *Assume that the code $\mathscr{C}$ is chosen by picking for it an $(n - k) \times n$ binary parity-check matrix uniformly at random. Let $\mathcal{N}$ be a fixed set of $n-s$ positions in $[\![1,n]\!]$ which is partitioned in two sets $\mathcal{N}_1$ and $\mathcal{N}_2$ and $\mathbf{e}$ be some error of weight u_i on $\mathcal{N}_i$ for $i \in \{1,2\}$. For $i \in \{1,2\}$, choose $\mathbf{h}$ uniformly at random among the parity-checks of $\mathscr{C}$ of weight w_i on the $\mathcal{N}_i$'s and $\mathbf{h}'$ uniformly at random among the words of weight w_i on the $\mathcal{N}_i$'s. For $i \in \{1,2\}$, let*

$$\delta_i \triangleq \mathrm{bias}\left(\langle \mathbf{e}_{\mathcal{N}_i}, \mathbf{h}'_{\mathcal{N}_i} \rangle\right) \ and \ \delta \triangleq \delta_1 \delta_2$$

If the parameters k, s, u_i, w_i are chosen as functions on n so that for n going to infinity, the expected number N of parity-checks of $\mathscr{C}$ of respective weight w_i on $\mathcal{N}_i$ for $i \in \{1, 2\}$, satisfies $N = \omega\left(1/\delta^2\right)$ then for all but a proportion $o(1)$ of codes we have

$$\text{bias}\left(\langle \mathbf{e}_{\mathcal{N}}, \mathbf{h}_{\mathcal{N}} \rangle\right) = (1 + o(1))\delta.$$

With the collision method we use, the parity-checks we produce have actually a slightly more specific form, since $\mathcal{N}_2$ is partitioned in two sets of (almost) the same size on which $\mathbf{h}$ has weight $w_2/2$. It is not difficult to turn such a generation of parity-checks at the cost of a polynomial overhead into a generation of uniformly distributed parity-checks of weight w_2 on $\mathcal{N}_2$. We leave out the details for doing this here. Under such an assumption, we have

Lemma 4.2. *With the same assumptions as in Proposition 4.1,*

$$\mathbb{P}_{\mathbf{h}}(\langle \mathbf{e}_{\mathcal{N}}, \mathbf{h}_{\mathcal{N}} = 1 \rangle) = \frac{1 - \varepsilon}{2} \quad \text{where} \quad \varepsilon = \delta_1 \delta_2 (1 - o(1))$$

$$\delta_1 \overset{\triangle}{=} \frac{K_{w_1}^{k-\ell-s}(u_1)}{\binom{k-\ell-s}{w_1}}, \quad \delta_2 \overset{\triangle}{=} \frac{K_{w_2}^{n-k+\ell}(u_2)}{\binom{n-k+\ell}{w_2}}, \quad u_1 \overset{\triangle}{=} |\mathbf{e}_{\mathcal{N}_1}|, \quad u_2 \overset{\triangle}{=} |\mathbf{e}_{\mathcal{N}_2}|, \quad w_1 \overset{\triangle}{=} |\mathbf{h}_{\mathcal{N}_1}| \quad \text{and}$$

$$w_2 \overset{\triangle}{=} |\mathbf{h}_{\mathcal{N}_2}|.$$

Proof. This is an application of the previous proposition and Lemma 3.3.   □

All these considerations lead to a slight variation of the RLPN decoder given in Algorithm 3.1. Let us make now a bet on the weight u_i of the error restricted to $\mathcal{N}_i$ for $i \in \{1, 2\}$ and use Dumer's [11] collision low-weight codeword generator to produce N parity-checks $\mathbf{h}$ such that $|\mathbf{h}_{\mathcal{N}_i}| = w_i$ for $i \in \{1, 2\}$. We call the associated function $\text{CREATE}(N, w_1, w_2, \mathscr{P})$.

Proposition 4.3. *If Assumption 3.7 holds and assuming that $\text{CREATE}(N, w_1, w_2, \mathscr{P})$ produces N parity-check equations in space S_{eq} and time T_{eq} that are of weight w_i on $\mathcal{N}_i$ for $i \in \{1, 2\}$. The probability P_{succ} (over the choice of $\mathcal{N}_1$ and $\mathcal{N}_2$) that there are exactly u_1 errors in $\mathcal{N}_1$ and u_2 errors in $\mathcal{N}_2$ is given by*

$$P_{succ} = \frac{\binom{s}{t-u_1-u_2}\binom{k-\ell-s}{u_1}\binom{n-k+\ell}{u_2}}{\binom{n}{t}}.$$

The space complexity $S_{Dumer89}$ and time complexity $T_{Dumer89}$ of the RLPN-decoder are given by

$$\textbf{Space}: S_{Dumer89} = O\left(S_{eq} + 2^s\right), \quad \textbf{Time}: T_{Dumer89} = \widetilde{O}\left(\frac{T_{eq} + 2^s}{P_{succ}}\right).$$

under the constraint on the parameters s, ℓ, u_1, u_2, w_1 and w_2 given by

$$N \leq 2^s \tag{4.3}$$

$$N \leq \frac{\binom{k-\ell-s}{w_1}\binom{n-k+\ell}{w_2}}{2^{k-s}} \tag{4.4}$$

$$N = \omega\left(\left(\frac{\binom{k-\ell-s}{w_1}\binom{n-k+\ell}{w_2}}{K_{w_1}^{k-\ell-s}(u_1) K_{w_2}^{k-\ell-s}(u_2)}\right)^2\right). \tag{4.5}$$

We have found out that choosing w_1 carefully is unnecessary and simply setting it to it its expected value is sufficient, *i.e.* $w_1 = \frac{k-\ell-s}{2}$. Again, the same discussion as in the previous section applies and if Conjecture 3.11 applies then the asymptotic form of the complexity is the same as if we use Proposition 4.3 and we get the following asymptotic form

Proposition 4.4. *If Conjecture 3.11 holds, the asymptotic complexity exponent of the RLPN decoder based on Dumer's collision low weight dual codeword generator is given by*

$$\alpha_{Dumer89}(R) \triangleq \min_{(\sigma,\nu_1,\nu_2,\lambda,\omega_1,\omega_2)\in\mathscr{R}} \beta(R,\sigma,\nu_1,\nu_2,\lambda,\omega_1,\omega_2) \qquad (4.6)$$

$$\beta \triangleq \max\left(\sigma,\nu'\right) + \pi,$$

$$\nu' \triangleq \max\left(\frac{(1-R+\lambda)}{2}h\left(\frac{\omega_2}{1-R+\lambda}\right),\nu\right), \quad \nu \triangleq (1-R+\lambda)h\left(\frac{\omega_2}{1-R+\lambda}\right) - \lambda,$$

$$\pi \triangleq 1 - R - \sigma h\left(\frac{\tau-\nu_1-\nu_2}{\sigma}\right) - (R-\lambda-\sigma)h\left(\frac{\nu_1}{R-\lambda-\sigma}\right) - (1-R+\lambda)h\left(\frac{\nu_2}{1-R+\lambda}\right),$$

$$\tau \triangleq \delta_{\mathrm{GV}}(R) = h^{-1}(1-R)$$

and the constraint region $\mathscr{R}$ is defined by the subregion of non-negative tuples $(\sigma,\nu_1,\nu_2,\lambda,\omega_1,\omega_2)$ such that $\omega_1 = \frac{R-\lambda-\sigma}{2}$ and

$$\sigma \leq R - \lambda, \ \ \nu_1 \leq R - \lambda - \sigma, \ \ \nu_2 \leq 1 - R + \lambda, \ \ \tau - \sigma \leq \nu_1 + \nu_2 \leq \tau, \ \ \nu \leq \sigma,$$

$$\nu = -(R-\lambda-\sigma)\tilde{\delta}\left(\frac{\nu_1}{R-\lambda-\sigma},\frac{\omega_1}{R-\lambda-\sigma}\right) - (1-R+\lambda)\tilde{\delta}\left(\frac{\nu_2}{1-R+\lambda},\frac{\omega_2}{1-R+\lambda}\right)$$

where $\tilde{\delta}$ is the function defined in Proposition 3.6.

5   Using Advanced Collision Techniques

ISD techniques have evolved [3,4,11,19,26] by first introducing [26] collision techniques whose purpose is to produce for codes of rate close to 1, all codewords of some small weight, and later on by substantially improving them by using on top of that for instance representation techniques [19]. These algorithms come very handy in our case for devising the function CREATE($N, w, \mathscr{P}$) that we need. In the previous section, we have explored what could be achieved by the very first techniques of this type taken from [10,11]. We are going to explain now what can be gained by using [3,19]. It is convenient here to formalize the basic step used in the previous section which can be explained by the function of Algorithm 5.1. It creates codewords of weight w in a code of parity-check matrix **H** as sums $\mathbf{x}_1 + \mathbf{x}_2$ of two lists $\mathscr{L}_1$ and $\mathscr{L}_2$ with a complexity which is of the form $O\left(\max\left(\#\mathscr{L}_1, \#\mathscr{L}_2, \frac{\#\mathscr{L}_1 \cdot \#\mathscr{L}_2}{2^\ell}\right)\right)$ if the $\mathbf{Hx}_i^\mathsf{T}$'s are distributed uniformly at random and independently (we will make this assumption from now on). It is clear that [10] and [11] is more or less a direct application of this method. [19] and [3] use several layers of this function. [19] starts by partitioning the set of

---

Algorithm 5.1. Merging two lists for producing low weight codewords

---

Input: $\mathscr{L}_1 \subseteq \mathbb{F}_2^n$, $\mathscr{L}_2 \subseteq \mathbb{F}_2^n$, $w \in [\![1, n]\!]$, $\mathbf{H} \in \mathbb{F}_2^{\ell \times n}$

Output: a list $\mathscr{L} = \{\mathbf{x} = \mathbf{x}_1 + \mathbf{x}_2 : \mathbf{x}_i \in \mathscr{L}_i, \ i \in \{1, 2\}, \ |\mathbf{x}| = w, \ \mathbf{H}\mathbf{x}^\mathsf{T} = \mathbf{0}\}$ of elements of the form $\mathbf{x}_1 + \mathbf{x}_2$ with $\mathbf{x}_i$ belonging to $\mathscr{L}_i$ of weight w belonging to the code of parity-check matrix $\mathbf{H}$

function MERGE($\mathscr{L}_1, \mathscr{L}_2, w, \mathbf{H}$)

$\quad$ $\mathscr{L} \leftarrow \emptyset$

$\quad$ **for all** $\mathbf{x}_1 \in \mathscr{L}_1$ **do**

$\quad\quad$ Store $\mathbf{x}_1$ in a hashtable $\mathscr{T}$ at address $\mathbf{H}\mathbf{x}_1^\mathsf{T}$

$\quad$ **end for**

$\quad$ **for all** $\mathbf{x}_2 \in \mathscr{L}_2$ **do**

$\quad\quad$ **if** $\exists \mathbf{x}_1$ in $\mathscr{T}$ at address $\mathbf{H}\mathbf{x}_2^\mathsf{T}$ and $|\mathbf{x}_1 + \mathbf{x}_2| = w$ **then**

$\quad\quad\quad$ Put $\mathbf{x}_1 + \mathbf{x}_2$ in $\mathscr{L}$

$\quad\quad$ **end if**

$\quad$ **end for**

$\quad$ **return** $\mathscr{L}$

end function

---

positions of the vectors of $\mathbb{F}_2^n$ which are considered in two sets $\mathscr{I}_1$ and $\mathscr{I}_2$ of about the same size. Then it starts with two lists $\mathscr{L}_1^0$ and $\mathscr{L}_2^0$ of all elements of weight p_0 and support $\mathscr{I}_1$ and $\mathscr{I}_2$ respectively. It merges them in a list $\mathscr{L}^1$ of elements of weight p_1 in the kernel of a parity-check matrix $\mathbf{H}_1$. Since the elements of $\mathscr{L}_1^0$ and $\mathscr{L}_2^0$ have disjoint supports by construction, we necessarily have that $p_1 = 2p_0$. List $\mathscr{L}^1$ is then merged with itself to yield elements which are in the kernel of another matrix $\mathbf{H}_2$ (see Fig. 7). Since these are sums of elements of $\mathscr{L}^1$ they are also in the kernel of $\mathbf{H}_1$, so that the elements of the final list are of weight p_2 and belong to the code of parity-check $\mathbf{H} = \begin{pmatrix} \mathbf{H}_1 \\ \mathbf{H}_2 \end{pmatrix}$. The size of $\mathbf{H}_1$ is chosen such that an element $\mathbf{x}$ of weight p_2 and $\mathbf{H}_1\mathbf{x}^\mathsf{T} = \mathbf{0}$ is typically the sum of only two elements of $\mathscr{L}^1$ (this is the point of the representation technique). [3] is similar to [19] with one layer which is added. In this case, we create at the end a list of elements of weight p_3 which are in the code of parity-check matrix

$$\mathbf{H} \stackrel{\triangle}{=} \begin{pmatrix} \mathbf{H}_1 \\ \mathbf{H}_2 \\ \mathbf{H}_3 \end{pmatrix}. \tag{5.1}$$

The sizes of $\mathbf{H}_1$ in the [19] case, and of $\mathbf{H}_1$ and $\mathbf{H}_2$ in [3] are chosen to ensure unicity of the representation of an element of a list as the sum of two elements of the lists used for the merge (this is the representation technique).

$\quad$ We use these two techniques as we used the [10] technique inside the [11] technique, namely to generate codewords of $\mathscr{C}^\perp$ (*i.e.* $\mathbf{H}\mathbf{x}^\mathsf{T} = \mathbf{0}$ for $\mathbf{H}$ given by (5.1)) which are of weight p_3 on a set of indices of size $n - k + \ell$ (see Fig. 8).

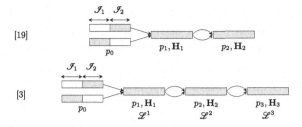

Fig. 7. This figure represents the successive lists obtained in [19] and [3]. The support of the elements of the list are represented in pink. Arrows point from the lists which are merged to the result of the merge and if two arrows depart from a list and arrive at another list, this means that the departure list is merged with itself. The weights of the elements are indicated for each level and the matrix $\mathbf{H}_i$ used for the merge is also given at the level of the result of the merge.

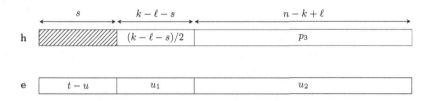

Fig. 8. The form of the parity-checks produced by this method [3], *vs.* the bet made on the error. The hatched rectangle of size s for $\mathbf{h}$ indicates that the weight is arbitrary on this part.

If we let ℓ_1 be the number of rows of $\mathbf{H}_1$, ℓ_2 be the number of rows of the matrix of $\mathbf{H}'_2 \triangleq \begin{pmatrix} \mathbf{H}_1 \\ \mathbf{H}_2 \end{pmatrix}$, then the fact that the elements of $\mathscr{L}^2$ should have a unique representation in terms of a sum of a pair of elements of $\mathscr{L}^1$ respectively and that they are all elements $\mathbf{x}$ of weight p_1 and p_2 respectively which satisfy $\mathbf{H}'_2\mathbf{x}^\mathsf{T} = \mathbf{0}$ and $\mathbf{H}\mathbf{x}^\mathsf{T} = \mathbf{0}$ respectively, imposes conditions (5.2) which follow. The S_i represent the space complexity of the successive lists (*i.e.* $\mathscr{L}^0$, $\mathscr{L}^1$, $\mathscr{L}^2$ and $\mathscr{L}^3$) used in the [3] algorithm, whereas the T_i's denote the complexity of each merge and T_{eq} is the final complexity.

$$2^{\ell_1} = \binom{p_2}{p_2/2}\binom{n-k+\ell-p_2}{p_1-p_2/2}, \quad 2^{\ell_2} = \binom{p_3}{p_3/2}\binom{n-k+\ell-p_3}{p_2-p_3/2} \quad (5.2)$$

$$S_0 = \binom{\frac{n-k+\ell}{2}}{\frac{p_1}{2}}, \quad S_1 = \frac{\binom{n-k+\ell}{p_1}}{2^{\ell_1}}, \quad S_2 = \frac{\binom{n-k+\ell}{p_2}}{2^{\ell_2}}, \quad S_3 = \frac{\binom{n-k+\ell}{p_3}}{2^{\ell}} \quad (5.3)$$

$$T_0 = S_0, \ T_1 = S_0 + \frac{S_0^2}{2^{\ell_1}}, \ T_2 = S_1 + \frac{S_1^2}{2^{\ell_2-\ell_1}}, \ T_3 = S_2 + \frac{S_2^2}{2^{\ell-\ell_2}}, \ T_{\text{eq}} = \sum_i T_i \quad (5.4)$$

There is a similar proposition as Proposition 4.4 which gives the asymptotic complexity of the RLPN decoder used in conjunction with the [19] or [3] techniques for producing low weight codewords. For [19] it is given by

Proposition 5.1. *If conjecture 3.11 applies, the asymptotic complexity exponent of the RLPN decoder based on [19] is given by*

$$\alpha_{MMT}(R) \triangleq \min_{(\sigma,\nu_1,\nu_2,\lambda,\lambda_1,\omega_1,\omega_2,\pi_1)\in\mathscr{R}} \beta(R,\sigma,\nu_1,\nu_2,\lambda,\lambda_1,\omega_1,\omega_2,\pi_1) \tag{5.5}$$

$$\beta \triangleq \max(\sigma,\nu') + \pi, \quad \nu' \triangleq \max(\gamma_1,\gamma_2), \quad \nu \triangleq (1-R+\lambda)h\left(\frac{\omega_2}{1-R+\lambda}\right) - \lambda$$

$$\gamma_1 \triangleq \max\left(\frac{1-R+\lambda}{2}h\left(\frac{\pi_1}{1-R+\lambda}\right), (1-R+\lambda)h\left(\frac{\pi_1}{1-R+\lambda}\right) - \lambda_1\right),$$

$$\gamma_2 \triangleq 2(1-R+\lambda)h\left(\frac{\pi_1}{1-R+\lambda}\right) - \lambda_1 - \lambda,$$

$$\rho \triangleq 1 - R - \sigma h\left(\frac{\tau-\nu_1-\nu_2}{\sigma}\right) - (R-\lambda-\sigma)h\left(\frac{\nu_1}{R-\lambda-\sigma}\right) - (1-R+\lambda)h\left(\frac{\nu_2}{1-R+\lambda}\right),$$

$$\tau \triangleq \delta_{\mathrm{GV}}(R) = h^{-1}(1-R)$$

and the constraint region $\mathscr{R}$ is defined by the subregion of non-negative tuples $(\sigma,\nu_1,\nu_2,\lambda,\lambda_1,\pi,\omega_1,\omega_2)$ such that

$$\sigma \le R-\lambda, \quad \lambda_1 \le \lambda, \quad \pi_1 \le \omega_2, \quad \nu_1 \le R-\lambda-\sigma, \quad \nu_2 \le 1-R+\lambda, \quad \nu \le \sigma,$$

$$\tau - \sigma \le \nu_1 + \nu_2 \le \tau, \quad \omega_1 = \frac{R-\lambda-\sigma}{2}, \quad \omega_2 < 1-R+\lambda,$$

$$\frac{\omega_2}{2} < \pi_1 < 1-R+\lambda, \quad \lambda_1 = \omega_2 + (1-R+\lambda-\omega_2)h\left(\frac{\pi_1-\omega_2/2}{1-R+\lambda-\omega_2}\right),$$

$$\nu = -(R-\lambda-\sigma)\widetilde{\delta}\left(\frac{\nu_1}{R-\lambda-\sigma}, \frac{\omega_1}{R-\lambda-\sigma}\right) - (1-R+\lambda)\widetilde{\delta}\left(\frac{\nu_2}{1-R+\lambda}, \frac{\omega_2}{1-R+\lambda}\right)$$

where $\widetilde{\delta}$ is the function defined in Proposition 3.6.

A proposition for the asymptotic behavior of RLPN decoding used together with [3] can be found in the full version of the paper [8, Ap. A]. We have used them for producing the complexity curves given in Fig. 9 which display the various complexities of the RLPN decoders we have presented. Even if there is a tiny improvement by using [3] instead of [19] the two curves are nearly indistinguishable. A perspective of improvement of our algorithm could be to produce the parity-check equations by using more recent ISD techniques than [3], in particular [5,20] or [6] which all use nearest-neighbor search. Our preliminary results using in particular [20] do not provide significant improvement, we have only been able to achieve a very slightly better complexity for rates close to 0.2.

6   A Lower Bound on the Complexity of RLPN Decoders

As pointed out all along the paper, RLPN decoding needs a large number N of parity-check equations to work *but* of some shape as indicated below

where the hatched area indicates that the weight is arbitrary on this part while **h** restricted on the other positions needs to have Hamming weight w. The number N of such parity-checks has to verify (see Proposition 3.10)

$$N = \omega \left(n \left(\frac{\binom{n-s}{w}}{K_w^{n-s}(u)} \right)^2 \right) \tag{6.1}$$

in order to be able to solve the underlying LPN problem. It can be verified that the smaller w is (the bigger is the bias ε), the smaller is N and the more efficient is our algorithm. Obviously if w is too small, there are not enough such parity-checks. It can be verified that the expected number of parity-checks of the aforementioned shape is given by $2^s \binom{n-s}{w}/2^k$ in a random code (which is our assumption). Therefore we need

$$N = O \left(\frac{2^s \binom{n-s}{w}}{2^k} \right). \tag{6.2}$$

Given this picture it is readily seen that the complexity of RLPN decoding is always lower-bounded by N (which is at least the cost to produce N parity-checks) but we can be more accurate on the lower-bound over the complexity. Recall that we first need to solve an underlying LPN problem and that we make a bet on the number of errors u in $\mathcal{N}$. Therefore, *assuming* that we can compute a parity-check of the aforementioned shape in time $O(1)$, the complexity of this genie-aided RLPN decoding is given by

$$\tilde{O} \left(\frac{1}{P_{\text{succ}}} \max \left(2^s, N \right) \right) \tag{6.3}$$

where P_{succ} is given in Proposition 3.10. Our only constraints are given by (6.1) and (6.2). By optimizing (6.3) over s, u and w, we can give a lower-bound on the complexity of RLPN decoding. However notice that our lower-bound applies to a partition of parity-checks in two parts (s and $n - s$). We do not consider here finer partitions. This method for lower bounding the complexity of RLPN decoding is very similar to the technique used in [9, §7] to lower bound the complexity of statistical decoding. All in all, we give in Fig. 9 this lower-bound of the complexity. The optimal parameters computed for each RLPN algorithms can be found on https://github.com/tillich/RLPNdecoding. As we see our RLPN decoders meet this lower-bound for small rates and we can hope to outperform significantly ISD's for code rates smaller than ≈ 0.45.

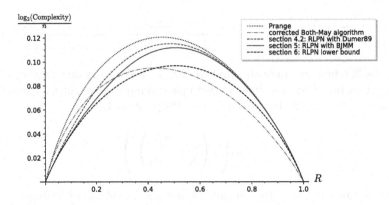

Fig. 9. Complexity exponents of our different RLPN decoders, ISD's and the genie-aided RLPN algorithm when splitting parity-checks in two parts.

7 Concluding Remarks

Since Prange's seminal work [24] in 1962, ISD algorithms have played a predominant role for assessing the complexity of code-based cryptographic primitives. In the fixed rate regime, they have been beaten only once in [10] with the help of collision techniques, and this only for a tiny code rate range ($R \in (0.98, 1)$) and for a short period of time [11, 26] until these collision techniques were merged with the collision techniques to yield modern ISD's. Surprisingly enough, these improved ISD have resulted in decoding complexity curves tilting more and more to the left (*i.e.* with a maximum which is attained more and more below $\frac{1}{2}$) instead of being symmetric around $\frac{1}{2}$ as it could have been expected. It is precisely for rates below $\frac{1}{2}$ that RLPN decoding is able to outperform the best ISD's. This seems to point to the fact that it is precisely for this regime of parameters that we should aim for improving them. Interestingly enough, even if there is some room of improvement for RLPN decoding by using better strategies for producing the needed low weight parity-checks, there is a ceiling that this technique can not break (at least if we just split the parity-checks in two parts) and which is extremely close at rate $R = 0.45$ to the best ISD algorithm [6]. The RLPN decoding algorithm presented here has not succeeded in changing the landscape for very tiny code rates (R going to 0), since the complexity exponent of RLPN decoding approaches the one of exhaustive search on codewords, but the speed at which this complexity approaches exhaustive search is much smaller than for ISD's in the full decoding regime (*i.e.* at the GV distance). The success of RLPN decoding for $R < 0.3$ could be traced back precisely to this behaviour close to 0. An interesting venue for research could be to try to explore if there are other decoding strategies that would be candidate for beating exhaustive search in the tiny code rate regime.

Note however that like dual attacks in lattice based cryptography, the success of this algorithm relies on assumptions of the noise model we get from the low weight parity-check equations we produce (which is similar to the vectors in the dual lattice of small norm we use for dual attacks). The strict LPN model for this noise (Assumption 3.7) has been found out not to be completely accurate for the large Fourier coefficients obtained during decoding the $[N, s]$-code with Fourier techniques (see Subsect. 3.4). However, a weaker conjecture, namely Conjecture 3.11, is enough for guaranteeing the success of this decoding method and is compatible with the experiments we have made. There is a rather clear path for verifying at least semi-heuristically this conjecture and this will be the object of further studies about this algorithm.

Acknowledgement. We would like to express our warmest gratitude to Elena Kirshanova for all her work and comments on an earlier version of this paper which helped us a great deal in improving the quality of this submission. We would also thank the Asiacrypt 22' reviewers for all their comments and their scientific rectitude. We thank Ilya Dumer for his very insightful thoughts about decoding linear codes in the low rate regime. The work of TDA was funded by the French Agence Nationale de la Recherche through ANR JCJC COLA (ANR-21-CE39-0011). The work of CMH was funded by the French Agence de l'innovation de Défense and by Inria.

References

1. Aguilar, C., Gaborit, P., Schrek, J.: A new zero-knowledge code based identification scheme with reduced communication. In: Proceedings of IEEE Information Theory Workshop- ITW 2011, pp. 648–652. IEEE, October 2011
2. Barg, A.: Complexity issues in coding theory. Electronic Colloquium on Computational Complexity, October 1997
3. Becker, A., Joux, A., May, A., Meurer, A.: Decoding random binary linear codes in $2^{n/20}$: how $1 + 1 = 0$ improves information set decoding. In: Pointcheval, D., Johansson, T. (eds.) EUROCRYPT 2012. LNCS, vol. 7237, pp. 520–536. Springer, Heidelberg (2012). https://doi.org/10.1007/978-3-642-29011-4_31
4. Bernstein, D.J., Lange, T., Peters, C.: Smaller decoding exponents: ball-collision decoding. In: Rogaway, P. (ed.) CRYPTO 2011. LNCS, vol. 6841, pp. 743–760. Springer, Heidelberg (2011). https://doi.org/10.1007/978-3-642-22792-9_42
5. Both, L., May, A.: Optimizing BJMM with nearest neighbors: full decoding in $2^{2/21n}$ and McEliece security. In: WCC Workshop on Coding and Cryptography, September 2017
6. Both, L., May, A.: Decoding linear codes with high error rate and its impact for LPN security. In: Lange, T., Steinwandt, R. (eds.) PQCrypto 2018. LNCS, vol. 10786, pp. 25–46. Springer, Cham (2018). https://doi.org/10.1007/978-3-319-79063-3_2
7. Canto Torres, R., Sendrier, N.: Analysis of information set decoding for a sub-linear error weight. In: Takagi, T. (ed.) PQCrypto 2016. LNCS, vol. 9606, pp. 144–161. Springer, Cham (2016). https://doi.org/10.1007/978-3-319-29360-8_10
8. Carrier, K., Debris-Alazard, T., Meyer-Hilfiger, C., Tillich, J.: Statistical decoding 2.0: reducing decoding to LPN. Cryptology ePrint Archive, Report 2022/1000 (2022)
9. Debris-Alazard, T., Tillich, J.-P.: Statistical decoding. preprint, January 2017. arXiv:1701.07416

10. Dumer, I.: On syndrome decoding of linear codes. In: Proceedings of the 9th All-Union Symposium on Redundancy in Information Systems, Abstracts of Papers (in Russian), Part 2 (Leningrad, 1986), pp. 157–159

11. Dumer, I.: Two decoding algorithms for linear codes. Probl. Inf. Transm. **25**(1), 17–23 (1989)

12. Dumer, I.: On minimum distance decoding of linear codes. In: Proceedings of 5th Joint Soviet-Swedish International Workshop Information Theory (Moscow, 1991), pp. 50–52 (1991)

13. Feneuil, T., Joux, A., Rivain, M.: Shared permutation for syndrome decoding: new zero-knowledge protocol and code-based signature. IACR Cryptology ePrint Archive, p. 1576 (2021)

14. Finiasz, M., Sendrier, N.: Security bounds for the design of code-based cryptosystems. In: Matsui, M. (ed.) ASIACRYPT 2009. LNCS, vol. 5912, pp. 88–105. Springer, Heidelberg (2009). https://doi.org/10.1007/978-3-642-10366-7_6

15. Fossorier, M.P.C., Kobara, K., Imai, H.: Modeling bit flipping decoding based on nonorthogonal check sums with application to iterative decoding attack of McEliece cryptosystem. IEEE Trans. Inform. Theory **53**(1), 402–411 (2007)

16. Gaborit, P., Girault, M.: Lightweight code-based authentication and signature. In: Proceedings of IEEE International Symposium Information Theory - ISIT (Nice, France), pp. 191–195, June 2007

17. Jabri, A.A.: A statistical decoding algorithm for general linear block codes. In: Honary, B. (ed.) Cryptography and Coding 2001. LNCS, vol. 2260, pp. 1–8. Springer, Heidelberg (2001). https://doi.org/10.1007/3-540-45325-3_1

18. Kirshner, N., Samorodnitsky, A.: A moment ratio bound for polynomials and some extremal properties of Krawchouk polynomials and hamming spheres. IEEE Trans. Inform. Theory **67**(6), 3509–3541 (2021)

19. May, A., Meurer, A., Thomae, E.: Decoding random linear codes in $\tilde{\mathcal{O}}(2^{0.054n})$. In: Lee, D.H., Wang, X. (eds.) ASIACRYPT 2011. LNCS, vol. 7073, pp. 107–124. Springer, Heidelberg (2011). https://doi.org/10.1007/978-3-642-25385-0_6

20. May, A., Ozerov, I.: On computing nearest neighbors with applications to decoding of binary linear codes. In: Oswald, E., Fischlin, M. (eds.) EUROCRYPT 2015. LNCS, vol. 9056, pp. 203–228. Springer, Heidelberg (2015). https://doi.org/10.1007/978-3-662-46800-5_9

21. McEliece, R.J.: A public-key system based on algebraic coding theory. . DSN Progress Report 44, pp. 114–116. Jet Propulsion Lab (1978)

22. Misoczki, R., Tillich, J.-P., Sendrier, N., Barreto, P.S.L.M.: MDPC-McEliece: new McEliece variants from moderate density parity-check codes. In: Proceedings of IEEE International Symposium Information Theory - ISIT, pp. 2069–2073 (2013)

23. Overbeck, R.: Statistical decoding revisited. In: Batten, L.M., Safavi-Naini, R. (eds.) ACISP 2006. LNCS, vol. 4058, pp. 283–294. Springer, Heidelberg (2006). https://doi.org/10.1007/11780656_24

24. Prange, E.: The use of information sets in decoding cyclic codes. IRE Trans. Inf. Theory **8**(5), 5–9 (1962)

25. Richardson, T., Urbanke, R.: Modern Coding Theory. Cambridge University Press, Cambridge (2008)

26. Stern, J.: A method for finding codewords of small weight. In: Cohen, G., Wolfmann, J. (eds.) Coding Theory 1988. LNCS, vol. 388, pp. 106–113. Springer, Heidelberg (1989). https://doi.org/10.1007/BFb0019850

27. Stern, J.: A new identification scheme based on syndrome decoding. In: Stinson, D.R. (ed.) CRYPTO 1993. LNCS, vol. 773, pp. 13–21. Springer, Heidelberg (1994). https://doi.org/10.1007/3-540-48329-2_2

28. Wagner, D.: A generalized birthday problem. In: Yung, M. (ed.) CRYPTO 2002. LNCS, vol. 2442, pp. 288–304. Springer, Heidelberg (2002). https://doi.org/10. 1007/3-540-45708-9_19

A Third is All You Need: Extended Partial Key Exposure Attack on CRT-RSA with Additive Exponent Blinding

Yuanyuan Zhou[1] , Joop van de Pol[2], Yu Yu[3,4](✉) ,
and François-Xavier Standaert[1]

[1] Crypto Group, ICTEAM Institute, UCLouvain, Louvain-la-Neuve, Belgium
zhou.yuanyuan@gmail.com, fstandae@uclouvain.be
[2] Delft, Netherlands
csjhvdp@my.bristol.ac.uk
[3] Shanghai Jiao Tong University, Shanghai 200240, China
[4] Shanghai Qi Zhi Institute, 701 Yunjin Road, Shanghai 200232, China
yuyu@yuyu.hk

Abstract. At Eurocrypt 2022, May et al. proposed a partial key exposure (PKE) attack on CRT-RSA that efficiently factors N knowing only a $\frac{1}{3}$-fraction of either most significant bits (MSBs) or least significant bits (LSBs) of private exponents d_p and d_q for public exponent $e \approx N^{\frac{1}{12}}$. In practice, PKE attacks typically rely on the side-channel leakage of these exponents, while a side-channel resistant implementation of CRT-RSA often uses additively blinded exponents $d'_p = d_p + r_p(p-1)$ and $d'_q = d_q + r_q(q-1)$ with unknown random blinding factors r_p and r_q, which makes PKE attacks more challenging.

Motivated by the above, we extend the PKE attack of May et al. to CRT-RSA with additive exponent blinding. While admitting $r_p e \in (0, N^{\frac{1}{4}})$, our extended PKE works ideally when $r_p e \approx N^{\frac{1}{12}}$, in which case the entire private key can be recovered using only $\frac{1}{3}$ known MSBs or LSBs of the blinded CRT exponents d'_p and d'_q. Our extended PKE follows their novel two-step approach to first compute the key-dependent constant k' ($ed'_p = 1 + k'(p-1)$, $ed'_q = 1 + l'(q-1)$), and then to factor N by computing the root of a univariate polynomial modulo $k'p$. We extend their approach as follows. For the MSB case, we propose two options for the first step of the attack, either by obtaining a single estimate $k'l'$ and calculating k' via factoring, or by obtaining multiple estimates $k'l'_1, \ldots, k'l'_z$ and calculating k' probabilistically via GCD.

For the LSB case, we extend their approach by constructing a different univariate polynomial in the second step of the LSB attack. A formal analysis shows that our LSB attack runs in polynomial time under the standard Coppersmith-type assumption, while our MSB attack either runs in sub-exponential time with a reduced input size (the problem is reduced to factor a number of size $e^2 r_p r_q \approx N^{\frac{1}{6}}$) or in probabilistic polynomial time under a novel heuristic assumption. Under the settings of the most common key sizes (1024-bit, 2048-bit, and 3072-bit) and blinding factor lengths (32-bit, 64-bit, and 128-bit), our experiments verify the

S. Agrawal and D. Lin (Eds.): ASIACRYPT 2022, LNCS 13794, pp. 508–536, 2022.
https://doi.org/10.1007/978-3-031-22972-5_18

validity of the Coppersmith-type assumption and our own assumption, as well as the feasibility of the factoring step.

To the best of our knowledge, this is the first PKE on CRT-RSA with experimentally verified effectiveness against 128-bit unknown exponent blinding factors. We also demonstrate an application of the proposed PKE attack using real partial side-channel key leakage targeting a Montgomery Ladder exponentiation CRT implementation.

Keywords: Partial key exposure · Additive blinding · CRT-RSA · Coppersmith method

1 Introduction

1.1 Partial Key Exposure Attacks on (CRT-)RSA

As one of the longest-serving and the most widely used public-key cryptosystems, RSA can use the Chinese Remainder Theorem (CRT) optimization to speed up exponentiation operations, which is especially favored by power-constrained embedded systems. To mitigate side-channel attacks [35], a real implementation of (CRT-)RSA often adopts blinding countermeasures such as message blinding, modulus blinding and exponent blinding [15,19,22,35,40], of which additive exponent blinding [35] was referred to by the BSI as the "classical exponent blinding" [11] and is widely deployed, e.g., in open source cryptographic libraries MbedTLS [44], Libgcrypt [37], and Botan [9]. Throughout this work, we consider CRT-RSA with additive exponent blinding as the main target of our research.

At Eurocrypt'96, Coppersmith presented a novel lattice-based method to find small solutions of univariate modular polynomials with some applications to cryptanalysis of RSA [17], and he [16] extended this method to bivariate equations to factor RSA modulus N with half MSBs of one of its prime factors. Boneh et al. [6] introduced PKE attacks to recover the full RSA private key using a few consecutive MSBs or LSBs of the private key based on the Coppersmith method. Many subsequent works continued the research on PKE, but most do not take into account the widely deployed exponent blinding countermeasure [3,7,23,28,38,42,43,50,56–59], with only a couple of exceptions to the best of our knowledge [24,32]. Fouque et al. [24] investigated PKE attacks on an additively blinded private exponent with up to 32-bit blinding factors and very small e values for RSA without CRT. They showed that non-consecutive known bits—which could realistically result from SCA (Side-Channel Analysis) leakage of sliding-window exponentiation implementations—of the additively blinded private exponent could be used to recover the private exponent. However, their attack relies on the fact that both the public exponent e and the blinding factor are small to enable brute force, and requires multiple traces to gradually retrieve the entire private key. In particular, the retrieval requires several (50 in their experiments) instantiations of the recovered non-consecutive exponent bits (when $e = 3$) or 2-bit consecutive exponent bits (when $e = 2^{16} + 1$), each providing a $\frac{1}{64}$ to $\frac{1}{16}$ (depending on the public exponent, key length) non-consecutive or consecutive portion of the blinded exponents. Further, it works with very small e values (the cases of $e = 3$ and $2^{16} + 1$ were experimentally verified) and up to 32-bit blinding factors. Joye and Lepoint [32] also focused on PKE on RSA with additive exponent blinding. They constructed trivariate or bivariate polynomials based on Coppersmith's lattice techniques to recover the whole key with partial known blinded exponent MSBs/LSBs. Their attack requires in the best case more than half of the known MSBs or LSBs of the blinded private exponent, which was experimentally verified. In addition to the aforementioned works that assume some **partial** bits of the (blinded) private exponent(s) known with certainty, another line of works considers the case where **all** bits of the blinded private exponent(s) are classified, but where they can be wrongly classified with some error probability, e.g. [4,52–54]. In summary, previous PKE attacks on (CRT-)RSA with additive exponent blinding mostly consider restricted cases of e and small blinding factors using special-structured partial key leakages from multiple observations, or need more than half of blinded private exponent from a single observation of the partial key leakage, or need a full recovery of the (blinded) exponent bits with errors.

1.2   Our Contribution

In this work, we aim to answer the question: *how and to which extent can we extend the PKE attack to CRT-RSA with additive exponent blinding (ideally using as few as possible consecutive MSBs/LSBs of the private CRT exponent from a single observation of the partial key leakage) both theoretically and empirically?*

Our contributions in this context are summarized as follows.

First, we extend the PKE attack on CRT-RSA with unblinded exponents (d_p and d_q) [43] to that with additively blinded ones, i.e., $d'_p = d_p + r_p(p - 1)$ and $d'_q = d_q + r_q(q - 1)$ for unknown random blinding factors r_p and r_q.[1] Instead of restricting r_p and r_q to 32 bits or any lengths within the reach of brute force [24], we allow the blinding factors up to some exponential size N^γ, and concretely 128 bits or even more. Our extended PKE works ideally when the products of public exponent $e = N^\alpha$ and the blinding factors (i.e., $e \cdot r_p$ and $e \cdot r_q$ in the LSB case; $e \cdot r_p^{\frac{2}{3}}$ and $e \cdot r_q^{\frac{2}{3}}$ in the MSB case) are roughly $N^{\frac{1}{12}}$, i.e., $\alpha + \gamma \approx \frac{1}{12}$ or $\alpha + \frac{2}{3}\gamma \approx \frac{1}{12}$. In this setting, the attackers/evaluators need only a $\frac{1}{3}$-fraction of MSBs or LSBs of d'_p and d'_q to recover the entire private key. In general, as for [43], our extended PKE attack works in the small e regime (albeit with more MSBs/LSBs), i.e., $0 < e < N^{\frac{1}{4} - \gamma}$, which arguably covers most common choices in practice (e.g., NIST mandates $e \in (2^{16}, 2^{256})$ [45]).

Second, we formally analyze the asymptotic time complexity of the proposed PKE attack. In the LSB case, it runs in polynomial time under the standard

---

[1] We argue that the extension is non-trivial as, intuitively (from an information theoretic point of view), the random unknown blinding factors (r_p and r_q) effectively reduce the information on d_p, d_q, k, and l that can be obtained directly from partial key exposure.

Coppersmith-type heuristic assumption. In the MSB case, it either runs in sub-exponential time with a reduced input size (i.e., the number to factor in this case is of size $e^2 \cdot r_p \cdot r_q$, significantly smaller than the RSA modulus N), or runs in probabilistic polynomial time (PPT) under a novel assumption that certain values corresponding to the blinded exponents are coprime with a certain probability, but with the additional cost that, for one of the exponents, multiple observations of the blinded execution are needed. We implement the proposed PKE attack for the most common key sizes (1024-bit, 2048-bit, and 3072-bit) and blinding factor lengths (32-bit, 64-bit, and 128-bit), and our extensive experiments not only confirm the effectiveness of the Coppersmith-type heuristic (in the LSB case), but also that of our own assumption and the feasibility of the sub-exponential (in $e^2 \cdot r_p \cdot r_q$) time complexity (in the MSB case). In particular, the MSB attack succeeds with the probability that randomly distributed numbers are coprime (using multiple observations of the blinded exponents), or completes mostly in seconds or minutes for most parameter settings (using single observation of the blinded exponents). In the most challenging case occasionally observed for 2048-bit (resp., 3072-bit) key with 128-bit additive blinding exponent, it finishes in less than 1.5 (resp., 50) hours. To the best of our knowledge, this is the first[2] PKE on CRT work that experimentally verifies the effectiveness using 128-bit additive exponent blinding factors. The experiment parameters also provide hands-on references (such as lattice dimensions, and required running time) to the attackers/evaluators for applying PKE attacks.

Third, the extended PKE attack can be combined with various forms of side-channel attacks, e.g., cold boot attacks [27,61], cache-timing micro-architectural attacks [2,62], and timing, power or electromagnetic analysis attacks on CRT-RSA [13,29,35,51,64], to significantly enhance the applicability of these attacks (by reducing the goal of full key recovery to obtaining only a $\frac{1}{3}$-fraction of leakage). Note that this PKE attack can tolerate some errors of the partial key leakage,[3] i.e., combining the error-free MSBs or LSBs of d'_p from one observation of the partial key leakage, and those of d'_q from another one. To this end, we demonstrate an application of the extended PKE attacks on deep learning-based partial side-channel leakage from a typical real-world target, i.e., a Montgomery Ladder exponentiation CRT implementation with 2048-bit key and 64-bit additive exponent blinding on a 45 nm secure microcontroller with RSA co-processor.

Several preliminaries and proofs in this work closely follow the corresponding versions in [43]. In those cases, the contributions of May et al. are included here in full such that this work is self-contained and easier to read.

1.3 Organization of the Paper

The rest of this paper is organized as follows. Section 2 introduces the necessary background information about the Coppersmith method and the state-of-the-art

---

[2] The work [54] estimates the effort for 128-bit blinding factors with error probability 0.05, but only verifies the estimates experimentally for 32-bit blinding factors.

[3] It is a commonly used strategy also for error-tolerant lattice-based attacks on (EC)DSA as pointed out in [1].

PKE attack on unblinded CRT exponents published at Eurocrypt'22. Section 3 provides a mathematical proof of the extended PKE attack in the additive blinding scenario. Afterwards, we experimentally verify the effectiveness and time complexity of this approach in Sect. 4. Finally, in Sect. 5, an application of the extended PKE attack is demonstrated using partial side-channel key leakage of a typical real-world Montgomery Ladder exponentiation implementation with additive exponent blinding countermeasure.

2   Preliminaries

2.1   Notations

By 'log' we denote the base 2 logarithm, 'ln' denotes the natural logarithm, and $\zeta(.)$ denotes Riemann's zeta function. We use capital letters for random variables and small caps for their realizations. We use capital bold font letters for matrices (e.g., $\mathbf{M}$) and small bold caps for vectors (e.g., $\mathbf{v}$). We use $|\det \mathbf{M}|$ to denote the absolute value of the *determinant* of the matrix $\mathbf{M}$, which corresponds to the determinant of the lattice spanned by this matrix.

2.2   Coppersmith's Method

Similar to many previous PKE works, we rely on Coppersmith's method to find small modular roots of multivariate polynomials [18]. We first give a simple introduction to the multivariate Coppersmith's lattice-based method.

Let $f \in \mathbb{Z}[x_1, ..., x_j]$ be a j-variate polynomial over the integers with maximum degree δ in each variable separately, this polynomial has a small root $r = (r_1, ..., r_j)$ modular an integer M and let $U_i \in \mathbb{Z}$ denote some known bounds. The goal is to find integers $|r_i| \le U_i$ such that $f(r_1, ..., r_j) = 0$ in polynomial time.

To this end, a series of so-called *shift-polynomials* with a chosen sufficiently big positive integer $m \in \mathbb{N}$ and the indices $i_0, ..., i_j \in \mathbb{N}$ is constructed as below:

$$s_{[i_0,...,i_j]}(x_1, ..., x_j) = f^{i_0}(x_1, ..., x_j) \cdot x_1^{i_1} \cdot ... \cdot x_n^{i_j} \cdot M^{m-i_0}.$$

Those polynomials have the root r modulo M^m by construction. A subset of the constructed shift-polynomials $s_{[i_0,...,i_j]}(U_1 x_1, ..., U_j x_j)$ is selected to generate an l-dimensional lattice $\mathcal{L}$ with their coefficient vectors such that the lattice $\mathcal{L}$ has a triangular basis matrix $\mathbf{B}$. Given a large enough chosen integer m and the determinant of $\mathcal{L}$ fulfilling the *enabling condition*, i.e., $|\det \mathbf{B}| \le M^{ml}$, then a collection of j polynomials $p_1(x_1, ..., x_j), ..., p_j(x_1, ..., x_j)$ can be computed in polynomial time. This is due to the fact that the coefficient vectors of the polynomials $p_j(U_1 x_1, ..., U_j x_j)$ are elements of $\mathcal{L}$, which is generated by the coefficient vectors of the polynomials $s_i(U_1 x_1, ..., U_j x_j)$. Therefore, the computation of $p_1(x_1, ..., x_j), ..., p_j(x_1, ..., x_j)$ can be done with the widely used LLL lattice basis reduction algorithm [36]. Those computed polynomials have the root r not only modulo M^m but also over the integers as proved by Howgrave-Graham in [30] as stated below.

Lemma 1 (Howgrave-Graham [30]). *Let $h(x_1, ..., x_k) \in \mathbb{Z}[x_1, ..., x_k]$ be a polynomial in at most ω monomials. Suppose that $h(r_1, ..., r_k) \equiv 0 \mod M^m$ for some positive integer m. Also let $|r_i| < X_i$ for $1 \leq i \leq k$ and*

$$\|h(x_1 X_1, ..., x_k X_k)\| < \frac{M^m}{\sqrt{\omega}}.$$

Then, $h(r_1, ..., r_k) = 0$ holds over the integers.

In the case of $j = 1$, i.e., the polynomial f is univariate, the root r can be straightforwardly resolved from p_1 using standard techniques, e.g., Newton's method. In the case of $j > 1$, if such (computed) polynomials generate an ideal $(p_1, ..., p_j)$ of zero-dimensional variety, we can use a Gröbner basis to resolve their root, it means that the RSA modulus N can be efficiently factored in our context. However, the existence of such a zero-dimensional variety relies on the standard Coppersmith-type heuristic assumption (see also [43, Assumption 1]) as below:

Assumption 1. *In the multivariate setting, Coppersmith's method yields polynomials that generate an ideal of zero-dimensional variety.*

It is worth mentioning that it is essential to experimentally verify the validity of this assumption because it might fail in some cases, e.g., in the small e regime of the TK attack [57] as pointed out in [43].

2.3 PKE Attack on Unblinded CRT Exponents

We first briefly recall the PKE attack on unblinded CRT private exponents in [43]. We denote an RSA public key as (N, e), where $N = pq$ and $e = N^\alpha$. In practice, p and q usually have the same bit-length, so they are bounded as $p, q = \Theta(\sqrt{N})$. The unblinded CRT exponents are marked as d_p and d_q, without loss of generality, which are assumed to be full-size, i.e., $d_p, d_q = \Theta(\sqrt{N})$. The CRT private key exponentiation is executed as

$$M = (C^{d_q} \mod q) + q \cdot ((q^{-1} \mod p) \cdot ((C^{d_p} \mod p) - (C^{d_q} \mod q)) \mod p) ,$$

where C is the ciphertext to be decrypted and M is the plaintext. The definition of PKE attacks on RSA is, that the RSA private key can be fully recovered in polynomial time given only a constant fraction of the secret exponent(s). This recent work put forward the state-of-the-art PKE attack on CRT exponents in small e regime from $\frac{1}{2}$ known LSBs of d_p (or d_q, see [7, Fig. 4]) to $\frac{1}{3}$ known LSBs (or MSBs) of both d_p and d_q (see [43, Fig. 1]) when $e \approx N^{\frac{1}{12}}$. It is a novel two-step (both steps can finish in polynomial time) approach as below:

- **Step 1:** Compute CRT key constants k ($ed_p = 1 + k(p - 1)$) and l ($ed_q = 1 + l(q - 1)$) based on the known parts of d_p and d_q and the public key (N, e). If the MSBs of d_p and d_q are known, this step is trivial to solve a quadratic polynomial equation. In the LSB case (the LSBs are known),

Coppersmith's lattice-based method [18] is involved so this step relies on a standard Coppersmith-type heuristic assumption as mentioned above in Assumption 1. They experimentally verified this heuristic in addition to the mathematical proof.

- **Step 2:** Recover the unknown bits of d_p and subsequently the factor p of N using the previously calculated k. The authors considered it as an extension of Howgrave-Graham's *approximate divisor* algorithm [31] to the case of *approximate divisor multiples* for some known multiple k of an unknown divisor p of N. They mathematically proved that this unknown divisor can be recovered in polynomial time.

3   Extended PKE Attack on Additively Blinded CRT Exponents

As discussed in Subsect. 1.2, the problem to be solved in this work is: to which extent can one reveal the whole private key when only part of the additively blinded CRT exponent bits is disclosed. In the following, we describe the extended PKE attack on additively blinded CRT exponents based on [43].

May et al. only considered the PKE attack on unblinded CRT private exponents in [43], we extend their work to cover the additively blinded CRT private exponents, and it is called EPKE (Extended Partial Key Exposure) attack in the rest of this paper.

Using the additive blinding factors r_p and r_q, the blinded CRT exponents are $d_p' = d_p + r_p(p-1)$ and $d_q' = d_q + r_q(q-1)$, where $r_p, r_q = N^\gamma$. Let $(d_p'^{(M)}, d_q'^{(M)})$ be the MSBs of d_p' and d_q', and $(d_p'^{(L)}, d_q'^{(L)})$ be the LSBs. So, we have:

$$d_p' = d_p'^{(M)} 2^i + d_p'^{(L)},$$

$$d_q' = d_q'^{(M)} 2^i + d_q'^{(L)}.$$

Hereafter, we label it as the MSB case if $(d_p'^{(M)}, d_q'^{(M)})$ are known (e.g., by side-channel attacks), or as the LSB case if $(d_p'^{(L)}, d_q'^{(L)})$ are known. In addition to the Coppersmith-type assumption required for the LSB case in [43], our algorithm in the MSB case has two options with different requirements:

- Given only parts of two blinded exponents d_p' and d_q', a factoring step of a number roughly $\frac{1}{6}$ the size of N is required, leading to a sub-exponential time complexity.
- Given parts of one blinded exponent d_p' and multiple blinded exponents $d_{q,i}'$, the time complexity remains polynomial, with a success probability according to the additional heuristic Assumption 2 defined below (which will be experimentally verified).

Assumption 2. *For z distinct blinded exponents $d_{q,i}' = d_q + r_{q,i}(q-1)$, the corresponding values $l_i' = l + r_{q,i}e$ are coprime with probability $1/\zeta(z)$.*

According to [20, (1.2) and (3.1)], this assumption holds if the values $l'_i = l + r_{q,i}e$ are distributed uniformly. However, the assumption that these values are distributed uniformly is too strong. In any case, Assumption 2 is sufficient and is experimentally validated as described in Sect. 4.

Our main result of EPKE regarding factoring N is the extension of [43, **Theorem 1**] as follows:

Theorem 1. *Let (N, e) be the public key and N be large enough with $e = N^\alpha$. Given the MSBs $(d_p'^{(M)}, d_{q,1}'^{(M)}, \ldots, d_{q,z}'^{(M)})$ or the LSBs $(d_p'^{(L)}, d_q'^{(L)})$ of the additively blinded CRT exponents (d_p', d_q') with blinding factors $r_p, r_{q,i} = N^\gamma$. If the unknown parts of d_p' and $d_{q(,i)}'$ are upper bounded by N^δ and $\delta \geq \gamma$ (which already holds for commonly used up to 128-bit additive blinding factors), where*

$$\gamma \leq \delta < \min\{\frac{1}{4} + \alpha + \gamma, \frac{1}{2} - 2\alpha - \gamma\}$$

for the MSB case, or

$$\delta < \min\{\frac{1}{4} + \alpha + \gamma, \frac{1}{2} - 2\alpha - 2\gamma\}$$

for the LSB case, then N can be factored

- *in polynomial time under Coppersmith's heuristic assumption (see Assumption 1) for the LSB case,*
- *in sub-exponential time $\exp(c(\ln(N^{2\alpha+2\gamma}))^t(\ln\ln(N^{2\alpha+2\gamma}))^{1-t})$ for the MSB case $(z = 1)$ with constants c and t dependent on the underlying integer factorization algorithm, or*
- *in probabilistic polynomial time under Assumption 2 for the MSB case $(z > 1)$.*

Proof Outline. The additively blinded CRT exponents d_p', d_q' satisfy the equations

$$ed_p' = 1 + k'(p - 1), \tag{1}$$
$$ed_q' = 1 + l'(q - 1), \tag{2}$$

where $k' = k + r_p e$ and $l' = l + r_q e$ as we have

$$ed_p = 1 + k(p - 1),$$
$$ed_q = 1 + l(q - 1).$$

Similar to [43], we use a two-step method to factor N.

Step 1: Given the unknown parts of d_p' and d_q' being upper bounded by $N^{\frac{1}{2}-2\alpha-\gamma}$ (MSB case) or $N^{\frac{1}{2}-2\alpha-2\gamma}$ (LSB case),

- in Sect. 3.1 we prove that k' can be calculated in sub-exponential time $\exp(c(\ln(N^{2\alpha+2\gamma}))^t(\ln\ln(N^{2\alpha+2\gamma}))^{1-t})$ using a single known MSBs of d_q' in the MSB case,

- in Sect. 3.2 we prove that k' can be calculated in probabilistic polynomial time using multiple known MSBs of d'_q in the MSB case under Assumption 2, and
- in Sect. 3.3 we prove that k' can be calculated in polynomial time under the Coppersmith-type heuristic Assumption 1 for multivariate polynomials in the LSB case.

Step 2: With the computed k' and the unknown MSBs or LSBs of d'_p bounded by $N^{\frac{1}{4}+\alpha+\gamma}$, we provide an algorithm for factoring N in polynomial time based on the novel result of May et al. of *approximate divisor multiples* [43, **Theorem 3**]. ∎

Note that the proof outline for Theorem 1 and the proofs of Lemmas 2, 4 and 5 follow the work of May et al. [43] and only differ in handling those two random blinding factors r_p and r_q.

3.1   Step 1a: Computing (k', l') from MSB Using Factoring

In the MSB case, to compute k' using known MSBs of two blinded exponents d'_p and d'_q, the basic idea is to compute the product $k'l'$ followed by a factorization of this product to find the candidates of k' using the modular sum of $k'+l' \mod e$. The time complexity here is determined by the factorization of the product $k'l'$, which is sub-exponential according to [8, **Formula 3.10**]. The time complexities of the state-of-the-art fastest known integer factorization algorithms are of the form $\exp(c(\ln n)^t(\ln\ln n)^{1-t})$ for some constants $c > 0$ and $0 < t < 1$, in which n is the number to be factored. For QS (Quadratic Sieve) and ECM (Elliptic-Curve Method) factorization algorithms, $t = \frac{1}{2}$; for NFS (Number Field Sieve), $t = \frac{1}{3}$. Note that, in practice, this sub-exponential time complexity is affordable because of the small size of e and commonly used small sizes (very often 64 bits or even 32 bits, at most 128 bits) of exponent blinding factors r_p and r_q. We also experimentally verify this in Sect. 4. Most of the experiments take seconds or minutes for the factorization step and occasionally need up to one and a half hours (resp., fifty hours) for 2048-bit (resp., 3072-bit) key with a regular PC.

Lemma 2 ($((k',l')$ from MSB). *Let (N, e) be the public key and N be large enough with $e = N^\alpha$. Given the MSBs $(d_p'^{(M)}, d_q'^{(M)})$, if the unknown parts $(d_p'^{(L)}, d_q'^{(L)})$ are upper bounded by N^δ, where*

$$\gamma \le \delta < \frac{1}{2} - 2\alpha - \gamma,$$

then (k',l') can be computed in time $\exp(c(\ln(N^{2\alpha+2\gamma}))^t(\ln\ln(N^{2\alpha+2\gamma}))^{1-t})$.

Proof. The first steps of the proof are completely analogous to the proof of [43, Lemma 1], where k, l, d_p, and d_q are replaced by k', l', d'_p, and d'_q, respectively. Similarly, the following quantity can be computed efficiently from the known MSBs:

$$\widetilde{A} = \frac{2^{2i}e^2 d_p'^{(M)} d_q'^{(M)}}{N}.$$

Considering

$$d_p', d_q' = \Theta(N^{\frac{1}{2}+\gamma}), d_p'^M, d_q'^M = \Theta(N^{\frac{1}{2}+\gamma-\delta}), d_p'^{(L)}, d_q'^{(L)}, 2^i = \Theta(N^\delta), k', l' = \Theta(N^{\alpha+\gamma}),$$

we have

$$k'l'N - \tilde{A}N = \mathcal{O}(N^{2\alpha+2\gamma}) + \mathcal{O}(N^{2\alpha+\frac{1}{2}+2\gamma}) + \mathcal{O}(N^{2\alpha+\frac{1}{2}+\gamma+\delta}) + \mathcal{O}(N^{2\alpha+2\delta})$$
$$= \mathcal{O}(N^{2\alpha+\frac{1}{2}+\gamma+\delta}),$$

and further we obtain

$$k'l' - \tilde{A} = \mathcal{O}(N^{\delta+2\alpha+\gamma-\frac{1}{2}}) = o(1).$$

In conclusion, the product $k'l'$ can be calculated in polynomial time $\mathcal{O}(\log^2 N)$.

Further we can deduce the analogue of [43, Equation (7)], i.e.,

$$k' + l' \equiv 1 - k'l'(N-1) \mod e, \tag{3}$$

where the right-hand side can be computed with the obtained product $k'l'$ and the public key (N, e).

To compute k', the product $k'l'$ is factored using the state-of-the-art integer factorization algorithms [8] to get all its factors in sub-exponential time $\exp(c(\ln(N^{2\alpha+2\gamma}))^t(\ln\ln(N^{2\alpha+2\gamma}))^{1-t})$. Then, the search for a combination of those factors that satisfies Eq. 3 will reveal two values corresponding to k' and l'. Putting all together, the time complexity of computing k' in the MSB case is $\exp(c(\ln(N^{2\alpha+2\gamma}))^t(\ln\ln(N^{2\alpha+2\gamma}))^{1-t})$. ∎

As opposed to the proof in [43], it is not trivial to recover k' and l' from one product $k'l'$ in polynomial time. Trying to use Eq. (3) to compute a univariate polynomial with k' and l' as roots will fail because, unlike $0 < k+l < 2e$, there is no small interval that $k'+l'$ will fall into to derive $k'+l'$ from $k'+l' \mod e$, which is due to the blinding factors r_p and r_q. Since $k = k' \mod e$ and $l = l' \mod e$, it may seem feasible to find k and l instead, but the method from [43] will not work as it is non-trivial to derive the required product kl from $kl \mod e = k'l' \mod e$. Constructing a multivariate polynomial as in the LSB case to recover k and l using Coppersmith's method is also non-trivial, as the modulus e is not large enough compared to roots k and l. Regardless, the factoring method is fast enough in practice shown by the experimental results in Sect. 4.

In the end, two candidates for k' are found because the modular sum cannot tell which of those two possible values is k' and which is l'. The fact that two candidates are found for k' means that Step 2 may have to be repeated for both candidates. However, it is not described in [43] how the two values k and l can be distinguished in the MSB case, while they are two equivalent roots of a univariate polynomial (as opposed to the LSB case, where they together form one root of a bivariate polynomial).

3.2   Step 1b: Computing $(k', l'_1, \ldots, l'_z)$ from MSB Using GCD

This section describes how to compute, in the MSB case, k' using known MSBs of one blinded exponent d'_p and multiple blinded exponents $d'_{q,i}$ in heuristic probabilistic polynomial time. Rather than using factorization methods to determine the factors of $k'l'$, it is possible to use the fact that l' is different in every execution of the CRT exponentiation due to the random blinding factor. An attacker can recover partial information on two different exponentiation executions with blinded d_q, i.e., $d'_{q,1}$ and $d'_{q,2}$, compute the products $k'l'_1$ and $k'l'_2$, and recover k' by computing the GCD (Greatest Common Divisor). It may be that l'_1 and l'_2 are not coprime, in which case the GCD will comprise $k' \cdot f$ where $f = \gcd(l'_1, l'_2)$. This happens with some probability, and can be solved by capturing additional exponentiation executions and successively computing the GCD with more products that include k'. Alternatively, the additional factor f is likely small (experimentally verified as shown in Fig. 3) in practice and can be recovered using a small brute-force with only two instantiations. The attacker can guess f, derive the corresponding k', l'_1, and l'_2, and verify whether both pairs satisfy Eq. (3).

Lemma 3 ($(k', l'_1, \ldots, l'_z)$ from MSB). *Let (N, e) be the public key and N be large enough with $e = N^\alpha$. Given the MSBs $(d'^{(M)}_p, d'^{(M)}_{q,1}, \ldots, d'^{(M)}_{q,z})$, if the unknown parts $(d'^{(L)}_p, d'^{(L)}_{q,1}, \ldots, d'^{(L)}_{q,z})$ are upper bounded by N^δ, where*

$$\gamma \le \delta < \frac{1}{2} - 2\alpha - \gamma,$$

then $(k', l'_1, \ldots, l'_z)$ can be computed in time $\mathcal{O}(\log^2 N)$ with probability $1/\zeta(z)$ under Assumption 2.

Proof. In this case, to compute k', we use one observation $d'^{(M)}_p$ combined with z observations $d'^{(M)}_{q,1}, \ldots, d'^{(M)}_{q,z}$. To this end, we first calculate all the products $k'l'_1, \ldots, k'l'_z$, using the process described in the proof of Lemma 2 and then compute $k^* = \gcd(k'l'_1, \ldots, k'l'_z)$. According to Sect. 3.1, all the products $k'l'_i$ can be calculated in polynomial time $\mathcal{O}(\log^2 N)$ using the already known MSBs $(d'^{(M)}_p, d'^{(M)}_{q,1}, \ldots, d'^{(M)}_{q,z})$ and public key (N, e). Now, $k^* = k'$ if and only if $\gcd(l'_1, \ldots, l'_z) = 1$, which, according to Assumption 2 occurs with probability $1/\zeta(z)$. Upon obtaining k', it can be verified that this is correct by computing a corresponding l'_i and verify that they satisfy Eq. (3). The complexity of the GCD computation is $\mathcal{O}((\log z) \cdot M((2\alpha + 2\gamma) \log N) \log((2\alpha + 2\gamma) \log N)$ considering the state-of-the-art quasi-linear time recursive algorithm [55, **Theorem 4**]. Putting all together, the time complexity of computing k' in the MSB case using multiple known MSBs is $\mathcal{O}(\log^2 N)$. ∎

3.3   Step 1c: Computing (k', l') with Known LSBs

As mentioned above, in the LSB case, the approach to computing k' using Coppersmith's lattice-based method relies on the standard heuristic Assumption 1. In Sect. 4, we will verify the efficiency of this heuristic method in practice.

Lemma 4 ((k', l') from LSB). *Let (N, e) be the public key and N be large enough with $e = N^\alpha$. Given the LSBs $(d_p'^{(L)}, d_q'^{(L)})$, if the unknown parts $(d_p'^{(M)}, d_q'^{(M)})$ are upper bounded by N^δ, where*

$$\delta < \frac{1}{2} - 2\alpha - 2\gamma,$$

then (k', l') can be computed in polynomial time under Assumption 1.

Proof. The first steps of the proof are completely analogous to the proof of [43, Lemma 2], where k, l, d_p, and d_q are replaced by k', l', d_p', and d_q', respectively. Specifically, the polynomials f and g are defined analogously.

We know that k', l' are upper bounded by $N^\gamma e$, and it is also known that, under Assumption 1, all roots (x_0, y_0) of g modulo $2^i e$ that satisfy $|x_0|, |y_0| < N^\gamma e$ can be solved in polynomial time if

$$(N^\gamma e)^2 < (2^i e)^{\frac{2}{3}}. \tag{4}$$

Because $e = N^\alpha$ and $2^i = \Theta(N^{\frac{1}{2} + \gamma - \delta})$, the inequality 4 is actually asymptotically equivalent to

$$\delta < \frac{1}{2} - 2\alpha - 2\gamma,$$

which completes the proof. ∎

3.4 Step 2: Factoring N with Computed k'

After computing k' as described in Sects. 3.1 and 3.2 for the MSB case or in Sect. 3.3 for the LSB case, the second step is to factor N in polynomial time using the computed k' and the known part of d_p'. Please keep in mind that, in the MSB case when factoring is used, this step occasionally has to be performed twice because we do not know which of the two factors obtained in Step 1 corresponds to k' (as opposed to l'). Our Step 2 is similar to [43] and based on their **Theorem 3** as below:

Theorem 2 (May-Nowakowski-Sarkar [43]). *Suppose we are given a polynomial $f(x) = x + a$ and integers $k, N \in \mathbb{N}$, where $k = N^\mu$ for some $\mu \geq 0$. Let $p > N^\beta \in \mathbb{N}, \beta \in [0, 1]$ be an unknown divisor of N. In time polynomial in $\log N, \log k$ and $\log a$, we can compute all integers x_0, satisfying*

$$f(x_0) \equiv 0 \mod kp \quad and \quad |x_0| \leq N^{\beta^2 + \mu}.$$

To factor N with the computed k' and the known parts of (d_p', d_q'), we have the following Lemma 5, which is a direct application of Theorem 2.

Lemma 5. *Let (N, e) be the public key and N be large enough with $e = N^\alpha$. Given the value k' and the MSBs $(d_p'^{(M)}, d_q'^{(M)})$ or the LSBs $(d_p'^{(L)}, d_q'^{(L)})$. If the* *unknown parts of (d_p', d_q') are upper bounded by N^δ for $\delta < \frac{1}{4} + \alpha + \gamma$, then N can be factored in time polynomial in $\log N, \log k'$ and $\log a$, where*

$$a = (ed_p'^{(M)}2^i + k' - 1) \cdot (e^{-1} \mod k'N)$$

in the MSB case, or

$$a = \left(\frac{ed_p'^{(L)} + k' - 1}{\gcd(2^i e, k'N)} \right) \cdot \left(\left(\frac{2^i e}{\gcd(2^i e, k'N)} \right)^{-1} \mod \frac{k'N}{\gcd(2^i e, k'N)} \right)$$

in the LSB case.

Proof. In the MSB case, the first steps of the proof are completely analogous to the proof of [43, Lemma 3], where k, l, d_p, and d_q are replaced by k', l', d_p', and d_q', respectively.

Since $k' = \Theta(N^{\alpha+\gamma})$ and $p = \Theta(\sqrt{N})$, it is concluded from [43, **Theorem 3**] that the unknown part $d_p'^{(L)}$ can be solved in polynomial time if $d_p'^{(L)} < N^{\frac{1}{4}+\alpha+\gamma}$. This condition is already fulfilled because $d_p'^{(L)} \leq N^\delta$. The last step to factor N is to get $p = \gcd\left(f_{MSB}(d_p'^{(L)}), N\right)$.

In the LSB case, similarly we construct a polynomial

$$f_{LSB}(x) = x + (ed_p'^{(L)} + k' - 1) \cdot ((2^i e)^{-1} \mod k'N),$$

however, it is slightly different from the MSB case (and from [43]) that the modular multiplicative inverse $(2^i e)^{-1} \mod k'N$ does not always exist because $\gcd(2^i e, k'N) = 1$ does not always hold. To this end, we slightly change the polynomial to

$$f_{LSB}(x) = x + \left(\frac{ed_p'^{(L)} + k' - 1}{\gcd(2^i e, k'N)} \right) \cdot \left(\left(\frac{2^i e}{\gcd(2^i e, k'N)} \right)^{-1} \mod \frac{k'N}{\gcd(2^i e, k'N)} \right),$$

in this way, it is guaranteed that the modular multiplicative inverse $\left(\frac{2^i e}{\gcd(2^i e, k'N)} \right)^{-1} \mod \frac{k'N}{\gcd(2^i e, k'N)}$ exists. The rest is the same as the MSB case to factor N to get $p = \gcd\left(f_{LSB}(d_p'^{(M)}), N\right)$ and that finishes our proof. ∎

It is worth noting that our EPKE also does not work if $e \geq N^{\frac{1}{4}-\gamma}$, unless factoring is easy, according to [43, **Corollary 1**].

4   Experimental Results

As aforementioned, it is critical to experimentally verify the validity of Assumption 1 in the LSB case, as well as the validity of Assumption 2 and the subexponential time of factoring $k'l'$ in the MSB case. To assess the effectiveness of the EPKE attacks, we first conduct the EPKE attacks to recover the entire private exponent with $\frac{1}{3}$ known blinded MSBs or LSBs of d_p' and d_q', with different

Table 1. Summary of the EPKE experiments - MSB case with single $d_q'^{(M)}$

Len(N)	Len(e)	Len(r_p, r_q)	Len(UnknownLSB)	Step 1a Factoring time	Step 2 Lattice Dim.	LLL time
1024	64	32	336/**352**	<1 s	21	1 s
1024	43	64	347/**362**	<1 s	21	1 s
1024	17*	128	347/**401**	2 s	21	2 s
2048	149	32	665/**693**	42 s	21	4 s
2048	128	64	677/**704**	175 s	21	4 s
2048	85	128	697/**725**	340 s	21	4 s
3072	235	32	1008/**1034**	1787 s	31	60 s
3072	213	64	1014/**1045**	5993 s	31	60 s
3072	171	128	1032/**1066**	6651 s	31	60 s

Table 2. Summary of the EPKE experiments - MSB case with multiple $d_q'^{(M)}$

Len(N)	Len(e)	Len(r_p, r_q)	Len(UnknownLSB)	Step 1b Success Prob.
1024	64	32	336/**352**	0.67/0.89/0.93/0.97/0.98/0.99/0.98/0.98/1.00
1024	43	64	347/**362**	0.65/0.89/0.91/0.98/0.97/0.99/0.99/1.00/0.99
1024	17*	128	347/**401**	0.65/0.78/0.94/0.99/0.96/0.99/0.99/1.00/1.00
2048	149	32	665/**693**	0.67/0.79/0.89/0.95/0.99/1.00/0.98/0.99/1.00
2048	128	64	677/**704**	0.73/0.86/0.92/0.93/0.98/1.00/1.00/1.00/1.00
2048	85	128	697/**725**	0.73/0.86/0.92/0.95/0.99/1.00/0.99/1.00/1.00
3072	235	32	1008/**1034**	0.69/0.81/0.93/0.98/0.98/0.99/1.00/1.00/1.00
3072	213	64	1014/**1045**	0.72/0.82/0.94/0.98/0.98/0.99/1.00/1.00/1.00
3072	171	128	1032/**1066**	0.67/0.81/0.93/1.00/0.99/1.00/1.00/1.00/1.00

key and additive blinding factor lengths. To this end, we consider the commonly used key length of 1024-bit, 2048-bit and 3072-bit, the commonly used additive blinding factor length of 32-bit, 64-bit and 128-bit, and both MSB and LSB cases. Rather than executing the EPKE attacks on real or simulated side-channel leakage, known keys are generated and a fraction of the known bits of the blinded private exponents are used directly. Since our bounds depend on both the length of e and the length of the additive blinding factor, we choose the length of e based on the length of the additive blinding factor such that $r_p^{\frac{2}{3}} e \approx N^{\frac{1}{12}}$ in the MSB case and such that $r_p e \approx N^{\frac{1}{12}}$ in the LSB case. In these cases, we can use only $\frac{1}{3}$-part of known bits to recover the full key. More precisely, $\alpha = \frac{1}{12} - \frac{2}{3}\gamma$ according to our bounds $\min\{\frac{1}{4} + \alpha + \gamma, \frac{1}{2} - 2\alpha - \gamma\}$ for the MSB case, and $\alpha = \frac{1}{12} - \gamma$ according to our bounds $\min\{\frac{1}{4} + \alpha + \gamma, \frac{1}{2} - 2\alpha - 2\gamma\}$ for the LSB case. If $\gamma = 0$, i.e., without exponent blinding, our bounds are the same as [43] for both MSB and LSB cases, i.e., our bounds are the generalization of their work. The experimental EPKE attack results are summarized in Table 1 and Table 2 for the MSB case and Table 3 for the LSB case. The experiments are repeated 100 times for each setting by randomly generating a CRT key pair including e, so the time values in each table correspond to the average time over 100 experiments of each setting. We have implemented the experiments in SAGE 9.5 and YAFU [5] 2.08 factorization toolkit (Ubuntu 20.04.4) with an Intel® Core™ i5-7500 CPU 3.40 GHz.

Table 3. Summary of the EPKE experiments - LSB case

Len(N)	Len(e)	Len(r_p, r_q)	Len(UnknownMSB)	Step 1c Lattice Dim.	LLL time	Step 2 Lattice Dim.	LLL time
1024	53	32	320/**341**	121	216 s	21	<1 s
1024	21	64	320/**341**	121	202 s	21	<1 s
1024	17*	128	191/**222**	121	461 s	21	4 s
2048	139	32	648/**682**	121	487 s	21	4 s
2048	107	64	647/**682**	121	470 s	21	4 s
2048	43	128	649/**682**	121	419 s	21	4 s
3072	224	32	978/**1024**	121	1104 s	31	90 s
3072	192	64	978/**1024**	121	1110 s	31	90 s
3072	128	128	976/**1024**	121	991 s	31	87 s

The fourth column shows two values, the ones in bold font correspond to the theoretical bounds, and the others correspond to the experimental results. In the MSB case, with a public exponent e of size $\alpha = \frac{1}{12} - \frac{2}{3}\gamma$, we nearly reach the asymptotic bound using a $\min\{\frac{1}{4} + \alpha + \gamma, \frac{1}{2} - 2\alpha - \gamma\}$-part MSBs of blinded CRT exponents (d'_p, d'_q) to recover the entire private key.

In the LSB case, with a public exponent e of size $\alpha = \frac{1}{12} - \gamma$, we succeeded in computing (k', l') in each performed experiment, affirming the validity of Assumption 1. We closely reach the asymptotically bound using a $\min\{\frac{1}{4} + \alpha + \gamma, \frac{1}{2} - 2\alpha - 2\gamma\}$-part LSBs of blinded CRT exponents (d'_p, d'_q) to recover the entire private key. We need more known bits to reveal the key compared with the MSB case.

It has to be mentioned that the fourth row (1024-bit key with 128-bit blinding factor) in both MSB and LSB cases is different from the other settings. Because the chosen e should be 1 (resp., $N^{-\frac{1}{24}}$) for the MSB (resp., LSB) case if we want to use $\frac{1}{3}$ known MSBs/LSBs of blinded CRT exponents (d'_p, d'_q) to recover the full private key. However, those two e values are not realistic, instead, we choose a very widely-used (e.g., $2^{16} + 1$) size of e, i.e., 17-bit, which complies with the NIST's recommendation of e and is also close to those two values. Our experiments suggest that in the MSB case the required known bits are close to the optimum value, i.e., $\frac{1}{3}$ MSBs of blinded exponents. While in the LSB case we need more than $\frac{2}{3}$ LSBs of blinded exponents, because the used e value is too far away from the expected value $e = N^{-\frac{1}{24}}$.

Another critical point to be verified is the required sub-exponential factoring time to compute k' in Step 1a (see Sect. 3.1), as shown in Fig. 1, clearly it can be observed that the required factoring time for all the settings is certainly affordable even with an average PC. Mostly, the factoring finishes within seconds or minutes, but on very few occasions it requires between one hour and one and a half hours (resp., fourteen hours and fifty hours) for 2048-bit (resp., 3072-bit) key with 128-bit blinding. It is worth noting that the 1024-bit key with the 32-bit blinding factor case requires slightly more time than the 1024-bit key with the 64-bit blinding factor case, because the former case uses SAGE's internal factorization function while all other cases utilize YAFU's factorization functions.

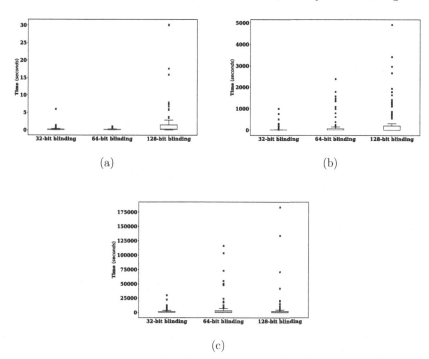

Fig. 1. Step 1a Factoring Time for: (a) 1024-bit key; (b) 2048-bit key; (c) 3072-bit key.

Finally, the success probability of the probabilistic method to obtain k' in Step 1b (see Sect. 3.2) is shown in Fig. 2. For all parameter sets in Tables 1, 2 and 3, 100 RSA key pairs were generated, and for each key pair, 1,000 sets of values $(l'_1, \ldots, l'_{10})$ were generated based on blinded exponents. The number of values required to obtain a GCD of 1 was computed for each set, in order to determine the estimated success probability of the attack depending on z. Our experimental results in Table 2 also validate the estimated probability here as part of the full attack path, as the last column indicates the successful EPKE attack probability with $2 \sim 10$ different randomly generated l'_z values for each setting of key size and blinding factor length. As can be observed, the successful EPKE attack probability is already above 0.65 using only two l'_z values, and it reaches up to almost 1 using five l'_z values. Therefore, we experimentally verify the validity of Assumption 2. In addition, as mentioned above, the f factor can be recovered using only two l'_z values with a small brute-force because it is expected to be small in practice. We also empirically confirm that the f factor is indeed pretty small as shown in Fig. 3. Mostly it is smaller than 100 for different key sizes and exponent blinding factor lengths, the brute-force effort is affordable to compute k' with only two l'_z values to achieve the successful EPKE attack probability of 1.

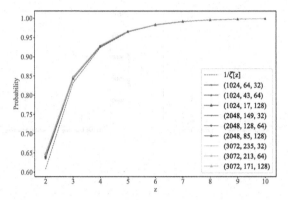

Fig. 2. Step 1b Estimated versus assumed probability that $l'_1, \ldots, l'_z$ are coprime.

A somewhat surprising observation is, from a PKE attack perspective, comparing to without additive exponent blinding, CRT-RSA with additive exponent blinding of size N^γ and public exponents $e \leq N^{\frac{1}{12}-\gamma}$ becomes easier to attack with larger exponent blinding factors. For instance, CRT-RSA with 2048-bit N and widely used 17-bit public exponent e. Without exponent blinding, the PKE attack can efficiently break the scheme with roughly 48% (492 bits) of the LSBs of the CRT exponents. On the contrary, given a 153-bit exponent blinding, then roughly only 33% (389 bits) are required. However, from an SCA attack point of view, it is other way around. The additive exponent blinding limits an attacker to use only a single attack trace to get the partial key information instead of using multiple attack traces without exponent blinding.

In both cases, we verified the effectiveness of the proposed EPKE attacks using partially known blinded CRT exponents to disclose the entire private key. Next, we will demonstrate an application of this EPKE attack using the obtained partial side-channel key leakage via profiled attacks in a realistic context.

5   A Use Case of EPKE on Real SCA Partial Key Leakage

In the following, we first introduce our profiled attacks-based experimental verification methodology concerning the EPKE attacks for an attacker/evaluator to disclose the full private key based on partially recovered CRT exponents. It includes the metrics used for training neural networks and the knowledge of points of interest (POIs) assumption. In the end, we present the experimental results rendering this verification methodology.

5.1   Deep Learning Profiled Attack

Since the seminal work of Kocher [35], side-channel analysis (SCA) has been a powerful and de facto tool to evaluate the physical security of various cryptographic implementations, especially on embedded devices. There is a

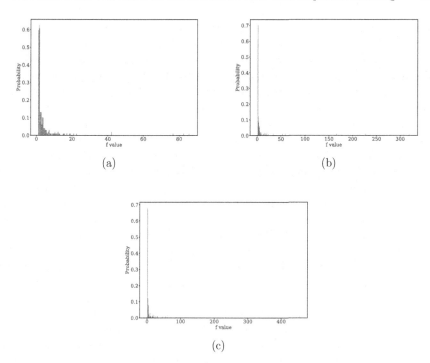

Fig. 3. Step 1b Histogram of f values with two l'_z values for: (a) 1024-bit key; (b) 2048-bit key; (c) 3072-bit key.

rich body of literature about SCA on RSA implementations. Some of these works [13,15,48,60,64] concentrated on RSA implementations with additive blinding. In particular, Carbone et al. [13] conducted profiled attacks, which is considered the most powerful SCA, on an RSA implementation with all afore-mentioned blinding countermeasures on a CC EAL4+ certified IC. Zaid et al. [64] improved the profiled attack by introducing a new ensembling loss function.

Since the introduction of template attacks [14], the SCA community has considered profiled attacks as the most powerful side-channel attacks. Profiled attacks have two stages, i.e., the profiling stage and the attack stage. In the profiling stage, an attacker/evaluator uses a profiling device (and has control of the key or at least knows the key) to model the leakage characteristic of the target key-dependent sensitive data (exponent bits in this work) with the side-channel traces of the target implementation. The built leakage characteristic models for every possible target sensitive data value are the outcome of the profiling stage. In the attack (also called online) stage, the victim device is used to measure the side-channel traces of the target implementation. Afterwards, the attack traces are matched with the previously built leakage characteristic models of the target sensitive data (exponent bits in this work). For each attack trace, a probability is computed for each possible guessed key unit value (2 possible values for one exponent bit) per each trace. Finally, for each hypothesised key unit value, the probabilities for all the attack traces are combined using, e.g., the maximum likelihood method to get a combined probability of that specific guessed key unit value. The combined probability of each possible hypothesised key unit value is compared to find the highest one. The hypothesised key unit value with the highest probability is considered the recovered key unit. This attack process is repeated for all key units to reveal the complete key. In this work, the combination of probabilities is skipped because only single-trace attacks are in scope due to the exponent blinding countermeasure.

We use deep learning profiled attacks (DL) to experimentally investigate the efficiency of our proposed extended PKE attack in the additive exponent blinding scenario. In this regard, the deep learning model is used to extract the required partial MSBs or LSBs of blinded CRT exponents as the input to our extended PKE attack to reveal the entire private key. We use a published MLP (Multi-Layer Perceptron) [39] neural network model for our DL profiled attacks. The structure of this model is very simple and shallow, but it showed pretty good performance. We will describe the parameters-setting in Sect. 5.6.

Unlike the classical profiled attacks (e.g., template attacks), DL makes no assumption of the leakage characteristic. It exploits the features (sample points for side-channel traces) to classify the labels (sensitive data in the SCA context) using neural networks (details followed in Subsect. 5.6). The training process of neural networks (i.e., the profiling) aims to construct a classifier function $F(.) : \mathbb{R}^d \to \mathbb{R}^{|S|}$. The input trace $l \in R^d$ is mapped to the output vector $\mathbf{p} \in R^{|S|}$ of scores via this function. During the training, the backpropagation method [25,34] is used for each training batch to update the trainable parameters of the neural network model aiming at minimizing the loss, which is computed to quantize the classification error over each training batch. Then in the attack stage, the built trained model (i.e., $F(.)$ with all the final updated trainable parameters) is used to classify each attack trace to obtain its probability vector $\mathbf{p}[s_g]$. Afterwards, the final probability vector $\mathbf{p}[g]$ of each key candidate g is calculated using all the attack traces. Note that, in this work only a single attack trace is used to decide the final probability of each attacked exponent bit. The key candidate $g^* = \text{argmax } \mathbf{p}[g]$ is considered the right one.

5.2   Knowledge of POIs Assumption

There is an implicit assumption about the knowledge of the POIs to apply the profiled attacks to CRT exponentiation implementations. That is, the attackers/evaluators can determine the rough timing interval of each exponent bit calculation in the side-channel traces. It is feasible for most of security products in a grey-box testing context via SPA (Simple Power Analysis)/SEMA (Simple Electromagnetic Analysis) and CPA (Correlation Power Analysis)/CEMA (Correlation Electromagnetic Analysis) (or similar techniques) as shown in [13,21]. For instance, one can vary the key length, perform correlation analyses on the input and output data, make use of the design information such as the location of the RSA co-processor in the glue logic area or temporarily switch off some side-channel countermeasures like jitters. The additive exponent blinding countermeasure will not make this harder, because it only adds more patterns corresponding to exponent bit calculations in the side-channel traces. If the patterns of one exponent bit calculation without exponent blinding can be identified in a side-channel trace, it is the same to identify the exponent bit calculation patterns given the presence of an additive exponent blinding countermeasure.

5.3 Metrics

We use the most common machine learning metric accuracy [25] to monitor and evaluate our deep learning profiled attacks. Its definition is the successful classification rate obtained over a dataset. Accordingly, the training accuracy, the validation accuracy and the test accuracy correspond to the reached successful classification rates respectively over the training, the validation and the test sets. The training and validation accuracy metrics are used to monitor the performance of the neural network training, and we use the test accuracy to evaluate the trained model. The accuracy is suitable for our experiments because we focus on the successful classification rate of each exponent bit, and we use a balanced dataset (the number of profiling traces of each class is the same) to avoid the potential deceptive impact of the accuracy metric. Concerning the metrics used to train the neural networks, we use the Negative Log-Likelihood (NLL) loss function [12] for DL profiled attacks. It is a loss function calculated as $-\log y$ used in multi-class classification, where y is a prediction corresponding to the ground-truth label after the softmax [25] activation function is applied. The loss for a mini-batch is computed by taking the mean or sum of all items in the batch. Because it is proved that minimizing the NLL loss is equivalent to maximizing the Perceived Information [10,49] and thus minimizing the online attack complexity, thanks to the recent work [41].

5.4 Montgomery Ladder Exponentiation Implementation

Our target is a Montgomery Ladder exponentiation CRT-RSA implementation on a modern 45 nm secure microcontroller equipped with an RSA co-processor running at 100 MHz. This is a typical real-world target from a side-channel attack viewpoint due to the implemented side-channel countermeasures, that is, SPA/DPA-resistant atomic Montgomery Ladder exponentiation with additive message and exponent blinding and multiplicative modulus blinding. Moreover, the 32-bit CPU also has variable internal clock, random branch insertion, memory encryption and physical address scrambling countermeasures to enhance the side-channel resistance.

Algorithm 1 illustrates the implemented left-to-right Montgomery Ladder exponentiation [33]. It is a well-known and widely used SPA-resistant regular exponentiation algorithm without using dummy operations to defeat SPA/SEMA and safe-error attacks [63]. We view the n-bit private exponent as a binary vector

$\mathbf{d} = (d_{n-1}, ..., d_0)$ (where d_0 is the LSB). N is the modulus used for the exponentiation, and C is the message to be decrypted using the private exponent.

Algorithm 1. Montgomery Ladder.

Require: $C, N, \mathbf{d} = (d_{n-1}, ..., d_0)$
Ensure: $M = C^d \mod N$
1: $R_0 \leftarrow 1$
2: $R_1 \leftarrow C$
3: **for** $i = n - 1$ *downto* 0 **do**
4:     $R_{\neg d_i} \leftarrow R_{d_i} \times R_{\neg d_i} \mod N$
5:     $R_{d_i} \leftarrow R_{d_i} \times R_{d_i} \mod N$
6: **end for**
7: **return** R_0

5.5 EPKE Attack on SCA Partial Key Leakage Verification Strategy

To represent a realistic scenario of EPKE attack on CRT using SCA partial key leakage, we follow the verification strategy as below:

1. Determine the Montgomery Ladder exponentiation interval using the SPA technique as discussed in Sect. 5.2.
2. Measure a set of 5,000 profiling traces focusing on the exponentiation interval using a CRT key pair labelled as K_{Prof0}.
3. Randomly generate ten different CRT key pairs with 128-bit e values (considering a 64-bit additive blinding factor used by the target CRT implementation) to measure the attack traces for the MSB case, denote those ten attack key pairs as $K_{MSB1}, K_{MSB2}, ..., K_{MSB10}$. Similarly, for the LSB case, randomly generate another ten different CRT key pairs $K_{LSB1}, K_{LSB2}, ..., K_{LSB10}$ with 107-bit e values to acquire the corresponding attack traces.
4. Measure ten attack traces for each of those 20 attack keys.
5. Train the neural network model using the profiling traces to save the best model with the highest test accuracy.
6. Perform the profiled attack on all the attack traces using the saved best neural network model to recover the MSBs or LSBs of CRT exponents. More precisely, recover 411 (= 1024+64−677, according to the sixth row in Table 1) MSBs of d_p' and d_q' for each attack trace with $K_{MSB1}, K_{MSB2}, ..., K_{MSB10}$. Similarly, recover 441 (= 1024+64−647, according to the sixth row in Table 3) LSBs of d_p' and d_q' for each attack trace with $K_{LSB1}, K_{LSB2}, ..., K_{LSB10}$.
7. Conduct the EPKE attack using the recovered 411 MSBs of d_p' and d_q' to disclose the full private key for $K_{MSB1}, K_{MSB2}, ..., K_{MSB10}$ and verify the required sub-exponential time. To this end, we benefit from the previously mentioned combination of the recovered MSBs of d_p' from one attack trace

and the recovered MSBs of d'_q from another attack trace. For each MSB attack key K_{MSBi}, we have 100 different combinations, using those combinations to tolerate potential SCA errors. We do the same for the LSB attack keys. In this case we need to verify the validity of the Coppersmith-type heuristic assumption.

We acquired power consumption traces with a Lecroy WaveRunner 8254 oscilloscope at a sampling rate of 500 MS/s. For each exponentiation execution, we triggered the oscilloscope at its end and recorded the processing of the entire exponentiation. Each trace consists of 16,000,000 sample points. Each exponent bit processing corresponds to two Montgomery modular multiplications as shown in Algorithm 1, and it contains about 6,074 sample points illustrated in the full version.

While we recorded the entire exponentiation for this experiment, it is worth mentioning that an extra advantage of our EPKE attack is that the recovered MSBs or LSBs of d'_p and the MSBs or LSBs of d'_q can come from different observations of the partial key leakage. An attacker can, at his own convenience, capture and combine the error-free MSBs or LSBs of d'_p from one observation of the partial key leakage, and those of d'_q from another one, while the remaining parts can be arbitrarily erroneous or not captured at all (i.e., only capture one-third of the execution of one of the two CRT exponentiations).

5.6   Attack Results

We have implemented the DL profiled attacks in Python and PyTorch [46] version 1.10.1 with an NVIDIA GTX 1080Ti GPU. We use the *Adadelta* optimizer [65] and utilize the adaptive learning rate policy *ReduceLROnPlateau* to gradually decrease the learning rate (with the default Adadelta optimizer initial learning rate of 1.0) with a factor of 0.05 if the training stagnates. We use a batch size of 512 and 100 as the number of epochs. All profiling and attack traces are normalized using the *StandardScalar* function from the Scikit-learn [47] library by removing the mean and scaling to unit variance. 20% of profiling traces compose a validation set. A validation data set is crucial to DL performance because it provides a way of instantly detecting over-fitting [26]. The DL attacks utilize the trained model with the highest validation accuracy. As mentioned above, we use the NLL loss for the model training. Table 4 summarizes the details of the used DL model and the corresponding hyperparameters.

We first train the model using the profiling traces to save the best model based on the highest validation accuracy depicted in Fig. 4, in which the best model corresponds to a validation accuracy of 100%.

The saved best model is then used to retrieve the 411 (resp., 441) MSBs (resp., LSBs) of d'_p and d'_q for all the 10 MSB-case (resp., LSB-case) attack traces with attack key K_{MSBi} (resp., K_{LSBi}). For each attack key, there are 100 combinations of recovered MSBs (resp., LSBs) of d'_p from one attack trace and recovered MSBs (resp., LSBs) of d'_q from another attack trace. We conduct the EPKE attacks using those combinations to recover the prime factor p as

Table 4. MLP model details

MLP
nb_epoch = 100
batch_size_training = 512
Dense(50, activation="relu", input_shape=(nb_samples,))
BatchNormalization()
Dense(100, activation="relu")
BatchNormalization()
Dense(2, activation="softmax")
compile(loss='categorical-crossentropy', optimizer='adadelta', metrics=['accuracy'])
learning_rate_policy = ReduceLROnPlateau(optimizer, 'min', factor=0.05, verbose=True)

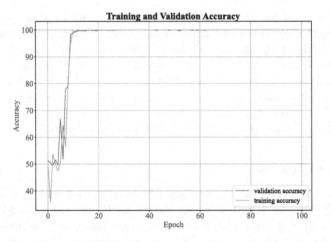

Fig. 4. Training and validation accuracy.

described in Sect. 3.4. The second column of Tables 5 and 6 presents the number of successful recovery of the prime factor out of 100 combinations for each attack key. The last three (resp., four) columns indicate the time cost and lattice dimensions of the two-step EPKE attack on the MSB (resp., LSB) cases. In the third column of Table 5, we present the average factoring time to compute k' and the corresponding minimum and maximum time (in the brackets).

The results further confirm the effectiveness of our EPKE attack in a realistic context, that is, disclosing a fraction of blinded CRT exponents via SCA followed by an EPKE attack to reveal the entire private key. In addition, the SCA experiments show that the proposed EPKE attack can tolerate slight SCA errors as demonstrated by our proposed verification strategy, i.e., combining the recovered error-free partial MSBs or LSBs of d'_p from one trace and MSBs or LSBs of d'_q from another one. When considering real-world CRT implementations, SCA attacks will often result in errors, which is why it is essential for an attacker/evaluator to be able to apply (E)PKE attacks.

Table 5. Summary of the real SCA data EPKE experiments - MSB case

Attack Key	Success Nr.	Step 1a Factoring time	Step 2 Lattice Dim.	LLL time
K_{MSB1}	26	110 s ([0.93 s, 599.7 s])	21	6 s
K_{MSB2}	35	90 s ([0.5 s, 1379.7 s])	21	6 s
K_{MSB3}	15	176 s ([1.0 s, 1817.7 s])	21	6 s
K_{MSB4}	3	10 s ([6.1 s, 16.4 s])	21	6 s
K_{MSB5}	9	202 s ([1.5 s, 1211.8 s])	21	6 s
K_{MSB6}	4	251 s ([59.7 s, 477.9 s])	21	6 s
K_{MSB7}	4	65 s ([2.1 s, 235.7 s])	21	6 s
K_{MSB8}	4	212 s ([1.6 s, 775.2 s])	21	6 s
K_{MSB9}	4	969 s ([764.4 s, 1373.7 s])	21	6 s
K_{MSB10}	12	21 s ([2.6 s, 60.7 s])	21	6 s

Table 6. Summary of the real SCA data EPKE experiments - LSB case

Attack Key	Success Nr.	Step 1c Lattice Dim.	LLL time	Step 2 Lattice Dim.	LLL time
K_{LSB1}	6	121	388 s	21	2 s
K_{LSB2}	2	121	404 s	21	2 s
K_{LSB3}	4	121	407 s	21	3 s
K_{LSB4}	3	121	421 s	21	3 s
K_{LSB5}	8	121	410 s	21	3 s
K_{LSB6}	5	121	407 s	21	3 s
K_{LSB7}	9	121	399 s	21	3 s
K_{LSB8}	12	121	405 s	21	3 s
K_{LSB9}	16	121	442 s	21	3 s
K_{LSB10}	9	121	433 s	21	3 s

6   Conclusion and Future Work

Many existing PKE works focused on implementations of RSA and its CRT variant without exponent blinding countermeasures. The state-of-the-art PKE attack on CRT without exponent blinding [43] can recover the whole CRT private key with only a third MSBs or LSBs of CRT exponents when the public exponent $e \approx N^{\frac{1}{12}}$. In this work, we showed that it can be extended to CRT implementations with additive exponent blinding, which is the most widely deployed exponent blinding countermeasure in real-world products. We proposed an extended PKE attack to recover the full CRT private key using partial disclosed MSBs or LSBs of additively blinded CRT exponents. It follows a two-step approach, first computing the key-dependent constant k' and then factoring the N using partial MSBs or LSBs of blinded CRT exponents d'_p and d'_q.

The mathematical proof and time-complexity analyses suggest that a third MSBs or LSBs of blinded CRT exponents d'_p and d'_q are enough to recover the entire CRT private key: in polynomial time based on the standard Coppersmith-type heuristic assumption in the LSB case when $e \approx N^{\frac{1}{12}-\gamma}$, as well as in sub-exponential (yet practically feasible) time or in probabilistic polynomial time under a heuristic assumption in the MSB case when $e \approx N^{\frac{1}{12}-\frac{2}{3}\gamma}$. Under different settings of typical key size and exponent blinding factor length, our extensive experiments verify the validity of the Coppersmith-type heuristic for the LSB case, as well as the affordability of the required sub-exponential time and the heuristic assumption for the MSB case. More precisely, in practice, using an average PC, the required sub-exponential time is mostly in seconds and minutes, the worst-case occasionally observed is less than one and a half hours.

Moreover, as an application of the proposed EPKE attack in real life, utilizing real SCA partial key leakage of a real-world SPA/DPA-resistant Montgomery Ladder CRT implementation on a 45 nm secure microcontroller with an RSA co-processor, our SCA experimental results suggest that the EPKE attack can tolerate slight SCA errors of the recovered MSBs or LSBs of the blinded CRT exponents. Such errors are expected to occur in a realistic scenario, especially when only a single attack trace is available. It sheds some light on the error-tolerant potential of the EPKE attack, and points out a possible future direction of our work, i.e., how to improve the EPKE to tolerate more generic SCA errors of the recovered MSBs or LSBs, e.g., in the binary symmetric model where every recovered exponent bit will be "flipped" with a crossover probability (i.e., the Bernoulli distribution).

Acknowledgements. We would like to express our gratitude to the anonymous reviewers for their insightful comments. Yu Yu was supported by the National Key Research and Development Program of China (Grant Nos. 2020YFA0309705 and 2018YFA0704701) and the National Natural Science Foundation of China (Grant Nos. 62125204 and 61872236). Yu Yu also acknowledges the support from the XPLORER PRIZE and Shanghai Key Laboratory of Privacy-Preserving Computation. François-Xavier Standaert is a senior research associate of the Belgian Fund for Scientific Research (F.R.S.-FNRS). This work has been funded in parts by the ERC project SWORD (Grant Number 724725).

References

1. Albrecht, M.R., Heninger, N.: On bounded distance decoding with predicate: breaking the "lattice barrier" for the hidden number problem. In: Canteaut, A., Standaert, F.-X. (eds.) EUROCRYPT 2021, Part I. LNCS, vol. 12696, pp. 528–558. Springer, Cham (2021). https://doi.org/10.1007/978-3-030-77870-5_19
2. Aldaya, A.C., García, C.P., Tapia, L.M.A., Brumley, B.B.: Cache-timing attacks on RSA key generation. IACR TCHES **2019**(4), 213–242 (2019). https://doi.org/10.13154/tches.v2019.i4.213-242. https://tches.iacr.org/index.php/TCHES/article/view/8350
3. Aono, Y.: A new lattice construction for partial key exposure attack for RSA. In: Jarecki, S., Tsudik, G. (eds.) PKC 2009. LNCS, vol. 5443, pp. 34–53. Springer, Heidelberg (2009). https://doi.org/10.1007/978-3-642-00468-1_3

4. Bauer, S.: Attacking exponent blinding in RSA without CRT. In: Schindler, W., Huss, S.A. (eds.) COSADE 2012. LNCS, vol. 7275, pp. 82–88. Springer, Heidelberg (2012). https://doi.org/10.1007/978-3-642-29912-4_7
5. bbuhrow: YAFU, Automated integer factorization Version: 2.0.8 (2022). https://github.com/bbuhrow/yafu
6. Boneh, D., Durfee, G., Frankel, Y.: An attack on RSA given a small fraction of the private key bits. In: Ohta, K., Pei, D. (eds.) ASIACRYPT 1998. LNCS, vol. 1514, pp. 25–34. Springer, Heidelberg (1998). https://doi.org/10.1007/3-540-49649-1_3
7. Blömer, J., May, A.: New partial key exposure attacks on RSA. In: Boneh, D. (ed.) CRYPTO 2003. LNCS, vol. 2729, pp. 27–43. Springer, Heidelberg (2003). https://doi.org/10.1007/978-3-540-45146-4_2
8. Bos, J., Stam, M. (eds.): Computational Cryptography: Algorithmic Aspects of Cryptology. London Mathematical Society Lecture Note Series. Cambridge University Press, Cambridge (2021). https://doi.org/10.1017/9781108854207
9. Botan: Botan, a Crypto and TLS for Modern C++ library, Version: 2.19.1 (2022). https://github.com/randombit/botan. https://github.com/randombit/botan/blob/master/src/lib/pubkey/rsa/rsa.cpp
10. Bronchain, O., Hendrickx, J.M., Massart, C., Olshevsky, A., Standaert, F.-X.: Leakage certification revisited: bounding model errors in side-channel security evaluations. In: Boldyreva, A., Micciancio, D. (eds.) CRYPTO 2019, Part I. LNCS, vol. 11692, pp. 713–737. Springer, Cham (2019). https://doi.org/10.1007/978-3-030-26948-7_25
11. BSI: BSI AIS46 RSA SCA Resistance Guideline, Minimum Requirements for Evaluating Side-Channel Attack Resistance of RSA, DSA and Diffie-Hellman Key Exchange Implementations Version: 1.0 (2013). https://www.bsi.bund.de/SharedDocs/Downloads/DE/BSI/Zertifizierung/Interpretationen/AIS_46_BSI_guidelines_SCA_RSA_V1_0_e_pdf.pdf?__blob=publicationFile&v=1
12. Cagli, E., Dumas, C., Prouff, E.: Convolutional neural networks with data augmentation against jitter-based countermeasures. In: Fischer, W., Homma, N. (eds.) CHES 2017. LNCS, vol. 10529, pp. 45–68. Springer, Cham (2017). https://doi.org/10.1007/978-3-319-66787-4_3
13. Carbone, M., et al.: Deep learning to evaluate secure RSA implementations. IACR TCHES 2019(2), 132–161 (2019). https://doi.org/10.13154/tches.v2019.i2.132-161. https://tches.iacr.org/index.php/TCHES/article/view/7388
14. Chari, S., Rao, J.R., Rohatgi, P.: Template attacks. In: Kaliski, B.S., Koç, K., Paar, C. (eds.) CHES 2002. LNCS, vol. 2523, pp. 13–28. Springer, Heidelberg (2003). https://doi.org/10.1007/3-540-36400-5_3
15. Clavier, C., Feix, B., Gagnerot, G., Roussellet, M., Verneuil, V.: Horizontal correlation analysis on exponentiation. In: Soriano, M., Qing, S., López, J. (eds.) ICICS 2010. LNCS, vol. 6476, pp. 46–61. Springer, Heidelberg (2010). https://doi.org/10.1007/978-3-642-17650-0_5
16. Coppersmith, D.: Finding a small root of a bivariate integer equation; factoring with high bits known. In: Maurer, U. (ed.) EUROCRYPT 1996. LNCS, vol. 1070, pp. 178–189. Springer, Heidelberg (1996). https://doi.org/10.1007/3-540-68339-9_16
17. Coppersmith, D.: Finding a small root of a univariate modular equation. In: Maurer, U. (ed.) EUROCRYPT 1996. LNCS, vol. 1070, pp. 155–165. Springer, Heidelberg (1996). https://doi.org/10.1007/3-540-68339-9_14
18. Coppersmith, D.: Small solutions to polynomial equations, and low exponent RSA vulnerabilities. J. Cryptol. 10(4), 233–260 (1997). https://doi.org/10.1007/s001459900030

19. Coron, J.-S.: Resistance against differential power analysis for elliptic curve cryptosystems. In: Koç, Ç.K., Paar, C. (eds.) CHES 1999. LNCS, vol. 1717, pp. 292–302. Springer, Heidelberg (1999). https://doi.org/10.1007/3-540-48059-5_25

20. Diaconis, P., Erdös, P.: On the distribution of the greatest common divisor. In: A Festschrift for Herman Rubin, pp. 56–61. Institute of Mathematical Statistics (2004)

21. Diop, I., Linge, Y., Ordas, T., Liardet, P.-Y., Maurine, P.: From theory to practice: horizontal attacks on protected implementations of modular exponentiations. J. Cryptogr. Eng. 9(1), 37–52 (2018). https://doi.org/10.1007/s13389-018-0181-1

22. Dugardin, M., Schindler, W., Guilley, S.: Stochastic methods defeat regular RSA exponentiation algorithms with combined blinding methods. J. Math. Cryptol. 15(1), 408–433 (2021). https://doi.org/10.1515/jmc-2020-0010

23. Ernst, M., Jochemsz, E., May, A., de Weger, B.: Partial key exposure attacks on RSA up to full size exponents. In: Cramer, R. (ed.) EUROCRYPT 2005. LNCS, vol. 3494, pp. 371–386. Springer, Heidelberg (2005). https://doi.org/10.1007/11426639_22

24. Fouque, P.-A., Kunz-Jacques, S., Martinet, G., Muller, F., Valette, F.: Power attack on small RSA public exponent. In: Goubin, L., Matsui, M. (eds.) CHES 2006. LNCS, vol. 4249, pp. 339–353. Springer, Heidelberg (2006). https://doi.org/10.1007/11894063_27

25. Goodfellow, I., Bengio, Y., Courville, A.: Deep Learning. MIT Press, Cambridge (2016). http://www.deeplearningbook.org

26. Guyon, I.: A scaling law for the validation-set training-set size ratio. In: AT & T Bell Laboratories (1997)

27. Halderman, J.A., et al.: Lest we remember: cold boot attacks on encryption keys. In: van Oorschot, P.C. (ed.) USENIX Security 2008, San Jose, CA, USA, 28 July–1 August 2008, pp. 45–60. USENIX Association (2008)

28. Heninger, N., Shacham, H.: Reconstructing RSA private keys from random key bits. In: Halevi, S. (ed.) CRYPTO 2009. LNCS, vol. 5677, pp. 1–17. Springer, Heidelberg (2009). https://doi.org/10.1007/978-3-642-03356-8_1

29. Hlaváč, M.: Known–plaintext–only attack on RSA–CRT with montgomery multiplication. In: Clavier, C., Gaj, K. (eds.) CHES 2009. LNCS, vol. 5747, pp. 128–140. Springer, Heidelberg (2009). https://doi.org/10.1007/978-3-642-04138-9_10

30. Howgrave-Graham, N.: Finding small roots of univariate modular equations revisited. In: Darnell, M. (ed.) Cryptography and Coding 1997. LNCS, vol. 1355, pp. 131–142. Springer, Heidelberg (1997). https://doi.org/10.1007/BFb0024458

31. Howgrave-Graham, N.: Approximate integer common divisors. In: Silverman, J.H. (ed.) CaLC 2001. LNCS, vol. 2146, pp. 51–66. Springer, Heidelberg (2001). https://doi.org/10.1007/3-540-44670-2_6

32. Joye, M., Lepoint, T.: Partial key exposure on RSA with private exponents larger than N. In: Ryan, M.D., Smyth, B., Wang, G. (eds.) ISPEC 2012. LNCS, vol. 7232, pp. 369–380. Springer, Heidelberg (2012). https://doi.org/10.1007/978-3-642-29101-2_25

33. Joye, M., Yen, S.-M.: The montgomery powering ladder. In: Kaliski, B.S., Koç, K., Paar, C. (eds.) CHES 2002. LNCS, vol. 2523, pp. 291–302. Springer, Heidelberg (2003). https://doi.org/10.1007/3-540-36400-5_22

34. Kelley, H.J.: Gradient theory of optimal flight paths. Ars J. 30(10), 947–954 (1960)

35. Kocher, P.C.: Timing attacks on implementations of Diffie-Hellman, RSA, DSS, and other systems. In: Koblitz, N. (ed.) CRYPTO 1996. LNCS, vol. 1109, pp. 104–113. Springer, Heidelberg (1996). https://doi.org/10.1007/3-540-68697-5_9

36. Lenstra, A., Lenstra, H., Lovász, L.: Factoring polynomials with rational coefficients. Math. Ann. **261**, 515–534 (1982)
37. Libgcrypt: Libgcrypt, the gnu crypto library, Version: 1.9.0 (2021). https://github.com/gpg/libgcrypt. https://github.com/gpg/libgcrypt/blob/master/cipher/rsa.c
38. Lu, Y., Zhang, R., Lin, D.: New partial key exposure attacks on CRT-RSA with large public exponents. In: Boureanu, I., Owesarski, P., Vaudenay, S. (eds.) ACNS 2014. LNCS, vol. 8479, pp. 151–162. Springer, Cham (2014). https://doi.org/10.1007/978-3-319-07536-5_10
39. Maghrebi, H.: Deep learning based side-channel attack: a new profiling methodology based on multi-label classification. Cryptology ePrint Archive, Report 2020/436 (2020). https://eprint.iacr.org/2020/436
40. Mangard, S., Oswald, E., Popp, T.: Power Analysis Attacks - Revealing the Secrets of Smart Cards. Springer, New York (2007). https://doi.org/10.1007/978-0-387-38162-6
41. Masure, L., Dumas, C., Prouff, E.: A comprehensive study of deep learning for side-channel analysis. IACR TCHES **2020**(1), 348–375 (2019). https://doi.org/10.13154/tches.v2020.i1.348-375. https://tches.iacr.org/index.php/TCHES/article/view/8402
42. May, A., Nowakowski, J., Sarkar, S.: Partial key exposure attack on short secret exponent CRT-RSA. In: Tibouchi, M., Wang, H. (eds.) ASIACRYPT 2021, Part I. LNCS, vol. 13090, pp. 99–129. Springer, Cham (2021). https://doi.org/10.1007/978-3-030-92062-3_4
43. May, A., Nowakowski, J., Sarkar, S.: Approximate divisor multiples - factoring with only a third of the secret CRT-exponents. In: Dunkelman, O., Dziembowski, S. (eds.) EUROCRYPT 2022, Part III. LNCS, vol. 13277, pp. 147–167. Springer, Cham (2022). https://doi.org/10.1007/978-3-031-07082-2_6
44. MbedTLS: MbedTLS, a TLS and SSL library, Version: 3.1.0 (2021). https://github.com/Mbed-TLS/mbedtls. https://github.com/Mbed-TLS/mbedtls/blob/development/library/rsa.c
45. NIST: FIPS PUB 186-4, Digital Signature Standard (DSS) (FIPS 186-4) (2013). https://nvlpubs.nist.gov/nistpubs/FIPS/NIST.FIPS.186-4.pdf
46. Paszke, A., et al.: Pytorch: an imperative style, high-performance deep learning library. In: Wallach, H.M., Larochelle, H., Beygelzimer, A., d'Alché-Buc, F., Fox, E.B., Garnett, R. (eds.) Advances in Neural Information Processing Systems 32: Annual Conference on Neural Information Processing Systems 2019, NeurIPS 2019, 8–14 December 2019, Vancouver, BC, Canada, pp. 8024–8035 (2019). https://proceedings.neurips.cc/paper/2019/hash/bdbca288fee7f92f2bfa9f7012727740-Abstract.html
47. Pedregosa, F., et al.: Scikit-learn: machine learning in Python. J. Mach. Learn. Res. **12**, 2825–2830 (2011)
48. Perin, G., Chmielewski, Ł: A semi-parametric approach for side-channel attacks on protected RSA implementations. In: Homma, N., Medwed, M. (eds.) CARDIS 2015. LNCS, vol. 9514, pp. 34–53. Springer, Cham (2016). https://doi.org/10.1007/978-3-319-31271-2_3
49. Renauld, M., Standaert, F.-X., Veyrat-Charvillon, N., Kamel, D., Flandre, D.: A formal study of power variability issues and side-channel attacks for nanoscale devices. In: Paterson, K.G. (ed.) EUROCRYPT 2011. LNCS, vol. 6632, pp. 109–128. Springer, Heidelberg (2011). https://doi.org/10.1007/978-3-642-20465-4_8
50. Sarkar, S., Venkateswarlu, A.: Partial key exposure attack on CRT-RSA. In: Meier, W., Mukhopadhyay, D. (eds.) INDOCRYPT 2014. LNCS, vol. 8885, pp. 255–264. Springer, Cham (2014). https://doi.org/10.1007/978-3-319-13039-2_15

51. Schindler, W.: A timing attack against RSA with the Chinese remainder theorem. In: Koç, Ç.K., Paar, C. (eds.) CHES 2000. LNCS, vol. 1965, pp. 109–124. Springer, Heidelberg (2000). https://doi.org/10.1007/3-540-44499-8_8

52. Schindler, W., Itoh, K.: Exponent blinding does not always lift (partial) spa resistance to higher-level security. In: Lopez, J., Tsudik, G. (eds.) ACNS 2011. LNCS, vol. 6715, pp. 73–90. Springer, Heidelberg (2011). https://doi.org/10.1007/978-3-642-21554-4_5

53. Schindler, W., Wiemers, A.: Power attacks in the presence of exponent blinding. J. Cryptogr. Eng. **4**(4), 213–236 (2014). https://doi.org/10.1007/s13389-014-0081-y

54. Schindler, W., Wiemers, A.: Generic power attacks on RSA with CRT and exponent blinding: new results. J. Cryptogr. Eng. **7**(4), 255–272 (2017). https://doi.org/10.1007/s13389-016-0146-1

55. Stehlé, D., Zimmermann, P.: A binary recursive Gcd algorithm. In: Buell, D. (ed.) ANTS 2004. LNCS, vol. 3076, pp. 411–425. Springer, Heidelberg (2004). https://doi.org/10.1007/978-3-540-24847-7_31

56. Takayasu, A., Kunihiro, N.: Partial key exposure attacks on RSA: achieving the Boneh-Durfee bound. In: Joux, A., Youssef, A. (eds.) SAC 2014. LNCS, vol. 8781, pp. 345–362. Springer, Cham (2014). https://doi.org/10.1007/978-3-319-13051-4_21

57. Takayasu, A., Kunihiro, N.: Partial key exposure attacks on CRT-RSA: better cryptanalysis to full size encryption exponents. In: Malkin, T., Kolesnikov, V., Lewko, A.B., Polychronakis, M. (eds.) ACNS 2015. LNCS, vol. 9092, pp. 518–537. Springer, Cham (2015). https://doi.org/10.1007/978-3-319-28166-7_25

58. Takayasu, A., Kunihiro, N.: Partial key exposure attacks on RSA: achieving the Boneh-Durfee bound. Theor. Comput. Sci. **761**, 51–77 (2019). https://doi.org/10.1016/j.tcs.2018.08.021

59. Takayasu, A., Lu, Y., Peng, L.: Small CRT-exponent RSA revisited. J. Cryptol. **32**(4), 1337–1382 (2018). https://doi.org/10.1007/s00145-018-9282-3

60. Walter, C.D.: Sliding windows succumbs to big mac attack. In: Koç, Ç.K., Naccache, D., Paar, C. (eds.) CHES 2001. LNCS, vol. 2162, pp. 286–299. Springer, Heidelberg (2001). https://doi.org/10.1007/3-540-44709-1_24

61. Wang, T., Cui, X., Ni, Y., Yu, D., Cui, X., Qu, G.: A practical cold boot attack on RSA private keys. In: 2017 Asian Hardware Oriented Security and Trust Symposium, AsianHOST 2017, Beijing, China, 19–20 October 2017, pp. 55–60. IEEE Computer Society (2017). https://doi.org/10.1109/AsianHOST.2017.8353995

62. Yarom, Y., Genkin, D., Heninger, N.: CacheBleed: a timing attack on OpenSSL constant time RSA. In: Gierlichs, B., Poschmann, A.Y. (eds.) CHES 2016. LNCS, vol. 9813, pp. 346–367. Springer, Heidelberg (2016). https://doi.org/10.1007/978-3-662-53140-2_17

63. Yen, S., Joye, M.: Checking before output may not be enough against fault-based cryptanalysis. IEEE Trans. Computers **49**(9), 967–970 (2000). https://doi.org/10.1109/12.869328

64. Zaid, G., Bossuet, L., Habrard, A., Venelli, A.: Efficiency through diversity in ensemble models applied to side-channel attacks. IACR TCHES **2021**(3), 60–96 (2021). https://doi.org/10.46586/tches.v2021.i3.60-96. https://tches.iacr.org/index.php/TCHES/article/view/8968

65. Zeiler, M.D.: ADADELTA: an adaptive learning rate method. CoRR abs/1212.5701 (2012). http://arxiv.org/abs/1212.5701

Stretching Cube Attacks: Improved Methods to Recover Massive Superpolies

Jiahui He[1,4] , Kai Hu[2] , Bart Preneel[3], and Meiqin Wang[1,4,5(✉)]

[1] School of Cyber Science and Technology, Shandong University, Qingdao, Shandong, China
hejiahui2020@mail.sdu.edu.cn, mqwang@sdu.edu.cn
[2] School of Physical and Mathematical Sciences, Nanyang Technological University, Singapore, Singapore
kai.hu@ntu.edu.sg
[3] imec-COSIC, KU Leuven, Leuven, Belgium
bart.preneel@esat.kuleuven.be
[4] Key Laboratory of Cryptologic Technology and Information Security, Ministry of Education, Shandong University, Jinan, China
[5] Quan Cheng Shandong Laboratory, Jinan, China

Abstract. Cube attacks exploit the algebraic properties of symmetric ciphers by recovering a special polynomial, the superpoly, and subsequently the secret key. When the algebraic normal forms of the corresponding Boolean functions are not available, the division property based approach allows to recover the exact superpoly in a clever way. However, the computational cost to recover the superpoly becomes prohibitive as the number of rounds of the cipher increases. For example, the nested monomial predictions (NMP) proposed at ASIACRYPT 2021 stuck at round 845 for TRIVIUM. To alleviate the bottleneck of the NMP technique, i.e., the unsolvable model due to the excessive number of monomial trails, we shift our focus to the so-called valuable terms of a specific middle round that contribute to the superpoly. Two new techniques are introduced, namely, Non-zero Bit-based Division Property (NBDP) and Core Monomial Prediction (CMP), both of which result in a simpler MILP model compared to the MILP model of MP. It can be shown that the CMP technique offers a substantial improvement over the monomial prediction technique in terms of computational complexity of recovering valuable terms. Combining the divide-and-conquer strategy with these two new techniques, we catch the valuable terms more effectively and thus avoid wasting computational resources on intermediate terms contributing nothing to the superpoly. As an illustration of the power of our techniques, we apply our framework to TRIVIUM, Grain-128AEAD, Kreyvium and ACORN. As a result, the computational cost of earlier attacks can be significantly reduced and the exact ANFs of the superpolies for 846-, 847- and 848-round TRIVIUM, 192-round Grain-128AEAD, 895-round Kreyvium and 776-round ACORN can be recovered

Due to page limits, all appendixes and some tables of this paper are provided in our full version [13].

S. Agrawal and D. Lin (Eds.): ASIACRYPT 2022, LNCS 13794, pp. 537–566, 2022.
https://doi.org/10.1007/978-3-031-22972-5_19

in practical time, even though the superpoly of 848-round TRIVIUM contains over 500 million terms; this corresponds to respectively 3, 1, 1 and 1 rounds more than the previous best results. Moreover, by investigating the internal properties of Möbius transformation, we show how to perform key recovery using superpolies involving full key bits, which leads to the best key recovery attacks on the targeted ciphers.

Keywords: Cube attack · Superpoly · TRIVIUM · Grain-128AEAD · ACORN · Kreyvium · Division property · Monomial prediction

1   Introduction

The cube attack, proposed by Dinur and Shamir at EUROCRYPT 2009 [8], is one of the most powerful cryptanalytic techniques against symmetric ciphers. Typically, any output bit of a cipher can be regarded as a polynomial of the public input $\boldsymbol{x} = (x_0, x_1, \ldots, x_{n-1})$ and the secret input $\boldsymbol{k} = (k_0, k_1, \ldots, k_{m-1})$, denoted by $f(\boldsymbol{x}, \boldsymbol{k})$. For a chosen term $\boldsymbol{x}^{\boldsymbol{u}} = \prod_{u_i=1} x_i, \boldsymbol{u}, \boldsymbol{x} \in \mathbb{F}_2^n$, $f(\boldsymbol{x}, \boldsymbol{k})$ can be uniquely expressed as

$$f(\boldsymbol{x}, \boldsymbol{k}) = p(\boldsymbol{x}[\bar{\boldsymbol{u}}], \boldsymbol{k}) \cdot \boldsymbol{x}^{\boldsymbol{u}} + q(\boldsymbol{x}, \boldsymbol{k}) \ ,$$

where $p(\boldsymbol{x}[\bar{\boldsymbol{u}}], \boldsymbol{k})$ is a Boolean function of $\boldsymbol{k}$, $\boldsymbol{x}[\bar{\boldsymbol{u}}] = \{x_i : u_i = 0\}$ and each term in $q(\boldsymbol{x}, \boldsymbol{k})$ misses at least one variable from $\{x_i : u_i = 1\}$. The polynomial $p(\boldsymbol{x}[\bar{\boldsymbol{u}}], \boldsymbol{k})$ is called the superpoly of the cube term $\boldsymbol{x}^{\boldsymbol{u}}$. After assigning a static value to $\boldsymbol{k}$ and $\boldsymbol{x}[\bar{\boldsymbol{u}}]$, the value of $p(\boldsymbol{x}[\bar{\boldsymbol{u}}], \boldsymbol{k})$ can be computed by summing $f(\boldsymbol{x}, \boldsymbol{k})$ over a structure called *cube*, denoted as $\mathbb{C}_{\boldsymbol{u}}$, composed of all possible 0/1 combinations of $\{x_i : u_i = 1\}$.

To mount a cube attack, one first recovers the superpoly in an offline phase. Then, the value of the superpoly is obtained by querying the encryption oracle and computing the summation. From the equation between the superpoly and its value, information of the secret key can be revealed. Therefore, the superpoly recovery is a central step in the cube attack.

Traditional cube attacks [8,9,20,35] regard ciphers as black boxes so the superpolies are recovered experimentally. Only linear or quadratic superpolies are applicable. In [25], Todo et al. introduced cube attacks based on the Conventional Bit-based Division Property (CBDP). New methods based on CBDP [27] were proposed to efficiently identify secret variables that are not involved in the superpoly. After removing these uninvolved key bits and collecting the remaining key bits into a set J, the truth table of the superpoly can be recovered with time complexity $2^{|I|+|J|}$, where the set $I = \{i : u_i = 1\}$ is called *cube indices*. In [28], Wang et al. improved the precision of CBDP by considering cancellation characteristics of constant 1 bits, thus further lowering the complexity.

Exact Superpoly Recovery. Although the CBDP never produces a false positive error [17], it cannot accurately predict the existence of a monomial in the superpoly. A substantial amount of works have been carried out to get around this point. At Asiacrypt 2019, Wang et al. [29] managed to recover the exact superpoly for the first time with the pruning technique combined with the three-subset bit-based division property. However, the value of this technique is limited as it requires the assumption that almost all elements in the so-called 1-subset can be pruned. In [30], Ye and Tian introduced the recursively-expressing method, which recursively splits the output bits into intermediate terms of smaller rounds and filters out these useless terms that contribute nothing to the superpoly. As a result, several superpolies recovered in [28] are proved to degenerate to constants. In [11,12], Hao et al. proposed the three-subset division property without unknown subsets (3SDPwoU) to recover the exact superpolies from the perspective of counting the number of three-subset trails. In [17], Hu et al. established the equivalence between monomial prediction and 3SDPwoU from the viewpoint of monomial propagations. In [36], Ye and Tian also developed a pure algebraic method to recover the exact superpoly. However, as the number of rounds of the cipher increases, such useful cubes are hard to find. Last year, Hu el al. embedded the monomial prediction technique into a nested framework, which allows them to recover massive superpolies [16] that contain almost 20 million terms.

Nested Monomial Predictions. In terms of structure, the nested monomial prediction [16] consists of two components, namely the *coefficient solver* and the *term expander*. Given a cube term x^u, the coefficient solver is designed to compute the superpoly of x^u for a term of the current round, and the term expander is responsible for expressing unsolved terms as terms of a deeper round. At first, from top to bottom, the target output bit is expressed as a polynomial of the state bits of an intermediate round, then by iteratively calling the coefficient solver and expanding unsolved terms into terms of deeper rounds, the final superpoly can be recovered.

As mentioned, the cube attack is one of the powerful tools to evaluate the security of stream ciphers. It is important to explore its limits by recovering superpolies for as many rounds as possible. While the nested monomial predictions is efficient for massive superpolies (e.g., it can recover a superpoly for 845-round TRIVIUM that contains 19,967,968 terms), it has been stuck at 845 rounds of TRIVIUM. In order to recover superpolies for more rounds, novel techniques are required.

Contributions. This paper provides new efficient methods to recover superpolies for more initialization rounds of stream ciphers such as TRIVIUM [5], Grain-128AEAD [15], Kreyvium [6] and the authenticated encryption algorithm ACORN [31].

Recall that the framework of nested monomial predictions consists of two components, i.e., the coefficient solver and the term expander; we design two algorithms to greatly improve the efficiency of both of them.

- *Two-step strategy for the coefficient solver.* Unlike the monomial prediction, our coefficient solver takes two steps to compute the superpoly. During the first stage, the intermediate monomials related to the superpoly are determined utilizing a new technique called core monomial prediction. Next, by applying the monomial prediction to these intermediate monomials and collecting the results, the final superpoly can be recovered quickly.

Table 1. Verification and comparison of superpolies for 843-, 844- and 845-round Trivium[†] from [16].

I	Round	Status	TimeCost ([16])	TimeCost (ours)
I_0	843	Verified ✓	Less than 2 weeks	2 h
I_1	843	Verified ✓		4 h
I_2	843	Verified ✓		1 h
I_3	843	Verified ✓		1.5 h
I_4	843	Verified ✓		1 day and 17 h
I_2	844	Verified ✓	17 h	5 h
I_3	844	Verified ✓	6 h	2.5 h
I_2	845	Verified ✓	about 16 days	19.5 h
I_3	845	Verified ✓	4 days and 9 h	8.5 h

†: The time consumption of the superpoly recovery of 843-, 844-round Trivium is stated as 'less than two weeks' in [16]. The concrete time cost for 844- and 845-round Trivium was obtained by rerunning the code provided by [16] on our platform.

– *Fast-descent algorithm for the term expander.* Instead of expressing the current terms as a polynomial of indistinguishable terms of a deeper round and then testing them one by one, our term expander uses Gurobi's callback function to automatically filter out the useless terms internally during each expansion, which makes the number of rounds drop faster and reduces the time spent on useless terms.

Our new framework offers substantial efficiency improvements in recovering superpolies compared to the nested monomial prediction. We verified superpolies for Trivium recovered in [16]. As a result, our framework allows to recover superpolies in a few hours rather than in weeks. The comparison is illustrated in Table 1.

More importantly, our framework is able to recover superpolies for more initialization rounds of high profile symmetric-key ciphers including Trivium (ISO/IEC standard [3,5]), Grain-128AEAD (a member of the ten finalist candidates of the NIST LWC standardization process [15]), Kreyvium (designed for Fully Homomorphic Encryption [6]) and Acorn (a member of the final portfolio of the CAESAR competition for Lightweight applications [31]). For Trivium, we are the first to obtain superpolies for up to 848-round Trivium. We also recovered the superpolies of 192-round Grain-128AEAD, 895-round Kreyvium and 776-round Acorn, all penetrating one more round than the previous best results. By investigating the internal properties of Möbius transformation, we propose a novel method to perform key recovery inside Möbius transformation. The summary of our cube attack results and the previous best results are provided in Table 2.

All source codes for recovering the superpolies in this paper are provided in the public git repository https://github.com/viocently/ekignrb9lc.git.

Table 2. Summary of our cube attack results and the previous best results. #Cube means the number of cubes whose superpolies are recovered.

Cipher	Rounds	#Cube	Cube size	Time complexity	Attack types	Reference
TRIVIUM	≤ 806	–	–	Practical	key recovery	[8,9,20,23,37]
	808	37	39–41	Practical	Key recovery	[23]
	≤ 844	–	–	$2^{75} \sim 2^{79.6}$	Key recovery	[11,12,16,17,19,23]
						[9,26,29,35,37,38]
	845	2	54–55	2^{78}	Key recovery	[16]
	846	6	51–54	2^{79}	Key recovery	Sect. 6.1
	847	2	52–53	2^{79}	Key recovery	Sect. 6.1
	848	1	52	2^{79}	Key recovery	Sect. 6.1
Grain‡	169	–	–	Practical	Condit. Diff.	[18]
	–	–	–	Practical	State recovery	[7]
	≤ 190	–	–	$2^{123} \sim 2^{129}$	Key recovery	[11,12,25,26,28]
	191	2	95–96	2^{127}	Key recovery	[16]
	192	1	94	2^{127}	Key recovery	Sect. 6.2
Kreyvium	≤ 893	–	–	$2^{119} \sim 2^{127}$	Key recovery	[10–12,23,26,28]
	894	1	119	2^{127}	Key recovery	[16]
	895	1	120	2^{127}	Key recovery	Sect. 6.3
ACORN	≤ 774	–	–	2^{127}	Key recovery	[10,11,26,28]
	775	6	127	2^{127}	Distinguisher	[34]
	775	5	126	2^{126}	Distinguisher	[33]
	775	1	126	2^{127}	Key recovery	[33]
	776	2	126	2^{127}	Key recovery	Sect. 6.4

$\ddagger$: Grain-128a or Grain-128AEAD.

2 Division Property and Monomial Prediction

2.1 Notations and Definitions

We use bold italic lowercase letters to represent bit vectors. For an n-bit vector $\boldsymbol{u} = (u_0, \cdots, u_{n-1}) \in \mathbb{F}_2^n$, its complementary vector is denoted by $\bar{\boldsymbol{u}}$, where $u_i \oplus \bar{u}_i = 1$ for $0 \leq i < n$. The Hamming weight of $\boldsymbol{u}$ is $wt(\boldsymbol{u}) = |\{i : u_i = 1\}|$. The concatenation of $\boldsymbol{u}_0$ and $\boldsymbol{u}_1$ is denoted by $\boldsymbol{u}_0 \| \boldsymbol{u}_1$. For $\boldsymbol{u}, \boldsymbol{x} \in \mathbb{F}_2^n$, $\boldsymbol{x}[\boldsymbol{u}]$ denotes a sub-vector of $\boldsymbol{x}$ with respect to $\boldsymbol{u}$ as $\boldsymbol{x}[\boldsymbol{u}] = (x_{i_0}, x_{i_1}, \ldots, x_{i_{wt(\boldsymbol{u})-1}}) \in \mathbb{F}_2^{wt(\boldsymbol{u})}$, where $i_j \in \{0 \leq i \leq n - 1 : u_i = 1\}$ and $(i_0, \ldots, i_{wt(\boldsymbol{u})-1})$ is arranged from the least to the greatest. For any n-bit vectors $\boldsymbol{u}$ and $\boldsymbol{u}'$, we define $\boldsymbol{u} \succeq \boldsymbol{u}'$ if $u_i \geq u_i'$ for all i. Similarly, we define $\boldsymbol{u} \preceq \boldsymbol{u}'$ if $u_i \leq u_i'$ for all i. Bold italic lowercase letters with superscript are used to represent the bitvector in a certain round. Particularly, $\boldsymbol{u}^{(i)}$ represents a bitvector in round i. We use $\boldsymbol{0}^n$ or $\boldsymbol{1}^n$ to represent an all-zeros or all-ones vector of length n.

Blackboard bold uppercase letters (e.g. $\mathbb{S}, \mathbb{K}, \mathbb{U}, \ldots$) are used to represent sets of bit vectors. In the propagation of some algebraic properties such as CBDP, the set generated in the i-th round is denoted as $\mathbb{S}^{(i)}$.

Boolean Function. Let $f : \mathbb{F}_2^n \to \mathbb{F}_2$ be a Boolean function whose *algebraic normal form* (ANF) is

$$f(\boldsymbol{x}) = f(x_0, x_1, \ldots, x_{n-1}) = \bigoplus_{u \in \mathbb{F}_2^n} a_u \prod_{i=0}^{n-1} x_i^{u_i} \;,$$

where $a_u \in \mathbb{F}_2$, and

$$\boldsymbol{x}^u = \pi_u(\boldsymbol{x}) = \prod_{i=0}^{n-1} x_i^{u_i} \text{ with } x_i^{u_i} = \begin{cases} x_i, \text{ if } u_i = 1 \;, \\ 1, \text{ if } u_i = 0 \;, \end{cases}$$

is called a monomial. If the coefficient of $\boldsymbol{x}^u$ in f is 1, i.e., $\boldsymbol{x}^u$ is contained by f, then we denote it by $\boldsymbol{x}^u \to f$. Otherwise, we denote the absence of $\boldsymbol{x}^u$ in f by $\boldsymbol{x}^u \not\to f$. In this work, we will use $\boldsymbol{x}^u$ and $\pi_u(\boldsymbol{x})$ interchangeably to avoid using the awkward notation $\boldsymbol{x}^{(i)^{u^{(j)}}}$ when both $\boldsymbol{x}$ and $\boldsymbol{u}$ have superscripts.

Vectorial Boolean Function. Let $\boldsymbol{f} : \mathbb{F}_2^m \to \mathbb{F}_2^n$ be a vectorial Boolean function with $\boldsymbol{y} = (y_0, y_1, \ldots, y_{m-1}) = \boldsymbol{f}(\boldsymbol{x}) = (f_0(\boldsymbol{x}), f_1(\boldsymbol{x}), \ldots, f_{n-1}(\boldsymbol{x}))$. For $v \in \mathbb{F}_2^n$, we use $\boldsymbol{y}^v$ to denote the product of some coordinates of $\boldsymbol{y}$:

$$\boldsymbol{y}^v = \prod_{i=0}^{m-1} y_i^{v_i} = \prod_{i=0}^{m-1} (f_i(\boldsymbol{x}))^{v_i},$$

which is a Boolean function in $\boldsymbol{x}$.

2.2   Conventional Bit-Based Division Property

The word-based division property [24] was proposed by Todo originally as a generalization of integral attack. Subsequently, by shifting the propagation of the division property to the bit level, Todo and Morii [27] introduced the bit-based division property (CBDP).

Definition 1 (Conventional bit-based division property (CBDP) [27]). *Let $\mathbb{X}$ be a multiset whose elements take a value of $\mathbb{F}_2^m$ and $\boldsymbol{k} \in \mathbb{F}_2^m$. When the multiset has the division property $\mathcal{D}_{\mathbb{K}}^{1^m}$, the following conditions are fulfilled:*

$$\bigoplus_{\boldsymbol{x} \in \mathbb{X}} \boldsymbol{x}^u = \begin{cases} \text{unknown,} & \text{if there exists } \boldsymbol{k} \in \mathbb{K} \text{ s.t. } \boldsymbol{u} \succeq \boldsymbol{k}, \\ 0, & \text{otherwise.} \end{cases}$$

In [32], Xiang et al. introduced the mixed integer linear programming (MILP) method to search for integral distinguishers of block ciphers based on CBDP. They first introduced the division trail as follows.

Definition 2 (Division Trail of CBDP [32]). *Let $\mathbb{D}_{\mathbb{K}^{(i)}}$ be the division property of the input for the ith round function. Consider the propagation of the division property $\{k\} = \mathbb{K}^{(0)} \rightarrow \mathbb{K}^{(1)} \rightarrow \mathbb{K}^{(2)} \rightarrow \cdots \rightarrow \mathbb{K}^{(r)}$. For any bitvector $k^{(i+1)} \in \mathbb{K}^{(i+1)}$, there must exist a bitvector $k^{(i)} \in \mathbb{K}^{(i+1)}$ such that $k^{(i)}$ can propagate to $k^{(i+1)}$ by the propagation rules of CBDP. Furthermore, for $(k^{(0)}, k^{(1)}, ..., k^{(r)}) \in (\mathbb{K}^{(0)} \times \mathbb{K}^{(1)} \times \cdots \times \mathbb{K}^{(r)})$, we call $(k^{(0)} \rightarrow k^{(1)} \rightarrow \cdots \rightarrow k^{(r)})$ an r-round division trial if $k^{(i)}$ can propagate to $k^{(i+1)}$ for all $i \in \{0, 1, \cdots, r-1\}$.*

For a stream cipher, three fundamental operations, i.e., COPY, AND, and XOR are sufficient to cover all division trails. Xiang et al. showed how to model these three operations by inequalities. We present their MILP models in [13, Sup.Mat. B].

In our work, we use $k^{(0)} \overset{\mathbb{K}_f}{\rightsquigarrow} k^{(r)}$ to denote the existence of at least one division trail from $k^{(0)}$ to $k^{(r)}$ through the function f. The set of all division trails from $k^{(0)}$ to $k^{(r)}$ is denoted as $k^{(0)} \overset{\mathbb{K}_f}{\bowtie} k^{(r)}$, whose size is denoted by $|k^{(0)} \overset{\mathbb{K}_f}{\bowtie} k^{(r)}|$. When f is not explicitly given or can be inferred from the context, we use $k^{(0)} \overset{\mathbb{K}}{\rightsquigarrow} k^{(r)}$ and $k^{(0)} \overset{\mathbb{K}}{\bowtie} k^{(r)}$ for simplicity.

2.3 Monomial Prediction

Let $f : \mathbb{F}_2^{n_0} \rightarrow \mathbb{F}_2^{n_r}$ be a composite vectorial Boolean function built by composition from a sequence of vectorial Boolean functions $f^{(i)} : \mathbb{F}_2^{n_i} \rightarrow \mathbb{F}_2^{n_{i+1}}, 0 \leq i \leq r - 1$ whose ANFs are known, i.e.,

$$f = f^{(r-1)} \circ f^{(r-2)} \circ \cdots \circ f^{(0)}. \tag{1}$$

Let $x^{(i)} \in \mathbb{F}_2^{n_i}$ and $x^{(i+1)} \in \mathbb{F}_2^{n_{i+1}}$ be the input and output variables of $f^{(i)}$ respectively. We call an i-round monomial $\pi_{u^{(i)}}(x^{(i)})$ $(1 \leq i \leq r - 1)$ an *intermediate monomial* or an *intermediate term*[1]. Starting from a monomial of $x^{(0)}$, say $\pi_{u^{(0)}}(x^{(0)})$, all monomials of $x^{(1)}$ satisfying $\pi_{u^{(0)}}(x^{(0)}) \rightarrow \pi_{u^{(1)}}(x^{(1)})$ can be derived; for every such $\pi_{u^{(1)}}(x^{(1)})$, we then find all $\pi_{u^{(2)}}(x^{(2)})$ satisfying $\pi_{u^{(1)}}(x^{(1)}) \rightarrow \pi_{u^{(2)}}(x^{(2)})$; such forward expansions continue until we arrive at the monomials of $x^{(r)}$. Each transition from $\pi_{u^{(0)}}(x^{(0)})$ to $\pi_{u^{(r)}}(x^{(r)})$ denoted by

$$\pi_{u^{(0)}}(x^{(0)}) \rightarrow \pi_{u^{(1)}}(x^{(1)}) \rightarrow \cdots \rightarrow \pi_{u^{(r)}}(x^{(r)}).$$

is called a monomial trail [17], denoted by $\pi_{u^{(0)}}(x^{(0)}) \rightsquigarrow \pi_{u^{(r)}}(x^{(r)})$, which is also used to indicate the existence of at least one monomial trail from $\pi_{u^{(0)}}(x^{(0)})$ to $\pi_{u^{(r)}}(x^{(r)})$. All the trails from $\pi_{u^{(0)}}(x^{(0)})$ to $\pi_{u^{(r)}}(x^{(r)})$ are denoted by $\pi_{u^{(0)}}(x^{(0)}) \bowtie \pi_{u^{(r)}}(x^{(r)})$, which is the set of all trails. Whether $\pi_{u^{(0)}}(x^{(0)}) \rightarrow \pi_{u^{(r)}}(x^{(r)})$ is determined by the size of $\pi_{u^{(0)}}(x^{(0)}) \bowtie \pi_{u^{(r)}}(x^{(r)})$, represented as $|\pi_{u^{(0)}}(x^{(0)}) \bowtie \pi_{u^{(r)}}(x^{(r)})|$. If there is no trail from $\pi_{u^{(0)}}(x^{(0)})$ to $\pi_{u^{(r)}}(x^{(r)})$, we say $\pi_{u^{(0)}}(x^{(0)}) \not\rightsquigarrow \pi_{u^{(r)}}(x^{(r)})$ and accordingly $|\pi_{u^{(0)}}(x^{(0)}) \bowtie \pi_{u^{(r)}}(x^{(r)})| = 0$.

---

[1] In this paper, 'monomial' and 'term' have the same meaning.

Theorem 1 (Integrated from [11,12,14,17]). *Let $f = f^{(r-1)} \circ f^{(r-2)} \circ \cdots \circ f^{(0)}$ defined as above. $\pi_{u^{(0)}}(x^{(0)}) \rightarrow \pi_{u^{(r)}}(x^{(r)})$ if and only if*

$$|\pi_{u^{(0)}}(x^{(0)}) \bowtie \pi_{u^{(r)}}(x^{(r)})| \equiv 1 \pmod 2.$$

Propagation Rules of the Monomial Prediction. Each symmetric cipher can be decomposed into a sequence of the basic operations XOR, AND and COPY, hence it is sufficient to give propagation rules of the monomial prediction for these basic operations. To model the propagation of the monomial prediction for a vectorial Boolean function, a common method is to list all the possible (input, output) tuples according to the definition of the monomial prediction [17]. These tuples can be transformed into a set of linear inequalities [4,21,22], which are suitable for MILP modeling. The concrete propagation rules and models of the monomial prediction are provided in [13, Sup.Mat. B].

Gurobi's PoolSearchMode and Callback Functions. In our work, we choose the Gurobi solver [1] as our MILP tool. Since our coefficient solver follows the idea of counting propagation trails similar to [11,12,17], we turn on Gurobi's PoolSearchMode with $\mathcal{M}.\text{PoolSearchMode} \leftarrow 1$ to extract all possible solutions of a model. By adding a lazy constraint to the MILP model from within a callback function, Gurobi allows users to cut off a feasible solution during the search. We use $\mathcal{M}.\text{LazyConstraints} \leftarrow 1$ to turn on lazy constraints. For more on Gurobi's callback functions and PoolSearchMode, readers are requested to refer to the Gurobi manual [2]. We would like to mention that the callback function is also used in the code provided by [11,12].

2.4   Cube Attack

In the context of the cube attack, the output bit of a symmetric cipher is typically regarded as a parameterized Boolean function $f : \mathbb{F}_2^{n+m} \rightarrow \mathbb{F}_2$ whose inputs are the public variables $x \in \mathbb{F}_2^n$ and the secret ones $k \in \mathbb{F}_2^m$. For a constant bitvector $u \in \mathbb{F}_2^n$ indexed by $I = \{0 \le i \le n - 1 : u_i = 1\} \subseteq \{0, 1, \ldots, n - 1\}$, the ANF of $f(x, k)$ can be uniquely represented as

$$f(x, k) = p(x[\bar{u}], k) \cdot x^u + q(x, k),$$

where each term of $q(x, k)$ misses at least one variable from $\{x_i : u_i = 1\}$. x^u is called a *cube term*, and $\mathbb{C}_u$ (or $\mathbb{C}_I$) is called a *cube*, which is the set $\{x \in \mathbb{F}_2^n : x \preceq u\}$. The sum of f over all values of the cube $\mathbb{C}_u$ is

$$\bigoplus_{x \in \mathbb{C}_u} f(x, k) = \bigoplus_{x \in \mathbb{C}_u} (p(x[\bar{u}], k) \cdot x^u \oplus q(x, k)) = p(x[\bar{u}], k),$$

which is exactly the coefficient of x^u in $f(x, k)$, denoted by $\text{Coe}\,(f(x, k), x^u)$ in our work. If we assign a fixed value to $x[\bar{u}]$, then $\text{Coe}\,(f(x, k), x^u)$ becomes a Boolean function of k.

As mentioned, the superpoly recovery is of significant importance in the cube attack. If the recovered superpoly is constant 0 or 1, we actually find a distinguisher for the cipher. If the superpoly is a Boolean function of k, then key bits can be extracted. In particular, a balanced superpoly always contains one bit of information on average. The remaining key bits can be recovered through exhaustive search.

2.5 Superpoly Recovery with the Monomial Prediction/3SDPwoU

To the best of our knowledge, monomial prediction/3DSPwoU [11,12,17] can reach the perfect accuracy in determining the existence of a certain monomial in f. To recover the superpoly of a cube term x^u with the monomial prediction/3DSPwoU, the initial state variables of the MILP model are divided into three parts: the public input (plaintext, IV or tweak), the secret input (the key bits) and the constant input.

The public input variables are constrained to be equal to u. The secret input variables are left as free variables without any constraints. For the constant 0 bits, we constrain the corresponding MILP variables to 0, while for the constant 1 bits, we let their variables be free. We then model the propagation of monomial trails to f. Each solution of the model is a valid monomial trail of the form $k^w x^u \leadsto f$. By collecting monomials $k^w x^u$ occurring an odd number of times in all solutions and adding them, we can obtain the superpoly of x^u as

$$\mathsf{Coe}\,(f, x^u) = \bigoplus_{|k^w x^u \bowtie f| \equiv 1 \pmod 2} k^w.$$

In [17], Hu et al. observed that for the composite function f, where

$$f = f^{(r-1)} \circ f^{(r-2)} \circ \cdots \circ f^{(0)},$$

if $\pi_{u^{(0)}}(x^{(0)}) \leadsto f$, then for $0 < i < r$,

$$|\pi_{u^{(0)}}(x^{(0)}) \bowtie f| \equiv \sum_{\pi_{u^{(r-i)}}(x^{(r-i)}) \to f} \left|\pi_{u^{(0)}}(x^{(0)}) \bowtie \pi_{u^{(r-i)}}(x^{(r-i)})\right| \pmod 2.$$

Instead of computing $|\pi_{u^{(0)}}(x^{(0)}) \bowtie f|$ for a large r, we can compute $|\pi_{u^{(0)}}(x^{(0)}) \bowtie \pi_{u^{(r-i)}}(x^{(r-i)})|$ for all $\pi_{u^{(r-i)}}(x^{(r-i)})$ satisfying $\pi_{u^{(r-i)}}(x^{(r-i)}) \to f$ with a lower computational difficulty. In practice, such a divide-and-conquer strategy resulted in a significant speed-up of the search.

3 Nested Monomial Predictions (NMP)

At Asiacrypt 2021, Hu et al. proposed a nested framework, called Nested Monomial Predictions, to recover the superpoly of TRIVIUM up to 845 rounds. In this section, we briefly introduce the workflow of this framework and divide the structure of this framework into two parts, namely the *coefficient solver* and the *term expander*.

3.1 The Workflow

Given a parameterized Boolean function which consists of a sequence of simple vectorial Boolean functions as

$$f(x, k) = f^{(r-1)} \circ f^{(r-2)} \circ \cdots \circ f^{(0)}(x, k),$$

let the output of $f^{(i)}$ be $s^{(i+1)}$. Assume we want to compute $\mathsf{Coe}(f, x^u)$. The nested monomial predictions works as follows:

1. Initialize a variable $r_l = r$ and a set $\mathbb{S}_u^{(r_l)} = \{f\}$.
2. Choose r_n such that $0 < r_n < r_l$ according to some criterion.
3. Express each term in $\mathbb{S}_u^{(r_l)}$ as a polynomial of $s^{(r_n)}$ using the monomial prediction technique and save the terms of this polynomial in a multiset $\mathbb{T}^{(r_n)}$.
4. Count the number of occurrences for each element in $\mathbb{T}^{(r_n)}$ and add the elements occurring an odd number of times to a set $\mathbb{S}^{(r_n)}$.
5. For each term $\pi_{t(r_n)}(s^{(r_n)}) \in \mathbb{S}^{(r_n)}$, construct a MILP model of the monomial prediction and invoke Gurobi to solve it. If the model has solutions and is successfully solved, then this term is partitioned into $\mathbb{S}_p^{(r_n)}$ and we can compute $\mathsf{Coe}(\pi_{t(r_n)}(s^{(r_n)}), x^u)$, which is collected as a part of $\mathsf{Coe}(f, x^u)$; if the model has no solutions, then this term is partitioned into $\mathbb{S}_0^{(r_n)}$ and discarded; if the model isn't solved in limited time, we partition this term into the set $\mathbb{S}_u^{(r_n)}$.
6. If the set $\mathbb{S}_u^{(r_n)}$ is not empty, we update the variable $r_l = r_n$ and regard the set $\mathbb{S}_u^{(r_n)}$ as $\mathbb{S}_u^{(r_l)}$, then jump to step 2. Otherwise we have successfully compute $\mathsf{Coe}(f, x^u)$.

In step 2 of NMP, r_n is chosen as the round that makes the size of $\mathbb{T}^{(r_n)}$ larger than N for the first time, where N can take the value $10\,000$ or $100\,000$. Interested readers can refer to [16] for more details.

3.2 The Structure of the Nested Monomial Prediction

In terms of the structure, the nested monomial prediction consists of two components. In Sect. 3.1, step 3 and 4 are responsible for expanding terms in $\mathbb{S}_u^{(r_l)}$ into terms of a deeper round r_n represented by $\mathbb{S}^{(r_n)}$, while the step 5 attempts to compute $\mathsf{Coe}(\pi_{t(r_n)}(s^{(r_n)}), x^u)$ for each term $\pi_{t(r_n)}(s^{(r_n)})$ in $\mathbb{S}^{(r_n)}$. This leads to the following two concepts.

Term Expander. For an algorithm $\mathcal{H}$ of a specific cryptographic algorithm X, if given the last round r_l, the set $\mathbb{S}_u^{(r_l)}$ containing terms of round r_l, the next round r_n and other auxiliary parameters as input, the algorithm $\mathcal{H}$ can always output all $\pi_{t(r_n)}(s^{(r_n)})$s satisfying $\sum_{\pi_{t(r_l)}(s^{(r_l)}) \in \mathbb{S}_u^{(r_l)}} |\pi_{t(r_n)}(s^{(r_n)}) \bowtie \pi_{t(r_l)}(s^{(r_l)})| \equiv 1$ (mod 2), then we say $\mathcal{H}$ is a term expander of X.

Coefficient Solver. For an algorithm $\mathcal{H}$ of a specific cryptographic algorithm X, if given the last round r_l, a term $\pi_{t(r_l)}(s^{(r_l)})$ of round r_l, u indicating the

---

Algorithm 1: Generic structure of the nested monomial predictions [16]

---

1 **Procedure** SuperpolyRecFramework(*the target output bit* $f(\boldsymbol{x}, \boldsymbol{k})$, *the target round* r, $\boldsymbol{u}$ *indicating the cube term*):

2   Prepare a polynomial $p = 0$

3   Initialize $r_l = r, \mathbb{S}_u^{(r_l)} = \{f\}$

4   **while** $\mathbb{S}_u^{(r_l)} \neq \emptyset$ **do**

5        $r_n = $ ChooseRiX$(\mathbb{S}_u^{(r_l)}, r_l, ...)$

6        $\mathbb{S}^{(r_n)} = $ TermExpanderX$(\mathbb{S}_u^{(r_l)}, r_l, r_n, ...)$

7   **for** $\pi_{t(r_n)}(\boldsymbol{s}^{(r_n)}) \in \mathbb{S}^{(r_n)}$ **do**

8           $\tau = $ ChooseTiX(r_n)

9           $(status, p^{(r_n)}) = $ CofSolverX$(\pi_{t(r_n)}(\boldsymbol{s}^{(r_n)}), r_n, \boldsymbol{u}, \tau, ...)$

10   **if** $status = $ SOLVED **then**

11              $p = p \oplus p^{(r_n)}$

12   **else if** $status = $ TIMEOUT **then**

13   Insert $\pi_{t(r_n)}(\boldsymbol{s}^{(r_n)})$ into $\mathbb{S}_u^{(r_n)}$

14        $r_l \leftarrow r_n$

15        $\mathbb{S}_u^{(r_l)} \leftarrow \mathbb{S}_u^{(r_n)}$

16   **return** p

---

cube term $\boldsymbol{x}^u$ (or other parameters that can identify the cube), the time limit τ and other auxiliary parameters as input, the algorithm $\mathcal{H}$ can always output either $\mathsf{Coe}\left(\pi_{t(r_l)}(\boldsymbol{s}^{(r_l)}), \boldsymbol{x}^u\right)$, no solution or timeout, then we say $\mathcal{H}$ is a coefficient solver of X.

In this paper, we denote the term expander and the coefficient solver by TermExpanderX$(\mathbb{S}_u^{(r_l)}, r_l, r_n, ...)$ and CofSolverX$(\pi_{t(r_l)}(\boldsymbol{s}^{(r_l)}), r_l, \boldsymbol{u}, \tau, ...)$ respectively, where we use ... to represent arbitrary auxiliary parameters. TermExpanderX returns a set containing all $\pi_{t(r_n)}(\boldsymbol{s}^{(r_n)})$s satisfying $\sum_{\pi_{t(r_l)}(\boldsymbol{s}^{(r_l)}) \in \mathbb{S}_u^{(r_l)}} |\pi_{t(r_n)}(\boldsymbol{s}^{(r_n)}) \bowtie \pi_{t(r_l)}(\boldsymbol{s}^{(r_l)})| \equiv 1 \pmod 2$. CofSolverX returns a 2-tuple $(status, result)$, where $status$ takes SOLVED, NOSOLUTION or TIMEOUT and $result$ represents $\mathsf{Coe}\left(\pi_{t(r_l)}(\boldsymbol{s}^{(r_l)}), \boldsymbol{x}^u\right)$ only when $status = $ SOLVED. Using these notions, the generic structure of the nested monomial predictions can be described in Algorithm 1, where ChooseRiX and ChooseTiX represent the process of selecting r_n and τ.

Following the generic structure, the nested monomial predictions utilizes the monomial prediction technique to build the term expander and the coefficient solver. As a result, the superpoly recovery of the target output bit is divided into superpoly recoveries of thousands of terms of fewer rounds, thereby reducing the computational difficulty. Our work in this paper also follows the generic structure, but with a more efficient term expander and coefficient solver.

4 New Coefficient Solver

4.1 Motivation

Although the monomial prediction technique can reach perfect accuracy in detecting if $\boldsymbol{k}^w \boldsymbol{x}^u \rightarrow f$, it requires counting the number of monomial trails.

Such a task is impractical for a high number of rounds of a well-designed crypto-graphic algorithms, as the number of monomial trails grows almost exponentially with the number of rounds.

As mentioned in Sect. 2.5, the divide-and-conquer strategy can speed up the search compared with counting the number of monomial trails directly. Inspired by this, we construct a new coefficient solver that first divides the output bit of the current round into terms of a quite deep round, then solve these terms using the monomial prediction technique.

4.2 The Theory

For simplicity, we assume the term of the current round is $\pi_{t^{(r)}}(s^{(r)})$ and we want to compute $\mathsf{Coe}\left(\pi_{t^{(r)}}(s^{(r)}), x^u\right)$ with the coefficient solver. We divide $\pi_{t^{(r)}}(s^{(r)})$ into terms of a reduced number $r_m < r$ of rounds. Naturally, we introduce the concept of valuable terms to capture those terms in round r_m that contribute to $\mathsf{Coe}\left(\pi_{t^{(r)}}(s^{(r)}), x^u\right)$.

Valuable Terms. According to the divide-and-conquer strategy, the monomial trails of the form $k^w x^u \rightsquigarrow \pi_{t^{(r)}}(s^{(r)})$ can be divided into monomial trails of the form $k^w x^u \rightsquigarrow \pi_{t^{(r_m)}}(s^{(r_m)})$ for each $\pi_{t^{(r_m)}}(s^{(r_m)})$ satisfying $\pi_{t^{(r_m)}}(s^{(r_m)}) \rightarrow \pi_{t^{(r)}}(s^{(r)})$, e.g.,

$$|k^w x^u \bowtie \pi_{t^{(r)}}(s^{(r)})| \equiv \sum_{\pi_{t^{(r_m)}}(s^{(r_m)}) \rightarrow \pi_{t^{(r)}}(s^{(r)})} |k^w x^u \bowtie \pi_{t^{(r_m)}}(s^{(r_m)})| \pmod 2 \quad (2)$$

Note that if $|k^w x^u \bowtie \pi_{t^{(r_m)}}(s^{(r_m)})| = 0$, $\pi_{t^{(r_m)}}(s^{(r_m)})$ contributes nothing to $|k^w x^u \bowtie \pi_{t^{(r)}}(s^{(r)})|$. Therefore, to make it precise we rewrite the Eq. (2) as

$$|k^w x^u \bowtie \pi_{t^{(r)}}(s^{(r)})| \equiv \sum_{\substack{\pi_{t^{(r_m)}}(s^{(r_m)}) \rightarrow \pi_{t^{(r)}}(s^{(r)}) \\ k^w x^u \rightsquigarrow \pi_{t^{(r_m)}}(s^{(r_m)})}} |k^w x^u \bowtie \pi_{t^{(r_m)}}(s^{(r_m)})| \pmod 2 \quad (3)$$

Terms satisfying (A) $\pi_{t^{(r_m)}}(s^{(r_m)}) \rightarrow \pi_{t^{(r)}}(s^{(r)})$, (B) $\exists k^w$ such that $k^w x^u \rightsquigarrow \pi_{t^{(r_m)}}(s^{(r_m)})$ are called *valuable terms* of round r_m, denoted by $VT^{(r_m)}$. Usually r_m is chosen not too large, say 90 for TRIVIUM. Once we have recovered all $VT^{(r_m)}$s, we can compute $\mathsf{Coe}\left(\pi_{t^{(r)}}(s^{(r)}), x^u\right)$ easily by applying the monomial prediction to compute $\mathsf{Coe}\left(VT^{(r_m)}, x^u\right)$ for each $VT^{(r_m)}$. Briefly speaking, the workflow of our coefficient solver is as follows:

1. Develop a method to recover $VT^{(r_m)}$s within the time limit τ. If it times out, return TIMEOUT; else if no $VT^{(r_m)}$ could be recovered, return NOSOLU-TION; otherwise, if $VT^{(r_m)}$s are recovered successfully, go to step 2.
2. Apply the monomial prediction to each $VT^{(r_m)}$ to compute $\mathsf{Coe}\left(VT^{(r_m)}, x^u\right)$.
3. Sum all $\mathsf{Coe}\left(VT^{(r_m)}, x^u\right)$s to compute $\mathsf{Coe}\left(\pi_{t^{(r)}}(s^{(r)}), x^u\right)$ and return SOLVED.

How to Recover $VT^{(r_m)}$. If a term $\pi_{t^{(r_m)}}(s^{(r_m)})$ is a $VT^{(r_m)}$, then two condi-tions are necessary and sufficient, namely $\pi_{t^{(r_m)}}(s^{(r_m)}) \rightarrow \pi_{t^{(r)}}(s^{(r)})$ (Condition

A) and $\exists \boldsymbol{k}^w$ s.t. $\boldsymbol{k}^w \boldsymbol{x}^u \rightsquigarrow \pi_{t^{(r_m)}}(\boldsymbol{s}^{(r_m)})$ (Condition B). We need to construct a MILP model to describe these two conditions simultaneously.

At a first glance, both conditions can be described by the monomial prediction with the following structure

$$\overbrace{\boldsymbol{k}^w \boldsymbol{x}^u \xrightarrow{\text{MP}} \pi_{t^{(r_m)}}(\boldsymbol{s}^{(r_m)})}^{r_m \ rounds} = \pi_{t^{(r_m)}}(\boldsymbol{s}^{(r_m)}) \overbrace{\xrightarrow{\text{MP}} \pi_{t^{(r)}}(\boldsymbol{s}^{(r)})}^{r - r_m \ rounds} , \qquad (4)$$

where $\xrightarrow{\text{MP}}$ means the propagation is described according to the propagation rules of MP. However, since we need to incorporate these two conditions into one MILP model, such a structure is equivalent to computing $\mathsf{Coe}\left(\pi_{t^{(r)}}(\boldsymbol{s}^{(r)}), \boldsymbol{x}^u\right)$ by the monomial prediction directly. We do not gain efficiency improvement from valuable terms.

Note that when describing Condition B, the monomial prediction is so accurate that we can even determine whether $\exists \boldsymbol{k}^w$ s.t. $\boldsymbol{k}^w \boldsymbol{x}^u \to \pi_{t^{(r_m)}}(\boldsymbol{s}^{(r_m)})$. Therefore, a natural idea is to sacrifice some accuracy in exchange for efficiency. In next section, we provide two variants of bit-based division properties for efficient descriptions of Condition B. The first variant is called non-zero bit-based division property (NBDP): it simply excludes the propagation of CBDP related to constant 0 bits. The second is called the core monomial prediction (recall that the monomial prediction is an explanation of division properties): it ignores the role of constant bits and attempts to establish a set of rules to characterize those non-constant bits. Both variants play important roles in our new algorithms for recovering superpolies.

5 Two Variants of the Division Property for Describing Condition B

In this section, we present two techniques to describe Condition B under the assumption that non-cube public variables are set to 0. For convenience, we always consider an r_m-round cryptographic function $\boldsymbol{f} : \mathbb{F}_2^{n_0} \to \mathbb{F}_2^{n_1} \to \cdots \to \mathbb{F}_2^{n_{r_m}}$ ($n_0 = n + m$) with $\boldsymbol{x}, \boldsymbol{k}$ as input and $\boldsymbol{s}^{(i+1)}$ as output of the i-th round ($0 < i \leq r_m - 1$), where $\boldsymbol{x} \in \mathbb{F}_2^n$ and $\boldsymbol{k} \in \mathbb{F}_2^m$ denote the public and secret variables, respectively. Let the cube term be $\boldsymbol{x}^u$. The output term of round r_m is represented as $\pi_{t^{(r_m)}}(\boldsymbol{s}^{(r_m)})$. Correspondingly, Condition B should be expressed as $\exists \boldsymbol{k}^w$ s.t. $\boldsymbol{k}^w \boldsymbol{x}^u \rightsquigarrow \pi_{t^{(r_m)}}(\boldsymbol{s}^{(r_m)})$.

Flag Technique. Similar to [28], we propose a flag technique to classify bits. In our work, we treat $\boldsymbol{k}$ as non-zero constants and set $\boldsymbol{x}[\bar{\boldsymbol{u}}]$ to 0, then each bit involved in the round function of $\boldsymbol{f}$ can be represented as an ANF of $\boldsymbol{k}$ and $\boldsymbol{x}[\boldsymbol{u}]$. For each involved bit b, we assign it an additional flag $b.F \in \{1_c, 0_c, \delta\}$. 0_c means b is constant 0; δ means the ANF of b involves $\boldsymbol{x}[\boldsymbol{u}]$, i.e., it contains a monomial associated with at least one cube variable; 1_c means b is non-zero and its ANF doesn't involve $\boldsymbol{x}[\boldsymbol{u}]$. Since the ANF will become intractable as the number of rounds increases, these flags are precomputed according to COPY, XOR and

AND without considering the effect of cancellation characteristics. Note that the computation of our flags does not require the help of MILP models, and the flags in [28] can be handled in the same way, although the authors of [28] encoded the flags into their MILP models. We define $=$, $\oplus$ and $\times$ operations for the elements of set $\{1_c, 0_c, \delta\}$ corresponding to the basic operations COPY, XOR and AND, respectively. The $=$ operation sets one element equal to another element. The $\oplus$ operation follows the rules:

$$\begin{cases} 1_c \oplus 1_c = 1_c \ , \\ 0_c \oplus x = x \oplus 0_c = x \text{ for arbitrary } x \in \{1_c, 0_c, \delta\} \ , \\ \delta \oplus x = x \oplus \delta = \delta \text{ for arbitrary } x \in \{1_c, 0_c, \delta\} \ . \end{cases}$$

The $\times$ operation follows the rules:

$$\begin{cases} 1_c \times x = x \times 1_c = x \text{ for arbitrary } x \in \{1_c, 0_c, \delta\} \ , \\ 0_c \times x = x \times 0_c = 0_c \text{ for arbitrary } x \in \{1_c, 0_c, \delta\} \ , \\ \delta \times \delta = \delta \ . \end{cases}$$

Bits flagged by x ($x \in \{1_c, 0_c, \delta\}$) are referred to as x bits in this paper. For a bit vector $\boldsymbol{t}^{(j)}$, suppose the state bits in the j-th round are denoted by $\boldsymbol{s}^{(j)}$, we use $\Lambda^{1_c}(\boldsymbol{t}^{(j)})$, $\Lambda^{0_c}(\boldsymbol{t}^{(j)})$, $\Lambda^{\delta}(\boldsymbol{t}^{(j)})$ to divide $\boldsymbol{t}^{(j)}$ into three bit vectors according to the $1_c, 0_c, \delta$ part of $\boldsymbol{s}^{(j)}$ respectively, i.e.,

$$\Lambda^x_i(\boldsymbol{t}^{(j)}) = t^{(j)}_i \ \forall \ s^{(j)}_i . F = x, \text{ otherwise } \Lambda^x_i(\boldsymbol{t}^{(j)}) = 0$$

for arbitrary $x \in \{1_c, 0_c, \delta\}$. When introducing MILP models, for a MILP variable $v \in \mathcal{M}.var$ assigned to the bit b, we may use $v.F$ to represent $b.F$ implicitly. Once the cube term is given, the flags of all state bits of $\boldsymbol{f}$ are determined. A specific example of our flag computation can be found in Example 1.

5.1 Non-zero Bit-Based Division Property (NBDP)

First, we revisit the roles of CBDP in recovering the superpoly from a perspective of the monomial propagation.

Proposition 1. *Given a term $\pi_{\boldsymbol{t}^{(r_m)}}(\boldsymbol{s}^{(r_m)})$ of round r_m. Assuming the initial CBDP $\mathcal{D}^{1^{m+n}}_{\{0^m \| u\}}$ propagates to $\mathcal{D}^{1^{r_m}}_{\mathbb{K}^{(r_m)}}$ after evaluating $\boldsymbol{f}$ through r_m rounds, if $\exists \boldsymbol{k}^{(r_m)} \in \mathbb{K}^{(r_m)}$ such that $\boldsymbol{k}^{(r_m)} \preceq \boldsymbol{t}^{(r_m)}$, then there must $\exists \boldsymbol{w} \succeq 0^m, \boldsymbol{u}' \succeq \boldsymbol{u}$ s.t. $\boldsymbol{k}^{\boldsymbol{w}} \boldsymbol{x}^{\boldsymbol{u}'} \rightsquigarrow \pi_{\boldsymbol{t}^{(r_m)}}(\boldsymbol{s}^{(r_m)})$. The converse is also true.*

Proof. Let the input and output multisets of CBDP be $\mathbb{X}^{(0)}$ and $\mathbb{X}^{(r)}$ respectively. According to the definition of CBDP, we assume $\sum_{\boldsymbol{k} \| \boldsymbol{x} \in \mathbb{X}^{(0)}} \boldsymbol{k}^{\boldsymbol{w}} \boldsymbol{x}^{\boldsymbol{u}'}$ is unknown for any $\boldsymbol{w} \| \boldsymbol{u}' \succeq 0^m \| \boldsymbol{u}$ and $\sum_{\boldsymbol{k} \| \boldsymbol{x} \in \mathbb{X}^{(0)}} \boldsymbol{k}^{\boldsymbol{w}} \boldsymbol{x}^{\boldsymbol{u}'} = 0$ for any $\boldsymbol{w} \| \boldsymbol{u}' \not\succeq 0^m \| \boldsymbol{u}$.

If $\exists \boldsymbol{w} \succeq 0, \boldsymbol{u}' \succeq \boldsymbol{u}$ s.t. $\boldsymbol{k}^{\boldsymbol{w}} \boldsymbol{x}^{\boldsymbol{u}'} \rightsquigarrow \pi_{\boldsymbol{t}^{(r_m)}}(\boldsymbol{s}^{(r_m)})$, then $\sum_{\boldsymbol{s}^{(r_m)} \in \mathbb{X}^{(r_m)}} \pi_{\boldsymbol{t}^{(r_m)}}(\boldsymbol{s}^{(r_m)})$ must be unknown, which means $\exists \boldsymbol{k}^{(r_m)} \in \mathbb{K}^{(r_m)}$ such that

$k^{(r_m)} \preceq t^{(r_m)}$. Conversely, if $\exists k^{(r_m)} \in \mathbb{K}^{(r_m)}$ such that $k^{(r_m)} \preceq t^{(r_m)}$, then $\sum_{s^{(r_m)} \in \mathbb{X}^{(r_m)}} \pi_{t^{(r_m)}}(s^{(r_m)})$ must be unknown. We can deduce there exists $w \succeq 0^m, u' \succeq u$ s.t. $k^w x^{u'} \rightsquigarrow \pi_{t^{(r_m)}}(s^{(r_m)})$, because otherwise $\sum_{s^{(r_m)} \in \mathbb{X}^{(r_m)}} \pi_{t^{(r_m)}}(s^{(r_m)})$ would be 0 rather than unknown. $\qquad \square$

Based on Proposition 1, a natural idea to describe Condition B is to exclude all division trails related to $x[\bar{u}]$. Since $x[\bar{u}]$ is set to constant 0, we only need to handle constant 0 bits during the propagation of CBDP. A lot of work has been conducted on this research line ([25,28]). In our work, to deal with constant 0 bits, we follow three rules that are described in [28] for Copy, And and Xor, but with our flag technique. These three rules are slightly adjusted and listed in [13, Sup.Mat. C], together with some additional constraints that can be added to remove redundancy.

In addition, to describe Condition B, the partial order in CBDP should also consider the effect of constant 0 bits, so we modify the partial order in CBDP.

Definition 3 (The Partial Order). *Let v' and v be two bit vectors. We say $v' \succeq v$ on y or simply $y^{v'} \succeq y^v$, if*

$$\begin{cases} v'_i = v_i = 0 & y_i.F = 0_c \\ v'_i \geq v_i & y_i.F \neq 0_c \end{cases}.$$

We denote this variant of CBDP as *non-zero bit-based division property* (NBDP). Using NBDP, if $\exists k^w$ such that $k^w x^u \rightsquigarrow \pi_{t^{(r_m)}}(s^{(r_m)})$, then there must exist $k^{(r_m)}$ propagated from $0^m \| u$ such that $k^{(r_m)} \hat{\preceq} t^{(r_m)}$ on $s^{(r_m)}$. Hence, we can construct a MILP model to recover $VT^{(r_m)}$s as follows:

$$k^0 x^u \xrightarrow[]{\overbrace{\text{NBDP}}^{r_m \ rounds}} \pi_{k^{(r_m)}}(s^{(r_m)}) \hat{\preceq} \pi_{t^{(r_m)}}(s^{(r_m)}) \xrightarrow[]{\overbrace{\text{MP}}^{r-r_m \ rounds}} \pi_{t^{(r)}}(s^{(r)}), \qquad (5)$$

where NBDP propagates from $0^m \| u$ to $k^{(r_m)}$ in the first r_m rounds. Such a MILP model is described as `NBDP-MPModelX` in [13, Algorithm 4]. After extracting all solutions of this MILP model, for each $\pi_{t^{(r_m)}}(s^{(r_m)})$ we can count the number of monomial trails between $\pi_{t^{(r_m)}}(s^{(r_m)})$ and $\pi_{t^{(r)}}(s^{(r)})$ to determine if $\pi_{t^{(r_m)}}(s^{(r_m)}) \rightarrow \pi_{t^{(r)}}(s^{(r)})$, then determine if this term $\pi_{t^{(r_m)}}(s^{(r_m)})$ is a $VT^{(r_m)}$. In this way, a new coefficient solver can be developed by first recovering $VT^{(r_m)}$s and then applying the monomial prediction to each $VT^{(r_m)}$, as stated in Sect. 4. We did test such a new coefficient solver for 846-round TRIVIUM by setting $r_m = 90$, combined with the term expander used in NMP. As a result, the superpoly of the cube term I_3 in [13, Table 5] is recovered in about two days on our platform. However, apart from this result, no other superpolies were recovered.

The Bottleneck of Recovering $VT^{(r_m)}$s Based on Eq. (5). The number of solutions of `NBDP-MPModelX` can be expressed as

$$\sum_{\substack{k^{(r_m)} \in \mathbb{F}_2^{n_{r_m}}, t^{(r_m)} \in \mathbb{F}_2^{n_{r_m}} \\ k^{(r_m)} \hat{\preceq} t^{(r_m)} \text{ on } s^{(r_m)}}} |0^m \| u \overset{\mathbb{K}}{\bowtie} k^{(r_m)}| \cdot |\pi_{t^{(r_m)}}(s^{(r_m)}) \bowtie \pi_{t^{(r)}}(s^{(r)})|,$$

where $\boldsymbol{k}^{(r_m)}$ and $\boldsymbol{t}^{(r_m)}$ take all allowed values. Note that for a specific $\boldsymbol{t}^{(r_m)}$ satisfying $|\pi_{t^{(r_m)}}(\boldsymbol{s}^{(r_m)}) \bowtie \pi_{t^{(r)}}(\boldsymbol{s}^{(r)})| > 0$ with a high hamming weight, the sum of all $|\boldsymbol{0}^m || \boldsymbol{u} \overset{K}{\bowtie} \boldsymbol{k}^{(r_m)}|$ satisfying $\boldsymbol{k}^{(r_m)} \overset{\sim}{\preceq} \boldsymbol{t}^{(r_m)}$ on $\boldsymbol{s}^{(r_m)}$ may be extraordinarily large, which makes it hard to extract all solutions of NBDP-MPModelX within limited time.

5.2   Core Monomial Prediction (CMP)

To overcome the bottleneck of recovering $VT^{(r_m)}$s based on Eq. (5), we next propose an alternative approach to characterize Condition B from the perspective of monomial propagation. This new technique is called *Core Monomial Prediction (CMP)*, which can be regarded as a relaxed version of monomial prediction.

Generalization of Condition B. Notice that given a non-zero term $\pi_{t^{(r_m)}}(\boldsymbol{s}^{(r_m)})$, what determines whether Condition B holds is $\Lambda^\delta(\boldsymbol{t}^{(r_m)})$. Moreover, denoting the initial term $\boldsymbol{k}^w || \boldsymbol{x}^u$ in Condition B by $\pi_{t^{(0)}}(\boldsymbol{s}^{(0)})$, notice that $\pi_{\Lambda^\delta(t^{(0)})}(\boldsymbol{s}^{(0)}) = \boldsymbol{k}^0 || \boldsymbol{x}^u$ and $\pi_{\Lambda^{1c}(t^{(0)})}(\boldsymbol{s}^{(0)}) = \boldsymbol{k}^w || \boldsymbol{x}^0$. Let $\Lambda^{1c}(\boldsymbol{1}^{n_0})$ indicate the 1_c bits of the initial state (round 0), that is, $\Lambda_i^{1c}(\boldsymbol{1}^{n_0}) = 1$ if $s_i^{(0)}.F = 1_c$, otherwise $\Lambda_i^{1c}(\boldsymbol{1}^{n_0}) = 0$. Obviously $\Lambda^{1c}(\boldsymbol{1}^{n_0}) = \boldsymbol{1}^m || \boldsymbol{0}^n$. Considering in Condition B we only require the existence of $\boldsymbol{w}$, $\boldsymbol{w}$ can be any vector satisfying $\boldsymbol{w} \preceq \Lambda^{1c}(\boldsymbol{1}^{n_0})$. Therefore, we can give a generalization of Condition B by

$$\exists \boldsymbol{w} \preceq \Lambda^{1c}(\boldsymbol{1}^{n_0}), \text{ such that } \pi_{\Lambda^\delta(t^{(0)})\oplus w}(\boldsymbol{s}^{(0)}) \rightsquigarrow \pi_{\Lambda^\delta(t^{(r_m)})}(\boldsymbol{s}^{(r_m)}). \quad (6)$$

Naturally, we study how to describe

$$\exists \boldsymbol{w} \preceq \Lambda^{1c}(\boldsymbol{1}^{n_i}), \text{ such that } \pi_{\Lambda^\delta(t^{(i)})\oplus w}(\boldsymbol{s}^{(i)}) \rightsquigarrow \pi_{\Lambda^\delta(t^{(j)})}(\boldsymbol{s}^{(j)})$$

for arbitrary $i < j$. Note that in the process of generalizing Condition B, we aggressively assume that $\pi_{t^{(r_m)}}(\boldsymbol{s}^{(r_m)}) \neq 0$, whereas in practice, it is entirely possible that $\pi_{t^{(r_m)}}(\boldsymbol{s}^{(r_m)})$ equals to 0. Recalling that NBDP is derived by considering the effect of constant 0 bits in the propagation and partial order of CBDP, whose propagation rules are established first, it is reasonable that we first study the case where constant 0 bits are not taken into account.

The Definition and Propagation of CMP. Let $\boldsymbol{g} : \mathbb{F}_2^{n_{in}} \rightarrow \mathbb{F}_2^{n_{out}}$ be a vectorial Boolean function mapping $\boldsymbol{z} = (z_0, \cdots, z_{n_{in}-1})$ to $\boldsymbol{y} = (y_0, \cdots, y_{n_{out}-1})$ with $y_i = g_i(\boldsymbol{z})$. In [17], the monomial prediction is defined as the problem of determining the presence or absence of a particular monomial $\boldsymbol{z}^u$ in $\boldsymbol{y}^v$, that is, whether $\boldsymbol{z}^u \rightarrow \boldsymbol{y}^v$. Similarly, the *core monomial prediction* is defined as the problem of determining whether $\pi_{\Lambda^\delta(v)}(\boldsymbol{y})$ contains at least one monomial, say $\boldsymbol{z}^u$, whose δ part $(\pi_{\Lambda^\delta(u)}(\boldsymbol{z}))$ is a particular monomial. We denote this problem by whether $\pi_{\Lambda^\delta(u)}(\boldsymbol{z}) \overset{\text{Core}}{\rightarrow} \pi_{\Lambda^\delta(v)}(\boldsymbol{y})$. Similar to the monomial trail, the definition of CMP gives rise to the concept of the *core monomial trail*.

Definition 4 (Core Monomial Trail). *Given the cube term $\boldsymbol{x}^u$, let* $\pi_{\Lambda^\delta(t^{(0)})}(\boldsymbol{s}^{(0)}) = \boldsymbol{k}^0 || \boldsymbol{x}^u$ *and* $\boldsymbol{s}^{(i+1)} = \boldsymbol{f}^{(i)}(\boldsymbol{s}^{(i)})$ *for* $0 \leq i < r$. *We call a sequence* of monomials $(\pi_{\Lambda^\delta(t^{(0)})}(s^{(0)}), \pi_{\Lambda^\delta(t^{(1)})}(s^{(1)}), \ldots, \pi_{\Lambda^\delta(t^{(r)})}(s^{(r)}))$ an r-round core monomial trail connecting $\pi_{\Lambda^\delta(t^{(0)})}(s^{(0)})$ and $\pi_{\Lambda^\delta(t^{(r)})}(s^{(r)})$ with respect to the composite function $f = f^{(r-1)} \circ f^{(i-2)} \circ \cdots \circ f^{(0)}$ if

$$\pi_{\Lambda^\delta(t^{(0)})}(s^{(0)}) \xrightarrow{Core} \cdots \xrightarrow{Core} \pi_{\Lambda^\delta(t^{(i)})}(s^{(i)}) \xrightarrow{Core} \cdots \xrightarrow{Core} \pi_{\Lambda^\delta(t^{(r)})}(s^{(r)}),$$

If there is at least one core monomial trail connecting $\pi_{\Lambda^\delta(t^{(0)})}(s^{(0)})$ to $\pi_{\Lambda^\delta(t^{(r)})}(s^{(r)})$, we write $\pi_{\Lambda^\delta(t^{(0)})}(s^{(0)}) \overset{Core}{\rightsquigarrow} \pi_{\Lambda^\delta(t^{(r)})}(s^{(r)})$. All core monomial trails between $\pi_{\Lambda^\delta(t^{(0)})}(s^{(0)})$ and $\pi_{\Lambda^\delta(t^{(r)})}(s^{(r)})$ are denoted by the set $\pi_{\Lambda^\delta(t^{(0)})}(s^{(0)}) \overset{Core}{\bowtie} \pi_{\Lambda^\delta(t^{(r)})}(s^{(r)})$.

The monomial prediction determines whether $\pi_{t^{(0)}}(s^{(0)}) \rightarrow \pi_{t^{(r)}}(s^{(r)})$ by counting the number of monomial trails between $\pi_{t^{(0)}}(s^{(0)})$ and $\pi_{t^{(r)}}(s^{(r)})$. However, the number of core monomial trails between $\pi_{\Lambda^\delta(t^{(0)})}(s^{(0)})$ and $\pi_{\Lambda^\delta(t^{(r)})}(s^{(r)})$ can not reflect precisely whether $\pi_{\Lambda^\delta(t^{(0)})}(s^{(0)}) \overset{Core}{\rightarrow} \pi_{\Lambda^\delta(t^{(r)})}(s^{(r)})$, i.e., whether there exists a $w \preceq \Lambda^{1_c}(1^{n_0})$ such that $\pi_{\Lambda^\delta(t^{(0)})\oplus w}(s^{(0)}) \rightarrow \pi_{\Lambda^\delta(t^{(r)})}(s^{(r)})$. Since the information of 1_c bits is ignored by the core monomial trail, we can only draw a weaker conclusion from the existence of a core monomial trail, that is, $\exists w \preceq \Lambda^{1_c}(1^{n_0})$ such that $\pi_{\Lambda^\delta(t^{(0)})\oplus w}(s^{(0)}) \rightsquigarrow \pi_{\Lambda^\delta(t^{(r)})}(s^{(r)})$. Notice that this is exactly the generalization of Condition B, which means the existence of a core monomial trail between $\pi_{\Lambda^\delta(t^{(0)})}(s^{(0)})$ and $\pi_{\Lambda^\delta(t^{(r_m)})}(s^{(r_m)})$ is another equivalent description of Condition B.

To better understand how core monomial trails are generated, we give a concrete example.

Example 1. Let $z = (z_0, z_1) = f^{(1)}(y_0, y_1) = (y_0 y_1, y_0 + y_1 + 1)$, $y = (y_0, y_1) = f^{(0)}(x_0, x_1, x_2, k_0, k_1) = (k_0 x_0 + k_1 x_0 x_2 + k_0 + k_1, k_0 k_1 x_1 + k_0 k_1 x_0 + k_0)$. Consider the cube term $(x_0, x_1, x_2)^{(1,1,0)} = x_0 x_1$. First, we can compute the flags of x, k, y, z, i.e.,

$$x_0.F = x_1.F = \delta, x_2.F = 0_c. \; k_0.F = k_1.F = 1_c.$$
$$y_0.F = 1_c \times \delta \oplus 1_c \times \delta \times 0_c \oplus 1_c \oplus 1_c = \delta.$$
$$y_1.F = 1_c \times 1_c \times \delta \oplus 1_c \times 1_c \times \delta \oplus 1_c = \delta.$$
$$z_0.F = \delta \times \delta = \delta. \; z_1.F = \delta \oplus \delta \oplus 1_c = \delta.$$

Since the ANF of $f^{(0)}$ is available, we can compute all monomials of y (x_2 is set to 0), i.e.,

$$(y_0, y_1)^{(0,0)} = 1, (y_0, y_1)^{(1,0)} = y_0 = k_0 x_0 + k_0 + k_1.$$
$$(y_0, y_1)^{(0,1)} = y_1 = k_0 k_1 x_1 + k_0 k_1 x_0 + k_0.$$
$$(y_0, y_1)^{(1,1)} = y_0 y_1 = k_0 k_1 \underline{x_0 x_1} + k_0 k_1 x_0 + k_0 x_0 + k_0 + k_0 k_1.$$

Considering $(y_0, y_1)^{\Lambda^\delta((1,1))} = y_0 y_1$, then $x_0 x_1 \overset{Core}{\to} y_0 y_1$ is the only core monomial trail of $\boldsymbol{f}^{(0)}$ connecting $x_0 x_1$ and the δ part of monomials of $\boldsymbol{y}$. Similarly, we can compute all monomials of $\boldsymbol{z}$ as follows,

$$(z_0, z_1)^{(0,0)} = 1, (z_0, z_1)^{(1,0)} = z_0 = \underline{y_0 y_1}, (z_0, z_1)^{(0,1)} = z_1 = y_0 + y_1 + 1,$$

$$(z_0, z_1)^{(1,1)} = z_0 z_1 = \underline{y_0 y_1}.$$

Since $z_0.F = z_1.F = \delta$, we have $(z_0, z_1)^{\Lambda^\delta((1,0))} = z_0$ and $(z_0, z_1)^{\Lambda^\delta((1,1))} = z_0 z_1$. Finally, we obtain two core monomial trails of $\boldsymbol{f}$ connecting $x_0 x_1$ and the δ part of monomials of $\boldsymbol{z}$:

$$x_0 x_1 \overset{Core}{\to} y_0 y_1 \overset{Core}{\to} z_0, \quad x_0 x_1 \overset{Core}{\to} y_0 y_1 \overset{Core}{\to} z_0 z_1.$$

Recalling in [17], the propagation rules of 3SDPwoU are revisited from the algebraic perspective according to the definition of the monomial prediction. In a similar way, the propagation rules of the core monomial prediction can be derived from its definition. And we only give the rule of COPY an algebraic proof, as the others can be interpreted in a same way. As mentioned, we do not take constant 0 bits into account, so we assume the bits of $\boldsymbol{z}$ and $\boldsymbol{y}$ below are all non-zero, i.e., their flags are not 0_c.

Rule 1 (COPY). *Let* $\boldsymbol{z} = (z_0, z_1, \ldots, z_{n-1})$ *and* $\boldsymbol{y} = (z_0, z_0, z_1, z_2, \ldots, z_{n-1})$ *be the input and output vector of a COPY function. Let* $\Lambda^\delta(\boldsymbol{u}) = (u_0', \ldots, u_{n-1}')$ *and* $\Lambda^\delta(\boldsymbol{v}) = (v_0', \ldots, v_n')$. $\pi_{\Lambda^\delta(\boldsymbol{u})}(\boldsymbol{z}) \overset{Core}{\to} \pi_{\Lambda^\delta(\boldsymbol{v})}(\boldsymbol{y})$ *only when* $\Lambda^\delta(\boldsymbol{v})$ *satisfies*

$$\Lambda^\delta(\boldsymbol{v}) = \begin{cases} (0, 0, \ldots, u_{n-1}'), & \text{if } u_0' = 0 \ , \\ (0, 1, \ldots, u_{n-1}'), (1, 0, \ldots, u_{n-1}'), (1, 1, \ldots, u_{n-1}'), & \text{if } u_0' = 1 \ . \end{cases}$$

Proof. Let $\boldsymbol{z}.F = (z_0.F, \ldots, z_{n-1}.F)$ and $\boldsymbol{y}.F = (y_0.F, \ldots, y_n.F)$. $\pi_{\Lambda^\delta(\boldsymbol{v})}(\boldsymbol{y})$ can be expressed as $\pi_{\Lambda^\delta(\boldsymbol{v})}(\boldsymbol{y}) = z_0^{v_0' \vee v_1'} z_1^{v_2'} \cdots z_{n-1}^{v_n'}$. $\pi_{\Lambda^\delta(\boldsymbol{u})}(\boldsymbol{z}) \overset{Core}{\to} \pi_{\Lambda^\delta(\boldsymbol{v})}(\boldsymbol{y})$ only when $\Lambda^\delta((v_0' \vee v_1', v_2', \ldots, v_n')) = (u_0', u_1', \ldots, u_{n-1}')$, where $\Lambda^\delta((v_0' \vee v_1', v_2', \ldots, v_n'))$ depends on $\boldsymbol{z}.F$.

Notice that $\Lambda^\delta((v_0', \ldots, v_n')) = (v_0', \ldots, v_n')$ according to $\boldsymbol{y}.F$ and $y_i.F = z_{i-1}.F$ for $2 \le i \le n$, therefore $v_i' = u_{i-1}'$ for $2 \le i \le n$. Next we consider $z_0.F$. If $z_0.F = y_0.F = y_1.F = 1_c$, then $v_0' = v_1' = 0$ and $u_0' = 0$; otherwise if $z_0.F = y_0.F = y_1.F = \delta$, we can deduce that $v_0' \vee v_1' = u_0'$. To sum up, the propagation rule of COPY can be concluded as $v_0' \vee v_1' = u_0'$ and $v_i' = u_{i-1}'$ for $2 \le i \le n$. □

Rule 2 (AND). *Let* $\boldsymbol{z} = (z_0, z_1, \ldots, z_{n-1})$ *and* $\boldsymbol{y} = (z_0 \wedge z_1, z_2, \ldots, z_{n-1})$ *be the input and output vector of an AND function. Let* $\Lambda^\delta(\boldsymbol{u}) = (u_0', \ldots, u_{n-1}')$ *and* $\Lambda^\delta(\boldsymbol{v}) = (v_0', \ldots, v_{n-2}')$. $\pi_{\Lambda^\delta(\boldsymbol{u})}(\boldsymbol{z}) \overset{Core}{\to} \pi_{\Lambda^\delta(\boldsymbol{v})}(\boldsymbol{y})$ *only when* $\Lambda^\delta(\boldsymbol{u}), \Lambda^\delta(\boldsymbol{v})$ *satisfies*

$$(v_0', v_1', \ldots, v_{n-2}') = (u_0' \vee u_1', u_2', \ldots, u_{n-1}') \ ,$$
$$v_0' = u_0', \text{ if } z_0.F = \delta \ ,$$
$$v_0' = u_1', \text{ if } z_1.F = \delta \ .$$

Rule 3 (XOR). *Let* $z = (z_0, z_1, \ldots, z_{n-1})$ *and* $y = (z_0 \oplus z_1, z_2, \ldots, z_{n-1})$ *be the input and output vector of a XOR function. Let* $\Lambda^\delta(u) = (u'_0, \ldots, u'_{n-1})$ *and* $\Lambda^\delta(v) = (v'_0, \ldots, v'_{n-2})$. $\pi_{\Lambda^\delta(u)}(z) \xrightarrow{Core} \pi_{\Lambda^\delta(v)}(y)$ *only when* $\Lambda^\delta(v)$ *satisfies*

$$
\Lambda^\delta(v) = \begin{cases} (v'_0, u'_2, \ldots, u'_{n-1}) \text{ with } v'_0 \geq u'_0 + u'_1, & \text{if } \{z_0.F, z_1.F\} = \{1_c, \delta\} , \\ (u'_0 + u'_1, u'_2, \ldots, u'_{n-1}), & \text{otherwise} . \end{cases}
$$

The MILP models corresponding to propagation rules can be easily derived, as shown in [13, Sup.Mat. D]. Next we consider the effect of constant 0 bits. In the propagation of CMP, we treat constant 0 bits in the same way as NBDP. Namely, we follow the rules listed in [13, Sup.Mat. C]. Recall in the generalization of Condition B, we assume $\pi_{t^{(r_m)}}(s^{(r_m)})$ is non-zero. However, $\pi_{\Lambda^\delta(t^{(0)})}(s^{(0)}) \xrightarrow{Core} \pi_{\Lambda^\delta(t^{(r_m)})}(s^{(r_m)})$ cannot guarantee $\pi_{t^{(r_m)}}(s^{(r_m)}) \neq 0$. Therefore, like the proposal of the new partial order in NBDP, we propose a new partial order to impose stricter constraints on $\pi_{t^{(r_m)}}(s^{(r_m)})$.

Definition 5 (New Partial Order of CMP). *Let* v' *and* v *be two bit vectors. We say* $v' \stackrel{\sim}{\succeq} v$ *on* y *or simply* $y^{v'} \stackrel{\sim}{\succeq} y^v$, *if*

$$
\begin{cases} v'_i = v_i = 0 & y_i.F = 0_c , \\ v'_i \geq v_i & y_i.F = 1_c , \\ v'_i = v_i & y_i.F = \delta . \end{cases}
$$

Then, the generalization of Condition B (6) holds if and only if $\pi_{\Lambda^\delta(t^{(0)})}(s^{(0)})$ $\xrightarrow{Core} \pi_{\Lambda^\delta(t^{(r_m)})}(s^{(r_m)})$ and $\pi_{t^{(r_m)}}(s^{(r_m)}) \stackrel{\sim}{\succeq} \pi_{\Lambda^\delta(t^{(r_m)})}(s^{(r_m)})$.

Recovering $VT^{(r_m)}$s with CMP. Based on the discussion above, we can construct a MILP model using CMP to recover $VT^{(r_m)}$s as follows:

$$
k^0 x^u \xrightarrow[\overbrace{}^{r_m \text{ rounds}}]{CMP} \pi_{\Lambda^\delta(t^{(r_m)})}(s^{(r_m)}) \stackrel{\sim}{\preceq} \pi_{t^{(r_m)}}(s^{(r_m)}) \xrightarrow[\overbrace{}^{r-r_m \text{ rounds}}]{MP} \pi_{t^{(r)}}(s^{(r)}). \tag{7}
$$

A MILP model based on the structure in Eq. (7) is described as `CMP-MPModelX` in [13, Algorithm 5].

CMP versus MP. We can prove that the MILP model based on Eq. (7) has fewer solutions than the MILP model based on Eq. (4). The number of solutions of the MILP model based on Eq. (7) can be represented by

$$
\sum_{t^{(r_m)} \in \mathbb{F}_2^{n_{r_m}}} |k^0 x^u \xrightarrow[\bowtie]{Core} \pi_{\Lambda^\delta(t^{(r_m)})}(s^{(r_m)})| \cdot |\pi_{t^{(r_m)}}(s^{(r_m)}) \bowtie \pi_{t^{(r)}}(s^{(r)})|.
$$

The number of solutions of the MILP model based on Eq. (4) can be represented by

$$
\sum_{t^{(r_m)} \in \mathbb{F}_2^{n_{r_m}}, w \in \mathbb{F}_2^m} |k^w x^u \bowtie \pi_{t^{(r_m)}}(s^{(r_m)})| \cdot |\pi_{t^{(r_m)}}(s^{(r_m)}) \bowtie \pi_{t^{(r)}}(s^{(r)})|.
$$

Notice that we can always map a r_m-round monomial trail $\boldsymbol{k}^w \boldsymbol{x}^u \to \pi_{t^{(1)}}(\boldsymbol{s}^{(1)}) \to$ $\cdots \to \pi_{t^{(r_m)}}(\boldsymbol{s}^{(r_m)})$ to a r_m-round core monomial trail $\boldsymbol{k}^0 \boldsymbol{x}^u \overset{\text{Core}}{\to} \pi_{\Lambda^\delta(t^{(1)})}(\boldsymbol{s}^{(1)})$ $\overset{\text{Core}}{\to} \cdots \overset{\text{Core}}{\to} \pi_{\Lambda^\delta(t^{(r_m)})}(\boldsymbol{s}^{(r_m)})$. Furthermore, notice that whether Condition B holds can be determined by checking whether $\boldsymbol{k}^0 \boldsymbol{x}^u \overset{\text{Core}}{\rightsquigarrow} \pi_{\Lambda^\delta(t^{(r_m)})}(\boldsymbol{s}^{(r_m)})$, which means this mapping is surjective. As a result, for a specific non-zero monomial $\pi_{t^{(r_m)}}(\boldsymbol{s}^{(r_m)})$, we have

$$\sum_{w \in \mathbb{F}_2^m} |\boldsymbol{k}^w \boldsymbol{x}^u \bowtie \pi_{t^{(r_m)}}(\boldsymbol{s}^{(r_m)})| \geq |\boldsymbol{k}^0 \boldsymbol{x}^u \overset{\text{Core}}{\bowtie} \pi_{\Lambda^\delta(t^{(r_m)})}(\boldsymbol{s}^{(r_m)})|,$$

meaning the model based on Eq. (7) has fewer solutions.

In addition, recall that when modeling Condition B, the propagation model of CMP only describes the δ part of monomials, and the 1_c or 0_c bits are constrained to 0, while the propagation model of MP needs to consider not only the δ part, but it also need to track the propagation of the 1_c bits. The difference between CMP and MP can be seen most intuitively from their algebraic interpretation, which was described earlier in this paper.

Naturally, we believe the MILP model based on Eq. (7) can be solved faster than the model based on Eq. (4). Indeed, taking the MILP model based on Eq. (7) as the core component of our coefficient solver, we successfully recovered the superpoly of 848-round TRIVIUM, a result that can not be achieved by the model based on Eq. (4).

The MILP models based on Eq. (7) can be further optimized using [13, Proposition 2], where the XOR propagation rule (Rule 3) of CMP is reduced to

$$\Lambda^\delta(\boldsymbol{v}) = (u'_0 + u'_1, u'_2, \ldots, u'_{n-1}).$$

Moreover, when constructing the MILP models based on Eq. (7) and Eq. (5) for ACORN, this proposition helps to exclude some redundant propagation trails, thus simplifying the models.

Towards New Coefficient Solver and Term Expander. Finally, we choose the MILP model based on Eq. (7) to recover $VT^{(r_m)}$s in a more efficient way than the monomial prediction. Notice that if $\pi_{t^{(r_m)}}(\boldsymbol{s}^{(r_m)})$ is a $VT^{(r_m)}$, we can split $\pi_{t^{(r_m)}}(\boldsymbol{s}^{(r_m)})$ into 1_c part and δ part, namely

$$\pi_{t^{(r_m)}}(\boldsymbol{s}^{(r_m)}) = \pi_{\Lambda^\delta(t^{(r_m)})}(\boldsymbol{s}^{(r_m)}) \cdot \pi_{\Lambda^{1_c}(t^{(r_m)})}(\boldsymbol{s}^{(r_m)}).$$

$\pi_{\Lambda^{1_c}(t^{(r_m)})}(\boldsymbol{s}^{(r_m)})$ is the product of some 1_c bits whose ANFs can be computed beforehand, hence the monomial prediction technique is only applied to δ part of $\pi_{t^{(r_m)}}(\boldsymbol{s}^{(r_m)})$ to compute $\mathsf{Coe}\left(\pi_{\Lambda^\delta(t^{(r_m)})}(\boldsymbol{s}^{(r_m)}), \boldsymbol{x}^u\right)$. Such a strategy can speed up the coefficient solver for some ciphers.

Combined with the callback function interface provided in Gurobi, MILP models based on Eq. (7) and Eq. (5) can also be extended to construct a new term expander. However, we prefer this to be an implementation improvement rather than a theoretical innovation. In other words, even if we use the term expander in NMP with our new coefficient solver, we can still get the results listed in this paper, but it might take slightly more time. For this reason, we put the introduction of our term expander in [13, Sup.Mat. E].

6 Applications

Using our designed term expander and coefficient solver, we can assemble a new nested framework according to Algorithm 1. We apply this new nested framework to four NLFSR-based ciphers, namely TRIVIUM, Grain-128AEAD, Kreyvium and ACORN. As a result, the exact ANFs of the superpolies for 846-, 847- and 848-round TRIVIUM, 192-round Grain-128AEAD, 895-round Kreyvium and 776-round ACORN are recovered. All experiments are performed using Gurobi Solver (version 9.1.2) on a work station with high-speed processors, (totally 32 cores and 64 threads). The source code (as well as some superpolies we recovered) is available in our git repository.

In [11, 12, 16], the MILP models of TRIVIUM, Grain-128AEAD, Kreyvium, and ACORN for tracing the three-subset division/monomial trails are proposed. In this section, the propagation models of monomial trails in [13, Sup.Mat. G] are directly borrowed from [11, 12, 16] and we adjust them slightly to fit our new framework. The MILP models of basic operations that NBDP and CMP rely on are provided in [13, Sup.Mat. F]. As pointed out before, NBDP-MPModelX in [13, Algorithm 4] and CMP-MPModelX in [13, Algorithm 5] are the most important parts in the framework, so next we only describe how to construct these two MILP models for a specific cipher, along with the selection of related parameters.

6.1 Superpoly Recovery for TRIVIUM up to 848 Rounds

As shown in [13, Sup.Mat. H], we applied our framework to TRIVIUM and verified the correctness of some previous superpolies with significantly less time cost.

Superpoly Recovery for 846-, 847- and 848-Round Trivium. To the best of our knowledge, currently there is no effective method for choosing a good cube, hence we heuristically choose cubes with similar structure to I_0–I_4. Finally, we find some other cubes applicable to TRIVIUM up to 848 rounds. They are listed in Table 3. Since the sizes of these superpolies are too large, we only provide our codes in the git repository. The details of these superpolies are given in Table 4. The balancedness of each superpoly is estimated by testing 2^{15} random keys.

6.2 Superpoly Recovery for 192-Round Grain-128AEAD

In [13, Sup.Mat. I], we introduce the specification of Grain-128AEAD and apply our new framework to it. We successfully verified the results given in [16]. For 192-round Grain-128AEAD, we heuristically choose a 94-dimensional cube indexed by $\{0, 1, 2, \ldots, 95\} \backslash \{42, 43\}$. The superpoly of this cube for 192-round Grain-128AEAD is recovered in about 45 days using our new framework. The

Table 3. Cube indices for the superpoly recovery of TRIVIUM up to 848 rounds

I	$|I|$	Indices
I_5	53	0, 1, 2, 3, 4, 5, 6, 7, 8, 9, 10, 11, 12, 13, 14, 15, 16, 17, 18, 19, 20, 21, 22, 23, 24, 25, 26, 27, 28, 29, 32, 34, 36, 38, 40, 42, 45, 47, 49, 51, 53, 55, 57, 60, 62, 64, 66, 68, 70, 72, 77, 75, 79
I_6	52	0, 1, 2, 3, 4, 5, 6, 7, 8, 9, 10, 11, 12, 13, 14, 15, 16, 17, 18, 19, 20, 21, 22, 23, 24, 25, 26, 28, 30, 32, 34, 36, 38, 40, 42, 45, 47, 49, 51, 53, 55, 57, 60, 62, 64, 66, 68, 70, 72, 77, 75, 79
I_7	51	0, 1, 2, 3, 4, 5, 6, 7, 8, 9, 10, 11, 12, 13, 14, 15, 16, 17, 18, 19, 20, 21, 22, 23, 24, 26, 28, 30, 32, 34, 36, 38, 40, 42, 45, 47, 49, 51, 53, 55, 57, 60, 62, 64, 66, 68, 70, 72, 77, 75, 79
I_8	53	0, 1, 2, 3, 4, 5, 6, 7, 8, 9, 10, 11, 12, 13, 14, 15, 16, 17, 18, 19, 20, 21, 22, 23, 24, 25, 26, 27, 28, 30, 32, 34, 36, 38, 40, 42, 45, 47, 49, 51, 53, 55, 57, 60, 62, 64, 66, 68, 70, 72, 77, 75, 79
I_9	53	0, 1, 2, 3, 4, 5, 6, 7, 8, 9, 10, 11, 12, 13, 14, 15, 16, 17, 18, 19, 20, 21, 22, 23, 24, 25, 26, 28, 30, 31, 32, 34, 36, 38, 40, 42, 45, 47, 49, 51, 53, 55, 57, 60, 62, 64, 66, 68, 70, 72, 77, 75, 79

Table 4. Details related to the superpolies of 846-, 847- and 848-round TRIVIUM.

I	Round	Status	#Involved key bits	Balancedness	TimeCost
I_3	846	New	80	0.50	1 day and 12 h
I_5	846	New	80	0.50	16 h
I_6	846	New	80	0.50	5 h
I_7	846	New	80	0.50	11 h
I_8	846	New	80	0.50	5 h
I_9	846	New	80	0.50	1 day and 17.5 h
I_6	847	New	80	0.50	9 days and 20.5 h
I_7	847	New	80	0.50	2 days
I_6	848	New	80	0.50	11 days

superpoly is a 34-degree polynomial involving 534 077 971 terms and 128 key bits. The balancedness is estimated to be 0.49 after testing 2^{15} random keys. Since the size of this superpoly is too large, we only provide our codes in the git repository.

6.3 Superpoly Recovery for 895-Round Kreyvium

As can be seen in [13, Sup.Mat. J], we verified the superpoly of the 119-dimensional cube given in [16] with our new framework. For 895-round Kreyvium, we heuristically choose a 120-dimensional cube indexed by

$$I_2 = \{0, 1, \ldots, 127\} \setminus \{66, 72, 73, 78, 101, 106, 109, 110\}.$$

The superpoly of I_2 for 895-Round Kreyvium is recovered in about two weeks using our nested framework. The superpoly is a 7-degree polynomial that involves

19411 terms and 128 key bits. The balancedness is estimated to be 0.50 after testing 2^{15} random keys.

6.4 Superpoly Recovery for ACORN up to 776 Rounds

As can be seen in [13, Sup.Mat. K], we verified the results given in [33] with our new framework. For 776-round ACORN, we heuristically choose two 127-dimensional cubes indexed by $I_1 = \{0, 1, \ldots, 127\} \backslash \{1, 28\}$ and $I_2 = \{0, 1, \ldots, 127\} \backslash \{2, 28\}$. The superpoly recoveries of these two cubes are completed after about 8 days using our nested framework.

The superpoly of I_1 is an 8-degree polynomial involving 123 key bits and $2\,464\,007$ terms, with k_{104}, k_{105} and k_{115} as single balanced bits. Bits not involved are $k_{100}, k_{103}, k_{106}, k_{114}$ and k_{126}. The superpoly of I_2 is an 8-degree polynomial involving 121 key bits and $2\,521\,399$ terms, with k_{104} and k_{126} as single balanced bits. Bits not involved are $k_{99}, k_{100}, k_{101}, k_{103}, k_{106}, k_{110}$ and k_{112}. The concrete expressions of these two superpolies, denoted by p_{I_1} and p_{I_2}, are shown in [13, Sup.Mat. N], where they are represented by 1_c bits of 256th round.

7 Towards Efficient Key-Recovery Attacks

Though we have recovered more than one superpolies for 846- and 847-round TRIVIUM, how to recover the information of key bits from multiple superpolies remains a problem. We briefly discuss several previous approaches to this problem in [13, Sup.Mat. L].

Cube Attacks Against 776-Round Acorn. Since the two superpolies of 776-round ACORN do not involve full key bits, we can mount a key recovery attack against 776-round ACORN as follows:

1. We can obtain the real values of the two superpolies during the online phase, which requires 2^{127} ACORN calls.
2. We guess the values of $\{k_0, ..., k_{127}\} \backslash \{k_{100}, k_{103}, k_{106}\}$ and check if the values of the two superpolies are correct. As mentioned in [13, Sup.Mat. K], one evaluation of the superpoly of ACORN is equivalent to one 256-round ACORN call or approximately $\frac{1}{3}$ 776-round ACORN call, so the complexity of this step is about $2 \times 2^{125} \times \frac{1}{3} \approx 2^{124.4}$ 776-round ACORN calls.
3. For the remaining 2^{126} candidates of key bits, we can find the correct key by an exhaustive search with time complexity of 2^{126} 776-round ACORN calls.

Therefore, the final complexity is slightly more than 2^{127} 776-round ACORN calls to recover all the secret key bits. Next we show how to mount the cube attack using the superpoly involving full key bits.

Revisiting Möbius Transformation. Let $f(x_0, x_1, \ldots, x_{n-1})$ be a Boolean function on $x_0, x_1, ..., x_{n-1}$. The ANF of f is obtained by writing:

$$f = \bigoplus_{(c_0, \ldots, c_{n-1}) \in \mathbb{F}_2^n} g_0(c_0, \ldots, c_{n-1}) \cdot \prod_{i=0}^{n-1} x_i^{c_i}. \tag{8}$$

The process of Möbius transformation on f from ANF to truth table can be represented by Algorithm 2, where t represents the t-th step and g_n is exactly f. For simplicity, we also use $g_t(e)(0 \leq t \leq n)$ to represent $g_t(c_0, \ldots, c_{n-1})$, where $e = c_0 + c_1 2^1 + \cdots + c_{n-1} 2^{n-1}$ and $(c_0, \ldots, c_{n-1})$ is called the binary representation of e. We assume in this paper that Möbius transformation requires $n \times 2^{n-1}$ bitwise XORs and 2^n-bits memory complexity.

Algorithm 2: Möbius transformation on f in Eq. (8)

1 **Procedure** MobiusTransformation(The ANF of f):
2   **for** $t = 1$ to n **do**
3   Initialize g_t to be the same as g_{t-1}
4   **for** $j = 0$ to $2^{n-t} - 1$ **do**
5   **for** $k = 0$ to $2^{t-1} - 1$ **do**
6              $g_t(2^t j + 2^{t-1} + k) = g_{t-1}(2^t j + 2^{t-1} + k) + g_{t-1}(2^t j + k)$

7   **return** g_n

Proposition 3. *Let $f, g_0, g_1, \ldots, g_n$ be defined as above. After the t-th $(1 \leq t \leq n-1)$ step of Möbius transformation on the ANF of f, if we represent f as*

$$f = \sum_{(c_t, \ldots, c_{n-1}) \in \mathbb{F}_{n-t}} p_{(c_t, \ldots, c_{n-1})}(x_0, \ldots, x_{t-1}) \cdot \prod_{i=t}^{n-1} x_i^{c_i}, \tag{9}$$

where $p_{(c_t, \ldots, c_{n-1})}(x_0, \ldots, x_{t-1})$ is a Boolean polynomial of $(x_0, \ldots, x_{t-1})$ determined by $(c_t, \ldots, c_{n-1})$, then for any value of $(c_t, \ldots, c_{n-1})$,

$$g_t(x_0, \ldots, x_{t-1}, c_t, \ldots, c_{n-1}) = p_{(c_t, \ldots, c_{n-1})}(x_0, \ldots, x_{t-1}).$$

An intuitive description of Eq. (9) is, we regard $(x_t, \ldots, x_{n-1})$ as variables and $(x_0, \ldots, x_{t-1})$ as constants, then $p_{(c_t, \ldots, c_{n-1})}(x_0, \ldots, x_{t-1})$ is exactly the coefficient of the monomial $\prod_{i=t}^{n-1} x_i^{c_i}$.

Proof. It can be easily verified that when $t = 1$, the conclusion holds. Assume the conclusion holds for $t = l$ $(1 \leq l \leq n-2)$, next we prove that the conclusion is also true for $t = l+1$.

According to Eq. (9), $p_{(c_{l+1}, \ldots, c_{n-1})}(x_0, \ldots, x_l)$ can be expressed as the sum of $p_{(0, c_{l+1}, \ldots, c_{n-1})}(x_0, \ldots, x_{l-1})$ and $p_{(1, c_{l+1}, \ldots, c_{n-1})}(x_0, \ldots, x_{l-1}) \cdot x_l$, that is,

$$g_l(x_0, \ldots, x_{l-1}, 0, c_{l+1}, \ldots, c_{n-1}) + g_l(x_0, \ldots, x_{l-1}, 1, c_{l+1}, \ldots, c_{n-1}) \cdot x_l.$$

Considering that x_l takes 0 or 1, $p_{(c_{l+1}, \ldots, c_{n-1})}(x_0, \ldots, x_l)$ is equal to

$$\begin{cases} g_l(x_0, \ldots, x_{l-1}, 0, c_{l+1}, \ldots, c_{n-1}), & \text{if } x_l = 0, \\ g_l(x_0, \ldots, x_{l-1}, 0, c_{l+1}, \ldots, c_{n-1}) + g_l(x_0, \ldots, x_{l-1}, 1, c_{l+1}, \ldots, c_{n-1}), & \text{if } x_l = 1. \end{cases}$$

This is the same as how $g_{l+1}(x_0, \ldots, x_l, c_{l+1}, \ldots, c_{n-1})$ is generated during the process of Möbius transformation. Hence, $g_{l+1}(x_0, \ldots, x_l, c_{l+1}, \ldots, c_{n-1})$ is exactly $p_{(c_{l+1}, \ldots, c_{n-1})}(x_0, \ldots, x_l)$. By mathematical induction, the conclusion is true for all t ($1 \le t \le n-1$). □

Example 2. Let $f(x_0, x_1, x_2, x_3) = x_0 x_1 x_2 + x_2 x_3 + x_1 x_3 + x_2$. The process of Möbius transformation on the ANF of f is shown in the following table, where each row is the truth table of g_t ($0 \le t \le 4$).

	0	1	2	3	4	5	6	7	8	9	10	11	12	13	14	15
g_0	0	0	0	0	1	0	0	1	0	0	1	0	1	0	0	0
g_1	0	0	0	0	1	1	0	1	0	0	1	1	1	1	0	0
g_2	0	0	0	0	1	1	1	1	0	0	0	1	1	1	1	1
g_3	0	0	0	0	1	1	1	1	0	0	0	1	1	1	0	0
g_4	0	0	0	0	1	1	1	1	0	0	0	1	1	0	0	1	0

Consider g_2. We regard (x_0, x_1) as constants and (x_2, x_3) as variables, f can be expressed as $f = (x_0 x_1 + 1) \cdot x_2 + x_1 \cdot x_3 + 1 \cdot x_2 x_3$. Then $g_2(x_0, x_1, 0, 0) = 0$, which is the coefficient of $x_2^0 x_3^0$ in f; $g_2(x_0, x_1, 1, 0) = x_0 x_1 + 1$, which is the coefficient of $x_2^1 x_3^0$; $g_2(x_0, x_1, 0, 1) = x_1$, which is the coefficient of $x_2^0 x_3^1$; $g_2(x_0, x_1, 1, 1) = 1$, which is the coefficient of $x_2^1 x_3^1$. This corresponds to truth table of g_2. Note that $g_2(j) = g_2(x_0, x_1, x_2, x_3)$, where $j = x_0 + x_1 2^1 + x_2 2^2 + x_3 2^3$.

We can further simplify Möbius transformation exploiting Proposition 3 and the degree of f. Since this would not affect our final complexity, we discuss it in [13, Sup.Mat. M]

Key Recovery During Möbius Transformation. Let f be as defined in Eq. (8) and $(x_0, \ldots, x_{n-1})$ be n secret key variables. It can be deduced from Proposition 3 that if $(c_t, \ldots, c_{n-1}) = (0, \ldots, 0)$, $f(x_0, \ldots, x_{t-1}, 0, \ldots, 0)$ is equal to $g_t(x_0, \ldots, x_{t-1}, 0, \ldots, 0)$, therefore after t steps of Möbius transformation, we can already obtain the function values of $f(x_0, \ldots, x_{t-1}, 0, \ldots, 0)$. Using this property, we can recover the key during Möbius transformation. We use Example 3 to illustrate our basic idea.

Example 3. Let f and its Möbius transformation be as defined in Example 2. Now we want to recover the key from the equation $f(x_0, x_1, x_2, x_3) = a$.
1. At the beginning, $f(0) = g_0(0)$. If $f(0) = a$, we test whether $(0, 0, 0, 0)$ is the correct key by one encryption call. And if it is incorrect, we go to next step.
2. Compute $g_1(1) = g_0(0) + g_0(1)$, $g_1(0) = g_0(0)$, then $f(1) = g_1(1)$. If $f(1) = a$, we test whether $(1, 0, 0, 0)$ is the correct key by one encryption call. And if it is incorrect, go to next step.
3. First, we compute $g_1(3) = g_0(2) + g_0(3)$, $g_1(2) = g_0(2)$. Compute $g_2(2) = g_1(2) + g_1(0)$, $g_2(3) = g_1(3) + g_1(1)$, $g_2(0) = g_1(0)$, $g_2(1) = g_1(1)$, then $f(2) = g_2(2)$, $f(3) = g_2(3)$. If $f(2) = a$, we test if $(0, 1, 0, 0)$ is the correct key by one

encryption call; if $f(3) = a$, we test if $(1, 1, 0, 0)$ is the correct key by one encryption call. And if none of them is correct, go to next step.

4. First, we compute $g_1(i)$ $(i = 4, 5, 6, 7)$ from $g_0(i)$ $(i = 4, 5, 6, 7)$ and $g_2(i)$ $(i = 4, 5, 6, 7)$ from $g_1(i)$ $(i = 4, 5, 6, 7)$. Compute $g_3(j)$ $(j = 0, \ldots, 7)$ from $g_2(j)$ $(j = 0, \ldots, 7)$, then $f(i) = g_3(i)$ $(i = 4, 5, 6, 7)$. If $f(i) = a$ $(i = 4, 5, 6, 7)$, we test if the binary representation of i is the correct key by one encryption call. And if none of them is correct, go to next step.

5. First, we compute $g_1(i)$ $(i = 8, \ldots, 15)$ from $g_0(i)$ $(i = 8, \ldots, 15)$, $g_2(i)$ $(i = 8, \ldots, 15)$ from $g_1(i)$ $(i = 8, \ldots, 15)$ and $g_3(i)$ $(i = 8, \ldots, 15)$ from $g_2(i)$ $(i = 8, \ldots, 15)$. Compute $g_4(j)$ $(j = 0, \ldots, 15)$ from $g_3(j)$ $(j = 0, \ldots, 15)$, then $f(i) = g_4(i)$ $(i = 8, \ldots, 15)$. If $f(i) = a$ $(i = 8, \ldots, 15)$, we test if the binary representation of i is the correct key by one encryption call. And if none of them is correct, we claim this equation has no solution.

In each step, we use the minimum memory and the least XOR operations to calculate the necessary bits. In step 1, only 1-bit memory $(g_0(0))$ is sufficient. In step 2, 1 XOR and 2-bits memory $(g_1(1), g_1(0))$ are sufficient. In step 3, $2 + 1$ XORs and 4-bits memory $(g_2(i)$ $(i = 1, 2, 3, 4))$ are sufficient. In step 4, $2 + 2 + 4$ XORs and 8-bits memory $(g_3(j)$ $(j = 0, \ldots, 7))$ are sufficient. Finally in step 5, $4 + 4 + 4 + 8$ XORs and 16-bits memory $(g_4(j)$ $(j = 0, \ldots, 15))$ are sufficient. Note that in each step, the first computation can be regarded as performing Möbius transformation on part of the ANF of f. For example, in step 4, we first compute $g_2(i)$ $(i = 4, 5, 6, 7)$ iteratively from $g_0(i)$ $(i = 4, 5, 6, 7)$. This can be regarded as performing Möbius transformation on the ANF of $p_{(1,0)}(x_0, x_1)$, namely $x_0 x_1 + 1$.

We summarize our key recovery strategy in Algorithm 3, which can be seen as embedding the key testing procedure into a Möbius transformation with an adjusted computational order. Though a more accurate estimation of the average complexity can be given, here we roughly estimate the time cost (only considering the loop starting at Line 8) of Algorithm 3 as one Möbius transformation together with required encryption calls, that is, $q \cdot 2^n$ encryption calls $+ n \cdot 2^{n-1}$ XORs, where q denotes the probability that $f(x_0, \ldots, x_{n-1}) = a$. The cost of the comparison is ignored. The memory complexity in the worst case is 2^n bits. Comparing with the traditional key recovery method of first constructing a large truth table and then performing queries, our method naturally saves the query cost.

Key Recovery Attacks on 848-Round Trivium. Our further evaluation shows that the superpoly of 848-round TRIVIUM, denoted by $p(k_0, \ldots, k_{79})$, is a polynomial whose degree is upper bounded by 25. It contains about $2^{30.5}$ terms, but is still very sparse compared with a random polynomial (a random polynomial may contain about 2^{79} terms). A natural idea is to treat $p(k_0, \ldots, k_{79})$ as f in Algorithm 3. However, Möbius transformation also incurs memory access cost. In the worse case, Algorithm 3 requires 2^{80}-bits memory and the memory access cost of such a big table is unbearable. To address this difficulty, we propose the following strategies:

Algorithm 3: Recover the key from the equation $f(x_0, \ldots, x_{n-1}) = a$

---

1   **Procedure** RecoverKey(The ANF of f):
2   **for** $t = 1$ to n **do**
3     $\lfloor$ Precompute the ANF of $p_{(1,0,\ldots,0)}(x_0, \ldots, x_{t-2})$ from the ANF of f

4   **if** $g_0(0, \ldots, 0) = a$ **then**
5   Check if $(0, \ldots, 0)$ is the correct key by calling the encryption oracle once
6   **if** The check passes **then**
7      $\lfloor$ **return** $(0, \ldots, 0)$

8   **for** $t = 1$ to n **do**
9   Perform Möbius transformation on the ANF of $p_{(1,0,\ldots,0)}(x_0, \ldots, x_{t-2})$ to obtain the truth table of $g_{t-1}(x_0, \ldots, x_{t-2}, 1, 0, \ldots, 0)$
     /* When $t = 1$, we assume $p_{(c_{t-1}, \ldots, c_{n-1})}(x_0, \ldots, x_{t-2}) = g_0(c_{t-1}, \ldots, c_{n-1})$ */
10   **for** $k = 0$ to $2^{t-1} - 1$ **do**
11      $g_t(2^{t-1} + k) = g_{t-1}(2^{t-1} + k) + g_{t-1}(k)$
12   **if** $g_t(2^{t-1} + k) = a$ **then**
13   Let $(c_0, \ldots, c_{n-1})$ be the binary representation of $2^{t-1} + k$
14   Check if $(c_0, \ldots, c_{n-1})$ is the correct key by calling the encryption oracle once
15   **if** The check passes **then**
16        $\lfloor$ **return** $(c_0, \ldots, c_{n-1})$

17     $\lfloor g_t(k) = g_{t-1}(k)$

18   $\lfloor$ **return** no solution found

---

1. We guess the values of $(k_{40}, \ldots, k_{79})$. Let $(v_{40}, \ldots, v_{79})$ denote the values of $(k_{40}, \ldots, k_{79})$, then the equation $p(k_0, \ldots, k_{79}) = a$ can be reduced to $p'(k_0, \ldots, k_{39}) = p(k_0, \ldots, k_{39}, v_{40}, \ldots, v_{79}) = a$.
2. For each guess, treat $p'(k_0, \ldots, k_{39})$ as f and apply Algorithm 3 to it. Once Algorithm 3 returns the correct values of $(k_0, \ldots, k_{39})$, denoted by $(v_0, \ldots, v_{39})$, the correct key is found as $(v_0, \ldots, v_{79})$.

Assuming reducing $p(k_0, \ldots, k_{79})$ to $p'(k_0, \ldots, k_{39})$ for all guesses requires $2^{40} \times 2^{30.5} = 2^{70.5}$ XORs, the final time complexity is approximately 2^{79} TRIVIUM calls and 40×2^{79} XORs. Assuming one 848-round TRIVIUM call is equivalent to $848 \times 9 = 7632$ XORs, finally our key recovery strategy requires slightly more than 2^{79} 848-round TRIVIUM calls, but only about 2^{40}-bits memory. Similarly, we can recover the key of 192-round Grain-128AEAD and 895-round Kreyvium with time complexity 2^{127} and 2^{127}, respectively.

8   Conclusion

In this paper, we revisit the two core components of nested monomial predictions, namely the coefficient solver and the term expander. The coefficient solver is responsible for performing the superpoly recovery for a given term, while the term expander is used to transform output bits into multiple terms of fewer rounds. We try to improve the coefficient solver by first recovering valuable intermediate terms of a middle round, then applying the monomial prediction to each of them. This idea gives rise to two techniques called NBDP and core monomial prediction that identify the necessary condition that a valuable intermediate term should satisfy. The core monomial prediction presents a substantial improvement over monomial prediction in terms of efficiency of enumerating solutions, hence we choose it to build our coefficient solver. Besides, we construct an improved term expander using NBDP in order to spend less time on useless terms of fewer rounds. We apply our new framework to TRIVIUM, Grain-128AEAD, ACORN and Kreyvium and recover superpolies for reduced-round versions of the four ciphers with 848, 192, 776 and 895 rounds. This results in attacks that are more efficient and cover more rounds than earlier work.

Acknowledgment.. The authors would like to thank the anonymous reviewers for their valuable comments and suggestions to improve the quality of the paper. The research leading to these results has received funding from the National Natural Science Foundation of China (Grant No. 62002201, Grant No. 62032014), the National Key Research and Development Program of China (Grant No. 2018YFA0704702), and the Major Basic Research Project of Natural Science Foundation of Shandong Province, China (Grant No. ZR202010220025). Bart Preneel was supported by CyberSecurity Research Flanders with reference number VR20192203. Kai Hu is supported by the "ANR-NRF project SELECT". The scientific calculations in this paper have been done on the HPC Cloud Platform of Shandong University.

References

1. Gorubi Optimization. https://www.gurobi.com
2. Gorubi Optimization Reference Manual. https://www.gurobi.com/wp-content/plugins/hd_documentations/documentation/9.1/refman.pdf
3. ISO/IEC 29192-3:2012: Information technology—Security techniques—Lightweight cryptography—part 3: Stream ciphers. https://www.iso.org/standard/56426.html
4. Boura, C., Coggia, D.: Efficient MILP modelings for sboxes and linear layers of SPN ciphers. IACR Trans. Symmetric Cryptol. **2020**(3), 327–361 (2020)
5. De Cannière, C., Preneel, B.: Trivium. In: Robshaw, M., Billet, O. (eds.) New Stream Cipher Designs. LNCS, vol. 4986, pp. 244–266. Springer, Heidelberg (2008). https://doi.org/10.1007/978-3-540-68351-3_18
6. Canteaut, A., et al.: Stream ciphers: a practical solution for efficient homomorphic-ciphertext compression. J. Cryptol. **31**(3), 885–916 (2018)
7. Chang, D., Turan, M.S.: Recovering the key from the internal state of Grain-128AEAD. IACR Cryptology ePrint Archive 2021:439 (2021)
8. Dinur, I., Shamir, A.: Cube attacks on tweakable black box polynomials. In: Joux, A. (ed.) EUROCRYPT 2009. LNCS, vol. 5479, pp. 278–299. Springer, Heidelberg (2009). https://doi.org/10.1007/978-3-642-01001-9_16
9. Fouque, P.-A., Vannet, T.: Improving key recovery to 784 and 799 rounds of Trivium using optimized cube attacks. In: Moriai, S. (ed.) FSE 2013. LNCS, vol. 8424, pp. 502–517. Springer, Heidelberg (2014). https://doi.org/10.1007/978-3-662-43933-3_26
10. Hao, Y., Jiao, L., Li, C., Meier, W., Todo, Y., Wang, Q.: Links between division property and other cube attack variants. IACR Trans. Symmetric Cryptol. **2020**(1), 363–395 (2020)

11. Hao, Y., Leander, G., Meier, W., Todo, Y., Wang, Q.: Modeling for three-subset division property without unknown subset - improved cube attacks against Trivium and grain-128AEAD. In: Canteaut, A., Ishai, Y. (eds.) EUROCRYPT 2020. LNCS, vol. 12105, pp. 466–495. Springer, Cham (2020). https://doi.org/10.1007/978-3-030-45721-1_17

12. Hao, Y., Leander, G., Meier, W., Todo, Y., Wang, Q.: Modeling for three-subset division property without unknown subset. J. Cryptol. **34**(3), 22 (2021)

13. He, J., Hu, K., Preneel, B., Wang, M.: Stretching cube attacks: improved methods to recover massive superpolies. Cryptology ePrint Archive, Paper 2022/1218 (2022). https://eprint.iacr.org/2022/1218

14. Hebborn, P., Lambin, B., Leander, G., Todo, Y.: Lower bounds on the degree of block ciphers. In: Moriai, S., Wang, H. (eds.) ASIACRYPT 2020. LNCS, vol. 12491, pp. 537–566. Springer, Cham (2020). https://doi.org/10.1007/978-3-030-64837-4_18

15. Hell, M., Johansson, T., Meier, W., Sönnerup, J., Yoshida, H.: Grain-128AEAD - a lightweight AEAD stream cipher. NIST Lightweight Cryptography, Round, 3 (2019)

16. Hu, K., Sun, S., Todo, Y., Wang, M., Wang, Q.: Massive superpoly recovery with nested monomial predictions. In: Tibouchi, M., Wang, H. (eds.) ASIACRYPT 2021. LNCS, vol. 13090, pp. 392–421. Springer, Cham (2021). https://doi.org/10.1007/978-3-030-92062-3_14

17. Hu, K., Sun, S., Wang, M., Wang, Q.: An algebraic formulation of the division property: revisiting degree evaluations, cube attacks, and key-independent sums. In: Moriai, S., Wang, H. (eds.) ASIACRYPT 2020. LNCS, vol. 12491, pp. 446–476. Springer, Cham (2020). https://doi.org/10.1007/978-3-030-64837-4_15

18. Lehmann, M., Meier, W.: Conditional Differential Cryptanalysis of Grain-128a. In: Pieprzyk, J., Sadeghi, A.-R., Manulis, M. (eds.) CANS 2012. LNCS, vol. 7712, pp. 1–11. Springer, Heidelberg (2012). https://doi.org/10.1007/978-3-642-35404-5_1

19. Meicheng Liu. Degree evaluation of NFSR-based cryptosystems. In Jonathan Katz and Hovav Shacham, editors, CRYPTO 2017, volume 10403 of LNCS, pages 227–249. Springer, 2017

20. Mroczkowski, P., Szmidt, J.: The cube attack on stream cipher Trivium and quadraticity tests. Fundam. Informaticae **114**(3–4), 309–318 (2012)

21. Sasaki, Yu., Todo, Y.: New algorithm for modeling S-box in MILP based differential and division trail search. In: Farshim, P., Simion, E. (eds.) SecITC 2017. LNCS, vol. 10543, pp. 150–165. Springer, Cham (2017). https://doi.org/10.1007/978-3-319-69284-5_11

22. Sun, S., Hu, L., Wang, P., Qiao, K., Ma, X., Song, L.: Automatic security evaluation and (related-key) differential characteristic search: application to SIMON, PRESENT, LBlock, DES(L) and other bit-oriented block ciphers. In: Sarkar, P., Iwata, T. (eds.) ASIACRYPT 2014. LNCS, vol. 8873, pp. 158–178. Springer, Heidelberg (2014). https://doi.org/10.1007/978-3-662-45611-8_9

23. Sun, Y.: Automatic search of cubes for attacking stream ciphers. IACR Trans. Symmetric Cryptol. **2021**(4), 100–123 (2021)

24. Todo, Y.: Structural evaluation by generalized integral property. In: Oswald, E., Fischlin, M. (eds.) EUROCRYPT 2015. LNCS, vol. 9056, pp. 287–314. Springer, Heidelberg (2015). https://doi.org/10.1007/978-3-662-46800-5_12

25. Todo, Y., Isobe, T., Hao, Y., Meier, W.: Cube attacks on non-blackbox polynomials based on division property. In: Katz, J., Shacham, H. (eds.) CRYPTO 2017. LNCS, vol. 10403, pp. 250–279. Springer, Cham (2017). https://doi.org/10.1007/978-3-319-63697-9_9

26. Todo, Y., Isobe, T., Hao, Y., Meier, W.: Cube attacks on non-blackbox polynomials based on division property. IACR Cryptology ePrint Archive 2017:306 (2017)

27. Todo, Y., Morii, M.: Bit-based division property and application to SIMON family. In: Peyrin, T. (ed.) FSE 2016. LNCS, vol. 9783, pp. 357–377. Springer, Heidelberg (2016). https://doi.org/10.1007/978-3-662-52993-5_18

28. Wang, Q., Hao, Y., Todo, Y., Li, C., Isobe, T., Meier, W.: Improved division property based cube attacks exploiting algebraic properties of superpoly. In: Shacham, H., Boldyreva, A. (eds.) CRYPTO 2018. LNCS, vol. 10991, pp. 275–305. Springer, Cham (2018). https://doi.org/10.1007/978-3-319-96884-1_10

29. Wang, S., Hu, B., Guan, J., Zhang, K., Shi, T.: MILP-aided method of searching division property using three subsets and applications. In: Galbraith, S.D., Moriai, S. (eds.) ASIACRYPT 2019. LNCS, vol. 11923, pp. 398–427. Springer, Cham (2019). https://doi.org/10.1007/978-3-030-34618-8_14

30. Wang, S.P., Bin, H., Guan, J., Zhang, K., Shi, T.: A practical method to recover exact superpoly in cube attack. IACR Cryptology ePrint Archive 2019:259 (2019)

31. Wu, H.: Acorn v3. Submission to CAESAR competition (2016)

32. Xiang, Z., Zhang, W., Bao, Z., Lin, D.: Applying MILP method to searching integral distinguishers based on division property for 6 lightweight block ciphers. In: Cheon, J.H., Takagi, T. (eds.) ASIACRYPT 2016. LNCS, vol. 10031, pp. 648–678. Springer, Heidelberg (2016). https://doi.org/10.1007/978-3-662-53887-6_24

33. Yang, J., Lin, D.: Searching cubes in division property based cube attack: applications to round-reduced acorn. Cryptology ePrint Archive, Report 2020/1128 (2020). https://ia.cr/2020/1128

34. Yang, J., Liu, M., Lin, D.: Cube cryptanalysis of round-reduced acorn. Cryptology ePrint Archive, Report 2019/1226 (2019). https://ia.cr/2019/1226

35. Ye, C., Tian, T.: A new framework for finding nonlinear superpolies in cube attacks against Trivium-like ciphers. In: Susilo, W., Yang, G. (eds.) ACISP 2018. LNCS, vol. 10946, pp. 172–187. Springer, Cham (2018). https://doi.org/10.1007/978-3-319-93638-3_11

36. Ye, C.-D., Tian, T.: Algebraic method to recover superpolies in cube attacks. IET Inf. Secur. 14(4), 430–441 (2020)

37. Ye, C.-D., Tian, T.: A practical key-recovery attack on 805-round trivium. IACR Cryptology ePrint Archive 2020:1404 (2020)

38. Ye, C., Tian, T.: Revisit division property based cube attacks: key-recovery or distinguishing attacks? IACR Trans. Symmetric Cryptol. 2019(3), 81–102 (2019)

Quantum Cryptography

Functional Encryption with Secure Key Leasing

Fuyuki Kitagawa$^{(\boxtimes)}$ and Ryo Nishimaki

NTT Social Informatics Laboratories, Tokyo, Japan
{fuyuki.kitagawa.yh,ryo.nishimaki.zk}@hco.ntt.co.jp

Abstract. Secure software leasing is a quantum cryptographic primitive that enables us to lease software to a user by encoding it into a quantum state. Secure software leasing has a mechanism that verifies whether a returned software is valid or not. The security notion guarantees that once a user returns a software in a valid form, the user no longer uses the software.

In this work, we introduce the notion of secret-key functional encryption (SKFE) with secure key leasing, where a decryption key can be securely leased in the sense of secure software leasing. We also instantiate it with standard cryptographic assumptions. More specifically, our contribution is as follows.

- We define the syntax and security definitions for SKFE with secure key leasing.
- We achieve a transformation from standard SKFE into SKFE with secure key leasing *without using additional assumptions*. Especially, we obtain bounded collusion-resistant SKFE for P/poly with secure key leasing based on post-quantum one-way functions since we can instantiate bounded collusion-resistant SKFE for P/poly with the assumption.

Some previous secure software leasing schemes capture only pirate software that runs on an *honest* evaluation algorithm (on a legitimate platform). However, our secure key leasing notion captures arbitrary attack strategies and does not have such a limitation. As an additional contribution, we introduce the notion of single-decryptor FE (SDFE), where each functional decryption key is copy-protected. Since copy-protection is a stronger primitive than secure software leasing, this notion can be seen as a stronger cryptographic primitive than FE with secure key leasing. More specifically, our additional contribution is as follows.

- We define the syntax and security definitions for SDFE.
- We achieve collusion-resistant single-decryptor PKFE for P/poly from post-quantum indistinguishability obfuscation and quantum hardness of the learning with errors problem.

1 Introduction

1.1 Background

Functional encryption (FE) [BSW11] is an advanced encryption system that enables us to compute on encrypted data. In FE, an authority generates a mas-

S. Agrawal and D. Lin (Eds.): ASIACRYPT 2022, LNCS 13794, pp. 569–598, 2022.
https://doi.org/10.1007/978-3-031-22972-5_20

ter secret key and an encryption key. An encryptor uses the encryption key to generate a ciphertext ct_x of a plaintext x. The authority generates a functional decryption key fsk from a function f and the master secret key. When a decryptor receives fsk and ct_x, it can compute $f(x)$ and obtains nothing beyond $f(x)$. In secret-key FE (SKFE), the encryption key is the same as the master secret key, while the encryption key is public in public-key FE (PKFE).

FE offers flexible accessibility to encrypted data since multiple users can obtain various processed data via functional decryption keys. Public-key encryption (PKE) and attribute-based encryption (ABE) [SW05] do not have this property since they recover an entire plaintext if decryption succeeds. This flexible feature is suitable for analyzing sensitive data and computing new data from personal data without compromising data privacy. For example, we can compute medical statistics from patients' data without directly accessing individual data. Some works present practical applications of FE (for limited functionalities): non-interactive protocol for hidden-weight coin flips [CS19], biometric authentication, nearest-neighbor search on encrypted data [KLM+18], private inference on encrypted data [RPB+19].

One issue is that once a user obtains fsk, it can compute $f(x)$ from a ciphertext of x forever. An authority may not want to provide users with the permanent right to compute on encrypted data. A motivative example is as follows. A research group member receives a functional decryption key fsk to compute some statistics from many encrypted data for their research. When the member leaves the group, an authority wants to prevent the member from doing the same computation on another encrypted data due to terms and conditions. However, the member might *keep a copy* of their functional decryption key and penetrate the database of the group to do the same computation. Another motivation is that the subscription business model is common for many services such as cloud storage services (ex. OneDrive, Dropbox), video on demand (ex. Netflix, Hulu), software applications (ex. Office 365, Adobe Photoshop). If we can keep a copy of functional decryption keys, we cannot use FE in the subscription business model (for example, FE can be used as broadcast encryption in a video on demand). We can also consider the following subscription service. A company provides encrypted data sets for machine learning and a functional decryption key. A researcher can perform some tasks using the encrypted data set and the key.

Achieving a revocation mechanism [NP01] is an option to solve the issue above. Some works propose revocation mechanisms for advanced encryption such as ABE [SSW12] and FE [NWZ16]. However, revocation is not a perfect solution since we need to update ciphertexts to embed information about revoked users. We want to avoid updating ciphertexts for several reasons. One is a practical reason. We possibly handle a vast amount of data, and updating ciphertexts incurs significant overhead. Another one is more fundamental. Even if we update ciphertexts, *there is no guarantee that all old ciphertexts are appropriately deleted*. If some user keeps copies of old ciphertexts, and a data breach happens after revocation, another functional decryption key holder whose key was revoked still can decrypt the old ciphertexts.

This problem is rooted in classical computation since we cannot prevent copying digital data. Ananth and La Placa introduce the notion of secure software leasing [AL21] to solve the copy problem by using the power of quantum computation. Secure software leasing enables us to encode software into a leased version. The leased version has the same functionality as the original one and must be a quantum state to prevent copying. *After a lessor verifies that the returned software from a lessee is valid (or that the lessee deleted the software)*, the lessee cannot execute the software anymore. Several works present secure software leasing for simple functionalities such as a sub-class of evasive functions (subEVS), PKE, signatures, pseudorandom functions (PRFs) [AL21, ALL+21, KNY21, BJL+21, CMP20]. If we can securely implement leasing and returning mechanisms for functional decryption keys, we can solve the problem above. Such mechanisms help us to use FE in real-world applications.

Thus, the main question in this work is as follows.

Can we achieve secure a leasing mechanism for functional decryption keys of FE?

We can also consider copy-protection, which is stronger security than secure leasing. Aaronson [Aar09] introduces the notion of quantum copy-protection. Copy-protection prevents users from creating a pirate copy. *It does not have a returning process*, and prevents copying software. If a user returns the original software, no copy is left behind on the user, and it cannot run the software. Coladangelo, Liu, Liu, and Zhandry [CLLZ21] achieve copy-protected PRFs and single-decryptor encryption (SDE)[1]. Our second question in this work is as follows.

Can we achieve copy-protection for functional decryption keys of FE?

We affirmatively answer those questions in this work.

1.2   Our Result

Secure Key Leasing. Our main contributions are introducing the notion of SKFE with secure key leasing and instantiating it with standard cryptographic assumptions. More specifically,

- We define the syntax and security definitions for SKFE with secure key leasing.
- We achieve a transformation from standard SKFE into SKFE with secure key leasing *without using additional assumptions.*

In SKFE with secure key leasing, a functional decryption key is a quantum state. More specifically, the key generation algorithm takes as input a master secret key, a function f, and an availability bound n (in terms of the number of ciphertexts), and outputs a quantum decryption key fsk tied to f. We can generate a *certificate for deleting* the decryption key fsk. If the user of this decryption key deletes fsk

---

[1] SDE is PKE whose decryption keys are copy-protected.

within the declared availability bound n and the generated certificate is valid, the user cannot compute $f(x)$ from a ciphertext of x anymore. We provide a high-level overview of the security definition in Sect. 1.3.

We can obtain bounded collusion-resistant SKFE for P/poly with secure key leasing from OWFs since we can instantiate bounded collusion-resistant SKFE for P/poly with OWFs.[2] Note that all building blocks in this work are post-quantum secure since we use quantum computation and we omit "post-quantum".

Our secure key leasing notion is similar to but different from secure software leasing [AL21] for FE because adversaries in secure software leasing (for FE) must run their pirate software by an *honest* evaluation algorithm (on a legitimate platform). This is a severe limitation. In our FE with secure key leasing setting, adversaries do *not* necessarily run their pirate software (for functional decryption) by an honest evaluation algorithm and can take arbitrary attack strategies.

We develop a transformation from standard SKFE into SKFE with secure key leasing by using quantum power. In particular, we use (reusable) secret-key encryption (SKE) with certified deletion [BI20,HMNY21], where we can securely delete *ciphertexts*, as a building block. We also develop a technique based on the security bound amplification for FE [AJL+19, JKMS20] to amplify the availability bound, that is, the number of encryption queries before ct* is given. This technique deviates from known multi-party-computation-based techniques for achieving bounded many-ciphertext security for SKFE [GVW12, AV19].[3] The security bound amplification-based technique is of independent interest since the security bound amplification is not directly related to the amplification of the number of queries. These are the main technical contributions of this work. See Sect. 1.3 and main sections for more details.

Copy-Protected Functional Decryption Keys. The other contributions are copy-protected functional decryption keys. We introduce the notion of single-decryptor FE (SDFE), where each functional decryption key is copy-protected. This notion can be seen as a stronger cryptographic primitive than FE with secure key leasing, as we argued in Sect. 1.1.

- We define the syntax and security definitions for SDFE.
- We achieve collusion-resistant public key SDFE for P/poly from subexponentially secure indistinguishability obfuscation (IO) and the subexponential hardness of the learning with errors problem (QLWE assumption).

First, we transform single-key PKFE for P/poly into *single-key* SDFE for P/poly by using SDE. Then, we transform single-key SDFE P/poly into collusion-resistant

---

[2] If we start with fully collusion-resistant SKFE, we can obtain fully collusion-resistant SKFE with secure key leasing.

[3] These techniques [GVW12, AV19] work as transformations from single-key FE into bounded collusion-resistant FE. However, they also work as transformations from single-ciphertext SKFE into bounded many-ciphertext SKFE. Many-ciphertext means that SKFE is secure even if adversaries can send unbounded polynomially many queries to an encryption oracle.

SDFE for P/poly by using an IO-based key bundling technique [KNT21, BNPW20]. We can instantiate SDE with IO and the QLWE assumption [CLLZ21, CV21] and single-key PKFE for P/poly with PKE [SS10, GVW12].

1.3   Technical Overview

We provide a high-level overview of our techniques. Below, standard math font stands for classical algorithms and classical variables, and calligraphic font stands for quantum algorithms and quantum states.

Syntax of SKFE with Secure Key Leasing. We first recall a standard SKFE scheme. It consists of four algorithms (Setup, KG, Enc, Dec). Setup is given a security parameter 1^λ and a collusion bound 1^q and generates a master secret key msk. Enc is given msk and a plaintext x and outputs a ciphertext ct. KG is given msk and a function f and outputs a decryption key fsk tied to f. Dec is given fsk and ct and outputs $f(x)$. Then, the indistinguishability-security of SKFE roughly states that any QPT adversary cannot distinguish encryptions of x_0 and x_1 under the existence of the encryption oracle and the key generation oracle. Here, the adversary can access the key generation oracle at most q times and can query only a function f such that $f(x_0) = f(x_1)$.

An SKFE scheme with secure key leasing (SKFE-SKL) is a tuple of six algorithms (Setup, $\mathcal{KG}$, Enc, $\mathcal{Dec}$, Cert, Vrfy), where the first four algorithms form a standard SKFE scheme except the following difference on $\mathcal{KG}$. In addition to a function f, $\mathcal{KG}$ is given an availability bound 1^n in terms of the number of ciphertexts. Also, given those inputs, $\mathcal{KG}$ outputs a verification key vk together with a decryption key fsk tied to f encoded in a quantum state, as $(\mathit{fsk}, \text{vk}) \leftarrow \mathcal{KG}(\text{msk}, f, 1^n)$. By using Cert, we can generate a (classical) certificate that a quantum decryption key fsk is deleted, as cert $\leftarrow \mathit{Cert}(\mathit{fsk})$. We check the validity of certificates by using vk and Vrfy, as $\top/\bot \leftarrow \text{Vrfy}(\text{vk}, \text{cert})$. In addition to the decryption correctness, an SKFE-SKL scheme is required to satisfy the verification correctness that states that a correctly generated certificate is accepted, that is, $\top = \text{Vrfy}(\text{vk}, \text{cert})$ for $(\mathit{fsk}, \text{vk}) \leftarrow \mathcal{KG}(\text{msk}, f, 1^n)$ and cert $\leftarrow \mathit{Cert}(\mathit{fsk})$.

Security of SKFE-SKL. The security notion of SKFE-SKL we call lessor security intuitively guarantees that if an adversary given fsk deletes it and the generated certificate is accepted within the declared availability bound, the adversary cannot use fsk any more. The following indistinguishability experiment formalizes this security notion. For simplicity, we focus on a selective setting where the challenge plaintext pair (x_0^*, x_1^*) and the collusion bound q are fixed outside of the security experiment in this overview.

1. Throughout the experiment, $\mathcal{A}$ can get access to the following oracles, where $L_{\mathcal{KG}}$ is a list that is initially empty.

   $O_{\text{Enc}}(x)$: This is the standard encryption oracle that returns $\text{Enc}(\text{msk}, x)$ given x.

   $O_{\mathcal{KG}}(f, 1^n)$: This oracle takes as input a function f and an availability bound 1^n, generate $(\mathit{fsk}, \text{vk}) \leftarrow \mathcal{KG}(\text{msk}, f, 1^n)$, returns fsk to $\mathcal{A}$, and adds

$(f, 1^n, \mathsf{vk}, \perp)$ to $L_{\mathcal{KG}}$. Differently from the standard SKFE, $\mathcal{A}$ can query a function f such that $f(x_0^*) \neq f(x_1^*)$. $\mathcal{A}$ can get access to the key generation oracle at most q times.

$O_{\mathsf{Vrfy}}(f, \mathsf{cert})$: Also, $\mathcal{A}$ can get access to the verification oracle. Intuitively, this oracle checks that $\mathcal{A}$ deletes leased decryption keys correctly within the declared availability bounds. Given (f, cert), it finds an entry $(f, 1^n, \mathsf{vk}, M)$ from $L_{\mathcal{KG}}$. (If there is no such entry, it returns $\perp$.) If $\top = \mathsf{Vrfy}(\mathsf{vk}, \mathsf{cert})$ and the number of queries to O_{Enc} at this point is less than n, it returns $\top$ and updates the entry into $(f, 1^n, \mathsf{vk}, \top)$. Otherwise, it returns $\perp$.

2. When $\mathcal{A}$ requests the challenge ciphertext, the challenger checks if $\mathcal{A}$ has correctly deleted all leased decryption keys for functions f such that $f(x_0^*) \neq f(x_1^*)$. If so, the challenger gives the challenge ciphertext $\mathsf{ct}^* \leftarrow \mathsf{Enc}(\mathsf{msk}, x_{\mathsf{coin}}^*)$ for random bit $\mathsf{coin} \leftarrow \{0, 1\}$ to $\mathcal{A}$, and otherwise the challenger output 0. Hereafter, $\mathcal{A}$ is not allowed to send a function f such that $f(x_0^*) \neq f(x_1^*)$ to $O_{\mathcal{KG}}$.

3. $\mathcal{A}$ outputs a guess coin' of coin.

We say that the SKFE-SKL scheme is lessor secure if no QPT adversary can guess coin significantly better than random guessing. We see that if $\mathcal{A}$ can use a decryption key after once $\mathcal{A}$ deletes and the deletion certificate is accepted, $\mathcal{A}$ can detect coin with high probability since $\mathcal{A}$ can obtain a decryption key for f such that $f(x_0^*) \neq f(x_1^*)$. Thus, this security notion captures the above intuition. We see that *lessor security implies standard indistinguishability-security for SKFE*.

We basically work with the above indistinguishability based selective security for simplicity. In the full version, we also provide the definitions of adaptive security and simulation based security notions and general transformations to achieve those security notions from indistinguishability based selective security.

Dynamic Availability Bound vs. Static Availability Bound. In SKFE-SKL, we can set the availability bound for each decryption key differently. We can also consider a weaker variant where we statically set the single availability bound applied to each decryption key at the setup algorithm. We call this variant SKFE with static bound secure key leasing (SKFE-sbSKL). In fact, by using a technique developed in the context of dynamic bounded collusion FE [AMVY21, GGLW21], we can generically transform SKFE-sbSKL into SKFE-SKL if the underlying SKFE-sbSKL satisfies some additional security property and efficiency requirement. For the overview of this transformation, see Sect. 2.2. Therefore, we below focus on how to achieve SKFE-sbSKL. For simplicity, we ignore those additional properties required for the transformation to SKFE-SKL.

SKFE-sbSKL with the Availability Bound 0 from Certified Deletion. We start with a simple construction of an SKFE-sbSKL scheme secure for the availability bound 0 based on an SKE scheme with certified deletion [BI20, HMNY21]. The availability bound is 0 means that it is secure if an adversary deletes decryption keys without seeing any ciphertext.

SKE with certified deletion consists of five algorithms $(\mathsf{KG}, \mathcal{E}nc, \mathcal{D}ec, \mathcal{D}el, \mathsf{Vrfy})$. The first three algorithms form a standard SKE scheme except that $\mathcal{E}nc$ output a verification key vk together with a ciphertext encoded in a quantum state ct. By using $\mathcal{D}el$, we can generate a (classical) certificate that ct is deleted. The certificate is verified using vk and Vrfy. In addition to the decryption correctness, it satisfies the verification correctness that guarantees that a correctly generated certificate is accepted. The security notion roughly states that once an adversary deletes a ciphertext ct and the generated certificate is accepted, the adversary cannot obtain any plaintext information encrypted inside ct, even if the adversary is given the secret key after the deletion.

We now construct an SKFE-sbSKL scheme zSKFE-sbSKL that is secure for the availability bound 0, based on a standard SKFE scheme SKFE = (Setup, KG, Enc, Dec) and an SKE scheme with certified deletion CDSKE = (CD.KG, CD.$\mathcal{E}nc$, CD.$\mathcal{D}ec$, CD.$\mathcal{D}el$, CD.Vrfy). In the setup of zSKFE-sbSKL, we generate msk $\leftarrow$ Setup$(1^\lambda, 1^q)$ and cd.sk $\leftarrow$ CD.KG(1^λ), and the master secret key of zSKFE-sbSKL is set to zmsk = (msk, cd.sk). To generate a decryption key for f, we generate a decryption key for f by SKFE as fsk $\leftarrow$ KG(msk, f) and encrypt it by CDSKE as (cd.ct, vk) $\leftarrow$ CD.$\mathcal{E}nc$(cd.sk, fsk). The resulting decryption key is $zfsk := $ cd.ct and the corresponding verification key is vk. To encrypt a plaintext x, we just encrypt it by SKFE as ct $\leftarrow$ Enc(msk, x) and append cd.sk contained in zmsk, as zct := (ct, cd.sk). To decrypt zct with $zfsk$, we first retrieve fsk from cd.ct and cd.sk, and compute $f(x) \leftarrow$ Dec(fsk, ct). The certificate generation and verification are simply defined as those of CDSKE since $zfsk$ is a ciphertext of CDSKE.

The security of zSKFE-sbSKL is easily analyzed. Let (x_0^*, x_1^*) be the challenge plaintext pair. When an adversary $\mathcal{A}$ queries f to $O_{\mathcal{KG}}$, $\mathcal{A}$ is given $zfsk := $ cd.ct, where fsk $\leftarrow$ KG(msk, f) and (cd.ct, vk) $\leftarrow$ CD.$\mathcal{E}nc$(cd.sk, fsk). If $f(x_0^*) \neq f(x_1^*)$, $\mathcal{A}$ is required to delete $zfsk$ without seeing any ciphertext. This means that $\mathcal{A}$ cannot obtain cd.sk before $zfsk$ is deleted. Then, from the security of CDSKE, $\mathcal{A}$ cannot obtain any information of fsk. This implies that $\mathcal{A}$ can obtain a decryption key of SKFE only for a function f such that $f(x_0^*) = f(x_1^*)$, and thus the lessor security of zSKFE-sbSKL follows form the security of SKFE.

How to Amplify the Availability Bound? We now explain how to amplify the availability bound from 0 to any polynomial n. One possible solution is to rely on the techniques for bounded collusion FE [GVW12, AV19]. Although the bounded collusion techniques can be used to amplify "1-bounded security" to "poly-bounded security", it is not clear how to use it starting from "0-bounded security". For more detailed discussion on this point, see Remark 2.3. Therefore, we use a different technique from the existing bounded collusion FE. At a high level, we reduce the task of amplifying the availability bound to the task of amplifying the security bound, which has been studied in the context of standard FE [AJL+19, JKMS20].

We observe that we can obtain an SKFE-sbSKL scheme with availability bound n for any n that is secure with only inverse polynomial probability by just using many instances of zSKFE-sbSKL in parallel. Concretely, suppose we use $N = \alpha n$ instances of zSKFE-sbSKL to achieve a scheme with availability bound n, where $\alpha \in \mathbb{N}$. To generate a decryption key for f, we generate $(zfsk_j, vk_j) \leftarrow z\mathcal{KG}(zmsk_j, f)$ for every $j \in [N]$, and set the resulting decryption key as $(zfsk_j)_{j\in[N]}$ and the corresponding verification key as $(vk_j)_{j\in[N]}$. To encrypt x, we randomly choose $j \leftarrow [N]$, generate $zct_j \leftarrow zEnc(zmsk_j, x)$, and set the resulting ciphertext as (j, zct_j). To decrypt this ciphertext with $(zfsk_j)_{j\in[N]}$, we just compute $f(x) \leftarrow zDec(zfsk_j, zct_j)$. The certification generation and verification are done by performing them under all N instances. The security of this construction is analyzed as follows. The probability that the j^* chosen when generating the challenge ciphertext collides with some of n indices $j_1, \cdots, j_n$ used by the first n calls of the encryption oracle, is at most $n/N = 1/\alpha$. If such a collision does not happen, we can use the security of j^*-th instance of zSKFE-sbSKL to prove the security of this construction. Therefore, this construction is secure with probability roughly $1 - 1/\alpha$ (denoted by $1/\alpha$-secure scheme).

Thus, all we have to do is to convert an SKFE-sbSKL scheme with inverse polynomial security into one with negligible security. As stated above, such security amplification has been studied for standard FE. In this work, we adopt the amplification technique using homomorphic secret sharing (HSS) [AJL+19, JKMS20].

Amplification Using HSS. In this overview, we describe our construction using HSS that requires the LWE assumption with super-polynomial modulus to give a high-level intuition. However, our actual construction uses a primitive called set homomorphic secret sharing (SetHSS) [JKMS20], which is a weak form of HSS and *can be based on OWFs*.[4] See Sect. 4 for our construction based on OWFs.

An HSS scheme consists of three algorithms (InpEncode, FuncEncode, Decode). InpEncode is given a security parameter 1^λ, a number 1^m, and an input x, and outputs m input shares $(s_i)_{i\in[m]}$. FuncEncode is given a security parameter 1^λ, a number 1^m, and a function f, and outputs m function shares $(f_i)_{i\in[m]}$. Decode takes a set of evaluations of function shares on their respective input shares $(f_i(s_i))_{i\in[m]}$, and outputs a value $f(x)$. Then, the security property of an HSS scheme roughly guarantees that for any (i^*, x_0^*, x_1^*), given a set of input shares $(s_i)_{i\in[m]\setminus\{i^*\}}$ for some i^*, an adversary cannot detect from which of the challenge inputs they are generated, under the existence of function encode oracle that is given f such that $f(x_0^*) = f(x_1^*)$ and returns $(f_i(s_i))_{i\in[m]}$.

We describe SKFE-sbSKL scheme SKFE-sbSKL with the availability bound $n \geq 1$ of our choice using a HSS scheme HSS = (InpEncode, FuncEncode, Decode). In the setup of SKFE-sbSKL, we first set up $1/2$-secure SKFE-sbSKL scheme SKFE-sbSKL$'$ with the availability bound n. This is done by parallelizing $2n$ instances of zSKFE-sbSKL as explained before. We generate m master secret keys $msk_1, \cdots, msk_m$ of SKFE-sbSKL$'$. Then, to generate a decryption key for f by SKFE-sbSKL, we first generate $(f_i)_{i\in[m]} \leftarrow FuncEncode(1^\lambda, 1^m, f)$, and generate a decryption key fsk_i tied to f_i under msk_i for each $i \in [m]$. To encrypt x by SKFE-sbSKL, we first generate $(s_i)_{i\in[m]} \leftarrow InpEncode(1^\lambda, 1^m, x)$ and generate a ciphertext ct_i of s_i under msk_i for each $i \in [m]$. The certification generation and

---

[4] The definition of HSS provided below is not standard. We modify the definition to be close to SetHSS. Note that HSS defined below can be constructed from multi-key fully homomorphic encryption with simulatable partial decryption property [MW16].

verification are done by performing those of SKFE-SKL′ for all of the m instances. When decrypting the ciphertext $(\mathsf{ct}_i)_{i \in [m]}$ by $(\mathit{fsk}_i)_{i \in [m]}$, we can obtain $f_i(s_i)$ by decrypting ct_i with fsk_i for every $i \in [m]$. By combining $(f_i(s_i))_{i \in [m]}$ using Decode, we can obtain $\hat{f}(x)$.

The lessor security of SKFE-sbSKL can be proved as follows. Each of m instances of SKFE-sbSKL′ is secure independently with probability $1/2$. Thus, there is at least one secure instance without probability $1/2^m$, which is negligible by setting $m = \omega(\log \lambda)$. Suppose i^*-th instance is a secure instance. Let (x_0^*, x_1^*) be the challenge plaintext pair, and let $(s_i^*)_{i \in [m]} \leftarrow \mathsf{InpEncode}(1^\lambda, 1^m, x_{\mathsf{coin}}^*)$ for $\mathsf{coin} \leftarrow \{0,1\}$. In the security experiment, from the security of SKFE-sbSKL′ under msk_{i^*}, an adversary cannot obtain the information of s_{i^*} except for its evaluation on function shares for a function f queried to $O_{\mathcal{KG}}$ that satisfies that $f(x_0^*) = f(x_1^*)$. Especially, from the security of SKFE-sbSKL′ under msk_{i^*}, the adversary cannot obtain an evaluation of s_{i^*} on function shares for a function f such that $f(x_0^*) \neq f(x_1^*)$, though $\mathcal{A}$ can query such a function to $O_{\mathcal{KG}}$. Then, we see that the lessor security of SKFE-sbSKL can be reduced to the security of HSS.[5]

In the actual construction, we use SetHSS instead of HSS, as stated before. Also, in the main body, we abstract the parallelized zSKFE-sbSKL as index-based SKFE-sbSKL. This makes the security proof of our construction using SetHSS simple. Moreover, in the actual construction of an index-based SKFE-sbSKL, we bundle the parallelized instances of zSKFE-sbSKL using a PRF. This modification is necessary to achieve the efficiency required for the above transformation into SKFE-SKL.

Goyal et al. [CGO21] use a similar technique using HSS in a different setting (private simultaneous message protocols). However, their technique relies on the LWE assumption unlike ours.

Single Decryptor PKFE. In this work, we also define the notion of single decryptor PKFE, which is PKFE whose functional decryption key is copy-protected. The definition is a natural extension of SDE (PKE with copy-protected decryption keys). An adversary $\mathcal{A}$ tries to copy a target functional decryption key sk_{f^*}. More specifically, $\mathcal{A}$ is given sk_{f^*} and outputs two possibly entangled quantum distinguishers $\mathcal{D}_1$ and $\mathcal{D}_2$ and two plaintexts (x_0, x_1) such that $f^*(x_0) \neq f^*(x_1)$. If $\mathcal{D}_1$ or $\mathcal{D}_2$ cannot distinguish a given ciphertext is encryption of x_0 or x_1, sk_{f^*} is copy-protected. If both $\mathcal{D}_1$ and $\mathcal{D}_2$ have sk_{f^*}, they can trivially distinguish the challenge ciphertext. Thus, the definition guarantees copy-protection security. We provide a collusion-resistant single-decryptor PKFE scheme, where adversaries obtain polynomially many functional decryption keys, based on IO.

We first show that a single-key single-decryptor PKFE can be constructed from a single-key standard PKFE scheme and SDE scheme. The construction is simple nested encryption. Namely, when encrypting a plaintext x, we first encrypt it by the standard PKFE scheme and then encrypt the ciphertext by

---

[5] Actual construction and security proof needs to use a technique called the trojan method [ABSV15]. We ignore the issue here for simplicity.

the SDE scheme. The secret key of the SDE scheme is included in the functional decryption key of the resulting single-decryptor PKFE scheme. Although a PKFE functional decryption key can be copied, the SDE decryption key cannot be copied and adversaries cannot break the security of PKFE. This is because we need to run the SDE decryption algorithm before we run the PKFE decryption algorithm.

The security notion for SDE by Coladangelo et al. [CLLZ21] is not sufficient for our purpose since SDE plaintexts are ciphertexts of the standard PKFE in the construction. We need to extend the security notion for SDE to prove the security of this construction because we need to handle randomized messages (the PKFE encryption is a randomized algorithm). Roughly speaking, this new security notion guarantees that the security of SDE holds for plaintexts of the form $g(x; r)$, where g and x respectively are a function and an input chosen by an adversary and r is a random coin chosen by the experiment. We can observe that the SDE scheme proposed by Coladangelo et al. [CLLZ21] based on IO satisfies this security notion. Then, by setting g as the encryption circuit of the standard PKFE, the security of the single-key single-decryptor PKFE scheme above can be immediately reduced to the security of the SDE scheme. We also extend adversarial quantum decryptors, which try to output an entire plaintext, to adversarial quantum distinguishers, which try to guess a 1-bit coin used to generate a ciphertext. We need this extension to use SDE as a building block. It is easy to observe the SDE scheme by Coladangelo et al. [CLLZ21] is secure even against quantum distinguishers.

Once we obtain a single-key single-decryptor PKFE scheme, we can transform it into a collusion-resistant single-decryptor PKFE scheme by again using IO. This transformation is based on one from a single-key standard PKFE scheme into a collusion-resistant standard PKFE scheme [BNPW20,KNT21]. The idea is as follows. We need to generate a fresh instance of the single-key scheme above for *each random tag* and bundle (unbounded) polynomially many instances to achieve collusion-resistance. We use IO to bundle multiple instances of single-key SDFE. More specifically, a public key is an obfuscated circuit of the following setup circuit. The setup circuit takes a public tag τ as input, generates a key pair $(\mathsf{pk}_\tau, \mathsf{msk}_\tau)$ of the single-key SDFE scheme using PRF value $\mathsf{F}_\mathsf{K}(\tau)$ as randomness, and outputs only pk_τ. The master secret key is the PRF key K. We can generate a functional decryption key for f by choosing a random tag τ and generating a functional decryption key $sk_{f,\tau}$ under msk_τ. A functional decryption key of our collusion-resistant scheme consists of $(\tau, sk_{f,\tau})$. A ciphertext is an obfuscated circuit of the following encryption circuit, where a plaintext x is hardwired. The encryption circuit takes a public tag τ, generates pk_τ by using the public key explained above, and outputs a ciphertext of x under pk_τ. Due to this mechanism, only one functional decryption key $sk_{f,\tau}$ under msk_τ is issued for each τ, but we can generate polynomially many functional decryption keys by using many tags. If we use a different tag τ', an independent key pair $(\mathsf{pk}_{\tau'}, \mathsf{msk}_{\tau'})$ is generated and it is useless for another instance under $(\mathsf{pk}_\tau, \mathsf{msk}_\tau)$. The IO security guarantees that the information about K (and msk_τ) is hidden.[6] Thus, we can reduce the collusion-resistance to the single-key security of the underlying single-decryptor PKFE. Note that we need to consider super-polynomially many hybrid games to complete the proof since the tag space size must be super-polynomial to treat *unbounded* polynomially many tags. This is the reason why we need the sub-exponential security for building blocks.

1.4   Organization

Due to the space limitation, we focus on SKFE-SKL in the rest of this version, and we provide results on single decryptor FE in the full version. For the high-level overview of our single-decryptor FE, please see Sect. 1.3. Also, please refer the full version for preliminaries including notations.

In Sect. 2, we provide the definition of SKFE-SKL, and its variants SKFE-sbSKL and index-based SKFE-sbSKL. In Sect. 3, we construct an index-based SKFE-sbSKL scheme. In Sect. 4, we show how to transform an index-based SKFE-sbSKL scheme into an SKFE-sbSKL scheme. In Sect. 5, we show how to construct an SKFE-SKL scheme from an SKFE-sbSKL scheme.

2   Definition of SKFE with Secure Key Leasing

We introduce the definition of SKFE with secure key leasing and its variants.

2.1   SKFE with Secure Key Leasing

We first define SKFE with secure key leasing (SKFE-SKL).

Definition 2.1 (SKFE with Secure Key Leasing). *An SKFE-SKL scheme* SKFE-SKL *is a tuple of six algorithms* (Setup, $\mathcal{KG}$, Enc, $\mathcal{Dec}$, $\mathcal{Cert}$, Vrfy). *Below, let* $\mathcal{X}$, $\mathcal{Y}$, *and* $\mathcal{F}$ *be the plaintext, output, and function spaces of* SKFE-SKL, *respectively.*

Setup$(1^\lambda, 1^q) \to$ msk: *The setup algorithm takes a security parameter* 1^λ *and a collusion bound* 1^q, *and outputs a master secret key* msk.

$\mathcal{KG}$(msk, f, 1^n) $\to$ (fsk, vk): *The key generation algorithm takes a master secret key* msk, *a function* $f \in \mathcal{F}$, *and an availability bound* 1^n, *and outputs a functional decryption key* fsk *and a verification key* vk.

Enc(msk, x) $\to$ ct: *The encryption algorithm takes a master secret key* msk *and a plaintext* $x \in \mathcal{X}$, *and outputs a ciphertext* ct.

$\mathcal{Dec}(\mathit{fsk}, \mathsf{ct}) \to \widetilde{x}$: *The decryption algorithm takes a functional decryption key* fsk *and a ciphertext* ct, *and outputs a value* $\widetilde{x}$.

$\mathcal{Cert}(\mathit{fsk}) \to$ cert: *The certification algorithm takes a function decryption key* fsk, *and outputs a classical string* cert.

---

[6] We use puncturable PRFs and the puncturing technique here as the standard technique for cryptographic primitives based on IO [SW21].

Vrfy(vk, cert) → ⊤/⊥: *The certification-verification algorithm takes a verification key* vk *and a string* cert, *and outputs* ⊤ *or* ⊥.

Decryption correctness: *For every* $x \in \mathcal{X}$, $f \in \mathcal{F}$, *and* $q, n \in \mathbb{N}$, *we have*

$$\Pr\left[\mathcal{D}ec(\textit{fsk}, \text{ct}) = f(x) \; \middle| \; \begin{array}{l} \text{msk} \leftarrow \text{Setup}(1^\lambda, 1^q) \\ (\textit{fsk}, \text{vk}) \leftarrow \mathcal{KG}(\text{msk}, f, 1^n) \\ \text{ct} \leftarrow \text{Enc}(\text{msk}, x) \end{array}\right] = 1 - \text{negl}(\lambda).$$

Verification correctness: *For every* $f \in \mathcal{F}$ *and* $q, n \in \mathbb{N}$, *we have*

$$\Pr\left[\text{Vrfy}(\text{vk}, \text{cert}) = \top \; \middle| \; \begin{array}{l} \text{msk} \leftarrow \text{Setup}(1^\lambda, 1^q) \\ (\textit{fsk}, \text{vk}) \leftarrow \mathcal{KG}(\text{msk}, f, 1^n) \\ \text{cert} \leftarrow \mathcal{C}ert(\textit{fsk}) \end{array}\right] = 1 - \text{negl}(\lambda).$$

Definition 2.2 (Selective Lessor Security). *We say that* SKFE-SKL *is a selectively lessor secure SKFE-SKL scheme for* $\mathcal{X}, \mathcal{Y}$, *and* $\mathcal{F}$, *if it satisfies the following requirement, formalized from the experiment* $\text{Exp}^{\text{sel-lessor}}_{\mathcal{A}, \text{SKFE-SKL}}(1^\lambda, \text{coin})$ *between an adversary* $\mathcal{A}$ *and a challenger:*

1. *At the beginning,* $\mathcal{A}$ *sends* $(1^q, x_0^*, x_1^*)$ *to the challenger. The challenger runs* msk $\leftarrow$ Setup$(1^\lambda, 1^q)$. *Throughout the experiment,* $\mathcal{A}$ *can access the following oracles.*

   $O_{\text{Enc}}(x)$: *Given* x, *it returns* Enc(msk, x).

   $O_{\mathcal{KG}}(f, 1^n)$: *Given* $(f, 1^n)$, *it generates* $(\textit{fsk}, \text{vk}) \leftarrow \mathcal{KG}(\text{msk}, f, 1^n)$, *sends* fsk *to* $\mathcal{A}$, *and adds* $(f, 1^n, \text{vk}, \bot)$ *to* $L_{\mathcal{KG}}$. $\mathcal{A}$ *can access this oracle at most* q *times.*

   $O_{\text{Vrfy}}(f, \text{cert})$: *Given* (f, cert), *it finds an entry* $(f, 1^n, \text{vk}, M)$ *from* $L_{\mathcal{KG}}$. *(If there is no such entry, it returns* $\bot$.*) If* $\top = \text{Vrfy}(\text{vk}, \text{cert})$ *and the number of queries to* O_{Enc} *at this point is less than* n, *it returns* $\top$ *and updates the entry into* $(f, 1^n, \text{vk}, \top)$. *Otherwise, it returns* $\bot$.

2. *When* $\mathcal{A}$ *requests the challenge ciphertext, the challenger checks if for any entry* $(f, 1^n, \text{vk}, M)$ *in* $L_{\mathcal{KG}}$ *such that* $f(x_0^*) \neq f(x_1^*)$, *it holds that* $M = \top$. *If so, the challenger generates* ct* $\leftarrow$ Enc(msk, x^*_{coin}) *and sends* ct* *to* $\mathcal{A}$. *Otherwise, the challenger outputs* 0. *Hereafter,* $\mathcal{A}$ *is not allowed to sends a function* f *such that* $f(x_0^*) \neq f(x_1^*)$ *to* $O_{\mathcal{KG}}$.

3. $\mathcal{A}$ *outputs a guess* coin′ *for* coin. *The challenger outputs* coin′ *as the final output of the experiment.*

For any QPT $\mathcal{A}$, *it holds that*

$$\text{Adv}^{\text{sel-lessor}}_{\text{SKFE-SKL}, \mathcal{A}}(\lambda) := \left| \Pr[\text{Exp}^{\text{sel-lessor}}_{\text{SKFE-SKL}, \mathcal{A}}(1^\lambda, 0) = 1] - \Pr[\text{Exp}^{\text{sel-lessor}}_{\text{SKFE-SKL}, \mathcal{A}}(1^\lambda, 1) = 1] \right|$$
$$\leq \text{negl}(\lambda).$$

Remark 2.1 (On the adaptive security). We can similarly define adaptive lessor security where we allow $\mathcal{A}$ to adaptively choose the challenge plaintext pair (x_0^*, x_1^*). For standard FE, we can generically convert a selectively secure one into an adaptively secure one without any additional assumption [ABSV15]. We observe that a similar transformation works for SKFE with secure key leasing. Thus, for simplicity, we focus on selective lessor security in this work. See the full version for the definition and transformation.

Remark 2.2 (On the simulation-based security). We can also define a simulation-based variant of selective/adaptive lessor security where a simulator simulates a challenge ciphertext without the challenge plaintext x^* as the simulation-based security for standard FE [BSW11, GVW12]. We can generically convert indistinguishability-based lessor secure SKFE with secure key leasing into a simulation-based lessor secure one without any additional assumptions as standard FE [DIJ+13]. See the full version for the simulation-based definition and the transformation.

2.2 SKFE with Static-Bound Secure Key Leasing

In this section, we define SKFE with static-bound secure key leasing (SKFE-sbSKL). It is a weaker variant of SKFE-SKL in which a single availability bound n applied to every decryption key is fixed at the setup time. We design SKFE-sbSKL so that it can be transformed into SKFE-SKL in a generic way. For this reason, we require an SKFE-sbSKL scheme to satisfy an efficiency requirement called weak optimal efficiency and slightly stronger variant of the lessor security notion.[7]

Below, we first introduce the syntax of SKFE-sbSKL. Then, before introducing the definition of (selective) lessor security for it, we provide the overview of the transformation to SKFE-SKL since we think the overview makes it easy to understand the security notion.

Definition 2.3 (SKFE with Static-Bound Secure Key Leasing). *An SKFE-sbSKL scheme* SKFE-sbSKL *is a tuple of six algorithms* (Setup, $\mathcal{KG}$, Enc, $\mathcal{Dec}$, $\mathcal{Cert}$, Vrfy). *The only difference from a normal SKFE scheme with secure key leasing is that* $\mathcal{KG}$ *does not take as input the availability bound n, and instead,* Setup *takes it as an input. Moreover,* Setup *takes it in binary as* Setup$(1^\lambda, 1^q, n)$, *and we require the following weak optimal efficiency.*

Weak Optimal Efficiency: *We require that the running time of* Setup *and* Enc *is bounded by a fixed polynomial of λ, q, and $\log n$.*

Overview of the Transformation to SKFE-SKL. As seen above, Setup and Enc of an SKFE-sbSKL scheme SKFE-sbSKL is required to run in time $\log n$. This is because, in the transformation to SKFE-SKL, we use λ instances of SKFE-sbSKL where the k-th instance is set up with the availability bound 2^k for every $k \in [\lambda]$. The weak optimal efficiency ensures that Setup and Enc of all λ instances run in polynomial time. The details of the transformation are as follows.

We construct an SKFE-SKL scheme SKFE-SKL from an SKFE-sbSKL scheme SKFE-sbSKL = (Setup, $\mathcal{KG}$, Enc, $\mathcal{Dec}$, $\mathcal{Cert}$, Vrfy). When generating a master secret key skl.msk of SKFE-SKL, we generate $\mathsf{msk}_k \leftarrow$ Setup$(1^\lambda, 1^q, 2^k)$ for every $k \in [\lambda]$, and set skl.msk := $(\mathsf{msk}_k)_{k \in [\lambda]}$. To encrypt x by SKFE-SKL, we encrypt it by all

---

[7] We borrow the term weak optimal efficiency from the paper by Garg, Goyal, Lu, and Waters [GGLW21], which studies dynamic bounded collusion security for standard FE.

λ instances, that is, generate $\mathsf{ct}_k \leftarrow \mathsf{Enc}(\mathsf{msk}_k, x)$ for every $k \in [\lambda]$. The resulting ciphertext is $\mathsf{skl.ct} := (\mathsf{ct}_k)_{k \in [\lambda]}$. To generate a decryption key of SKFE-SKL for a function f and an availability bound n, we first compute $k' \in [\lambda]$ such that $2^{k'-1} \leq n \leq 2^{k'}$. Then, we generate $(\mathit{fsk}_{k'}, \mathsf{vk}_{k'}) \leftarrow \mathcal{KG}(\mathsf{msk}_{k'}, f)$. The resulting decryption key is $\mathsf{skl.fsk} := (k', \mathit{fsk}_{k'})$ and the corresponding verification key is $\mathsf{vk} := \mathsf{vk}_{k'}$. Decryption is performed by decrypting $\mathsf{ct}_{k'}$ included in $\mathsf{skl.ct} := (\mathsf{ct}_k)_{k \in [\lambda]}$ by $\mathit{fsk}_{k'}$. The certification generation and verification of SKFE-SKL are simply those of SKFE-SKL.

We now consider the security proof of SKFE-SKL. In the experiment $\mathsf{Exp}^{\mathsf{sel\text{-}lessor}}_{\mathcal{A}, \mathsf{SKFE\text{-}SKL}}(1^\lambda, 0)$, an adversary $\mathcal{A}$ is given the challenge ciphertext $\mathsf{skl.ct}^* := (\mathsf{ct}_k^*)_{k \in [\lambda]}$, where $\mathsf{ct}_k^* \leftarrow \mathsf{Enc}(\mathsf{msk}_k, x_0^*)$ for every $k \in [\lambda]$. The proof is done if we can switch all of ct_k^* into $\mathsf{Enc}(\mathsf{msk}_k, x_1^*)$ without being detected by $\mathcal{A}$. To this end, the underlying SKFE-sbSKL needs to satisfy a stronger variant of lessor security notion where an adversary is allowed to declare the availability bound such that $\mathcal{KG}$ does not run in polynomial time, if the adversary does not make any query to the key generation oracle. For example, to switch ct_λ^*, the reduction algorithm attacking SKFE-sbSKL needs to declare the availability bound 2^λ, under which $\mathcal{KG}$ might not run in polynomial time. Note that Setup and Enc run in polynomial time even for such an availability bound due to the weak optimal efficiency. Thus, we formalize the security notion of SKFE-sbSKL as follows.

Definition 2.4 (Selective Strtong Lessor Security). *We define selective strong lessor security for SKFE-sbSKL in the same way as that for SKFE-SKL defined in Definition 2.2 , except the following changes for the security experiment.*

– *$\mathcal{A}$ outputs n at the beginning, and the challenger generates $\mathsf{msk} \leftarrow \mathsf{Setup}(1^\lambda, 1^q, n)$. If $\mathcal{A}$ makes a query to $O_{\mathcal{KG}}$ or O_{Vrfy}, $\mathcal{A}$ is required to output n such that $\mathcal{KG}$ and Vrfy run in polynomial time.*
– *$O_{\mathcal{KG}}$ does not take 1^n as an input.*

Remark 2.3 (Insufficiency of existing bounded collusion techniques). In Sect. 1.3, we stated that it is not clear how to use the existing bounded collusion techniques [GVW12, AV19] for constructing SKFE-sbSKL. We provide a more detailed discussion on this point.

The bounded collusion technique essentially enables us to increase the number of decryption keys that an adversary can obtain. Thus, to try to use the bounded collusion technique in our context, imagine the following naive construction using standard SKFE SKFE and SKE with certified deletion CDSKE. This construction is a flipped version of the naive construction provided in Sect. 1.3. In the construction, we encrypt a ciphertext of SKFE by CDSKE, and we include the key of CDSKE into the decryption key of the resulting scheme. The construction can be seen as an SKFE scheme with certified deletion (for ciphertexts) that is secure if an adversary deletes the challenge ciphertext before seeing any decryption key. The roles of ciphertexts and decryption keys are almost symmetric in SKFE [BS18]. Thus, if we can amplify the security of this construction so that it is secure if an adversary sees some decryption keys before deleting the challenge ciphertext, it would lead to SKFE-sbSKL. The question is whether we can perform such an amplification using the existing bounded collusion techniques [GVW12, AV19]. We observe that it is highly non-trivial to adapt the existing bounded collusion technique starting from "0-bounded" security. Especially, it seems difficult to design such a transformation so that the resulting SKFE-sbSKL obtained by flipping the roles of ciphertexts and decryption keys satisfies weak optimal efficiency and security against unbounded number of encryption queries such as Definition 2.4.

We develop a different technique due to the above reason. Namely, we reduce the task of amplifying the availability bound of SKFE-sbSKL into the task of amplifying the security bound of it. In fact, our work implicitly shows that security bound amplification for FE can be used to achieve bounded collusion-resistance. We see that we can construct bounded collusion secure FE from single-key FE by our parallelizing then security bound amplification technique.

2.3 Index-Based SKFE with Static-Bound Secure Key Leasing

We define index-based SKFE-sbSKL. Similarly to SKFE-sbSKL, it needs to satisfy weak optimal efficiency and (selective) strong lessor security.

Definition 2.5 (Index-Base SKFE with Static-Bound Secure Key Leasing). *An index-base SKFE-sbSKL scheme* iSKFE-sbSKL *is a tuple of six algorithms* (Setup, $\mathcal{KG}$, iEnc, $\mathcal{Dec}$, $\mathcal{Cert}$, Vrfy). *The only difference from an SKFE-sbSKL scheme is that the encryption algorithm* iEnc *additionally takes as input an index* $j \in [n]$.

Decryption correctness: *For every* $x \in \mathcal{X}$, $f \in \mathcal{F}$, $q, n \in \mathbb{N}$, *and* $j \in [n]$, *we have*

$$\Pr\left[\mathcal{Dec}(\mathit{fsk}, \mathsf{ct}) = f(x) \;\middle|\; \begin{array}{l} \mathsf{msk} \leftarrow \mathsf{Setup}(1^\lambda, 1^q, n) \\ (\mathit{fsk}, \mathsf{vk}) \leftarrow \mathcal{KG}(\mathsf{msk}, f) \\ \mathsf{ct} \leftarrow \mathsf{Enc}(\mathsf{msk}, j, x) \end{array}\right] = 1 - \mathsf{negl}(\lambda).$$

Verification correctness: *For every* $f \in \mathcal{F}$ *and* $q, n \in \mathbb{N}$, *we have*

$$\Pr\left[\mathsf{Vrfy}(\mathsf{vk}, \mathsf{cert}) = \top \;\middle|\; \begin{array}{l} \mathsf{msk} \leftarrow \mathsf{Setup}(1^\lambda, 1^q, n) \\ (\mathit{fsk}, \mathsf{vk}) \leftarrow \mathcal{KG}(\mathsf{msk}, f) \\ \mathsf{cert} \leftarrow \mathcal{Cert}(\mathit{fsk}) \end{array}\right] = 1 - \mathsf{negl}(\lambda).$$

Weak Optimal Efficiency: *We require that the running time of* Setup *and* Enc *is bounded by a fixed polynomial of* λ, q, *and* $\log n$.

Definition 2.6 (Selective Strong Lessor Security). *We say that* iSKFE-sbSKL *is a selectively strong lessor secure index-based SKFE-sbSKL scheme for* $\mathcal{X}, \mathcal{Y}$, *and* $\mathcal{F}$, *if it satisfies the following requirement, formalized from the experiment* $\mathsf{Exp}^{\mathsf{sel\text{-}s\text{-}lessor}}_{\mathcal{A}, \mathsf{iSKFE\text{-}sbSKL}}(1^\lambda, \mathsf{coin})$ *between an adversary* $\mathcal{A}$ *and a challenger:*

1. *At the beginning, $\mathcal{A}$ sends $(1^q, n, \mathcal{KG}j^*, x_0^*, x_1^*)$ to the challenger. If $\mathcal{A}$ makes a query to $O_{\mathcal{KG}}$ or O_{Vrfy}, $\mathcal{A}$ is required to output n such that $\mathcal{KG}$ and Vrfy run in polynomial time. The challenger runs $\mathsf{msk} \leftarrow \mathsf{Setup}(1^\lambda, 1^q, n)$. Throughout the experiment, $\mathcal{A}$ can access the following oracles.*
   $O_{\mathsf{Enc}}(j, x)$: *Given j and x, it returns $\mathsf{Enc}(\mathsf{msk}, j, x)$.*
   $O_{\mathcal{KG}}(f)$: *Given f, it generates $(\mathit{fsk}, \mathsf{vk}) \leftarrow \mathcal{KG}(\mathsf{msk}, f)$, sends fsk to $\mathcal{A}$, and adds $(f, \mathsf{vk}, \bot)$ to $L_{\mathcal{KG}}$. $\mathcal{A}$ can access this oracle at most q times.*
   $O_{\mathsf{Vrfy}}(f, \mathsf{cert})$: *Given (f, cert), it finds an entry (f, vk, M) from $L_{\mathcal{KG}}$. (If there is no such entry, it returns $\bot$.) If $\top = \mathsf{Vrfy}(\mathsf{vk}, \mathsf{cert})$, it returns $\top$ and updates the entry into $(f, \mathsf{vk}, \top)$. Otherwise, it returns $\bot$.*
2. *When $\mathcal{A}$ requests the challenge ciphertext, the challenger checks if for any entry (f, vk, M) in $L_{\mathcal{KG}}$ such that $f(x_0^*) \neq f(x_1^*)$, it holds that $M = \top$, and $\mathcal{A}$ does not make a query with $\mathsf{Enc}j^*$ to O_{Enc} at this point. If so, the challenger generates $\mathsf{ct}^* \leftarrow \mathsf{Enc}(\mathsf{msk}, j^*, x_{\mathsf{coin}}^*)$ and sends ct^* to $\mathcal{A}$. Otherwise, the challenger outputs 0. Hereafter, $\mathcal{A}$ is not allowed to sends a function f such that $f(x_0^*) \neq f(x_1^*)$ to $O_{\mathcal{KG}}$.*
3. *$\mathcal{A}$ outputs a guess coin' for coin. The challenger outputs coin' as the final output of the experiment.*

For any QPT $\mathcal{A}$, it holds that

$$\mathsf{Adv}_{\mathsf{iSKFE\text{-}sbSKL},\mathcal{A}}^{\mathsf{sel\text{-}s\text{-}lessor}}(\lambda) := \left| \Pr[\mathsf{Exp}_{\mathsf{iSKFE\text{-}sbSKL},\mathcal{A}}^{\mathsf{sel\text{-}s\text{-}lessor}}(1^\lambda, 0) = 1] - \Pr[\mathsf{Exp}_{\mathsf{iSKFE\text{-}sbSKL},\mathcal{A}}^{\mathsf{sel\text{-}s\text{-}lessor}}(1^\lambda, 0) = 1] \right|$$
$$\leq \mathsf{negl}(\lambda).$$

3   Index-Base SKFE with Static-Bound Secure Key Leasing

We present our index-based SFFE-sbSKL scheme in this section.

Tool. First, we introduce the definitions for reusable SKE with certified deletion introduced by Hiroka et al. [HMNY21]

Definition 3.1 (Reusable SKE with Certified Deletion (Syntax)). *A secret key encryption scheme with certified deletion is a tuple of quantum algorithms $(\mathsf{KG}, \mathcal{E}nc, \mathcal{D}ec, \mathcal{D}el, \mathsf{Vrfy})$ with plaintext space $\mathcal{M}$ and key space $\mathcal{K}$.*

$\mathsf{KG}(1^\lambda) \to \mathsf{sk}$: *The key generation algorithm takes as input the security parameter 1^λ and outputs a secret key $\mathsf{sk} \in \mathcal{K}$.*
$\mathcal{E}nc(\mathsf{sk}, m) \to (\mathsf{vk}, \mathit{ct})$: *The encryption algorithm takes as input sk and a plaintext $m \in \mathcal{M}$ and outputs a verification key vk and a ciphertext ct.*
$\mathcal{D}ec(\mathsf{sk}, \mathit{ct}) \to m'$: *The decryption algorithm takes as input sk and ct and outputs a plaintext $m' \in \mathcal{M}$ or $\bot$.*
$\mathcal{D}el(\mathit{ct}) \to \mathsf{cert}$: *The deletion algorithm takes as input ct and outputs a certification cert.*
$\mathsf{Vrfy}(\mathsf{vk}, \mathsf{cert}) \to \top$ or $\bot$: *The verification algorithm takes vk and cert and outputs $\top$ or $\bot$.*

Decryption correctness: *There exists a negligible function* negl *such that for any* $m \in \mathcal{M}$,

$$\Pr\left[\mathcal{Dec}(\mathsf{sk}, ct) = m \,\middle|\, \begin{array}{l} \mathsf{sk} \leftarrow \mathsf{KG}(1^\lambda) \\ (\mathsf{vk}, ct) \leftarrow \mathcal{Enc}(\mathsf{sk}, m) \end{array}\right] = 1 - \mathsf{negl}(\lambda).$$

Verification correctness: *There exists a negligible function* negl *such that for any* $m \in \mathcal{M}$,

$$\Pr\left[\mathsf{Vrfy}(\mathsf{vk}, \mathsf{cert}) = \top \,\middle|\, \begin{array}{l} \mathsf{sk} \leftarrow \mathsf{KG}(1^\lambda) \\ (\mathsf{vk}, ct) \leftarrow \mathcal{Enc}(\mathsf{sk}, m) \\ \mathsf{cert} \leftarrow \mathcal{Del}(ct) \end{array}\right] = 1 - \mathsf{negl}(\lambda).$$

We introduce a variant of certified deletion security where the adversary can send many verification queries, called indistinguishability against Chosen Verification Attacks (CVA). We use this security notion to achieve SKFE with secure key leasing in this section.

Definition 3.2 (IND-CVA-CD Security for Reusable SKE with Certified Deletion). *Let* $\Sigma = (\mathsf{KG}, \mathcal{Enc}, \mathcal{Dec}, \mathcal{Del}, \mathsf{Vrfy})$ *be a secret key encryption with certified deletion. We consider the following security experiment* $\mathsf{Exp}_{\Sigma, \mathcal{A}}^{\mathsf{sk\text{-}cert\text{-}vo}}(\lambda, b)$.

1. *The challenger computes* $\mathsf{sk} \leftarrow \mathsf{KG}(1^\lambda)$.
2. $\mathcal{A}$ *sends an encryption query* m *to the challenger. The challenger computes* $(\mathsf{vk}, ct) \leftarrow \mathcal{Enc}(\mathsf{sk}, m)$ *to* $\mathcal{A}$ *and returns* (vk, ct) *to* $\mathcal{A}$. *This process can be repeated polynomially many times.*
3. $\mathcal{A}$ *sends* $(m_0, m_1) \in \mathcal{M}^2$ *to the challenger.*
4. *The challenger computes* $(\mathsf{vk}_b, ct_b) \leftarrow \mathcal{Enc}(\mathsf{sk}, m_b)$ *and sends* ct_b *to* $\mathcal{A}$.
5. *Again,* $\mathcal{A}$ *can send encryption queries.* $\mathcal{A}$ *can also send a verification query* cert *to the challenger. The challenger returns* sk *if* $\top = \mathsf{Vrfy}(\mathsf{vk}_b, \mathsf{cert})$, $\bot$ *otherwise. This process can be repeated polynomially many times.*
6. $\mathcal{A}$ *outputs* $b' \in \{0, 1\}$.

We say that Σ *is IND-CVA-CD secure if for any QPT* $\mathcal{A}$, *it holds that*

$$\mathsf{Adv}_{\Sigma, \mathcal{A}}^{\mathsf{sk\text{-}cert\text{-}vo}}(\lambda) := \left| \Pr[\mathsf{Exp}_{\Sigma, \mathcal{A}}^{\mathsf{sk\text{-}cert\text{-}vo}}(\lambda, 0) = 1] - \Pr[\mathsf{Exp}_{\Sigma, \mathcal{A}}^{\mathsf{sk\text{-}cert\text{-}vo}}(\lambda, 1) = 1] \right| \leq \mathsf{negl}(\lambda).$$

Theorem 3.1. *Known reusable SKE with certified deletion scheme [HMNY21] satisfies IND-CVA-CD security.*

We prove this theorem in the full version.

Scheme Description. We construct an index-based SKFE-sbSKL scheme iSKFE-sbSKL = (iSetup, $i\mathcal{KG}$, iEnc, $i\mathcal{Dec}$, $i\mathcal{Cert}$, iVrfy) using the following tools:

- An SKFE scheme SKFE = (Setup, KG, Enc, Dec).
- An SKE scheme with Certified Deletion CDSKE = (CD.KG, CD.$\mathcal{Enc}$, CD.$\mathcal{Dec}$, CD.$\mathcal{Del}$, CD.Vrfy).

- A PRF F.

The description of iSKFE-sbSKL is as follows.

iSetup($1^\lambda, 1^q, n$):
  - Generate $K \leftarrow \{0,1\}^\lambda$.
  - Output skl.msk $:= (q, n, K)$.
i$\mathcal{KG}$(msk, f):
  - Parse $(q, n, K) \leftarrow$ skl.msk.
  - Compute $r_j \| w_j \leftarrow$ F$_K(j)$, msk$_j \leftarrow$ Setup($1^\lambda, 1^q; r_j$), and cd.sk$_j \leftarrow$ CD.KG($1^\lambda; w_j$) for every $j \in [n]$.
  - Generate fsk$_j \leftarrow$ KG(msk$_j, f$) for every $j \in [n]$.
  - Generate (cd.ct$_j$, vk$_j$) $\leftarrow$ CD.$\mathcal{E}nc$(cd.sk$_j$, fsk$_j$) for every $j \in [n]$.
  - Output skl.$fsk := ($cd.ct$_j)_{j \in [n]}$ and vk $:= ($vk$_j)_{j \in [n]}$.
iEnc(skl.msk, j, x):
  - Parse $(q, n, K) \leftarrow$ skl.msk.
  - Compute $r_j \| w_j \leftarrow$ F$_K(j)$, msk$_j \leftarrow$ Setup($1^\lambda, 1^q; r_j$), and cd.sk$_j \leftarrow$ CD.KG($1^\lambda; w_j$).
  - Generate ct$_j \leftarrow$ Enc(msk$_j, x$).
  - Output skl.ct $:= (j, ct_j, $cd.sk$_j)$.
i$\mathcal{D}ec$(skl.fsk, skl.ct):
  - Parse (cd.ct$_j)_{j \in [n]} \leftarrow$ skl.fsk and $(j, ct_j, $cd.sk$_j) \leftarrow$ skl.ct.
  - Compute fsk$_j \leftarrow$ CD.$\mathcal{D}ec$(cd.sk$_j$, skl.fsk_j).
  - Output $y \leftarrow$ Dec(fsk$_j$, ct$_j$).
i$\mathcal{C}ert$(skl.fsk):
  - Parse (cd.ct$_j)_{j \in [n]} \leftarrow$ skl.fsk.
  - Compute cert$_j \leftarrow$ CD.$\mathcal{D}el$(cd.ct$_j$) for every $j \in [n]$.
  - Output cert $:= ($cert$_j)_{j \in [n]}$.
iVrfy(vk, cert):
  - Parse (vk$_j)_{j \in [n]} \leftarrow$ vk and (cert$_j)_{j \in [n]} \leftarrow$ cert.
  - Output $\top$ if $\top =$ CD.Vrfy(vk$_j$, cert$_j$) for every $j \in [n]$, and otherwise $\bot$.

It is clear that iSKFE-sbSKL satisfies correctness and weak optimal efficiency. For security, we have the following theorem.

Theorem 3.2. *If* SKFE *is selective indistinguishability-secure,* CDSKE *is IND-CVA-CD secure,*[8] *and* F *is a secure PRF, then* iSKFE-sbSKL *satisfies selective strong lessor security.*

Proof of Theorem 3.2. We define a sequence of hybrid games to prove the theorem.

Hyb$_0$: This is the same as Exp$^{\text{sel-s-lessor}}_{\mathcal{A}, \text{iSKFE-sbSKL}}(1^\lambda, 0)$.
  1. At the beginning, $\mathcal{A}$ sends $(1^q, n, qj^*, x_0^*, x_1^*)$ to the challenger. The challenger generates $K \leftarrow \{0,1\}^\lambda$. Below, we let $r_j \| w_j \leftarrow$ F$_K(j)$, msk$_j \leftarrow$ Setup($1^\lambda, 1^q; r_j$), and cd.sk$_j \leftarrow$ CD.KG($1^\lambda; w_j$) for every $j \in [n]$. Throughout the experiment, $\mathcal{A}$ can access the following oracles.

---
[8] see Definition 3.2 for the defition of IND-CVA-CD.

$O_{\mathsf{Enc}}(j, x)$: Given j and x, it generates $\mathsf{ct}_j \leftarrow \mathsf{Enc}(\mathsf{msk}_j, x)$ and returns $\mathsf{skl.ct} := (j, \mathsf{ct}_j, \mathsf{cd.sk}_j)$.

$O_{\mathcal{KG}}(f)$: Given f, it does the following.
- Compute $\mathsf{fsk}_j \leftarrow \mathsf{KG}(\mathsf{msk}_j, f)$ for every $j \in [n]$.
- Compute $(\mathsf{cd}.ct_j, \mathsf{vk}_j) \leftarrow \mathsf{CD}.\mathcal{Enc}(\mathsf{cd.sk}_j, \mathsf{fsk}_j)$ for every $j \in [n]$.
- Sets $\mathsf{skl}.\mathit{fsk} := (\mathsf{cd}.ct_j)_{j \in [n]}$ and $\mathsf{skl.vk} := (\mathsf{vk}_j)_{j \in [n]}$.

It sends $\mathsf{skl}.\mathit{fsk}$ to $\mathcal{A}$ and adds $(f, \mathsf{skl.vk}, \perp)$ to $L_{\mathcal{KG}}$. $\mathcal{A}$ is allowed to make at most q queries to this oracle.

$O_{\mathsf{Vrfy}}(f, \mathsf{cert} := (\mathsf{cert}_j)_{j \in [n]})$: Given $(f, \mathsf{cert} := (\mathsf{cert}_j)_{j \in [n]})$, it finds an entry (f, vk, M) from $L_{\mathcal{KG}}$. (If there is no such entry, it returns $\perp$.) If $\top = \mathsf{Vrfy}(\mathsf{vk}_j, \mathsf{cert}_j)$ for every $j \in [n]$, it returns $\top$ and updates the entry into $(f, \mathsf{vk}, \top)$. Otherwise, it returns $\perp$.

2. When $\mathcal{A}$ requests the challenge ciphertext, the challenger checks if for any entry (f, vk, M) in $L_{\mathcal{KG}}$ such that $f(x_0^*) \neq f(x_1^*)$, it holds that $M = \top$, and $\mathcal{A}$ does not make a query with $\mathsf{Enc}j^*$ to O_{Enc} at this point. If so, the challenger generates $\mathsf{ct}_{j^* j^*}^* \leftarrow \mathsf{Enc}(\mathsf{msk}_{j^* j^*}, x_0^*)$ and sends $\mathsf{skl.ct}^* := (j^*, \mathsf{ct}_{j^* j^*}^*, \mathsf{cd.sk}_{\mathcal{KG}j^*})$ to $\mathcal{A}$. Otherwise, the challenger outputs 0. Hereafter, $\mathcal{A}$ is not allowed to sends a function f such that $f(x_0^*) \neq f(x_1^*)$ to $O_{\mathcal{KG}}$.

3. $\mathcal{A}$ outputs coin'. The challenger outputs coin' as the final output of the experiment.

Hyb_1: This is the same as Hyb_0 except that $r_j \| w_j$ is generated as a uniformly random string for every $j \in [n]$.

We have $|\Pr[\mathsf{Hyb}_0 = 1] - \Pr[\mathsf{Hyb}_1 = 1]| = \mathsf{negl}(\lambda)$ from the security of F.

Hyb_2: This hybrid is the same as Hyb_1 except that when $\mathcal{A}$ sends f to $O_{\mathcal{KG}}$, if $f(x_0^*) \neq f(x_1^*)$, the challenger generates $\mathsf{cd}.ct_{j \in [n]j^*}$ included in $\mathsf{skl}.\mathit{fsk} := (\mathsf{cd}.ct_j)_{j \in [n]}$ as $(\mathsf{cd}.ct_{j^* j^*}, \mathsf{vk}_{j^* j^*}) \leftarrow \mathsf{CD}.\mathcal{Enc}(\mathsf{cd.sk}_{0j^*}, \mathbf{0})$.

We can show that $|\Pr[\mathsf{Hyb}_1 = 1] - \Pr[\mathsf{Hyb}_2 = 1]| = \mathsf{negl}(\lambda)$ from the security of CDSKE as follows. We say $\mathcal{A}$ is valid if when $\mathcal{A}$ requests the challenge ciphertext, for any entry (f, vk, M) in $L_{\mathcal{KG}}$ such that $f(x_0^*) \neq f(x_1^*)$, it holds that $M = \top$, and $\mathcal{A}$ does not make a query with $\mathsf{Enc}j^*$ to O_{Enc} at this point. In the estimation of $|\Pr[\mathsf{Hyb}_1 = 1] - \Pr[\mathsf{Hyb}_2 = 1]|$, we have to consider the case where $\mathcal{A}$ is valid since if $\mathcal{A}$ is not valid, the output of the experiment is 0. In this transition of experiments, we change a plaintext encrypted under $\mathsf{cd.sk}_{j^*}$. If $\mathcal{A}$ is valid, $\mathcal{A}$ cannot obtain $\mathsf{cd.sk}_{j^* j^*}$ before $\mathcal{A}$ is given $\mathsf{skl.ct}^*$, and $\mathcal{A}$ returns all ciphertexts under $\mathsf{cd.sk}_{j^* j^*}$ before it gets $\mathsf{cd.sk}_{j^*}$. Although the reduction does not have vk_{j^*} here, it can simulate O_{Vrfy} by using the verification oracle in IND-CVA-CD game. Then, we see that $|\Pr[\mathsf{Hyb}_1 = 1] - \Pr[\mathsf{Hyb}_2 = 1]| = \mathsf{negl}(\lambda)$ follows from the security of CDSKE under the key $\mathsf{cd.sk}_{j^*}$.

Hyb_3: This hybrid is the same as Hyb_2 except that the challenger generates $\mathsf{ct}_{j^* j^*}^*$ included in $\mathsf{skl.ct}^*$ as $\mathsf{ct}_{j^* j^*}^* \leftarrow \mathsf{Enc}(\mathsf{msk}_{j^*}, x_1^*)$.

By the previous transition, in Hyb_2 and Hyb_3, $\mathcal{A}$ can obtain a decryption key under msk_{j^*} for a function f such that $f(x_0^*) = f(x_1^*)$. Thus, $|\Pr[\mathsf{Hyb}_2 = 1] - \Pr[\mathsf{Hyb}_3 = 1]| = \mathsf{negl}(\lambda)$ holds from the security of SKFE.

Hyb_4: This hybrid is the same as Hyb_3 except that we undo the changes from Hyb_0 to Hyb_2. Hyb_4 is the same as $\mathsf{Exp}^{\text{sel-s-lessor}}_{\mathcal{A},\text{iSKFE-sbSKL}}(1^\lambda, 1)$.

$|\Pr[\mathsf{Hyb}_3 = 1] - \Pr[\mathsf{Hyb}_4 = 1]| = \mathsf{negl}(\lambda)$ holds from the security of F and CDSKE.

From the above discussions, iSKFE-sbSKL satisfies selective lessor security. ∎

4   SKFE with Static-Bound Secure Key Leasing

We construct an SKFE-sbSKL scheme SKFE-sbSKL = (sbSKL.Setup, sbSKL.$\mathcal{KG}$, sbSKL.Enc, sbSKL.$\mathcal{Dec}$, sbSKL.$\mathcal{Cert}$, sbSKL.Vrfy) from the following tools:

- An index-based SKFE-sbSKL scheme iSKFE-sbSKL = (iSetup, i$\mathcal{KG}$, iEnc, i$\mathcal{Dec}$, i$\mathcal{Cert}$, iVrfy).
- A set homomorphic secret sharing SetHSS = (SetGen, InpEncode, FuncEncode, Decode).
- An SKE scheme SKE = (E, D).

The description of SKFE-sbSKL is as follows.

sbSKL.Setup($1^\lambda, 1^q, n$):
- Generate params $:= (p, \ell, (T_i)_{i \in [m]}) \leftarrow$ SetGen(1^λ).
- Generate $\mathsf{msk}_i \leftarrow$ iSetup($1^\lambda, 1^q, N$) for every $i \in [m]$, where $N = n/p$.
- Generate $K \leftarrow \{0, 1\}^\lambda$.
- Output sbskl.msk $:= (\mathsf{params}, N, (\mathsf{msk})_{i \in [m]}, K)$.

sbSKL.$\mathcal{KG}$(sbskl.msk, f):
- Parse $(\mathsf{params}, N, (\mathsf{msk})_{i \in [m]}, K) \leftarrow$ sbskl.msk.
- Generate $\mathsf{sct}_i \leftarrow$ E($K, \mathbf{0}$) for every $i \in [m]$.
- Generate $(f_i)_{i \in [m]} \leftarrow$ FuncEncode(params, f).
- Generate $(\mathit{fsk}_i, \mathsf{vk}_i) \leftarrow$ i$\mathcal{KG}$($\mathsf{msk}_i, F[f_i, \mathsf{sct}_i]$) for every $i \in [m]$, where the circuit F is described in Fig. 1.
- Output sbskl.$\mathit{fsk} := (\mathit{fsk}_i)_{i \in [m]}$ and sbskl.vk $:= (\mathsf{vk}_i)_{i \in [m]}$.

sbSKL.Enc(sbskl.msk, x):
- Parse $(\mathsf{params}, N, (\mathsf{msk})_{i \in [m]}, K) \leftarrow$ sbskl.msk.
- Generate $(s_i)_{i \in [m]} \leftarrow$ InpEncode(params, x).
- Generate $i \leftarrow [N]$ for every $i \in [m]$.
- Generate $\mathsf{ct}_i \leftarrow$ iEnc($\mathsf{msk}_i, i, (s_i, \mathbf{0}, 0)$) for every $i \in [m]$.
- Output sbskl.ct $:= (\mathsf{ct}_i)_{i \in [m]}$.

sbSKL.$\mathcal{Dec}$(sbskl.fsk, sbskl.ct):
- Parse $(\mathit{fsk}_i)_{i \in [m]} \leftarrow$ sbskl.fsk and $(\mathsf{ct}_i)_{i \in [m]} \leftarrow$ sbskl.ct.
- Compute $y_I \leftarrow$ i$\mathcal{Dec}$($\mathit{fsk}_i, \mathsf{ct}_i$) for every $i \in [m]$.
- Output $y \leftarrow$ Decode($(y_i)_{i \in [m]}$).

sbSKL.$\mathcal{Cert}$(sbskl.fsk):
- Parse $(\mathit{fsk}_i)_{i \in [m]} \leftarrow$ sbskl.fsk.
- Compute $\mathsf{cert}_i \leftarrow$ i$\mathcal{Cert}$(fsk_i) for every $i \in [m]$.
- Output sbskl.cert $:= (\mathsf{cert}_i)_{i \in [m]}$.

sbSKL.Vrfy(sbskl.vk, sbskl.cert):

- Parse $(\mathsf{vk}_i)_{i \in [m]} \leftarrow \mathsf{sbskl.vk}$ and $(\mathsf{cert}_i)_{i \in [m]} \leftarrow \mathsf{sbskl.cert}$.
- Output $\top$ if $\top = \mathsf{iVrfy}(\mathsf{vk}_i, \mathsf{cert}_i)$ for every $i \in [m]$, and otherwise $\bot$.

We show the correctness of SKFE-sbSKL. Let $\mathsf{sbskl}.\mathit{fsk} := (\mathit{fsk}_i)_{i \in [m]}$ be a decryption key for f and let $\mathsf{sbskl.ct} := (\mathsf{ct}_i)_{i \in [m]}$ be a ciphertext of x. From the correctness of iSKFE-sbSKL, we obtain $f_i(s_i)$ by decrypting ct_i with fsk_i for every $i \in [m]$, where $(f_i)_{i \in [m]} \leftarrow \mathsf{FuncEncode}(\mathsf{params}, f)$ and $(s_i)_{i \in [m]} \leftarrow \mathsf{InpEncode}(\mathsf{params}, x)$. Thus, we obtains $f(x) \leftarrow \mathsf{Decode}((f_i(s_i))_{i \in [m]})$ from the correctness of SetHSS. It is clear that SKFE-sbSKL also satisfies verification correctness.

Circuit $F[f_i, \mathsf{sct}_i](s_i, K, b)$

Hardwired: A function share f_i and an SKE's ciphertext sct_i.
Input: an input share s_i, an SKE's secret key K, and a bit b.

1. If $b = 1$, output $\mathsf{D}(K, \mathsf{sct}_i)$.
2. Otherwise, output $f_i(s_i)$.

Fig. 1. Description of $F[f_i, \mathsf{sct}_i](s_i, K, b)$.

Also, the weak optimal efficiency of SKFE-sbSKL easily follows from that of iSKFE-sbSKL since the running time of algorithms of SetHSS is independent of n. Note that sbSKL.Enc samples indices from $[N] = [n/p]$, but it can be done in time $\log n$.

For security, we have the following theorems.

Theorem 4.1. *If* iSKFE-sbSKL *is a selectively strong lessor secure index-based SKFE-sbSKL scheme and* SetHSS *is a set homomorphic secret sharing scheme, and* SKE *is a CPA secure SKE scheme, then* SKFE-sbSKL *is selectively strong lessor secure.*

Proof of Theorem 4.1. We define a sequence of hybrid games to prove the theorem.

Hyb_0: This is the same as $\mathsf{Exp}^{\mathsf{sel\text{-}s\text{-}lessor}}_{\mathcal{A}, \mathsf{SKFE\text{-}sbSKL}}(1^\lambda, 0)$.
1. At the beginning, $\mathcal{A}$ sends $(1^q, n, x_0^*, x_1^*)$ to the challenger. The challenger generates $\mathsf{params} := (p, \ell, (T_i)_{i \in [m]}) \leftarrow \mathsf{SetGen}(1^\lambda)$, $\mathsf{msk}_i \leftarrow \mathsf{iSetup}(1^\lambda, 1^q, N)$ for every $i \in [m]$, and $K \leftarrow \{0, 1\}^\lambda$, where $N = n/p$. Throughout the experiment, $\mathcal{A}$ can access the following oracles.
   $\mathcal{O}_{\mathsf{Enc}}(x^k)$: Given the k-th query x^k, it returns $\mathsf{sbskl.ct}^k$ generated as follows.
     - Generate $(s_i^k)_{i \in [m]} \leftarrow \mathsf{InpEncode}(\mathsf{params}, x^k)$.
     - Generate $k_i \leftarrow [N]$ for every $i \in [m]$.
     - Generate $\mathsf{ct}_i^k \leftarrow \mathsf{iEnc}(\mathsf{msk}, i, k_i, (s_i^k, \mathbf{0}, 0))$ for every $i \in [m]$.
     - Set $\mathsf{sbskl.ct}^k := (\mathsf{ct}_i^k)_{i \in [m]}$.
   $\mathcal{O}_{\mathcal{KG}}(f)$: Given f, it generates $\mathsf{sbskl}.\mathit{fsk}$ and $\mathsf{sbskl.vk}$ as follows.

- Generate $(f_i)_{i \in [m]} \leftarrow \mathsf{FuncEncode}(\mathsf{params}, f)$.
- Generate $\mathsf{sct}_i \leftarrow \mathsf{E}(K, \mathbf{0})$ for every $i \in [m]$.
- Generate $(\mathit{fsk}_i, \mathsf{vk}_i) \leftarrow i\mathcal{KG}(\mathsf{msk}_i, F[f_i, \mathsf{sct}_i])$ for every $i \in [m]$.
- Set $\mathsf{sbskl}.\mathit{fsk} := (\mathit{fsk}_i)_{i \in [m]}$ and $\mathsf{sbskl}.\mathsf{vk} := (\mathsf{vk}_i)_{i \in [m]}$.

It sends $\mathsf{sbskl}.\mathit{fsk}$ to $\mathcal{A}$ and adds $(f, \mathsf{sbskl}.\mathsf{vk}, \bot)$ to $L_{\mathcal{KG}}$.

$O_{\mathsf{Vrfy}}(f, \mathsf{cert} := (\mathsf{cert}_i)_{i \in [m]})$: Given $(f, \mathsf{cert} := (\mathsf{cert}_i)_{i \in [m]})$, it finds an entry (f, vk, M) from $L_{\mathcal{KG}}$. (If there is no such entry, it returns $\bot$.) If $\top = \mathsf{Vrfy}(\mathsf{vk}_i, \mathsf{cert}_i)$ for every $i \in [m]$, it returns $\top$ and updates the entry into $(f, \mathsf{vk}, \top)$. Otherwise, it returns $\bot$.

2. When $\mathcal{A}$ requests the challenge ciphertext, the challenger checks if for any entry (f, vk, M) in $L_{\mathcal{KG}}$ such that $f(x_0^*) \neq f(x_1^*)$, it holds that $M = \top$, and the number of queries to O_{Enc} at this point is less than n. If so, the challenger sends $\mathsf{sbskl}.\mathsf{ct}^*$ computed as follows to $\mathcal{A}$.
   - Generate $(s_i^*)_{i \in [m]} \leftarrow \mathsf{InpEncode}(\mathsf{params}, x_0^*)$.
   - Generate $*_i \leftarrow [N]$ for every $i \in [m]$.
   - Generate $\mathsf{ct}_i^* \leftarrow i\mathsf{Enc}(\mathsf{msk}_i, (s_i^*, \mathbf{0}, 0))$ for every $i \in [m]$.
   - Set $\mathsf{sbskl}.\mathsf{ct}^* := (\mathsf{ct}_i^*)_{i \in [m]}$.

   Otherwise, the challenger outputs 0. Hereafter, $\mathcal{A}$ is not allowed to sends a function f such that $f(x_0^*) \neq f(x_1^*)$ to $O_{\mathcal{KG}}$.

3. $\mathcal{A}$ outputs coin'. The challenger outputs coin' as the final output of the experiment.

Below, we call $i \in [m]$ a *secure instance index* if $i^* \neq i^k$ holds for every $k \in [n]$. We also call $i \in [m]$ an *insecure instance index* if it is not a secure instance index. Let $S_{\mathsf{secure}} \subseteq [m]$ be the set of secure instance indices, and $S_{\mathsf{insecure}} = S \setminus S_{\mathsf{secure}}$. Since each i^k is sampled from $[N] = [n/p]$, for each $i \in [m]$, i is independently included in S_{insecure} with probability at most $n/N = p$. Then, from the existence of unmarked element property of SetHSS, without negligible probability, there exists $e \in [\ell]$ such that $e \notin \bigcup_{i \in S_{\mathsf{insecure}}} T_i$. Below, for simplicity, we assume that there always exists at least one such instance index, and we denote it as e^*.

Hyb_1: This is the same as Hyb_0 except that we generate i^k for every $i \in [m]$ and $k \in [n]$ and i^* for every $i \in [m]$ at the beginning of the experiment. Note that by this change, secure instance indices and i^* are determined at the beginning of the experiment.

$|\Pr[\mathsf{Hyb}_0 = 1] - \Pr[\mathsf{Hyb}_1 = 1]| = 0$ holds since the change at this step is only conceptual.

Hyb_2: This is the same as Hyb_1 except that when $\mathcal{A}$ makes a query f to $O_{\mathcal{KG}}$, if $f(x_0^*) = f(x_1^*)$, it generates sct_i as $\mathsf{sct}_i \leftarrow \mathsf{E}(K, f_i(s_i^*))$ for every $i \in S_{\mathsf{secure}}$.

$|\Pr[\mathsf{Hyb}_1 = 1] - \Pr[\mathsf{Hyb}_2 = 1]| = \mathsf{negl}(\lambda)$ holds from the security of SKE.

Hyb_3: This is the same as Hyb_2 except that the challenger generates ct_i^* as $\mathsf{ct}_i^* \leftarrow i\mathsf{Enc}(\mathsf{msk}_i, i*_i, (\mathbf{0}, K, 1))$ for every $i \in S_{\mathsf{secure}}$.

$|\Pr[\mathsf{Hyb}_2 = 1] - \Pr[\mathsf{Hyb}_3 = 1]| = \mathsf{negl}(\lambda)$ holds from the selective lessor security of iSKFE-sbSKL. We provide the proof of it in Proposition 4.1.

Hyb_4: This is the same as Hyb_3 except that the challenger generates $(s_i^*)_{i \in [m]}$ as $(s_i^*)_{i \in [m]} \leftarrow \mathsf{InpEncode}(\mathsf{params}, x_1^*)$.

$|\Pr[\mathsf{Hyb}_3 = 1] - \Pr[\mathsf{Hyb}_4 = 1]| = \mathsf{negl}(\lambda)$ holds from the selective indistinguishability-security of SetHSS. We provide the proof of it in Proposition 4.2.

Hyb_5: This is the same as Hyb_4 except that we undo the changes from Hyb_0 to Hyb_3. This is the same experiment as $\mathsf{Exp}^{\mathsf{sel\text{-}s\text{-}lessor}}_{\mathcal{A},\mathsf{SKFE\text{-}sbSKL}}(1^\lambda, 1)$.

$|\Pr[\mathsf{Hyb}_4 = 1] - \Pr[\mathsf{Hyb}_5 = 1]| = \mathsf{negl}(\lambda)$ holds from the security of SKE and iSKFE-sbSKL.

Proposition 4.1. $|\Pr[\mathsf{Hyb}_2 = 1] - \Pr[\mathsf{Hyb}_3 = 1]| = \mathsf{negl}(\lambda)$ holds if iSKFE-sbSKL is selectively lessor secure.

Proof of Proposition 4.1. We define intermediate experiments $\mathsf{Hyb}_{2,i'}$ between Hyb_2 and Hyb_3 for $i' \in [m]$.

$\mathsf{Hyb}_{2,i'}$: This is the same as Hyb_2 except that the challenger generates ct_i^* as $\mathsf{ct}_i^* \leftarrow \mathsf{iEnc}(\mathsf{msk}_i, i *_i, (\mathbf{0}, K, 1))$ for every i such that $i \in S_{\mathsf{secure}}$ and $i \leq i'$.

Then, we have

$$|\Pr[\mathsf{Hyb}_2 = 1] - \Pr[\mathsf{Hyb}_3 = 1]|$$

$$\leq \sum_{i' \in m} \left| \Pr[\mathsf{Hyb}_{2,i'-1} = 1 \wedge i' \in S_{\mathsf{secure}}] - \Pr[\mathsf{Hyb}_{2,i} = 1 \wedge i' \in S_{\mathsf{secure}}] \right|, \quad (1)$$

where we define $\mathsf{Hyb}_{2,0} = \mathsf{Hyb}_2$ and $\mathsf{Hyb}_{2,m} = \mathsf{Hyb}_3$. To estimate each term of Equation (1), we construct the following adversary $\mathcal{B}$ that attacks selective lessor security of iSKFE-sbSKL.

1. $\mathcal{B}$ executes $\mathcal{A}$ and obtains $(1^q, n, x_0^*, x_1^*)$. $\mathcal{B}$ generates $\mathsf{params} := (p, \ell, (T_i)_{i \in [m]}) \leftarrow \mathsf{SetGen}(1^\lambda)$. $\mathcal{B}$ generates $i^k \leftarrow [N]$ for every $i \in [m]$ and $k \in [n]$ and $i^* \leftarrow [N]$ for every $i \in [m]$, and identifies S_{secure} and S_{insecure}, where $N = n/p$. If $i' \notin S_{\mathsf{secure}}$, $\mathcal{B}$ aborts with output 0. Otherwise, $\mathcal{B}$ behaves as follows. Below, we let $S_{\mathsf{secure},<i'} = S_{\mathsf{secure}} \cap [i'-1]$. $\mathcal{B}$ computes $(s_i^*)_{i \in [m]} \leftarrow \mathsf{InpEncode}(\mathsf{params}, x_0^*)$. $\mathcal{B}$ also generates $K \leftarrow \{0,1\}^\lambda$. $\mathcal{B}$ sends $(1^q, N, i'^*, (s_{i'}^*, \mathbf{0}, 0), (\mathbf{0}, K, 1))$. $\mathcal{B}$ also generates $\mathsf{msk}_i \leftarrow \mathsf{iSetup}(1^\lambda, 1^q, N)$ for every $i \in [m] \setminus \{i'\}$. $\mathcal{B}$ simulates oracles for $\mathcal{A}$ as follows.
   $O_{\mathsf{Enc}}(x^k)$: Given the k-th query x^k, $\mathcal{B}$ returns $\mathsf{sbskl}.\mathsf{ct}^k$ generated as follows.
   – Generate $(s_i^k)_{i \in [m]} \leftarrow \mathsf{InpEncode}(\mathsf{params}, x^k)$.
   – If $k \leq n$, use $(i^k)_{i \in [m]}$ generated at the beginning. Otherwise, Generate $k_i \leftarrow [N]$ for every $i \in [m]$.
   – Query $(k_{i'}, (s_{i'}^k, \mathbf{0}, 0))$ to its encryption oracle and obtain $\mathsf{ct}_{i'}^k$.
   – Generate $\mathsf{ct}_i^k \leftarrow \mathsf{iEnc}(\mathsf{msk}_i, i^k, (s_i^k, \mathbf{0}, 0))$ for every $i \in [m] \setminus \{i'\}$.

- Set sbskl.ct^k := $(\text{ct}_i^k)_{i\in[m]}$.

$O_{\mathcal{KG}}(f)$: Given f, $\mathcal{B}$ returns sbskl.fsk computed as follows.

- Generate $(f_i)_{i\in[m]} \leftarrow \mathsf{FuncEncode}(\mathsf{params}, f)$.
- Generate $\mathsf{sct}_i \leftarrow \mathsf{E}(K, \mathbf{0})$ for every $i \in S_{\mathsf{insecure}}$. Generate also $\mathsf{sct}_i \leftarrow \mathsf{E}(K, f_i(s_i^*))$ for every $i \in S_{\mathsf{secure}}$ if $f(x_0^*) = f(x_1^*)$, and otherwise generate $\mathsf{sct}_i \leftarrow \mathsf{E}(K, \mathbf{0})$ for every $i \in S_{\mathsf{secure}}$.
- Query $F[f_{i'}, \mathsf{sct}_{i'}]$ to its key generation oracle and obtain $(fsk_{i'}, \mathsf{vk}_{i'})$.
- Generate $(fsk_i, \mathsf{vk}_i) \leftarrow i\mathcal{KG}(\mathsf{msk}_i, F[f_i, \mathsf{sct}_i])$ for every $i \in [m] \setminus \{i'\}$.
- Set sbskl.fsk := $(fsk_i)_{i\in[m]}$.

Also, $\mathcal{B}$ adds $(f, (\mathsf{vk}_i)_{i\in[m]\setminus\{i'\}}, \perp)$ to $L_{\mathcal{KG}}$.

$O_{\mathsf{Vrfy}}(f, \mathsf{cert} := (\mathsf{cert}_i)_{i\in[m]})$: Given $(f, \mathsf{cert} := (\mathsf{cert}_i)_{i\in[m]})$, it finds an entry $(f, (\mathsf{vk}_i)_{i\in[m]\setminus\{i'\}}, \perp)$ from $L_{\mathcal{KG}}$. (If there is no such entry, it returns $\perp$.) $\mathcal{B}$ sends $(f, \mathsf{cert}_{i'})$ to its verification oracle and obtains $M_{i'}$. If $M = \top$ and $\top = \mathsf{Vrfy}(\mathsf{vk}_i, \mathsf{cert}_i)$ for every $i \in [m] \setminus \{i'\}$, $\mathcal{B}$ returns $\top$ and updates the entry into $(f, (\mathsf{vk}_i)_{i\in[m]\setminus\{i'\}}, \top)$. Otherwise, $\mathcal{B}$ returns $\perp$.

2. When $\mathcal{A}$ requests the challenge ciphertext, $\mathcal{B}$ checks if for any entry $(f, (\mathsf{vk}_i)_{i\in[m]\setminus\{i'\}}, M)$ in $L_{\mathcal{KG}}$ such that $f(x_0^*) \neq f(x_1^*)$, it holds that $M = \top$. If so, $\mathcal{B}$ requests the challenge ciphertext to its challenger and obtains $\mathsf{ct}_{i'}^*$. $\mathcal{B}$ also generates $\mathsf{ct}_i^* \leftarrow i\mathsf{Enc}(\mathsf{msk}_i, 0i^*, (\mathbf{0}, K, 1))$ for every $i \in S_{\mathsf{secure}, <i'}$ and $\mathsf{ct}_i^* \leftarrow i\mathsf{Enc}(\mathsf{msk}_i, 0i^*, (s_i^*, \mathbf{0}, 0))$ for every $i \in [m] \setminus (S_{\mathsf{secure}, <i'} \cup \{i'\})$. $\mathcal{B}$ sends sbskl.ct := $(\mathsf{ct}_i^*)_{i\in[m]}$ to $\mathcal{A}$. Hereafter, $\mathcal{B}$ rejects $\mathcal{A}$'s query f to $O_{\mathcal{KG}}$ such that $f(x_0^*) \neq f(x_1^*)$.

3. When $\mathcal{A}$ outputs coin', $\mathcal{B}$ outputs coin'.

$\mathcal{B}$ simulates $\mathsf{Hyb}_{2,i'-1}$ (resp. $\mathsf{Hyb}_{2,i'}$) if $\mathcal{B}$ runs in $\mathsf{Exp}_{\mathcal{B}, \mathsf{SKFE\text{-}sbSKL}}^{\mathsf{sel\text{-}s\text{-}lessor}}(1^\lambda, 0)$ (resp. $\mathsf{Exp}_{\mathcal{B}, \mathsf{SKFE\text{-}sbSKL}}^{\mathsf{sel\text{-}s\text{-}lessor}}(1^\lambda, 1)$) and $i' \in S_{\mathsf{secure}}$. This completes the proof. ∎

Proposition 4.2. $|\Pr[\mathsf{Hyb}_3 = 1] - \Pr[\mathsf{Hyb}_4 = 1]| = \mathsf{negl}(\lambda)$ holds if SetHSS is a set homomorphic secret sharing.

Proof (of Proposition 4.2). We construct the following adversary $\mathcal{B}$ that attacks the selective indistinguishability-security of SetHSS.

1. Given $\mathsf{params} := (p, \ell, (T_i)_{i\in[m]})$, $\mathcal{B}$ executes $\mathcal{A}$ and obtains $(1^q, n, x_0^*, x_1^*)$. $\mathcal{B}$ generates $i^k \leftarrow [N]$ for every $i \in [m]$ and $k \in [n]$ and $i^* \leftarrow [N]$ for every $i \in [m]$, and identifies $S_{\mathsf{secure}}, S_{\mathsf{insecure}}$, and the unmarked element e^*, where $N = n/p$. $\mathcal{B}$ sends (e^*, x_0^*, x_1^*) to the challenger and obtains $(s_i^*)_{i\in[m]_{e^*} \notin}$, where $[m]_{e^* \notin}$ denotes the subset of $[m]$ consisting of i such that $e^* \notin T_i$. $\mathcal{B}$ also generates $\mathsf{msk}_i \leftarrow i\mathsf{Setup}(1^\lambda, 1^q, N)$ for every $i \in [m]$ and $K \leftarrow \{0,1\}^\lambda$. $\mathcal{B}$ simulates oracles for $\mathcal{A}$ as follows.

   $O_{\mathsf{Enc}}(x^k)$: Given the k-th query x^k, $\mathcal{B}$ returns sbskl.ct^k generated as follows.
   - Generate $(s_i^k)_{i\in[m]} \leftarrow \mathsf{InpEncode}(\mathsf{params}, x^k)$.
   - If $k \leq n$, use $(i^k)_{i\in[m]}$ generated at the beginning. Otherwise, Generate $k_i \leftarrow [N]$ for every $i \in [m]$.
   - Generate $\mathsf{ct}_i^k \leftarrow i\mathsf{Enc}(\mathsf{msk}_i, k_i, (s_i^k, \mathbf{0}, 0))$ for every $i \in [m]$.
   - Set sbskl.ct^k := $(\mathsf{ct}_i^k)_{i\in[m]}$.

$O_{\mathcal{KG}}(f)$: Given f, $\mathcal{B}$ returns sbskl.fsk computed as follows.

- Queries f to its function encode oracle and obtain $(f_i, y_i := f_i(s_i^*))_{i \in [m]}$ if $f(x_0^*) = f(x_1^*)$. Otherwise, compute $(f_i)_{i \in [m]} \leftarrow$ FuncEncode(params, f).
- Generate $\mathsf{sct}_i \leftarrow \mathsf{E}(K, \mathbf{0})$ for every $i \in S_{\mathsf{insecure}}$. Generate also $\mathsf{sct}_i \leftarrow \mathsf{E}(K, f_i(s_i^*))$ for every $i \in S_{\mathsf{secure}}$ if $f(x_0^*) = f(x_1^*)$, and otherwise generate $\mathsf{sct}_i \leftarrow \mathsf{E}(K, \mathbf{0})$ for every $i \in S_{\mathsf{secure}}$.
- Generate $(\mathit{fsk}_i, \mathsf{vk}_i) \leftarrow i\mathcal{KG}(\mathsf{msk}_i, F[f_i, \mathsf{sct}_i])$ for every $i \in [m]$.
- Set sbskl.$\mathit{fsk} := (\mathit{fsk}_i)_{i \in [m]}$.

Also, $\mathcal{B}$ adds $(f, (\mathsf{vk}_i)_{i \in [m]}, \perp)$ to $L_{\mathcal{KG}}$.

$O_{\mathsf{Vrfy}}(f, \mathsf{cert} := (\mathsf{cert}_i)_{i \in [m]})$: Given $(f, \mathsf{cert} := (\mathsf{cert}_i)_{i \in [m]})$, it finds an entry $(f, (\mathsf{vk}_i)_{i \in [m]}, \perp)$ from $L_{\mathcal{KG}}$. (If there is no such entry, it returns $\perp$.) If $\top = \mathsf{Vrfy}(\mathsf{vk}_i, \mathsf{cert}_i)$ for every $i \in [m]$ and the number of queries to O_{Enc} at this point is less than n, $\mathcal{B}$ returns $\top$ and updates the entry into $(f, (\mathsf{vk}_i)_{i \in [m]}, \top)$. Otherwise, $\mathcal{B}$ returns $\perp$.

2. When $\mathcal{A}$ requests the challenge ciphertext, $\mathcal{B}$ checks if for any entry $(f, (\mathsf{vk}_i)_{i \in [m] \setminus \{i'\}}, M)$ in $L_{\mathcal{KG}}$ such that $f(x_0^*) \neq f(x_1^*)$, it holds that $M = \top$. If so, $\mathcal{B}$ generates $\mathsf{ct}_i^* \leftarrow \mathsf{iEnc}(\mathsf{msk}_i, i*_i, (\mathbf{0}, K, 1))$ for every $i \in S_{\mathsf{secure}}$ and $\mathsf{ct}_i^* \leftarrow \mathsf{iEnc}(\mathsf{msk}_i, i*_i, (s_i^*, \mathbf{0}, 0))$ for every $i \in S_{\mathsf{insecure}}$, and $\mathcal{B}$ sends sbskl.ct := $(\mathsf{ct}_i^*)_{i \in [m]}$ to $\mathcal{A}$. Otherwise, $\mathcal{B}$ outputs 0 and terminates. Hereafter, $\mathcal{B}$ rejects $\mathcal{A}$'s query f to $O_{\mathcal{KG}}$ such that $f(x_0^*) \neq f(x_1^*)$.

3. When $\mathcal{A}$ outputs coin′, $\mathcal{B}$ outputs coin′.

$\mathcal{B}$ simulates Hyb_3 (resp. Hyb_4) if $\mathcal{B}$ runs in $\mathsf{Exp}^{\mathsf{sel\text{-}ind}}_{\mathsf{SetHSS}, \mathcal{B}}(1^\lambda, 0)$ (resp. $\mathsf{Exp}^{\mathsf{sel\text{-}ind}}_{\mathsf{SetHSS}, \mathcal{B}}(1^\lambda, 1)$). This completes the proof. ∎

From the above discussions, SKFE-sbSKL satisfies selective strong lessor security. ∎

Remark 4.1 (Difference from FE security amplification). A savvy reader notices that although we use the technique used in the FE security amplification by Jain et al. [JKMS20], we do not use their probabilistic replacement theorem [JKMS20, Theorem 7.1 in eprint ver.] and the nested construction [JKMS20, Section 9 in eprint ver.] in the proofs of Theorem 4.1. We do not need them for our purpose due to the following reason.

Jain et al. need the nested construction to achieve a secure FE scheme whose adversary's advantage is less than $1/6$ from one whose adversary's advantage is any constant $\epsilon \in (0, 1)$. We do not need the nested construction since we can start with a secure construction whose adversary's advantage is less than $1/6$ by setting a large index space in the index-based construction.

Jain et al. need the probabilistic replacement theorem due to the following reason. We do not know which FE instance is secure at the beginning of the FE security game in the security amplification context, while the adversary in set homomorphic secret sharing must declare the index of a secure instance at the beginning. In our case, whether each index-based FE instance is secure or not depends on whether randomly sampled indices collide or not. In addition, we can sample all indices used in the security game at the beginning of the game, and a secure FE instance is fixed at the beginning. Thus, we can apply the security of set homomorphic secret sharing without the probabilistic replacement theorem.

5   SKFE with Secure Key Leasing

We construct an SKFE-SKL scheme SKFE-SKL = (SKL.Setup, SKL.$\mathcal{KG}$, SKL.Enc, SKL.$\mathcal{Dec}$, SKL.$\mathcal{Cert}$, SKL.Vrfy) from an SKFE-sbSKL scheme SKFE-sbSKL = (sbSKL.Setup, sbSKL.$\mathcal{KG}$, sbSKL.Enc, sbSKL.$\mathcal{Dec}$, sbSKL.$\mathcal{Cert}$, sbSKL.Vrfy). The description of SKFE-SKL is as follows.

SKL.Setup($1^\lambda, 1^q$):
  - Generate $\mathsf{msk}_k \leftarrow$ sbSKL.Setup($1^\lambda, 1^q, 2^k$) for every $k \in [\lambda]$.
  - Output skl.msk := $(\mathsf{msk}_k)_{k \in [\lambda]}$.
SKL.$\mathcal{KG}$(skl.msk, $f, 1^n$):
  - Parse $(\mathsf{msk}_k)_{k \in [\lambda]} \leftarrow$ skl.msk.
  - Compute k' such that $2^{k'-1} \leq n \leq 2^{k'}$.
  - Generate $(\mathit{fsk}_{k'}, \mathsf{vk}_{k'}) \leftarrow$ sbSKL.$\mathcal{KG}$($\mathsf{msk}_{k'}, f$).
  - Output skl.fsk := $(k', \mathit{fsk}_{k'})$ and $\mathsf{vk}_{k'}$.
SKL.Enc(skl.msk, x):
  - Parse $(\mathsf{msk}_k)_{k \in [\lambda]} \leftarrow$ skl.msk.
  - Generate $\mathsf{ct}_k \leftarrow$ sbSKL.Enc(msk_k, x) for every $k \in [\lambda]$.
  - Output skl.ct := $(\mathsf{ct}_k)_{k \in [\lambda]}$.
SKL.$\mathcal{Dec}$(skl.sk_f, skl.ct):
  - Parse $(k', \mathit{fsk}_{k'}) \leftarrow$ skl.fsk and $(\mathsf{ct}_k)_{k \in [\lambda]} \leftarrow$ skl.ct.
  - Output $y \leftarrow$ sbSKL.$\mathcal{Dec}$($\mathit{fsk}_{k'}, \mathsf{ct}_{k'}$).
SKL.$\mathcal{Cert}$(skl.sk_f):
  - Parse $(k', \mathit{fsk}_{k'}) \leftarrow$ skl.sk_f.
  - Output cert $\leftarrow$ sbSKL.$\mathcal{Cert}$($\mathit{fsk}_{k'}$).
SKL.Vrfy(vk, cert):
  - Output $\top/\bot \leftarrow$ sbSKL.Vrfy(vk, cert).

The correctness of SKFE-SKL follows from that of SKFE-sbSKL. Also, we can confirm that all algorithms of SKFE-SKL run in polynomial time since sbSKL.Setup and sbSKL.Enc of SKFE-sbSKL run in polynomial time even for the availability bound 2^λ due to its weak optimal efficiency. For security, we have the following theorem.

Theorem 5.1. *If* SKFE-sbSKL *satisfies selective strong lessor security, then* SKFE-SKL *satisfies selective lessor security.*

Proof of Theorem 5.1. We define a sequence of hybrid games to prove the theorem.

Hyb$_0$: This is the same as $\mathsf{Exp}^{\mathsf{sel\text{-}lessor}}_{\mathcal{A}, \mathsf{SKFE\text{-}SKL}}(1^\lambda, 0)$.
  1. At the beginning, $\mathcal{A}$ sends $(1^q, x_0^*, x_1^*)$ to the challenger. The challenger runs $\mathsf{msk}_k \leftarrow$ sbSKL.Setup($1^\lambda, 1^q, 2^k$) for every $k \in [\lambda]$. Throughout the experiment, $\mathcal{A}$ can access the following oracles.

$O_{\mathsf{Enc}}(x)$: Given x, it generates $\mathsf{ct}_k \leftarrow \mathsf{sbSKL.Enc}(\mathsf{msk}_k, x)$ for every $k \in [\lambda]$ and returns $\mathsf{skl.ct} := (\mathsf{ct}_k)_{k\in[\lambda]}$.

$O_{\mathcal{KG}}(f, 1^n)$: Given $(f, 1^n)$, it computes k such that $2^{k-1} \leq n \leq 2^k$, generates $(\mathit{fsk}_k, \mathsf{vk}_k) \leftarrow \mathsf{sbSKL.KG}(\mathsf{msk}_k, f)$, and sets $\mathsf{skl.fsk} := (k, \mathit{fsk}_k)$. It returns $\mathsf{skl.fsk}$ to $\mathcal{A}$ and adds $(f, 1^n, \mathsf{vk}_k, \bot)$ to $L_{\mathcal{KG}}$. $\mathcal{A}$ can access this oracle at most q times.

$O_{\mathsf{Vrfy}}(f, \mathsf{cert})$: Given (f, cert), it finds an entry $(f, 1^n, \mathsf{vk}, M)$ from $L_{\mathcal{KG}}$. (If there is no such entry, it returns $\bot$.) If $\top = \mathsf{Vrfy}(\mathsf{vk}, \mathsf{cert})$ and the number of queries to O_{Enc} at this point is less than n, it returns $\top$ and updates the entry into $(f, 1^n, \mathsf{vk}, \top)$. Otherwise, it returns $\bot$.

2. When $\mathcal{A}$ requests the challenge ciphertext, the challenger checks if for any entry $(f, 1^n, \mathsf{vk}, M)$ in $L_{\mathcal{KG}}$ such that $f(x_0^*) \neq f(x_1^*)$, it holds that $M = \top$. If so, the challenger generates $\mathsf{ct}_k^* \leftarrow \mathsf{sbSKL.Enc}(\mathsf{msk}_k, x_0^*)$ for every $k \in [\lambda]$ and sends $\mathsf{skl.ct}^* := (\mathsf{ct}_k^*)_{k\in[\lambda]}$ to $\mathcal{A}$. Otherwise, the challenger outputs 0. Hereafter, $\mathcal{A}$ is not allowed to sends a function f such that $f(x_0^*) \neq f(x_1^*)$ to $O_{\mathcal{KG}}$.

3. $\mathcal{A}$ outputs a guess coin' for coin. The challenger outputs coin' as the final output of the experiment.

We define $\mathsf{Hyb}_{k'}$ for every $k' \in [\lambda]$.

$\mathsf{Hyb}_{k'}$: This hybrid is the same as $\mathsf{Hyb}_{k'-1}$ except that $\mathsf{ct}_{k'}^*$ is generated as $\mathsf{ct}_{k'}^* \leftarrow \mathsf{Enc}(\mathsf{msk}_{k'}, x_1^*)$.

Hyb_λ is exactly the same experiment as $\mathsf{Exp}_{\mathcal{A},\mathsf{SKFE\text{-}SKL}}^{\mathsf{sel\text{-}lessor}}(1^\lambda, 1)$.

For every $k' \in [\lambda]$, we let $\mathsf{SUC}_{k'}$ be the event that the output of the experiment $\mathsf{Hyb}_{k'}$ is 1. Then, we have

$$\mathsf{Adv}_{\mathsf{SKFE\text{-}SKL},\mathcal{A}}^{\mathsf{sel\text{-}lessor}}(\lambda) = |\Pr[\mathsf{Hyb}_0 = 1] - \Pr[\mathsf{Hyb}_\lambda = 1]| \leq \sum_{k'=1}^{\lambda} \left| \Pr[\mathsf{SUC}_{k'-1}] - \Pr[\mathsf{SUC}_{k'}] \right|.$$

Proposition 5.1. *It holds that* $\left|\Pr[\mathsf{Hyb}_{k'-1} = 1] - \Pr[\mathsf{Hyb}_{k'} = 1]\right| = \mathsf{negl}(\lambda)$ *for every* $k' \in [\lambda]$ *if* $\mathsf{SKFE\text{-}sbSKL}$ *is selectively lessor secure.*

Proof (of Proposition 5.1). We construct the following adversary $\mathcal{B}$ that attacks selective lessor security of $\mathsf{SKFE\text{-}sbSKL}$ with respect to $\mathsf{msk}_{k'}$.

1. $\mathcal{B}$ executes $\mathcal{A}$ and obtains $(1^q, x_0^*, x_1^*)$ from $\mathcal{A}$. $\mathcal{B}$ sends $(1^q, x_0^*, x_1^*, 2^{k'})$ to the challenger. $\mathcal{B}$ generates $\mathsf{msk}_k \leftarrow \mathsf{sbSKL.Setup}(1^\lambda, 1^q, 2^k)$ for every $k \in [\lambda]\setminus\{k'\}$. $\mathcal{B}$ simulates queries made by $\mathcal{A}$ as follows.

$O_{\mathsf{Enc}}(x)$: Given x, $\mathcal{B}$ generates $\mathsf{ct}_k \leftarrow \mathsf{sbSKL.Enc}(\mathsf{msk}_k, x)$ for every $k \in [\lambda] \setminus \{k'\}$. $\mathcal{B}$ also queries x to its encryption oracle and obtains $\mathsf{ct}_{k'}$. $\mathcal{B}$ returns $\mathsf{skl.ct} := (\mathsf{ct}_k)_{k\in[\lambda]}$.

$O_{\mathcal{KG}}(f, 1^n)$: Given $(f, 1^n)$, $\mathcal{B}$ computes k such that $2^{k-1} \leq n \leq 2^k$. If $k \neq k'$, $\mathcal{B}$ generates $(\mathit{fsk}_k, \mathsf{vk}_k) \leftarrow \mathsf{sbSKL.KG}(\mathsf{msk}_k, f)$, and otherwise $\mathcal{B}$ queries f to its key generation oracle and obtains fsk_k and sets $\mathsf{vk}_k := \bot$. $\mathcal{B}$ returns $\mathsf{skl.fsk} := \mathit{fsk}_k$. $\mathcal{B}$ adds $(f, 1^n, \mathsf{vk}_k, \bot)$ to $L_{\mathcal{KG}}$.

$O_{\mathsf{Vrfy}}(f, \mathsf{cert})$: Given (f, cert), it finds an entry $(f, 1^n, \mathsf{vk}, M)$ from $L_{\mathcal{KG}}$. (If there is no such entry, it returns $\bot$.) If $\mathsf{vk} = \bot$, $\mathcal{B}$ sends cert to its verification oracle and obtains M, and otherwise it computes $M = \mathsf{Vrfy}(\mathsf{vk}, \mathsf{cert})$. If $M = \top$ and the number of queries to O_{Enc} at this point is less than n, it returns $\top$ and updates the entry into $(f, 1^n, \mathsf{vk}, \top)$. Otherwise, it returns $\bot$.

2. When $\mathcal{A}$ requests the challenge ciphertext, the challenger checks if for any entry $(f, 1^n, \mathsf{vk}, M)$ in $L_{\mathcal{KG}}$ such that $f(x_0^*) \neq f(x_1^*)$, it holds that $M = \top$. If so, $\mathcal{B}$ requests the challenge ciphertext to its challenger and obtains $\mathsf{ct}_{k'}^*$, generates $\mathsf{ct}_k^* \leftarrow \mathsf{sbSKL.Enc}(\mathsf{msk}_k, x_1^*)$ for every $1 \leq k < k'$ and $\mathsf{ct}_k^* \leftarrow \mathsf{sbSKL.Enc}(\mathsf{msk}_k, x_0^*)$ for every $k' < k \leq \lambda$, and sends $\mathsf{skl.ct}^* := (\mathsf{ct}_k^*)_{k \in [\lambda]}$ to $\mathcal{A}$. Otherwise, the challenger outputs 0. Hereafter, $\mathcal{A}$ is not allowed to sends a function f such that $f(x_0^*) \neq f(x_1^*)$ to $O_{\mathcal{KG}}$.

3. When $\mathcal{A}$ outputs coin', $\mathcal{B}$ outputs coin' and terminates.

$\mathcal{B}$ simulates $\mathsf{Hyb}_{k'-1}$ (resp. $\mathsf{Hyb}_{k'}$) for $\mathcal{A}$ if $\mathcal{B}$ runs in $\mathsf{Exp}_{\mathcal{B}, \mathsf{SKFE\text{-}sbSKL}}^{\mathsf{sel\text{-}lessor}}(1^\lambda, 0)$ (resp. $\mathsf{Exp}_{\mathcal{B}, \mathsf{SKFE\text{-}sbSKL}}^{\mathsf{sel\text{-}lessor}}(1^\lambda, 1)$.). This completes the proof. ∎

From the above discussions, SKFE-SKL satisfies selective lessor security. ∎

By Theorem 5.1, 4.1 and 3.2 and the fact that all building blocks used to obtain these theorems can be based on OWFs, we obtain the following theorem.

Theorem 5.2. *If there exist OWFs, there exists selectively lessor secure SKFE-SKL for P/poly (in the sense of Definition 2.2).*

Although we describe our results on SKFE-SKL in the bounded collusion-resistant setting, our transformation from standard SKFE to SKFE-SKL also works in the fully collusion-resistant setting. The fully collusion-resistance guarantees that the SKFE scheme is secure even if an adversary accesses the key generation oracle a-priori unbounded times. Namely, if we start with fully collusion-resistant SKFE, we can obtain fully collusion-resistant SKFE-SKL by our transformations.

References

[Aar09] Aaronson, S.: quantum copy-protection and quantum money. In: Proceedings of the 24th Annual IEEE Conference on Computational Complexity, CCC 2009, Paris, France, 15–18 July 2009, pp 229–242 (2009)

[ABSV15] Ananth, P., Brakerski, Z., Segev, G., Vaikuntanathan, V.: From selective to adaptive security in functional encryption. In: CRYPTO 2015, Part II, pp. 657–677 (2015)

[AJL+19] Ananth, P., Jain, A., Lin, H., Matt, C., Sahai, A.: Indistinguishability obfuscation without multilinear maps: new paradigms via low degree weak pseudorandomness and security amplification. In: CRYPTO 2019, Part III, pp. 284–332 (2019)

[AL21] Ananth, P., La Placa, R.L.: Secure software leasing. In: EUROCRYPT 2021, Part II, pp. 501–530 (2021)

[ALL+21] Aaronson, S., Liu, J., Liu, Q., Zhandry, M., Zhang. R.: New approaches for quantum copy-protection. In: CRYPTO 2021, Part I, pp. 526–555, Virtual Event (2021)

[AMVY21] Agrawal, S., Maitra, M., Vempati, N.S., Yamada, S.: Functional encryption for turing machines with dynamic bounded collusion from LWE. In: CRYPTO 2021, Part IV, pp. 239–269, Virtual Event (2021)

[AV19] Ananth, P., Vaikuntanathan, V.: Optimal bounded-collusion secure functional encryption. In: TCC 2019, Part I, pp. 174–198 (2019)

[BI20] Broadbent, A., Islam, R.: Quantum encryption with certified deletion. In: TCC 2020, Part III, pp. 92–122 (2020)

[BJL+21] Broadbent, A., Jeffery, S., Lord, S., Podder, S., Sundaram, A.: Secure software leasing without assumptions. In:: TCC 2021, Part I, pp. 90–120 (2021)

[BNPW20] Bitansky, N., Nishimaki, R., Passelègue, A., Wichs, D.: From Cryptomania to Obfustopia through secret-key functional encryption. J. Cryptol. 33(2), 357–405 (2020)

[BS18] Brakerski, Z., Segev, G.: Function-private functional encryption in the private-key setting. J. Cryptol. 31(1), 202–225 (2018)

[BSW11] Boneh, D., Sahai, A., Waters, B.: Functional encryption: definitions and challenges. In: Ishai, Y. (ed.) TCC 2011. LNCS, vol. 6597, pp. 253–273. Springer, Heidelberg (2011). https://doi.org/10.1007/978-3-642-19571-6_16

[CGO21] Ciampi, M., Goyal, V., Ostrovsky. R.: Threshold garbled circuits and ad hoc secure computation. In: EUROCRYPT 2021, Part III, pp. 64–93 (2021)

[CLLZ21] Coladangelo, A., Liu, J., Liu, Q., Zhandry. M.: Hidden Cosets and applications to unclonable cryptography. In: CRYPTO 2021, Part I, pp. 556–584, Virtual Event (2021)

[CMP20] Coladangelo, A., Majenz, C., Poremba. A.: Quantum copy-protection of compute-and-compare programs in the quantum random oracle model. Cryptology ePrint Archive, Report 2020/1194 (2020). https://eprint.iacr.org/2020/1194

[CS19] Connor, R.J., Schuchard, M.: Blind Bernoulli trials: a noninteractive protocol for hidden-weight coin flips. In: USENIX Security, pp. 1483–1500 (2019)

[CV21] Culf, E., Vidick, T.: A monogamy-of-entanglement game for subspace Coset states. arXiv (CoRR), abs/2107.13324 (2021)

[DIJ+13] De Caro, A., Iovino, V., Jain, A., O'Neill, A., Paneth, O., Persiano, G.: On the achievability of simulation-based security for functional encryption. In: CRYPTO 2013, Part II, pp. 519–535 (2013)

[GGLW21] Garg, R., Goyal, R., Lu, G., Waters, B.: Dynamic collusion bounded functional encryption from identity-based encryption. Cryptology ePrint Archive, Report 2021/847 (2021) https://eprint.iacr.org/2021/847

[GVW12] Gorbunov, S., Vaikuntanathan, V., Wee, H.: Functional encryption with bounded collusions via multi-party computation. In: Safavi-Naini, R., Canetti, R. (eds.) CRYPTO 2012. LNCS, vol. 7417, pp. 162–179. Springer, Heidelberg (2012). https://doi.org/10.1007/978-3-642-32009-5_11

[HMNY21] Hiroka, T., Morimae, T., Nishimaki, R., Yamakawa, T.: Quantum encryption with certified deletion, revisited: public key, attribute-based, and classical communication. In: ASIACRYPT 2021, Part I, pp. 606–636 (2021)

[JKMS20] Jain, A., Korb, A., Manohar, N., Sahai, A.: Amplifying the security of functional encryption, unconditionally. In: CRYPTO 2020, Part I, pp. 717–746 (2020)

[KLM+18] Kim, S., Lewi, K., Mandal, A., Montgomery, H., Roy, A., Wu, D.J.: Function-hiding inner product encryption is practical. In SCN **18**, 544–562 (2018)

[KNT21] Kitagawa, F., Nishimaki, R., Tanaka, K.: Simple and generic constructions of succinct functional encryption. J. Cryptol. **34**(3), 1–46 (2021). https://doi.org/10.1007/s00145-021-09396-x

[KNY21] Kitagawa, F., Nishimaki, R., Yamakawa, T.: Secure software leasing from standard assumptions. In: TCC 2021, Part I, pp. 31–61 (2021)

[MW16] Mukherjee, P., Wichs, D.: Two round multiparty computation via multi-key FHE. In: EUROCRYPT 2016, Part II, pp. 735–763 (2016)

[NP01] Naor, M., Pinkas, B.: Efficient trace and revoke schemes. In: FC , pp. 1–20 (2001)

[NWZ16] Nishimaki, R., Wichs, D., Zhandry, M.: Anonymous traitor tracing: how to embed arbitrary information in a key. In: EUROCRYPT 2016, Part II, pp. 388–419 (2016)

[RPB+19] Ryffel, T., Pointcheval, D., Bach, F.R., Dufour-Sans, E., Gay, R.: Partially encrypted deep learning using functional encryption. In: NeurIPS, pp. 4519–4530 (2019)

[SS10] Sahai, A., Seyalioglu, H.: Worry-free encryption: functional encryption with public keys. In: ACM CCS, pp. 463–472 (2010)

[SSW12] Sahai, A., Seyalioglu, H., Waters, B.: Dynamic credentials and ciphertext delegation for attribute-based encryption. In: Safavi-Naini, R., Canetti, R. (eds.) CRYPTO 2012. LNCS, vol. 7417, pp. 199–217. Springer, Heidelberg (2012). https://doi.org/10.1007/978-3-642-32009-5_13

[SW05] Sahai, A., Waters, B.: Fuzzy identity-based encryption. In: Cramer, R. (ed.) EUROCRYPT 2005. LNCS, vol. 3494, pp. 457–473. Springer, Heidelberg (2005). https://doi.org/10.1007/11426639_27

[SW21] Sahai, A., Waters, B.: How to use indistinguishability obfuscation: deniable encryption, and more. SIAM J. Comput. **50**(3), 857–908 (2021)

Classically Verifiable NIZK for QMA with Preprocessing

Tomoyuki Morimae[1]([✉]) and Takashi Yamakawa[1,2]

[1] Yukawa Institute for Theoretical Physics, Kyoto University, Kyoto, Japan
tomoyuki.morimae@yukawa.kyoto-u.ac.jp
[2] NTT Social Informatics Laboratories, Tokyo, Japan
takashi.yamakawa.ga@hco.ntt.co.jp

Abstract. We propose three constructions of classically verifiable non-interactive zero-knowledge proofs and arguments (CV-NIZK) for **QMA** in various preprocessing models.

1. We construct a CV-NIZK for **QMA** in the quantum secret parameter model where a trusted setup sends a quantum proving key to the prover and a classical verification key to the verifier. It is information theoretically sound and zero-knowledge.
2. Assuming the quantum hardness of the learning with errors problem, we construct a CV-NIZK for **QMA** in a model where a trusted party generates a CRS and the verifier sends an instance-independent quantum message to the prover as preprocessing. This model is the same as one considered in the recent work by Coladangelo, Vidick, and Zhang (CRYPTO '20). Our construction has the so-called dual-mode property, which means that there are two computationally indistinguishable modes of generating CRS, and we have information theoretical soundness in one mode and information theoretical zero-knowledge property in the other. This answers an open problem left by Coladangelo et al., which is to achieve either of soundness or zero-knowledge information theoretically. To the best of our knowledge, ours is the first dual-mode NIZK for **QMA** in any kind of model.
3. We construct a CV-NIZK for **QMA** with quantum preprocessing in the quantum random oracle model. This quantum preprocessing is the one where the verifier sends a random Pauli-basis states to the prover. Our construction uses the Fiat-Shamir transformation. The quantum preprocessing can be replaced with the setup that distributes Bell pairs among the prover and the verifier, and therefore we solve the open problem by Broadbent and Grilo (FOCS '20) about the possibility of NIZK for **QMA** in the shared Bell pair model via the Fiat-Shamir transformation.

1 Introduction

1.1 Background

The zero-knowledge [GMR89], which ensures that the verifier learns nothing beyond the statement proven by the prover, is one of the most central

S. Agrawal and D. Lin (Eds.): ASIACRYPT 2022, LNCS 13794, pp. 599–627, 2022.
https://doi.org/10.1007/978-3-031-22972-5_21

concepts in cryptography. Recently, there have been many works that constructed non-interactive zero-knowledge (NIZK) [BFM88] proofs or arguments for **QMA**, which is the "quantum counterpart" of **NP**, in various kind of models [ACGH20, CVZ20, BG20, Shm21, BCKM21, BM21]. We note that we require the honest prover to run in quantum polynomial-time receiving sufficiently many copies of a witness when we consider NIZK proofs or arguments for **QMA**. All known protocols except for the protocol of Broadbent and Grilo [BG20] only satisfy computational soundness. The protocol of [BG20] satisfies information theoretical soundness and zero-knowledge in the *secret parameter (SP) model* [Ps05] where a trusted party generates proving and verification keys and gives them to the corresponding party while keeping it secret to the other party as setup.[1] A drawback of their protocol is that the prover sends a quantum proof to the verifier, and thus the verifier should be quantum. Therefore it is natural to ask the following question.

Can we construct a NIZK proof for **QMA** *with classical verification assuming a trusted party that generates proving and verification keys?*

In addition, the SP model is not a very desirable model since it assumes a strong trust in the setup. In the classical literature, there are constructions of NIZK proofs for **NP** in the common reference string (CRS) model [BFM88, FLS99, PS19] where the only trust in the setup is that a classical string is chosen according to a certain distribution and then published. Compared to the SP model, we need to put much less trust in the setup in the CRS model. Indeed, several works [BG20, CVZ20, Shm21] mention it as an open problem to construct a NIZK proofs (or even arguments) for **QMA** in the CRS model. Though this is still open, there are several constructions of NIZKs for **QMA** in different models that assume less trust in the setup than in the SP model [CVZ20, Shm21, BCKM21]. However, all of them are arguments. Therefore, we ask the following question.

Can we construct a NIZK proof for **QMA** *with classical verification in a model that assumes less trust in the setup than in the SP model?*

The Fiat-Shamir transformation [FS87] is one of the most important techniques in cryptography that have many applications. In particular, NIZK can be constructed from a Σ protocol: the prover generates the verifier's challenge β by itself by applying a random oracle H on the prover's first message α, and then the prover issues the proof $\pi = (\alpha, \gamma)$, where γ is the third message generated from α and $\beta = H(\alpha)$. It is known that Fiat-Shamir transform works in the post-quantum setting where we consider classical protocols secure against quantum adversaries [LZ19, DFMS19, DFM20]. On the other hand, it is often pointed out that (for example, [Shm21, BG20]) this standard technique cannot be used in the fully quantum setting. In particular, due to the no-cloning, the application of random oracle on the first message does not work when the first message is quantum like so-called the Ξ-protocol constructed by Broadbent and Grilo [BG20]. Broadbent and Grilo left the following open problem:

---

[1] The SP model is also often referred to as *preprocessing model* [DMP90].

Is it possible to construct NIZK for **QMA** *in the CRS model (or shared Bell pair model) via the Fiat-Shamir transformation?*

Note that the shared Bell pair model is the setup model where the setup distributes Bell pairs among the prover and the verifier. It can be considered as a "quantum analogue" of the CRS [Kob03].

1.2   Our Results

We answer the above questions affirmatively.

1. We construct a classically verifiable NIZK (CV-NIZK) for **QMA** in the QSP model where a trusted party generates a quantum proving key and classical verification key and gives them to the corresponding parties. We do not rely on any computational assumption for this construction either, and thus both soundness and the zero-knowledge property are satisfied information theoretically. This answers our first question. Compared with [BG20], ours has an advantage that verification is classical at the cost of making the proving key quantum. The proving key is a very simple state, i.e., a tensor product of randomly chosen Pauli X, Y, or Z basis states. We note that we should not let the verifier play the role of the trusted party for this construction since that would break the zero-knowledge property.

2. Assuming the quantum hardness of the learning with errors problem (the LWE assumption) [Reg09], we construct a CV-NIZK for **QMA** in a model where a trusted party generates a CRS and the verifier sends an instance-independent quantum message to the prover as preprocessing. We note that the CRS is reusable for generating multiple proofs but the quantum message in the preprocessing is not reusable. In this model, we only assume a trusted party that just generates a CRS once, and thus this answers our second question. This model is the same as one considered in [CVZ20] recently, and we call it the CRS + $(V \rightarrow P)$ model. Compared to their work, our construction has the following advantages.

   (a) In their protocol, both soundness and the zero-knowledge property hold only against quantum polynomial-time adversaries, and they left it open to achieve either of them information theoretically. We answer the open problem. Indeed, our construction has the so-called dual-mode property [GOS12, PS19], which means that there are two computationally indistinguishable modes of generating CRS, and we have information theoretical soundness in one mode and information theoretical zero-knowledge property in the other. To the best of our knowledge, ours is the first dual-mode NIZK for **QMA** in any kind of model.

   (b) Our protocol uses underlying cryptographic primitives (which are lossy encryption and oblivious transfer with certain security) only in a black-box manner whereas their protocol heavily relies on non-black-box usage of the underlying primitives. Indeed, their protocol uses fully homomorphic encryption to homomorphically runs the proving algorithm of a NIZK for **NP**, which would make the protocol extremely inefficient. On

Table 1. Comparison of NIZKs for **QMA**.

Reference	Soundness	ZK	Ver.	Model	Assumption	Misc
[ACGH20]	comp.	comp.	C	SP	LWE + QRO	
[CVZ20]	comp.	comp.	Q+C	CRS + $(V \to P)$	LWE	AoQK
[BG20]	stat.	stat.	Q	SP	None	
[Shm21]	comp.	comp.	Q	MDV	LWE	Reusable
[BCKM21]	comp.	comp.	Q	MDV	LWE	Reusable and single-witness
[BM21]	comp.	stat.	C	CRS	iO + QRO (heuristic)	
Section 3	stat.	stat.	C	QSP	None	
Section 4	stat. comp.	comp. stat.	Q+C	CRS + $(V \to P)$	LWE	Dual-mode
Section 5	comp. (query)	comp. (query)	C	$V \to P$/Bell pair	QRO	

In column "Soundness" (resp. "ZK"), stat., and comp. mean statistical, and computational soundness (resp. zero-knowledge), respectively. Also, comp.(query) means that only the number of queries should be polynomial. In column "Ver.", "Q" and "C" mean that the verification is quantum and classical, respectively, and "Q+C" means that the verifier needs to send a quantum message in preprocessing but the online phase of verification is classical. QRO means the quantum random oracle.

the other hand, our construction uses the underlying primitives only in a black-box manner, which results in a much more efficient construction. We note that black-box constructions have been considered desirable for both theoretical and practical reasons in the cryptography community (e.g., see introduction of [IKLP06]).

(c) The verifier's quantum operation in our preprocessing is simpler than that in theirs: in the preprocessing of our protocol, the verifier has only to do single-qubit gate operations (Hadamard, bit-flip or phase gates), while in the preprocessing of their protocol, the verifier has to do five-qubit (entangled) Clifford operations. In their paper [CVZ20], they left the following open problem: how far their preprocessing phase could be weakened? Our construction with the weaker verifier therefore partially answers the open problem.

On the other hand, Coladangelo et al. [CVZ20] proved that their protocol is also an *argument of quantum knowledge (AoQK)*. We leave it open to study if ours is also a proof/argument of knowledge.

3. We construct a CV-NIZK for **QMA** with quantum preprocessing in the quantum random oracle model. This quantum preprocessing is the one where the verifier sends a random Pauli-basis states to the prover. Our construction uses the Fiat-Shamir transformation. Importantly, the quantum preprocessing can be replaced with the setup that distributes Bell pairs among the prover and the verifier. The distribution of Bell pairs by the setup can be considered as a "quantum analogue" of the CRS. This result gives an answer to our third question (and the second question as well). (Note that both the soundness and zero-knowledge property of the construction are computational one, but it does not mean that we use some computational assumptions: just the oracle query is restricted to be polynomial time.)

Comparison Among NIZKs for **QMA**. We give more comparisons among our and known constructions of NIZKs for **QMA**. Since we already discuss comparisons with ours and [BG20, CVZ20], we discuss comparisons with other works. A summary of the comparisons is given in Table 1.

Alagic et al. [ACGH20] gave a construction of a NIZK for **QMA** in the SP model. Their protocol has an advantage that both the trusted party and verifier are completely classical. On the other hand, the drawback is that only computational soundness and zero-knowledge are achieved, whereas our first two constructions achieve (at least) either statistical soundness or zero-knowledge. Their protocol also uses the Fiat-Shamir transformation with quantum random oracle like our third result, but their setup is the secret parameter model, whereas ours can be the sharing Bell pair model, which is a quantum analogue of the CRS model.

Shmueli [Shm21] gave a construction of a NIZK for **QMA** in the malicious designated-verifier (MDV) model, where a trusted party generates a CRS and the verifier sends an instance-independent classical message to the prover as preprocessing. In this model, the preprocessing is *reusable*, i.e., a single preprocessing can be reused to generate arbitrarily many proofs later. This is a crucial advantage of their construction compared to ours. On the other hand, in their protocol, proofs are quantum and thus the verifier should perform quantum computations in the online phase whereas the online phase of the verifier is classical in our constructions. Also, their protocol only satisfies computational soundness and zero-knowledge whereas we can achieve (at least) either of them statistically.

Recently, Bartusek et al. [BCKM21] gave another construction of a NIZK for **QMA** in the MDV model that has an advantage that the honest prover only uses a single copy of a witness. (Note that all other NIZKs for **QMA** including ours require the honest prover to take multiple copies of a witness if we require neglible completeness and soundness errors.) However, their construction also requires quantum verifier in the online phase and only achieves computational soundness and zero-knowledge similarly to [Shm21].

Subsequently to our work, Bartusek and Malavolta [BM21] recently constructed the first CV-NIZK argument for **QMA** in the CRS model assuming the LWE assumption and ideal obfuscation for classical circuits. An obvious drawback is the usage of ideal obfuscation, which has no provably secure instantiation.[2] They also construct a witness encryption scheme for **QMA** under the same assumptions. They use the verification protocol of Mahadev [Mah18] and therefore the LWE assumption is necessary. If our CV-NIZK in the QSP model is used, instead, a witness encryption for **QMA** (with quantum ciphertext) would be constructed without the LWE assumption, which is one interesting application of our results.

---

[2] In the latest version, they give a candidate instantiation based on indistinguishability obfuscation and random oracles. However, the instantiation is heuristic since they obfuscate circuits that involve the random oracle, which cannot be done in the quantum random oracle model.

1.3 Technical Overview

Classically Verifiable NIZK for **QMA** *in the QSP Model.* Our starting point is the NIZK for **QMA** in [BG20], which is based on the fact that a **QMA** language can be reduced to the 5-local Hamiltonian problem with *locally simulatable* history states [BG20,GSY19]. (We will explain later the meaning of "locally simulatable".) An instance x corresponds to an N-qubit Hamiltonian $\mathcal{H}_x$ of the form $\mathcal{H}_x = \sum_{i=1}^{M} p_i \frac{I + s_i P_i}{2}$, where $N = \text{poly}(|x|)$, $M = \text{poly}(|x|)$, $s_i \in \{+1, -1\}$, $p_i > 0$, $\sum_{i=1}^{M} p_i = 1$, and P_i is a tensor product of Pauli operators (I, X, Y, Z) with at most 5 nontrivial Pauli operators (X, Y, Z). There are $0 < \alpha < \beta < 1$ with $\beta - \alpha = 1/\text{poly}(|x|)$ such that if x is a yes instance, then there exists a state ρ_{hist} (called the *history state*) such that $\text{Tr}(\rho_{\text{hist}}\mathcal{H}_x) \le \alpha$, and if x is a no instance, then for any state ρ, we have $\text{Tr}(\rho\mathcal{H}_x) \ge \beta$.

The completeness and the soundness of the NIZK for **QMA** in [BG20] is based on the posthoc verification protocol [FHM18], which is explained as follows. To prove that x is a yes instance, the prover sends the history state to the verifier. The verifier first chooses P_i with probability p_i, and measures each qubit in the Pauli basis corresponding to P_i. Let $m_j \in \{0, 1\}$ be the measurement result on jth qubit. The verifier accepts if $(-1)^{\oplus_j m_j} = -s_i$ and rejects otherwise. The probability that the verifier accepts is $1 - \text{Tr}(\rho\mathcal{H}_x)$ when the prover's quantum message is ρ, and therefore the verifier accepts with probability at least $1 - \alpha$ if x is a yes instance and the prover is honest whereas it accepts with probability at most $1 - \beta$ if x is a no instance. (See Lemma 2.3 and [FHM18].) The gap between completeness and soundness can be amplified by simple parallel repetitions.

The verifier in the posthoc protocol is, however, not classical, because it has to receive a quantum state and measure each qubit. Our first idea to make the verifier classical is to use the quantum teleportation. Suppose that the prover and verifier share sufficiently many Bell pairs at the beginning. Then the prover can send the history state to the verifier with classical communication by the quantum teleportation. Though this removes the necessity of quantum communication, the verifier still needs to be quantum since it has to keep halves of Bell pairs and perform a measurement after receiving a proof.

To solve the problem, we utilize our observation that the verifier's measurement and the prover's measurement commute with each other, which is our second idea. In other words, we can let the verifier perform the measurement at the beginning without losing completeness or soundness. In the above quantum-teleportation-based protocol, when the prover sends its measurement outcomes $\{(x_j, z_j)\}_{j \in [N]}$ to the verifier, the verifier's state collapses to $X^x Z^z \rho_{\text{hist}} Z^z X^x$ where ρ_{hist} denotes the history state and $X^x Z^z$ means $\prod_{j=1}^{N} X_j^{x_j} Z_j^{z_j}$. Then the verifier applies the Pauli correction $X^x Z^z$ and then measures each qubit in a Pauli basis. We observe that the Pauli correction can be applied even after the verifier measures each qubit because $X_j^{x_j} Z_j^{z_j}$ before a Pauli measurement on the jth qubit has the same effect as XOR by z_j or x_j after the measurement (see Lemma 2.2). Therefore, if a trusted party generates Bell pairs and measures half of them in random Pauli basis and gives the unmeasured halves to the prover as a proving key while the measurement outcomes to the verifier as a verification key, a completely classical verifier can verify the **QMA** promise problem.

The last remaining issue is that the distribution of bases that appear in P_i depends on the instance x, and thus we cannot sample the distribution at the setup phase where x is not decided yet. To resolve this issue, we use the following idea (which was also used in [ACGH20]). The trusted party just chooses random bases, and the verifier just accepts if they are inconsistent to P_i chosen by the verifier in the online phase. Since there are only 3 possible choices of the bases and P_i non-trivially acts on at most 5 qubits, the probability that the randomly chosen bases are consistent to P_i is at least 3^{-5}.[3] Therefore we can still achieve inverse-polynomial gap between completeness and soundness.

The zero-knowledge property of the NIZK for **QMA** in [BG20] uses the local simulatability of the history state. It roughly means that a classical description of the reduced density matrix of the history state for any 5-qubit subsystem can be efficiently computable without knowing the witness. Broadbent and Grilo [BG20] used this local simulatability to achieve the zero-knowledge property as follows. A trusted party randomly chooses $(\widehat{x}, \widehat{z}) \xleftarrow{\$} \{0,1\}^N \times \{0,1\}^N$, and randomly picks a random subset $S_V \subseteq [N]$ such that $1 \leq |S_V| \leq 5$. Then it gives $(\widehat{x}, \widehat{z})$ to the prover as a proving key and gives $\{(\widehat{x}_j, \widehat{z}_j)\}_{j \in S_V}$ to the verifier as a verification key where $\widehat{x}_j$ and $\widehat{z}_j$ denote the j-th bits of $\widehat{x}$ and $\widehat{z}$, respectively. The prover generates the history state ρ_{hist} and sends $\rho' = X^{\widehat{x}} Z^{\widehat{z}} \rho_{\text{hist}} Z^{\widehat{z}} X^{\widehat{x}}$ to the verifier as a proof. The verifier then measures each qubit as is done in the posthoc verification protocol. This needs the quantum verifier, but as we have explained, we can make the verifier classical by using the teleportation technique.

An intuitive explanation of why it is zero-knowledge is that the verifier can access at most five qubits of the history state, because other qubits are quantum one-time padded. Due to the local simulatability of the history state, the information that the verifier gets can be classically simulated without the witness. This results in our classically verifiable NIZK for **QMA** in the QSP model. In our QSP model, the trusted setup sends random Pauli basis states to the prover and their classical description to the verifier. Furthermore, the trusted setup also sends randomly chosen $(\widehat{x}, \widehat{z}) \xleftarrow{\$} \{0,1\}^N \times \{0,1\}^N$ to the prover, and $\{(\widehat{x}_j, \widehat{z}_j)\}_{j \in S_V}$ to the verifier with randomly chosen subset S_V.

Classically Verifiable NIZK for QMA in the CRS $+ (V \to P)$ *Model.* We want to reduce the trust in the setup, so let us first examine what happens if the verifier runs the setup as preprocessing. Unfortunately, such a construction is not zero-knowledge since the verifier can know whole bits of $(\widehat{x}, \widehat{z})$ and thus it may obtain information of qubits of ρ_{hist} that are outside of S_V, in which case we cannot rely on the local simulatability. Therefore, for ensuring the zero-knowledge property, we have to make sure that the verifier only knows $\{(\widehat{x}_j, \widehat{z}_j)\}_{j \in S_V}$. Then suppose that the prover chooses $(\widehat{x}, \widehat{z})$ whereas other setups are still done by the verifier. Here, the problem is how to let the verifier know $\{(\widehat{x}_j, \widehat{z}_j)\}_{j \in S_V}$. A naive

---

[3] There is a subtle issue that the probability depends on the number of qubits on which P_i non-trivially acts. We adjust this by an additional biased coin flipping.

solution is that the verifier sends S_V to the prover and then the prover returns $\{(\widehat{x}_j, \widehat{z}_j)\}_{j \in S_V}$. However, such a construction is not sound since it is essential that the prover "commits" to a single quantum state independently of S_V when reducing soundness to the local Hamiltonian problem. So what we need is a protocol between the prover and verifier where the verifier only gets $\{(\widehat{x}_j, \widehat{z}_j)\}_{j \in S_V}$ and the prover does not learn S_V. We observe that this is exactly the functionality of 5-*out-of-N oblivious transfer* [BCR87].

Though it may sound easy to solve the problem by just using a known two-round 5-out-of-N oblivious transfer, there is still some subtlety. For example, if we use an oblivious transfer that satisfies only indistinguishability-based notion of receiver's security (e.g., [NP01,BD18]),[4] which just says that the sender cannot know indices chosen by the receiver, we cannot prove soundness. Intuitively, this is because the indistinguishability-based receiver's security does not prevent a malicious sender from generating a malicious message such that the message derived on the receiver's side depends on the chosen indices, which does not force the prover to "commit" to a single state.

If we use a *fully-simulatable* [Lin08] oblivious transfer, the above problem does not arise and we can prove both soundness and zero-knowledge. However, the problem is that we are not aware of any efficient fully-simulatable 5-out-of-N oblivious transfer based on post-quantum assumptions (in the CRS model). The LWE-based construction of [PVW08] does not suffice for our purpose since a CRS can be reused only a bounded number of times in their construction. Recently, Quach [Qua20] resolved this issue, and proposed an efficient fully-simulatable 1-out-of-2 oblivious transfer based on the LWE assumption.[5] We can extend his construction to a fully-simulatable 1-out-of-N oblivious transfer efficiently. However, we do not know how to convert this into 5-out-of-N one efficiently without losing the full-simulatability. We note that a conversion from 1-out-of-N to 5-out-of-N oblivious transfer by a simple 5-parallel repetition loses the full-simulatability against malicious senders since a malicious sender can send different inconsistent messages in different sessions, which should be considered as an attack against the full-simulatability. One possible way to prevent such an inconsistent message attack is to let the sender prove that the messages in all sessions are consistent by using (post-quantum) CRS-NIZK for **NP** [PS19]. However, such a construction is very inefficient since it uses the underlying 1-out-of-N oblivious transfer in a non-black-box manner, which we want to avoid.

We note that the parallel repetition construction preserves indistinguishability-based receiver's security and fully-simulatable sender's security for two-round protocols. Therefore, we have an efficient (black-box) construction of 5-out-of-N oblivious transfer if we relax the receiver's security to the indistinguishability-based one. As already explained, such a security does not suffice for proving soundness. To resolve this issue, we add an additional mechanism to force the prover to "commit" to a single state. Specifically, instead of

---

[4] The indistinguishability-based receiver's security is also often referred to as half-simulation security [CNs07].

[5] Actually, his construction satisfies a stronger UC-security [Can20,PVW08].

directly sending (x, z) by a 5-out-of-N oblivious transfer, the prover sends a commitment of (x, z) and then sends (x, z) and the corresponding randomness used in the commitment by a 5-out-of-N oblivious transfer. When the verifier receives $\{x_j, z_j\}_{j \in S_V}$ and corresponding randomness, it checks if it is consistent to the commitment by recomputing it, and immediately rejects if not. This additional mechanism prevents a malicious prover's inconsistent behavior, which resolves the problem in the proof of soundness.

Finally, our construction satisfies the dual-mode property if we assume appropriate dual-mode properties for building blocks. A dual-mode oblivious transfer (in the CRS model) has two modes of generating a CRS and it satisfies statistical (indistinguishability-based) receiver's security in one mode and statistical (full-simulation-based) sender's security in the other mode. The construction of [Qua20] is an instantiation of a 1-out-of-2 oblivious transfer with such a dual-mode property, and this can be converted into 5-out-of-N one as explained above. We stress again that it is important to relax the receiver's security to the indistinguishability-based one to make the conversion work. A dual-mode commitment (in the CRS model) has two modes of generating a CRS and it is statistically binding in one mode and statistically hiding in the other mode. We can use lossy encryption [BHY09, Reg09] as an instantiation of such a dual-mode commitment. Both of dual-mode 5-out-of-N oblivious transfer and lossy encryption are based on the LWE assumption (with super-polynomial modulus for the former) and fairly efficient in the sense that they do not rely on non-black-box techniques. Putting everything together, we obtain a fairly efficient (black-box) construction of a dual-mode NIZK for **QMA** in the CRS + $(V \to P)$ model.

NIZK for **QMA** *via Fiat-Shamir Transformation.* Finally, let us explain our construction of NIZK for **QMA** via the Fiat-Shamir transformation. It is based on so-called the Ξ-protocol for **QMA** [BG20], which is equal to the standard Σ-protocol except that the first message is quantum. Because the first message is quantum, the Fiat-Shamir technique cannot be directly applied. Our idea is again to use the teleportation technique: if we introduce a setup that sends random Pauli basis states to the prover and their classical description to the verifier, the first message can be classical. We thus obtain a (classical) Σ-protocol in the QSP model, where the trusted setup sends random Pauli basis states to the prover and their classical description to the verifier. This task can be, actually, done by the verifier, not the trusted setup, unlike our first construction. We therefore obtain a (classical) Σ-protocol with quantum preprocessing (Definition 5.2), where the verifier sends random Pauli basis states to the prover as the preprocessing.

We then apply the (classical) Fiat-Shamir transformation to the Σ-protocol with quantum preprocessing, and obtain the CV-NIZK for **QMA** in the quantum random oracle plus $V \to P$ model (Definition 5.1), where $V \to P$ means the communication from the verifier to the prover as the preprocessing. Note that we are considering a classical Σ-protocol with quantum preprocessing differently from previous works. By a close inspection, we show that an existing security proof for classical Σ-protocol in the QROM [DFM20] also works in our setting.

Importantly, in this case, unlike the previous two constructions, the quantum preprocessing can be replaced with the setup that distributes Bell pairs among the prover and the verifier. As a corollary, we therefore obtain NIZK for **QMA** in the shared Bell pair model (plus quantum random oracle). The distribution of Bell pairs by a trusted setup can be considered as a "quantum analogue" of the CRS, and therefore we can say that we obtain NIZK for **QMA** in the "quantum CRS" model via the Fiat-Sharmir transformation.

2   Preliminaries

2.1   Quantum Computation Preliminaries

Here, we briefly review basic notations and facts on quantum computations.

For any quantum state ρ over registers $\mathbf{A}$ and $\mathbf{B}$, $\mathrm{Tr}_{\mathbf{A}}(\rho)$ is the partial trace of ρ over $\mathbf{A}$. We use I to mean the identity operator. (For simplicity, we use the same I for all identity operators with different dimensions, because the dimension of an identity operator is clear from the context.) We use X, Y, and Z to mean Pauli operators i.e., $X := \begin{pmatrix} 0 & 1 \\ 1 & 0 \end{pmatrix}$, $Z := \begin{pmatrix} 1 & 0 \\ 0 & -1 \end{pmatrix}$, and $Y := iXZ$. We use H to mean Hadamard operator, i.e., $H := \frac{1}{\sqrt{2}} \begin{pmatrix} 1 & 1 \\ 1 & -1 \end{pmatrix}$. We also define the T operator by $T := \begin{pmatrix} 1 & 0 \\ 0 & e^{i\pi/4} \end{pmatrix}$. The $CNOT := |0\rangle\langle 0| \otimes I + |1\rangle\langle 1| \otimes X$ is the controlled-NOT operator.

We define $V(Z) := I$, $V(X) := H$, and $V(Y) := \frac{1}{\sqrt{2}} \begin{pmatrix} 1 & 1 \\ i & -i \end{pmatrix}$ so that for each $W \in \{X, Y, Z\}$, $V(W)|0\rangle$ and $V(W)|1\rangle$ are the eigenvectors of W with eigenvalues $+1$ and -1, respectively. For each $W \in \{X, Y, Z\}$, we call $\{V(W)|0\rangle, V(W)|1\rangle\}$ the W-basis.

When we consider an N-qubit system, for a Pauli operator $Q \in \{X, Y, Z\}$, Q_j denotes the operator that acts on j-th qubit as Q and trivially acts on all the other qubits. Similarly, $V_j(W)$ denotes the operator that acts on j-th qubit as $V(W)$ and trivially acts on all the other qubits. For any $x \in \{0,1\}^N$ and $z \in \{0,1\}^N$, $X^x Z^z$ means $\prod_{j=1}^{N} X_j^{x_j} Z_j^{z_j}$.

We call the state $\frac{1}{\sqrt{2}} (|0\rangle \otimes |0\rangle + |1\rangle \otimes |1\rangle)$ the Bell pair. We call the set $\{|\phi_{x,z}\rangle\}_{(x,z)\in\{0,1\}^2}$ the Bell basis where $|\phi_{x,z}\rangle := (X^x Z^z \otimes I) \frac{|0\rangle\otimes|0\rangle+|1\rangle\otimes|1\rangle}{\sqrt{2}}$. Let us define $U(X) := V(X)$, $U(Y) := V(Y)X$, and $U(Z) := V(Z)$.

Lemma 2.1. (State Collapsing). *If we project one qubit of a Bell pair onto $V(W)|m\rangle$ with $W \in \{X, Y, Z\}$ and $m \in \{0,1\}$, the other qubit collapses to $U(W)|m\rangle$.*

Lemma 2.2. (Effect of $X^x Z^z$ before measurement). *For any N-qubit state ρ, $(W_1, ..., W_N) \in \{X, Y, Z\}^N$, and $(x, z) \in \{0,1\}^N \times \{0,1\}^N$, the distributions of $(m'_1, ... m'_n)$ sampled in the following two ways are identical.*

1. For $j \in [N]$, measure j-th qubit of ρ in W_j basis, let $m_j \in \{0,1\}$ be the outcome, and set

$$m'_j := \begin{cases} m_j \oplus x_j & (W_j = Z), \\ m_j \oplus z_j & (W_j = X), \\ m_j \oplus x_j \oplus z_j & (W_j = Y). \end{cases}$$

2. For $j \in [N]$, measure j-th qubit of $X^x Z^z \rho Z^z X^x$ in W_j basis and let $m'_j \in \{0,1\}$ be the outcome.

The proofs of the above lemmas are straightforward. The following lemma is implicit in previous works, e.g., [MNS18, FHM18].

Lemma 2.3. Let $\mathcal{H} := \frac{1}{2} \left[I + s(\prod_{j \in S_X} X_j)(\prod_{j \in S_Y} Y_j)(\prod_{j \in S_Z} Z_j) \right]$ be an N-qubit projection operator, where $s \in \{+1, -1\}$, and S_X, S_Y, and S_Z are disjoint subsets of $[N]$. For any N-qubit quantum state ρ, suppose that for all $j \in S_W$, where $W \in \{X, Y, Z\}$, we measure j-th qubit of ρ in the W-basis, and let $m_j \in \{0,1\}$ be the outcome. Then we have $\Pr \left[(-1)^{\bigoplus_{j \in S_X \cup S_Y \cup S_Z} m_j} = -s \right] = 1 - \mathrm{Tr}(\rho \mathcal{H})$.

2.2   QMA and Local Hamiltonian Problem

For any **QMA** promise problem $L = (L_{\mathsf{yes}}, L_{\mathsf{no}})$ and $\mathbf{x} \in L_{\mathsf{yes}}$, we denote by $R_L(\mathbf{x})$ to mean the (possibly infinite) set of all quantum states $\mathbf{w}$ such that $\Pr[V(\mathbf{x}, \mathbf{w}) = 1] \geq 2/3$.

Recently, Broadbent and Grilo [BG20] showed that any **QMA** problem can be reduced to a 5-local Hamiltonian problem with *local simulatability*. (See also [GSY19].) Moreover, it is easy to see that we can make the Hamiltonian $\mathcal{H}_{\mathbf{x}}$ be of the form $\mathcal{H}_{\mathbf{x}} = \sum_{i=1}^{M} p_i \frac{I + s_i P_i}{2}$ where $s_i \in \{+1, -1\}$, $p_i \geq 0$, $\sum_{i=1}^{M} p_i = 1$, and P_i is a tensor product of Pauli operators (I, X, Z, Y) with at most 5 nontrivial Pauli operators (X, Y, Z). Then we have the following lemma.

Lemma 2.4. (QMA-completeness of 5-local Hamiltonian problem with local simulatability [BG20]). *For any* **QMA** *promise problem* $L = (L_{\mathsf{yes}}, L_{\mathsf{no}})$, *there is a classical polynomial-time computable deterministic function that maps* $\mathbf{x} \in \{0,1\}^*$ *to an N-qubit Hamiltonian $\mathcal{H}_{\mathbf{x}}$ of the form* $\mathcal{H}_{\mathbf{x}} = \sum_{i=1}^{M} p_i \frac{I + s_i P_i}{2}$, *where $N = \mathsf{poly}(|\mathbf{x}|)$, $M = \mathsf{poly}(|\mathbf{x}|)$, $s_i \in \{+1, -1\}$, $p_i > 0$, $\sum_{i=1}^{M} p_i = 1$, and P_i is a tensor product of Pauli operators (I, X, Z, Y) with at most 5 nontrivial Pauli operators (X, Y, Z), and satisfies the following: There are $0 < \alpha < \beta < 1$ such that $\beta - \alpha = 1/\mathsf{poly}(|\mathbf{x}|)$ and*

- *if $\mathbf{x} \in L_{\mathsf{yes}}$, then there exists an N-qubit state ρ such that $\mathrm{Tr}(\rho \mathcal{H}_{\mathbf{x}}) \leq \alpha$, and*
- *if $\mathbf{x} \in L_{\mathsf{no}}$, then for any N-qubit state ρ, we have $\mathrm{Tr}(\rho \mathcal{H}_{\mathbf{x}}) \geq \beta$.*

Moreover, for any $\mathbf{x} \in L_{\mathsf{yes}}$, we can convert any witness $\mathbf{w} \in R_L(\mathbf{x})$ into a state ρ_{hist}, called the history state, such that $\mathrm{Tr}(\rho_{\mathsf{hist}} \mathcal{H}_{\mathbf{x}}) \leq \alpha$ in quantum polynomial time. Moreover, there exists a classical deterministic polynomial time algorithm $\mathsf{Sim}_{\mathsf{hist}}$ *such that for any $\mathbf{x} \in L_{\mathsf{yes}}$ and any subset $S \subseteq [N]$ with $|S| \leq 5$,*

$\mathsf{Sim}_{\mathsf{hist}}(\mathbf{x}, S)$ *outputs a classical description of an* $|S|$-*qubit density matrix* ρ_S *such that* $\|\rho_S - \mathrm{Tr}_{[N]\backslash S}\rho_{\mathsf{hist}}\|_{tr} = \mathsf{negl}(\lambda)$ *where* $\mathrm{Tr}_{[N]\backslash S}\rho_{\mathsf{hist}}$ *is the state of* ρ_{hist} *in registers corresponding to* S *tracing out all other registers.*

2.3 Classically-Verifiable Non-interactive Zero-Knowledge Proofs

Definition 2.1. (CV-NIZK in the QSP model). *A classically-verifiable non-interactive zero-knowledge proof (CV-NIZK) for a* **QMA** *promise problem* $L = (L_{\mathsf{yes}}, L_{\mathsf{no}})$ *in the quantum secret parameter (QSP) model consists of algorithms* $\Pi = (\mathsf{Setup}, \mathsf{Prove}, \mathsf{Verify})$ *with the following syntax:*

$\mathsf{Setup}(1^\lambda)$: *This is a QPT algorithm that takes the security parameter* 1^λ *as input and outputs a quantum proving key* k_P *and a classical verification key* k_V.

$\mathsf{Prove}(k_P, \mathbf{x}, \mathbf{w}^{\otimes k})$: *This is a QPT algorithm that takes the proving key* k_P, *a statement* $\mathbf{x}$, *and* $k = \mathsf{poly}(\lambda)$ *copies* $\mathbf{w}^{\otimes k}$ *of a witness* $\mathbf{w} \in R_L(\mathbf{x})$ *as input and outputs a classical proof* π.

$\mathsf{Verify}(k_V, \mathbf{x}, \pi)$: *This is a PPT algorithm that takes the verification key* k_V, *a statement* $\mathbf{x}$, *and a proof* π *as input and outputs* $\top$ *indicating acceptance or* $\bot$ *indicating rejection.*

We require Π *to satisfy the following properties for some* $0 < s < c < 1$ *such that* $c - s > 1/\mathsf{poly}(\lambda)$. *Especially, when we do not specify* c *and* s, *they are set as* $c = 1 - \mathsf{negl}(\lambda)$ *and* $s = \mathsf{negl}(\lambda)$.

*c-**Completeness.** For all* $\mathbf{x} \in L_{\mathsf{yes}} \cap \{0,1\}^\lambda$, *and* $\mathbf{w} \in R_L(\mathbf{x})$, *we have*

$$\Pr\left[\mathsf{Verify}(k_V, \mathbf{x}, \pi) = \top : (k_P, k_V) \xleftarrow{\$} \mathsf{Setup}(1^\lambda), \pi \xleftarrow{\$} \mathsf{Prove}(k_P, \mathbf{x}, \mathbf{w}^{\otimes k})\right] \geq c.$$

*(**Adaptive Statistical**) s-**Soundness.** For all unbounded-time adversary* $\mathcal{A}$, *we have*

$$\Pr\left[\mathbf{x} \in L_{\mathsf{no}} \wedge \mathsf{Verify}(k_V, \mathbf{x}, \pi) = \top : (k_P, k_V) \xleftarrow{\$} \mathsf{Setup}(1^\lambda), (\mathbf{x}, \pi) \xleftarrow{\$} \mathcal{A}(k_P)\right] \leq s.$$

*(**Adaptive Statistical Single-Theorem**) Zero-Knowledge. There exists a PPT simulator* Sim *such that for any unbounded-time distinguisher* $\mathcal{D}$, *we have*

$$\left|\Pr\left[\mathcal{D}^{\mathcal{O}_P(k_P, \cdot, \cdot)}(k_V) = 1\right] - \Pr\left[\mathcal{D}^{\mathcal{O}_S(k_V, \cdot, \cdot)}(k_V) = 1\right]\right| = \mathsf{negl}(\lambda)$$

where $(k_P, k_V) \xleftarrow{\$} \mathsf{Setup}(1^\lambda)$, $\mathcal{D}$ *can make at most one query, which should be of the form* $(\mathbf{x}, \mathbf{w}^{\otimes k})$ *where* $\mathbf{w} \in R_L(\mathbf{x})$ *and* $\mathbf{w}^{\otimes k}$ *is unentangled with* $\mathcal{D}$'s *internal registers,*[6] $\mathcal{O}_P(k_P, \mathbf{x}, \mathbf{w}^{\otimes k})$ *returns* $\mathsf{Prove}(k_P, \mathbf{x}, \mathbf{w}^{\otimes k})$, *and* $\mathcal{O}_S(k_V, \mathbf{x}, \mathbf{w}^{\otimes k})$ *returns* $\mathsf{Sim}(k_V, \mathbf{x})$.

---

[6] Though our protocols are likely to remain secure even if they can be entangled, we assume that they are unentangled for simplicity. To the best of our knowledge, none of existing works on interactive or non-interactive zero-knowledge for **QMA** [BJSW20,CVZ20,BS20,BG20,Shm21,BCKM21] considered entanglement between a witness and distinguisher's internal register.

It is easy to see that we can amplify the gap between completeness and soundness thresholds by a simple parallel repetition. Moreover, we can see that this does not lose the zero-knowledge property. Therefore, we have the following lemma.

Lemma 2.5. (Gap Amplification for CV-NIZK). *If there exists a CV-NIZK for L in the QSP model that satisfies c-completeness and s-soundness, for some $0 < s < c < 1$ such that $c - s > 1/\mathsf{poly}(\lambda)$, then there exists a CV-NIZK for L in the QSP model (with $(1 - \mathsf{negl}(\lambda))$-completeness and $\mathsf{negl}(\lambda)$-soundness).*

3   CV-NIZK in the QSP Model

In this section, we construct a CV-NIZK in the QSP model (Definition 2.1). Specifically, we prove the following theorem.

Theorem 3.1. *There exists a CV-NIZK for* **QMA** *in the QSP model (without any computational assumption).*

Our construction of a CV-NIZK for a **QMA** promise problem L is given in Fig. 1 where $\mathcal{H}_\mathsf{x}$, N, M, p_i, s_i, P_i, α, β, and ρ_hist are as in Lemma 2.4 for L and $V_j(W_j)$ is as defined in Sect. 2.1.

To show Theroem 3.1, we prove the following lemmas.

Lemma 3.1. (Completeness and Soundness). Π_NIZK *satisfies* $\left(1 - \frac{\alpha}{N'}\right)$-*completeness and* $\left(1 - \frac{\beta}{N'}\right)$-*soundness where* $N' := 3^5 \sum_{i=1}^5 \binom{N}{i}$.

Lemma 3.2. (Zero-Knowledge). Π_NIZK *satisfies the zero-knowledge property.*

Since $\left(1 - \frac{\alpha}{N'}\right) - \left(1 - \frac{\beta}{N'}\right) = \frac{\beta - \alpha}{N'} \geq 1/\mathsf{poly}(\lambda)$, by combining Lemmas 2.5, 3.1 and 3.2 and Theorem 3.1 follows.

In the following, we give proofs of Lemmas 3.1 and 3.2.

Proof. of Lemma 3.1. We prove this lemma by considering virtual protocols that do not change completeness and soundness. First, we consider the virtual protocol 1 described in Fig. 2. There are two differences from the original protocol. The first is that k_V includes the whole $(\widehat{x}, \widehat{z})$ instead of $\{\widehat{x}_j, \widehat{z}_j\}_{j \in S_V}$. This difference does not change the (possibly malicious) prover's view since k_V is not given to the prover. The second is that the setup algorithm generates N Bell pairs and gives each halves to the prover and verifier, and the verifier obtains $(m_1, ..., m_N)$ by measuring his halves in Pauli basis. Because the verifier's measurement and the prover's measurement commute with each other, in the virtual protocol 1, the verifier's acceptance probability does not change even if the verifier chooses $(W_1, ..., W_N)$ and measures ρ_V in the corresponding basis to obtain outcomes $(m_1, ..., m_N)$ before ρ_P is given to the prover. Moreover, conditioned on the above measurement outcomes, the state in **P** collapses to $\bigotimes_{j=1}^N (U(W_j)|m_j\rangle)$ (See Lemma 2.1). Therefore, the virtual protocol 1 is exactly the same as the

Setup(1^λ): The setup algorithm chooses $(W_1, ..., W_N) \xleftarrow{\$} \{X, Y, Z\}^N$, $(m_1, ..., m_N) \xleftarrow{\$}$ $\{0,1\}^N$, $(\widehat{x}, \widehat{z}) \xleftarrow{\$} \{0,1\}^N \times \{0,1\}^N$, and a uniformly random subset $S_V \subseteq [N]$ such that $1 \leq |S_V| \leq 5$, and outputs a proving key $k_P := \left(\rho_P := \bigotimes_{j=1}^N (U(W_j)|m_j\rangle), \widehat{x}, \widehat{z}\right)$ and a verification key $k_V :=$ $(W_1, ..., W_N, m_1, ..., m_N, S_V, \{\widehat{x}_j, \widehat{z}_j\}_{j \in S_V})$.

Prove($k_P, \mathbf{x}, \mathbf{w}$): The proving algorithm parses $(\rho_P, \widehat{x}, \widehat{z}) \leftarrow k_P$, generates the history state ρ_{hist} for $\mathcal{H}_{\mathbf{x}}$ from $\mathbf{w}$, and computes $\rho'_{\text{hist}} := X^{\widehat{x}} Z^{\widehat{z}} \rho_{\text{hist}} Z^{\widehat{z}} X^{\widehat{x}}$. It measures j-th qubits of ρ'_{hist} and ρ_P in the Bell basis for $j \in [N]$. Let $x := x_1 \| x_2 \| ... \| x_N$, and $z := z_1 \| z_2 \| ... \| z_N$ where $(x_j, z_j) \in \{0,1\}^2$ denotes the outcome of j-th measurement. It outputs a proof $\pi := (x, z)$.

Verify($k_V, \mathbf{x}, \pi$): The verification algorithm parses $(W_1, ..., W_N, m_1, ..., m_N, S_V, \{\widehat{x}_j, \widehat{z}_j\}_{j \in S_V}) \leftarrow k_V$ and $(x, z) \leftarrow \pi$, chooses $i \in [M]$ according to the probability distribution defined by $\{p_i\}_{i \in [M]}$ (i.e., chooses i with probability p_i). Let

$$S_i := \{j \in [N] \mid j\text{th Pauli operator of } P_i \text{ is not } I\}.$$

We note that we have $1 \leq |S_i| \leq 5$ by the 5-locality of $\mathcal{H}_{\mathbf{x}}$. We say that P_i is consistent to $(S_V, \{W_j\}_{j \in S_V})$ if and only if $S_i = S_V$ and the jth Pauli operator of P_i is W_j for all $j \in S_i$. If P_i is not consistent to $(S_V, \{W_j\}_{j \in S_V})$, it outputs $\top$. If P_i is consistent to $(S_V, \{W_j\}_{j \in S_V})$, it flips a biased coin that heads with probability $1 - 3^{|S_i|-5}$. If heads, it outputs $\top$. If tails, it defines

$$m'_j := \begin{cases} m_j \oplus x_j \oplus \widehat{x}_j & (W_j = Z), \\ m_j \oplus z_j \oplus \widehat{z}_j & (W_j = X), \\ m_j \oplus x_j \oplus \widehat{x}_j \oplus z_j \oplus \widehat{z}_j & (W_j = Y) \end{cases}$$

for $j \in S_i$, and outputs $\top$ if $(-1)^{\oplus_{j \in S_i} m'_j} = -s_i$ and $\bot$ otherwise.

Fig. 1. CV-NIZK Π_{NIZK} in the QSP model.

original protocol from the prover's view, and the verifier's acceptance probability of the virtual protocol 1 is the same as that of the original protocol Π_{NIZK} for any possibly malicious prover.

Next, we further modify the protocol to define the virtual protocol 2 described in Fig. 3. The difference from the virtual protocol 1 is that instead of setting m'_j, the verification algorithm applies a corresponding Pauli $X^{x \oplus \widehat{x}} Z^{z \oplus \widehat{z}}$ on ρ_V, and then measures it to obtain m'_j. By Lemma 2.2, this does not change the distribution of $(m'_1, ..., m'_N)$. Therefore, the verifier's acceptance probability of the virtual protocol 2 is the same as that of the virtual protocol 1 for any possibly malicious prover.

Therefore, it suffices to prove $(1 - \frac{\alpha}{N'})$-completeness and $(1 - \frac{\beta}{N'})$-soundness for the virtual protocol 2. When $\mathbf{x} \in L_{\text{yes}}$ and π is honestly generated, then ρ'_V is the history state ρ_{hist}, which satisfies $\text{Tr}(\rho_{\text{hist}} \mathcal{H}_{\mathbf{x}}) \leq \alpha$, by the correctness of quantum teleportation. For any fixed P_i, the probability that P_i is consistent to

Setup$_{\text{vir-1}}(1^\lambda)$: The setup algorithm generates N Bell-pairs between registers **P** and **V** and lets ρ_P and ρ_V be quantum states in registers **P** and **V**, respectively. It chooses $(\widehat{x}, \widehat{z}) \xleftarrow{\$} \{0,1\}^N \times \{0,1\}^N$. It chooses a uniformly random subset $S_V \subseteq [N]$ such that $1 \leq |S_V| \leq 5$, and outputs a proving key $k_P := (\rho_P, \widehat{x}, \widehat{z})$ and a verification key $k_V := (\rho_V, S_V, \widehat{x}, \widehat{z})$.

Prove$_{\text{vir-1}}(k_P, \mathbf{x}, \mathbf{w})$: This is the same as Prove$(k_P, \mathbf{x}, \mathbf{w})$ in Figure 1.

Verify$_{\text{vir-1}}(k_V, \mathbf{x}, \pi)$: The verification algorithm chooses $(W_1, ..., W_N) \xleftarrow{\$} \{X, Y, Z\}^N$, and measures j-th qubit of ρ_V in the W_j basis for all $j \in [N]$, and lets $(m_1, ..., m_N)$ be the measurement outcomes. The rest of this algorithm is the same as Verify$(k_V, \mathbf{x}, \pi)$ given in Figure 1.

Fig. 2. The virtual protocol 1 for Π_{NIZK}

Setup$_{\text{vir-2}}(1^\lambda)$: This is the same as Setup$_{\text{vir-1}}(1^\lambda)$ in Figure 2.

Prove$_{\text{vir-2}}(k_P, \mathbf{x}, \mathbf{w})$: This is the same as Prove$(k_P, \mathbf{x}, \mathbf{w})$ in Figure 1.

Verify$_{\text{vir-2}}(k_V, \mathbf{x}, \pi)$: The verification algorithm parses $(\rho_V, S_V, \widehat{x}, \widehat{z}) \leftarrow k_V$ and $(x, z) \leftarrow \pi$, computes $\rho'_V := X^{x \oplus \widehat{x}} Z^{z \oplus \widehat{z}} \rho_V Z^{z \oplus \widehat{z}} X^{x \oplus \widehat{x}}$, chooses $(W_1, ..., W_N) \xleftarrow{\$} \{X, Y, Z\}^N$, measures j-th qubit of ρ'_V in the W_j basis for all $j \in [N]$, and lets $(m'_1, ..., m'_N)$ be the measurement outcomes.

It chooses $i \in [M]$ and defines $S_i \subseteq [N]$ similarly to Verify$(k_V, \mathbf{x}, \pi)$ in Figure 1. If P_i is not consistent to $(S_V, \{W_j\}_{j \in S_V})$, it outputs $\top$. If P_i is consistent to $(S_V, \{W_j\}_{j \in S_V})$, it flips a biased coin that heads with probability $1 - 3^{|S_i| - 5}$. If heads, it outputs $\top$. If tails, it outputs $\top$ if $(-1)^{\oplus_{j \in S_i} m'_j} = -s_i$ and $\bot$ otherwise.

Fig. 3. The virtual protocol 2 for Π_{NIZK}

$(S_V, \{W_j\}_{j \in S_V})$ and the coin tails is $\frac{1}{N'}$. Therefore, by Lemma 2.3 and Lemma 2.4, the verifier's acceptance probability is $1 - \frac{1}{N'}\text{Tr}(\rho_{\text{hist}}\mathcal{H}_{\mathbf{x}}) \geq 1 - \frac{\alpha}{N'}$.

Let $\mathcal{A}$ be an adaptive adversary against soundness of virtual protocol 2. That is, $\mathcal{A}$ is given k_P and outputs $(\mathbf{x}, \pi)$. We say that $\mathcal{A}$ wins if $\mathbf{x} \in L_{\text{no}}$ and Verify$(k_V, \mathbf{x}, \pi) = \top$. For any $\mathbf{x}$, let $\mathsf{E}_{\mathbf{x}}$ be the event that the statement output by $\mathcal{A}$ is $\mathbf{x}$, and $\rho'_{V,\mathbf{x}}$ be the state in **V** right before the measurement by Verify conditioned on $\mathsf{E}_{\mathbf{x}}$. Similarly to the analysis for the completeness, by Lemma 2.3 and Lemma 2.4, we have

$$\Pr[\mathcal{A} \text{ wins}] = \sum_{\mathbf{x} \in L_{\text{no}}} \Pr[\mathsf{E}_{\mathbf{x}}] \left(1 - \frac{1}{N'}\text{Tr}(\rho'_{V,\mathbf{x}}\mathcal{H}_{\mathbf{x}})\right) \leq \sum_{\mathbf{x} \in L_{\text{no}}} \Pr[\mathsf{E}_{\mathbf{x}}] \left(1 - \frac{\beta}{N'}\right) \leq 1 - \frac{\beta}{N'}.$$

Proof. of Theorem 3.2. We describe the simulator Sim below.

Sim$(k_V, \mathbf{x})$: The simulator parses $(W_1, ..., W_N, m_1, ..., m_N, S_V, \{\widehat{x}_j, \widehat{z}_j\}_{j \in S_V}) \leftarrow k_V$ and does the following.

1. Generate the classical description of the density matrix $\rho_{S_V} := \mathsf{Sim}_{\mathrm{hist}}(\mathbf{x}, S_V)$ where $\mathsf{Sim}_{\mathrm{hist}}$ is as in Lemma 2.4.
2. Sample $\{x_j, z_j\}_{j \in S_V}$ according to the probability distribution of outcomes of the Bell-basis measurements of the corresponding pairs of qubits of $\left(\prod_{j \in S_V} X_j^{\widehat{x}_j} Z_j^{\widehat{z}_j}\right) \rho_{S_V} \left(\prod_{j \in S_V} Z_j^{\widehat{z}_j} X_j^{\widehat{x}_j}\right)$ and $\bigotimes_{j \in S_V} (U(W_j)|m_j\rangle)$. We emphasize that this measurement can be simulated in a classical probabilistic polynomial time since $|S_V| \le 5$.
3. Choose $(x_j, z_j) \xleftarrow{\$} \{0,1\}^2$ for all $j \in [N] \setminus S_V$.
4. Output $\pi := (x, z)$ where $x := x_1\|x_2\|...\|x_N$ and $z := z_1\|z_2\|...\|z_N$.

We prove that the output of this simulator is indistinguishable from the real proof. For proving this, we consider the following sequences of modified simulators. We note that these simulators may perform quantum computations unlike the real simulator.

$\mathsf{Sim}_1(k_V, \mathbf{x})$: The simulator parses $(W_1, ..., W_N, m_1, ..., m_N, S_V, \{\widehat{x}_j, \widehat{z}_j\}_{j \in S_V}) \leftarrow k_V$ and does the following.
1. Generate the classical description of the density matrix $\rho_{S_V} := \mathsf{Sim}_{\mathrm{hist}}(\mathbf{x}, S_V)$ where $\mathsf{Sim}_{\mathrm{hist}}$ is as in Lemma 2.4. (This step is the same as the step 1 of $\mathsf{Sim}(k_V, \mathbf{x})$.)
2. Generate $\widetilde{\rho}'_{\mathrm{hist}} := \left(\prod_{j \in S_V} X_j^{\widehat{x}_j} Z_j^{\widehat{z}_j}\right) \rho_{S_V} \left(\prod_{j \in S_V} Z_j^{\widehat{z}_j} X_j^{\widehat{x}_j}\right) \otimes \frac{I_{[N] \setminus S_V}}{2^{|[N] \setminus S_V|}}$.
3. Measure j-th qubits of $\widetilde{\rho}'_{\mathrm{hist}}$ and $\rho_P := \bigotimes_{j=1}^N (U(W_j)|m_j\rangle)$ in the Bell basis for $j \in [N]$, and let (x_j, z_j) be the j-th measurement result.
4. Output $\pi := (x, z)$ where $x := x_1\|x_2\|...\|x_N$ and $z := z_1\|z_2\|...\|z_N$.

Clearly, the distributions of $\{x_j, z_j\}_{j \in S_V}$ output by $\mathsf{Sim}(k_V, \mathbf{x})$ and $\mathsf{Sim}_1(k_V, \mathbf{x})$ are the same. Moreover, the distributions of $\{x_j, z_j\}_{j \in [N] \setminus S_V}$ output by $\mathsf{Sim}(k_V, \mathbf{x})$ and $\mathsf{Sim}_1(k_V, \mathbf{x})$ are both uniformly and independently random. Therefore, output distributions of $\mathsf{Sim}(k_V, \mathbf{x})$ and $\mathsf{Sim}_1(k_V, \mathbf{x})$ are exactly the same.

Next, we consider the following modified simulator that takes a witness $\mathbf{w} \in R_L(\mathbf{x})$ as input.

$\mathsf{Sim}_2(k_V, \mathbf{x}, \mathbf{w})$: The simulator parses $(W_1, ..., W_N, m_1, ..., m_N, S_V, \{\widehat{x}_j, \widehat{z}_j\}_{j \in S_V}) \leftarrow k_V$ and does the following.
1. Generate the history state ρ_{hist} for $\mathcal{H}_\mathbf{x}$ from $\mathbf{w}$.
2. Generate $(\widehat{x}_j, \widehat{z}_j) \xleftarrow{\$} \{0,1\}^2$ for $j \in [N] \setminus S_V$ and let $\widehat{x} := \widehat{x}_1\|...\|\widehat{x}_N$ and $\widehat{z} := \widehat{z}_1\|...\|\widehat{z}_N$.
3. Compute $\rho'_{\mathrm{hist}} := X^{\widehat{x}} Z^{\widehat{z}} \rho_{\mathrm{hist}} Z^{\widehat{z}} X^{\widehat{x}}$.
4. Measure j-th qubits of ρ'_{hist} and $\rho_P := \bigotimes_{j=1}^N (U(W_j)|m_j\rangle)$ in the Bell basis for $j \in [N]$, and let (x_j, z_j) be the j-th measurement result.
5. Output $\pi := (x, z)$ where $x := x_1\|x_2\|...\|x_N$ and $z := z_1\|z_2\|...\|z_N$.

We have $\rho'_{\mathrm{hist}} = \left(\prod_{j \in S_V} X_j^{\widehat{x}_j} Z_j^{\widehat{z}_j}\right) \mathrm{Tr}_{N \setminus S_V}[\rho_{\mathrm{hist}}] \left(\prod_{j \in S_V} Z_j^{\widehat{z}_j} X_j^{\widehat{x}_j}\right) \otimes \frac{I_{[N] \setminus S_V}}{2^{|[N] \setminus S_V|}}$ from the view of a distinguisher that has no information on $\{\widehat{x}_j, \widehat{z}_j\}_{j \in [N] \setminus S_V}$. By Lemma 2.4, we have $\|\rho_{S_V} - \mathrm{Tr}_{[N] \setminus S_V} \rho_{\mathrm{hist}}\|_{\mathrm{tr}} = \mathsf{negl}(\lambda)$. Therefore, we have

$\|\tilde{\rho}'_{\text{hist}} - \rho'_{\text{hist}}\|_{tr} = \mathsf{negl}(\lambda)$. This means that $\mathsf{Sim}_1(k_V, \mathbf{x})$ and $\mathsf{Sim}_2(k_V, \mathbf{x}, \mathbf{w})$ are statistically indistinguishable from the view of a distinguisher that makes at most one query.

Finally, noting that the output distribution of $\mathsf{Sim}_2(k_V, \mathbf{x}, \mathbf{w})$ is exactly the same as that of $\mathsf{Prove}(k_P, \mathbf{x}, \mathbf{w})$, the proof of Lemma 3.2 is completed.

4   Dual-Mode CV-NIZK with Preprocessing

In this section, we extend the CV-NIZK given in Sect. 3 to reduce the amount of trust in the setup at the cost of introducing a quantum preprocessing and relying on a computational assumption. In the construction in Sect. 3, we assume that the trusted setup algorithm honestly generates proving and verification keys, which are correlated with each other, and sends them to the prover and verifier, respectively, without revealing them to the other party. Here, we give a construction of CV-NIZK with preprocessing that consists of the generation of common reference string by a trusted party and a single instance-independent quantum message from the verifier to the prover. We call such a model the CRS $+ (V \rightarrow P)$ model. We note this is the same model as is considered in [CVZ20]. Moreover, our construction has a nice feature called the dual-mode property, which has been considered for NIZKs for **NP** [GS12, GOS12, PS19].

4.1   Definition

We give a formal definition of a dual-mode CV-NIZK in the CRS $+ (V \rightarrow P)$ model.

Definition 4.1. (Dual-Mode CV-NIZK in the CRS $+ (V \rightarrow P)$ Model). *A dual-mode CV-NIZK for a* **QMA** *promise problem* $L = (L_{\mathsf{yes}}, L_{\mathsf{no}})$ *in the CRS $+ (V \rightarrow P)$ model consists of algorithms* $\Pi = (\mathsf{CRSGen}, \mathsf{Preprocess}, \mathsf{Prove}, \mathsf{Verify})$ *with the following syntax:*

$\mathsf{CRSGen}(1^\lambda, \mathsf{mode})$*: This is a PPT algorithm that takes the security parameter* 1^λ *and a mode* $\mathsf{mode} \in \{\mathsf{binding}, \mathsf{hiding}\}$ *as input and outputs a classical common reference string* crs*. We note that* crs *can be reused and thus this algorithm is only needed to run once by a trusted third party.*

$\mathsf{Preprocess}(\mathsf{crs})$*: This is a QPT algorithm that takes the common reference string* crs *as input and outputs a quantum proving key* k_P *and a classical verification key* k_V*. We note that this algorithm is supposed to be run by the verifier as preprocessing, and* k_P *is supposed to be sent to the prover while* k_V *is supposed to be kept on verifier's side in secret. We also note that they can be used only once and cannot be reused unlike* crs*.*

$\mathsf{Prove}(\mathsf{crs}, k_P, \mathbf{x}, \mathbf{w}^{\otimes k})$*: This is a QPT algorithm that takes the common reference string* crs*, the proving key* k_P*, a statement* $\mathbf{x}$*, and* $k = \mathsf{poly}(\lambda)$ *copies* $\mathbf{w}^{\otimes k}$ *of a witness* $\mathbf{w} \in R_L(\mathbf{x})$ *as input and outputs a classical proof* π*.*

$\mathsf{Verify}(\mathsf{crs}, k_V, \mathbf{x}, \pi)$*: This is a PPT algorithm that takes the common reference string* crs*, the verification key* k_V*, a statement* $\mathbf{x}$*, and a proof* π *as input and outputs* $\top$ *indicating acceptance or* $\bot$ *indicating rejection.*

We require Π to satisfy the following properties for some $0 < s < c < 1$ such that $c - s > 1/\mathsf{poly}(\lambda)$. Especially, when we do not specify c and s, they are set as $c = 1 - \mathsf{negl}(\lambda)$ and $s = \mathsf{negl}(\lambda)$.

c-Completeness. *For all* $\mathsf{mode} \in \{\mathsf{binding}, \mathsf{hiding}\}$, $\mathsf{x} \in L_{\mathsf{yes}} \cap \{0,1\}^\lambda$, *and* $\overline{\mathsf{w} \in R_L(\mathsf{x})}$, *we have*

$$\Pr\left[\mathsf{Verify}(\mathsf{crs}, k_V, \mathsf{x}, \pi) = \top : \begin{array}{c} \mathsf{crs} \xleftarrow{\$} \mathsf{CRSGen}(1^\lambda, \mathsf{mode}) \\ (k_P, k_V) \xleftarrow{\$} \mathsf{Preprocess}(\mathsf{crs}) \\ \pi \xleftarrow{\$} \mathsf{Prove}(\mathsf{crs}, k_P, \mathsf{x}, \mathsf{w}^{\otimes k}) \end{array}\right] \geq c.$$

(Adaptive) Statistical s-Soundness in the Binding Mode. For   all *unbounded-time adversary $\mathcal{A}$, we have*

$$\Pr\left[\mathsf{x} \in L_{\mathsf{no}} \wedge \mathsf{Verify}(\mathsf{crs}, k_V, \mathsf{x}, \pi) = \top : \begin{array}{c} \mathsf{crs} \xleftarrow{\$} \mathsf{CRSGen}(1^\lambda, \mathsf{binding}) \\ (k_P, k_V) \xleftarrow{\$} \mathsf{Preprocess}(\mathsf{crs}) \\ (\mathsf{x}, \pi) \xleftarrow{\$} \mathcal{A}(\mathsf{crs}, k_P) \end{array}\right] \leq s.$$

(Adaptive Multi-theorem) Statistical Zero-Knowledge in the Hiding Mode. *There exists a PPT simulator Sim_0 and a QPT simulator Sim_1 such that for any unbounded-time distinguisher $\mathcal{D}$, we have*

$$\left| \Pr\left[\mathcal{D}^{\mathcal{O}_P(\mathsf{crs}, \cdot, \cdot, \cdot)}(\mathsf{crs}) = 1 : \mathsf{crs} \xleftarrow{\$} \mathsf{CRSGen}(1^\lambda, \mathsf{hiding})\right] \right.$$
$$\left. - \Pr\left[\mathcal{D}^{\mathcal{O}_S(\mathsf{td}, \cdot, \cdot, \cdot)}(\mathsf{crs}) = 1 : (\mathsf{crs}, \mathsf{td}) \xleftarrow{\$} \mathsf{Sim}_0(1^\lambda)\right] \right| \leq \mathsf{negl}(\lambda)$$

where $\mathcal{D}$ can make $\mathsf{poly}(\lambda)$ queries, which should be of the form $(k_P, \mathsf{x}, \mathsf{w}^{\otimes k})$ where $\mathsf{w} \in R_L(\mathsf{x})$ and $\mathsf{w}^{\otimes k}$ is unentangled with $\mathcal{D}$'s internal registers,[7] $\mathcal{O}_P(\mathsf{crs}, k_P, \mathsf{x}, \mathsf{w}^{\otimes k})$ returns $\mathsf{Prove}(\mathsf{crs}, k_P, \mathsf{x}, \mathsf{w}^{\otimes k})$, and $\mathcal{O}_S(\mathsf{td}, k_P, \mathsf{x}, \mathsf{w}^{\otimes k})$ returns $\mathsf{Sim}_1(\mathsf{td}, k_P, \mathsf{x})$.

Computational Mode Indistinguishability. *For any non-uniform QPT distinguisher $\mathcal{D}$, we have*

$$\left| \Pr\left[\mathcal{D}(\mathsf{crs}_{\mathsf{binding}}) = 1\right] - \Pr\left[\mathcal{D}(\mathsf{crs}_{\mathsf{hiding}}) = 1\right] \right| \leq \mathsf{negl}(\lambda)$$

where $\mathsf{crs}_{\mathsf{binding}} \xleftarrow{\$} \mathsf{CRSGen}(1^\lambda, \mathsf{binding})$ and $\mathsf{crs}_{\mathsf{hiding}} \xleftarrow{\$} \mathsf{CRSGen}(1^\lambda, \mathsf{hiding})$.

Though Definition 4.1 does not explicitly require anything on soundness in the hiding mode or the zero-knowledge property in the binding mode, we can easily prove that they are satisfied in a computational sense.

Finally, we note that we can amplify the gap between the thresholds for completeness and soundness by parallel repetitions similarly to CV-NIZK in the QSP model as discussed in Sect. 2.3. As a result, we obtain the following lemma.

---

[7]   We remark that k_P is allowed to be entangled with $\mathcal{D}$'s internal registers unlike $\mathsf{w}^{\otimes k}$. See also footnote 6.

Lemma 4.1. (Gap amplification for dual-mode CV-NIZK in the CRS + $(V \to P)$ model). *If there exists a dual-mode CV-NIZK for L in the CRS + $(V \to P)$ model that satisfies c-completeness and s-soundness, for some $0 < s < c < 1$ such that $c - s > 1/\mathsf{poly}(\lambda)$, then there exists a dual-mode CV-NIZK for L in the CRS + $(V \to P)$ model (with $(1 - \mathsf{negl}(\lambda))$-completeness and $\mathsf{negl}(\lambda)$-soundness).*

Since this can be proven similarly to Lemma 2.5, we omit a proof.

4.2 Building Blocks

We introduce two cryptographic building blocks for our dual-mode CV-NIZK in the CRS + $(V \to P)$ model.

Lossy Encryption. Intuitively, a lossy encryption scheme is a public key encryption scheme with a special property that we can generate a *lossy key* that is computationally indistinguishable from an honestly generated public key, for which there is no corresponding decryption key.

Dual-Mode Oblivious Transfer. The second building block is a k-out-of-n *dual-mode oblivious transfer*. Though this is a newly introduced definition in this paper, 1-out-of-2 case is already implicit in existing works on universally composable (UC-secure) [Can20] oblivious transfers [PVW08, Qua20]. Due to the space limitation, we only give its syntax and intuitive explanations for the security requirements.

Definition 4.2. (Dual-mode oblivious transfer (sketch)). *A (2-round) k-out-of-n dual-mode oblivious transfer with a message space $\mathcal{M}$ consists of PPT algorithms $\Pi_{\mathsf{OT}} = (\mathsf{CRSGen}, \mathsf{Receiver}, \mathsf{Sender}, \mathsf{Derive})$.*

$\mathsf{CRSGen}(1^\lambda, \mathsf{mode})$*: This is an algorithm supposed to be run by a trusted third party that takes the security parameter 1^λ and a mode $\mathsf{mode} \in \{\mathsf{binding}, \mathsf{hiding}\}$ as input and outputs a common reference string crs.*

$\mathsf{Receiver}(\mathsf{crs}, J)$*: This is an algorithm supposed to be run by a receiver that takes the common reference string crs and an ordered set of k indices $J \in [n]^k$ as input and outputs a first message ot_1 and a receiver's state st.*

$\mathsf{Sender}(\mathsf{crs}, \mathsf{ot}_1, \boldsymbol{\mu})$*: This is an algorithm supposed to be run by a sender that takes the common reference string crs, a first message ot_1 sent from a receiver and a tuple of messages $\boldsymbol{\mu} \in \mathcal{M}^n$ as input and outputs a second message ot_2.*

$\mathsf{Derive}(\mathsf{crs}, \mathsf{st}, \mathsf{ot}_2)$*: This is an algorithm supposed to be run by a receiver that takes a receiver's state st and a second message ot_2 as input and outputs a tuple of messages $\boldsymbol{\mu}' \in \mathcal{M}^k$.*

We require the following properties.

Correctness. *For all* mode $\in \{\text{binding}, \text{hiding}\}$, $J = (j_1, ..., j_k) \in [n]^k$, *and* $\boldsymbol{\mu} = (\mu_1, ..., \mu_n) \in \mathcal{M}^n$, *we have*

$$\Pr \left[\text{Derive}(\text{crs}, \text{st}, \text{ot}_2) = (\mu_{j_1}, ..., \mu_{j_k}) : \begin{array}{l} \text{crs} \xleftarrow{\$} \text{CRSGen}(1^\lambda, \text{mode}) \\ (\text{ot}_1, \text{st}) \xleftarrow{\$} \text{Receiver}(\text{crs}, J) \\ \text{ot}_2 \xleftarrow{\$} \text{Sender}(\text{crs}, \text{ot}_1, \boldsymbol{\mu}) \end{array} \right] \geq 1 - \text{negl}(\lambda).$$

Statistical Receiver's Security in the Binding Mode. *Intuitively, this security requires that the indices chosen by a receiver are information theoretically hidden from a sender in the binding mode.*

Statistical Sender's Security in the Hiding Mode. *Intuitively, this security requires that we can extract the indices of messages which a (possibly malicious) receiver tries to learn by using a trapdoor in the hiding mode.*

Computational Mode Indistinguishability. *This requires that common reference strings generated in binding and hiding modes are computationally indistinguishable.*

Lemma 4.2. *If the LWE assumption holds, then there exists k-out-of-n dual-mode oblivious transfer for arbitrary $0 < k < n$ that are polynomial in λ.*

Proof. (sketch). First, we can see that the LWE-based UC-secure OT by Quach [Qua20] can be seen as a 1-out-of-2 dual-mode oblivious transfer. This construction can be converted into 1-out-of-n dual-mode oblivious transfer by using the generic conversion for an ordinary oblivious transfer given in [BCR86] observing that the conversion preserves the dual-mode property.[8] By k-parallel repetition of the 1-out-of-n dual-mode oblivious transfer, we obtain k-out-of-n dual-mode oblivious transfer.

4.3   Construction

In this section, we construct a dual-mode CV-NIZK in the CRS + $(V \rightarrow P)$ model. As a result, we obtain the following theorem.

Theorem 4.1. *If the LWE assumption holds, then there exists a dual-mode CV-NIZK in the CRS + $(V \rightarrow P)$ model.*

Let L be a **QMA** promise problem, and $\mathcal{H}_x$, N, M, p_i, s_i, P_i, α, β, and ρ_{hist} be as in Lemma 2.4 for the language L. We let $N' := 3^5 \sum_{i=1}^5 \binom{N}{i}$ similarly to Lemma 3.1. Let $\Pi_{\text{LE}} = (\text{InjGen}_{\text{LE}}, \text{LossyGen}_{\text{LE}}, \text{Enc}_{\text{LE}}, \text{Dec}_{\text{LE}})$ be a lossy encryption scheme over the message space $\mathcal{M}_{\text{LE}} = \{0,1\}^2$ and the randomness space $\mathcal{R}_{\text{LE}}$. Let $\Pi_{\text{OT}} = (\text{CRSGen}_{\text{OT}}, \text{Receiver}_{\text{OT}}, \text{Sender}_{\text{OT}}, \text{Derive}_{\text{OT}})$ be a 5-out-of-N dual-mode oblivious transfer over the message space $\mathcal{M}_{\text{OT}} = \mathcal{M}_{\text{LE}} \times \mathcal{R}_{\text{LE}}$. Then our dual-mode CV-NIZK $\Pi_{\text{DM}} = (\text{CRSGen}_{\text{DM}}, \text{Preprocess}_{\text{DM}}, \text{Prove}_{\text{DM}}, \text{Verify}_{\text{DM}})$ for L is described in Fig. 4.

Then we prove the following lemmas.

---

[8] Alternatively, it may be possible to directly construct 1-out-of-n dual-mode oblivious transfer by appropriately modifying the construction by Quach [Qua20].

CRSGen$_{\text{DM}}(1^\lambda, \text{mode})$: The CRS generation algorithm generates $\text{crs}_{\text{OT}} \xleftarrow{\$}$ CRSGen$_{\text{OT}}(1^\lambda, \text{mode})$.

- If mode = binding, then it generates $(\text{pk}, \text{sk}) \xleftarrow{\$} \text{InjGen}_{\text{LE}}(1^\lambda)$.
- If mode = hiding, then it generates $\text{pk} \xleftarrow{\$} \text{LossyGen}_{\text{LE}}(1^\lambda)$.

Then it outputs $\text{crs}_{\text{DM}} := (\text{crs}_{\text{OT}}, \text{pk})$.

Preprocess$_{\text{DM}}(\text{crs}_{\text{DM}})$: The preprocessing algorithm parses $(\text{crs}_{\text{OT}}, \text{pk}) \leftarrow \text{crs}_{\text{DM}}$ and chooses $(W_1, ..., W_N) \xleftarrow{\$} \{X, Y, Z\}^N$, $(m_1, ..., m_N) \xleftarrow{\$} \{0, 1\}^N$, and a uniformly random subset $S_V \subseteq [N]$ such that $1 \leq |S_V| \leq 5$. Let $J = (j_1, ..., j_5) \in [N]^5$ be the elements of S_V in the ascending order where we append arbitrary indices when $|S_V| < 5$. It generates $(\text{ot}_1, \text{st}) \xleftarrow{\$} \text{Receiver}_{\text{OT}}(\text{crs}_{\text{OT}}, J)$ and outputs a proving key $k_P := \left(\rho_P := \bigotimes_{j=1}^{N}(U(W_j)|m_j\rangle), \text{ot}_1 \right)$ and a verification key $k_V := (W_1, ..., W_N, m_1, ..., m_N, S_V, \text{st})$.

Prove$_{\text{DM}}(\text{crs}_{\text{DM}}, k_P, \mathbf{x}, \mathbf{w})$: The proving algorithm parses $(\text{crs}_{\text{OT}}, \text{pk}) \leftarrow \text{crs}_{\text{DM}}$ and $(\rho_P, \text{ot}_1) \leftarrow k_P$, generates $(\hat{x}, \hat{z}) \xleftarrow{\$} \{0, 1\}^N \times \{0, 1\}^N$, generates the history state ρ_{hist} for $\mathcal{H}_x$ from $\mathbf{w}$, and computes $\rho'_{\text{hist}} := X^{\hat{x}} Z^{\hat{z}} \rho_{\text{hist}} Z^{\hat{z}} X^{\hat{x}}$. It measures j-th qubits of ρ'_{hist} and ρ_P in the Bell basis for $j \in [N]$. Let $x := x_1 \| x_2 \| ... \| x_N$, and $z := z_1 \| z_2 \| ... \| z_N$ where (x_j, z_j) denotes the outcome of j-th measurement. For $j \in [N]$, it generates $\text{ct}_j := \text{Enc}_{\text{LE}}(\text{pk}, (\hat{x}_j, \hat{z}_j); R_j)$ where $R_j \xleftarrow{\$} \mathcal{R}_{\text{LE}}$ and $\hat{x}_j$ and $\hat{z}_j$ denote the j-th bits of $\hat{x}$ and $\hat{z}$, respectively. It sets $\mu_j := ((\hat{x}_j, \hat{z}_j), R_j)$ for $j \in [N]$ and generates $\text{ot}_2 \xleftarrow{\$} \text{Sender}_{\text{OT}}(\text{crs}_{\text{OT}}, \text{ot}_1, (\mu_1, ..., \mu_N))$. It outputs a proof $\pi := (x, z, \{\text{ct}_j\}_{j \in [N]}, \text{ot}_2)$.

Verify$_{\text{DM}}(\text{crs}_{\text{DM}}, k_V, \mathbf{x}, \pi)$: The verification algorithm parses $(\text{crs}_{\text{OT}}, \text{pk}) \leftarrow \text{crs}_{\text{DM}}$, $(W_1, ..., W_N, m_1, ..., m_N, S_V, \text{st}) \leftarrow k_V$, and $(x, z, \{\text{ct}_j\}_{j \in [N]}, \text{ot}_2) \leftarrow \pi$. It runs $\mu' \xleftarrow{\$} \text{Derive}_{\text{OT}}(\text{crs}_{\text{OT}}, \text{st}, \text{ot}_2)$ and parses $(((\hat{x}'_1, \hat{z}'_1), R'_1), ..., ((\hat{x}'_5, \hat{z}'_5), R'_5)) \leftarrow \mu'$. If $\text{Enc}_{\text{LE}}(\text{pk}, (\hat{x}'_i, \hat{z}'_i); R'_i) \neq \text{ct}_{j_i}$ for some $i \in [5]$, it outputs $\bot$. Otherwise, it recovers $\{\hat{x}_j, \hat{z}_j\}_{j \in S_V}$ by setting $(\hat{x}_{j_i}, \hat{z}_{j_i}) := (\hat{x}'_i, \hat{z}'_i)$ for $i \in [|S_V|]$. It chooses $i \in [M]$ according to the probability distribution defined by $\{p_i\}_{i \in [M]}$ (i.e., chooses i with probability p_i). Let

$$S_i := \{j \in [N] \mid j\text{th Pauli operator of } P_i \text{ is not } I\}.$$

We note that we have $1 \leq |S_i| \leq 5$ by the 5-locality of $\mathcal{H}_x$. We say that P_i is consistent to $(S_V, \{W_j\}_{j \in S_V})$ if and only if $S_i = S_V$ and the jth Pauli operator of P_i is W_j for all $j \in S_i$. If P_i is not consistent to $(S_V, \{W_j\}_{j \in S_V})$, it outputs $\top$. If P_i is consistent to $(S_V, \{W_j\}_{j \in S_V})$, it flips a biased coin that heads with probability $1 - 3^{|S_i|-5}$. If heads, it outputs $\top$. If tails, it defines

$$m'_j := \begin{cases} m_j \oplus x_j \oplus \hat{x}_j & (W_j = Z), \\ m_j \oplus z_j \oplus \hat{z}_j & (W_j = X), \\ m_j \oplus x_j \oplus \hat{x}_j \oplus z_j \oplus \hat{z}_j & (W_j = Y) \end{cases}$$

for $j \in S_i$, and outputs $\top$ if $(-1)^{\oplus_{j \in S_i} m'_j} = -s_i$ and $\bot$ otherwise.

Fig. 4. Dual-Mode CV-NIZK Π_{DM}.

Lemma 4.3. Π_{DM} *satisfies* $\left(1 - \frac{\alpha}{N'} - \mathsf{negl}(\lambda)\right)$-*completeness.*

Proof. By the correctness of Π_{OT}, it is easy to see that the probability that an honestly generated proof passes the verification differs from that in Π_{NIZK} in Fig. 1 only by $\mathsf{negl}(\lambda)$. Since Π_{NIZK} satisfies $\left(1 - \frac{\alpha}{N'}\right)$-completeness as shown in Lemma 3.1, Π_{DM} satisfies $\left(1 - \frac{\alpha}{N'} - \mathsf{negl}(\lambda)\right)$-completeness.

Lemma 4.4. Π_{DM} *satisfies the computational mode indistinguishability.*

Proof. This can be reduced to the computational mode indistinguishability of Π_{OT} and Π_{LE} in a straightforward manner.

Lemma 4.5. Π_{DM} *satisfies statistical* $\left(1 - \frac{\beta}{N'} + \mathsf{negl}(\lambda)\right)$-*soundness in the binding mode.*

Lemma 4.6. Π_{DM} *satisfies the statistical zero-knowledge property in the hiding mode.*

By combining Lemmas 4.1 to 4.6 and

$$\left(1 - \frac{\alpha}{N'} - \mathsf{negl}(\lambda)\right) - \left(1 - \frac{\beta}{N'} + \mathsf{negl}(\lambda)\right) = \frac{\beta - \alpha}{N'} - \mathsf{negl}(\lambda) = \frac{1}{\mathsf{poly}(\lambda)},$$

we obtain Theorem 4.1.

In the following, we give proof sketches of Lemmas 4.5 and 4.6.

Soundness in the Binding Mode. For a cheating prover, we consider a modified soundness game where the challenger extracts $\{\widehat{x}_j, \widehat{z}_j\}_{j \in S_V}$ from $\{\mathsf{ct}_j\}_{j \in S_V}$ by just decrypting them instead of deriving $\{(\widehat{x}_j, \widehat{z}_j), R_j\}_{j \in S_V}$ from ot_2 and then checking the consistency to $\{\mathsf{ct}_j\}_{j \in S_V}$ as in the actual verification algorithm. This does not decrease adversary's winning probability since $\{\widehat{x}_j, \widehat{z}_j\}_{j \in S_V}$ derived from ot_2 should be equal to decryption of $\{\mathsf{ct}_j\}_{j \in S_V}$ or otherwise the verification algorithm immediately rejects. In this game, the challenger does not use st of Π_{OT}. Therefore, by the receiver's security of Π_{OT}, adversary's winning probability changes negligibly even if we generate ot_1 by the simulator $\mathsf{Sim}_{\mathsf{rec}}$. At this point, the challenger obtain no information about S_V. Then soundness in this game can be reduced to the soundness of Π_{NIZK} in Fig. 1 against augmented cheating provers with an additional capability to choose $\{\widehat{x}_j, \widehat{z}_j\}_{j \in [N]}$. By carefully examining the proof of the soundness of Π_{NIZK}, one can see that the proof works against such augmented cheating provers as well. (Note that what is essential for the soundness of Π_{NIZK} is that S_V is hidden from the cheating prover.)

Zero-Knowledge in the Hiding Mode. In the hiding mode, pk of Π_{LE} is in the lossy mode, and thus $\{\mathsf{ct}_j\}_{j \in [N]}$ can be simulated only from pk by encrypting all 0 message. Moreover, by sender's security in the hiding mode of Π_{OT}, ot_2 can be simulated from $\{\widehat{x}_j, \widehat{z}_j\}_{j \in S_V}$ where S_V is a subset such that $|S_V| = 5$ extracted from ot_1. Therefore, the zero-knowledge property of Π_{DM} can be reduced to the zero-knowledge property of Π_{NIZK} in Fig. 1 against augmented malicious verifiers with an additional capability to choose S_V and ρ_P. By carefully examining the proof of the zero-knowledge property of Π_{NIZK}, one can see that the proof works against such augmented malicious verifiers as well. (Note that what is essential for the zero-knowledge property of Π_{NIZK} is that $\{\widehat{x}_j, \widehat{z}_j\}_{j \notin S_V}$ is hidden from the malicious verifier.)

5   CV-NIZK via Fiat-Shamir Transformation

In this section, we construct CV-NIZK in the quantum random oracle model via the Fiat-Shamir transformation.

5.1   Definition

We give a formal definition of CV-NIZK in the QRO + $(V \to P)$ model.

Definition 5.1. (CV-NIZK in the QRO + $(V \to P)$ Model). *A CV-NIZK for a* **QMA** *promise problem $L = (L_{\mathsf{yes}}, L_{\mathsf{no}})$ in the QRO + $(V \to P)$ model w.r.t. a random oracle distribution* ROdist *consists of algorithms* $\Pi = (\mathsf{Preprocess}, \mathsf{Prove}, \mathsf{Verify})$ *with the following syntax:*

$\mathsf{Preprocess}(1^\lambda)$: *This is a QPT algorithm that takes the security parameter 1^λ as input, and outputs a quantum proving key k_P and a classical verification key k_V. We note that this algorithm is supposed to be run by the verifier as preprocessing, and k_P is supposed to be sent to the prover while k_V is supposed to be kept on verifier's side in secret. We also note that they can be used only once and cannot be reused.*

$\mathsf{Prove}^H(k_P, \mathsf{x}, \mathsf{w}^{\otimes k})$: *This is a QPT algorithm that is given quantum oracle access to the random oracle H. It takes the proving key k_P, a statement x, and $k = \mathsf{poly}(\lambda)$ copies $\mathsf{w}^{\otimes k}$ of a witness $\mathsf{w} \in R_L(\mathsf{x})$ as input, and outputs a classical proof π.*

$\mathsf{Verify}^H(k_V, \mathsf{x}, \pi)$: *This is a PPT algorithm that is given classical oracle access to the random oracle H. It takes the verification key k_V, a statement x, and a proof π as input, and outputs $\top$ indicating acceptance or $\bot$ indicating rejection.*

We require Π to satisfy the following properties.

Completeness. *For all $\mathsf{x} \in L_{\mathsf{yes}} \cap \{0,1\}^\lambda$, and $\mathsf{w} \in R_L(\mathsf{x})$, we have*

$$\Pr\left[\mathsf{Verify}^H(k_V, \mathsf{x}, \pi) = \top : \begin{array}{c} H \xleftarrow{\$} \mathsf{ROdist} \\ (k_P, k_V) \xleftarrow{\$} \mathsf{Preprocess}(1^\lambda) \\ \pi \xleftarrow{\$} \mathsf{Prove}^H(k_P, \mathsf{x}, \mathsf{w}^{\otimes k}) \end{array}\right] \geq 1 - \mathsf{negl}(\lambda).$$

Adaptive Statistical Soundness. *For all adversaries $\mathcal{A}$ that make at most* $\text{poly}(\lambda)$ *quantum random oracle queries, we have*

$$\Pr\left[\mathbf{x} \in L_{\text{no}} \wedge \mathsf{Verify}^H(k_V, \mathbf{x}, \pi) = \top : \begin{array}{c} H \xleftarrow{\$} \mathsf{ROdist} \\ (k_P, k_V) \xleftarrow{\$} \mathsf{Preprocess}(1^\lambda) \\ (\mathbf{x}, \pi) \xleftarrow{\$} \mathcal{A}^H(k_P) \end{array}\right] \leq \mathsf{negl}(\lambda).$$

Adaptive Multi-theorem Zero-Knowledge. *For defining the zero-knowledge property in the QROM, we define the syntax of a simulator in the QROM following [Unr15]. A simulator is given quantum access to the random oracle H and classical access to reprogramming oracle* $\mathsf{Reprogram}$*. When the simulator queries (x, y) to* $\mathsf{Reprogram}$*, the random oracle H is reprogrammed so that $H(x) := y$ while keeping the values on other inputs unchanged. Then the adaptive multi-theorem zero-knowledge property is defined as follows:*

There exists a QPT simulator Sim *with the above syntax such that for any QPT distinguisher $\mathcal{D}$, we have*

$$\left| \Pr\left[\mathcal{D}^{H, \mathcal{O}_P^H(\cdot, \cdot, \cdot)}(1^\lambda) = 1 : H \xleftarrow{\$} \mathsf{ROdist} \right] \right.$$
$$\left. - \Pr\left[\mathcal{D}^{H, \mathcal{O}_S^{H, \mathsf{Reprogram}}(\cdot, \cdot, \cdot)}(1^\lambda) = 1 : H \xleftarrow{\$} \mathsf{ROdist} \right] \right| \leq \mathsf{negl}(\lambda)$$

where $\mathcal{D}$'s queries to the second oracle should be of the form $(k_P, \mathbf{x}, \mathbf{w}^{\otimes k})$ where $\mathbf{w} \in R_L(\mathbf{x})$ and $\mathbf{w}^{\otimes k}$ is unentangled with $\mathcal{D}$'s internal registers,[9] $\mathcal{O}_P^H(k_P, \mathbf{x}, \mathbf{w}^{\otimes k})$ returns $\mathsf{Prove}^H(k_P, \mathbf{x}, \mathbf{w}^{\otimes k})$*, and $\mathcal{O}_S^{H, \mathsf{Reprogram}}(k_P, \mathbf{x}, \mathbf{w}^{\otimes k})$ returns* $\mathsf{Sim}^{H, \mathsf{Reprogram}}(k_P, \mathbf{x})$*.*

Remark 5.1. Remark that the "multi-theorem" zero-knowledge does not mean that a preprocessing can be reused many times. It rather means that a single random oracle can be reused as long as a fresh preprocessing is run every time. This is consistent to the definition in the CRS + $(V \to P)$ model (Definition 4.1) if we think of the random oracle as replacement of CRS.

5.2   Building Blocks

We use the two cryptographic primitives, a non-interactive commitment scheme and a Σ-protocol with quantum preprocessing, for our construction.

Definition 5.2. (Σ-protocol with Quantum Preprocessing). *A Σ-protocol with quantum preprocessing for a* **QMA** *promise problem $L = (L_{\text{yes}}, L_{\text{no}})$ consists of algorithms $\Pi = (\mathsf{Preprocess}, \mathsf{Prove}_1, \mathsf{Verify}_1, \mathsf{Prove}_2, \mathsf{Verify}_2)$ with the following syntax:*

---

[9] We remark that k_P is allowed to be entangled with $\mathcal{D}$'s internal registers unlike $\mathbf{w}^{\otimes k}$. See also footnote 6.

Preprocess(1^λ): *This is a QPT algorithm that takes the security parameter 1^λ as input, and outputs a quantum proving key k_P and a classical verification key k_V. We note that this algorithm is supposed to be run by the verifier as preprocessing, and k_P is supposed to be sent to the prover while k_V is supposed to be kept on verifier's side in secret. We also note that they can be used only once and cannot be reused.*

Prove$_1$($k_P, \mathrm{x}, \mathrm{w}^{\otimes k}$): *This is a QPT algorithm that takes the proving key k_P, a statement x, and $k = \mathsf{poly}(\lambda)$ copies $\mathrm{w}^{\otimes k}$ of a witness $\mathrm{w} \in R_L(\mathrm{x})$ as input, and outputs a classical message msg_1 and a state st.*

Verify$_1$(1^λ): *This is a PPT algorithm that takes the security parameter 1^λ, and outputs a classical message msg_2, which is uniformly sampled from a certain set.*

Prove$_2$($\mathsf{st}, \mathsf{msg}_2$) *We use the two cryptographic primitives This is a QPT algorithm that takes the state st and the message msg_2 as input, and outputs a classical message msg_3.*

Verify$_2$($k_V, \mathrm{xx}, \mathsf{msg}_1, \mathsf{msg}_2, \mathsf{msg}_3$): *This is a PPT algorithm that takes the verification key k_V, the statement x, and classical messages $\mathsf{msg}_1, \mathsf{msg}_2, \mathsf{msg}_3$ as input, and outputs $\top$ indicating acceptance or $\bot$ indicating rejection.*

We require Π to satisfy the following properties.

c-*Completeness*. *For all $\mathrm{x} \in L_{\mathsf{yes}} \cap \{0,1\}^\lambda$, and $\mathrm{w} \in R_L(\mathrm{x})$, we have*

$$\Pr\left[\mathsf{Verify}_2(k_V, \mathrm{x}, \mathsf{msg}_1, \mathsf{msg}_2, \mathsf{msg}_3) = \top : \begin{array}{c} (k_P, k_V) \xleftarrow{\$} \mathsf{Preprocess}(1^\lambda) \\ (\mathsf{msg}_1, \mathsf{st}) \xleftarrow{\$} \mathsf{Prove}_1(k_P, \mathrm{x}, \mathrm{w}^{\otimes k}) \\ \mathsf{msg}_2 \xleftarrow{\$} \mathsf{Verify}_1(1^\lambda) \\ \mathsf{msg}_3 \xleftarrow{\$} \mathsf{Prove}_2(\mathsf{st}, \mathsf{msg}_2) \end{array}\right] \geq c.$$

(*Adaptive Statistical*) s-*soundness*. *For all adversary $(\mathcal{A}_1, \mathcal{A}_2)$, we have*

$$\Pr\left[\mathrm{x} \in L_{\mathsf{no}} \wedge \Sigma.\mathsf{Verify}_2(k_V, \mathrm{x}, \mathsf{msg}_1, \mathsf{msg}_2, \mathsf{msg}_3) = \top : \begin{array}{c} (k_P, k_V) \xleftarrow{\$} \mathsf{Preprocess}(1^\lambda) \\ (\mathrm{x}, \mathsf{st}, \mathsf{msg}_1) \xleftarrow{\$} \mathcal{A}_1(k_P) \\ \mathsf{msg}_2 \xleftarrow{\$} \mathsf{Verify}_1(1^\lambda) \\ \mathsf{msg}_3 \xleftarrow{\$} \mathcal{A}_2(\mathsf{st}, \mathsf{msg}_2) \end{array}\right] \leq s.$$

Special Zero-Knowledge. *There exists a QPT algorithm Sim such that for any $\mathrm{x} \in L_{\mathsf{yes}}$, $\mathrm{w} \in R_L(\mathrm{x})$, msg_2, and QPT adversary $(\mathcal{A}_1, \mathcal{A}_2)$, we have*

$$\left| \Pr\left[\mathcal{A}_2(\mathsf{st}_\mathcal{A}, \mathrm{x}, \mathsf{msg}_1, \mathsf{msg}_2, \mathsf{msg}_3) = 1 : \begin{array}{c} (k_P, \mathsf{st}_\mathcal{A}) \xleftarrow{\$} \mathcal{A}_1(1^\lambda) \\ (\mathsf{msg}_1, \mathsf{st}) \xleftarrow{\$} \mathsf{Prove}_1(k_P, \mathrm{x}, \mathrm{w}^{\otimes k}) \\ \mathsf{msg}_3 \xleftarrow{\$} \mathsf{Prove}_2(\mathsf{st}, \mathsf{msg}_2) \end{array}\right] \right.$$
$$\left. - \Pr\left[\mathcal{A}_2(\mathsf{st}_\mathcal{A}, \mathrm{x}, \mathsf{msg}_1, \mathsf{msg}_2, \mathsf{msg}_3) = 1 : \begin{array}{c} (k_P, \mathsf{st}_\mathcal{A}) \xleftarrow{\$} \mathcal{A}_1(1^\lambda) \\ (\mathsf{msg}_1, \mathsf{msg}_3) \xleftarrow{\$} \mathsf{Sim}(k_P, \mathrm{x}, \mathsf{msg}_2) \end{array}\right] \right| \leq \mathsf{negl}(\lambda).$$

High Min-Entropy. *Prove$_1$ can be divided into the "quantum part" and "classical part" as follows:*

$\mathsf{Prove}_1^Q(k_P, \mathsf{x}, \mathsf{w}^{\otimes k})$: *This is a QPT algorithm that outputs a classical string* st$'$. $\mathsf{Prove}_1^C(\mathsf{st}')$: *This is a PPT algorithm that outputs* msg$_1$ *and* st.

Moreover, for any st$'$ *generated by* Prove_1^Q, *we have*

$$\max_{\mathsf{msg}_1^*} \Pr[\mathsf{Prove}_1^C(\mathsf{st}') = \mathsf{msg}_1^*] = \mathsf{negl}(\lambda).$$

Lemma 5.1. (Gap Amplification for Σ-protocol with quantum preprocessing). *If there exists a Σ-protocol with quantum preprocessing for a promise problem L that satisfies c-completeness, s-soundness, special zero-knowledge, and high min-entropy for some $0 < s < c < 1$ such that $c - s > 1/\mathsf{poly}(\lambda)$, then there exists a Σ-protocol with quantum preprocessing for L with $(1 - \mathsf{negl}(\lambda))$-completeness, $\mathsf{negl}(\lambda)$-soundness, special zero-knowledge, and high min-entropy.*

Proof. It is clear that the parallel repetition can amplify the completeness-soundness gap, and that the high min-entropy is preserved under the parallel repetition. We can also show that parallel repetition preserves the special zero-knowledge property by a standard hybrid argument.

By applying a similar trick as in Sect. 3 to the quantum Σ-protocol of [BG20], we obtain the following theorem.

Theorem 5.1. *If a non-interactive commitment scheme exists, then there exists a Σ-protocol with quantum preprocessing for* **QMA**.

As mentioned in Sect. 5.1, a non-interactive commitment scheme unconditionally exists in the QROM. Therefore, the above theorem implies the following corollary.

Corollary 5.1. *There exists a Σ-protocol with quantum preprocessing for* **QMA** *in the QROM.*

5.3   Construction

In this section, we construct a CV-NIZK in the QRO + $(V \rightarrow P)$ model. As a result, we obtain the following theorem.

Theorem 5.2. *There exists a CV-NIZK for* **QMA** *in the QRO + $(V \rightarrow P)$ model.*

Let $L = (L_\mathsf{yes}, L_\mathsf{no})$ be a **QMA** promise problem, H be a random oracle, and $\Pi_\Sigma = (\Sigma.\mathsf{Preprocess}, \Sigma.\mathsf{Prove}_1, \Sigma.\mathsf{Verify}_1, \Sigma.\mathsf{Prove}_2, \Sigma.\mathsf{Verify}_2)$ be a Σ-protocol with quantum preprocessing (with $(1 - \mathsf{negl}(\lambda))$-completeness and $\mathsf{negl}(\lambda)$-soundness). Then our CV-NIZK in the QRO + $(V \rightarrow P)$ model $\Pi_\mathsf{QRO} = (\mathsf{Preprocess}_\mathsf{QRO}, \mathsf{Prove}_\mathsf{QRO}, \mathsf{Verify}_\mathsf{QRO})$ for L is described in Fig. 5.

Lemma 5.2. *Π_QRO satisfies $(1 - \mathsf{negl}(\lambda))$-completeness and adaptive $\mathsf{negl}(\lambda)$-soundness.*

Correctness is clear. Soundness is shown by using the measure-and-reprogram lemma shown in [DFM20].

Lemma 5.3. *Π_QRO satisfies adaptive multi-theorem zero-knowledge property.*

This is proven by using adaptive reprogramming lemma shown in [GHHM20].

$\mathsf{Preprocess}_{\mathsf{QRO}}(1^\lambda)$: It runs $\Sigma.\mathsf{Preprocess}(1^\lambda) \to (\Sigma.k_V, \Sigma.k_P)$, and outputs $k_V := \Sigma.k_V$ and $k_P := \Sigma.k_P$.

$\mathsf{Prove}_{\mathsf{QRO}}^{H}(k_P, \mathbf{x}, \mathbf{w}^{\otimes k})$: It parses $\Sigma.k_P \leftarrow k_P$, and runs $\Sigma.\mathsf{Prove}_1(k_P, \mathbf{x}, \mathbf{w}^{\otimes k}) \to (\mathsf{msg}_1, \mathsf{st})$. It computes $\mathsf{msg}_2 := H(\mathbf{x}, \mathsf{msg}_1)$. It runs $\Sigma.\mathsf{Prove}_2(\mathsf{st}, \mathsf{msg}_2) \to \mathsf{msg}_3$. It outputs $\pi := (\mathsf{msg}_1, \mathsf{msg}_3)$.

$\mathsf{Verify}_{\mathsf{QRO}}^{H}(k_V, \mathbf{x}, \pi)$: It parses $\Sigma.k_V \leftarrow k_V$ and $(\mathsf{msg}_1, \mathsf{msg}_3) \leftarrow \pi$. It computes $\Sigma.\mathsf{Verify}_2(k_V, \mathbf{x}, \mathsf{msg}_1, H(\mathbf{x}, \mathsf{msg}_1), \mathsf{msg}_3)$. If the output is $\bot$, it outputs $\bot$. If the output is $\top$, it outputs $\top$.

Fig. 5. CV-NIZK in the QRO + $(V \to P)$ model Π_{QRO}.

Shared Bell-Pair Model. Remark that the verifier of Π_{QRO} just sends a state $\rho_P := \bigotimes_{j=1}^{N}(U(W_j)|m_j\rangle)$ for $(W_1, ..., W_N) \xleftarrow{\$} \{X, Y, Z\}^N$ and $(m_1, ..., m_N) \xleftarrow{\$} \{0, 1\}^N$ while keeping $(W_1, ..., W_N, m_1, ..., m_N)$ as a verification key. This step can be done in a non-interactive way if N Bell-pairs are a priori shared between the prover and verifier. That is, the verifier can measure his halves of Bell pairs in a randomly chosen bases $(W_1, ..., W_N)$ to get measurement outcomes $(m_1, ..., m_N)$. Apparently, this does not harm either of soundness or zero-knowledge since the protocol is the same as Π_{QRO} from the view of the prover and the malicious verifier's power is just weaker than that in Π_{QRO} in the sense that it cannot control the quantum state to be sent to the prover. Thus, we obtain the following theorem.

Theorem 5.3. *There exists a CV-NIZK for* **QMA** *in the QRO + shared Bell pair model.*

References

[ACGH20] Alagic, G., Childs, A.M., Grilo, A.B., Hung, S.-H.: Non-interactive classical verification of quantum computation. In: TCC 2020, Part III, pp. 153–180 (2020)

[BCKM21] Bartusek, J., Coladangelo, A., Khurana, D., Ma, F.: On the round complexity of secure quantum computation. In: CRYPTO 2021, Part I, pp. 406–435, Virtual Event (2021)

[BCR86] Brassard, G., Crépeau, C., Robert, J.-M.: Information theoretic reductions among disclosure problems. In: 27th FOCS, pp. 168–173 (1986)

[BCR87] Brassard, G., Crépeau, C., Robert, J.-M.: All-or-nothing disclosure of secrets. In: CRYPTO'86, pp. 234–238 (1987)

[BD18] Brakerski, Z., Döttling, N.: Two-message statistically sender-private OT from LWE. In: TCC 2018, Part II, pp. 370–390 (2018)

[BFM88] Blum, M., Feldman, P., Micali, S.: Non-interactive zero-knowledge and its applications (extended abstract). In: 20th ACM STOC, pp. 103–112 (1988)

[BG20] Broadbent, A., Grilo, A.B.: QMA-hardness of consistency of local density matrices with applications to quantum zero-knowledge. In: 61st FOCS, pp. 196–205 (2020)

[BHY09] Bellare, M., Hofheinz, D., Yilek, S.: Possibility and impossibility results for encryption and commitment secure under selective opening. In: Joux, A. (ed.) EUROCRYPT 2009. LNCS, vol. 5479, pp. 1–35. Springer, Heidelberg (2009). https://doi.org/10.1007/978-3-642-01001-9_1

[BJSW20] Broadbent, A., Ji, Z., Song, F., Watrous, J.: Zero-knowledge proof systems for QMA. SIAM J. Comput. 49(2), 245–283 (2020)

[BM21] Bartusek, J., Malavolta, G.: Candidate obfuscation of null quantum circuits and witness encryption for QMA. IACR Cryptology ePrint Archive 2021, 421 (2021)

[BS20] Bitansky, N., Shmueli, O.: Post-quantum zero knowledge in constant rounds. In: 52nd ACM STOC, pp. 269–279 (2020)

[Can20] Canetti, R.: Universally Composable Security. J. ACM 67(5), 28:1–28:94 (2020)

[CNs07] Camenisch, J., Neven, G., Shelat, A.: Simulatable adaptive oblivious transfer. In: EUROCRYPT 2007, pp. 573–590 (2007)

[CVZ20] Coladangelo, A., Vidick, T., Zhang, T.: Non-interactive zero-knowledge arguments for QMA, with preprocessing. In: CRYPTO 2020, Part III, pp. 799–828 (2020)

[DFM20] Don, J., Fehr, S., Majenz, C.: The measure-and-reprogram technique 2.0: multi-round Fiat-Shamir and more. In: CRYPTO 2020, Part III, pp. 602–631 (2020)

[DFMS19] Don, J., Fehr, S., Majenz, C., Schaffner, C.: Security of the Fiat-Shamir transformation in the quantum random-oracle model. In: CRYPTO 2019, Part II, pp. 356–383 (2019)

[DMP90] De Santis, A., Micali, S., Persiano, G.: Non-interactive zero-knowledge with preprocessing. In: CRYPTO'88, pp. 269–282 (1990)

[FHM18] Fitzsimons, J.F., Hajdušek, M., Morimae, T.: Post hoc verification with a single prover. Phys. Rev. Lett. 120, 040501 (2018)

[FLS99] Feige, U., Lapidot, D., Shamir, A.: Multiple non interactive zero knowledge proofs under general assumptions. SIAM J. Comput. 29(1), 1–28 (1999)

[FS87] Fiat, A., Shamir, A.: How to prove yourself: practical solutions to identification and signature problems. In: CRYPTO'86, pp. 186–194 (1987)

[GHHM20] Grilo, A.B., Hövelmanns, K., Hülsing, A., Majenz, C.: Tight adaptive reprogramming in the QROM. arXiv:2010.15103 (2020)

[GMR89] Goldwasser, S., Micali, S., Rackoff, C.: The knowledge complexity of interactive proof systems. SIAM J. Comput. 18(1), 186–208 (1989)

[GOS12] Groth, J., Ostrovsky, R., Sahai, A.: New techniques for noninteractive zero-knowledge. J. ACM 59(3), 11:1–11:35 (2012)

[GS12] Groth, J., Sahai, A.: Efficient noninteractive proof systems for bilinear groups. SIAM J. Comput. 41(5), 1193–1232 (2012)

[GSY19] Grilo, A.B., Slofstra, W., Yuen, H.: Perfect zero knowledge for quantum multiprover interactive proofs. In: 60th FOCS, pp. 611–635 (2019)

[IKLP06] Ishai, Y., Kushilevitz, E., Lindell, Y., Petrank, E.: Black-box constructions for secure computation. In: 38th ACM STOC, pp. 99–108 (2006)

[Kob03] Kobayashi, H.: Non-interactive quantum perfect and statistical zero-knowledge. In: Algorithms and Computation, 14th International Symposium, ISAAC 2003, Kyoto, Japan, 15–17 December 2003, Proceedings, pp. 178–188 (2003)

[Lin08] Lindell, A.Y.: Efficient fully-simulatable oblivious transfer. In: CT-RSA 2008, pp. 52–70 (2008)

[LZ19] Liu, Q., Zhandry, M.: Revisiting post-quantum Fiat-Shamir. In: CRYPTO 2019, Part II, pp. 326–355 (2019)

[Mah18] Mahadev, U.: Classical homomorphic encryption for quantum circuits. In: 59th FOCS, pp. 332–338 (2018)

[MNS18] Morimae, T., Nagaj, D., Schuch, N.: Quantum proofs can be verified using only single-qubit measurements. Phys. Rev. A **93**, 022326 (2018)

[NP01] Naor, M., Pinkas, B.: Efficient oblivious transfer protocols. In: Proceedings of the Twelfth Annual Symposium on Discrete Algorithms, 7–9 January 2001, Washington, DC, USA, pp. 448–457 (2001)

[Ps05] Pass, R., Shelat, A.: Unconditional characterizations of non-interactive zero-knowledge. In: CRYPTO 2005, pp. 118–134 (2005)

[PS19] Peikert, C., Shiehian, S.: Noninteractive zero knowledge for NP from (plain) learning with errors. In: CRYPTO 2019, Part I, pp. 89–114 (2019)

[PVW08] Peikert, C., Vaikuntanathan, V., Waters, B.: A framework for efficient and composable oblivious transfer. In: Wagner, D. (ed.) CRYPTO 2008. LNCS, vol. 5157, pp. 554–571. Springer, Heidelberg (2008). https://doi.org/10.1007/978-3-540-85174-5_31

[Qua20] Quach, W.: UC-Secure OT from LWE. Revisited. In SCN **20**, 192–211 (2020)

[Reg09] Regev, O.: On lattices, learning with errors, random linear codes, and cryptography. J. ACM **56**(6), 34:1–34:40 (2009)

[Shm21] Shmueli, O.: Multi-theorem designated-verifier NIZK for QMA. In: CRYPTO 2021 Part I, pp. 375–405, Virtual Event (2021)

[Unr15] Unruh, D.: Non-interactive zero-knowledge proofs in the quantum random oracle model. In: EUROCRYPT 2015, Part II, pp. 755–784 (2015)

General Properties of Quantum Bit Commitments (Extended Abstract)

Jun Yan[(✉)]

Jinan University, Guangzhou, China
tjunyan@jnu.edu.cn

Abstract. While unconditionally-secure quantum bit commitment (allowing both quantum computation and communication) is impossible, researchers turn to study the *complexity-based* one, a.k.a. *computational* quantum bit commitment. A computational *canonical* (non-interactive) quantum bit commitment scheme refers to a kind of schemes such that the commitment consists of just a single (quantum) message from the sender to the receiver that later can be opened by *uncomputing* the commit stage. In this work, we study general properties of computational quantum bit commitments through the lens of canonical quantum bit commitments. Among other results, we in particular obtain the following two:

1. Any computational quantum bit commitment scheme can be converted into the canonical (non-interactive) form (with its *sum-binding* property preserved).
2. Two flavors of canonical quantum bit commitments are *equivalent*; that is, canonical computationally-hiding statistically-binding quantum bit commitment exists if and only if the canonical statistically-hiding computationally-binding one exists. Combining this result with the first one, it immediately implies (unconditionally) that computational quantum bit commitment is *symmetric*.

Canonical quantum bit commitments can be based on quantum-secure one-way functions or pseudorandom quantum states. But in our opinion, the formulation of canonical quantum bit commitment is so clean and simple that itself can be viewed as a plausible complexity assumption as well. We propose to explore canonical quantum bit commitment from perspectives of both quantum cryptography and quantum complexity theory in the future.

Keywords: Quantum bit commitment · Quantum binding · Round complexity · Parallel composition

1 Introduction

In the classical world, bit commitment is an important cryptographic primitive. A bit commitment scheme defines a two-stage interactive protocol between

---

The full version of this paper is referred to [50].

© International Association for Cryptologic Research 2022
S. Agrawal and D. Lin (Eds.): ASIACRYPT 2022, LNCS 13794, pp. 628–657, 2022.
https://doi.org/10.1007/978-3-031-22972-5_22

a sender and a receiver, providing two security guarantees, hiding and binding. Informally, the *hiding* property states that the committed bit is hidden from the receiver during the *commit* stage and afterwards until it is opened, while the *binding* property states that the sender can only open the commitment as at most one bit value (0 or 1, exclusively) in the *reveal* stage later. Unfortunately, unconditionally (or information-theoretically)-secure bit commitment is impossible. As a compromise, we turn to consider complexity-based bit commitment, a.k.a. *computational* bit commitment. The one-way function assumption is a basic computational hardness assumption without any mathematical structure; it is the *minimum* assumption in complexity-based cryptography [25]. From a one-way function we can construct two flavors of bit commitments: computationally-hiding (statistically-binding) bit commitment [37] and (statistically-hiding) computationally-binding bit commitment [24,38]. However, a major disadvantage of these constructions is that they are *interactive*: at least two or even polynomial numbers of messages are needed to exchange in the commit stage, and which seems inherent [23,34].

As quantum technology develops, existing cryptosystems are facing possible quantum attacks in the near future. Regarding bit commitment, we thus have to study bit commitment secure against quantum attacks, a.k.a. *quantum bit commitment*. A *general* quantum bit commitment scheme itself could be a hybrid of classical and quantum computation and communication. When the construction is purely classical, we often call it "(classical) bit commitment scheme secure against quantum attacks" or "post-quantum bit commitment scheme"[1].

The concept of quantum bit commitment was proposed almost three decades ago, aiming to make use of quantum mechanics to realize bit commitments [6,10]. Unfortunately, unconditionally-secure quantum bit commitment is impossible either [33,35]. Based on complexity assumptions such as quantum-secure one-way permutations or functions, we can also construct two flavors of quantum bit commitments [2,14,17,30,31,52]. An interesting observation about these constructions is that almost all of them (except for the one in [14]) are *non-interactive* (in both the commit and the reveal stages). This is a great advantage over the classical bit commitment. And this motivates us to ask the following question:

Is quantum bit commitment inherently non-interactive? Or, can any quantum bit commitment scheme be "compressed" into a non-interactive one that is still useful in applications?

This possible non-interactivity of quantum bit commitment is intriguing: if it is true, then replacing post-quantum bit commitments with quantum bit commitments in applications can potentially reduce the *round complexity* of the whole construction.

While the idea of using quantum bit commitments in applications sounds wonderful, unfortunately, it is well-known that the *general* binding property of

---

[1] Even in case, it is still legal to call it "quantum bit commitment scheme". This is because classical computation and communication can be simulated by quantum computation and communication, respectively, in a standard way.

quantum bit commitment, i.e. *sum-binding*, is much weaker than the classical-style binding[2] [12,17,44,52], or *unique-binding* hereafter. This is because a quantum cheating sender may commit to a bit 0 and 1 in an arbitrary *superposition*, resulting in the committed value no longer unique. Thus, it is questionable *a priori* whether quantum bit commitments could be useful in cryptographic applications, let alone the notorious difficulty (or general impossibility) of quantum rewinding [21] in security analysis.

Canonical Quantum Bit Commitment. Motivated by the study of complete problems for quantum zero-knowledge [28,45,49] and more general quantum interactive proofs [11,41], the so-called *canonical* (non-interactive) quantum bit commitment[3] was proposed [18,52].

Roughly speaking, by a canonical quantum bit commitment scheme, the commitment consists of just a single (quantum) message from the sender to the receiver, which can be opened later by *uncompute* the commit stage. Its definition is sketched at the beginning of "Our contributions" shortly and given in Definition 2 formally. A canonical quantum bit commitment scheme satisfies the so-called *honest-binding* property, which guarantees that any cheating sender in the *reveal* stage cannot open an *honest* commitment to the bit 0 as 1, and vice versa. This honest-binding property appears even weaker than sum-binding. Both flavors of canonical quantum bit commitments can be constructed from quantum-secure one-way functions [30,31,52], or pseudorandom quantum states by a more recent result [36] and this work.

Though its binding property appears extremely weak, interestingly, it turns out that canonical quantum bit commitment is sufficient to construct quantum zero-knowledge [18,51,52] and quantum oblivious transfer[4] [18]. However, the corresponding security (that will be based on quantum bit honest-binding) there are more tricky to establish than the corresponding security based on unique-binding.

Other Quantum Commitments and Binding Properties. There are also other (classical or quantum) constructions of commitments that satisfy some stronger binding properties (but which may not hold for *general* quantum bit commitments) than sum-binding, including *collapse-binding* commitments [43, 44], and *extractable* commitments [5,22]; they are likely to be more versatile than general quantum bit commitments in applications. However, both of them need interactions in the standard model, losing the possible advantage of the non-interactivity of quantum bit commitments.

---

[2] That is, any quantum cheating sender cannot generate a commitment that can be opened as both 0 and 1 successfully with non-negligible probability.

[3] In the prior work (e.g. [18,51,52]) and an earlier draft of this paper (back in 2020), it is called "generic" form. However, this name is misleading as pointed out by Ananth, Qian, and Yuen [4], who also suggest the current name "canonical" to us. And we accept.

[4] In [18], a quantum oblivious transfer with a security that is weaker than the full simulation-security [5,22] but still very useful in many scenarios was achieved.

Restricting to quantum *statistically-binding* commitments, statistical *unique-binding* can be achieved based on quantum one-way permutations [2], or even functions by a recent result [7]. More recently, Ananth, Qian and Yuen [3] also propose an *extractor-based* quantum statistical-binding property, hereafter *AQY-binding*, and show that it can be satisfied by a construction of quantum bit commitment based on pseudorandom quantum states. Though these binding properties seem much stronger than the honest-binding property guaranteed by canonical statistically-binding quantum bit commitment (whose instantiations can be found either in [52], [50, Appendix D], or [36]), commitments satisfying these binding properties turn out to be *no more useful* (at least in theory, as far as we can tell) than canonical statistically-binding quantum bit commitments in applications [18]. More discussion on this point is referred to Subsect. 1.2 (where we will discuss the extractor-based AQY-binding property in greater detail.)

Yet in some other work certain strong quantum binding properties are proposed for applications [12,16], but no instantiations of the corresponding commitments based on well-founded complexity assumptions are known even today.

This Work. In this work, we show that the canonical quantum bit commitment *captures* the computational hardness underlying general computational quantum bit commitments, by providing a *compiler* that can transform any computational quantum bit commitment scheme into the canonical (non-interactive) form. This not only answer the motivating question aforementioned affirmatively, but also allows us to study general properties of quantum bit commitments through the lens of canonical quantum bit commitments.

We further propose to study canonical quantum bit commitment in the future not only as a cryptographic primitive in the MiniQCrypt world (named after [22]), but also as a basic (quantum) complexity-theoretic object whose existence is an interesting open problem in its own right. Our proposal is based on our current knowledge about canonical quantum bit commitment summarized as follows: (Refer to Subsect. 1.3 for more detail.)

1. Its formulation is clean and simple (Definition 2), inducing two basic quantum complexity-theoretic open questions: one is on the existence of quantum state ensembles that are computationally indistinguishable but far apart in the trace distance, while the other on the existence of unitaries that cannot be efficiently realized.
2. It is robust (Theorem 6), implying that the two basic open questions mentioned in the 1st item above are essentially the same question.
3. It captures the computational hardness underlying general computational quantum bit commitments (Theorem 4).
4. It is useful in quantum cryptography [3,5,18,51,52].
5. Conversely, it is also implied by some basic quantum cryptographic primitives such as quantum zero-knowledge [52] and quantum oblivious transfer [14].
6. It is implied by quantum complexity assumptions such as quantum-secure one-way functions and pseudorandom quantum states in the MiniQCrypt world [14,30,31,36,52]. But the converse is unknown.

Before introducing our contribution of this work in greater detail, we stress that in this paper when we talk about statistical or computational binding without explicitly mentioning other properties of binding, we mean the most general *sum-binding* property (or equivalently, honest-binding w.r.t. canonical quantum bit commitments, as will become clear shortly). In spite of this, we have already known that canonical quantum bit commitments can satisfy some stronger binding properties than sum-binding that are interesting and useful in applications [18,50,51]. We expect further exploration on the binding properties of canonical quantum bit commitments in the future.

1.1   Our Contribution

We first sketch what a *canonical* quantum bit commitment scheme looks like; its formal definition is given in Definition 2. Informally speaking, a canonical (non-interactive) quantum bit commitment scheme can be represented by an ensemble of unitary polynomial-time generated quantum circuit pair $\{(Q_0(n), Q_1(n))\}_n$, where n is the security parameter. For the moment, let us drop the security parameter n to simplify the notation. Both quantum circuits Q_0 and Q_1 perform on a quantum register pair (C, R), which are composed of qubits. To commit a bit $b \in \{0, 1\}$, the sender (of bit commitment) first initializes the register pair (C, R) in all $|0\rangle$'s state and then performs the quantum circuit Q_b on them, sending the *commitment* register C to the receiver. In the reveal stage, the sender sends the bit b together with the *decommitment* register R to the receiver, who will first perform the *inverse* of the quantum circuit Q_b (since it is unitary) on the register pair (C, R), and then measure each qubit of (C, R) in the computational basis. The receiver will accept (i.e. the opening is successful) if and only if the measurement outcome of each qubit is 0. We say that the scheme (Q_0, Q_1) is hiding if the reduced quantum state of $Q_0 |0\rangle$ in the register C and that of $Q_1 |0\rangle$ are indistinguishable, and that the scheme is binding if there does not exist a unitary performing on the register R that transforms the quantum state $Q_0 |0\rangle$ into $Q_1 |0\rangle$.

We obtain *four* main results on properties of canonical and more general quantum bit commitments as follows:

1. Honest-binding is equivalent to sum-binding (w.r.t. the canonical form)

Among various binding properties proposed for quantum (including post-quantum) commitments [2,12,16,17,44,51,52], *honest-binding* [52] is the weakest. Informally, it states that any cheating sender (in the reveal stage) cannot open an *honest* commitment to 0 (resp. 1) as 1 (resp. 0). Its formal definition w.r.t. a canonical quantum bit commitment scheme is given in Definition 2. A priori, honest-binding seems to be too weak to be useful: anyway, it is unrealistic to restrict a cheating sender's behavior to be honest in the commit stage!

Sum-binding is a general binding property of quantum bit commitment [17]. Roughly, let p_0 and p_1 denote the probability that a cheating sender (in the reveal stage) can open the commitment (generated in the commit stage in which the sender is also cheating) as 0 and 1, respectively. Then sum-binding requires that $p_0 + p_1 < 1 + negl(n)$, where $negl(\cdot)$ is some negligible function of the security parameter. The formal definition of sum-binding w.r.t. a canonical quantum bit commitment scheme is given in Definition 3.

While it is trivial that sum-binding implies honest-binding, in this work we show that the converse is also true w.r.t. canonical quantum bit commitments[5] (Theorem 2). This in turn establishes an *equivalence* between its semi-honest security (against an honest-but-curious attacker, i.e. honest-hiding and honest-binding; refer to Definition 2) and the full security (against an arbitrary attacker) (Theorem 3). This equivalence not only explains at a high level why previous applications of canonical quantum bit commitments only make use of its honest-binding property [18,51,52], but also enables us to simplify the security analysis of canonical quantum bit commitments schemes[6]. As an application, we can significantly simplify the DMS construction [17] of computationally-binding quantum bit commitment based on quantum-secure one-way permutations[7]. (The detail is referred to [50, Section 5]).

2. Quantum bit commitment is inherently non-interactive

We answer the motivating question raised before affirmatively, i.e. quantum bit commitment is inherently non-interacitve, by proving a *round-collapse* theorem (Theorem 4). This theorem can also be viewed as an extension of converting an arbitrary non-interactive quantum bit commitment scheme into the canonical form [18,52]. Its basic idea follows the non-interactive case, with the only *non-trivial* thing lying in identifying a sufficient yet as weak as possible condition under which the same idea works for such an extension. A priori, one may expect that for the compression of rounds, the original scheme itself should be firstly secure (against quantum attacks), with some additional structure requirements (if needed). Surprisingly, it turns out the condition for the round compression could be *extremely weak*: even the original quantum bit commitment scheme need not be fully secure; instead, it is sufficient that its *purification is semi-honest secure*! In greater detail, we construct a general *compiler* that can convert any (interactive) quantum bit commitment scheme whose purification is semi-honest secure into a quantum bit commitment scheme of the canonical form. This resulting scheme (of the canonical form), which will be referred to as the "compressed scheme", has *perfect completeness* and satisfies the *same flavor of hiding and binding properties* as the original scheme. This theorem is interesting by noting that we do not have a classical counterpart of it yet, which seems even unlikely [23,34]. An immediate consequence of the round-collapse theorem is that any known quantum bit commitment scheme (of either flavor

---

[5] We do not claim that this holds for a *general* quantum bit commitment; the two simple schemes presented in [50, Appendix C] also serve as two counterexamples in this regard.

[6] Then it suffices to show its semi-honest security.

[7] Strictly speaking, we simplify the security analysis of the DMS scheme *after* it is firstly converted into the canonical form (which is straightforward).

and based on any complexity assumption) can be converted into the canonical form (Theorem 5).

If we want to apply the round-collapse theorem in applications, (seeing from its statement) the relationship between the semi-honest security of the original scheme and its purification becomes important. We thus initiate a study towards this relationship. (The detail is referred to [50, Section 7, 9, and 10].) On one hand, we identify many situations in which the semi-honest security of the original scheme *extends* to its purification. On the other hand, we find two counterexamples for which such an extension is impossible. (The detail is referred to [50, Appendix C]). A *bridge* that connects these two notions of security is the security against a special kind of attack which we will refer to as the "purification attack", i.e. attacking by purifying all the party's (honest) operations prescribed by the protocol. A typical purification attack is *not* to perform the expected measurements. It turns out that an (interactive) quantum bit commitment scheme is secure against the purification attack *if and only if* its purification is semi-honest secure [50, Proposition 15]. But in comparison, the security against the purification attack is more convenient to work with in security analysis than the semi-honest security of the purified scheme. We believe that this security against the purification attack as well as techniques developed to establish it (refer to "Technical overview" for a discussion) are of independent interest.

As an interesting application, we apply the round-collapse theorem to compress the classical NOVY scheme [38], obtaining yet another construction (besides ones given in [17,30,31]) of non-interactive computationally-binding quantum bit commitment based on quantum-secure one-way permutations [50, Section 9]. This is interesting because we even do not know whether the original NOVY scheme itself is secure against quantum attacks (when the underlying quantum one-way permutation used is quantum secure). We also highlight that our quantum security analysis here is (interestingly) much simpler than the classical analysis of the NOVY scheme in [38]. This simplification mainly comes from that it suffices to show that the NOVY scheme is secure against the purification attack (for the purpose of round compression).

3. Quantum bit commitment is symmetric, or two flavors of quantum bit commitments are equivalent

Almost two decades ago, Crépeau, Légaré and Salvail [14] gave a way that virtually can transform any quantum bit commitment scheme that is computationally hiding and statistically unique-binding into another one of the opposite flavor, i.e. computationally binding and statistically hiding. In this work, we generalize this result significantly by proving a *symmetry*[8] in the sense as stated in the following (unconditional) theorem:

Theorem 1. *Computationally-hiding statistically-binding quantum bit commitments exist if and only if statistically-hiding computationally-binding quantum bit commitments exist.*

---

[8] This symmetry is in the same sense as that of oblivious transfer [48].

The *high-level idea* of proving the theorem above is as follows. By the virtue of the round-collapse theorem, it suffices to prove that the theorem holds w.r.t. canonical quantum bit commitments (Theorem 6). In greater detail, given a canonical quantum bit commitment scheme, we first feed it to a *somewhat simplified* CLS construction [14] to *convert* its flavor, and then feed the resulting scheme to the general compiler guaranteed by the round-collapse theorem to obtain the final scheme (which will be in the canonical form automatically).

Our security analysis are significantly simpler than the related ones given in [12,14]. Basically, the simplification comes from two aspects:

1. By the virtue of our round-collapse theorem (Theorem 4), the original CLS scheme (with a canonical quantum bit commitment scheme plugged in) can be simplified in the first place to just satisfy the security against the purification attack *before* the compression.
2. Proving the security against the purification attack turns out to be much easier than the full security.

Towards proving Theorem 6, we develop several techniques to establish the security against the purification attack. Most of these techniques are adapted from those used in [18,51]. Among others, we in particular show a *computational collapse* caused by canonical quantum computationally-binding commitments [50, Appendix F], which might be of independent interest. More discussion on our techniques is referred to "Technical overview".

We finally remark that as a by-product of the symmetry, we automatically obtain a construction of canonical statistically-hiding computationally-binding quantum bit commitment based on quantum-secure one-way functions or pseudorandom quantum states. This is achieved by first plugging in the somewhat simplified CLS construction a canonical computationally-hiding statistically-binding quantum bit commitment scheme that is either based on quantum-secure one-way functions or pseudorandom quantum states, and then compressing the resulting scheme. We remark that the construction of statistically-hiding computationally-binding quantum bit commitment based on pseudorandom quantum states is previously unknown.

4. Quantum statistical string sum-binding (w.r.t. the canonical form)

A natural way to commit a string is to commit it in a bitwise fashion using a quantum bit commitment scheme. So it is interesting to explore what binding property can be obtained if a quantum bit commitment scheme is composed in parallel. Since a canonical quantum bit commitment scheme satisfies the sum-binding property, ideally, we may hope to prove such a dream version of the quantum *string sum-binding* property as $\sum_{s \in \{0,1\}^m} p_s < 1 + negl(n)$, where p_s denotes the success probability that the cheating sender can open a (claimed) string commitment as the m-bit string s, and $negl(\cdot)$ denotes some negligible function of the security parameter n. However, this string sum-binding property seems too strong to be true generally when $m = poly(n)$, in which case the sender can attack by committing to a superposition of *exponentially* many m-

bit strings [12]. Then bounding the error induced by such a superposition by a negligible quantity becomes technically hard or even impossible[9].

In spite of the above, we manage to show that composing a canonical *statistically-binding* quantum bit commitment scheme in parallel indeed gives rise to a quantum string commitment scheme satisfying a dream version of the quantum statistical string sum-binding property (Theorem 7). Since our proof relies heavily on that the error (incurred by the statistical binding error) decreases *exponentially* in the Hamming distance between the committed string and the string to reveal, it does not extend to the case quantum computational binding.

1.2   Related (More Recent) Work

More recently[10], Bitansky and Brakerski [7] construct a non-interactive statistically-binding quantum bit commitment scheme based on quantum-secure one-way functions. Their scheme deviates from the canonical one given in [52], managing to achieve *unique-binding* and the *classical* reveal stage, but at the cost of more complex construction and analysis.

Morimae and Yamakawa [36] construct a statistically-binding quantum bit commitment scheme based on pseudorandom quantum states [26], a quantum complexity assumption arguably weaker than quantum-secure one-way functions [32]. Interestingly, we find their construction is just in the canonical form. So by results of this work, their security analysis of quantum statistical binding can be simplified to just show the quantum statistical honest-binding (rather than sum-binding) property. Moreover, combining results in this work (Theorem 6), it follows that both flavors of canonical quantum bit commitments can be constructed based on pseudorandom quantum states.

Ananth, Qian and Yuen [3] also construct a statistically-binding quantum bit commitment scheme based on pseudorandom quantum states, which has *two* messages in the commit stage and a single *classical* message in the reveal stage. Clearly, this scheme is not in the canonical form. But they show that it satisfies a strong (statistical) binding property such that an (inefficient) extractor is associated with scheme, which can be used to extract (and thus collapse) the committed value from the commitment at the end of the commit stage. We find[11] that this idea of introducing an extractor to quantum statistically-binding commitments is very similar in spirit to the analysis framework introduced in [18] but only for canonical perfectly/statistically-binding quantum bit commitments. More discussion on the comparison between them is referred to [50, Appendix B], where by tweaking techniques used in [18], we in particular prove that canonical statistically-binding quantum bit commitments automatically satisfy the AQY-binding property.

---

[9] To the best of our knowledge, however, no impossibility result is known yet. In [12], authors only vaguely argue that this seems impossible for quantum computationally-binding commitments.

[10] After the upload of the first preprint of this work to Cryptology ePrint Archive [50] in 2020.

[11] This is also observed in [36, Appendix B].

While the extractor-based AQY-binding definition is more readily usable by cryptographers, there seems no obvious way to extend it to the case of quantum computational binding (when the commitment is statistically hiding). This is because then the quantum commitments to different values are negligibly close (in the trace distance); we cannot hope that a similar extractor exists. In contrast, the formalization of canonical quantum bit commitment schemes provide a *uniform* way to capture both flavors of quantum bit commitments.

Moreover, Ananth, Qian and Yuen [3] propose studying pseudorandom quantum states, instead of quantum-secure one-way functions, as a basic quantum complexity assumption for quantum (rather than post-quantum) cryptography. In this regard, we feel that it would be equally interesting to study the existence of canonical quantum bit commitment schemes as a basic quantum complexity assumption for quantum cryptography. More discussion on this point is referred to the next subsection.

1.3 Quantum Bit Commitments: Seeing from Both Quantum Cryptography and Quantum Complexity Perspectives

Based on previous results and results in this paper, now let us give an overview of quantum bit commitments from quantum cryptography and quantum complexity perspectives, respectively.

Seeing from the *quantum cryptography perspective*, on one hand quantum bit commitment can be constructed from quantum-secure one-way functions/permutations [2,7,14,17,30,31,52], or pseudorandom quantum states [3, 26,36]. It is interesting to explore whether quantum bit commitments imply pseudorandom quantum states (of any sort) conversely[12]. On the other hand, quantum bit commitments are useful, and may help reduce the round complexity of cryptographic constructions [18,51,52]. In particular, there exists a certain *equivalence* between quantum bit commitment and quantum zero-knowledge [52], and an equivalence between quantum bit commitment and quantum oblivious transfer [3,5,14,18,54]. Thus, quantum bit commitment is likely to be an important primitive in the MiniQCrypt world [22]. It is interesting to explore more cryptographic applications of quantum bit commitments in the future.

Seeing from the *quantum complexity perspective*, whether computational quantum bit commitments exist is an interesting open problem. As mentioned, canonical quantum bit commitment are motivated by the study of complete problems for quantum zero-knowledge [45,49] and more general quantum interactive proofs [11,41]. The existence of canonical statistically-hiding computationally-binding quantum bit commitment schemes is closely related to the *quantum complexity of unitaries* [1]. In greater detail, suppose that (Q_0, Q_1) is a canonical statistically-hiding computationally-binding quantum bit commitment scheme. Then its statistical hiding property implies that quantum states $Q_0 |0\rangle^{CR}$ and

---

[12] We do not expect that quantum bit commitments can imply quantum-secure one-way functions, simply because a canonical quantum bit commitment scheme concerns quantum states rather than any sort of functions.

$Q_1 |0\rangle^{CR}$ only differ up to a unitary U performing on the decommitment register R. This is because restricting to the commitment register C, the corresponding two reduced quantum states are negligibly close in the trace distance. However, the computational binding property implies that this unitary U is *not* efficiently realizable!

We can motivate the study of canonical computationally-hiding statistically-binding quantum bit commitment by comparing it with a pair of efficiently constructible probability distributions that are *computationally indistinguishable* but *statistically far apart* in the classical setting. They look quite similar; we may view the former as the quantum counterpart of the latter. Goldreich shows that the existence of the latter implies one-way functions [20, an exercise in Chap. 3] and pseudorandom generators [19]. In a try to translate this result to the quantum setting, it brings us back to the open question of whether quantum bit commitments imply pseudorandom quantum states (which are the quantum analog of pseudorandom generators) [3,26,36].

We finally remark that the round-collapse theorem and the equivalence between two flavors of quantum bit commitments established in this paper indicate that the open question regarding the existence of computational quantum bit commitments is very *robust*. And it will be more robust if the answer to the following open question, which concerns *quantum hardness amplification*, is "yes": can the computational binding error of a canonical quantum bit commitment scheme be reduced by parallel repetition, say from $1/2$ or even inverse polynomial to some negligible quantity? This question looks very similar to the amplification of the hardness of inverting an arbitrary one-way function in classical cryptography [53]. More interestingly, if the answer to this question is indeed "yes", then combining it with results in [18,45,51,52] will complete a proof for an equivalence between quantum bit commitment and quantum zero-knowledge like in the classical setting [40].

1.4 Technical Overview

Honest-Binding Implies Sum-Binding. The proof is just a simple application of the quantum rewinding lemma (Lemma 1) once used in [18,51,52], which in a nutshell is another variant (other than the one used in [42] that is designed specific for sigma protocols) of the gentle measurement lemma [47].

Round Compression. Our compiler for the round compression is inspired by the equivalence between the semi-honest security and the full security w.r.t. canonical quantum bit commitments (Theorem 3).

Informally speaking, the *compiler* itself is extremely simple: in the new (non-interactive) commit stage, the sender will simulate an *honest* execution of the commit stage of the original (possibly interactive) scheme, and then send the original receiver's system as the commitment to the new receiver. Later in the reveal stage, the new sender will send the residual system to the new receiver, who will check the new sender's whole computation in the commit stage via the quantum *reversible* computation. For this construction to be legal, possible *irreversible* computation of both parties in the commit stage prescribed by the original scheme should be simulated by corresponding unitary computation (in a standard way) in the first place. This procedure of simulation is typically referred to as the "purification" (of a quantum protocol).

At the first glance, the compiler constructed as above seems too simple to be true: how can the idea of simply letting the new sender delegate all the computation in the commit stage of (the purification of) the original scheme work? After all, the new sender may deviate arbitrarily, and there seems no way of restricting its behavior by just exchanging a single message in the (non-interactive) commit stage! Clearly, this idea of compression does not work for commitments in classical cryptography.

The reason why our compiler works is by the virtue of Theorem 3: it suffices to show that the resulting *compressed* quantum bit commitment scheme (which is just in the canonical form by our construction) is semi-honest secure. This also provides some intuition why in the formal statement of our round-collapse theorem (Theorem 4), it requires that the *(*purification) of the original scheme (rather than the original scheme itself), or *purified scheme* hereafter, be semi-honest secure. As for the proof of the round-collapse theorem, while the honest-hiding property of the compressed scheme is trivial, its honest-binding property can be roughly argued in the below.

Suppose (for contradiction) that at the beginning of the reveal stage, there is a cheating sender who can transform the quantum state of the whole system when a bit 0 is committed to the state when a bit 1 is committed, by just performing some unitary operation U on its own system. This will gives rise to an attack against the honest-binding property of the purified scheme as follows: the sender commits to the bit 0 honestly following the purified scheme in the commit stage. In the reveal stage, it first performs the operation U on its own system, transforming the whole system to a state that is close to the state when the bit 1 is committed, and then proceeds honestly to open the commitment as 1. While the intuition underlying this reduction is simple, to turn it into a formal proof, we need a large amount of (and tedious) work in formalizing an execution of (the commit stage of) a general (interactive) quantum bit commitment scheme and its purification [50, Section 6], as well as their semi-honest security [50, Section 7].

Last, we would like to compare our round compression of a general interactive quantum bit commitment scheme with that of a quantum interactive proof [27] or a zero-knowledge proof [29]. Ideas in these two settings are very similar: both of them rely heavily on the *reversibility* of quantum computation. The *key difference* lies in that for the latter, since (even) the honest prover could be computationally unbounded, an (interactive) *swap test* is introduced for the purpose of checking the computation. In comparison, in our setting this test is not necessary; this is because (as typical in cryptography) both the honest sender and the honest receiver of bit commitment are polynomial-time bounded.

Proving an Equivalence Between Two Flavors of Canonical Quantum Bit Commitments. The basic idea to *convert* the flavor of a canonical quantum bit commitment scheme is to use the CLS construction [14]. In a nutshell, the original CLS scheme in [14] uses *classical* statistically unique-binding bit commitments (e.g. Naor's scheme [37]) to realize a 1-out-of-2 *quantum oblivious transfer* (QOT) [13], which in turn can be used to construct a computationally-binding quantum bit commitment scheme. In [18], it is shown that commitments used in the CLS scheme, or QOT subprotocol more precisely, can be replaced with canonical statistically/perfectly-binding quantum bit commitments. Then combined with the round-collapse theorem (Theorem 4), this already proves one direction of the equivalence.

For the other direction of the equivalence, however, it is still open whether one can use computationally-binding quantum bit commitments in the CLS scheme to obtain a statistically-binding quantum bit commitment scheme. Technically, this is because we do not know whether using computationally-binding quantum bit commitments can force the receiver of BB84 qubits in the QOT subprotocol to measure these qubits upon receiving them. (We note that this is not a big problem when statistically-binding quantum bit commitments are used [14,18]). To overcome this difficulty, in [12] a tailored quantum string binding property is proposed, by which they show that quantum commitments satisfying such binding property are sufficient to show the security of the QOT protocol. Unfortunately, we do not know whether quantum commitments satisfying such binding property are instantiatable even today. In this work, we overcome this technical difficulty by proving a *computational collapse theorem* [50, Appendix F], as will be discussed shortly.

Actually, for our purpose of converting the flavor of canonical quantum bit commitments, it suffices for us to use a *somewhat simplified CLS construction*: all *intermediate verifications of quantum commitments* within the original CLS scheme can be removed. We can do this is by the virtue of the round-collapse theorem, namely, we only need a scheme whose purification is semi-honest secure for the purpose of the round compression. In particular, we only need such a QOT that satisfies the following security property: after the interaction, the purified receiver of QOT does not know the other bit that the honest sender is given as input, while the purified sender of QOT does not know which input bit the honest receiver is aware of. This security is already much *weaker* than the security against an arbitrary quantum attack considered in [14,18,54], let alone the recently achieved simulation security [5,15,22]. Hence, one can imagine that it is much easier to establish.

For the formal security analysis, we will first prove the semi-honest security of this somewhat simplified CLS scheme, and then manage to extend it to its purification. For such an extension, a *crucial step* is to show that quantum commitments will cause an implicit collapse of the quantum state just like the measurements prescribed by the QOT subprotocol were really performed. To this end, we will use techniques introduced in the below.

Arguing the Security Against the Purification Attack. Seeing from the statement of our round-collapse theorem, to apply it, one needs first to show that the purification of the original (interactive) quantum bit commitment scheme is semi-honest secure, or equivalently, the original scheme is secure against the purification attack. It turns out that this security is closely related to the semi-honest security, thus often much easier to establish than the full security. In particular, we show that in many interesting scenarios, the semi-honest security of the original scheme *extends* to its purification. For such an extension, the *basic idea* is to show that collapses prescribed by the original scheme are *enforced* even *after* the purification. To have a taste of how to do this, note that messages sent through the classical channel automatically collapse; when a message is uniquely determined by some other collapsed messages, it can be viewed as having collapsed as well.

A non-trivial case in which collapses are enforced is by *quantum commitments*, as argued in [18] and within the proof of Theorem 6 in this paper. That is, committing to a *superposition* using canonical statistically- or computationally-binding quantum bit commitments (in a bitwise fashing) can be viewed as an *implicit* way of measuring it (but without leaking its value)! In greater detail, when canonical statistically-binding quantum bit commitments are used, collapses can be shown using techniques (i.e. *perturbation* and *commitment measurement*) developed in [18]. When canonical computationally-binding quantum bit commitments are used, we will show a "computational collapse" (named after [12]) by proving a *computational collapse theorem* [50, Appendix F] in this work. The technique used towards proving this theorem is inspired by the proof of the quantum computational string predicate-binding property in [51], which basically is a way of bounding exponentially many negligible errors in an arbitrary superposition by a negligible quantity. We remark that currently, this computational collapse theorem is only known to be suitable to apply when the security against the purification attack is considered; whether it can be extended to be suitable for the security analysis against an arbitrary quantum attack (like in [12]) is left as an interesting open problem.

Last, we stress that the semi-honest security of an arbitrary (interactive) quantum bit commitment scheme does *not* extend to its purification *generally*; two counterexamples are presented in [50, Appedix C].

1.5   Follow-Up Work

In preparing the camera-ready version of this extended abstract, we notice that there is a follow-up work [9].

After reading an earlier draft of the full version of this extended abstract [50] (the version uploaded to Cryptology ePrint Archive this February, 2022), authors of [9] call the two ensembles of efficiently-generated quantum state that are far in the trace distance but quantum computationally indistinguishable the "EFI pair". (As we have argued in this extended abstract, EFI pair and canonical statistically-binding quantum bit commitment are actually the same object seen from different perspectives). They further explore the connections between EFI pairs and some other cryptographic applications that are not discussed in this extended abstract, in particular multiparty secure computations for classical functionalities and quantum zero-knowledge proofs for languages *beyond* **NP**. (Note that within **NP**, an equivalence between (instance-dependent) canonical statistically-binding quantum bit commitments (hence EFI pairs) and quantum zero-knowledge proofs has already been established in [52] back in 2015).

Organization. The remainder of this paper is organized as follows. In Sect. 2, we review necessary preliminaries. In Sect. 3, we formally introduce the definition of a canonical quantum bit commitment scheme and its honest-hiding and honest-binding properties. In Sect. 4, we show that w.r.t. canonical quantum bit commitment, its honest-binding property is equivalent to the sum-binding property. This equivalence will be used to prove the round-collapse theorem in Sect. 5. As an application of the round-collapse theorem, in Sect. 6 we prove an equivalence between two flavors of quantum bit commitments. In Sect. 7, a very strong quantum string sum-binding property of the parallel composition of canonical statistically-binding quantum bit commitments is established. We conclude with Sect. 8, where several open problems are also raised.

2   Preliminaries

Notation. Denote $[n] = \{1, 2, \ldots, n\}$ for an integer n. Denote by U_n the uniform distribution/random variable ranging over the set $\{0, 1\}^n$, i.e. all binary strings of length n. We use "$\xleftarrow{\$}$" to denote the action of choosing an element uniformly random from a given set, e.g. $x \xleftarrow{\$} U_n$. Let $negl(n)$ denote an arbitrary *negligible* (i.e. asymptotically smaller than any inverse polynomial) function of the security parameter n. Given two strings $s, s' \in \{0, 1\}^n$, let $\mathrm{dist}(s, s')$ denote the Hamming distance between s and s'.

Quantum Formalism. Quantum registers/systems we use in this paper are composed of multiple qubits. We sometimes explicitly write quantum register(s) as a *superscript* of an operator or a quantum state to indicate on which register(s) this operator performs or which register(s) hold this quantum state, respectively. For example, we may write U^A, $|\psi\rangle^A$ or ρ^A, highlighting that the operator U performs on the register A, and the register A is in pure state $|\psi\rangle$ or mixed state ρ, respectively. When it is clear from the context, we often drop superscripts to simplify the notation.

We use $\mathrm{F}(\cdot, \cdot)$ to denote the *fidelity* of two quantum states [46]. Given a projector Π on a Hilbert space, we call $\{\Pi, \mathbb{1} - \Pi\}$ the *binary* measurement induced by Π. This binary measurement is typically induced by a *verification*, for which we call it *succeeds*, *accepts*, or the outcome is *one*, if the measured quantum state collapses to the subspace on which Π projects.

For a bit $b \in \{0, 1\}$, let $|b\rangle_+$ and $|b\rangle_\times$ be the qubits in the state $|b\rangle$ w.r.t. the standard basis and Hadamard basis, respectively. For the former, we often drop "+" and just write $|b\rangle$.

We work with the standard *unitary* quantum circuit model. In this model, a quantum algorithm can be formalized in terms of *uniformly generated* quantum circuit family, where the "uniformly generated" means the description of the quantum circuit coping with n-bit inputs can be output by *a single classical polynomial-time algorithm* on the input 1^n. We assume without loss of generality that each quantum circuit is composed of quantum gates chosen from some fixed universal, finite, and *unitary* quantum gate set [39]. Given a quantum circuit Q, we also overload the notation to use Q to denote its corresponding *unitary transformation*; $Q^\dagger$ denotes its *inverse*.

(In)distinguishability of Quantum State Ensembles

Definition 1 ((In)distinguishability of quantum state ensembles). *Two quantum state ensembles $\{\rho_n\}_n$ and $\{\xi_n\}_n$ are quantum statistically (resp. computationally) indistinguishable, if for any quantum state ensemble $\{\sigma_n\}_n$ and any unbounded (resp. polynomial-time bounded) quantum algorithm D which outputs a single classical bit,*

$$|\Pr[D(1^n, \rho_n \otimes \sigma_n) = 1] - \Pr[D(1^n, \xi_n \otimes \sigma_n) = 1]| < negl(n)$$

for sufficiently large n.

Remark. The quantum state ensemble $\{\sigma_n\}_n$ in the definition above plays the role of the *non-uniformity* given to the distinguisher D. Since a mixed quantum state can always be purified, we can assume without loss of generality that the state σ_n is *pure*.

A Quantum Rewinding Lemma

Lemma 1 (A quantum rewinding [18]). *Let $\mathcal{X}$ and $\mathcal{Y}$ be two Hilbert spaces. Unit vector $|\psi\rangle \in \mathcal{X} \otimes \mathcal{Y}$. Orthogonal projectors $\Gamma_1, \ldots, \Gamma_k$ perform on the space $\mathcal{X} \otimes \mathcal{Y}$, while unitary transformations $U_1, \ldots, U_k$ perform on the space $\mathcal{Y}$. If $1/k \cdot \sum_{i=1}^k \left\| \Gamma_i (U_i \otimes \mathbb{1}^\mathcal{X}) |\psi\rangle \right\|^2 \geq 1 - \eta$, where $0 \leq \eta \leq 1$, then*

$$\left\| (U_k^\dagger \otimes \mathbb{1}^\mathcal{X}) \Gamma_k (U_k \otimes \mathbb{1}^\mathcal{X}) \cdots (U_1^\dagger \otimes \mathbb{1}^\mathcal{X}) \Gamma_1 (U_1 \otimes \mathbb{1}^\mathcal{X}) |\psi\rangle \right\| \geq 1 - \sqrt{k\eta}. \quad (1)$$

3   Canonical (Non-interactive) Quantum Bit Commitment

The definition of a canonical (non-interactive) quantum bit commitment scheme is as follows.

Definition 2. *A canonical (non-interactive) quantum bit commitment scheme is represented by an ensemble of polynomial-time uniformly generated quantum circuit pair $\{(Q_0(n), Q_1(n))\}_n$ as follows, where we drop the security parameter n to simplify the notation:*

- *In the commit stage, to commit a bit $b \in \{0, 1\}$, the sender performs the quantum circuit Q_b on the quantum register pair (C, R)[13] initialized in all $|0\rangle$'s state. Then the sender sends the commitment register C to the receiver, whose state at this moment is denoted by ρ_b.*

---

[13] Their size depend on the security parameter n.

– *In the subsequent (canonical) reveal stage, the sender announces the bit b, and sends the decommitment register R to the receiver. The receiver will first perform $Q_b^\dagger$ on the quantum register pair (C, R) and then measure each qubit of (C, R) in the computational basis, accepting if measurement outcomes are all 0's.*

The hiding (or concealing) and the binding properties of the scheme are defined as follows:

– *(Honest)-**hiding**. We say that the scheme is statistically (resp. computationally) hiding if quantum states ρ_0 and ρ_1 are statistically (resp. computationally) indistinguishable[14].*
– *ϵ-(honest-)**binding**. First prepare the quantum register pair (C, R) in the state $Q_0 |0\rangle$[15]. We say that the scheme is computationally (resp. statistically) ϵ-binding if for any state $|\psi\rangle$ of an auxiliary register Z, and any polynomial-time (resp. physically) realizable unitary transformation U performing on registers (R, Z), the reduced state of the quantum register pair (C, R) after the transformation U is performed is far from the state $Q_1 |0\rangle$. Or formally,*

$$\left\| (Q_1 |0\rangle \langle 0| Q_1^\dagger)^{CR} U^{RZ} ((Q_0 |0\rangle)^{CR} |\psi\rangle^Z) \right\| < \epsilon. \qquad (2)$$

By the reversibility of quantum computation, this binding property can be equivalently defined by swapping the roles of Q_0 and Q_1, in which case the inequality (2) becomes

$$\left\| (Q_0 |0\rangle \langle 0| Q_0^\dagger)^{CR} U^{RZ} ((Q_1 |0\rangle)^{CR} |\psi\rangle^Z) \right\| < \epsilon. \qquad (3)$$

As typical in cryptography, We say that the scheme is computationally (resp. statistically) binding (without referring to the parameter ϵ) when the function $\epsilon(\cdot)$ is a negligible function (of the security parameter n).

Remark

1. We call the binding property defined above *honest-binding*, because informally it states that any cheating sender cannot open the *honest* commitment to a bit b as $1 - b$. That is, in the definition of honest-binding, a cheating sender is honest in the commit stage but may deviate arbitrarily in the reveal stage. In this regard, the attack $(U, |\psi\rangle)$ of the sender just happens in the reveal stage. Honest-binding is the *weakest* binding property that any meaningful quantum bit commitment scheme should satisfy. This definition will be generalized to the case of *interactive* quantum bit commitment schemes in [50, Section 7].

---

[14] Strictly speaking, it should be understood as the corresponding two quantum state ensembles indexed by the security parameter n are indistinguishable.

[15] Here the notation $|0\rangle$ should be understood as multiple $|0\rangle$'s, the number of which depends on the security parameter; we just write a single $|0\rangle$ to simplify the notation. We will follow this rule throughout this paper.

2. The hiding property of a bit commitment scheme is only defined w.r.t. the commit stage. For the hiding property defined above, since the commit stage is non-interactive (so that the receiver will send nothing during the commit stage), the hiding against a semi-honest (i.e. honest-but-curious) receiver and that against an arbitrary receiver are just the same security property. In this regard, the honest-hiding is also the hiding against an arbitrary quantum receiver. However, in the sequel when we consider a general (interactive) quantum bit commitment scheme, these two notions are not necessarily equivalent.

3. As commented in [52], the reveal stage in the definition above is *canonical* in the sense that it is similar to the canonical opening of a classical bit commitment: the sender sends all its *random coins* used in the commit stage to the receiver, who then checks that these coins *explain* (i.e. are consistent with) the conversation generated during the commit stage.

4. In [18,52], it is argued informally that any *non-interactive* statistically-binding quantum bit commitment scheme can be converted into a scheme of the canonical form. Actually, the same argument extends to the setting of non-interactive computationally-binding quantum bit commitment schemes in a straightforward way. In this work, we will further extend it, showing that any (interactive) quantum bit commitment scheme can be converted into this canonical form (Theorem 4).

5. In the sequel, to simplify the notation we often drop the security parameter n and just write (Q_0, Q_1) to represent a canonical quantum bit commitment scheme.

6. We can commit to a binary string $s \in \{0,1\}^m$ in a bitwise fashion using a canonical quantum bit commitment scheme (Q_0, Q_1). Then the corresponding quantum circuit is given by

$$Q_s \stackrel{def}{=} \bigotimes_{i=1}^{m} Q_{s_i}, \tag{4}$$

where s_i is the i-th bit of the string s and each quantum circuit Q_{s_i} performs on one copy of the quantum register pair (C, R).

7. As discussed in "Introduction", this definition of a canonical quantum bit commitment scheme can also be viewed as a quantum complexity assumption that is weaker than quantum-secure one-way functions and pseudorandom quantum states [26].

4   Honest-Binding is Equivalent to Sum-Binding

Sum-binding is a general binding property of quantum bit commitment. Its definition w.r.t. a canonical quantum bit commitment scheme is as follows.

Definition 3 (Sum-binding). *At the beginning of the commit stage, the cheating sender prepares the whole system (C, R, Z) in an arbitrary quantum state $|\psi\rangle$. Then it sends the commitment register C to the receiver. In the reveal stage,* *to open the bit commitment as 0 (resp. 1), the sender performs U_0 (resp. U_1) on the system (R, Z) and then send the decommitment register R to the receiver. Let p_0 (resp. p_1) be the success probability that the sender opens the bit commitment as 0 (resp. 1). The sum-binding requires that $p_0 + p_1 < 1 + negl(n)$.*

Compared with honest-binding (Definition 2), sum-binding is a security against an *arbitrary* quantum sender, who may deviate from the scheme in both the commit and the reveal stages. Clearly, sum-binding implies honest-binding, by noting that if we fix p_0 or p_1 in Definition 3 to be 1, then we end up with honest-binding. Interestingly, it turns out that the opposite direction is also true, i.e. the seemingly weaker honest-binding also implies sum-binding. Combining them we have the following theorem.

Theorem 2. *Honest-binding is equivalent to sum-binding w.r.t. a canonical quantum bit commitment scheme (of either flavors).*

Proof. It is left to prove that honest-binding implies sum-binding. It turns out that an attack which breaks the sum-binding property can be directly used to break the honest-binding property without much modification. Detail follows. We remark that the proof below holds for either flavors of canonical quantum bit commitment schemes.

Let n be the security parameter. According to its definition (Definition 3), an arbitrary attack of the sum-binding property of a canonical quantum bit commitment scheme (Q_0, Q_1) can be modeled by $(U_0, U_1, |\psi\rangle)$. Now assume that the attack $(U_0, U_1, |\psi\rangle)$ breaks the sum-binding property; that is,

$$\left\| (Q_0 |0\rangle \langle 0| Q_0^\dagger)^{CR} \cdot U_0^{RZ} |\psi\rangle \right\|^2 + \left\| (Q_1 |0\rangle \langle 0| Q_1^\dagger)^{CR} \cdot U_1^{RZ} |\psi\rangle \right\|^2 > 1 + \frac{1}{p},$$

where $p(\cdot)$ is some polynomial of the security parameter n. We apply the quantum rewinding lemma (Lemma 1) to the inequality above, with the parameters $k, \eta, U_1, U_2, \Gamma_1$ and Γ_2 in the lemma replaced by $2, 1/2 - 1/(2p), U_0, U_1, Q_0 |0\rangle \langle 0| Q_0^\dagger$ and $Q_1 |0\rangle \langle 0| Q_1^\dagger$, respectively. We obtain

$$\left\| (U_1^\dagger)^{RZ} (Q_1 |0\rangle \langle 0| Q_1^\dagger)^{CR} U_1^{RZ} (U_0^\dagger)^{RZ} \cdot (Q_0 |0\rangle \langle 0| Q_0^\dagger)^{CR} U_0^{RZ} |\psi\rangle^{CRZ} \right\|$$

$$\geq 1 - \sqrt{1 - \frac{1}{p}} > \frac{1}{2p}. \tag{5}$$

An intuitive interpretation of this inequality is that the success probability of first opening the bit commitment as 0 and then as 1 is at least some non-negligible quantity.

We are next to devise an attack of the honest-binding property of the scheme (Q_0, Q_1) given the attack $(U_0, U_1, |\psi\rangle)$. Specifically, suppose that in the commit stage, the sender (honestly) prepares the quantum state $Q_0 |0\rangle$ in the quantum register pair (C, R) and sends the commitment register C to the receiver. Later at the beginning of the reveal stage, the sender receives the quantum state $|\psi\rangle$, which is stored in quantum registers (C', R', Z') that are of the same size as registers (C, R, Z), respectively. Then the cheating sender S^* proceeds as follows to try to open the quantum bit commitment as 1:

1. Perform the unitary transformation U_0 on the quantum registers (R', Z').
2. Perform the binary measurement induced by the projector $Q_0 |0\rangle \langle 0| Q_0^\dagger$ on the quantum register pair (C', R'). (*Intuitively,* we expect that conditioned on its outcome being 1, the reduced state of the register Z' will help the sender S^* cheat.)
3. Perform the unitary transformation $U_1 U_0^\dagger$ on the registers (R, Z').
4. Send the decommitment register R to the receiver.

To show that S^* breaks the honest-binding property of the scheme (Q_0, Q_1), it suffices to prove a lower bound of the probability of both the following two events happening simultaneously: (1) the measurement outcome in the step 2 being 1; and (2) the cheating sender S^* succeeds. (Note that S^* may also cheat successfully while the measurement outcome of the step 2 is 0; but its probability can be ignored for a lower bound of S^*'s success probability.) This probability is given by the expression

$$\left\| (U_1^\dagger)^{RZ'} (Q_1 |0\rangle \langle 0| Q_1^\dagger)^{CR} U_1^{RZ'} \cdot (U_0^\dagger)^{RZ'} (Q_0 |0\rangle \langle 0| Q_0^\dagger)^{C'R'} U_0^{R'Z'} ((Q_0 |0\rangle)^{CR} |\psi\rangle^{C'R'Z'}) \right\|^2 .$$

A key observation is that conditioned on the measurement outcome in the step 2 being 1, both the quantum register pair (C, R) and (C', R') will be in the state $Q_0 |0\rangle$ at the end of the step 2. Thus, from then on, switching to perform unitaries U_0, U_1 on registers (R', Z') (as opposed to (R, Z')) and opening the commitment in the register C' will result in the same success probability. That is, the expression above is equal to

$$\left\| (U_1^\dagger)^{R'Z'} (Q_1 |0\rangle \langle 0| Q_1^\dagger)^{C'R'} U_1^{R'Z'} (U_0^\dagger)^{R'Z'} \cdot (Q_0 |0\rangle \langle 0| Q_0^\dagger)^{C'R'} U_0^{R'Z'} ((Q_0 |0\rangle)^{CR} |\psi\rangle^{C'R'Z'}) \right\|^2 .$$

Since now the quantum registers (C, R) are untouched, this expression will simplify to

$$\left\| (U_1^\dagger)^{R'Z'} (Q_1 |0\rangle \langle 0| Q_1^\dagger)^{C'R'} U_1^{R'Z'} (U_0^\dagger)^{R'Z'} \cdot (Q_0 |0\rangle \langle 0| Q_0^\dagger)^{C'R'} U_0^{R'Z'} |\psi\rangle^{C'R'Z'} \right\|^2 .$$

But this final expression can be lowerbounded by applying the inequality (5), if we identify registers (C, R, Z) in the l.h.s. of the inequality (5) with registers (C', R', Z') here, respectively. This will yield a lower bound $1/4p^2$, which is non-negligible.

Hence, S^* breaks the honest-binding property of the scheme (Q_0, Q_1).

Remark. We highlight that the security reduction above is *uniform*.

Combing the second remark following Definition 2 with Theorem 2, we have the following theorem as an immediate corollary.

Theorem 3. *A canonical quantum bit commitment scheme (Q_0, Q_1) (of either flavor) is secure if and only if it is semi-honest secure.*

5   A Round-Collapse Theorem

In this section, we will prove a round-collapse theorem (Theorem 4), which can be viewed as an extension of converting an arbitrary *non-interactive* quantum bit commitment scheme into the canonical form [18,52]. To understand the statement and the proof of this theorem, in the first place we should have given a formal treatment of a general quantum two-party interactive protocols, their purifications, as well as their semi-honest and related security. However, we cannot do this in this extended abstract due to the limited space. Now let us informally introduce these notions, while moving their formal treatments to [50, Section 6, 7].

Roughly, a *general quantum two-party interactive protocols* allows both classical and quantum computation and communication. We can assume without loss of generality that quantum computation is limited to measurements in the computational basis, as well as quantum operations realized by polynomial-size quantum circuits composed of unitary quantum gates. A *purification* of an interactive protocol refers to the protocol obtained by simulating all classical computation and communication, as well as quantum measurements of the original protocol, by unitary quantum operations in a standard way. The *purification attack* against one party of the protocol refers to the attack by *purifying* all this party's operations.

Restricting to quantum bit commitment schemes, for our purpose we will define their *semi-honest security* as that both the semi-honest sender and receiver will *follow* the protocol in the commit stage; but in the reveal stage later, the semi-honest sender may *deviate* the protocol. Correspondingly, the *purification attack against the receiver* refers to the attack by purifying all the honest receiver's operations in the commit stage. And the *purification attack against the sender* refers to the attack by purifying all the honest sender's operations in the commit stage; but the attack in the reveal stage could be arbitrary.

Theorem 4 (Round-collapse). *If a quantum bit commitment scheme is secure against the purification attack (or equivalently, its purification is semi-honest secure), then it can be compressed into a scheme of the canonical form (Definition 2) such that:*

1. *It has perfect completeness. That is, if both the sender and the receiver follow the scheme honestly, then the receiver will not reject or abort in both the commit and the reveal stages.*
2. *Both the hiding and binding properties of the original scheme are preserved after the compression. That is, if the original scheme is statistically (resp. computationally) hiding (resp. binding), then the new scheme is also statistically (resp. computationally) hiding (resp. binding) as well.*

At a high level, our *compiler* achieves the round-collapse by delegating the computation of both parties in the commit stage prescribed by the *purification* of the original scheme to the new sender. Later in the reveal stage, the new receiver will check this computation in the commit stage via the *reversible* quantum computation.

Due to the space limitation, the proof of the round-collapse theorem can be found in [50].

As a simple application of the round-collapse theorem, we can compress Naor's bit commitment scheme [37] to get a non-interactive one [50, Appendix D]. Nevertheless, this application seems not a big deal, since there already exists a more straightforward (and somewhat simpler) construction (also inspired by Naor's scheme [52]). Two non-trivial applications are referred to the subsequent section and [50, Section 9], respectively.

Since the purification attack is just a special kind of attack among all possible attacks, the following theorem is an immediate corollary of Theorem 4.

Theorem 5. *Any secure (against an arbitrary quantum attack) interactive quantum bit commitment scheme, in particular post-quantum secure (classical) bit commitment scheme, can be compressed into a non-interactive one of the canonical form (Definition 2) with perfect completeness and the same flavors of the hiding and binding properties.*

Remark. We stress again that in this work we consider *general* quantum binding properties that *all* quantum bit commitment schemes can satisfy, for which sum-binding is likely to be the strongest. A specific quantum bit commitment scheme may satisfy even stronger binding properties (e.g. [2, 5, 7, 22, 43, 44]) than sum-binding. But if we feed it into our compiler for the round-compression, these stronger binding properties may be lost; the resulting/compressed scheme is only guaranteed sum-binding (or equivalently honest-binding, since it is of the canonical form).

6   Application: An Equivalence Between Two Flavors of Quantum Bit Commitments

In this section, we show that quantum bit commitment is *symmetric*, or two flavors of quantum bit commitments are *equivalent* (Theorem 1). This is an immediate corollary of the following theorem combined with the round-collapse theorem (Theorem 4).

Theorem 6. *Canonical computationally-hiding statistically-binding quantum bit commitments exist if and only if canonical statistically-hiding computationally-binding quantum bit commitments exist.*

Towards establishing the equivalence above, our basic idea is first using a construction that is a simplification of the CLS scheme [14] to convert the flavor of the given quantum bit commitment scheme, and then compressing the resulting (interactive) scheme into a canonical one using the round-collapse theorem (Theorem 4).

In greater detail, our construction for the purpose of converting the flavor of quantum bit commitments is basically the *parallel composition* of the atomic (interactive) scheme as described in Fig. 1, which we denote by QBC(n), with the security parameter n (which we often drop to simplify the notation). Let QBC(n)$^{\otimes n}$ denote the *parallel* composition of n copies of the scheme QBC(n). This construction is almost the CLS scheme given in [14], but with a significant simplification: all *intermediate verifications* of the commitments by the sender are removed. In spite of this, we will still call it *CLS scheme* in this paper. Intuitively, these intermediate verifications can be removed because by the virtue of the round-collapse theorem (Theorem 4), we only need a scheme that is just secure against the purification attack for the purpose of the compression. That is, we only need to show that the CLS scheme QBC(n)$^{\otimes n}$ is secure against the purification attack, or the purified CLS scheme is both honest-hiding and honest-binding. This simplification of the construction will induce a significant simplification of the analysis of the original CLS scheme [14], which is for the full security and quite technically involved.

Security parameter: n

Commit stage: Let $b \in \{0, 1\}$ be the bit to commit.

- **(S1)** For $i = 1, 2, \ldots, n$, the sender chooses a bit $x_i \xleftarrow{\$} \{0, 1\}$ and a basis $\theta_i \xleftarrow{\$} \{+, \times\}$, sending the qubit $|x_i\rangle_{\theta_i}$ to the receiver.

- **(R2)** For $i = 1, 2, \ldots, n$, the receiver chooses a basis $\hat{\theta}_i \xleftarrow{\$} \{+, \times\}$ and measures each received qubit $|x_i\rangle_{\theta_i}$ in the basis $\hat{\theta}_i$, obtaining the outcome $\hat{x}_i$. Then commit to $(\hat{\theta}_i, \hat{x}_i)$ in a bitwise fashion using a canonical quantum bit commitment scheme (Q_0, Q_1). (We can assume that the bases "+" and "×" are encoded as 0 and 1, respectively.)

- **(S3)** The sender sends all θ_i's, $i = 1, 2, \ldots, n$, to the receiver.

- **(R4)** The receiver chooses a random bit $c \xleftarrow{\$} \{0, 1\}$, as well as two random subsets of indices $I_0, I_1 \subset [n]$ such that $|I_0| = |I_1| = n/3$, $I_0 \cap I_1 = \emptyset$, and $\theta_i = \hat{\theta}_i$ for each $i \in I_c$. Then send (I_0, I_1) to the sender.

- **(S5)** The sender chooses a bit $a_0 \xleftarrow{\$} \{0, 1\}$ and sets $a_1 = a_0 \oplus b$. Then compute $\hat{a}_0 = \bigoplus_{i \in I_0} x_i \oplus a_0$, $\hat{a}_1 = \bigoplus_{i \in I_1} x_i \oplus a_1$, and send $(\hat{a}_0, \hat{a}_1)$ to the receiver.

- **(R6)** The receiver computes the bit $d_c = \bigoplus_{i \in I_c} \hat{x}_i \oplus \hat{a}_c$.

Reveal stage:

- The sender sends the bits b and (a_0, a_1) to the receiver.
- The receiver verifies that $b = a_0 \oplus a_1$ and $d_c = a_c$.

Fig. 1. The atomic scheme QBC, which composed in parallel gives a scheme that is a somewhat simplification of the original CLS scheme

Due to the space limitation, the proof of Theorem 6 is referred to [50, Section 10].

7   Parallel Composition of a Canonical Statistically-Binding Quantum Bit Commitment Scheme

In cryptography, a typical way to commit a string is to commit it in a *bitwise* fashion using a bit commitment scheme. We naturally ask, what binding property can we obtain if we commit a string in a bitwise fashion using a canonical quantum bit commitment scheme? The answer to this question on the *parallel* composition of quantum bit commitments turns out to be elusive, especially w.r.t. *computationally-binding* quantum bit commitment [12].

In this section, we will study the parallel composition of a canonical *statistically-binding* quantum bit commitment scheme, establishing a very strong quantum string binding property. We also show that this binding property implies the CDMS-binding property of quantum string commitment (referred to [50, Section 11]), which is useful in quantum cryptography [12]. However, we do not expect the same binding property extends to canonical *computationally-binding* quantum bit commitment schemes.

We first define the sum-binding property of a general quantum string commitment scheme.

Definition 4 (Sum-binding). *Suppose that a possibly cheating sender interacts with an honest receiver prescribed by a quantum string commitment scheme, and completes the commit stage. For any string $s \in \{0,1\}^{m(n)}$, where $m(\cdot)$ is a polynomial of the security parameter n, let p_s denote the success probability that the sender can open the commitment as the string s in the reveal stage. We say that this quantum string commitment scheme is sum-binding if*

$$\sum_{s \in \{0,1\}^m} p_s < 1 + negl(n). \tag{6}$$

Remark. The sum-binding property defined above is very *strong* for quantum string commitment in the following sense. Note that a cheating sender can trivially achieve $\sum_{s \in \{0,1\}^m} p_s = 1$, by committing to an arbitrary superposition of the strings in $\{0,1\}^m$ honestly and then open the commitment honestly. But showing that the advantage of any cheating sender in opening a commitment is negligible is likely to be hard or even impossible [12]. Roughly speaking, the main difficulty comes from that there are *exponentially* many strings (2^m, exactly) in $\{0,1\}^m$, but we still hope to bound the sum of exponentially many advantages by a negligible quantity.

In spite of the difficulty mentioned above, we can prove the following parallel composition theorem w.r.t. a canonical statistically-binding quantum bit commitment scheme.

Theorem 7 (Parallel composition). *Suppose that a canonical quantum bit commitment scheme (Q_0, Q_1) is statistically binding. Then the quantum string commitment scheme obtained by composing it in parallel is statistically sum-binding. Formally, if the scheme (Q_0, Q_1) is statistically $\epsilon(n)$-binding where the* *function $\epsilon(\cdot)$ is negligible, then*

$$\sum_{s\in\{0,1\}^m} p_s \leq 1 + O(m^2\epsilon). \tag{7}$$

The proof of the theorem above will be information-theoretic, thus does not extend to the computational setting. Due to the space limitation, its proof is referred to [50, Section 11].

8 Conclusion and Open Problems

In this work, we study general properties of complexity-based/computational quantum bit commitments. Specifically, we show that any quantum bit commitment scheme can be compressed into the canonical form (Theorem 4), which is non-interactive and whose semi-honest security implies the full security (Theorem 3). This yields several applications [50, Appendix D and Section 9], allowing us to not only obtain new constructions of quantum bit commitment but also simplify the security analysis of existing ones. Moreover, it also enables us to establish an equivalence between two flavors of quantum bit commitments (Theorem 6). Regarding the parallel composition, we establish a very strong quantum statistical string sum-binding property by composing a canonical statistically-binding quantum bit commitment scheme in parallel (Theorem 7).

We propose to study quantum bit commitments in the future from both quantum cryptography and quantum complexity theory perspectives. In the below, we summarize and raise some open problems that are related to this work and beyond:

1. Can canonical quantum bit commitments satisfy any stronger binding properties than sum-binding that are interesting? The answer to this question is "yes" ([18,51] and [50, Appendix B]). We expect further exploration towards this open question in the future.

2. In this work, we plug a canonical computationally-binding quantum bit commitment scheme in a somewhat simplified CLS scheme for the purpose of converting its flavor (Sect. 6). This construction essentially realizes a quantum oblivious transfer (QOT) that satisfies the following security requirements: the purified receiver of QOT does not know the other bit that the honest sender is given as input , while the purified sender of QOT does not know which input bit the honest receiver is aware of. We highlight that this security is neither the security against an arbitrary quantum attack nor the *simulation security* [5,22] that is preferable in cryptography. Recall that we prove a computational collapse theorem ([50, Appendix F]) for the analysis this security. So a natural open question is, can this computational-collapse technique be extended to show the same security but against an arbitrary quantum attack (as opposed to against the purification attack) for the original QOT protocol (or some of its variant like the one considered in [12]) with a canonical computationally-binding quantum bit commitment scheme

plugged in [13]? Possibly combine it with the quantum sampling technique devised in [8]? Though this security is not as good as the simulation security, the corresponding construction is much simpler (in particular, consisting of constant number of rounds). And it might be sufficient in some interesting applications, just like [14] and here for the purpose of converting the flavor of quantum bit commitment.

3. In this work, we show that the NOVY bit commitment scheme can be compressed into the canonical form and shown secure against quantum attacks [50, Section 9]. A natural and interesting extension of this result would be compressing the construction of statistically-hiding computationally-binding (classical) bit commitment scheme based on one-way functions [24] into the canonical form and showing its quantum security (when the underlying one-way function used is quantum secure).

4. As mentioned in Sect. 1.3, it is interesting to explore whether quantum bit commitments conversely imply pseudorandom quantum states (of any sort).

5. This open question regards *quantum hardness amplification*. The big question here is, if a unitary operation U is hard to realize (e.g. requires super-polynomial number of elementary quantum gates), then is the unitary operation $U^{\otimes n}$ (i.e. perform the unitary operation U n times in parallel) harder? Specific to a canonical quantum bit commitment scheme, we ask: can the parallel composition of quantum bit commitments reduce the binding error? The answer is a trivial "yes" w.r.t. a canonical statistically-binding quantum bit commitment scheme, whose binding error can be captured by an information-theoretic notion known as *fidelity* [52]. However, the answer becomes unclear when it comes to a canonical computationally-binding quantum bit commitment scheme. In particular, can the parallel composition reduce the *computational* binding error from, say $1/2$ or even inverse polynomial, to a negligible quantity? This question looks very similar to the question of amplifying the one-wayness of one-way functions in classical cryptography [53]. If the answer to this question is "yes", then combining it with results in [18,45,51,52] will complete the proof for an equivalence between quantum bit commitment and quantum zero-knowledge like in the classical setting [40].

6. Some fancier open questions include: can quantum bit commitment find more applications in quantum cryptography? Are there any other quantum cryptographic applications (besides quantum zero-knowledge and quantum oblivious transfer) that also imply quantum bit commitment? That is, can quantum bit commitment serve as the foundation of quantum cryptography?

7. Finally, the perhaps biggest open question that is related to the quantum complexity theory is: do computational quantum bit commitments really exist?

Acknowledgements. We thank Dominique Unruh and Takeshi Koshiba for bringing the reference [48] to our attention. Many thanks also go to Dominique Unruh, Takeshi Koshiba, Prabhanjan Ananth, Luowen Qian, Henry Yuen, and the anonymous referees of ICALP 2021, Crypto 2022 and Asiacrypt 2022 for their useful suggestions and valuable comments on earlier drafts of this paper.

This work was supported by National Natural Science Foundation of China (Grant No. 61602208), by PhD Start-up Fund of Natural Science Foundation of Guangdong Province, China (Grant No. 2014A030310333), by Major Program of Guangdong Basic and Applied Research Project (Grant No. 2019B030302008), by National Joint Engineering Research Center of Network Security Detection and Protection Technology, and by Guangdong Key Laboratory of Data Security and Privacy Preserving. Any opinions, findings and conclusions or recommendations expressed in this material are those of the author(s) and do not necessarily reflect the views of funding agencies.

References

1. Aaronson, S.: The complexity of quantum states and transformations: from quantum money to black holes. arXiv:1607.05256 (2016)
2. Adcock, M., Cleve, R.: A quantum Goldreich-Levin theorem with cryptographic applications. In: Alt, H., Ferreira, A. (eds.) STACS 2002. LNCS, vol. 2285, pp. 323–334. Springer, Heidelberg (2002). https://doi.org/10.1007/3-540-45841-7_26
3. Ananth, P., Qian, L., Yuen, H.: Cryptography from pseudorandom quantum states. Cryptology ePrint Archive, Report 2021/1663 (2021). https://ia.cr/2021/1663
4. Ananth, P., Qian, L., Yuen, H.: (2022). Private communication
5. Bartusek, J., Coladangelo, A., Khurana, D., Ma, F.: One-way functions imply secure computation in a quantum world. In: Malkin, T., Peikert, C. (eds.) CRYPTO 2021. LNCS, vol. 12825, pp. 467–496. Springer, Cham (2021). https://doi.org/10.1007/978-3-030-84242-0_17
6. Bennett, C.H., Brassard, G.: Quantum cryptography: public key distribution and coin tossing. In: Proceedings of IEEE International Conference on Computers, Systems and Signal Processing, vol. 175 (1984)
7. Bitansky, N., Brakerski, Z.: Classical binding for quantum commitments. In: Nissim, K., Waters, B. (eds.) TCC 2021. LNCS, vol. 13042, pp. 273–298. Springer, Cham (2021). https://doi.org/10.1007/978-3-030-90459-3_10
8. Bouman, N.J., Fehr, S.: Sampling in a quantum population, and applications. In: Rabin, T. (ed.) CRYPTO 2010. LNCS, vol. 6223, pp. 724–741. Springer, Heidelberg (2010). https://doi.org/10.1007/978-3-642-14623-7_39
9. Brakerski, Z., Canetti, R., Qian, L.: On the computational hardness needed for quantum cryptography. Cryptology ePrint Archive, Paper 2022/1181 (2022). https://eprint.iacr.org/2022/1181
10. Brassard, G., Crépeau, C.: Quantum bit commitment and coin tossing protocols. In: Menezes, A.J., Vanstone, S.A. (eds.) CRYPTO 1990. LNCS, vol. 537, pp. 49–61. Springer, Heidelberg (1991). https://doi.org/10.1007/3-540-38424-3_4
11. Chailloux, A., Kerenidis, I., Rosgen, B.: Quantum commitments from complexity assumptions. In: Aceto, L., Henzinger, M., Sgall, J. (eds.) ICALP 2011. LNCS, vol. 6755, pp. 73–85. Springer, Heidelberg (2011). https://doi.org/10.1007/978-3-642-22006-7_7
12. Crépeau, C., Dumais, P., Mayers, D., Salvail, L.: Computational collapse of quantum state with application to oblivious transfer. In: Naor, M. (ed.) TCC 2004. LNCS, vol. 2951, pp. 374–393. Springer, Heidelberg (2004). https://doi.org/10.1007/978-3-540-24638-1_21
13. Crépeau, C., Kilian, J.: Achieving oblivious transfer using weakened security assumptions (extended abstract). In: FOCS, pp. 42–52 (1988)

14. Crépeau, C., Légaré, F., Salvail, L.: How to convert the flavor of a quantum bit commitment. In: Pfitzmann, B. (ed.) EUROCRYPT 2001. LNCS, vol. 2045, pp. 60–77. Springer, Heidelberg (2001). https://doi.org/10.1007/3-540-44987-6_5

15. Damgård, I., Fehr, S., Lunemann, C., Salvail, L., Schaffner, C.: Improving the security of quantum protocols via commit-and-open. In: Halevi, S. (ed.) CRYPTO 2009. LNCS, vol. 5677, pp. 408–427. Springer, Heidelberg (2009). https://doi.org/10.1007/978-3-642-03356-8_24

16. Damgård, I., Fehr, S., Salvail, L.: Zero-knowledge proofs and string commitments withstanding quantum attacks. In: Franklin, M. (ed.) CRYPTO 2004. LNCS, vol. 3152, pp. 254–272. Springer, Heidelberg (2004). https://doi.org/10.1007/978-3-540-28628-8_16

17. Dumais, P., Mayers, D., Salvail, L.: Perfectly concealing quantum bit commitment from any quantum one-way permutation. In: Preneel, B. (ed.) EUROCRYPT 2000. LNCS, vol. 1807, pp. 300–315. Springer, Heidelberg (2000). https://doi.org/10.1007/3-540-45539-6_21

18. Fang, J., Unruh, D., Yan, J., Zhou, D.: How to base security on the perfect/statistical binding property of quantum bit commitment? Cryptology ePrint Archive, Report 2020/621 (2020). https://ia.cr/2020/621

19. Goldreich, O.: A note on computational indistinguishability. Inf. Process. Lett. **34**(6), 277–281 (1990)

20. Goldreich, O.: Foundations of Cryptography, Basic Tools, vol. I. Cambridge University Press, Cambridge (2001)

21. van de Graaf, J.: Towards a formal definition of security for quantum protocols. Ph.D. thesis, Université de Montréal (1997)

22. Grilo, A.B., Lin, H., Song, F., Vaikuntanathan, V.: Oblivious transfer is in miniqcrypt. In: Canteaut, A., Standaert, F.-X. (eds.) EUROCRYPT 2021. LNCS, vol. 12697, pp. 531–561. Springer, Cham (2021). https://doi.org/10.1007/978-3-030-77886-6_18

23. Haitner, I., Hoch, J.J., Reingold, O., Segev, G.: Finding collisions in interactive protocols - a tight lower bound on the round complexity of statistically-hiding commitments. In: FOCS, pp. 669–679 (2007)

24. Haitner, I., Nguyen, M.H., Ong, S.J., Reingold, O., Vadhan, S.P.: Statistically hiding commitments and statistical zero-knowledge arguments from any one-way function. SIAM J. Comput. **39**(3), 1153–1218 (2009)

25. Impagliazzo, R., Luby, M.: One-way functions are essential for complexity based cryptography (extended abstract). In: FOCS, pp. 230–235 (1989)

26. Ji, Z., Liu, Y.-K., Song, F.: Pseudorandom quantum states. In: Shacham, H., Boldyreva, A. (eds.) CRYPTO 2018. LNCS, vol. 10993, pp. 126–152. Springer, Cham (2018). https://doi.org/10.1007/978-3-319-96878-0_5

27. Kitaev, A., Watrous, J.: Parallelization, amplification, and exponential time simulation of quantum interactive proof systems. In: STOC, pp. 608–617 (2000)

28. Kobayashi, H.: Non-interactive quantum perfect and statistical zero-knowledge. In: Ibaraki, T., Katoh, N., Ono, H. (eds.) ISAAC 2003. LNCS, vol. 2906, pp. 178–188. Springer, Heidelberg (2003). https://doi.org/10.1007/978-3-540-24587-2_20

29. Kobayashi, H.: General properties of quantum zero-knowledge proofs. In: TCC, pp. 107–124 (2008). arXiv:0705.1129

30. Koshiba, T., Odaira, T.: Statistically-hiding quantum bit commitment from approximable-preimage-size quantum one-way function. In: Childs, A., Mosca, M. (eds.) TQC 2009. LNCS, vol. 5906, pp. 33–46. Springer, Heidelberg (2009). https://doi.org/10.1007/978-3-642-10698-9_4

31. Koshiba, T., Odaira, T.: Non-interactive statistically-hiding quantum bit commitment from any quantum one-way function. arXiv:1102.3441 (2011)
32. Kretschmer, W.: Quantum pseudorandomness and classical complexity. In: Hsieh, M. (ed.) TQC. LIPIcs, vol. 197, pp. 2:1–2:20. Schloss Dagstuhl - Leibniz-Zentrum für Informatik (2021)
33. Lo, H.K., Chau, H.F.: Why quantum bit commitment and ideal quantum coin tossing are impossible. Phys. D 120(1), 177–187 (1998)
34. Mahmoody, M., Pass, R.: The curious case of non-interactive commitments – on the power of black-box vs. non-black-box use of primitives. In: Safavi-Naini, R., Canetti, R. (eds.) CRYPTO 2012. LNCS, vol. 7417, pp. 701–718. Springer, Heidelberg (2012). https://doi.org/10.1007/978-3-642-32009-5_41
35. Mayers, D.: Unconditionally secure quantum bit commitment is impossible. Phys. Rev. Lett. 78(17), 3414–3417 (1997)
36. Morimae, T., Yamakawa, T.: Quantum commitments and signatures without one-way functions. In: Dodis, Y., Shrimpton, T. (eds.) CRYPTO 2022. LNCS, vol. 13507, pp. 269–295. Springer, Cham (2021). https://doi.org/10.1007/978-3-031-15802-5_10, https://ia.cr/2021/1691
37. Naor, M.: Bit commitment using pseudorandomness. J. Cryptol. 4(2), 151–158 (1991)
38. Naor, M., Ostrovsky, R., Venkatesan, R., Yung, M.: Perfect zero-knowledge arguments for NP using any one-way permutation. J. Cryptol. 11(2), 87–108 (1998)
39. Nielsen, M.A., Chuang, I.L.: Quantum Computation and Quantum Informatioin. Cambridge University Press, Cambridge (2000)
40. Ong, S.J., Vadhan, S.: An equivalence between zero knowledge and commitments. In: Canetti, R. (ed.) TCC 2008. LNCS, vol. 4948, pp. 482–500. Springer, Heidelberg (2008). https://doi.org/10.1007/978-3-540-78524-8_27
41. Rosgen, B., Watrous, J.: On the hardness of distinguishing mixed-state quantum computations. In: CCC, pp. 344–354. IEEE Computer Society (2005)
42. Unruh, D.: Quantum proofs of knowledge. In: Pointcheval, D., Johansson, T. (eds.) EUROCRYPT 2012. LNCS, vol. 7237, pp. 135–152. Springer, Heidelberg (2012). https://doi.org/10.1007/978-3-642-29011-4_10
43. Unruh, D.: Collapse-binding quantum commitments without random oracles. In: Cheon, J.H., Takagi, T. (eds.) ASIACRYPT 2016. LNCS, vol. 10032, pp. 166–195. Springer, Heidelberg (2016). https://doi.org/10.1007/978-3-662-53890-6_6
44. Unruh, D.: Computationally binding quantum commitments. In: Fischlin, M., Coron, J.-S. (eds.) EUROCRYPT 2016. LNCS, vol. 9666, pp. 497–527. Springer, Heidelberg (2016). https://doi.org/10.1007/978-3-662-49896-5_18
45. Watrous, J.: Limits on the power of quantum statistical zero-knowledge. In: FOCS, pp. 459–468 (2002)
46. Watrous, J.: Theory of Quantum Information. Cambridge University Press, Cambridge (2018)
47. Winter, A.J.: Coding theorem and strong converse for quantum channels. IEEE Trans. Inf. Theory 45(7), 2481–2485 (1999)
48. Wolf, S., Wullschleger, J.: Oblivious transfer is symmetric. In: Vaudenay, S. (ed.) EUROCRYPT 2006. LNCS, vol. 4004, pp. 222–232. Springer, Heidelberg (2006). https://doi.org/10.1007/11761679_14
49. Yan, J.: Complete problem for perfect zero-knowledge quantum proof. In: Bieliková, M., Friedrich, G., Gottlob, G., Katzenbeisser, S., Turán, G. (eds.) SOFSEM 2012. LNCS, vol. 7147, pp. 419–430. Springer, Heidelberg (2012). https://doi.org/10.1007/978-3-642-27660-6_34

50. Yan, J.: General properties of quantum bit commitments. Cryptology ePrint Archive, Report 2020/1488 (2020). https://ia.cr/2020/1488
51. Yan, J.: Quantum computationally predicate-binding commitments with application in quantum zero-knowledge arguments for NP. In: Tibouchi, M., Wang, H. (eds.) ASIACRYPT 2021. LNCS, vol. 13090, pp. 575–605. Springer, Cham (2021). https://doi.org/10.1007/978-3-030-92062-3_20
52. Yan, J., Weng, J., Lin, D., Quan, Y.: Quantum bit commitment with application in quantum zero-knowledge proof (extended abstract). In: Elbassioni, K., Makino, K. (eds.) ISAAC 2015. LNCS, vol. 9472, pp. 555–565. Springer, Heidelberg (2015). https://doi.org/10.1007/978-3-662-48971-0_47
53. Yao, A.C.: Theory and applications of trapdoor functions (extended abstract). In: 23rd Annual Symposium on Foundations of Computer Science, Chicago, Illinois, USA, 3–5 November 1982, pp. 80–91 (1982)
54. Yao, A.C.C.: Security of quantum protocols against coherent measurements. In: STOC, pp. 67–75 (1995)

Author Index